Readings in Intelligent User Interfaces

Readings in Intelligent User Interfaces

Edited by

Mark T. Maybury
MITRE Corporation

Wolfgang Wahlster
University of Saarbrücken

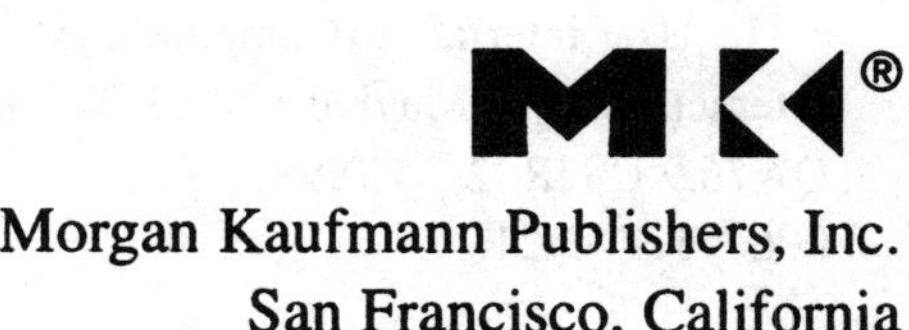

Morgan Kaufmann Publishers, Inc.
San Francisco, California

Senior Editor *Diane D. Cerra*
Director of Production and Manufacturing *Yonie Overton*
Production Editor *Cheri Palmer*
Production Assistant *Pamela Sullivan*
Assistant Editor *Marilyn Alan*
Cover Design *Ross Carron Design*
Text Design, Composition, and Pasteup *Susan M. Sheldrake*
Copyeditor *Jennifer McClain*
Proofreader *Pamela Sullivan*
Printer *Victor Graphics, Inc.*

Morgan Kaufmann Publishers, Inc.
Editorial and Sales Office
340 Pine Street, Sixth Floor
San Francisco, CA 94104-3205
USA

Telephone *415 / 392-2665*
Facsimile *415 / 982-2665*
Email *mkp@mkp.com*
WWW *www.mkp.com*
Order toll free *800 / 745-7323*

Printed in the United States of America

02 01 00 99 98 5 4 3 2 1

Library of Congress Cataloging-in-Publication Data

Readings in intelligent user interfaces / edited by Mark Maybury,
Wolfgang Wahlster.
p. cm.
Includes bibliographical references and index.
ISBN 1-55860-444-8
1. User interfaces (Computer systems) 2. Human-computer
interaction. I. Maybury, Mark T. II. Wahlster, Wolfgang.
QA76.9.U83R42 1998
006.3'37—dc21 98-16058
CIP

For their continuous support and encouragement,
we dedicate this collection to our families.

Contents

SECTION V: User and Discourse Modeling *325*

SECTION VI: Model-Based Interfaces *443*

Section VII: Agent Interfaces *521*

SECTION VIII: Evaluation *593*

Author Index 643

Keywords 645

Preface

PURPOSE

The increasing complexity of software and the proliferation of information makes this collection more relevant every day. The promise of interfaces that are knowledgeable, sensitive to our needs, agile, and genuinely useful has motivated research across the world, from academia to industry to governments, to seek to advance the state of the art and practice in user interfaces that exhibit intelligence. *Readings in Intelligent User Interfaces* (IUI) originates from the research and teaching experience of the editors, confirmed by that of their colleagues, that there exists no convenient and definitive source on the best research in intelligent user interfaces. This collection is the result of a rich collaboration between the editors, editorial review board, and many expert advisors.

CONTENTS

Readings in Intelligent User Interfaces represents the best classical and contemporary research in the field. The 44 articles in the collection represent the work of over 100 authors from 33 sites internationally. Following an introduction to the field, the collection is organized into eight sections as shown below.

Readings in Intelligent User Interfaces	
Section I	Multimedia Input Analysis
Section II	Multimedia Presentation Design
Section III	Automated Graphics Design
Section IV	Automated Layout
Section V	User and Discourse Modeling
Section VI	Model-Based Interfaces
Section VII	Agent Interfaces
Section VIII	Evaluation

The first section addresses systems that automatically process coordinated language, gesture, and gaze input. Multimodal output generation is addressed in the next three sections. Section II focuses on systems that automatically perform the tasks of content selection, media allocation, media realization, and layout. Section III focuses on the automated design of two- and three-dimensional graphics from structured data, whereas Section IV concerns designing the most efficacious layout of multimedia content in time and space. Section V considers systems that explicit build, maintain, and exploit models of the discourse and user during interactive sessions. Section VI addresses tools and techniques aimed at decreasing the time and expertise required to create interfaces through automation or design assistance. Section VI considers the role of agents in the interface, both in terms of anthropomorphic assistants or mediators, as well as the use of agent architectures for constructing intelligent user interfaces. While intelligent user interfaces remains a young and dynamic field in which innovation and exploration is necessary, a final section focuses on evaluation measures, metrics, and methods (e.g., corpus studies, benchmarking, error analysis). Our intent is to encourage the use of evaluation as an integral part of research and foster well-designed, focused, and repeatable science. Finally, in the introduction we point to additional resources such as bibliographical databases, tutorials, and major funding programs.

REFLECTIONS

To enhance the timeliness and relevancy of the collection, following each article is a short "reflection" written by the original author(s) commenting on their own work, citing important developments which influenced, have resulted from, and/or followed the publication of their work including key follow-up publications by the author and others. This can serve as an invaluable tool for the teacher, researcher, or practitioner to read a personal account by the principal investigator of what worked, what did not, and where opportunities remain.

TEACHING AND RESEARCH

To facilitate the use of the readings in teaching, this Readings provides several aids to the instructor, which will also benefit the researcher, student, and practitioner. While we expect this readings will be utilized, in part, for advanced undergraduate and graduate courses in computer science and artificial intelligence, the collection is highly relevant to courses in human-computer interaction. Following the *Readings in HCI*, we illustrate below how the content of this Readings relates to the ACM SIGCHI Curricula for Human-Computer Interaction developed by the Curriculum Development Group (CDG) *(http://www.acm.org/sigchi/cdg/)*. In some cases, articles addressing topics in the CDG's curricula are found throughout this collection, which we indicate by "entire collection."

In order to facilitate research, in the introduction to the readings following this preface we cross-index each chapter in the major sections (e.g., input analysis, presentation design, evaluation) by multiple dimensions such as the media data types investigated (e.g., text, speech, graphics, gesture), underlying models (e.g., of the user, discourse, task, situation), representational devices utilized (e.g., numerical-, rule-, plan-, model-, or agent-based processing), and application areas addressed (e.g., design/decision support, information access, training). This enables the reader rapid access to the most relevant chapters and also encourages interlinkage among the chapters. Finally, in the introduction we point to additional resources such as bibliographic databases and tutorials.

ACKNOWLEDGMENTS

Wolfgang and I would like to thank the editorial review board (Ed Hovy, Johanna Moore, Sharon Oviatt, Oliviero Stock, and Steve Roth) and the many expert reviewers who provided valuable commentary on earlier drafts, including Bob Neches, Elisabeth André, Thomas Rist, Tony Jameson, Lynette Hirschman, Joe Marks, Loren

Relationship to HCI Curriculum

ACM SIGCHI CDG Inventory of HCI Topics			Readings in IUI
N	The Nature of HCI		
	N1	(Meta-)Models of HCI	Introduction
U	Use and Context of Computers		
	U1	Human Social Organization and Work	Introduction
	U2	Application Areas	Introduction, Entire collection
	U3	Human-Machine Fit and Adaptation	Introduction, Section V
H	Human Characteristics		
	H1	Human Information Processing	Section V
	H2	Language, Communication, Interaction	Section I, II
	H3	Ergonomics	Section V
C	Computer System and Interface Architecture		
	C1	Input and Output Devices	Section I, II
	C2	Dialogue Techniques	Section V
	C3	Dialogue Genre	Section V, VII
	C4	Computer Graphics	Section III, IV
	C5	Dialog Architecture	Section VI
D	Development Process		
	D1	Design Approaches	Introduction, Section VI, VII
	D2	Implementation Techniques	Sections I–VII, especially VI
	D3	Evaluation Techniques	Section VIII
	D4	Example Systems and Case Studies	Entire collection

Terveen, Angel Puerta, Peter Johnson, Hilary Johnson, Stu Shapiro, Peter Brusilovsky, Paul McKevitt, Gary Strong, David Benyon, Bonnie Webber, Candy Sidner, Alex Waibel, Barbara Grosz, Kathy McCoy, Noelle Carbonell, Eric Horvitz, Nick Belkin, Henry Lieberman, and Niels Ole Bernsen. We thank Paula MacDonald for her excellent administrative support, Diane Cerra for expert publishing advice, Antonia Richmond and Marilyn Uffner Alan for editorial assistance, and Cheri Palmer for production support.

Acknowledgments

Arens, Y., Miller, L., and Sondheimer, N. (1991) Presentation Design Using an Integrated Knowledge Base. Sullivan, J., and Tyler, S. (eds.). *Intelligent User Interfaces*. 241–258. © 1991 by the ACM Press, a division of the Association for Computing Machinery, Inc. Reprinted with permission.

Arens, Y., Hovy, E., Vossers, M. (1993) On the Knowledge Underlying Multimedia Presentations. Maybury, M. (ed.). *Intelligent Multimedia Interfaces*. 280–306. AAAI/MIT Press. © 1993 American Association for Artificial Intelligence. Reprinted with permission.

Bolt, R. A. (1980) "Put-That-There": Voice and Gesture at the Graphics Interface. *Computer Graphics*. 14(3), 262–270. © 1980 by the Association for Computing Machinery, Inc. Reprinted with permission.

Burger, J. D., and Marshall, R. J. (1993) The Application of Natural Language Models to Intelligent Multimedia. Maybury, M. T. (ed.). *Intelligent Multimedia Interfaces*. 174–196. AAAI/MIT Press. © 1993 American Association for Artificial Intelligence. Reprinted with permission.

Card, S. K., Mackinlay, J. D., and Robertson, G. G. (1991) A Morphological Analysis of the Design Space of Input Devices. *Transactions on Information Systems*. 9(2), 99–122. © 1991 by the Association of Computing Machinery, Inc. Reprinted with permission.

Casner, S. M. (1991) A Task-Analytic Approach to the Automated Design of Graphic Presentations. *Transactions on Graphics*. 10(2), 111–151. © 1991 by the Association of Computing Machinery, Inc. Reprinted with permission.

Cassell, J., Pelachaud, C., Badler, N., Steedman, M., Achorn, B., Becket, T., Douville, B., Prevost, S., and Stone, M. (1994) Animated Conversation: Rule-Based Generation of Facial Expression, Gesture and Spoken Intonation for Multiple Conversational Agents. SIG-GRAPH '94. 413–420. © 1994 by the Association of Computing Machinery, Inc. Reprinted with permission.

Cawsey, A. (1993) Planning Interactive Explanations. *International Journal of Man-Machine Studies*. 38,169–199. © 1993 Academic Press. Reprinted with permission.

Chin, D. (1991) Intelligent Interfaces as Agents. Sullivan, J. and Tyler, S. (eds.). *Intelligent User Interfaces*. 177–206. © 1991 by the ACM Press, a division of the Association of Computing Machinery, Inc. Reprinted with permission.

Christensen, J., Marks, J., Shieber, S. (1995) An Empirical Study of Algorithms for Point-Feature Label Placement. *Transactions on Graphics*. 14(3), 203–232. ACM Press. © 1995 by the Association of Computing Machinery, Inc. Reprinted with permission.

Cohen, P. R., Dalrymple, M., Moran, D. B., Pereira, F. C. N., Sullivan, J. W., Gargan, R. A., Jr., Schlossberg, J. L., and Tyler, S. W. (1989) Synergistic Use of Direct Manipulation and Natural Language. *Procceedings of the 1989 Conference on Human Factors in Computing Systems (CHI '89)*. 227–233. ACM Press. © 1989 by the Association of Computing Machinery, Inc. Reprinted with permission.

Cohen, P. R., Johnston, M., McGee, D., Oviatt, S., Pittman, J., Smith, I., Chen, L., and Clow, J. (1997) Multimodal Interaction for Distributed Interactive Simulation. *Proceedings of the 14th National Conference on Artificial Intelligence and 9th Innovative Applications of Artificial Intelligence Conference*. 978–985. AAAI/MIT Press. © 1997 American Association for Artificial Intelligence.

Dahlbäck, N., Jönsson, A., and Ahrenberg, L. (1993) Wizard of Oz Studies-Why and How. Gray, W., Hefley, W. E., and Murray, D. (eds.). *Proceedings of the 1993 International Workshop on Intelligent User Interfaces*. 193–199. © Association of Computing Machinery, Inc. Reprinted with permission.

Feiner, S. K. (1988) A Grid-Based Approach to Automating Display Layout. *Proceedings of the 1988 Graphics Interface Conference (GI '88).* 192–197. © 1988 Canadian Information Processing Society.

Feiner, S. K., and McKeown, K. R. (1991) Automating the Generation of Coordinated Multimedia Explanations. © 1991 IEEE. Reprinted, with permission, from *IEEE Computer*. 24(10), 33–41.

Fischer, G., Nakakoji, K., Ostwald, J., Stahl, G., and Sumner, T. (1993) Embedding Critics in Design Environments. *The Knowledge Engineering Review Journal, Special Issue on Expert Critiquing*. 8(4), 285–307. © 1993 Cambridge University Press. Reprinted with the permission of Cambridge University Press.

Foley, J., Gibbs, C., Kim, W. C., and Kovacevic, S. A. (1988) Knowledge-Based User Interface Management System. *Proceedings of the 1988 Conference on Human Factors in Computer Systems (CHI'88).* 67–72. © 1988 Association of Computing Machinery, Inc. Reprinted with permission.

Graf, W. H. (1992) Constraint-Based Graphical Layout of Multimodal Presentations. *Proceedings of Advanced Visual Interfaces (AVI'92).* 36, 365–385. © 1992 World Scientific Series in Computer Science. Reprinted with permission.

Hollan, J. D., Hutchins, E. L., and Weitzman, L. M. (1984) Steamer: An Interactive Inspectable Simulation-Based Training System. *AI Magazine*. 5(2), 15–28. © 1984 American Association for Artificial Intelligence. Reprinted with permission.

Hovy, E. H., and Arens, Y. (1991) Automatic Generation of Formatted Text. *Proceedings of the 10th National Conference on Artificial Intelligence*. 92–97. AAAI/MIT Press. © 1991 American Association for Artificial Intelligence.

Jacob, R. J. K. (1991) The Use of Eye Movements in Human-Computer Interaction Techniques: What You Look at Is What You Get. *Transactions on Information Systems*. 9(3), 152–169. © 1991 by the Association of Computing Machinery, Inc. Reprinted with permission.

Kobsa, A., Müller, D., and Nill, A. (1994) KN-AHS: An Adaptive Hypertext Client of the User Modeling System BGP-MS. Reprinted from *Proceedings of the Fourth International Conference on User Modeling*, Hyannis, MA. 99–105. © User Modeling, Inc. (http://www.um.org).

Koons, D. B., Sparrell, C. J., and Thórisson, K. R. (1993) Integrating Simultaneous Input from Speech, Gaze, and Hand Gestures. Maybury, M. T. (ed.). *Intelligent Multimedia Interfaces*. 257–276. AAAI/MIT Press. © 1993 American Association for Artificial Intelligence. Reprinted with permission.

Mackinlay, J. D. (1987) Automating the Design of Graphical Presentations of Relational Information. *Transactions on Graphics*. 5(2), 110–141. © 1987 by the Association of Computing Machinery, Inc. Reprinted with permission.

Maes, P. (1994) Agents That Reduce Work and Information Overload. *Communications of the ACM*. 37(7), 31–40, 146. © 1994 by the Association of Computing Machinery, Inc. Reprinted with permission.

Maybury, M. T. (1993) Planning Multimedia Explanations Using Communicative Acts. Maybury, M. T. (ed.). *Intelligent Multimedia Interfaces*. 59–74. AAAI/MIT Press. © 1993 American Association for Artificial Intelligence. Reprinted with permission.

Moore, J. D., and Paris, C. L. (1993) Planning Text for Advisory Dialogues: Capturing Intentional and Rhetorical Information. *Computational Linguistics*. 19(4), 651–695. © 1993 Association of Computational Linguistics. Reprinted with permission.

Nagao, K. and Takeuchi, A. (1994) Speech Dialogue with Facial Displays: Multimodal Human-Computer Conversation. *Proceedings of the 32nd Annual Meeting of the Association of Computational Linguistics*. 102–109. © 1994 Association of Computational Linguistics. Reprinted with permission.

Neal, J. G., Thielman, C. Y., Dobes, Z., Haller, S. M., and Shapiro, S. C. (1989) Natural Language with Integrated Deictic and Graphic Gestures. *Proceedings of the 1989 DARPA Workshop on Speech and Natural Language*. 410–423. © 1989 Defense Advanced Research Projects Agency (DARPA).

Oviatt, S. L. (1996) User-Centered Modeling for Spoken Language and Multimodal Interfaces. © 1996 IEEE. Reprinted, with permission, from *IEEE Multimedia*. 3(4), 26–35.

Puerta, A., Eriksson, H., Gennari, J. H., and Musen, M. A. (1994) Model-Based Automated Generation of User Interfaces. *Proceedings of the National Conference on Artificial Intelligence*. 471–477. © 1994 American Association for Artificial Intelligence. Reprinted with permission.

Reiter, E., Mellish, C., and Levine, J. (1995) Automatic Generation of Technical Documentation. *Applied Artificial Intelligence*. 9(3), 259–287. © 1995 Taylor & Francis. Reprinted with permission.

Rich, E. (1979) User Modeling via Stereotypes. *Cognitive Science*. 3, 329–354. © 1979 Ablex Press. Reprinted with permission.

Roth, S. F., and Mattis, J. (1990) Data Characterization for Intelligent Graphics Presentation. *Proceedings of the Conference on Human Factors in Computing Systems (CHI'90).* 193–200. © 1990 Association of Computing Machinery, Inc. Reprinted with permission.

Roth, S. F., Kolojejchick, J., Mattis, J., and Goldstein, J. (1994) Interactive Graphic Design Using Automatic Presentation Knowledge. *Proceedings of the Conference on Human Factors in Computing Systems (CHI '94).*

112–117. © 1994 by the Association of Computing Machinery, Inc. Reprinted with permission.

Seligmann, D. D., and Feiner, S. (1991) Automated Generation of Intent-Based 3D Illustrations. *Computer Graphics*. 25(4), 123–132. © 1991 by the Association of Computing Machinery, Inc. Reprinted with permission.

Stock, O. (1991) Natural Language and Exploration of an Information Space: The ALFresco Interactive System. *Proceedings of the 12th International Joint Conference on Artificial Intelligence (IJCAI '91)*. 972–978. © 1991 International Joint Conferences on Artificial Intelligence, Inc. Reprinted with permission.

Szekely, P., Luo, P., Neches, R. (1993) Beyond Interface Builders: Model-Based Interface Tools. *Proceedings of INTERCHI '93*. 383–390. © 1993 by the Association of Computing Machinery, Inc. Reprinted with permission.

Vanderdonckt, J. (1994) Automatic Generation of a User Interface for Highly Interactive Business-Oriented Applications. *Conference Companion of the 1994 Conference on Human Factors in Computing Systems (CHI '94)*. 123–124. © 1994 by the Association for Computing Machinery, Inc. Reprinted with permission.

Wahlster, W. (1991) User and Discourse Models for Multimodal Communication. Sullivan, J. and Tyler, S., (eds.). *Intelligent User Interfaces*. 45–67. © 1991 by the ACM Press, a division of the Association of Computing Machinery, Inc. Reprinted with permission.

Wahlster, W., André, E., Finkler, W., Profitlich, H.-J., and Rist, T. (1993) Plan-Based Integration of Natural Language and Graphics Generation. *Artificial Intelligence*. 63(1–2), 387–427. Reprinted with kind permission from Elsevier Science-NL. Sara Burgerhartstraat 25, 1055 KV Amsterdam, The Netherlands.

Walker, M. A., Litman, D. J., Kamm, C. A., and Abella, A. (1997) PARADISE: A Framework for Evaluating Spoken Dialogue Agents. *Proceedings of the 35th Annual Meeting of the ACL and 8th European Conference of the European Chapter of the ACL*. 271–280. © 1997 Association of Computational Linguistics. Reprinted with permission.

Weitzman, L., and Wittenburg, K. (1996) Grammar-Based Articulation for Multimedia Document Design. *Multimedia Systems Journal*. 4, 99–111. © 1996 Springer-Verlag. Reprinted with permission.

Wiecha, C., Bennett, W., Boies, S., Gould, J., and Greene, S. (1989) ITS: A Tool for Rapidly Developing Interactive Applications. *Transactions on Information Systems*. 8(3), 204–236. © 1989 by the Association of Computing Machinery, Inc. Reprinted with permission.

Intelligent User Interfaces: An Introduction

This introduction describes the need for intelligent user interfaces (IUIs), specifies the intended purpose and use of this collection, outlines the collection's scope, and defines basic terminology used in the field. After outlining the theoretical foundations of intelligent user interfaces, this introductory section describes the current state of the art and summarizes the structure and contents of this collection, which addresses some remaining fundamental problems in the field.

1. MOTIVATION

The explosion of available materials on corporate, national, and global information networks is driving the need for more effective, efficient, and natural interfaces to support access to information, applications, and people. This is exacerbated by the increasing complexity of systems, the shrinking of task time lines, and the need to reduce the cost of application and interface development. Fortunately, the basic infrastructure for advanced multimedia user interfaces is rapidly appearing or already available. In addition to traditional public telephone networks, cable, fiber-optic, wireless and satellite communications are rapidly evolving with the aim of serving many simultaneous users through a great variety of multimedia communications (e.g., video, audio, text, data). Rapidly advancing microprocessor and storage capabilities, coupled with multimedia input and output devices integrated into workstations and portable machines, provide a dizzying array of potential for personal and personalized multimedia interaction.

Interface technology has advanced from initial command line interfaces to the established use of direct manipulation or WIMP (windows, icons, menus, and pointing) interfaces in nearly all applications. Even some of the first computing systems incorporated graphical displays and light pens as pointing devices (Everett et al. 1957). The next generation of interfaces, often called "intelligent," will provide a number of additional benefits to users, including adaptivity, context sensitivity, and task assistance. As with traditional interfaces, principled intelligent interfaces should be learnable, usable, and transparent. In contrast, however, intelligent user interfaces promise to provide additional benefits to users that can enhance interaction, such as:

- Comprehension of possibly imprecise, ambiguous, and/or partial multimodal input
- Generation of coordinated, cohesive, and coherent multimodal presentations
- Semi- or fully automated completion of delegated tasks
- Management of the interaction (e.g., task completion, tailoring interaction styles, adapting the interface) by representing, reasoning, and exploiting models of the user, domain, task, and context

In addition to these end-user benefits, new model-based interface tools promise to help user interface designers and developers decrease the time, expense, and level of expertise necessary to construct successful user interfaces.

In search of these benefits, governments, industry, and academia have emphasized the importance of the human-machine interface in the global information economy. For example, the United States Digital Library, European Telematics, and the Japanese Human Interface Programs are all well funded in the long term, but their continued success will require researchers and managers to rapidly acquire the standard literature and train in the latest interface tools and techniques. As an example, the $500 million, 10-year Real World Computing (RWC) Program initiated in 1992 (Tsukuba, Japan) focuses on pattern/symbol processing and includes an emphasis on multimodal interfaces integrating gesture, speech, and body language. Academic and commercial advances in human-computer interface technology (Baecker, Grudin, Buxton, and Greenberg 1995) has dramatically improved interaction with computers; however, these efforts are necessary but not sufficient to address the preceding challenges. Instead, a new class of interfaces is required that goes beyond the current tripartite interface model of application, dialogue, and presentation. This collection of papers points the way toward interfaces that model the situation, task, user, discourse, and media and that enable model-based specification and generation of interfaces, agent-based interaction, and integrated multimodal input and output. Unlike traditional human-computer interfaces, intelligent interfaces are those that represent and reason about the user, domain, task, media, and situation. A number of applications are emerging, ranging from mail filters (Maes, Section VII of this volume) to office assistants (Horvitz 1997) to speaking and listening interface agents (Nagao and Takeuchi, Section VII of this volume).

2. PURPOSE AND USE

The purpose of this collection is multifold. First, it is intended to motivate and define the field of intelligent user interfaces. Second, it is intended to capture and place into context key developments in this field. Third, it is intended to serve as a stimulus for continued research into the many interesting and challenging problems that remain. Finally, a principal goal of this collection is to bridge the gap between scientists and engineers working in the distinct but interdependent fields of human-computer interaction and intelligent user interfaces/artificial intelligence. We hope the collection will also serve to foster scientific interchange among individuals working in both theory and applications, and, as such, the collection reflects a mix of these activities.

This collection can be used as: a key reference source for students, researchers, and practitioners of IUI or as a text in user interface classes or advanced graduate seminars. To satisfy these purposes, the book is organized around the key areas of IUI: input analysis, output generation, user- and discourse-adapted interaction, agent-based interaction, model-based interface design, and intelligent interface evaluation. In addition to a traditional author and keyword index, we also provide a two-dimensional content index in Section 5.7, to facilitate tailored access to relevant content for a range of purposes: research, analysis, or teaching.

Articles were chosen from a broad range of sources, including journals, conference proceedings, workshop notes, and previous book collections. Each article was nominated by a member of the editorial board and evaluated by multiple reviewers considering selection criteria of quality, significance, originality, clarity, and relevance as well as special considerations such as historical and sustained influence and difficulty of acquisition. Each article is followed by a brief reflection written by the original authors, indicating important developments that have influenced, have resulted from, and/or have followed the publication of their work, including key follow-up publications by the authors and others. After providing the scope and definitions of the field, we overview its brief history and then provide summaries of the key sections of the readings.

3. SCOPE AND DEFINITIONS

Intelligent user interfaces (IUIs) are human-machine interfaces that aim to improve the efficiency, effectiveness, and naturalness of human-machine interaction by representing, reasoning, and acting on models of the user, domain, task, discourse, and media (e.g., graphics, natural language, gesture). As a consequence, this interdisciplinary area draws upon research in and lies at the intersection of human-computer interaction, ergonomics, cognitive science, and artificial intelligence and its subareas (e.g., vision, speech and language processing, knowledge representation and reasoning, machine learning/knowledge discovery, planning and agent-modeling, user and discourse modeling). Whereas previous collections have focused on related enabling technologies such as text processing (Grosz, Sparck Jones, and Webber 1986; MUC-6 1995), spoken language processing (Waibel and Lee 1990), human-computer interaction (Baecker, Grudin, Buxton, and Greenberg 1995), user modeling (Kobsa and Wahlster 1989), artificial intelligence (Webber and Nilsson 1985), knowledge representation (Brachman and Levesque 1985), and planning (Allen and Hendler 1990), intelligent human-computer interaction requires a synergistic integration of these areas. This collection complements previous works focused on human-computer interaction, multimedia or intelligent interfaces (Blattner and Dannenberg 1992, Sullivan and Tyler 1991), and intelligent multimedia interfaces (Maybury 1993).

Figure 1 illustrates a high-level architecture of intelligent user interfaces and, as such, defines many of the subareas in the field. These include analyzing and interpreting input, designing and rendering output, managing the interaction, and representing and reasoning about models that support intelligent interaction. An example of a model is a user model, more generally, an agent model (e.g., that could represent the user, system, intermediary, addressee, etc.). The "intelligence" in IUIs that distinguishes them from traditional interfaces is indicated in bold in Figure 1—it includes mechanisms that perform automated media analysis, design, and interaction management. Thus, the collection does not address input and output devices and drivers for input processing and output rendering.

As the dotted regions in Figure 2 illustrate, traditional user interfaces distinguish only three models: presentation, dialog, and application. Refinements beyond these three models that are found in IUIs include explicit models of the user, discourse and domain, input analysis and output generation, and mechanisms to manage the interaction, such as fusing and interpreting imprecise, ambiguous, and/or inaccurate input, controlling the dialog progression, or tailoring presentation output to the current situation.

Research so far has shown that it is possible to adapt many of the fundamental concepts developed to date in computational linguistics and discourse theory in such a way that they become useful for multimedia user interfaces as well. In particular, semantic and pragmatic concepts like communicative acts, coherence, focus, reference, discourse model, user model, implicature, anaphora, rhetorical relations, and scope ambiguity take on an extended meaning in the context of multimodal communication. As Figure 3 illustrates, artificial intelligence has much to contribute to user interfaces, including the use of knowledge representations for model-based interface development tools, the

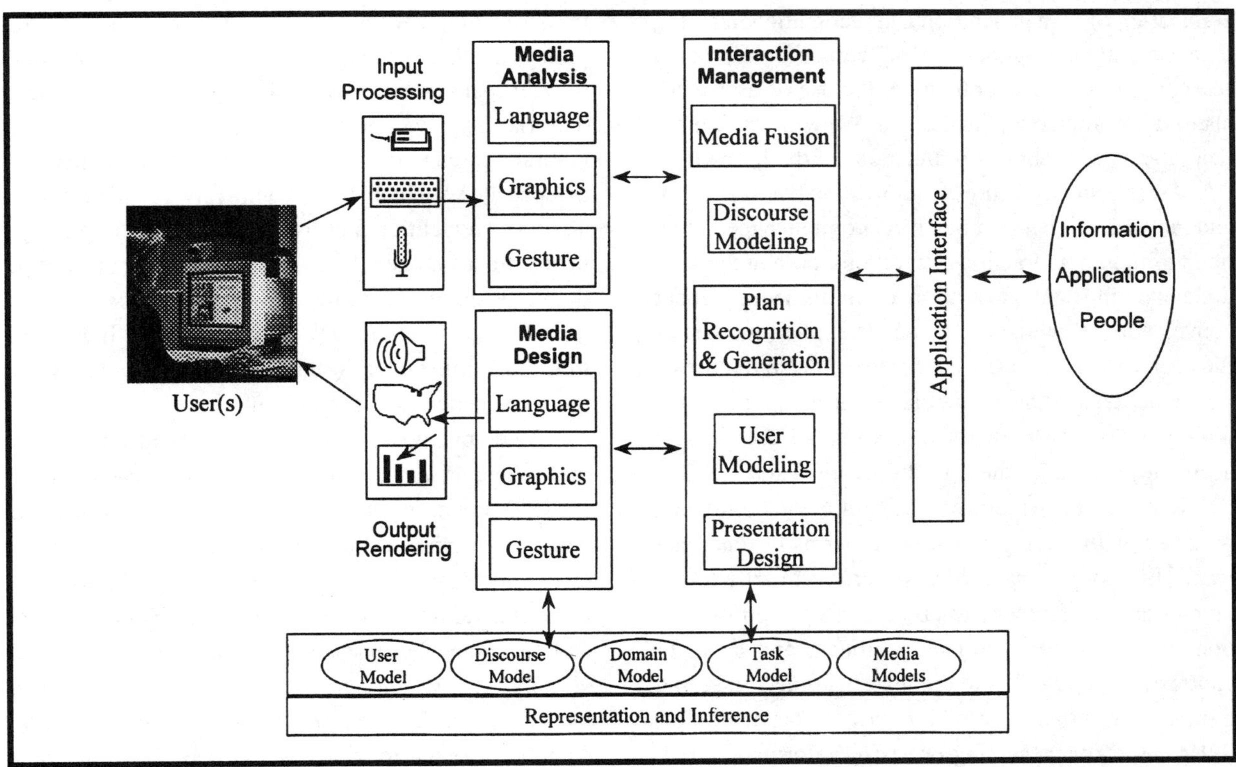

Figure 1. Architecture of Intelligent User Interfaces

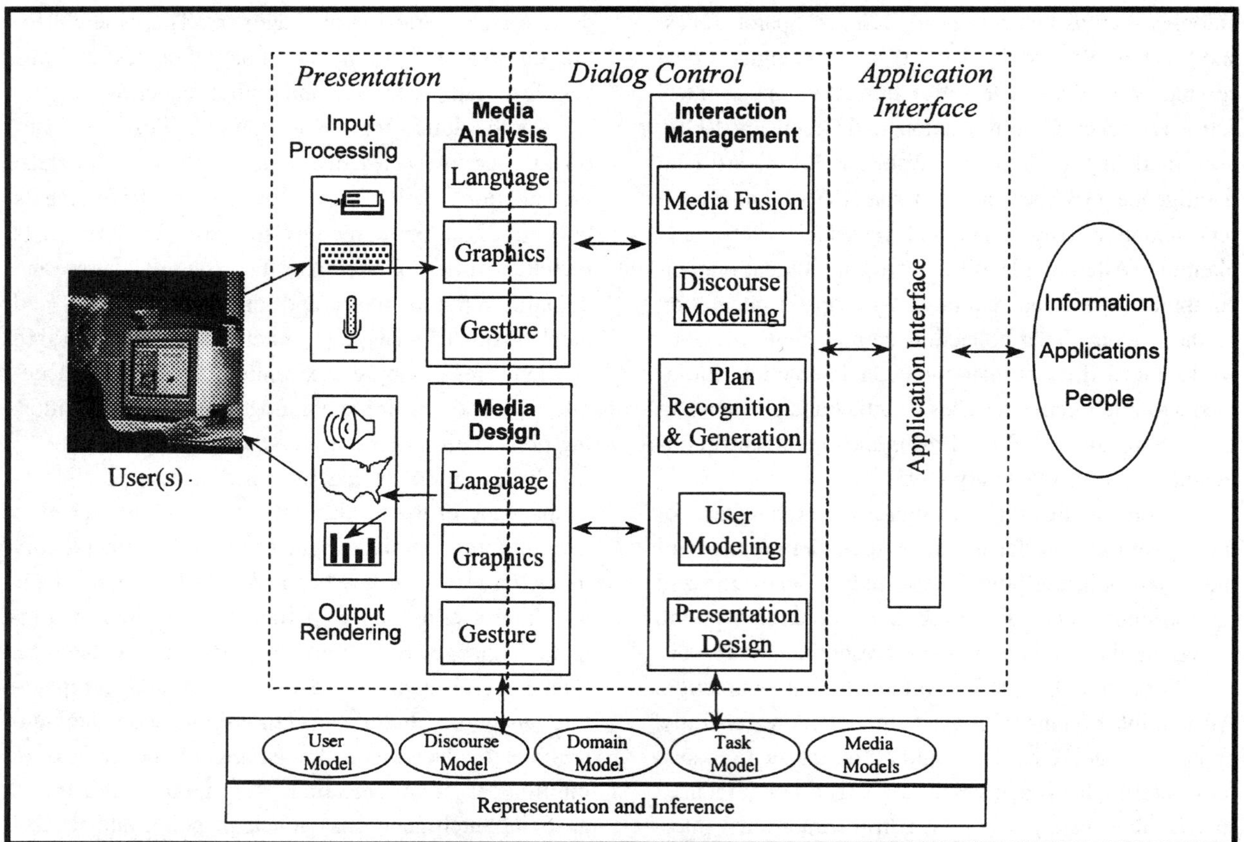

FIGURE 2. Current Interface Practice and Its Relation to IUI

application of plan generation and recognition in dialog management, the application of temporal and spatial reasoning to media coordination, the use of user models to tailor interaction, and so on. We will detail these theoretical and technical foundations in the following.

As shown in Figure 3, more effective, efficient, and natural human-computer or computer-mediated, human-human interaction will require both automated understanding and generation of multimedia. Fluent conversational interaction demands explicit models of the user, discourse, task, and context. It also requires a richer understanding of media in its use both in the interface to support interaction with the user and in access to content by the user during a session.

Because of widespread terminology confusion, we begin with a clarification of the terms *medium* and *mode*. By *mode* or *modality*, we refer primarily to the human senses employed to process incoming information: vision, audition, olfaction, touch, and taste. In contrast, *medium* refers to the material object (e.g., the physical carrier of information such as paper or CD-ROM) used for presenting or saving information and, particularly in the context of human-computer interaction, to computer input/output devices (e.g., microphone, speaker, screen, pointer). We use the term *code* to refer to a system of symbols (e.g., natural language, pictorial language, gestural language). For example, a natural language code might use typed or written text or speech, which in turn would rely upon visual or auditory modalities and associated media (e.g., keyboard, microphone). It is important to note, however, that especially the terms *media* and *mode* are frequently used ambiguously in the literature. Indeed, in this collection we will use them interchangeably when their distinction is not important.

Medium, mode, and code are related nontrivially (see Figure 4). First, a single medium may carry several modalities and, in turn, codes. For example, a piece of paper may support both language and graphics codes just as a visual display may support text, images, and video. Likewise, a single code may be supported by many media and modalities. For instance, language can be supported visually (i.e., written language) and aurally (i.e., spoken language)—in fact, spoken language can have a visual component (e.g., lip reading). Analogously, a user of a multimedia CD-ROM is interacting with a physical me-

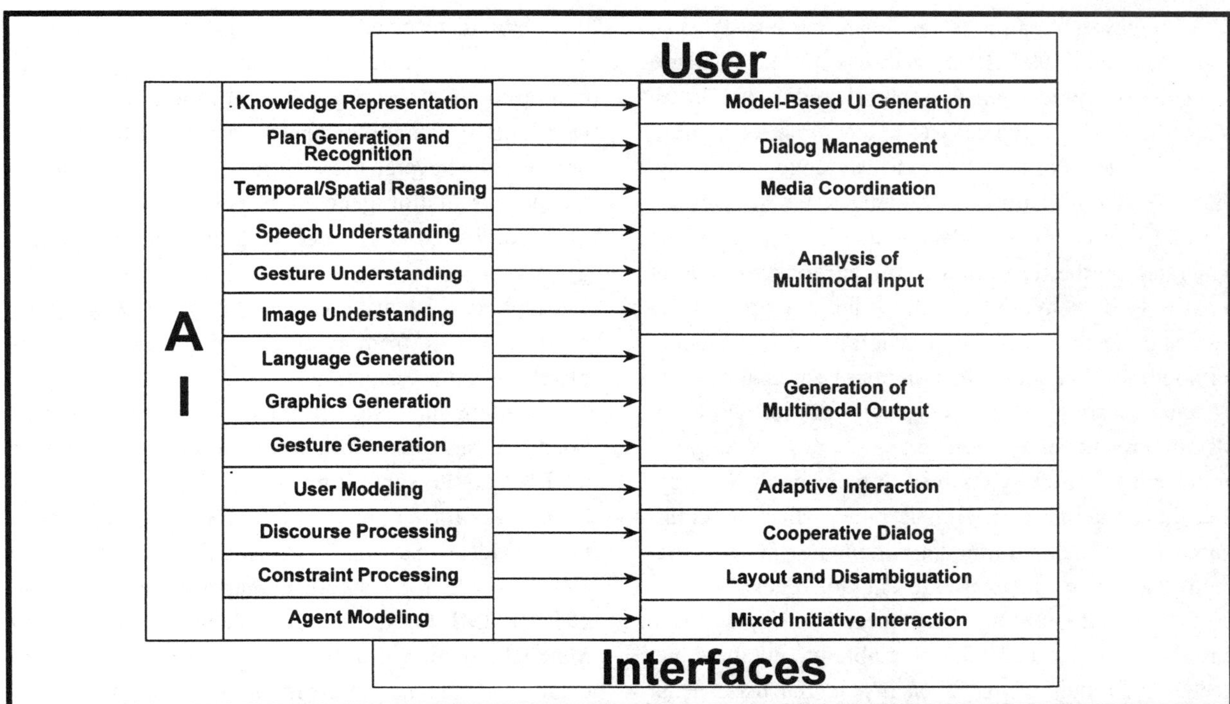

FIGURE 3. AI Meets User Interfaces

dium used to store information captured in a variety of codes (e.g., language, graphics) using multiple modalities (e.g., auditory, visual) and using various input/output media (e.g., mouse, display, speaker). A multimedia document on the CD-ROM might include text, graphics, speech, and video that affect several modalities, for example, visual and auditory perception of natural language, visual perception of images (still and moving), and auditory perception of sounds. Finally, this multimedia and multimodal interaction occurs over time. Therefore, it is necessary to account for the processing of discourse, context shifts, and changes in agent states over time.

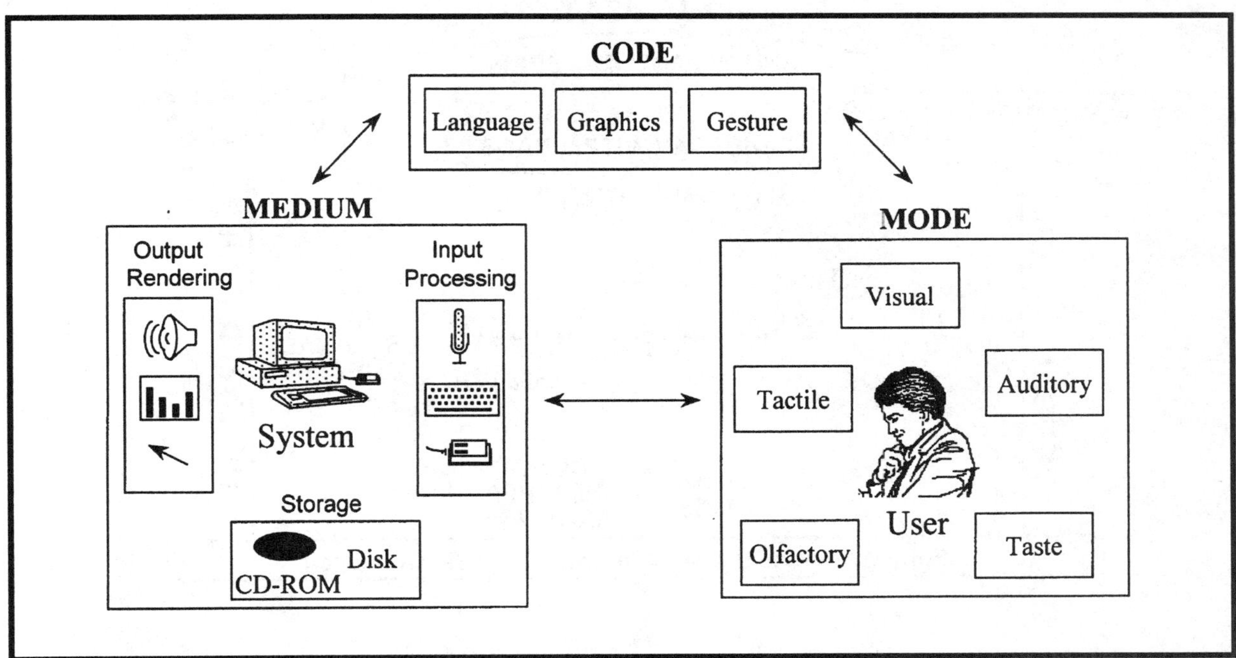

FIGURE 4. Medium, Mode, and Code

The new generation of intelligent multimodal systems (Maybury 1993, 1995) goes beyond the standard canned text, predesigned graphics, and prerecorded images and sounds typically found in commercial multimedia systems of today. A basic principle underlying these so-called intellimedia systems is that the various constituents of a multimodal communication should be generated on the fly from a common representation of what is to be conveyed without using any preplanned text or images; that is, the principle is "no generation without representation." It is an important goal of such systems not simply to merge the verbalization and visualization results of a text generator and a graphics generator but to carefully coordinate them in such a way that they generate a synergistic improvement in communication. Such multimodal presentation systems are highly adaptive since all presentation decisions are postponed until runtime. The quest for adaptation is based on the fact that it is impossible to anticipate the needs and requirements of each potential user in an infinite number of presentation situations.

Figure 5 indicates the key processes and exemplifies some systems that have addressed multimodal information processing, including media generation and media conversion. The large arrows indicate where processing typically begins, that is, from formal representations such as a data or knowledge base or from the media themselves (e.g., text, graphics, or images). Key processes include *verbalization* (moving from formal representations or graphics or images to text) and *visualization* (from representations or text to graphics or images). Several systems have focused on multimodal presentation generation, designing, and realizing coordinated text, speech, graphical, and cartographic presentations. As the dial in the middle indicates, these systems raise the opportunity to select between a scale from an entirely linguistic to a completely visual presentation.

Multimedia dialog prototypes have been developed in several application domains, including CUBRICON to support mission planning (Neal et al., Section I of this volume), XTRA for tax form preparation (Wahlster, Section V of this volume; Kobsa et al. 1986), MMI2 for network management (Binot et al. 1990), AIMI for air mission planning (Burger and Marshall, Section V of this volume), and ALFresco to enable art history information exploration (Stock, Section V of this volume). Typically, these systems parse mixed and asynchronous multimedia input and generate coordinated multimedia output. They also attempt to maintain coherency, cohesion, and consistency across both multimedia input and output. For example, these systems often support integrated language and deixis for both input and output. They

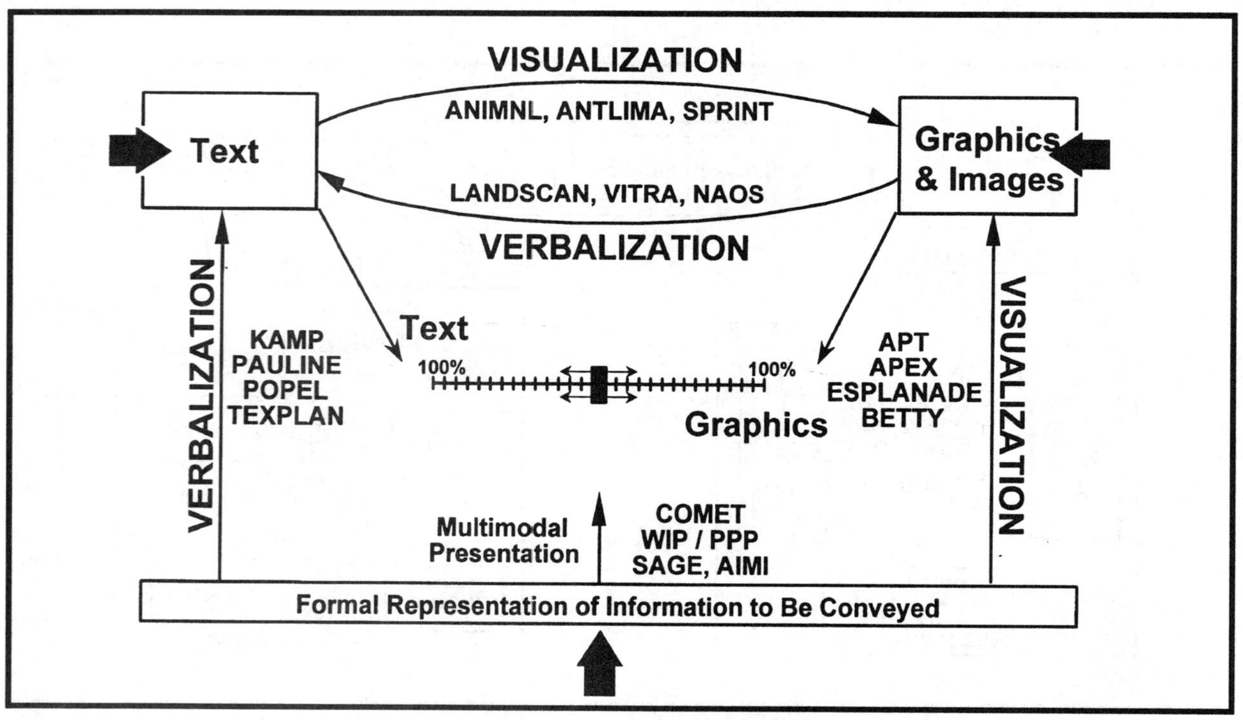

FIGURE 5. Key Processes in Multimedia Processing

extend research in discourse and user modeling (Kobsa and Wahlster 1989) by incorporating representations of media to enable media reference, cross-reference, and reuse over the course of a session with a user. These enhanced representations support the exploitation of user perceptual abilities and media preferences as well as the resolution of multimedia references (e.g., "Send this plane there" articulated with synchronous gestures on a map).

The details of discourse models in these systems, however, differ significantly. For example, CUBRICON represents a global focus space ordered by recency whereas AIMI represents a focus space segmented by the intentional structure of the discourse (i.e., a model of the domain tasks to be completed). Although intelligent multimedia interfaces promise natural and personalized interaction, they remain complicated and require specialized expertise to build. One practical approach to achieving some of the benefits of these more sophisticated systems without the expense of developing full multimedia interpretation and generation components was achieved in ALFresco (Stock, Section V of this volume), a multimedia information kiosk for Italian art exploration. By adding natural language processing to a traditional hypermedia system, ALFresco achieved the benefits of hypermedia (e.g., organization of heterogeneous and unstructured information via hyperlinks, direct manipulation to facilitate exploration) together with the benefits of natural language parsing (e.g., direct query of nodes, links, and subnetworks, which provides rapid navigation). Providing a user with natural language query within a hypertext system helps overcome the indirectness of the hypermedia web as well as disorientation and cognitive overhead caused by large amounts of semantically heterogeneous links (e.g., part-of, class-of, instance-of, or elaboration-of). In addition, as in other systems previously mentioned (e.g., CUBRICON, XTRA), ambiguous gesture and language can yield a unique referent through mutual constraint. Finally, ALFresco incorporates simple natural language generation that can be combined with more complex canned text (e.g., art critiques) and images. Reiter, Mellish, and Levine (Section II of this volume) analogously integrate traditional language generation with hypertext to produce hypertext technical manuals.

Whereas practical systems are possible today, the multimedia interface of the future may have facilities that are much more sophisticated. These interfaces may include humanlike agents that converse naturally with users, monitoring their interaction with the interface (e.g., keystrokes, gestures, facial expressions) and the properties of those interactions (e.g., conversational syntax and semantics, dialog structure) over time and for different tasks and contexts. Equally, future interfaces will likely incorporate more sophisticated presentation mechanisms. For example, Pelachaud, Badler, and Steedman (1996) characterize spoken language intonation and associated emotions (anger, disgust, fear, happiness, sadness, and surprise) and from these use rules to compute facial expressions, including lip shapes, head movements, eye and eyebrow movements, and blinks. Finally, future multimedia interfaces should support richer interactions, including user and session adaptation (Schneider-Hufschmidt et al. 1993), dialog interruptions, follow-up questions, and management of the focus of attention.

In summary, as Figures 1 through 5 illustrate, principal areas of intelligent interface research include

- *Analysis* of input (e.g., spoken, typed, and hand-written language; gestures, including hand, eye, and body states and motion)
- *Generation* (planning or realization) of coordinated output
- *Modeling* of the user, discourse, task, and situation and *interaction management*, including possible tailoring of interaction to the user, task, and/or situation

As such, we distinguish these functions in the organization of this collection, described later in this introductory section.

4. THE ROOTS OF INTELLIGENT USER INTERFACES

Enabling conversational interaction with computers has been a vision since the creation of the first computers. In part stimulated by attempts to pass the Turing test, a number of initial efforts attempted to literally simulate conversation with computers using pattern matching to select possible responses from a conversational database (e.g., McCarthy's ADVICE, Weizenbaum's ELIZA, Colby's PARRY). Other efforts focused on specific aspects of conversation, most notably the focus on natural language interfaces. We refer the reader to *Readings in Natural Language Processing* (Grosz, Sparck Jones, and Webber 1986), which outlines the history of natural language processing research, including theoretical and computational investigations into tasks, discourse, attention, beliefs, and plans in support of both analysis and generation of natural language. Intelligent user interfaces have benefited from a rich interaction between theoretical developments, such as Grice's work on implicatures and Austin and Searle's work on speech acts, as well as practical application areas, such as interfaces to data bases, intelligent tutoring, and automated interface design. Figure 6 captures some of the important events in the emergence of the discipline of IUIs, including the appearance of the first international workshops and conferences, specialized collections, and the emergence of commercial products and standards. Depicted is the creation of natural language interfaces in the seventies and eighties (including natural language processing toolkits), agents in commercial products in the nineties, and a standard reference model (SRM) for intelligent multimodal presentation systems (IMMPS) in 1998 (Bordegoni et al. 1998). The nineties are also characterized by increasing scientific advances (many captured in this collection), tool developments (e.g., Kobsa et al.'s BGP-MS user modeling shell (Section V of this volume)), and commercial applications such as e-mail filters (Maes, Section VII of this volume) and Bayesian-based user models for Microsoft's Office Assistant (Horvitz 1997).

5. STATE OF THE ART: AN OVERVIEW OF THE READINGS

This readings collection is organized around solutions to the key elements introduced in the architecture outlined at the beginning of this introductory section: input analysis, output generation, user and discourse modeling, model-based interfaces, agent interaction, and evaluation. We briefly describe each of these in turn, referring the reader to the section introductions for summary overviews of the included papers.

5.1. Analysis of Input

The chapters in Section I of the collection focus on supporting intelligent input processing. Motivated by the observation that human-human communication is multimedia, multimodal, and multicodal (including spoken and written language, gesture, gaze), these papers investigate enriching human-machine interactions using such capabilities. Collectively, the authors illustrate how supporting integrated input from multiple sources can simultaneously enhance communication efficiency, effectiveness (e.g., speed and accuracy), and naturalness. They provide technical solutions that support interpretation of parallel, imprecise, and ambiguous multimedia input. The papers also illustrate the context-dependent, multifunctional nature of multimodal input, providing rich ground for future research. Taken together, these papers advance our ability to enable humans to utilize the full extent of their linguistic, gestural, and gaze input, with the attendant benefits.

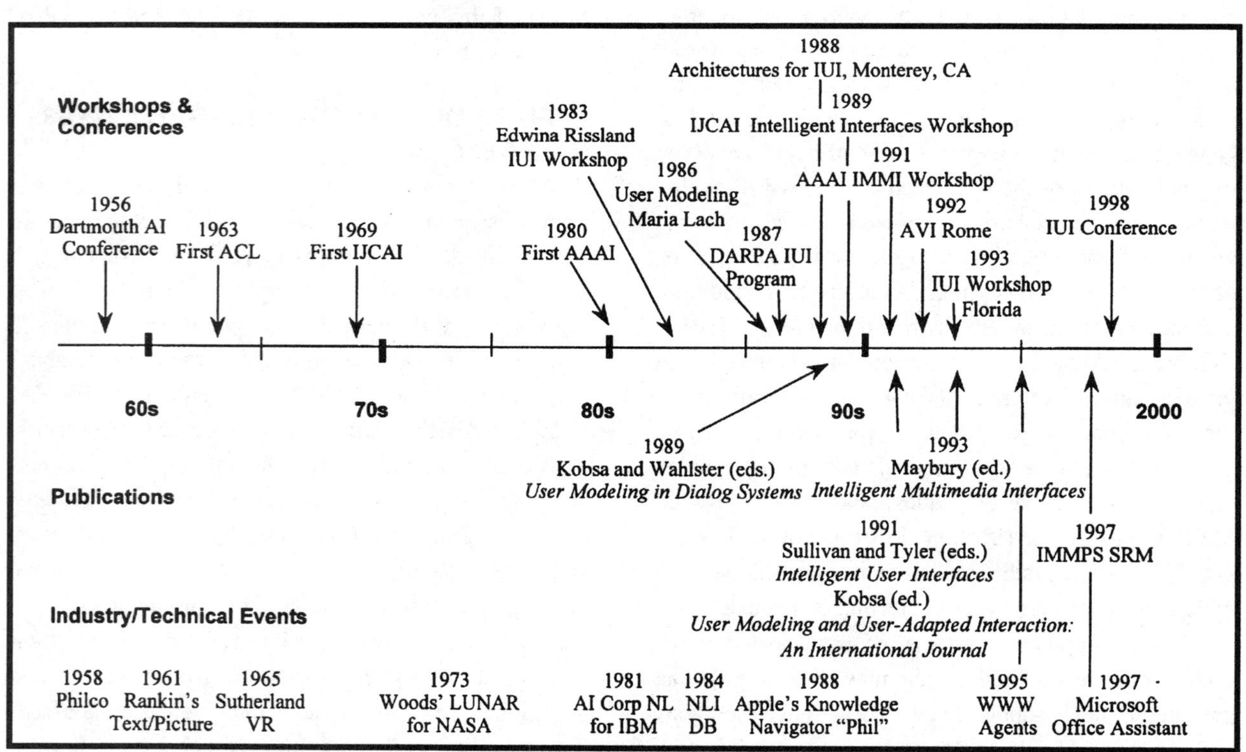

FIGURE 6. Historical Emergence of Intelligent User Interfaces

5.2. Generation of Output

The next three sections of the book address semi- or fully automatic generation of coordinated multimedia output. Designing and realizing coherent and cohesive multimedia presentations can be subdivided into several co-constraining processes, which include the determination of communicative intent, the selection of content to achieve this, its grouping/structuring and ordering, its allocation to a particular code (e.g., text versus graphics), its realization in a coordinated fashion across media, and finally its layout. Ideally, the generation process is tailored to the context, task, and user. Investigators have explored these processes in several domains using a range of algorithms. This area is accordingly divided into three sections: "Multimedia Presentation Design," "Automated Graphics Design," and "Automated Layout."

5.2.1. Multimedia Presentation Design

The second section of the book addresses multimedia presentation design, which encompasses the tasks of content selection, media allocation, media realization, and layout. The papers suggest these processes are interdependent and must be closely coordinated during generation to ensure cohesive and coherent output. Together, the papers also argue for the importance of key knowledge sources in these processes, including models of the information and media, the user, the discourse context, the producer, and the interface itself. They further demonstrate generalizations of text-linguistic notions, such as coherence, speech acts, anaphora, and rhetorical relations for multimedia presentation design. Each paper contributes concrete but widely ranging technical approaches and solutions to these tasks (e.g., employing templates, rules, plans, constraints).

5.2.2. Automated Graphics Design

Whereas several articles in Section II address automated generation of natural language text, this third section looks at the automatic design and realization of two- and three-dimensional graphics from structured data (see Maybury 1994 for pointers to eight surveys and six specialized collections on natural language generation and Grosz, Sparck Jones, and Webber 1986).

These papers collectively aim to elucidate not only how but why graphics should be designed. Moving beyond descriptive works of graphical design practice that consider examples of successful graphics and make observations on how to avoid ambiguous, confusing, or imprecise and misleading graphics, these efforts aim at formal and prescriptive theories of graphics design.

A number of factors have motivated researchers to seek automated graphic designers. Currently, application designers are forced to anticipate and predesign every possible data and presentation situation. Moreover, in order to create effective graphics, developers need to be design experts, which is often not the case.

Several features characterize the papers. First, they all focus on a move toward explicit representation of graphical presentation knowledge. Second, they support explicit choices among graphical encoding mechanisms that reason about the expressiveness and effectiveness of underlying representations and resulting presentations. Finally, the authors increasingly focus on representation of knowledge of the user, task, and context and its exploitation to generating more effective, tailored presentations while decreasing required user expertise. Whereas some papers focus principally on information characteristics and data graphics, others consider how differences in users' goals impact the effectiveness of designed graphics. Still others exploit perceptual operations that yield more rapid results than cognitive operations (e.g., arithmetic, comparison); for example, grouping and ordering information as well as encoding it using color, shading, and layout to support "preattentive" and sometimes parallel visual search to enable both more accurate and more efficient task performance.

5.2.3. Automated Layout

The fourth section of the book addresses the layout of media objects, which has a strong influence on the attentional structure of multimodal communication. A change in the layout of a multimedia document does not necessarily change the meaning of the document but certainly changes the focus of attention of the reader. Multimedia presentations are too dynamic and come too fast to have the layout of every visual presentation designed manually so that automated layout becomes a necessity. In addition, automated layout may help to adapt an interface to the screen or window size of a user as well as to the user's perceptual abilities and preferences. The articles in this section survey the most important techniques for automated multimedia layout, including approaches based on rules, constraints, or simulated annealing.

5.3. User and Discourse Models

Section V of the collection addresses the adaptation of interfaces to the user and context of the interaction, specifically addressing the acquisition, tracking, and utilization of models of the user and discourse. The articles address user modeling issues, including stereotypes, plan- and goal-based user models, system initiative, and user modeling shells. The articles also address the modeling and use of models of discourse for such tasks as planning explanations, answering follow-up questions in the context of prior discourse, and supporting interruption. The articles cover a wide range of application areas, including interactive consultation (e.g., recommending books or guiding software use), user- and context-adaptive hypertext (e.g., art exploration), and multimedia interfaces to decision support. A number of innovations in these systems include the extension of user and discourse models to multimedia interfaces (e.g., to process multimodal deixis), the use of incremental explanation planning, and interleaved design and realization.

5.4. Model-Based Interfaces

Section VI of the collection describes efforts to create tools that decrease both the time and the expertise required to create interfaces through automation or design assistance. These efforts go beyond user interface toolkits by separating dialog control from application code and teasing out presentation and style decisions from the toolkit code libraries. They are also distinct from user interface management systems in that they make finer-grained distinctions and provide more powerful design tools to interface developers. Much research effort has been focused on more crisply defining the functional areas of the interface in order to support declarative expression and modularization of interface functionality.

These papers make a few key contributions. First, they move toward declarative specifications of interfaces, refining the distinctions among models and processes associated with the domain, the application, the user-machine dialog control, and the presentation. Second, they promise increased portability and ease of evolution as maintenance and extension is done within a more formal framework. Finally, they enable new forms of designer support, such as automated design critique, refinement, and implementation.

5.5. Agent-Based Interaction

The papers in Section VII consider the use of agents in the interface. Important questions explored include, What can and should an agent do? How they should do it? and How, when, and why should they interact with the user when doing it? Agents promise to decrease human workloads and make the overall experience of interaction less stressful and more productive. Agents may assist by decreasing task complexity, bringing expertise to the user (in the form of expert critiquing, task completion, coordination), or simply providing a more natural environment with which to interact. The papers in this section report examples of each of these and also describe open architectures for building agent-based multimodal interfaces, the use of agents to express system and discourse status via facial displays, and the multimodal communication between animated computer agents.

5.6. Empirical Evaluation

The final section focuses on IUI evaluation. Whereas community-based evaluation using standard corpora and tasks has been applied in several areas related to intelligent interfaces (most notably, DARPA evaluations in speech, starting with Hirschman 1989; information extraction, e.g., MUC-6 1995; and information retrieval, e.g., TREC-1, Harmon 1993), relatively little evaluation has been systematically performed on IUIs. This section attempts to collect the best examples to foster more rigorous development of and widespread use of evaluation in the future. Important dimensions of the problem include considering human-human versus human-computer communication, spoken versus written communication, unimodal versus multimodal communication, and direct versus mediated communication.

As the papers in this section illustrate, the evaluator and analyst have at their disposal a range of tools, such as Wizard-of-Oz experiments, simulations, and instrumentation of live environments to evaluate a range of metrics using a variety of quantitive and qualitative measures and evaluation methodologies (e.g., corpus based, task based).

5.7. Content Index

Because many of the papers address issues that cut across section distinctions, Table 1 provides cross-references to facilitate access to chapters according to the following categories:

1. Media input and output data types investigated (e.g., text, speech, graphics, gesture), which, as a result, indicate if the investigations examine cross-stream or multiple media processing
2. The underlying models (e.g., of the user, discourse, task, situation) that are created, maintained, and exploited
3. Representational devices utilized, such as numerical-, rule-, plan-, model-, or agent-based processing
4. Application areas addressed, (e.g., decision/design support, information access or creation, training)

SECTION	Input Analysis					Presentation Design						Graphics Design					Layout					User & Discourse Models								Model-Based Design						Agents					Evaluation			
CHAPTER	**1.1**	**1.2**	**1.3**	**1.4**	**1.5**	**2.1**	**2.2**	**2.3**	**2.4**	**2.5**	**2.6**	**3.1**	**3.2**	**3.3**	**3.4**	**3.5**	**4.1**	**4.2**	**4.3**	**4.4**	**4.5**	**5.1**	**5.2**	**5.3**	**5.4**	**5.5**	**5.6**	**5.7**	**5.8**	**6.1**	**6.2**	**6.3**	**6.4**	**6.5**	**6.6**	**7.1**	**7.2**	**7.3**	**7.4**	**7.5**	**8.1**	**8.2**	**8.3**	**8.4**
Text	✖	✖	✖	✖		✖	✖	✖	✖	✖	✖	✖					✖	✖	✖			✖	✖	✖	✖	✖	✖	✖	✖		✖	✖	✖	✖	✖		✖	✖	✖	✖		✖	✖	✖
Speech	✖	✖	✖	✖																																		✖	✖	✖		✖	✖	✖
Audio/Music																													✖															
Graphics	✖	✖	✖	✖	✖	✖	✖	✖	✖	✖	✖	✖	✖	✖	✖	✖	✖		✖	✖	✖			✖	✖		✖	✖	✖	✖	✖	✖	✖	✖	✖		✖	✖	✖		✖	✖	✖	✖
Maps																													✖									✖				✖	✖	✖
Gesture	✖	✖	✖	✖		✖	✖	✖																✖				✖	✖									✖	✖	✖	✖		✖	
Gaze				✖	✖																																		✖	✖				
Discourse		✖	✖	✖	✖	✖	✖	✖					✖											✖		✖	✖	✖	✖		✖	✖	✖	✖	✖				✖	✖				✖
User			✖	✖	✖		✖	✖		✖				✖	✖	✖						✖	✖	✖	✖	✖	✖	✖	✖										✖	✖				
Task			✖	✖		✖	✖	✖		✖				✖	✖	✖						✖	✖	✖	✖	✖	✖		✖	✖	✖	✖	✖	✖	✖	✖	✖		✖	✖	✖			✖
Media						✖	✖	✖	✖	✖	✖								✖		✖			✖					✖										✖		✖		✖	
Statistical					✖				✖																✖																			
Rule-Based	✖					✖			✖	✖	✖	✖	✖	✖	✖	✖	✖		✖	✖	✖	✖			✖			✖	✖								✖			✖				
Plan-Based		✖	✖	✖			✖	✖										✖					✖			✖	✖																	
Model-Based																								✖	✖					✖	✖	✖	✖	✖					✖	✖	✖			✖
Agent-Based																																				✖		✖	✖	✖			✖	
Design Assist												✖	✖	✖		✖	✖	✖	✖	✖	✖									✖	✖	✖	✖	✖	✖		✖							
Decision Support	✖	✖	✖	✖	✖																	✖		✖		✖	✖		✖									✖			✖	✖	✖	✖
Help						✖	✖		✖	✖	✖												✖		✖											✖			✖					
Info Access					✖	✖	✖	✖	✖	✖	✖													✖	✖			✖								✖		✖	✖	✖	✖	✖	✖	✖
Training						✖			✖		✖		✖																	✖								✖						

TABLE 1. Content-Based Index

6. CONCLUSION

Intelligent interfaces promise to improve the quality of interaction for all who interact with computers—at work and at play. They promise

- more *efficient* interaction—enabling more rapid task completion with less work.
- more *effective* interaction—doing the right thing at the right time, tailoring the content and form of the interaction to the context of the user, task, dialog.
- more *natural* interaction—supporting spoken, written, and gestural interaction, ideally as if interacting with a human interlocutor.

When these interfaces are created in a model-based fashion, modifying their behavior will require model changes, not reprogramming. This will reduce the time, cost, and expertise required to develop interfaces and, at the same time, will facilitate the creation of more principled interfaces. Intelligent interface technology will be essential to effective information interaction in the future. For example, better interaction via the web (Brusilovsky 1996) has been identified as a challenging problem, and intelligent web sites in the future promise to discover user and group skills and interests, tailor presentations, and automatically improve web site interfaces (Perkowitz and Etzioni 1997). In short, this area has the potential to improve the quality and effectiveness of interaction for everyone who communicates with a machine in the future. To achieve these benefits, however, we must overcome the remaining fundamental problems outlined in the chapters herein.

7. RESOURCES

A number of resources for teachers, students, and researchers contain additional information about this subject area. Several relevant collections of papers are cited in the references at the end of this introductory section, notably, *Intelligent User Interfaces* (Sullivan and Tyler 1991), *Intelligent Multimedia Interfaces* (Maybury 1993), and *Readings in Human-Computer Interaction* (Baecker et al. 1995). Maybury (1995) provides a summary of research in multimedia parsing and generation. Key journals (and associated World Wide Web sites) in which new results in intelligent user interfaces appear include the international journals of *Human-Computer Interaction* (*www.parc.xerox.com/istl/projects/HCI*), including a special issue on multimedia interfaces (Oviatt and Wahlster 1997), *User Modeling and User-Adapted Interaction* (*umuai.informatik.uni-essen.de*), *Artificial Intelligence* (*www.elsevier.com/locate/artint*), *Cognitive Science,* and *ACM Transactions on Graphics* as well as more general forums such as *Communications of the ACM* and *IEEE Computer.*

In addition to journals and books, a series of conferences and workshops can provide additional sources, such as the annual ACM-sponsored International Conference on Intelligent User Interfaces (*sigart.acm.org/iui99/*), the International Conference on User Modeling, the International Workshop on Advanced Visual Interfaces (AVI), and the User Interface Systems Technology (UIST Conference). Proceedings from a number of annual or semiannual conferences typically contain sessions on intelligent user interfaces, such as the conference of the Association for Computing Machinery Special Interest Group on Computer Human Interaction (*www.acm.org/sigchi*), the American Association of Artificial Intelligence (AAAI) National Conference on Artificial Intelligence, the European Conference on Artificial Intelligence (ECAI), and the International Joint Conference on Artificial Intelligence (IJCAI). There are also many related conferences and specialized workshops in subdisciplines, including speech and language processing, user and discourse modeling, multimedia, and intelligent training systems.

Finally, materials are increasingly available on-line, such as an on-line tutorial on intelligent multimedia interfaces (*www.mitre.org/resources/centers/advanced_info/mark.html*); an on-line survey, "State of the Art in Human Language Technology" (*www.cse.ogi.edu/CSLU/HLTsurvey*); a study by the National Research Council on Every Citizen Interfaces (*www.nap.edu/readingroom/books/screen*); a human-computer interaction index (*is.twi.tudelft.nl/hci*); and the Electronic Transactions on Artificial Intelligence (*www.ida.liu.se/ext/etai/indexframe.html*), which includes a special area on intelligent user interfaces (*www.dfki.de/~andre/etai/colloqb.html*). Additional pointers are available from the ACL SigMedia special interest group in multimedia language processing (*www.dfki.de/sigmedia*). Related government initiatives include the European Intelligent Information Interfaces program (*www.i3net.org*) and DARPA's Intelligent Collaboration and Visualization program (*snad.ncsl.nist.gov/~icv-ewg/*).

8. REFERENCES

Allen, J., and Hendler, J. (eds.). 1990. *Readings in Planning*. San Francisco: Morgan Kaufmann.

Arens, Y.; Feiner, S.; Foley, J.; Hovy, E.; John, B.; Neches, R.; Pausch, R.; Schorr, H.; and Swartout, W. 1991.

Intelligent User Interfaces. (ISI/RR-91-288). University of Southern California Information Sciences Institute Research Report, Marina del Rey, CA.

Baecker, R.; Grudin, J.; Buxton, W.; and Greenberg, S. 1995. *Readings in Human-Computer Interaction: Toward the Year 2000* (second edition). San Francisco: Morgan Kaufmann.

Binot, J-L.; Falzon, P.; Perez, R.; Peroche, B.; Sheehy, N.; Rouault, J.; and Wilson, M. D. 1990. Architecture of a Multimodal Dialogue Interface for Knowledge-Based Systems. In *Proceedings of Esprit '90 Conference*, 412–433. Dordrecht, Netherlands: Kluwer Academic Publishers.

Blattner, M., and Dannenberg, R. (eds.). 1992. *Multimedia Interface Design*. New York: ACM Press.

Bordegoni, M.; Faconti, G.; Feiner, S.; Maybury, M.; Rist, T.; Ruggieri, S.; Trahanias, P.; and Wilson, M. 1997. A Standard Reference Model for Intelligent Multimedia Presentation Systems. *The International Journal on the Development and Application of Standards for Computers, Data Communications and Interfaces, Special Issue on Intelligent Multimedia Presentation Systems*. Vol. 18, Nos. 6 and 7. Amsterdam: Elsevier Science.

Brachman, R. J., and Levesque, H. J. (eds.) 1985. *Readings in Knowledge Representation*. San Francisco: Morgan Kaufmann.

Brusilovsky, P. 1996. Methods and Techniques of Adaptive Hypermedia. In Brusilovsky, P., and Vassileva, J., (eds.), *Special Issue on Adaptive Hypertext and Hypermedia, User Modeling and User-Adapted Interaction* 6 (2–3): 87–129.

Everett, R.; Zraket, C. A.; and Bennington, H. 1957. SAGE: A Data Processing System for Air Defense, In *Proceedings of the Eastern Joint Computer Conference*, Washington, DC, December. IRE (now IEEE), 148–155. Reprinted in Everett, R.; Zraket, C. A.; and Bennington, H. 1983. SAGE: A Data Processing System for Air Defense. *Annals of the History of Computing*, 5(4): 330–339. October.

Grosz, B. J., Sparck Jones, K., and Webber, B. 1986. *Readings in Natural Language Processing*. San Francisco: Morgan Kaufmann.

Hirschman, L. (chair), *Proceedings of the Speech and Natural Language Workshop*, February 1989. San Francisco: Morgan Kaufmann.

Horvitz, E. 1997. Agents with Beliefs: Reflections on Bayesian Methods for User Modeling. Invited Talk, Sixth International Conference on User Modeling, Chia Laguna, Sardinia, June 2–5. (*http://www.research.microsoft.com /research/dtg/horvitz/lum.htm*)

Kobsa, A.; Allgayer, J.; Reddig, C.; Reithinger, N.; Schmaucks, D.; Harbusch, K.; and Wahlster, W. 1986. Combining Deictic Gestures and Natural Language for Referent Identification. In *Proceedings of 11th International Conference on Computational Linguistics*, Bonn, Germany, 356–361.

Kobsa, A., and Wahlster, W. (eds.). 1989. *User Models in Dialog Systems*. Berlin: Springer-Verlag.

Maybury, M. T. 1993. *Intelligent Multimedia Interfaces*. Menlo Park, CA/Cambridge, MA: AAAI/MIT Press.

Maybury, M. T. 1994. Automated Explanation and Natural Language Generation. In Sabourin, C., (ed.), *Computational Text Generation*, Bibliography, Montreal: Infolingua, 1–88.

Maybury, M. T. 1995. Research in Multimedia Parsing and Generation. In McKevitt, P. (ed.), *Artificial Intelligence Review: Special Issue on the Integration of Natural Language and Vision Processing*, 9(2–3): 103–127.

Maybury, M. T. 1997. *Intelligent Multimedia Information Retrieval*. Menlo Park, CA/Cambridge, MA: AAAI/MIT Press.

MUC-6. 1995. *Proceedings of the Sixth Message Understanding Conference*. Advanced Research Projects Agency Information Technology Office, Columbia, MD, November 6–8.

Oviatt, S., and Wahlster, W. (eds.). 1997. *Special Issue on Multimodal Interfaces. Human-Computer Interaction: A Journal of Theoretical, Empirical, and Methodological Issues, of User Science and of System Design*, 12(1, 2). Mahwah, NJ: Lawrence Erlbaum Associates.

Pattabhiraman, T., and Cercone, N. (eds.). 1991. *Computational Intelligence: Special Issue on Natural Language Generation*, 7(4) November. National Research Council of Canada.

Pelachaud, C.; Badler, N. I.; and Steedman, M. 1996. Generating Facial Expressions for Speech. *Cognitive Science*, 20(1): 1–46.

Perkowitz, M., and Etzioni, O. 1997. Adaptive Web Sites: An AI Challenge. In *Proceedings of Fifteenth International Joint Conference on Artificial Intelligence (IJCAI '97)*, Nagoya, Japan, August 23–29, 16–21.

Schneider-Hufschmidt, M.; Kühme, T.; and Malinowski, U. (eds.). 1993. *Adaptive User Interfaces: Principles and Practice*. Amsterdam: Elsevier.

Sullivan, J., and Tyler, S. (eds.). 1991. *Intelligent User Interfaces*. New York: ACM Press.

TREC-1. 1993. First Text REtrieval Conference (TREC-1), NIST, Harmon, Donna K. (ed.). NIST Special Publication 500-207, March.

Waibel, A., and Lee, K. 1990. *Readings in Speech Recognition*. San Francisco, CA: Morgan Kaufmann.

Webber, B. L., and Nilsson, N. J. (eds.). 1985. *Readings in Artificial Intelligence: A Collection of Articles*. San Francisco: Morgan Kaufmann.

SECTION I

Multimedia Input Analysis

When humans converse with one another, they utilize multiple channels of communication, including spoken and written language, gesture, and gaze. Each of these channels draws upon differing perceptual modalities, including the auditory, visual, and tactile senses, and different codes, including linguistic, graphical, and gestural. Just as human-human communication exploits multiple modalities, researchers have investigated the utility of enriching human-machine interactions with such capabilities.

This section considers techniques developed to support integrated input from multiple sources (e.g., typed and spoken language, gesture, eye/lip movements). The benefits of providing multiple means of communication include the following:

- *Efficiency*—for example, objects with geospatial extent are efficiently identified with a map and gesture; identifying sets of objects with abstract properties is done more quickly linguistically
- *Redundancy*—for example, conveying the location of an entity both in language and gesture can increase the likelihood of reference identification
- *Perceptability*—for example, certain tasks such as feature detection, orientation, and/or reference identification may be facilitated in spatial context
- *Naturalness*—for example, empowering the user to use those forms of communication chosen in human-human interaction
- *Accuracy*—for example, gesture may enable more precise spatial indication over voice
- *Synergy*—for example, one channel of communication can help refine imprecision, modify the meaning, and/or resolve ambiguities in another

The first paper in this section is by Dick Bolt and represents some of the first research to investigate these issues. In his classic "Put-That-There" paper, Bolt describes an application in which a user situated in a mixed virtual/real space manipulates displayed blocks-world shapes around a large-screen graphics display using both spoken language and gestural input. The user can create, modify, move, and delete objects and in the process use pronouns such as "that" or "there" to refer to objects or their locations, which are resolved by corresponding gestural input. The user can further name objects, switching the speech recognizer from recognition to training mode. Although the application used a small vocabulary by today's standards, the synergistic use of voice and gesture was groundbreaking.

Like Bolt's novel work, the second paper by Phil Cohen, Mary Dalrymple, Douglas Moran, Fernando Pereira, Joseph Sullivan, Robert Gargan Jr., Jon Schlossberg, and Sherman Tyler reports on the synergistic use of direct manipulation and natural language, also arguing that the use of both overcomes some of the limitations of each. The authors indicate the strengths of direct manipulation (e.g., visibility of options, direct access) and natural language (e.g., expression of quantification, the use of context to abbreviate expression using devices such as pronouns, definite noun phrases, and tense). They also point out their individual weaknesses. Challenges associated with language processing include anaphoric resolution, sense disambiguation, phrasal attachment, reasoning about quantification, and the opacity of linguistic coverage. In contrast, direct manipulation suffers from limited expressiveness and the need to navigate through menus to select objects because of the inability to directly describe and/or access them. The authors describe experiences with two systems that extend the natural language question-answering system, Chat, in the domain of manufacturing process decision support (in particular, the SHOPTALK (SRI) and CHORIS (Lockheed Space) systems). They demonstrate how the ability to specify objects and actions by natural language description complements direct manipulation (e.g., sequential but mixed pointing and typing), whereas direct manipulation facilitates learning and selection of available objects and actions as well as the establishment of context that can be exploited during anaphoric resolution. In particular, answers to questions are presented in their own window, enabling interpretation of follow-up questions within this constrained context. Users can also graphically view the discourse as a tree of queries from which the user can select to return to particular contexts. Further, a user can invoke "natural language forms" by selecting from a menu of actions and then fill in the graphically presented arguments using natural language.

The CUBRICON system described in the third paper, by Jeanette Neal, Carol Thielman, Zuzana Dobes, S. M. Haller, and Stuart Shapiro, goes beyond this work to investigate the integration of natural language and gesture for both user input and system output. The authors report the ability to interpret typed or spoken natural language together with *simultaneous* gesture on one of two graphical displays (a map and a forms/table-based interface). CUBRICON interprets simultaneous input using a multimodal (generalized augmented transition network) grammar and is able to both disambiguate multimodal references as well as infer the intended referent of a point gesture that is inconsistent with associated natural language input. After an input is interpreted and executed (e.g., performing a database retrieval, a mission planning system action, or simply an interface manipulation), a multimodal response is composed and generated to potentially include coordinated natural language, gesture, and graphical expressions. CUBRICON exploits several knowledge sources for both parsing and generation, including a lexicon, multimodal grammar, task/domain model, user model, and discourse model. In this last case, the discourse model includes both a focus list of expressed entities and propositions as well as a display model representing visible windows and their contents. These models are exploited, for example, to handle the ambiguity and imprecision of pointing, for example, performing a bounded incremental search around an imprecise gesture to find the closest object that satisfies semantic constraints expressed in any accompanying language. They also are exploited by an intelligent window manager (IWM), which utilizes a number of quantitative metrics (e.g., recency of window creation, number and importance of objects in a window, recency of last interaction with and frequency of use of window), as well as the discourse model to dynamically apportion generated media to screen real estate using placement heuristics (e.g., prefer placing maps on the color monitor).

Whereas prior efforts at multistream input integration have assumed sequential, nonoverlapping input, the chapter by David Koons, Carlton Sparrell, and Kristinn R. Thórisson reports on integrating simultaneous input from speech, gaze, and hand gestures in the context of interactions with a two-dimensional firefighting map and a three-dimensional virtual reality blocks world. In the latter domain, the three modes are processed into a common frame-based encoding and jointly interpreted to resolve references. In one example, the user says "that blue square below the red triangle" and looks in the upper right quadrant of the screen and points in that direction. The system identifies multiple blue squares in that region of the map and resolves the linguistic reference using information from the gesture and gaze channels.

This cross-channel integration is enabled by representing and processing each channel at multiple levels of abstraction. For example, the low-level data from the gesture input device (a data glove that outputs x, y, z, pitch, yaw, and roll) is first characterized into features of posture (straight, relaxed, or closed fingers), orientation (normal and longitudinal vectors from palm), and motion (moving, stopped). This stream of features is grouped by rules into structures termed "gestlets," which characterize higher-level gestures, such as attack, sweep, or end reference. Additional processing recognizes not only deictic but also iconic gestures (representing object shape, spatial relations, and actions) and pantomimic gestures (representing manipulation of objects or tools).

Analogous to the gesture recognizer, the eye tracker classifies input into fixations, saccades, and blinks. Speech-related hand movements are processed to an intermediate level of representation without automatically assigning a deictic or symbolic meaning. Simultaneous channel processing enables cross-channel cueing and constraint for referent determination (e.g., use of deictic linguistic expressions suggests deictic gestures). Interpretation from within a frame-based representation occurs later and takes advantage of information from the other modes and from the context. In addition to aiding interpretation, gesture and gaze information has future utility beyond input disambiguation, such as indicating interest, suggesting turn-taking in dialog, and indicating fatigue.

The paper by Rob Jacob further explores interaction techniques that incorporate natural eye movement into human-computer dialog in an unobtrusive manner. In Jacob's experiments with a naval ship display, a nonintrusive eye tracker measures the visual line of gaze by simultaneously tracking corneal reflection and pupil outline using a light shown at the eye. A servo-controlled mirror compensates for user head motion. The most common eye movements are saccades (sudden movements) and fixations (200–600 ms) on a particular region or object during which the eye actually makes small movements of less than one degree width of the fovea, a small region at the center of the retina. Continuous, raw data from the eye tracker is first filtered for noise, fixations are detected, and discrete tokens are output as a result. In practice, Jacob found the need to provide calibration local to particular areas of the screen that enhance object selection and other interaction techniques. Further, he reports a fixation recognition algorithm (that detects sequences of 100 ms during which eye position changes no more than 0.5 degrees) that better reflects user-visible behavior in the interface (reported as start, 50-ms continuation, and end of fixation). These tokens are multiplexed together with keyboard and mouse events and input into the user interface management system. Jacob explores several gaze-driven interaction techniques in which he observes that gaze enhances interaction in tasks such as object selection (e.g., selection after a 150–200-ms dwell time); selection of the active or "listener" window (providing a short delay following fixation to filter out brief, cross-window glances); text scrolling; continuous attribute display (e.g., gazing at objects that results in a display of their attributes in an adjacent display); and object movement (e.g., eyes-based selection coupled with mouse gesture movement or an eyes-only selection and movement, the latter of which users prefer, although destination selection is more difficult with the eyes when no object is present). Jacob also observed that eye input alone is appropriate for menu pull-down (after a 400-ms dwell) and command highlighting (following a 100-ms dwell); however, a button-down was more effective for menu selection because a 1-second dwell was required on menu items to enable users to recognize unfamiliar items. As these experiments illustrate, in spite of the fact that human eye gaze is less accurate than, for example, gestural input, this additional channel promises benefits such as nonintrusiveness and positive user experiences with an interface that responds to indirect rather than direct input. Jacob's careful incorporation of eye tracking into interaction techniques followed by task-based evaluation presents an important approach to the incremental incorporation of supporting behavior—intelligent or otherwise—into the interface.

Taken together, these papers advance our ability to enable humans to utilize the full extent of their linguistic, gestural, and gaze input, with the benefits outlined at the beginning of this section. The papers demonstrate mechanisms to support interpretation of parallel, imprecise, and ambiguous multimedia input; they demonstrate more natural, efficient interaction, synergistically processing multimodal input. The papers also illustrate the context-dependent, multifunctional nature of multimodal input, providing rich ground for future research.

Remaining research issues include providing users with sensors that are less obtrusive than current gloves and head-borne eye trackers. These untethered eye and gesture trackers might use, for example, image processing to detect gesture and gaze or gloveless electric field sensing of gesture. Another important area is moving beyond hand gesture to address full arm and full body descriptions as well as more complex gestures (e.g., iconic, pantomimic) in more complex situations. More sophisticated analysis of other modalities (e.g., speech, gaze) will be required as well. The early systems raise fundamental questions about the relationship to, and need for, extension of attentional and intentional models (e.g., relating gestural actions to states of attention). The need to extend traditional representations with syntactic and semantic characterization of input streams raises the need for appropriate cross-media representations. It is also important to ensure consistency of input and output, the latter of which is the focus of the next section.

"Put-That-There": Voice and Gesture at the Graphics Interface

Richard A. Bolt

Architecture Machine Group
Massachusetts Institute of Technology
Cambridge, Massachusetts 02139

ABSTRACT

Recent technological advances in connected-speech recognition and position sensing in space have encouraged the notion that voice and gesture inputs at the graphics interface can converge to provide a concerted, natural user modality.

The work described herein involves the user commanding simple shapes about a large-screen graphics display surface. Because voice can be augmented with simultaneous pointing, the free usage of pronouns becomes possible, with a corresponding gain in naturalness and economy of expression. Conversely, gesture aided by voice gains precision in its power to reference.

Key Words: Voice input; speech input; gesture; space sensing; spatial data management; man-machine interfaces; graphics; graphics interface.

Category Numbers: 8.2, 6.9.

The work reported herein has been supported by the Cybernetics Technology Division of the Defense Advanced Research Projects Agency, under Contract No. MDA-903-77-C-0037.

INTRODUCTION

Recently, the Architecture Machine Group at the Massachusetts Institute of Technology has been experimenting with the conjoint use of voice-input and gesture-recognition to command events on a large format raster-scan graphics display.

Of central interest is how voice and gesture can be made to inter-orchestrate, actions in one modality amplifying, modifying, disambiguating, actions in the other. The approach involves the significant use of pronouns, effectively as "temporary variables" to reference items on the display.

The interactions to be described are staged in the MIT Architecture Machine Group's "Media Room," a physical facility where the user's terminal is literally a room into which one steps, rather than a desk-top CRT before which one is perched.

The Media Room Sketched in Figure 1, is the size of a personal office: about sixteen feet long, eleven feet wide, and about eight feet from floor to ceiling. The floor is raised to accommodate cabling from an ensemble of mini-computers which drives displays and devices resident in the Media Room. The walls, finished in dark brown pile fabric, house banks of loudspeakers on either side of a wall-sized, frosted-glass projection screen, and on either side and a bit to the rear of the user's chair.

The user's chair is a vinyl-covered Eames-type chair, exactly as comes from the furniture store, except for two types of instumentation based in its arms. Either arm bears a small, one-inch high joystick, of the non-displacing variety, sensitive to pressure and direction. Nearby each joystick is a two-inch on edge, square-shaped touch sensitive pad.

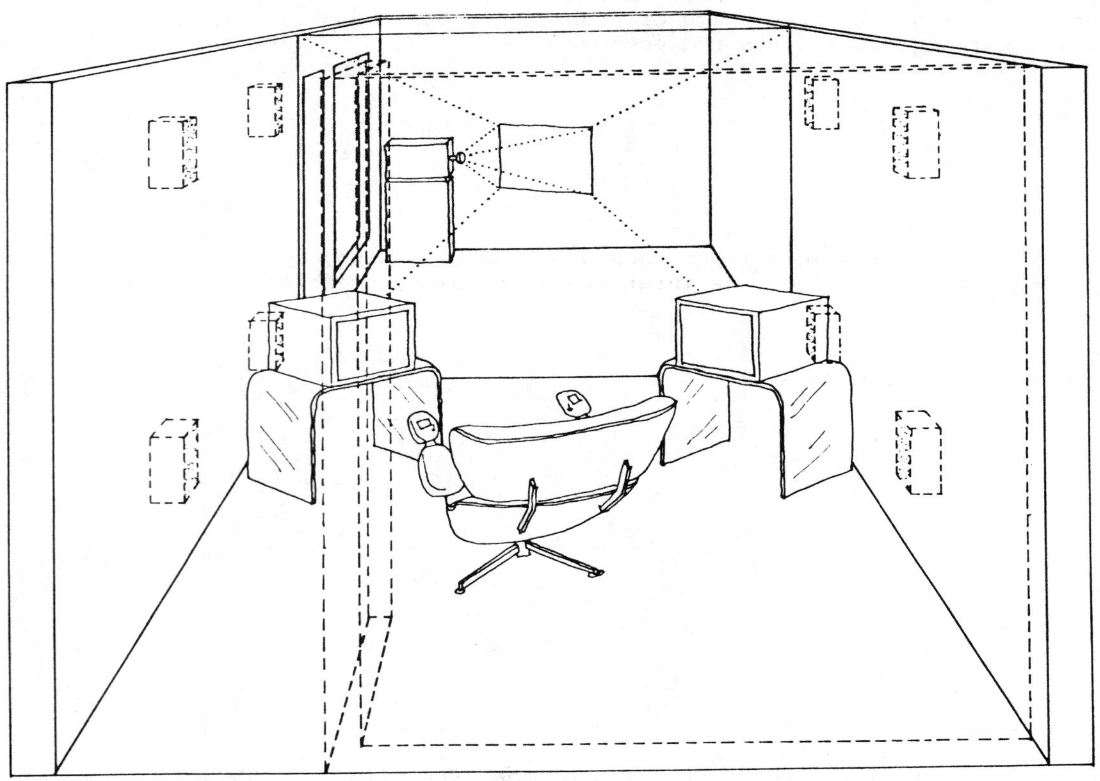

Figure 1

Sketch of Media Room

The wall-sized screen, about eight feet to the user's front, is served by back-projection from a color TV light-valve projector situated in an adjoining room. Color TV monitors are situated on either side of the user's chair, each with its tube face overlain with a transparent, touch-sensitive pad.

Apart from its role as an embodiment of the user terminal as an "informational surround [1]," the Media Room with its user chair has played a key role in our researches into a "Spatial Data-Management System, or SDMS [2]."

The specific rationale for spatially indexing data derives from our everyday experience of retrieving items, say, from our desktop: the phone to the right and above the blotter; the appointment calendar in the lower right; the "in-box" nearby the ashtray at the lower left, and so forth. Retrieval is natural and automatic for these items, with even an apparently "messy" desk having a spatial logic well-known to its creator and user, the knowledge of where this and that item are located being encoded conjointly in mental and motor models of the layout of the desktop.

The user of SDMS retrieves information not by typing names, i.e., alphanumeric strings on a keyboard terminal, but instead uses joystick and, occasionally, touch controls to navigate about in a helicopter-like manner to where specific caches of information reside in a rich graphics world of color and sound.

The world of information in SDMS, dubbed "Dataland," appears in its entirety upon one of the color TV monitors near-by the user chair. A small transparent rectangular overlay, a "you-are-here" marker, can be moved and positioned about Dataland by the user's managing of the chair's right-hand joystick (or by direct touch on the TV screen, if desired). That sub-portion of the Dataland surface indicated by the "you-are-here" rectangle is portrayed with increased detail on the large screen, effectively a magnifying window onto Dataland. The left-hand joystick on the user chair enables the user to zoom-in upon information to get a closer look at any of a number of multi-media data-types (e.g., maps, electronic "books," videodisc episodes), and perhaps to peruse them with the aid of an associated touch-sensitive "Key-map" which comes up on the other TV monitor by the user chair.

The Media Room setting, in addition to its power to generate a convincing impression of interacting with an implicit, "virtual" world of data behind the frame of the physical interface, implies yet another realm or order of space rife with possibilities for interaction: the actual space of the Media Room itself.

The sheer extent of the Media Room's physical interface creates a "real-space" environment. The user's focal situation amidst an ensemble of several screens of various sizes creates a set of geometrical relationships quite apart from any purely logical relationship between any one screen's content and that of any other.

Properly orchestrated, the two spatial orders, virtual graphical space, and the user's immediate real space in the Media Room, can converge to become effectively one continuous interactive space.

User awareness of this common space is implicit: the user points, gestures, references "up," "down," "...to the left of...," and so on, freely and naturally, precisely because the user is situated in a real space. Tapping this interactive potential is rooted in two new technical offerings in the areas of: 1) connected speech recognition; 2) position sensing in space.

SPEECH AND SPACE: THE TECHNOLOGIES

Two broad categories of currently commercially available speech recognizers may be distinguished: those which recognize discrete or isolated utterances, and those which recognize connected speech.

With those speech recognition systems restricted to discrete utterances, parsing of the speech signal into word-by-word tokens, is not done. The human speaker must talk to the system in a "clipped" or word-by-word style.

The recognition of connected speech has been a classic challenge in the field of speech recognition generally [3]. The DP-100 Connected Speech Recognition System (CSRS) by NEC (Nippon Electric Company) America, Inc. is capable of a limited amount of recognition of connected speech [4]. No pause between words is necessary, and up to five words or "utterances" are permitted per spoken sentence.

The recognition response time at the end of each sentence is about 300 milliseconds. Output is a display of the text of the utterance on an alphanumeric visual display, and/or a set of ASCII codes (numbers or letters) to be received by a processor interfaced with the NEC system.

The device's vocabulary, held in the recognizer's active memory as a set of word reference patterns, is a maximum of 120 words. With an optional "discrete utterance" mode, the size of the active vocabulary in the system's memory may be larger, about 1000 words. Except for the digits "one" to "ten," which must be spoken twice by the user when "training" the machine, each word in training mode need be spoken only once. The standard system comes with a lightweight, head-mounted microphone. We look forward to eventual use of a "shotgun" microphone in the Media Room, remote from but aimed at the speaker.

A space position and orientation sensing technology suitable for our intentions was found to be made by Polhemus Navigation Science, Inc., of Essex, Vermont. This system, called ROPAMS (Remote Object Position Attitude Measurement System) is based on measurements made of a nutating magnetic field. Essentials of the system are as follows.

Three coils are epoxied into a plastic cube, their mountings mutually orthogonal to correspond to x,y, and z spatial axes. Two such cubes are involved: one, about 1.5 inches on edge which acts as a transmitter, and another, 0.75 inches on edge, which functions as a sensor. The arrangement of coils in either cube essentially creates an antenna that is sensitive in all three orientations.

The transmitter cube radiates a nutating dipole field pointed at the sensor cube. When the pointing vector is correct, the field strength received will be constant. When it is not, there will be an error signal consisting of the nutation frequency. This error is used to generate the output pointing angles, and to re-aim the transmitter.

The orientation in space of the sensor cube is determined by transforming the differential signals from the three individual orthogonal coils in the sensor cube. The sensor cube's distance from the transmitter cube is computed by the $1/R^3$ fall-off of signal strength from the radiating dipole, or by triangulation with an additional radiator.

The sensor cube is very lightweight, and although it has a small cord running out of it, it is not an especially troublesome item to handle. Such sensors can readily be wrist-mounted, worn as finger rings, mounted on the visor of baseball caps, or put on a sort of "lab jacket" in lieu of cuff and collar buttons or epaulets.

COMMANDS

Suppose the user seated before the Media Room's large screen, with a space-sensing cube attached to a watchband on his wrist, and that the system's microphone is ready and listening. Some commands from the system's current repertoire illustrative of voice and pointing in concert are the following:

"Create . . ."

In our demonstration system, the large screen is initially either clear, or bears some simple backdrop such as a map. Against this background, simple items are called into existence, moved about, replicated, their attributes altered, and then may be ordered to vanish.

The items used are basic shapes: circles, squares, diamonds. They are non-representational in that the thing *is* the shape. Variable attributes are: *color* (red, yellow, orange, green, blue. . .), and *size* (large, medium, small).

For example, the user points to some spot on the large screen. A small, white "x" cursor on the screen provides running visual feedback for pointing. The user then says:

"Create a blue square there."

The size of the square is not given explicitly in this example command; the default size, "medium," is used. A blue square appears on the spot where the user is pointing. There is no default color; some color from the pre-programmed parent ensemble of color names must be given. The same is true for shape.

Where the feed-back cursor is residing on the screen at the time the spoken "there" occurs becomes the spot where the to-be-created item is placed. The occurrence of the spoken "there" is thus functionally a "when"; that is, it serves as a "voice button" for the x,y cursor action of the pointing gesture.

Accordingly, a considerable pause before the occurrence of the "there" is permissible, i.e.:

"Create a blue square . . . there."

The complete utterance in effect is a "call" to a Create routine, which routine expects certain parameters to be supplied. Before the user recites "there," the routine is parameter hung. The awaited parameter is input, completing the conjunction of x,y pointing input from the wrist-borne space sensor with the utterance "there."

Figure 2 shows the user having created a number of items on the screen before him.

"Move . . ."

The user can readily move items about the screen, and has available a variety of ways in which to express the complete "move" command.

Consider the user command:

"Move the blue triangle to the right of the green square."

This example command relies on voice mode only. Should, for example, there exist only one triangle on the screen at the time the command is given, the adjective "blue" bears no information, and could be omitted; the same logic applies for the qualifier green in "green square."

We note in passing that in the phrase ". . . the green square," the attribute "green" as voiced is treated simply as part of the name of the item as originally created. That is, the color name is used in a nominal sense, as in Moscow's "Red Square," where "Red" is functionally part of a proper name, not a signal that we should expect a city square to be painted all in red.

Apropos of color, a more ambitious "interpretive" approach might be to map the utterance "green" to pixel values, the matching mediated through the classical CIE color space, partitioned into a number of referenceable regions. The partitioning of the CIE color space on the basis of an ensemble of color names could be programmer determined on an ad hoc basis, or the partitioning might involve a quite sophisticated calibration on the basis of having subject observers name or classify displayed colors. The essential point is that the mapping from attribute-name to item-attribute can be well defined, even though it may be as complex as one cares to attempt.

In any event, the result of the above command is that the blue triangle upon "hearing" its name, de-saturates as immediate feedback that it has been "addressed," disappears from its present site to re-appear centered in a spot to the right of the green square.

The exact positioning "to the right" is programmer determined in our version; some reasonable placement is executed. The meaning, intent and interpretation of relational expressions in graphic space is a complex issue [5,6]; the

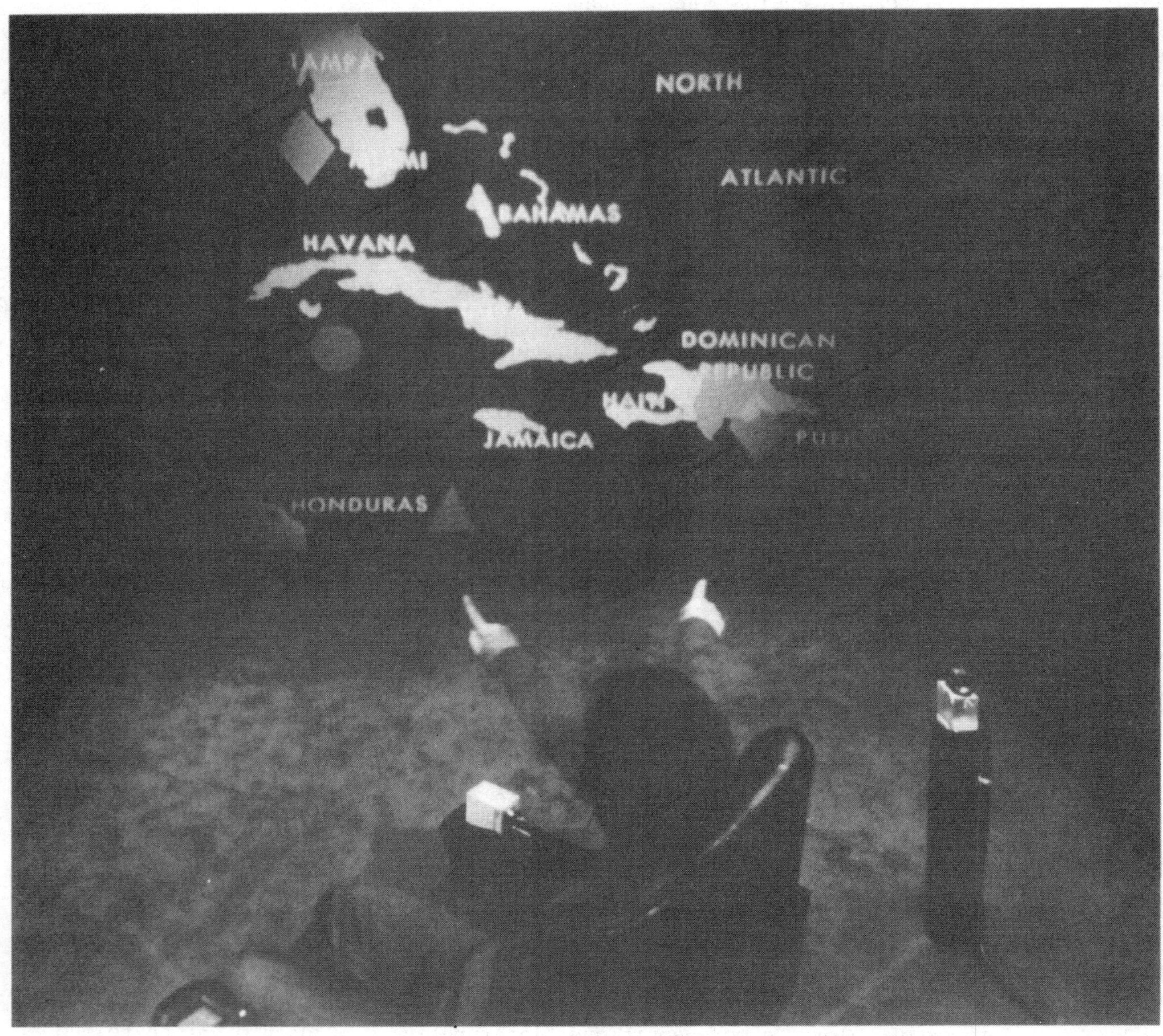

Figure 2

Talking and pointing to items on the Media Room's large screen. Here, the items are circle and diamond shapes being moved about against a backdrop of a Caribbean map. A double exposure effect catches two images of the user's right arm, strapped to which is the smaller of the pair of space-sensing cubes (covered by the user's cuff). On a pedestal to the right of the user chair is a lucite block, and to the top of this block is attached the larger transmitter cube.

important thing is that the item is now where the user has ordered it to be, and he can make minor modifications in position later.

Now, in our example action, the user might equally well have said:

"Move that to the right of the green square."

In this option, the user employs the pronoun "that," simultaneously pointing to what is intended, the pointing act being a motor analogue to the speech string: ". . . the blue triangle . . . "

Notice that in this mode of giving the command, the user may not only omit the words "blue" and "triangle," he need not even know what the thing is, or what it is called. In our simple graphics world, what anything is, is in a subtle and interesting sense, where it is.

"That" is thus defined as whatever is pointed out; effectively, it is "ostensively defined" [7]. For the namer, at least, the process is not unlike that of telling a small child what things "are": for example, pointing at a cat, and saying "cat" or "kitty." The meaning of the word is given by indicating what is the intended referent in the context of alternatives, namely, whatever else is in the scene.

This process of "pronomialization" can readily be extended in our simple graphical example. The intended target spot to which the item is to be moved can be rendered as

"Put that there"

where there, now indicated by gesture, serves in lieu of the entire phrase ". . . to the right of the green square." The power of this function is even more general. The place description ". . . to the right of the green square" presupposes an item in the vicinity for reference: namely, the green square. There may be no plausible reference frame in terms of already extant items for a word description of where the moved item is to go. The intended spot, however, may readily be indicated by voice-and-pointing: there. In this function, as well as others, some variation in expression is understandably a valuable option; thus, a mini-thesaurus of common synonyms, such as "move," "put," "place," etc., is built into the vocabulary.

"Copy . . ." as a command is simply a variant of the move action, except that the image of the item to be moved also remains in place at the original spot.

"Make that . . ."

The attributes of any item in this graphic mini-universe that the user has called into existence by voice and gesture can be modified. Here, the attributes are those of color and size.

For example, the utterance:

"Make the blue triangle smaller"

causes the referenced item to become reduced in size. The mode of reference in this instance is via voice alone, but the user could as well have said, pointing to the desired item:

"Make that smaller . . ."

The command:

"Make that a large blue diamond"

uttered while the user points at a small yellow circle causes the indicated transformation.

Extrapolations readily suggest themselves, e.g., the command line:

"Make that (indicating some item) like that (indicating some other item).

The second "that" is, functionally, a when to read the x,y coordinate of pointing. The item indicated when the second "that" is uttered becomes the "model" for change, and internally, the action is an expunging of the first referenced item, to be replaced in a "copy"-like fashion by the second referenced item.

"Delete . . ."

The "delete" command (synonyms: "erase; expunge; take out. . . ," etc.) allows the user to drop selected items from display.

As before, the "operand" of the command can be:

". . . the large blue circle"

or

". . .that" (pointing to some item).

Again, variations and extrapolations of the basic notion suggest themselves: global expunging, "clear" or "delete everything," in order to wipe the graphical slate clean; or "Detete everything to the left of this (drawing a line vertically down the face of the screen)."

NAMING

Consider a blue square that is present upon the screen. The user points to it, saying:

"Call that . . . the calendar"

with the intention of later somehow elaborating the blue square at that node into a graphical "appointment book."

The initial portion of this utterance, "Call that . . .," when processed by the recognizer unit results in codes being sent over to the host system signalling that a "naming" command has been issued. The x,y coordinates of what item is singled out by pointing are noted by the host system.

The host system then immediately directs the speech recognition unit to switch from "recognition mode" to "training mode" so that the recognizer will add the latter part of the utterance, ". . . the calendar," as a new entry in its file of word reference patterns. Upon completion of this action, the recognizer is directed to go back into recognition mode, to be ready for the next verbal input.

As the communications for switching the recognizer under host-system control between recognition and training modes currently takes a finite amount of real-time, a brief pause (indicated in the command above by three dots) must occur in the spoken command line to accommodate the time taken for the mode shift. However, the user tends to pause at precisely that point in the command line anyway, waiting for momentary desaturation of the blue square. This quick desaturation of an addressed item was noted earlier in this paper as being the system's way of giving visual feedback that the user has indeed "contacted" the item.

This spontaneous pause for feedback fortunately operates in this context to "mask" for the user the system's need for a pause in input. However, the obligation to pause represents to the system designer something of a break-down in the general convenience of continuous vs discrete speech input. An eventual strategy for relieving the necessity for a user pause in speech is the augmentation of the "intelligence" resident in a speech recognizer unit so that it to some extent interprets as well as recognizes.

For example, upon the recognition of certain "key" words or phrases within the input utterance, the recognizer itself switches directly from recognition to training mode so that sub-portions of the input utterance are handled appropriately.

In the case of the "Call that . . ." or naming command, the action of the now "intelligent" recognizer would be in effect to truncate-off from the "front-end" of the original input speech signal that span of signal corresponding to successive recognized words of the command, the non-recognized residue of the speech line to be then assumed as the new name to be assimilated by the recognizer to its internal reference pattern lexicon. In order to maintain overall coordination with the host system, the recognizer would of course simultaneously transmit ASCII codes for recognized or learned words, together with any relevant "control" codes.

While such a strategy may eliminate the need for a within-sentence speaker pause, the general problem of "coarticulation" remains: the phonemic properties of the speech signal for any word are influenced by what words are spoken with it, what particular words precede or follow the word in question (Cf. reference 3, p. 518). Thus, while not required to pause, the speaker yet must enunciate very clearly, particularly when about to utter the new name to be added.

SUMMARY

The foregoing rudimentary set of commands, concerning themselves with the simple management of a limited ensemble of non-representative objects, is intended to suggest the versatility and ease of use that can enter upon the management of graphic space with voice and gesture. More real-life examples of commanding about "things" in a more meaningful space come readily to mind: moving ships about a harbor map in planning a harbor facility; moving battalion formations about as overlays on a terrain map; facilities planning, where rooms and hallways as rectangles are tried out "here" and "there."

The power of the described technique is that indications of what is to be done with these visible, out-there-on-view items can be expressed spontaneously and naturally in ways which are compatible with the spirit and nature of the display: one is pointing to them, addressing them in *spoken* words, not typed symbols.

Further, the *pronoun* as verbal tag achieves in the graphical world the same high usefulness it has in ordinary discourse by being pronounced in the presence of a pointed to, visible graphic which functionally defines its meaning.

ACKNOWLEDGEMENTS

The programming and systems expertise of Chris Schmandt and Eric Hulteen underlay the implementation and development of the concepts described in this paper. Their efforts are duly appreciated.

REFERENCES

1. Negroponte, N *The Media Room*. Report for ONR and DARPA. MIT, Architecture Machine Group, Cambridge, MA, December 1978.

2. Bolt, R.A. *Spatial Data-Management*. DARPA Report. MIT, Architecture Machine Group, Cambridge, MA, March 1979.

3. Reddy, D.R. Speech recognition by machine: a review. *Proceeding of the IEEE*, *64*, 4 (April 1976), 501-531.

4. Robinson, A.L. More people are talking to computers as speech recognition enters the real world. (Research News) (First of two articles) *Science*, *203*, (16 February 1979), 634-638.

5. Sondeheimer, N.K. Spatial reference and natural-language machine control. *International Journal of Man-Machine Studies*, *8*, (1976), 329-336.

6. Winston, P. Learning structural descriptions from examples. MIT Project MAC, TR-76, 1970.

7. Olson, D.R. Language and thought: Aspects of a cognitive theory of semantics. *Psychological Review*, *77*, (1970), 257-273.

"Put-That-There": Voice and Gesture at the Graphics Interface

Richard A. Bolt

Over a weekend in mid-May 1979, I outlined an approach to creating and manipulating items on a graphics display using a magnetic space-sensing cube in concert with connected speech recognition technology. I presented my thoughts in a memo to my colleagues at the MIT Architecture Machine Group (precursor of today's MIT Media Lab). The scheme seemed plausible, and we decided to go ahead and build a demonstration prototype. While we already had a couple of space-sensing cubes in-house, we had to place a rush order for the speech recognizer—an item, in those days, by no means inexpensive.

Things moved fast after the recognizer arrived. In less than two weeks, Chris Schmandt (then a grad student, now leading speech research at the Media Lab) had designed, written, and debugged an initial version of the program—by then dubbed "Put-That-There." Even in its first form (the items created and manipulated being simple squares, circles, triangles, and rectangles), the demo had undeniable impact. You saw immediately what was going on: a person addressing a computer display using everyday speech and gesture. Chris proceeded to create a second, more elaborate version of Put-That-There—one that let you create and direct a fleet of ships about the Caribbean; a variant of this second version involved icons of forts, campsites, and meetinghouses set against a map of colonial Boston.

In the years since, as part of an extended agenda in multimodal natural dialog, my students and I have developed prototype systems, demonstrating, for example, two-handed freehand gestural input with accompanying speech (Bolt and Herranz 1992) as well as concurrent speech, gesture, and gaze input (Koons et al. 1993). But even though these systems were vastly more sophisticated in both instrumentation and software intelligence than was Put-That-There, that earlier demo yet retains a certain éclat. Even after 17 years, looking at a video of the demo, you sense something special when Chris, seated before our media room's large screen, raises his hand, points, and says "Put that (pointing at a blue triangle) . . . there (pointing to a spot above and to the left)," and lo, the triangle moves where he told it to. I have yet to see an interface demo that makes its point as cleanly and succinctly as did that very first version of Put-That -There.

REFERENCES

Bolt, R. A., and Herranz, E. 1992. Two-Handed Gesture in Multimodal Natural Dialog. In *Proceedings of UIST '92, Fifth Annual Symposium on User Interface Software and Technology*, Monterey, CA, November 15–18, 7–14.

Koons, D. B.; Sparrell, C. J.; and Thorisson, K. R. 1993. Integrating Simultaneous Input from Speech, Gaze, and Hand Gestures. In Maybury, M. (ed.), *Intelligent Multi-Media Interfaces*, 257–276. Menlo Park, CA: AAAI Press.

Synergistic Use of Direct Manipulation and Natural Language

Philip R. Cohen
Mary Dalrymple
Douglas B. Moran
Fernando C.N. Pereira
Artificial Intelligence Center
SRI International
333 Ravenswood Ave
Menlo Park, CA 94025

Joseph W. Sullivan
Robert A. Gargan Jr
Jon L. Schlossberg
Sherman W. Tyler
Artificial Intelligence Center
Lockheed Missiles and Space Co
2710 Sand Hill Road
Menlo Park, CA 94025

KEYWORDS: User Interfaces, Natural Language, Direct Manipulation

Abstract

This paper shows how the integration of natural language with direct manipulation produces a multimodal interface that overcomes limitations of these techniques when used separately. Natural language helps direct manipulation in being able to specify objects and actions by description, while direct manipulation enables users to learn which objects and actions are available in the system. Furthermore, graphical rendering and manipulation of context provides a partial solution to difficult problems of natural language anaphora.

1 Introduction

In this paper, we show how a multimodal interface integrating natural language and direct manipulation can provide advantages over the pure use of either technology. The overriding goal of our work is to provide the user the power and flexibility of natural language as well as the use of direct manipulation in a decision-support environment. We will demonstrate throughout this paper that by integrating the two technologies, we are simplifying the system's job of understanding users' queries, and that users will have an easier and more expressive means of achieving their goals. Ultimately, the utility of the technology needs to be borne out empirically. This paper does not present empirical results, but rather an implemented approach that generates a space of possible system designs that will be investigated empirically.

Direct manipulation is appropriate when the task is such that a limited number of actions can be taken at a given time, and the objects to which the actions are applied can be made visible on the screen in a coherent fashion. Natural language is particularly appropriate for describing objects and time periods that cannot be referred to directly (e.g., in environments in which it is inconvenient or impossible to provide screen representation of all user options). Another strength of natural language is its convenience for expressing quantificational information. Finally, the use of pronouns, definite noun phrases, and tense allows speakers' utterances to depend on context for their interpretation. Use of context often makes interaction much more efficient.

A number of problems pose difficulties for each approach, however. For natural language interaction, these problems include the use of context in resolving anaphoric reference, word sense disambiguation, and the attachment of prepositional phrases, as well as the ability to reason efficiently with quantified statements. Another often-cited weakness of "pure" natural language systems is the opacity of the system's linguistic and conceptual coverage. Although users know the system cannot understand everything, they do not know precisely what it can understand.

On the other hand, direct manipulation interfaces have difficulties allowing users to apply selected functions to unknown arguments. This weakness is a symptom of their inability to express procedures or general information directly, such as quantificational information, and an inability to describe objects rather than merely select or name them. Yet another weakness arises from the necessity of using hierarchies of menus that stand between a user and one action he/she wants to perform. When many actions are possible, it is cumbersome to have to navigate a menu tree to invoke a particular one.

There is clearly a spectrum of possibilities for integrating natural language and direct manipulation. At one end is the NL Menu system at Texas Instruments [16]. Users of that system are able to compose a query by incrementally selecting the set of words from among those that would correctly complete that query given the previously selected words. There is not space here to provide an in-depth discussion of the advantages and disadvantages of NLMenu. Several intelligent interface systems use natural language and direct manipulation components (CUBRICON [11], XTRA [18]), but they are just beginning to explore the integration of these technologies. Like the systems we will describe, CUBRICON and XTRA allow the insertion of a selected object within a natural language query (i.e., a form of deictic reference), but they do not allow the use of natural language with forms nor use the direct manipulation mechanism to constrain context (see section 3).

The techniques described here have been implemented using various versions of Chat [13, 19], a natural-language question-answering system implemented in Prolog. Two systems exist: the SHOPTALK system at SRI, and the CHORIS system at Lockheed. The similarities and differences between the systems are described as needed throughout the paper.

2 Application Domains

We have experimented with a number of application domains, primarily in manufacturing. SHOPTALK is being developed in the domains of semiconductor and circuit-board manufacturing. Data have been gathered from a factory being developed by the South Carolina Research Authority (SCRA), under contract from the Navy. The current application for CHORIS (Computer-Human Object-oriented Reasoning Interface System) is the Automated Center for Electronics (ACE) facility in Lockheed Space Systems Division. Both ACE and the SCRA factory are manufacturing environments consisting of automated electronic insertion and test machines, and stations where operators manually insert components and perform various inspection procedures on assembled circuit boards. The varied nature of the users of such factory systems (e.g., managers, floor supervisors, product assurance inspectors, and operators) make them fertile environments for the study of a variety of issues related to intelligent interfaces to complex systems Figures 1 and 2 are layouts of the factory floors.

The systems allow users to manipulate the manufacturing objects (such as circuit-boards or machines) on the screen through "mouse" operations to invoke commands relevant to those objects. Sample commands might be to move boards from one place to another, or to take a machine offline.

At any time, users can ask English questions about the current state of the factory, and can take actions in which the arguments can either be described or pointed at. CHORIS adapts to particular users by, in part, determining what subsets of commands and which portion of the factory to present. The result of Chat's analysis of the user's question is a logical form and a set

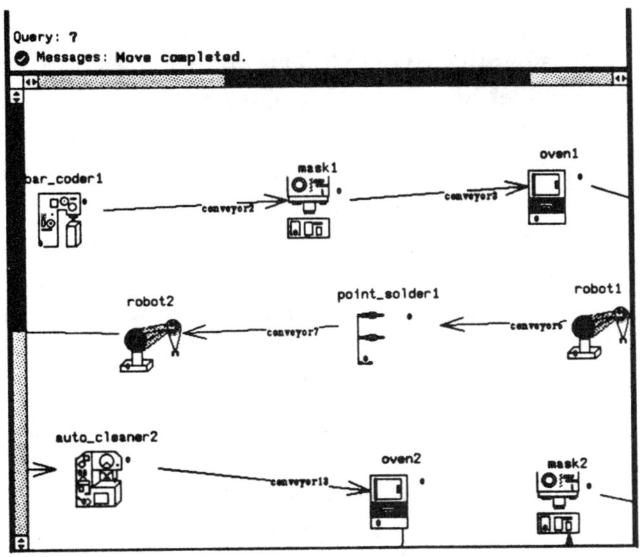

Figure 1: Main window depicting a portion of the SHOPTALK factory floor

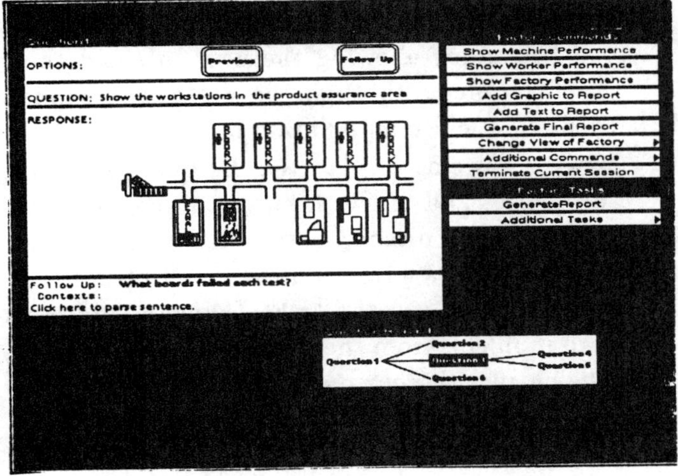

Figure 2: Main screen of CHORIS showing adapted view of ACE factory to a product assurance inspector

of answers that can be rendered as tables, histograms, and other display forms [10, 17]. The display forms presented offer facilities for the user to ask *follow-up* questions, as will be described in detail below.

The remainder of this paper describes three ways in which we have integrated and extended natural language and direct manipulation to support the user better: anaphora and the direct manipulation of context, deixis, and forms.

3 Anaphora and the Direct Manipulation of Context

No one wants to ask just one question. During problem-solving, answers to questions lead the questioner to think of still other required information, and this leads him to ask "follow-up" questions. A characteristic of such questions is the use of anaphora. To date, the determination of the referents for anaphoric noun phrases has been extremely difficult. This paper illustrates a technique that alleviates some of the difficulty. For the present purposes anaphora will be treated as a unitary phenomenon, although it is well-known that pronouns and definite noun phrases behave differently. Many writers have remarked on the need for a pragmatic approach that can draw the needed referent identification inferences from a substantive knowledge base [2, 8]. Others have attempted to constrain that inference process by using *focus spaces* [5], a *focus machine* [15], *centering* [1, 6], and even a purely syntactic approach that is reputed to derive 80-90% correct pronominal referent identifications [9]. In general, the effectiveness of any of the above approaches for resolving anaphoric reference is unknown, and the topic of anaphora in discourse is a locus of substantial research.

3.1 Anaphora and Context

We have integrated a number of anaphoric reference techniques by adapting Hobbs' method [9] for use with Chat in resolving intrasentential anaphora, and by providing a technique for us-

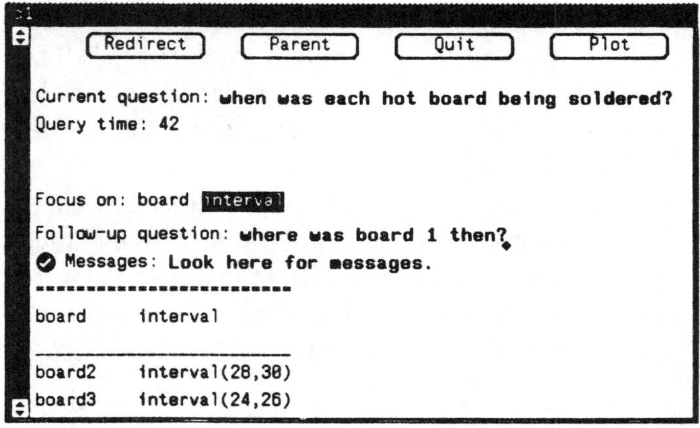

Figure 3: A Follow-up Window

ing and manipulating focus spaces via windows. In particular, answers to questions are presented in their own window, thereby graphically limiting context. To ask a follow-up question to a given question, a user must ask the follow-up in the latter's answer window.

To see the utility of this technique, consider the following example: The user knows that Board1 is defective and that the defect was caused by during the soldering step. One way to determine which high priority (or "hot") boards might have the same defect would be to ask first "When was each hot board being soldered?", to which the system (for this example we will use SHOPTALK) answers with the table in Figure 3. The window shows a table whose columns indicate a set of boards that were soldered, and the time interval for each soldering event. On the window panel are "focus buttons" Board and Interval, indicating that the user can refer to those boards or those intervals anaphorically if he presses the relevant button. In the example, to refer to the time intervals, the user might select the Interval button, and type "Where was board 1 then?" SHOPTALK interprets "then" as anaphorically referring to the selected time intervals.

Both systems constrain the answer to follow-up questions by adding predicates into the questions' logical forms indicating the types of entities being focused upon, and a constraint that the set of entities will be in the given context. We are experimenting with two representations of context—intensional (SHOPTALK), and extensional (CHORIS). The intensional approach provides additional flexibility at the cost of having to retrieve the answers to the previous query again. The extensional approach caches the answers to the previous question and applies further restrictions only to those, but has the limitation that two sets of entities of the same type in the same answer window cannot be distinguished.

3.2 Direct Manipulation of Context

Most natural-language database query systems now allow some limited form of anaphoric reference. However, the context mechanisms developed do not provide a full tree structure, as researchers have argued is needed [5, 14], but rather a bounded linear structure in which users can make anaphoric reference to entities brought into focus by some small number of prior questions and/or answers. A full tree structure is not maintained in part because the semantics of discourse markers (such as "Ok, now"), whose use enables speakers and listeners to navigate the implicit discourse structure tree, is still unclear. We have developed a simple technique allowing the user to avoid these hard problems through the use of the explicit depiction and manipulation of context.

Our systems display the discourse as a tree of queries and allow the user to view and manipulate the discourse graphically (Figure 2). A return to a prior context is effected by selecting a node in the tree. Doing so addresses two problems from the user's perspective: First, the current discourse context is made apparent to the user, allowing him/her to decide explicitly whether or not the present question should follow-up on the answer to a prior one. Second, displaying the discourse as a tree allows the user to follow-up on any query in the discourse, not just those recently asked. As a result, users need not be impeded by the lack of a semantics for "cue phrases"; they can be served adequately by graphically navigating the discourse tree.

4 Pointing and Deixis

The desire to point while speaking is often irresistible. Although not as obvious, users would also like to point along with typing natural language expressions. Pointing allows users to take advantage of the graphical environment of the display to reduce the verbosity of their natural language input, increase the specificity of their requests, and increase the naturalness of the interaction.

Hayes [7] has explored deictic phrases (e.g., "this," "these") and proposed three issues to be addressed. First, the interface must determine when pointing events are related to natural-language input. In our interfaces, pointing events are associated with natural-language input if the user's focus of attention is in a natural-language input window (focus of attention is indicated, in this case, by the blinking of a cursor). Second, the interface must try to minimize the ambiguity of the object being pointed to (e.g., when the graphic items are nested within each other or overlap on the screen). Since deictic references in our system will occur in the midst of typing a natural-language query, the context of the linguistic input will often clarify the intended referent. Finally, a representation of the referent must be integrated into the natural-language string. A preprocessor underlying the natural-language window handles the insertion of the deictics into the text string, and the Chat semantic interpretation module provides a lambda-expression describing the set of entities selected. A restriction placed on a user of the present system is that he/she must point at the referent(s) for a given deictic before typing another deictic word.

To demonstrate these capabilities, Figure 4 depicts a CHORIS response window for the query, "How many boards were processed at these **[rework1] [rework2]** stations?" To produce this query, the user first typed, "How many boards were processed at these" into the natural-language input window. The user then selected two stations from the graphic depiction of the factory floor, and so that names of these stations were inserted into the query. Finally, the user typed "stations" to complete the query. The bar graph is the system's response to the query. Alternatively, the user could have typed in the names of the stations in lieu of selecting them from the factory-floor image. We have attempted to exploit the available screen environment (e.g., windows, graphics, items, menus) to support system interaction, thereby making user actions and their intention as explicit as possible.

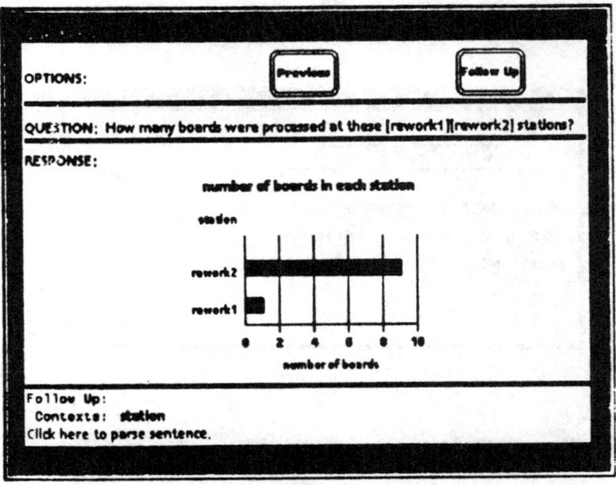

Figure 4: A response window to a follow-up deictic question

5 Natural-Language Forms

A third area of integration between natural-language and direct manipulation is natural-language forms. With this facility, the user can supply arguments to commands either in terms of natural language phrases or by selecting graphic screen elements. By allowing users this capability, we overcome some of the frequently cited limitations of direct manipulation interfaces: arguments that are not known or not visible can be entered in textual form and complex quantificational relations can be expressed more readily in natural language.

Figure 5 shows how a user can move boards from each down (nonworking) machine to a manual station by: (1) invoking **MOVE** from a menu, (2) typing the description "each board at a down machine" to the **what** prompt, and

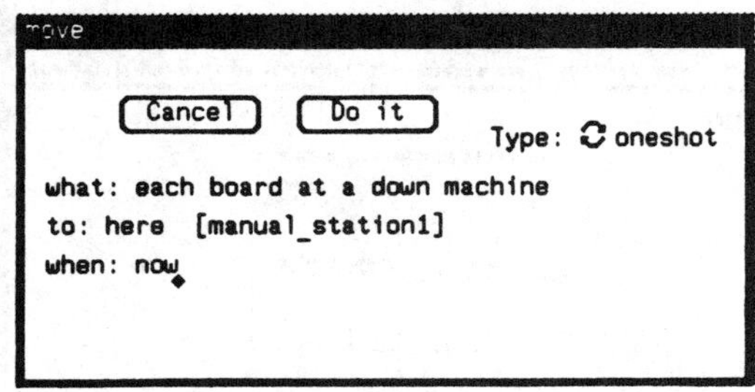

Figure 5: A Completed Move Action-Form

(3) pointing at the relevant destination machine, typing "here," and (4) "depositing" the selected machine into the **to** slot. Another benefit of the use of these forms is the opportunity to specify certain prepositional phrase attachments by filling-in explicitly marked case roles. This cuts down the number of parses substantially [3].

6 Implementation

Both systems described here employ versions of the Chat natural language system [13, 19] that have been extended with the capabilities discussed in the previous sections. Under development since 1983, SHOPTALK extends Chat with capabilities for handling time and tense [4], anaphora (following Hobbs [9]), and declarative graphics [12]. The system is integrated with discrete-event simulation. CHORIS extends Chat-80 as described above for input and also includes adaptation relative to the user and task being performed [17], dynamic multimodal response planning [10], and a discrete-event simulation of the ACE factory as its underlying application.

7 Conclusion

This research has explored the issues of what natural language and direct manipulation are good for. Their integration produces a multimodal interface that overcomes the limitations of the component technologies. Natural language helps direct manipulation in describing arguments to selected actions, and direct manipulation enables users to learn the relevant conceptual coverage for those actions. Similarly, the graphical rendering and manipulation of context provides a partial solution to difficult problems of natural language anaphora. Much future work remains, but we believe that these complementary interface approaches may forge a happy and productive working relationship.

8 Acknowledgments

This research was supported by SRI International and by the Lockheed Missiles and Space Company. We would like to thank Bill Mark and Martha Pollack for valuable commentary on the paper.

References

[1] S. Brennan, M. Friedman, and C. Pollard. A centering approach to pronouns. In *Proceedings of the 25th Annual Meeting of the Association for Computational Linguistics*, Stanford, California, 1987.

[2] E. Charniak. Jack and Janet in search of a theory of knowledge. In *Advance Papers of the Third Meeting of the International Joint Conference on Artificial Intelligence*, William Kaufman, Inc., Los Altos, California, 1973.

[3] K. Church and R. Patil. Coping with syntactic ambiguity or how to put the block in the box on the table. *American Journal of Computational Linguistics*, 8(3-4):139 – 149, 1982.

[4] M. Dalrymple. The interpretation of tense and aspect in English. In *Proceedings of the 26th Annual Meeting of the Association for Computational Linguistics*, Buffalo, New York, 1988.

[5] B. J. Grosz. Focusing and description in natural language dialogues, In *Elements of Discourse Understanding*, Cambridge University Press, 1981.

[6] B.J. Grosz, A.K. Joshi, and S. Weinstein. Providing a unified account of definite noun phrases in discourse. In *Proceedings of the 21st Annual Meeting of the Association for Computational Linguistics*, Cambridge, Massachusetts, 1983.

[7] P. J. Hayes. Using a knowledge base to drive an expert system interface with a natural language component. In J. A. Hendler, editor, *Expert Systems: The User Interface*, pages 153 – 182, Ablex, Norwood, NJ, 1988.

[8] J. R. Hobbs and P. Martin. Local pragmatics. In *Proceedings of the Ninth International Joint Conference on Artificial Intelligence*, Morgan Kaufman Publishers, Los Altos, California, August 1987.

[9] J.R. Hobbs. Resolving pronoun reference. *Lingua*, 44, 1978.

[10] R.A. Gargan Jr., J.W. Sullivan, and S.W. Tyler. Multimodal response planning: an adaptive rule based approach. In *CHI 1988 Proceedings*, May 1988.

[11] J.G. Neal and S.C. Shapiro. Intelligent multi-media interface technology. In *Architectures for Intelligent Interfaces: Elements and Prototypes*, Monterey, CA, March 1988.

[12] F.C.N. Pereira. Can drawing be liberated from the Von Neumann style? *Proceedings of the 1983 ACM Database Week, ACM*, 1983.

[13] F.C.N. Pereira. *Logic for natural language analysis.* SRI Technical Note #275, Artificial Intelligence Center, SRI International, Menlo Park, Calif.

[14] R. Reichman. *Plain-speaking: A theory and grammar of spontaneous discourse.* Ph.D. thesis, Department of Computer Science, Harvard University, 1981.

[15] C.L. Sidner. *Towards a computational theory of definite anaphora comprehension in English discourse.* Technical Report 537, Artificial Intelligence Laboratory, Massachusetts Institute of Technology, 1979.

[16] H. R. Tennant, K. M. Ross, R. M. Saenz, C. W. Thompson, and J. R. Miller. Menu-based natural language understanding. In *Proceedings of the 21st Annual Meeting of the Association for Computational Linguistics*, pages 151 – 158, Cambridge, Massachusetts, June 1983.

[17] S.W. Tyler, R.A. Gargan Jr., and J.W. Sullivan. Adaptation and response planning: elements of an intelligent interface architecture. In *Third Annual Rocky Mountain Conference Proceedings*, June 1988.

[18] W. Wahlster. User and discourse models for multimodal communication. In J.W. Sullivan and S.W. Tyler, editors, *Architectures for Intelligent Interfaces: Elements and Prototypes*, Addison-Wesley, Palo Alto, CA, 1989.

[19] D. Warren and F. Pereira. An efficient easily adaptable system for interpreting natural language queries. *American Journal of Computational Linguistics*, 8(3):110 – 123, 1982.

Synergistic Use of Direct Manipulation and Natural Language

Philip R. Cohen

This paper marked the first of numerous research efforts by us to address multimodal communication. We were inspired by the observation that the two reigning interface camps—direct manipulation/graphical user interface and natural language—unfortunately viewed themselves as providing the complete interface solution. Numerous papers were then in the literature arguing about the relative advantages of the two modalities, but none had as yet truly integrated them in a principled way that allowed each modality to contribute its strengths and to overcome weaknesses of the other.

A number of avenues of research were in part stimulated by this paper and the system it presented. Whereas strengths and weaknesses of interface modalities were identified conceptually in this paper, subsequent work with Sharon Oviatt strove to identify and quantify modality characteristics empirically. For example, this paper identified user interface "forms" as offering advantages for both natural language processing and graphical user interfaces. Subsequently, Oviatt and colleagues (Oviatt et al. 1994) compared spoken and written language to such forms and found threefold reductions in bigram perplexity, syntactic complexity, semantic integration, and spoken disfluencies when users spoke phrases and sentences to fill a slot in a form as compared to speech or writing to an open workspace. Thus, it was demonstrated that the user interface could have a rather large impact on the processibility of utterances, overcoming some of the weaknesses of communication via language. A subsequent summary of argumentation for the complementarity of direct manipulation and natural language can be found in (Cohen 1992), and Cohen and Oviatt (1994, 1995) review the role of speech in human-computer interaction.

The Shoptalk system was greatly expanded and became the basis of a number of other multimodal applications, ranging from military command-and-control to mail management. In addition, it was incorporated as a core component of the Distant Mentor collaboration system at SRI International. The graphical depiction of discourse history offered a solution to the difficult problem of providing to late-joiners a view of what has transpired during an individual or collaborative session. Here, the late-joining "mentor" could simply read the sequence of questions (rather than review the sequence of mouse clicks) in order to understand what the user was trying to do.

The topic of multimodal control of simulators has been a constant in our research, most recently in our development of QuickSet, a multimodal interface for setting up and controlling distributed military simulations (Cohen et al. 1997; Johnston et al. 1997; Pittman et al. 1996). Here speech is used to create and name entities and describe their movements, and pen-based gestures are used to indicate locations, draw objects, and invoke simple commands. Speech and pen can be used together, for example, with the user drawing a line and telling a given entity to follow that route. Whereas Shoptalk's multimodal integration process assumed language was "in control," such that selected items were only sought if a deictic expression was parsed, QuickSet's multimodal integration via a statistically based unification component allows any modality to contribute to an interpretation, with no one modality guiding the process.

Sullivan's work on intelligent interfaces focused on adaptation, task support, and multimodal communications within an otherwise more traditional human interface paradigm. He is currently looking at expanding this approach to include embodying this software in a more animate and lifelike form, expanding its sense of agency, and including social/emotional communications capabilities.

REFERENCES

Cohen, P. R. 1992. The role of Natural Language in a Multimodal Interface. In *Proceedings of the User Interface Software Technology Conference*, 143–149. Monterey, CA: ACM Press.

Cohen, P. R.; Johnston, M.; McGee, D.; Oviatt, S. L.; Pittman, J.; Smith, I.; Chen, L.; and Clow, J., 1997. Multimodal Interaction for Distributed Interactive Simulation. In *Proceedings of the Conference on Innovative Applications of Artificial Intelligence*, July. Menlo Park, CA: AAAI Press.

Cohen, P. R., and Oviatt, S. L., 1994. The Role of Voice in Human-Computer Communication. In Roe, D., and Wilpon, J. (eds.), *Human-Computer Interaction by Voice*, 34–75. Chapter 3. Washington, DC: National Academy of Sciences Press.

Cohen, P. R., and Oviatt, S. L. 1995. The Role of Voice Input for Human-Machine Communication. In *Proceedings of the National Academy of Sciences*, October, 92.

Johnston, M.; Cohen, P. R.; McGee, D.; Oviatt, S. L.; Pittman, J.; and Smith, I., 1997. Unification-Based Multimodal Integration. In *Proceedings of the 35th Annual Meeting of the Association for Computational Linguistics and Meeting of the European Association of Computational Linguistics* (ACL-97/EACL-97), Madrid, July.

Oviatt, S. L.; Cohen, P. R.; and Wang, M. Q. 1994. Toward Interface Design for Human Language Technology: Modality and Structure as Determinants of Linguistic Complexity. *Speech Communication*, 15: 283–300.

Pittman, J.; Smith, I.; Cohen, P. R.; Oviatt, S. L.; and Yang, T. C. 1996. QuickSet: A Multimodal Interface for Military Simulation. In *Proceedings of the Sixth Conference on Computer Generated Forces and Behavioral Representation*, University of Central Florida, Orlando, 217–224.

Natural Language with Integrated Deictic and Graphic Gestures [1]

J.G. Neal[2], C.Y. Thielman[2], Z. Dobes[3]
S.M. Haller[3], S.C. Shapiro[3]
Calspan-UB Research Center (CUBRC)
P.O. Box 400, 4455 Genesee Street
Buffalo, NY 14225

ABSTRACT

People frequently and effectively integrate deictic and graphic gestures with their natural language (NL) when conducting human-to-human dialogue. Similar multi-modal communication can facilitate human interaction with modern sophisticated information processing and decision-aiding computer systems. As part of the CUBRICON project, we are developing NL processing technology that incorporates deictic and graphic gestures with simultaneous coordinated NL for both user inputs and system-generated outputs. Such multi-modal language should be natural and efficient for human-computer dialogue, particularly for presenting or requesting information about objects that are visible, or can be presented visibly, on a graphics display. This paper discusses unique interface capabilities that the CUBRICON system provides including the ability to: (1) accept and understand multi-media input such that references to entities in (spoken or typed) natural language sentences can include coordinated simultaneous pointing to the respective entities on a graphics display; use simultaneous pointing and NL references to disambiguate one another when appropriate; infer the intended referent of a point gesture which is inconsistent with the accompanying NL; (2) dynamically compose and generate multi-modal language that combines NL with deictic gestures and graphic expressions; synchronously present the spoken natural language and coordinated pointing gestures and graphic expressions; discriminate between spoken and written NL.

1 INTRODUCTION

One of the strong arguments in favor of using Natural Language (NL) processing systems as front-ends to sophisticated application systems is that if human-computer communication is conducted in an NL that most users know, then the cost of training a user to use the system

[1] This research was supported, in part, by the Defense Advanced Research Projects Agency and monitored by the Rome Air Development Center under Contract No. F30603-87-C-0136 and the National Science Foundation grant No. SES-88-10917 to The National Center for Geographic Information and Analysis

[2] Calspan Corporation

[3] State University of New York at Buffalo

should be greatly reduced. Human-computer communication can be made even more natural and effective for the user if deictic gestures and drawing expressions are incorporated into the language, since people very commonly and effectively augment their NL with deictic gestures, drawing, and other modes of communication when engaged in human-human dialogue. As part of the CUBRICON project, we are developing NL processing technology that incorporates deictic and graphic gestures with simultaneous coordinated NL for both user inputs and system-generated outputs.

The CUBRICON project [Neal88a, Neal88b, Neal89] is devoted to the development of knowledge-based interface technology that integrates speech input, speech output, natural language text, geographic maps, tables, graphics, and pointing gestures for interactive dialogues between human and computer. The objective is to provide both the user and system with modes of expression that can be combined and used in a natural and efficient manner, particularly when presenting or requesting information about objects that are visible, or can be presented visibly, on a graphics display. The goal of the project is to develop interface technology that uses its media/modalities intelligently in a flexible, highly integrated manner modelled after the manner in which humans converse in simultaneous coordinated multiple modalities.

The interface technology developed as part of this project has been implemented in the form of a prototype system, called CUBRICON (the CUBRC Intelligent CONversationalist). Although the application domain used to drive the research for the CUBRICON project is that of tactical Air Force mission planning, the interface technology incorporated in CUBRICON is applicable to domains with similar communication characteristics and requirements.

This paper discusses the research effort within the CUBRICON project that has focused on integrating NL with deictic and graphic gestures for user inputs and system-generated outputs. The unique interface capabilities that have been developed and implemented in the CUBRICON system include the ability to: (1) accept and understand multi-media input such that references to entities in (spoken or typed) natural language sentences can include coordinated simultaneous pointing to the respective entities on a graphics display; use simultaneous pointing and NL references to disambiguate one another when appropriate; infer the intended referent of a point gesture which is inconsistent with the accompanying NL; (2) dynamically compose and generate multi-modal language that combines NL with deictic gestures and graphic expressions; synchronously present the spoken natural language and coordinated pointing gestures and graphic expressions; discriminate between spoken and written NL.

2 SYSTEM OVERVIEW

The CUBRICON design provides for the use of a unified multi-media language, by both the user and system, for communication in a dialogue setting. Input and output streams are treated as compound streams with components corresponding to different media. This approach is intended to imitate, to a certain extent, the ability of humans to simultaneously accept input from different sensory devices (such as eyes and ears), and to simultaneously produce output in different media (such as voice, pointing motions, and drawings).

An overview of the CUBRICON software system and hardware I/O devices is presented in Figure 1. CUBRICON accepts input from three input devices: speech input device, keyboard, and mouse. CUBRICON produces output for three output devices: high-resolution color-graphics display, high-resolution monochrome display, and speech production device. The primary path that the input data follows is indicated by the modules that are numbered in the figure: (1) Input Coordinator, (2) Multi-Media Parser Interpreter, (3) Executor/Communicator to Target System, (4) Multi-Media Output Planner, and (5) the Coordinated Output Generator. The Input Coordinator module accepts input from the three input devices and fuses the input streams into a single compound stream, maintaining the temporal order of tokens in the original streams. The Multi-Media Parser/Interpreter is a generalized augmented transition network (GATN) that has been extended to accept the compound stream produced by the Input Coordinator and produce an interpretation of this compound stream. Appropriate action is then taken by the Executor module. This action may be a command to the mission planning system, a database query, or an action that entails participation of the interface system only. An expression of the results of the action is then planned by the Multi-Media Output Planner for communication to the user. The Output Planner uses a GATN that produces a multi-media output stream representation with components targeted for the different output devices. This output representation is translated into visual/auditory output by the Output Generator module. This module is responsible for producing the multi-media output in a coordinated manner in real time (e.g., the Planner module can specify that a certain icon on the color-graphics display must be highlighted when the entity represented by the icon is mentioned in the simultaneous natural language output).

The CUBRICON system includes several knowledge sources that are used for both understanding input and composing output. The knowledge sources include: a lexicon, a grammar defining the multi-modal language used by the system for input and output, a discourse model, a user model, and a knowledge base of task domain and interface information. The latter knowledge sources are discussed briefly in the following paragraphs.

The *knowledge base* consists of information about the task domain of tactical Air Force mission planning. This knowledge base includes information about concepts such as SAMs, air bases, radars, and missions as well as related HCI concepts such as verbal/graphical expressions for the domain concepts.

The *discourse model* is a representation of the attentional focus space [Grosz86] of the dialogue carried out in multi-modal language. It consists of (1) a main focus list that includes those entities and propositions that have been explicitly expressed (by the user or by CUBRI-

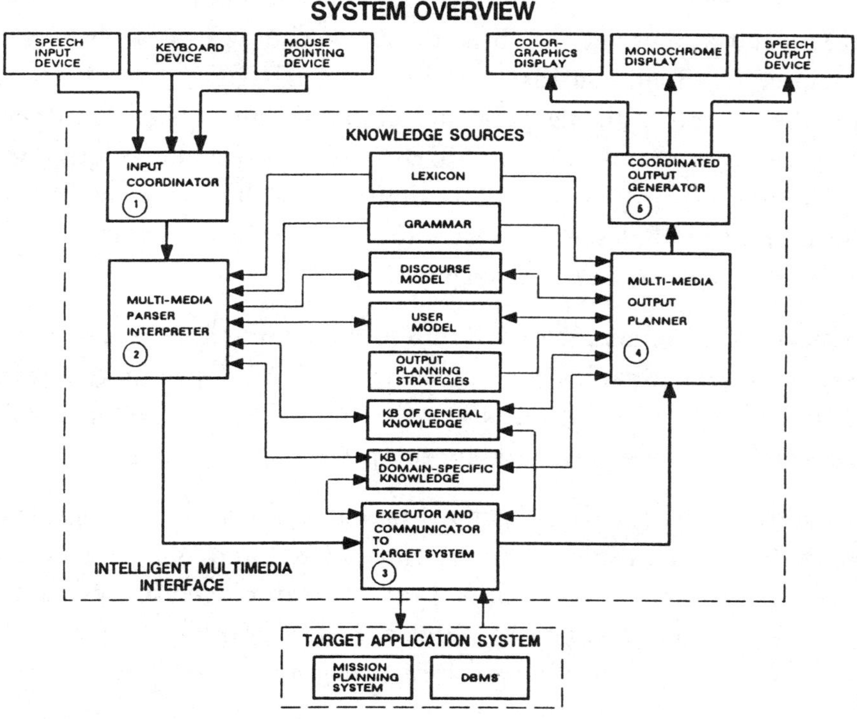

Figure 1: System Overview

CON) via natural language and/or graphic/pointing gestures and (2) a display model that includes a representation of all the objects (windows and their contents) that are "in focus" because they are visible on one of the two CRT screens.

The *user model* [Kobsa88] consists of an *entity rating module* that includes a task-dependent representation of the relative importance of all the entity types known to the system and an algorithm for modifying these ratings depending on task and dialogue activity.

Key features of the CUBRICON design, discussed in this paper, include the integration of NL and graphics in a unified language that is defined by a multi-modal grammar and the generation of synchronized speech and graphics in real time. The integration of NL and graphics in a unified language distinguishes this research from other approaches to multi-modal interface technology [Sullivan88, Arens89]. The Integrated Interface system [Arens88] and the XTRA system [Kobsa86, Allgayer89] are two of the most relevant. The Integrated Interface system is a multi-modal system in that it uses both maps and NL for the presentation of information to the user. The system provides information about the status and movements of naval platforms and groups in the Pacific Ocean. The system displays NL in text boxes positioned on a map display near the relevant objects. The system does not use a multi-modal language, however. The language generated is purely NL with no integrated graphics. The XTRA system is a multi-modal interface system which accepts and generates NL with accompanying point gestures for input and output, respectively. In contrast to the XTRA system, however, CUBRICON supports a greater number of different types of pointing gestures and does not restrict the user to pointing at form slots alone, but enables the user to point at a variety of objects such as windows, table entries, icons on maps, and geometric points. In added contrast to XTRA, CUBRICON provides for multiple point gestures per NL phrase and multiple point-accompanied phrases per sentence during both user input and system-generated output. CUBRICON also includes graphic gestures (i.e., certain types of simple drawing) as part of its multi-modal language, in addition to pointing gestures. Furthermore, CUBRICON addresses the problem of coordinating NL (speech) and graphic gestures during both input and output.

CUBRICON software is implemented on a Symbolics Lisp Machine using the SNePS semantic network processing system [Shapiro79, Shapiro87], a GATN parser-generator [Shapiro82], and Common Lisp. Speech recognition is handled by a Dragon Systems VoiceScribe 1000. Speech output is produced by a DECtalk speech production system.

As stated previously, CUBRICON is a multi-modal system that integrates the following modalities: geographic maps, tables, forms, printed text, and NL with graphic and deictic gestures. Subsequent sections of this paper present example sentences that include simultaneous coordinated pointing gestures to objects on the graphics displays. Figure 2 shows example CUBRICON displays containing a form, geographic map, table, part-whole decomposition.

The following sections discuss CUBRICON's input understanding and output composition processes and their use of the knowledge sources discussed above.

3 MULTI-MODAL LANGUAGE UNDERSTANDING

People commonly and naturally use coordinated simultaneous natural language and graphic gestures when working at graphic displays. These modes of communication combine synergistically to form an efficient language for expressing definite references and locative adverbials. One of the benefits of this multi-modal language is that it eliminates the need for the lengthy definite descriptions that would be necessary for unnamed objects if only natural language were used. Instead, a terse reference such as "this SAM" (surface-to-air missile system) accompanied by a point to an entity on the display can be used. CUBRICON accepts such NL accompanied by simultaneous coordinated pointing gestures. The NL can be input via the keyboard, the speech recognition system, or a mixture of both. CUBRICON provides

- variety in the object types that can be targets of point gestures; these object types include windows, form slots, table entries, icons, and geometric points;
- variety in the number of point gestures allowed per phrase; each noun phrase can be accompanied by zero or more point gestures; such a phrase may contain no words, just the pointing gestures;

PACKAGE WORKSHEET

PKG#	0023	Preparer's Name		Date Prepared		Priority	

OFFENSIVE COUNTER AIR MISSIONS

Mission	OCA#	Origin	TOD	#AC	AC Type	SCL	AC Pool
1	345	Nurnberg Fighter Base	06:00				49tfu-F-1
2	445	Rhein Main Fighter Bas	05:45				45tfu-Ef-
3							
4							

PRE-TARGET REFUELING

SVC#	STN#	Start	Dur.	Disbur.

TARGET STRIKE MISSION

Mission	Aim Point	TOT
1	6-24-Dresden Runway	07:02
2	6-24-Merseberg Runway	06:50
3		
4		

POST-TARGET REFUELING

SVC#	STN#	Start	Dur.	Disbur.
345	244	07:45	00:10	20942 lbs
445	244	07:25	00:10	21960 lbs

REFUELING MISSION

RFL#	345	TOD	07:00	AC Type	Kc-135	Load		Origin	Rhein Main Fighter Base

Station	STN#	Start Time	Stop Time	Orbit Location
1	244	07:20	07:55	50.75 N Latitude, 13.55 E Longitude
2				

AIR ESCORT MISSIONS

Mission	AEM#	Origin	TOD	#AC	ACT	SCL	Remarks
1							
2							

Mission	SSM#	Origin	TOD	#AC	ACT	SCL	Target	TOT
1								
2								

=>> Display the forms window.
=>> Make PKG0023 the current package.
I understand, assigning newly created mission (PKG0023) as the current package.
=>>

[Tue 23 May 12:07:25] Keyboard CL SNEPS: User Input SLNR

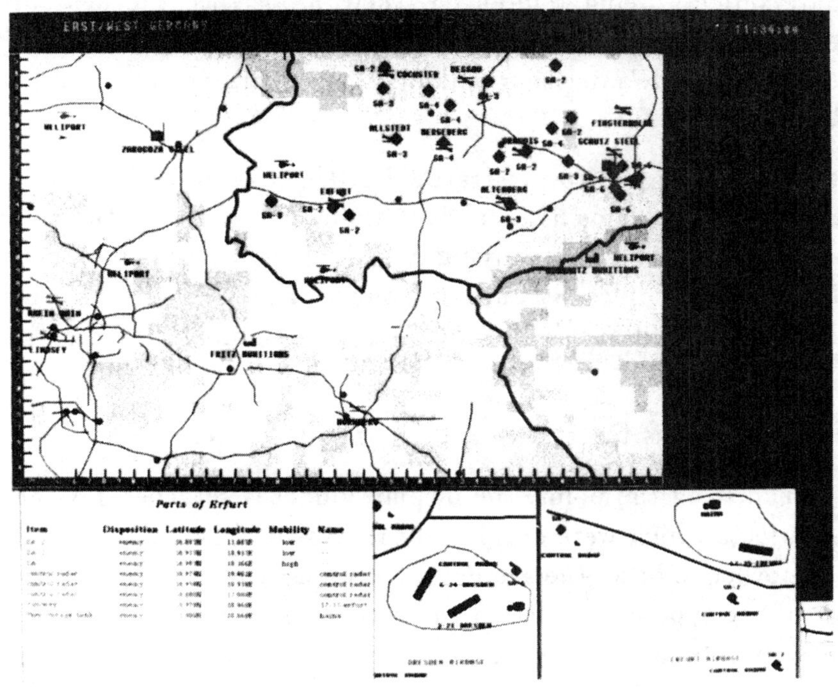

Figure 2: Example CUBRICON Displays

- variety in the number of multi-modal phrases allowed per sentence; deictic gestures can accompany more than one phrase per sentence.

Just as natural language used alone has shortcomings, so also does the use of pointing gestures alone. Pointing used alone has the following problems: (1) a point gesture can be ambiguous if the point touches the area where two or more graphical figures or icons overlap or (2) the user may inadvertently miss the object at which he intended to point. To handle these pointing problems, some systems use default techniques such as having a point handler return the entity represented by (a) the "top" or "foremost" icon where the system has a data structure it uses to remember the order in which icons are "painted" on the display (i.e., which are further in the background and which are foremost in the foreground) or (b) the icon whose "center" is closest to the location on the screen/window touched by the point. A serious disadvantage of such default point-interpretation techniques is that it is difficult, if not impossible, for certain icons to be selected via a point reference.

CUBRICON's acceptance of dual-media input (NL accompanied by coordinated pointing gestures) overcomes the limitations of the above weak default techniques and provides an efficient expressive referencing capability. The CUBRICON methodology for handling dual-media input is a decision-making process that depends on a variety of factors such as the *types* of candidate objects being referenced, their *properties*, the *sentential context*, and the *constraints on the participants* or fillers of the semantic case frame for the verb of any given sentence. CUBRICON's decision-making process draws upon it's knowledge sources discussed briefly in Section 2.

We present a few brief examples to illustrate CUBRICON's referent determination process. This process handles the problems listed above: ambiguous point gestures and point gestures that are inconsistent with the accompanying NL. First we discuss ambiguous point gestures. In each of the following examples, assume that the <point> represents a point gesture with a device such as a mouse and each point gesture can be ambiguous (i.e., it can touch more than one icon).

Example 1: USER: "What is the status of this <point> airbase?"

From the icons touched by the point, the display model is searched for the semantic representation of the objects which were graphically represented by the touched icons. From the hierarchy of the knowledge base, the system determines which of the objects selected by the point gesture are of the type mentioned in the accompanying verbal phrase ("airbase" in the example sentence) and discards the others.

Example 2: USER: "What is the mobility of these <point>$_1$ <point>$_2$ <point>$_3$?"

Example 2 illustrates that CUBRICON enables the user to use more than one point gesture per phrase. Also, in contrast to Example 1, no object type is mentioned in the noun phrase corresponding to the point gestures. In this case, CUBRICON can use a mentioned property (e.g., mobility) to select from among the candidate referents of the point gesture. CUBRICON accesses the display model to retrieve the semantic representations of the objects touched by each of the user's point gestures, and then determines which of these objects have property "mobility" using the knowledge base of application information.

Example 3: USER: "Enter this <point-map-icon> here <point-form-slot>."

Example 3 illustrates that CUBRICON enables the user to use point gestures in conjunction with more than just one phrase of a sentence and that the point gestures may access different types of windows, even on different CRTs. In Example 3, the user's first point gesture touches an object on a map display on the color-graphics CRT and the second selects a slot of the mission planning form on the monochrome CRT. Two of CUBRICON's features are critical to its ability to process the sentence of Example 3: First, the display model contains semantic representations of all the objects displayed visually in each of the windows of each CRT, and second, all objects and concepts in the CUBRICON system are represented in a single knowledge representation language, namely the formalism of the SNePS knowledge base. This knowledge base is shared by all the modules of the CUBRICON system. Suppose that the <point-map-icon> selects the Nuernberg airbase on the map and the <point-form-slot> touches the "origin airbase" slot on the mission planning form. CUBRICON's response to the input of Example 3 would be to build the knowledge base structure which represents the assertion that Nuernberg is the airbase from which the particular mission will be flown.

As mentioned previously in this section, in addition to being ambiguous, another problem that can arise with point gestures is that the user may inadvertently miss the object at which he intended to point. In this case, the point gesture will be inconsistent with the accompanying natural language phrase, meaning that the natural language part of the expression and the accompanying point cannot be interpreted as referring to the same object(s) (e.g., the user says "this airbase" and points to a factory or points at nothing, missing all the icons). CUBRICON includes methodology to infer the intended referent in this case. CUBRICON uses the information from the sentence, parsed and interpreted thus far, as filtering criteria for candidate objects. The system performs a bounded incremental search around the location of the user's point to find the closest object(s) that satisfy the filtering criteria. If one is found, then the system responds to the user's input (e.g., command or request) and also issues an advisory statement concerning the inconsistency. In the event that no qualified object is found in the vicinity of the user's point, then a response is made to the user to this effect.

4 MULTI-MODAL LANGUAGE GENERATION

Just as CUBRICON accepts NL accompanied by deictic and graphic gestures during input, CUBRICON can generate multi-modal language output that combines NL with *deictic gestures* and *graphic expressions*. An important feature of the CUBRICON design is that NL and graphics are incorporated in a single language generator providing a unified multi-modal language with speech and graphics synchronized in real time.

Another important aspect of the CUBRICON system is that it distinguishes between spoken and written (to a CRT display) NL. CUBRICON uses graphic and deictic gestures with *spoken NL* only (not with written NL), since a pointing or graphic gesture needs to be temporally synchronized with the corresponding verbal phrase, allowing for multiple graphic gestures within any individual sentence. The coordination between a graphic gesture and its co-referring verbal phrase is lost if printed text is used instead of speech. As mentioned in Section 3, a pointing gesture can be used very effectively with a terse NL phrase (e.g., "this SAM") to reference an object that is visible on one of the displays (by the system as well as the user). When CUBRICON generates *written NL*, however, deictic/graphic expressions are not used, but, instead, definite descriptions are generated as noun phrases with sufficient specificity to hopefully avoid ambiguous references. CUBRICON's use of deictic gestures and graphic expressions are discussed in the following paragraphs.

Deictic gestures are combined with appropriate NL during output to guide the user's visual focus of attention. During language generation, in order to compose a reference for an object,

1. if the object is represented by an icon on the display, then CUBRICON generates a NL expression for the object and a simultaneous coordinated graphic gesture that points to its icon.

   If the object has an individual name or identifier, then CUBRICON uses its name or identifier (e.g., "the Merseberg airbase") as the NL expression

   else CUBRICON generates an expression consisting of a demonstrative pronoun followed by the name of an appropriate class to which the object belongs (e.g., "this SAM", "these SAMs") as the NL expression.

2. if the object (call it X) is not represented by an icon on the display, but is a component of such a visible object (call it Y), then CUBRICON generates a phrase that expresses object X as a component of object Y and uses a combined deictic-verbal expression for object Y as described in the above case. For example, if CUBRICON is generating a reference for the runway of an airbase called Merseberg and an icon for the airbase is visible on the map (the airbase as a whole is represented visibly, but not its parts), then CUBRICON generates the phrase "the runway of the Merseberg Airbase" with a simultaneous point gesture that is directed at the Merseberg airbase icon on the map.

It is frequently the case that an object to which CUBRICON wants to point has a visible representation in more than one window on the CRTs. Therefore the system must select the visual representation(s) of the object (e.g., an icon, table entry, form slot entry) that it will use in its point gesture(s) from among the several candidates. The current CUBRICON methodology is to point out all the object's visible representations, but to use a strong pointing gesture (e.g., blink the icon to attract the user's attention and add a pointing text-box) for the most significant or relevant representations and weak non-distracting gestures (e.g., just highlight the visible representation) for the less significant ones. In order to select the most relevant visible representations from among all the candidates, CUBRICON:

1. selects all the windows which contain a visible representation of the object.
2. filters out any windows which are not active or not exposed.
3. if there are exposed windows containing a visible representation of the object, then CUBRICON uses all of these representations as objects of weak diectic gestures and selects the visible representation in the most important or salient window [Neal89b] as the target of a strong diectic gesture.
4. if there are no exposed windows displaying the object's visible representation, then CUBRICON determines the most important active de-exposed window [Neal89b] displaying the object. CUBRICON exposes this window and uses the representation of the object in this window in a strong deictic gesture.

CUBRICON combines *graphic expressions* with NL output when the information to be expressed is, at least partially, amenable to graphic presentation. In the current CUBRICON implementation, the type of information that falls in this category includes (1) locative information and (2) path traversal information. We discuss only the locative case in this paper.

When generating locative information about some object (call it the figure object [Herskovits85]), CUBRICON selects an appropriate landmark as the ground object [Herskovits85], determines a spatial relationship between the figure and ground object, and generates a multi-modal expression for the locative information including the spatial relationship. When selecting the ground object, CUBRICON selects a landmark such as a city, border, or region, that is within the current map display (i.e., does not require a map transformation). If possible, CUBRICON uses a landmark that is in focus by virtue of its having been already used recently as a ground object. CUBRICON's discourse model, discussed briefly in Section 2, includes a representation of the attentional focus space of the dialogue, including a main focus list of entities and propositions that have been expressed by CUBRICON or by the user via multi-modal language. If a new landmark must be used as a ground object, then CUBRICON selects the landmark that is nearest the figure object. CUBRICON derives a spatial relation between the ground object and figure object that it represents in its knowledge base. This relation includes (1) the direction from the ground object to the figure object and (2) the distance if the distance is greater than 0.04 of the window width. If the distance is less than 0.04 of the window width, then the figure object appears to be right next to the ground object. This criterion for deciding whether to include distance as part of the relation reflects the tendency for people to omit a distance measure when the distance is small relative to the geographic area under discussion and to say something like "just northeast of" instead of stating a distance explicitly.

As an illustrative example, the user may ask about the location of a particular object, such as the Fritz Steel plant. The system then uses the steel plant as the figure object, selects a ground object, and derives a spatial relation between ground object and figure object as discussed above. The multi-modal response is given below.

USER: "Where is the Fritz Steel plant?"

CUBRICON: "The Fritz Steel plant is located here <point>, 45 miles southwest of Dresden <graphic-expression>."

The <point> consists of a gesture that points out the Fritz Steel plant icon to the user via a gesture that uses a combination of blinking, highlighting, circling the icon and the attachment of a pointing label-box that identifies the icon. The <graphic-expression> is a visual presentation of the spatial relation between the figure object (Fritz steel plant) and the ground object (Dresden city), consisting of an arrow drawn from the Dresden city icon to the steel plant icon, a label stating the distance, and a label identifying the city (the steel plant should already be labeled).

CUBRICON's multi-modal language generation is also discussed in [Neal89].

5 FUTURE DIRECTIONS

There are numerous worthwhile areas and ideas to be investigated and developed to advance this research. We briefly discuss two of these areas:

CUBRICON is currently being extended so that it accepts a larger vocabulary of graphic drawing gestures as part of the user's multi-modal input. An integrated language consisting of both verbal and graphic "tokens" can be used for both referencing objects that the system already knows about as well as explaining and defining new concepts to the system. Such a multi-modal input language should be especially useful for the definition and explanation of geographical and spatial concepts to a system that would then use the concepts for geographical applications. We are currently focusing on adding polylines to the set of graphic gestures that CUBRICON accepts. Polylines can be used to approximate free-hand drawing and thereby give the user great expressive power.

We are also planning to conduct a research program to investigate the problem of user gestures that are not synchronized with their corresponding NL phrases. We are interested in the characteristics of the phenomenon: to what degree are gestures of different types not synchronized with their corresponding NL phrase, how frequently does the phenomenon occur, is there a correlation between characteristics of the phenomenon and characteristics of the corresponding natural language? We also plan to investigate methods that would enable the system to decide which phrase of the accompanying natural language input is the co-referring phrase for any pointing gesture that is not synchronized with its co-referring phrase.

6 SUMMARY

People frequently augment their NL with deictic gestures, drawing, and other modes of communication when engaged in human-human dialogue. The CUBRICON project is devoted to the development of knowledge-based interface technology that integrates speech input, speech output, natural language text, geographic maps, tables, graphics, and pointing gestures for interactive communication between human and computer. The objective is to provide both the user and system with modes of expression that are combined and used in a natural and efficient manner, particularly when presenting or requesting information about objects that are visible, or can be presented visibly, on a graphics display.

As part of the CUBRICON project, we are developing NL processing technology that integrates deictic and graphic gestures with simultaneous coordinated NL to form a multi-modal language for human-computer dialogues. CUBRICON's main I/O processing modules have access to several knowledge sources or data structures, including one modeling each of (1) the application domain, (2) the discourse, and (3) the user.

This paper discussed the unique interface capabilities that the CUBRICON system provides including the ability to: (1) accept and understand multi-media input such that references to entities in (spoken or typed) natural language sentences can include coordinated simultaneous pointing to the respective entities on a graphics display; use simultaneous pointing and NL references to disambiguate one another when appropriate; infer the intended referent of a point gesture which is inconsistent with the accompanying NL; (2) dynamically compose and generate multi-modal language that combines NL with deictic gestures and graphic expressions; synchronously present the spoken natural language and coordinated pointing gestures and graphic expressions; discriminate between spoken and written NL.

7 REFERENCES

[**Allgayer89**] Allgayer, J., Jansen-Winkeln, R., Reddig, C., & Reithinger, N. 1989. Bidirectional Use of Knowledge in the Multi-Modal NL Access System XTRA. *Proc. of IJCAI-89*, Detroit, MI, pp. 1492-1497.

[**Arens88**] Arens, Y., Miller, L., & Sondheimer, N.K. 1988. Presentation Planning Using an Integrated Knowledge Base, in *Architectures for Intelligent Interfaces: Elements and Prototypes*, J.W. Sullivan & S.W. Tyler (eds.), Addison-Wesley, pp. 93-108.

[Arens89] Arens, Y., Feiner, S., Hollan, J., & Neches, R. (eds.) 1989. *A New Generation of Intelligent Interfaces, IJCAI-89 Workshop*, Detroit, MI.

[Grosz86] Grosz, B.J. 1986. The Representation and Use of Focus in a System for Understanding Dialogs, in *Readings in Natural Language Processing*, B.J. Grosz, K.S. Jones, & B.L. Webber (eds.), Morgan Kaufmann Pub., pp. 353-362.

[Haller89] Haller, S.M. 1989. Technical Report: Spatial Relations and Locative Phrase Generation in a Map Context. Computer Science Department, State University of New York at Buffalo.

[Herskovits85] Herskovits, A. 1985. Semantics and Pragmatics of Locative Expressions. *Cognitive Science*, 9:341-378.

[Kobsa86] Kobsa, A., Allgayer, J., Reddig, C., Reithinger, N., Schmauks, D., Harbusch, K., & Wahlster, W. 1986. Combining Deictic Gestures and Natural Language for Referent Identification, *Proc. of the 11th International Conf. on Computational Linguistics*, Bonn, FR Germany.

[Kobsa88] Kobsa, A. & Wahlster, W. (eds.), 1988. *Computational Linguistics*, Special Issue on User Modeling, MIT Press.

[Neal88a] Neal, J.G. & Shapiro, S.C. 1988. Intelligent Multi-Media Interface Technology, in *Architectures for Intelligent Interfaces: Elements and Prototypes*, J.W. Sullivan & S.W. Tyler (eds.), Addison-Wesley, pp. 69-91.

[Neal88b] Neal, J.G., Dobes, Z., Bettinger, K.E., & Byoun, J.S. 1988. Multi-Modal References in Human-Computer Dialogue, *Proc. AAAI-88*, St. Paul, MN, pp. 819-823.

[Neal89a] Neal, J.G., Thielman, C.Y., Funke, D.J., & Byoun, J.S. 1989. Multi-Modal Output Composition for Human-Computer Dialogues. *Proc. of the AI Systems in Government Conference*, George Washington Univ., Wash. D.C., pp. 250-257.

[Neal89b] Neal, J.G. et. al. 1989. The CUBRICON Multi-Modal Interface System. (Journal paper in preparation).

[Shapiro79] Shapiro, S.C. 1979. The SNePS Semantic Network Processing System, in *Associative Networks - The Representation and Use of Knowledge by Computers*, N. Findler (ed.), Academic Press, pp. 179-203.

[Shapiro82] Shapiro, S.C. 1982. Generalized Augmented Transition Network Grammars for Generation from Semantic Networks. *AJCL*, Vol. 8, No. 1, pp. 12-25.

[Shapiro87] Shapiro, S.C. & Rapaport, W.J. 1987. SNePS Considered as a Fully Intensional Propositional Semantic Network, in *The Knowledge Frontier, Essays in the Representation of Knowledge*, N. Cercone & G. McCalla (eds.), Springer-Verlag, pp. 263-315.

[Sullivan88] Sullivan, J.W. & Sherman, W.T. (eds.) 1988. *Architectures for Intelligent Interfaces: Elements and Prototypes*, Addison-Wesley Pub. Co.

Natural Language with Integrated Deictic and Graphic Gestures

Stuart C. Shapiro, Jeannette G. Neal, and Susan M. Haller

The CUBRICON project was active during the years 1987–1989. General papers on CUBRICON published subsequent to the one in this collection include (Neal and Shapiro 1991, 1994). Although no major advances were made to CUBRICON itself afterward, some of the themes examined in the CUBRICON project were extended in various ways.

A continuation of the aspect of CUBRICON in which windows are placed intelligently and without user intervention is described in (Funke, Neal, and Paul 1993). That work carried on the theme of the CUBRICON project that a user should only have to be concerned with the problem being worked on with an intelligent user interface, not with the interface itself.

A significant part of the CUBRICON language, used both for user input and system output, was its use of references to geographical locations on the maps. Additional work on such expressions is reported in (Haller and Ali 1990) and (Haller and Mark 1990). Since a major aspect of CUBRICON is to discuss objects and locations on a map, it may be viewed as a geographic information system. A start to this connection is reported in (Shapiro et al. 1992).

The CUBRICON project investigated the use of deictic gestures during on-line computer-human interaction, when both computer and human point to objects displayed on a computer screen. Indexical terms are generally explained as getting their meanings from the occasion of their use in such on-line interactions (usually between two humans). However, indexicals are also used in third-person, generally past-tense, narratives, when "the occasion of their use" is hard—or even impossible—to specify. A major interdisciplinary study of the use of deixis in narrative is reported in (Duchan, Bruder and Hewitt 1995).

REFERENCES

Duchan, J. F.; Bruder, G. A.; and Hewitt, L. E. (eds.). 1995. *Deixis in Narrative: a Cognitive Science Perspective*. Hillsdale, NJ: Lawrence Erlbaum.

Funke, D. J.; Neal, J. G; and Paul, R. D. 1993. An Approach to Intelligent Automated Window Management. *International Journal of Man-Machine Studies*, 38: 949–983.

Haller, S. M., and Ali, S. 1990. Using Focus for Generating Felicitous Locative Expressions. In *Proceedings of the Third International Conference on Industrial and Engineering Applications of Artificial Intelligence and Expert Systems*, Charleston, 472–477.

Haller, S. M., and Mark, D. M. 1990. Knowledge Representation for Understanding Geographical Locatives. In *Proceedings of the 4th International Symposium on Spatial Data Handling*, Zurich, 465–477.

Neal, J. G., and Shapiro, S. C. 1991. Intelligent Multi-Media Interface Technology. In Sullivan, J. W., and Tyler, S. W. (eds.), *Intelligent User Interfaces*, 11–43. Reading, MA: Addison-Wesley.

Neal, J. G., and Shapiro, S. C. 1994. Knowledge-Based Multimedia Systems. In Koegel Buford, J. F. (ed.), *Multimedia Systems*, 403–438. Reading, MA: ACM Press/Addison-Wesley.

Shapiro, S. C.; Chalupsky, H.; Chou, H.-C.; and Mark, D. M. 1992. Intelligent User Interfaces: Connecting ARC/INFO and SNACTor. In *Proceedings of the Twelfth Annual ESRI User Conference*, Vol. 3, 151–165. Redlands, CA: Environmental Systems Research Institute.

Chapter 11

Integrating Simultaneous Input from Speech, Gaze, and Hand Gestures

David B. Koons, Carlton J. Sparrell, and Kristinn R. Thorisson

Abstract

The focus of this chapter is the integration of information from speech, gestures, and gaze at the computer interface. We describe two prototype systems that accept simultaneous speech, gestural and eye movement input from a user. The three modes are processed to a common frame-based encoding and interpreted together to resolve references to objects in the map. In the first prototype, a user can interact with a simple two-dimensional map. The computer responds in synthesized speech and by manipulating the map display. The second system uses a three-dimensional blocks world and demonstrates a more flexible interpretation strategy for handling full-hand gestures. Speech-related hand movements are processed to an intermediate level of representation without automatically assigning a deictic or symbolic meaning. Interpretation occurs later and takes advantage of information from the other modes and from the context.

1. Introduction

With increasing computer and robot intelligence, it is becoming more desirable to *communicate* with machines rather than *operating* them. We have at our disposal a wealth of techniques to communicate our thoughts and intentions. To get ideas across quickly, our communication system relies on a very efficient mix of spatial and semantic knowledge. We can switch instantly between various modes for communicating the same ideas: speech, hand gestures, facial gestures, intonation, etc. Together, these features significantly increase the "bandwidth" between two communicating parties.

One of the problems encountered when interpreting simultaneous input from multiple modes is the timing of events. With a free mix of input modes, actions are not coordinated according to a script or a set sequence. This puts a higher burden on the interpretation methods used. A second problem is the level of abstraction. If the signals from the disjoint modes are separate pieces of a particular message, the question becomes how far we should process the given "evidence" in each mode before trying to integrate it with the information from the other modes. A related problem is *how* to combine the information once it has been extracted. In this paper, we focus on integrating information from speech, gestures, and gaze at the computer interface. We have built two prototype systems that accept speech, gestural and eye movement input from a user. The first one allows interaction with a simple two-dimensional map (for an overview and hardware description, see [Thorisson et al. 1992]). Through a free mixture of speech, deictic gestures and glances the user can request information or give commands to modify the contents of the map database. The second system extends the repertoire of free gestures to include iconic and pantomimic gestures and replaces the two-dimensional graphics with a three-dimensional blocks world.

2. Related Research

2.1. Multi-Modal Interfaces

The most widespread example of a computer interface that offers multiple input channels is the combination of keyboard and mouse found on most modern workstations. These systems offer the user a choice of modes for many tasks: entering text is best accomplished with the keyboard; moving the cursor or other objects around on the screen is easily carried out with the mouse or other pointing device. Interface designers must constrain the possible actions that a user may carry out and develop an unambiguous mapping between the context of an action and its interpretation. In addition to a highly-constrained interaction, these interfaces do not allow the use of the multiple input channels in parallel (except for a few cases such as the click-drag).

"Put That There" [Bolt 1980] used speech-recognition and a three-dimensional sensing device to simultaneously gather input from a user's speech and the location of a cursor on a wall-sized display. CUBRICON, a more recent multi-modal interface prototype, provides for simultaneous speech, keyboard and mouse input [Neal and Shapiro 1991]. Although these are important contributions to the development of multi-modal interfaces, both systems reduce gestures to the location of a simple two-dimensional cursor. Hauptman [1989] conducted a "Wizard of Oz" study (a person monitors the user's actions and translates them into computer commands) and found that, when given the task of manipulating objects displayed on a computer display, there is an advantage in allowing a person to communicate using a free mixture of speech and gestures. However, the study also showed that two-dimensional input devices severely restricted the types of gestures that could be made by the person.

2.2. Gestures

Human hands are powerful tools for directly interacting with the environment and exerting influence on it. This may be one of the reasons why research on hand gestures (both in three-dimensional interactive graphics and computer generated environments as well as telerobotics) has focused on *tool-level* manipulation (e.g., [Butterworth et al. 1992; Sheridan 1992; Sturman 1992; Weimer and Ganapathy 1989; Fisher et al. 1986]). In these interfaces, gestures either imitate real-world actions (like grasping and throwing) or are purely symbolic, with a single and complete meaning attached to a pre-defined motion, posture, or combination of the two. While tool-level interfaces can be very efficient and sometimes intuitive, they often become unwieldy when functionality is hidden under layers of hierarchical modes and menus.

Another characteristic of these interfaces is their limitation to a small set of gestures [Tyler et al. 1991b; Wahlster 1991] that the user sometimes has to learn, and even train for, to be able to apply. Wahlster [1991] has a good example of such a system using deictic gestures. In his interface the user selects the desired type of gesture from a menu of icons; the interpretation of the subsequent deictic gesture (a mouse click in a chosen region of the screen) is based on the type of icon selected. While the interpretation is context dependent, the interface still forces the user to learn specific rules for operating the computer.

In addition to tool-level manipulation our hands play a large role in communication because of their natural link to the spatio-temporal world in which we live [Rimé and Sachiaratura 1991]. People use their hands to show three-dimensional relationships between objects and temporal sequences of events: a hand can in one instance take the role of an object and in the next, serve as a pointer to fictional constructs created in the gesture space. These types of gestures at the interface have received very little attention.

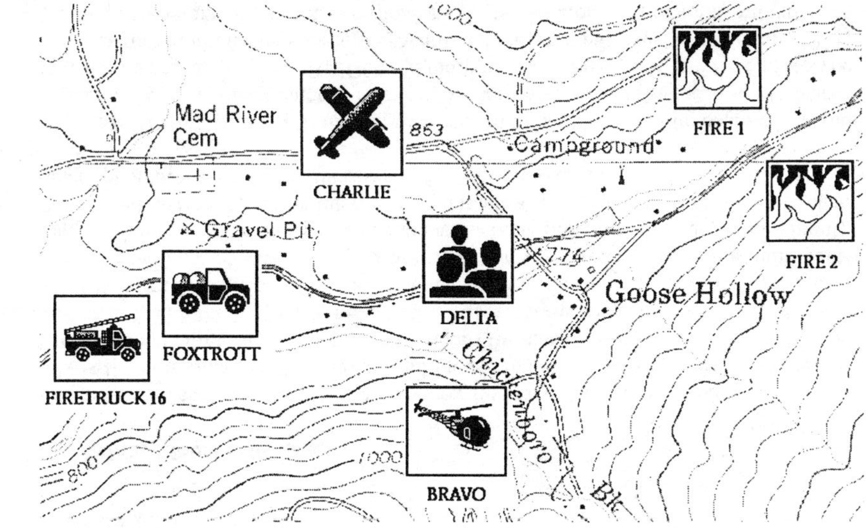

Figure 1. A section of the screen with icons representing helicopters, airplanes, trucks, fire crews and fire locations. The user can move, create and change these objects by referring to them in a free mixture of speech, gaze, and gestures.

2.3. Eyes

If an object of discussion is in someone's vicinity there is a natural tendency to glance in its direction, make gestures toward it, and to look directly at it, in coherence with the flow of the conversation [Kahneman 1973]. This feature of gaze can augment the interpretation of deictic references when the input from other modes is partial or segmented. Starker and Bolt [1990] describe an interface that bases its output on the data from a user's looking behavior. Whereas their system used only eyes as input, they made an effort to interpret the deictic behavior of the eye on more than one level, making the interface potentially more responsive to the user's looking. Jacob [1990] devised an eye tracking interface that allows a person to use gaze, or gaze and keyboard input in combination, to make selections on a computer screen. However, in this system, eye tracking plays a role similar to a mouse or other pointing device. In our system, the user is not required to use eyes as a pointer. We are specifically looking to incorporate eyes into the interaction process in a non-intrusive manner.

3. Prototype for Three Modes

To explore the issues related to multi-modal interpretation, we designed a prototype system that can gather input from speech, gestures and eye movements. The primary goal was to design a computer interface that could collect, process and interpret the different channels into a single integrated meaning.

A simple two-dimensional map is used as the subject of the interaction with the computer (Figure 1). Through a free mixture of speech, gestures and glances the user can request information or give commands to modify the contents of the map database. The prototype is composed of three major components: the input system, the map database, and the interpretation module (Figure 2).

Figure 2. The interpretation module receives information from both the user's actions and the map database, which allows it to interpret the actions in the context of the map.

3.1. Input System

The user's speech is recognized using a PC-based discrete word recognition system. Hand and arm movements are sampled using full hand sensing hardware, and data on eye movements is collected using a corneal-reflection eye tracker. All three streams of data, the words from the speech recognizer, the position and posture of the hand and the point of gaze, are collected on a central workstation (Figure 3). Each incoming data record is assigned a time stamp as it arrives on the host computer. This timing information is later used to realign data from the different sources.

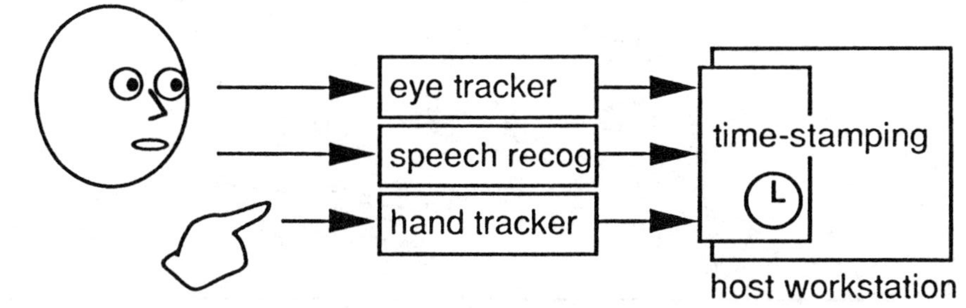

Figure 3. The data from speech, eye and hands are collected and sent to a real- time interface where they are time stamped. The time stamping allows for a later reconstruction of the input based on the exact time of occurrence.

3.2. Map Database

The map, displayed on the workstation display, serves as the shared subject for the human-computer interaction. The graphic presented is a simple two-dimensional color map and a number of colored icons representing objects. An object-oriented database manages the attributes and locations of the map objects. A command-language interface allows the interpretation module (and external simulation modules) to make queries to the database contents or to modify selected objects. When the system is initiated, the map database reads a stored configuration and displays the map for the user.

3.3. Interpretation Module

Based on the observation that a message is often composed of at least two very different kinds of information, the interpretation module includes two different representational systems that are interconnected: the first system is used to encode categorical information; the other is used to encode geometrical or spatial information. Information from the map database is used to build and maintain a knowledge base that spans the two representational systems. Map objects are represented both as nodes in a semantic network within the categorical system and as models in the spatial system. The interpretation module's task is to gather information from the input system and match the message to elements within the knowledge base.

The user input is processed in two major steps. First, the three input streams are parsed to produce a frame-like description of the structure of the incoming data. Second, the frames are interconnected and evaluated. Some frames can be encoded and evaluated in the categorical system where others find values in the spatial system. Together the expression guides the evaluation of the user's utterance. Once the expression is completely evaluated and all references have been resolved, the computer can then respond to the user's request. An example of this process is given in Section 3.6.

3.4. Parsing

Each mode has its own parser that takes advantage of the structure or syntax inherent in the corresponding data stream. The output of the three parsers is an expression in a common intermediate frame-based representation.

A parse tree is produced from the incoming words in the speech channel (Figure 4). As syntactic tokens are created and added to the parse tree, frames associated with those tokens are created and arranged into nested expressions. The timing information of individual words is carried up through the syntactic tokens and into the frames.

For this prototype, gestures and eye movements are treated in a simplified way and have only deictic interpretations. Posture and movement data from the hand-sensing hardware are processed to recognize postures and movements directed at the workstation display. When such a movement is detected, a frame is created with the glove and time data. Data from the eye tracker is analyzed to detect characteristic features in the motion of the eyes: fixations, saccades and blinks. A frame is created for each fixation containing the associated tracking data and time stamp.

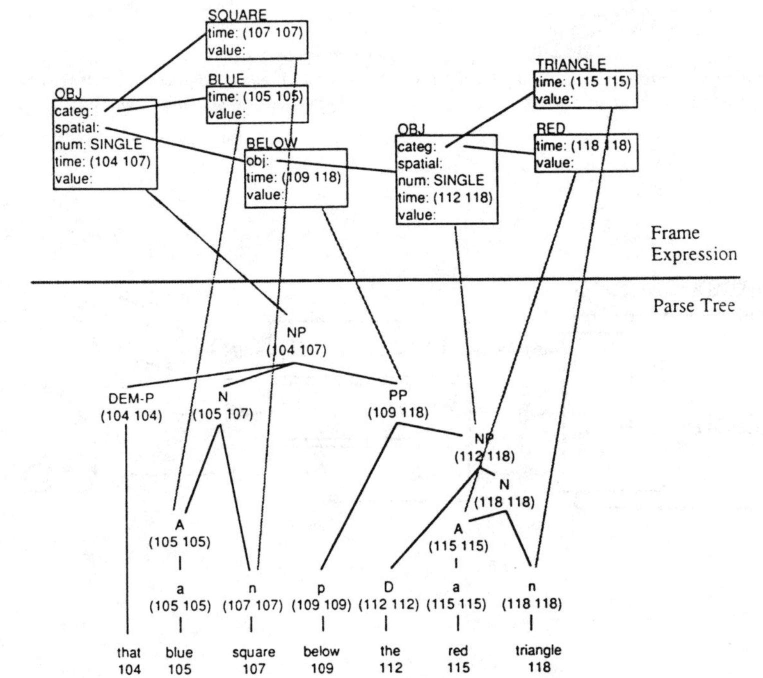

Figure 4. A parse tree is built from the incoming speech and then connected to the frame-based system. Here the parsed utterance is "... that blue square below the red triangle." Figure 5 shows frames produced from the other two modes.

3.5. Evaluation

Each frame produced during parsing has a corresponding "evaluation method" that controls the search for that frame's value within the knowledge base. Depending on the type of frame, values can range from *nodes* in the propositional system (representing attributes or individual objects) to *points* or *regions* in the spatial system. When an evaluation method is successful, the resulting value for the corresponding frame is now available to other evaluation methods. (Frames can serve as slot values in other frames, creating nested expressions similar to LISP functions.) If a problem arises in the evaluation of a frame, a "problem method" is started. A new subgoal is then created that attempts to find the missing information in other modes or by asking the user for additional information.

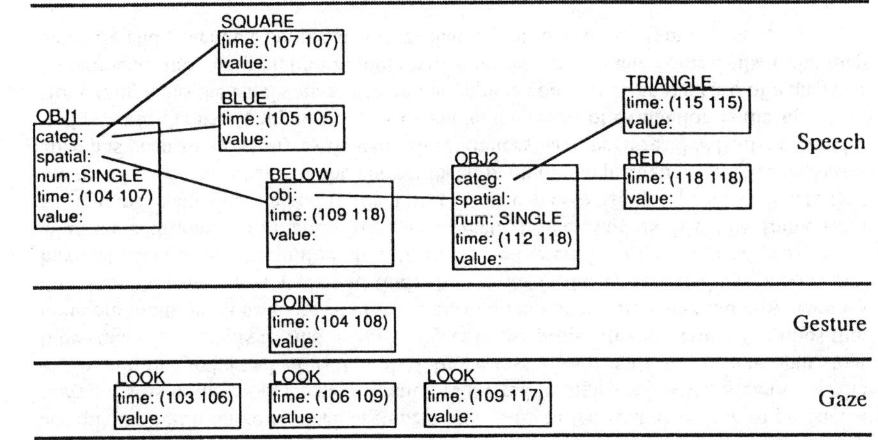

Figure 5. An idealized example of the frames produced from all three input modes during utterance "...that blue square below the red triangle"

3.6. Example Evaluation

Suppose the user is sitting in front of the display. He now says, "That blue square below the red triangle" while looking at the upper right quadrant of the screen and pointing in a similar direction. After this speech input is parsed, a nested expression of frames will be produced (Figure 5). Parsing the hand data and eye tracking data will produce additional, but at this time, disjoint frames. The evaluation methods attached to each of the frames begin to search for values for their frames in the representational systems. Because all gestures in this prototype are treated as deictic, an evaluation method attached to a gesture frame will produce a *point* in the spatial system; this *point* is the frame's value. The fixation frames are treated in a similar manner.

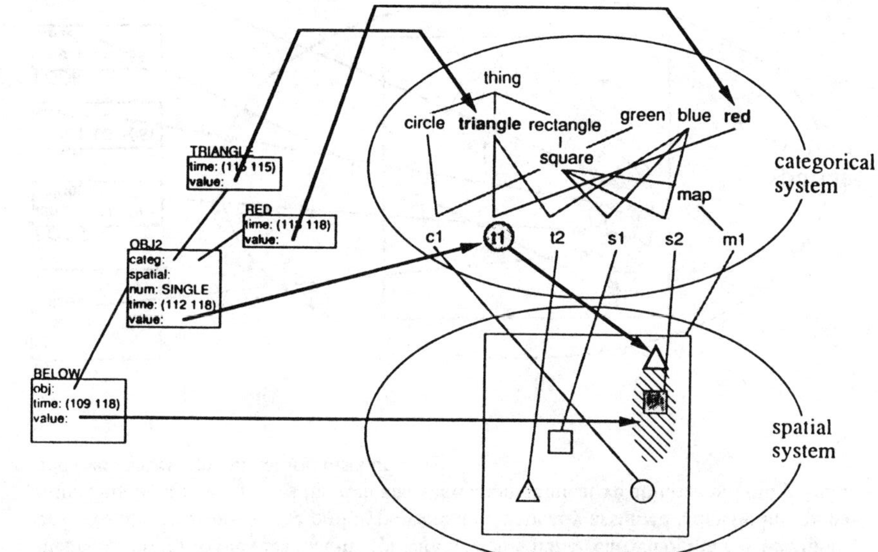

Figure 6. The expression associated with "below the red triangle" is evaluated by finding values for each frame. Frame values include object models and regions in the spatial system as well as nodes in the categorical system.

The evaluation method attached to the speech frame labeled OBJ2 (and associated with the speech input "the red triangle") in Figure 6 first attempts to use the propositional system to find an object that is both *red* and a *triangle.* This object, represented as a node in the propositional system (with links into its representation in the spatial system), is now available to the evaluation method attached to the BELOW frame. This method accepts the *red* triangle *t1* as an argument and shifts to the spatial system to produce a region that is in the proper spatial relation to the red triangle (below it). Meanwhile, the evaluation method attached to the OBJ1 frame (associated with the speech input "that blue square") attempts to find a single object in the propositional system but finds that there are multiple blue squares within the current map. A problem method now searches the other information sources and finds the frames in the gesture and eye modes that have an acceptable temporal relation to its frame (determined by temporal proximity). With the additional information from these deictic frames, and the BELOW frame from speech, the evaluation method for the OBJ1 frame can now use the spatial system to find the only blue square that is in the correct location on the map (Figure 7). Once the utterance has been successfully evaluated (all references have been resolved), the computer will react to the user's input. For this example, the result of evaluation is the square *s2* (for example, as the user's answer to an incomplete command). In the case of a query or a command, the interpretation module will send the appropriate commands to the map database and generate a simple statement that is sent to a speech synthesizer.

3.7. Discussion

This prototype system highlights many important points in attempting to interpret simultaneous multi-modal inputs. First and most obviously, this interface is a departure from current computer interface design. Unlike the interaction on a modern workstation, the user is able to use any combination of modes to communicate the request. For example, the user can choose to use speech alone with a request like "Delete all the blue squares." Or, speech can be reduced to "Move that to here" with gestures or glances filling in the necessary information. This opens up a highly flexible communication style for the user (and the interface designer).

A related point demonstrated in the prototype is that the interpretation of multi-modal input must be handled in a way that takes advantage of the interdependencies between the information supplied by each mode. While one mode may carry a significant portion of the information (usually speech), most messages cannot be interpreted without using the information from the other modes. These interdependencies require an interpretation process that is able to build up a single meaning by using all the modes simultaneously in a process similar to constraint satisfaction.

A shortcoming of this first prototype is its oversimplification of gestures and eye movements. Contrary to the idea that interpretation should not be carried out in any one mode, gestures and fixations in the prototype were automatically assigned a deictic interpretation. This treatment ignores the rich and subtle communicative abilities of both gestures and eye movements in natural discourse.

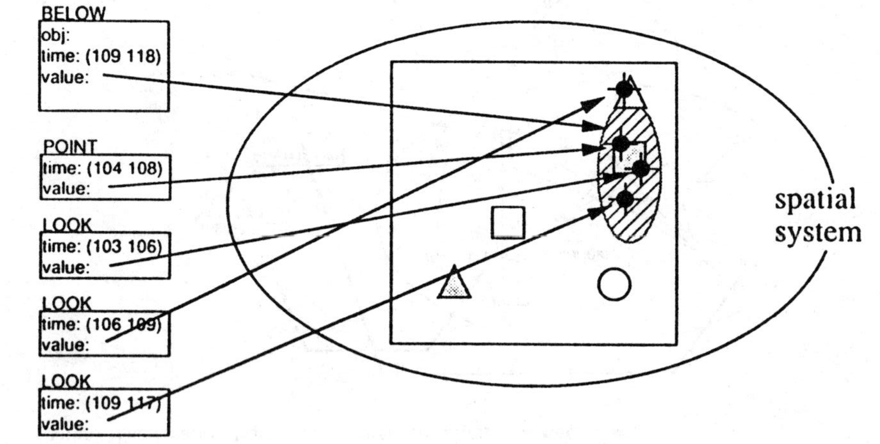

Figure 7. Spatial values for frames originating in the speech, gesture and eye tracking channels are compared in the spatial representation system.

4. Beyond Pointing

Gestures are most often integrated with our speech and other channels of communication. We fluidly switch context in the process of communicating a message, such that two identical hand movements might represent different actions, objects or ideas even when performed in the space of one verbal phrase. What are the different ways that a speech-related movement might be interpreted? Several taxonomies have been proposed for categorizing gestures that occur with speech. The taxonomy proposed by Rimé and Schiaratura [1991], which is a revision of the Efron classification system, proposes the following gesture types:

> *Symbolic gestures* can be translated directly to some verbal meaning (such as the "OK" *posture* made by touching the forefinger to the thumb and extending the other fingers). Gestures such as these are normally part of a culture and have come to represent a single unambiguous meaning within that culture.
>
> *Deictic gestures* include pointing or motioning to direct the listener's attention to objects or events in the surrounding environment.
>
> *Iconic gestures* are used by a speaker to display information about the shape of objects, spatial relations, and actions.
>
> *Pantomimic gestures* usually involve the manipulation of some invisible object or tool in contact with the speaker's hand.

Of these possible interpretations of speech-related hand movements, only the symbolic gestures can be interpreted immediately (within a given cultural context). Deictic, iconic and pantomimic gestures usually cannot stand alone and must be interpreted with additional information from the other channels and/or the surrounding context.

4.1. Representational Level

In order to extract meaning from the streams of gestural data, an appropriate level of abstraction must be chosen. At the lowest level, we have the constant flow of raw data from the full-hand input device hardware. At the highest level of abstraction would be a pure symbolic language (such as American Sign Language) in which complete gestures are specifically categorized to have an exact meaning.

It has been previously stated that using the highest level of abstraction, as in a symbolic language, limits the flexibility of the hands. This method changes the hands into "tools" and restricts their communicative power, creating problems such as the "Midas Touch." We have tried to find an intermediate level of abstraction that refines and reduces the information from the raw data and faciltates interpretation in the broader context of information available from other sources.

4.2. Gesture Features

Two layers of abstraction are built before the final interpretation of the gestures (Figures 8 and 9). First, the hand data is classified into features of *posture, orientation*, and *motion* at each discrete sample point. Currently, the posture features for each finger are *straight, relaxed*, or *closed*. For orientation of the hand, we look at the direction of two vectors coming out of the hand. The first is a normal vector out of the palm (vector A in Figure 10). The second is a longitudinal vector indicating where the hand is pointing (vector B in Figure 10). The general direction of both vectors is quantized into the values *up, down, left, right, forward*, or *back* (relative to the person's trunk). Hand motion is currently only specified as *moving* or *stopped*. While relatively crude, these descriptive tags are useful in detecting important changes in the hand data.

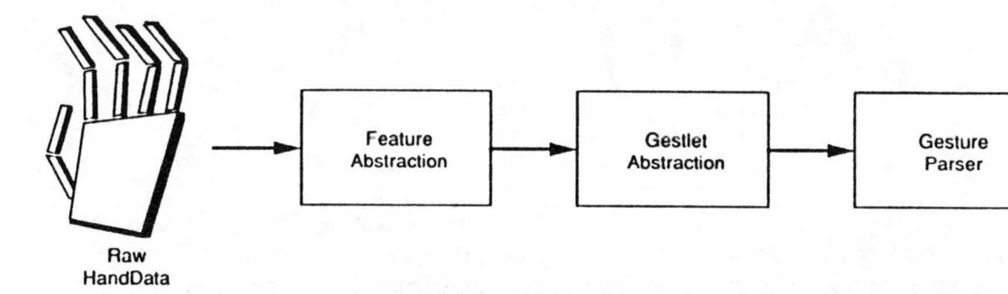

Figure 8. Raw hand data are processed successively on three separate representational levels.

The features are first used for data reduction: when a record is received with one or more of the values differing from the preceding record, it is extracted for further processing. These extracted records are passed to the next abstraction layer. Subsequent identical records are saved but not processed. (The unprocessed records are preserved for cases where the exact path is important, such as in the case of a person drawing out a detailed shape with their hand.)

4.3. Gestlets

A second layer of abstraction is created by collapsing the stream of features into structures similar to speech phrases (Figure 9). We refer to these structures as *gestlets*. The gestlets are pieces of gestures that have been formed by grouping portions of the feature stream together using certain rules. The most useful rule for this purpose has been to group all contiguous data sets where the hand is moving together with the preceding and following records when the hand is stopped.

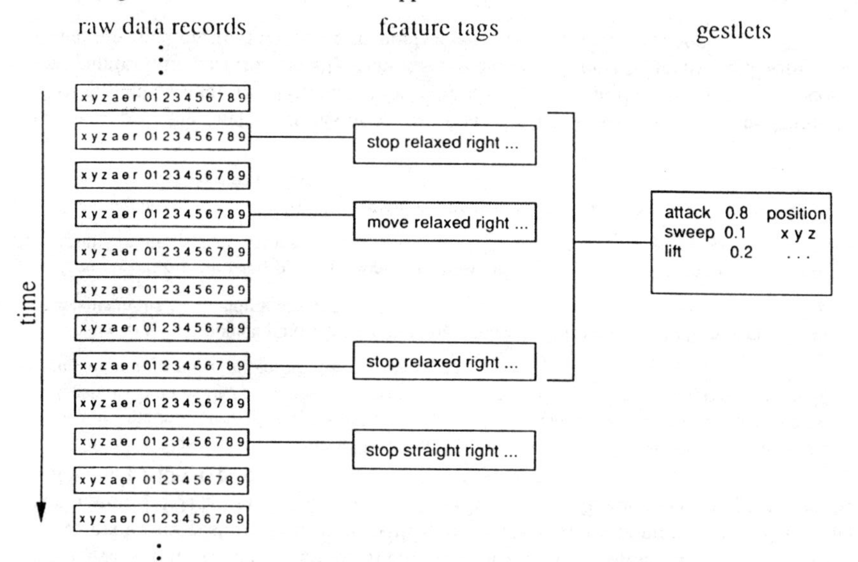

Figure 9. Parsing the raw hand data involves extracting features (feature tags) and combining these into meaningful units to produce gestlets.

The resulting stream of gestlets is buffered. If evidence in the speech channel suggests that important informaion may be found in gestures, the interpretation module searches the gestlet buffer for specific categories of gestures. The gesture parsing routines produce a broad description of the hand motion that occurred, using various weighted parameters. A pointing gesture, for example, would include *attack* (motion towards the gesture space), *sweep* (motion from side to side), and *end reference space* (position of hand at the end of the motion). By adding up the parameter weights, and looking for various logical combinations of gestlets, the parameters provide a way to estimate the likelihood that a certain categry of gesture happened. For this specific example, if a deictic gesture is gound, the hand orientation would be used to find a vector in three-space that intersects the screen.

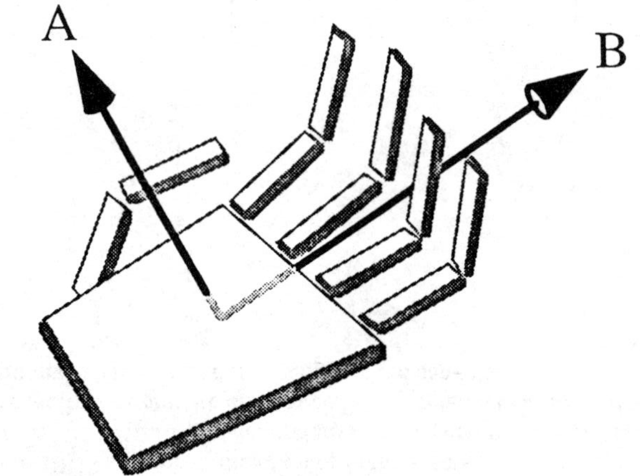

Figure 10. Normal and Longitudinal Vectors from Palm

4.4. Example Evaluation

A second prototype system, based on these modifications, enables a user to manipulate objects in a simple "blocks world" by using not only deictic but iconic and pantomimic gestures as well. A typical interaction is shown in Figure 11. The user in this example wishes to move and rotate a cylinder so that it ends up in a particular orientation next to a cube. It is important to note that gesture types are fluidly mixed in situations such as this. The raw data must be processed in a way that these motions can be separated and interpreted in the context of the accompanying speech.

While the hand data is being processed into gestlets, the speech recognizer is converting the voice input into words. The eye tracking module is also working in parallel determining fixations, saccades and blinks. Each channel of information is brought to a similar level of abstraction allowing for close examination of the interdependencies of the modalities.

Figure 11. Typical Interaction

Processing the speech produces a structure as shown in Figure 12. The first part of the command to be resolved is the reference with the phrase "that cylinder." The use of "that" in the utterance *"Place that cylinder"* strongly suggests a deictic gesture. The speech and gesture phrases are tied together and interpreted in the spatial representational system to determine a referent in the environment. The remainder of the directive, "next to the red cube," indicates the possibility of either a deictic or an iconic gesture.

The phrase "next to the red cube" allows for several interpretations. The first might be that the user doesn't care about the exact location and orientation of the cylinder, only that it is in close proximity to the cube. In that case, no gesture information would have been given, and the exact placement of the cylinder could be arbitrary. Alternatively, the person might use a deictic gesture and point to a location near the cube where the cylinder should be placed.

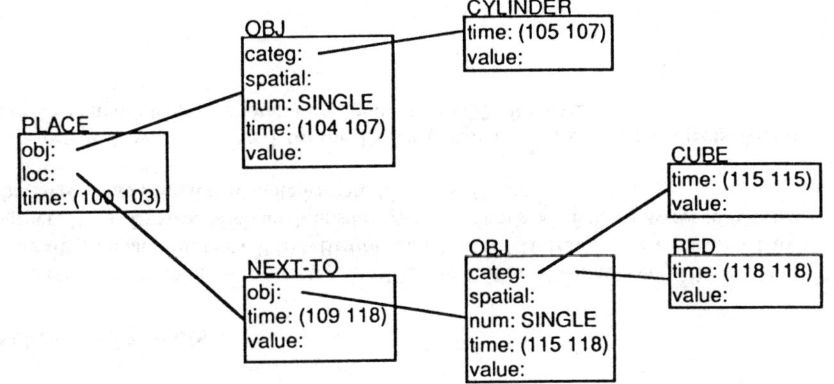

Figure 12. Structure After Speech Processing

A third possibility is the one shown in Figure 11. The person has used a two-handed iconic gesture to indicate not only the relative position of the cylinder with respect to the cube but also the orientation. The movement of both hands is important. First, the left hand is brought up to represent the cube. Then the right hand is moved in next to it to show the relative positioning of the two objects. Orientation information is provided by the right hand: it is placed in a curled posture suggesting that an invisible cylinder is being held.[1] With one command the user has accomplished a selection, a three-dimensional translation, and a rotation around all three axes.

5. Beyond Looking as Deixis

Most uses of gaze at the computer interface have been interpreted as deictic gestures indicating the user's interest [Thorisson et al. 1992; Starker and Bolt 1990; Jacob 1990]. However, like gestures, eye movements can be interpreted in many different ways, depending on the context in which they are performed. For example, gaze is a good indicator of a person's attention over time [Kahneman 1973] and could be useful in predicting the user's behavior in the context of a broader task. The eyes also play a very special role in social interaction; they are important in the regulation of turn-taking between participants in a dialog (who has control of the "floor") [Argyle and Cook 1976]. Turn taking is crucially important in both clarification and negotiation [Whittaker and Walker 1991]. Additionally, eye movements have been found to play a significant role in conveying personality, emotional states, and interpersonal attitudes [Argyle et al. 1974; Kleinke 1986].

Future work should include the ability to incorporate this eye behavior information in an integrated interpretation process. Someday, significant looks, tired stares, winks and rapid searches can all be useful in our interaction with machines.

6. Summary

We have shown a frame-based method of interpreting multi-modal input. The system takes into account various types of gestures, fairly complex speech and deictic gaze. By bringing gestures to an intermediate representational level, interpretation of hand data is made more flexible. The gesture parsing method described can currently handle deictic references, pantomimic and iconic gestures, but should be easily extended to accommodate other categories as well.

Future work should include extensions such as full-arm and full-body descriptions. We are currently working on methods to accommodate more complex interpretations of looking and are exploring other gesture categories in a variety of contexts.

Acknowledgments

We would like to thank our director, Dr. Richard Bolt, and acknolwedge the contributions of graduate students Brent Britton and Edward Herranz, and assistants David Berger, Brian Brown, Michael Johnson, Mathew Kaminski, Brian Lawrence, Christopher Wren, and research affiliate Masaru Sugai, NEC, Japan.

This research was supported by the Defense Advanced Research Projects Agency (DARPA) under Rome Laboratories, contract F30602-89-C-0022.

[1] The point might also be argued that the user is representing the cylinder by the shape of his hand. According to Rimé and Schiaratura's modified Efron classification, this would be an iconic gesture. In many cases this distinction will not make a difference for interpretation.

Reflections on. . .

Integrating Simultaneous Input from Speech, Gaze, and Hand Gestures

Dave Koons

A few months following the orginal publication of this chapter, a prototype system was completed that brought together much of the work described herein. ICONIC (Koons and Sparrell 1994) was developed to explore the use of speech and "depictive" gestures in a three-dimensional blocks world. The user can speak and gesture in any free combination to describe some action on the objects in the displayed scene.

ICONIC includes an object-oriented 3-D graphics/animation module built on top of SGI/Inventor, a pair of VPL data gloves with two Polhemus space-sensing cubes attached to the backs of the user's hands, and a BBN Hark connected speech recognition system. The system consists of three major modules: (1) the 3-D blocks world that serves as the shared context, (2) a gesture segmentation and parsing module, and (3) multimodal interpretation module.

A significant new feature of ICONIC is the development of an incremental parser and interpretation module. As new information becomes available from the input sources, the interpreter attempts to construct the best interpretation from the available data. This allows for a very flexible scheme that permits the evaluation to "anneal" from the provided multimodal inputs and the current graphical context or configuration.

The processing of gestures into the intermediate "gestlet" encoding was implemented as described in the chapter (Sparrell and Koons 1994). However, segmenting gestures using only the position of the user's hands proved to be sensitive to only large, sweeping-type movements. Almost immediately after the ICONIC system was completed, work began on a new gesture segmentation scheme that used a more complete model of the user's body. A pair of Virtual Technologies CyberGloves and a four-cube Ascension Flock replaced the previous hands-only sensing equipment. The four space-sensing cubes were distributed to key locations on the user's upper body: one each on the forearm (the CyberGloves include two bend sensors for the wrist), one on the head, and one on the back. By placing the cubes at these locations and using a model of the structure of the human body, inverse kinematics could then be used to give a complete description of the location/orientation of major segments of the user's upper body. The end result was a body-centered encoding of body postures and movements independent of the underlying sensing technology. A new segmentation scheme based on changes in computed joint angles has proven to be very robust and allows for very sensitive detection and segmentation of the user's movements into key gestural phases.

My current research is guided by three observations. First, traditional symbolic representational schemes, although well suited to capturing the content of speech, tend to miss much of the content of other modes, especially gestures. Second, multimodal communication is particularly powerful when dealing with topics or domains that include significant spatiotemporal components (e.g., describing a car accident or discussing an architectural design). Third, a subtle and complex relationship often exists between the information carried in the different modes: information in one mode tends to complement the information carried in other modes. From these observations, I have proposed a representational system composed of multiple encoding schemes: a traditional symbolic scheme combined with a specialized representation for encoding spatiotemporal structure (Koons 1994). This multi-representational system supports the encoding and interpretation of a person's multimodal descriptions by capturing information in different formats and affording a wide range of operations and inferences. Resolving references in the user's input is seen as a process of reestablishing the relations between information in the different modes and simultaneously defining a mapping between the user's description and the system's knowledge about the context. A successful interpretation is represented as an interconnected set of elements that allows the identification of the referenced element or the specification of an action.

REFERENCES

Koons, D. B. 1994. Capturing and Interpreting Multi-Modal Descriptions with Multiple Representations. *In Proceedings of the AAAI 1994 Spring Symposium: Intelligent Multi-Media Multi-Modal Systems*, Stanford University.

Koons, D. B., and Sparrell, C. J. 1994. ICONIC: Speech and Depictive Gestures at the Human-Machine Interface. In *Proceedings of CHI '94* (SIGRAPH/SIGCHI video review), Boston, MA.

Sparrell, C. J., and Koons, D. B. 1994. Interpretation of Coverbal Depictive Gestures. In *Proceedings of the AAAI 1994 Spring Symposium: Intelligent Multi-Media Multi-Modal Systems*, Stanford University.

The Use of Eye Movements in Human-Computer Interaction Techniques: What You Look At is What You Get

ROBERT J. K. JACOB
Naval Research Laboratory

In seeking hitherto-unused methods by which users and computers can communicate, we investigate the usefulness of eye movements as a fast and convenient auxiliary user-to-computer communication mode. The barrier to exploiting this medium has not been eye-tracking technology but the study of interaction techniques that incorporate eye movements into the user-computer dialogue in a natural and unobtrusive way. This paper discusses some of the human factors and technical considerations that arise in trying to use eye movements as an input medium, describes our approach and the first eye movement-based interaction techniques that we have devised and implemented in our laboratory, and reports our experiences and observations on them.

Categories and Subject Descriptors: D.2.2 [**Software Engineering**]: Tools and Techniques—*user interfaces*; H.1.2 [**Models and Principles**]: User/Machine Systems—*human factors*; H.5.2 [**Information Interfaces and Presentation**]: User Interfaces—*input devices and strategies, interaction styles, user interface management system*

General Terms: Design, Human Factors

Additional Key Words and Phrases: Eye movements, eye tracking, human-computer interaction, state transition diagram, UIMS, input

1. INTRODUCTION

Current user-computer dialogues tend to be one sided, with the bandwidth from the computer to the user far greater than that from user to computer. A fast and effortless mode of communication from a user to a computer would help redress this imbalance. We therefore investigate the possibility of introducing the movements of a user's eyes as an additional input medium. While the technology for measuring eye movements and reporting them in real time has been improving, what is needed is appropriate *interaction techniques* that incorporate eye movements into the user-computer dialogue in a convenient and natural way. This paper describes research at NRL on developing such interaction techniques. It discusses some of the human factors and technical considerations that arise in trying to use eye movements as an input medium, describes our approach and the first eye

This work was sponsored by the Office of Naval Research.
Author's address: Human-Computer Interaction Lab., Naval Research Laboratory, Washington, D.C. 20375.

movement-based interaction techniques that we have devised and implemented in our laboratory, and reports our experiences and observations on them.

2. BACKGROUND

Methods for Measuring Eye Movements

Available techniques for measuring eye movements vary considerably; while none is perfect, some are considerably more suitable for user-computer interaction than others. First, note that our goal is to measure *visual line of gaze*, that is, the absolute position in space at which the user's eyes are pointed, rather than, for example, the position of the eye in space or the relative motion of the eye within the head; not all eye tracking techniques do this [16]. Since both eyes generally point together, it is customary to track only one eye.

The simplest eye tracking technique is electronic recording, using electrodes placed on the skin around the eye to measure changes in the orientation of the potential difference that exists between the cornea and the retina. However, this method is more useful for measuring relative eye movements than absolute position. Perhaps the least user-friendly approach uses a contact lens that fits precisely over the corneal bulge and is held in place with a slight suction. This method is extremely accurate, but suitable only for laboratory studies. More practical methods use remote imaging of a visible feature located on the eye, such as the boundary between the sclera and iris, the outline of the pupil, or the corneal reflection of a light shone at the eye. All these require the head to be held absolutely stationary (a bite board is customarily used), to be sure that any measured movement represents movement of the eye, not the head. However, by simultaneously tracking two features of the eye that move differentially (because of the difference in radius of curvature of the cornea and sclera), it is possible to distinguish head movements (the two features move together) from eye movements (the two move with respect to one another), and the head need not be rigidly fixed. This is currently the most practical method for use in a conventional computer-and-user setting, since the eye tracker sits several feet from the user, nothing contacts him or her, and the head need not be clamped. In our laboratory, we use an Applied Science Laboratories (Waltham, Mass.) Model 3250R eye tracker [10, 16]. Figure 1 shows the components of this type of eye tracker. It simultaneously tracks the corneal reflection (from an infrared light shining on eye) and the outline of the pupil (illuminated by same light). Visual line of gaze is computed from the relationship between the two tracked points.

Previous Work

While current technology for measuring visual line of gaze is adequate, there has been little research on *using* this information in real-time. There is a considerable body of research using eye tracking, but it has concentrated on

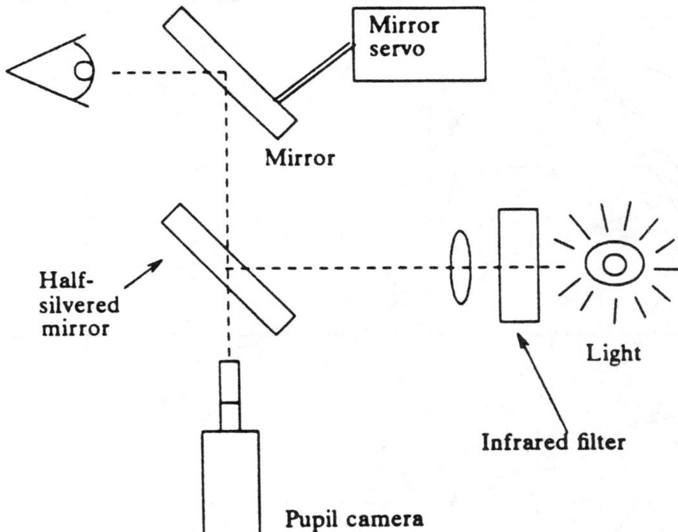

Fig. 1. Illustration of components of a corneal reflection-plus-pupil eye tracker. The pupil camera and illuminator operate along the same optical axis, via a half-silvered mirror. The servo-controlled mirror is used to compensate for the user's head motions.

eye movement data as a tool for studying motor and cognitive processes [8, 11]. Such work involves recording the eye movements and then analyzing them subsequently; the user's eye movements do not have any effect on the computer interface while it is in operation.

Real-time eye input has been used most frequently for disabled (quadriplegic) users, who can use only their eyes for input (e.g., Hutchinson et al. and Levine [6, 9] report work for which the primary focus was disabled users). Our interest is, instead, on dialogues that combine real-time eye movement data with other, more conventional modes of user-computer communication. Bolt did some of the earliest work in this particular area and demonstrated several innovative uses of eye movements [1, 2, 14]. Glenn [5] used eye movements for several tracking tasks involving moving targets. Ware and Mikaelian [15] reported an experiment in which simple target selection and cursor positioning operations were performed approximately twice as fast with an eye tracker than with any of the more conventional cursor positioning devices. Fitt's law relationship as seen in experiments with other cursor positioning devices [4] remained true of the eye tracker; only the speed was different.

Characteristics of Eye Movements

To see an object clearly, it is necessary to move the eye so that the object appears on the fovea, a small area at the center of the retina. Because of this, a person's eye position provides a rather good indication (to within the

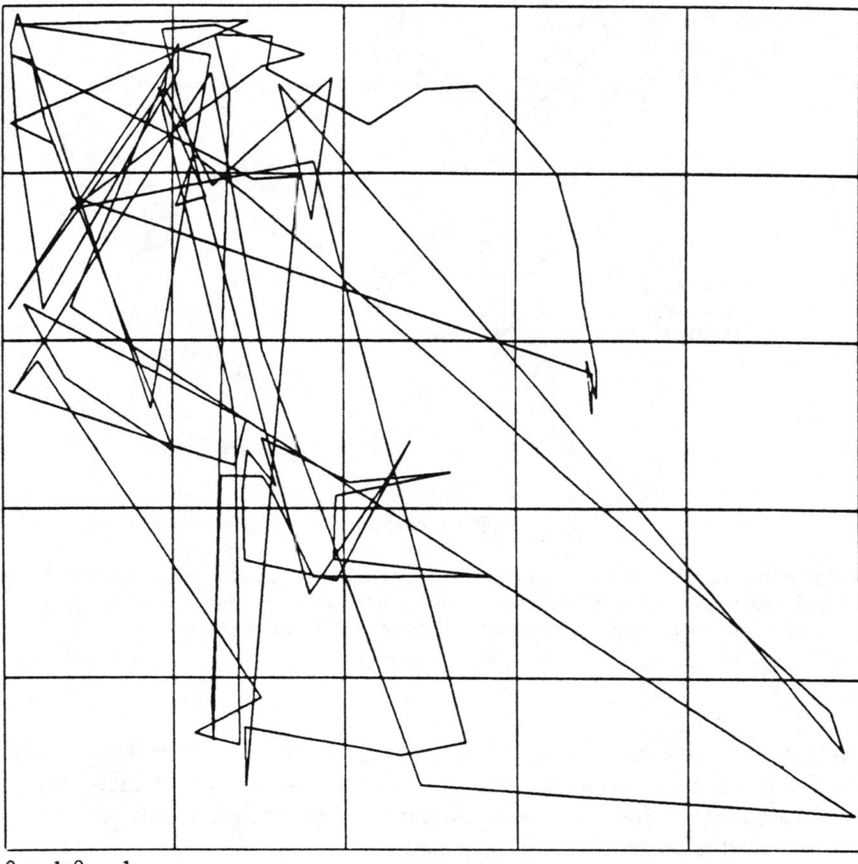

Fig. 2. A trace of a computer user's eye movements over approximately 30 seconds, while performing normal work (i.e., no eye-operate interfaces) using a windowed display. Jitter within each fixation has been removed from this plot.

one-degree width of the fovea) of what specific portion of the scene before him he is examining. The most common way of moving the eyes is a sudden, ballistic, and nearly instantaneous *saccade*. It is typically followed by a *fixation*, a 200-600 ms. period of relative stability during which an object can be viewed. During a fixation, however, the eye does not remain still; it still makes small, jittery motions, generally covering less than one degree. Smooth eye motions, less sudden than saccades, occur only in response to a moving object in the visual field. Other eye movements, such as nystagmus, vergence, and torsional rotation are relatively insignificant in a user-computer dialogue.

The overall picture of eye movements for a user sitting in front of a computer is a collection of steady (but slightly jittery) fixations connected by sudden, rapid saccades. The eyes are rarely entirely still. They move during a fixation, and they seldom remain in one fixation for long. Figure 2 shows a trace of eye movements (with intra-fixation jitter removed) for a user using a computer for 30 seconds. Compared to the slow and deliberate way people operate a mouse or other manual input device, eye movements careen madly about the screen. During a fixation, a user generally thinks he is looking steadily at a single object—he is not consciously aware of the small, jittery motions. This suggests that the human-computer dialogue should be constructed so that it, too, ignores those motions, since, ultimately, it should correspond to what the user *thinks* he is doing, rather than what his eye muscles are actually doing. This will require filtering of the raw eye position data to eliminate the high-frequency jitter, but at the same time we must not unduly slow response to the high-frequency component of a genuine saccade.

"Midas Touch" Problem

The most naive approach to using eye position as an input might be to use it as a direct substitute for a mouse: changes in the user's line of gaze would cause the mouse cursor to move. This is an unworkable (and annoying) approach, because people are not accustomed to operating devices just by moving their eyes. They expect to be able to look at an item without having the look "mean" something. Normal visual perception requires that the eyes move about, scanning the scene before them. It is not desirable for each such move to initiate a computer command.

At first, it is empowering to be able simply to look at what you want and have it happen, rather than having to look at it (as you would anyway) and then point and click it with the mouse or otherwise issue a command. Before long, though, it becomes like the Midas Touch. Everywhere you look, another command is activated; you cannot look anywhere without issuing a command. The challenge in building a useful eye tracker interface is to avoid this Midas Touch problem. Ideally, the interface should act on the user's eye input when he wants it to and let him just look around when that's what he wants, but the two cases are impossible to distinguish in general. Instead, we investigate interaction techniques that address this problem in specific cases.

3. EXPERIENCE WITH EYE MOVEMENTS

Configuration

We use an Applied Science Laboratories corneal reflection eye tracker. The user sits at a conventional (government-issue) desk, with a Sun computer display, mouse, and keyboard, in a standard chair and office. The eye tracker camera/illuminator sits on the desk next to the monitor. Other than the illuminator box with its dim red glow, the overall setting is thus far just like that for an ordinary office computer user. In addition, the room lights are dimmed to keep the user's pupil from becoming too small. The eye tracker transmits the x and y coordinates for the user's visual line of gaze every $\frac{1}{60}$ second, on a serial port, to a Sun 4/260 computer. The Sun performs all further processing, filtering, fixation recognition, and some additional calibration. Software on the Sun parses the raw eye tracker data stream into tokens that represent events meaningful to the user-computer dialogue. Our User Interface Management System [7] multiplexes these tokens with other inputs (such as mouse and keyboard) and processes them to implement the user interfaces under study.

Observation. The eye tracker is, strictly speaking, nonintrusive and does not touch the user in any way. Our setting is almost identical to that for a user of a conventional office computer. Nevertheless, we find it is difficult to ignore the eye tracker. It is noisy; the dimmed room lighting is unusual; the dull red light, while not annoying, is a constant reminder of the equipment; and, most significantly, the action of the servo-controlled mirror, which results in the red light following the slightest motions of user's head gives one the eerie feeling of being watched. One further wrinkle is that the eye tracker is designed for use in experiments, where there is a "subject" whose eye is tracked and an "experimenter" who monitors and adjusts the equipment. Operation by a single user playing both roles simultaneously is somewhat awkward because, as soon as you look at the eye tracker control panel to make an adjustment, your eye is no longer pointed where it should be for tracking.

Accuracy and Range

A user generally need not position his eye more accurately than the width of the fovea (about one degree) to see an object sharply. Finer accuracy from an eye tracker might be needed for studying the operation of the eye muscles but adds little for our purposes. The eye's normal jittering further limits the practical accuracy of eye tracking. It is possible to improve accuracy by averaging over a fixation, but not in a real-time interface.

Observation. Despite the servo-controlled mirror mechanism for following the user's head, we find that the steadier the user holds his head, the better the eye tracker works. We find that we can generally get two degrees accuracy quite easily, and sometimes can achieve one degree (or approximately 0.4″ on the screen at a 24″ viewing distance). The eye tracker should thus be viewed as having a resolution much coarser than that of a mouse or other typical devices, perhaps more like a traditional touch screen. A further problem is that the range over which the eye can be tracked with this equipment is fairly limited. In our configuration, it can barely cover the surface of a 19″ monitor at a 24″ viewing distance.

Using the Eye Tracker Data

Our approach to processing eye movement data is to partition the problem into two stages. First we process the raw data from the eye tracker in order to filter noise, recognize fixations, compensate for local calibration errors, and generally try to reconstruct the user's more conscious intentions from the available information. This processing stage converts the continuous, somewhat noisy stream of raw eye position reports into discrete tokens that we claim more closely approximate the user's intentions in a higher-level user-computer dialogue. Then, we design generic interaction techniques based on these tokens as inputs.

Observation. Because eye movements are so different from conventional computer inputs, we achieve success with a philosophy that tries, as much as possible, to use natural eye movements as an implicit input, rather than to train a user to move the eyes in a particular way to operate the system. We try to think of eye position more as a piece of information available to the user-computer dialogue involving a variety of input devices than as the intentional actuation of an input device.

Local Calibration

The eye tracker calibration procedure produces a mapping that is applied uniformly to the whole screen. Ideally, no further calibration or adjustment is necessary. In practice, we found small calibration errors appear in portions of the screen, rather than systematically across it. We introduced an additional layer of calibration into the chain, outside of the eye tracker computer, which allows the user to make local modifications to the calibration, based on arbitrary points he inputs whenever he feels it would be helpful. If the user feels the eye tracker is not responding accurately in some area of the screen, he can at any point move the mouse cursor to that area, look at the cursor, and click a button.

Observation. Surprisingly, this had the effect of increasing the apparent response speed for object selection and other interaction techniques. The reason is that, if the calibration is slightly wrong in a local region and the user stares at a single target in that region, the eye tracker will report the eye position somewhere slightly outside the target. If he continues to stare at it, though, his eyes will in fact jitter around to a spot that the eye tracker will report as being on the target. The effect feels as though the system is responding too slowly, but it is a problem of local calibration. The local calibration procedure results in a marked improvement in the apparent responsiveness of the interface as well as an increase in the user's control over the system (since he can recalibrate when and where desired).

Fixation Recognition

After improving the calibration, we still observed what seemed like erratic behavior in the user interface, even when the user thought he was staring perfectly still. This was caused by both natural and artificial sources: the normal jittery motions of the eye during fixations as well as artifacts introduced when the eye tracker momentarily fails to obtain an adequate video image of the eye.

Figure 3 shows the type of data obtained from the eye tracker. It plots the x coordinate of the eye position output against time over a relatively jumpy three second period. (A plot of the y coordinate for the same period would show generally the same areas of smooth versus jumpy behavior, but differ-

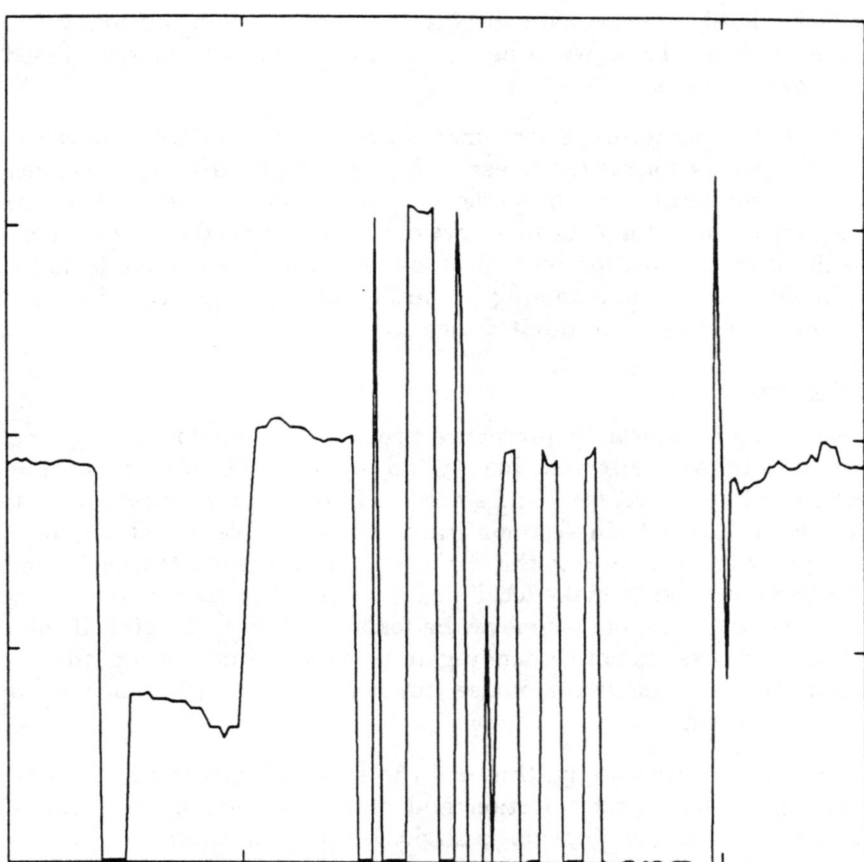

Fig. 3. Illustration of erratic nature of raw data from the eye tracker. The plot shows one coordinate of eye position versus time, over a somewhat worse-than-typical three second period.

ent absolute positions.) Zero values on the ordinate represent periods when the eye tracker could not locate the line of gaze, due either to eye tracker artifacts, such as glare in the video camera, lag in compensating for head motion, or failure of the processing algorithm, or by actual user actions, such as blinks or movements outside the range of the eye tracker. Unfortunately, the two cases are indistinguishable in the eye tracker output. During the period represented by Figure 3, the subject thought he was simply looking around at a few different points on a CRT screen. Buried in these data, thus, are a few relatively long gazes along with some motions to connect the gazes. Such raw data are quite unusable as input to a human-computer dialogue: while the noise and jumpiness do partly reflect the actual motion of the user's eye muscles, they do not reflect his intentions nor his impression of what his eyes were doing. The difference is attributable not only to the eye tracker artifacts but to the fact that much of the fine-grained behavior of the eye muscles is not intentional.

The problem is to extract from the noisy, jittery, error-filled stream of position reports produced by the eye tracker some "intentional" components of the eye motions, which make sense as tokens in a user-computer dialogue. Our first solution was to use a simple moving average filter to smooth the data. It improves performance during a fixation, but tends to dampen the sudden saccades that move the eye from one fixation to the next. Since one of the principal benefits we hope to obtain from eye motions as input is speed, damping them is counterproductive. Further, the resulting smoothed data do not correctly reflect the user's intentions. The user was not slowly gliding from one fixation to another; he was, in fact, fixating a spot and then jumping ballistically to a new fixation.

Instead, we return to the picture of a computer user's eye movements as a collection of jittery fixations connected by essentially instantaneous saccades. We start with an *a priori* model of such saccades and fixations and then attempt to recognize those events in the data stream. We then identify and quickly report the start and approximate position of each recognized fixation. We ignore any reports of eye position during saccades themselves, since they are difficult for the eye tracker to catch and their dynamics are not particularly meaningful to the user-computer dialogue.

Specifically, our algorithm, which is based on that used for retrospective analysis of eye tracker data and on the known properties of fixations and saccades, watches the input data for a sequence of 100 milliseconds during which the reported eye position remains within approximately 0.5 degrees. As soon as the 100 milliseconds have passed, it reports the start of a fixation and takes the mean of the set of data collected during the 100 milliseconds duration as the location of that fixation. A better estimate of the location of a fixation could be obtained by averaging over more eye tracker data, but this would mean a longer delay before the fixation position could be reported to the user interface software. Our algorithm implies a delay of 100 milliseconds before reporting the start of a fixation, and, in practice this delay is nearly undetectable to the user. Further eye positions within approximately one degree are assumed to represent continuations of the same fixation (rather than a saccade to a new one). To terminate a fixation, 50 milliseconds of data lying outside one degree of the current fixation must be received. Blinks or artifacts of up to 200 milliseconds may occur during a fixation without terminating it. (These occur when the eye tracker reports a "no position" code.) At first, blinks seemed to present a problem, since, obviously, we cannot obtain eye position data during a blink. However (equally obviously in retrospect), the screen need not respond to the eye during that blink period, since the user can't see it anyway.

After applying this algorithm, the noisy data shown in Figure 3 are found to comprise about 6 fixations, which more accurately reflects what the user thought he was doing (rather than what his eye muscles plus the eye tracking equipment actually did). Figure 4 shows the same data, with a horizontal line marking each recognized fixation at the time and location it would be reported.

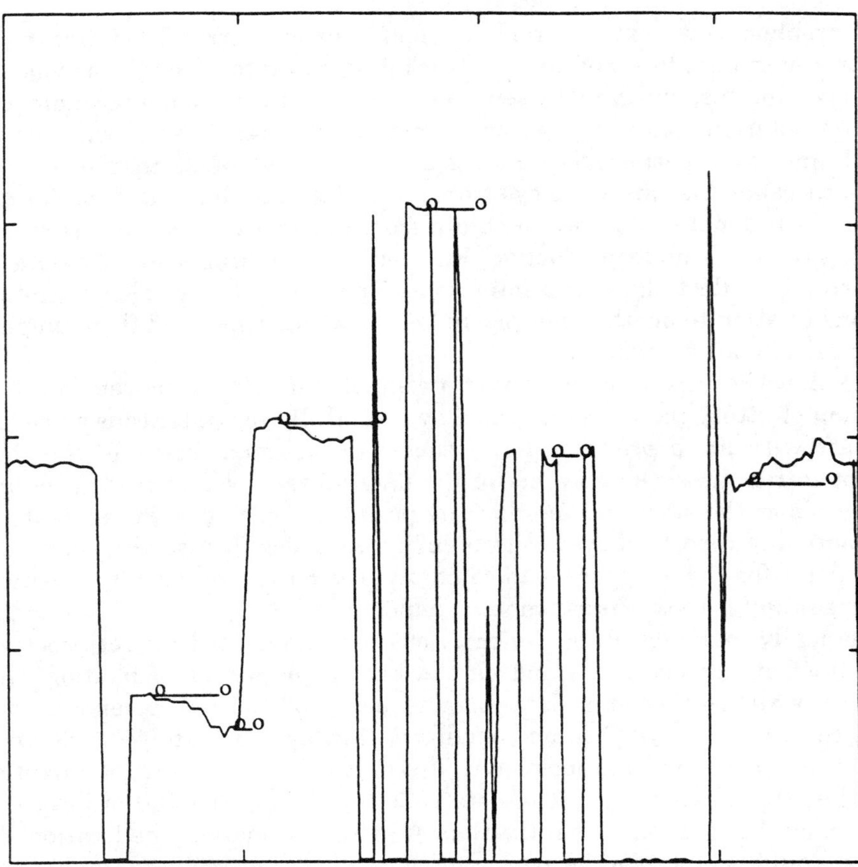

Fig. 4. Result of applying the fixation recognition algorithm to the data of Figure 3. A horizontal line beginning and ending with an o marks each fixation at the time and coordinate position it would be reported.

Observation. Applying the fixation recognition approach to the real-time data coming from the eye tracker yielded a significant improvement in the user-visible behavior of the interface. Filtering the data based on an *a priori* model of eye motion is an important step in transforming the raw eye tracker output into a user-computer dialogue.

User Interface Management System

In order to make the eye tracker data more tractable for use as input to an interactive user interface, we turn the output of the recognition algorithm into a stream of *tokens*. We report tokens for eye events considered meaningful to the user-computer dialogue, analogous to the way that raw input from a keyboard (shift key went down, letter *a* key went down, etc.) is turned into meaningful events (one ASCII upper case *A* was typed). We report tokens for the start, continuation (every 50 milliseconds, in case the dialogue is waiting to respond to a fixation of a certain duration), and end of each detected fixation. Each such token is tagged with the actual fixation duration to date, so an interaction technique that expects a fixation of a particular length will not be skewed by delays in UIMS processing or by the delay inherent in the fixation recognition algorithm. In between fixations, we periodically report a nonfixation token indicating where the eye is, although our current interaction techniques ignore this token in preference to the more processed fixation tokens. A token is also reported whenever the eye tracker fails to determine eye position for 200 milliseconds and again when it resumes tracking. These tokens, having been processed by the algorithms described above, are suitable for use in a user-computer dialogue in the same way as tokens generated by mouse or keyboard events.

We then multiplex the eye tokens into the same stream with those generated by the mouse and keyboard and present the overall token stream as input to our User Interface Management System. The desired user interface is specified to the UIMS as a collection of concurrently executing interaction objects [7]. The operation of each such object is described by a state transition diagram that accepts the tokens as input. Each object can accept any combination of eye, mouse, and keyboard tokens, as specified in its own syntax diagram.

4. INTERACTION TECHNIQUES

An interaction technique is a way of using a physical input device to perform a generic task in a human-computer dialogue [12]. It represents an abstraction of some common class of interactive task, for example, choosing one of several objects shown on a display screen. This section describes the first few eye movement-based interaction techniques that we have implemented and our initial observations from using them.

Object Selection

The task here is to select one object from among several displayed on the screen, for example, one of several file icons on a desktop or, as shown in Figure 5, one of several ships on a map in a hypothetical "command and control" system. With a mouse, this is usually done by pointing at the object and then pressing a button. With the eye tracker, there is no natural counterpart of the button press. We reject using a blink for a signal because it detracts from the naturalness possible with an eye movement-based dialogue by requiring the user to think about when he or she blinks. We tested two alternatives. In one, the user looks at the desired object then presses a button on a keypad to indicate that the looked-at object is his choice. In Figure 5, the user has looked at ship "EF151" and caused it to be selected (for attribute display, described below). The second uses dwell time—if the user continues to look at the object for a sufficiently long time, it is selected without further operations. The two techniques are actually implemented simultaneously, where the button press is optional and can be used to avoid

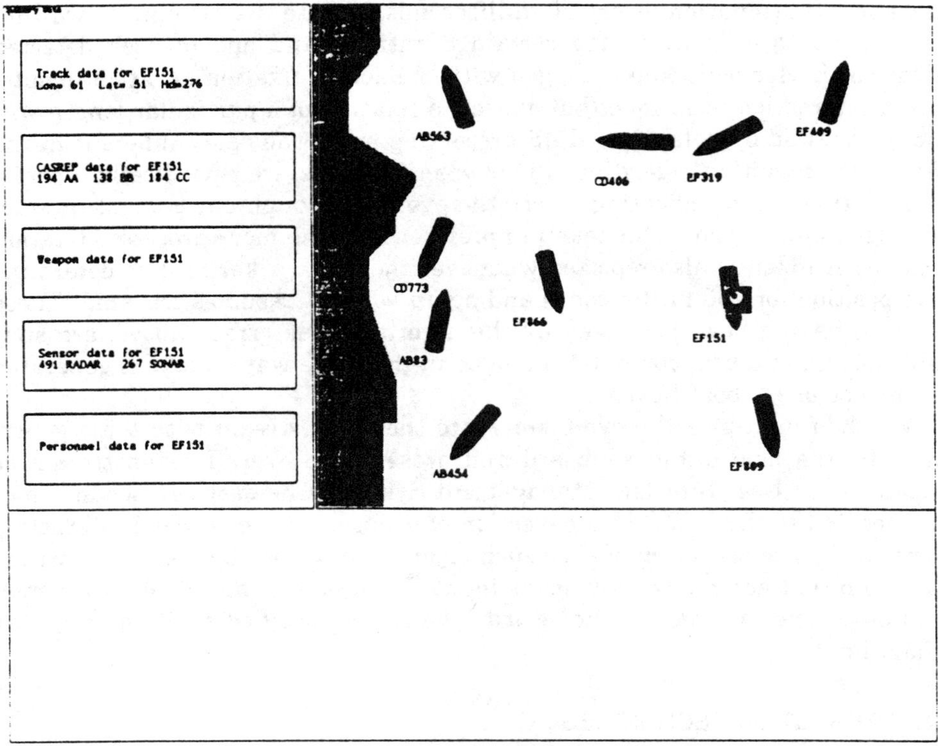

Fig. 5. Display from eye tracker testbed, illustrating object selection technique. Whenever the user looks at a ship in the right window, the ship is selected and information about it is displayed in left window. The square eye icon at the right is used to show where the user's eye was pointing in these illustrations; it does not normally appear on the screen. The actual screen image uses light figures on a dark background to keep the pupil large.

waiting for the dwell time to expire, much as an optional menu accelerator key is used to avoid traversing a menu.

Observation. At first this seemed like a good combination. In practice, however, the dwell time approach is much more convenient. While a long dwell time might be used to ensure that an inadvertent selection will not be made by simply "looking around" on the display, this mitigates the speed advantage of using eye movements for input and also reduces the responsiveness of the interface. To reduce dwell time, we make a further distinction. If the result of selecting the wrong object can be undone trivially (selection of a wrong object followed by a selection of the right object causes no adverse effect—the second selection instantaneously overrides the first), then a very short dwell time can be used. For example, if selecting an object causes a display of information about that object to appear and the information display can be changed instantaneously, then the effect of selecting wrong objects is immediately undone as long as the user eventually reaches the right one. This approach, using a 150–250 milliseconds dwell time gives excellent results. The lag between eye movement and system response (required to reach the dwell time) is hardly detectable to the user, yet long enough to accumulate sufficient data for our fixation recognition and processing. The subjective feeling is of a highly responsive system, almost as though the system is executing the user's intentions before he expresses them. For situations where selecting an object is more difficult to undo, button confirmation is used. We found no case where a long dwell time (over $\frac{3}{4}$ second) alone was useful, probably because it does not exploit natural eye movements (people do not normally fixate one spot for that long) and also creates the suspicion that the system has crashed. Pilot studies for an experiment that will compare response time for object selection by dwell time versus conventional selection by mouse pick, using the more abstract display shown in Figure 6, suggest a 30 percent decrease in time for the eye over the mouse, although the eye trials show more variability.

Continuous Attribute Display

A good use of this object selection interaction technique is for requesting further details or attributes of one of the objects on a display. Our approach is to provide a separate area of the display where such attributes are always shown. In Figure 5, the window on the right is a geographic display of ships, while the text window on the left shows some attributes of one of the ships, the one selected by the user's eye movement. The idea behind this is that the user can look around the ship window as desired. Whenever he looks over to the text window, he will always find there the attribute display for the last ship looked at—presumably the one he is interested in. (The ship remains selected when he looks away from the ship window to the text window.) However, if he simply looks at the ship window and never looks at the text area, he need not be concerned that his eye movements are causing commands in the text window. The text window is double-buffered, so that changes in its contents could hardly be seen unless the user were looking directly at it at the time it changed (which, of course, he is not—he must be looking at the ship window to effect a change).

Moving an Object

Another important interaction technique, particularly for direct manipulation systems, is moving an object on the display. We have experimented with two methods. Our initial notion was that, in a direct manipulation system, a mouse is typically used for two distinct operations—selecting an object to be manipulated and performing the manipulation. The two functions could be separated and each assigned to an appropriate input device. In particular, the selection could be performed by eye position, while the hand input device is devoted exclusively to the manipulations. We therefore implemented a technique whereby the eye selects an object (ship) to be manipulated (moved on the map, in this case) and then the mouse is used to move it. The eye selection is made precisely as in the previously-described interaction techniques. Then, the user grabs the mouse, presses a button, drags the mouse in

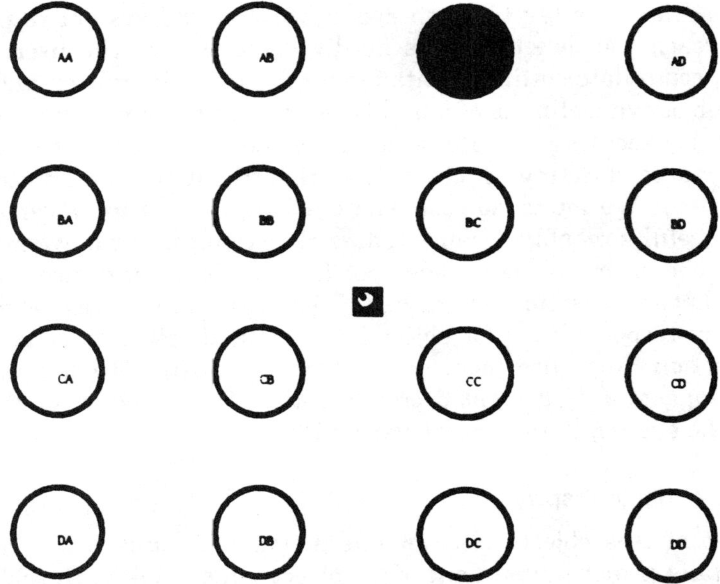

Fig. 6. Display for experimental study of the object selection interaction technique. Item "AC" near the upper right has just become highlighted, and the user must now select it (by eye or mouse).

the direction the object is to be moved, and releases the button. There is no visible mouse cursor in this scheme, and the mouse is used as a relative position device—it starts moving from wherever the eye-selected ship was. Our second approach used the eye to select and drag the ship, and a pushbutton to pick it up and put it down. The user selects a ship, then presses a button; while the button is depressed, the ship drags along with the user's eye. When it is released, the ship remains in its new position. Since the processing described previously is performed on the eye movements, the ship actually jumps to each fixation after about 100 milliseconds and then remains steadily there—despite actual eye jitter—until the next fixation.

Observation. Our initial guess was that the second method would be difficult to use: eye movements would be fine for selecting an object, but picking it up and having it jump around on the screen in response to eye movements would be annoying—a mouse would give more concrete control. Once again, our initial guess was not borne out. While the eye-to-select/mouse-to-drag method worked well, the user was quickly spoiled by the eye-only method. Once you begin to expect the system to know where you are looking, the mouse-to-drag operation seems awkward and slow. After looking at the desired ship and pressing the "pick up" button, the natural thing to do is to look at where you are planning to move the ship. At this point, you feel, "I'm looking right at the destination I want, why do I now have to go get the mouse to drag the ship over here?" With eye movements

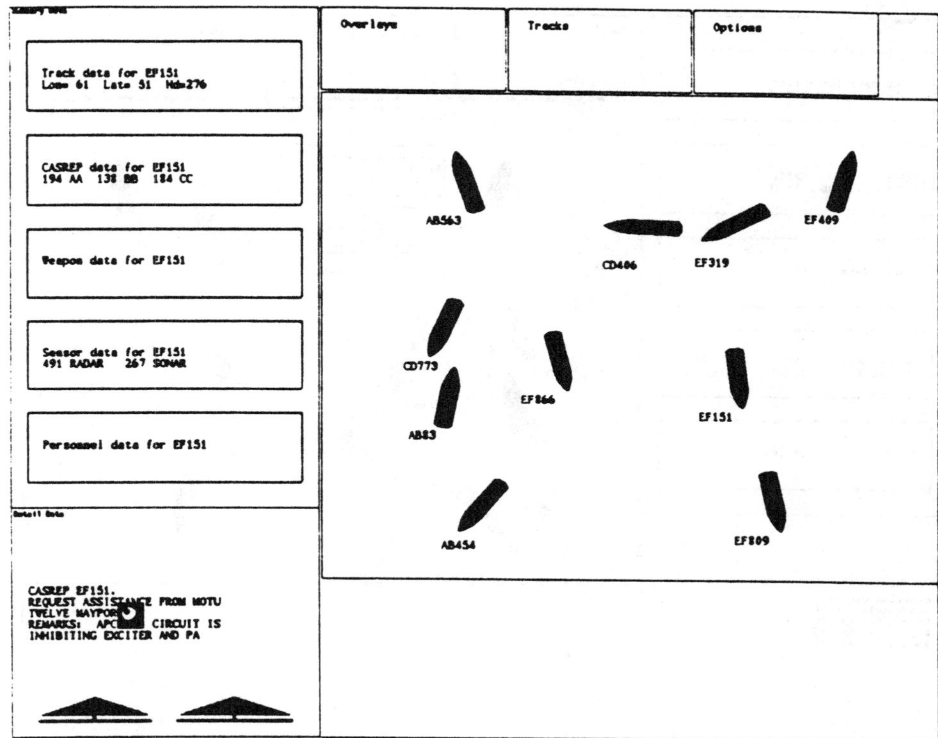

Fig. 7. Another display from the testbed, showing the scrolling text and other windows.

processed to suppress jitter and respond only to recognized fixations, the motion of the dragging ship is reasonably smooth and predictable and yet appears subjectively instantaneous. It works best when the destination of the move is a recognizable feature on the screen (another ship, or a harbor on a map); when the destination is an arbitrary blank spot, it is more difficult to make your eye look at it, as the eye is always drawn to features.

Eye-Controlled Scrolling Text

A window of text is shown, but not all of the material to be displayed can fit. As shown at the bottom left of Figure 7, arrows appear below the last line of the text and above the first line, indicating that there is additional material not shown. If the user looks at an arrow, the text itself starts to scroll. Note, though, that it never scrolls when the user is actually reading the text (rather than looking at the arrow). The assumption is that, as soon as the text starts scrolling, the user's eye will be drawn to the moving display and away from the arrow, which will stop the scrolling. The user can thus read down to the end of the window, then, after he finishes reading the last line, look slightly below it, at the arrow, in order to retrieve the next part of the

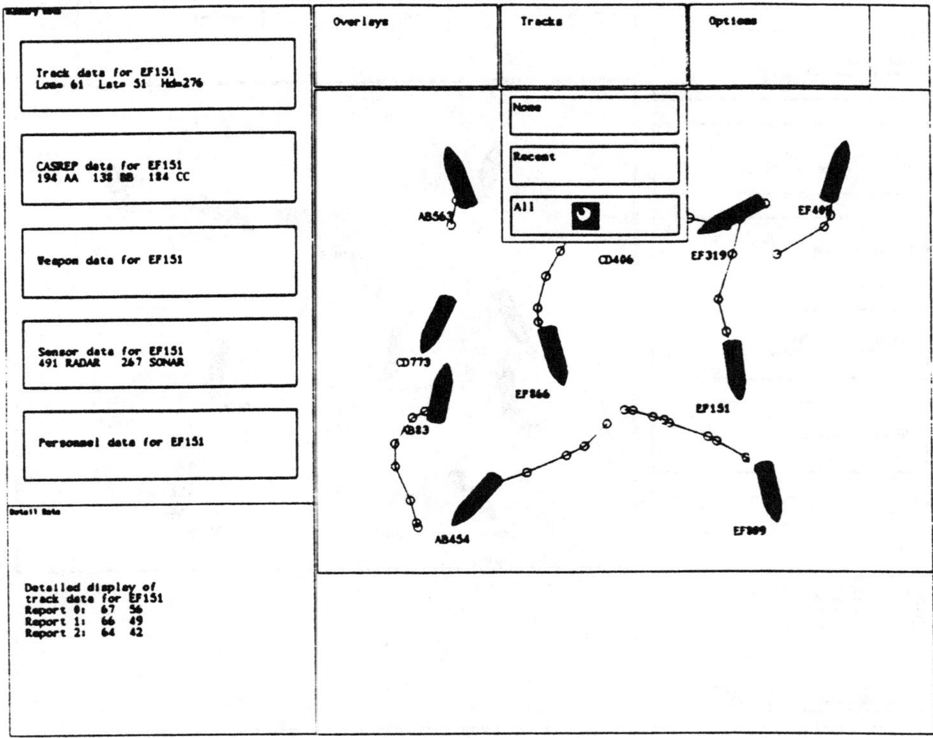

Fig. 8. Testbed display showing eye-controlled pull-down menu.

text. The arrow is visible above and/or below text display only when there is additional scrollable material in that direction.

Menu Commands

Another interaction technique is for choosing a command from a menu. Since pop-up menus inherently assume a button, we experimented with an eye-operated pull-down menu. In Figure 8, if the user looks at the header of a pull-down menu for a given dwell time (400 milliseconds), the body of the menu will appear on the screen. Next, he can look at the items shown on the menu. After a brief look at an item (100 milliseconds), it will be highlighted, but its command will not yet be executed. This allows the user time to examine the different items on the menu. If the user looks at one item for a much longer time (1 second), its command will be executed and the menu erased. Alternatively, once the item is highlighted, pressing a button will execute its command immediately and erase the menu. If the user looks outside the menu (for 600 milliseconds), the menu is erased without any command executed.

Observation. Our initial experience with this interaction technique suggests that the button is more convenient than the long dwell time for executing a menu command. This is because the dwell time necessary before executing a command must be kept quite high, at least noticeably longer than the time required to read an unfamiliar item. This is longer than people normally fixate on one spot, so selecting such an item requires an unnatural sort of "stare." Pulling the menu down and selecting an item to be highlighted are both done very effectively with short dwell times, as with object selection.

Listener Window

In a window system, the user must designate the active or "listener" window, that is, the one that receives keyboard inputs. Current systems use an explicit mouse command to designate the active window; in some, the command is simply pointing, in others, it is pointing and clicking. Instead, we use eye position—the listener window is simply the one the user is looking at. A delay is built into the system, so that the user can look briefly at other windows without changing the listener window designation. Fine cursor motions within a window are still handled with the mouse, which gives an appropriate partition of tasks between eye tracker and mouse, analogous to that between speech and mouse used by Schmandt [13]. A possible extension to this approach is for each window to remember the location of the mouse cursor within it when the user last left that window. When the window is reactivated (by looking at it), the mouse cursor is restored to that remembered position.

5. OBSERVATIONS

Following Brooks' taxonomy [3], we present "observations," rather than more formal "findings" of our research at this point:

An eye tracker as an input device is far from "perfect," in the sense that a mouse or keyboard is, and that is caused both by the limitations of current equipment and, more importantly, by the nature of human eye movements. Accuracy obtainable is more similar to a traditional touch screen than a mouse, and the range can barely cover a single CRT display. The equipment, while nonintrusive and noncontacting, is still difficult to ignore. Nevertheless, it is perhaps amazing that this can be done at all; and, when the system is working well, it can give the powerful impression of responding to its user's intentions rather than his explicit inputs.

To achieve this, our overall approach in designing interaction techniques is, wherever possible, to obtain information from a user's *natural* eye movements while viewing the screen rather than requiring the user to make specific eye movements to actuate the system. We also found it important to search for and recognize fixations in the raw eye tracker data stream and construct our dialogue around these higher-level events.

In our initial interaction techniques, we observed the value of short dwell time eye-only object selection for cases where a wrong pick immediately followed by a correct pick is acceptable. For moving an object we found filtered eye movements surprisingly effective, even though a mouse initially seemed more appropriate for this task. For menu commands, we found the eye alone appropriate for popping up a menu or tentatively choosing an item, but executing an item requires a button for confirmation rather than a long dwell time.

ACKNOWLEDGMENTS

I want to thank my colleagues, Robert Carter, Connie Heitmeyer, Preston Mullen, Linda Sibert, Stan Wilson, and Diane Zimmerman, for all kinds of help with this research.

REFERENCES

1. Bolt, R. A. Gaze-orchestrated dynamic windows. *Comput. Graph. 15*, 3 (Aug. 1981), 109-119.
2. Bolt, R. A. Eyes at the interface. In *Proceedings of the ACM Human Factors in Computer Systems Conference* (Gaithersburg, MD, Mar. 15-17, 1982), pp. 360-362.
3. Brooks, F. P. Grasping reality through illusion-interactive graphics serving science. In *Proceedings of the ACM CHI'88 Human Factors in Computing Systems Conference* (Washington, D.C., May 15-19, 1988), Addison-Wesley/ACM Press, pp. 1-11.
4. Card, S., English, W., and Burr, B. Evaluation of mouse, rate-controlled isometric joystick, step keys, and text keys for text selection on a CRT. *Ergonomics 21*, 8 (1978), 601-613.
5. Glenn, F. A., Iavecchia, H. P., Ross, L. V., Stokes, J. M., Weiland, W. J., Weiss, D., and Zaklad, A. L. Eye-voice-controlled interface. In *Proceedings of the 30th Annual Meeting of the Human Factors Society* (Santa Monica, Calif., 1986), pp. 322-326.
6. Hutchinson, T. E., White, K. P., Martin, W. N., Reichert, K. C., and Frey, L. A. Human-computer interaction using eye-gaze input. *IEEE Trans. Syst. Man and Cybern. 19*, 6 (Nov. 1989), 1527-1534.
7. Jacob, R. J. K. A specification language for direct manipulation user interfaces. *ACM Trans. Graph. 5*, 4 (1986), 283-317. Special Issue on User Interface Software.
8. Just, M. A., and Carpenter, P. A. A theory of reading: From eye fixations to comprehension. *Psychological Rev. 87*, 4 (Jul. 1980), 329-354.
9. Levine, J. L. An eye-controlled computer. IBM Thomas J. Watson Research Center, Res. Rep. RC-8857, Yorktown Heights, N.Y., 1981.
10. Merchant, J., Morrissette, R., and Porterfield, J. L. Remote measurement of eye direction allowing subject motion over one cubic foot of space. *IEEE Trans. Biomed. Eng. BME-21*, 4 (Jul. 1974), 309-317.
11. Monty, R. A., and Senders, J. W. *Eye Movements and Psychological Processes*. Lawrence Erlbaum, Hillsdale, N.J., 1976.
12. Myers, B. A. User-interface tools: Introduction and survey. *IEEE Softw. 6*, 1 (Jan. 1989), 15-23.
13. Schmandt, C., Ackerman, M. S., and Hindus, D. Augmenting a window system with speech input. *IEEE Comput. 23*, 8 (Aug. 1990), 50-56.
14. Starker, I., and Bolt, R. A. A gaze-responsive self-disclosing display. In *Proceedings of the ACM CHI'90 Human Factors in Computing Systems Conference* (Seattle, Wash., Apr. 1-5, 1990), Addison-Wesley/ACM Press, pp. 3-9.
15. Ware, C., and Mikaelian, H. T. An evaluation of an eye tracker as a device for computer input. In *Proceedings of the ACM CHI + GI'87 Human Factors in Computing Systems Conference* (Toronto, Canada, Apr. 5-9, 1987), pp. 183-188.
16. Young, L. R., and Sheena, D. Survey of eye movement recording methods. *Behav. Res. Meth. Instrument. 7*, 5 (1975), 397-429.

The Use of Eye Movements in Human-Computer Interaction Techniques: What You Look at Is What You Get

Robert Jacob

When I began this work, eye trackers were expensive, cumbersome, and performed poorly for interactive use (they were better suited—and more widely used—for retrospective analysis in psychological or physiological experiments). We expected eye tracking technology to get better and cheaper over the years. Meanwhile, we explored how you might use eye movements as an element of a user-computer dialog in order to create faster, more natural, more convenient user interfaces—interfaces that almost anticipate the user's intentions without requiring explicit input.

We simulated the good, cheap eye tracker, which we hoped would become available in the future, with the expensive, imperfect eye tracker we used (the best available at that time) and were able to create elements of the fast and effortless eye-movement-based interface we sought. We hoped that, while we proceeded with our research on interaction techniques and software, eye tracker hardware technology would improve, and we would meet at the finish line, prepared to exploit the emerging technology. Unfortunately, so far, we are winning this race.

Our more recent research confirms with formal experimental results the promise we found in incorporating natural eye movements into a user interface, but useful application of this work requires technological improvements in the underlying hardware. The fact that workstations are beginning to incorporate small cameras and frame grabbers (usually intended for teleconferencing) along with DSP (digital signal processing) or other high-speed multimedia processing engines is very promising since these are also the main hardware components of an eye tracker. Perhaps the widely deployed, good, cheap eye tracker will emerge piggybacked on this teleconferencing hardware.

Our current work at Tufts is extending eye movement interaction by applying it in virtual reality interfaces, where there is particularly high value to rapid pointing over long distances, and by developing more subtle interaction techniques that respond to the accumulated recent history of the user's eye movements rather than to the current instantaneous position of the eye.

Some more recent publications that expanded upon this paper are listed in the references that follow.

REFERENCES

Jacob, R. J. K. 1993. Eye Movement-Based Human-Computer Interaction Techniques: Toward Non-Command Interfaces. In Hartson, H.R., and Hix, D. (eds.), *Advances in Human-Computer Interaction*, Vol. 4, 151–190. Norwood, NJ: Ablex Publishing Co. (*http://www.eecs.tufts.edu /~jacob/papers/hartson.txt or hartson.ps*)

Jacob, R. J. K. 1995. Eye Tracking in Advanced Interface Design. In Barfield, W., and Furness, T. A. (eds.), *Virtual Environments and Advanced Interface Design*, 258–288. New York: Oxford University Press. (*http://www.eecs.tufts.edu /~jacob/papers/barfield.html or barfield.ps*)

Jacob, R. J. K. 1995. Natural Dialogue in Modes Other Than Natural Language. In Beun, R.-J., Baker, M., and Reiner, M. (eds.), *Dialogue and Instruction*, 289–301. Berlin: Springer-Verlag. (*http://www.eecs.tufts.edu /~jacob/papers/como.html or como.ps*)

Jacob, R. J. K. 1996. Input Devices and Techniques. In Tucker, A. B. (ed.), *The Computer Science and Engineering Handbook*, 1494–1511. Boca Raton, FL: CRC Press. (*http://www.eecs.tufts.edu/~jacob/papers/crc.html* or *crc.txt or crc.ps*)

Jacob, R. J. K.; Leggett, J. J.; Myers, B. A.; and Pausch, R. 1993. Interaction Styles and Input/Output Devices. *Behaviour and Information Technology*, 12(2): 69–79. (*http://www.eecs.tufts.edu/~jacob/papers/bit.txt or bit.ps*)

Sibert, L. E. and Jacob, R. J. K. 1997. Evaluation of Eye Gaze Interaction Techniques. Submitted for publication.

SECTION II

Multimedia Presentation Design

This section covers efforts at semi- or fully automated design and realization of coherent and cohesive multimedia presentations. The generation process can be subdivided into several co-constraining processes, which include the determination of communicative intent, the selection of content to achieve this, its grouping/structuring and ordering, its allocation to particular media (e.g., text versus graphics), its realization in a coordinated fashion across media, and finally its layout. Ideally, the generation process is tailored to the context, task, and user. Investigators have explored these processes in several domains using a range of algorithms. We consider these, leaving investigations into media layout for Section IV.

The first paper by Steven Feiner and Kathy McKeown investigates the automated generation of coordinated multimedia (text and three-dimensional graphic) presentations that explain the operation and maintenance of complex devices such as military radios. Drawing information from an underlying knowledge base, their COMET (Coordinated Multimedia Explanation Testbed) system performs content selection, media selection, media generation, and coordinated layout to achieve complementary text/picture combinations. COMET extends rhetorical schemata used previously by McKeown et al. (1990) for text generation to address multimedia artifacts. Upon receiving an explanation request, COMET uses text plans or schemata to determine which information to select from underlying knowledge sources, exploiting models of the domain, user, and previous discourse. Given a list of logical forms output from the content planner, COMET's media coordinator selects which items should be expressed in text (e.g., causal relations or abstract actions), graphics (e.g., physical properties such as shape and location), or both (e.g., compound actions). Coordinated text and graphics generators realize these logical forms, the results of which are laid out and then rendered. Coordination includes the use of picture breaks synchronized with sentence breaks. A common underlying content representation of the presentation supports consistency and cross-generator communication, enables cross-media references (e.g., "the highlighted object," "in the left picture"), and simplifies control by separating communicative goals from resources. Future work includes supporting feedback from the media generators to affect assignments made by the media coordinator and selection of goals made by the content planner.

In contrast to the schema-based approach to content selection employed in COMET, the second article by Mark Maybury introduces the use of planning technology to represent and reason about communicative actions to generate presentations. Moving beyond static text/picture presentations to address animated route narrations, the paper argues for a hierarchy of media- and modality-independent communicative acts (e.g., identify, describe, narrate, argue) that can be realized by media- and code-specific acts (e.g., linguistic acts, graphical acts). Maybury formalizes these communicative actions as plan operators, identifying the necessary and sufficient constraints and preconditions for effective performance, any necessary subactions, and the expected effect of each action. Hierarchies of communicative actions have the advantage that more abstract actions (e.g., attentional actions in text, graphics, gesture) can be realized in a variety of manners (e.g., visual highlighting versus use of prosodics for acoustic emphasis). Communicative actions were implemented in TEXPLAN (Textual EXplanation PLANner) and are illustrated in use in the paper to plan the narrated animation of integrated linguistic and graphical routes in an object-oriented geographic information system. Choices among alternative communicative actions are based on (1) the contents of the application knowledge base, (2) a model of the user's knowledge, beliefs, and plans, (3) a model of discourse, and (4) the complexity of the actions themselves. When developing the linguistic realizer for route plans, Maybury discovered the need to create a more generalized notion of focus of attention and extended models of linguistic and temporal focus to include spatial focus.

The third article by Wolfgang Wahlster, Elisabeth André, Wolfgang Finkler, Hans-Jürgen Profitlich, and Thomas Rist also addresses plan-based multimedia presentation authoring in the WIP system. WIP (German for knowledge-based presentation of information) generates multimodal explanations for assembling, using, maintaining, or repairing physical devices such as espresso machines, lawn mowers, or modems, demonstrating language and application independence. WIP investigates the incremental and coordinated design and realization of presentations from a common representation, adapting these to the addressee and situation to achieve particular communicative goals. The authors focus on the generalization of text-linguistic notions such as coherence, speech acts, anaphora, and rhetorical relations to multimedia presentations. For example, the authors slightly extend Rhetorical Structure Theory to capture relations not only between text fragments but also picture elements, pictures, and text or sequences of text-picture combinations. The WIP architecture supports bidirectional communication between the presentation planner and layout manager as well as interleaved mode selection and content selection, instead of these being strictly sequential as in COMET. Importantly, WIP does not use plan operators at all levels of the system, instead relying on, for example, expert design rules for routine tasks such as annotation, grid determination, and font selection. The authors emphasize cross-modal referring expressions to establish coherence (e.g., "The on/off switch is located in the upper left part of the picture."). More recent work of the authors focuses on interactive presentations, the application of an animated character to navigate the presentation (personalized plan-based presenter), and monitoring presentation effectiveness.

Yigal Arens, Lawrence Miller, and Norman Sondheimer move beyond the realm of presentation design to apply similar techniques to the automated creation of interfaces, historically a timely and expensive activity. In the Integrated Interfaces system, the authors investigate the dynamic construction of multimedia displays (e.g., natural language, maps, menus, forms) using rules. The authors' paper focuses on the presentation designer within Integrated Interfaces that automatically creates displays using a hybrid reasoning system consisting of a frame-based (NIKL) and theorem-proving (PENNI) systems. It is further an integration of several subsystems, notably, Penman (text generation), QFORMS (forms generation), and GDA (Geographic Display Agent for map and graphic generation). The presentation designer operates using formal models of the domain (Pacific naval forces), visual displays (structure and graphical features), underlying application (e.g., database, expert system), and interface. It uses antecedent-consequence rules to perform tasks such as determining output modalities, structuring content, and realizing it. The authors investigate what constitutes a "good" presentation and attempt to capture this in design heuristics. For example, they describe the automated generation of a naval situation report. Models of domain objects (e.g., carriers, repair activities) are mapped onto interface objects (e.g., maps, icons, points) using three design processes: realization of the abstract classes that specific facts belong to, selection of the most specific design rules that apply to those classes, and redescription of those classes into textual and visual presentation elements. The authors present sample presentation rules that specify realization or layout implications (e.g., highlight mobile missions with a special icon and orient that in the direction of the ship's course). In addition to output displays, the authors describe the generation of displays for soliciting user input (e.g., a form requesting a world region and ship selection) from rules that drive a separate forms management package (QFORMS). Like Mackinlay's APT system for data graphics generation appearing in the next section, Integrated Interfaces investigates a broader set of display types and attempts to re-create standard displays to facilitate coherent presentations for trained Navy users whenever possible.

However, unlike APT and other systems, the premise of the authors' work here is to simplify the production of multimodal interfaces (e.g, Pacific fleet status display) by reasoning about formal models of the application domain and interface to create a description of the desired interface. The authors point to a need for and plans to extend their work to include explicit user, dialog, and display models.

The next chapter by Ehud Reiter, Chris Mellish, and John Levine focuses on the automatic generation of hypertext documentation; their IDAS system dynamically generates both text and hyperlinks from a knowledge base. They argue that users prefer hypertext documentation and that it is not difficult to add simple hypertext capabilities to a document generation system. They also argue that different applications should use different generation techniques, depending on their characteristics; for example, it often makes sense to use some canned text in monolingual systems, but this is more difficult to justify in systems that produce output in multiple languages. Interestingly, the authors discovered that tailoring text to the user task, expertise, and discourse context did not seem to help users as much as expected since the hypertext links allowed readers of nontailored text to get additional information or clarifications if they believed they needed this. Further evaluation is required to understand this preliminary finding; however, it is noteworthy that industrial participants stated that variable (i.e., tailored) output was undesirable because it resulted in more difficult and expensive quality assurance. However, industrial collaborators in this project pointed to reduced costs, consistency, conformance to standards (e.g., linguistic simplicity), multimodality, and multilinguality as important benefits. The authors argue for the need for more cost-effective knowledge acquisition and model-building mechanisms to minimize knowledge base development cost.

The final chapter by Yigal Arens, Ed Hovy, and Mira Vossers focuses on a core problem for presentation analysis and design: the representation of knowledge underlying multimedia presentations. They describe four principal classes of knowledge required: characteristics of the information to be communicated, the media through which it can be conveyed, the nature of the producer, and, finally, that of the perceiver. The authors argue against mapping information (e.g., a ship's location) directly to types of media (e.g., tables, maps) but propose instead that properties of information (e.g., two-dimensional geospatial coordinates) should be matched to properties of media (e.g., planar media, which include graphs, tables, and maps). The authors define properties of information, media, producer, and perceiver and discuss their formalization using systemic networks. The authors exemplify their application to modality selection and rule generalization, demonstrating how these knowledge sources can be used to interpret and generate multimedia displays.

Collectively, these papers recognize some fundamental tasks in presentation design, including content selection, media allocation, media realization, and layout. They suggest these processes are interdependent and must be closely coordinated during generation to ensure cohesive and coherent output. Together, the papers also argue for the importance of key knowledge sources in these processes, including models of the information and media, the user, the discourse context, the producer, and the interface itself. They contribute some concrete but widely varying algorithms (templates, rules, plans, constraints) that offer solutions to these tasks.

Many open research issues remain. First, whereas the basic processes are beginning to be understood (e.g., reasoning about communicative intentions, content selection, rhetorical structuring, realization, layout), we are only beginning to understand their interdependencies (e.g., cross-media references). Researchers are also searching for "cheaper" techniques for generating multimodal documents, which require less computation time and less knowledge. To achieve further progress, we need to move toward understanding of the principles of effective communication design.

REFERENCES

McKeown, K.; Elhadad, M.; Fukumoto, Y.; Lim, J.; Lombardi, C.; and Smadja, F. 1990. Language Generation in COMET. In Mellish, C., Dale, R., and Zock, M. (eds.), *Current Research in Natural Language Generation*, 103–140. London: Academic Press.

Automating the Generation of Coordinated Multimedia Explanations

Steven K. Feiner and Kathleen R. McKeown
Columbia University

We developed an explanation system to overcome the disadvantages of conventional authoring in multimedia applications. COMET not only determines what to say, but how to say it.

Sometimes a picture is worth the proverbial thousand words; sometimes a few well-chosen words are far more effective than a picture. Pictures often describe objects or diagram physical actions more clearly than words do. In contrast, language often conveys information about abstract objects, properties, and relations more effectively than pictures can. Pictures and language used together can complement and reinforce each other to enable more effective communication than can either medium alone. In this sense, multimedia information systems may greatly increase effective communications.

Fortunately, technical advances are beginning to reduce the cost of hardware for computer-based multimedia and hypermedia. First-generation authoring facilities let users create presentations that include text, graphics, animation, and video. Regardless of the basic functionality or interface provided, however, multimedia authoring systems require authors to possess even more skills than do single-medium authoring systems. Not only must authors be skilled in the conventions of each medium, but they must also be able to coordinate multiple media in a coherent presentation, determining where and when to use different media, and referencing material in one medium from another. Furthermore, since the presentation must be authored in advance, the ways in which it can be customized for an individual user or situation are limited to those built in by the author.

To overcome the disadvantages of this predesigned authoring, we have developed an experimental test bed for the automated generation of multimedia explanations. COMET (Coordinated Multimedia Explanation Testbed)[1] has as its goal the coordinated, interactive generation of explanations that combine text and three-dimensional graphics, all of which is generated on the fly.

In response to a user request for an explanation, COMET dynamically determines the explanation's content using constraints based on the type of request, the information available in a set of underlying knowledge bases, and information about the user's background and goals. Having determined *what* to say, COMET also determines *how* to express it at the time of generation. The pictures and text that it uses are not "canned": COMET does not select from a database of conventionally authored text, preprogrammed graphics, or prerecorded video.

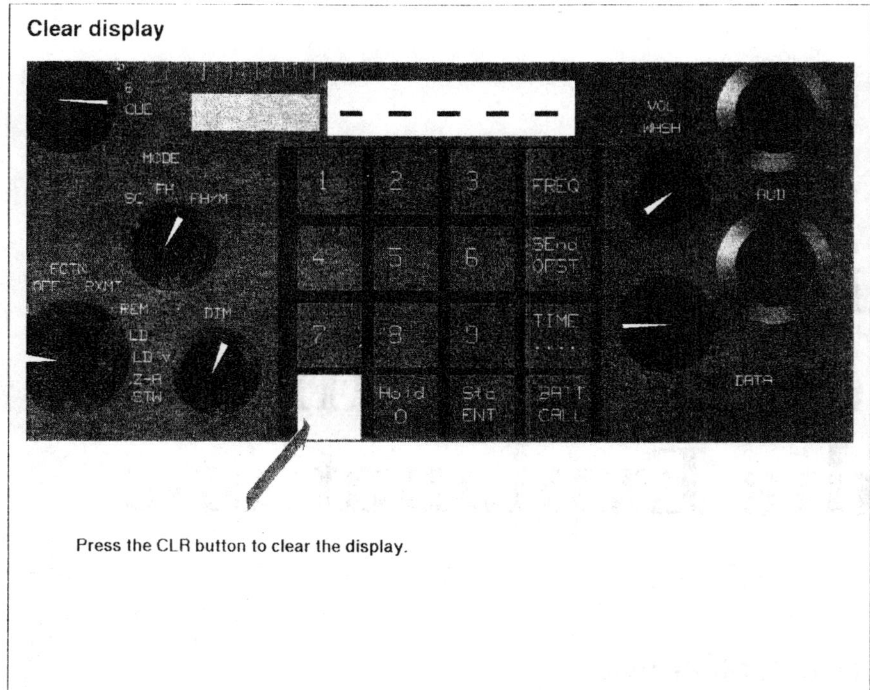
Clear display
Press the CLR button to clear the display.

Figure 1. COMET's directions for clearing the radio display.

Instead, COMET decides which information should be expressed in each medium, which words and syntactic structures best express the portion to be conveyed textually, and which graphical objects, graphical style, and picture structure best express the portion to be conveyed graphically. COMET's text and graphics are created by separate *media generators*, each of which can communicate with the other.

We first provide a brief overview of COMET's domain and architecture. Then we focus on the specific ways in which COMET can coordinate its text and graphics. *Coordination* begins with the choice of media in which specific information is communicated. For example, an object's complex shape may be shown in a picture, rather than described in text, while a sentence may describe a causal relation between several actions involving the object. Coordination also means applying knowledge about what information is expressed in text to influence the generation of graphics, and vice versa. Thus, the graphics generator may use the fact that a causal relation is being communicated in text to determine how it depicts other information, even though the relation itself is not depicted. Finally, coordination means using knowledge about how information is expressed in other media in decision-making. For example, if the graphics generator shows the location of an object by highlighting it, the text generator can refer to "the highlighted object."

Overview

Much of our work on COMET is being done in a field maintenance and repair domain for a military radio receiver-transmitter. When provided with a set of symptoms, COMET generates multimedia explanations that instruct the user in how to carry out diagnostic tests. The user interacts with COMET by means of a simple menu and can initially choose to request instructions for a specific procedure or to invoke the diagnostic component. In the latter case, an underlying expert system is called to determine the problems that the radio is experiencing and to identify their causes.

The user selects symptoms from a menu. If the expert system decides that a set of diagnostic tests must be run to determine the cause of the problem, it calls the explanation component to tell the user how to carry out these tests. Explanations consist of one or more steps that are presented in a series of displays. Although our emphasis thus far has been on generating explanations, rather than on navigating through them, COMET's menu interface also provides rudimentary facilities for exploring the explanation by paging for-

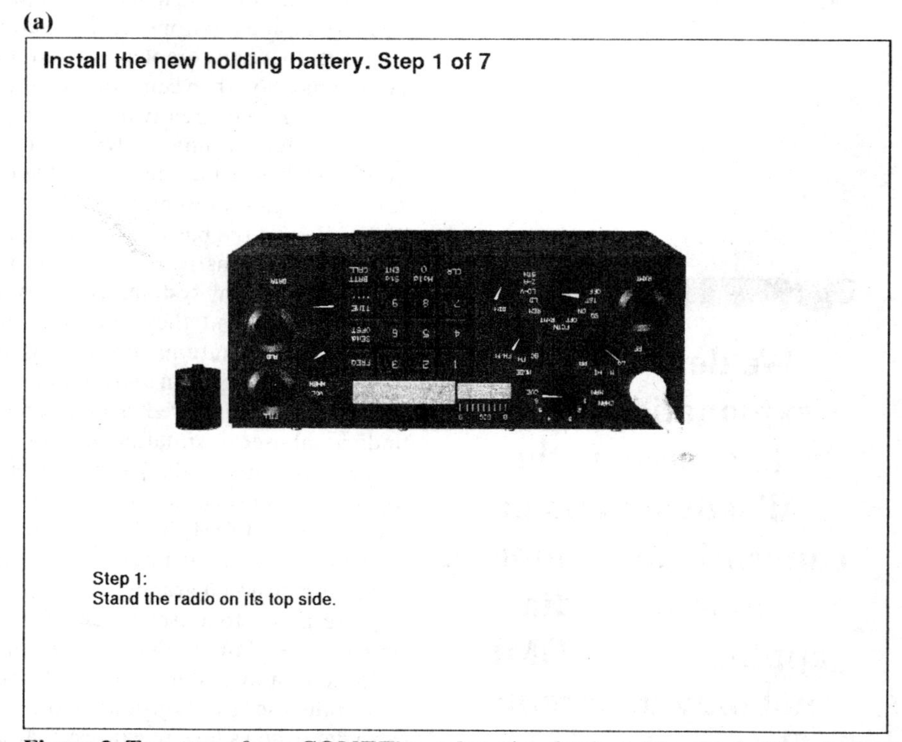
(a)
Install the new holding battery. Step 1 of 7
Step 1:
Stand the radio on its top side.

Figure 2. Two steps from COMET's explanation for installing the holding battery.

ward and backward through its steps. It can also access steps by name.

Figure 1 shows COMET's explanation for clearing the radio's display. Figure 2 shows the beginning of COMET's multistep explanation for installing a new "holding battery." (The holding battery provides power for the radio's memory when the main battery has been removed.) In these first two steps, the user is instructed to turn the radio upside down and remove the cover plate from the battery compartment. Replacing the holding battery is the first of a series of actions that COMET instructs the user to perform in the course of troubleshooting loss of radio memory, a symptom that the user selected from COMET's menu.

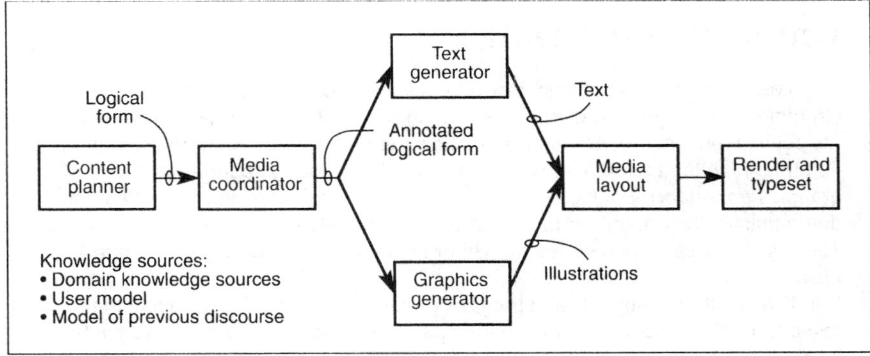

Figure 3. System architecture.

System organization. COMET consists of a set of parallel processes that cooperate in the design of an explanation, as shown in Figure 3. On receiving a request for an explanation, the content planner uses text plans, or schemas,[2] to determine which information from the underlying knowledge sources should be included in the explanation. COMET uses three different domain knowledge sources: a static representation of domain objects and actions encoded in the Loom knowledge representation language,[3] a diagnostic rule base, and a detailed geometric knowledge base needed for graphics generation. It also maintains a user model and a model of the previous discourse. These knowledge sources are used by all system components to construct the explanation, not just by the content planner. Consequently, they are shown separately at the bottom of the figure without arrows to each module.

The *content planner* produces the full content for the explanation, represented as a hierarchy of logical forms[4] (LFs), as explained in the sidebar titled "Unification in COMET." The LFs then are passed to the *media coordinator*. This component refines each LF by annotating it with directives that indicate which portions are to be produced by each of the media-specific generation systems. The *text generator* and *graphics generator* each process the same LFs, producing fragments of text and graphics that are keyed to the LFs they instantiate. The output from both generators is processed by the *media-layout component*, which formats the final presentation for the low-level *rendering-and-typesetting* software.

COMET's major components run in parallel on up to five networked workstations. Text and menus are displayed through the X Window System, while 3D shaded graphics are rendered by Hewlett-Packard's Starbase graphics package. Each example shown in the figures takes approximately 10-20 seconds to generate and display following the initial user request.

One main feature of COMET's architecture is the use of the LF as a type of blackboard facility. (A *blackboard*[5] is a central repository in which a system component can record its intermediate decisions and examine those of other components.) Each component reads and annotates its LF, continually enriching it with further decisions and finer specifications until the explanation is complete. Annotations include directives (like the media coordinator's choice of medium) and details about how a piece of information will be realized in text or graphics (like the proper verb to convey an action). While the annotated LF serves as a blueprint for the final explanation, it also allows for communication between media-specific components. For example, when deciding which expressive possibilities best con-

(b)

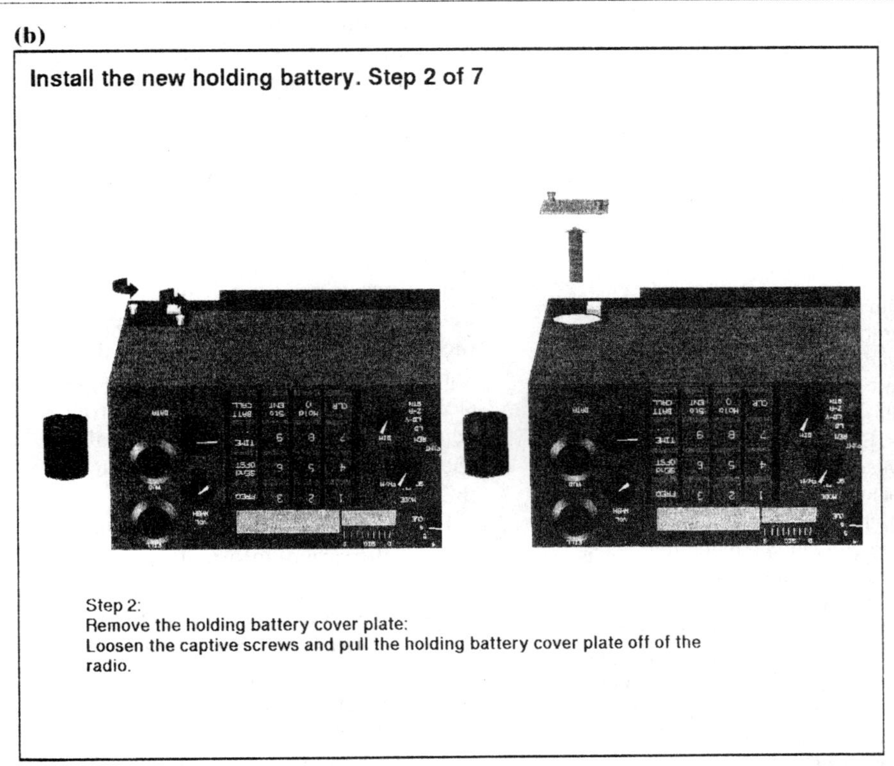

vey the specified content, a media generator can examine decisions made in other media by reading their annotated LFs and use that information to influence its own choices. COMET uses a single mechanism, FUF (Functional Unification Formalism), to make annotations throughout the system. This allows for additional bidirectional interaction between COMET's components through the use of unification, as described in the sidebar. Before describing coordination in more detail, we briefly discuss some of COMET's key components, focusing on their individual capabilities.

Media coordinator. This component performs a fine-grained analysis of an input LF to decide whether each portion should be realized in either or both media. After conducting a series of informal experiments and a survey of literature on media effectiveness, we distinguished six different types of information that can appear in an LF. We have categorized each type as to whether it is more appropriately presented in text or graphics. We use graphics alone for location and physical attributes, and text alone for communicating abstract actions and expressing connectives that indicate relationships among actions, such as causality. Both text and graphics represent simple and compound actions. The media coordinator has a FUF grammar that maps these information types to media.

Figure 4 shows a representative portion of the annotated LF produced by the media coordinator for Figure 1. The part of the LF in roman font was generated by the content planner, while the annotations added by the media coordinator are in boldface. This LF specifies a single substep and its effect, where the substep is a simple action (c-push) and the effect is also a simple action (c-clear). The c-push substep has one role (the medium, c-button-clr), and it also specifies that the location and size of the button should be included.

Figures 1 and 4 illustrate the fine-grained division of information among media. For example, location information is portrayed in graphics only, while the actions are realized in both text and graphics. In contrast, other information in the LF is communicated only in text, such as the causal relation between pushing the button and clearing the display.

Unification in COMET

COMET uses FUF, an efficient extended version of Functional Unification Grammar,[6] for media coordination. FUF also performs two text-generation tasks (selecting words and generating syntactic structure) and part of graphics generation (mapping the LFs to a communicative goal language supported by the graphics generator). Each component has its own "grammar" that is unified nondeterministically with the LF to annotate it with directives or further specifications. The result is a cascaded series of FUF grammars, each handling a separate task.

In FUF, both the input LF and the task grammar are represented using the same formalism, a set of attribute-value pairs. A value can be an atomic symbol or, recursively, a set of attribute-value pairs. For example, consider the following fragment of an input LF:

```
(substeps
 [((process-type action)
   (process-concept c-push)
   (roles ( . . . )) . . . ])
```

This fragment contains a single attribute, substeps, whose value is a set of attribute-value pairs. It contains three subattributes. The first, process-type, specifies the type of substep process as an action. The second, process-concept, indicates that the specific action is a knowledge-base concept called c-push that represents the action of pushing. The third, roles, specifies the actors and objects that participate in the action. The value of the roles attribute is a set (not shown here). Additional attribute-value pairs occur in a full LF.

Annotation is accomplished by *unifying* the task grammar with the input and is controlled by the grammar. For each attribute in the grammar that has an atomic value, any corresponding input attribute must have the same value. (Technically, it must have a compatible[6] value. As one example, when the grammar attribute has the value Any, the input attribute can have any value.) When the values are different, unification fails. When the attributes match and both values are sets, unification is applied recursively to the values, and the result replaces the input value. When the input LF does not contain the grammar attribute, the attribute and its value are added to the input. Any attributes that occur in the input but not in the grammar remain in the input after unification. Thus, unification matches only the relevant subsections of the input. Note that unification is similar to set union, since enriched attribute-value pairs from both input and grammar are merged.

A fragment of the media coordinator's grammar states that an action should be realized in both graphics and text:

```
(((process-type action)  ;; If process is an action
  (media-graphics yes) ;;        Use graphics
  (media-text yes)     ;;        Use text
  . . .))
```

On unifying this fragment of the grammar with the value of the substeps fragment of the input LF, FUF first checks whether the attribute process-type occurs in the input. Since it does and the value following it is action, FUF now checks whether the attribute media-graphics occurs in the input. Since it does not, FUF adds to the input the attribute-value pair (media-graphics yes), a directive indicating that the action is to be realized in graphics. Similarly, it adds the directive (media-text yes), specifying that the action is also to be realized in text. Thus, the first attribute-value pair is used as a test for this grammar portion. When it matches the input (the input LF describes an action), the input is annotated with the remaining attribute-value pairs. If the input LF had contained a different process-type (like abstract), unification with this portion of the grammar would have failed and FUF would have attempted unification with a new portion.

In most uses of the media coordinator grammar, a fragment is recursively applied to small nested segments of the input LF at least once. For example, the input LF can contain a causal relation, with two roles, both of which are actions. In this case, the grammar fragment as shown matches each role. A different fragment matches the causal relation (one that annotates it to be realized in text only). The roles of the actions are annotated recursively, as are their modifiers.

Text generator. COMET's text generator[2] realizes the LF segments it has been assigned in text. It must determine both the number of sentences needed to realize the segments and their type (compound, simple, declarative, or imperative). It must select verbs to express LF actions, and nouns and modifiers to refer to LF objects. Finally, it must construct the syntactic structure for each sentence and linearize the resulting tree as a sentence.

The text generator divides into two modules that carry out these functions: the *Lexical Chooser* and the *Sentence Generator*. The Lexical Chooser selects the overall sentence type and the words, while the Sentence Generator produces individual sentences. Both modules are implemented using FUF.

The text generator can select words based on a variety of underlying constraints. This enables it to use a number of different words for the same LF concepts, depending on the context. The result is a wider variety of more appropriate output. COMET can use constraints from the underlying knowledge base, from previous discourse, from a user model, and from syntax. For example, for the knowledge-base concept c-install, the text generator can use "install," "reinstall," or "return." It makes a choice based on previous discourse (that is, what it has already told the user). Thus, after the user has installed the new holding battery, COMET instructs the user to remove the radio's main battery to check the new holding battery's functionality. At this point, COMET uses the previous discourse to select the verbs "reinstall" and "return" when instructing the user to put the main battery back in the radio. If the user had not been previously instructed to remove the battery, COMET would have selected the verb "install."

COMET can also avoid words that the user does not know. For example, it generates "Make sure the plus lines up with the plus" instead of "Check the polarity" when describing battery installation to a user not familiar with the word "polarity." The novel use of FUF to represent the lexicon efficiently provides a variety of different interacting constraints on word choice.

```
((cat lf)
 (directive-act substeps)
 (substeps
  [((process-type action)
    (process-concept c-push)
    (mood non-finite)
    (speech-act directive)
    (function ((type substeps)
               (media-text yes)
               (media-graphics no)))
    (roles
     ((medium
       ((object-concept c-button-clr)
        (roles
         ((location ((object-concept c-location)
                     (media-graphics yes)
                     (media-text no)))
          (size     ((object-concept c-size)
                     (media-graphics yes)
                     (media-text no)))))))
        . . .
        ))
    (cat lf)
    (media-graphics yes)
    (media-text yes))])
 (effects
  [((process-type action)
    (process-concept c-clear)
    (mood non-finite)
    (function ((type effects)
               (media-text yes)
               (media-graphics no)))
    (speech-act assertive)
    (roles
     ((agent
       ((object-concept c-display)
        (roles
         ((location ((object-concept c-location)
                     (media-graphics yes)
                     (media-text no)))
          (size     ((object-concept c-size)
                     (media-graphics yes)
                     (media-text no)))))))
        . . .
        ))
    (cat lf)
    (media-text yes)
    (media-graphics yes))]))
```

Figure 4. Logical form for Figure 1.

Graphics generator. IBIS (Intent-Based Illustration System[7]) generates illustrations designed to satisfy the communicative goals specified in the annotated LFs that it receives as input. The communicative goals that IBIS currently supports include showing absolute and relative locations of objects, physical properties (such as size, shape, material, and color), state (such as a knob setting), change of state (such as the change in a knob setting), and a variety of actions (such as pushing, pulling, turning, and lifting). In designing an illustration, IBIS controls all aspects of the picture-making process: the objects included and their visual attributes, the lighting specification, the graphical style used in rendering the objects, the viewing specification, and the structure of the picture itself.

IBIS uses a generate-and-test approach. The IBIS rule base contains at least one design rule for each communicative goal that can appear in an input LF. Each design rule invokes a set of stylistic strategies that specify high-level visual effects, such as highlighting an object. These strategies are in turn accomplished by still lower level rules that realize the strategies. The lower level rules create and manipulate the graphical depictions of objects included in the illustration and modify the illustration's lighting specification, viewing specification, and rendering information.

For example, IBIS uses a combination of techniques to portray the location of the button in Figure 1, as requested in the LF of Figure 4. It selects a viewing specification that (1) locates the button panel centrally in the illustration, (2) makes additional, surrounding context visible, and (3) ensures that both the object and context are recognizable. It highlights the button by modifying the intensity of the lights that illuminate the objects in the illustration.

IBIS rules evaluate the success of each task that it performs. This is important because of the complex interactions that can occur in an illustration. Consider object visibility. Each object may be obscured by or obscure other objects. IBIS must determine whether visibility constraints are violated and address these by modifying the illustration. If an IBIS strategy doesn't succeed, it can backtrack and try another one. For example, if illuminating an object doesn't make it brighter than surrounding objects, IBIS can try to decrease the intensity of the lights illuminating the surrounding objects.

Media coordination

A multimedia explanation system must coordinate the use of different media in a single explanation. It must determine how to divide explanation content between different media such as pictures and text. Moreover, once the content has been divided, the system must determine how material can be generated in each medium to complement that of the other media.

A few researchers are addressing the automated generation of coordinated multimedia explanations with emphasis on how the media can complement each other. Integrated Interfaces[8] produces US Navy briefing charts, using rules to map objects in the application domain (a database of information about ships) into objects in the presentation. Sage[9] explains how and why quantitative models change over time, while Wip[10] explains physical actions like those of COMET's domain.

Integrated Interfaces and Sage operate in a two-dimensional world of charts and graphs, and do not address the problems of describing objects and actions in 3D. Integrated Interfaces also uses many design rules specific to the particular kind of briefing chart it produces. Although Wip also emphasizes tight media coordination in application to 3D domains, its content planner takes an incremental approach. Each piece of information to be communicated is assigned sequentially to its generators. Evaluations of potential success are returned to the planner to help determine media assignments even before enough information is provided for an entire sentence or illustration.

In contrast, COMET provides its media generators with more information at a time in a common LF that describes what the other generators have been assigned. The LF can also be enriched with accomplishments of the other generators. Thus COMET gives its media generators more context from which to work in making their initial decisions, while still allowing feedback.

Here we focus on two aspects of media coordination in COMET. First, we show how the use of a common content-description language allows for more flexible interaction between media, making it possible for each generator to query and reference other generators. By passing the same annotated description of what is to be described to each generator, we permit each generator to use information about what the other generators present to influence its own presentation. Then, we show how bidirectional interaction between the media-specific generators is necessary for certain kinds of coordination. Bidirectional interaction allows COMET to generate explanations that are structurally coordinated and that contain cross-references between media.

Common content description

All components in COMET following the content planner share a common description of what is to be communicated. Just as modules accept input in the same formalism, they can also annotate the description as they carry out its directives. This design has the following ramifications:

- It lets text and graphics influence each other.
- Communicative goals are separated from the resources used to carry them out.
- It provides a mechanism for text and graphics generators to communicate.

Mutual influence. Since both the text generator and graphics generator receive the same annotated content description as input, each knows which goals are to be expressed in text, in graphics, or both. Even when a media-specific generator does not communicate a piece of information, it knows that the information is to be conveyed to the user; thus, it can use this knowledge to influence its presentation. Consider a portion of the explanation that COMET generates to instruct the user in how to install the holding battery. The second step of the explanation (Figure 2b) was generated from a complex LF that consists of one goal (to remove the holding battery cover plate) and two complex substeps that carry out that goal. As Figure 2b illustrates, the media coordinator determines that the goal is to be generated only in text ("Remove the holding battery cover plate:") and that the substeps are to be shown in both media.

Although IBIS depicts only the substeps of the LF, it receives the entire annotated LF as input. Since it receives the full LF, and not just the pieces assigned to graphics, IBIS knows that the actions to be depicted are steps that achieve a higher level goal. Although this goal is not itself realized in graphics, IBIS uses this information to create a composite illustration.[7] This type of illustration consists of an integrated set of pictures that work together to achieve a common set of goals that cannot be accomplished in a single "simple" illustration. In this case, IBIS rules do not include any satisfactory way to show the radio with its cover plate and captive screws in different positions in one illustration.

If IBIS were to receive only the substeps, it would have no way of knowing that the substeps are being described in relation to a higher level goal. It may end up producing two separate illustrations, just as it does for each simple LF, such as that shown in Figure 2a. Thus, information conveyed in the explanation as a whole, but not in graphics, influences how IBIS depicts other information.

Separation of goals from resources. Because we are using a common content-description language, content must be specified at a level that is appropriate for all generators. We have found that by expressing content as a combination of communicative goals and the information needed to achieve these goals, each generator can select the resources it has at hand for accomplishing its assigned goals. In text generation, this means the selection of specific syntactic or lexical resources (using passive voice to indicate focus, for example). In graphics generation, it means the selection of a conjunction of visual resources (modifying an object's material and the lights that illuminate it to highlight it, for example).

Consider again the explanation shown in Figure 1 and its associated annotated LF in Figure 4. The main goal of the first part of the LF is to describe an action (c-push) and its role (medium). Subgoals include referencing an object (for example, c-button-clr, the clear button) and conveying its location and size. IBIS and the text generator use different resources to achieve these goals. For example, the text generator selects a lexical item, the verb "press," to describe the action. "Press" can be used instead of other verbs because of the characteristics of the medium, c-button-clr. If the medium were a slider, a verb such as "push" or "move" would be required. In contrast, IBIS uses a *metaobject*, an object that does not itself represent any of the objects in the world being depicted. In this case, the metaobject is an arrow that IBIS generates to depict the action of pushing the button. To refer to the clear button itself, the Sentence Generator uses a definite noun phrase, whereas IBIS highlights the object in the picture.

A mechanism for communication. Since both generators understand the same formalism, they can provide more information to each other about the resources they have selected simply by annotating the content description. Thus, the content description serves as a blackboard to which all processes can write messages. We use this facility for coordinating the internal text structure with pictures.

Bidirectional interaction

Certain types of coordination between media can only be provided by incorporating interacting constraints between text and graphics. Two-way communication between the media-specific generators may be required as they carry out their individual realizations. Furthermore, coordination may only be possible once partial decisions have been made by the media-specific generators. For example, the text generator needs to know how the graphics generator has depicted an object before it can refer to the object's visual properties in the illustration. Here we discuss two types of coordination that require bidirectional interaction: coordination of sentence breaks with picture breaks, and cross-referencing text and graphics.

Coordinating sentence breaks with picture breaks. In addition to revealing several dimensions along which to assign information to media, our media coordination experiments also demonstrated a strong preference for tight structural coordination between text and graphics. Our subjects much preferred sentence breaks that coincided with picture breaks. While multiple sentences accompanying one picture were found satisfactory, subjects strongly objected to a single sentence that ran across several pictures.

Including this type of coordination in COMET requires two-way interaction between text and graphics. Both text and graphics have hard and fast constraints that must be taken into account to achieve sentence-picture coordination. IBIS uses a variety of constraints to determine picture size and composition, including how much information can easily fit into one picture, the size of the objects being represented, and the position of the objects and their relationship to each other. Some of these constraints cannot be overridden. For example, if too many objects are depicted in one picture, individual objects may be too small for clarity.

This situation suggests that constraints from graphics be used to determine sentence size and thereby achieve coordination between picture and sentence breaks. However, some grammatical constraints on sentence size cannot be overridden without creating ungrammatical — or at least very awkward — text. Each verb takes a required set of inherent roles. For example, "put" takes a medium and to-location. Thus, "John put." and "John put the book." are both ungrammatical. Once a verb is selected for a sentence, this can in turn constrain minimal picture size; the LF portion containing information for all required verb roles should not be split across two pictures. Consequently, constraints from text must also be taken into account.

In COMET we incorporate this interaction by maintaining two separate tasks that run independently, each annotating its own copy of the LF when a decision is made and querying the other when a choice about sentence or picture structure must be made. Once a verb is selected for a sentence, the text generator annotates its copy of the LF by noting the roles that must be included to make a complete sentence. At the same time, the graphics generator annotates its LF with the mapping from the pieces of information to be communicated by graphics to the identifiers of the illustrations in which it intends to communicate the information.

When different sentence structures are possible, the text generator uses the graphics generator's annotations to make a choice by unifying the graphics generator's LF with its own. Consider the example of clearing the display shown in Figure 1. IBIS generates one picture showing the action and its effect; the text generator produces one sentence incorporating the effect as a purpose role of the action ("... to clear the display"). IBIS could depict this action in many ways, depending on the situation. For example, a pair of "before" and "after" pictures can be used, the first showing the action "push" about to occur and the second showing the cleared display. This picture structure can be especially useful in locating the objects participating in the action by showing their appearance prior to this event. Figure 5 (on the next page) shows what happens when IBIS's style rule base is modified so that a composite "before" and "after" pair is preferred. After consulting the annotated logical form, the text generator produces two separate sentences.

Cross-references. One important goal of media coordination is to allow material in one medium to cross-reference material in another. COMET provides for two kinds of cross-referencing: structural and content. The former refers to the coarse structure of the material being referenced. For example, a sentence could refer to an action by mentioning that it is depicted in one of the two pictures on the display. In contrast, a content cross-reference refers to the material's content, such as an object's position in a picture or the way in which the object is highlighted. Structural cross-references require only high-level knowledge of how the material being referenced is structured, whereas content cross-references require low-level

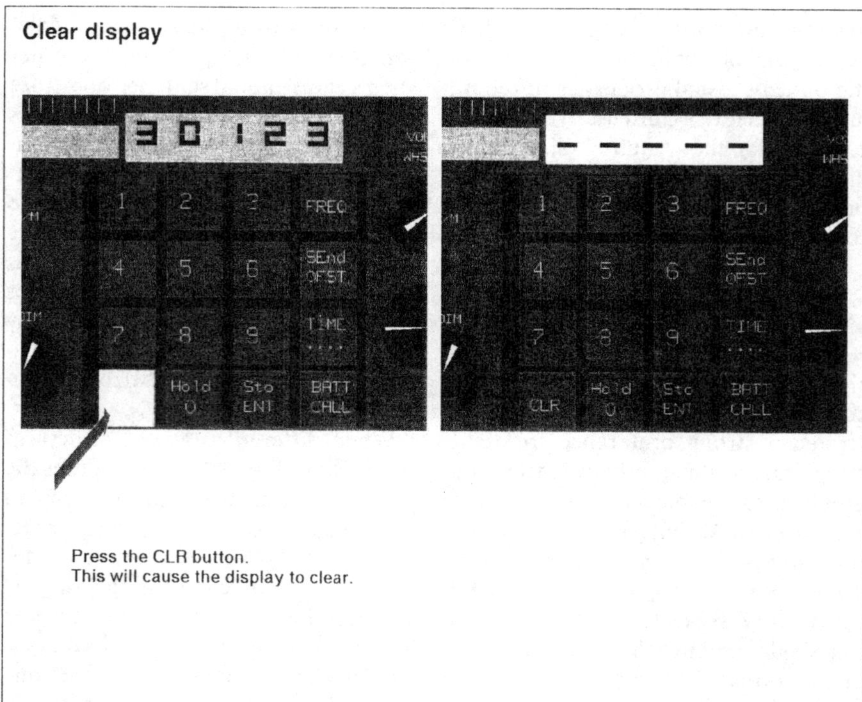

Clear display
Press the CLR button.
This will cause the display to clear.

Figure 5. An alternative explanation for clearing the radio display. A composite illustration containing two pictures is generated with coordinated text (compare with Figure 1).

knowledge of how the material's communicative goals are realized.

COMET's text generator can make both structural and content cross-references to IBIS illustrations. IBIS constructs a representation of each illustration it generates that is indexed by the LF. This representation contains information about the illustration's hierarchical structure, the identity and position of the objects that it depicts, and the kinds of illustrative effects used in constructing the illustration (like highlighting or cut-away views). The text generator queries this representation to generate cross-references. For example, it can refer to information that is communicated "... in the left picture" (structural cross-reference) or mention "... the old holding battery shown in the cut-away view" (content cross-reference).

Current status and limitations

COMET can provide instructions for maintenance and repair procedures in two different contexts. A user can directly request instructions for a specific procedure through a menu interface (essentially, asking "How do I do *x*?"). Alternatively, during symptom diagnosis, the user can request an explanation for any diagnostic procedure the system specifies must be carried out. COMET can explain over 40 complex procedures represented in the knowledge base. A variety of explanations are provided for a single procedure, depending on user background, explanation context, or previous discourse. For example, COMET can vary the vocabulary (like not using the word "polarity" if it isn't in the user's vocabulary), the illustration design (like attempting to reuse the preceding illustration's viewing specification for the next illustration to avoid confusing camera motion), or the information communicated (like omitting an explanation for a procedural step if it was explained recently). COMET also has preliminary facilities for answering follow-up questions of the form: "What is an *x*?", "Where is the *x*?", or "Why should I do *x*?"

COMET was designed to be as domain independent as possible. It can be adapted with minimum effort to a new task-based domain when tasks and actions are encoded using a standard plan-based representation[11] and objects are represented using frames. The content planner can produce the content for explanations of tasks or actions represented as plans, as well as for follow-up questions. Because many artificial intelligence systems use plans and frame-based representations, COMET's explanation facilities can be used in a wide range of applications. Similarly, the Sentence Generator grammar, the Lexical Chooser rules, and IBIS rules apply to any domain, task-based or not. In fact, these components have already been used in a number of applications under development at Columbia University. The media coordination rules we developed also apply to any domain that includes actions, physical objects, and abstract relations.

To handle a new domain, it would be necessary to augment the lexicon (adding new vocabulary), the Loom knowledge base (adding new plans and objects), and the graphics knowledge base (adding the new objects' detailed geometry and physical properties). These are currently substantial tasks, but so is the effort required to create conventionally authored explanations for a new domain. Also, note that some domain-dependent information, such as the graphics knowledge base, would ideally be available in CAD/CAM databases created when the objects to be documented were designed. COMET's rule bases were designed for domains involving physical objects. Therefore, handling domains that stress abstract relations among abstract concepts (like statistical analyses of numeric variables) would require major changes. The changes include different content-planning strategies, a different media coordinator grammar, and new graphics generation approaches (for example, adding a method for designing quantitative data displays[9,12]).

The COMET testbed has allowed us to explore many ways to coordinate the generation of text and graphics. Our present and future work on COMET and its components includes the development of additional generators that support the temporal media of speech and animation. (IBIS already allows for direct, dynamic user control of the viewing specification.[7]) Our work also includes the design of a browsing/navigation facility for COMET's explanations. We are developing a media layout component that will rely on the media generators' annotations to determine the relationships among pieces of text and graphics. This will allow COMET to group related items spatially.

We plan to allow feedback from the media generators to affect assignments made by the media coordinator and the selection of communicative goals made by the content planner. Our use of unification has the potential to make such feedback possible. Currently, we use an overall control structure for efficiency, calling the unifier separately for each grammar. Instead, we could call the unifier once for the combined series of grammars, thus allowing complete interaction through unification among the types of constraints. In this scenario, a decision made at a later stage of processing can propagate back to undo an earlier one. For example, information about the syntactic form selected can propagate back to the lexical chooser to influence verb choice.

While COMET is a research prototype, we believe that far more powerful systems will someday generate high-quality multimedia explanations for users in a variety of domains. Potential applications include education (explaining scientific phenomena) or even basic home repairs (coaching the user through troubleshooting a broken appliance). Although the hardware needed to run our current system is beyond the reach of most users, rapid improvements in the price-performance ratio will soon make high-performance real-time 3D graphics a fundamental capability of any computer system. In our work on COMET, we have attempted to lay some of the groundwork for the kinds of knowledge-based user interfaces that technological advances will soon make feasible. ■

Acknowledgments

Research on COMET is partly supported by Defense Advanced Research Projects Agency Contract N00039-84-C-0165, the Hewlett-Packard Company AI University Grants Program, National Science Foundation Grant IRT-84-51438, New York State Center for Advanced Technology Contract NYSSTF-CAT(88)-5, and Office of Naval Research Contracts N00014-82-K-0256, N00014-89-J-1782, and N00014-91-J-1872. COMET's development is an ongoing group effort and has benefited from the contributions of Michael Elhadad (FUF), Dorée Seligmann (IBIS), Andrea Danyluk (diagnostic rule base), Yumiko Fukumoto (media coordinator), Jong Lim (static knowledge base and content planner), Christine Lombardi (media coordinator), Jacques Robin (Lexical Chooser), Michael Tanenblatt (knowledge base), Michelle Baker, Cliff Beshers, David Fox, Laura Gabbe, Frank Smadja, and Tony Weida.

References

1. S. Feiner and K. McKeown, "Coordinating Text and Graphics in Explanation Generation," *Proc. Eighth Nat'l Conf. Artificial Intelligence*, AAAI Press/MIT Press, Menlo Park, Calif., 1990, pp. 442-449.

2. K.R. McKeown et al., "Language Generation in COMET," in *Current Research in Language Generation*, C. Mellish, R. Dale, and M. Zock, eds., Academic Press, London, 1990.

3. R. MacGregor and R. Bates, "The Loom Knowledge Representation Language," Tech. Report ISI/RS-87-188, Information Sciences Institute, University of Southern California, 1987.

4. J. Allen, *Natural Language Understanding*, Benjamin Cummings Publishing Company Inc., Menlo Park, Calif., 1987.

5. R. Reddy et al., "The Hearsay Speech Understanding System: An Example of the Recognition Process," *Proc. IJCAI 73*, Morgan Kaufmann Publishers, Palo Alto, Calif., 1973, pp. 185-193.

6. M. Kay, "Functional Grammar," *Proc. Fifth Mtg. Berkeley Linguistics Soc.*, Berkeley Linguistics Society, Berkeley, Calif., 1979.

7. D. Seligmann and S. Feiner, "Automated Generation of Intent-Based 3D Illustrations," *Computer Graphics* (*Proc. SIGgraph 91*), Vol. 25, No. 4, July 1991, pp. 123-132.

8. Y. Arens, L. Miller, and N. Sondheimer, "Presentation Design Using an Integrated Knowledge Base," in *Intelligent User Interfaces*, J. Sullivan and S. Tyler, eds., Addison-Wesley, Reading, Mass., 1991, pp. 241-258.

9. S. Roth, J. Mattis, and X. Mesnard, "Graphics and Natural Language as Components of Automatic Explanation," in *Intelligent User Interfaces*, J. Sullivan and S. Tyler, eds., Addison-Wesley, Reading, Mass., 1991, pp. 207-239.

10. W. Wahlster et al., "Designing Illustrated Texts: How Language Production is Influenced by Graphics Generation," *Proc. European Chapter Assoc. Computational Linguistics*, 1991, pp. 8-14.

11. E. Sacerdoti, *A Structure for Plans and Behavior*, American Elsevier, New York, 1977.

12. J. Mackinlay, "Automating the Design of Graphical Presentations of Relational Information," *ACM Trans. Graphics*, Vol. 5, No. 2, Apr. 1986, pp. 110-141.

Automating the Generation of Coordinated Multimedia Explanations

Steven K. Feiner and Kathleen R. McKeown

Our work on COMET stressed the coordination between static written text and 3-D graphics. Since this paper was published, we refined COMET's capabilities for generating cross-references between text and graphics (McKeown et al. 1992). COMET's cross-references could refer to spatial relations between objects shown in an illustration (e.g., "the top left of the radio"), spatial relations relative to the illustration itself (e.g., "the top right of the picture"), and special graphical features of the illustration (e.g., "the cutaway view" or "the highlighted knob in the inset").

To incorporate cross-references, we modified COMET's architecture by adding a new *cross-reference generator* module to the media coordinator and by changing the unidirectional interfaces between the content planner and media coordinator and between the media coordinator and media-specific generators (shown in the paper's Figure 3) into bidirectional interfaces. A cross-reference is called for by either the content planner (to show where an object is located) or the text generator's lexical chooser (to disambiguate an unfamiliar description of an object). The cross-reference generator uses a representation of the illustration, maintained by the graphics generator, which specifies its objects and their visibility, the special graphics features used, and the techniques used to communicate each of the illustration's goals. Cross-referencing in COMET not only involves generating text but can also require modifying or generating an illustration. For example, if the lexical chooser determines that a description will be unfamiliar to the user, it can request that the cross-reference generator reinvoke the content planner to show the object graphically. After the illustration has been generated (or regenerated) by the graphics generator, the cross-reference generator accesses the graphics generator's representation of the illustration to determine the specific cross-reference to use and provides this information to the lexical chooser, which selects the cross-reference's wording.

After finishing COMET, we began to explore the coordinated generation of temporal media, including spoken language and animated graphics. We are currently working on MAGIC (Multimedia Abstract Generation for Intensive Care) (Dalal et al. 1997), which generates multimedia briefings for hospital caregivers. Coordination in MAGIC requires negotiation about ordering and synchronization of spoken and graphical actions. Negotiation is a two-phase process, arbitrated by the media coordinator. In the first (ordering) phase, the spoken language and graphics generators each provide a ranked list of preferred orderings to the media coordinator, which uses a temporal constraint solver to determine a compatible ordering. In the second (timing) phase, the spoken language and graphics generators plan duration constraints for the chosen ordering and pass their duration constraints back to the media coordinator. The media coordinator then uses the temporal constraint solver to compute the action durations.

REFERENCES

Dalal, M.; Feiner, S.; McKeown, K.; Pan, S.; Zhou, M.; Höllerer, T.; Shaw, J.; Feng, Y.; and Fromer, J. 1996. Negotiation for Automated Generation of Temporal Multimedia Presentations. In *Proceedings of ACM Multimedia '96*, 55–64. New York: Association for Computing Machinery.

McKeown, K.; Feiner, S.; Robin, J.; Seligmann, D.; and Tanenblatt, M. 1992. Generating Cross-References for Multimedia Explanation. In *Proceedings of the Tenth National Conference on Artificial Intelligence*, 9–16. Menlo Park, CA: AAAI Press.

Chapter 2

Planning Multimedia Explanations Using Communicative Acts

Mark T. Maybury

Abstract

A number of researchers have investigated the use of plan-based approaches to generate textual explanations (e.g., [Appelt 1985; Hovy 1988a; Moore 1989; Maybury 1990]). This chapter extends this approach to generate multimedia explanations by defining three types of communicative acts: linguistic acts (illocutionary and locutionary speech acts), graphical acts (e.g., deictic acts), and media-independent rhetorical acts (e.g., identify, describe). This chapter formalizes several of these communicative acts as operators in the library of a hierarchical planner. We illustrate the use of these plan operators to compose route plans in coordinated natural language and graphics in the context of a cartographic information system.

1. Introduction

The notion of communication as an action-based endeavor dates to Austin's [1962] view of language as purposeful behavior. Searle [1969] extended this view with his formalization of speech acts. Bruce's [1975] suggestion of a plan-based model of speech acts was followed by computational investigations into planning speech acts [Cohen 1978], planning referring expressions [Appelt 1985], and planning multisentential text to achieve particular communicative goals (e.g., [Hovy 1988a; Moore 1989; Maybury 1990]). Just as Grosz and Sidner [1986] argued that discourses have purposes and particular discourse segments have purposes, in Maybury [1990, 1992b] we claim that texts (spoken or written) in and of themselves are composed of a hierarchy of communicative acts, each of which are aimed at achieving particular effects on the addressee, independently and in conjunction.

Figure 1 gives a sense of our approach, which was embodied in the text planning system, TEXPLAN (Textual EXplanation PLANner). TEXPLAN reasoned about a hierarchy of communicative actions to accomplish particular discourse goals. Space does not permit the presentation of or support for the broad range of communicative actions that we formalized as plan operators, so we will exemplify them here and define some below. TEXPLAN planned higher level rhetorical actions such as; identify a given entity, compare two entities, or explain a process, in terms of more primitive illocutionary speech acts [Searle 1969] which in turn were further specified as locutionary or surface speech acts [Appelt 1985]. For example, to get a hearer to perform an action (i.e., argue that they do it), the system might plan to first request that they perform the action (which in turn might be accomplished by asking them nicely to do it or commanding them to do it), and subsequently tell them how to do it and/or motivate them to do it. Each communicative act has necessary conditions which must hold before its execution and specific intended effects which are achieved by its execution. Choices among alternative actions could be made guided by a number of factors including (1) the contents of the application knowledge base, (2) a model of the user's knowledge, beliefs, and plans, (3) a model of discourse, (4) the complexity of the actions (e.g., number of items in the decomposition), and so on. Rhetorical acts usually spanned more than one utterance and could be composed of one another (e.g., an explanation might require the narration of a set of events preceded by a description of key parts) or of more primitive speech acts. This enabled a hierarchical and compositional approach to planning multisentential text (for details see Maybury [1990, 1992b]).

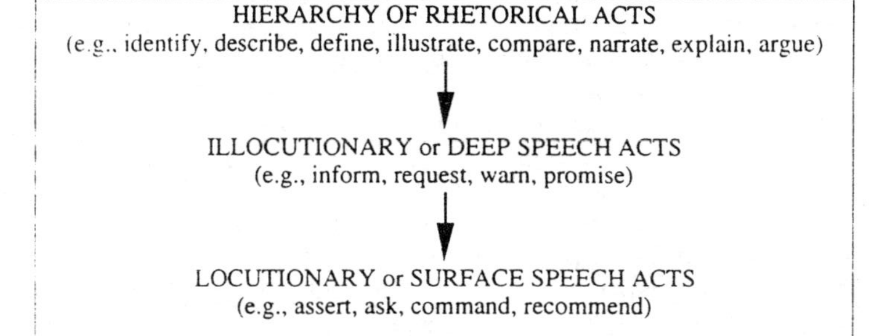

Figure 1. Integrated, Hierarchical Theory of Communicative Acts

In the remainder of this chapter we describe the extension of this approach to incorporate multimedia actions in order to generate coordinated language and graphics. We first define several communicative acts, including linguistic and graphical ones, in a common plan operator language. Next, we use these operators to plan coordinated texts and graphics which identify objects and convey route plans from the Map Display System [Hilton and Anken 1990], a knowledge-based cartographic information system. A final section identifies limitations and areas for further research.

2. Multimedia as Communicative Acts

Just as text can be viewed as consisting of a hierarchy of intentions, similarly, multimedia communication can be viewed as consisting of linguistic and graphical acts that, appropriately coordinated, can perform some communicative goal such as describing an object, narrating a sequence of events, or explaining how a complex process functions. For example, when giving directions on how to get from one place to another, if possible, humans will often utilize maps, gestures, and language to explain a route.

Just as humans communicate using multiple media (i.e., language, graphics, gestures) in multiple modes (i.e., language can be written or spoken), we have implemented an explanation planner that represents and reasons about multimedia *communicative acts* (see Figure 2). Communicative acts include rhetorical, linguistic, and graphical acts as well as non-linguistic auditory acts (e.g., snap, ring) and physical acts (e.g., gestures). A *rhetorical act* [Maybury 1990] is a sequence of linguistic or graphical acts which are used to achieve certain media-independent rhetorical goals such as identifying an entity, describing it, dividing it into its subparts or subtypes, narrating events and situations explaining a complex operation, and arguing to support a conclusion or to persuade someone to act.

In contrast, a *linguistic act* is a speech act [Searle 1969] such as INFORM or REQUEST which characterizes the illocutionary force of a single utterance. These illocutionary speech acts can be accomplished by *locutionary* or *surface speech acts* [Appelt 1985] such as ASSERT, ASK, and COMMAND which are associated with particular grammatical structures (declarative, imperative, and interrogative mood, respectively). While illocutionary speech acts are useful for plan abstraction (e.g., a REQUEST can be achieved by asking, commanding, recommending, etc.), we focus here on locutionary acts.

PHYSICAL ACT	LINGUISTIC ACT	GRAPHICAL ACT
DEICTIC ACT	*REFERENTIAL/ ATTENTIONAL ACT*	*DEICTIC ACT*
point, tap, circle		*highlight, blink, circle etc.*
indicate direction	*ILLOCUTIONARY ACT*	*indicate direction*
	inform	
ATTENTIONAL ACT	*request*	*DISPLAY CONTROL ACT*
pound fist/stomp foot	*warn*	*display-region*
snap/tap fingers, clap hands	*concede*	*zoom (in, out)*
		pan (left, right, up, down)
BODY LANGUAGE ACT	*LOCUTIONARY ACT*	
facial expressions	*assert (declarative)*	*DEPICT ACT*
gestures	*ask (interrogative)*	*depict image*
sign-language	*command (imperative)*	*draw (line, arc, circle)*
	recommend ("should")	*animate-action*
	exclaim (exclamation)	

Figure 2. Communicative Acts: Rhetorical, Linguistic, and Graphical

In contrast to linguistic acts, *graphical acts* include graphical deictic gestures (e.g., pointing, highlighting, blinking, circling), display control (e.g., zooming, panning), and image depiction. In the current implementation deictic gestures are considered primitive acts. In contrast, depiction can include depictions of primitive images (e.g., a point or line), composite images (e.g., a tree with arcs and nodes), and complex images (e.g., a picture of a location). Thus, depiction itself can be viewed as a plan-based endeavor (e.g., composing and rendering a bar graph) [Feiner 1985; Burger 1989]. The next section details several of these communicative acts for identifying locations.

Before doing so, however, we note that communication can occur not only via graphical and linguistic actions, but also via physical ones. For example, pointing to a group of people is a perfectly acceptable response to the request "Which soccer team do you want to be on?" I term this *physical deixis* (in contrast to linguistic deixis, as in "I want the one I just described"). As with other communicative acts, physical deixis might be performed in support of some higher level domain activity, such as selecting members for a soccer team, using a touch screen to select a part from an inventory system, or indicating a heading when giving directions.

In contrast to physical deixis, two other classes of physical communicative actions are *attentional actions* and body *language actions*. Attentional actions include snapping fingers or banging a shoe on a table and are performed with the purpose of managing focus of attention. More complex physical actions include facial expressions, gestures (e.g., a peace sign), and, closely related sign language. Physical actions may have linguistic and non-linguistic correlates, indeed the very name of sign-language suggests a connection not only between physical actions and language but also between physical actions and graphics or pictures. Formalizing "body language" actions would prove useful to virtual interfaces, which often incorporate gesture recognition from data gloves but also include full body suits. Each of these actions have constraints and enablements (e.g., facial expressions are not effective if they cannot be viewed by the addressee) and are performed to achieve particular effects (e.g., to gain attention, to offend). To

illustrate how these kinds of actions can be formalized in plan operators, we next detail graphical, linguistic, and higher level communicative actions for identifying locations.

3. Multimedia Plans for Location Identification

Similar to physical actions, communicative acts (rhetorical, linguistic, and graphical) can be formalized as plans. Communicative acts are represented as operators in the plan library of a hierarchical planner [Sacerdoti 1977]. Each plan operator defines the *constraints* and *preconditions* that must hold before a communicative act applies, its intended *effects* (also known as postconditions), and the refinement or *decomposition* of the act into subacts. Preconditions and constraints encode conditions concerning both physical states (e.g., is an object too large to be displayed) as well as cognitive states (e.g., does the hearer believe some proposition). Constraints, unlike preconditions, cannot be achieved or planned for if they are false. The decomposition of a plan operator defines how higher level communicative acts (e.g., describing an object) are divisible into potentially coordinated lower level actions (e.g., describing it in natural language, depicting an image of it, or both).

For example, the uninstantiated `Identify-location-linguistically` plan operator shown in Figure 3 is one of several methods of performing the communicative action `Identify`. As defined in the HEADER of the plan operator, the `Identify` act takes three arguments, the speaker (S), the hearer (H), and an entity. The English translation of Figure 3 is as follows: Provided the third argument is indeed an entity[1] (CONSTRAINTS) and the speaker wants the hearer to know about it (PRECONDITIONS), the speaker (S) will identify the location of the entity by informing the hearer (H) of its location (DECOMPOSITION), which has the intended effect that the hearer knows about it (EFFECTS).

NAME	Identify-location-linguistically
HEADER	Identify(*S*, *H*, *entity*)
CONSTRAINTS	Entity?(*entity*)
PRECONDITIONS	WANT(*S*, KNOW(*H*, Location(*entity*)))
EFFECTS	KNOW(*H*, Location(*entity*))
DECOMPOSITION	Assert(*S*, *H*, Location(*entity*))

Figure 3. Uninstantiated Linguistic Plan Operator

Plan operators are encoded in an extension of first order predicate calculus which allows for optionality within the decomposition. Predicates (which have true/false values (e.g., `Entity?`)), functions (which return values), and communicative acts (e.g., `Identify`, `Assert`, `Blink`) appear in lower-case type with their initial letter capitalized. Arguments to predicates, functions, and communicative acts include variables and constants. Variables are italicized (e.g., *S*, *H*, and *entity*) and constants appear in upper-case plain type.

Intentional operators, such as WANT, KNOW, and BELIEVE appear in capitals. KNOW details an agent's specific knowledge of the truth-values of propositions (e.g., `KNOW(H, Red(ROBIN-1))` or `KNOW(H, ¬Yellow(ROBIN-1)))` where truth or falsity is defined by the propositions in the knowledge base. That is, `KNOW(H, P)` implies `P ∧ BELIEVE(H, P)`. Agents can hold an invalid belief (e.g., `BELIEVE(JOHN, Yellow(ROBIN-1)))`. KNOW-ABOUT is a predicate that is an abstraction of a set of epistemic attitudes of some agent toward an individual. An agent can KNOW-ABOUT an object or event (e.g., `KNOW-ABOUT(H, ROBIN-1)` or KNOW-

[1] An entity is an object or event (e.g., a process or an action).

ABOUT(H, EXPLOSION-445)) if they KNOW its characteristics, components, subtypes, or purpose. KNOW-HOW indicates an agent's ability to perform an action.

If the object we are identifying has an associated graphical presentation in the backend cartographic display, we can augment natural language with visual identification. The `Identify-location-linguistically-&-visually` plan operator in Figure 4 is selected only if its constraints are satisfied (i.e., the given entity is a cartographic entity such as a town, road, lake, etc.). If these constraints are satisfied, the plan operator then ensures that the entity is visible. If the designated entity is out of the currently visible region or too small to be seen, this can be achieved by either panning, jumping, or zooming to the region around the designated entity. For example, Figure 5 illustrates the map display action, `Make-entity-visible`, which displays the region surrounding a given entity. Note that the precondition of this plan operator will ensure the entity is displayed. If it is not already displayed on the map, this will be planned for.

NAME	Identify-location-linguistically-&-visually
HEADER	Identify(*S*, *H*, *entity*)
CONSTRAINTS	Cartographic-Entity?(*entity*)
PRECONDITIONS	Visible(*entity*) ∧ WANT(*S*, KNOW(*H*, Location(*entity*)))
EFFECTS	KNOW(*H*, Location(*entity*))
DECOMPOSITION	Indicate-Deictically(*S*, *H*, *entity*) Assert(*S*, *H*, Location(*entity*))

Figure 4. Plan Operator for Graphical/Textual Display

After the entity is visible, the decomposition of the identify action of Figure 4 deictically indicates the entity and then describes its location in natural language (as above). There are several plan operators for deictic indication available including highlighting (a permanent indication of an entity), blinking (intermittent highlighting), and circling. These forms of visual deixis can be used to indicate individual objects (e.g., roads, towns, dams), groups of objects, or geographical regions. While the current implementation simply defaults to highlighting, the choice among different deictic techniques could be motivated by a number of considerations including the number and kind of entities visible in the region, their visual properties (e.g., size, color, shading) in order to maximize the distinction of the given entity and its background, and the kind of communication being generated (e.g., highlighting may be preferred when communicating route plans so that upon completion the entire route is visible). We next illustrate these plans in action.

NAME	Make-entity-visible
HEADER	Make-Visible(*entity*)
CONSTRAINTS	Cartographic-Entity?(*entity*)
PRECONDITIONS	Displayed(*entity*)
EFFECTS	Visible(*entity*)
DECOMPOSITION	Display-Region(*entity*)

Figure 5. Plan Operator for Map Display Control

4. Multimedia Identification Exemplified

To illustrate these and other communicative acts, we detail the planning of multimedia directions for the Map Display System [Hilton and Anken 1990], a knowledge-based cartographic information system which represents over 600 European towns, 227 airbases, 40 lakes, 14 dams, as well as other objects. The road network in the map includes 233 roads (divided up into 4,607 road segments) and 889 intersections.

If the user queries the system "Where is Chemnitz?," this is simulated by posting the goal `Identify(SYSTEM, USER, #<Chemnitz>)` to the explanation planner. The planner then uses a unification algorithm to find all operators from the library whose HEADER portion matches the current goal. This includes the identification plan operators in Figures 3 and 4. Next all operators whose header matches this goal are found and instantiated with the bindings of the variables that match the header. Figure 6 shows the plan operator for linguistic and visual identification instantiated with bindings. When the action `Identify(SYSTEM, USER, #<Chemnitz>)` unifies against the header of the plan operator in Figure 4, the variable *S* is bound to SYSTEM, *H* is bound to USER, and *entity* is bound to the object `#<Chemnitz>`. These bindings are used to instantiate the entire plan operator to that shown in Figure 6.

Because there may be many methods of achieving a given goal, those operators that satisfy the constraints and essential preconditions are then prioritized using *preference metrics*. For example, operators that utilize both text and graphics are preferred over simply textual operators. Also, those operators with fewer subgoals are preferred (where this does not conflict with the previous preference). The preference metric prefers plan operators with fewer subplans (cognitive economy), with fewer new variables (limiting the introduction of new entities in the focus space of the discourse), those that satisfy all preconditions (to avoid backward chaining for efficiency), and those plan operators that are more common or preferred in naturally-occurring explanations (e.g., certain kinds of communicative acts occur more frequently in human-produced text or are preferred by rhetoricians over other methods). While the first three preferences are explicitly inferred, the last preference is implemented by the sequence in which operators appear in the plan library.

NAME	Identify-location-linguistically-&-visually
HEADER	Identify(SYSTEM, USER, #<Chemnitz>)
CONSTRAINTS	Cartographic-Entity?(#<Chemnitz>)
PRECONDITIONS	Visible(#<Chemnitz>) ∧ WANT(SYSTEM, KNOW(USER, Location(#<Chemnitz>)))
EFFECTS	KNOW(USER, Location(#<Chemnitz>))
DECOMPOSITION	Indicate-Deictically(SYSTEM, USER, #<Chemnitz>) Assert(SYSTEM, USER, Location(#<Chemnitz>))

Figure 6. Instantiated identify *Plan Operator*

Working from this prioritized list of operators, the planner ensures preconditions are satisfied and tries to execute the decomposition of each until one succeeds. This involves processing any special operators (e.g., optionality is allowed in the decomposition) or quantifiers (∀ or ∃) as well as distinguishing between subgoals and primitive acts. For example, if the planner chooses the plan operator in Figure 6 from those that satisfy their constraints, it first ensures its preconditions hold (i.e., by making sure the entity is visible through other graphical acts).

Next, the planner attempts to execute the two subacts in its decomposition, Indicate-Deictically(SYSTEM, USER, #<Chemnitz>) and Assert(SYSTEM, USER, Location(#<Chemnitz>). Assert is a primitive act and so decomposition halts here. In contrast, Indicate-Deictically is not a primitive act and so the planner is reinvoked. As indicated in the previous section, in the current implementation deictic indication defaults to highlighting, which is also a primitive act.

Thus, our original simulated user query, "Where is Chemnitz?", results in the hierarchical decomposition shown in Figure 7. This tree is linearized by a depth-first search and the resulting sequence of linguistic and graphical primitive actions is executed. The surface speech act, Assert, together with the Location predicate and its argument, #<Chemnitz>, are passed to the linguistic realization component. Using this information, the realizer fills a semantic case role associated with the Location predicate to yield a semantic specification #<Assert location-predicate Chemnitz>, which contains the following information:

```
ACTION:      #<be-copula>
AGENT:       #<Chemnitz>
PATIENT:     #<town>
MODIFIERS:   (location (latitude 50.82) (longitude 12.88))
```

This specification is used to build grammatical relations (subject, object), then syntactic constituents (noun, verb, adverbial, and prepositional phrases), and finally a surface tree which is realized as (see [Maybury 1991b]):

```
Chemnitz is a town located at 50.82° latitude 12.88° longitude.
```

This is uttered after the map displays the region around Chemnitz and highlights its icon.

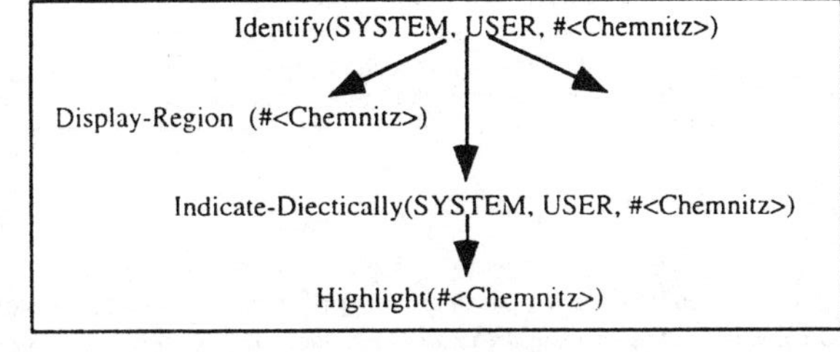

Figure 7. Hierarchical Multimedia Plan to Identify Chemnitz

5. Extended Multimedia Directions

While the above coordinated graphical and linguistic identification of Chemnitz may satisfy the user's query, often a cartographic information system must communicate a route between distant points. This can be accomplished in language alone, or by coordinating language and map displays. The communicative act `Explain-Route`, formalized in Figure 8, does the latter, the former being a simplification thereof. The constraints of this operator first test if both objects are cartographic ones and that there exists a path between them in the underlying Map Display System [Hilton and Anken 1990]. The function `cartographic-path` which is used in the plan operator takes as arguments two objects from the cartographic knowledge base and, using a branch and bound search strategy, explores the road network to return the "best" route between the two points (if one exists). The path returned by the function is an ordered list of roads, intersections, and towns indicating the preferred route from one entity to another, as defined by the rewrite rules:

```
path     ->   segment + (path)
segment  ->   point + road-segment + point
point    ->   intersection | city | town | bridge
```

where "()" indicates optionality and "|" indicates logical disjunction. For any given segment, the functions `source`, `link`, and `destination` return the source and destination point and the link that connects them (i.e., a road segment).

If the constraints on the `Explain-Route` action are satisfied, then the planner attempts to achieve its preconditions. The first precondition requires the source location to be visible. If not currently the case, this can be achieved using graphical actions like the make-visible act defined in Figure 5. If the constraints and preconditions can be satisfied, then the decomposition first visually identifies the source of the next segment, next linguistically requests the hearer to move from the source to the destination of that segment, then visually identifies the link of the next segment, and lastly visually indicates the direction of the movement along the link between the two (using an arrow). (The initial source location is not *linguistically* identified because we assume the hearer is traveling from that location and thus is familiar with it.) After repeating this for all segments, the plan concludes by identifying the ultimate destination using actions like those of Figures 3 and 4. The effect of explaining the route is that the hearer knows how to get from origin to destination and the hearer knows the segments of that route.

For example, assume the user asks "How do I get from Wiesbaden to Frankfurt?", simulated by posting the discourse goal `Explain-Route(SYSTEM, USER, #<Wiesbaden>, #<Frankfurt-am-Main>)`. The planner uses the `Explain-Route` act of Figure 8 to build the explanation plan shown in Figure 9. This plan is realized as (graphical acts indicated parenthetically in italics):

> *(Display map region around Wiesbaden) (highlight Wiesbaden)* From Wiesbaden take Autobahn A66 Northeast for thirty-one kilometers to Frankfurt-am-Main. *(highlight Autobahn A66) (indicate direction with blinking arrow) (highlight Frankfurt-am-Main)* Frankfurt-am-Main is located at 50.11° latitude and 8.66° longitude.

NAME	Explain-route-linguistically-and-visually
HEADER	Explain-Route(*S, H, from-entity, to-entity*)
CONSTRAINTS	Cartographic-entity?(*from-entity*) $\wedge$ Cartographic-entity?(*to-entity*) $\wedge$ *path*
PRECONDITIONS	visible(*from-entity*) $\wedge$ WANT(*S*, KNOW-HOW(*H*, Go(*from-entity, to-entity*)))
EFFECTS	KNOW-HOW(*H*, Go(*from-entity, to-entity*)) $\wedge$ $\forall$*segment* $\in$ *path* KNOW(*H*, Subpath(*segment, path*))
DECOMPOSITION	$\forall$*segment* $\in$ *path* Indicate-Deictically(*S, H*, source(*segment*)) Command(*S, H*, Do(*H*, Go(source(*segment*), link(*segment*), destination(*segment*)))) Indicate-Deictically(*S, H*, link(*segment*)) Indicate-Direction(*S, H*, source(*segment*), link(*segment*), destination(*segment*)) Identify(*S, H, to-entity*)
WHERE	*path* = cartographic-path(*from-entity, to-entity*)

Figure 8. `Explain-Route` *Plan Operator*

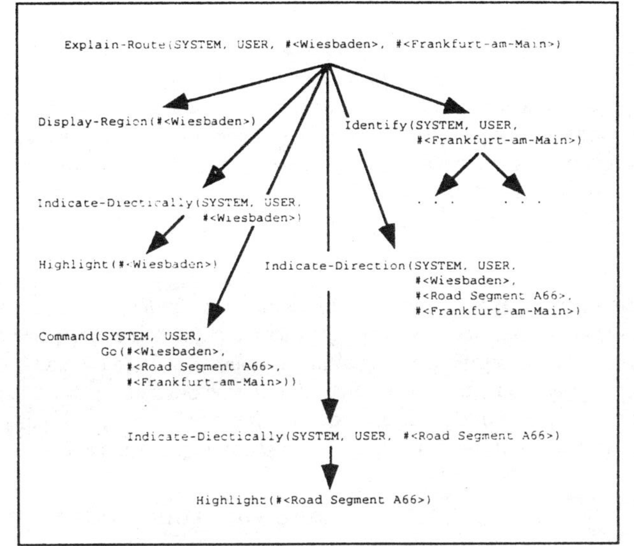

Figure 9. Hierarchical Plan for Locational Instructions

A slightly more complex locational instruction results if the user asks how to get from Mannheim to Heidelberg, initiated by posting the discourse goal `Explain-Route(SYSTEM, USER, #<Mannheim>, #<Heidelberg>)`. The resulting multimedia explanation is realized as:

> (Display map region around Mannheim) (highlight Mannheim) From Mannheim take Route 38 Southeast for four kilometers to the intersection of Route 38 and Autobahn A5. (highlight Route 38) (indicate direction with blinking arrow) (highlight intersection of Route 38 and Autobahn A5) From there take Autobahn A5 Southeast for seven kilometers to Heidelberg. (highlight Autobahn A5) (indicate direction with blinking arrow) (highlight Heidelberg) Heidelberg is located at 49.39° latitude and 6.68° longitude, four kilometers Northwest of Dossenheim, six kilometers Northwest of Edingen, and five kilometers Southwest of Eppelheim.

The linguistic realization component keeps track of the relationship of the current *spatial focus* (the current visited segment) to the previous spatial focus (the previously visited segment). This relationship constrains the choice of surface choices [Maybury 1991b] such as demonstrative pronouns ("this" versus "that"; "here" versus "there") as well as the generation of spatial directionals (e.g., "Southeast", "West") and durationals (e.g., "seven kilometers"). This focus-based choice contrasts with the use of heuristic approaches based on rules (e.g., describe an entity using a demonstrative noun phrase if there is no proper name for that entity [Neal et al. 1989]).

6. Contrast with Related Research

As noted in the introduction, in recent years a number of advances have been made in the area of text planning. At the same time, others have made progress in graphical design. For example, mechanisms have been developed to design graphical presentations of relational information [Mackinlay 1986b], to design network diagrams [Marks 1991b], and to automatically create business graphics displays [Roth and Mattis 1990]. Others began investigating the automatic generation of coordinated multimedia explanations. Some have focused on the knowledge underlying mixed media presentations [Arens et al., this volume], on media-independent representations of intentions [Elhadad et al. 1989], or on the psycho perception of verbal and pictorial elements [Guastello and Traut 1989]. Others have investigated selecting and designing integrated information displays including maps, text, tables, and graphics (e.g., [Arens 1991; Burger and Marshall, this volume]).

Recently, however, there is a move to an even tighter coupling of text and graphics design. For example, COMET [Feiner and McKeown, this volume; Feiner et al., this volume] uses rhetorical schema to select content independent of media and then apportion this to text and three dimensional graphics to design coordinated multimedia presentations concerning the operation and maintenance of an Army field radio. Unlike COMET, mode allocation in our approach occurs during not after content selection so that content selection and mode allocation can co-constrain. More closely related to our approach, WIP [André and Rist, this volume; André et al., this volume] uses plan operators to design presentations. In contrast to WIP, however, our approach is based on a generalization of a set of rhetorical acts used previously for multisentential text planning in the TEXPLAN system [Maybury 1990, 1992b]. This accounts, for example, for the distinction between illocutionary and locutionary acts in TEXPLAN (see Section 2).

WIP, on the other hand, claims roots in rhetorical structure theory-based (RST) text planners [Hovy 1988a; Moore 1989]. See Maybury [1992a] for a contrast of these two approaches and Hovy et al. [1992] for a discussion of a more integrated approach. Another difference is that WIP focuses on the generation of static illustrated instructions (i.e., picture sequences) whereas our multimedia extension to TEXPLAN focuses on the design of dynamic, narrated animation of routes over an object-oriented cartographic information system. Also, WIP includes a fine-grained constraint-based layout mechanism [Graf 1992] whereas our approach controls only coarse-grained layout by way of display control actions (see Figure 2). Also, WIP's tree adjoining grammar approach supports incremental generation below the clause level whereas TEXPLAN can only generate incrementally at the clause level. Finally, WIP and COMET address the challenging problem of cross-modal references. Nevertheless, COMET, WIP, and the extended TEXPLAN all raise issues central to multimedia design such as: how do we select and apportion content to different media, how do we coordinate media, and how do we ensure that our communicative goals are achieved by the resulting artifact?

7. Conclusion and Future Directions

This chapter proposes a number of communicative acts — linguistic, graphical, and rhetorical — that can be exploited to plan and coordinate multimedia explanations. We first formalize several linguistic acts and graphical acts as plan operators. These are abstracted into higher level, media-independent actions called rhetorical acts. A computational implementation is described which identifies locations and composes route plans in coordinated natural language text and graphics in the context of a cartographic information system.

We are currently extending the implementation to incorporate other types of graphical acts. For example, the system is able to divide an entity linguistically in two ways: by detailing its constituents or subparts (e.g., "The United Kingdom contains England, Scotland, Wales, and Northern Ireland.") or if the entity is an abstract concept, by indicating its subtypes or subclasses (e.g., "There are three Baltic languages: Old Prussian, Lithuanian, and Latvian."). Graphically, subpart division can be accomplished, for example, by depicting subcomponents or hierarchical trees.

Similarly, subtype division can be accomplished graphically using trees (which indicate parent/child relations) or Venn diagrams (indicating set relationships). Also, while the system can linguistically characterize an entity (e.g., "The pancreas is a long, soft, irregular shaped gland located behind the stomach."), entities which have visual attributes such as size, shape, color and location can be depicted, perhaps with greater effect than the corresponding linguistic description. Finally, the system can generate paragraph-length comparisons of entities, and we intend to compose tabular comparisons of attributes and values, although this will require planning of more sophisticated composite graphs [Feiner 1985; Burger 1989]. Other composite graphical acts also require further investigation (e.g., circling a group of objects and indicating their movement with an arrow).

There are several issues which require further investigation. These include the relationship of deictic and display control acts to the model of the user's attention (i.e., salient objects, events, and regions). Another important issue concerns coordinating graphical and linguistic acts at the clausal and lexical level (e.g., referring expressions coordinated with deixis). One approach would be to extend paragraph planning below the sentence level [Appelt 1985]. Much more difficult is how to narrate events and situations in multiple media, which requires communication of temporal, spatial, and causal information (i.e., story telling coupled with graphical animation).

Finally, we need to investigate the relation of linguistic and graphical acts to other non-speech audio acts. For example, there are analogs between mediums such as linguistic, graphical, and auditory warnings (exclaiming, flashing, and beeping), graphical and auditory icons (e.g., using sirens to indicate danger), and graphical and auditory motion (e.g., using the perception of Doppler effects to indicate motion). Lastly, we are also investigating the utility of probabilistic media allocation algorithms that might overcome some of the inflexibility of rule-based approaches and also augment the formal plan-based approach we have detailed. These remain interesting avenues for future research.

8. Acknowledgments

I thank the reviewers for their comments and Karen Sparck Jones, John Burger, Sam Bayer, and Marc Vilain for stimulating discussions on related issues.

Reflections on. . .

Planning Multimedia Explanations Using Communicative Acts

Mark T. Maybury

This work was inspired by Austin's view of communication as an action-based endeavor and subsequent attempts by Searle and others to formalize communicative actions, their associated applicability conditions, constraints, and effects on the cognitive state of the addressee. Initial investigations focused on analysis of a broad range of multisentential text, including description, comparison, narration, exposition, and argument (Maybury 1991a, 1993a). In the process of corpus analysis, it became clear that multiple media (e.g., text, graphics, imagery) associated with multiple sensory modalities (e.g., auditory, visual, haptic) could be utilized to more effectively convey certain classes of information (e.g., quantitative/qualitative, geospatial, ordinal) for different purposes, audiences, and contexts. Motivated by related work in discourse processing, Maybury (in press) extends this communicative action approach to incorporate interactive dialog actions (e.g., open/close, interrupt/resume).

During our investigations, we discovered the need for a more generalized notion of focus of attention and extended models of linguistic and temporal focus to include spatial focus (Maybury 1991b). We also found an important role for condensed communication and began investigating narrative summary generation, developing the SumGen system (Maybury 1995b). In an evaluation of information extraction by 22 human subjects from both source and summary texts, SumGen demonstrated a 15% reduction in average sentence length, a 70% reduction in document length, and a 58% reduction in time to perform information extraction tasks in two diverse application domains.

Following an AAAI workshop on intelligent multimedia interfaces and a resulting collection (Maybury 1993b), we identified key multimedia presentation processes (Maybury 1995a), including communication/interaction management, content selection, media allocation, media realization, media coordination, and media layout. Together these works specify knowledge sources (e.g., models of the user, discourse, task, and media) and their relationship to the identified fundamental processes. Current efforts aim to establish a common multimedia reference architecture from these and other early efforts (Bordegoni et al., 1998).

Just as media can play a significant role in interfaces, retrieval of multiple media require enhanced processing algorithms to support efficient content-based access to audio, graphics, imagery, and video. Our current efforts include a collection (Maybury 1997) motivated by an IJCAI '95 workshop addressing intelligent indexing of multiple media, including the exploitation of additional media sources (e.g., processing written or spoken language information associated with still or moving images to provide content-based imagery access). Indeed, just as integrated gesture, gaze, and speech may need support upon input, these same media become paramount when analyzing a complex artifact such as video, which may require simultaneous speech, nonspeech audio, closed-caption text, and imagery processing to address ambiguity, imprecision, or errors in the content. We have accordingly applied our ideas to broadcast news on demand embodied in the Broadcast News Navigator (BNN) System.

REFERENCES

Bordegoni, M.; Faconti, G.; Feiner, S.; Maybury, M.; Rist, T.; Ruggieri, S.; Trahanias, P.; and Wilson, M., 1998. A Standard Reference Model for Intelligent Multimedia Presentation Systems. *International Journal on the Development and Application of Standards for Computers, Data Communications and Interfaces*, Vol. 18, Nos. 6 and 7, 477–496. Amsterdam: Elsevier Science.

Maybury, M. T. 1991a. Planning Multisentential English Text Using Communicative Acts. Ph.D. dissertation, University of Cambridge, England, (TR-239).

Maybury, M. T. 1991b. Topical, Temporal and Spatial Constraints on Linguistic Realization. *Computational Intelligence: Special Issue on Natural Language Generation,* 7(4): 266–275.

Maybury, M. T. 1993a. Communicative Acts for Generating Natural Language Arguments. In *Proceedings of the Eleventh AAAI*, Washington, D.C., 357–364. Menlo Park, CA: AAAI/MIT Press.

Maybury, M. T. (ed.) 1993b. *Intelligent Multimedia Interfaces*. Cambridge, MA: AAAI/MIT Press. (*http://www.aaai.org:80/Press/Books/Maybury-1 /maybury.html*)

Maybury, M. T. 1995a. Research in Multimedia Parsing and Generation. In McKevitt, P. (ed.), *Artificial Intelligence Review: Special Issue on the Integration of Natural Language and Vision Processing*, 9(2–3): 103–127.

Maybury, M. T. 1995b. Generating Summaries from Event Data. *International Journal of Information Processing and Management: Special Issue on Text Summarization*, 31(5): 735–751.

Maybury, M. T. (ed.) 1997. *Intelligent Multimedia Information Retrieval*. Cambridge, MA: AAAI/MIT Press. (*http://www.aaai.org:80/Press/Books/Maybury-2/*)

Maybury, M. T. (in press). Communicative Acts for Multimedia and Multimodal Dialog. In Taylor, M. M., Néel, F., and Bouwhuis, D. G. (eds.), *The Structure of Multimodal Dialog II*. Amsterdam: John Benjamin.

Maybury, M.; Merlino, A.; and Morey, D. 1997. Broadcast News Navigator Using Story Segments. In *ACM International Multimedia Conference*, Seattle, WA, November 8–14. New York: ACM Press. 381–391.

Plan-based integration of natural language and graphics generation

Wolfgang Wahlster, Elisabeth André, Wolfgang Finkler, Hans-Jürgen Profitlich and Thomas Rist

German Research Center for Artificial Intelligence (DFKI), Stuhlsatzenhausweg 3, D-66123 Saarbrücken 11, Germany

Abstract

Wahlster, W., E. André, W. Finkler, H.-J. Profitlich and T. Rist, Plan-based integration of natural language and graphics generation, Artificial Intelligence 63 (1993) 387–427.

Multimodal interfaces combining natural language and graphics take advantage of both the individual strength of each communication mode and the fact that several modes can be employed in parallel. The central claim of this paper is that the generation of a multimodal presentation can be considered as an incremental planning process that aims to achieve a given communicative goal. We describe the multimodal presentation system WIP which allows the generation of alternate presentations of the same content taking into account various contextual factors. We discuss how the plan-based approach to presentation design can be exploited so that graphics generation influences the production of text and vice versa. We show that well-known concepts from the area of natural language processing like speech acts, anaphora, and rhetorical relations take on an extended meaning in the context of multimodal communication. Finally, we discuss two detailed examples illustrating and reinforcing our theoretical claims.

1. Introduction

When explaining how to use a technical device, humans will often utilize a combination of language and graphics. It is a rare instruction manual that does not contain illustrations. Multimodal presentation systems combining natural language and graphics take advantage of both the individual strength of each communication mode and the fact that both modes can be employed in parallel. Allowing all of the modalities to refer to and depend upon each other is a key to the richness of multimodal communication.

In this paper, we describe the basic methods used in our attempt to integrate multiple AI components such as planning, knowledge representation, natural language generation, and graphics generation into a functioning prototype called WIP that plans and coordinates multimodal presentations in which all material is generated by the system. We will concentrate on the intercomponent interactions and synergies that arise from combining components.

A basic principle underlying the WIP model is that the various constituents of a multimodal presentation should be generated from a common representation of what is to be conveyed. This raises the question of how to decompose a given communicative goal into subgoals to be realized by the mode-specific generators, so that the modes[1] complement each other.

1.1. Major design goals of WIP

The major design goals of WIP are the generation of coordinated multimodal presentations from a common representation, the adaptation of these presentations to the intended target audience and situation, and the incrementality of all processes constituting the design and realization of the multimodal output.

1.1.1. Generating coordinated presentations

It is an important goal of this research not simply to merge the verbalization results of a natural language generator and the visualization results of a knowledge-based graphics design component, but to carefully coordinate natural language and graphics in such a way that they generate a multiplicative improvement in communication capabilities. Enforcing a consistent, harmonious and aesthetic integration of text and graphics is an essential subtask in automating the synthesis of multimodal presentations. To address this problem, we explored computational models of the cognitive decision process, coping with questions such as what should go into text, what should go into graphics, and which kinds of links between the verbal and non-verbal fragments are necessary.

In addition, WIP deals with page layout as a rhetorical force, influencing the intentional and attentional state of the reader. In summary, systems like WIP shift the metaphor of "computer as author" used in natural language

[1] Since one of the generation parameters of WIP is the specification of the output device, we use the term "medium" in the sense of a physical carrier of information. In contrast, the term "mode" is used throughout this paper to refer to the particular sign system. We are aware of the fact that other authors use these terms differently.

generation to the broader view of "computer as desktop publisher" (cf. [14]).

1.1.2. *Generating situated presentations*

WIP is a highly adaptive interface since all of its output is generated on the fly and customized for the intended target audience and situation. The quest for adaptation is based on the fact that it is impossible to anticipate the needs and requirements of each potential user in an infinite number of presentation situations. Thus all presentation decisions are postponed until runtime. In contrast to hypermedia-based approaches to adaptive information presentation, WIP does not use any predesigned texts or graphics. That is, each presentation is designed from scratch by reasoning from first principles using common-sense presentation knowledge. Through its clear separation of content and form WIP goes well beyond hypermedia systems.

The concept of tailoring presentations to the user can be seen as an extended version of the view concept known from database technology. One step on the way to intelligent interfaces for computer-supported collaborative work (CSCW) is to use multimodal systems like WIP as presentation experts that map fragments of a shared knowledge-base onto a variety of presentations satisfying the information needs of the individual group members.

1.1.3. *Incremental generation*

An important design goal of WIP was that the incremental generation of a multimodal presentation should be supported. Incremental generation is the immediate realization of parts of a stepwise provided input. This means that most of the computations relevant to a text or picture element are performed not long before this element is output (see [66]). This is in contrast to non-incremental systems that rely heavily on pre-planning or lookahead and plan the whole multimodal presentation at once. While incremental generation is not always needed, we claim that for systems like WIP incrementality is essential:

On the one hand, WIP must be able to begin outputting words and graphical elements before the input is complete, when the information to be expressed arrives in a stream from the back-end system, as when reporting about simultaneous events (e.g., in a control panel situation). On the other hand, WIP should be prepared for cases when the presentation goal and the input to the generator are changed in the course of generation. Such a change might be due to new high priority goals in the back-end system or the addressee's reaction to the output generated so far. Whereas a non-incremental system is only able to react to unexpected events after the complete realization of a particular presentation plan, an incremental system is able to respond more promptly. It is obvious that in most situations, human presenters follow such an incremental processing strategy (cf. [37]).

Since, in an interactive setting, a multimodal presentation system should reply fast, incrementality is useful for the sake of decreasing response time, even if the entire input is available before generation.

Of course, WIP cannot be completely incremental in the sense that it converts an element in the input stream completely in a text or picture fragment before moving on to the next element of the input stream, since this would not allow for the necessary dependencies among choices.

1.2. *The current prototype of WIP*

The current prototype of WIP generates multimodal explanations and instructions on assembling, using, maintaining or repairing physical devices. WIP is currently able to generate simple German or English explanations on using an espresso machine, assembling a lawn-mower, or installing a modem, demonstrating our claim of language and application independence.

We view the design of multimodal presentations including text and graphics design as a subarea of general communication design. We approximate the fact that communication is always situated by introducing generation parameters in our model. The current system includes a choice between user stereotypes (e.g., novice, expert), target languages (German versus English), layout formats (e.g., hardcopy of instruction manual, screen display), and output modes (incremental output versus complete output only). The set of generation parameters is used to specify design constraints that must be satisfied by the final presentation. A diverse set of evaluation knowledge for text, graphics and layout is necessary to select a particular design that satisfies the design specifications stated as generation parameters. WIP provides computationally tractable evaluations of candidate designs at various levels of the incremental generation process.

In summary, WIP allows the generation of alternate presentations of the same content taking into account various contextual factors such as the user's degree of expertise and preferences for a particular output medium or mode.

One of the important insights we gained from building the WIP system is that it is actually possible to extend and adapt many of the fundamental concepts developed to date in AI and computational linguistics for the generation of natural language in such a way that they become useful for the generation of graphics and text–picture combinations as well. This means that an interesting methodological transfer from the area of natural language processing to a much broader computational model of multimodal communication seems possible. In particular, semantic and pragmatic concepts like coherence, speech acts, anaphora, and rhetorical relations take on an extended meaning in the context of text–picture combinations.

The rest of the paper is organized as follows: Section 2 provides a survey of related research and highlights the distinguishing features of the WIP approach. Sections 3 and 4 introduce the functionality and the architecture of the WIP system, respectively. In Section 5, we show that techniques for planning text and discourse can be generalized to plan the structure and content of multimodal communications. Section 6 introduces an RST-based presentation planner for communicating domain plans in multimodal documents. Section 7 provides a description of WIP's mode-specific generators. While in Section 8 the interplay between presentation planning, design and realization will be discussed and illustrated by means of examples, Section 9 concentrates on our model for the coordination of text and graphics generation. Finally, we discuss limitations of the current WIP system and give an outlook for our future research directions.

2. Related research

Over the past several years, a number of projects have entered the area between natural language processing and multimodal communication, often focusing on a single specific functionality, such as the use of pointing gestures parallel to verbal descriptions for referent identification (e.g., [13,36,43]). The automatic design of complete multimodal presentations has only recently received significant attention in artificial intelligence research. The most extensive discussion of active research in this field can be found in the proceedings of a series of workshops on intelligent multimedia interfaces (e.g., [6,40,60]).

We have been engaged in work in the area of multimodal communication for several years now, starting with the HAM-ANS (cf. [65]) and VITRA systems (cf. [1,27]), which automatically create natural language descriptions of pictures and image sequences shown on the screen. These projects resulted in a better understanding of how perception interacts with language production.

Since then, we have been investigating ways of integrating tactile pointing with natural language understanding and generation in the XTRA project (cf. [36,62]). WIP grew out of the results of our previous research into multimodal interaction, particularly in the VITRA and XTRA projects.

Various user interfaces to date combine natural language and graphics, but only a few of them (cf. [34,41,52,63]) generate both forms of presentation from a common representation and therefore can explicitly address the problem of media choice and coordination.

For example, Kerpedjiev has designed a system that transforms a dataset about a particular weather situation into a multimodal weather report consisting of a text illustrated by tables and weather maps with various icons and annotations (cf. [34]).

Whereas most systems combine text with informational graphics (e.g., maps, diagrams, charts), COMET [41] and WIP [2] generate text illustrated by 3D graphics of physical objects.

The work closest to our own is being carried out in the COMET project (cf. [18,19]). Both projects share a strong research interest in the coordination of text and graphics. COMET generates directions for the maintenance and repair of a portable radio using text coordinated with 3D graphics. In spite of many similarities, there are major differences between COMET and WIP, e.g., in the systems' processing strategies, representation languages, and architectures.

COMET uses a schema-based content planner while WIP uses an operator-based approach to planning. As was shown in [45], information concerning the effects of the individual parts of a schema is compiled out. If it turns out that a particular schema fails, the system may use a different schema, but it is impossible to extend or modify only one part of the schema. In contrast, an operator-based approach enables more local revisions by explicitly representing the effects of each section of the presentation. Another advantage of an operator-based approach is that mode information can be easily incorporated and propagated during the content selection process.[2] This method facilitates the coordination of the two processes as mode selection can take place during content selection and not only after as in COMET.

Another distinguishing feature of WIP's architecture is its function of supporting incrementality, thus insuring a more fine-grained division of work between the selected presentation modes.

In contrast to COMET, WIP allows for bidirectional communication between the presentation planner and the layout manager. While COMET's layout component is supposed to combine text and graphics fragments produced by mode-specific generators during one of the final processing steps, WIP's layout manager interacts with a presentation planner before text and graphics are generated so that layout considerations can influence the early stages of the planning process and constrain the mode-specific generators. In WIP, we view layout as an important carrier of meaning.

The importance of the layout dimension is also stressed by recent work at ISI that involves the generation of formatted text exploiting the communicative function of headings, enumerations, and footnotes (cf. [30]).

Whereas the majority of work has concentrated on combining static media, the VITRA-Soccer project (cf. [27], for details of VITRA's animation

[2] This also applies to temporal information in the case of animated presentations.

	Informational Graphics	3D Graphics of Physical Objects
Static Media	Maps, Charts, Diagrams Example Systems: SAGE, FNN	Rendered Pictures Example Systems: WIP, COMET
Dynamic Media	Hypermedia Presentations Example Systems: AlFresco, IDAS	Animation Example Systems: VITRA-SOCCER, AnimNL

Fig. 1. Combining text production with four types of graphics generation.

component see [56]), the AnimNL project (cf. [10]) and recent extensions of COMET (cf. [17]) and WIP also deal with dynamic media, such as animation. Systems like AlFresco (cf. [59]) and IDAS (cf. [47]) demonstrate that natural language generation can be enhanced by integration with hypermedia systems. In such systems, the generated text may contain links to hypercards, and canned text or images can be combined with generated text for a hypermedia presentation.

Figure 1 summarizes the various types of graphical presentations that have been combined with generated text in recent research prototypes. In all these projects, the generation system is no longer only the author of a text, but also plays the role of a desktop publisher, a hypertext designer, a multimodal interface designer, or a commentator of animations.

Whereas the projects mentioned above focus on computational methods for the automatic synthesis of multimodal presentations, [7] concentrates on the analysis and representation of presentation knowledge.

3. A functional view of WIP

The task of the knowledge-based presentation system WIP is the context-sensitive generation of a variety of multimodal documents from an input including a presentation goal. The presentation goal is a formal representation of the communicative intent specified by the back-end application system.

The example of a presentation goal in Fig. 2 represents the system's assumption about the mutual belief (BMB) of the presenter P and the addressee A, that it is P's goal that A carries out a plan denoted by the constant FILL-IN-128. This is a concrete domain plan specified as part of

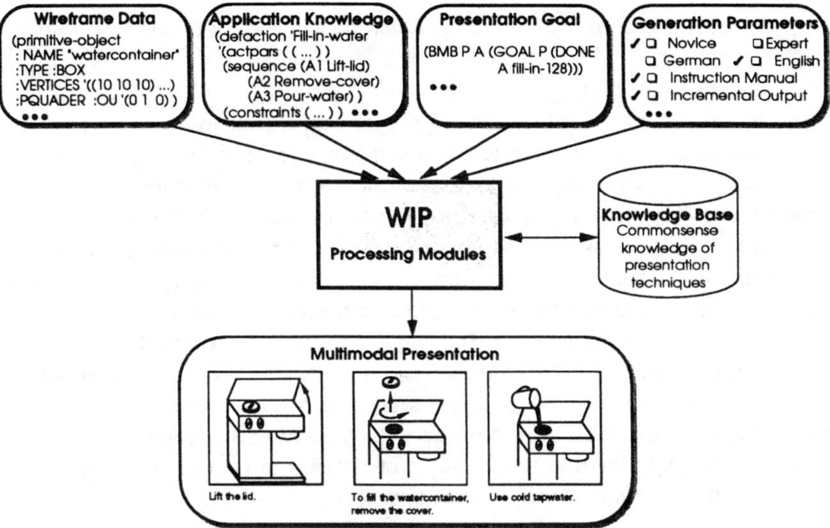

Fig. 2. WIP—a functional view.

WIP's application knowledge. In this case, the plan is a fully instantiated sequence of actions represented in the assertional part of the hybrid knowledge representation system RAT (Representation of Actions in Terminological logics, see Section 6.1). The terminological part of RAT is used to represent the ontology and abstract plans for a particular application domain (see Fig. 2).

In addition to this propositional representation, that includes the relevant information about the structure, function, behavior, and use of the technical device, WIP has access to an analogical representation of the geometry of the machine in the form of a wireframe model (see Fig. 2).

WIP is a transportable interface based on processing schemes, independent of any particular back-end system and so requires only a limited effort to adapt to a new application. Obviously, for a new domain the application knowledge and the wireframe model must be transformed into WIP's representation schemes. In order to validate WIP's transportability we tested the system in three different application domains (espresso machine, lawnmower, and modem). Starting from the original espresso-machine domain we did not have to change a single line of code in going to the two new domains. Only the declarative knowledge sources coded in RAT, the lexicon, and the geometric information are different. While for each domain the application knowledge and the wireframe model are fixed, the presentation goal and the generation parameters can be varied to tailor WIP's results for a particular communicative situation.

WIP is designed for interfacing with heterogeneous back-end systems such as expert systems, tutoring systems, intelligent control panels, on-line documentation, and help systems, which supply the presentation system with the necessary input. However, the current prototype has been tested with manually coded domain plans only. The presentation goal and the generation parameters have been set interactively in these test runs.

Note that the incremental output mode mentioned in Section 1.2 as one of the options for the generation of multimodal output, characterizes a likely application scenario for systems like WIP, since the intended use includes intelligent control panels and active help systems, where the timeliness and fluency of output is critical, e.g., when generating a warning. In such a situation, the presentation system must be able to start with an incremental output although it has not yet received all the information to be conveyed from the back-end system (cf. [22]). To adapt a generator to work incrementally usually complicates it, but WIP is designed right from the beginning with the incrementality of all processing stages in mind (see Section 1.1).

WIP can also be used in a stand-alone fashion, where an author specifies the necessary domain information. This leads to the long-term vision of an intelligent authoring system, that forces one to specify information only once in a formal way and then allows the generation of a possibly infinite variety of presentations of this information tailored to various audiences and media. In contrast to the current situation in technical writing and document preparation, this approach—similar to the view concept in database design—could ensure consistency across all derived presentations, since the underlying content is stored in only one place.

4. Structuring a multimodal presentation system

4.1. The need for an interleaved processing scheme

Most multimodal generation systems consist of three different kinds of processes: a content planning process, a mode selection process, and content realization processes. When designing an architecture for a multimodal presentation system, the question arises of how to organize these processes. Previous work on natural language generation has shown that content selection and content realization should not be treated independently of each other (see also [29,48]). A strictly sequential model in which data flow only from the "what to present" to the "how to present" part has proven inappropriate because the components responsible for selecting the contents would have to anticipate all decisions of the realization components. This problem is compounded if, as in WIP, content realization is done by separate components (currently a text and a graphics generator) of which the content planner has only limited knowledge.

It seems even inappropriate to sequentialize content planning and mode selection although mode selection is only a very rough decision about content realization. Selecting a mode of presentation depends to a large extent on the nature of the information to be conveyed. On the other hand, content planning is strongly influenced by previously selected mode combinations. For example, to graphically refer to a physical object, we need visual information that may be irrelevant to textual references.

A better solution is to interleave content planning, mode selection, and content realization. In the WIP system, we interleave content and mode selection using a uniform planning mechanism. In contrast to this, presentation planning and content realization are performed by separate components that access various knowledge sources. This modularization enables parallel processing, but makes interaction between the single components necessary.

Interactions are, however, only useful if the realization components are able to process information in an incremental manner. As soon as the content planner has decided which generator should encode a certain piece of information, this piece should be passed on to the respective generator. Conversely, the content planner should incorporate the results of the realization components as soon as possible.

4.2. The cascaded architecture of the WIP system

These considerations have led to the architecture shown in Fig. 3. The major components of the WIP system[3] are: a presentation planner that is responsible for determining the contents and selecting an appropriate mode combination, mode-specific generators (currently for text and graphics) and a layout manager (cf. [23]) that arranges the generated output in a document. Each generator consists of an incremental design and realization component which form a cascade. Thus the basic modularization is the same both for text and graphics generation, resulting in two parallel cascades.

The presentation planner and the mode-specific generators interact incrementally in a pipelined mode. In other words, text and graphics design and even the verbalization and visualization can start, before the presentation plan is completed. The text and graphics design components can be seen as micro-planners of the "what to say" and "what to show" parts of the mode-specific generators. For example, lexical choice is not carried out by the presentation planner on the macro-plan level, but by the text design component.

[3] As the result of a 30-man-year effort the WIP prototype is fully implemented, comprising 5.5 MB of Common Lisp and CLOS source code.

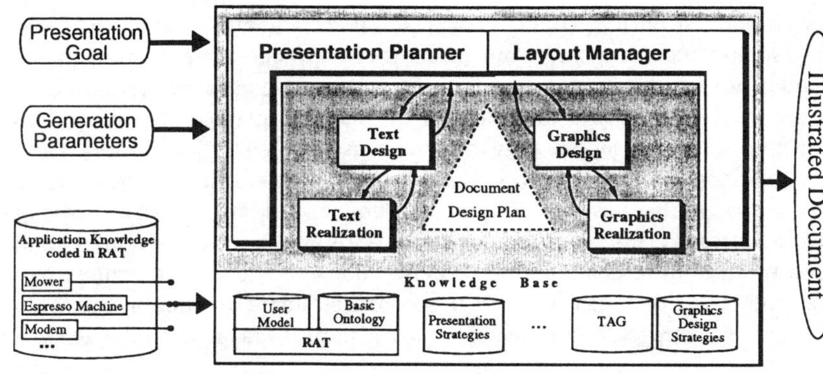

Fig. 3. The architecture of the WIP system.

There is no direct communication from a mode-specific realization module back to the presentation planner or layout manager, but all such communication is mediated by the corresponding design module. As soon as the presentation planner and the layout manager have made enough commitments to allow the mode-specific generators to start work, the text and/or graphics design components are activated. Then the control passes back and forth between the modules of the cascade, interleaving their execution.

To prevent disconcerting or incoherent output, the document design plan keeps the history of the design decisions on all levels of the incremental generation process. This means that decisions of the language generator may influence graphics generation and that graphical constraints may sometimes force decisions in the language production process.

The incremental processing mode with feedback and negotiation among the components supports self-monitoring and the anticipation of the addressee's interpretation (see [62]).

WIP's basic ontology and user model are represented in the terminological logic RAT (cf. [26] and Section 6.1). In addition, WIP's knowledge base includes declaratively coded presentation strategies (see Section 6.2.1), graphical design strategies (see Section 7.1) and a lexicalized Tree Adjoining Grammar (TAG, see [25] and Section 7.2).

5. Generalizing language generation to multimodal presentations

Since a lot of progress has been achieved in natural language generation, it is quite natural to wonder whether it is possible to generalize the underlying concepts and methods in such a way that they become useful in the broader context of multimodal presentations. Although new questions arise, e.g., how to optimally divide the work between the available presentation modes, a lot of tasks in multimodal generation bear much resemblance to problems occurring in natural language generation, in particular, the structuring of the presentation in a coherent manner and the establishment of cohesive links by appropriate cross-references.

5.1. The generation of multimodal documents as a goal-directed activity

Our approach is based on the assumption that not only the generation of text, but also the generation of multimodal documents can be considered as a goal-directed activity (cf. [4]). We presume that there is at least one act that is central to the goal of the whole document. This act is referred to as the *main act.* Acts supporting the main act are called *subsidiary acts.* This distinction between main and subsidiary acts essentially corresponds to the distinction between *global* and *subsidiary speech acts* in [57], *main speech acts* and *subordinate speech acts* in [61], and between *nucleus* and *satellites* in the Rhetorical Structure Theory (RST) proposed in [39]. Since main and subsidiary acts can, in turn, be composed of main and subsidiary acts, a hierarchical document structure results. While the root of the hierarchy generally corresponds to a complex communicative act such as describing a process, the leaves are elementary acts, i.e., speech acts (cf. [57]) or pictorial acts (cf. [35]).

5.2. An extended notion of coherence for multimodal documents

A number of textlinguists have characterized coherence in terms of semantic and pragmatic coherence relations that hold between the parts of the text (e.g., see [24,28]). Semantic relations, such as *Sequence*, directly correspond to the structure of the domain whereas pragmatic relations, such as *Motivation*, refer to the communicative function of document parts. Perhaps the most elaborated set of coherence relations is presented in RST (cf. [39]). Examples of RST relations are *Sequence*, *Motivation*, *Elaboration*, *Enablement*, *Interpretation*, and *Summary.* Text–picture researchers have investigated the role a particular picture plays in relation to accompanying text passages. E.g., Levin has found five primary functions (cf. [38]): *Decoration*, *Representation*, *Organization*, *Interpretation*, and *Transformation.* Hunter and colleagues distinguish between: *Embellish*, *Reinforce*, *Elaborate*, *Summarize*, and *Compare* (cf. [31]). An attempt at a transfer of the relations proposed by Hobbs to pictures and text–picture combinations has been made in [11]. Unfortunately, text–picture researchers only consider the communicative functions of whole pictures, i.e., they do not address the question of how a picture is organized. To get an informative description of the whole document structure, one has to consider relations between picture parts or between picture parts and text passages, too. E.g., a portion of a picture can serve as background for the rest of the picture or a text passage can elaborate on a particular section of a picture. We have analyzed several illustrated documents in order to find out which relations occur between textual and pictorial document parts (cf. [3]). In particular, we have examined the relations found by text–picture researchers (cf. [38]) and those proposed in RST (cf. [39]). To ensure that the user recognizes how document parts relate to others, a multimodal presentation system has to know which mode combination conveys a certain relationship most effectively.

6. Plans for communicating plans

A basic assumption behind the WIP model is that not only the generation of text and dialog contributions, but also the design of graphics and multimodal presentations are planning tasks (cf. [5]). When explaining how a complex process functions, WIP generates and realizes plans for communicating domain plans provided by the back-end system. The elements of the plans generated by WIP are communicative acts that verbalize and visualize the physical acts specified in a given domain plan.

6.1. Representing domain plans

As WIP is designed as a presentation system, our research is focused on the generation of presentation plans, not domain plans. Nevertheless, domain plans are an essential part of WIP's input and therefore must be made accessible to the presentation system. Moreover, for the design of presentations WIP must be able to perform certain reasoning tasks on domain plans—although domain plans are not generated by WIP, but by application systems. In order to have a well defined interface between the application system and WIP, we assume that domain plans are represented in RAT terms.

The RAT module (cf. [26]) is used both for the generation of text and graphics as the main source of knowledge about the domain. Besides the domain plans the entire information concerning the domain terminology is represented in RAT. In order to support the user modeling RAT provides partitioning mechanisms to reason about the potentially conflicting views of the world the user and the system may have.

The architecture of RAT was inspired by the need for a tool for the reasoning about concepts and instances of the domain as well as actions, plans, and relations between them. Terminological representation systems have proven to be adequate formalisms for the representation of ontologies in various applications [46]. However, besides their abilities of managing concept and instance descriptions, they do not provide any meaningful way of representing temporal or causal relationships. On the other hand various STRIPS-like systems have been developed that provide powerful tools to synthesize and retrieve plans (cf. [12]). The shortcomings of these systems, however, are their limited services concerning the reasoning about the objects in the domain and relations between plans. In order to merge the advantages of both types of systems, RAT was designed as an extension on top of the terminological logic KRIS [9] with close links between action and concept representation.

The presentation planner can make use of a number of reasoning services provided by RAT, e.g., temporal projection, plan subsumption, or the simulated execution of plans. For instance, suppose the domain plan is nonlinear, i.e., some subplans P1 and P2 can be executed in any order and P1 needs a longer explanation than P2 (because its explanation should contain an illustration, for instance). Now suppose that the layout manager informs the presentation planner that only a little space is left on the current document page. In this case the presentation planner would decide first to present P2 and then P1. In order to reason about the world state after the user's execution of P2 the presentation planner can make use of RAT's inference services, namely, the simulated plan execution. This is critical for the design of the illustration used for P1 since the shown state of the world should include the effects of P2. In some cases it might be helpful to explain a sequence of several subactions on a more abstract level. RAT supports such an abstraction by finding a plan sequence which is composed of these subactions. In other cases the explanation of a later subplan can be shortened by referring to a subplan which has already been presented if RAT detects that they subsume each other.

Like in other state-based formalisms RAT actions are defined by the change they cause in the world state. We distinguish between *atomic actions*, which are non-decomposable and defined by a pre- and postcondition and *plan schemata*, which represent sequences of actions with possible constraints on the objects involved. In contrast to other STRIPS-like formalisms the pre- and postconditions of atomic actions are described by using a subset of the underlying terminological logic, namely, conjunctions of feature restrictions, agreements, and disagreements. By that the underlying terminological logic provides a limited form of a background theory and, as a consequence, predicates are not unrelated but ordered by the subsumption relation. In addition, a set of feature restrictions interpreted as *action parameters* is specified that play the role of "formal parameters" of the action.

Formally, an atomic action is a triplet $\langle pars, pre, post \rangle$ where *pars* is a conjunction of restrictions on feature atoms: $f_1 : C_1 \sqcap \cdots \sqcap f_n : C_n$, which is interpreted as a set of (typed) *action parameters*; *pre* is a conjunction of feature (or feature chain) restrictions $(p : C)$, agreements $(p \stackrel{\downarrow}{=} q)$, and disagreements $(p \stackrel{\downarrow}{\neq} q)$, and is interpreted as the *precondition* of the action; *post* has the same form as *pre* and is interpreted as the *postcondition* of the action.[4]

In order to illustrate the definition, let us consider the following two example actions:

$$
\begin{aligned}
&\texttt{put-cup-under-water-outlet} =\\
&\quad\langle(\text{agent}:\text{person} \sqcap \text{object}:\text{cup} \sqcap \text{machine}:\text{espresso-machine}),\\
&\quad\ (\text{object.position} \stackrel{\downarrow}{=} \text{agent.has-hand.inside-region}),\\
&\quad\ (\text{object.position} \stackrel{\downarrow}{=} \text{machine.has-water-outlet.under-region})\rangle
\end{aligned}
$$

$$
\begin{aligned}
&\texttt{turn-switch-to-espresso} =\\
&\quad\langle(\text{agent}:\text{person} \sqcap \text{machine}:\text{espresso-machine}),\\
&\quad\ (\text{machine.has-switch.position}:\text{off-position} \sqcap\\
&\quad\quad \text{machine.state}:(\text{off} \sqcap \text{ready})),\\
&\quad\ (\text{machine.has-switch.position}:\text{espresso-position} \sqcap\\
&\quad\quad \text{machine.state}:\text{on})\rangle
\end{aligned}
$$

In plain words, the action `put-cup-under-water-outlet` has the action parameters agent, object, and machine, the precondition is that the cup is held by the agent's hand, and the postcondition is that the cup is located under the water outlet. Note that, e.g., agent.has-hand.inside-region is not a single, primitive feature, but the composition of the three features agent, has-hand, and inside-region, which are defined in the taxonomy. Similarly, the action `turn-switch-to-espresso` has two action parameters agent and machine, the precondition is that the switch is in the "off" position and that the machine is off and ready, and the postcondition is that the switch is in the "espresso" position and the machine is running.

Atomic actions can be composed to form plan schemata, which are specified by a set of action parameters, a sequence of actions, and, in contrast to similar formalisms, equality constraints on the action parameters of the plan schema and the actions involved. Formally, a plan schema is a triplet $\langle pars, seq, constr\rangle$, where *pars* represents the action parameters of the plan schema in the same way as for atomic actions, *seq* is a sequence of pairs consisting of *labels* and *actions*, which may be either atomic actions or plan schemata, and *constr* is a conjunction of agreements expressing equality constraints on the action parameters. Consider as an example an excerpt of the plan schema for making espresso:

$$
\begin{aligned}
&\texttt{make-espresso} =\\
&\quad\langle(\text{agent}:\text{person} \sqcap \text{object1}:\text{cup} \sqcap\\
&\quad\quad \text{object2}:\text{espresso-machine} \sqcap \cdots),\\
&\quad\ (\ldots,\\
&\quad\quad \text{A5: put-cup-under-water-outlet},\\
&\quad\quad \text{A6: turn-switch-to-espresso},\\
&\quad\quad \ldots),\\
&\quad\ (\text{object2} \stackrel{\downarrow}{=} \text{A5.machine} \sqcap\\
&\quad\quad \text{object2} \stackrel{\downarrow}{=} \text{A6.machine} \sqcap \cdots)\rangle
\end{aligned}
$$

The precondition of an action must be satisfied by the current world state to allow the execution of the action. This is checked by mapping this problem into the underlying terminological logic and testing if the subsumption relation holds between the precondition and the current world state. The postconditions are asserted to be valid after the successful execution by interpreting their restrictions on the world state as assignments. Note that by allowing equations between feature chains in the postcondition we permit structural changes as opposed to simple changes in truth-values of atomic formulae, as in STRIPS-like systems.

RAT shows that the design of a plan representation system as an extension of a terminological logic can be successfully exploited to provide a variety of interesting and new reasoning services like plan subsumption, temporal projection of conditions, or the simulated execution of plans. In contrast to other approaches which combine terminological and temporal reasoning like CLASP [16] or T-REX [68] whose focus is on plan recognition, the RAT system additionally allows for detailed descriptions of states as pre- and postconditions. On the other hand, these systems currently provide a much richer language to combine actions to plans (regular expressions and temporal constraints, respectively).

6.2. *Plan-based mode selection, content determination, and organization*

As argued in Section 5, text–picture combinations follow similar structuring principles as text. In particular, a document is characterized by its intentional structure that is reflected by the presenter's intentions and by its rhetorical structure that is reflected by various coherence relations. Therefore, it was quite natural to extend methods for text planning in such a way that they become also useful for multimodal presentations.

6.2.1. *Representing presentation knowledge*

In order to generate multimodal presentations, we have defined a set of presentation strategies that can be selected and combined according to

[4] The formal notation follows [8].

a particular presentation task. Such presentation strategies reflect general presentation knowledge or they embody more specific knowledge of how to present a certain subject.

To represent presentation strategies, we follow the approach proposed by Moore and Paris (cf. [42]) to operationalize RST for text planning. However, an additional slot for the presentation mode must be introduced. The strategies are represented by a name, a header, an effect, a set of applicability conditions and a specification of main and subsidiary acts. Whereas the header of a strategy is a complex communicative act (e.g., to enable an action), its effect refers to an intentional goal (e.g., the user knows a particular object).[5] After the successful execution of a strategy, the user model is updated by adding the effect to the knowledge base via RAT's TELL language. The applicability conditions specify when a strategy may be used, and constrain the variables to be instantiated. To evaluate an applicability condition, knowledge represented in RAT is accessed via the ASK language. Example requests are: finding all instances of a certain concept, finding role fillers, realizing object or domain action instances or finding all subactions of a domain plan. We would like to stress that some requests go beyond pure knowledge retrieval. For example, when describing a complex domain plan, a presenter often relies on presentation strategies which involve the depiction of intermediate world states after the execution of certain actions. Since the RAT representation of a complex domain plan does not comprise intermediate world states, they have to be inferred using RAT's inferential services (see Section 6.1).

The kernel of the presentation strategies is formed by main and subsidiary acts. For example, the strategies below can be used to show the orientation of an object in a picture and to ensure that it is identifiable. Whereas graphics must be used to carry out the main acts in these strategies, the mode for the subsidiary acts is still open.

```
(def-presentation-strategy
  :Header (Describe P A (Orientation ?orientation) G)
  :Effect (BMB P A (Has-Orientation ?x ?orientation))
  :Applicability-Conditions
    (Bel P (Has-Orientation ?x ?orientation))
  :Main-Acts
    (S-Depict P A (Orientation ?orientation) ?p-ori ?picture)
  :Subsidiary-Acts
    (Achieve P (BMB P A (Identifiable A ?x ?px ?picture))
             ?mode))
```

[5]In [42], this distinction between header and effect is not made because the effect of their strategies may be an intentional goal as well as a rhetorical relation.

```
(def-presentation-strategy
  :Header (Background P A ?x ?px ?picture G)
  :Effect (BMB P A (Identifiable A ?x ?px ?picture))
  :Applicability-Conditions
    (AND (Bel P (Image-of ?x ?px ?picture))
         (Bel P (Perceptually-Accessible A ?x))
         (Bel P (Part-of ?x ?z)))
  :Main-Acts (S-Depict P A (Object ?z) ?pz ?picture)
  :Subsidiary-Acts
    (Achieve P (BMB P A (Identifiable A ?z ?pz ?picture))
             ?mode))
```

Since there may be several strategies for achieving a certain goal, criteria for ranking the effectiveness, the side-effects, and costs of executing presentation strategies are needed.

To formulate selection criteria, we use meta-rules. For example, the meta-rule below suggests the use of graphics rather than text when presenting spatial information.

```
IF (IS-A ?current-attribute-value Spatial-Concept)
  THEN (Dobefore *graphics-strategies* *text-strategies*)
```

A basis for our meta-rules and presentation strategies form extended studies of relevant psychological literature and our own analyses of various illustrated documents. In particular, we identified seven information types (concrete, abstract, spatial, covariant, temporal, quantification, negation) with several subtypes and ten communicative functions (attract-attention, compare, elaborate, enable, elucidate, label, motivate, evidence, background, summarize) and examined which mode or mode combination conveys them best. For example, it is very difficult or even impossible to graphically depict quantifiers (such as *some* or *a few*) whereas graphics are in general the preferred modality for communicating visual attributes (concrete information), for more details see [5]. Although we focused on the nature of information and the communicative function of a document, there is no doubt that other criteria (e.g., user characteristics and resource limitations) are also important.

6.2.2. The presentation planning process

At the heart of the presentation system is a parallel top-down planner and a constraint-based layout manager. The presentation planner receives as input a high-level presentation goal (see Fig. 4). It then tries to find a presentation strategy whose effect or header match the presentation goal and generates a refinement-style plan in the form of a directed acyclic graph (DAG). The leaves of the planned DAG are specifications for elementary

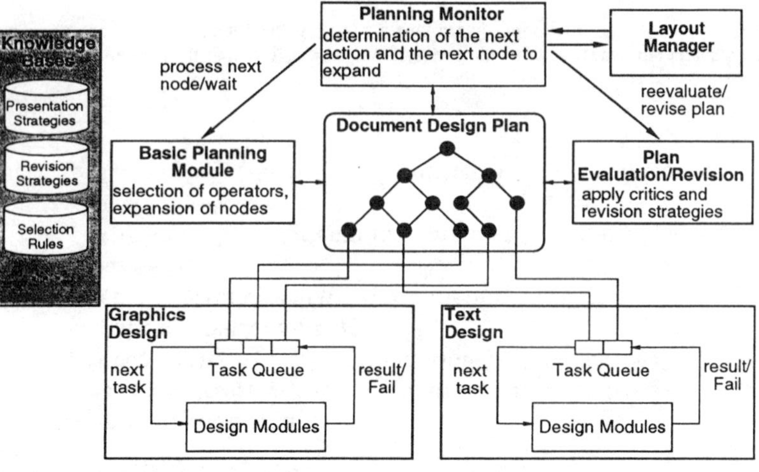

Fig. 4. The presentation planner of WIP.

acts of presentation. They are sent to the appropriate task queue (see Fig. 4). The text designer handles elementary speech acts, such as s-assert (generate a surface structure for an assertion) or s-request (generate a surface structure of a request), the graphics designer executes pictorial acts, such as s-depict (depict an object) or s-annotate (label an object). During the text and graphics generation processes, further refinements of individual presentation goals are possible.

Since the presentation planner has no direct access to knowledge concerning mode-specific realization, it cannot consider this information when building up a candidate document structure. Consequently, it may happen that the results provided by the generators deviate to a certain extent from the initial document plan. Such deviations are reflected in the DAG by *output sharing*, *structure sharing*, and *structure adding*. Output sharing occurs when parts of the generated output are reused for different purposes, e.g., as part of a labeling relation and as part of a background relation (see also Section 8). Structure sharing is similar to output sharing. It occurs when not only parts of the output, but also a more complex part of the DAG are shared. For example, let us assume the presentation planner decides to show an action and its result by means of two pictures. To orientate the user, it is planned to show background objects in both pictures. If the graphics designer is able to convey the requested information in a single picture, the background for the actions has, however, to be included only once. Consequently, the structure of the document can be simplified by factoring out the background branch. Whereas structure sharing leads to simplifications of the initial document plan, structure adding results in a more complex plan. It occurs, e.g., if the graphics generator is expected to integrate information in a single picture, but is only able to convey the information by generating several pictures.

Restructuring methods are applied when the results of the generators do not correspond to the initial document plan. However, it may also happen that the generators are not able to accomplish a task. In such situations, restructuring methods do not lead to a result. Instead, the planner will have to revise its initial proposal by choosing another presentation strategy or by instantiating variables differently. To ensure consistency of the document, all changes have to be propagated to other parts of the document.

Information must flow not only between the content planner and the generators, but also from one generator to the other. Let us suppose the text generator has generated a referring expression for an object shown in a picture. If the picture is changed due to graphical constraints, it might happen that the referring expression no longer fits. Thus, the planner will have to create a new object description and pass this description on to the text generator, which will have to replace the initial referring expression by a new one. As shown in Fig. 4, the leaves of the document plan are connected to entries in the task queues of the mode-specific generators. Thus, the document design plan serves not only as an interface between the planner and the generators, but also enables a two-way exchange of information between the generators.

Furthermore, the need for propagating data during presentation planning arises when dealing with dependencies between presentation strategies. For example, a decision about mode selection often depends on earlier decisions. Assume the system decides to compare two objects by describing the different values of a common attribute. At this time, the only restriction is that both descriptions should be realized in the same mode. Once the system has decided on the mode for the attribute value of the first object, the result of this decision must be made available for describing the value of the second object. This problem can be handled by passing mode information during the planning process both from top to bottom and from bottom to top. Mode information is propagated via the header of a strategy. Depending on whether the main acts of a strategy are to be realized in text, graphics, or both modes, the values T(ext), G(raphics), or M(ixed) are assigned. The mode remains unspecified until mode decisions are made for the main acts of a strategy. By deferring mode decisions for as long as possible, the planner is able to continue planning without making selections that are too specific.

Due to the distributed processing scheme of WIP, there is no guarantee that the results of the individual components will always be available at a given time. In some situations, it might happen that the planner is not able to expand a node because it is still waiting for a generator to supply results. To avoid processing delays, WIP's presentation planner does not always expand nodes in a depth-first fashion, but selects the nodes to be expanded in a flexible way, considering heuristics, such as the number of assumptions to be made. To allow for alternating revision and expansion processes, WIP's presentation planner is controlled by a plan monitor that determines the next action and the next nodes to be expanded.

7. Mode-specific content realization

7.1. The graphics generator

In illustrated instructions for technical equipment, graphics are used in order to accomplish presentation tasks, such as depicting a domain object in a certain state, showing an object's location, or visualizing the course of an action. As a starting point, we operationalized certain 2D and 3D illustration techniques frequently used by human illustrators. Inspired by the compositional approach to computational semantics of natural language, our formalization is based on a compositional semantics of pictures. A picture is regarded as a composition of a picture frame and a set of images located within this frame. Each image is treated as an object that is characterized by a restricted 2D region and a set of attributes including visual properties, such as shape, color/gray pattern. In accordance with the underlying source from which an image is derived (cf. Fig. 5), we can distinguish between several basic image types:

- images that result from mapping a 3D model of an object or an object configuration onto a plane 2D region;
- images of 2D concepts such as point, line, arrow, rectangle, etc., which are often used in 3D illustrations as metagraphical objects. These images are considered as instantiations of generic 2D concepts;
- images that are created by typesetting character strings or symbols.

To produce graphics including different image types, we have developed a graphics realization component, comparable to an object-oriented graphics editor (cf. [51]). The operators handled by this component fall into three classes:

(1) operators for creating and manipulating wireframe models of 3D objects; examples include: adding an object to a configuration, spatially separating object parts in order to construct exploded views, and cutting away object faces to make opaque parts visible;
(2) operators which constrain projection parameters and map wireframe models onto images, e.g., it is possible to map models onto schematic line drawings or to produce more realistic looking depictions using rendering techniques;

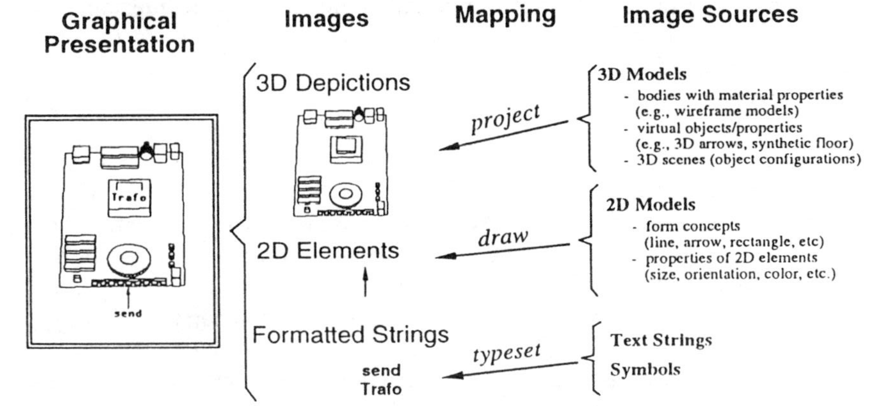

Fig. 5. Graphics as compositions of images from different sources.

(3) operators that are defined on the picture level, e.g., annotating an object image with a text label, or scaling/framing/coloring picture parts.

The annotated modem shown in the left part of Fig. 5 can be created with the realization component through the following sequence of operators: take a wireframe model of the modem circuit board, choose a viewing specification so that the whole object is in the view-volume and the top part of the circuit board is visible, take a schematic perspective projection as mapping function, apply the projection and paste the resulting image into a picture frame, then make an arrow-annotation to relate the formatted string "send" to the image of the modem's LED indicating the send mode, finally annotate the transformer image with the string "Trafo" by writing it onto the image.

In the WIP system, operator sequences, as in the example above, are generated by the graphics design component (cf. [50,51]) starting with presentation tasks forwarded by the presentation planner. A basic idea which underlies our representation of design knowledge, is that we do not directly relate presentation tasks to graphical presentations. Instead we associate presentation tasks with a set of constraints. These constraints place restrictions on image sources (e.g., 3D models), mappings and images in a picture. Thus, they eventually constrain the set of graphical presentations in a way that a presentation task can be achieved. This enables us to cover a variety of plausible designs for one and the same presentation task with a single set of constraints. Among others, this has the advantage that the graphics designer can flexibly carry out several presentation tasks with a single graphics—provided the graphics satisfies all constraints associated with the presentation tasks. Such flexibility is particularly needed, if the graphics generator receives input from the presentation planner in a piecemeal fashion, as is the case in the WIP system. Recognizing whether or not new information can be incorporated into an already designed picture is done by checking whether the picture already meets the new constraints or whether it can be modified in such a way that the new constraints can be met.

While the presentation strategies introduced in Section 6.2.1 serve to decompose communicative goals into elementary presentation tasks, we use *graphical design strategies* in order to relate elementary tasks to constraints on the graphics to be generated. Some of these constraints are directly related to operators which are to be executed by the realization component, others lead to the application of further design strategies. For example, a graphical design strategy to depict a physical object in a picture embodies the following constraints: there must be a wireframe model of the object that is to serve as an image source. If the object is to be shown with further objects, there must be a viewing specification such that the object is visible. The resulting image must be included in a picture, and the image must not be obstructed by any other picture elements.

Using graphical design strategies, graphics design is in principle a goal-driven planning process, i.e., presentation tasks are related to constraints and after several refinement steps a sequence of instructions for the realization component is obtained. However, it does not seem feasible to strictly separate a graphics design and a realization phase as some realization operators have side effects which are difficult (i.e., computationally expensive) to anticipate in advance. For example, minor changes in a 3D configuration may dramatically affect the visibility of objects and the discriminability of object images. A solution to this problem is to interleave graphics design with graphics realization and to allow for feedback. During the design process we have to check whether constraints have already been satisfied and if they are still being met even after further realization operators have been applied. Therefore, the realization component provides not only *achievement* operators which produce effects on models, mappings or pictures, but also provides *evaluation* operators[6] (e.g., in checking if an object as part of an object configuration is visible from a given viewing specification, or in checking if a picture part can be discriminated from other picture components). Evaluation operators are also useful in coping with phenomena that cannot be properly described by our compositional semantics. For example, using reverse video is a means for highlighting an item. However, applying this technique too frequently in a single picture will weaken the intended effect.

[6]Achievement operators and evaluation operators are comparable to *style methods* and *style evaluators* in the IBIS system (cf. [58]).

To enable the graphics designer to flexibly combine design strategies, the strategies should only contain a minimal set of graphical constraints associated with a single presentation task. For example, the task of depicting an object does not prescribe how to encode particular object attributes (such as shape, size or surface structure); therefore, a graphical design strategy should not include any corresponding constraints. In some situations the set of constraints placed on a picture may be augmented by further presentation tasks. In situations where several choices remain, the graphics designer uses heuristics to make the necessary decisions, e.g., to choose among a set of possible view directions (cf. [49]). Heuristics are also needed in finding a priority order if several design strategies apply, or if more than one realization operator can be used to satisfy a constraint. For example, to establish a labeling relation between an image and a text string in a picture the graphics designer's repertoire of annotation techniques currently covers 33 variations of three basic annotation techniques (writing on an object image, along an object image and annotating with an arrow). Which annotation technique applies depends on syntactic criteria (e.g., formatting restrictions) as well as semantic criteria. For example, in order to avoid confusion, the same annotation technique should be used for all instances of the same basic concept. The current WIP prototype relies on about 50 rules in order to select an appropriate annotation technique (cf. [69]). This shows that WIP does not use planning operators or schemata on all levels of the design process, but exploits expert design knowledge for routine subtasks like annotation, grid determination and font selection.

7.2. The text generator

As for the graphics generator the design of the text generator was strongly influenced by the quest for incremental processing. Thus the form and size of basic processing units, data flow, and the interaction between the components of the text generator were determined by this incremental processing scheme.

This section focuses on principles of the inner working of the generator, especially on the interrelations between the levels of generation resulting from dependencies among choices (see Fig. 6).

The first component that is activated during natural language generation in WIP is the *text design* component. As soon as the presentation planner decides, in its mode selection process, that a particular element should be presented as part of a text, the element is handed over as input to this component. The main task of the text design component is the organization of the input elements into clauses. This comprises for example the determination of the order in which the given input elements can be realized in the text, the control of the use of anaphora to obtain a coherent text, and lexical

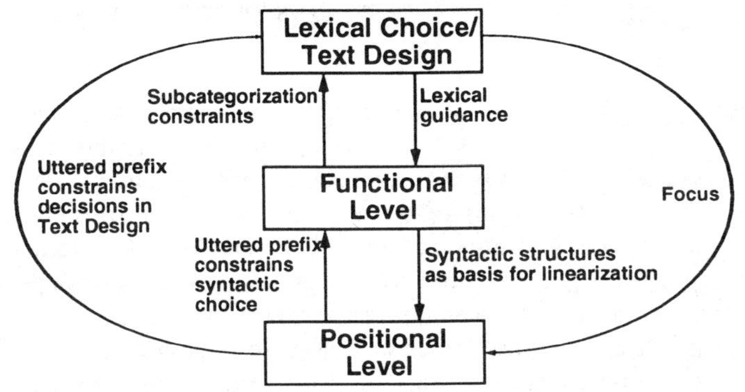

Fig. 6. Design of a system with incremental output.

choice. The resulting preverbal message is input to the *text realization* component in a piecemeal fashion where grammatical encoding, linearization, and inflection take place.

In accordance with the requirement of lexical guidance of the generation process (cf. [33,44]) the process of lexical choice for an input element is made within the text design component before the element is handed over to the text realization component. The text realization component consists of a functional and a positional level (see Fig. 6). Lexemes in the input to the text realization component direct the choice of syntactic structures. To facilitate this selection process, WIP uses a lexicalized grammar where each syntactic rule is associated with at least one lexeme serving as head element in the represented phrase. These anchors of the grammar in the lexicon can be utilized to select the elementary structures for grammatical encoding (cf. [25]). A second dependency between text design and text realization results from the subcategorization constraints of the previously chosen lexemes. They provide a syntactic context for the further lexical choice. In order to be able to report this additional syntactic information to the text design component, the cascaded architecture of the text generator allows for feedback between the two components.

The granularity of the processing units is especially important in the text realization component that is conceived as a distributed parallel model, because the simultaneous activity on existing parts of the syntactic structure supports the incremental processing of these parts (cf. [21,55]). These structures must be small enough to avoid redundancy and to allow the specification of input in a piecemeal fashion. They must be large enough to be operated on relatively independently from other structures. We use a lexicalized TAG (LTAG, cf. [53]) for the syntactic level of description. Its extended domain of locality (cf. [32]) and the flexible expansion of partial structures by substitution and adjunction (cf. [15]) make it a good candidate for incremental syntactic generation (cf. [20,54]).

The separation of knowledge concerning dominance and linear precedence relations (see Fig. 6) is a result of the assumption that the chronological order in which syntactic segments are attached does not correspond to the linear order of the resulting utterance. This separation results in another bidirectional dependency between processing levels: On the one hand, the syntactic structures at the functional level are the data to be linearized at the positional level. On the other hand, in a system with incremental output it is no longer guaranteed that a correct position can be found for each syntactic structure that can be integrated at the functional level (cf. [22]). For example, it is always possible to realize a modifying adjective as an attribute in an NP at the functional level. This results in phrases such as "the big switch". If however, the noun was already uttered, then for example the realization of "big" in a relative clause as in "the switch ... that is big" should be preferred. In this case, knowledge at the positional level orders the selection of structures at the functional level.[7]

Furthermore, dependencies exist between decisions in the text design component and the positional level of the text realization component: the interpretation of semantic and pragmatic criteria by the text design component may influence the selection of linearization rules. Conversely, the prefix, which has already been uttered, may constrain the realization of further input elements, directed by the text design component. An example of this dependency is depicted in the following situation: suppose WIP has already output the fragment "Then the modem sends you". If the text design component decides to reduce the NP "the return code" to "it", the pronominalization has to be rejected by the positional level. There are two options: performing a repair like "... sends it to you" or ignoring the demand for pronominalization as in "... the return code".

8. Interleaving presentation planning, design, and realization

In this section, the planning process and the interplay of the planner and the generation components for text and graphics are discussed in more detail. Let us assume the presentation planner intends to describe a sequence of two actions PUT-1 and TURN-1. Figure 7 shows the DAG that has been produced by the presentation planner. The presentation goal

(DESCRIBE P A (SEQUENCE PUT-1 TURN-1) T)

[7]Note, that this construction is only possible if in the meantime nothing was uttered after the noun. For more details about synchronization and effects of incremental output on incremental natural language generation, see [22].

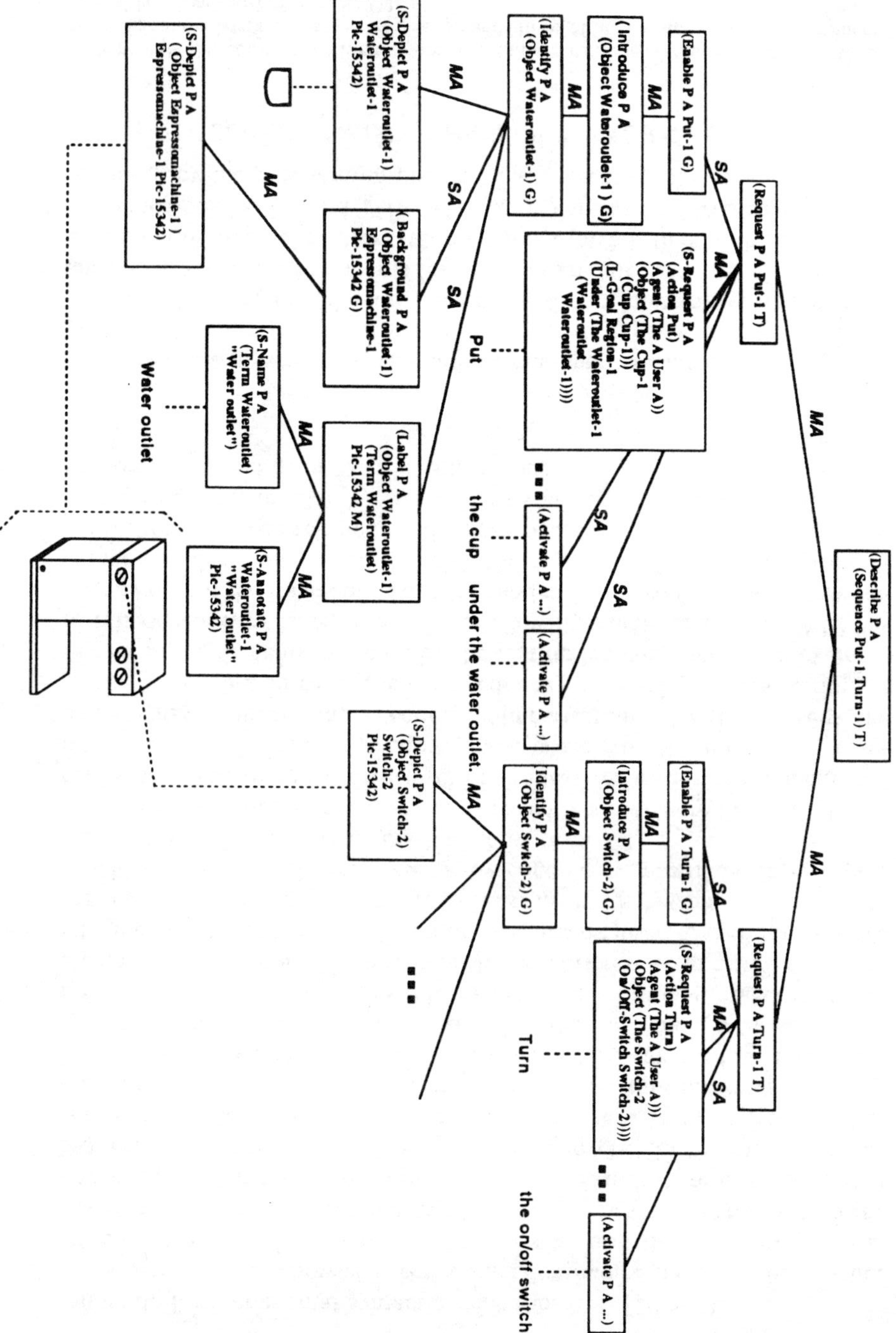

Fig. 7. DAG representation of the planned multimodal document.

has been decomposed into two subgoals: (REQUEST P A PUT-1 T) and (REQUEST P A TURN-1 T). After the refinement of (REQUEST P A PUT-1 T), five acts[8] have been posted as new subgoals: a complex communicative act (ENABLE) which has to be further expanded, an elementary speech act (S-REQUEST) which is passed onto the text designer and four referential acts (ACTIVATE) for filling the semantic case roles associated with the action PUT-1.

As mentioned above, the planner passes a certain piece of information onto the respective generator as soon as it has decided which component should encode it. In the example, (S-REQUEST P A ...) is sent to the text designer although the semantic case roles have not yet been filled at that stage. The text designer attempts to generate input for the TAG generator which starts processing this input, but is not able to produce any output before a content word of the utterance has been determined. While the text generator is still working on the realization of the actual request, the presentation planner already expands the ENABLE act. Since it assumes that the user is not able to localize the water outlet, it decides to introduce it by annotating it in a picture that includes the water outlet and the espresso machine as background. As a first presentation task, the graphics designer receives

(S-DEPICT P A (OBJECT WATEROUTLET-1)
(? PX) (? PICTURE)).

The graphics design component has to map this presentation task onto a sequence of operators to be executed by the graphics realization component.

Note that the graphics designer receives the presentation tasks in a piecemeal fashion. As a consequence, the graphics generator must be able to process new input depending on what has been generated before. Among other things, this includes recognizing whether new information can be incorporated into previously designed pictures or not (cf. Section 7.1). In our example, the graphics designer receives the task of depicting the espresso machine as background while processing the first presentation task. To accomplish the new presentation task, the same graphical design strategy as before may be applied. However, the graphics generator has to check after each step whether previously satisfied constraints are still being fulfilled; e.g., it might happen that objects which were previously visible are obstructed by objects that are added at a later stage. In the example, the perspective has been constrained in such a way that both the entire espresso machine and the water outlet are visible.

While the graphics generator is still concerned with depicting the espresso

[8] In Fig. 7, MA stands for main act, SA for subsidiary act (cf. Section 5.1).

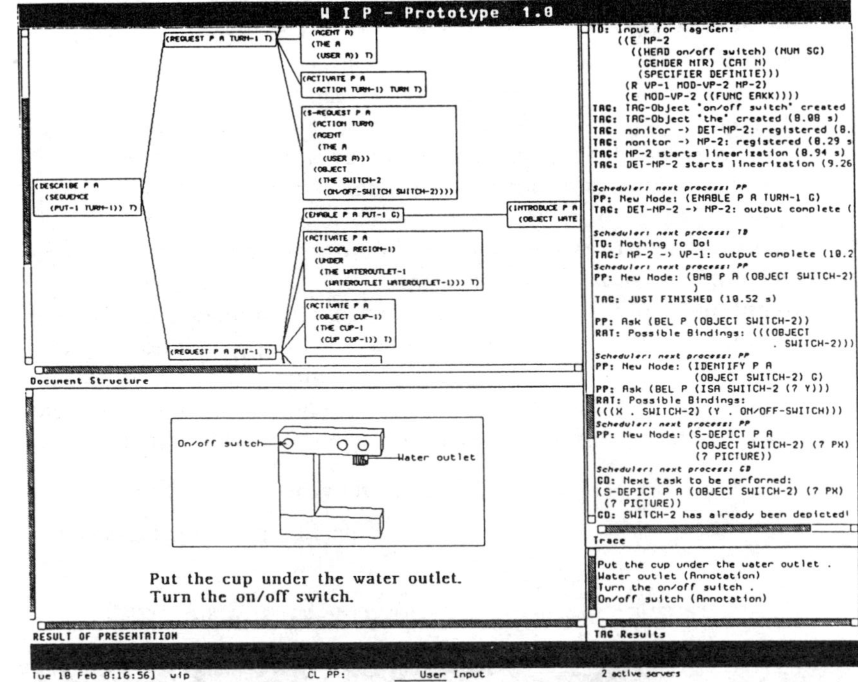

Fig. 8. Generating a multimodal presentation.

machine as background, the TAG generator produces a natural language expression for the label which later has to be pasted as part of an arrow annotation into the picture.

Figure 8 shows a screen copy of a session with the WIP prototype. The snapshot of the system trace was taken immediately after the second request was verbalized and the on/off switch was annotated in the picture. In the upper part of the trace pane, one can see the input specification for a noun phrase that the text designer has sent to the TAG generator. Note that the specification for other parts of the sentence have already been sent and processed earlier.

In the third last line of the trace pane, the graphics designer selects

(S-DEPICT P A (OBJECT SWITCH-2) (? PX) (? PICTURE))

from the task queue. Since it finds out that the switch has already been depicted, no further picture generation is necessary (see the last line in the trace pane). The presentation planner registers this by linking the corresponding parts with each other in the DAG (cf. Fig. 7) that forms a part of the document design plan.

The above example is a kind of visual anaphora. As for a linguistic anaphora, such as (1), the antecedent of the anaphora is part of an object that was previously mentioned in the discourse.

The machine is running. The on/off switch was turned on. (1)

In the case discussed here, a projection of SWITCH-2 has already been displayed as part of the background provided for the picture of the water outlet (see Fig. 7). The multimodal document design plan plays the role of a discourse model in traditional natural language systems. It helps to determine whether or not an anaphoric reference is possible. In the example presented above, the metagraphical arrow generated by WIP's annotation component is the equivalent of a pronoun since it focuses attention on a specific part of the visual antecedent. Mixed anaphoric reference generation is also supported by WIP's architecture. In a sequence like (2), the antecedent of the anaphora "the on/off switch" is a visual object stored in the document design plan and focused by the cross-modal reference in the sentence preceding the anaphora.

Fig. 3 provides a survey. The on/off switch ... (2)

Note that the final result shown in the lower left pane was produced incrementally. The incrementality of the overall generation process that was initiated by expanding the presentation goal

(DESCRIBE P A (SEQUENCE (PUT-1 TURN-1)) T)

(see Fig. 8) is illustrated in the TAG Results pane. The generation component first verbalizes the PUT-1 request and forwards the label "Water outlet" to the graphics designer. The second request is then verbalized and the corresponding label "On/off switch" is produced and inserted in the previously generated picture. In addition to this incrementality across generation components, there is another level of incrementality in the individual generation components.

9. Coordinating text and graphics generation

In a multimodal presentation, cross-modal expressions establish referential relationships of representations in one modality to representations in another modality. The use of cross-modal deictic assertions such as (3) is essential for the efficient coordination of text and graphics in illustrated documents (see Fig. 9).

The on/off switch is located in the upper left part of the picture. (3)

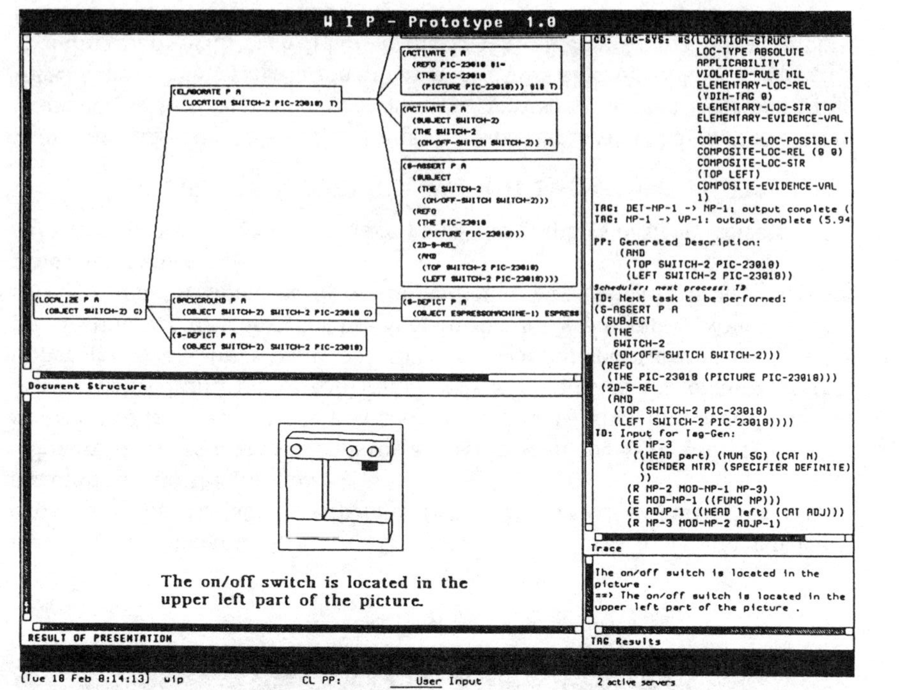

Fig. 9. Incremental generation of a cross-modal reference.

Given the presentation goal

(BMB P A (LOCATION SWITCH-2 (? LOCATION))),

the presentation planner designs the text–picture combination in the bottom left pane of Fig. 9 communicating the relevant information about the spatial position of the on/off switch.

In this example, WIP uses a spatial description to refer to an object shown in a synthetic picture of the espresso machine. Note that the multimodal referential act can only be successful if the addressee is able to identify the intended knob of the real espresso machine. It is clear that the depiction of the switch cannot be used as an on/off switch, but only the physical object identified as the result of a multi-level reference resolution (see Fig. 10). The cross-modal assertion in the text refers to a pictorial element that visualizes an instance of a concept represented by a RAT term as part of WIP's application knowledge. An additional coreferentiality relation exists between the individual constant SWITCH-2 in the ABox of RAT and an object in the wireframe model of the machine providing a description of the geometry of that knob. Finally, the depiction of the knob generated by

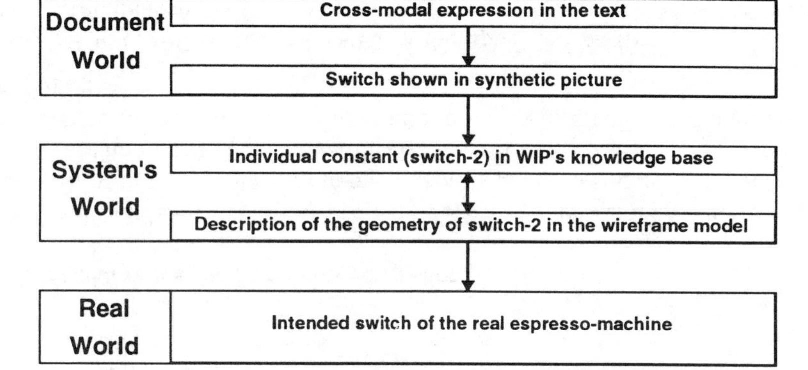

Fig. 10. WIP's multi-level reference process.

WIP's graphics design component in turn refers to the corresponding switch of the real machine.

The generation of cross-modal expressions highlights the tight interaction between various components of WIP and the cross dependencies among decisions of the mode-specific generators. In our example the text design component, that is activated by the presentation planner after a first draft of the picture has been completed by the graphics designer, calls the graphics component once again to ask for a localization of a pictorial element.

The top left pane in Fig. 9, labelled "Document Structure", shows a fragment of the DAG produced by the presentation planner. Note that the LOCALIZE act is decomposed into three acts. The main act specifies the task for the graphics designer to depict SWITCH-2 in a picture. One subsidiary act tries to provide background information for the generated depiction by showing other salient parts of the machine as the visual context of the switch. The other subsidiary act is supposed to generate text that elaborates on the picture. Further refinements using presentation strategies for textual elaboration finally lead to the cross-modal expression discussed above. Although the mode flag is set to TEXT for this elaboration (coded as T in the corresponding node of the presentation plan, see Fig. 9), the evaluation facilities of the graphics generator are used to compute a spatial relation describing the absolute localization of the switch in the picture.

The most important steps in the design process leading to the cross-modal assertion (3) are shown in the top right pane of Fig. 9 that displays a partial trace of the interaction between the major components of the presentation system. After the presentation planner (PP in the trace) has established a new node in the DAG that contains an unbound variable representing a description of the location of the switch in the picture, the graphics designer

(GD in the trace) calls its localization component to determine the value of that variable.

One of the basic ideas behind this component is that absolute localizations like "in the upper left part of the picture" can be derived from relative spatial predicates like LEFT-OF(X,Y) and ON-TOP-OF(X,Y) through the use of virtual reference objects induced by the page layout. This means that objects depicted in a figure can be spatially related to the center, the corners, the borderline and even to the caption of that figure.

In the example shown, the rectangular picture region, in which the image of the espresso machine is displayed by the graphics component, is used as a frame of reference for the spatial description encoding the position of SWITCH-2's depiction (see the bottom left pane of Fig. 9). The relative location of the on/off switch is described by the conjunction of the literals LEFT-OF(SWITCH-2, CENTER(PIC-23018)) and ON-TOP-OF(SWITCH-2, CENTER(PIC-23018)) that use the center of the figure as a reference object. In WIP, the center of a picture is approximated by a virtual rectangle in the middle with one third of the horizontal and vertical extension of the whole figure (for more details see [67]).

These relative localizations are then transformed into absolute ones through deleting the second argument. The presentation planner forwards the result of the localization process to the text design (TD) component for lexical choice (see top left pane of Fig. 9).

The generation of cross-modal expressions can involve various levels of recursion. One subtlety not illustrated by the example above is the use of different frames of reference for spatial relations in a single cross-modal expression. Suppose that in addition to the picture discussed in the previous example, another figure is placed on the same page. Then the generic localization methods of WIP will generate another relative description like RIGHT-OF(PIC-23018, CENTER(PAGE-1)) leading to a recursive spatial reference such as "in the upper left part of the figure on the right".

Since the layout constraints specified in WIP's input together with revisions of the presentation planner force the layout manager to backtrack from time to time during the incremental design of a multimodal presentation, it may turn out that a figure has to be repositioned and thus parts of the cross-modal expression have to be revised. For example, "the figure on the right" may become "the figure on the top".

Another level of recursion in the localization process is introduced by dealing with groups of objects. In this case, a group can serve at the same time as a frame of reference for one of its elements and as a perceptual unit that itself must be localized using other reference objects in the figure (cf. [64]). For example, the generation of a localization for the group of two switches on the right part of the machine in Fig. 9 leads to a cross-modal expression like "The left button on the right part of the picture is the selector switch" (see [67] for further details).

As illustrated by this example such verbal descriptions can get quite long-winded. Therefore WIP's presentation strategies include alternate methods to establish cross-modal referential relations. As mentioned in Section 7.1, the graphics generator supports various labeling techniques for placing text strings in a figure so that they annotate the parts of a composite object in an illustration. The generation of labels as a part of the graphics design is an example where in comparison to the previous discussions concerning the localization component, the dependency between graphics generation and text generation is reversed. In this case the text generator is activated during the graphics design process in order to produce a string that can be used for labeling a picture element. Note that one has to ensure that the same description is used for referring to the object in the text, as it would lead to an incoherent text–picture combination, if a switch that is labelled "on/off switch" in a picture is referred to as "starting switch" in the corresponding text. This means that for the generation of multimodal presentations the document design plan plays the same role as the discourse model for verbal communication, namely allowing the presentation planner to ensure the consistent use of referential expressions across modes.

Suppose that in our example, the text generator is asked to find a lexical realization for the concept EM-SELECTOR-SWITCH and comes up with the description "selector switch for coffee and steam". When trying to annotate the switch with this text string, the graphics generator finds out that none of the available annotation techniques apply. Placing the string close to the corresponding depiction causes ambiguities. The string also cannot be placed onto the projection of the object without occluding other parts of the picture. For the same reason, annotations with arrows fail. Therefore, the text generator is asked to produce a shorter formulation. Unfortunately, it is not able to do so without reducing the contents. Thus, the presentation planner is informed that the required task cannot be accomplished. The presentation planner then tries to reduce the contents by omitting attributes or by selecting more general concepts from the subsumption hierarchy encoded in terms of the terminological logic. Given that EM-SELECTOR-SWITCH is a compound description which inherits information from the concepts SWITCH and EM-SELECTOR, the planner has to decide which component of the contents specification should be reduced. As the concept SWITCH contains less discriminating information than the concept EM-SELECTOR and the concept SWITCH is at least partially inferable from the picture, the planner first tries to reduce the component SWITCH by replacing it by PHYSICAL-OBJECT. Thus, the text generator has to find a sufficiently short definite description containing the components PHYSICAL-OBJECT and EM-SELECTOR. Since this fails, the planner has to propose another

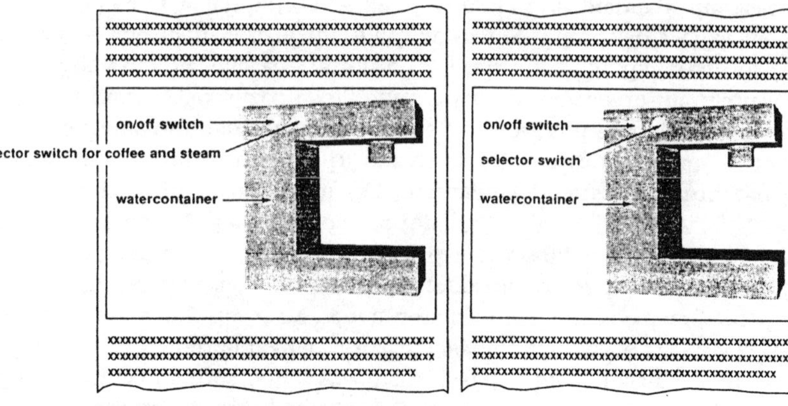

Fig. 11. Annotating a rendered picture.

reduction. It now tries to reduce the component EM-SELECTOR by omitting the coffee/steam mode. The text generator then tries to construct a NP combining the concepts SWITCH and SELECTOR. This time it succeeds and the annotation string can be put into place.

Figure 11 is a hardcopy produced by WIP showing the rendered espresso machine after the required annotations have been carried out.

No serial architecture with a total ordering of the components for text and graphics generation would be adequate in this case. On the one hand, the text strings have to be produced by the TAG generator before they are put into place by the graphics generator. On the other hand, graphical knowledge is necessary to determine how long a text string may be. Since determining the maximal admissible length of a text string is no local decision, but depends, among others, on the position of other picture elements, the processes for text and graphics generation cannot be sequentialized.

10. Future research

It is obvious that the current WIP system has serious shortcomings with respect to the interactive aspects of multimodal presentations. In our future research, much more attention will be placed on the following problems:

Interactive multimodal presentations

WIP's most significant current limitation is that it does not support user interaction during the multimodal presentation. An interactive user may want to interrupt the presentation before it is completed for one of the following reasons:

- he is dissatisfied with the current style of presentation,
- he has a question about the presentation generated so far.

Since WIP's output is generated incrementally, much of the machinery is already in place to accommodate such interruptions. However, the presentation planner has to be extended so that it allows for the necessary reactive planning. Clearly, the next step is to allow the user to change the generation parameters during the presentation, e.g., by demanding the system to change the level of detail or the speed of the current presentation. Probably the greatest opportunity lies in the generalization of methods, which generate cooperative responses to follow-up questions in natural language dialog systems, to the broader domain of multimodal communication.

Planning multimodal presentation acts

Another important deficiency of the current WIP system is that it merely generates coordinated language and graphics according to a particular presentation goal, rather than planning when and how to present this material to a particular user. We expect more efficient presentations from an augmented version of WIP, in which an animated character called PPP (Personalized Plan-based Presenter) will play the role of a presenter, showing, commenting and explaining the generated material. This means that the system should be able to plan presentations as well as presentation acts and their temporal coordination. For example, PPP could point to a particular section of an illustrated explanation and, at the same time, produce an utterance highlighting the importance of a particular instruction step.

Monitoring the effectiveness of a presentation

A further limitation of the current version of WIP is that it has no means to check whether the user really has understood the presentation and has followed the instructions correctly. In a follow-up project to WIP, we plan to provide the presentation system with an indirect feedback on the user's physical behavior after he has received the instructions, by evaluating the state changes caused by his actions. A simple method to obtain such a feedback, without relying on a sophisticated vision system, is to use a data bus to physically connect the technical device, which is to be serviced by the user, with the presentation system. The presentation system could, based on such a connection, keep track of the relevant behavior of the user, monitor the effectiveness of the presentation and continuously adapt its presentations to the current situation. Our main interest here is the close integration of presentation planning and plan monitoring, in order to improve the effectiveness of the generated multimodal presentations.

11. Conclusions

The central claim of this paper is that the generation of a multimodal presentation can be considered as an incremental planning process that aims to achieve a given communicative goal.

We have shown how techniques for planning text and discourse can be generalized to allow the structure and content of multimodal communications to be planned as well. When explaining how a complex process functions, WIP generates and realizes plans for communicating domain plans provided by the back-end system. While the root of the hierarchical plan structure for a particular presentation corresponds to a complex communicative act such as describing a process, the leaves are elementary acts that verbalize and visualize the physical acts specified in a given domain plan.

A key observation is that it is possible to use a slightly extended version of RST to describe important semantic and pragmatic coherence relations not only between text fragments, but also picture elements, pictures, and text or sequences of text–picture combinations. We have explored the question of how the presentation planner can decide what should go into text, what should go into graphics, and how to link verbal and non-verbal fragments by cross-modal references. We have formalized the knowledge needed for the planning of coordinated multimedia presentations, thereby introducing new concepts like presentation strategies, design strategies, and meta-rules for mode selection.

Since one of the design principles behind WIP is that the theoretical basis of all components should be sound enough to allow scale-up, we have combined and extended only formalisms that have reached a certain level of maturity, in particular terminological logics, RST-based planning, constraint processing techniques, and tree adjoining grammars with feature unification.

One of the surprises from our research is that it is actually possible to extend and adapt many of the fundamental concepts developed to date in AI and computational linguistics for the generation of natural language in such a way that they become useful for the generation of graphics and text–picture combinations as well. In particular, we have shown that well-known concepts from the area of natural language processing like speech acts, anaphora, and rhetorical relations take on an extended meaning in the context of multimodal communication.

The experience we gained from the design and implementation of the WIP prototype provides a good starting point for a deeper understanding of the interdependencies of language and graphics in coordinated multimodal communication.

Acknowledgements

The WIP project is supported by the German Ministry of Research and Technology under grant ITW8901 8. The development of WIP has been a group effort and has benefited from the contributions of our collaborators Winfried Graf, Karin Harbusch, Jochen Heinsohn, Anne Kilger, and Bernhard Nebel as well as our students Jochen Bedersdorfer, Andreas Butz, Bernd Herrmann, Antonio Krüger, Daniel Kudenko, Peter Poller, Thomas Schiffmann, Georg Schneider, Frank Schneiderlöchner, Christoph Schommer, Dudung Soetopo, Martin Weiler, and Detlev Zimmermann. We would like to thank the anonymous referees for helpful comments on an earlier draft of this paper.

References

[1] E. André, G. Bosch, G. Herzog and T. Rist, Characterizing trajectories of moving objects using natural language path descriptions, in: *Proceedings Seventh European Conference on Artificial Intelligence, Vol. 2*, Brighton, England (1986) 1–8.

[2] E. André, W. Finkler, W. Graf, T. Rist, A. Schauder and W. Wahlster, WIP: the automatic synthesis of multimodal presentations, in: M. Maybury, ed., *Intelligent Multimedia Interfaces* (AAAI Press, Cambridge, MA, 1993).

[3] E. André and T. Rist, Synthesizing illustrated documents: a plan-based approach, in: *Proceedings InfoJapan*, Tokyo, Japan (1990) 163–170.

[4] E. André and T. Rist, Towards a plan-based synthesis of illustrated documents, in: *Proceedings Ninth European Conference on Artificial Intelligence*, Stockholm, Sweden (1990) 25–30.

[5] E. André and T. Rist, The design of illustrated documents as a planning task, in: M. Maybury, ed., *Intelligent Multimedia Interfaces* (AAAI Press, Cambridge, MA, 1993).

[6] Y. Arens, S.K. Feiner, J. Hollan and B. Neches, A new generation of intelligent interfaces, Workshop IJCAI-89, Detroit, MI (1989).

[7] Y. Arens, E.H. Hovy and M. Vossers, The knowledge underlying multimedia presentations, in: M. Maybury, ed., *Intelligent Multimedia Interfaces* (AAAI Press, Cambridge, MA, 1993).

[8] F. Baader, H.-J. Bürckert, J. Heinsohn, B. Hollunder, J. Müller, B. Nebel, W. Nutt and H.-J. Profitlich, Terminological knowledge representation: a proposal for a terminological logic, Tech. Memo TM-90-04 DFKI Saarbrücken, Germany (1990).

[9] F. Baader and B. Hollunder, KRIS: Knowledge representation and inference system, *SIGART Bull.* **2** (3) (1991) 8–14.

[10] N. Badler, B. Webber, J. Kalita and J. Esakov, Animation from instructions, in: N. Badler, B. Barsky and D. Zeltzer, eds., *Making Them Move: Mechanics, Control and Animation of Articulated Figures* (Morgan Kaufmann, San Mateo, CA, 1991) 51–93.

[11] S. Bandyopadhyay, Towards an understanding of coherence in multimodal discourse, Tech. Memo TM-90-01, DFKI, Saarbrücken, Germany (1990).

[12] D. Chapman, Planning for conjunctive goals, *Artif. Intell.* **32** (3) (1987) 333–377.

[13] P.R. Cohen, J.W. Sullivan, M. Dalyrymple, R.A. Gargan, D.B. Moran, J.O. Schlossberg, F.C.N. Perreira and S.W. Tyler, Synergistic use of direct manipulation and natural language, in: *Proceedings CHI-89*, Austin, TX (1989) 227–233.

[14] R. Dale, Visible language: multimodal constraints in information presentation, in: R. Dale, E.H. Hovy, D. Rösner and O. Stock, eds., *Aspects of Automated Natural Language Generation*, Lecture Notes in Artificial Intelligence **587** (Springer, New York, 1992) 281–283; also in: *Proceedings Sixth International Workshop on Natural Language Generation*, Trento, Italy (1992).

[15] K. De Smedt and G. Kempen, Incremental sentence production, self-correction and coordination, in: G. Kempen, ed., *Natural Language Generation: New Results in Artificial Intelligence, Psychology and Linguistics*, NATO ASI Series E **135** (Martinus Nijhoff, Dordrecht, Netherlands, 1987) 365–376 (Chapter 23).

[16] P.T. Devanbu and D.J. Litman, Plan-based terminological reasoning, in: J.F. Allen, R.E. Fikes and E. Sandewall, eds., *Proceedings Second International Conference on Principles of Knowledge Representation and Reasoning*, Cambridge, MA (1991) 128–138.

[17] S.K. Feiner, D.J. Litman, K.R. McKeown and R.J. Passonneau, Towards coordinated temporal multimedia presentations, in: M. Maybury, ed., *Intelligent Multimedia Interfaces* (AAAI Press, Cambridge, MA, 1993).

[18] S.K. Feiner and K.R. McKeown, Coordinating text and graphics in explanation generation, in: *Proceedings AAAI-90*, Boston, MA (1990) 442–449.

[19] S.K. Feiner and K.R. McKeown, Automating the generation of coordinated multimedia explanations, *IEEE Computer* **24** (10) (1991) 33–41.

[20] W. Finkler, Incremental natural language generation with TAGs in the WIP-project, in: W. Wahlster and K. Harbusch, eds., *First International Workshop on Tree Adjoining Grammars*, Dagstuhl, Germany (1990) 64–70.

[21] W. Finkler and G. Neumann, POPEL-HOW—a distributed parallel model for incremental natural language production with feedback, in: *Proceedings IJCAI-89*, Detroit, MI (1989) 1518–1523.

[22] W. Finkler and A. Schauder, Effects of incremental output on incremental natural language generation, in: B. Neumann, ed., *Proceedings Tenth European Conference on Artificial Intelligence*, Vienna, Austria (1992) 505–507.

[23] W. Graf, Constrained-based graphical layout of multimodal presentations, in: *Proceedings Advanced Visual Interfaces (AVI) Workshop*, Rome, Italy (1992).

[24] J.E. Grimes, *The Thread of Discourse* (Mouton/de Gruyter, The Hague, Netherlands, 1975).

[25] K. Harbusch, W. Finkler and A. Schauder, Incremental syntax generation with tree adjoining grammars, in: W. Brauer and D. Hernández, eds., *Proceedings Fourth International GI Congress on Knowledge-Based Systems*, Munich, Germany (1991) 363–374.

[26] J. Heinsohn, D. Kudenko, B. Nebel and H.-J. Profitlich, RAT—representation of actions using terminological logics, Research Report, DFKI, Saarbrücken, Germany (1992).

[27] G. Herzog, C.-K. Sung, E. André, W. Enkelmann, H.-H. Nagel, T. Rist, W. Wahlster and G. Zimmermann, Incremental natural language description of dynamic imagery, in: W. Brauer and C. Freksa, eds., *Proceedings Third International GI Congress*, Munich, Germany (1989) 153–162.

[28] J.R. Hobbs, Why is a discourse coherent?, Tech. Report 176, SRI, Menlo Park, CA (1978).

[29] E.H. Hovy, *Generating Natural Language under Pragmatic Constraints* (Lawrence Erlbaum, Hillsdale, NJ, 1988).

[30] E.H. Hovy and Y. Arens, Automatic generation of formatted text, in: *Proceedings AAAI-91*, Anaheim, CA (1991) 92–94.

[31] B. Hunter, A. Crismore and P.D. Pearson, Visual displays in basal readers and social studies textbooks, in: D.M. Willows and H.A. Houghton, eds., *The Psychology of Illustration* **2**, *Basic Research* (Springer, New York, 1987) 116–135.

[32] A.K. Joshi, How much context-sensitivity is necessary for characterization structural descriptions—tree adjoining grammar, in: D. Dowty, L. Karttunen and A. Zwicky, eds., *Natural Language Processing—Theoretical, Computational and Psychological Perspective* (Cambridge University Press, New York, 1985).

[33] G. Kempen and E. Hoenkamp, An incremental procedural grammar for sentence formulation, *Cogn. Sci.* **2** (11) (1987) 201–258.

[34] S. Kerpedjiev, Automatic generation of multimodal weather reports from datasets, in: *Proceedings Third Conference on Applied Natural Language Processing (ANLP-92)*, Trento, Italy (1992) 48–55.

[35] S. Kjorup, Pictorial speech acts, *Erkenntnis* **12** (1978) 55–71.

[36] A. Kobsa, J. Allgayer, C. Reddig, N. Reithinger, D. Schmauks, K. Harbusch and W. Wahlster, Combining deictic gestures and natural language for referent identification, in: *Proceedings Eleventh COLING*, Bonn, Germany (1986) 356–361.

[37] W.J.M. Levelt, *Speaking: From Intention to Articulation* (MIT Press, Cambridge, MA, 1989).

[38] J.R. Levin, G.J. Anglin and R.N. Carney, On empirically validating functions of pictures in prose, in: D.M. Willows and H.A. Houghton, eds., *The Psychology of Illustration* **1** (Springer, New York, 1987) 51–85.

[39] W.C. Mann and S.A. Thompson, Rhetorical structure theory: description and construction of text structures, in: G. Kempen, ed., *Natural Language Generation: New Results in Artificial Intelligence, Psychology and Linguistics*, NATO ASI Series E **135** (Martinus Nijhoff, Dordrecht, Netherlands, 1987) 85–95.

[40] M. Maybury, ed., *Intelligent Multimedia Interfaces* (AAAI Press, Cambridge, MA, 1993); Workshop Notes from AAAI-91, Anaheim, CA (1991).

[41] K.R. McKeown and S.K. Feiner, Interactive multimedia explanation for equipment maintenance and repair, in: *Proceedings DARPA Speech and Language Workshop* (1990) 42–47.

[42] J.D. Moore and C.L. Paris, Planning text for advisory dialogues, in: *Proceedings 27th Annual Meeting of the Association for Computational Linguistics*, Vancouver, BC (1989).

[43] J.G. Neal and S.C. Shapiro, Intelligent multi-media interface technology, in: J.W. Sullivan and S.W. Tyler, eds., *Intelligent User Interfaces* (Addison-Wesley, Reading, MA, 1991) 11–43.

[44] G. Neumann and W. Finkler, A head-driven approach to incremental and parallel generation of syntactic structures, in: *Proceedings Thirteenth COLING*, Helsinki, Finland (1990) 288–293.

[45] C.L. Paris, Generation and explanation: building an explanation facility for the explainable expert systems framework, in: C.L. Paris, W.R. Swartout and W.C. Mann, eds., *Natural Language Generation in Artificial Intelligence and Computational Linguistics* (Kluwer, Boston, MA, 1991) 49–82.

[46] P.F. Patel-Schneider, B. Owsnicki-Klewe, A. Kobsa, N. Guarino, R. MacGregor, W.S. Mark, D. McGuinness, B. Nebel, A. Schmiedel and J. Yen, Term subsumption languages in knowledge representation, *AI Mag.* **11** (2) (1990) 16–23.

[47] E. Reiter, C. Mellish and J. Levine, Automatic generation of on-line documentation in the IDAS project, in: *Proceedings Third Conference on Applied Natural Language Processing (ANLP-92)*, Trento, Italy (1992) 64–71.

[48] N. Reithinger, A parallel and incremental natural language generation system, in: C.L. Paris, W.R. Swartout and W.C. Mann, eds., *Natural Language Generation in Artificial Intelligence and Computational Linguistics* (Kluwer, Boston, MA, 1991) 179–200.

[49] T. Rist and E. André, Wissensbasierte Perspektivenwahl für die automatische Erzeugung von 3D-Objektdarstellungen, in: K. Kansy and P. Wißkirchen, eds., *Graphik und KI*, Informatik Fachberichte **239** (Springer, Berlin, 1991) 48–57.

[50] T. Rist and E. André, From presentation tasks to pictures: towards an approach to automatic graphics design, in: B. Neumann, ed., *Proceedings Tenth European Conference on Artificial Intelligence*, Vienna, Austria (1992) 764–768.

[51] T. Rist and E. André, Incorporating graphics design and realization into the multimodal presentation system WIP, in: *Proceedings Advanced Visual Interfaces (AVI) Workshop*, Rome, Italy (1992).

[52] S. Roth, J. Mattis and X. Mesnard, Graphics and natural language as components of automatic explanation, in: J.W. Sullivan and S.W. Tyler, eds., *Intelligent User Interfaces* (Addison-Wesley, Reading, MA, 1991) 207–239.

[53] Y. Schabes, A. Abeillé and A.K. Joshi, Parsing strategies with lexicalized grammars: application to tree adjoining grammar, in: *Proceedings Twelfth COLING*, Budapest, Hungary (1988).

[54] A. Schauder, Inkrementelle syntaktische Generierung natürlicher Sprache mit Tree Adjoining Grammars, Master's Thesis, Fachbereich Informatik, Universität des Saarlandes, Saarbrücken, Germany (1990).

[55] A. Schauder, Incremental syntactic generation of natural language with tree adjoining grammars, Document D-92-21, DFKI, Saarbrücken, Germany (1992).

[56] J. Schirra, A contribution to reference semantics of spatial prepositions: the visualization problem and its solution in VITRA, in: C. Zelinsky-Wibbelt, ed., *The Semantics of Prepositions—From Mental Processing to Natural Language Processing* (Mouton/de Gruyter, Berlin, 1992).

[57] J.R. Searle, *Speech Acts: An Essay in the Philosophy of Language* (Cambridge University Press, Cambridge, England, 1969).

[58] D.D. Seligmann and S.K. Feiner, Automated generation of intent-based 3D illustrations, *Comput. Graph.* **25** (4) (1991) 123–132.

[59] O. Stock, Natural language and exploration of an information space: the AlFresco interactive system, in: *Proceedings IJCAI-91*, Sydney, Australia (1991) 972–978.

[60] J.W. Sullivan and S.W. Tyler, eds., *Intelligent User Interfaces* (Addison-Wesley, Reading, MA, 1991).

[61] T.A. van Dijk, *Textwissenschaft* (DTV, Munich, Germany, 1980).

[62] W. Wahlster, User and discourse models for multimodal communication, in: J.W. Sullivan and S.W. Tyler, eds., *Intelligent User Interfaces* (Addison-Wesley, Reading, MA, 1991) 45–67.

[63] W. Wahlster, E. André, S. Bandyopadhyay, W. Graf and T. Rist, WIP: the coordinated generation of multimodal presentations from a common representation, in: A. Ortony, J. Slack and O. Stock, eds., *Communication from an Artificial Intelligence Perspective: Theoretical and Applied Issues* (Springer, Heidelberg, 1992) 121–144.

[64] W. Wahlster, A. Jameson and W. Hoeppner, Glancing, referring and explaining in the dialogue system HAM-RPM, *Amer. J. Comput. Ling.*, Microfiche 77 (1978) 53–67.

[65] W. Wahlster, H. Marburger, A. Jameson and S. Busemann, Over-answering yes–no questions: extended responses in a NL interface to a vision system, in: *Proceedings IJCAI-83*, Karlsruhe, Germany (1983) 643–646.

[66] N. Ward, A flexible, parallel model of natural language generation, Ph.D. Thesis, Report No. UCB/CSD 91/629, Computer Science Division (EECS), University of California, Berkeley, CA, (1991),

[67] P. Wazinski, Generating spatial descriptions for cross-modal references, in: *Third Conference on Applied Natural Language Processing (ANLP-92)*, Trento, Italy (1992) 56–63.

[68] R. Weida and D.J. Litman, Terminological reasoning with constraint networks and an application to plan recognition, in: B. Nebel, W. Swartout and C. Rich, eds., *Principles of Knowledge Representation and Reasoning: Proceedings Third International Conference* (Morgan Kaufmann, San Mateo, CA, 1992) 282–293.

[69] D. Zimmermann, Anna: Ein wissensbasiertes System zur automatischen Annotation von Graphiken, Document, DFKI, Saarbrücken, Germany (1993).

Plan-Based Integration of Natural Language and Graphics Generation

Wolfgang Wahlster

In a follow-up project called "Personalized Plan-Based Presenter" (PPP), we continued the work done in WIP along the lines discussed in Section 10 of this paper, entitled "Future Work." PPP extends WIP by allowing user interaction during the multimedia presentation. The user can change presentation parameters, ask follow-up questions, and control the graphical output by menu-based interaction designed by PPP. Thus, the user can direct the system as to how to continue the presentation or can ask for more detail about objects described or shown in the presentation. WIP's planning approach could be extended to conditional presentation plans, depending on the dialog behavior of the user. PPP plans and schedules interaction steps during the ongoing multimedia presentation. For PPP, the presentation strategies of WIP have been augmented by qualitative and metric temporal constraints so that an automatic synchronization of all presentation acts became possible. Since the time consumed by user interactions cannot be predicted reliably, PPP is able to revise and adapt its preliminary presentation schedule according to the user's interactive behavior.

With the user modeling component PEDRO, the decodability of PPP's planned presentations can be anticipated. If it becomes obvious from the predictions that a particular presentation may not be understood correctly by the user, the PPP system can try to find an alternative way to present the intended information. PEDRO's predictions of the user's interpretation of multimedia presentations are based on Bayesian networks (van Mulken 1996).

The CATHI system (Butz 1997) is an incremental animation component that enables PPP to present information not only by coordinated text and graphics but also by 3-D animation clips. Starting from a communicative subgoal such as enabling the user to localize a particular domain object, CATHI computes a complete animation script, including camera motions, cuts, lighting setup, and various visual effects.

In contrast to WIP, the PPP system not only synthesizes multimedia documents but also plans how this material is to be presented in a personalized way to a specific user. PPP personalizes a presentation in two respects: On the one hand, PPP makes a presentation personal by tailoring its content, verbalization, visualization, and layout to a specific user. On the other hand, it personifies the presentation system and the user model as a virtual interface agent called Persona (Rist et al. 1997) that appears as an animated character and highlights, comments, and explains the generated multimodal presentations. The behavior of the PPP Persona is automatically planned and coordinated with the display acts for the generated media objects.

The WIP results have been successfully exploited in various industrial application projects at DFKI, such as YPPS and FLUIDS. In November 1995, the European Council of Applied Sciences and Engineering announced that WIP had won one of the Information Technology European Awards (ITEA'95) on the basis of its technical excellence and innovative content.

REFERENCES

Butz, A. 1997. Animation with CATHI. In *Proceedings of AAAI/IAAI '97*, Providence, RI, 957–962. Menlo Park, CA: AAAI Press.

Rist, T.; André, E.; and Müller, J. 1997. Adding Animated Presentation Agents to the Interface. In *Proceedings of the 1997 International Conference on Intelligent User Interfaces*, Orlando, FL, 79–86.

van Mulken, S. 1996. Reasoning about the User's Decoding of Presentations in a Multimedia Presentation System. In Carberry, S., and Zuckerman, I. (eds.), *Proceedings of the Fifth International Conference on User Modeling*, Kailua Kona, Hawaii, 67–74.

CHAPTER 11

PRESENTATION DESIGN USING AN INTEGRATED KNOWLEDGE BASE

YIGAL ARENS, LAWRENCE MILLER,
and **NORMAN SONDHEIMER**
USC/Information Sciences Institute

ABSTRACT

In spite of the development of user interface tool kits, construction and enhancement of user interfaces for most computer applications remains time consuming and difficult. This is particularly true when the user interface systems must dynamically create displays. This chapter shows how artificial intelligence knowledge base and rule technology can be used to solve this problem.

A prototype model-driven user interface management system has been created using a hybrid knowledge representation system, KL-TWO, combining a frame-based representation system, NIKL, with a propositional logic theorem prover, PENNI. NIKL is used to model the entities of the application domain and the facilities of the user interface. Rules are written connecting the two models. These rules range from application specific to general rules of presentation. The situation to be displayed is asserted into the PENNI database. A *presentation designer* interprets this data using the domain model, chooses the appropriate rules to use in creating the display, and creates a description of the desired display in terms of the interface model. A system, *Integrated Interfaces,* using this design for a multimodal map graphics, natural-language, menu, and form interface has been created and applied to a database-reporting application.

This research was supported by the Defense Advanced Research Projects Agency under Contract No. N0014-87-K-0130. Views and conclusions contained herein are the authors' and should not be interpreted as representing the official opinion or policy of DARPA, the U.S. Government, or any person or agency connected with them.

11.1 INTRODUCTION

ISI is involved in user interface research aimed at bringing together multiple input and output modes in a way that handles mixed-mode input (commands, menus, forms, natural language), interacts with a diverse collection of underlying software utilities in a uniform way, and presents the results through a combination of output modes including natural-language text, maps, and other graphics, tables, and forms.

Our system, **Integrated Interfaces,** supports dynamic presentations, where displays are driven by the information that is available at the time they are produced. Determination of the best way to present information is made at run time when the actual data is available as opposed to being precompiled by the interface designer.

Much of Integrated Interfaces' ability to interact uniformly with the user and the underlying services and to build its presentations derives from the availability of a central knowledge base. This knowledge base integrates models of the application domain (Navy ships in the Pacific region, in the current demonstration version), the structure of visual displays and their graphical features, the underlying services (databases and expert systems), and interface functions. The emphasis in this paper is on a presentation designer that uses the knowledge base to produce multimodal output.

There has been a flurry of recent work in user interface management systems (we list several recent examples in the references). Existing work is characterized by an attempt to relieve the software designer of the burden of handcrafting an interface for each application. The work has generally focused on intelligently handling input. In our paper we deal with the other end of the pipeline—presentations.

The overall runtime architecture of the Integrated Interfaces system is given in Figure 11.1. Input is provided via the mouse and keyboard through forms and menus (produced by QFORMS). Output is provided via a combination of natural-language generation (produced by PENMAN), maps and graphics (produced by the Geographic Display Agent), and forms. Drivers have been written for each of these media, which translate from the language of the Integrated Interfaces rules (KL-TWO) to the input language they respectively require. QFORMS, PENMAN, and the GDA were all developed at ISI.

FIGURE 11.1
ARCHITECTURE OF INTEGRATED INTERFACES SYSTEM

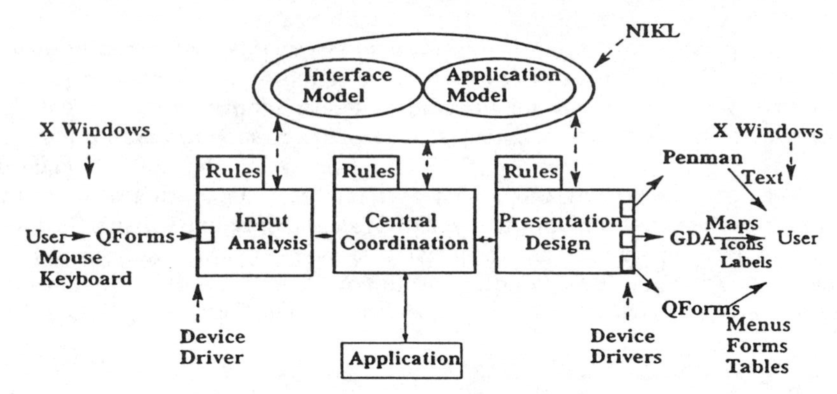

Presentations are put together by a **presentation designer.** The presentation designer decides what output mode or combinations of output modes to use for each piece of information. This involves recognition of the topic of the information, classification of the topic, a check of the user's preferences for presentation, and a coordinated delegation activity to assign tasks to the various output modes. This is done by rules that map between concepts and display modes.

In moving from an interface with a single-output device to an integrated multiple-output device interface output processing changes substantially. Even in single-mode systems, we find that some preparation is necessary beyond the mere determination of the contents of presentations. For example, an information retrieval system may use tables exclusively for the display of retrieved data. Such a system may still decide to split information between tables in a report to control the length of the tables before the final output is generated. In an integrated presentation system, such design activity grows considerably. The system must be able to decide what output mode to use for each piece of information.

The research issues that must be addressed in this context include determining what constitutes a good presentation of information, how to recognize information presentation situations, how to build knowledge that can be shared across several modalities, and how to choose the mode and form of output.

11.2 THE PROCESS OF PRESENTATION DESIGN

We call our method of developing and operating a user interface, **model-driven programming.** A model is a description of objects of the application and the interface and their classes, relationships among them, behaviors they can engage in, and the effects of such behaviors. Actions are associated with these classes. When new data (e. g., the existence of a new ship) is introduced into the system, it is classified, any implications that can be drawn from it are propagated, and actions associated with it are triggered—usually resulting in a potential change or addition to the display.

Presentation design is achieved by the application of a system of antecedent-consequent rules, the actions associated with certain objects. The rules are used to map types of information to appropriate types of presentations. Specifically, presentation design involves *realizing* the categories that a given piece of information fits within, that is, finding the classes to which the information belongs and thus the rules whose antecedents describe the information; *selecting* the most germane category for the information, that is, finding the most specific rules; and *redescribing* the information in appropriate textual and visual forms, that is, using the consequents of the rules to structure the presentation.

We cannot at this point claim that we have a complete theory of what constitutes a good presentation, since such a theory would have to explain aesthetic considerations involved in the preparation of presentations. While we cannot handle such considerations in general, we have been able to provide heuristics useful in certain situations. The Integrated Interfaces system contains rules that structure forms so that they contain what we consider appropriate amounts of information. Users whose aesthetic judgements differ from ours can modify these explicit rules to achieve different behavior. In this sense our system can be considered a presentation *shell.*

11.2.1. Example

The U.S. Navy's Pacific Fleet prepares a daily report on the situation and plans of the fleet. This report conveys current ship locations, courses, current activities, and the activities planned for ships in the near future. The person putting this situation report together has available for presentation a graphics system for ocean surface maps, a business graphics system for time tables, and methods for adding text to maps and tables.

Such a report could be presented in many ways: a map with lines showing each ship's course with a label at each point where the ship starts a new activity; or a map with points showing each ship's initial location and a timetable for each ship; or a map with points showing each ship's initial location and a label in English explaining its sailing plans. The Pacific Fleet uses the third form.

The Navy's report-generating activities can be described as following a process and rules similar to those encoded in our system. Information concerning ships is realized as belonging to certain known categories (e.g., the ship's planned activities). Rules for translating such information into a component of a report (e.g., an indication on a map or a textual description) are then examined, and a rule appropriate for the desired mode of presentation is selected. The information about the ships is then redescribed as part of the presentation being prepared.

A typical presentation generated by the Integrated Interfaces system is shown in Figure 11.2.

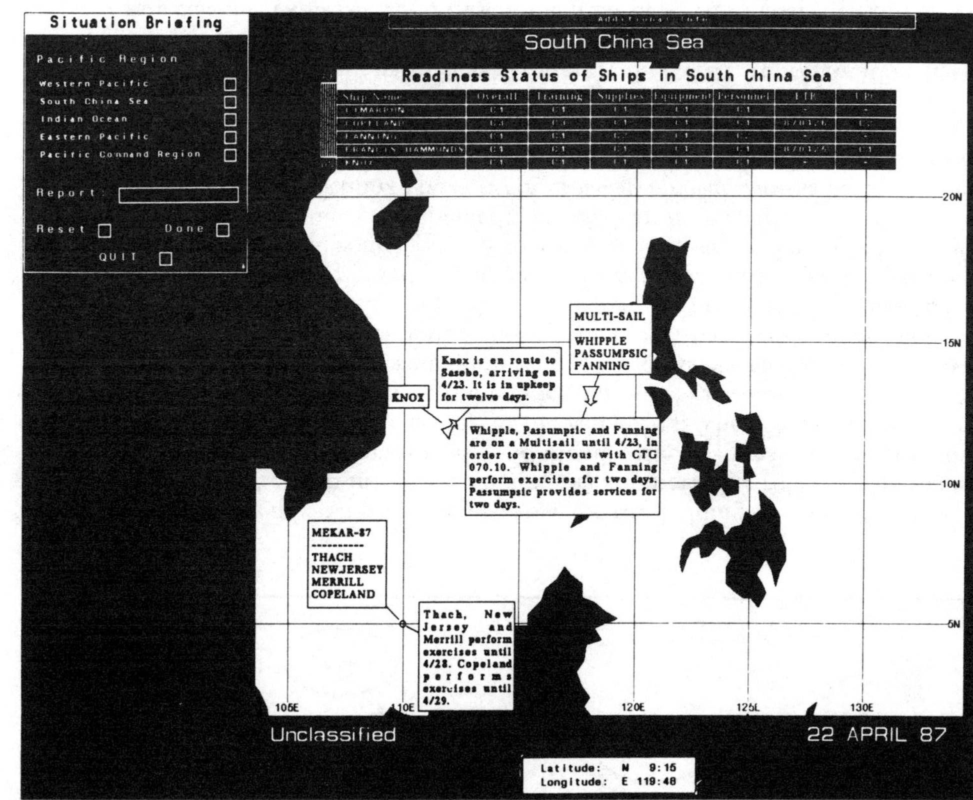

FIGURE 11.2
SOUTH CHINA SEA SITUATION DISPLAY

11.2.2. Design

Models

Our models characterize or define the categories of *entities* our user interface can deal with. One of the models identifies the categories of objects and actions in a common-sense view of the domain of our system. We indicate subclass relations present between categories, as well as relationships between objects and actions. For the Navy application we described above, we include the various categories of ships and sailing activities. We also include specific knowledge, such as that *tankers* are a type of *ship,* and that a *repair* activity involves a *disabled-ship*.

Another model describes the categories of objects and actions of the interface world. The objects here include windows, tables, maps, text strings, and icons. The actions here include creation, deletion, movement, and structure of displays.

A final model (not crucial for this discussion) describes the functions and data structures of the available application services. Included here are descriptions of underlying application software, and any database schemas.

When converting the interface to a new application, the existing interface model can be shared and need not be rewritten. Although some sharing may be possible with the application model, considerable work on a new application model will most probably be necessary. The interface designer will be aided, however, by the higher-level structures of the model containing abstract concepts such as "action," "event," and the like, which already exist and can be used to guide the design of a model for a new application.

Rules

The presentation rules are simple: They map objects from the application domain model into objects in the interface model. Hence, the entity that describes a daily status report may be mapped into a map. A position report may be mapped onto a point. A ship's planned future activities may be mapped onto a text string. These rules are arranged according to the class subsumption hierarchy of the models, so the rules applicable to all ships are further up the hierarchy than those applying only to tankers.

A system that constructs a visual display based entirely on an analysis of the details of the data to be presented [Mackinlay86] holds considerable appeal. However, in a domain as complex as ours, it is probably impossible to design such a presentation system. We thus allow both low-level rules that map details of the domain to details of the presentations, such as those that map the various types of ships to their icons, and high-level ones of wider scope that, given a particular type of presentation request, provide a script to be followed in fulfilling the request.

Rule Application

Presentation design can now be described as the task of recognizing the domain categories within which a request for information presentation falls, selection of the appropriate rules that apply to those categories, and mapping of the domain terms in the request into appropriate presentation terms.

The three phases that we refer to as *realization, selection,* and *redescription* are implemented in our system as described below. Realization relates the facts about instances to the abstract categories of the model. For example, the concrete facts about *Sprite,* a ship with a malfunctioning radar, must lead to the realization that it is a *disabled-ship* (assuming *disabled-ship* is defined in the domain model). Selection works by allowing for the appropriate mapping rules to be chosen, allowing for additivity. Selection also ensures that all aspects of the demand for presentation are met by some rule. Redescription applies the rules, mapping each aspect of a common-sense view of a presentation into an equivalent presentation form.

The forms produced by rule application are not actually the commands to the output subsystems (i.e., the map graphics system, text generator, and the business forms system). Instead, they are interpretable by *device drivers* that control these systems. This design allows the forms produced by the rules to serve as a model for the contents of the screen. Although we do not currently do so, user input activity on the screen could be interpreted with this screen model serving as a context. So, our design has the additional advantage of allowing, in principle, the use of the same knowledge base and many of the same inference mechanisms for analysis and presentation design.

11.3 KNOWLEDGE REPRESENTATION TOOLS

Our implementation of presentation design depends on two knowledge representation systems: NIKL and KL-TWO. NIKL holds our models; KL-TWO automatically carries out realization. KL-TWO also holds the demands for presentation and receives the forms read by the device drivers. This section provides a brief introduction to these tools.

11.3.1. NIKL

NIKL [Kaczmarek86] is a network knowledge-base system descended from KL-ONE [Brachman85]. This type of system supports description of the entities that make up a domain. The central components of the notation are sets of concepts and roles organized in *is-a* hierarchies. These hierarchies identify when membership in one category (or the holding of one relationship) entails membership in (or the holding of) another. The roles are associated with concepts (as *role restrictions*), and identify the relationships that can hold between individuals that belong to the categories. The role restrictions also hold number restrictions on the entities that fill these roles.

FIGURE 11.3
FRAGMENT OF DOMAIN MODEL CONTAINING SHIP

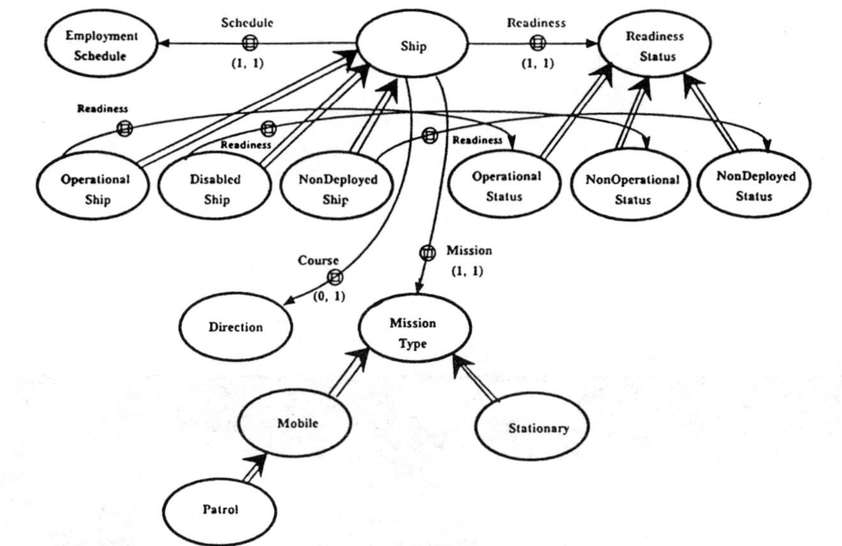

We have been experimenting with a naval assets model for the naval briefing application mentioned above. The model has a concept *disabled-ship* that is meant to identify ships that are unable to carry out their missions. A *disabled-ship is-a* type of *ship* distinguished from *ship* by having a role restriction *readiness* that relates *disabled-ship* to *nonoperational-status* (i.e., all ships with nonoperational status are disabled). All *ships* can have exactly one filler of the *readiness* role restriction. The concept of *nonoperational-status* is partly defined through the *is-a* relation to a concept *readiness-status*. This situation is shown graphically in Figure11.3 in a notation used for KL-ONE knowledge bases.

In flavor, NIKL is a frame system with the concepts equivalent to frames and the role restrictions to slots. However, the NIKL representation has a formal semantics. We could translate our NIKL knowledge bases into predicate calculus expressions and use a theorem prover to make the same inferences; however, NIKL is optimized for the limited inferences it makes, and a general-purpose theorem prover would be less efficient.

11.3.2. KL-TWO

KL-TWO is a hybrid knowledge representation system that takes advantage of NIKL's formal semantics [Vilain85]. KL-TWO links a reasoner, PENNI, to NIKL. PENNI, an enhanced version of RUP [McAllester82], reasons using propositional logic. It is more restricted than systems that use first-order logic and a general-purpose theorem prover.

PENNI manages a database of propositions of the form (P_a) and $(Q_{a,b})$, where the forms are variable free. The first item in each ordered pair is the name of a concept in an associated NIKL network, and the first item in each ordered triple is the name of a role in the network. The assertion of any form (P_a) is a statement that the individual a is a thing described by the concept P. The assertion $(Q_{a,b})$ states that individuals a and b are related by the abstract relation described by Q.

NIKL adds to PENNI the ability to do taxonomic reasoning. Assume the NIKL database contains the concepts described above. Assume that we assert just the following three facts: (*Ship Sprite*), (*readiness Sprite C4*), and *nonoperational-Status C4)* (*C4* is a U.S. Navy readiness code). Using the knowledge base, PENNI is able to deduce that any *Ship* whose *readiness* is a *nonoperational-status* is a *disabled-ship*. So, if we ask if (*disabled-ship Sprite*) is true, KL-TWO will reply positively.

PENNI also provides a truth maintenance system that keeps track of the facts used to deduce others. When our rules are used to determine aspects of a presentation from facts about the world, the truth maintenance system records the dependencies between the domain and the presentation. For example, *readiness Sprite C4* triggers a rule that asserts *disabled-ship Sprite*. If *readiness Sprite C4* is retracted, PENNI's truth maintenance system will automatically retract the assertion that the Sprite is a disabled ship.

11.4 EXAMPLES

The power of presentation design is in its flexibility. The designer of a system does not specify rigidly in advance what form information will be requested from the user and how data and results will be displayed. Instead, our models contain descriptions of the types of information the application programs deal with and the types of graphical tools and instruments available. The rules for presentation enable the system to generate on demand displays appropriate for given needs. Here are some concrete examples.

11.4.1. Construction of a Visual Representation of an Object

Consider the knowledge about ships and about graphical instruments encoded in the NIKL models in Figures 11.3 and 11.4. Besides the aspects of Figure 11.3 already indicated, note that *ships* have *missions* and that *patrol* missions are a subclass of *mobile* missions. Note also that all *ships* have *schedules*.

FIGURE 11.4
FRAGMENT OF INTERFACE MODEL CONTAINING GRAPHICAL-INSTRUMENT

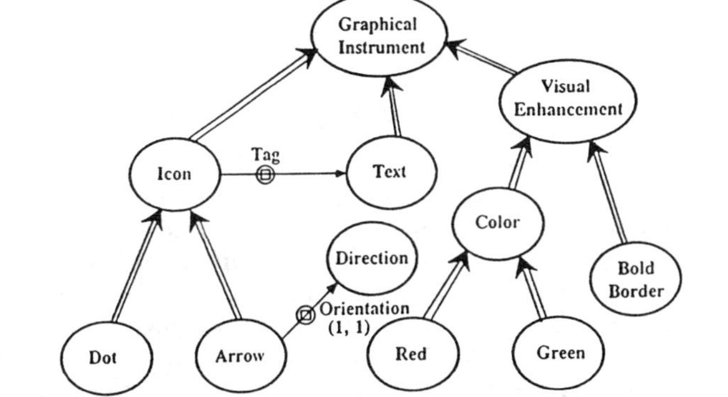

Figure 11.4 describes some *graphical-instruments*. This includes *text* for language output, *icons* for maps and isolated forms, and *visual-enhancements* that could apply to icons and text. *Icons* have *text* as their *tag*. Several specific *icons* and *visual-enhancements* are included.

Let us assume that the user wishes to show ships engaged in a *mobile* mission with a special *icon*, and that the icon should be oriented in a direction identical to the ship's course. In addition, assume that *disabled-ships* are to be shown with *red* icons and that the *schedule* of a ship is to be shown in the natural-language *tag* of the *icon* representing it. A version of the rules that we would use to achieve this is shown in Figure 11.5.

FIGURE 11.5
SAMPLE PRESENTATION RULES

1. IF (operational-ship **x**) or (nondeployed-ship **x**)
   THEN (icon-color image (**x**) green)
2. IF (disabled-ship **x**)
   THEN (icon-color image (**x**) red)
3. IF (ship **x**) and (mission **x y**) and (course **y z**)
   THEN (orientation image (**x**) **z**)
4. IF (ship **x**) and (mission **x,y**) and
   (Mobile **y**) THEN (Icon-Type image(**x**) arrow)
5. IF (ship **x**) and (schedule **x,y**)
   THEN (tag image(**x**) textual-description(**y**))

The antecedent considers the categories of one or more individuals and their relationships, all in terms of the NIKL models. The consequents provide assertions about the graphic representation of objects for the PENNI database. These rules are asserted into PENNI so that the truth maintenance system may keep track of the dependencies between antecedent facts and their resultant consequents, as explained in the previous section.

The functions *image* and *textual-description* map the constants of the common sense world into constants of the visual and textual world, respectively. For example, rule 5 in Figure 11.5 states that if some individual **x** is a *ship* and another individual **y** is its *schedule,* then the *tag* of the image of **x** is the textual description of **y.** The textual description of **y** will be created by the invocation of our text generator.

To complete the example, suppose that the following set of facts was asserted into the PENNI database: (*ship Sprite*), (*readiness Sprite C4*), (*nonoperational-status C4*), (*mission Sprite X37*), (*patrol X37*), (*schedule Sprite U46*), (*course X37 220*), and (*employment-schedule U46*). Suppose further that the NIKL model defined *patrol* to be a subclass of *mobile* missions. Then realization would recognize the *Sprite* as a *disabled-Ship* and one engaged in a *mobile* mission on a course of 220 degrees. Selection would identify that rules 2, 3, 4 and 5 apply. Redescription would result in the addition to the PENNI database of the description of the image of the *Sprite* as a red arrow with an orientation of 220, and with a textual representation of its schedule as its label.

If any of the facts about *Sprite* are retracted, an automatic change in the description of its graphic image will occur.

11.4.2. Recognizing Special Cases

For many requests for information encountered in our domain, the presentation required is far more complex than the rules of the kind listed could provide. The construction of these complex presentations requires an evaluation of the coherence of the display. It would therefore be hopeless at this point to attempt writing rules for deriving an elaborate presentation entirely from low-level information about the objects to be described. Our approach provides us a partial solution to this problem.

The availability of models of the domain and of displays to our presentation designer allows it to recognize collections of data as representing information of a certain known type. The presentation designer can then make use of presentation techniques specialized for this type of data to provide the user with more appropriate displays.

For example, Figure 11.6 provides portions of our model that include the class *Pacific situation,* a display of data about ships and ports in the *Pacific region,* which includes certain specific information from the ships' employment schedule.

When provided with data about ships in the Pacific region and their employments, the presentation designer would classify the data in its model of the domain. A spatial reasoner deduces the region containing all of the ships that would be included in the *Pacific region,* and the presentation designer recognizes that it has received a collection of data belonging to the class *Pacific situation.* Once the classification of the data is accomplished, the presentation designer will use specific presentation rules appropriate for displaying the information. In the domain we have considered there is a preferred way for presenting this information, to which we try to conform. This preferred presentation has developed in the Navy after years of handcrafted situation briefings. The specific presentation rules appropriate only for a situation briefing will combine the entities created by more general rules, of the kind described in the previous section, to produce the final presentation.

FIGURE 11.6
FRAGMENT OF DOMAIN MODEL INCLUDING SITUATION

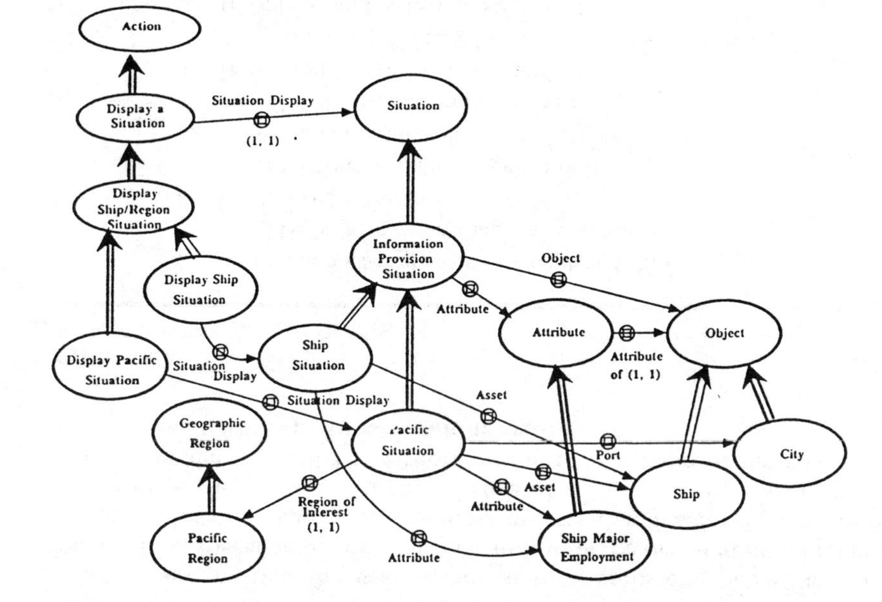

11.4.3. Generation of an Input Display

The presentation designer must also deal with the preparation of displays for soliciting information from the user. Here, again, the task and domain models are indispensable.

At some point the user may want to view data about ships in some region. In terms of our model (see Figure 11.6), that would mean *display a situation.* As it turns out, the presentation designer does not have any rules that can be used to redescribe this general request into a presentation, but there exist ways of satisfying more specific requests. For example, requests to have the *Pacific region* or any of its subregions displayed can be satisfied. As we see in Figure 11.6, the situation involves specific ships and ports, which may also be displayed.

The presentation designer collects all options the user can choose among to construct an executable request. The presentation designer then constructs a display form that will be used to present these options to the user. The result of this is a set of assertions in PENNI that the device driver for a separate forms-management package (Qforms [Kaczmarek84]) uses to prepare the input form.

The form below, presented to the user, allows the user to make one of several specific choices:

Pacific Regions:
- Western Pacific ☐
- South China Sea ☐
- Indian Ocean ☐
- Easter Pacific ☐
- Pacific Command Region ☐

Ship: ____________

It is instructive to examine precisely how this form is created. Specifically, how does the choice *Ship* become part of the form? It is not a Pacific region, but Navy personnel request that this possibility be supported.

We included in our model the concept *display-ship/region situation*. Since this has two subclasses of actions, namely *display ship situation* and *display regional situation* our system could have generated an intermediate two-item submenu, something like:

Situation in Pacific Region ☐
Situation of Ship ☐

We consider this unsatisfactory from a human-factor standpoint. We formulated a rule that if the choices on a proposed menu can be further subdivided, and if the number of choices is less than N, then the proposed menu should not be displayed. Instead, a more detailed form should be generated, based on the subchoices. Our prototype uses the value 3 for N, so in this case the rule causes the presentation designer to immediately generate the more specific form. A user is free to change the value of N in the rule, modifying the design of forms the system generates in situations such as this.

Note that the regions available were specified by name in the form, while ships were not; the user specifies a ship by typing on the form (Figure 11.2). This distinction in selection methods is a result of information about the cardinality of the relevant collections of objects—information encoded in our models. Since the number of possible choices for region is small, they are enumerated. However, the number of ships is large, so the user is provided with a way to specify a choice explicitly instead. Cardinality is information attached to concepts in the model and is specified at the time the model is created.

Generating interfaces by models and rules is time consuming and tedious, but it forces designers to think out every aspect of an interface. The decisions are not hidden in the code; they are explicit—observable and modifiable—in the rules and the model.

11.5 RELATED WORK

11.5.1. Related Work in Integrated Interfaces

The literature contains numerous examples of user interface management systems. However, we see our contribution as being our emphasis on *presentation design*, and very few systems are concerned with this aspect of the interface. Perhaps the best-known previous work dealing with this issue is that of [Mackinlay ([Mackinlay86] and Chapter 13 in this volume).

Much like part of our system, Mackinlay's *APT* uses information about characteristics of data it is provided to produce a graphical representation of that data. The differences between the two systems become clear when we consider the variety of data each deals with and the variety of presentations they produce. *APT* produces graphs of various kinds, and much of its effort goes into deciding which axes to choose and how to indicate the values along each axis. Data that can be dealt with is limited to what can be presented using such graphs. Consequently, Mackinlay has succeeded in producing a system that can generate graphical presentations automatically using only low-level information about the objects and their attributes.

Our system is expected to generate a much wider variety of displays, many that would require considerable design work even from an expert human graphic artist.[1] In addition, certain display layouts are often chosen simply to conform to pre-existing preferences of Navy personnel. Consequently, unlike Mackinlay we are required to provide for the possibility of following preset stereotypical instructions in certain cases. We must therefore devote considerable effort to recognizing which cases require these special displays.

A further significant difference between the systems is the complexity of the data we are required to present. In order to handle this range of data, we must represent it using a sophisticated knowledge-representation language, NIKL, a facility which Mackinlay finds unnecessary in APT. Both systems make use of sophisticated reasoning facilities.

Neal and Shapiro (see Chapter 2 in this volume) present a system with several superficial similarities to ours, due mostly to the choice of a simi-

[1] As in fact they do. Maps of the kind produced by our system take Navy personnel approximately four hours to produce every day.

lar domain and the common use of maps. However, the systems have emphases that differ considerably. Integrated Interfaces has devoted considerable effort to the integration of several different subsystems—the GDA, QFORMS, PENMAN—while Neal and Shapiro's only external system is the map-drawing one. Map-drawing itself is only a minor part of the functionality of the GDA. More significantly, Integrated Interfaces has a strong UIMS emphasis. We view our effort as an attempt to simplify the production of multimodal interfaces. Neal and Shapiro, on the other hand, have emphasized research into new integrated communication modalities, taking an intelligent systems approach.

It is interesting to compare the architecture of the Integrated Interfaces system to that proposed by Feiner (Chapter 12 in this volume). Our version of Feiner's *media experts* are external systems, integrated into the interface with the use of device drivers. All our models are written in a single knowledge-representation language, NIKL.

11.5.2. Coordinated Work at ISI

At ISI we have been working closely with the Services and Information Management for Decision Systems[2] (SIMS) project [Arens90; Pavlin88a; Pavlin 88b]. The goal of SIMS is to provide a wrapper around a diverse collection of underlying software. Input is transformed into a canonical representation, then passed to a planning agent that attempts to piece together the most appropriate subsystem, or combination of subsystems, to respond. If the response does not meet some a priori criteria, the request may be reiterated with other subsystems until it is satisfied. Finally, the output may be packaged in a form for the Integrated Interface's presentation planner.

11.6 CURRENT STATUS

A demonstration version of the Integrated Interfaces system is now available at ISI. The current version models the domain of Navy ships in the Pacific Ocean. A user may use the system to access information about ships' locations, tasks, readiness status, and more. The resulting information is displayed using combinations of maps, menus, tables, and natural-language output (Figure 11.2).

The system is written in Common Lisp and runs in the *X*-windows environment under UNIX on HP 9000 Model 350 workstations. Displays are presented on a Renaissance color graphics monitor. The map graphic modality is supported by ISI's Graphics Display Agent. Menus and forms are created using QFORMS [Kaczmarek84]. Natural-language output is produced by ISI's Penman system [Sondheimer86].

[2] Formerly called the Single Interface to Multiple Systems

11.7 FUTURE WORK

We believe our approach to the problem of presentation design is a viable one. Indeed, as illustrated in the examples of the previous section, we are using it to generate various interesting displays. However, there are still several problems that remain to be solved. Below we list three structures that we plan to add to our system.

- *User model:* enhances the presentation designer by allowing it to tailor presentations to individual user preferences. For example, it would enable the system to label only ports and regions unfamiliar to a user, thereby reducing screen clutter.
- *Dialogue model:* allows the presentations to be more closely tailored to specific users' requests. Currently, the presentation designer is simply provided with data to display. It is not aware of the purpose of the display.
- *Screen model:* the screen display is more than a bitmap; it is viewed by a user as containing icons and text that have real-world denotations. The interface's internal description of the display must be rich enough to allow a user to alternate between references to screen entities and their denotations. A screen model will make such relationships explicit.

11.8 CONCLUSIONS

We have realized the process of presentation design in a system that utilizes natural language, graphics, menus, and forms. Specifically, the Integrated Interfaces system can create maps containing icons with string tags and natural-language descriptions attached to them. It can further combine such maps with forms and tables presenting additional, related information. In addition, the system is capable of dynamically creating menus for choosing among alternative actions and of creating more complicated forms for specifying desired information.

To support this activity, we have constructed application models describing concepts in an important real-world domain—the naval situation briefing. We have implemented rules that enable the creation of different types of integrated multimodal output displays based on the Navy's current manual practices. We have represented large enough portions of both the general and application-specific domains to demonstrate that a model-driven presentation design approach is potentially useful in real-world situations.

In achieving this result, we have done more than produce a system for constructing and controlling multimodal application interfaces. We have shown that what would otherwise appear to be distinct communication mechanisms (viz., graphics, natural language, tables, etc.) can be treated as part of an integrated whole, all relating to a common level of meaning representation. We have further shown that the decisions on the use of the appropriate mode can be represented straightforwardly by explicit rules relating information to be presented to the method of presentation. We believe that this work can serve as the basis of a comprehensive theory of multimodal communication.

Acknowledgments

We wish to acknowledge the crucial help provided by others working on the Integrated Interface project. Stu Shapiro helped in developing the general framework of the system and contributed to its implementation. Paul Raveling has developed the graphical interface and continues to maintain the GDA. Chin Chee has ported QFORMS and PENMAN to the HP workstation and is responsible for coordinating the various parts of the system. Jim Geller has contributed to the implementation of the spatial reasoner.

The final form of this paper was enhanced by many useful comments provided by an anonymous reviewer.

References

[Arens90] Arens, Y. 1990. Services and Information Management for Decision Support. *AISIG-90: Proceedings of the Annual AI Systems in Government Conference.* George Washington University, Washington, DC, May 7–11.

[Brachman85] Brachman, R. J., and Schmolze, J. G. 1985. An Overview of the KL-ONE Knowledge Representation System. *Cognitive Science,* 9(2), 171–216.

[Feiner88] Feiner, S. 1988. An Architecture for Knowledge-Based Graphical Interfaces. *Proceedings, Architectures for Intelligent Interfaces: Elements and Prototypes,* Monterey, CA, March, pp. 129–140. Also available as Chapter 12 in present volume.

[Kaczmarek84] Kaczmarek, T. 1984. *CUE Forms Description,* ISI Internal Report, USC/ISI, Marina del Rey, CA.

[Kaczmarek86] Kaczmarek, T., Bates, R. and Robins, G. 1986. Recent Developments in NIKL. *Proceedings, AAAI '86,* Philadelphia, PA, pp. 978–985.

[Mackinlay86] Mackinlay, J. D. 1986. *Automatic Design of Graphical Presentations.* Ph.D. thesis, Department of Computer Science, Stanford University, Stanford, CA.

[McAllester82] McAllester, D. A. 1982. *Reasoning Utility Package User's Manual,* Massachusetts Institute of Technology, AI Memo 667, Cambridge, MA, April.

[Neal88] Neal, J. G., and Shapiro, S. 1988. Intelligent Multi-Media Interface Technology. *Proceedings, Architectures for Intelligent Interfaces: Elements and Prototypes,* Monterey, CA, March, pp. 69–91. Also available as Chapter 2 in present volume.

[Pavlin88a] Pavlin, J. and Bates, R. L. 1988. SIMS: Single Interface to Multiple Systems. Invited paper presented at *Tenth International Computer Symposium,* University of Dubrovnik, Yugoslavia. Also available as ISI Research Report ISI/RR-88-200.

[Pavlin88b] Pavlin, J. and Bates, R. L. 1988. SIMS: A Uniform Environment for Planning and Performing User's Tasks. *Proceedings of First International Conference on Industrial and Engineering Applications of AI and Expert Systems,* Tullahoma, TN, pp. 195–200.

[Sondheimer86] Sondheimer, N. K. and Nebel, B. 1986. A Logical-Form and Knowledge-Base Design For Natural Language Generation. *Proceedings, AAAI '86,* Philadelphia, pp. 612–618.

[Vilain85] Vilain, M. 1985. The Restricted Language Architecture of a Hybrid Representation System. *Proceedings of the Ninth International Joint Conference on Artificial Intelligence,* Los Angeles, pp. 547–551.

Presentation Design Using an Integrated Knowledge Base

Yigal Arens, Lawrence Miller, and Norm Sondheimer

The central notion put forward in the original paper was that interface displays could be generated dynamically by taking into account information stored in a central knowledge base. At the time the paper was written, we considered that knowledge base to include models of the application domain, the structure of visual displays and their graphical features, the underlying services, and interface functions. A *presentation design* process would assemble presentations based on that knowledge.

Although the specific project described in this paper came to an end shortly after the paper was written (1989), the ideas developed in the integrated interfaces project formed the basis for work along similar lines that did continue at ISI for several years. The new group of researchers included Yigal Arens and Eduard Hovy with contributions from Mira Vossers and Susanne van Mulken. The early notion of *model-based presentation design* described in this paper was expanded upon in several ways. Specifically, we made the categories of the knowledge underlying multimedia presentations more explicit, and we devoted more work to understanding the kind of planning process that was required in order to actually generate a multimedia display. The initial expansion of our modeling ideas was described in (Arens and Hovy 1990).

These early ideas were eventually developed into the theory described in the paper by Arens, Hovy, and Vossers (2.6 in this volume). See the discussion that follows it for further references. Our ideas regarding the planning required for multimedia display design were described in (Hovy and Arens 1993).

REFERENCES

Arens, Y., and Hovy, E. H. 1990. How to Describe What? Towards a Theory of Modality Utilization. In *Proceedings of the Twelfth Annual Conference of the Cognitive Science Society*, Ann Arbor, MI. Hillsdale, NJ: Lawrence Erlbaum Associates.

Hovy, E. H., and Arens, Y. 1993. The Planning Paradigm Required for Automated Multimedia Presentation Planning. In *Human-Computer Collaboration: Reconciling Theory, Synthesizing Practice*. Papers from the 1993 Fall Symposium Series, AAAI Technical Report FS-93-05.

AUTOMATIC GENERATION OF TECHNICAL DOCUMENTATION

EHUD REITER, CHRIS MELLISH, and JOHN LEVINE
Department of Artificial Intelligence, University of Edinburgh, Edinburgh, Scotland

Natural-language generation (NLG) techniques can be used to automatically produce technical documentation from a domain knowledge base and linguistic and contextual models. We discuss this application of NLG technology from both a technical and a usefulness (costs and benefits) perspective. This discussion is based largely on our experiences with the Intelligent Documentation Advisory System (IDAS) documentation-generation project, and the reactions that various interested people from industry have had to IDAS. We hope that this summary of our experiences with IDAS and the lessons we have learned from it will be beneficial for other researchers who wish to build technical documentation-generation systems.

Natural-language generation (NLG) is a young but growing research field, whose goal is to build computer systems that can automatically produce fluent texts in English, French, and other human languages. To date, NLG has mainly been of interest to academic researchers, but fielded application systems based on this technology have recently begun to appear (e.g., Goldberg et al., 1994).

In this article, we discuss one particular application of NLG technology, automatic generation of technical documentation, mostly from the perspective of "what can the technology do and what are its costs and benefits?" rather than "how does it work?" Our discussion is general, but much of it is based on our experiences with the Intelligent Documentation Advisory System (IDAS) technical-documentation generation project, which we worked on from 1990 until 1993. Project IDAS was a partial success, and we will discuss its weaknesses as well as its strengths, and the lessons we have learned both from building IDAS and from the reactions interested people from industry have had to the system; these lessons will hopefully be of use in future attempts to build technical documentation-generation systems.

Technical documentation refers to the extensive design, maintenance, and operations documents that must be supplied with complex machinery; we are primarily interested here in documents that are intended to be read by technicians and other experts, as opposed to "the man in the street" (e.g., aircraft maintenance manuals, not VCR operations manuals). Producing technical documentation is a very expensive process and, furthermore, one that is relatively unautomated in comparison with other aspects of the design process. In other words, there is as yet no equivalent in the technical documentation field of the computer-aided design (CAD) tools that have significantly enhanced the productivity of design engineers. One potential candidate for the "CAD tool for technical authors" is systems that use NLG technology to automatically produce technical documents from various data and knowledge bases (KBs). The potential effectiveness and appropriateness of such tools is the subject of this article.

The IDAS was a 3-year collaborative effort between the University of Edinburgh, Racal Instruments Ltd., Racal Research Ltd., and Inference Europe Ltd. Its goal was to build an advanced on-line documentation system for users of Racal automatic test equipment (ATE), which could give ATE users help messages tailored to the context and the user. Part of the project involved an attempt to build what might be called an "advanced canned-text system," which used hypertext and object-oriented techniques to make a "conventional" canned-text help and on-line-documentation system both more effective (for users) and easier to create, update, and otherwise modify (for authors). The rest of the project was more ambitious and attempted to automatically generate documentation from a domain KB and contextual models, using NLG techniques; this is the part of the project that the group at Edinburgh was most involved with, and is the focus of this article. At the time of this writing, the NLG system seems less likely to be incorporated into Racal and Inference products than the advanced canned-text system, essentially because it does not offer sufficient benefits to make its extra cost worthwhile. This is largely because when we started the project, we had only a very vague idea about what the actual costs and benefits of using NLG in document-generation applications were, and therefore did not emphasize the benefits that turned out to be most significant. Thanks largely to the valuable comments and criticisms about IDAS that we have obtained from various interested people in industry, we now have a much better idea of potential NLG costs and benefits and their relative importance. We hope that our presentation here of the lessons we have learned from IDAS will help future researchers who are interested in building technical documentation-generation systems.

The rest of this article discusses these points in more detail. We will first examine the general idea of producing technical documentation from a KB with NLG techniques, including a summary of the costs and benefits of this approach. Subsequent sections present a summary of IDAS (what it does, how it works, etc.,) and an

The IDAS project was partially funded by UK SERC grant GR/F/36750 and UK DTI grant IED 4/1/1072, and we are grateful to SERC and DTI for their support of this work. We would especially like to thank the IDAS industrial collaborators—Inference Europe Ltd.; Racal Instruments Ltd.; and Racal Research Ltd.—for all the help they have given us in performing this research. We would also like to thank the many interested people from other industrial organizations (including Andersen Consulting, British Aerospace, COWIconsult, Dassault Aviation, General Motors, and Sun Microsystems), who have spent significant amounts of time discussing IDAS and natural-language generation with us; the first author would also like to thank the people at CoGenTex (especially Richard Kittredge and Tanya Korelsky) for their comments and advice. We are also very grateful for the effort contributed by the visitors and MSc students who worked on IDAS, including Ilona Bellos, Dan Cristea, Colin Dick, Sam Marshall, and Michael Pake. It goes without saying, of course, that all opinions expressed in this paper are our own, and we are solely responsible for any errors or mistakes in the text.

Address correspondence to Dr. Ehud Reiter, Department of Computing Science, University of Aberdeen, King's College, Aberdeen AB9 2UE United Kingdom; E-mail:ereiter@csd.abdn.ac.uk; or to Dr. Chris Mellish, Department of Artificial Intelligence, University of Edinburgh, 80 South Bridge, Edinburgh EH1 1HN, United Kingdom; E-mail: c.mellish@ed.ac.uk.

evaluation of the NLG-from-KB system, including the reactions of our collaborators and other interested potential users as well as a summary of our user trials. In the final section we will try to summarize the lessons that we think are most important for future efforts to build technical documentation-generation systems.

TECHNICAL DOCUMENTATION

The Problem

Complex machinery, of necessity, requires complex documentation, and producing technical documentation is a time-consuming and expensive task for many corporations. Stories abound, for example, of engineers who spend 5 hours documenting for every hour they spend designing, or of airplane documentation sets that weigh more than the plane they document. In many cases, technical documents also must meet externally imposed writing or content standards, be translated into several languages, and be written for easy maintenance and updating. All of these factors make the documentation yet more expensive and time consuming to produce.

The problem of generating technical documentation in a cost-effective manner is becoming even more critical because advanced CAD tools are reducing the time required to design objects. However, no equivalent tools have been developed to reduce the time required to document designs. Tools that could reduce document-creation time in a fashion similar to the way CAD tools have reduced design-creation times would be of tremendous value to numerous organizations, and also a boon to engineers (many of whom find designing a more interesting and enjoyable task than documenting!).

The NLG Approach

Much of the information presented in technical documentation is already present in machine-readable form in CAD systems, component-description databases, KBs created for expert-system applications, etc. This suggests attempting to automatically create at least a portion of the relevant technical document from these data, using NLG techniques. The NLG approach has several potential advantages, which are described below.

Reduced Cost to Generate and Maintain Documentation

If most of the information required to generate the documentation is already present in a database or KB of some kind, then the NLG approach can reduce the time and effort required to produce documentation. This should be the case even if the system's output needs to be postedited by a human, or if additional information needs to be entered into the system to support document generation, provided the amount of postediting and extra information required is not overly large.

Cost savings may be even more significant for document maintenance than initial document creation. As with software, maintaining and updating a document can be more costly than initially creating it; the problem here is not so much fixing spelling and grammatical mistakes in a document, but rather keeping a document up to date when the machine it describes is upgraded or released in a new configuration. In many cases, such upgrades and new configurations can be represented by very simple changes to a design database that describes the machine, and the NLG approach allows the new documentation to be produced automatically once the design has been upgraded in this manner.

For example, if a machine is upgraded by installing a higher-capacity power supply, the NLG approach allows the specifications of the new power supply to be loaded into a single well-defined place in the domain KB, from which they will be automatically propagated to all relevant documentation texts. In many cases, this can be significantly easier than manually making such changes, particularly if references to the power supply are scattered throughout the documentation set.

Guaranteed Consistency between Documentation and Design

Current practice often requires engineers to instantiate their designs twice: once in a design database (e.g., CAD system), which may be used to drive automated computer-aided-manufacturing (CAM) equipment; and once in a human-readable document, where maintainers and users can learn about it. This duplicate instantiation is, of course, expensive, but perhaps even more significant is the danger of inconsistencies. If the design described in the document is not exactly the same as the design entered in the design database, the user may misuse the machine, and the manufacturing company will be held legally liable. The NLG approach allows the designer to instantiate his or her design once into a design database or KB that is augmented to also represent the extra data needed for document generation; this greatly reduces the possibility of errors due to inconsistency between the machine- and human-readable representations (as well as potentially reducing effort, since designers only have to instantiate their designs once instead of twice).

As with the reduced cost benefit (see previous section), guaranteed consistency can be especially important for document maintenance. If a machine is upgraded or released in a new configuration, it is very easy for the documenter to forget to make some of the necessary changes in the documentation, especially if the current document maintainer is not the original author. The NLG approach can significantly reduce the risk of this eventuality.

Guaranteed Conformance to Standards

Many documents are required to obey writing or content standards. Writing standards are usually intended to ensure that the language used in a document is unambiguous and easily comprehensible, especially for non-native-English speakers. Examples of such standards include AECMA Simplified English (AECMA,

1986) and Perkins Approved Clear English (Pym, 1993). AECMA Simplified English, for example,

- imposes a fixed unambiguous lexicon,
- prohibits potentially confusing syntactic constructs, such as gerunds or complex tenses, and
- imposes general stylistic guidelines, such as requesting that sentences be kept under 20 words if possible.

Content standards, such as the U.K. Army Equipment Support Publication rules and the U.S. Defense Department 2167A standard for software documentation, specify what information must be included in various documents (e.g., required maintenance procedures and safety information). Content standards are often less precise than writing standards, which can make them harder to automate.

NLG systems can be set up to automatically enforce most rules found in writing standards, by programming an appropriate grammar and lexicon into the system. NLG systems can also be set up to obey content standards if the relevant information is available in the KB and can print a warning message if it is not, provided that the standard is precise enough to be computationally interpretable.

Multilinguality

If the relevant domain and contextual models are language independent, then the NLG system can be modified to produce texts in multiple output languages; NLG systems with multilingual output have, in fact, been built since the NLG field began (Hovy et al., 1992). Producing multilingual output is not a trivial technical problem, but it is perhaps less complex for technical documentation than for other kinds of text for the following reasons.

- Complex and difficult-to-translate syntax, lexemes, tenses, etc., are prohibited by most technical documentation writing standards (see previous section) and hence the system does not have to worry about correctly using such complex linguistic constructs in multiple languages.
- Achieving complex pragmatic and stylistic effects (e.g., making the reader laugh, or indirectly informing them of a fictional character's mental state) is not generally a goal of technical documentation; these are some of the most difficult things to get right in multilingual texts.

Multilingual output reduces document translation costs, but it probably will not eliminate it completely, since it is likely that human quality assurance and postediting will still need to be performed for texts in all output languages.

Tailoring

The NLG approach allows a documentation text to be dynamically tailored to the context (e.g., the user's task, the user's expertise level, and the discourse history). Among the many kinds of tailoring that have been discussed in the literature are

- tailoring rhetorical (Paris, 1988) and syntactic (Bateman & Paris, 1989) structures according to a user's expertise,
- choosing different lexical units (words) depending on the user's vocabulary and background knowledge (Reiter, 1991),
- generating helpful responses that communicate the information the user needs to execute his or her current plan (Allen & Perrault, 1980), and
- choosing appropriate referring expressions for the current environment and discourse context (e.g., Reiter & Dale, 1992).

The research literature on this topic is extensive, and the above list is by no means complete.

Multimodality

Information can be communicated to (and from) the user with graphics as well as text. Ideally, a document generation and presentation system should be able to interact with the user in whatever modality is most suitable for the task at hand. It is useful to distinguish between three kinds of multimodality, as follows.

Visual formatting. Text can be much more effective if it is presented with appropriate visual formatting devices, such as bullets, font changes, and indentation. An NLG system can produce visually formatted text by treating such formatting devices as an additional "resource" that can be used to communicate and structure information (e.g., Hovy & Arens, 1991).

Hypertext input. Text can be generated with hypertext-like links that allow a user to issue clarification, elaboration, and other kinds of follow-up questions simply by clicking the mouse on an appropriate word (Carenini et al., 1993; Reiter et al., 1992; Moore & Swartout, 1990). This is obviously only useful in an on-line system.

Graphics output. Much research has been done on generating diagrams (and other graphical presentations of data) and text from a single-domain KB (e.g., Feiner & McKeown, 1990; Wahlster et al., 1993). Graphics output requires a different low-level "realization/rendering" module than text output, but in some cases, high-level content-oriented modules can be used for both text and graphics output (Wahlster et al., 1993).

NLG techniques can be adapted to the problem of producing appropriate visual formatting and hypertext links, and to determining the content (although not the layout) of associated diagrams. When doing so, many of the advantages mentioned in the previous sections also apply to these multimedia "extensions." For example, AECMA Simplified English (see section above, Guaranteed Conformance to Standards) has standards for the use of visual formatting, which an NLG system can ensure are obeyed; hypertext links can be automatically updated if the text they point to is changed; and generated diagrams can be modified according to the user's goals (Roth et al., 1991).

With hypertext in particular, it is also possible that automatic generation of hypertext links may produce a hypertext network that is more consistent and therefore easier to navigate. This currently remains an interesting but unproven hypothesis; more research needs to be done on the acceptability of automatically generated hypertext networks.

It is also worth noting that NLG systems will be much more useful in practice if they can include visual formatting, hypertext links, and associated diagrams in their output. An NLG system that has no multimodal abilities may only be useful in a limited number of applications in real-world document generation.

Costs of NLG

Against the potential benefits must be weighed the costs of the NLG approach. NLG will, of course, only be worth using in real applications if its benefits outweigh its costs.

Increased CAD/KB Creation Time

In general, design and other databases do not contain all the information needed to produce the relevant documentation, which means the designer/engineer will need to enter additional information into the design database or knowledge base (KB) when creating the design, in order to give the NLG system sufficient information. This extra information can, however, be used for many purposes other than document generation, such as consistency, correctness, and completeness checks on the design. The cost of creating an appropriate model of a system in a CAD or KB framework should thus be evaluated in light of all the benefits it can potentially bring, not just document generation.

Fixed Overhead for KB Creation

The NLG system will also require KBs that describe the sublanguage used in the documentation (which is often specified in a writing standard), and user and contextual models (if tailoring is being done). The per-application cost of building these KBs will be decreased if the KBs can be shared among several applications, which is certainly possible to some degree (e.g., a grammar and lexicon for the AECMA Simplified English sublanguage can probably be used for most documents about aerospace systems).

Quality Assurance

Many organizations require documents to pass through a quality assurance (QA) procedure, which usually means being checked and perhaps edited by a separate group of people (this last procedure is sometimes called *postediting*). It seems likely that computer-generated documents will also have to pass through this QA process, at least until users are confident that generated documents are both linguistically correct and a faithful rendition of the relevant KB or database. Such checking and postediting can cost significant amounts of money (e.g., see the costs reported by Isabelle and Bourbeau (1985) for postediting in a machine translation project).

Computation Time

A certain amount of computer time will obviously be required to generate text using NLG techniques. While the monetary cost of computer time is fairly low (and getting lower), NLG systems must satisfy response-time constraints. In particular, interactive systems must be able to generate text within a few seconds in order to be useful. The response-time constraints on off-line (batch) generation are looser, but they exist; a batch system that required several days to generate a document, for example, would probably be considered of limited usefulness.

Related Approaches

There is some overlap between generating documentation from a KB with NLG techniques, and using knowledge-based machine translation (KBMT) (Goodman & Nirenburg, 1991) techniques to translate documents. KBMT systems take an input document written in one language, process that document with an NL understanding system to produce an "interlingua representation" that essentially contains the same information as a pure NLG system would hope to extract from its various knowledge and databases, and then use NLG to produce an output text from the "interlingua." From a technical perspective, the main difference between the KBMT and pure NLG approaches is that the former expects its input data to be expressed as NL text (in a different language), while the latter expects it to be present as design information in a database of some kind. From an applications perspective, it is worth noting that KBMT is generally viewed only as an aid to document translation, while NLG can be used to improve productivity throughout the document-creation process.

IDAS

Goals

The goal of the IDAS project was to build a better on-line documentation system for Racal automatic test equipment (ATE). ATEs are complex machines used to test potentially faulty circuit boards and determine if they are, in fact, malfunctioning. IDAS was intended to produce short on-line help messages (as opposed to complete paper documents) for three kinds of ATE users: operators, maintenance technicians, and programmers. Two systems were built, as follows.

- A hypertext documentation system mainly relied on canned texts, but used a domain KB to enhance the effectiveness of the system in various ways [somewhat similar to the system proposed, but not implemented by Hayes and Pepper (1989)]. The system used object-oriented techniques to make the documents easier to update and otherwise modify.
- An NLG-based system, in addition to the above qualities, attempted to generate the hypertext nodes (both text and links) from a domain KB and various contextual models.

Our group at the University of Edinburgh was primarily concerned with the second system, which is the one on which this article focuses.

In relation to the benefits described in the section The NLG Approach, the initial goals of the IDAS NLG system could be characterized as follows.

Reduced cost. The main interest was in reducing document maintenance costs. ATE designs were not available in machine-readable databases, which meant that special KBs would need to be constructed for the NLG system, and this would probably cost more than simply directly authoring the documentation. The hope, though, was that once an NLG KB had been built, changes to reflect new ATE configurations, or upgraded ATE components, could be made easily in the KB, and this would reduce document maintenance costs. Maintenance costs are high because ATEs are sold in many different configurations, and are continually being upgraded to utilize the most up-to-date components.

Guaranteed consistency. Consistency was a significant goal, especially for document maintenance. It was not possible to ensure consistency between the document and the design (since the design was not present in a CAD system), but it was hoped to increase the likelihood of consistency by making it more straightforward to update the documentation. With IDAS, the designer or technical author could update the documentation to reflect modified hardware simply by changing the KB to reflect the changes in the hardware, and all necessary documentation changes would then be made automatically.

Standards and multilinguality. Not emphasized.

Tailoring. Tailoring was also important, in that a primary goal of the system was to be able to tailor its output to at least the three classes of users mentioned above, namely, operators, maintenance technicians, and programmers.

Multimodality. Hypertext was central to the project. Some importance was also attached to being able to use canned graphics.

With regard to cost, the main concern was to reduce the cost of authoring the domain KB as much as possible. This was especially critical because it was not possible to extract any information from existing databases. Less emphasis was placed on reducing the cost of constructing fixed KBs, since it was felt that this cost could be amortized over several projects if IDAS was successful. The main computation constraint was that response texts should be generated in an acceptable time for an interactive system. Quality assurance was not originally regarded as a significant cost, although in retrospect, it did have an impact, especially when considering the amount of tailoring that was desirable.

Some "intermediate" techniques were developed that attempted to reduce domain-KB authoring costs at the expense of making some relatively unimportant benefits (e.g., multilingual generation) more difficult to achieve; these are discussed in the section below, Intermediate Techniques.

The System

Input

The prototype IDAS NLG system built by Edinburgh is described by Reiter et al. (1992). The system's input is a "question-space" point that specifies five parameters, as follows.

Basic question. The basic system supported seven questions: What-is-it, Where-is-it, What-are-its-parts, What-are-its-specs, What-is-its-purpose, What-does-it-connect-to, and How-do-I-perform-the-current-task. This list was modified for some of the non-ATE KBs.

Component. The KB contained a Part-of component hierarchy of the target machine (the ATE in the main IDAS application), and queries could be issued for components at any level (from the ATE as a whole down to individual switches and levers).

User-task. The user-task model told IDAS (in very rough terms) what kind of task the user was performing. The tasks were represented in an Is-a taxonomy.

User-expertise. The user-expertise model told the system how much the user knew about the domain, and what some of his or her stylistic preferences were. The former included what technical vocabulary the user knew and what actions he or she could perform. The latter included, for example, whether contractions should be used (e.g., *it's* versus *it is*).

Discourse. The discourse parameter told the system what objects were salient and hence could be referred to by simple noun phrases; this follows a much simplified version of the discourse model proposed by Grosz and Sidner (1986).

For example, the question-space point ⟨What-is-it, DC-Power-Supply-23, Operations, Skilled, {VXI-Chassis-36, DC-Power-Supply-23}⟩ represents the query "What is the DC power supply?", when asked by a user of skilled expertise who is engaged in an operations task with the discourse context containing the objects

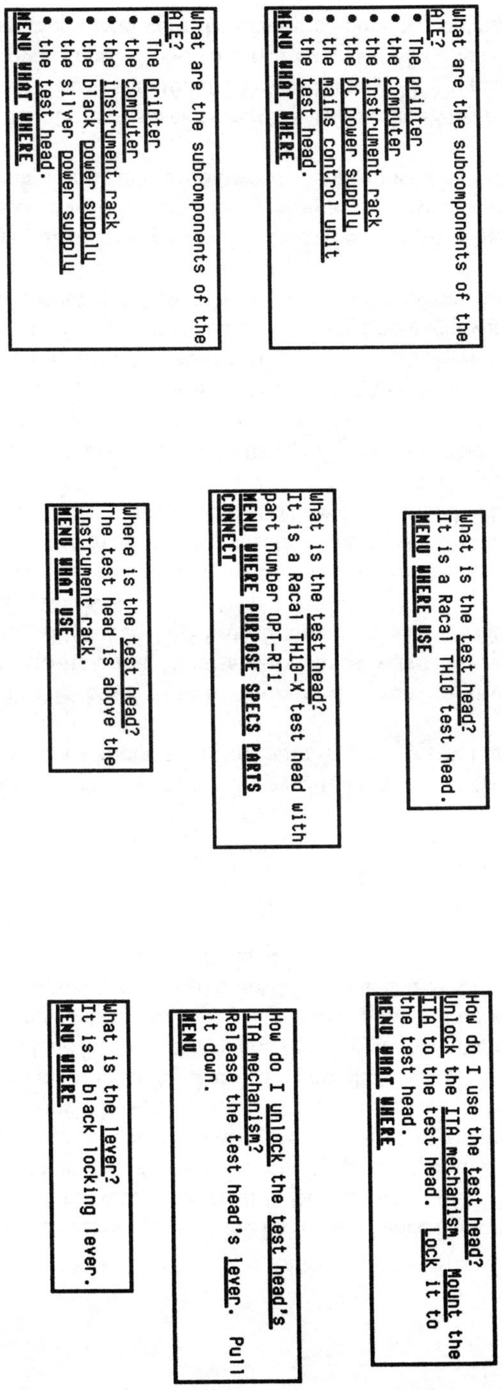

What are the subcomponents of the ATE?
• The printer
• the computer
• the instrument rack
• the DC power supply
• the mains control unit
• the test head.
MENU WHAT WHERE

What are the subcomponents of the ATE?
• The printer
• the computer
• the instrument rack
• the black power supply
• the silver power supply
• the test head.
MENU WHAT WHERE

What is the test head?
It is a Racal TH10 test head.
MENU WHERE USE

What is the test head?
It is a Racal TH10-X test head with part number OPT-RT1.
MENU WHERE PURPOSE SPECS PARTS CONNECT

Where is the test head?
The test head is above the instrument rack.
MENU WHAT USE

How do I use the test head?
Unlock the ITA mechanism. Mount the ITA to the test head. Lock it to the test head.
MENU WHAT WHERE

How do I unlock the test head's ITA mechanism?
Release the test head's lever. Pull it down.
MENU

What is the lever?
It is a black locking lever.
MENU WHERE

Figure 1. Example screen dump.

VXI-Chassis-36 and DC-Power-Supply-23. The NLG component would in this case produce the response

It is a black Elgar AT-8000 dc power supply.

More example IDAS outputs, including those that show the effect of changing the user-task or user-expertise models, are shown in Figure 1, and described in the section below, Example.

Knowledge Base

A KL-ONE (Brachman & Schmolze, 1985) type knowledge representation (KR) language called I1 was used as IDAS's knowledge representation system. I1 included support for Is-a and Part-of hierarchies, default attribute inheritance (along the Is-a hierarchy), and automatic classification of new classes into the correct position in the Is-a taxonomy. In addition to the basic KR support functions, I1 also included a graphical browser that could be used to examine the KB.

I1 proved surprisingly powerful and versatile; IDAS used it to represent many kinds of information, including

- domain knowledge,
- grammatical rules,
- the lexicon,
- user-task and user-expertise models, and
- content-determination rules.

IDAS also used I1 classification and inheritance mechanisms to perform most of the reasoning needed to generate text (Reiter & Mellish, 1992). The use of a single KR system for so many kinds of knowledge and so many kinds of reasoning is perhaps the most theoretically interesting feature of IDAS.

From a practical perspective, the use of an object-oriented KR system that supported taxonomies and inheritance made it significantly easier to create the necessary KBs. For example, the procedure for removing a circuit board from a VXI chassis (a type of backplane used in ATE systems) was only specified once, at the level VXI-Chassis-Board, and then inherited by all the specific boards (digital multimeter, counter timer, etc). Inheritance was also used within the linguistic KBs; the definition of the grammatical rule for Imperative-Sentence, for example, was relatively short because it could inherit most of the necessary information from its parent class Sentence. It is unclear to what extent the presence of a default inheritance system added to the theoretical expressive power of I1, but it certainly proved to be a significant convenience to KB authors.

Most of the KBs that IDAS was used with were created by hand; our experience showed that a domain KB for a machine with 50 subcomponents could be created in a few weeks by someone familiar with the system and knowledgeable in AI techniques (see section below, The Experiment). Two of our industrial collaborators, Inference Europe and Racal Instruments, developed a graphically oriented KB authoring tool that could be used by people less familiar with AI techniques. This tool, for example, used the terms Parts Stores and Family Trees, which are standard Racal terminology, instead of Is-a taxonomy and Part-of hierarchy (AI terminology); it also attempted to use some of Racal's standard presentation techniques for describing Parts Stores and Family Trees.

Unfortunately, the Inference/Racal authoring tool was not developed until fairly late in the project, and therefore it has not yet been used to construct a nontrivial IDAS KB. There was also a feeling that the authoring tool would be more useful if it could be used to build up a general-purpose design description that could be used for other tasks as well as document generation. As this article is being written, further research is being considered to extend the authoring tool in this manner and to investigate how it would best fit into the Racal design and documentation environment.

Operations

IDAS, like many other applied NLG systems (Reiter, 1994), generates texts in three stages: content determination, sentence planning, and surface realization.

Content determination. The basic-question, component, and user-task components of the question-space tuple are used to pick a *content-determination rule*. This rule specifies

- the basic structure of the response, i.e., the *schema* used to build it [see McKeown (1985), although our schemas have a somewhat different structure than McKeown's],
- the information from the KB that will be included in the response text, and
- hypertext follow-up buttons that will be displayed at the bottom of the response text (the idea is that information that is immediately relevant should be presented in the response text, while possibly relevant information should be accessible by clicking on a follow-up button).

We used a rule-based content-determination system in IDAS because we believed rules would be relatively easy for domain experts to create (Reiter & Mellish, 1993). The rule-based system was also very fast, which was important in ensuring acceptable response times.

Sentence planning. A Sentence Planning Language (SPL) (Kasper, 1989) expression (i.e., a semantic form) is constructed from the output of the content-determination system. This process is sensitive to the user-expertise and discourse components of the question-space tuple, and involves in particular,

- Aggregation (Dalianis & Hovy, 1993). This includes deciding how many sentences to use and which information should be conveyed by each sentence. This is currently done fairly simplistically; a more complex aggregation and optimization module was developed as an MSc project (Pake, 1992), but it was not reliable enough to be used in the main version of the system.
- Generating referring expressions. Pronouns were generated by a simplified version of the centering algorithm (Grosz et al., 1983); definite noun phrases were generated with the algorithm described by Reiter and Dale (1992).
- Choosing appropriate open-class lexical items (words). This was based on the ideas presented by Reiter (1991) and involved, for example, trying to use basic-level terms (Rosch, 1978) whenever possible.

Surface realization. The SPL term is converted into a surface form, that is, a set of words with formatting and hypertext annotations. This process involves

- Syntactic processing. The IDAS grammar is represented as a series of I1 classes, and classification is used to apply the grammar to the SPL produced by the sentence planner (Reiter & Mellish, 1992; Mellish, 1991). The IDAS grammar is small when compared with, for example, the NIGEL (Mann, 1983) or the SURGE (Elhadad, 1992) grammars, but it is adequate for IDAS's needs (remember that writing standards for technical documentation generally prohibit complex syntactic structures in any case).
- Morphology. Morphological processing in IDAS is again done with classification; some of the specific rules are taken from Ritchie et al. (1992). A morphological processor for Romanian (which is much more complex in morphological terms than English) was also built within the IDAS/I1 framework (Cristea, 1993).
- Postprocessing. This module handles capitalizing initial words of the sentence, inserting the right spacing around punctuation (e.g., *My dog (Spotty) is here*, not *My dog(Spotty)is here*), and other such details of the written form of English.

IDAS's NLG system was only designed to be able to generate small pieces of text (a few sentences, a paragraph at most). This was because IDAS's hypertext system enabled users to dynamically select the paragraphs they wish to read, that is, to perform their own high-level text planning (Levine et al., 1991), thereby eliminating the need for the generation system to perform such planning.

Example

Figure 1 shows several complete IDAS texts (including hypertext follow-up buttons). The texts are shown in a simple hypertext display system developed at Edinburgh; a more sophisticated hypertext delivery system was built by our industrial collaborators. The initial query was What-are-its-parts, asked about the complete ATE by a skilled-expertise person performing an operations task; this produces the text shown in Response 1. The underlined names (which are, in fact, referring expressions) are all mousable, as is ATE in the title question and the buttons on the bottom line. Response 2 shows how the system would respond to the same query issued under a naive user-expertise model. Note in particular, that the components described in Response 1 as the *DC power supply* and the *mains control unit* are described in Response 2 as the *black power supply* and the *silver power supply*. This is a consequence of the fact that naive users are not expected to have as rich a technical vocabulary as skilled users.

Response 3 was produced by clicking on *test head* in Response 1, and selecting What-is-it from a pop-up menu of basic questions; this response was generated using the same user-task, user-expertise, and discourse-in-focus question-space components as Response 1. The What-Operations-Rule content rule used to generate Response 3 specifies that Where-is-it and How-do-I-use-it should be added as hypertext follow-ups, so Where and Use buttons are presented below the text. Other questions, such as What-are-its-parts, can be asked by clicking on *test head* in the title question, and selecting from the pop-up menu. The Menu button allows the user to change the contextual models (user-task, user-expertise, etc). Response 4 shows the response for the same query under a Repair-Part task. More information is given in the response text (for example, a reorder Part-Number is included in the Repair-Part response but not the operations response), and also more follow-up buttons are created, for instance, Specs (specifications) are assumed to potentially be of interest to a maintenance engineer, but not to an operator.

Response 5 was obtained by clicking on Where; it answers *Where is the test head?* Response 6 comes from clicking on the Use button in Response 3; it is a response to *How do I use the test head?* In this response the underlined nouns *test head, ITA mechanism,* and *ITA* are all linked to pop-up menus of basic questions about these components, while the verbs *unlock, mount,* and *lock* are all linked to How-do-I-perform queries for the relevant action. Clicking on *unlock* produces Response 7, which presents a step-by-step decomposition of the action of unlocking the ITA mechanism. Response 8 was obtained by clicking on *lever* in Response 7 and selecting What-is-it from the pop-up menu.

Figure 2 shows a trace of IDAS generating Response 8 in Figure 1. The initial query can be textually represented as *What is the lever?,* but is represented internally as a What-is-it query about the Test-Head's Locking-Lever under the context of an operations task undertaken by a skilled user; the default discourse context is used.

```
; The initial query
; This is the 'What is the lever' query in Figure 1
Basic question is WHAT
Component is LLEVER-TEST-HEAD12
Task is OPERATIONS
User-model is SKILLED
Focus-list is NIL

; The output of content-determination
Schema function is
  (IDENTIFY-SCHEMA :BULLET? NIL :UNABBREVIATE? T)
Schema properties are ((COLOUR BLACK))
Followups are (WHERE)

; The output of sentence planning
SPL is

  (S1543 / IDENTITY
    :DOMAIN (LLEVER-TEST-HEAD12 /
              |locking lever| :PRONOUN YES)
    :RANGE (R1542 /
              |locking lever| :DETERMINER INDEFINITE
              :RELATIONS
               ((R1545 / |colour| :DOMAIN R1542
                 :RANGE (R1544 / BLACK)))))

; The output of surface realisation
It is a black locking lever.
```

Figure 2. A trace of Response 8 in Figure 1.

This input triggers the What-Operations-Rule content-determination rule. This specifies that text should be structured by the Identify-Schema (which basically means a single Is-a sentence will be generated), with no bulletization being performed, and with no abbreviations allowed (e.g., *digital multimeter* would be used instead of *DMM*). The text should directly inform the user that Llever-Test-Head12 has the property (Color Black), and Where-is-it should be presented as a hypertext follow-up button. What-Operations-Rule was also used to generate Response 3 in Figure 1. The difference between the information conveyed in Responses 3 and 8, and the follow-up buttons shown, is due to the presence/absence of knowledge in the KB; for example, the Use button is present in Response 3 but not in Response 8 because the KB does not have information about how people use levers.

This output is given to the sentence planner, which generates the SPL shown in Figure 2. (Our version of SPL differs from the original PENMAN version (Penman Natural Language Group, 1989). Note that the referring-expression module has decided to pronominalize the subject (i.e., :Domain filler), based on its discourse model and centering rules, and that the lexical choice module has decided to use the noun Locking Lever for Llever-Test-Head12, instead of just Lever.

The final stage is converting the SPL into a surface form, that is, the actual text. The output of the surface realization module is "It-is-a-black-locking-lever."

Each of the responses in Figure 1 was produced in less than 2 seconds on a SUN IPX (Sparc 2) workstation, measured from the initial click on a hypertext follow-up button to the appearance of the response box on the user's screen. Almost all IDAS responses are, in fact, produced within 2 seconds, and this seems acceptable to users.

Intermediate Techniques

Since not all of the benefits listed in the section The NLG Approach were deemed important in IDAS, we decided to search for generation techniques that "cheated" in certain ways and hence sacrificed some of the benefits listed in this section, but in return lowered some of the costs listed in the section Costs of NLG. If we could sacrifice benefits that were unimportant in IDAS and as a result decrease costs that were deemed quite important, this would make the system more useful and valuable. Reiter and Mellish (1993) describe our search for such intermediate techniques in more detail. In this article, we will just describe one such technique, the use of *hybrid action representations,* to give readers a feel for what an intermediate technique consists of and how it is motivated.

One of IDAS's tasks is to tell the user how to perform actions (e.g., Response 6 in Figure 1). IDAS can perform this in a "deep" manner by generating text from a case-frame representation of the action to be performed. It is, however, impractical to expect domain experts or technical authors, who in general have minimal experience with AI techniques, to create such case frames by hand. Such authors find writing text easier than building case frames, so the ideal solution would be to have the authors write text and then convert this text into case frames with an NL understanding system. Given the state of the art in NL understanding, it is difficult to reliably and unambiguously translate arbitrary texts into IDAS's internal case-frame notation, but some processing can certainly be done. This has led to the notion of hybrid action representations, which mix proper KB structures with canned-text fragments. The former represent pieces of the input text that the analysis system can confidently analyze, while the latter are used for unanalyzable portions of the text.

More specifically, we support two hybrid representations in IDAS: canned text with embedded KB references (EKR), and case frames with textual case fillers (TCF). In the EKR representation, references to machine components and other KB entities can be embedded in a canned-text action representation. The generation system then generates appropriate referring expressions for these references when it processes the EKR form (this is somewhat similar to the system described by Springer et al. (1991)). In the TCF representation, the IDAS case-frame representation is used, but case fillers are allowed to be canned text; these are then inserted into the generated sentences in appropriate positions. Examples of these representations are as follows.

Canned text: *Remove any connections to the board*

EKR: *Carefully slide* `[Board21]` *out along its guides*

TCF: `REMOVE(actor=User, actee=Board21, source=Instrument-Rack1, manner=`"*gently*")

Case frame: `PUT(actor=User, actee=Board21, destination=Faulty-Board-Tray3)`

Along with our industrial collaborators and an MSc student, we have developed authoring tools that can produce EKR or TCF representations from textual input; one of these tools also has some support for graphical authoring of actions (Marshall, 1992). Entering an EKR or TCF action specification with one of these tools (or indeed by hand) is usually quicker than manually building up a case-frame structure. It also requires less detailed knowledge of how information is represented in IDAS and I1. The cost of using these techniques is that some of the potential NLG benefits are lost. In particular, multilingual generation is impossible, and standards conformance cannot be guaranteed in the canned portions of the representation. On the other hand, a significant amount of tailoring can still be done in the noncanned portions of the text. Consistency between the design in the KB and the documentation text can still largely be guaranteed, and reduced costs may still be the case for document creation and maintenance. Some multimodality can also be introduced, that is, hypertext links can still be automatically added to referring expressions.

Thus, hybrid action representations reduce the cost of creating a domain KB for an NLG system, at the price of sacrificing some potential benefits (most notably multilingual generation and guaranteed standards conformance). Hybrid action representations are still superior to canned text, however, since they allow some amount of tailoring, make it easier to enforce consistency within and between documents and a machine-readable design database, allow hypertext links to be automatically added to texts, and so forth. Whether hybrid action representations are appropriate in a particular NLG application depends on the goals of that application and, in particular, which of the potential benefits of NLG are felt to be most important.

Some of the other intermediate techniques we developed in IDAS are described by Reiter and Mellish (1993). The basic idea is the same as presented above; the goal of intermediate techniques is to reduce the costs of using NLG by sacrificing NLG benefits that are not regarded as important in the current application.

```
A quoi sert le carburateur?
• Il contrôle l'arrivée d'air dans
le cylindre
• il contrôle l'arrivée d'essence
dans le gicleur.
MENU QUOI OU PIECES REGLER
```

```
Comment régler le carburateur?
Dévissez le papillon des gaz du
volet de départ. Jaugez la cuve de
pression.
MENU QUOI OU PIECES FONCTION
```

```
De quoi se compose le carburateur?
• La cuve de pression
• la pompe de reprise
• le gicleur
• le cylindre
• l'enrichisseur a 110
• le volet de départ.
MENU QUOI OU FONCTION REGLER
```

```
What is the purpose of the
carburettor?
• It controls the air intake in
the cylinder
• it controls the fuel intake in
the fuel duct.
MENU WHAT WHERE PARTS ADJUST
```

```
How do I adjust the carburettor?
Unscrew the starter cam's throttle
butterfly. Gauge the pressure
valve.
MENU WHAT WHERE PARTS PURPOSE
```

```
What are the components of the
carburettor?
• The pressure valve
• the pump
• the fuel duct
• the cylinder
• the rich fuel valve
• the starter cam.
MENU WHAT WHERE PURPOSE ADJUST
```

Figure 3. Bilingual system.

Multilingual IDAS

Ilona Bellos, an MSc student, built a variant of IDAS that could produce output in both French and English (Bellos, 1992), if no hybrid action representations were used in the KB (see previous section). A screen dump of the output of her system (Figure 3) shows three IDAS responses (in a KB documenting Renault cars instead of ATEs) in both French and English. The French responses appear above the corresponding English responses. The user switches between languages simply by changing the user-expertise model; this loads in an appropriate lexicon and grammar and also sets some flags for the sentence planner. Colin Dick, another MSc student, worked on a Turkish version of IDAS; and Dan Cristea, a visitor from Romania, built a morphology module for Romanian within the IDAS framework (Cristea, 1993).

Such a multilingual adaptation of an NLG system is not unusual; as Rösner (1992) points out, it has been common practice since NLG research began for generators to be adapted to produce output in multiple languages.

EVALUATION

User Trials

We were not able to perform any evaluation of IDAS using the ATE KB, for various reasons. We were, however, able to perform some user-effectiveness trials with another KB that we built, which described a racing bicycle. The results of this evaluation are reported in this section. Only a small number of people (three) were tested in the trials, so the results should be considered as suggestive rather than statistically significant.

The Experiment

Three subjects, none of whom had much previous knowledge of bicycles, were asked to carry out the evaluation exercise. The exercise had three parts, as follows.

1. Subjects were given instructions on how to use IDAS and shown how to navigate around the question-space.
2. Subjects were asked to answer 15 questions about the bicycle, using information obtained from IDAS. Example questions include

- What is the cost of the front brake cable?
- Imagine that you are selling this bicycle to someone who does not know how to use the gear levers. Use IDAS to find out how this is done, and then explain this in your own words to the customer.
- True or false, the front wheel has fewer spokes than the back wheel?

Subjects were timed, and all queries they issued to IDAS were recorded.

3. Subjects were asked to complete a questionnaire that asked for both general opinions about IDAS and specific suggestions for how it might be improved.

The bicycle KB, incidentally, described about 50 components of the bicycle and was constructed (by hand) in about 2 weeks by a person who was familiar with IDAS but had not previously constructed any IDAS KBs.

Analysis of Subjects' Performance

The general result of the evaluation exercise was encouraging; out of 45 total responses, there were only 2 mistakes. One involved a misinterpretation of the phrase *It is a Cinelli Super Record saddle;* the subject thought that Cinelli Super Record was the name of the manufacturer, whereas in fact, Cinelli was the name of the manufacturer and Super Record was the saddle's model name. The other mistake involved an incorrect description of how the gear levers worked; the relevant information was in this case being communicated unambiguously by IDAS, but it probably would have been easier to understand if accompanied by a diagram.

It was also encouraging that users managed to navigate through IDAS's hyperspace very efficiently, despite not having much experience with the system. Of the 132 queries issued to IDAS by the users, the following results were found.

- 57 (43%) conveyed information needed to respond to a question.
- 29 (22%) were intermediate nodes that a user had to pass through in order to get to an information-presenting node.
- 27 (20%) were unnecessary and did not contribute to responding to a question.
- 19 (15%) were repeats of a previous query.

Subjects were not asked to attempt to minimize the number of queries, and some of the "unnecessary" queries were, in fact, due to subjects randomly browsing through the KB. An analysis of the remaining unnecessary queries suggests that many were due to the fact that the subjects were unfamiliar with IDAS in general and the bicycle KB in particular. Experienced IDAS users would presumably be more efficient in their use of the system.

Subjects in some cases went down a wrong path in hyperspace when attempting to get information but in all cases managed to quickly recover. Subjects were also able to combine information from several IDAS queries in a single multisentence response. This supports the claim [see Levine et al. (1991), Reiter et al. (1992), and the section, Operations] that it is sufficient for IDAS to generate short responses and rely on the user to be able to put them together as necessary.

In summary, there is clearly room for improvement in both the way IDAS uses text to present information, and in its use of hypertext mechanisms. Nevertheless, the system's performance seems to be quite reasonable. The fact that subjects answered 95% of the questions correctly suggests that, in the great majority of cases, IDAS is presenting information in a clear and accessible manner. The fact that only one-third of the queries were unnecessary indicates that subjects in most cases managed to navigate around IDAS's hyperspace without excessive difficulty.

Subject's Comments

After completing the exercise, subjects were asked for comments and suggestions about IDAS. In general, the comments were quite favorable and supportive. More specifically, some of the responses were as follows.

- There were several complaints about the details of the IDAS hypertext interface (use of mouse buttons, positioning of windows, etc). These problems could easily be fixed by building a better user interface.
- Some subjects wanted to be able to ask more questions (e.g., *how does it work?*).
- Subjects commented that IDAS's texts were very concise but, in general, agreed that this was appropriate in the context of helping users perform specific tasks (as opposed to teaching them general information about a bicycle).
- Subjects felt that finding information by searching through IDAS's question-space (hyperspace) was quicker and easier than finding it in paper documentation.
- Subjects commented that having some graphics output (in particular, a picture of the bicycle) would have been useful (the version of IDAS used in the evaluation trial was not able to display diagrams of any kind).

Industrial Reaction

In addition to the quantitative user-evaluation trials, we also solicited informal reactions and comments from our industrial collaborators, and from interested people in other industrial R&D establishments. Although these are not as rigorous as the data from our user-evaluation trials, they are valuable in helping to answer broader questions, including in particular, what potential benefits of NLG are most likely to be useful in the real world.

These reactions can perhaps best be summarized by going over the benefits described in the section above, The NLG Approach. The following are reconstructed comments from many people over the course of numerous meetings and demonstrations; we are not claiming that they represent any opinion except our own.

Reduced Cost

In retrospect, we underestimated the cost of building a KB that can support NLG. This is not a cheap endeavor, and it may be unrealistic to hope that its cost will be less than the cost of simply writing documentation directly. Even if some information can be extracted from an existing database or KB (e.g., a CAD system), additional information will almost certainly be required for NLG, and entering it will not be cheap. No existing CAD system that we are aware of, for example, includes the kind of design rationale information that an NLG system would need in order to be able to respond to a What-is-its-purpose question (which was one of IDAS's basic questions).

It may, however, be more realistic to expect that the NLG approach can reduce the cost of document maintenance, even if it does not reduce the cost of initial document creation. Document maintenance can be a larger proportion of total life-cycle cost than initial document production. By document maintenance, we primarily mean the cost of updating documentation when the hardware being documented changes, not the cost of fixing spelling and grammatical errors. Once the initial machine design has been entered into the CAD or KR systems, many of the most common changes to that design (e.g., a new configuration or an upgraded component) can be made fairly easily and in a manner that can be well supported by authoring tools such as the one developed by our industrial collaborators (see section above, Knowledge Base). Making changes in this manner and then re-generating the documentation may well be more economical than revising the documentation by hand.

Many of the enhanced maintenance advantages of the IDAS NLG system, however, were also present in the object-oriented canned-text system, which also supported creating new configurations and upgrading components in existing configurations. So, while maintenance is extremely important and should be kept in mind for all documentation systems, it is hard to claim that it is a particular benefit of NLG systems. At least in the ATE domain, most of the benefits we observed could be obtained simply by building an object-oriented KB that can represent Is-a and Part-of hierarchies of components, and then associating canned texts with the objects represented in this KB.

Perhaps a more promising way of justifying the expense of creating a KB is to ensure that the design knowledge it contains is used in many ways, not just for document generation. If KB authoring is thought of merely as a replacement for document authoring, then indeed it might seem to require unreasonable resources. However, if the knowledge base + NLG architecture is presented as a solution to a wider need to design, reason about, and present products, and if this can be integrated with the normal product development process, then it looks much more attractive. In a follow-on project to IDAS (Levine & Mellish, 1994), we are hoping to evolve our authoring tool into a general requirements capture tool to be used by engineers right from the start of the design process. In such a situation, we hope that the cost of a small amount of extra authoring (largely collaborative) will be amply repaid by advantages gained by a number of sections of the company.

Another point that was raised in our discussions was that it was desirable to have a single tool capture both the "normal" design information, and the "extra" information needed for NLG or other knowledge-based processing. This may require more work from the design engineer than just entering design information and letting someone else enter documentation-related information. However, the total amount of effort will be less with an integrated tool, and there will be far fewer opportunities for inconsistencies. Also, if the KB is being used to support many kinds of reasoning, it may be hard in any case to make a clear distinction between design and extra information.

In summary, we would now be cautious about claiming that generating documentation from a KB will reduce direct document-creation costs if a special KB has to be created for the NLG system. Cost reduction is perhaps only likely if most of the information needed for NLG can be extracted from information that is being used for other purposes, and cost reduction may be more likely for document maintenance than initial document creation.

Consistency

Ensuring that a document is in fact consistent with a design is a very important benefit to industry, and one that we did not fully appreciate when we started IDAS. It is difficult to ensure that the design described in a human-readable text document is the same as the design described in a machine-readable design database, and this problem becomes especially severe when a document is being updated (e.g., to reflect changes in the hardware), and the document updater is not the original document author. Furthermore, inaccuracies in documentation are very worrisome to companies because they can cause customers to become annoyed and consider switching to another supplier, and because they may result in a company being legally liable if customers misuse a product. Our discussions suggested that many companies might be willing to accept higher costs for document production if the resultant documents had fewer inaccuracies. Increased document accuracy may be, in fact, one of the most important potential benefits of using NLG to produce technical documentation. Indeed, for some applications, accuracy is much more important than the quality of the text.

Guaranteed Conformance to Standards

Ensuring that a document conforms to relevant standards is another important potential benefit of NLG that we did not initially appreciate, and that proved to be extremely important to many of the industrial people we talked to. Writing standards, in particular, can seem unnatural to human authors [e.g., AECMA Simplified English (AECMA, 1986) prohibits *Test the power supply* and requires *Do a test on the power supply,* instead], and training authors to obey the standards can be a nontrivial task. With NLG systems, however, the relevant standard can simply be incorporated into the system's grammar, lexicon, and planning rules, and then all output will be guaranteed to meet the standard. Indeed, it is probably easier to generate Simplified English than full English because many of the syntactic, lexical, and other choices that have to be made when generating full English are already specified in the Simplified English standard. Hence the NLG system does not have to worry about them.

One thing that was clear from talking to our industrial contacts, incidentally, is that no one wanted systems that produced linguistically complex output. All potential users we talked to preferred to have technical documentation presented as simply as possible; the use of complex syntactic or lexical constructions, which has been the focus of much academic research, was considered a minus, not a plus.

Multilinguality

Producing documents in several languages from a single-domain KB is certainly technically possible (Hovy et al., 1992), and indeed a bilingual French/English version of IDAS was built by one of our MSc students (see section above, Multilingual IDAS). Perhaps the main disadvantage of multilingual generation (in addition to the need to create multiple lexicons and grammars) is that it disallows the use of hybrid action representations and similar, otherwise useful intermediate techniques (see section above, Intermediate Techniques). All knowledge to be communicated must be properly encoded in the underlying deep representation, and this can make the domain KB authoring task more difficult.

The level of interest in multilingual generation varied greatly among our industrial contacts. Some people (especially those working for firms that produced consumer goods) thought this was potentially very valuable. People working for aerospace and other heavy industrial firms, however, often felt that a better way to reach international customers was to produce documents in Simplified English (AECMA, 1986) and similar English dialects that are designed to be easily readable by nonnative speakers. The cost of generating documents in multiple languages is not zero, after all. Even if a proper KB exists, it will probably still be necessary for human editors and quality-assurance personnel to check the translated documents before they are sent out to customers.

There are also cases where multilingual output is required by law. This is part of the justification of the FoG weather-report-generation system (Goldberg et al., 1994) (weather reports in Canada must be distributed in both French and English).

Tailoring

One of the initial goals of IDAS was to be able to tailor its output to different kinds of users, including operators, maintenance engineers, and programmers. There has been a substantial amount of research in user-tailoring in the NLG community (e.g., Paris, 1988; McCoy, 1988; Wilensky et al., 1988; Breuker, 1990). Following this research and incorporating some ideas of our own, we built into IDAS separate user-task, user-expertise, and discourse models. As a result, in some cases, perhaps 50 different responses could potentially be produced for 1 query, depending on the value of these contextual parameters.

Unfortunately, it turned out that such a high degree of variability was *not* desirable for our industrial collaborators because it made quality assurance more difficult and expensive. All responses generated by our system would need to be examined by the quality-assurance department before our system could be sent to customers, and having 50 variants of a response made that task 50 times more difficult. A small number of variations was thus perhaps useful, but utilizing a rich fine-grained contextual model to produce many response variants was definitely not desirable.

We also observed that IDAS users often used the hypertext follow-up mechanism to clarify terms or actions they did not understand; they simply clicked on unfamiliar words or actions, and in most cases got sufficient information from the follow-up text to enable them to continue with their original task (even though IDAS hypertext follow-ups were not originally designed or intended to serve as a glossary or term-explanation mechanism). Many commercial on-line help systems, of course, use hypertext in this way; the user clicks on a word he or she does not understand, and a glossary entry or new help window appears. The hypertext approach both gives the user more direct control over what he or she sees, and also avoids the quality-assurance costs of the text-modifying tailoring that we performed in IDAS. In many applications, hypertext mechanisms may turn out to be the most appropriate technique for supporting users with different tasks and expertise levels.

One final point is that most of the people from industry whom we talked to (besides our direct industrial collaborators) did not seem very interested in tailoring responses, perhaps because they were more interested in cutting the life-cycle costs of documentation (e.g., including maintenance, translation, and editing for standards conformance) than in improving documentation effectiveness.

Multimodality

Both our discussions and our user-effectiveness trials emphasized that any useful technical documentation-generation system *must* be able to produce output that includes visual formatting, hypertext links, and diagrams whenever appropriate (and when allowed by the medium). A system that generates technical documentation that consists only of a sequence of words and sentences may be an interesting academic exercise, but it is unlikely to be useful in real applications.

IDAS did produce hypertext; this was one of its original design goals. Indeed, our experience has been that if one is going to all the trouble to generate NL text from a KB, adding hypertext follow-up links to this text is a relatively low-cost increment to the basic NLG system (Reiter et al., 1992). IDAS can also use some visual formatting devices; this capability is not as extensive as it should be, but the proper use of such formatting devices is an underresearched area in NLG.

The Edinburgh IDAS system is not able to perform any kind of graphic generation, although one version of the system can display canned bitmaps in response to certain queries. This is a definite weakness of the system, and an automatic technical documentation-generation system that is used in real applications may need to possess more sophisticated graphics abilities. There has been some research on combining text and graphics generation (e.g., Feiner & McKeown, 1990; Wahlster et al., 1993), but this work has tended to stress very "principled" methods, which may be too costly (in terms of both the amount of domain knowledge and the amount of computer time required) to be practical in realistically sized systems. Further research probably needs to be done on "cheaper" ways of combining text and graphics generation.

LESSONS LEARNED

Perhaps the most important lessons we have learned from IDAS are the following.

- Document production should, as much as possible, utilize information in existing design (and other) databases; if more information is needed, it should ideally be useful for other purposes in addition to document generation (e.g., consistency checks). The capture of the necessary information, and the production of documents, should be an integral part of the design environment.
- The output text should be kept as linguistically simple as possible, with relevant writing and content standards being followed. Graphical mechanisms (including visual formatting and hypertext input as well as diagram production) should be used when they are appropriate.
- Automatic document generation is probably best justified in terms of guaranteeing consistency of documents with the actual designs, guaranteeing that relevant standards are followed, and simplifying the process of updating documents to reflect changes in the documented hardware. It may be more difficult to justify automatic document generation on the basis of reducing the costs of initially creating a document.
- Multimodal techniques (such as automatic insertion of hypertext links) hold promise as a way of increasing the effectiveness of generated documentation; user-tailoring may be less promising, unless a way can be found to solve the quality-assurance problem.

In conclusion, we believe that there is great potential in using natural-language generation to automate the process of producing technical documentation, if the developers of such systems have a clear idea of the costs and benefits of NLG and, hence, of the niches in which it might most usefully be applied. The technology is not a panacea that will instantly cut document-production costs to zero, but when used appropriately, it has great promise in reducing the total life-cycle costs of documentation, in making documentation more accurate and effective, and in enabling design engineers to spend more of their time on designing and less on documenting.

REFERENCES

AECMA. 1986. *A guide for the preparation of aircraft maintenance documentation in the international aerospace maintenance language*. Derby, UK: BDC Publishing Services.

Allen, J., and C. R. Perrault. 1980. Analyzing intention in utterances. *Artificial Intelligence* 15:143–78.

Bateman, J., and C. Paris. 1989. Phrasing a text in terms the user can understand. In *Proceedings of the 11th international joint conference on artificial intelligence, IJCAI-1989*, vol. 2, pp. 1511–17. Cambridge, Mass.: MIT Press.

Bellos, I. 1992. Towards a multilingual IDAS. Master's thesis, Department of Artificial Intelligence, University of Edinburgh, Edinburgh, Scotland.

Brachman, R., and J. Schmolze. 1985. An overview of the KL-ONE knowledge representation system. *Cognitive Science* 9:171–216.

Breuker, J., ed. 1990. *EUROHELP: Developing intelligent help systems*. Technical report on the P280 ESPRIT project EUROHELP. Department of Social Science Informatics, University of Amsterdam.

Carenini, G., F. Pianesi, M. Ponzi, and O. Stock. 1993. Natural language generation and hypertext access. *Applied Artificial Intelligence* 7:135–64.

Cristea, D. 1993. Romanian morphological generation through classification. Department of Computer Science, University "A1.I.Cuza" of Iasi, Romania.

Dalianis, H., and E. Hovy. 1993. Aggregation in natural language generation. In *Proceedings of the fourth European workshop on natural language generation*, pp. 67–78.

Elhadad, M. 1992. Using argumentation to control lexical choice: A functional unification implementation. PhD thesis, Columbia University, New York.

Feiner, S., and K. McKeown. 1990. Coordinating text and graphics in explanation generation. In *Proceedings of the 8th national conference on artificial intelligence, AAAI-1990*, vol. 1, pp. 442–49. Cambridge, Mass.: MIT Press.

Goldberg, E., N. Driedger, and R. Kittredge. 1994. Using natural-language processing to produce weather forecasts. *IEEE Expert* 9(2):45–53.

Goodman, K., and S. Nirenburg, eds. 1991. *The KBMT project: A case study in knowledge-based machine translation*. San Mateo, Calif.: Morgan Kaufmann.

Grosz, B., A. Joshi, and S. Weinstein. 1983. Providing a unified account of definite noun phrases in discourse. In *Proceedings of the 21st annual meeting of the Association for Computational Linguistics, ACL-1983, Cambridge, Mass.*, pp. 44–50. Association for Computational Linguistics. Available from MIT Press.

Grosz, B., and C. Sidner. 1986. Attention, intention, and the structure of discourse. *Computational Linguistics* 12:175–206.

Hayes, P., and J. Pepper. 1989. Towards an integrated maintenance advisor. In *Hypertext 1989 proceedings, Pittsburgh*, pp. 119–27. New York: Association for Computing Machinery. Cambridge, Mass.: MIT Press.

Hovy, E., and Y. Arens. 1991. Automatic generation of formatted text. In *Proceedings of ninth national conference on artificial intelligence (AAAI-1991)*, pp. 92–97.

Hovy, E., R. Kittredge, C. Matthiessen, S. Nirenburg, and D. Rösner. 1992. Multilinguality and generation. In *Aspects of automated natural language generation: Proceedings of the sixth international natural language generation workshop*, pp. 293–308. Edited by R. Dale et al. Lecture Notes in Artificial Intelligence 587. New York: Springer-Verlag.

Isabelle, P., and L. Bourbeau. 1985. TAUM-AVIATION: Its technical features and some experimental results. *Computational Linguistics* 11:18–27.

Kasper, R. 1989. A flexible interface for linking applications to Penman's sentence generator. In *Proceedings of the 1989 DARPA speech and natural language workshop, Philadelphia*, pp. 153–58. Marina del Ray, Calif.: USC/Information Sciences Institute.

Levine, J., A. Cawsey, C. Mellish, L. Poynter, E. Reiter, P. Tyson, and J. Walker. 1991. IDAS: Combining hypertext and natural language generation. In *Proceedings of the third European workshop on natural language generation, Innsbruck, Austria*, pp. 55–62. Department of Artificial Intelligence, University of Edinburgh.

Levine, J., and C. Mellish. 1994. CORECT: Combining CSCW with natural language generation for collaborative requirements capture. In *Proceedings of the seventh international workshop on natural language generation (INLGW-1994)*, pp. 236–39. Department of Artificial Intelligence, University of Edinburgh.

Mann, W. 1983. An overview of the NIGEL text generation grammar. In *Proceedings of the 21st annual meeting of the Association for Computational Linguistics (ACL-1983)*, pp. 79–84. Association for Computational Linguistics. Available from MIT Press.

Marshall, S. 1992. The IDAS action authoring tool. Master's thesis, Department of Artificial Intellligence, University of Edinburgh, Edinburgh, Scotland.

McCoy, K. 1988. Reasoning on a highlighted user model to respond to misconceptions. *Computational Linguistics* 14(3):52–63.

McKeown, K. 1985. *Text generation*. New York: Cambridge University Press.

Mellish, C. 1991. Approaches to realization in natural language generation. In *Natural language and speech*. Edited by E. Klein and F. Veltman. New York: Springer-Verlag.

Moore, J., and W. Swartout. 1990. Pointing: A way toward explanation dialogue. In *Proceedings of the eighth national conference on artificial intelligence (AAAI-1990)*, pp. 457–64. Cambridge, Mass.: MIT Press.

Pake, M. 1992. An optimiser for an SPL based text generator. Master's thesis, Department of Artificial Intelligence, University of Edinburgh, Edinburgh, Scotland.

Paris, C. 1988. Tailoring object descriptions to the user's level of expertise. *Computational Linguistics* 14(3):64–78.

Penman Natural Language Group. 1989. The Penman user guide. Technical Report, Information Sciences Institute, Marina del Rey, California.

Pym, P. 1993. Perkins engines and publications. Paper presented at Technology and Language in Europe 2000: The UK Perspective, London, January 1993.

Reiter, E. 1991. A new model of lexical choice for nouns. *Computational Intelligence* 7(4):240–51.

Reiter, E. 1994. Has a consensus NL Generation architecture appeared, and is it psycholinguistically plausible? In *Proceedings of the seventh international workshop on natural language generation (INLGW-1994)*, pp. 163–70. Department of Computing Science, University of Aberdeen.

Reiter, E., and R. Dale. 1992. A fast algorithm for the generation of referring expressions. In *Proceedings of the fourteenth international conference on computational linguistics (COLING-1992)*, vol. 1, pp. 232–38. Association for Computational Linguistics. Available from MIT Press.

Reiter, E., and C. Mellish. 1992. Using classification to generate text. In *Proceedings of the 30th annual meeting of the Association for Computational Linguistics (ACL-1992)*, pp. 265–72. Association for Computational Linguistics. Available from MIT Press.

Reiter, E., and C. Mellish. 1993. Optimising the costs and benefits of natural language generation. In *Proceedings of the 13th international joint conference on artificial intelligence (IJCAI-1993)*, vol. 2, pp. 1164–69. San Mateo, Calif.: Morgan Kaufmann.

Reiter, E., C. Mellish, and J. Levine. 1992. Automatic generation of on-line documentation in the IDAS project. In *Proceedings of the third conference on applied natural language processing (ANLP-1992), Trento, Italy*, pp. 64–71.

Ritchie, G., G. Russell, A. Black, and S. Pulman. *Computational morphology: Practical mechanisms for the English lexicon*. Cambridge, Mass.: MIT Press.

Rosch, E. 1978. Principles of categorization. In *Cognition and categorization*, pp. 27–48. Edited by E. Rosch and B. Lloyd. Hillsdale, N.J.: Lawrence Erlbaum.

Rösner, D. 1992. Remarks on multilinguality and generation. In *Aspects of automated natural language generation: Proceedings of the sixth international natural language generation workshop*, pp. 306–308. Edited by R. Dale et al. Lecture Notes in Artificial Intelligence 587. New York: Springer-Verlag.

Roth, S., J. Mattis, and X. Mesnard. 1991. Graphics and natural language as components of automatic explanation. In *Intelligent user interfaces*, pp. 207–39. Edited by J. Sullivan and S. Tyler. Reading, Mass.: ACM Press.

Springer, S., P. Buta, and T. Wolf. 1991. Automatic letter composition for customer service. In *Innovative applications of artificial intelligence 3 (Proceedings of CAIA-1991)*. Edited by R. Smith and C. Scott. Menlo Park, Calif.: AAAI Press. Available from MIT Press.

Wahlster, W., E. André, W. Finkler, H.-J. Profitlich, and T. Rist. 1993. Plan-based integration of natural language and graphics generation. *Artificial Intelligence* 63:387–427.

Wilensky, R., D. Chin, M. Luria, J. Martin, J. Mayfield, and D. Wu. 1988. The Berkeley UNIX consultant project. *Computational Linguistics* 14(4):35–85.

Reflections on. . .

Automatic Generation of Technical Documentation

Ehud Reiter, Chris Mellish, and John Levine

It is difficult to precisely quantify IDAS's contributions, but certainly many ideas that were new and unusual in IDAS are now widely accepted in the natural language generation (NLG) field. These include

- using simple "intermediate" techniques, justified by an analysis of the requirements of the application; see (Reiter 1995) for more recent work comparing different techniques.
- generating dynamic hypertext instead of linear text. Knott et al. (1996) gives some pointers to more recent work on generating dynamic hypertext.
- using NLG to generate technical documentation. More recent projects include GhostWriter (Marchant, Cerbah, and Mellish 1996) and CogentHelp (White and Caldwell 1997).

An important lesson of IDAS was that it is essential to minimize the cost of building the domain knowledge base (KB). Newer systems such as CogentHelp place much more emphasis than IDAS on extracting information from existing sources and providing good authoring tools. Another approach is to use the same KB for many tasks, so users are more willing to spend time building it. The CORECT system (Levine et al. 1996), for example, uses the KB to support requirements capture, solution design, and consistency checking as well as NLG.

A perhaps less successful aspect of IDAS was its extensive contextual tailoring of texts, based on models of the user's expertise, the user's task, and the discourse context. As we describe in the paper, the IDAS evaluation showed that detailed contextual tailoring was less useful than we had hoped and perhaps did not offer much advantage over giving users nontailored texts with plenty of hyperlinks that users could follow to get additional information or explanations. We have continued in subsequent years to work on automatic user tailoring of generated texts, but we have focused on applications where the system's goal is more complex than simply assisting the user, and hence (we believe) explicit tailoring cannot be replaced by user-controlled hypertext clicks. Examples of this work include the ILEX museum information system (Knott et al. 1996) and a new project to generate tailored smoking cessation letters (Reiter et al. 1997).

REFERENCES

Knott, A.; Mellish, C.; Oberlander, O; and O'Donnell, M. 1996. Sources of Flexibility in Dynamic Hypertext Generation. In *Proceedings of the Eighth International Natural Language Generation Workshop*, 151–160.

Levine, J.; Rogers, I.; Bennington, A.; and Pattison, C. 1996. Class Hierarchies as a Multi-Purpose Knowledge Representation in a Requirements Capture and Design Tool. In Nealon, J., and Hunt, J. (eds.), *Proceedings of Expert Systems 96, Technical Stream*, 255–272. Cambridge, England: SGES Publications.

Marchant, B.; Cerbah, F.; and Mellish, C. 1996. The GhostWriter Project: A Demonstration of the Use of AI Techniques in the Production of Technical Publications. In Macintosh, A. and Cooper, C. (eds.), *Proceedings of Expert Systems 96, Application Stream*, 9–25. Cambridge, England: SGES Publications.

Reiter, E. 1995. NLG vs. Templates. In *Proceedings of the Fifth European Workshop on Natural Language Generation*, 95–105.

Reiter, E.; Cawsey, A.; Osman, L.; and Roff, Y. 1997. Knowledge Acquisition for Content Selection. In *Proceedings of the Sixth European Workshop on Natural Language Generation*, 117–126.

White, M., and Caldwell, D. 1997. CogentHelp: NLG Meets SE in a Tool for Authoring Dynamically Generated On-Line Help. In *Proceedings of the Fourth Conference on Applied Natural-Language Processing*, 257–264.

Chapter 12

On the Knowledge Underlying Multimedia Presentations

Yigal Arens, Eduard Hovy, and Mira Vossers[1]

Abstract

We address one of the problems at the heart of automated multimedia presentation production and interpretation. The media allocation problem can be stated as follows: how does the producer of a presentation determine which information to allocate to which medium, and how does a perceiver recognize the function of each part as displayed in the presentation and integrate them into a coherent whole? What knowledge is used, and what processes? We describe the four major types of knowledge that play a role in the allocation problem as well as interdependencies that hold among them. We discuss two formalisms that can be used to represent this knowledge and, using examples, describe the kinds of processing required for the media allocation problem.

1. The General Problem of Presentations Using Multiple Media

When communicating, people almost always employ multiple media. Even natural language, which is after all the most powerful representational medium developed by humankind, is usually augmented by pictures, diagrams, etc., when written, or by gestures, hand and eye movements, intonational variations, etc., when spoken. And this preference for multimedia carries over to communication with computational systems, as evidenced by the explosive growth of the field of Human-Computer Interfaces. Since the early dream of Artificial Intelligence – of creating fully autonomous intelligent agents that would interact with people as equals – has proved impossible to achieve in the near term, the thrust of much AI work is on the construction of semi-intelligent machines operating in close symbiosis with humans, forming units. For maximum ease of communication within such units, natural language and other human-oriented media are the prime candidates (after all, computers are easier to program than humans are).

How then can computers construct and analyze such multimedia presentations? A survey of the literature on the design of presentations (book design, graphic illustration, etc., see [Tufte 1990; Bertin 1983; Tufte 1983]) underscores how this area of communication remains an art and shows how hard it is to describe the rules that govern presentations. But people clearly do follow rules when they use several media to construct communications; textbooks, for example, are definitely not illustrated randomly. Psychologists have been studying multimedia issues such as the effects of pictures in text, design principles for multimedia presentation, etc. for many years [Hartley 1985; Twyman 1985; Dwyer 1978; Fleming and Levie 1978], although most of their results are too general to be directly applicable in work that is to be computationalized. On the other hand, cognitive science studies of the past few years have provided results which can be incorporated into theories about good multimedia design [Petre and Green 1990; Roth and Mattis 1990a; Mayer 1989; Larkin and Simon 1987]. They address questions such as whether graphical notations are really superior to text, what makes a picture worth (sometimes) a thousand words, how illustration affects thinking, the characterization of data, etc.

Artificial Intelligence (AI) researchers and other computer scientists have been addressing aspects of the problem of automatically constructing multimedia presentations as well. Mackinlay [1986a] describes the automatic generation of a variety of tables and charts; the WIP system [Wahlster et al. 1991b; André et al., this volume; André and Rist, this volume] plans a text/graphics description of the use of an espresso machine, starting with a database of facts about the machine and appropriate communicative goals, and using text and presentation plans. The COMET system [Feiner 1991; Feiner and McKeown 1990b] plans text/graphic presentations of a military radio using text schemas and pictorial perspective presentation rules. The TEXPLAN [Maybury 1991a,

[1]The first author was supported in part by Rome Laboratory of the Air Force Systems Command and the Defense Advanced Research Projects Agency under contract no. F30602-91-C-0081. The second author was supported in part by Rome Laboratory of the Air Force Systems Command under RL contract no. FQ7619-89-03326-0001. The third author, a graduate student at the University of Nijmegen, Nijmegen, The Netherlands, spent six months at USC/ISI and has since graduated. Views and conclusions contained in this report are the authors' and should not be interpreted as representing the official opinion or policy of DARPA, RL, the U.S. Government, or any person or agency connected with them.

this volume] and AIMI [Burger and Marhsall 1991, this volume] systems plan text/map/table presentations of military information, also using presentation plans. Similarly, the INTEGRATED INTERFACES system [Arens et al. 1988] and the CUBRICON system [Neal 1990] plan and produce presentations involving maps, text, and menus. Other work is reported in the collections [Sullivan and Tyler 1991; Ortony et al. 1992].

One lesson that is clear from all this work is the need for a detailed study of the major types of knowledge required for multimedia presentations, encoded in a formalism that supports both their analysis and generation. For the past few years, we have been involved in various studies of one aspect or another of this problem. In particular, we ask: why and how do people apportion the information to be presented to various media? And how do they reassemble the portions into a single message again? This paper contains an overview of some of our results. Section 2 describes our methodology and formalisms. Section 3 provides details about the features and their interdependencies that we have managed to collect, and Section 4 provides some examples of the use of this knowledge.

2. Our Approach and Methodology

2.1. The Problem of Media Allocation

In order to focus our efforts, we have concentrated on the media allocation problem: given arbitrary information and any number of media, how, and on what basis, is a particular medium selected for the display of each portion of the information? This question, a particularization of the question why people use different media and other gestures and movements when they communicate, in our opinion lies at the heart of the general multimedia issue.

Rather than start with a literature study, we here describe the problem from the computational side. In most systems, the media allocation problem is addressed simply by the use of fixed rules that specify exactly what medium is to be used for each particular data type. This is clearly not a satisfactory solution, given the inflexibility and non-portability of such systems. Our approach is a *two-stage generalization* of this straightforward approach. We take an example from a hypothetical data base about ships in a Navy to illustrate. Under the straightforward approach, a typical rule may be:

1. Ships' locations are presented on maps.

Our first generalization is to assign a medium not to each data type, but instead to each feature that characterizes data types. Thus instead of rule 1, we write the rule:

1. Data duples (of which ships' locations are an example) are presented on maps, graphs, or tables.

Of course, when considering subsets of features, one invariably gets under-specific rules. To provide more specificity we formulate such additional rules as:

2. Data with spatial denotations (such as locations) are presented on media with spatial denotations (such as maps).

However, note that this rule deals not with the medium of maps but instead with a characteristic of this medium. It suggests the second step of the generalization.

The second generalization is to assign characteristics of data not to media, but instead to characteristics of media. The two example rules now become:

1'. Data duples (of which locations are an example) are presented on planar media (such as graphs, tables, and maps).

2'. Data with spatial denotations (such as locations) are presented on media with spatial denotations (such as maps).

In this example, the two rules together suffice to specify maps uniquely as the appropriate medium for location coordinates. Of course, though, one can present the same information using natural language, as in "*the ship is at 15N 79E*". Thus one is led to rephrase rule 2' to arrive at a more general but very powerful formulation:

2" Data with specific denotations are presented on media which can convey the same denotations.

Since language, pictures, and maps can carry spatial denotations (while, say, graphs or histograms usually do not), we once again require additional rules in order to specify a unique medium. However, since each of the three mentioned media can be perfectly suitable in the right context, the rules we formulate might not absolutely prohibit a medium; rather, the rules should be context-dependent in ways which enable the selection of the most appropriate medium. Thus we are led to rules such as:

3. If more than one medium can be used, and there is an existing presentation, prefer the medium/a that is/are already present as exhibits in the presentation.

4. If more than one media can be used, and there is additional information to be presented as well, prefer medium/a that can accommodate the other information too.

Rule 4 has important consequences. If one is to present not only the location of a ship, but also its heading, then both language and a map would do, since both media have facilities for indicating direction (in the case of language, an appositive phrase with the value *"heading SSW"* and in the case of a map, an icon with an elongation or an arrow). If in addition to this now one adds the requirement to present the nationality of the ship, natural language has such a capability (the adjective *"Swiss"*, say) but due to limitations of the map medium, one of the icon's independent characteristics (say, its color) must be allocated to convey nationality. Of course, this requires the addition of a description of the meaning of the different values the icon's independent characteristic can have (for example, a table of color for nationality). Such additional presentational overhead makes a map a less attractive medium than natural language for presenting a single ship's location/heading/nationality (though possibly not that of several ships together).

We formalize and discuss this point later in more detail. Here it is enough to note that the two-stage generalizations provide collections of rules that relate characteristics of information and characteristics of media in service of good multimedia presentations. In general terms, the medium allocation algorithm required can be described as a constraint satisfaction system, where the constraints arise from rules requiring the features of the information to be presented (i.e., the data) to be matched up optimally with the features of the media at hand.

2.2. The Four Types of Knowledge Required

We illustrated the use of knowledge about media and information type. But what additional factors play a role in multimedia communication?

In our previous work in multimedia human-computer interactions [Arens et al. 1993; Vossers 1991; Hovy and Arens 1991; Hovy 1990a; Arens and Hovy 1990a,b], we addressed this question from several angles, trying to build up a library of terms that capture all the factors that play a role in multimedia human-human and human-computer communication. Drawing from an extensive survey of literature from Psychology, Human-Computer Interfaces, Natural Language Processing, Linguistics, Human Factors, and Cognitive Science, (see [Vossers 1991] as well as from several small analyses of pages from newspapers such as the *USA Today* and instruction manuals for appliances such as user manuals for a motor car, a sewing machine, a VCR, and a cookbook, we collected well over a hundred distinct features that play a role in the higher-level aspects of the production and interpretation processes, as well as over fifty rules that express the interdependencies among these features. Where appropriate, we applied the two-step generalization method to come up with features of the right type and at the right level of detail.

These features classify naturally into four major groups:

- the characteristics of the media used,
- the nature of the information to be conveyed,
- the goals and characteristics of the producer, and
- the characteristics of the perceiver and the communicative situation.

Section 3 provides more details about each type of knowledge resource and the rules interlinking them. Before getting to this seyction, however, we describe our attempts to find an adequately flexible and powerful representation formalism for the knowledge.

2.3. An Adequate Representation Formalism

Though we did not study all four aspects iny equal detail, we needed a representation formalism that could capture the requisite individual distinctions as well as their underlying interdependencies, that was extensible, and that did not hamper our research methodology.

As illustrated in Section 2.1, the two-step generalization process provides features and rules simultaneously. Features and their values we tried to tabulate straightforwardly, until we discovered that the underlying intyerdependencies between features – for example, the subclassification of some but not all values for a feature into finer classes, or the combination of values from several features to give rise to a new feature – and the interdependencies between rules made the simple tabular format cumbersome. In the spirit of our work on various media, we decided to codify our results in a more visual way, following the paradigm of AND-OR networks of features and values used in Systemic Functional Linguistics to analyze language and write grammars [Halliday 1985]. This is the notation used in the network fragments that appear in this chapter. The tables in this chapter can be drawn as networks as well, but more clearly illustrate the points being made here.

Processing of the networks is to be understood as similar to discrimination net traversal; one enters the network, makes the appropriate selection(s) at the first choice point(s), records the feature(s) so chosen, and moves along the connecting path(s) to the next choice point(s). In the network, curly brackets mean AND (that is, when entering one, all paths should be followed in parallel) and square brackets EXCLUSIVE OR (that is, at most one path must be selected and followed). Square brackets with slanted serifs are INCLUSIVE OR (that is, zero or more paths may be selected and followed). Whenever a feature is encountered during traversal, it is recorded; the final collection of features uniquely specifies the eventual result.

Using this notation, we follow a three-step research methodology: First, we identify the phenomena in some aspect of a presentation (e.g., the fact that the producer usually wants to affect the perceiver's future goals, or the fact that different media utilize different numbers of presentation 'dimensions'); second, we characterize the variability involved in each phenomenon (e.g., a producer may want to affect the perceiver's goals through warnings, suggestions, hints, requests, etc., or language is expressed 'linearly' while diagrams are two-dimensional); and third, we map out the interdependencies among the values of all the phenomena (e.g., the goal to warn selects a feature value 'urgent', and this value is interdependent with values such as 'high noticeability' which are tied to appropriate media such as sound or flashing icons). In the resulting AND-OR networks of interdependencies, each node represents a single phenomenon and each arc a possible value for it together with its interdependencies with other values.

One advantage of the network notation is its independence of process; one can implement the knowledge contained directly in network form, in a traditional rule-based system, or a connectionist one. We maintain the network form because several other presentation-related software at USC/ISI use the same formalism. The Penman sentence generator [Mann and Matthiessen 1983; Penman 1988] and associated text planning system [Hovy et al. 1992] contain a grammar of English and various factors influencing text structure all represented as AND-OR networks; sentence generation proceeds by traversing the grammar network from 'more semantic' toward 'more syntactic' nodes, collecting at each node features that instruct the system how to build the eventual sentence (see [Matthiessen 1984]). Parsing proceeds by traversing the same network 'backwards', eventually arriving at the 'more semantic' nodes and their associated features, the set of which constitutes the parse and determines the parse tree (see [Kasper 1989; Kasper and Hovy 1990]). This bi-directionality of processing is an additional advantage of the network formalism.

With respect to multimedia presentation planning and analysis, our overall conceptual organization of the knowledge resources is shown in Figure 1. Each knowledge resource appears as a separate network; the central network houses the interlinkages between the other ones. When producing a communication, the communicative goals and situational features cause appropriate features of the upper three networks to be selected, and information then propagates through the interlinkage network (the system's 'rules') to the appropriate medium networks at the bottom, causing appropriate values to be set, which in turn are used to control the low-level generation modules (the language generator, the diagram constructor, etc.). For multimedia input, a communication is analyzed by identifying its features in the relevant bottom networks for each portion of the communication, and propagating the information upward along the internetwork linkage to select appropriate 'high-level' features that describe the producer's goals, the nature of the information mentioned in that portion, etc. Examples appear in Section 4.

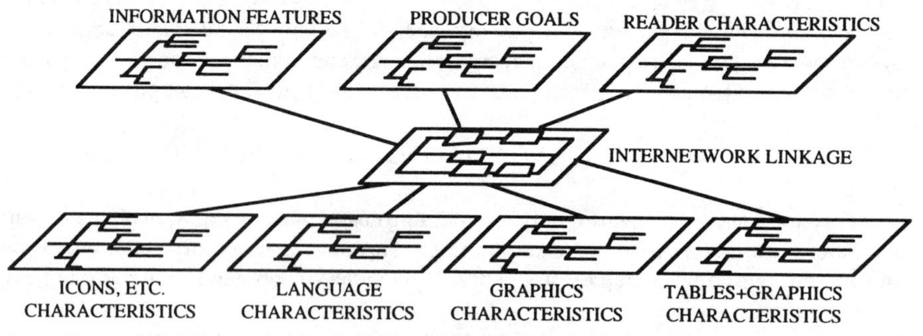

Figure 1. Knowledge Resources that Support Multimedia Communication.

3. The Knowledge Resources

In this section we describe the four major classes of features that influence multimedia presentation planning. In the fifth section we discuss the rules expressing interdependencies among the features in the four classes.

3.1. Characterization of Media

3.1.1. Definition of Terms

The following terms are used to describe presentation-related concepts. We take the point of view of the communicator (indicating where the consumer's subjective experience may differ).

Consumer: A person interpreting a communication.

Medium: A single mechanism by which to express information. Examples: spoken and written natural language, diagrams, sketches, graphs, tables, pictures.

Exhibit: A complex exhibit is a collection, or composition, of several simple exhibits. A simple exhibit is what is produced by one invocation of one medium. Examples of simple exhibits are a paragraph of text, a diagram, a computer beep. Simple exhibits involve the placement of one or more Information Carriers on a background Substrate.

Substrate: The background to a simple exhibit. That which establishes, to the consumer, physical or temporal location, and often the semantic context, within which new information is presented to the information consumer. The new information will often derive its meaning, at least in part, from its relation to the substrate. Examples: a piece of paper or screen (on which information may be drawn or presented); a grid (on which a marker might indicate the position of an entity); a page of text (on which certain words may be emphasized in red); a noun phrase (to which a prepositional phrase may be appended). An empty substrate is possible.

Information Carrier: That part of the simple exhibit which, to the consumer, communicates the principal piece of information requested or relevant in the current communicative context. Examples: a marker on a map substrate; a prepositional phrase within a sentence predicate substrate. A degenerate carrier is one which cannot be distinguished from its background (in the discussion below the degenerate carrier is a special case, but we do not bother explicitly to except it where necessary. Please assume it excepted).

Carried Item: That piece of information represented by the carrier; the 'denotation' of the carrier.

For purposes of rigor, it is important to note that a substrate is simply one or more information carrier(s) superimposed. This is because the substrate carries information as well.[2] In addition, in many cases the substrate provides an internal system of semantics which may be utilized by the carrier to convey information. Thus, despite its name, not all information is transmitted by the carrier itself alone; its positioning (temporal or spatial) in relation to the substrate may encode information as well. This is discussed further below.

Channel: An independent dimension of variation of a particular information carrier in a particular substrate. The total number of channels gives the total number of independent pieces of information the carrier can convey. For example, a single mark or icon can convey information by its shape, color, and position and orientation in relation to a background map. The number and nature of the channels depend on the type of the carrier and on the exhibit's substrate.

3.1.2. Internal Semantic Systems

Some information carriers exhibit an internal structure that can be assigned a 'real-world' denotation, enabling them subsequently to be used as substrates against which other carriers can acquire information by virtue of being interpreted within the substrate. For example, a map used to describe a region of the world possesses an internal structure – points on it correspond to points in the region it charts. When used as a background for a ship icon, one may indicate the location of the ship in the world by placing

[2]Note that from the information consumer's point of view, Carrier and Substrate are subjective terms; two people looking at the same exhibit can interpret its components as carrier and substrate in different ways, depending on what they already know. For example, different people may interpret a graph tracking the daily value of some index differently as follows: someone who is familiar with the history of the index may call only the last point of the graph, that is, its most recent addition, the information carrier, and call all the rest of the graph the substrate. Someone who is unfamiliar with the history of the index may interpret the whole line plotted out as the information carrier, and the graph's axes and title, etc., as substrate. Someone who is completely unfamiliar with the index may interpret the whole graph, including its title and axis titles, as information carrier, and interpret the screen on which it is displayed as substrate.

its icon in the corresponding location on the map substrate. Examples of such carriers and their internal semantic systems are shown in Table 1.

Other information carriers exhibit no internal structure. Examples: icon, computer beep, and unordered list. An internal semantic system of the type described is always intrinsic to the item carried.

Carrier	Internal Semantic System
Picture	'real-world' spatial location based on picture denotation
NL Sentence	'real-world' sentence denotation
Table	categorization according to row and column
Graph	coordinate values on graph axes
Map	'real-world' spatial location based on map denotation
Ordered list	ordinal sequentiality

Table 1. Internal Semantic Systems

3.1.3. Characteristics of Media

In addition to the internal semantics listed above, media differ in a number of other ways which can be exploited by a presenter to communicate effectively and efficiently. The values of these characteristics for various media are shown in Table 2.

Carrier Dimension: Values: *0D, 1D, 2D.* A measure of the number of dimensions usually required to exhibit the information presented by the medium.

Internal Semantic Dimension: Values: *0D, 1D, 2D, >2D, 3D, #D, ∞D.* The number of dimensions present in the internal semantic system of the carrier or substrate.

Temporal Endurance: Values: *permanent, transient.* An indication whether the created exhibit varies during the lifetime of the presentation.

Granularity: Values: *continuous, discrete.* An indication of whether arbitrarily small variations along any dimension of presentation have meaning in the denotation or not.

Medium Type: Values: *aural, visual.* What type of medium is necessary for presenting the created exhibit.

Default Detectability: Values: *low, medlow, medhigh, high.* A default measure of how intrusive to the consumer the exhibit created by the medium will be.

Baggage: Values: *low, high.* A gross measure of the amount of extra information a consumer must process in order to become familiar enough with the substrate to correctly interpret a carrier on it.

Generic Medium	Carrier Dimension	Internal Semantic Dimension	Temporal Endurance	Granularity	Medium Type	Default Detectability	Baggage
Beep	0D		transient	N/A	aural	high	
Icon	0D		permanent	N/A	visual	low	
Map	2D	>2D	permanent	continuous	visual	low	high
Picture	2D	∞D	permanent	continuous	visual	low	high
Table	2D	2D	permanent	discrete	visual	low	high
Form	2D	>2D	permanent	discrete	visual	low	high
Graph	2D	1D	permanent	continuous	visual	low	high
Ordered List	1D	#D	permanent	discrete	visual	low	low
Unordered List	0D	#D	permanent	N/A	visual	low	low
Written Sentence	1D	∞D	permanent	discrete	visual	low	low
Spoken Sentence	1D	∞D	transient	discrete	aural	medhigh	low
Animated Material	2D	∞D	transient	continuous	visual	high	high
Music	1D	∞D	transient	continuous	aural	medhigh	low

Table 2. Media characteristics

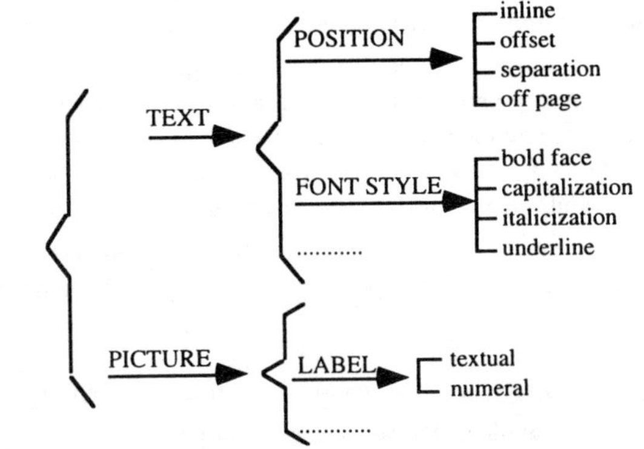

Figure 2. Portion of the Media Network: Values for some Text Channels

3.1.4. How Carriers Convey Information

As part of an exhibit, a carrier can convey information along one or more *channels*. For example, with an icon carrier, one may convey information by the icon's shape, color, and possibly through its position in relation to a background map. The number and nature of the channels depends on the type of carrier and the substrate. The semantics of a channel may be *derived* from the carrier's spatial or temporal relation to a substrate which possesses an internal semantic structure; e.g., placement on a map of a carrier representing an object which exists in the charted area. Otherwise we say the channel is *free*.

Among *free* channels we distinguish between those whose interpretation is *independent* of the carried item (e.g., color, if the carrier does not represent an object for which color is relevant); and those whose interpretation is *dependent* on the carried item (e.g., shape, if the carrier represents an object which has some shape).

Most of the carrier channels can be made to vary their presented value in time. Time variation can be seen as an additional channel which provides yet another degree of freedom of presentation to most of the other channels. The most basic variation is the alternation between two states, in other words, a flip-flop, because this guarantees the continued (though intermittent) presentation of the original basic channel value.

The fonts and positions of letters and words in a text are also free channels for the words as carriers. Figure 2 contains a fragment of the network describing some possible values for these channels.

3.2. Characterization of Information

In this section we develop a vocabulary of presentation-related characteristics of information.

Broadly speaking, as shown in Table 3, three subcases must be considered when choosing a presentation for an item of information: intrinsic properties of the specific item; properties associated with the class to which the item belongs; and properties of the collection of items that will eventually be presented, and of which the current item is a member. These characteristics are explained in the remainder of this section.

Type	Characteristic	Values
Intrinsic Property	Dimensionality	0D, 1D, 2D, >2D, ∞D
	Transience	live, dead
	Urgency	urgent, routine
Class Property	Order	ordered, nominal, quantitative
	Density	dense, discrete, N/A
	Naming	identification, introduction
Set Property	Volume	singular, little, much

Table 3. Information characteristics by type.

Dimensionality: Some single items of information, such as a database record, can be decomposed as a vector of simple components; others, such as a photograph, have a complex internal structure which is not decomposable. We define the *dimensionality* of the latter as *complex*, and of the former as the dimension of the vector.

Since all the information must be represented in some fashion, the following rule must hold (where *simple* dimensionality has a value of 0, *single* the value 1, and so on, and *complex* the value ∞):

The Basic Dimensionality Rule of Presentations

$$\text{Dim (Info)} \leq \text{Dim (Carrier)} + \text{Free Channels (Carrier)} + \text{Internal Semantic Dim (Substrate)}$$

In addition, we have found that different rules apply to information of differing dimensions. With respect to dimensionality, we divide information into several classes as follows:

- *Simple:* Simple atomic items of information, such as an indication of the presence or absence of email.
- *Single:* The value of some meter, such as the amount of gasoline left.
- *Double:* Pairs of information components, such as coordinates (graphs, map locations), or domain-range pairs in relations (automobile × satisfaction rating, etc.).
- *Multiple:* More complex information structures of higher dimension, such as home addresses. It is assumed that information of this type requires more time to consume.
- *Complex:* Information with internal structure that is not decomposable this way, such as photographs.

Transience: Transience refers to whether the information to be presented expresses some current (and presumably changing) state or not. Presentations may be:

- *Live:* The information presented consists of a single conceptual item of information (that is, one carried item) that varies with time (or in general, along some linear, ordered, dimension), and for which the history of values is not important. Examples are the amount of money owed while pumping gasoline or the load average on a computer. Most appropriate for *live* information is a single exhibit.
- *Dead:* The other case, in which information does not reflect some current state, or in which it does but the history of values is important. An example is the history of some stock on the stock market; though only the current price may be important to a trader, the history of the stock is of import to the buyer.

Urgency: Some information may be designated *urgent*, requiring presentation in such a way that the consumer's attention is drawn. This characteristic takes the values *urgent* and *routine*:

- *Urgent:* This information relates to the user's persistent goals (involving actions which could cause personal injury or property damage, whether an imminent meltdown or a warning to a person crossing the road in front of a car) and must therefore be reinforced by textual devices such as 'boldface', 'capitalization', etc. For more details see [Hovy and Arens 1991].
- *Routine:* The normal, non-distinguished case.

Order: Order is a property of a collection of items all displayed together as a group of some kind. Values here are:

- *Quantitative:* This characterizes items belonging to a conceptually and/or syntactically regular but not presentationally ordered set, such as temperature readings for various parts of the country.
- *Ordinal:* This characterizes items of a set ordered according to their semantic denotations (e.g., steps in a recipe).
- *Nominal:* The items are not ordered.

Density: The difference between information that is presented equally well on a graph and a histogram and information that is not well presented on a histogram is a matter of the density of the class to which the information belongs. The former case is *discrete* information; an example is the various types of car made in Japan. The latter is *dense* information; an example is the prices of cars made in Japan.

- *Dense:* A class in which arbitrary small variations along a dimension of interest carry meaning. Information in such a class is best presented by a medium that supports continuous change.
- *Discrete:* A class in which there exists a lower limit to variations on the dimension of interest.

Naming (function): The role information plays may be defined relative to other information present. A good example is the information that names and introduces, such as that in headings of text sections, titles of diagrams, and labels in pictures. We identify just two of the many types here:

- *Identification:* This information identifies a portion of the presentation, based on an appropriate underlying semantic relation such as between a text label and a picture part; see [Hovy et al. 1992].
- *Introduction:* This information identifies and introduces other information by appearing first and standing out positionally.

Volume: A batch of information may contain various amounts of information to be presented. If it is a single fact, we call it *singular*: if more than one fact but still little relative to some task- and user-specific threshold, we call it *little*; and if not, we call it *much*. This distinction is useful because not all media are suited to present *much* information.

- *Much*: The relatively permanent media such as written text or graphics leave a trace to which the consumer can refer if he or she gets lost doing the task or forgets, while transient media such as spoken sentences and beeps do not. Thus the former should be preferred in this case.
- *Little*: There is no need to avoid the more transient media when the amount of information to present is *little*.
- *Singular*: A single atomic item of information. A transient medium can be used. However, one should not overwhelm the consumer with irrelevant information. For example, to display information about a single ship, one need not draw a map.

The features listed here are only the tip of a large iceberg. They can be subclassified in several ways. One way is by whether the feature is apparent by virtue of the information itself or by its juxtaposition with others, as in Table 3; another way is by its teleological status, as partially shown in Figure 3.

3.3. The Producer's Intentions

Particularly in the field of natural language research, there has been much work identifying and classifying the possible goals of a producer of an utterance – work which can quite easily be applied to multimedia presentations in general.

Automated text generators, when possessing a rich grammar and lexicon, typically require several producer-related aspects to specify their parameters fully. For example, the PAULINE generator [Hovy 1988b] produced numerous variations from the same underlying representation depending on its input parameters, which included the following presenter-oriented features:

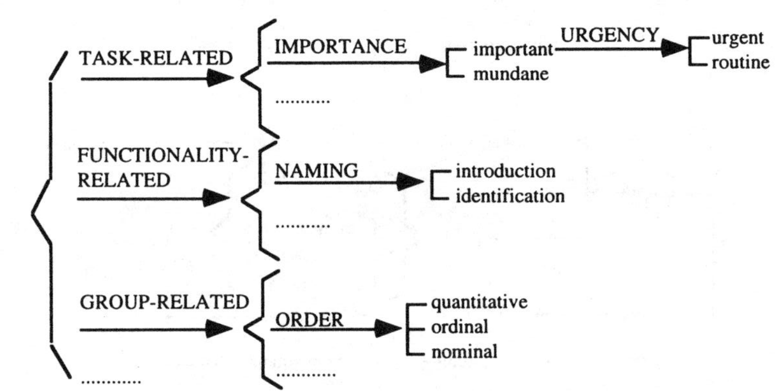

Figure 3. Fragment of the Information Features Network.

Producer's goals with respect to perceiver: These goals all address some aspect of the perceiver's mental knowledge or state, such as:

Affect perceiver's knowledge. This feature takes such values as teach, inform, and confuse.

Affect perceiver's opinions of topic: Values include switch, reinforce.

Involve perceiver in the conversation: Involve, repel.

Affect perceiver's emotional state: Of the hundreds of possibilities we list simply anger, cheer up, calm.

Affect perceiver's goals: Values include activate and deactivate. These goals cover warnings, orders, etc.

Producer's goals with respect to the producer-perceiver relationship: These address both producer and perceiver, for example:

Affect perceiver's emotion toward producer: Values include respect, like, dislike.

Affect relative status: Values here determine formality of address forms in certain languages, etc.: dominant, equal, subordinate.

Affect interpersonal distance: Values such as intimate, close, distant.

For our purposes, we have chosen to borrow and adapt a partial classification of a producer's communicative goals from existing work on Speech Acts. Figure 4 provides a small portion of the network containing aspects of a producer's communicative intentions that may affect the appearance of a presentation (see [Vossers 1991] for more details). In this network fragment *warn* is distinguished from *inform* because, unlike inform speech acts, the semantics of warnings involve capturing the attention of the reader in order to affect his/her goals or actions. To achieve this, a warning must be realized using presentation features that distinguish it from the background presentation.

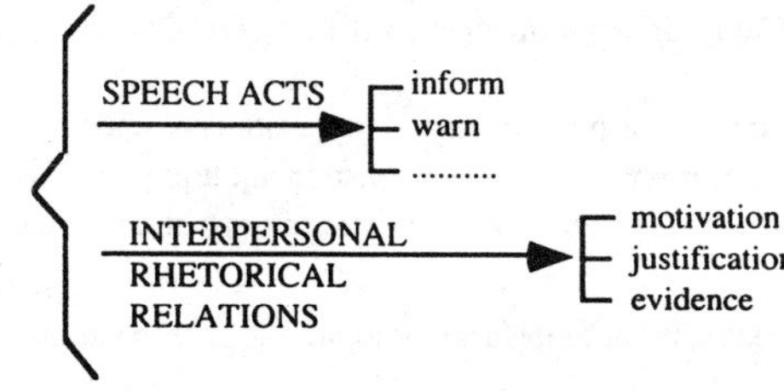

Figure 4. Portion of the Producer Goals Network.

3.4. The Perceiver's Nature and Situation

Our work has only begun to address this issue. Existing research provides considerable material with a bearing on the topic, including especially the work in Cognitive Psychology on issues of human perception which influence the appropriateness of media choices for presentation of certain types of data. A survey and discussion of these results is presented in [Vossers 1991]. On the computational side, the abovementioned text generation system [Hovy 1988b] contains several categories of characteristics of the perceiver, including (with example values):

- *Knowledge of the topic:* Expert, student, novice.
- *Interest in the topic:* High, low.
- *Opinions of the topic:* Good, neutral, bad.
- *Language ability:* High, low.
- *Emotional state:* Calm, angry, agitated.

3.5. Interdependencies and Rules

The factors that affect multimedia presentations are not independent. Their interdependencies can be thought of as rules which establish associations between the goals of the producer, the content of the information, and surface features of presentations to constrain the options for presenting information (during generation) and disambiguate alternative readings (during interpretation). A small portion of these rules, also represented in network form, appears in Figure 5. Moving from left to right through the network (that is, in the direction of presentation interpretation), one first finds the presentation forms which express the information, then features of the information which are linked to various presentation forms, and finally the producer goals. That formalism is essentially equivalent to standard "Rule" writing, as below. We use one formalism or the other, depending on what we feel is most suitable to the task being addressed.

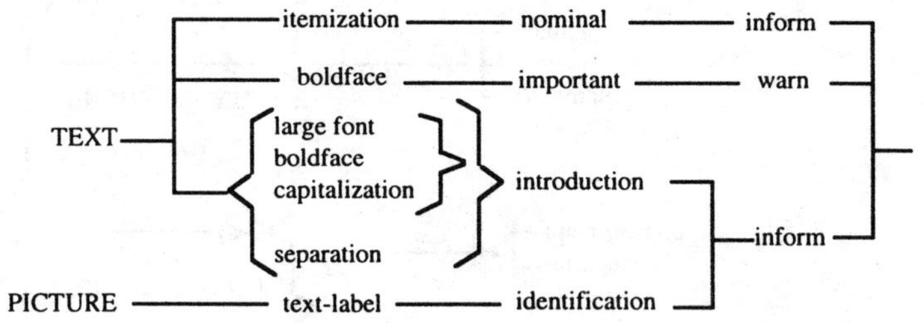

Figure 5. Portion of the Internetwork Linkage.

Below, in traditional form, is a more comprehensive list of rules, organized by characteristics of data being considered for presentation. The terminology is defined in Section 3.2.

Dimensionality

- Simple:
  - ◊ Rule: As carrier, use a medium with a dimension value of 0D.
  - ◊ Rule: No special restrictions on substrate.

- Single:
  - ◊ Rule: No special restrictions on substrate.

- Double:
  - ◊ Rule: As substrate, use media with internal semantic dimension of 2D.
  - ◊ Rule:As substrate, use media with discrete granularity (e.g., forms and tables) if information-class of both components is discrete.
  - ◊ Rule: As substrate, use media with continuous granularity (e.g., graphs and maps) if information-class of either component is dense.
  - ◊ Rule: As carrier, use a medium with a dimension value of 0D.

- Multiple:
  - ◊ Rule: As substrate, use media with discrete granularity if information-class of all components is discrete.
  - ◊ Rule: As substrate, use media with continuous granularity if the information-class of some component is dense.
  - ◊ Rule: As carrier, use a medium with a dimension value of at least 1D.
  - ◊ Rule: As substrate and carrier, do not use media with the temporal endurance value transient.

- Complex:
  - ◊ Rule: Check for the existence of specialized media for this class of information.

Transience

- Live:
  - ◊ Rule: As carrier, use a medium with the temporal endurance characteristic transient if the update rate is comparable to the lifetime of the carrier signal.
  - ◊ Rule: As carrier, use a medium with the temporal endurance characteristic permanent if update rate is much longer.
  - ◊ Rule: As substrate, unless the information is already part of an existing exhibit, use the neutral substrate.

- Dead:
  - ◊ Rule: As carrier, use ones that are marked with the value permanent temporal endurance.

Urgency

- Urgent:
  - ◊ Rule: If the information is not yet part of a presentation instance, use a medium whose default detectability has the value high (such as an aural medium) either for the substrate or the carrier.
  - ◊ Rule: If the information is already displayed as part of a presentation instance, use the present medium but switch one or more of its channels from fixed to the corresponding temporally varying state (such as flashing, pulsating, or hopping).

- Routine
  - ◊ Rule: Choose a medium with low default detectability and a channel with no temporal variance.

Density

- Dense:
  - ◊ Rule: As substrate, use a medium with granularity characteristic continuous (e.g., graphs, maps, animations).

- Discrete:
  - ◊ Rule: As substrate, use a medium with granularity characteristic discrete (e.g., tables, histograms, lists).

Volume

- Much:

◊ Rule: As carrier, do not use a medium with the temporal endurance value transient.

◊ As substrate, do not use a medium with the temporal endurance value transient.

- Little:

  ◊ Rule: No need to avoid transient media.

- Singular:

  ◊ Rule: As substrate, if possible use a medium whose internal semantic system has low baggage.

4. Some Examples

In this section we present a few simple examples of how the knowledge and rules outlined earlier can be applied to produce and interpret sample displays. Each example utilizes only a portion of the knowledge resources we have collected.

4.1. Example 1: Identification of Appropriate Media

We present three simple tasks in parallel. Given the following:

- **Task:** the task of presenting Paris (as the destination of a flight, say).
- **Available information** (three separate examples): the coordinates of the city, the name *Paris*, and a photograph of the Eiffel Tower.
- **Available media:** maps, spoken and written language, pictures, tables, graphs, ordered lists.

The characteristics of the media available appear in Table 2, and the characteristics of the information to be presented appear in Table 4.

The allocation algorithm classifies information characteristics with respect to characteristics of media, according to the rules outlined in Section 3.2. The medium with the most desired characteristics is then chosen to form the exhibit.

	Coordinates	**Name**	**Photograph**
Information	48N 2E	Paris	Eiffel Tower
Dimensionality	double	single	single
Volume	little	singular	singular
Density	dense	discrete	discrete
Transience	dead	dead	dead
Urgency	routine	routine	routine

Table 4. Example information characteristics.

4.1.1. Handling the coordinates

As given by the rules mentioned in Section 3.2, information with a *dimensionality* value of *double* is best presented in a substrate with a *dimension* value of *2D*. This means that candidate substrates for the exhibit are maps, pictures, tables, and graphs. Since the *volume* is *little*, *transient* media are not ruled out. The value *dense* for the characteristic *density* rules out tables. The values for *transience* and *urgency* have no further effect. This leaves tables, maps, and graphs as possible media. Next, taking into account the rules dealing with the internal semantics of media, immediately everything but maps are ruled out (maps' internal semantics denote spatial locations, which matches up with the denotation of the coordinates). If no other information is present, a map medium is selected to display the location of Paris.

4.1.2. Handling the name

The name Paris, being an atomic entity, has the value *single* for the *dimensionality* characteristic. By the appropriate rule (see Section 3.2), the substrate should be the neutral substrate or natural language and the carrier one with *dimension* of *0D*. Since the *volume* is *singular*, a *transient* medium is not ruled out. None of the other characteristics have any effect, leaving the possibility of communicating the single word `Paris` or of speaking or writing a sentence such as *"The destination is Paris"*.

4.1.3. Handling the photograph

The photograph has a *dimensionality* value *complex*, for which appropriate rules specify media with *internal semantic dimension* of ∞D, and with *density* of *dense* (see Section

3.2) – animation or pictures. Since no other characteristic plays a role, the photograph can simply be presented.

This example illustrated how data characteristics can help limit the selection of media appropriate for displaying a particular item. The features we discussed can be used to establish a number of possible display media (or media combinations). Further knowledge can then be applied to make the final media determination.

4.2. Example 2: Rule Simplification and Generalization

This example involves the analysis of a figure taken from the 1990 Honda Accord Owner's Manual page explaining how to adjust the front seat [Honda 1990].

On first inspection, the section heading **Front Seat** and the label **Pull up** in Figure 6 look very different; indeed, the heading is analyzed as including the features *text-in-text*, *boldface*, *large-font*, *separation*, and *short*, while the label includes the features *text-in-picture* and *short*. But upon following the internetwork linkage rules in Figure 5, both items are seen to serve almost-identical producer goals: *introduce* and *identify*, respectively. Thus they are both instances of the *naming* function (see Figure 3); the features that differ are simply those required to differentiate each item from its background. Thus the operative rule can concisely be expressed as:

◊ Rule: To indicate the *naming* function, use *short* text which is *distinct* from the background presentation object.

How to achieve distinction is a matter for the individual presentation media, and has nothing to do with the communicative function of *naming* per se. Within a picture, *distinction* is achieved by the mere use of text, while within text, *distinction* must be achieved by varying the features of the surrounding rendering of the language, for example by changing the font type and size or the position of the item in relation to the general text body.

The notion of *distinction*, having crystallized out of the above two presentations, somewhat unexpectedly turns out to be quite generally applicable. Consider the text bullets at the bottom of the figure. Since their function is to *warn* (and not merely to *inform*, which is the purpose of the preceding paragraphs), the text has the feature *bold*. This serves to *distinguish* the warning text from the background, thereby signaling the special force required for a warning. Using the rule stated above, we can now predict that, within the context of a diagram or picture, one can effect a warning simply by placing text within the non-textual substrate.

Thus, though the notion of *distinction* was not explicitly developed for the individual networks influencing presentations, Figure 5 suggested its utility with an appropriate collection of specific features. Its importance was discerned in the course of investigating the internetwork linkage rules and their application to presentations such as this manual page.

The example illustrates the generality of the rules that can be used to generate and parse multimedia presentations, but, when described, it may seem obvious. However, it can only be explained by using such notions as *distinguished/separated* (both the positional/off-text distinctiveness and the realizational/text-vs-graphics distinctiveness) and *communicative function* (one part of the communication serves to name/introduce/identify another part). When one constructs a vocabulary of terms on this level of description, one finds unexpected overlaps in communicative functionality across media.

In the domain of presentations containing text and line drawings, we demonstrated that media selection rules can be written so that the same rule can be used to control the analysis and generation of some aspect of both a diagram and a piece of text. This is extremely significant, in that the resulting parsimony and expressive power of these rules simultaneously motivates the particular representational level we have used and also suggests how the complex task of multimedia communication is achieved with less overhead than at first seemed necessary. The assembly of a vocabulary of media-independent (or at least shared by multiple media) features of the kind we discuss is an important future research task.

5. Conclusion

The enormous numbers of possibilities that appear when one begins to deal with multiple media, as illustrated by the psychology, cognitive science, and automated text generation and formatting work mentioned above, is daunting. We believe that systematic analysis of the factors influencing presentations, such as the types described here, is required before powerful general-purpose multimedia human-computer interfaces can be built. Appropriate formalisms for representing the underlying knowledge may serve to uncover unexpected overlaps of functionality which serve to simplify the rules upon which such interface systems will depend. It appears that the dependency network formalism and feature-based analysis methodology described in this paper hold some promise for untangling the complex issues involved, and, perhaps, may one day help explain why multimedia communication is so pervasive in human interaction.

Reflections on. . .

On the Knowledge Underlying Multimedia Presentations

Yigal Arens, Eduard Hovy, and Mira Vossers

The main idea put forward in this paper was that multimedia presentations are generated based on knowledge that can be divided into five categories:

- media characteristics and capabilities,
- information characteristics,
- application tasks and interlocutor goals,
- communicative goals and discourse structure, and
- the user's capabilities and preferences.

Research based on this insight and further refining it continued at ISI for several years. The work expanded particularly on the design processing that takes place given this information and on the standardization that must be agreed on before it would be possible to incorporate program components and models developed at different sites into a single system for multimedia presentation design. Our subsequent work was described in a series of papers, including (Hovy and Arens 1991, 1993, 1996; Arens et al. 1993; Arens and Hovy 1995).

Although the authors are no longer actively pursuing research in this area because of other commitments, the work referenced above appears to have influenced research by others. From personal communications, we know it has played a role in the development of theories by Bernsen at Roskilde University (Denmark), by Oberlander and colleagues at the University of Edinburgh, at the Royal Technical Institute of the University of Stockholm, and by a group of researchers at the Free University of Amsterdam.

REFERENCES

Arens, Y., and Hovy, E. H. 1995. The Design of a Model-Based Multimedia Interaction Manager. In McKevitt, P. (guest ed.), *Artificial Intelligence Review* 9(2–3), 167–188, Special Issue on Integration of Natural Language and Vision.

Arens, Y.; Hovy, E. H.; and van Mulken, S. 1993. A Tree-Traversing Prototype That Allocates Presentation Media. In *Proceedings of the 13th International Joint Conference on Artificial Intelligence (IJCAI-93)*, Chambéry, Savoie, France.

Hovy, E. H., and Arens, Y. 1991. Automatic Generation of Formatted Text. In *Proceedings of the Tenth National Conference on Artificial Intelligence (AAAI-91)*, Anaheim, CA. (Also in this volume, Section IV)

Hovy, E. H., and Arens, Y. 1993. The Planning Paradigm Required for Automated Multimedia Presentation Planning. In *Human-Computer Collaboration: Reconciling Theory, Synthesizing Practice*. Papers from the 1993 Fall Symposium Series, AAAI Technical Report FS-93-05.

Hovy, E. H. and Arens, Y. 1996. Virtual Devices: An Approach to Standardizing Multimedia System Components. In *Proceedings of ECAI-96 Workshop: Towards a Standard Reference Model for Intelligent Multimedia Presentation Systems*. Budapest, Hungary: John Wiley & Sons Ltd.

SECTION III

Automated Graphics Design

This section addresses efforts aimed at the semi- and fully automatic design and realization of two- and three-dimensional graphics from structured data. The research described by these papers attempts to go beyond descriptive works of graphical design practice (e.g., Tufte 1983) that consider examples of successful graphics and make observations on how to avoid ambiguous, confusing, or imprecise/misleading graphics. In contrast, these papers aim to elucidate both why and how graphics should be designed; that is, they aim at formal and prescriptive theories of graphics design.

A number of factors have motivated researchers to seek automated graphic designers. Currently, application designers are forced to anticipate and predesign every possible data and presentation situation. Moreover, in order to create effective graphics, developers need to be design experts, which is often not the case. Thus, it would be valuable to have mechanisms to assist users in authoring effective graphics or to tailor graphics automatically to given data, users, and contexts.

The first paper by Jock Mackinlay represents some of the first research to investigate the automatic design of two-dimensional, static graphical presentations of relational information such as bar charts, scatter plots, and connected graphs. Mackinlay addresses the problems of codifying graphic design criteria formally (both syntax and semantics) in order to support the generation of and choice from a range of potential designs. Mackinlay distinguishes between *expressiveness* criteria and *effectiveness* criteria, which characterize the ability of a graphical language to represent desired information in the former case, and the ability of a graphical language to exploit characteristics of the output media and the human visual system to achieve an intended effect in the latter case. Mackinlay describes effectiveness orderings based on empirical studies of perceptual tasks (e.g., perceptions of position and length encodings are accomplished more accurately than volume or density). He extends these using psychophysical results (not claimed to be empirically verified) beyond quantitative information to include nonquantitative information.

Using a *composition algebra*—a collection of graphical languages together with composition operators—Mackinlay implemented the prototype system, APT (A Presentation Tool), an approximately 200-rule-based program that automatically generates a range of useful graphic designs. Mackinlay argues for the importance of encoding more important information more effectively and describes the composition of two designs by merging parts that encode the same information. APT's generation algorithm, based on a divide-and-conquer search strategy, has three steps: partition, selection, and composition. Partitioning involves dividing relations to be expressed into groups that match the expressiveness criteria of the primitive languages. Next, selection uses expressivness criteria to generate a list of candidate designs for each partition. Finally, composition performs pairwise comparison of designs to see if one of three composition operators applies.

Like Mackinlay's APT system, the SAGE system described in the second paper by Steven Roth and Joe

Mattis also designs 2-D static presentations of relational data. In contrast to the first paper, SAGE generates text as well as graphics. The authors present a more detailed and complete taxonomy of data characteristics and go beyond APT's use of relation ordering to choose among graphical encoding techniques. Like APT, SAGE characterizes three kinds of relation-ordering techniques: quantitative, ordinal, and nominal (APT also distinguishes uniqueness, which is described in database terms as a functional dependency). SAGE further distinguishes amounts from coordinates (e.g., in time or space) and recognizes distinct domains of time, space, temperature, and mass. Whereas the first dimension of information characterization pertains to the properties of the relation itself, the second dimension relates to the properties of the structure of relations, that is, the way relations map from elements of one set to another. For example, relational coverage characterizes the degree to which each element in a set can be mapped to at least one element of another (e.g., data might be missing, not applicable, or nonexistent). In contrast, cardinality expresses the number of elements in a set to which a relation can map from an element of another set (i.e., the number of values that can occur for an attribute of an entity). Finally, uniqueness indicates whether a relation maps to a unique value or values for each element of a set.

A third information dimension is the expression of relationships among relations. In contrast to binary relations (e.g., mapping a population to a location), *n*-ary relations map to multiple values (e.g., an activity having a start date, stop date, and duration). A system that does not represent these relations richly is likely to generate fragmented, less effective displays that separate otherwise possibly integrable displays. Another factor that can affect presentation design is dependencies that can occur among attributes (relations) or among values in data sets that can serve as opportunities for integration/aggregation. For example, a stacked bar chart can be used to represent quantitative component values, with the bar in its entirety representing the aggregate of the component values. The paper characterizes how each of these properties influences the appropriateness of different types of graphics (e.g., node-link diagrams, bar charts, scatter plots).

Finally, and significantly, whereas APT focused principally on information characteristics and data graphics, Roth and Mattis consider how differences in users' goals impact the effectiveness of designed graphics. The authors describe how information-seeking goals (e.g., value lookup, comparison, correlation) can be supported by different data displays. For example, text tables are most effective for accurate value lookup, independent graphics are most effective for value comparison within one relation, and composite graphics are most effective for interrelation value comparison. Composite graphics where two or more properties of a single mark (e.g., color, size, shape, location) convey different relations can enhance display of correlation among attributes.

Stephen Casner furthers the notions of user-centered design with his automated graphic design and presentation tool, BOZ, which takes a task-analytic approach. His paper utilizes a unifying example of presentations generated to enable airline trip planning. Specifically, Casner focuses on the design of graphics that optimize human performance in information processing tasks by (1) designing them to enable users to substitute "perceptual inferences" in place of more cognitively demanding "logical inferences" and (2) streamlining users' information search through task-custom design. In the former case, perceptual inferences such as distance and size determinations, spatial collocation, and color comparison yield more rapid results than cognitive operations (e.g., arithmetic, comparison). In the latter case, group and ordering information as well as encoding using color, shading, and layout can support "preattentive and sometimes parallel visual search." Casner's system, BOZ, contains five main components: a logical task description language, perceptual operator substitution, perceptual data structuring, perceptual operator selection, and rendering. BOZ represents and reasons about "perceptual operators," such as searching for visual characteristics of objects (e.g., location, size, color, shape) or making computations about graphical properties (e.g., determining horizontal distance or slope difference). Casner develops the notion of "equivalence classes" for perceptual operators that enables their grouping into classes such as search operations or computational operations (e.g., equivalence, subtraction), which in turn enables the substitution of logical operators (e.g., "compute airline trip layover") for equivalent perceptual ones (e.g., "determine horizontal distance") since both operators compute the subtraction function.

In its perceptual data structuring module, BOZ aggregates information shared across operators and graphically encodes these together (e.g., grouping attributes that pertain to the same object, keeping together objects needed to draw particular inferences such as a flight and a seat) but also partitions unique information into distinct presentations (e.g., nested presentations for "part-of" relationships). Finally, BOZ uses three criteria to select among perceptual operators: (1) relative performance efficiency and accuracy, (2) the expressiveness or representational power of the associated primitive graphical language, and (3) the ability of the primitive graphical language associated with the perceptual operators to be combined to create coherent presentations. The paper includes rankings for human performance for perceptual operators (e.g., arithmetic operators take more effort to perform than lookup operators; horizontal distance calculation is faster and more accurate than area difference calculation). Casner briefly presents the results of empirical reaction time studies that demonstrate reductions in time to complete tasks using BOZ-generated informational graphics, lending credence to the value of streamlining task performance through the substitution of perceptual operators for logical operators.

In the next paper, Dorée Seligmann and Steven Feiner are similarly concerned with generating presentations tailored to particular user needs in their Intent-Based Illustration System (IBIS), a subcomponent of the COMET multimedia generation system described in the first paper in Section II of this collection. Unlike previous systems, IBIS generates 3-D illustrations of army field radio operations and supports "metaobjects" such as arrows that indicate state changes. The authors argue for the need to formalize not only the (linguistic and graphical) language to be used in the presentation but also the audience and context of the communication as well as its purpose or intent (e.g., locate, indicate property, show state, show change). Like BOZ, IBIS supports "subordinate" or embedded illustrations. Like APT, SAGE, and BOZ, IBIS uses a generate-and-test approach, however, IBIS breaks the presentation generation task into a design (illustrator) stage followed by a style (drafter) stage. Design rules specify how to achieve communicative goals. For example, one design specifies that locating an object can be achieved by making sure the object and its context are visible, highlighted, recognizable, and so on. Style rules then map stylistic choices onto visual effects (e.g., highlighting can be achieved by increasing an object's intensity or decreasing the intensity of surrounding objects). Associated with both design and style rules are evaluators that support the choice among competing rules. Illustrative styles include cutaways, transparency, and ghosting, all of which can be used to depict obscured objects more clearly. IBIS supports interactive illustrations. In one example, if a user continually zooms in on the army radio function button, eventually IBIS will generate and position an inset (thus resulting in a composite illustration) to show the user the location during navigation.

The next paper by Steven Roth, John Kolojejchick, Joe Mattis, and Jade Goldstein also focuses on the interactive design of two-dimensional informational graphics. Building upon the earlier SAGE system (described in the previously mentioned Roth and Mattis paper), the authors describe SAGEBook and SAGEBrush, which support, respectively, design as construction and design as customization of retrieved, previously created artifacts. Users interact with SAGEBrush to sketch designs that are translated into *design directives*—specifications expressed in SAGE's graphic representation language, which has a rich syntax and semantics that enable the expression of items such as grapheme and property choices (e.g., color and size of circles, lines, text), frame of references (e.g., two-axis chart, table, map, network), layout constraints (e.g., alignment, ordering), grouping, and mappings between data and these graphic elements. These design directives serve both to guide SAGE's automatic design processes and to provide criteria for the search of a library of previously designed presentations. The authors illustrate the application of their system to interactively design a new version of the famous graphic by Minard showing Napoleon's 1812 campaign. Some of the benefits of their approach include the reduction of the effort required to convey design choices and map them to data, the ability to construct composite graphics (e.g., an indented chart sharing an axis with a color-coded bar chart), and the provision of design expertise to novice users. One issue raised by the authors is that of exploring cognitive models for similarity criteria for defining (partial) match criteria. The authors suggest that users apply different criteria for different search purposes; for example, retrieving pictures whose name has been forgotten, discovering how generic frames of reference can be expanded with additional graphical elements, or minimizing design effort through retrieval of designs similar to required ones.

Taken together, these papers make three principal contributions. First, they all focus on a move toward explicit representation of graphical presentation knowledge. Second, they support explicit choices among graphical encoding mechanisms that reason about the expressiveness and effectiveness of underlying representations and resulting presentations. Finally, the authors focus increasingly on representation of knowledge of the user, task, and context and its exploitation to generate more effective, tailored presentations while at the same time decreasing required user expertise.

A number of open research issues remain. With regard to the design process itself, one key issue is whether the generate-and-test approach represented in all these systems is the most appropriate, or if other methods (e.g., constraint based, case based) might yield new insights. A related question is if the pipeline approach to design (e.g., illustrators followed by drafters) needs to be replaced with a co-constraining cascaded and/or distributed model. In addition, the mining, visualization, and animation of massive and composite data sets requires further investigation. Additional engineering efforts remain to make all of this research computationally efficient.

With regard to human perception and comprehension, many issues require further investigation. One issue is the representation of high-level user goals (e.g., data extraction, comparison, correlation) and communicative actions (e.g., warn, remind) and their relation to stylistic choices (e.g., color, orientation). A significant amount of empirical investigation is needed to better understand human perceptual and cognitive processes, including motor skills and ergonomic issues, in order to decrease the need for design expertise and enable better design of graphics and, increasingly, mixed media presentations.

REFERENCES

Tufte, E. 1983. *The Visual Display of Quantitative Information*. Cheshire, CT: Graphics Press.

Automating the Design of Graphical Presentations of Relational Information

JOCK MACKINLAY
Stanford University

The goal of the research described in this paper is to develop an application-independent presentation tool that automatically designs effective graphical presentations (such as bar charts, scatter plots, and connected graphs) of relational information. Two problems are raised by this goal: The codification of graphic design criteria in a form that can be used by the presentation tool, and the generation of a wide variety of designs so that the presentation tool can accommodate a wide variety of information. The approach described in this paper is based on the view that graphical presentations are sentences of graphical languages. The graphic design issues are codified as expressiveness and effectiveness criteria for graphical languages. Expressiveness criteria determine whether a graphical language can express the desired information. Effectiveness criteria determine whether a graphical language exploits the capabilities of the output medium and the human visual system. A wide variety of designs can be systematically generated by using a composition algebra that composes a small set of primitive graphical languages. Artificial intelligence techniques are used to implement a prototype presentation tool called APT (A Presentation Tool), which is based on the composition algebra and the graphic design criteria.

Categories and Subject Descriptors: D.2.2 [**Software Engineering**]: Tools and Techniques—*user interfaces*; H.1.2 [**Models and Principles**]: User/Machine Systems—*human information processing*; H.3.4 [**Information Storage and Retrieval**]: Systems and Software; I.2.1 [**Artificial Intelligence**]: Applications and Expert Systems; I.3.6 [**Computer Graphics**]: Methodology and Techniques—*device independence*; *ergonomics*

General Terms: Algorithms, Design, Human Factors, Languages, Theory

Additional Key Words and Phrases: Automatic generation, composition algebra, effectiveness, expressiveness, graphic design, information presentation, presentation tool, user interface

1. INTRODUCTION

Computer-based information plays a crucial role in our society. As a result, an important responsibility of a user interface is to make intelligent use of human visual abilities and output media whenever it presents information to the user. For example, a color medium makes it possible to use graphical techniques based on the fact that the human visual system is very effective at distinguishing a small number of distinct colors [13, 23]. A monochrome medium requires other graphical techniques that utilize other capabilities of the human visual system.

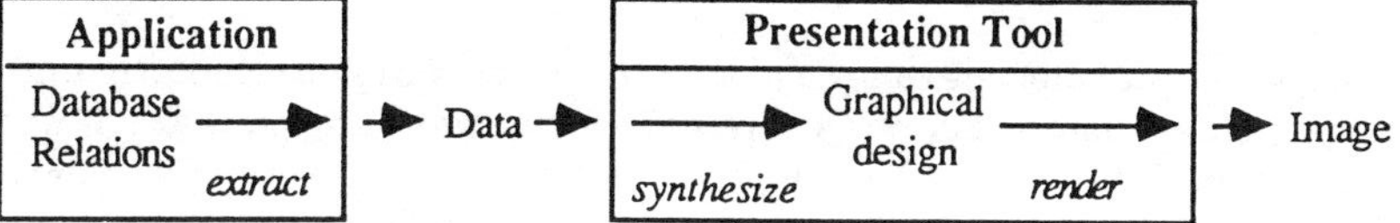

Fig. 1. A linear model for generating presentations. This simplified model, which does not include feedback loops that are required for difficult design problems, describes the fundamental process of generating a graphical presentation. A graphical design synthesized by a presentation tool describes the basic structure and meaning of a graphical presentation. The rendering process fills in the details that are required to form the final image.

Building user interfaces that intelligently present information is a difficult task. At the current time, application designers are forced to anticipate every presentation situation that might arise in an application and decide which graphical techniques are most effective in each situation. Not only do application designers have to "predesign" the presentations, but they must be graphic design experts to ensure that the resulting presentations are effective.

An obvious solution is to build a system, called a presentation tool, that automatically designs graphical presentations of information. Using such a system, application designers need not predesign the presentations, and the graphic design issues are the responsibility of the presentation tool. Figure 1 illustrates how application designers would use such a tool. The application extracts some information from its database (perhaps using statistical analysis). The presentation tool then synthesizes a graphical design and renders an image that presents this information. A *graphical design* is an abstract description of an image that indicates the graphical techniques (such as color variation or position on an axis) that are used to encode information.

There are two open problems that must be solved before such a presentation tool can be constructed: Graphic design criteria must be codified before the presentation tool can synthesize effective designs, and a wide variety of designs must be generated before the presentation tool can handle a wide variety of input.

This paper describes research that begins to solve these problems by focusing on automating the design of two dimensional (2-D) static presentations (such as bar charts, scatter plots, and connected graphs) of relational information. The cornerstone of this research is the development of precise definitions of graphical languages that describe the syntactic and semantic properties of graphical presentations. The framework established by these definitions addresses the two problems mentioned above. Graphic design issues are codified with expressiveness and effectiveness criteria. *Expressiveness criteria* identify graphical languages that express the desired information. *Effectiveness criteria* identify which of these graphical languages, in a given situation, is the most effective at exploiting the capabilities of the output medium and the human visual system. A wide variety of designs is systematically generated using a *composition algebra*, which is a collection of primitive graphical languages and composition operators that can form complex presentations. This framework is implemented with artificial intelligence techniques. A prototype application-independent presentation tool called APT (A Presentation Tool) has been built. Even though only the basic

This work was supported in part by grant N00014-81-K-0004 from the Office of Naval Research.
Author's current address: Xerox PARC, 3333 Coyote Hill Rd., Palo Alto, CA 94304.

framework has been implemented, APT can synthesize a wide variety of useful designs.

The paper is a top-down description of the two types of graphic design criteria and the composition algebra mentioned above. Related work is described in Section 2. Section 3 uses three examples to motivate the development of the criteria and algebra. Section 4 gives a detailed overview of the results described in this paper. The core of the paper is contained in Sections 5–7, which describe the details of the expressiveness and effectiveness criteria and the composition algebra. Sections 8 and 9 describe how APT uses these results to synthesize presentations. Finally, Section 10 considers how the research can be extended.

2. RELATED WORK

The automatic design of graphical presentations of information is a relatively unexplored research area. As a result, existing work has focused on restricted aspects of the problem. Aside from the early unfocused work, the following three foci categorize the existing work: content issues, graphic design issues, and design variation issues. Content issues are central to systems that automatically determine the content of presentations, such as adding or removing details to generate an effective presentation or developing a sequence of related presentations. The graphic design and design variation issues have already been described. Another useful categorization is the graphical techniques used by the system (2-D, 3-D, animation).

Two of the early, less focused pieces of work deserve mention. The first developed the AIPS system, which was one of the earliest attempts to separate the presentation process from the rest of an application [24]. AIPS used the KLONE representation system to specify and refine a high-level specification of a 2-D information display. The second piece of early work studied automatic animation scripting and the rule-based layout of node-link diagrams [12].

Content issues were the primary focus for the work on two systems. The first was the VIEW system developed by Friedell, which automatically generated 2-D icons describing the properties of ships stored in a naval database [10]. A stepwise refinement of icon templates, using subicon templates, terminated when sufficient detail was generated for a given icon size. The templates were designed by hand rather than by the system. The second was the APEX system developed by Feiner, which automatically generated a sequence of images that describe actions in a 3-D world consisting of some sonar cabinets [8]. The system carefully tailored the sequence of images to omit irrelevant or redundant details. The graphic design issues surrounding the merging of icons and 3-D images were also considered.

Two other pieces of work focused on graphic design issues. The first was the BHARAT system developed by Gnanamgari, which was an early effort at the automatic generation of 2-D presentation graphics [11]. It selected a pie chart, bar chart, or line chart design for a single unary function, which could have multiple numeric ranges. BHARAT was based on a simple design algorithm. When the function was continuous, a line chart design was used. When the user indicated that the range sets could be summed to a meaningful total, a pie chart design was used. Bar chart designs were used in the remaining cases. Although multiple designs were generated, BHARAT's range of designs was limited. It could not present a collection of relations or nonfunctional relations. Gnanamgari's discussion focused on graphic design issues. However, her effectiveness criteria about issues such as font and color choice were "wired" into the code that rendered the design, making it difficult to extend the system to a broader range of input.

The second piece of work that focused on graphic design issues was Beach's system, which automated the low-level layout and design of 2-D tables whose high-level topology was specified by the user as a matrix of rows and columns [1]. This research utilized a specification called a *graphical style* [2], which allowed the explicit description of the graphic design properties of the table, such as line widths, background tints, and size constraints. As a result, the user could control parts of the design while the remainder was controlled by the existing default style. Explicit graphical styles made it possible for the system to format the table in different ways for different output media. Although the graphical styles had to be specified by hand, care was taken to make sure that graphic design issues could be addressed in the specification.

Design variation and graphic design are the primary foci of the work described in this paper. This work differs from the previous work in that it focuses directly on the generation of a comprehensive variety of designs for 2-D static presentations of relational information. The APT system uses artificial intelligence techniques to implement a "generate and test" search for a design: The composition algebra generates design alternatives, and the graphic design criteria test the generated alternatives.

3. THE GRAPHICAL PRESENTATION PROBLEM

The graphical presentation problem is to synthesize a graphical design that expresses a set of relations and their structural properties effectively. This problem is illustrated in this section by three examples that describe the desired behavior of a presentation tool. These examples describe the basic concerns that led to the criteria and algebra discussed in the remainder of the paper.

Given the process model in Figure 1, the examples of presentation tool behavior begin with the application's database. Figure 2 describes a collection of relation tuples about automobiles that might be contained in such a database. The structural properties of these relations, which might be in the database schema, are shown in Figure 3 using standard database notation [22]. Structural properties include the domain sets and their functional relationships. Given such a database, a typical input from the application to the presentation tool would be the following:

Present the Price and Mileage relations.
The details about the set of Cars can be omitted.

Note that the application can include additional requests, such as asking that the *Cars* details be omitted.

Given this input, a presentation tool produces two outputs: a graphical design and an image rendered from that graphical design. A graphical design, which is the primary concern of this paper, consists of a set of encoding relations between

Price(Accord, 5799)	*Price*(AMC Pacer, 4749)
Mileage(Accord, 25)	*Mileage*(AMC Pacer, 17)
Weight(Accord, 2240)	*Weight*(AMC Pacer, 3350)
Repair(Accord, Great)	*Repair*(AMC Pacer, Terrible)
Nation(Accord, Germany)	*Nation*(AMC Pacer, USA)
Price(Audi 5000, 9690)	*Price*(BMW 320i, 9735)
⋮	⋮

Fig. 2. Relation tuples about 1979 automobiles. This is an example of a table of relation tuples that might be generated by a database system in response to a query. A presentation tool can do much better than this.

Price:	*Cars* → [3500, 13000]
Mileage:	*Cars* → [10, 40]
Weight:	*Cars* → [1500, 5000]
Repair:	*Cars* → ⟨Great, Good, OK, Bad, Terrible⟩
Nation:	*Cars* → {USA, Germany, France, ...}

Cars = {Accord, AMC Pacer, Audi 5000, BMW 320i, ...}

Fig. 3. Structural properties of the automobile relations. The arrow (→) indicates a functional dependency between domain sets. The square brackets ([ ]) describe domain sets that are quantitative ranges, the angle brackets (⟨ ⟩) describe domain sets that are ordered sets, and the curly braces ({ }) describe domain sets that are unordered sets.

a graphical image and the information it presents. For example, Figure 4 describes a scatter plot design for the price/mileage input. Graphical objects, such as points and line segments, encode the domains of the relations. Properties of those objects, such as their position, encode the functional information. The *Encodes* predicate is used to indicate these encoding relationships for both the graphical objects and their properties. Figure 5 contains the scatter plot image that APT rendered from this design.[1]

The following three price/mileage examples illustrate the expressiveness, effectiveness, and design variation concerns mentioned above. The scatter plot in Figure 5 illustrates the importance of the expressiveness concern. If the application had not requested that the details about the cars be omitted, the scatter plot in Figure 5 would not have expressed all the input. Without this request, the scatter plot would have had to include labels, as shown in Figure 6. These scatter plot labels, however, illustrate the importance of the effectiveness concern. The labels obscure the mark positions, and it is difficult to find individual cars. If the details about the cars are important, there are more effective design alternatives. For example, when the details of the cars are to be presented, the presentation tool should synthesize the aligned bar chart design

Encodes(*VertAxis*, [3500, 13000], *ScatterPlot*)
Encodes(*HorzAxis*, [10, 40], *ScatterPlot*)
Encodes(*Points*, *Cars*, *ScatterPlot*)
Encodes(*Position*(*Points*, *VertAxis*), *Price*(*Cars*), *ScatterPlot*)
Encodes(*Position*(*Points*, *HorzAxis*), *Mileage*(*Cars*), *ScatterPlot*)

Fig. 4. The graphical design for a scatter plot of the price mileage input. The *Encodes* relation indicates the relationship between graphical objects or properties and the information encoded. For example, the first line says that the vertical axis encodes the range of prices, and the fourth line says that the position of the points on the vertical axis encodes the prices of cars. The input relations are written as functions to simplify the description.

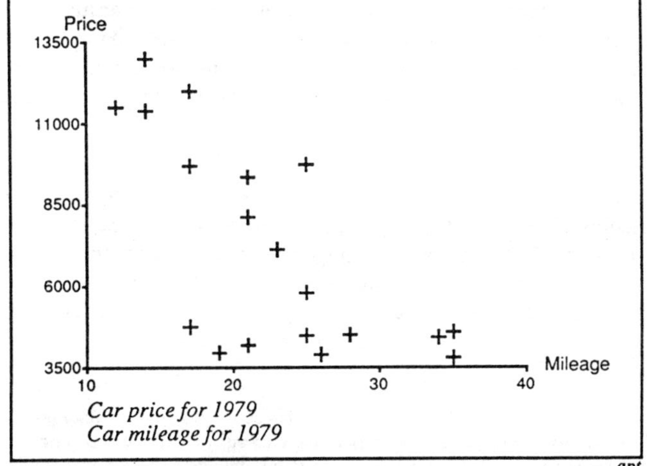

Fig. 5. Scatter plot of the price/mileage input. The graphical design for this image is in Figure 4. The design expresses the relations only if the application permits the details about the cars to be omitted. The *apt* in the lower right corner indicates that APT designed and rendered this diagram.

used to render Figure 7, rather than the scatter plot design. The aligned bar chart design makes it easy to find values associated with an individual car. The existence of this alternative design illustrates the importance of the design variation concern. A presentation tool should be able to generate an expressive and effective design for each presentation situation.

The following rough estimate indicates that there are many possible inputs to a presentation tool. The price/mileage input consists of two binary relations that share the same first domain set and are functional dependencies from a qualitative domain to a numeric range. The structural properties of the input relations are important factors for designing a graphical presentation. Different structural properties require the presentation tool to synthesize different designs. Furthermore, the ability to vary these properties independently leads to a combinatorial

[1] In this paper, an *apt* in the lower right corner of a figure indicates that APT designed and rendered the diagram. Such diagrams are intended to illustrate APT's ability to deal with coarse-grained graphic design issues, such as the choice of the graphical techniques to encode information. Fine-grained rendering issues, such as line width, font choice, and precise graphical object placement are not a focus of this research. A production presentation tool will certainly be able to generate more graphically interesting diagrams than the ones shown here.

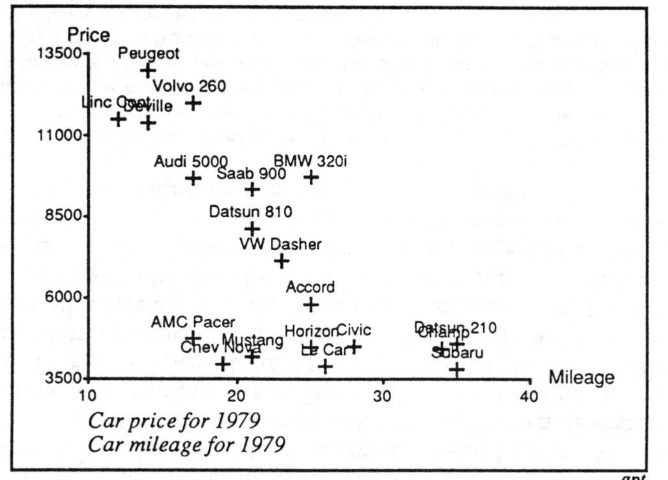

Fig. 6. Labeled scatter plot for the price/mileage input. Although a more sophisticated rendering could avoid the overlapping of the labels, two basic problems of a labeled scatter plot design reduce its effectiveness. First, labels make it difficult to perceive the positions of the points. Second, a given label is difficult to find.

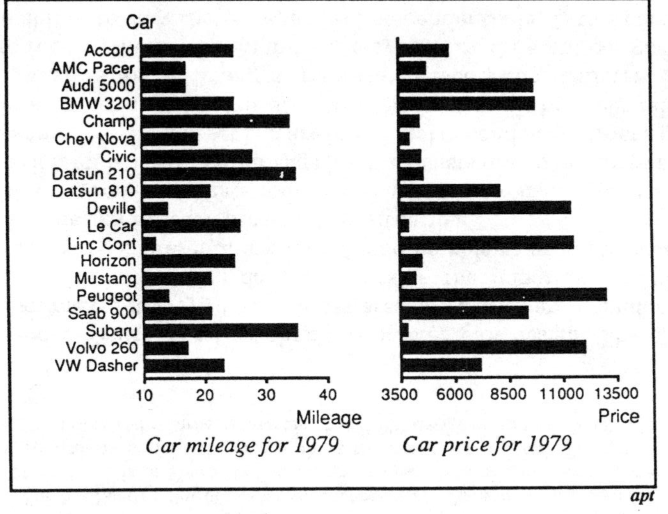

Fig. 7. Aligned bar chart for the price/mileage input. This diagram shows the detailed properties of the cars better than a scatter plot. However, the general relationships are not so easy to see.

explosion in the number of inputs that might be given to a presentation tool. To see this, abstract the two binary relations by ignoring the functional dependencies, the sharing of domain sets, and the properties of the domain sets:

$$\left.\begin{matrix} R\colon & \overbrace{A \quad B}^{d} \\ S\colon & C \quad D \end{matrix}\right\} r.$$

Given that there are on the average d domain sets for each relation and r relations in the input, there are

$$(2^d - 1)^r \times (dr)! \times 3^{dr}$$

different possible design problems. The $(2^d - 1)^r$ factor is based on the fact that each relation can be a functional dependency from 1 through d domain sets to the remaining domain sets and is equivalent to the number of nonempty subsets of the set of domain sets of the relation. The $(dr)!$ factor is based on the number of canonical permutation cycles that can be formed by the sharing of all the domain sets [14]. The 3^{dr} factor is based on the fact that each domain set can be one of the following three types [20]: A domain set is *nominal* when it is a collection of unordered items, such as {`Jay, Eagle, Robin`}. A domain set is *ordinal* when it is an ordered tuple, such as ⟨`Monday, Tuesday, Wednesday`⟩. A domain set is *quantitative* when it is a range, such as [`0, 273`].

The preceding formula indicates that there can be many inputs to the presentation tool. For two binary relations, there are over 17,000 possibilities. However, the input can include more relations or relations with more domain sets. For example, four binary relations (similar to the automobile data presented in Figure 30) can generate over 21 billion different inputs. Furthermore, this estimate does not include other factors that increase the number of designs that must be generated by a presentation tool, such as application requests or properties of the output media.

4. APPROACH

The fundamental assumption of the approach described in this paper is that graphical presentations are sentences of graphical languages, which are similar to other formal languages in that they have precise syntactic and semantic definitions. The three concerns described in the previous section are handled by a careful analysis of the properties of these definitions. This analysis leads to expressiveness and effectiveness criteria for evaluating graphical designs and a composition algebra for generating design alternatives.

An expressiveness criterion, which is derived from a precise language definition, is associated with each graphical language. A graphical language can be used to present some information when it includes a graphical sentence that expresses *exactly* the input information, that is, all the information and only the information. Expressing additional information is potentially dangerous because it may not be correct.

Effectiveness criteria can be based on a number of different factors. For example, a design can be judged effective when it can be interpreted accurately or quickly, when it has visual impact, or when it can be rendered in a

Fig. 8. Bertin's graphical objects and graphical relationships.

Marks:	Points, lines, and areas
Positional:	1-D, 2-D, and 3-D
Temporal:	Animation
Retinal:	Color, shape, size, saturation, texture, and orientation

cost-effective manner. This paper concentrates on generating designs that can be accurately interpreted. Dealing with multiple, perhaps conflicting, effectiveness criteria is beyond the scope of this research.

Given the focus on accuracy, effectiveness criteria are based on the observation that a graphical language uses specific graphical techniques to encode information. When interpreting a graphical sentence, a person is confronted with perceptual tasks that correspond to these graphical encoding techniques. Since some perceptual tasks are accomplished more accurately than others, effectiveness criteria can be based on the comparison of the perceptual tasks required by alternative graphical languages.

Since most graphical presentations of relational information are based on a general vocabulary of graphical techniques, a wide variety of designs can be generated with a composition algebra that describes this graphical vocabulary. Figure 8 summarizes graphic designer Jacques Bertin's vocabulary of the graphical techniques commonly used to encode information in presentation graphics [3]. Graphical presentations use graphical marks, such as points, lines, and areas, to encode information via their positional, temporal, and *retinal* properties.[2] The composition algebra consists of a *basis set* that contains primitive graphical languages, each of which embodies one of Bertin's graphical techniques for encoding information, and *composition operators* that are able to generate a wide range of presentations by composing the primitive languages.

5. EXPRESSIVENESS

All communication is based on the fact that the participants share conventions that determine how messages are constructed and interpreted. For graphical communication these conventions indicate how arrangements of graphical objects encode information. This section shows how to formalize these conventions by taking the view that graphical presentations are actually sentences of graphical languages that have precise syntactic and semantic definitions. Such definitions make it possible to determine the expressiveness and effectiveness properties of graphical languages.

Intuitively, a set of facts is expressible in a language if there is a sentence of the language that encodes every fact in the set. The difficulty with this intuition is that the sentence may encode additional incorrect facts (this is discussed in detail elsewhere [17]). Therefore, the expressiveness criteria for languages contain two conditions:

A set of facts is *expressible* in a language if it contains a sentence that
(1) encodes all the facts in the set,
(2) encodes only the facts in the set.

This section presents two examples that demonstrate the importance of these two conditions. The first example shows a case in which position on an axis cannot express a one-to-many relation. The second example shows a case in which a bar chart expresses additional incorrect facts. Before the examples can be given, however, it is necessary to develop some formal machinery for defining the syntax and semantics of graphical languages. Such machinery makes it possible to determine what information is encoded by the sentences of a language. Evaluating expressiveness requires this ability.

The formal machinery required to define a graphical language is fairly straightforward. A *graphical sentence s* is defined to be a collection of tuples:

$$s \subset \{\langle o, l \rangle \mid o \in O \wedge l \in L\},$$

where O is a set of graphical objects and L is a set of locations. Each tuple, which is called a *located object*, indicates the placement of an object at a given location. The syntax of a *graphical language* is defined to be a set of well-formed graphical sentences. This paper assumes that O and L are restricted to the standard 2-D Cartesian plane, such that the objects in O are 2-D graphical objects that have a finite, nonzero height and width, and the locations in L are the conventional binary tuples that represent the x and y positions in the Cartesian plane.[3] The height and width of a sentence is determined in the normal manner from the size and location of the objects that make up that sentence. This paper uses a variety of intuitively named functions to describe geometric properties. For example, the functions *Xmin*, *Xpos*, and *Xmax* identify the x position of the left, center, and right of a located object. Precise definitions of these functions can be found elsewhere [16].

The syntax of a language can be described with a predicate that identifies the well-formed sentences of the language. Systematic syntactic conventions can be captured by conditions that indicate when this predicate is true. For example, consider the diagram in Figure 9 that encodes the *Price* relation. Intuitively, it is an example of a set of graphical sentences (i.e., a graphical language) that is based on the syntactic convention of placing a plus object above an axis. The syntax of this "horizontal position" language can be formalized with the unary predicate *HorzPos*, which is true for any graphical sentence that consists of a horizontal axis and a set of tuples placing a plus object at a constant height somewhere above the axis.

More formally, a graphical sentence s is a legal sentence of the horizontal position language when it consists of the union of a horizontal axis set h and a set of marks m such that each located object $\langle o, l \rangle$ in m is a plus object *plusobj*

[2] The *retinal* properties are so called because the retina of the eye is sensitive to them, independent of the position of the object. Although they are included in the list of encoding relationships, 3-D position and animation are beyond the scope of this research.

[3] The resolution of a device can be represented by replacing the Cartesian plane with a grid of pixels [16].

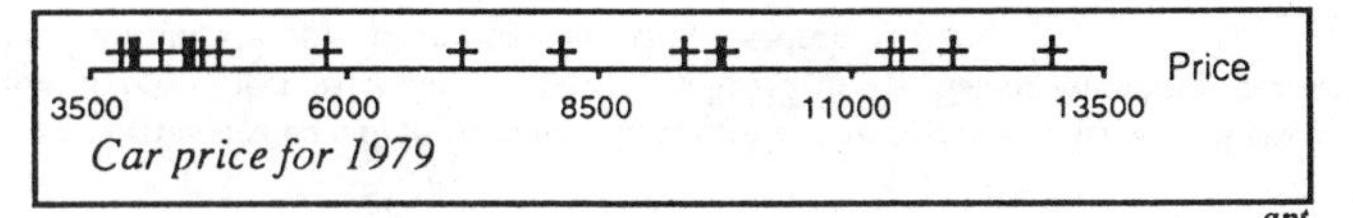

Fig. 9. The horizontal position sentence of the *Price* relation.

located at a constant height *const* above the axis:

$$
\begin{aligned}
&HorzPos(s) \Leftrightarrow \\
&\quad s = h \cup m \wedge \langle o, l \rangle \in m \Rightarrow [\\
&\qquad o = plusobj \wedge \\
&\qquad Ymax(h) \leq Ypos(l) = const \wedge \\
&\qquad Xmin(h) \leq Xpos(l) \leq Xmax(h)].
\end{aligned}
$$

The symbols in this formula are used in a similar manner throughout the paper. In particular, the symbol h always stands for a horizontal axis,[4] and the symbol m always stands for a set of located objects (called *marks*) that have a related set of properties, such as objects positioned against the same axis.

Given a precise syntactic definition, the semantics of a graphical language can be specified using established formal techniques, such as denotational semantics [7]. A collection of located objects representing a graphical sentence can have a denotation in the same way as a collection of characters representing a logic formula. However, a presentation tool designs graphical sentences. It must be able to describe the semantic relationships between a graphical sentence and the encoded facts. For example, the *HorzPos* language encodes a binary relation with an axis, a set of marks, and the position of the marks on the axis. Formally, a relation called *Encodes*$(s, facts, lang)$ is used to describe the semantic relationship between the objects and properties of a graphical sentence s and the set of *facts* that are encoded, given the semantic conventions of the language *lang*.[5] For example, given a relation r consisting of tuples $r(a_i, b_i)$, the following is a formal description of the three basic *Encodes* relationships for a sentence of the *HorzPos* language (see Figure 10 for an abstract description of these encodes relations). The axis h encodes the second domain of the relation, $Dom_2(r)$:

$$Encodes(h, Dom_2(r), HorzPos). \tag{1}$$

For the *Price* relation, the horizontal axis encodes the range [3500, 13000] of prices. Each located object o_i of the set of marks m encodes a unique domain value a_i of the first domain set of the relation $Dom_1(r)$:

$$Encodes(o_i, a_i, HorzPos). \tag{2}$$

Since this is true for every located object in the mark set m, the *Encodes* relation can be extended to the entire set:

$$Encodes(m, Dom_1(r), HorzPos).$$

For the *Price* relation, the marks encode the set of *Cars*.

[4] The symbol v stands for a vertical axis.

[5] Since an image might be a well-formed graphical sentence of more than one language, the *Encodes* relation includes the name of the language to indicate which semantic conventions are being described.

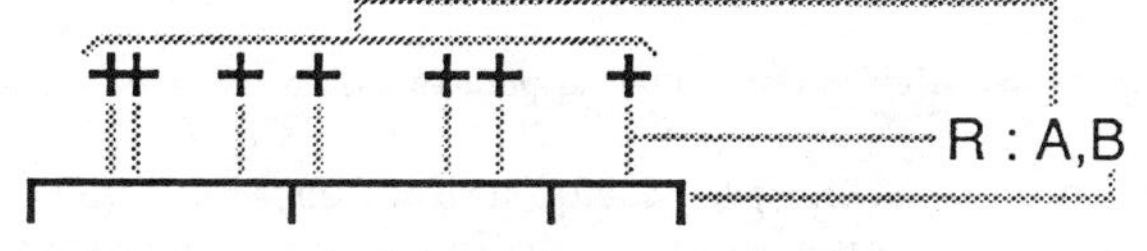

Fig. 10. The *Encodes* relationships for the horizontal position language. The graphical sentence is on the left, and the relation is on the right. The gray lines indicate that the domain sets are encoded by the objects, and the tuples of the relation are encoded by the relative positions of the marks.

Given the semantics for the objects in a graphical sentence, it is straightforward to describe the semantics for arrangements of objects. For the *HorzPos* language, the position of marks on the axis encodes the tuples of the r relation. That is, the first domain value a_i of a tuple $r(a_i, b_i)$ corresponds to a mark o_i as described in (2), and the second domain value b_i corresponds to the position of the mark o_i on the axis h, which is described with the binary function $Position(o_i, h)$. More formally, there exist two constants, *scale* and *offset*, that equate the domain value b_i with the axis position of the mark o_i for the domain value a_i:

$$
\begin{aligned}
&Encodes(o_i, a_i, HorzPos) \Rightarrow \\
&\quad b_i = scale \times (Position(o_i, h) + offset) \wedge \\
&\quad Encodes(Position(o_i, h), r(a_i, b_i), HorzPos).
\end{aligned}
\tag{3}
$$

Since this is true for every mark in the mark set m, the *Encodes* relation can be extended to the domain sets. The positional encoding for the entire relation r can be described as follows:

$$Encodes(Position(m, h), r, HorzPos).$$

The presentation tool APT uses the domain set versions of these *Encodes* relations in the designs that it develops.

The formal machinery for describing the syntax and semantics of a graphical language leads to a precise statement of expressiveness:

$$
\begin{aligned}
&Expressible(facts, lang) \Leftrightarrow \exists s[lang(s) \wedge \forall f[\\
&\quad f \in facts \Rightarrow Encodes(s, f, lang) \wedge \\
&\quad f \notin facts \Rightarrow \neg Encodes(s, f, lang)]].
\end{aligned}
\tag{4}
$$

The remainder of this section gives two examples that illustrate these two conditions of expressiveness.

The first example, which focuses on expressing all the facts, is based on the *HorzPos* language. It turns out that it is possible to prove that one-to-many relations cannot be expressed in the *HorzPos* language.

Theorem 1. *When r is a one-to-many relation, it cannot be expressed in the HorzPos language*:

$$
\begin{aligned}
&r(a_i, b_j) \wedge r(a_i, b_k) \wedge b_j \neq b_k \Rightarrow \\
&\quad \neg Expressible(r, HorzPos).
\end{aligned}
$$

Proof. A proof by contradiction is straightforward, given the obvious geometric fact that a mark cannot have two positions on an axis. Assume that there

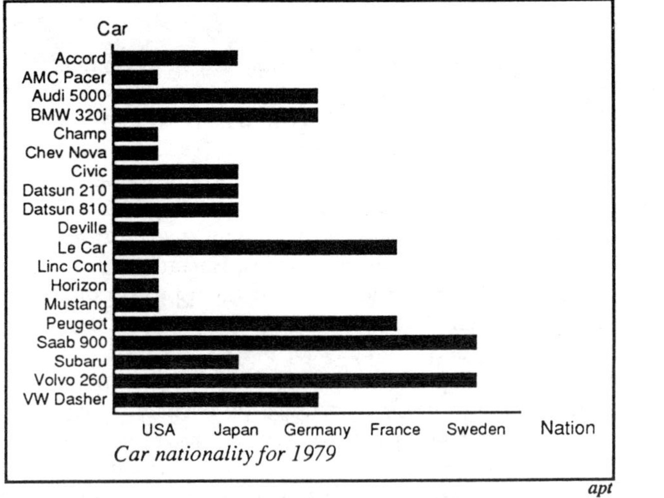

Fig. 11. Incorrect use of a bar chart for the *Nation* relation. The lengths of the bars suggest an ordering on the vertical axis, as if the USA cars were longer or better than the other cars, which is not true for the *Nation* relation.

exists a sentence s that satisfies (4) for the *HorzPos* language and relation r, which means that both tuples mentioned above are encoded in s. In particular, (2) indicates that there exists a mark o_i that is paired with the domain value a_i, and (3) indicates that $b_j = scale \times (Position(o_i, h) + offset) = b_k$, which contradicts the assumed inequality of the two domain values in the one-to-many relation. □

Although the previous theorem is not particularly deep, it illustrates the importance of precise definitions of the graphical conventions used to design and interpret information presentations. Not only do precise definitions make theorems possible, but they make clear which conventions are being used. Different conventions lead to different theorems. For example, the *HorzPos* language is based on the convention that the marks are uniquely paired with the domain values of the first domain set. Occasionally, graphical presentations use a different convention, that of pairing marks with the tuples rather than with the domain values of the first domain set. Given such a convention, the previous theorem is no longer valid because $r(a_i, b_j)$ and $r(a_i, b_k)$ can be encoded by the positions of different marks. However, this alternative convention is not so common as the *HorzPos* convention because it is natural to assume that marks are associated with domain values. For example, it is natural to assume that each mark in Figure 9 represents a unique car.

A second example, which focuses on the second expressiveness condition, illustrates the fact that some graphical languages encode additional information in the geometric relationships of the objects in a graphical sentence. Consider the bar chart diagram of the *Nation* relation in Figure 11. Most people perceive the lengths of the bars as an encoding of an ordered or quantitative set. That is, given domain tuples $r(a_i, b_i)$ and $r(a_j, b_j)$ and the corresponding bar objects bar_i

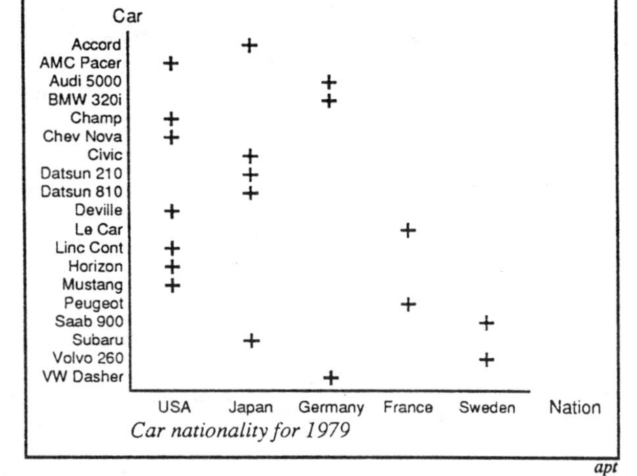

Fig. 12. Correct use of a plot chart for the *Nation* relation. Since bar charts encode ordered domain sets, plot charts are conventionally used to encode nominal domain sets. The ordering of the labels on the axes is ignored.

and bar_j, an ordering relationship among the bar lengths encodes an ordering relation among the domain values b_i and b_j:

$$Encodes(Length(bar_i) > Length(bar_j),\ b_i > b_j,\ BarChart),$$

where the rest of the *Encodes* relations for the *BarChart* language are similar to the ones for *HorzPos*. Given this *Encodes* relation, it is easy to prove that the bar chart in Figure 11 does not express the *Nation* relation because it expresses the fact that the countries are ordered, which is not correct (see Figure 3).

The plot chart of the *Nation* relation in Figure 12, which is an alternative design for encoding the *Nation* relation that avoids the bar length problem, also illustrates the importance of precise language definitions. Sometimes, people use the convention that the sequence of labels on an axis indicates an ordered domain set, which would ruin the expressiveness of the scatter plot design for Figure 12. However, the standard convention is to ignore this sequencing encoding. After all, when the second domain set is ordered, a bar chart can be used. This means that the precise definition for a plot chart language should not include an *Encodes* predicate for the ordering of the second domain set. Therefore, the plot chart in Figure 12 does *not* encode additional incorrect facts.[6]

[6] The rendering of the plot chart in Figure 12 has the independent domain set of the *Nation* function on the vertical axis, which does not conform to the often ignored convention of encoding the independent domain set of a function with the horizontal axis. In this case the rendering code flipped the axes to make the rendering of the car labels more legible, and it did not take into account the fact that such a flip might confuse the reader of the diagram about which domain set was the independent one. (The recent development of the Dot Chart design deals with this problem [5].) Trade-offs between conventions and rendering constraints often occur. In the future, the rendering component will also have to be involved in the search for the most effective design.

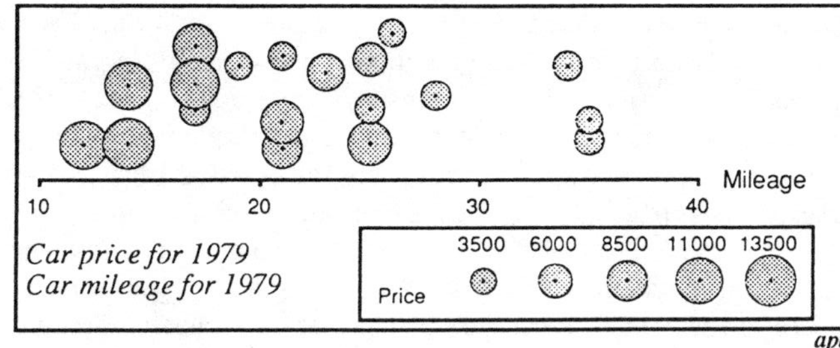

Fig. 13. Area/position presentation of the *Price* and *Mileage* relations. The vertical positioning of the marks reduces the chance that a mark is covered. This technique is called jittering; the vertical positioning does not encode any information.

6. EFFECTIVENESS

Given two graphical languages that express some information, the obvious question is which language involves a design that specifies the more effective presentation. For example, Figure 13 expresses the same price/mileage input as the scatter plot in Figure 5, but the prices are encoded with the area of the marks rather than with their position on a vertical axis. Which presentation is more effective?

Unlike expressiveness, which only depends on the syntax and semantics of the graphical language, effectiveness also depends on the capabilities of the perceiver. The difficulty is that there does not yet exist an empirically verified theory of human perceptual capabilities that can be used to prove theorems about the effectiveness of graphical languages. Therefore, one must conjecture a theory of effectiveness that is both intuitively motivated and consistent with current empirically verified knowledge about human perceptual capabilities. This section describes such a conjectural theory.

The core of this conjectural theory is an observation, made by Cleveland and McGill, that people accomplish the perceptual tasks associated with the interpretation of graphical presentations with different degrees of accuracy [6]. Cleveland and McGill focused on the presentation of quantitative information. They identified and ranked the tasks shown in Figure 14. Higher tasks are accomplished more accurately than lower tasks. Furthermore, they have some experimental evidence that supports the basic properties of this ranking.

Although the ranking in Figure 14 can be used to compare alternative graphical languages that encode quantitative information, it does not address the encoding of nonquantitative information, which involves additional perceptual tasks and different task rankings. For example, texture is not mentioned in Figure 14, and color, which is at the bottom of the quantitative ranking, is a very effective way of encoding nominal sets [23]. Therefore, it was necessary to extend Cleveland and McGill's ranking, as shown in Figure 15. Although this extension was developed using existing psychophysical results and various analyses of the different perceptual tasks, it has not been empirically verified [16].

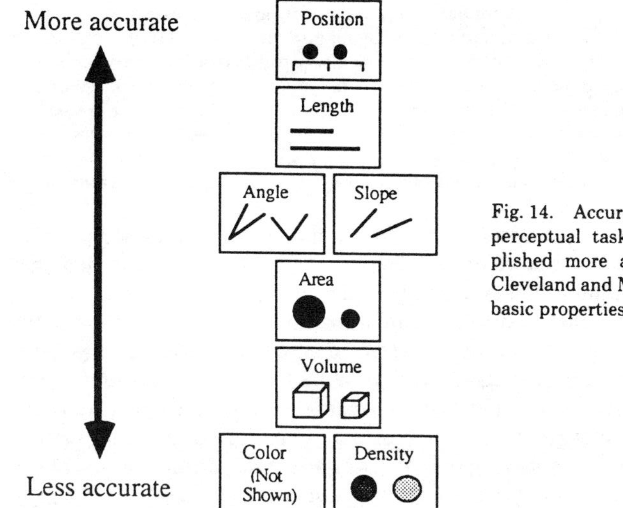

Fig. 14. Accuracy ranking of quantitative perceptual tasks. Higher tasks are accomplished more accurately than lower tasks. Cleveland and McGill empirically verified the basic properties of this ranking.

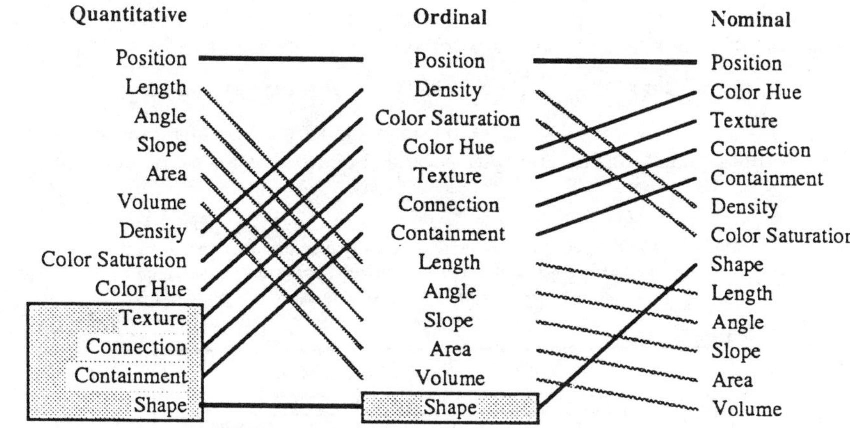

Fig. 15. Ranking of perceptual tasks. The tasks shown in the gray boxes are not relevant to these types of data.

An example analysis for area perception is shown in Figure 16. The top line shows that a series of decreasing areas can be used to encode a tenfold quantitative range. Of course, in a real diagram such as Figure 13, the areas would be laid out randomly, making it more difficult to judge the relative sizes of different areas accurately (hence, area is ranked fifth in Figure 14). Nevertheless, small misjudgments about the size of an area only leads to small misperceptions about the corresponding quantitative value that is encoded. The middle line shows that area can encode three ordinal values. However, one must be careful to make sure

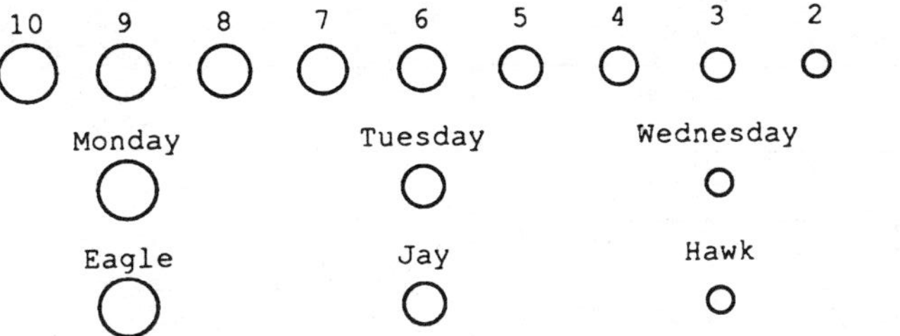

Fig. 16. Analysis of the area task. The top case shows that area is moderately effective for encoding quantitative information. The middle case shows that it is possible to encode ordinal information as long as the step size between areas is large enough so that the values are not confused. The bottom case shows that it is possible to encode nominal information, but people may perceive an ordinal encoding.

that ordinal areas are different enough so that they are not confused with each other. This is indicated by the fact that only three days of the week are encoded. If more days of the week were encoded, the step size between Tuesday's area and Monday's area would get small enough for people to start confusing them, which is quite different from confusing two quantitative values that are almost equal. The bottom line shows that area can encode three nominal values. Besides the fact that stepping is also required for nominal information, this case illustrates the additional problem that people often perceive area as an encoding of ordinal information. This analysis indicates that area should have a moderate quantitative ranking and a low nonquantitative ranking.

The ranking in Figure 15 can often be used to determine the relative effectiveness of different graphical languages. For example, Figure 17 compares the scatter plot and area/position designs for the price/mileage input. Since position has a higher ranking than area for quantitative data, it is clear that the scatter plot is a more effective design.

	Price	*Mileage*
Scatter plot	position	position
Area/Position	area	position

Fig. 17. Comparison of perceptual tasks for the price/mileage designs.

The ranking in Figure 15, however, does not specify a total ordering on the effectiveness of graphical languages. For example, Figure 18 compares two encodings of the *Price*, *Mileage*, and *Weight* relations. Both designs are scatter plots with information also encoded in the area of the marks. Since both designs require the same perceptual tasks, the ranking in Figure 15 does not indicate which design is more effective. The ranking can be extended to generate a lexicographic ordering with the following principle:

	Price	*Mileage*	*Weight*
Scatter plot 1	position	position	area
Scatter plot 2	area	position	position

Fig. 18. Example of designs not ordered by the effectiveness ranking.

Principle of Importance Ordering: Encode more important information more effectively.

That is, the input to the presentation tool is actually a tuple of relations that indicates the relative importance of the relations. For example, the input

⟨*Price*, *Mileage*, *Weight*⟩

should be presented with scatter plot 1, which has the *Weight* relation encoded with area.

7. COMPOSITION

Expressiveness and effectiveness criteria, which were described in the previous two sections, are not very useful without a method for generating alternative designs. The naïve approach is simply to develop an ad hoc list of graphical languages that can be filtered with the expressiveness criteria and ordered with the effectiveness criteria for each input. The major difficulty with this approach is that there is no guarantee that there will exist appropriate designs for a wide variety of presentation situations. A minor difficulty is that the entire list must always be considered, even when only a few alternatives are suitable for a given input. This section describes an alternative approach based on the idea of a composition algebra. Such an algebra consists of a basis set containing primitive graphical languages and some composition operators that can generate composite designs. Described is a specific choice of basis set and composition operators that generate many of the designs commonly found in presentation graphics [3–5, 15, 19, 21]. The study of alternative composition algebras is an open area of research.

The idea of a composition algebra occurred to me when I looked at a diagram that was very similar in design to the diagram in Figure 19. The design used in Figure 19 combines two encoding techniques that are generally not seen together. First, the prerequisites among computer science classes are encoded with links that connect nodes that encode the classes. Second, a class schedule is encoded by the position of the nodes on a vertical axis. This diagram is an example of a composite design. The primitive languages used to form this composite design are a node/link language (see Figure 20) and a vertical-axis language (see Figure 21). Given this unusual example of a composite design, I realized that many presentations could be described as compositions of a set of primitive languages.

7.1 A Basis Set of Primitive Graphical Languages

A basis set of primitive graphical languages derived from Bertin's vocabulary of graphical encoding techniques (see Figure 8) is listed in Figure 22. The primitive languages have been classified by their primary encoding technique. *Single-position languages* encode information by the position of a mark set on one axis. *Apposed-position languages* encode information by a mark set that is positioned

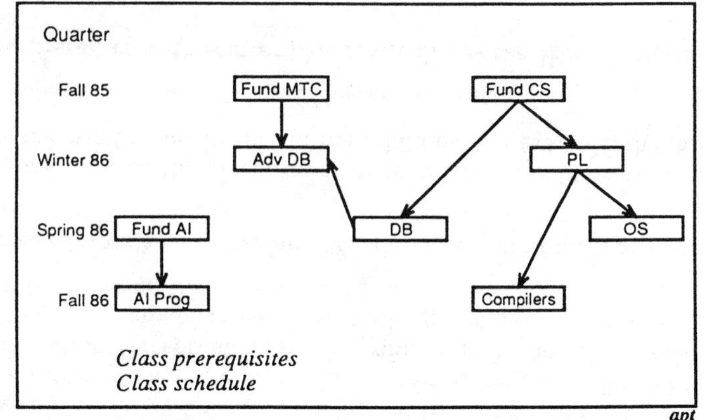

Fig. 19. Composite presentation for the prerequisite and schedule relations. The links encode the prerequisite relationships between computer science classes. The position on the vertical axis encodes the scheduling of the classes. Note that the advanced database class is scheduled before its prerequisite.

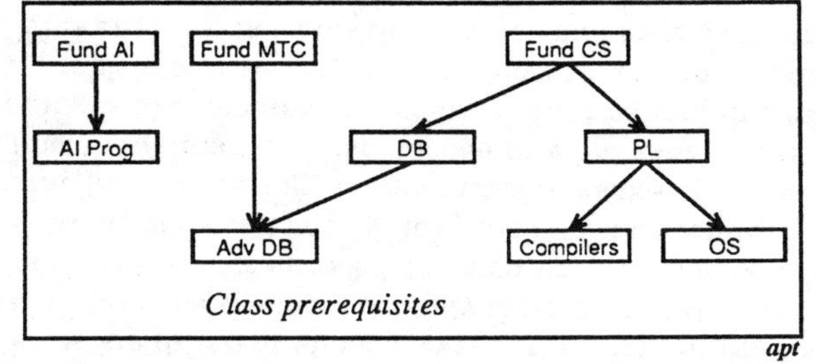

Fig. 20. Network presentation for the prerequisite relation.

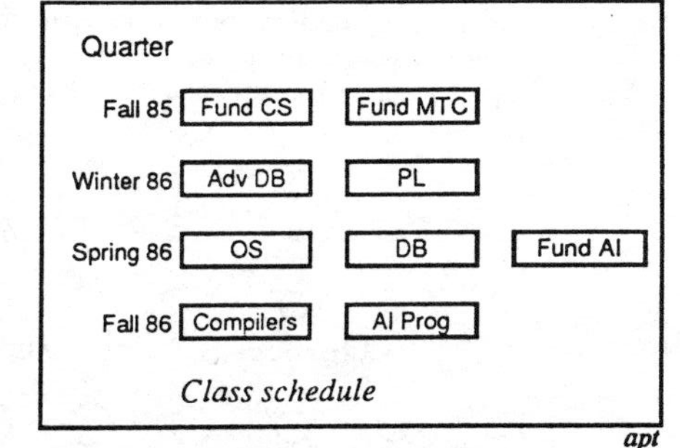

Fig. 21. Vertical-axis presentation for the schedule relation.

Encoding Technique	Primitive Graphical Language
Single-position	Horizontal axis, vertical axis
Apposed-position	Line chart, bar chart, plot chart
Retinal-list	Color, shape, size, saturation, texture, orientation
Map	Road map, topographic map
Connection	Tree, acyclic graph, network
Misc. (angle, contain, . . .)	Pie chart, Venn diagram, . . .

Fig. 22. A basis set of primitive graphical languages.

Encoding Technique	Syntactic Structure
Single-position	$h(m)$ or $v(m)$
Apposed-position	$vh(m)$
Retinal-list	m
Map	$vh(m)$
Connection	$m_n(m_l)$
Miscellaneous	$vh(m)$

Fig. 23. Syntactic structure of primitives. The notation is described in the text.

between two axes.[7] *Retinal-list languages* use one of the six retinal properties of the marks in a mark set to encode information. Since the positions of these marks do not encode anything, the marks can be moved when retinal list designs are composed with other designs. *Map languages*, which have fixed positions, encode information with graphical techniques that are specific to maps. *Connection languages* encode information by connecting a set of node objects with a set of link objects. *Miscellaneous languages* encode information with a variety of additional graphical techniques.

Figure 23 summarizes the basic syntactic structure of the primitive languages. The notation used in this figure is based on the fact that graphical sentences are sets of located object tuples. Except for connection languages, it turns out that every sentence of the primitive languages described in Figure 22 can be divided into the disjoint subsets

$$m \cup v \cup h,$$

where m is a set of marks, v contains at most a vertical axis, and h contains at most a horizontal axis. Furthermore, both the objects and positions of the mark sets have additional properties. The objects are either a collection of points, lines, or areas, and their positions are always fixed relative to the existing axes.[8] The notation always uses m for a set of marks, v for a vertical axis, and h for a

[7] It turns out that apposed-position languages can be described as the composition of single-position languages [16].

[8] This assumes that languages that restrict the positions of mark sets without a visible axis object, such as maps, define their sentences as having invisible axis objects.

Encoding Technique	Expressiveness Criteria
Single-position	$X \to Y$ (X is nominal)
Apposed-position	$X \times Y$ (X, Y are not nominal)
Retinal-list	X, or $X \to Y$ (X is not quantitative)
Map	$L \to X_1, \ldots$ (L is a location)
Connection	$X \times X$ (X is nominal)
Miscellaneous (angle, contain, ...)	Generally, $X \times Y$

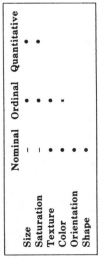

Fig. 24. Expressiveness criteria for the primitive languages. These are the general restrictions. Specific languages can have additional restrictions.

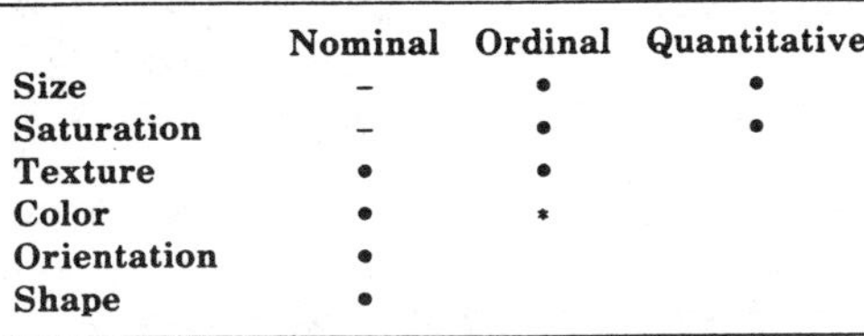

	Nominal	Ordinal	Quantitative
Size	–	•	•
Saturation	–	•	•
Texture	•	•	
Color	•	*	
Orientation	•		
Shape	•		

Fig. 25. Expressiveness of retinal techniques. The – indicates that size and saturation should not be used for nominal measurements because they will probably be perceived to be ordered. The * indicates that the full color spectrum is not ordered. However, parts of the color spectrum are ordinally perceived [23].

horizontal axis. The notation also uses parentheses to indicate that there is a positional constraint on a set of marks. For example, the positional constraints of bar charts are described by $vh(m)$, where v and h are not empty. Sentences of connection languages consist of two sets of marks: the set of nodes m_n and the set of links m_l. The nodes constrain the position of links. The notation can also be extended to more complex designs. For example, the two bar charts in Figure 7 that are aligned on their vertical axes have the structure $v(h_i(m_i), h_j(m_j))$.

An analysis of the semantic properties of these languages leads to the expressiveness criteria shown in Figures 24 and 25. Figure 24 describes the basic expressiveness criteria for each type of primitive language. For example, single-position languages can only express binary relations that have a functional dependency. Figure 25 describes the expressiveness criteria of various retinal techniques for nominal, ordinal, and quantitative information. There are additional requirements not mentioned in Figures 24 and 25. For example, line charts can only be used when a relation describes values of a continuous function.

7.2 Some Composition Operators

The composition operators associated with the primitive languages in Figure 22 are based on a single principle:

Principle of Composition: Compose two designs by merging parts that encode the same information.

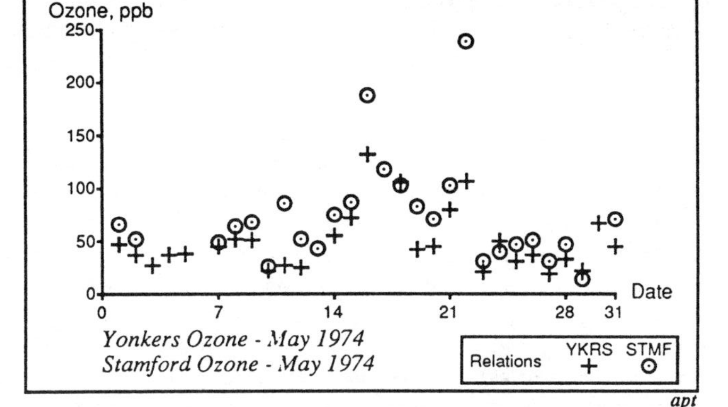

Fig. 26. Example of double-axes composition. The diagram describes a month of ozone measurements for two cities. The reason that a line chart design was not used for these data is that there are missing measurements for some of the days; a line chart is only used for continuous functions.

This principle leads to three composition operators that are based on the objects used by the primitive languages: *double-axes composition* $\bowtie_d$, *single-axis composition* $\bowtie_s$, and *mark composition* $\bowtie_m$. The following description of these composition operators gives an informal and formal definition of each of them.

Double-axes composition can compose graphical sentences that have identical horizontal and vertical axes. The multiple scatter plot in Figure 26 is an example of double-axes composition. The component designs are two plot charts that describe ozone measurements in two different cities. Since the measurements were taken in the same month, the axes of these two plot charts are identical. The composite is generated by merging the identical axes and copying the mark sets from the two component designs.

Formally, the double-axes composition $s_i \bowtie_d s_j$ is well defined if s_i contains $v_i h_i(m_i)$ and s_j contains $v_j h_j(m_j)$ such that the axis sets are not empty and encode the same information. That is, given that s_i is a sentence of language l_i and s_j is a sentence of language l_j, the *Encodes* relations indicate that both horizontal axes encode the same domain set x and both vertical axes encode the same domain set y:

$$v_i = v_j \neq \{\ \} \land h_i = h_j \neq \{\ \} \land$$
$$Encodes(h_i, x, l_i) \land Encodes(h_j, x, l_j) \land$$
$$Encodes(v_i, y, l_i) \land Encodes(v_j, y, l_j).$$

The composite contains $v_i h_i(m_i', m_j')$. The prime is required when the marks are changed by the composition. For example, composed bar charts move the bars next to each other. When the prime is not needed, double-axes composition is commutative. It is always associative.

Single-axis composition aligns two sentences that have identical horizontal or vertical axes. The diagram in Figure 7 is an example of single-axis composition.

The two component designs are bar charts that describe the price and mileage of some cars. Since the vertical axes encode the same set of cars, the composite can be generated by placing one diagram next to the other such that the vertical axes are aligned.

Formally, the single-axis composition $s_i \bowtie_s s_j$ is well defined if s_i contains $v_i h_i(m_i)$, s_j contains $v_j h_j(m_j)$, and the following condition is satisfied:

$$[v_i = v_j \neq \{\ \} \wedge Encodes(v_i, y, l_i) \wedge Encodes(v_j, y, l_j)] \vee$$
$$[h_i = h_j \neq \{\ \} \wedge Encodes(h_i, x, l_i) \wedge Encodes(h_j, x, l_j)],$$

where x, y, l_i, and l_j are defined in the same manner as for double-axes composition. The composite contains $v_i' h_i'(m_i')$ and $v_j' h_j'(m_j')$, where the positions of the objects are modified to place the diagrams next to each other in the viewing area. Single-axis composition is not commutative because the positions of the diagrams reverse. However, it is associative.

Mark composition is more complicated than the axis composition operators because it actually merges mark sets. For example, a mark set of uniform size that encodes information with color can be merged with a mark set of uniform color that encodes information with size. The resulting mark set uses both color and size to encode information (see Figure 30 for an example).

Mark composition merges mark sets by pairing each and every mark of one set with a compatible mark of the other set. The diagram in Figure 19 is an example of mark composition. The component design is a directed-acyclic-graph design for the prerequisite relation, which is rendered in Figure 20, and a vertical-axis design for the scheduling relation, which is rendered in Figure 21. The two mark sets are compatible because they encode the same information, and any shared positional or retinal constraints are identical. The composite is generated by merging the mark sets. That is, the composite includes a mark set that corresponds to the two mark sets of the components. The position and retinal properties of this composite mark set are based on the constrained position and retinal properties of the component mark sets. Compatibility makes sure that the component's properties do not conflict. Additional properties and objects in the component sentences are copied over into the composite. For example, the composite in Figure 19 includes the vertical-axis object from the diagram in Figure 21.

Formally, the mark composition $s_i \bowtie_m s_j$ is well defined if s_i contains $v_i h_i(m_i)$, and s_j contains $v_j h_j(m_j)$, and the marks in m_i and m_j can be paired such that each pair of located objects o_i and o_j encode the same domain value a:

$$[Encodes(o_i, a, l_i) \wedge Encodes(o_j, a, l_j)].$$

Furthermore, the position and retinal properties of these mark pairs must encode the same information. For position, an existing pair of axes means that the positions must be identical:

$$[v_i = v_j \neq \{\ \} \Rightarrow Position(o_i, v_i) = Position(o_j, v_j)] \wedge$$
$$[h_i = h_j \neq \{\ \} \Rightarrow Position(o_i, h_i) = Position(o_j, h_j)].$$

For the retinal properties, a little more formal machinery is required. A set of marks can have retinal constraints based on the six retinal properties identified by Bertin. For example, the size of the marks in Figure 13 encode the values of the *Price* relation. Six functions identify the six retianl values of an object. These functions can also be used to indicate when the retinal properties of a mark set are constrained. Given a retinal function f, a set of marks m, and a graphical sentence s that contains m, the relation $Rt(s, m, f)$ is true when the retinal properties corresponding to f encode information for the mark set m. Given this relation, the following indicates that the paired marks must have the same constraints on their retinal properties:

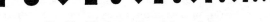

Fig. 27. The interaction of size and shape.

$$Rt(s_i, m_i, f) \wedge Rt(s_j, m_j, f) \Rightarrow$$
$$f(o_i) = f(o_j).$$

That is, when a retinal property is used by two mark sets to encode information, the objects for each pair of marks must have identical retinal properties.

The composite sentence $vh(m)$, generated by the mark composition $v_i h_i(m_i) \bowtie_m v_j h_j(m_j)$, is constructed in the following manner. The vertical axis v is v_i if it is not empty and v_j otherwise. The horizontal axis h is h_i if it is not empty and h_j otherwise. For each pair of marks, construct a composite mark from the constrained retinal and position properties of the component marks (which must be identical) and any remaining properties from m_i. The final condition means that $\bowtie_m$ is not commutative. It is easy to show that $\bowtie_m$ is associative.

The conditions for using these three composition operators are sufficiently general for them to be used together. The major difficulty is specifying exactly how the parts of the component sentences that are not part of the composition should be handled. The best approach is to merge pairs of axes or mark sets of the component sentence that satisfy the conditions of the composition operators. This will reduce redundancy in the composed diagram.

A rough effectiveness ranking can also be assigned to the composition operators. Mark composition is the most effective because it merges the component sentences in such a way that the number of graphical objects does not increase. Single-axis composition is the least effective because it does not actually merge the designs, which makes it harder to perceive all the information at once.

Composition can have side effects that must be addressed. For example, when size and shape are composed together, the perception of shape is made difficult when the sizes are small. For example, the marks in Figure 27 are a composition of shape and size. The shapes of the small objects begin to look the same. Therefore, care must be taken to avoid situations in which such interactions reduce the effectiveness of a composite design. APT's rendering component makes sure the marks do not get too small.

8. IMPLEMENTATION

The theoretical results described in the previous three sections have been combined in a synthesis algorithm that generates designs in order of the effectiveness criteria described above. The synthesis algorithm has been implemented in APT, which consists of a design component followed by a rendering component (see Figure 1). The design component uses logic programming techniques to implement the synthesis algorithm. The rendering component uses object-oriented programming techniques and a device-independent graphics package to render the resulting designs. The rendering component, which was not the focus of this research, places an implementation restriction on the set of primitive languages in Figure 22 that can be used by APT to generate presentations. As of this writing, the following primitive languages remain unimplemented: orientation, texture, line charts, maps, and miscellaneous. Even with these restrictions, the prototype can generate a wide range of useful presentations. The diagrams in this paper with *apt* in the lower right corner are examples of APT's output.

APT's synthesis algorithm is based on a divide-and-conquer search strategy. The algorithm has three steps: partition, selection, and composition. These steps, which are described below, involve choices. When a particular set of choices does not lead to a composite design, backtracking is used to consider other choices. APT uses depth-first search with simple backtracking.

(1) *Partitioning.* The set of relations to be presented is divided into partitions that match the expressiveness criteria of at least one of the primitive languages. This is done recursively. For example, the input

⟨*Price, Mileage, Repair, Weight*⟩

can be partitioned into the sets

⟨*Price*⟩ and ⟨*Mileage, Repair, Weight*⟩.

The right partition must be recursively divided because it does not match any of the primitive languages.

The principle of importance ordering is addressed by making sure that the choices among alternative partitionings give preference to the important information. The input shown above is a tuple that indicates the importance ordering for the automobile relations. It is partitioned so that the most important relation, which is the *Price* relation, will get first chance at being matched to an effective primitive language.

Since relations, as well as sets of relations, can be partitioned [16], it is possible for the input to include relations that have more than two domain sets. The cumulative bar chart in Figure 28 is an example of a design that is generated by relation partitioning. The input is a ternary relation, which is a function of years and quarters, to the Ph.D.s conferred in each quarter for a range of years. Binary relations are generated by fixing the year. The stacked bar designs corresponding to the binary relations are composed with single-axis composition to generate the cumulative bar chart.

(2) *Selection.* Given expressiveness and effectiveness criteria, selection is straightforward. For each partition generated by the previous step, the primitives are filtered, with their expressiveness criteria used to generate a list of candidate designs. For example, the list of candidate designs for the *Price* partition does not include maps because the *Price* relation does not satisfy the map expressiveness criterion (see Figure 24).

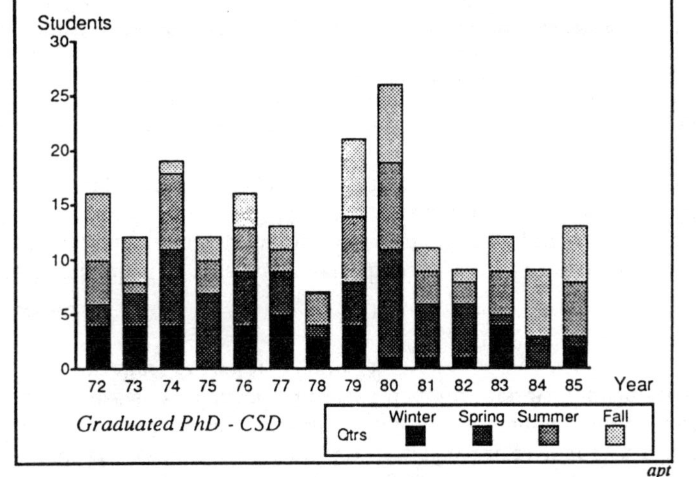

Fig. 28. A relation partitioning example. The cumulative bar chart describes the number of Ph.D. students that graduated each quarter for a range of years. The input is a relation of three domain sets, which are partitioned into a set of binary relations. The composite is generated by the single-axis composition of the stacked bar design chosen for each of these binary relations.

The effectiveness criteria are used to order the candidate designs so that the most effective design will be the first choice. For the *Price* relation the effectiveness ordering depends on whether the application has requested that the details about the cars be placed in the background. Apposed-position languages are the most effective when the details are required, and single-position languages are the most effective otherwise. The other primitive languages are less effective because position is at the top of the perceptual task ranking shown in Figure 15.

(3) *Composition.* Composition operators are used to compose the individual designs into a unified presentation of all the information. Given designs for two partitions, the three composition operators are checked to see if they can be applied. During the generation of the composite designs, additional conditions, such as the interaction of shape and size, can be checked.

The synthesis algorithm involves choices that might not lead to a design, which means that backtracking will occur. When backtracking occurs, the next most effective primitive language or composition operator is chosen until a design is found for all the information. For example, given a request to omit the details about the cars, APT processes the automobile input shown above as follows. The partitioning step generates a partition for the *Price* relation and a partition for the *Mileage* relation. The first selection choice is the vertical-axis primitive

$$
\left.\begin{array}{l}
rel = x \rightarrow y \wedge \neg Numeric(x) \wedge Numeric(y) \wedge \quad \} \text{ Expressiveness} \\
Cardinality(x) < 20 \wedge \quad \} \text{ Effectiveness} \\
LineObjs(barchart, lines) \wedge VertAxis(barchart, vaxis) \wedge \\
Encodes(lines, x) \wedge Encodes(vaxis, y) \wedge \\
Length(lines, len, vaxis) \wedge Encodes(len, rel(x)) \wedge \cdots \\
\quad \Rightarrow Presents(barchart, rel)
\end{array}\right.
$$

(The bracket labelled "Assumables" spans the LineObjs, Encodes and Length lines.)

Fig. 29. APT's bar-chart rule. The expressiveness conditions state that the relation must be a functional dependency from a nonnumeric set to a numeric set. The effectiveness condition limits the number of bars because too many bars make the presentation difficult to read. The assumables are *Encodes* relations that connect the relation and the presentation. The independent set is connected to the bar lines and the dependent set is connected to the vertical axis.

language for both of these partitions (because the relations have the same structure). However, the composition step fails to compose the resulting designs because mark composition, which is the only applicable operator, cannot merge marks that have two different positions on an axis. This failure triggers backtracking. The next most effective choice for the *Mileage* partition is the horizontal-axis primitive language. Mark composition succeeds for this choice, and the search proceeds to deal with the remaining relations in the input. (Given an indication from the application that the output medium includes color, the resulting design for the four automobile relations is the scatter plot rendered in Figure 30.)

The logic program implementing the synthesis algorithm is based on a depth-first[9] backward chaining version of a deductive algorithm called Residue [9]. Residue is useful for design problems because predicates describing the design can be declared to be assumable. During a deduction, an assumable predicate can be assumed to be true to make the deduction proceed. At the end of the deduction, all assumed predicates are returned as conditions that must be satisfied. For design problems, these conditions are exactly the design constraints. For example, Figure 29 describes APT's bar chart rule. The assumables are the *Encodes* relations of the bar-chart primitive language. When these predicates are assumed, they can be used to compose this design with others and to render the final image.

APT was deveoped on a Symbolics LISP Machine using MRS, a representation and logic programming system [18]. APT is a functional prototype, and no effort has been made to make it efficient, although designs are typically generated in 1–2 minutes, and images are rendered in less than a minute. The logic program is about 200 rules, and the rendering system is about 60 pages of LISP code.

APT demonstrates that a synthesis algorithm based on composition can be used to generate automatically effective designs that can express a wide variety of input. Although inefficient, the deductive search strategy used in APT has a number of advantages that recommend it over more procedural approaches. APT can be sensitive to many factors while generating designs. The next section describes how APT is sensitive to the output medium. APT is also sensitive to requests from the application. An application can indicate that a particular primitive language should be used, even when it contradicts the effectiveness ranking that APT would normally use. This makes it possible for an application to tailor a presentation to fit the profile of a particular user. Another advantage of the logic programming approach is that it is flexible. The range of designs that can be generated by APT can be modified by changing the rules associated with the primitive languages and the composition operators. The search order can also be modified by changing the expressiveness and effectiveness criteria. This is important because presentation graphics and human perceptual abilities are not yet well understood. As our understanding advances, it will be possible to make modifications to APT that will enable it to generate even more effective designs.

[9] Depth-first search can be used because the effectiveness criteria place a total ordering on designs that are understood by APT. As the theory of effectiveness becomes more sophisticated, it is likely that the control strategy will also have to become more sophisticated.

9. MEDIA SENSITIVITY

Since the synthesis algorithm searches for designs, it can be sensitive to the capabilities of the output medium. For example, when the application indicates that the output medium includes color, APT designs the scatter plot shown in Figure 30 for the automobile input, which is the mark composition of two single-position designs and two retinal-list designs. When the application restricts APT to a monochrome medium, APT designs the aligned bar chart shown in Figure 31, which is the single-axis composition of four bar-chart designs.[10] Given a color medium, the *Repair* relation can be encoded by the color-list primitive language. However, given a monochrome medium, the only available retinal-list primitive languages for ordinal information are texture, saturation, and size (see Figure 25). The texture primitive language was rejected because the rendering portion of APT does not implement texture. The saturation primitive language was rejected by its effectiveness criterion because five levels of gray blend together, making the repair values blend together. The size primitive language can be selected. However, the scatter plot design requires that size also be used for one of the other relations in the input, and mark composition cannot merge two designs that use size to encode different domain sets. APT ultimately settles on the aligned bar chart shown in Figure 31.

10. DISCUSSION

The research described in this paper sets the framework for the development of presentation tools that can automatically design effective graphical presentations for a wide variety of information. The formalization of graphical presentation as a collection of graphical languages makes it possible to develop expressiveness

[10] APT always generates the aligned bar design before the scatter plot design when the application does not indicate that the details about the cars can be omitted, because the bar charts contain the names of the cars. Labels on points in the scatter plot obscure information. When the output device is a computer monitor, however, it is generally better to omit detail, because omitted details can be obtained by interacting with the display through the use of techniques such as pick-sensitive objects and pop-up windows.

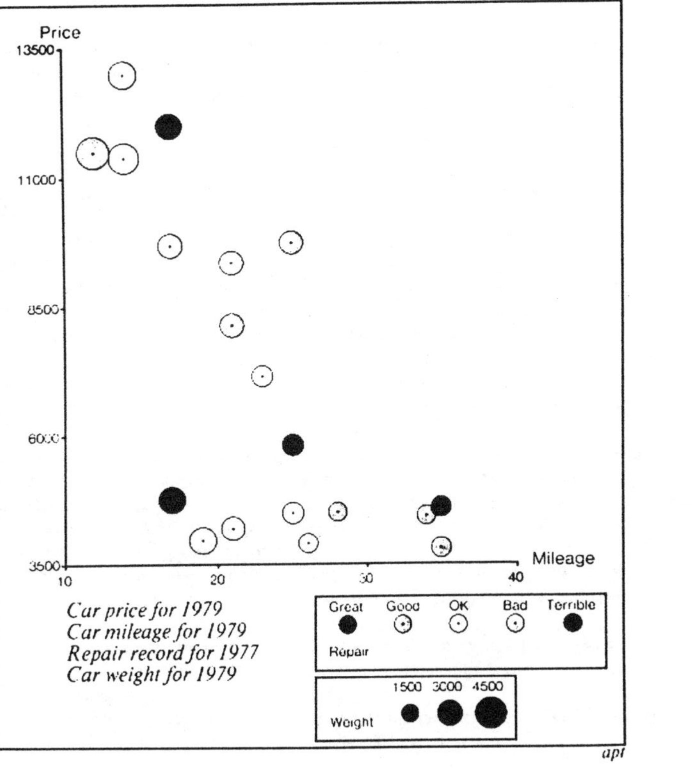

Fig. 30. Color scatter plot for four automobile relations. The design expresses the relations only if the application permits the details about the cars to be omitted.

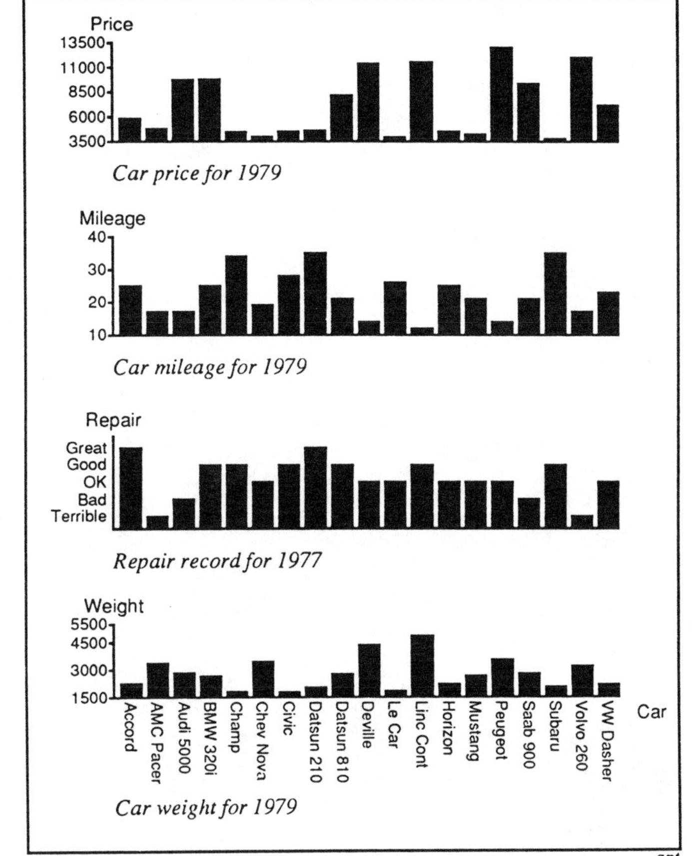

Fig. 31. Aligned bar chart of automobile data. This diagram shows the details about the car domain set. However, the general relationships are not so easy to see as in the scatter plot design.

and effectiveness criteria and a composition algebra. This formalization provides the basis of a logic program that designs presentations automatically. The prototype implementation, called APT, demonstrates the feasibility of this approach.

Many problems associated with the automatic generation of graphical designs remain to be solved. The engineering of robust presentation tools will raise many questions about the correct search criteria. Animation and 3-D presentation appear to be very powerful techniques for presenting symbolic information and should be incorporated into future tools. Larger search spaces, which can be generated with finer grained sets of primitive languages, make it more difficult to search for an appropriate choice in real time. However, it may be possible to build a discovery system that searches this larger space for unusual but effective designs. These designs can then be cached along with the primitive languages described in this paper to form a small but comprehensive search space.

This research on intelligent presentation applies artificial intelligence techniques to part of the user interface design problem—that of choosing an appropriate graphical presentation of relational data. Graphic design issues are an important concern of user interface design. This presentation research incorporates a formalized body of graphic design knowledge. Future work with these techniques can address other aspects of user interface management systems, perhaps choosing or adapting the dialogue specifications appropriate to the observed skill level of the user. When research develops theoretical results, such as the graphic design criteria and composition algebra described in this paper, from a careful analysis of user interface systems, artificial intelligence techniques can be used to develop an intelligent user interface.

ACKNOWLEDGMENTS

I would like to thank the following people: Polle Zellweger for her inspired suggestions that improved every draft of this paper, Rick Beach for his constructive suggestions just before the submission deadline, Matt Ginsberg and Eric Bier for their helpful suggestions on early drafts, and Michael Genesereth, my advisor, for his encouragement and suggestions throughout the research. The suggestions of the referees are also appreciated.

REFERENCES

1. BEACH, R. J. Setting tables and illustrations with style. Ph.D. dissertation, Dept. of Computer Science, Univ. of Waterloo, Waterloo, Ont., Canada, 1985. Also Xerox PARC Tech. Rep. CSL-85-3.
2. BEACH, R., AND STONE, M. Graphical style—towards high quality illustrations. *Computer Graph. (SIGGRAPH) 17*, 3 (1983), 127–135.
3. BERTIN, J. *Semiology of Graphics*, W. J. Berg, Tr. University of Wisconsin Press, Milwaukee, Wis., 1983.
4. BOWMAN, W. J. *Graphic Communication.* Wiley, New York, 1968.
5. CLEVELAND, W. S. *The Elements of Graphing Data.* Wadsworth Advanced Books and Software, Monterey, Calif., 1980.
6. CLEVELAND, W. S., AND MCGILL, R. Graphical perception: Theory, experimentation and application to the development of graphical methods. *J. Am. Stat. Assoc. 79*, 387 (Sept. 1984), 531–554.
7. ENDERTON, H. B. *A Mathematical Introduction to Logic.* Academic Press, Orlando, Fla., 1972.
8. FEINER, S. APEX: An experiment in the automated creation of pictorial explanations. *IEEE Comput. Graph. Appl. 5*, 11 (Nov. 1985), 29–37.
9. FINGER, J. J., AND GENESERETH, M. R. RESIDUE—A deductive approach to design synthesis. Tech. Rep. KSL-85-1, Computer Science Dept., Stanford Univ., Stanford, Calif., Jan. 1985.
10. FRIEDELL, M. Automatic graphics environment synthesis. Ph.D. dissertation, Dept. of Computer Engineering and Science, Case Western Reserve Univ., Cleveland, Ohio, 1983. Also Computer Corporation of America Tech. Rep. CCA-83-03.
11. GNANAMGARI, S. Information presentation through default displays. Ph.D. dissertation, Dept. of Decision Sciences, The Wharton School, Univ. of Pennsylvania, Philadelphia, Pa., May 1981.
12. KAHN, K. M. Creation of computer animation from story descriptions. Ph.D. dissertation, MIT-AI-540, Massachusetts Institute of Technology, Cambridge, Mass., Aug. 1979.
13. KAHNEMAN, D., AND HENIK, A. Perceptual organization and attention. In *Perceptual Organizaton.* M. Kubovy and J. R. Pomerantz, Eds. Lawrence Erlbaum, Hillsdale, N.J., 1981, pp. 181–211.
14. KNUTH, D. E. *The Art of Computer Programming*, vol. 1. Addison-Wesley, Reading, Mass., 1973, pp. 176–179.
15. LOCKWOOD, A. *Diagrams: A Visual Survey of Graphs, Maps, Charts and Diagrams for the Graphic Designer.* Watson-Guptill, 1969.
16. MACKINLAY, J. Automatic design of graphical presentations. Ph.D. dissertation, Computer Science Dept., Stanford Univ., Stanford, Calif., 1986. Also Tech. Rep. Stan-CS-86-1038.
17. MACKINLAY, J., AND GENESERETH, M. R. Expressiveness and language choice. *Data Knowl. Eng. 1*, 1 (June 1985), 17–29.
18. RUSSELL, S. The compleat guide to MRS. KSL-85-12, Computer Science Dept., Stanford Univ., Stanford, Calif., June 1985.
19. SCHMID, C. F. *Statistical Graphics: Design Principles and Practices.* Wiley, New York, 1983.
20. STEVENS, S. S. On the theory of scales of measurement. *Science, 103* 2684 (June 1946), 677–680.
21. TUFTE, E. R. *The Visual Display of Quantitative Information.* Graphics Press, Cheshire, Conn., 1983.
22. ULLMAN, J. D. *Principles of Database Systems.* Computer Science Press, Rockville, Md., 1980.
23. WARE, C., AND BEATTY, J. C. Using colour as a tool in discrete data analysis. Tech. Rep. CS-85-21, Computer Science Dept., Univ. of Waterloo, Waterloo, Ont., Canada, Aug. 1985.
24. ZDYBEL, F., GREENFELD, N. R., YONKE, M. D., AND GIBBONS, J. An information presentation system. In *7th International Joint Conference on Artificial Intelligence* (Vancouver, Canada, Aug.). AAAI, Menlo Park, Calif., 1981, pp. 978–984.

Reflections on. . .

Automating the Design of Graphical Presentations of Relational Information

Jock D. Mackinlay

When I finished my dissertation, there were two primary directions to take the research: (1) extend APT into a complete system or (2) shift from static presentation graphics to interactive 3-D graphics, a new medium being enabled by the emergence of graphically agile workstations. I chose to focus on the new medium. Meanwhile, during the last decade, other researchers have addressed some of the issues required to turn APT into a complete system.

Although the APT research developed expressiveness and effectiveness criteria for designing useful presentation, it did not have a good model of the user's task that was being supported by the presentation. Steve Casner's dissertation (1991) developed a task-oriented architecture that automatically designed presentations by substituting perceptual tasks for cognitive tasks.

The APT research and Casner's system focused on automatically deciding how to say some information graphically, leaving open the issue of deciding what to say. This has been the concern of computational linguistic research focusing on multimedia communication, including a team led by Wolfgang Wahlster at the Universität des Saarlandese (Wahlster et al. 1993) and a team led by Steven Feiner and Kathleen McKeown (1991) at Columbia University.

Rather than waiting for computational linguistics to tame the subtleties of multimedia communication, an interactive approach explored by Steve Roth's team at Carnegie Mellon University has been to support the human creation of presentation graphics. This approach seems quite promising to me. Unlike presentation graphics with its 200 years of development, there is no established body of knowledge for designing interactive 3-D graphical presentations of information. During the last decade, we have explored this new medium and coined the term *information visualization* (Robertson et al. 1993). Research on information visualization has now reached the point where a number of successful point designs have been proposed and a variety of techniques have been discovered. I have recently started to condense these examples into a framework for describing the structure of the information visualization design space (Card and Mackinlay 1997). This framework is similar to the one I used to develop APT. Ultimately, I hope to follow Roth's lead and develop a system that uses automatic design techniques to support people creating information visualizations.

REFERENCES

Card, S. K., and Mackinlay, J. 1997. The Structure of the Information Visualization Design Space. In *Proceedings of IEEE InfoVis'97*, Phoenix, AZ, October, 92–99.

Casner, S. M. 1991. A Task-Analytic Approach to the Automated Design of Graphic Presentations. *ACM Transactions of Graphics* 10(2) April: 111–151.

Feiner, S., and McKeown, K. 1991. Automating the Generation of Coordinated Multimedia Explanations. *IEEE Computer* 24(10) October: 33–41.

Robertson, G. G.; Card, S. K.; and Mackinlay, J. D. 1993. Information Visualization Using 3D Interactive Animation. *Communications of the ACM* 36(4) April: 57–71.

Roth, S.; Lucas, P.; Senn, J.; Gomberg, C.; Burks, M.; Stroffolino, P.; Kolojejchick, J.; and Dunmire, C. 1996. Visage: A User Interface Environment for Exploring Information. In *Proceedings of IEEE InfoVis'96*, San Francisco, October, 3–12.

Wahlster, W.; André, E.; Finkler, W.; Profitlich, H. J.; and Rist, T. 1993. Plan-Based Integration of Natural Language and Graphics Generation. *Artificial Intelligence* 63: 387–427.

DATA CHARACTERIZATION FOR INTELLIGENT GRAPHICS PRESENTATION

Steven F. Roth and Joe Mattis

Center for Integrated Manufacturing Decision Systems
The Robotics Institute
Carnegie Mellon University
Pittsburgh, PA 15213-3890
412-268-7690, roth@isl1.ri.cmu.edu

ABSTRACT

An automatic presentation system is an intelligent interface component which receives information from a user or application program and designs a combination of graphics and text that effectively conveys it. It is a facility that assumes the presentation responsibilities for other programs. An important research question has been how information should be specified or described by an application program for it to be presented by an automatic presenter. This paper proposes a taxonomy of **information characteristics** which would need to be provided to either human or computer designers for them to create presentations reflecting the individual needs of a diverse group of users. The proposed taxonomy of characteristics defines the representational goals for intelligent interfaces which reason about graphical displays.

INTRODUCTION: AUTOMATING THE PRESENTATION OF INFORMATION

The goal of an automatic presentation system would be to eliminate the need for end-users and application programmers to specify, design and arrange a display each time output is needed from a program. Instead, users would focus their attention more appropriately on the tasks of determining and describing the informational **content** to be presented in a display.

An important research problem for those interested in developing automatic presentation systems has been how it would interact and communicate with application programs. Specifically, what kinds of information about a user's data must be communicated to a system for it to design an effective presentation?

Figure 1 illustrates this question with an architectural description of a system called SAGE, which automatically designs both graphical and textual presentations [9]. The architecture is similar in philosophy to several other intelligent systems (e.g. [4], [6], [7]) in which an application program must provide information to a presentation system. For simplicity, the figure refers only to graphics presentation.

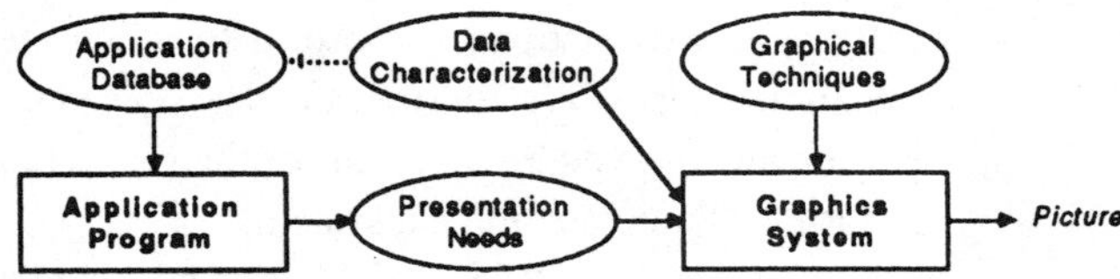

Figure 1: Automatic Presentation System Architecture

The application program in this architecture might be a query interface to a database system or any program that retrieves information within a spreadsheet, accounting, inventory, scheduling, project management or statistical package. Applications must communicate presentation needs in the form of particular database facts to the graphics system. The latter applies its design knowledge to select and synthesize appropriate graphical techniques to best convey the facts. Design knowledge must not be application-specific and therefore cannot depend on recognizing specific database relations or data sets contained in the presentation needs. Design knowledge must be expressed in terms of more general characterizations of information.

To preserve this generality, each application must provide a *data characterization*, which is a description of the semantic and structural properties of its information that are relevant to presentation design. Some of these characteristics are easily understood and communicated by human graphics designers. Others are often neglected and lead to inappropriate displays. In either case, it is necessary to define and represent explicitly all relevant characteristics of data for a computer system to make appropriate presentation decisions. The goal of this paper is to outline a taxonomy of characteristics which must be communicated to either human or computer designers for them to create effective presentations in an application independent fashion.

DIMENSIONS FOR DATA CHARACTERIZATION

The set of characteristics we propose has been used to design presentations with SAGE, a system for automatic and graphical explanation [9]. They also are generalizations of a smaller, less complete set of data characteristics implicit in other work in this area by [6] on APT, an automatic presentation tool. SAGE and APT are both concerned with presenting relational data using numerous variations and syntheses of 2-D static displays found in business and statistical graphics packages (e.g. bar and plot charts, node-link graphs, gauges, techniques using shape, color or size, tables).

The types of information with which these systems are concerned are the relations among data values contained in relational database or frame-based representations. For example, an entry from SAGE's testbed (a frame-based project management database) might specify a project activity, *build-roof*, a time-quantity, *12 days*, and a *duration* relationship between the two values. The *duration* relation maps between a set of activities and a set of time-quantities.

Similarly, SAGE's test-bed contained other information about a company's *activities*, *resources*, *products*, and *departments* and their *costs*, *dates*, *durations*, *precedence*, and *part-whole relations*. Information was expressed as object-attribute-value tuples (e.g. *design-activity cost $3000*), where objects and values correspond to set elements and attributes correspond to relations. Frames and relation-tuples among sets are equivalent informationally, but in this paper we will use the set and relational terminology.

There were several criteria by which we judged the relevance of different data characteristics. First, we included characteristics which were necessary for distinguishing the kinds of information that each graphical technique could *express*. We also included data characteristics which helped order graphical techniques based on how *effective* they were at conveying different information (following the [6] distinction between expressiveness and effectiveness). Third, we included characteristics which could be used to determine how information could be integrated within a display. Finally, characteristics were needed which could be applied easily by users.

Each of the following sub-sections describes a dimension along which data can be characterized to support presentation design. In addition, we describe several examples of graphical decisions which depend on each dimension and which motivated its inclusion.

Data Types

The building-blocks of a graphical presentation are the techniques for identifying a single element from a set of possible values. For example, the *horizontal position* technique uses a marker's X-location to identify a single value from among those listed on the graph's X-axis. *Retinal* techniques [2] use a marker's size, shape, or color to identify a value from a set described in a corresponding *key*. *Textual* techniques identify an element by displaying a sequence of letters and numbers which are usually its *name*. Several characteristics of a set are relevant to choosing an appropriate graphical technique.

Set Ordering. The nature of the ordering relationship among a data set's elements was the predominant criteria used in APT and one criteria in SAGE for choosing graphical techniques. An ordering technique can be characterized as either quantitative, ordinal, or nominal.

In ***quantitative*** sets, the elements are ordered numerically (e.g., the set of *dollar amounts* ranging from $0.01 to $50.00). Knowing that a data-set is quantitative tells a system that the elements can be conveyed effectively by a graphical technique with a quantitatively varying visual dimension, such as position along an axis, angles in a pie chart, the areas of circles, or the brightness of gray-scale levels. Users can easily transform these quantitative perceptual properties to the values of corresponding data-set elements. In contrast, a technique which expresses elements of a set with different shapes (e.g. star, circle, square, triangle) cannot express quantitative data because perceptual differences amongs shapes cannot be easily transformed to quantities.

In ***ordinal*** sets, element ordering is peculiar to the semantics of the set, as in *performance-ratings: {poor, fair, good, excellent}*. In contrast to quantitative sets, presentations of ordinal sets require techniques which can enumerate explicitly every element along an axis or key (since intermediate values cannot be interpolated).

In ***nominal*** sets, elements are unordered (e.g., the set of *computer-brands*). These can be expressed effectively using colors or shapes, which don't vary quantitatively, providing the set size is small. In contrast to quantitative sets, nominals may be misperceived as ordered if techniques are used which employ a quantitative dimension to convey elements (e.g. bar-charts, circle-size).

Coordinates Vs. Amounts. In order to capture some subtle distinctions relevant to SAGE's project management database, it was necessary to go beyond the Set-Ordering characteristic which was the predominant property used in APT. In particular, it was necessary to recognize that elements of ordered sets are *coordinates* if each element specifies a point or location temporally, spatially, or otherwise (e.g. *calendar-date, latitude, time-zone, congressional-district*). In contrast, *amounts* are not embedded in particular frames of reference (e.g. *number of days, dollar-amounts, weight*).

To understand the usefulness of this distinction, consider the graphs in Figure 2 and Figure 3, which express the *start-dates of activities*. The bar-chart is awkward because it suggests that *amounts* of time are being expressed. The plot-chart is superior, since it reinforces the idea that *start-dates* are *coordinates* in time. Other techniques (e.g. gauges, grey-scale) are likewise inappropriate for coordinates.

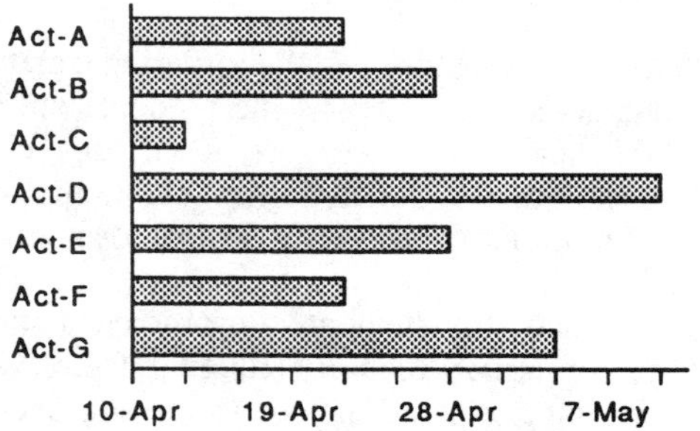

Figure 2: Inappropriate Use of Bar Chart for Coordinates

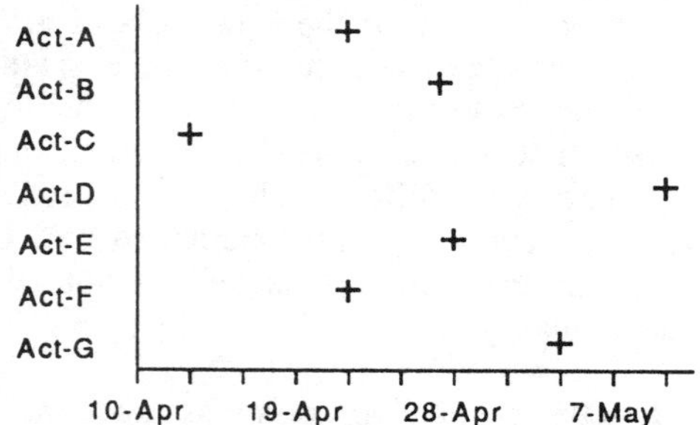

Figure 3: Effective Use of Plot Chart for Coordinates

Domain Of Membership. SAGE's characterization went beyond APT's by recognizing that sets can belong to the different domains of *time*, *space*, *temperature*, or *mass*. This information helps to preserve subtle stylistic conventions, such as using a horizontal axis for time coordinates and a vertical axis for temperature. This characterization can also be helpful for judging how to group and integrate relations within pictures (e.g. displays of *dates* and *durations* for *activities* might be grouped separately from data unrelated to time).

Properties Of Relational-Structure

The second dimension along which information was characterized describes the way relations map from elements of one set to another. Mackinlay distinguished relations having functional dependency as those for which each element of a domain maps to only one value in another domain. For example, the *cost* relation is a functional dependency, mapping from each activity in a set to exactly one dollar amount. In contrast, the has-part relation is not a functional dependency, since it maps from each organizational group to a variable number of sub-groups (or none at all). The functional dependency distinction helped determine the appropriateness of different techniques (e.g. networks do not require functional dependency, while bar charts do).

We refined and extended this distinction to handle a number of questions regarding the appropriateness of data - picture combinations not handled in APT. We defined three properties which describe the way relations map from elements of one set to another: *Coverage, Cardinality* and *Uniqueness*.

Relational Coverage. This characteristic conveys whether every element of a set can be mapped to at least one element of another. Recall that a relation like *start-date* maps from a set of *activities* to a set of *calendar-dates*. If the *start-date* relation has coverage, then every *activity* has a *calendar-date*.

We distinguish several types of Non-coverage, which occur when

1. data is missing (some *activities* have missing *start-dates*, a realistic situation in many database applications),
2. a relation is *not-applicable* to some elements (e.g. a relation called *cost-of-automatic-transmission*, which maps from *car-models* to *dollar-amounts*, won't apply to *car-models* without this option),
3. *no-value* is informative (e.g. some *departments* in a company may have no *organizational-parts*).

One example of the relevance of this distinction for graphical design is the fact that bar- and plot-charts do not express relations to quantitative sets effectively when there is non-coverage. The reason for this is that there is no way to express the absence of data without adding a special mark or leaving a blank space instead of a bar, either of which can be misperceived as low values (i.e. short bars). Figure 4 illustrates the potential misperception caused by missing values, when for example, a user needs to find the 3 or 4 *activities* with the smallest *labor-costs*. Placing an asterisk in the space still leaves this problem and also adds clutter.

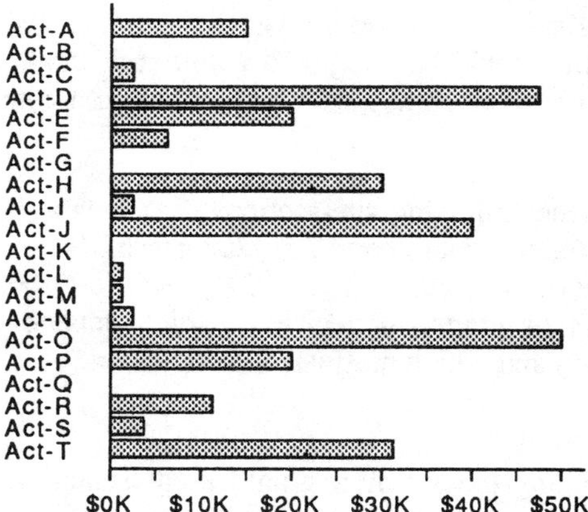

Figure 4: Inappropriate Use of Bar Chart for Data with Non-Coverage

In contrast, plot-charts have fewer problems with non-coverage with nominal sets because missing values can be explicitly marked on the unordered axis, as in Figure 5.

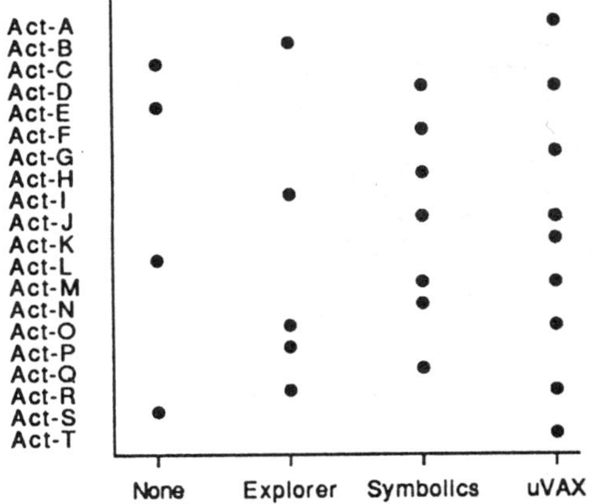

Figure 5: Effective Use of Plot Chart for Data with Non-Coverage

Node-link diagrams (trees or directed graphs) effectively convey relations involving *no-values* with the absence of a link from a node. For example, the *organizational-entities* which are the leaves of the tree in Figure 6 have no parts. In other words, the *has-part* relation does not show coverage for some of the *organizational-entities*. While node-link techniques are expressive for *no-values*, they are ineffective when non-coverage is due to missing data. The absence of a link below a node always implies there is no relation between the element represented by the node and other elements.

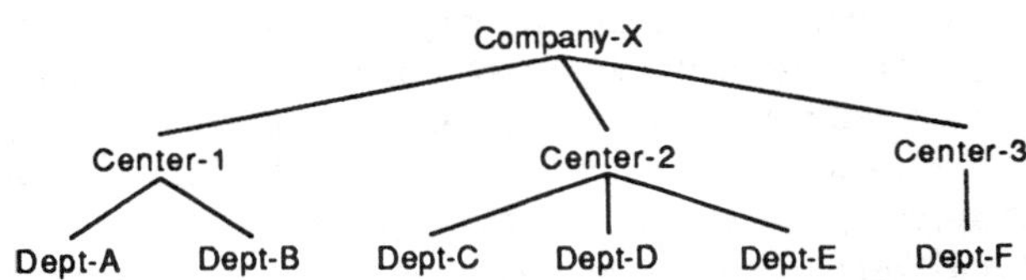

Figure 6: Node-Link Diagram

Cardinality. This characteristic expresses the number of elements of a set to which a relation can map from an element of another set. In frame terminology, it expresses the number of values that can occur for an attribute of an object: **single-valued, fixed-multiple-valued, variably-valued**. Examples are *activity start-date* (single-valued), *quality ratings by three inspectors* for a set of *product parts* (fixed-multiple values), and *organizational parts for groups in a company* (variably-valued). Cardinality should not be confused with the concept of arity [10], which refers to the number of different domains in a relation, where each domain (value) plays a different *role*.

As with coverage, the quality of displays using different techniques is influenced by cardinality. For example, as Figure 6 indicates, node-link diagrams express variably-valued and fixed-multiple-valued relations adequately. The *has-part* relation maps from one *organization-entity* to a variable number of others. Node-link techniques can also express single-values, but these result in a chain of nodes, which conveys little information. This problem is even greater for an indentation technique (Figure 7), which expresses multiple-values well but would be ineffective for some single-valued relations.

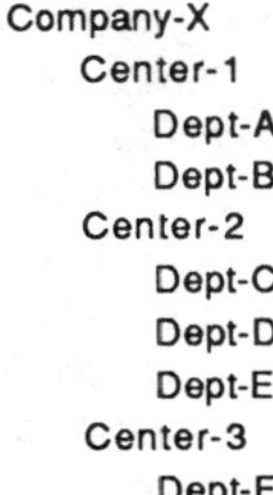

Figure 7: Indentation Diagram

Bar-charts are also affected by cardinality and are confusing for variably-valued relations which map to a quantitative data set. Consider a relation called *available-baud-rates* mapping *modem-models* to *rates* (110,300,1200,2400,3600), where *Brand-X* has 3 adjustable rates (300,1200,2400) and *Brand-Y* has only one rate (1200). Displaying variably-valued attributes in a bar chart would be unconventional and potentially confusing because multiple bars are typically used to express two or more different relations consistently for each object. In contrast, plot-charts express variably-valued relations effectively. For example, notice that some *activities* in Figure 5 require several *computers*.

Finally, gauges and retinal techniques like color or circle-area are restricted to single-valued relations because of the difficulty of associating more than one graphical object with each label.

Uniqueness. This characteristic refers to whether a relation maps to a unique value(s) for each element of a set. The *start-date* relation is non-unique because two activities can have the same *date*. The *has-part* relation (Figure 6) maps uniquely since each *organizational-entity* has a set of unique parts (i.e. nodes in the tree have only one parent).

Graphical techniques are differentially sensitive to the characteristic of uniqueness. Bar- and plot-charts are uninfluenced by this characteristic. Indentation techniques (Figure 7) require uniqueness because each node must have one parent. Repeating a node in different places in the display can lead to extreme duplication and confusion. In contrast, node-link diagrams can express relations which map non-uniquely with multiple links to a node (e.g. directed graphs).

Expressing Relationships Among Relations

Complex Data Types. While previous examples all involve simple, binary relations, some applications may have relations which map to multiple values, each *playing a different role*. For example, the *geographic-location* relation maps between *cities* and two coordinate values: *latitude* and *longitude*. The *period-of-employment* relation maps between *employees* and two *years*: *first-year* and *last-year*.

A first attempt to handle these complex relations (i.e. relations of arity > 2) was suggested by [6], but was based strictly on syntactic transformations. For example, it is possible to transform the *period-of-employment* relation into two simple relations, *first-year-employment* and *last-year-employment* which both map between *employees* and *years*. One can then design displays treating them as independent relations and ignoring the relationship between them. However, to design a presentation which integrates the relations appropriately requires a presentation system to have more knowledge of the semantics of data than provided in APT.

For example, Figure 8 illustrates a graphical style for displaying time intervals, which would require an automatic designer to understand the relationship among three relations for *activities*: *start-date, end-date* and *duration*. Using this graphical style requires understanding that these relations involve end-points of intervals.

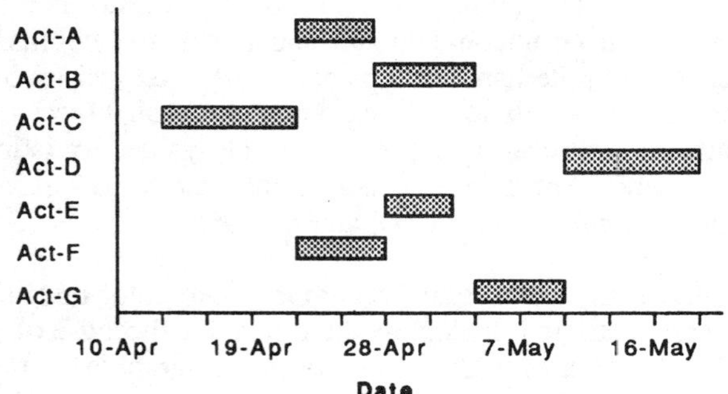

Figure 8: Expressing Complex Data: An Interval Chart

A similar understanding is necessary for displaying the *period-of-employment* relation. Intervals are important in other domains as well (e.g. the high, low and closing quotes for daily stock-market prices; minimum, maximum and mean for statistical ranges; mean and error ranges for measurement data). A system which does not understand these interval relationships is likely to generate the fragmented displays in Figure 9 rather than the more effective display of Figure 8.

Our approach to this problem is to develop a set of complex data-types which define roles to characterize the relationships among simple binary relations or arguments of complex (N-ary) relations in databases. The set of available data-types has been motivated by the common relationships found in various domains, as well as the existence of popular graphical styles for presenting them. Examples include *intervals, statistical abstractions (Mean, Standard Deviation)*, and *2-D coordinate-locations*.

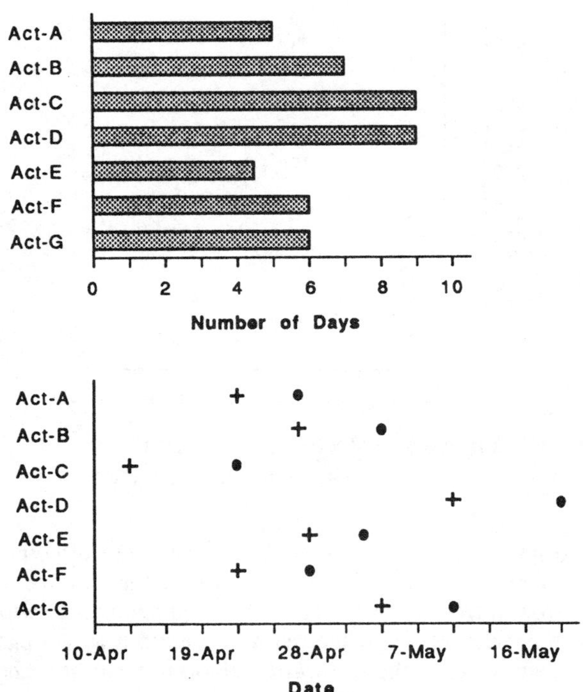

Figure 9: Fragmented Interval Presentation Due to Poor Data Characterization

Algebraic Dependencies. Algebraic dependencies among database elements suggest another dimension which can affect presentation design. Dependencies can occur among attributes (relations) or among values within data sets. For example, an *organizational* database may contain three relations mapping *departments* to *dollar-amounts*: *materials-costs, labor-costs,* and *total-costs*, where *total-costs = materials-costs + labor-costs*. Armed with this information, a designer can integrate the presentation, as in Figure 10. These dependencies can be characterized by representing the underlying semantics, noting that *Total-costs is aggregational* of the others, or with algebraic equations. Some representation is necessary if a system is to automatically generate this picture rather than depend exclusively on a user's request to do so, as was the case in APT.

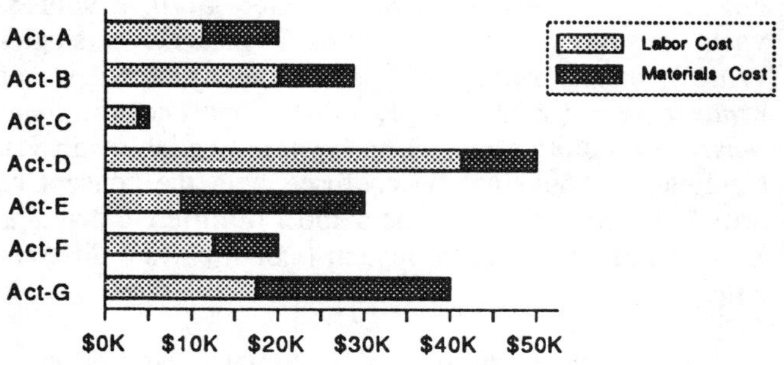

Figure 10: Algebraic Dependencies: A Stacked Bar Chart

Algebraic dependencies can also involve the elements of a single data-set and relation. Figure 11 shows an inappropriate synthesis of pictures of two relations relevant to *organizational-entities*: the *has-part* relation and the *budget-overrun* relation, the latter mapping to the amount by which expenses were under- or overestimated. The display is inappropriate because the value for each organizational-entity is actually the sum of the values of its parts. As a result, it is difficult to compare values for entities at the same level in the organization. In general, charts do not express dependencies and can be confusing when dependencies exist.

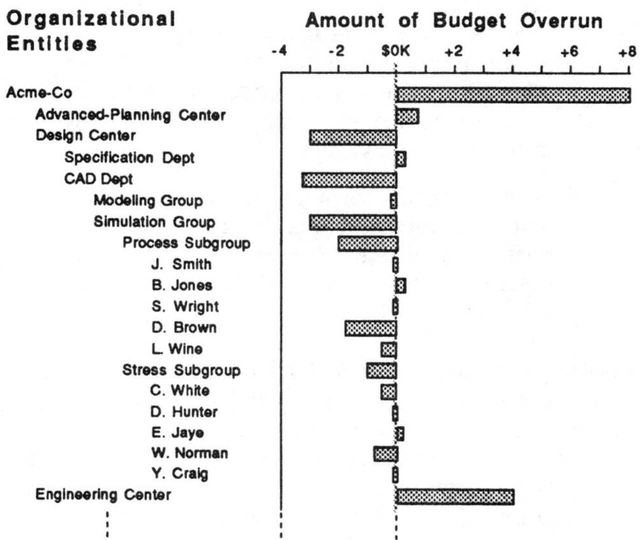

Figure 11: Problems Due to Algebraic Dependencies within Data Sets

These dependencies are common in the databases used for SAGE's testbed. They can be captured by enumerating the equations among elements of a database (as would be the case for variables in a spreadsheet), or by expressing the fact that the *has-part* relation aggregates *budget-overrun* (and perhaps many other relations involving *organizational-entities*).

Arity: Distinguishing Unary From Binary And N-ary Relations

Most of the data and graphical styles with which we are concerned involve the representation of binary or N-ary relations, i.e. relations which map from one domain to one or several other domains. These relations may be thought of as expressing a value for an attribute for each element of a domain (e.g. the *duration* relation attributes a *time-quantity* to each *activity*). There are cases, however, in which a relation serves simply to distinguish a subset of entities. Relations like these express a single property possessed by some elements of a set but not others. In relational terms, these can be considered *unary* relations: those with arity equal to one (arity referring to the number of domains or arguments in a relation) [10].

For example, the *significant* relation distinguishes variables from a set passing some statistical test. The *critical* relation distinguishes risky project *activities*. It is possible to represent these as binary relations by constructing a second domain for each with two elements. For example, one could convert the *significant* relation to the *significance* relation, the latter mapping from a set of *variables* to a set of *statistical-evaluations: {significant, insignificant}*. Similarly, frame-based representations force unary relations into a binary form by creating attributes like *critical* whose values are *{true, false}*. However, treating unary relations as binary, regardless of how the implementation expresses them, does not capture a user's intent of distinguishing members of a set, as opposed to expressing alternative values. This distinction was necessary for SAGE to select appropriate graphical techniques.

Figure 12 is an example of an appropriate technique for expressing the *critical* unary relation for elements represented along the vertical axis of another graph. Using an adjacent shape is just one technique for highlighting some members of a set. Other techniques in SAGE's library include darkening the background of a string, italicizing or making its font bold, or outlining it.

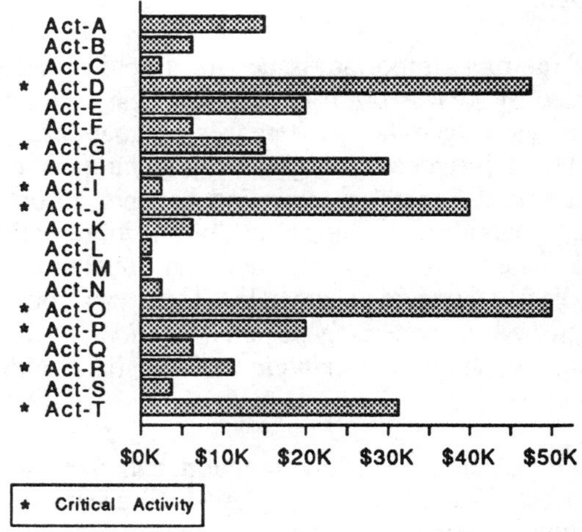

Figure 12: Expressing a Unary Relation

Figure 13 shows a technique which inappropriately expresses the *critical* relation as binary. The cluttered, redundant marks prevent rapid identification of the *critical* subset. Also, because the application does not give any indication of the different salience of *non-critical* and *critical*, the symbols (* -) are arbitrarily assigned to *(No Yes)*. It is clear that explicit characterization of the relation as unary is needed, so that a system can choose a graphical technique that distinguishes set elements rather than expresses binary relations.

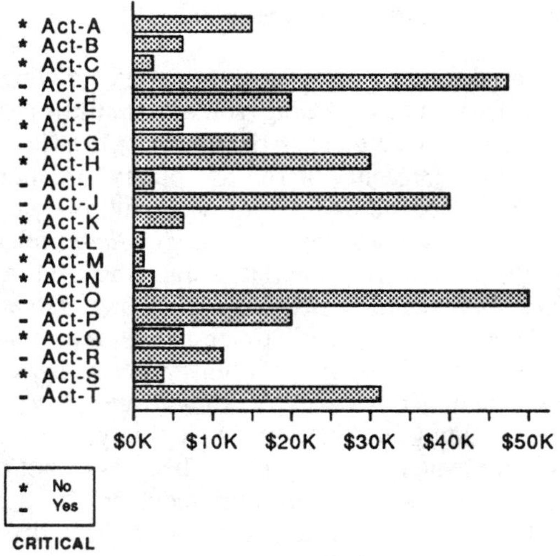

Figure 13: Inappropriately Use of a Binary Technique with a Unary Relation

Data Characteristics Based On User Information Seeking Goals

Thus far, we have discussed static database characteristics. A presentation system must also consider other properties of data which are specified dynamically either by an application program or an end-user when presentations are requested.

One of the most important issues for graphical design not addressed in APT is the role of an application's or user's goals in viewing data. Differences in goals can greatly alter the effectiveness of graphical techniques or their combinations. Several domain-independent information-seeking goals became apparent in our observations of typical graphical display variations and analytic tasks in the project management domain. They can roughly be distinguished as referring to the *function* of the data presentation and the *distribution* of the data within the presentation.

Display Function. Display function can vary for each relation or object set to be displayed. Presentations vary depending on whether goals emphasize:

1. accurate value lookup (which favors selection of text tables and makes stricter judgements about the acceptability of other techniques),
2. comparison of values *within*, but not *among* different relations, which results in evaluation criteria favoring separate pictures rather than a single *composite* for several relations (e.g. presenting separate charts for the *expected-cost* and *actual-cost* relations, rather than merging them into a single picture),
3. pairwise or n-wise comparison of relations for the same data set (which favors using the same technique to encode *expected-cost* and *actual-cost* and to position objects to be compared adjacently and in the same composite picture),
4. distributions of values for a relation, (e.g. where concern for the number of *employees at each salary level and not for individual salaries* requires graphics for frequency distributions),
5. functional correlations among attributes (e.g. observing the correlation between *Length-of-Employment and Salary for a set of Employees* as shown by scatter plot or other composite techniques for which two or more properties of a single mark convey different relations), and
6. indexing-needs for one or both data sets within a relation (e.g. different indexing goals will dictate whether the activities in Figure 8 are sorted alphabetically or by *start-date*).

Information Relatedness And Distribution. Finally, a user's immediate goals may determine the *relatedness* of different relations and thereby affect how they should be integrated in the presentation. For example, deciding how to group *start-date, labor-cost, end-date, and materials-cost* depends not only on the types of data, but also on the user's immediate view of which are related. Our approach is for applications to supply optional **relatedness** information by segmenting the total presentation request into sub-requests which group information by relation or data-set.

[9] has used this technique to coordinate text and graphics displays by converting a topic outline prepared by a discourse processor into a serial list of sub-requests. This indicates to the graphics system that information expressed in contiguous portions of the text should be considered more related, and therefore displayed together. As a result, the serial structure of information in the text corresponds well to the spatial integration of that information across several displays.

More generally, this characteristic provides a vehicle for expressing two, often competing, informational goals: the need to express as much information as possible and the need for selected partitions of sets or relations to be easily and cohesively viewed. A graphics system needs a characterization of the user's informational goals to determine how to distribute information across several displays.

SUMMARY AND CONCLUSION

The goal of this paper was to present several dimensions along which information can be characterized to support automatic presentation. The dimensions of Data Types, Relational-structure, Arity and Relationships among Relations are static and can be supplied by database creators or application programmers in advance. This is a plausible scenario for large systems with many long-term users. Other dimensions reflect a user's immediate information-seeking goals, including the functional goal of the display and the relatedness of different information subsets.

We have attempted to describe the rationale for these characteristics in terms of common presentation decisions. The strongest motivation was to improve the quality of displays generated by automatic presentation systems. Ultimately, the validity of this taxonomy will depend on its impact on presentation quality. This work must also be integrated with other research tasks described in recent papers ([1], [3], [4], [5], [6], [8], [9]), including:

- representing the structure and expressiveness of graphical techniques,
- developing graphical display evaluation criteria,
- extracting and implementing graphical design, synthesis and rendering knowledge,
- identifying and responding to information-seeking goals,
- coordinating text and graphics, and
- integrating presentation design with knowledge of a domain.

ACKNOWLEDGEMENTS

This research is supported by Digital Equipment Corporation. The views and conclusions contained in this document are those of the authors, and should not be interpreted as representing the official policies, either expressed or implied, of Digital Equipment Corporation.

REFERENCES

1. Arens, Y., Miller, L., and Sondheimer, N. Presentation Planning Using an Integrated Knowledge Base. In *Architectures for Intelligent Interfaces: Elements and Prototypes*, Sullivan, J. and Tyler, S., Ed., Addison-Wesley, Reading, Mass, 1990.

2. Bertin, Jacques. *Semiology of Graphics.* The University of Wisconsin Press, 1983.

3. Feiner, S. An Architecture for Knowledge-Based Graphical Interfaces. In *Architectures for Intelligent Interfaces: Elements and Prototypes*, Sullivan, J. and Tyler, S., Ed., Addison-Wesley, Reading, Mass, 1990.

4. Gargan, R.A., Sullivan, J.W., and Tyler, S.W. Multimodal Response Planning: An Adaptive Rule Based Approach. CHI '88 - Human Factors in Computing Systems, ACM/SIGCHI, Washington, D.C., May, 1988, pp. 229-234.

5. Kosslyn, S.M. "Graphics and Human Information Processing - A Review of Five Books". *Journal of the American Statistical Association 80*, 391 (September 1985), 499-512.

6. Mackinlay, J.D. "Automating the Design of Graphical Presentations of Relational Information". *ACM Transactions on Graphics 5*, 2 (April 1986), 110-141.

7. McKeown, K.R. "Discourse Strategies for Generating Natural-Language Text". *Artificial Intelligence 27* (1985), 1-41.

8. Neal, J. and Shapiro, S. Intelligent Multi-Media Interface Technology. In *Architectures for Intelligent Interfaces: Elements and Prototypes*, Sullivan, J. and Tyler, S., Ed., Addison-Wesley, Reading, Mass, 1990.

9. Roth, S.F., Mattis, J.A., and Mesnard, X.A. Graphics and Natural Language as Components of Automatic Explanation. In *Architectures for Intelligent Interfaces: Elements and Prototypes*, Sullivan, J. and Tyler, S., Ed., Addison-Wesley, Reading, Mass, 1990.

10. Ullman, Jeffrey. *Principles of Database Systems.* Computer Science Press, 1982.

Data Characterization for Intelligent Graphics Presentation

Stephen Roth

All the work on automated presentation design has addressed the problem of characterizing knowledge relevant to making design decisions. This consisted of characterizing data, the tasks that presentations are designed to support, and the structure and function of graphical primitives used to compose presentations. In fact, a relatively small representational vocabulary of these three components has made it feasible to create design mechanisms for mapping data to combinations of graphics that support tasks.

We've been steadily expanding the data and task characterizations as we apply automatic presentation technology to new domains (e.g., logistics and transportation scheduling, project management, real estate sales, marketing research). We have also found this approach to characterization to be useful in several other contexts:

- User-initiated searches of portfolios of visualizations based on abstract characteristics of data to find one useful for current goals
- Automating the generation of user-selectable options for aggregating and summarizing attributes of data sets
- Multimedia presentation design, in which a domain-independent vocabulary based on data and task characterizations bridges goal-based, domain- and media-independent presentation planning with media-specific (i.e., visualization and text) design components
- Generation of captions explaining the structure of graphics and how they encode data guided by heuristics for judging their complexity

Although progress has been made in these areas using general classifications related to database structure, it has also become clear that a richer semantics is needed similar to that used in natural language processing (e.g., the Penman upper model) in order to effectively generate text that explains and refers to graphics. A good example is how we refer to lines on maps, as in the redesign of the Minard graphic in the paper 3.5 Roth et al.. Lines on a map can refer to regions (e.g., paths or roads), static physical objects (e.g., phone lines), abstract relations between pairs of geographic points (e.g., reciprocal trade relationships among cities), or movements (e.g., troops). A complete approach to caption generation and coordinated text and graphic presentations will require a richer characterization that makes these distinctions. Perhaps explorations of new visualization techniques will require these distinctions as well. For example, animated lines moving across a map are more likely to be appropriate for temporally varying locational information like troop movements than for static or abstract relationships among locations. Certainly, automated design of visualizations that are interactive will require richer characterizations of both graphic structure and function and their relation to tasks. Some initial attempts in these directions can be found in the references that follow. (See also *http://www.cs.cmu.edu/~sage.*)

REFERENCES

Beshers, C., and Feiner, S. 1993. AutoVisual: Rule-Based Design of Interactive Multivariate Visualizations. *IEEE Computer Graphics and Applications* 13(4) July: 41–49.

Chuah, M. C., and Roth, S. F. 1996. On the Semantics of Interactive Visualizations. In *Proceedings of Information Visualization, IEEE*, San Francisco, October, 29–36.

Chuah, M. C.; Roth, S. F.; and Kerpedjiev, S. 1997. Sketching, Searching, and Customizing Visualizations: A Content-based Approach to Design Retrieval. In Maybury, M. (ed.), *Intelligent Multimedia Information Retrieval*, 83–111. Menlo Park, CA: AAAI/MIT Press.

Chuah, M. C.; Roth, S. F.; Kolojejchick, J.; Mattis, J.; and Juarez, O. 1995. SageBook: A System for Searching Datagraphics by Content. In *Proceedings SIGCHI'95 Human Factors in Computing Systems*, Denver, CO, May, 338–345.

Goldstein, J.; Roth, S. F.; Kolojejchick, J.; and Mattis, J. 1994. A Framework for the Automatic Design of Large Data Set Displays. *Journal of Visual Languages in Computing* 5 (December): 339–363.

Mittal, V.; Roth, S. F.; Moore, J.; and Mattis, J. 1995. Generating Explanatory Captions for Information Graphics. In *Proceedings International Joint Conference on Artificial Intelligence*, Montreal, Canada, August, 1276–1283.

Zhou, M. X., and Feiner, S. K. 1996. Data Characterization for Automatically Visualizing Heterogeneous Information. In *Proceedings of Information Visualization, IEEE*, San Francisco, October, 13–20.

A Task-Analytic Approach to the Automated Design of Graphic Presentations

STEPHEN M. CASNER
University of Pittsburgh

BOZ is an automated graphic design and presentation tool that designs graphics based on an analysis of the task for which a graphic is intended to support. When designing a graphic, BOZ aims to optimize two ways in which graphics help expedite human performance of information-processing tasks: (1) allowing users to substitute simple perceptual inferences in place of more demanding logical inferences, and (2) streamlining users' search for needed information. BOZ analyzes a logical description of a task to be performed by a human user and designs a provably equivalent perceptual task by substituting perceptual inferences in place of logical inferences in the task description. BOZ then designs and renders an accompanying graphic that encodes and structures data such that performance of each perceptual inference is supported and visual search is minimized. BOZ produces a graphic along with a perceptual procedure describing how to use the graphic to complete the task. A key feature of BOZ's approach is that it is able to design different presentations of the same information customized to the requirements of different tasks. BOZ is used to design graphic presentations of airline schedule information to support five different airline reservation tasks. Reaction time studies done with real users for one task and graphic show that the BOZ-designed graphic significantly reduces users' performance time to the task. Regression analyses link the observed efficiency savings to BOZ's two key design principles: perceptual inference substitutions and pruning of visual search.

Categories and Subject Descriptors: D.2.2 **[Software Engineering]**: Tools and Techniques—*user interfaces*; H.1.2 **[Models and Principles]**: User/Machine Systems—*human information processing*; I.2.1 **[Artificial Intelligence]**: Applications and Expert Systems; I.3.6 **[Computer Graphics]**: Methodology and Techniques—*ergonomics*

General Terms: Algorithms, Design, Human Factors, Theory

Additional Key Words and Phrases: Automated design, graphic design, graphic user interface, task analysis, visual languages

1. THE COGNITIVE UTILITY OF GRAPHIC PRESENTATIONS

Studies of people using graphics for the purpose of solving problems or performing information-processing tasks find little evidence to support the claim that graphics are superior to other types of presentations such as tables, lists, outlines, or text [19]. This is in striking contrast to the popular belief that graphics are the preferred medium for information presentation. These studies do not reject our intuitions about the usefulness of graphics but rather find that the utility of any information presentation is a function of the *task* that the presentation is being used to support. Graphics appear to succeed in practice when they have been designed to directly support a specific task, the success arising out of a judicious combination of task to be performed and particular graphic used. Generalizations made about the observed usefulness of a graphic for one task are highly inappropriate since using the same graphic for different tasks often causes the usefulness of the graphic to disappear. These results further suggest that graphic design principles that do not take into account the nature of the task to be supported (e.g., "line graphs are best for continuous data") are too underspecified to be useful in general. That is, empirical studies have shown that line graphs are supportive of some tasks that manipulate continuous data and are detrimental to the performance of others. The implication is that effective graphic design should begin with the task that a graphic is intended to support and be focused on finding those parts of the task, if any, that might be performed more efficiently within the context of a graphic.

Psychological studies concerned with how and why graphics are useful demonstrate two task-specific ways in which graphics can help expedite human performance of information-processing tasks [24, 34].

(1) *Computation.* Graphics sometimes allow users to substitute quick perceptual inferences in place of more difficult logical inferences. Perceptual inferences such as distance and size determinations, spatial coincidence judgments, and color comparisons, allow users to obtain the same information as more demanding logical inferences such as mental arithmetic or numerical comparisons.

(2) *Search.* Graphics sometimes reduce users' search for needed information by grouping related information in a single spatial locality, and by employing encoding techniques such as color, shading, and spatial arrangement that support preattentive and sometimes parallel visual search.

The following examples present combinations of tasks and graphics to illustrate the task-specific advantages that graphics can offer. The examples demonstrate two important consequences of the task-dependent usefulness of graphics. First, *different presentations of the same information best support different tasks.* That is, there is no such thing as the "most effective" way to display a data set. Graphic designs fall in and out of usefulness depending on the task a user wishes to perform using a data set. Consequently, there seems to be no way of designing an effective presentation without first considering the task for which the presentation will be used. Second, *what makes a presentation interesting are the efficient perceptual procedures that users can perform using the presentation to quickly arrive at a desired result.* In the examples below, the graphic designed for each task greatly simplifies the task by reducing the amount of cognitive work (computation and search)

This work was supported by the Office of Naval Research, University Research Initiative, under Contract N00014-86-K-0678, and is based on parts of the author's Ph.D. dissertation, Intelligent Systems Program, University of Pittsburgh.
Author's address: S. M. Casner, NASA Ames Research Center, Mail Stop 262-4, Moffetfield, Calif., 94035-1000. e-mail: Internet: casner@eos.arc.nasa.gov

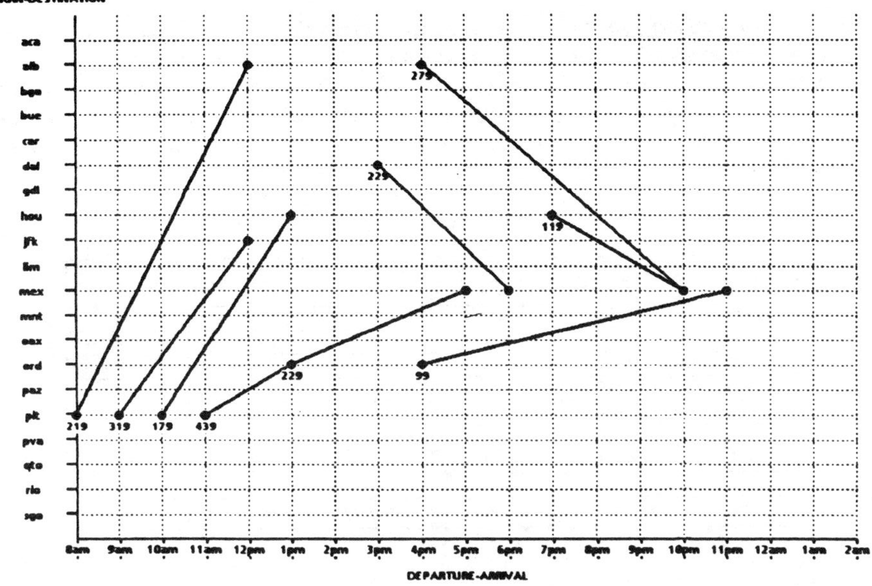

Fig. 1. Graphic for specific layover task.

the user must perform. To fully appreciate the task-specific advantages of each graphic, try performing each different task with each different graphic. The examples all pertain to the problem of using airline schedule information to locate flights obeying certain criteria. Each different task imposes different demands on the user, requiring the user to approach the same set of information in different ways. The graphic presentation for each task was designed by BOZ, the automated tool described throughout the paper.

(1) *Schedule Specific Layover*. Suppose you must travel from Pittsburgh to Mexico City but have to keep an afternoon business appointment in Albuquerque. Using the graphic in Figure 1 you can quickly locate your appointment time along the horizontal axis and locate Albuquerque (ALB) along the vertical axis. Running your fingers up and across the graphic to find the intersection of these two positions, you can now look for two flights that fall the closest to the right and to the left of the point of intersection. Note that this graphic allows you to immediately access exactly those flights that optimally satisfy your city and time constraints, reducing your search to a minimum. This graphic also lets you quickly figure your total "downtime" in the airport by simply judging the horizontal distance between the inside ends of each flight, and to figure your total travel time by judging the distance between the outer ends of each flight.

(2) *Find Cheapest Flight*. Suppose you wanted to find the cheapest flight going from Chicago to Mexico City. Using the graphic in Figure 2 you can

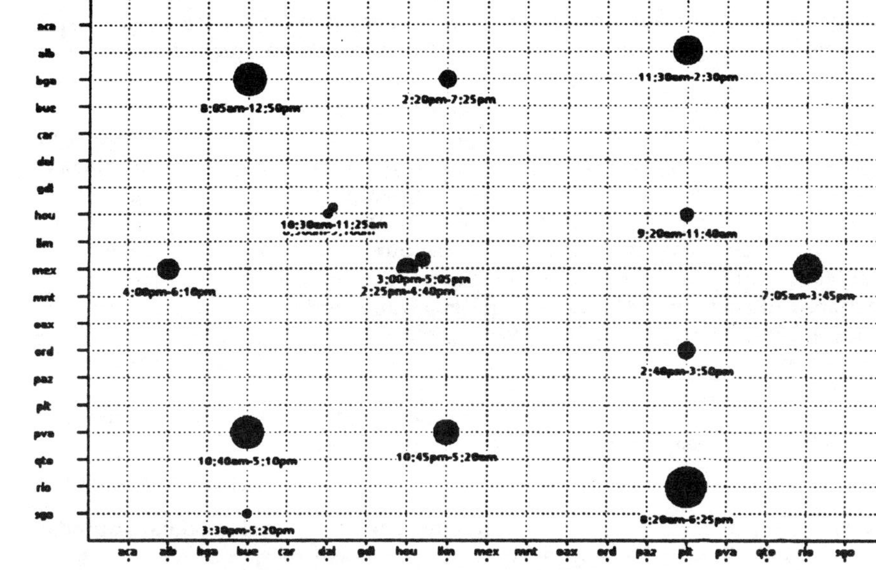

Fig. 2. Graphic for find cheapest flight task.

locate Chicago (ORD) and Mexico (MEX) on the horizontal and vertical axes, find the intersection of these positions, and choose the smallest circle present at that location since the size of the circle representing each flight encodes the airfare.

(3) *Find Most Direct Route*. Suppose you wanted to find the most direct route between two cities, minimizing the number of takeoffs and landings. Using the graphic in Figure 3 you can find your origin and destination cities around the perimeter of the circle and perform a simple connect the dots task, finding the shortest path between the two points. To be sure that the flights connect you must compare the departure and arrival times of each leg of the flight.

(4) *Look Up Flight Information*. Suppose you just wanted to know the time or cost of a flight. The tabular presentation in Figure 4 lets you locate your flight by city in the leftmost column and read off the required information in the corresponding row. In this case the best graphic is no graphic! If your task is to simply read the information, no encoding scheme is likely to prove superior to text.

Overview. The research described in this paper explores an approach to the design of graphic presentations based on an analysis of the tasks for which they are intended to support. The design approach is implemented in an automated graphic design and presentation tool called BOZ. BOZ designs graphic presentations that are customized to the requirements of a stated task. The core idea behind BOZ can be summarized as follows: *since the*

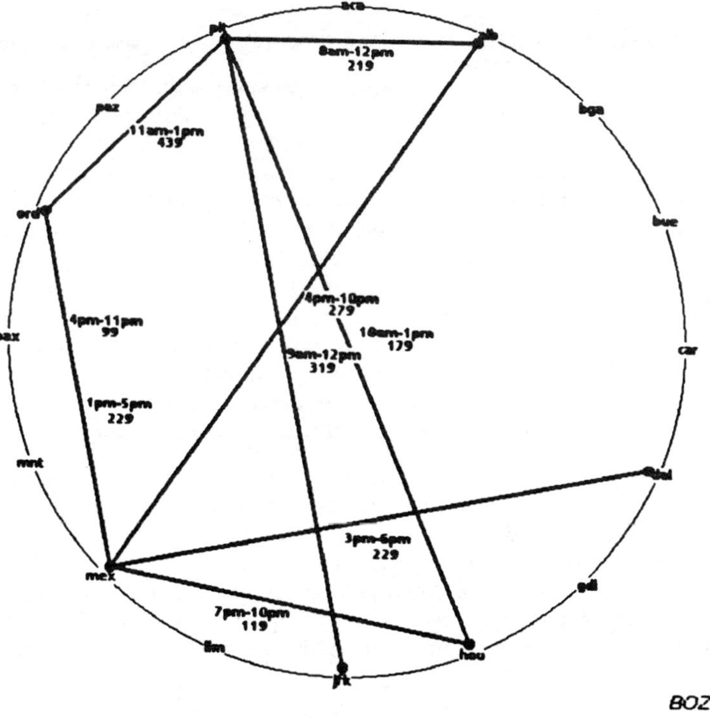

Fig. 3. Graphic for find most direct route task.

ORIGIN	DESTINATION	AVAILABILITY	COST	DEPARTURE	ARRIVAL
pit	hou	ok	179	10am	1pm
pit	alb	ok	219	8am	12pm
pit	jfk	ok	319	9am	12pm
pit	ord	ok	439	11am	1pm
ord	mex	full	99	4pm	11pm
ord	mex	full	229	1pm	5pm
hou	mex	ok	119	7pm	10pm
alb	mex	ok	279	4pm	10pm
dal	mex	ok	229	3pm	6pm

Fig. 4. Graphic for look up information task.

usefulness of a graphic presentation is a function of the task that the graphic will be used to support, graphic design should focus on designing efficient perceptual procedures to be performed by human users. Decisions made about how to encode and structure information in an accompanying graphic should be based primarily on supporting efficient and accurate performance of the perceptual procedure. The enabling step in the task-analytic approach is to capture the notion of a perceptual procedure performed by human users within the context of a graphic presentation using the same formal framework used to describe abstract computational processes, allowing design decisions to follow formal criteria.

Section 2 reviews previous work related to the problem of designing graphic presentations. Section 3 overviews the five main components of BOZ and introduces a running example used throughout the paper to describe BOZ's approach. Section 4 describes a language used to create logical descriptions of user tasks that are submitted to BOZ as input. Section 5 shows how alternative perceptual procedures can be derived from a logical description of a user task by substituting perceptual inferences in place of logical inferences when the logical and perceptual inferences can be shown to yield the same result. Section 6 shows how an analysis of the relationships between task inferences can be used to determine how information can be structured within a graphic such that visual search is minimized when users perform a perceptual procedure. Section 7 describes three criteria used by BOZ when selecting a single perceptual procedure and graphic design that best supports performance of the user's task. Section 8 describes an automated rendering component that transforms logical facts to graphical facts and displays them on the screen. Section 9 analyzes the cognitive advantages of a perceptual procedure and graphic designed by BOZ. The analysis produces a set of specific hypotheses about the potential task performance efficiencies of the BOZ-designed procedure and graphic. Finally, Section 10 reviews an experiment reported in Casner and Larkin [8] in which participants performed a BOZ-designed perceptual procedure using a series of accompanying BOZ-designed graphics. Results show significant decreases in users' performance times and suggest that users obtained the efficiency savings through the hypothesized perceptual inference substitutions and visual search reductions.

2. PREVIOUS WORK

The following surveys theoretical and empirical work concerned with the problem of designing effective graphics.

2.1 Graphic Design Practices

Tufte [32, 33], Bertin [2], Cleveland [10], and Schmid [28] present many inviting examples of graphics and describe general graphic design practices. These practices help designers to make use of graphic techniques that have been observed to be useful and to avoid bad practices known to make graphics ambiguous, confusing, or generally less usable. There are two basic limitations of these works. First, since the works do not well articulate the reasons *why* graphics succeed in practice, the graphic design practices provide little prescriptive information about how to design a graphic from scratch. Stating that a graph "reveals" a data set in one case tells us little about how to go about designing a graphic that reveals other data sets. Second, the graphic design practices focus mainly on the information to be presented in a graphic and include less concern for the tasks for which the graphics are designed to support. This approach offers little guidance when designing different graphics to support different tasks.

2.2 Automated Graphic Presentation Systems

APT [26] is an automated graphic presentation tool that designs static, 2D presentations of relational information. A significant contribution of APT was to formally characterize something to which many previous investigators informally alluded. Graphic presentations can be expressed as sentences in formal graphical languages that have the same precise syntax and semantics as propositional formalisms. The advantage of having a formalism for graphic presentations is that it provides a set of criteria for deciding the role of each visible sign or symbol placed in a graphic and improves the integrity of a graphic presentation by using formal methods for transforming logical facts to graphical facts. APT's style of analysis for formal graphical languages has been used by nearly every graphic presentation tool designed after APT, including the one described in this paper. A second contribution of APT is that, unlike proposals for graphic design practices, APT designs graphics with a minimum amount of intervention on the part of the designer; that is, APT embodies a genuinely *prescriptive* theory of how to design a graphic. However, APT's design algorithm is based on an analysis of the information to be presented and does not explicitly consider the task for which a graphic is to be used. This prevents APT from directly exploiting the task-related advantages of graphics and from creating different presentations of the same information to support different tasks.

SAGE [27] is a hybrid, text, and graphics presentation system that generates explanations of changes that occur in quantitative modeling systems such as project modeling and financial spreadsheets. Graphic presentations are designed by SAGE in response to information queries made by the user. Through an analysis of user queries, SAGE's design of graphic presentations is sensitive to the goals of the user, taking an important step toward exploiting the task-related advantages of graphics. SAGE presently contains only a small set of primitive problem-solving operators and is not able to fashion presentations to support complex information-processing tasks involving combinations of many primitive operators.

AIPS [36] accepts descriptions of information encoded using the KL-ONE [3] knowledge representation language. AIPS matches the KL-ONE descriptions against a set of predefined presentation formats and chooses that format that best matches the characteristics of the data. AIPS is not able to design novel graphic presentations.

BHARAT [16] accepts descriptions of data sets and chooses display formats to present relations between the data. The presentation format chosen is determined by the characteristics of the data: line charts are used for continuous data, pie charts for proportional data, and bar charts for all others. Like AIPS, BHARAT chooses among existing presentations rather than designing new ones.

VIEW [15] creates graphic presentations of information about ships maintained in a naval database. VIEW's knowledge base contains information about particular users, a set of tasks for the domain and a set of predefined KL-ONE descriptions of possible presentation formats. By matching users' identities, tasks, and queries against the presentation format descriptions, VIEW is able to present different graphics in different contexts. As with AIPS and BHARAT, VIEW does not design its presentation formats.

APEX [14] creates graphical explanations of actions performed with physical devices in a three-dimensional world. Explanations are created by presenting sequences of static images depicting the individual steps in an action. APEX uses hierarchical descriptions of the objects that can appear in an explanation where each level in the hierarchy contains more detailed features of the object. A second mechanism allows APEX to determine how much detail is needed at each step and to display only that information. Since the objects that appear in explanations are highly domain specific, they must be hand created prior to using APEX.

2.3 Cognitive Research on the Utility of Graphic Presentations

Larkin and Simon's [24] studied the utility of graphics from a cognitive science perspective. Larkin and Simon built detailed cognitive simulations of human task performance with each simulation performing a task using equivalent logical and graphical representations of a set of data. Larkin and Simon's analysis yielded two ways in which graphic presentation-based procedures could be performed more efficiently by humans: (1) by allowing users to substitute quick perceptual inferences for more demanding logical inferences, and (2) by reducing search for needed information.

Several more recent studies have investigated other cognitive utilities of graphic presentations. Hegarty and Just [17] studied the use of diagrams in understanding complex machines. Fallside [13] investigated how learners make use of animated diagrams similar to those produced by Feiner's APEX program when understanding complex machines. Koedinger and Anderson [23] examined the role of diagrams in geometry learning and instruction. Many other cognitive advantages of graphics have been proposed. Graphics appear to help improve recall for presented data, reduce short-term memory loads during problem solving, provide information about the state of a problem solution, help users organize their knowledge about a problem, and increase motivation or user satisfaction. A future articulation of how these advantages relate to specific graphic design features may allow them to be incorporated in a prescriptive theory of graphic presentation design.

3. BOZ: AUTOMATED TASK-ANALYTIC DESIGN OF GRAPHIC PRESENTATIONS

The following describes a technique for designing graphic presentations of relational information based on an analysis of the task that a graphic is intended to support. The graphic design technique is articulated in an automated graphic design and presentation tool called BOZ. BOZ focuses on designing perceptual procedures, to be performed by human users, that allow users to accomplish a stated goal more efficiently than they would be able to without the benefit of a graphic presentation. BOZ's task-analytic approach uses the following five components.

(1) A *logical task description language* allows the user of BOZ to describe the information-processing task that she or he wishes to design a graphic to support. This language is used to enumerate the individual problem-solving steps (called logical operators) that are required for a user to complete a task without the benefit of any information presentation. Logical task descriptions must be prepared by hand and submitted to BOZ as input. The task description language is also used to describe the informtion manipulated by a task.

(2) A *perceptual operator substitution* component considers each operator in a logical task description looking for ways to substitute perceptual operators in place of logical operators when the operators can be shown to produce the same output given the same input. BOZ contains a catalog of perceptual operators describing problem-solving steps performed within the context of a graphic. Perceptual operator substitution is the mechanism used to streamline the inferencing done by the human user when performing a task. Several perceptual operators typically qualify as substitutes for each logical operator, yielding a set of possible perceptual procedures.

(3) A *perceptual data structuring* component examines the information manipulated by each logical operator and determines how information shared by several operators should be collected together to form complex graphical objects, and how unrelated information can be partitioned into distinct presentations. Perceptual data structuring is one mechanism used to minimize the amount of time the user spends searching for information in a graphic. The perceptual data structuring component determines the optimal grouping and distribution of information within a graphic. It does not determine how the information is to be perceptually encoded in the graphic.

(4) A *perceptual operator selection* component chooses a single perceptual operator to substitute each logical operator in a task description. The first criteria for perceptual operator selection is how efficiently and accurately each perceptual operator is likely to be performed by human users. Selecting each particular perceptual operator also decides the way that the information manipulated by that operator must be perceptually encoded in a graphic. A second criteria for operator selection is choosing a complete set of perceptual operators that results in a set of graphical encodings that can be combined according to the specification produced by the perceptual data structuring component. The perceptual operator selection component yields a detailed description of a single perceptual procedure and an accompanying graphic design that supports the performance of the perceptual procedure.

(5) A *rendering* component translates logical facts into graphical facts and displays them on the computer screen following the graphic design produced by BOZ. Graphics produced by the rendering component support two-way interactions that allow changes made in the internally stored logical facts to be automatically reflected in the graphic presentation and direct manipulations of the graphical objects in the presentation to be reflected in the internal set of logical facts.

The next five sections describe the components of BOZ in detail. To illustrate how BOZ works, a running example is developed throughout the discussion. In the example, a graphic presentation is designed to support one additional airline reservation task:

> *Find a pair of connecting flights that travel from Pittsburgh to Mexico City. You are free to choose any intermediate city as long as the layover in that city is no more than 4 hours. Both flights that you choose must be available. The combined cost of the flights cannot exceed* $500. *Find an available seat on each flight.*

This task differs from the previous four reservation tasks in that the user must now be concerned with obeying both time and cost constraints. We will see that the requirements of this task lead BOZ to produce a graphic presentation completely different from those designed for the four previous reservation tasks.

4. LOGICAL TASK DESCRIPTION LANGUAGE

The first component of BOZ provides a means of describing the information-processing activities that a graphic is intended to support. Task descriptions must presently be prepared in advance and submitted to BOZ as input.[1] BOZ's task description language contains two basic components: (1) a notation for describing logical procedures, and (2) a notation for expressing logical facts manipulated by a logical procedure.

Logical procedure definitions are similar to programs in conventional programming languages such as Pascal. Every logical procedure contains three parts: (1) a set of domain set definitions; (2) a set of logical operator definitions; and (3) a main body. *Domain sets* are the information types that define the universe of discourse for a task. Domain sets consist of a name, a type of information, and a (possibly infinite) set of data values of that type. Three types of domain sets are allowed by BOZ: *quantitative*, *nominal*, and *ordinal* [30]. A *logical operator* (LOP) is composed of an operator name, a list of arguments taken as input to the operator, and a single relation that the operator computes. Logical operators occur in two forms. A *search operator* uses one of the three meta-commands: ASK, TELL, and RETRACT to query, assert, and remove logical facts from a simple database of logical facts. Logical facts describe object-attribute-value relations and take the form: (⟨attribute⟩ ⟨object⟩ ⟨value⟩), where ⟨attribute⟩ names some property of ⟨object⟩, and ⟨value⟩ is the property value. The arguments ⟨object⟩ and ⟨value⟩ in a search operator may be instantiated or uninstantiated. *Uninstantiated arguments* (i.e., variables that have not yet been assigned a value) are capitalized. *Instantiated arguments* are variables that were previously uninstantiated but have since been assigned a value. Instantiated arguments appear in lower case. A *computation operator* describes computations performed on a

[1] Section 11 discusses prospects for automating the process by which users communicate their tasks and goals to BOZ.

set of arguments using one of a set of predefined arithmetic or logical predicates: +, −, *, /, AND, OR, and NOT. Note that only instantiated arguments may appear in a computation operator.

The following are two logical operators in the airline reservation procedure. The two operators determine the departure time of an airline flight (search) and the layover between two flights (computation), respectively:

```
(LOP determineDeparture (⟨flight⟩ ⟨DEPARTURE⟩)
   (ASK (Departure ⟨flight⟩ ⟨DEPARTURE⟩)))
(LOP computeLayover (⟨departure⟩ ⟨arrival⟩ ⟨LAYOVER⟩
   (– ⟨departure⟩ ⟨arrival⟩ ⟨LAYOVER⟩))
```

The keyword LOP is used to denote a logical operator. The lists (⟨flight⟩ ⟨DEPARTURE⟩) and (⟨departure⟩ ⟨arrival⟩ ⟨LAYOVER⟩) are the sets of arguments that the two operators receive as input. The ASK predicate states that a list of facts should be checked to see if the relation that follows can be shown to be true, namely, if there exists a fact expressing the departure time of the flight. The relation (– ⟨departure⟩ ⟨arrival⟩) specifies that the predefined subtraction predicate is to be computed given the values ⟨departure⟩ and ⟨arrival⟩ and the variable ⟨LAYOVER⟩ is to be instantiated with the result.

The *main body* of a logical procedure is an ordered sequence of calls to the set of defined logical operators. To express control information, the main body of a logical procedure may additionally contain any of the following control constructs: **while-do**, **for**, **repeat-until**, and **if-then**.

To illustrate how logical procedures are described using the task language, Figure 5 shows a complete procedure description for the airline reservation task.[2] The procedure in Figure 5 assumes that there are no direct flights from Pittsburgh to Mexico City.

Logical facts are used to describe relational information manipulated by a logical procedure. Logical facts state relations between values drawn from one or more domain sets. The airline reservation procedure manipulates information from the domain sets specified in the top portion of Figure 5. Figure 6 shows logical facts that describe a set of three airline flights.

5. PERCEPTUAL OPERATOR SUBSTITUTION

Perceptual operator substitution is the graphic design technique used to insure that a graphic presentation best exploits the first task-specific advantage of graphics: users can substitute efficiently performed perceptual inferences in place of more demanding logical inferences. The perceptual operator substitution component considers each logical operator appearing in a logical procedure looking for ways of substituting perceptual operators in place of logical operators when the logical and perceptual operators can be shown to be equivalent. The perceptual operator substitution component produces a set

```
(PROCEDURE
 (let ((found nil))
  (while (and found (findFlightWithOrigin FLIGHT 'pit)) do
   (if (available? flight 'T) then
    (findDestination flight LAYOVERCITY)
    (determineArrival flight ARRIVAL)
    (while (and found (findFlightWithOrigin CONNECTING layovercity)) do
       (if (available? connecting 'T) then
        (findDestination flight FINALDESTINATION)
        (if (landsInDestinationCity? finaldestination 'mex) then
         (determineDeparture connecting DEPARTURE)
         (computeLayover departure arrival LAYOVER)
         (if (and (connecting? departure arrival)
                (layoverLessThanX? layover '4)) then
          (determineCost flight COST1)
          (determineCost connecting COST2)
          (addCosts cost1 cost2 TOTAL)
          (if (costLessThanX? total '500) then
           (repeat
            (findSeat flight SEAT1)
           until (emptySeat? seat1 'T))
           (findSeatNumber seat1 SEATNUM1)
           (repeat
            (findSeat connecting SEAT2)
           until (emptySeat? seat2 'T))
           (findSeatNumber seat2 SEATNUM2)
           (if (and seat1 seat2)
            (setq found t)]
(DOMAINSETS
 (flight NOMINAL 50)
 (origin NOMINAL (pit hou dal ord alb mex gdl qto paz bga))
 (destination NOMINAL (pit hou dal ord alb mex gdl qto paz bga))
 (departure QUANTITATIVE 1440)
 (arrival QUANTITATIVE 1440)
 (layover (departure arrival))
 (cost QUANTITATIVE 1000)
 (availability NOMINAL (ok full))
 (seat NOMINAL 144)
 (seatnumber ORDINAL (1A 1B 1C 1D 1E 1F ... 24A 24B 24C 24D 24E 24F))

(OPERATORS
 (LOP findFlightWithOrigin (<FLIGHT> <origin>)
  (ASK (Origin <FLIGHT> <origin>)))
 (LOP findDestination (<flight> <DESTINATION>)
  (ASK (Destination <flight> <DESTINTATION>)))
 (LOP landsInDestinationCity? (<destination> <destination>)
  (= <destination> <destination>)))
 (LOP available? (<flight> <availability>)
  (ASK (Availability <flight> <availability>)))
 (LOP determineDeparture (<flight> <DEPARTURE>)
  (ASK (Departure <flight> <DEPARTURE>)))
 (LOP determineArrival (<flight> <ARRIVAL>)
  (ASK (Arrival <flight> <ARRIVAL>)))
 (LOP computeLayover (<departure> <arrival> <LAYOVER>)
  (- <departure> <arrival> <LAYOVER>))
 (LOP connecting? (<departure> <arrival>)
  (> <departure> <arrival>))
 (LOP layoverLessThanX? (<layover> <layover>)
  (< <layover> <layover>))
 (LOP determineCost (<flight> <COST>)
  (ASK (Cost <flight> <COST>)))
 (LOP addCosts (<cost> <cost> <COST>)
  (+ <cost> <cost> <COST>))
 (LOP costLessThanX? (<cost> <cost>)
  (< <cost> <cost>))
 (LOP findSeat (<flight> <SEAT>)
  (ASK (Seat <flight> <SEAT>)))
 (LOP emptySeat? (<seat> <availability>)
  (ASK (Availability <seat> <availability>)))
 (LOP findSeatNumber (<seat> <SEATNUMBER>)
  (ASK (Seatnumber <seat> <SEATNUMBER>))))
```

Fig. 5. Logical airline reservation procedure.

[2]Note that there exist many variations of the procedure shown in Figure 5. The user might alternatively start by searching for flights that terminate in Mexico City and work backwards, or start by choosing an intermediate city and then searching for two flights that arrive from Pittsburgh and leave for Mexico City.

```
(origin flight117 pit)                 (cost flight117 179)
(origin flight738 pit)                 (cost flight738 219)
(origin flight839 pit)                 (cost flight839 319)
(destination flight117 hou)            (departure flight117 10:00)
(destination flight738 alb)            (departure flight738 8:00)
(destination flight839 jfk)            (departure flight839 9:15)
(availability flight117 ok)            (arrival flight117 12:50)
(availability flight738 ok)            (arrival flight738 12:00)
(availability flight839 ok)            (arrival flight839 12:05)
```

Fig. 6. Logical facts for airline reservation tasks.

of perceptual operators that can potentially serve as substitutes for each logical operator. Decisions about which particular perceptual operator to substitute for each logical operator are subject to further design criteria described in Section 7.

Perceptual operator substitution relies on two important components: (1) a *catalog of perceptual operators* that describes information-processing activities that occur within the context of a graphic presentation; and (2) a *substitution algorithm* that considers each logical operator in a task and searches the catalog of perceptual operators for those perceptual operators that compute the same function as the logical operator. Since there are often several perceptual operators that qualify as substitutes for a logical operator, the perceptual operator substitution component produces a set of possible perceptual procedures equivalent to the logical procedure.

5.1 A Catalog of Perceptual Operators

Perceptual operators (*POPs*), analogous to logical operators, characterize information-processing activities performed within the context of a graphic presentation and whose performance depends on the use of a graphic presentation. Perceptual operators describe perceptual inferences or visual search performed using graphically expressed information. For example, judging the distance between two objects in a graphic and locating an object having a particular color are examples of perceptual operators.

Perceptual operators are organized around a set of *primitive graphical languages* available to the designer of a graphic presentation [26]. Primitive graphical languages comprise the designer's resources for encoding information graphically. The set of primitive graphical languages used by BOZ are shown in Table I. The parenthesized numbers in Table I indicate an upper limit on the number of distinct values that can be practically encoded in a single graphic presentation using each primitive graphical language. Associated with each of the primitive graphical languages is a set of perceptual operators that are admitted when the designer of a graphic presentation elects to use one or more of the primitive languages in a graphic. For example, if we elect to use the Horizontal Position language we admit a family of perceptual operators (POPs) such as determining the horizontal position of a graphical object, comparing two or more horizontal positions, and finding the midpoint of an interval defined by two horizontal positions.

Table I. Primitive Graphical Languages

Horizontal Position (100)	Color (12)
Vertical Position (100)	Labels (∞)
Height (50)	Line Thickness (3)
Width (50)	Line Dashing (2)
Line Length (50)	Shape (5)
Area (10)	Visibility (2)
Shading (4)	Tabular (∞)
Connectivity (8)	

Table II. Perceptual Operators (POPs)

Horizontal Position	Shading
`determine-horz-pos`	`determine-shade`
`search-object-at-horz-pos`	`search-object-with-shade`
`search-any-horz-pos-object`	`search-object-and-shade`
`verify-object-at-horz-pos`	`verify-object-and-shade`
`horz-coincidence?`	`darker?`
`left-of?`	`lighter?`
`right-of?`	`same-shade?`
`horz-forward-projection`	
`horz-backward-projection`	
`determine-horz-distance`	

Table II shows the set of perceptual operators admitted by the Horizontal Position and Shading primitive graphical languages. It is interesting to compare the perceptual operators associated with each primitive graphical language. This exercise helps make explicit the task-specific usefulness of each graphical encoding technique. Note the difference in the number of computation operators supported by the Horizontal Position and Shading primitive graphical languages. For instance, human users can easily determine the difference between two horizontal positions but are not generally able to determine the difference between two shades.

Equivalence Classes for Perceptual Operators. Every perceptual operator computes a function over relational information. An *equivalence class* of perceptual operators is a set of operators that can be shown to compute the same function over relational information. Table III describes eleven equivalence classes used to categorize the perceptual operators in the catalog. Every perceptual operator in the catalog is classified under exactly one operator equivalence class. Table IV shows the perceptual operators associated with

Table III. Perceptual Operator Equivalence Classes

SEARCH OPERATORS

search: Given a graphical property, search a set of objects for an object having that graphical property.
lookup: Given an object, determine a specific property of that object.
search and lookup: Search for any object and determine a specified property of that object.
verify: Given an object and property, verify that the object has that property.

COMPUTATION OPERATORS

equal: Do two objects have the same graphical property?
less than: Does one object have a lower valued graphical property than another?
greater than: Does one object have a lower valued graphical property than another?
plus: Compute the sum of two graphical properties.
difference: Compute the difference of two graphical properties.
times: Compute the product of two graphical properties.
quotient: Compute the quotient of two graphical properties.

Table IV. Members of Two Perceptual Operator Equivalence Classes

search	**subtraction**
search-object-at-horz-pos	determine-horz-distance
search-object-at-vert-pos	determine-vert-distance
search-object-with-height	determine-height-difference
search-object-with-width	determine-width-difference
search-line-with-length	determine-difference-in-line-length
search-object-with-area	determine-area-difference
search-connected-object	subtract-labels
search-object-with-shading	determine-slope-difference
search-object-with-color	subtract-table-entries
search-object-with-label	
search-line-with-thickness	
search-line-with-dashing	
search-line-with-slope	
search-object-with-shape	
search-visible-object	
search-entry-in-table	

the **search** and **subtraction** equivalence classes. Perceptual operators are formalized using the same notation used for logical operators. For example, the search-object-with-shade search operator and determine-horz-distance computation operator are defined as follows:

```
(POP search-object-with-shade (⟨OBJECT⟩ ⟨shade⟩)
    (ASK (Shading ⟨OBJECT⟩ ⟨shade⟩)))
(POP determine-horz-distance (⟨horzpos1⟩ ⟨horzpos2⟩ ⟨DISTANCE⟩)
    (DIFFERENCE ⟨horzpos1⟩ ⟨horzpos2⟩ ⟨DISTANCE⟩))
```

The search-object-with-shade operator searches for an object in a graphic having a shade equal to the value of ⟨shade⟩ and instantiates the variable ⟨OBJECT⟩ with the result. The determine-horz-distance operator determines the distance between two objects located at ⟨horzpos1⟩ and ⟨horzpos2⟩ in a graphic and instantiates the variable ⟨DISTANCE⟩ with the result.

5.2 Substituting Operators

The formal characterization of logical and perceptual operators using equivalent notations allows BOZ to design perceptual tasks that allow users to accomplish the same results as a logical task submitted to BOZ as input. The ultimate goal of BOZ is to arrive at that perceptual task that is equivalent to the original logical task, and that is most easily and efficiently performed by human users. To design a perceptual task, BOZ considers each logical operator in a task description and searches the catalog of perceptual operators attempting to locate those POPs that can be shown to compute the same function as a LOP. Insisting on operator equivalence insures that whatever perceptual procedure is followed in place of a corresponding logical procedure, it is guaranteed that the user will obtain the same results if the perceptual procedure is performed correctly.

A perceptual operator qualifies as a substitute for a logical operator if and only if the logical operator can be categorized in the same equivalence class (see Table III) as the perceptual operator. Categorization is determined by attempting to match an LOP to an arbitrary member of an equivalence class. If an LOP is successfully matched to a member of an equivalence class, all perceptual operators in that class initially qualify as substitutions for the LOP. For example, given the computeLayover logical operator in the airline reservation procedure:

```
(POP computeLayover (⟨departure⟩ ⟨arrival⟩ ⟨LAYOVER⟩)
    (− ⟨departure⟩ ⟨arrival⟩ ⟨LAYOVER⟩))
```

BOZ attempts to classify the LOP into each of the equivalence classes given in Table III until a class is found or the set of classes is exhausted. The computeLayover LOP can be successfully categorized into the **subtraction** class of search operators. One member of the **subtraction** class is the determine-horz-distance operator associated with the Horizontal Position language and shown above. Since both operators compute the subtraction function and we can map the arguments of the LOP onto those of the POP, any graphic that represents departure and arrival times as objects positioned along a horizontal axis will always allow the user to perform the determine-horz-distance operator and obtain the same answer produced by the computeLayover operator.

Figure 7 shows the classifications for the logical operators in the airline reservation task. Each operator in the task can be categorized into a single equivalence class. Consequently, a set of perceptual operators initially qualify as substitutions for each logical operator in the task. For example, the list of perceptual operators associated with the **search** equivalence class are proposed as substitutions for the findFlightWithOrigin and findSeat operators.

```
findFlightWithOrigin (search)
findDestination (lookup)
landsInDestinationCity? (verify)
available? (verify)
determineDeparture (lookup)
determineArrival (lookup)
computeLayover (subtraction)
connecting? (greaterthan)
layoverLessThanX? (lessthan)
determineCost (lookup)
addCosts (addition)
costLessThanX? (lessthan)
findSeat (search)
emptySeat (verify)
findSeatNumber (lookup)
```

Fig. 7. Operator classifications for airline reservation task.

Similarly, the operators of the **subtraction** class match the description of the computeLayover operator.

It is important to note that BOZ has not yet decided *which* perceptual operator to choose in each case. Decisions about which perceptual operators to match with each logical operator are subject to further constraints computed by the perceptual data structuring and perceptual operator selection components described in Sections 6 and 7. What BOZ has produced at this stage is a space of perceptual procedures that may be selected according to additional design criteria.

6. PERCEPTUAL DATA STRUCTURING

The perceptual data structuring component is the design technique used to implement the second type of cognitive advantage of graphic presentations: graphics sometimes allow users to spend less time searching for needed information. The perceptual data structuring component examines the information required to perform each logical operator in a task. Two types of analyses are performed using this information. First, by noting the domain sets that each logical operator manipulates, BOZ determines what information should appear in a graphic designed to support a task. Second, by analyzing the relationships between the operators in a task in terms of the domain sets of information they manipulate, BOZ determines: (a) how information shared by several operators should be collected in the same spatial locality and graphically encoded using the same primitive graphical language and (b) how information not shared among operators can be partitioned into distinct presentations. The perceptual data structuring component produces a *perceptual data structure specification* that outlines the presentations that will be used to support the task, the information that should appear in each presentation, and how the information is to be grouped within each presentation. The perceptual data structuring component does *not* decide how information is to be graphically encoded in the presentation. These decisions are made by the perceptual operator selection component (Section 7).

[flight] x [origin] x [destination] x [availability] x [departure] x [arrival] x [layover] x [cost] x [seat] x [seatnumber]

Fig. 8. Feature space for airline reservation task.

The remainder of the section describes a scheme that analyzes relationships between operators by representing each operator as a vector defined over the domain sets that the operator manipulates. Relationships between vectors are determined by identifying common domain sets occurring in vectors. A complete sketch of all relationships between vectors reveals how information is to be collected together into graphical objects and partitioned among presentations.

6.1 Operator Vectors

Recall that every task description is defined over a finite collection of domain sets. When taken together, all of the domain sets used by a task description form a feature space. A *feature space* is formally defined as the cross product of all domain sets spanned by a task description. Figure 8 shows an example of a feature space defined over the domain sets that pertain to the airline reservation task.

Each logical operator in a task description computes a relation over one or more domain sets in the feature space defined for that task. BOZ makes explicit the domain sets relevant to each logical operator in a task description using a construct called a *vector*. For every logical operator in a task, BOZ generates a corresponding vector that indicates the domain sets of information manipulated by that operator. There are two types of vectors that correspond to the two types of logical operators: search vectors and computation vectors. A *search vector* contains the names of the two domain sets from which the arguments of a search operator are drawn. The first element of a search vector is treated as the *object*, the second domain set as an *attribute* of the object. For example, the findFlightWithOrigin logical operator defines the vector: ⟨flight,origin⟩, where flight is the object, and origin is the attribute. A *computation vector* contains the names of all domain sets that appear as arguments to the computation operator. For example, the computeLayover operator defines the vector: ⟨departure,arrival,layover⟩ since it manipulates arguments drawn from these three domain sets. The complete set of vectors defined by the logical operators in the airline reservation task are shown in Figure 9.

6.2 Relationships Between Vectors

BOZ's next step is to examine the relationships between the vectors in terms of the domain sets they manipulate. There are four types of relationships that can hold between vectors. BOZ determines relationships between vectors

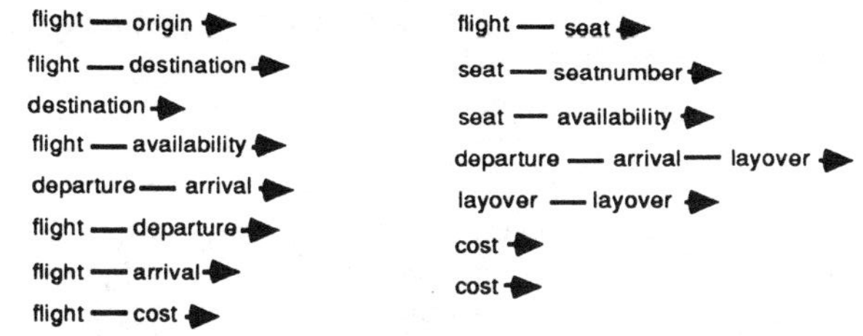

Fig. 9. Vectors for airline reservation task.

by applying an ordered set of four rules to the complete set of vectors for a task.

(1) *Conjoint*. Search vectors $s_1 = \langle o_1, a_1 \rangle$ and $s_2 = \langle o_2, a_2 \rangle$ are *conjoint* when they contain common objects, $o_1 = o_2$. For example, the vectors defined by the determineDeparture and determineArrival operators are conjoint. Conjoint vectors group together attributes that pertain to the same object. Consequently, these attributes should be encoded in a single graphical object in order to reduce eye movement over the presentation when searching for that object and its attributes.

(2) *Parallel*. Search vectors $s_1 = \langle o_1, a_1 \rangle$ and $s_2 = \langle o_2, a_2 \rangle$ are *parallel* when there exists a computation vector, $c = \langle a_1, a_2 \rangle$, that contains both a_1 and a_2. Parallel vectors indicate that some computation operator requires that two or more different objects (e.g., flight and seat) and their attributes be coordinated in order to draw a particular inference. Consequently, both objects should appear in the same graphic presentation and should be encoded using the same primitive graphical language. In the airline example, none of the vectors are parallel.

(3) *Orthogonal*. Search vector $s_2 = \langle o_2, a_2 \rangle$ is *orthogonal* to search vector $s_1 = \langle o_1, a_1 \rangle$ if the attribute of s_2 appears as the object in s_1, that is, $o_1 = a_2$. In the airline example, the search vectors corresponding to the seat object are orthogonal to the flight object vectors. Orthogonality indicates part-of relationships between objects. Domain sets manipulated by orthogonal vectors should appear in separate nested presentations. That is, the user should be able to view the part-of presentation by making an appropriate selection in the first presentation. Note that it is possible for two vectors to be orthogonal to each other.

(4) *Disjoint*. Search vectors s_1 and s_2 are *disjoint* when they share no common object or attribute. Disjoint vectors indicate that no computation operator requires that two or more objects be coordinated to draw an inference. Information relevant to disjoint vectors should appear in different presentations since the task does not require that the information be used together. None of the airline search vectors are disjoint.

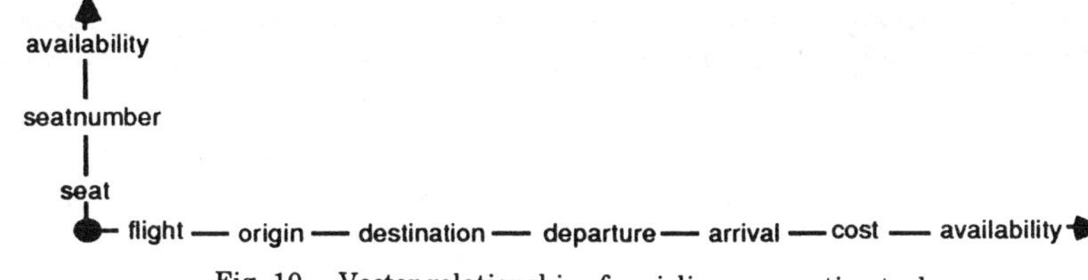

Fig. 10. Vector relationships for airline reservation task.

```
(NESTED (PRESENTATION1 (flight (Origin Destination Departure
                        Arrival Cost Availability))
        (PRESENTATION2 (seat (Seat Availability))))
```

Fig. 11. Initial perceptual data structure specification for airline reservation task.

Applying the vector relationship rules to the vectors in Figure 9 yields the arrangement shown in Figure 10. Since the vectors pertaining to origin, destination, departure, arrival, cost, and availability are conjoint, BOZ constrains them to be encoded in the same graphical object. Similarly, the vectors pertaining to seat number and availability are conjoint and thus form their own graphical object. The flight and seat vectors are not parallel since the task does not require the user to coordinate information about flights and seat (e.g., subtract seat number from arrival time). The seat vectors are orthogonal to the flight vectors indicating that the seat object is a part of the flight object. Hence, BOZ constrains the seat graphical objects to appear in a separate presentation that is nested inside each flight box.

BOZ uses the vector relationships shown in Figure 10 to specify how information will be grouped together into complex graphical objects and distributed among distinct graphic presentations. The initial perceptual data structure specification for the airline task is shown in Figure 11.

It is important to note that BOZ has not yet decided how facts about the origin, destination, departure, etc., of a flight are to be encoded in the graphic. That is, BOZ has not yet associated the names of primitive graphical languages with the predicate names appearing in the perceptual data structure specification. Which primitive graphical languages to associate with each predicate is determined by the perceptual operators selected to substitute the logical operators in the task. Note that information about flight numbers and layovers will not be encoded in any graphic. This has occurred since information about flight numbers is never used in the task and facts about layovers are produced as the results of the computeLayover computation operator.

7. PERCEPTUAL OPERATOR SELECTION

The perceptual operator selection component chooses a single perceptual operator to substitute each logical operator from the list of possibilities generated by the perceptual operator substitution component. Selecting a single perceptual operator to substitute each logical operator accomplishes two things: (1) reduces the space of possible perceptual procedures to a single perceptual procedure judged to be the most effective, and (2) allows BOZ to design a single accompanying graphic that supports human performance of the selected perceptual procedure.

Three important issues constrain the selection of perceptual operators. First, since the goal is to arrive at a perceptual procedure that minimizes the effort required to correctly complete a task, for each logical operator BOZ seeks to choose that perceptual operator that is performed most efficiently and accurately by human users. A first criteria for operator selection involves estimating the relative performance efficiency and accuracy of the perceptual operators. Second, recall that each perceptual operator is associated with a primitive graphical language that must be used to graphically encode information manipulated by that operator. A second criteria when selecting operators is that the representational power of the primitive graphical language associated with a candidate perceptual operator is sufficient to encode the logical facts manipulated by the operator. Third, recall that the perceptual data structure specification produced by the perceptual data structuring component constrains some domain sets of information to be represented in a single graphical object or using the same primitive graphical language. A third criteria for operator selection is that the primitive graphical languages associated with the selected perceptual operators be combinable such that they result in coherent graphic presentations that agree with the perceptual data structure specification for the task.

7.1 Human Performance Rankings for Perceptual Operators

The most important criteria when selecting a perceptual operator is choosing that operator that allows the human user to obtain the results of the operator most efficiently and accurately. To determine which of a set of perceptual operators is likely to be the most performance effective, BOZ uses a two-tier ranking system that is a generalization of the approach used in Mackinlay's APT program [26]. The first tier ranks the equivalence classes for logical operators in order of their relative difficulty. For instance, arithmetic operators require more effort to perform than lookup operators. Consequently, arithmetic operators are always awarded the most efficient perceptual operators. The second tier ranks the perceptual operators within each perceptual operator equivalence class. For instance, determining the horizontal distance between two points on a scale is generally performed more efficiently and accurately than determining the difference between two areas. Similarly, searching for an object having a particular color is performed more efficiently than searching for an object having a particular shape. An important observation is that the operators associated with each different primitive graphical language best support different tasks. That is, it is impossible to say that any one primitive graphical language is the most effective way to encode data in a graphic. Primitive graphical languages too fall in and out of usefulness with respect to the task to be supported.

Table V. Ranking of Perceptual Operators and Equivalence Classes

A. Class Rankings:

1. plus, difference, quotient, times
2. search
3. less than, greater than
4. equal
5. search and lookup
6. lookup
7. verify

B. Operator Rankings:

SEARCH OPERATORS

search: {Visibility, HorzPos, VertPos, Shape, Connectivity, Shading, Height, Width, LineDashing, LineLength, LineThickness, Labels, Area}

lookup, verify, search and lookup: {Shading, Shape, Labels, Height, Width, LineDashing, LineThickness, Connectivity, HorzPos, VertPos, LineLength, Area, Visibility}

COMPUTATION OPERATORS

equal: {Labels, Shading, HorzPos, VertPos, Shape, LineDashing, Height, Width, LineThickness, LineLength, Connectivity, Visibility, Area}

lessthan, greaterthan: {Shading, HorzPos, VertPos, Height, Width, LineThickness, LineLength, Labels, Connectivity, Shape, LineDashing, Visibility, Area}

plus, times: {Height, Width, LineLength, LineThickness, HorzPos, VertPos, Labels, Connectivity, Shading, LineDashing, Shape, Area}

difference, quotient: {HorzPos, VertPos, Height, Width, LineLength, LineThickness, Labels, Connectivity, Area, Shading, Shape}

BOZ's perceptual operator rankings were generated using a combination of two methods: (1) theoretical predictions based on a more fine-grained consideration of each perceptual operator [5, 34], and (2) experimental observations of human perceptual task performance [11, 12, 20, 31, 34]. Table V shows the rankings for perceptual operator equivalence classes and the rankings for the perceptual operators in each class.

7.2 Expressiveness

The second criterion used during operator selection is that a selected perceptual operator must be associated with a primitive graphical language that is powerful enough to encode the logical facts manipulated by that operator. For example, even though the search-shaded-object is the most efficiently performed search operator, it cannot be selected to substitute the findFlightWithOrigin logical operator since the number of different cities exceeds the number of different shades. When a selected perceptual operator fails to meet the expressiveness needs of a logical operator it is disqualified and the next highest ranking perceptual operator is considered. The interested reader can consult Mackinlay [26] for a thorough analysis of primitive graphical language expressiveness. Like all other recent presentation systems, BOZ adopts Mackinlay's technique for deciding expressiveness.

7.3 Perceptual Operator Combinability

The third criterion for operator selection concerns the combinability of perceptual operators. Suppose we have selected the stack-heights perceptual operator to substitute the addCosts logical operator in the airline reservation task and are currently selecting a perceptual operator to substitute the findFlightWithOrigin operator. Suppose that we are currently considering the determine-slope perceptual operator as a candidate selection. Recall that the perceptual data structuring component has indicated that the information relevant to these two operators should be encoded in the same graphical object. Every perceptual operator has associated with it a graphical presentation object (defined below) that is used to graphically encode the information manipulated by that object. For example, the graphical presentation object for the stack-heights and determine-slope operators are ⟨rectangle⟩ and ⟨line⟩, respectively. Note that the information relevant to the two operators cannot be encoded in the same graphical object. That is, it is meaningless to speak of the slope of a rectangle or the height of a line. Consequently, these two operators are not combinable and we must disqualify determine-slope as a candidate for selection. Now, suppose we move on and consider the read-label perceptual operator. Note that the two operators are indeed combinable. Even though the graphical presentation object for the read-label operator is ⟨label⟩ and the graphical presentation object for the stack-heights operator is ⟨rectangle⟩, the two graphical objects can be combined to form a labeled rectangle.

The next two sections describe how the set of graphical presentation objects and a set of graphical object composition rules are used by BOZ to decide combinability of perceptual operators.

7.3.1 *Graphical Presentation Objects.* Each primitive graphical language has a *graphical presentation object* associated with it, either: ⟨point⟩, ⟨line⟩, ⟨rectangle⟩, ⟨polygon⟩, or ⟨label⟩. The graphical presentation object for a primitive graphical language is that graphical object that supports the performance of the perceptual operators that are associated with that graphical language. For example, the graphical presentation object for the Height primitive graphical language is ⟨rectangle⟩. Note that only this object makes the perceptual operators associated with the Height language meaningful. That is, it would be impossible to determine the height of a point or a line since points and lines by definition have no height.[3] Table VI lists the graphical presentation objects associated with each of the primitive graphical languages. The first step in deciding perceptual operator combinability is to determine the graphical presentation object of a candidate perceptual operator.

7.3.2 *Composition Rules for Graphical Presentation Objects.* The second step in deciding operator combinability is to compare the graphical presentation object of the perceptual operator currently being considered with the presentation objects of all previously selected operators that appear in the same vector in the perceptual data structure specification. If the graphical presentation object matches those of the previously chosen operators then the

[3]In the case of the ⟨line⟩ object, it is important not to confuse the notion of height with that of line length for a vertically oriented line.

Table VI. Graphical Presentation Objects for the Primitive Graphical Languages

Horizontal Position = <point>	Shading = <polygon>
Vertical Position = <point>	Labels = <label>
Height = <rectangle>	Color = <point>
Width = <rectangle>	Line Thickness = <line>
Line Length = <line>	Line Dashing = <line>
Area = <polygon>	Shape = <polygon>
Connectivity = <line>	Visibility = <point>

new operator is combinable. If the presentation object does not match, BOZ attempts to show them combinable using the set of composition rules for graphical objects given in Table VII. Each composition rule describes how a set of individual presentation objects can be legally composed to form a single presentation object that inherits all of the graphical properties of the constituent objects. For any new perceptual operator and set of previously selected operators, the new operator is combinable if and only if a rule can be found that maps the set of presentation objects into another legal presentation object.

Applying the perceptual operator selection strategy to the set of possible perceptual operators obtained for the airline reservation procedure yields the perceptual procedure shown in Figure 12. For each logical operator, BOZ has selected the most efficient available perceptual operator as a substitute within the expressiveness and combinability constraints. It is interesting to note that the logical operator findFlightWithOrigin has been substituted by the search-object-with-label, a very low-ranking perceptual operator. This example illustrates how the expressiveness and combinability constrains operator selection. A more appealing substitution for findFlightWithOrigin would have been a perceptual operator in which the user locates a flight with a particular origin by searching a horizontal scale or by searching for an object having a particular shape. The reason that these two more attractive operators were not selected is because the higher-ranking computeLayover had already staked claim to the Horizontal Position operators and the Shape primitive graphical language unfortunately does not offer enough unique shapes to represent all ten different possible cities of origin. Consequently, due to these constraints imposed by the other competing operators, the findFlightWithOrigin operator was relegated to the more difficult perceptual task of searching for a labeled item.

Figure 13 shows the final perceptual data structure specification for the airline reservation task after perceptual operators have been selected. Note that each predicate appearing in the perceptual data structure specification has been associated with a single primitive graphical language. In each case the primitive graphical language chosen is precisely that language associated with the perceptual operators that have been selected to manipulate that type of information.

```
(let ((looking t))
  (while (and looking (search-object-with-label FLIGHT 'pit)) do
    (if (shaded? flight) then
      (read-label flight LAYOVERCITY)
      (determine-horz-pos flight ARRIVAL)
      (while (and looking (search-object-with-label CONNECTING layovercity)) do
         (if (shaded? connecting) then
           (read-label flight FINALDESTINATION)
           (if (same-labels? finaldestination 'mex) then
             (determine-horz-pos connecting DEPARTURE)
             (determine-horz-distance departure arrival LAYOVER)
             (if (and (right-of? departure arrival)
                      (left-of? layover '4)) then
               (determine-height flight COST1)
               (determine-height connecting COST2)
               (stack-heights cost1 cost2 TOTAL)
               (if (shorter? total '5) then
                 (repeat
                   (search-object-with-label flight SEAT1)
                  until (shaded? seat1))
                 (read-label seat1 SEATNUM1)
                 (repeat
                   (search-object-with-label connecting SEAT2)
                  until (shaded? seat2))
                 (read-label seat2 SEATNUM2)
                 (if (and seat1 seat2)
                   (setq looking nil)]
```

Fig. 12. Final perceptual airline reservation procedure.

```
(NESTED (PRESENTATION1 (flight ((Origin Labels) (Destination Labels)
                                (Departure HorzPos) (Arrival HorzPos)
                                (Cost Height) (Availability Shading))
                                <rectangle>)
          (PRESENTATION2 (seat ((Availability Shading)) <rectangle>)))
```

Fig. 13. Final perceptual data structure specification for airline reservation task.

7.4 Limitations of Automated Perceptual Operator Selection

It is important to note that there exists no algorithmic strategy that always chooses the most efficiently or accurately performed perceptual operators, including those based on experimental observations and detailed theoretical predictions. I am aware of no experimental result of people using graphics that has been successfully generalized across any one of the following: user [21], level of skill [17], practice [29], task [19], particular presentation used [25], age [9], culture [18], or even social situation [1]! Each of these factors have been shown to introduce variance strong enough to overturn the results of any particular experiment, making strong generalizations of these results inappropriate. What we can hope to achieve in an automated graphic design tool is a codified set of operational design principles that perform satisfactorily across interesting tasks and graphics.

Table VII. Composition Rules for Graphical Presentation Objects

Object Composition Rules:	Axis Composition Rules:
RULE 1: <point> + <point> = <point>	RULE 12: <horz-axis> + <horz-axis> = <horz-axis>
RULE 2: <point> + <line> = <line>	RULE 13: <vert-axis> + <vert-axis> = <vert-axis>
RULE 3: <line> + <line> = <line>	RULE 14: <horz-axis> + <vert-axis> = <cart-axis>
RULE 4: <rectangle> + <point> = <rectangle>	
RULE 5: <rectangle> + <rectangle> = <rectangle>	
RULE 6: <polygon> + <point> = <polygon>	
RULE 7: <polygon> + <polygon> = <polygon>	
RULE 8: <label> + <label> = <label>	
RULE 9: <label> + <line> = <line>	
RULE 10: <label> + <rectangle> = <rectangle>	
RULE 11: <label> + <polygon> = <polygon>	

Many task domains make use of standardized domain-specific graphic conventions that were originally designed using intuition or criteria other than cognitive efficiency. Without specific knowledge of a problem domain, an automated graphic design tool is unable to identify and select operators that correspond to existing graphic conventions and this is a second limitation of automated graph design. BOZ, like APT [26], allows the designer to intervene and manually select perceptual operators in order to support existing conventions.

The human performance efficiency of a perceptual operator may be sensitive to the particular data on which the operator is performed. For example, judging the distance between two points on scale that are aligned three units away from one another appears to be easier than if the points are aligned, say, 39 units apart. This phenomenon occurs because some input data allow the user to exploit more low-level perceptual capabilities such as *subitizing* [22]. A more reliable perceptual operator ranking system might be achieved by making the set of rankings functionally dependent on the set of logical facts to be displayed. That is, rather than using a fixed set of operator rankings, a different set of rankings would be computed for each different set of logical facts. The usefulness of such a scheme, along with its computational feasibility, is an open question.

BOZ's perceptual operator selection component proceeds under the assumption that the time to perform a perceptual operator is unaffected by any other perceptual operators that are performed before or after that operator. That is, the time to perform a perceptual operator is assumed to be context independent. There are two ways in which this assumption may be invalidated. First, while the questions of parallel perceptual operator performance remains open for debate, experimental observations suggest that human users are sometimes able to obtain the results of several perceptual operators in a time less than the sum of the observed performance times for each individual operator [34]. Furthermore, researchers have gained a partial understanding of which combinations of perceptual operators exhibit this property. Combinations of perceptual operators that achieve this property result in a greater savings in performance efficiency. Second, experimental observations of users in other task domains such as typing suggest that certain combinations of operators may sometimes result in a performance time that is greater than the sum of the individual performance times [35].

8. GRAPHIC PRESENTATION RENDERING

The rendering component translates logical facts to graphical facts and displays them on the computer screen. The form in which the graphical facts appear on the screen agrees precisely with the design described by the perceptual data structure specification along with a set of general rendering assumptions. The rendering component produces a fully rendered graphic presentation of the graphical facts. Graphic presentations produced by the rendering component support interactive manipulations of the graphical objects appearing in the presentation, allowing users to effect changes in the

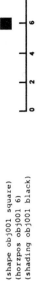

(shape obj001 square)
(horzpos obj001 6)
(shading obj001 black)

Fig. 14. Example graphical facts.

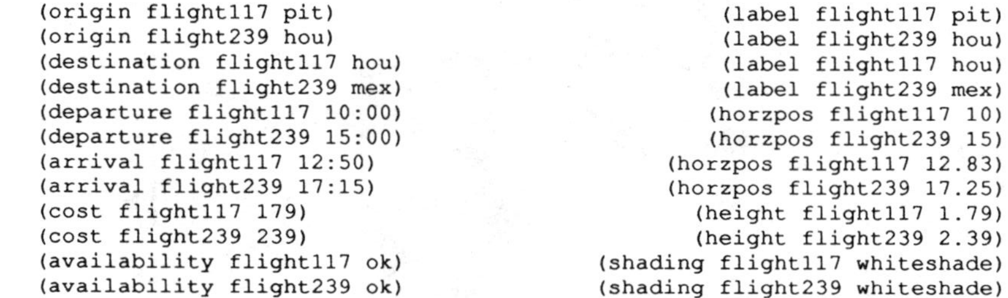

```
(origin flight117 pit)                          (label flight117 pit)
(origin flight239 hou)                          (label flight239 hou)
(destination flight117 hou)                     (label flight117 hou)
(destination flight239 mex)                     (label flight239 mex)
(departure flight117 10:00)                   (horzpos flight117 10)
(departure flight239 15:00)                   (horzpos flight239 15)
(arrival flight117 12:50)                  (horzpos flight117 12.83)
(arrival flight239 17:15)                  (horzpos flight239 17.25)
(cost flight117 179)                          (height flight117 1.79)
(cost flight239 239)                          (height flight239 2.39)
(availability flight117 ok)         (shading flight117 whiteshade)
(availability flight239 ok)         (shading flight239 whiteshade)
```

Fig. 15. Translated airline reservation facts.

internally stored logical facts by making changes to the graphical displayed facts.

8.1 Translating Logical Facts to Structured Graphical Facts

A prerequisite to graphically rendering arbitrary sets of logical facts on the computer screen is a notation for representing graphical facts that is equivalent to the notation used to express logical facts. To accomplish this, Mackinlay's formalism for expressing graphical facts is used and this has been shown to be equivalent to a logical representation of the same relational information [26]. Mackinlay's formulation allows logical facts to be expressed using each of the primitive graphical languages given in Table 1. Graphical facts expressed in a primitive graphical language take the following form: (PGL ⟨OBJECT⟩ ⟨VALUE⟩). For example, the facts in Figure 14 describe a square-shaped graphical object that is shaded black and positioned along a horizontal axis.

Figure 15 shows how logical facts (left side) about airline flights are translated to graphical facts (right side) when the mapping given in the perceptual data structure specification is applied. A final notation is needed for expressing collections of graphical facts whose structure agrees with the perceptual data structure specification for the task. A *structured graphical fact* corresponds to the "gestalt wholes" defined by the perceptual data structure specification. For example, the facts in Figure 16 show how the graphical facts (Figure 15) are structured according to the perceptual data structure specification for the airline task given in Figure 13. Each structured graphical fact in Figure 16 corresponds to a single flight.

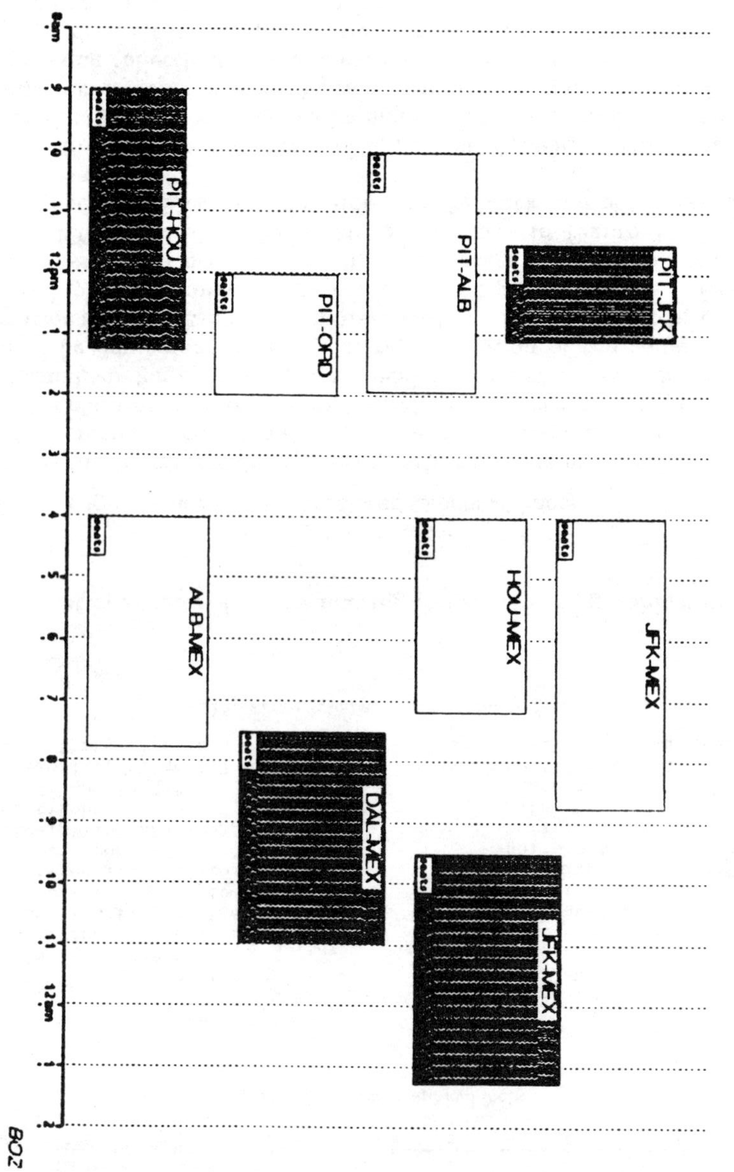

Fig. 17. Rendered airline schedule.

```
(((labels flight117 pit)
  (labels flight117 hou)
  (horzpos flight117 10)
  (horzpos flight117 12.83)
  (height flight117 1.79)
  (shading flight117 whiteshade))
((labels flight239 hou)
  (labels flight239 mex)
  (horzpos flight239 15.00)
  (horzpos flight239 17.25)
  (height flight239 2.39)
  (shading flight239 whiteshade)))
```

Fig. 16. Structured graphical facts.

8.2 Rendering Graphical Facts

The rendering component automatically displays arbitrary sets of structured graphical facts on the computer screen. This is accomplished by considering each structured fact, determining the form in which it is to be presented by consulting the perceptual data structure specification, and rendering the image of the fact on the screen. The rendering component uses an object-oriented approach to rendering structured graphical facts. For every type of graphical presentation object (i.e., ⟨point⟩, ⟨line⟩, ⟨rectangle⟩, ⟨polygon⟩, and ⟨label⟩) there exists a corresponding display object that can be rendered on the screen. Display objects can inherit one or more of a set of display methods that render the graphical properties of a display object. Display methods are defined for each of the primitive graphical languages in Table I. For presentations that do not use horizontal and vertical position to encode information, a simple displacement scheme is used to avoid occlusion of display objects by other display objects. Scales and guidelines are automatically computed, drawn, and labeled using the DOMAINSETS field in the logical procedure description. Fonts have been chosen arbitrarily and standardized. Nested graphics are implemented by mouse-sensitive buttons that are always placed in the lower left corner in rectangles and polygons and immediately on top of points and lines. Display methods are automatically attached to the buttons that cause the nested graphic to be rendered when the button is selected.

Figure 17 shows a fully rendered set of graphical airline facts. As specified by the perceptual data structure specification, the presentation consists of a single type of graphical object (i.e., a flight box) that inherits four graphical properties (i.e., horizontal position, shading, height, and labels). Selecting the seats button for any flight causes the nested seating chart for that flight to be rendered. A rendered seating chart is shown in Figure 18.

The graphics generated by the rendering component support two-way interactions between sets of logical facts and their graphical images. In addition to being able to effect changes in a graphic presentation through manipulations of the internally stored logical facts, the graphical objects in the presentations can be manipulated by the user to effect changes in the set of stored logical facts. For example, the upper, leftmost flight box in the presentation in Figure 17 indicates that there is a flight from Pittsburgh to JFK Airport (New York) leaving at 11:30 am, with no available seats, costing

Fig. 18. Rendered seating chart schedule.

$400. The user may simultaneously change the graphical and internal representation of this information by simply mouse-selecting the flight box and moving it to a new location, changing its shading, or increasing or decreasing its height. Casner [6] generalizes this technique in a tool that allows users to create customized diagramming languages that can be attached to and used to manipulate internally stored data and knowledge representation structures.

8.3 Limitations of Automated Rendering

There are several important limitations of the automated rendering component. First, the rendering component is incapable of rendering presentations that make use of domain-specific conventions. For example, airline seating charts typically orient the aircraft vertically with lower numbered seats appearing at the top and higher number seats at the bottom. Since BOZ's rendering component has no knowledge of this convention, the seats are arranged in increasing order from left to right as are the hours along the time scale. Second, many presentations depict realistic information such as spatial arrangements and shapes that do not encode information vital to the task at hand but preserve many features of a real-world artifact in an artificial representation. For example, airline seating charts typically depict the aisle separating the two halves of the plane. Some seating charts also use chair-shaped icons to represent seats instead of the generic box-shape used in BOZ's presentation. BOZ of course has no knowledge of these conventions. Note that despite these two limitations it is still possible to locate any seat. What may be lost is a familiarity and practice that users may have already acquired using other conventions. Third, the art of font, typeface, and color selection falls beyond the scope of BOZ's current design model. Consequently, BOZ chooses types and colors arbitrarily. This limitation is in part due to the lack of theoretical account of how type and color directly affect perceptual task performance. As theory-based typographic and color selection principles become available, they too could be integrated into BOZ's task-analytic design approach.

9. COGNITIVE ANALYSIS OF THE AIRLINE SCHEDULE GRAPHIC

Table VIII summarizes the potential cognitive advantages of the airline schedule graphic. The advantages occur in two forms that agree precisely with the design goals of BOZ: (1) substituting efficient perceptual inferences

Table VIII. Predicted Cognitive Efficiencies of the Airline Graphic

Computation

Substitutes a distance judgement (`determine-horz-pos`) in place of subtracting numerically expressed departure and arrival times (`computeLayover`).

Substitutes a shade judgement (`shaded?`) for reading the words "ok" and "full" (`available?`).

Substitutes judging the combined heights of two flight boxes (`stack-heights`) for adding two numerically expressed costs (`addCosts`).

Search

Eliminates eye movements when looking up time, city, cost, and availability information since this information is represented in the same spatial locality (a single flight box).

Allows users to limit their search for connecting flights to only those flights that appear to the right of the originating flight.

Since shading can be processed pre-attentively, users may immediately exclude from their search any flight square that has no available seats.

Allows users to immediately rule out "tall" flights from their search since these are likely to violate the cost constraint.

When looking for an available seat, users can immediately eliminate shaded seats. Users can also restrict their search to window or aisle seats by following simple eye movement patterns.

in place of more demanding logical inferences, and (2) reducing the number of items considered when searching for needed information. The advantages are explained by comparing how the task is performed using both the graphic presentation and a tabular presentation of the same information.

It is important to note that the hypothesized advantages of any BOZ-designed graphic depend on the user understanding and being able to perform the perceptual procedure supported by that graphic. Whether or not real users can or actually do follow the designed perceptual procedure and the extent to which the predicted efficiency advantages are reflected in users' performance is an empirical question to which we now turn our attention.

10. USERS' PERFORMANCE WITH THE AIRLINE GRAPHIC

Casner and Larkin [8] describe an experimental study designed to determine the extent to which the hypothesized advantages of the airline graphic listed in Table VIII were reflected in users' performance. To better understand the contribution made by each hypothesized advantage, a sequence of four graphics was designed in which each successive graphic provided an additional opportunity to substitute a perceptual for logical operator and an additional opportunity to reduce search. The final presentation in the sequence contained all of the efficiency advantages listed in Table VIII (except those pertaining to the seating chart presentation). The four experimental graphics, herein called Graphics 1, 2, 3, and 4, are shown in Figure 19.

Response times were collected from 7 participants who performed the airline reservation task using the four graphics a total of 10 times each (40 trials total). Users completed the task after receiving an explanation of the conventions used in each graphic and one practice trial. The order in which the graphics were presented to the users was varied systematically to evenly distribute effects due to learning and practice.

The results shown in the graphic in Figure 20 indicate significant differences in response times between Graphics 1 and 2, and between Graphics 2 and 3, but not between Graphics 3 and 4. The data suggest that time scale encoding used in Graphic 2 (and also in Graphics 3 and 4) reduced the amount of time required to locate two connecting flights and to determine whether or not two flights obey the layover constraint. Allowing users to perform the perceptual operator of determining the shade of a flight box (Graphic 3) also resulted in a significant savings. The perceptual task of determining whether or not two flights obey the cost constraint by judging the heights of the flight squares did not result in any reliable savings over the task of adding the two numbers or in narrowing down the search space of flights to consider. An analysis of the standard deviations in response times suggests that users exhibited significantly more stable performance between Graphics 1, 2, and 3 in that order.

Our next step was to understand how users obtained the efficiency savings we observed. We ran a regression analysis on the number of times each operator must be performed using each graphic, the number of facts searched, and the observed users' response times. We obtained the best fitting models when each graphic was combined with the procedures that used all of the operator substitutions and search reductions that were applicable to that graphic. This suggests that for each graphic users took advantage of all of the operator substitutions and search reductions that were possible with that graphic. The beta-coefficients in the regression model yielded estimates on performance time for several of the individual perceptual and logical operators.

—The time required to fix the eye on each item in a graphic was uniformly about 330 ms for all four graphics.

—Perceptually estimating layovers (determine-horz-distance) using Graphics 2, 3 and 4 proceeded about 2 s faster than subtracting the numerically expressed times (computeLayover).

—Judging the combined heights of two flight boxes (stack-heights) in Graphic 4 was negligibly 100 to 300 ms slower than adding the numerically expressed costs (addCosts).

The savings gained through substitution of perceptual for logical operators and use of search reductions match well with the global reductions observed in overall response times. Overall the results agree with users' comments after using all four graphics: Graphics 3 and 4 were the most effective. The interested reader can find details of the experimental design and methodology in Casner and Larkin [8].

Origin/ Destination	Availability	Price	Departure	Arrival
ALB-MEX	ok	$219	1:15pm	7:50pm
PIT-ORD	ok	$129	10:00am	12:00pm
PIT-HOU	full	$199	9:15am	2:05pm
ORD-DAL	full	$199	1:00pm	4:30pm
DAL-MEX	ok	$229	7:30pm	10:30pm
PIT-ALB	ok	$219	8:00am	11:50am
BAL-MEX	full	$279	3:50pm	9:50pm
JFK-MEX	ok	$229	3:00pm	6:00pm
PIT-JFK	full	$239	9:50am	12:30pm

(a)

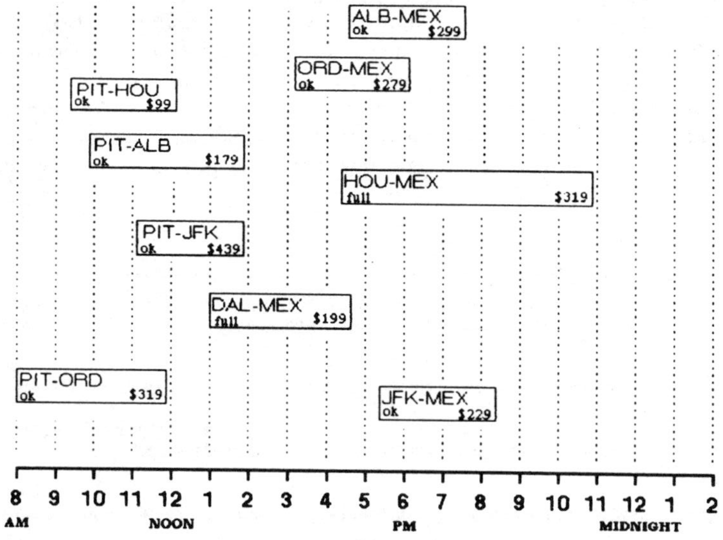

(b)

Fig. 19. Four experimental graphics for airline reservation. (a)Graphic. (b) Graphic 2. (c) Graphic 3. (d) Graphic 4.

11. GENERAL DISCUSSION

The research described above explores a task-analytic approach to the design of graphics in which graphic presentations are viewed as perceptually manipulated data structures that help streamline task performance in the same way that abstract data structures and their associated procedures help expedite abstract computational processes. The important distinction made in

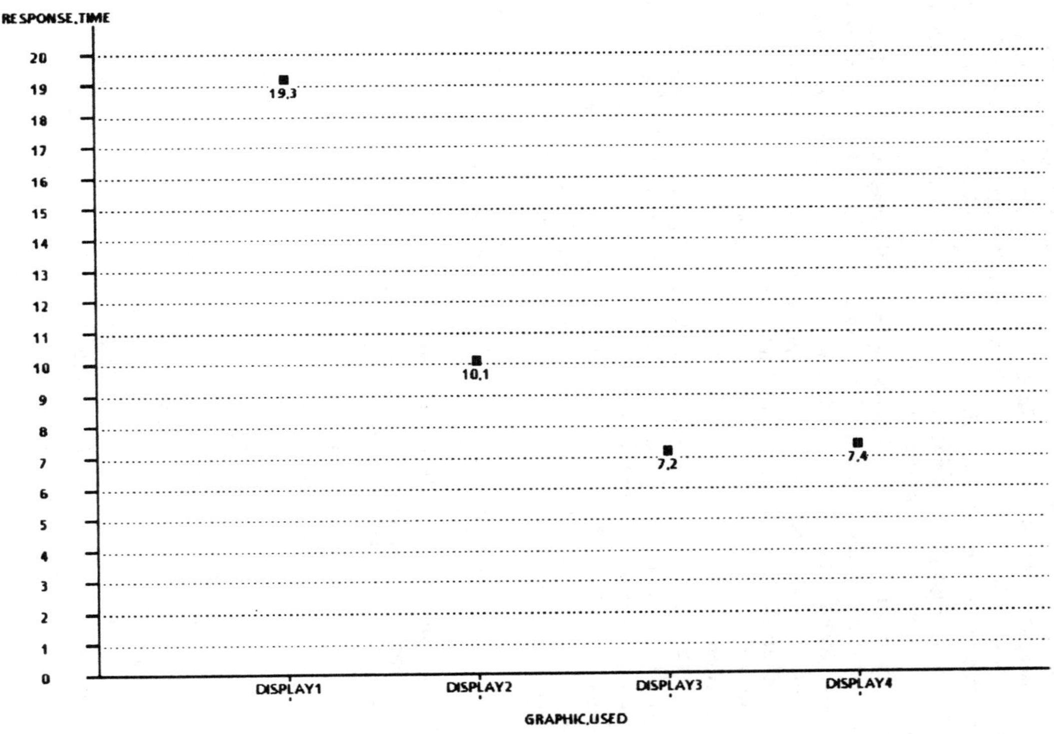

Fig. 20. Participants' mean response times for airline reservation task.

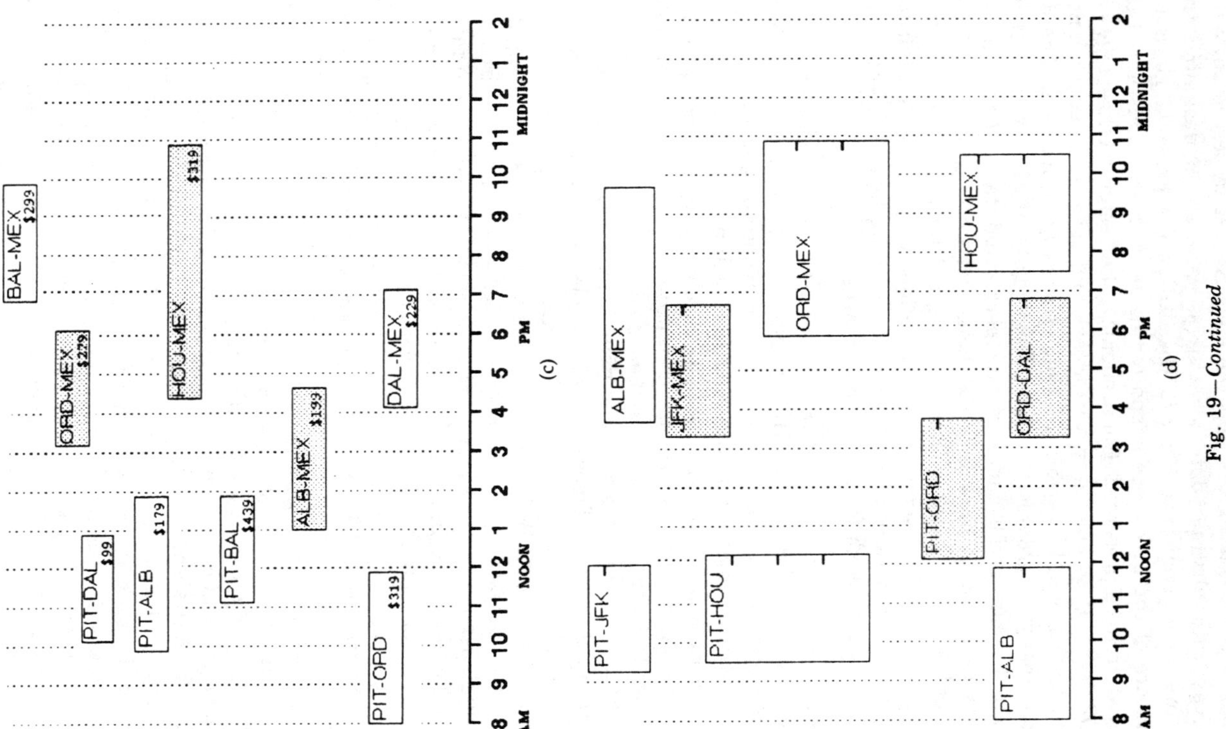

Fig. 19—*Continued*

task-based graphic design is that the effective use of perceptual data structures, as with abstract data structures, depends on designing the right structure for a given task. That is, the utility of a presentation is linked to the nature of the task to be supported more than the characteristics of the information to be presented. Consequently, the design methodology embodied in BOZ proceeds by analyzing a user task and generating equivalent perceptual tasks that can be performed more efficiently by humans. The design of an accompanying graphic is targeted primarily at supporting efficient and accurate human performance of the perceptual task. The examples and experimental results show how the task-analytic approach can be successfully applied to designing effective perceptual tasks and presentations that provide two types of advantages: (1) allowing users to substitute quick perceptual inferences in place of more demanding logical inferences, and (2) reducing user's search for needed information.

Design of Effective Graphic Presentations. What are the real graphic design successes of BOZ? Has BOZ produced a graphic that no one else has designed before? Given its current set of perceptual operators and graphical presentation objects it is unlikely that BOZ will produce new graphic designs that differ radically from existing designs. That is, in the examples developed in this paper, no graphic seems to contain a shape or a configuration of shapes that strikes the reader as being completely novel, or having never appeared in a graphic used in one domain or another. This comes as little surprise as the study of novel graphical elements and their mathematical properties enjoys centuries of prior investigation. Rather, the contribution of the present version of BOZ lies in forming compositions of existing designs to arrive at presentations that gather the task-supportive features of several individual designs in order to arrive at "customized" presentations that support the operators in a target user task. It is important to note that the degree of customization achieved by each presentation is more than a simple collection of useful presentations implicated by a task description. Rather, BOZ is additionally able to assign degrees of importance to the individual operators in a task and use this information to make sacrifices in less important aspects of a task to facilitate efficient perceptual processing in more demanding aspects of the same task.

BOZ has thus far been used to design graphics for the five airline reservation tasks given above, a computer operator task, a class scheduling problem, and simple charts and graphs such as those found in the popular literature. The interested reader can consult Casner [7] for these examples along with the complete task descriptions from which the graphics were generated. Future work will attempt to apply BOZ to more challenging information-processing tasks and in a wider variety of task domains. These efforts should lead to a more sophisticated understanding of how the problems of task analysis and graphic design interact, as well as novel ways of extending BOZ's capabilities.

Learning Graphical Conventions and Procedures. An important aspect of the utility of a graphic not addressed by BOZ is the time required to understand the procedures that must be followed to use that graphic successfully. There seem to be no inherent advantages of learning a perceptual procedure instead of a logical one even if that perceptual procedure is eventually performed more efficiently or accurately. The learning issue is relevant when graphics are presented in "walk up and use" situations where it is unsafe to assume prior knowledge or skill on the part of the user. Learning issues are less important in skilled performance task situations. The idea of using different graphics to support different tasks may further require the user to learn several different sets of graphic conventions. For example, the airline graphics in Figures 1, 2, 3, 4, and 17 all require the user to manipulate the same information in different ways.

Two arguments can be made in defense of BOZ with respect to the learning issue. First, the individual graphical conventions that follow from BOZ's current repertoire of graphical presentation objects and perceptual operators do not extend beyond what is used in popular graphic presentations in current use. Even though each of the airline schedule graphics are somewhat unique, they are all composed using familiar conventions such as aligning data values along horizontal and vertical scales, and color coding. Consequently, the learning requirements for BOZ-designed graphics extend beyond those of existing graphics only in that the user must understand novel combinations of familiar perceptual operators. Second, since there is a cost associated with learning to use any artifact, in each situation we must ask whether or not the artifact offers benefits to the user that justify the learning cost. Taking airline scheduling as a case in point, if the graphical airline schedules result in allowing customers to gain control of their own flight scheduling, the benefits may far outweigh the initial learning costs.

Real-Time Automated Graphical Presentation. Aside from an articulation of a cognitive theory of graphic presentation design, BOZ appears potentially useful as a tool for the automated design and generation of graphic presentations in computer information systems. However, two limitations of the present model prevent BOZ's current use in real-time applications. First, the logical task descriptions required by BOZ as input must presently be hand-generated. A future research topic is to investigate ways of automatically generating task descriptions and eliminating the need for human intervention. SAGE [27] uses a discourse processor that allows descriptions of simple operators to be generated by analyzing simple natural language queries made by the user. However, this approach is unable to generate descriptions of complex procedures defined using collections of many operators. Second, while the run time complexity of BOZ may theoretically be able to meet the demands of on-line information systems, the present implementation fails to produce graphics in a time that would be considered acceptable by computer users. The rendering component is particularly slow for graphics containing many graphical objects. The search complexity for BOZ's perceptual operator substitution component is presently: $T_{\text{operator substitution}} = n*c*t$, where n is the number of logical operators appearing in a procedure, c is the number of possible operator classes that each logical operator must be matched against, and t is the time required to find all matches for a single operator. The Xerox 1186 implementation of BOZ required about 9 s to classify the airline reservation task operators, as shown in Figure 7. BOZ's perceptual data structuring component is linear in the number of logical operators n and domain sets d: $T_{\text{data structuring}} = n*d$. BOZ required about 2 s to design the initial perceptual data structure shown in Figure 11. The perceptual operator selection component runs n^2 in the number of logical operators. The perceptual operator selection component required 7 s to select the perceptual procedure and data structure shown in Figures 12 and 13. The object-oriented rendering component is linear in the number of structured facts to be presented f and the number of primitive graphical languages p appearing in each structured fact: $T_{\text{rendering}} = f*p$. The rendering component required approximately 12 s to render the flights presentation in Figure 17 and approximately 1 min, 15 s to generate the seating chart presentation in Figure 18.

Overall, BOZ designed both presentations in about 18 s, rendering the flights and seating charts presentations after 30 s and 1 min, 45 s, respectively. BOZ's current run time does not fall within an acceptable standard for real-time data presentation. A future research topic is to investigate ways of making BOZ operate more efficiently.

Executable Logical and Perceptual Procedures. BOZ contains an additional component that allows the logical procedures and the perceptual procedures produced by BOZ to be compiled into executable simulations. These simulations manipulate databases of logical and graphical facts such as those shown in Figures 6 and 16. The simulation component allows alternative procedures to be executed while the number of operator firings and items searched are counted for any combination of logical or perceptual procedure and graphic. These measures can be used to obtain detailed quantitative predictions on the effectiveness of any procedure and graphic produced by BOZ and may avoid the need to perform time-consuming experimental studies with real users such as the one described in Section 10. Casner [7] uses the simulation component to explore other cognitive advantages of graphic presentation-based task performance and problem solving and to better understand the details of how efficiencies in inferencing and search are obtained through the use of graphic presentations.

ACKNOWLEDGMENTS

I thank Jill Larkin, Stellan Ohlsson, Ken Koedinger and three anonymous reviewers for their contributions to this research.

REFERENCES

1. Asch, S. E. Studies of independence and submission to group pressure: A minority of one against a unanimous majority. *Psychological Monographs*, 1956, 70.
2. Bertin, J. *Semiology of Graphics*, W. Berg (Transl). Univ. of Wisconsin Press, Madison, 1983.
3. Brachman, R. J., and Schmolze, J. G. An overview of the KL-ONE knowledge representation system. *Cognitive Sci. 9* 2, (1985), 171–216.
4. Brainerd, W. S., and Landweber, L. H. *Theory of Computation*, Wiley, New York, 1974.
5. Card, S. K., Moran, T. P., and Newell, A. *The Psychology of Human-Computer Interaction*. Lawrence Erlbaum, Hillsdale, N. J., 1983.
6. Casner, S. M. Building customized diagramming languages. In *Visual Languages and Visual Programming*, S. K. Chang Ed. Plenum Press, New York, 1990.
7. Casner, S. M. *Task-Analytic Design of Graphic Presentations*. Ph.D. dissertation, Intelligent Systems Program, Univ. of Pittsburgh, Aug. 1990.
8. Casner, S. M., and Larkin J. H. Cognitive efficiency considerations for good graphic design. In *Proc. 11th Annual Conf. Cognitive Science Society* (Ann Arbor, Mich., Aug. 1989).
9. Clancey, S. M., and Hoyer, W. J. Effects of age and skill on domain-specific visual search. In *Proc. 9th Annual Conf. Cognitive Science Society*, (Seattle, Wash., 1987), 398–404.
10. Cleveland, W. S. *Elements of Graphing Data*. Wadsworth Advanced Books and Software, Monterey, Calif., 1985.
11. Cleveland, W. S., and McGill, R. Graphical perception: Theory, experimentation, and application to the development of graphical methods. *J. Amer. Stat. Assoc. 79*, 387 (Sept. 1984), 531–554.
12. Davidoff, J. B. The role of colour in visual displays. *Int. Rev. Ergonomics 1*, (1987), 21–42.
13. Fallside, D. Understanding machines in motion. Ph.D. dissertation, Dept. of Psychology, Carnegie Mellon Univ., Pittsburgh, Pa., May 1988.
14. Feiner, S. APEX: An experiment in the automatic creation of pictorial explanations. *IEEE Comput. Graph. Appl.* (Nov. 1985), 29–37.
15. Friedell, M. Context-sensitive, graphic presentation of information. *Comput. Graphic. 16* 3, (July 1982), 181–188.
16. Gnanamgari, S. Information presentation through default displays. Ph.D. dissertation, Univ. of Pennsylvania, May 1981.
17. Hegarty, M., and Just, M. Understanding machines from text and diagram. In *Knowledge Acquisition from Text and Picture*, H. Mandl and J. Levin Eds., North-Holland, Amsterdam, 1988.
18. Hudson, W. The study of the problem of pictorial perception among accultured groups. *Int. J. Psychology 2* (1968), 89–107.
19. Jarvenpaa, S. L., and Dickson, G. W. Graphics and managerial decision making: Research Based Guidelines. *Commun. ACM 31*, 6 (June 1988), 764–774.
20. Jenks, C. F., and Knos, D. S. The use of shading patterns in graded series. *Ann. Assoc. Am. Geographers 51* (1961) 316–334.
21. Kieras, D., and Polson, P. G. An approach to the formal analysis of user complexity. *Int. J. Man-Mach. Stud. 22* (1985), 365–394.
22. Klahr, D. Quantification processes. In *Visual Information Processing*, W. G. Chase Ed., Academic Press, Orlando, Fla, 1973, pp. 3–34.
23. Koedinger, K. R., and Anderson, J. R. Abstract planning and perceptual chunks: Elements of expertise in geometry. *Cognitive Sci. 14*, 4 (1990), 511–550.
24. Larkin, J., and Simon, H. Why a diagram is (sometimes) worth 10,000 words. *Cognitive Sci. 11* (1987), 65–99.
25. Lusk, E. J., and Kersnick, M. The effect of cognitive style and report format on task performance: The MIS design consequences. *Manage. Sci. 22*, 3 (1979), 787–798.
26. Mackinlay, J. "Automating the design of graphical presentations of relational information." *ACM Trans. Graph. 5*, 2 (Apr. 1986), 110–141.
27. Roth, S. F., Mattis, J., and Mesnard, X. Graphics and natural language as components of automatic explanation. In *Architectures for Intelligent Interfaces: Elements and Prototypes*, J. Sullivan and S. Tyler Eds. Addison-Wesley, Reading, Mass., 1989.
28. Schmid, C. F. *Statistical Graphics: Design Principles and Practices*, Wiley, New York, 1983.
29. Schneider, W. Training high-performance skills: Fallacies and guidelines. *Hum. Factors 27*, 3 (1985), 285–300.

30. Stevens, S. S. On the theory of scales of measurement. *Science 103*, 2684 (June 1946), 677–680.
31. Teghtsoonian, J. The judgement of size. *Am. J. Psychology 78* (1965), 392–402.
32. Tufte, E. R. *Envisioning Information*. Graphics Press, Cheshire, Conn., 1990.
33. Tufte, E. R. *The Visual Display of Quantitative Information*. Graphics Press, Cheshire, Conn., 1983.
34. Ullman, S. Visual routines. *Cognition 18* (1984), 97–159.
35. Yamada, H. An analysis of the standard English keyboard. Tech. Rep. 80-11, Dept. of Information Science, Univ. of Tokyo, 1980.
36. Zdybel, F., Greenfield, N. R., Yonke, M.D., and Gibbons, J. An information presentation system. In *Proceedings of the 7th International Joint Conference on Artificial Intelligence* (Aug. 1981), 978–984.

A Task-Analytic Approach to the Automated Design of Graphic Presentations

Stephen M. Casner

BOZ was an interdisciplinary project that aimed to integrate some of what the field was learning, both about automated presentation design and about how humans interact with graphical presentations. BOZ was motivated by Larkin and Simon's earlier work that sought to explain why graphics are sometimes useful for information processing tasks. Moving beyond empirical tests in which one graphic is pitted against another, Larkin and Simon took a step-by-step look at the process of solving a problem using a graphic. Beginning with a problem and a graphic, Larkin and Simon's analysis aimed to understand the visual reasoning steps that were being used in combination with the graphic and how they contributed to solving the problem.

The aim of BOZ was to perform the converse of Larkin and Simon's analysis. If we begin with a problem and a specific understanding of how visual elements support specific solution steps, can we craft a set of visual reasoning steps and a supporting graphic that solves the problem and wins the advantages? Thus, rather than focus on the problem of designing a graphic, BOZ aimed to design an efficient set of visual reasoning steps that solved a stated problem. The graphics produced by BOZ were simply the collection of graphical elements required to perform the visual reasoning steps.

Of the limited successes of BOZ, perhaps the most important was that it began with psychological observations about the usefulness of graphics and cast them in prescriptive terms detailed enough to drive an automated design tool. Of the many discussions about why graphics are interesting, few spell out how to create the next interesting graphic. The combination of Larkin and Simon's work and Mackinlay's formalized graphical languages allowed BOZ to move one step closer to a theory of representation design that could produce graphics.

Perhaps the biggest limitation of BOZ was that it required users to enter formal descriptions of the task they needed a graphic to support. Early systems avoided this by allowing users to simply choose the data they wished to appear in the graphic. This strategy, however, prevents a design tool from considering the purposes for which a graphic is intended. The problem of inputting task descriptions is one part of a larger challenge: devising efficient ways that allow users to communicate their needs to an automated tool.

A second limitation of BOZ was its inability to evaluate and improve its own designs. As every graphic designer knows, in producing a work, the eye not only directs the hand but is also directed by it. Without this ability, automated graphic design tools are essentially feedforward systems that rely on empirical evaluation provided external to the program. Moreover, even if observations are made about how to improve a design, BOZ offers no mechanism for communicating them, aside from modifying the description of the task and information and rerunning BOZ. Roth and colleagues (last paper in this section) have attempted to work around this problem by decreasing the amount of automation and increasing the involvement of the user in producing a design.

Automated Generation of Intent-Based 3D Illustrations

Dorée Duncan Seligmann
Steven Feiner

Department of Computer Science
Columbia University
New York, New York 10027

Abstract

This paper describes an automated intent-based approach to illustration. An *illustration* is a picture that is designed to fulfill a *communicative intent* such as showing the location of an object or showing how an object is manipulated. An illustration is generated by implementing a set of stylistic decisions, ranging from determining the way in which an individual object is lit, to deciding the general composition of the illustration. The design of an illustration is treated as a goal-driven process within a system of constraints. The goal is to achieve communicative intent; the constraints are the illustrative techniques an illustrator can apply.

We have developed IBIS (Intent-Based Illustration System), a system that puts these ideas into practice. IBIS designs illustrations using a generate-and-test approach, relying upon a rule-based system of methods and evaluators. Methods are rules that specify how to accomplish visual effects, while evaluators are rules that specify how to determine how well a visual effect is accomplished in an illustration. Examples of illustrations designed by IBIS are included.

CR Categories and Subject Descriptors: I.3.3[**Computer Graphics**]: Picture/Image Generation–display algorithms, viewing algorithms; I.3.4[**Computer Graphics**]: Graphics Utilities–Picture description languages; I.3.7[**Computer Graphics**]: Three-dimensional graphics and realism; I.2.1[**Artificial Intelligence**]: Applications and Expert Systems.

Additional Keywords and Phrases: illustrations, automated picture generation, knowledge-based graphics, non-photorealistic rendering.

Introduction

The development over the last few centuries of printing and photographic technologies, and more recently of electronic mass media, has revolutionized communication by making the *exact same presentation* accessible to larger and larger groups of people. Nevertheless, communication involves both intent and interpretation. The same presentation, viewed by several people, may be interpreted to mean different things, while different presentations may be interpreted to mean the same thing. To further complicate matters, none of these interpretations may be the one intended by the presenter. With recent advances in computer technology, we may now embark upon a new phase of communication. By formalizing the intent of a communication, the language or medium to be used, the audience and context of the communication, and the way in which the language is used to achieve intent, we may create systems that generate presentations, each designed to satisfy the same communicative intent for a particular audience, thus making the *exact same meaning* accessible to many different people.

This paper describes the first steps in developing such a system for illustration. An *illustration* is a picture that has been designed to fulfill a communicative *intent*. For example, the intent of an illustration may be to show an object's material, size, or orientation. The intent might be more complex. It may, for example, be more important to show how to turn a dial, and less important to show where the dial is located.

Human illustrators plan and replan an illustration, considering at all times how the final illustration will look. An illustrator may try something on paper and then, after evaluating it, erase it and adopt another plan. Or, the illustrator may be so skilled that it is enough for her to simply imagine the consequences of a stylistic choice.

This characterization of illustration serves as the foundation for intent-based illustration. An *intent-based* illustration system designs illustrations to fulfill a high-level description of the communicative intent. The illustration process can be formalized as a goal-driven process: the goal is to achieve a specified communicative intent within a complex of stylistic choices. In order to use a generate-and-test approach, such a system must represent style in two ways. First, each stylistic choice represents a method for achieving a particular goal. For example, in order to highlight an object, it may be brightened or it may be colored in a special way. Second, each stylistic choice is associated with a set of criteria used to judge how well it has been accomplished.

This paper describes IBIS (Intent-Based Illustration System), concentrating on its rule base, architecture, and design process. It explains how IBIS both achieves and evaluates the highlighting, recognizability and visibility of objects using several examples.

IBIS

Overview

IBIS utilizes a generate-and-test approach to illustration design. Starting with a description of the communicative intent and a knowledge base representing the world to be depicted, IBIS begins to design an illustration. The communicative intent is specified using a language of *communicative goals*. For example, a communicative goal may be to show how an object has been moved or to show its color. For each communicative goal there exists at least one design rule in IBIS's rule base. A *design rule* specifies a prioritized set of style strategies. A *style strategy* specifies a visual effect, such as highlighting and is achieved by a set of style rules. A *style rule* determines some part of the traditional computer graphics specification of an image: a viewing specification, a lighting specification, the objects to be depicted, and rendering instructions. A style rule calls upon procedures that directly access and manipulate illustrations. Illustrators select style strategies by selecting design rules to accomplish communicative goals. Drafters select illustration methods by selecting style rules to accomplish style strategies.

The following subsections describe all the components of the system and their interaction.

Input: Communicative Goals

IBIS currently supports communicative goals that have been designed to satisfy the needs imposed by COMET, a knowledge-based multi-media explanation generation system for which IBIS generates graphics [Elhadad et al. 89, Feiner and McKeown 90a, Feiner and McKeown 90b]. COMET designs explanations for equipment maintenance and repair that include pictures and text. Its current domain is the army radio shown in the figures in this paper. The communicative goals that IBIS can satisfy are:

- *location*: show the location of an object in a context (either explicitly specified or derived by the system)
- *relative location*: show the relative location of two or more objects in terms of a specified or derived context
- *property*: show one of the following physical properties of an object: material, color, size, shape
- *state*: show an object's state
- *change*: show the difference between a set of states

Both the goals *state* and *change* may be further qualified by concepts that refer to how the object is manipulated or has changed. For example, the state of a dial can be shown in terms of an agent turning it. IBIS currently supports three dozen concepts useful to our maintenance and repair domain, among them, *pushing*, *pulling*, *loosening*, *lifting*, *inserting* and *blinking*.

In response to a user request for information, COMET's *content planner* generates a description of the communicative intent for an explanation that is sent to COMET's *media-coordinator*. The media-coordinator annotates the intent specification to indicate which generators should communicate which information and passes the same intent specification to COMET's *media generators*. All generators work from the same annotated intent specification [Elhadad et al. 89]. IBIS translates the intent description into a prioritized list of *communicative goals*. This translation is more or less direct; concepts such as *location* and *turn* are identified in the intent specification. IBIS associates with each goal an indication of its importance, which in turn is used to calculate an acceptable degree of success when the goals are evaluated.

Knowledge Base

IBIS has a knowledge base of the physical objects to be illustrated that includes not only geometric and material information, but also information about the object's features, physical properties, and abstract properties. Information about the features and abstract properties of physical objects is a superset of the information traditionally passed to a graphics system. It is, however, necessary to an intent-based system that designs its own pictures. For example, it may be important to represent how an object moves or its limits of articulation. IBIS currently utilizes a very simple model for object states. For example, the dials on the radio are represented as having discrete or continuous ranges with associated orientations; the latches have two states: snapped and unsnapped.

Design Rules: Mapping Intent to Stylistic Choice

Design rules describe on a high level how illustrations should be put together. A design rule consists of a communicative goal and a set of style strategies. There are two types of design rules: design methods and design evaluators. *Design methods* specify how to accomplish communicative goals; *design evaluators* determine how well communicative goals have been accomplished. A design method specifies what *style strategies* must be achieved, in addition to how well each should be achieved in order to accomplish a communicative goal. A design evaluator determines how well a communicative goal is achieved based on the achievement ratings of a collection of *style strategies*. Each communicative goal formalized in IBIS's intent-specification language [Seligmann 91] must have one or more design rule to accomplish and evaluate it.

Showing Location

Figure 1 lists two design rules for satisfying the communicative goal *location*. Figures 2 and 3 are illustrations that IBIS generated using design rules 1 and 2. In both illustrations, the location of the function dial is shown in context of the parent object, the radio. (How design rules are activated is described later.)

Design Rule 1 specifies that to show the location of an object (?object) in a specific context (?context-object), the following style strategies must be accomplished:

- The object must be *included* in the illustration. The achievement threshold "highest" indicates that this style strategy must be fully satisfied.
- The object must be recognizable.
- The context object must be included.
- The object must be visible.
- The object must be highlighted.
- The context object must also be recognizable, but with a lower threshold.
- The context object must also be visible, but with a lower threshold.

Design Rule 2 requires that a landmark object of the context object be visible and recognizable. A *landmark* is an object that serves as a key for identification, position, and/or location [Feiner 85]. IBIS uses a simplistic approach for identifying landmarks. It

Design Rule #1:

```
(method
(location ?object ?context-object highest)
=>
(include        ?object           highest)
(recognizable   ?object           high)
(include        ?context-object   highest)
(visible        ?object           high)
(highlight      ?object           high)
(recognizable   ?context-object   high)
(visible        ?context-object   medium-high))

(evaluator
(include        ?object           highest)
(recognizable   ?object           high)
(include        ?context-object   highest)
(visible        ?object           high)
(highlight      ?object           high)
(recognizable   ?context-object   high)
(visible        ?context-object   medium-high)
=>
(location ?object ?context-object highest))
```

Design Rule #2

```
(method
(location ?object ?context-object highest)
=>
(include        ?object           highest)
(recognizable   ?object           high)
(include        ?context-object   highest)
(visible        ?object           high)
(highlight      ?object           high)
?y <- (Landmark ?context-object)
(recognizable   ?y                high)
(visible        ?y                high))

(evaluator
(include        ?object           highest)
(recognizable   ?object           high)
(include        ?context-object   highest)
(visible        ?object           high)
(highlight      ?object           high)
?y <- (Landmark ?context-object)
(recognizable   ?y                high)
(visible        ?y                high)
=>
(location ?object ?context-object highest))
```

Figure 1. Two design rules for showing location

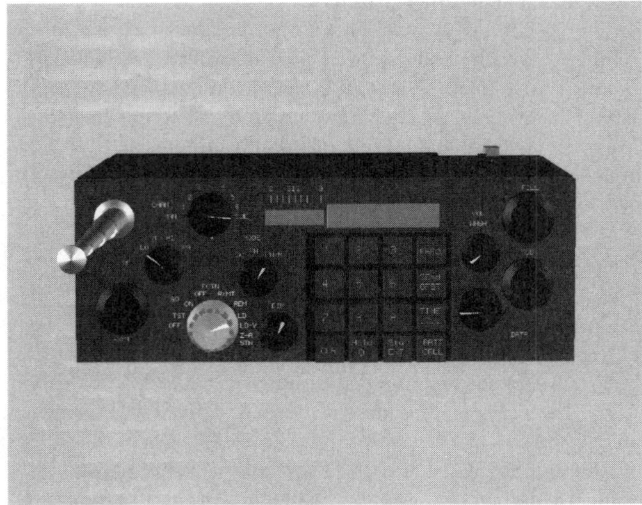

Figure 2. Showing location using Design Rule 1

Figure 3. Showing location using Design Rule 2

considers any object with a unique property (such as shape, material, or color) to be a landmark.

Style Rules: Mapping Stylistic Choice to Visual Effects

There are two types of *style rules*. *Style methods* accomplish visual effects specified by style strategies and *style evaluators* determine the success of style strategies in a given illustration. Style methods specify *illustration methods*, which are procedures to accomplish specific visual effects. Style evaluators match *illustration evaluators* which examine a representation of the planned illustration to determine how well a visual effect is accomplished. Illustration methods and illustration evaluators are the only components of IBIS that directly access the illustration.

A Style Strategy: Highlighting

Highlighting is a style strategy that can be accomplished by applying one of several style rules. The purpose of highlighting an object is to emphasize it and draw attention to it. This can be accomplished by rendering it in a manner that distinguishes it from all the surrounding objects. Consider the following two style methods and two style evaluators.

Style Methods: Highlight Object x

1. Brighten *x*: Increase the intensity of the lights shone on *x*.
2. Subdue other objects: Decrease the intensity of the lights shone on other objects.

Style Evaluators: Highlight Object x

1. For every object with modified lighting: Evaluate the contrast between the object before and after the modification.
2. Evaluate the contrast between *x* and other objects.

Figure 4. State of channel dial with no highlighting

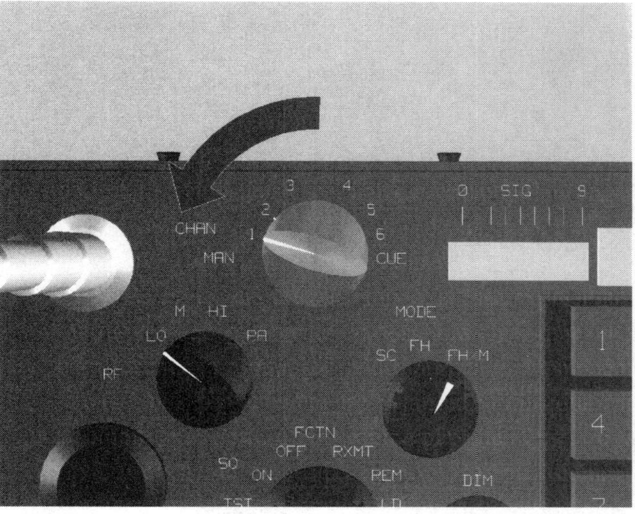

Figure 5. Highlighting by Style Method 1: Brighten object

Figure 6. Highlighting by Style Method 2: Subdue other objects

Figure 7. Highlighting: Combine Style Methods 1 and 2

Let us examine how IBIS uses these rules to highlight an object. At this point, a design rule has already been activated that asserts that the channel dial should be shown in addition to the other parts of the radio. This design rule also specifies that the channel dial should be highlighted.

Figure 4 shows the illustration IBIS would generate if highlighting were not specified. (Figures 4–6, which show intermediate states of the illustration during the illustration design process, were generated by requesting that IBIS render its intermediate results. They would not normally be rendered during the illustration design process.) The style rules are prioritized so that Style Method 1 is tried first, which executes illustration methods whose results are shown in Figure 5. Both style evaluators return unsatisfactory ratings. Style Evaluator 1 fails because its illustration evaluators detect that the dial's markings are brightest white, so increasing their lighting does not change their appearance. Style Evaluator 2 fails because its illustration evaluators detect that the other objects also have markings that are white and therefore do not contrast sufficiently with the channel dial's markings. Therefore, IBIS backtracks and returns the illustration to the state shown in Figure 4.

IBIS next tries Style Method 2, resulting in Figure 6. Style Evaluator 1 is successful, since the other markings are now darkened. Style Evaluator 2, however, returns a poor rating since the contrast between the channel dial and other objects is insufficient. Once again, IBIS backtracks and returns the illustration to the state shown in Figure 4.

IBIS now tries both style methods in combination, as specified by its search control strategy, with the results shown in Figure 7. Both style evaluators now return success. Therefore, IBIS asserts that the channel dial has been successfully highlighted.

Style Method 2 attempts to mute the objects at varying percentages, stopping at a prescribed threshold. In Figure 6, the global lighting is dimmed by 40%, the maximum allowed. In

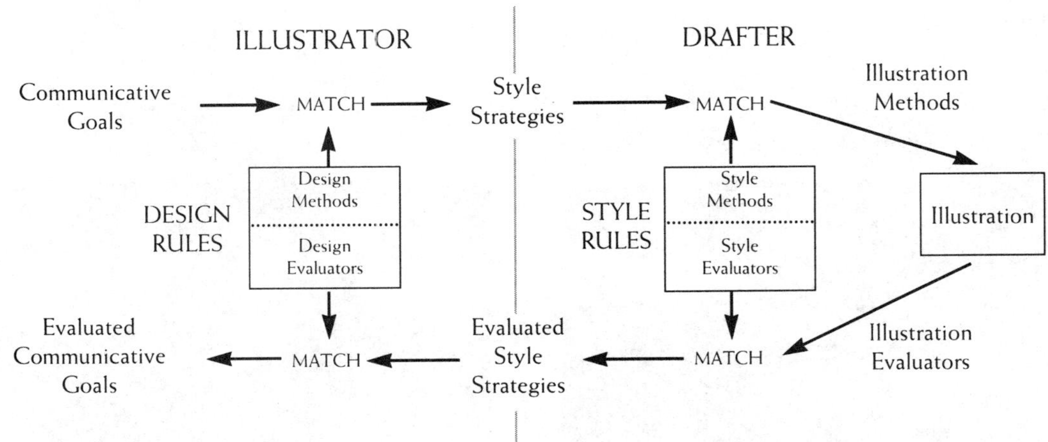

Figure 8. IBIS's illustration process

Figure 7, in which the global lighting is dimmed by 25%, IBIS decides that the brightened channel dial is sufficiently contrasted with other objects and that no additional muting is necessary.

Architecture

Illustrators

An IBIS illustration is designed by a component called an *illustrator*. An illustrator is assigned a set of communicative goals to fulfill. After trying the techniques at hand, an illustrator may detect that it cannot fulfill the complete set of communicative goals in just one illustration. For example, the communicative intent may be to show the opposite faces of the same object, or to show parts of an object in great detail, but also in context of a much larger object that must also be legible. No one view can satisfy these constraints. IBIS's rules allow it to create a *composite illustration*, which is defined as a set of related illustrations that in concert fulfill the communicative intent [Seligmann and Feiner 89]. Composite illustrations are made up of several sub-illustrations, each of which may be inside, overlapping, or next to others. The illustrator creates subordinate illustrators to which it contracts sets of communicative goals. One subordinate illustrator is responsible for the work already completed; the rest are assigned the remaining communicative goals. The original illustrator, which we call the *master illustrator*, is responsible for the work of the subordinates and the placement and sizing of their sub-illustrations. Although illustrations may have arbitrarily deep recursive hierarchies in theory, in practice the hierarchy is usually not very deep or broad.

While illustrators map communicative goals to style strategies with design methods and evaluate the success of communicative goals with design evaluators, they assign to *drafters* the task of accomplishing and evaluating style strategies.

Drafters

Drafters do not know about communicative intent. They are the unheralded workers who translate the illustrators' plans into reality. Drafters are tied to the hardware they utilize. For example, it is the drafters who apply the procedures that examine the contents of the framebuffer. Drafters share a body of style rules. Each style rule specifies illustration methods or evaluators to call in order to achieve or evaluate visual effects. Drafters report back to the illustrators with the achievement rating of the various style strategies they implement. Once an illustration has been approved by the master illustrator, it is the drafters who render the illustration.

Illustration Objects, Physical Objects, and their Relations

An illustration contains a set of *illustration objects*, each of which is created for that illustration. The drafter generates illustration objects when achieving style strategies. IBIS selects the objects to depict based on the communicative goals and design rules activated. Each illustration object usually depicts one or more corresponding physical objects in the knowledge base. Some illustration objects, however, may not correspond to any physical object, such as the arrow appearing in Figure 7. Such objects are called *meta-objects* [Feiner 85]. They are generated by the system to serve as visual annotations that illustrate those concepts that do not directly correspond to physical objects in the world being illustrated, such as the concept of turning in Figure 7.

An illustration includes a set of *object relations* that specifies the relationship between each illustration object and zero or more corresponding physical objects. Some physical objects have no corresponding illustration objects. These are the objects IBIS selects not to depict. In contrast, a physical object may correspond to several illustration objects. For example, two or more illustration objects can depict the same object in different states.

Generate and Test Approach

Figure 8 summarizes IBIS's illustration design process. Communicative goals match with a design method in the illustrator's design rule base. The design method asserts a set of style strategies. Style strategies match with style methods in the drafter's style rule base. This, in turn, activates a set of illustration methods that access the illustration object directly. Corresponding style evaluators activate a set of illustration evaluators that also access the illustration. The illustration evaluators match with style evaluators to assert the success ratings for style strategies. The evaluated style strategies match with design evaluators and assert the success ratings for communicative goals.

All illustrators share a set of design rules. All drafters share a set of style rules. Each illustrator or drafter, however, can be specified with a different illustrative style. An *illustrative style* is represented by ordering the rules so that preferred methods are always attempted first. When a preferred method fails, the illustrative style is overridden. The illustrations IBIS generates can combine different illustrative styles. The illustrations shown in the figures were generated using the illustrative style *realistic*. The *realistic* illustrative style favors methods that do not alter physical properties of objects. For example, highlighting methods that use lighting are preferred to methods that change the color of an object.

Evaluation is based on a system of ratings and thresholds. *Thresholds* are assigned by the illustrators and are inherited by the drafters for each style strategy. A threshold represents a minimum degree of success required for a method to be considered acceptable. Evaluators can directly assert that either a style strategy or communicative goal has been achieved.

Visibility and Recognizability

Style rules for evaluating and achieving highlighting were illustrated earlier. We now describe visibility and recognizability. First, we discuss the evaluators that the drafter uses to determine if objects are visible and recognizable in the current illustration. Then we discuss the methods the drafter uses to achieve visibility and recognizability.

Evaluating Visibility

Every IBIS illustration depicts at least one object that must be visible. We call an object that must be visible an *unoccludable object*. IBIS stores its objects in a parts hierarchy. An unoccludable object may be any node in the hierarchy. An object is considered completely visible if it resides entirely within the view volume and no other objects obscure it. Thus, an object is partially visible if it is obscured by other objects or if it is not completely within the view volume.

We use several approaches to determine visibility quickly, described in [Feiner and Seligmann 90]. One approach uses z-buffer picking [Foley et al. 90] to detect occlusion. The hardware z-buffer is loaded with an unoccludable object and the remainder of the z-buffer in the unoccludable object's bounding box is set to the closest possible z-value. For each remaining object, the system will determine if any part of the object is visible relative to the z-buffer, which occurs only if the object (partially) obscures the unoccludable object. This returns a binary occluding/non-occluding status. Another approach using shadow volumes [Chin and Feiner 89] returns a partially occluding/completely-occluding classification.

Evaluating Recognizability

An object is *recognizable* if its distinguishing features are shown. Some features depend upon the view; others depend on certain characteristics or attributes. We do not address the very difficult problem of determining or generating automatically *characteristic views* [Chakravarty 82, Kamada and Kawai 88] that ensure that an object's distinguishing characteristics are apparent. Instead each object is stored with an a priori characteristic view.

We represent a characteristic view as a union of volumes and a set of constraints. Each volume is specified by a ray originating from a point on the object. This volume represents a set of legal viewpoints that may be further restricted by the characteristic view's constraints. The constraints include a minimum screen size

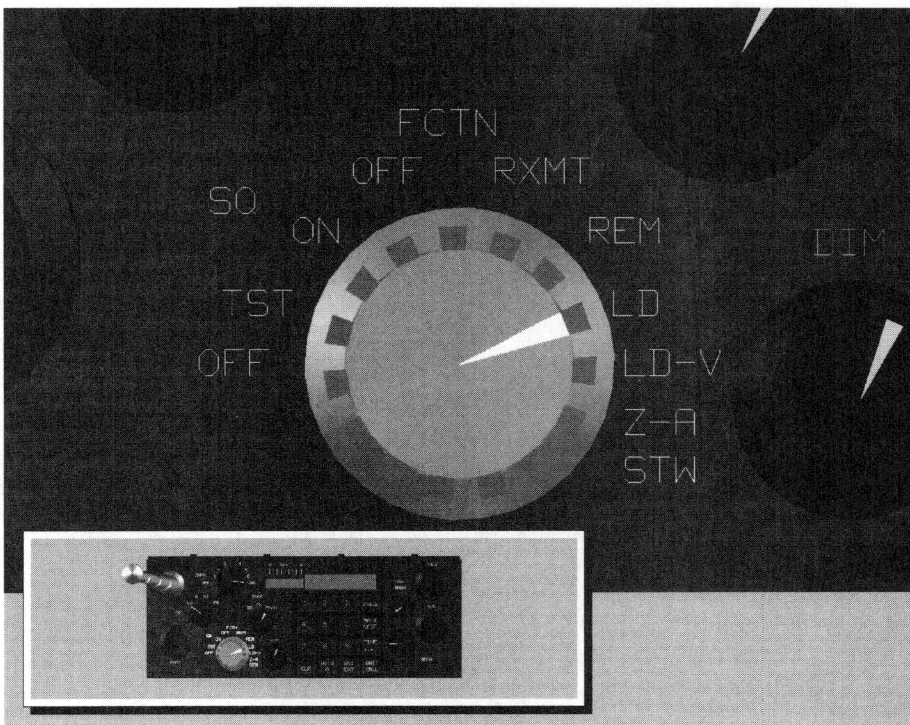

Figure 9. Automatically generated inset to show location during user navigation

the object must occupy and a list of properties that must be depicted.

Style Methods for Visibility and Recognizability

The drafter maintains a set of possible view specifications for every object that must be recognizable. A view specification satisfies the recognizability goals associated with these objects if the viewpoint lies within the intersection of the characteristic views' volumes and if the additional constraints are satisfied.

The visibility of each unoccludable object is maintained, if possible, by selecting a view in which unoccludable objects are not obscured. IBIS has several different methods for realizing visibility constraints when an unoccludable object is obscured by another object (that is not itself unoccludable). The first and simplest method is to remove from an illustration an object that obscures an unoccludable object. An object can be made visible by removing from the illustration all the objects that obscure it. This solution is problematic. In some cases, it would be misleading to remove objects from the scene. In other cases, it would be ideal.

A variety of illustrative styles have been developed by technical illustrators to depict obscured objects more clearly without completely eliminating those that obscure them [Giesecke et al. 36, Thomas 68, Martin 89]. These techniques include cutaways, transparency, and ghosting. We have developed several approaches for efficiently applying simple versions of these techniques interactively using z-buffer–based graphics systems [Seligmann and Feiner 89, Feiner and McKeown 90a, Feiner and Seligmann 91].

Interactive Illustrations

So far, we have treated IBIS's illustrations as static presentations. However, the same mechanisms that enable IBIS to design illustrations are utilized to maintain illustrations in their interactive state. An *interactive illustration* may be manipulated by a user. Currently, IBIS supports user-controlled view specification. In traditional user-controlled navigation, when the user specifies a new view, the same set of illustration objects is rendered from that view. In contrast, navigation in an illustrated 3D environment is more complex. The illustration is bound to the communicative goals with which it is specified. The illustration system's task is to satisfy continuously these communicative goals while the user changes the view specification. For example, consider an illustration in which the illustrator has determined that certain objects are unoccludable. As the user alters the view, these unoccludable objects may be obscured by other objects. The appearance of these otherwise occluding objects must be modified dynamically to maintain the unoccludable objects' visibility. (In [Feiner and Seligmann 91] we describe techniques for automatically maintaining visibility during an interactive session.)

Alternatively, different design rules may be activated to satisfy a communicative goal as the view specification changes. Consider an interactive session beginning with Figure 2, in which the communicative goal is to show the location of the function dial. Figure 2's view specification is generated by IBIS. As the user zooms in, using IBIS's interactive interface, Design Rule 1's evaluator is no longer satisfied: the context object is no longer completely recognizable and visible. However, Design Rule 2's evaluator is activated because the current view includes the keypad buttons, which are unique objects on the radio and considered landmarks of the radio. The communicative goal to show location is maintained and IBIS does not have to redesign the illustration. The user continues to zoom. Now, only the function dial is visible and recognizable. If design rules 1 and 2 are the only rules for showing location, then the communicative goal has been violated, since no design rule is satisfied. IBIS opts to generate a composite illustration, and designs and positions an inset illustration (using Design Rule 1), which pops up during the interactive session. The resulting illustration is shown in Figure 9.

Composite Illustrations

Here we describe some of the top-level decisions IBIS made when designing the illustration shown in Figure 10. The illustration is intended to show the user how to snap the latches of the primary battery box, as well as to indicate, with lesser importance, where another battery (the holding battery) is located. The master illustrator is assigned the following communicative goals:

(state latch1 snapped highest)
(state latch2 snapped highest)
(state latch3 snapped highest)
(state latch4 snapped highest)
(location holding-battery radio medium-low)

These communicative goals activate the following design rules that specify the following style strategies.

For each latch:
(include latch highest)
(context latch medium)
(recognizable latch high)
(visible latch high)
(highlight latch high)
(change latch snapped highest)
(meta-object latch snapped highest)

For the battery:
(include holding-battery highest)
(visible holding-battery medium-low)
(recognizable holding-battery low)
(context holding-battery medium-low)
(highlight holding-battery medium-low)

The illustrator's drafter tries to satisfy the highest priority style strategies first and begins by generating illustration objects for the latches, holding battery, and the rest of the radio. The recognizability constraints are set up for each object. The drafter fails when trying to make the fourth latch recognizable. Since all goal cannot be satisfied, IBIS decides that a composite illustration is needed. The master illustrator contracts two subordinate illustrators to handle the following communicative goals:

Illustrator One:
(state latch1 snapped highest)
(state latch2 snapped highest)
(state latch3 snapped highest)
(location holding-battery radio medium-low)

Illustrator Two:
(state latch4 snapped highest)

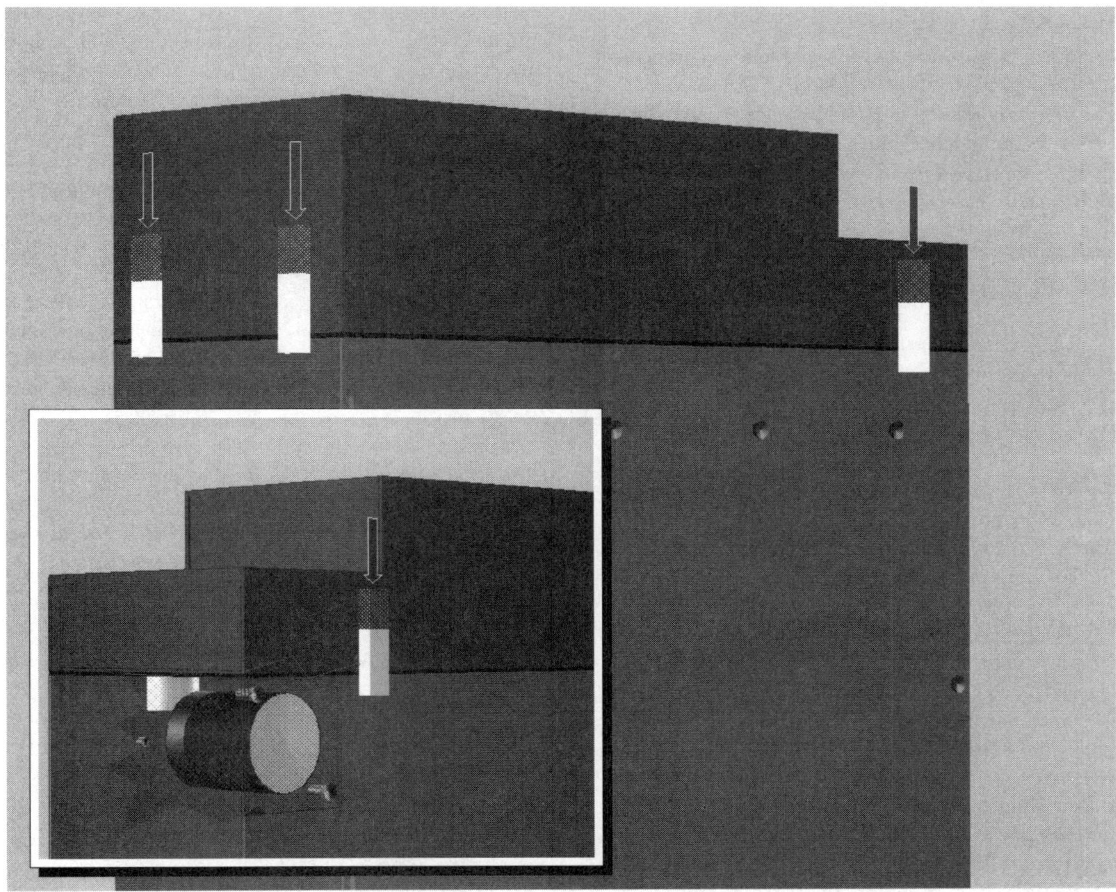

Figure 10. Showing snapping of latches and location of holding battery with a cutaway view

The latches are highlighted by increasing the intensity of their lighting. The drafter for Illustrator One reports failure for showing the battery—an unoccludable latch obscures it. Because the visibility goal for the holding battery is of low priority, the view specification that currently satisfies the high-priority recognizability and visibility goals associated with the latches is not altered. The master illustrator therefore assigns the holding battery's location goal to Illustrator Two:

Illustrator One:
(state latch1 snapped highest)
(state latch2 snapped highest)
(state latch3 snapped highest)

Illustrator Two:
(state latch4 snapped highest)
(location holding-battery radio medium-low)

Illustrator Two's drafter determines that the holding battery's recognizability and visibility goals can be achieved using the current view specification. The drafter then specifies a cutaway view for the holding battery. In the rule base for this illustration, a style method specifies that occluding objects be drawn using a wireframe style, and that the cutaway itself be semi-transparent. The concept of *snapping* is shown in the following way. The style rule specifies how to shape, position and orient an arrow meta-object based on the geometric information of the latch in the two states as well as the final view specification. The arrow begins at the previous state and points to the next state. The communicative goal to show the change of state is activated by a design rule that handles state and snapping. It activates a style strategy to show the object in both states. A style method specifies that a "ghost image" [Martin 89] be used to show the previous state of each latch. Illustration objects representing each latch in its previous state are generated. These ghost objects inherit the material and lighting from the illustration objects that are related to the same physical object, but their material is set to be partially transparent. The following constraints are added for each arrow and ghost object:

(visible ?object high)
(recognizable ?object high)

The master illustrator is notified that both illustrators have achieved the communicative goals they have been assigned. The master illustrator must now size and position the two illustrations. An inset style is selected for the illustration generated by Illustrator Two. The illustration must be sized so that the constraints are not violated (such as recognizability) and it must be positioned so that it does not obscure the unoccludable objects in Illustrator One's illustration. The resulting illustration is shown in Figure 10.

Related Work

Several researchers have addressed the problem of automatic picture generation. Simmons's CLOWNS [Simmons 75] generates simple line drawings of a 2D clown. Neiman's GAK [Neiman 82] generates animated pictures for a CAD system help facility. Both these systems, however, rely on predesigned vector objects. Friedell [Friedell 84] has generated synthesized 3D graphic environments using evaluators and backtracking, but this work emphasized modeling environments, rather than designing pictures. Feiner's APEX [Feiner 85] system designs pictures that depict actions performed in a 3D world, but without backtracking, self-evaluation, style combination, or visibility checks. Mackinlay's APT system [Mackinlay 86] designs 2D presentation graphics for quantitative data using a system of evaluation and backtracking, which enables the system to combine styles. Strothotte's chemistry explanation system [Strothotte 89] generates pictorial explanations automatically, but relies on handmade bitmapped images.

Other researchers have addressed rendering problems related to the illustration of objects. Kamada and Kawai [Kamada and Kawai 87] have developed techniques for generating line drawings that show the internal structure of complex objects. Saito and Takahashi [Saito and Takahashi 90] and Dooley and Cohen [Dooley and Cohen 90a, Dooley and Cohen 90b] have also developed non real–time techniques using transparency, cross-hatching, and different line styles to generate high-quality images that convey shape and construction.

The work described here differs from previous work in a number of ways emphasized in this paper. Our approach to automated illustration of 3D worlds is intent-based and depends upon a system of methods and evaluators that enables multi-level backtracking based on evaluations of a partially generated illustration. Illustration objects are generated based on both the representation of the physical object as well as the communicative intent. IBIS's evaluation process attempts to approximate the relationship between the visual appearance of an object in the real world (limited by the models used) and its appearance in the illustration. Finally, IBIS introduces an approach for generating composite illustrations, as well as semantically bound interactive illustrations.

Implementation

IBIS is written in C++ and the CLIPS production system language [Culbert 88]. It runs under UNIX on an HP 9000 375 TurboSRX workstation, which provides hardware support for realtime 3D shaded graphics. Drafters currently use the HP Starbase 3D graphics package, while the user interface is written in X.

The radio featured in the illustrations consists of over 8000 polygons rendered at 1280 x 1024 resolution. IBIS took .8 seconds to design Figure 7 and 7 seconds for IBIS to design Figure 10. It takes approximately .3 seconds to render either illustration.

Summary and Future Work

IBIS demonstrates an automated intent-based approach to illustration. Illustrations are designed by first considering a specified communicative intent and the world depicted. IBIS treats illustration as a goal-driven process using a generate–and–test approach and relies upon a rule base to make stylistic and design choices. These rules are represented as both methods for accomplishing visual effects and evaluators for determining how well visual effects have been accomplished in an illustration. Any choice may negatively affect the success of others; IBIS backtracks to find alternative solutions.

Our current efforts concentrate on the development of a visual language for 3D worlds [Seligmann 91] that will incorporate formalisms for communicative intent, style, design, viewer model, and session model. Communicative intent will be extended to include goals to represent the *purpose* of the communication, such as warnings and reminders. Style rules are being arranged into a hierarchy of constraints, ranging from those that identify conformant classes of illustration elements (e.g. colors and lines) to those that identify unaesthetic choices. We are also developing meta-rules to select methods based on the overall problem (rather than searching for the first adequate solution). For example, while IBIS currently generates composite illustrations only as a last resort, a meta-rule could allow them to be created as a regular design option. Finally, IBIS is being enhanced to allow for user control on all levels of specification, including the choice of design rules and style strategies.

Acknowledgments

This work is supported in part by the Defense Advanced Research Projects Agency under Contract N00039-84-C-0165 and the Hewlett-Packard Company under its AI University Grants Program. Esther Woo, John Edmark, Garry Johnson and Alan Waxman implemented portions of the system. Norman Chin developed the efficient procedures that we use to manipulate shadow volumes. Michael Elhadad is a a fellow comrade in arms in the COMET project. Conversations with Tom Ellman, J.R. Ensor, Allen Ginsberg, Jacques Robin, Frank Smadja have been more than helpful. Much appreciation is due to Suzanne Oboler and Cynthia King for their critical reading of this paper. Many thanks to David Kurlander and Rick Beach for help with the color separations.

References

Chakravarty, I., and Freeman, H. Characteristic Views as a Basis for Three-Dimensional Object Recognition. In *Proc. Society for Photo-Optical Instrumentation Engineers Conf. on Robot Vision*, Bellingham, WA, SPIE, vol. 336, 1982. 37–54.

Chin, N. and Feiner S. Near Real-Time Shadow Generation using BSP Trees. In *Proc. ACM SIGGRAPH 89 (Computer Graphics*, 23(3), July 1989), Boston, MA, July 31–August 4, 1989, 99–106.

Culbert, C. *CLIPS Reference Manual.* NASA/Johnson Space Center, TX, 1988.

Dooley, D. and Cohen, M. Automatic Illustration of 3D Geometric Models: Lines. In *Proc. 1990 Symp. on Interactive 3D Graphics (Computer Graphics 24(2)*, March 1990), Snowbird, UT, March 25–28, 1990, 77–82.

Dooley, D. and Cohen, M. Automatic Illustration of 3D Geometric Models: Surfaces. In *Proc. Visualization '90*, San Francisco, CA, October 23–26, 1990, 307–314.

Elhadad, M., Seligmann, D.D., Feiner, S., and McKeown, K. A Common Intention Description Language for Interactive Multi-

Media Systems. *IJCAI-89 Workshop on Intelligent Interfaces*, Detroit, MI, August 22, 1989, 46–52.

Feiner, Steven K. APEX: An Experiment in the Automated Creation of Pictoral Explanations. *IEEE Computer Graphics and Applications 5(11)*, November 1985, 29–38.

Feiner, S. and McKeown, K. Generating Coordinated Multimedia Explanations. In *Proc. CAIA90 (6th IEEE Conf. on Artificial Intelligence Applications)*, Santa Barbara, CA, March 5–9, 1990, 290–296.

Feiner, S. and McKeown, K. Coordinating text and graphics in explanation generation. In *Proc. AAAI-90*, Boston, MA, July 29–August 3,1990. 442–449.

Feiner, S. and Seligmann, D.D. Dynamic 3D Illustrations with Visibility Constraints. In *Proc. Computer Graphics International 91*, Cambridge, MA, June 24–28, 1991.

Foley, J., van Dam, A., Feiner, S., and Hughes, J. *Computer Graphics: Principles and Practice 2nd Edition*. Addison-Wesley, Reading, MA, 1990.

Friedell, M. Automatic Synthesis of Graphical Object Descriptions. *Computer Graphics 18(3)*, July 1984, 53–62.

Giesecke, F., Mitchell, A., and Spencer, H. *Technical Drawing*. New York, The Macmillan Co., 1936.

Kamada, T. and Kawai, S. An Enhanced Treatment of Hidden Lines. *ACM Trans. on Graphics* 6(4), October, 1987, 308–323.

Kamada, T. and Kawai, S. A Simple Method for Computing General Position in Displaying Three-Dimensional Objects. *Computer Vision, Graphics and Image Processing 41(1)*, January, 1988, 43–56.

Mackinlay, J. Automating the Design of Graphical Presentations of Relational Information. *ACM Trans. on Graphics 5(2)*, April 1986, 110–141.

Martin, J. *High Tech Illustration*. Cincinnati, OH, North Light Books, 1989.

Neiman, D. Graphical Animation from Knowledge. In *Proc. AAAI '82*, Pittsburgh, PA, August 18–20, 1982, 373–376.

Saito, T. and Takahashi, T. Comprehensible Rendering of 3-D Shapes. In *Proc. ACM SIGGRAPH '90 (Computer Graphics, 24(4)*, August 1990). Dallas, TX, August 6-10, 1990, 197–206.

Seligmann, D. D. Intent-Based Illustration: A Visual Language for 3D Worlds. Thesis Proposal. Department of Computer Science, Columbia University. New York, January 1991.

Seligmann, D. D., and Feiner, S. Specifying Composite Illustrations with Communicative Goals. In *Proc. UIST '89*. Williamsburg, VA, November 13–15, 1989, 1–9.

Simmons, R. F. The Clowns Microworld. In *Proc. TINLAP '75*, 17–19.

Strothotte, T. Pictures in Advice-Giving Dialog Systems: From Knowledge Representation to the User Interface. In *Proc. Graphics Interface '89*, London Ontario, June 19–23, 1989, 94–99.

Thomas, T.A. *Technical Illustration, 2nd. Edition*. McGraw-Hill, New York, NY. 1968.

Reflections on. . .

Automated Generation of Intent-Based 3D Illustrations

Dorée Duncan Seligmann and Steven K. Feiner

IBIS's architecture was extended to support changing goals, moving objects, and user interaction (Seligmann 1993; Seligmann and Feiner 1993). IBIS was also modified to generate overlaid animated graphics on a head-mounted display for KARMA (Feiner et al. 1993), illustrating tasks as they were performed. Using a new set of rules and an additional level of goals and evaluators to represent whole tasks, the user's head position constrains the illustration process while the user's actions trigger the evaluation process. Many of the ideas in IBIS have been applied in our work at Bell Labs. Archways (Seligmann and Edmark 1997) automatically generates a 3-D environment for multimedia communication. Its customized displays (consisting of 3-D sound and graphics) provide users with cues to enable them to interact more naturally (Seligmann et al. 1995). The virtual environment integrates visualization, content display, and user interface. Intelligent viewers are constrained to show specific information (such as the other people in a virtual place). User-sensitive objects are bound to low-level constraints (such as legibility). Environment-sensitive objects adapt to changes in the scene (such as a meeting table that grows in size to accommodate new participants).

Recent work on automated graphics generation at Columbia has also extended the ideas in IBIS. IMPROVISE (Zhou and and Feiner 1997b) uses a hierarchical-decomposition, partial-order planner to design heterogeneous graphical presentations whose elements range from static 2-D graphs to animated 3-D objects. A data characterization taxonomy (Zhou and Feiner 1996) expresses the relevant properties of the information to be presented, and a visual lexicon (Zhou and Feiner 1997a) contains parameterized visual objects that can potentially be used in a presentation. Each visual object is tagged with syntactic, semantic, and pragmatic information that IMPROVISE uses to determine the best visual object to express a given piece of data.

REFERENCES

Feiner, S.; MacIntyre, B.; and Seligmann, D. 1993. Knowledge-Based Augmented Reality. *Communications of the ACM* 36(7): 52–62.

Seligmann, D. D. 1993. Interactive Intent-Based Illustrations: A Visual Language for 3D Worlds. Ph.D. dissertation, Dept. of Computer Science, Columbia University.

Seligmann, D. D., and Edmark, J. T. 1997. Automatically Generated 3D Virtual Environments for Multimedia Communication. In *Proceedings of the Fifth International Conference in Central Europe on Computer Graphics and Visualization '97*, Plzen, Czech Republic, 494–503.

Seligmann, D. D., and Feiner, S. 1993. Supporting Interactivity in Automated 3D Illustrations, In *Proceedings of the 1993 International Workshop on Intelligent Interfaces*, Orlando, FL, 37–43.

Seligmann, D. D.; Mercuri, R. T.; and Edmark, J. T. 1995. Providing Assurances in a Multimedia Interactive Environment. In *Proceedings of ACM SIGCHI '95*, 250–256. New York: Association for Computing Machinery.

Zhou, M., and Feiner, S. 1996. Data Characterization for Automatically Visualizing Heterogeneous Information. In *Proceedings of IEEE Information Visualization '96*, 13–20. Los Alamitos, CA: IEEE Computer Society Press.

Zhou, M., and Feiner, S. 1997a. The Representation and Use of a Visual Lexicon for Automated Graphics Generation. In *Proceedings of the Fifteenth International Joint Conference on Artificial Intelligence*, 1056–1062. San Francisco: Morgan Kaufmann.

Zhou, M., and Feiner, S. 1997b. Top-Down Hierarchical Planning of Coherent Visual Discourse. In *Proceedings of the 1997 International Conference on Intelligent User Interfaces*, 129–136. New York: Association for Computing Machinery.

Interactive Graphic Design Using Automatic Presentation Knowledge

Steven F. Roth, John Kolojejchick, Joe Mattis, Jade Goldstein

School of Computer Science
Carnegie Mellon University
Pittsburgh, PA 15213
(412) 268-7690
Steven.Roth@cs.cmu.edu

ABSTRACT

We present three novel tools for creating data graphics: (1) SageBrush, for assembling graphics from primitive objects like bars, lines and axes, (2) SageBook, for browsing previously created graphics relevant to current needs, and (3) SAGE, a knowledge-based presentation system that automatically designs graphics and also interprets a user's specifications conveyed with the other tools. The combination of these tools supports two complementary processes in a single environment: design as a constructive process of selecting and arranging graphical elements, and design as a process of browsing and customizing previous cases. SAGE enhances *user-directed* design by completing partial specifications, by retrieving previously created graphics based on their appearance and data content, by creating the novel displays that users specify, and by designing alternatives when users request them. Our approach was to propose interfaces employing styles of interaction that appear to support graphic design. Knowledge-based techniques were then applied to enable the interfaces and enhance their usability.

KEYWORDS: Graphic Design, Data Visualization, Automatic Presentation Systems, Intelligent Interfaces, Design Environments, Interactive Techniques

INTRODUCTION

Graphic displays of information have been valuable for supporting data exploration, analysis, and presentation. Still, current graphics packages remain very limited because: (1) they do not provide *integrative* displays for viewing the relations among several data attributes or data sets, (2) they have time-consuming and complex interfaces, and (3) they provide little guidance for the majority of users who are not experienced graphic designers.

Consider these problems in the context of two graphics in Roth Color Plate 1. In 1a, a sequence of indented text, charts, and a table are aligned to integrate six attributes of *activities* (organization, start, end, status, cost, resource). All information about a single activity can be obtained by glancing horizontally across the graphic. Most packages do enable users to create charts and tables like these, but only as isolated displays. Even painstaking cutting, pasting, and resizing (usually the only means provided) are insufficient to layout and sort the bars and text in a coordinated way.

Similarly, current packages provide no way to create a single display with different graphical objects. In 1b, properties of lines, text strings and diamond-shaped marks vary to integrate ten data attributes. Also, graphical objects are *clustered* to express facts (i.e. each diamond is accompanied by two text labels to convey the geographic location, city, and date of battles). Together, these graphics illustrate the large number of possible combinations of object types, their graphical properties, the *encoding spaces* in which they occur (e.g. within a chart, map, table, or network), and the different ways they can be clustered and aligned. Clearly, current menu-style interfaces in spreadsheet packages would not support the creation of so many alternatives, nor could they help users assign data attributes to these graphics easily. Imagine the difficulty of conveying the relationship between data in spreadsheet columns and all the graphical objects and properties in 1b.

Furthermore, imagine the considerable design expertise required of users to produce these displays, including an awareness of the appropriateness of graphic choices for each data type. Even when users can judge the effectiveness of a particular display of their data, they often lack exposure to the many types and combinations of graphics that are possible. Systems that provide the ability to create new integrative designs will need to provide design guidance as well.

One approach to these problems is to build systems that are knowledgeable of graphic design, so they can generate a variety of effective displays based on descriptions of data and viewing goals [1,3,4,9,10]. This research has provided a vocabulary for describing the elements of graphics, knowledge about the appropriateness of their use for different data and tasks, and design operations for combining elements to form integrative displays.

Armed with this knowledge, automatic design systems should reduce the need for interaction and expertise, while providing great flexibility in customizing displays. However, previous automatic design research has not been concerned with supporting interaction with users and has focused on issues of identifying and encoding knowledge of data, tasks, and design. No paradigms have been developed for a collaborative process between human and automated designers.

This paper describes a novel approach to interactive graphic design, in which automatic mechanisms are used to support users, not replace them. The following sections describe an overview of our approach, two major components of the system that correspond to two complementary styles of design, and some sample design interactions which illustrate these capabilities.

OVERVIEW OF CURRENT APPROACH

Our approach to supporting design has been to integrate an evolving automatic presentation system called SAGE [9,10] with two new interactive design tools called SageBrush and SageBook. Both tools enable users to manipulate familiar objects in order to perform natural design operations, shielding users from the more complex representations and operations that SAGE uses to create graphics.

SageBrush (also called Brush) is representative of design tool interfaces in which users specify graphics by constructing sketches from a palette of primitives and/or partial designs. Our goal is to provide a flexible, generative, direct manipulation design interface, in which users can create a large number of possible combinations of graphical elements, customize their spatial and structural relationships, and map them to the data they wish to visualize.

SageBook (also called Book) is an interface for browsing and retrieving previously created pictures (i.e. complete, rendered designs) and utilizing them to visualize new data. Book supports an approach to design in which people remember or examine previous successful visualizations and use them as a starting point for designing displays of new data, extending and customizing them as needed. Our experiences in graphic design, as well as related research on engineering and software design [2,6], suggest that search and reuse of prior cases with customization is a common process. Therefore, our goal is to provide methods for searching through previously created pictures based on their graphical properties and/or the properties of the data they express. A picture found in this way can optionally be modified in Brush prior to sending it to SAGE, which creates a graphic for the new data.

SAGE is an automatic presentation system containing many features of related systems like APT, BOZ, and ANDD [1,3,4]. Inputs are a characterization of data to be visualized and a user's data viewing goals. Design operations include selecting techniques based on expressiveness and effectiveness criteria, and composing and laying out graphics appropriate to data and goals. A detailed discussion of automatic design capabilities, including the operations that produced Roth Color Plate 1a, can be found elsewhere [7,9].

The current version of SAGE goes beyond previous systems in several ways. SAGE can create graphics when users completely specify their designs as well as when they provide no specifications at all. Most importantly, it can accept *partial* specifications at any level of completeness between these two extremes and finish the design reasonably. User specifications serve as *design directives,* which constrain the path of a search algorithm that selects and composes graphics to create a design.

The ability to accept partial specifications from Brush is due to a rich *object representation* of the components of graphic displays, including their syntax (i.e. their spatial and structural relationships) and semantics (i.e. how they indicate the correspondence between data and graphics). The representation allows SAGE to produce combinations of a wide variety of 2D graphics (e.g. charts, tables, map-like coordinate systems, text-outlines, networks). It also enables SAGE to support Book's search for previous pictures with graphical elements specified by users.

The object representation is highly extensible, allowing new graphical objects (e.g. lines, polygons, custom icons) and encoder mechanisms (e.g. charts, color keys, maps) to be added incrementally. For example, when a line object is added to the library, each end-point is defined as having horizontal and vertical positions, enabling the line to be displayed against the axes of a chart. If a map-style is later defined in the library as an encoder that displays horizontal and vertical positions, then SAGE can automatically draw lines on maps (as in Roth Color Plate 1b).

SAGE also contains a richer representation of the *characteristics* of data (e.g. distinguishing scales of measurement, temperature, dates, spatial coordinates, etc). Data transformation operations enable the design of graphics without depending on the surface form of input data (e.g. in relational database terms, SAGE can display N-ary relations and is not dependent on whether data is expressed as multiple binary relations or as a single N-ary relation).

ARCHITECTURE

Figure 1 illustrates the conceptual relationships among SageBrush, SageBook, SAGE, and a Data Selector - a tool for indicating the mapping between data and graphics. The process of retrieving data needs to be integrated with graphic creation but is not the focus of this paper. We are exploring several interactive methods for retrieving and transferring data to the selector, where data appears as a table whose headers can be mapped to graphics (Figure 2).

Users interact with Brush to create graphic design *sketches,* which are schematic views of designs. These are translated into *design directives,* which are specifications expressed in SAGE's graphic representation language. Directives include:

- grapheme and property choices (e.g. color and size of circles, lines, text, and other graphical objects),
- encoding mechanisms that provide frames of reference against which properties of graphemes are interpreted (e.g. 2-axis chart, table, map, network),
- layout constraints (e.g. alignment of multiple charts horizontally; ordering of labels and graphemes),
- grouping constraints indicating that clusters of graphemes are being used to express a single fact (e.g. a bar annotated with a text string; a cluster of items around a city on a map),
- mappings between data and these graphic elements.

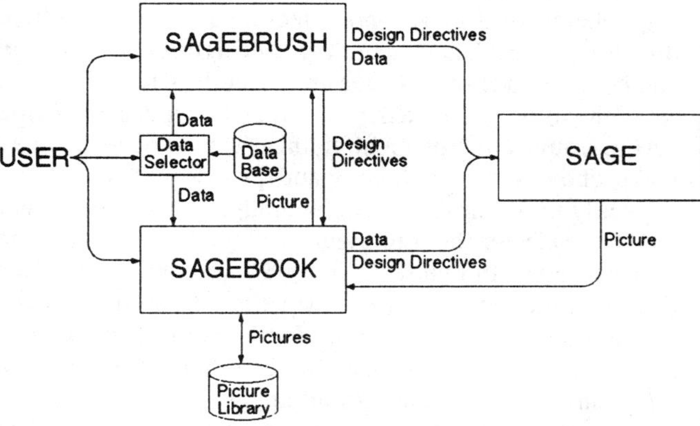

Figure 1: Architecture

Design directives from Brush serve two purposes: they guide SAGE's automatic processes and provide criteria for Book to use in searching its library of previously designed pictures. Brush can also translate graphics produced by SAGE back into sketches so that users can modify them.

Users interact with Book to view and save pictures created by SAGE. The saved information includes a bit map scaled to a browsable size, a sequence of design operations that SAGE can use to reconstruct the picture efficiently (i.e. without redesigning), the picture's data and data type characteristics, and a complete representation of the rendered graphic. Book searches its picture library based on data users specify with the Selector and/or design directives derived from sketches created in Brush's work area (Figure 2). Users request the creation of a graphic based on a previously found one by transferring it to Brush (where they modify it as a sketch) or directly to SAGE. The next sections describe these components in detail.

SAGEBRUSH

Brush is representative of tools with which users sketch or assemble graphical elements to create designs and map them to data. Brush provides users with an intuitive and efficient language for sketching their designs, and translates these sketches into a form that can be interpreted by SAGE. There are other possible styles of graphic design interface that could be coordinated with SAGE's internal design mechanisms. One alternative is the demonstrational approach proposed for Gold [5], in which users draw examples of displays. Our claim is that any interactive design interface that attempts to provide complete coverage of graphics will require a knowledgeable system behind it to be successful.

An example: Figures 2, 3, and Roth Color Plate 1b illustrate a sequence for creating a new version of the famous graphic by Minard showing Napoleon's 1812 Campaign [11]. One data set describes the march segments (start and end latitudes/longitudes of each segment, the number of troops remaining, and the temperature). The other data set contains the city, date, and location of each major battle. These will be visualized by composing multiple graphemes and their properties on a map.

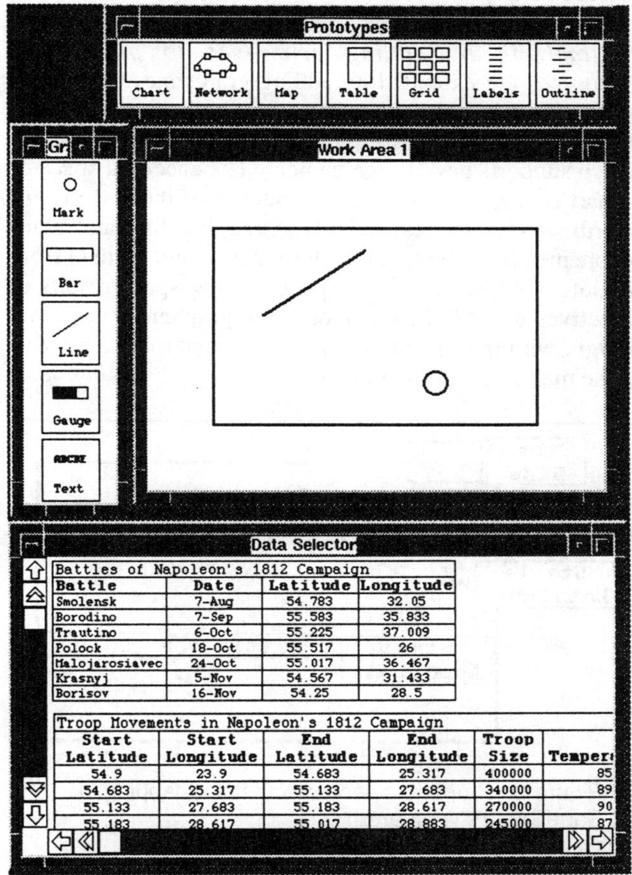

Figure 2: Starting a design sketch in SageBrush.

Anchoring new designs with partial prototypes. The creation of a new design begins with a user's selection of a partial prototype. As illustrated in Figure 2, Brush's interface consists of a design work area (center) into which users drag prototypes (top), graphemes (left), and data names (bottom). *Prototypes* are partial designs, each with a spatial organization, graphemes, and/or encoders that commonly occur together. Encoders are frames of reference for interpreting properties of graphemes. For example, axes enable us to interpret (i.e. derive a data value from) the position of a bar in a chart.

The choice of prototypes to include in the top menu can be customized to applications and could include previously designed graphics. Although primarily a constructive interface, Brush still allows design to be viewed as a process of refining prior, effective graphics. The first prototype in the top-left of Figure 2 is a general one for constructing all charts. It is actually a composite of horizontal and vertical axes. Although users could construct charts by assembling separate axes, doing so requires more steps and appears less intuitive than selecting a chart prototype. A similar rationale led to a network prototype, consisting of both graphemes (i.e. lines) and an encoder against which the graphemes are interpreted (i.e. the nodes). This eliminates the need for users to construct networks from primitives each time. In the example, a map prototype (more precisely, a 2D spatial coordinate display) was dragged to the design work area.

Customizing by adding primitives to prototypes. Prototypes are extended by adding graphemes. While the chart and map prototypes have no graphemes, dragging them into the design work area creates an *encoding space* which supports new design choices. The encoding space of a chart or map is defined by the interior of the two axes or coordinate-frame, respectively. Dragging line and mark graphemes (to represent march segments and battles) from the left window into the map's encoding space results in directives to SAGE to include these grapheme types in a design, with their positional properties interpreted relative to the map's coordinate system.

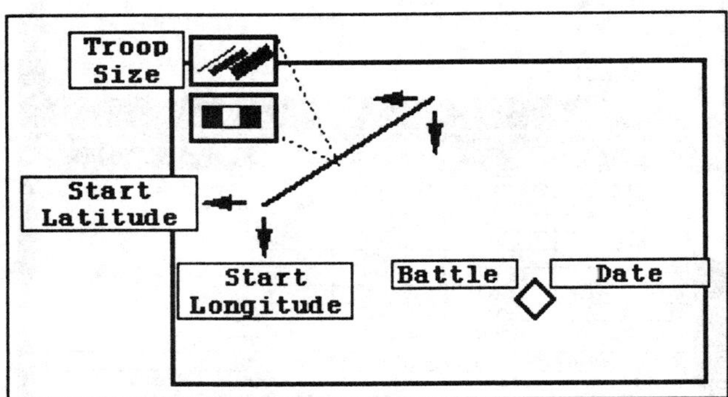

Figure 3: Property selection and data mapping in SageBrush's work area.

Customizing the properties of graphemes. Graphemes have other properties for encoding data besides position. Properties are chosen by selecting *property icons,* displayed by double-clicking a grapheme in the design work area. Double-clicking on the line in Figure 3 displays a menu of line properties (width and color) and arrows representing the positional properties of end-points. Selecting a property directs SAGE to use it to encode data in a design but does not indicate the data to which it corresponds. Double-clicking on a property icon allows users to convey specific directives (e.g. make all marks diamond-shaped or all lines blue; *reject* the use of color).

Completing the graphic requires a way to create *grapheme clusters*. As described above, dragging graphemes into an encoding space results in directives to use their positional properties in a design. When two or more graphemes are dropped close together in the same space, the position of one is interpreted relative to the axes or coordinate system, while the positions of others are interpreted to convey *association* by adjacency. In Figure 3, two text strings have been placed next to the mark (which has been customized to be diamond-shaped) to convey association. Note that Brush only determined that the two strings and diamond are associated. SAGE must infer which of the three is used to convey position in the coordinate system (using knowledge of data characteristics and graphic expressiveness criteria [8,9]). Of course, a user can explicitly double-click on the diamond and select its property icons for position (a pair of arrows).

Communicating the mapping of data to graphics. Dropping a grapheme in a chart and selecting its color result in directives to SAGE to generate a design where position and color encode data. It does not specify which data (i.e. relation domains) to assign to these properties. While SAGE could attempt to infer this (just as it could also make choices of graphemes and properties), users can explicitly make these choices by dragging data labels from the Data Selector (bottom Figure 2), and dropping them on property icons. In Figure 3, Troop Size was mapped to line thickness and Start Latitude and Start Longitude to the position of one end of the line. Battle and Date have been mapped to text labels adjacent to the diamond (dragging a data name into the space simultaneously specifies that a text grapheme be used and maps the data to it). The completed design resulting from this interaction is shown in Roth Color Plate 1b, which was generated by SAGE.

Coordinating multiple design spaces. In addition to defining encoding spaces, prototypes also define *layout spaces*, which enable users to specify the relative positions of prototypes with respect to each other. There are two types of layout spaces, reflecting adjacency and embedding relationships. Adjacency spaces enable horizontal and vertical alignments among charts, tables, maps and other prototypes. Two charts and a table in Figure 5 have been sequenced by placement adjacent to each others' layout spaces. Embedding spaces enable the placement of one prototype within another (e.g. a network placed within a map or chart; a list placed within a network node).

Finally, it is important to emphasize that all of these design choices are optional. Users only need to specify the data they wish to visualize, but may further specify (to any level of completion):

- prototypes only,
- prototypes and additional graphemes,
- graphemes and their properties,
- the mapping of data to graphemes, and
- the mapping of data to specific grapheme properties.

The Napoleon example illustrates that users needn't specify all mappings. The system inferred End Latitude, End Longitude, and Temperature (and could have made choices for the other data, possibly differing from those of the user). The strength of this approach is that it can (1) reduce the amount of work needed to convey design choices and map them to data, (2) enable the construction of composites that could not be created by menu-based approaches, (3) provide design expertise to supplement that of users, and (4) provide design directives for SageBook to use in searching its library of previously constructed pictures.

SAGEBOOK

The goal of Book is to provide users with the ability to create new pictures analogous to existing ones they consider useful. Our intent is to provide users with access to a growing portfolio of graphic designs to provide ideas for visualizing their data. Book capitalizes on the explicit representation of designs and data characteristics by SAGE to provide a vocabulary for expressing search criteria.

Book provides two mechanisms for browsing pictures. The first is a file-folder metaphor analogous to that used in the Macintosh system, in which pictures created by SAGE are named and stored in locations defined by users. The second mechanism provides browsing by two types of picture content: graphical elements and data. Search criteria are based on exact match or partial overlap with data in the Data Selector and/or design elements in Brush.

Figure 4 illustrates the interface for browsing pictures retrieved by a search based on data overlap. The data for the search were facts about activities in a project management database (the final picture is shown in Roth Color Plate 1a). Pictures in the library that expressed similar data were listed by the interface. As a user selects each picture name, its bitmap is displayed. Multiple full size pictures can be displayed and arranged by users for comparison.

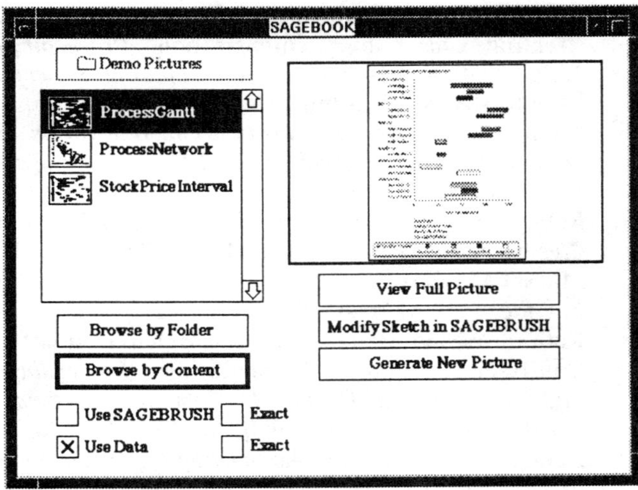

Figure 4: Browsing graphics by their data content in SageBook.

We have designed search criteria for several levels of match overlap based on data. These involve retrieving pictures which:

- show exactly the same data relations/attributes as in the data selector (e.g. find pictures of Activity End),
- contain the selected data in addition to other data,
- show different data that have the same underlying data characteristics.

For example, a *data relation* (to use relational database terms) representing quarterly expenses for a company's departments (Department, Business Quarter, Operating Cost) may have the same properties as another relation for stock market data (Stock, Calendar Date, Shares Traded). Both relations contain three domains with identical data characteristics: a nominal type, a temporal coordinate, and a quantity. There is also exactly one quantity for each nominal-time pair in both relations (i.e. functional dependency). See [8] for a more complete treatment of data characterization relevant to graphic design.

We have designed search criteria for several levels of match overlap based on graphical elements as well. These involve retrieving pictures that (1) show exactly the same design elements as those in the Brush sketch and (2) contain the Brush elements as a subset of a more complex design.

Our current work is addressing the problem of defining match criteria for combinations of data and graphical properties. We are also exploring similarity criteria for defining close matches with partial overlaps. For example, we need criteria for determining whether a network where the *color* of links encodes data is more similar to a chart using the color of bars or to another network where the *widths* of links encode data (i.e. what graphical elements are salient to users). Our intuitions suggest the latter, but a cognitive model based on user studies is needed to define similarity, as well as to verify the appropriate graphical primitives for the Book and Brush interfaces.

Our preliminary view is that searches based on different criteria serve different purposes for users, including:

- discovering how basic techniques can be expanded with additional graphical elements (e.g. how a network can encode using additional text or marks along its links or within its nodes),
- quickly retrieving a picture whose name has been forgotten, but some of whose elements are known,
- minimizing the effort of sketching a new design by retrieving a picture similar to the one desired and then modifying it in Brush.

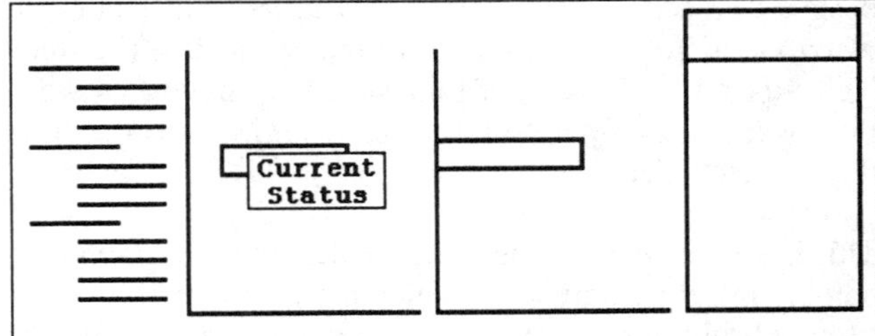

Figure 5: Adding graphics in SageBrush to a picture found using SageBook (see Figure 4).

The last case is illustrated in Figures 4 and 5. Book found an *indented chart* with *color-coded interval bars* for data matching only part of a large data selection (activity, organization, start, end, current-status, labor-cost, resource). The chart was converted to a sketch in Brush, and the user added a bar chart and table aligned with the original interval chart. The user also mapped Current-Status to the interval grapheme, leaving it to automatic mechanisms in SAGE to map it to color (because the original picture used color). SAGE can automatically assign Activity to the Y-axis, dates to the interval bar, and Labor-Cost to the horizontal position of the bars in the added chart, based on expressiveness rules for these graphical properties. The resulting picture is shown in Roth Color Plate 1a. SAGE integrated all design elements and determined appropriate data mappings. Notice that Resource is placed in the table, while Organization is placed in the indentation of the Y-axis...an arbitrary choice that a user can easily reverse. The operations that produced Roth Color Plate 1a can be found in [9].

SUMMARY AND CONCLUSIONS

Our approach views the task of creating visualizations of data as a combination of two interrelated processes:

- *constructing* designs from graphical elements, and
- finding and customizing relevant prior examples.

The extent to which each process occurs varies with user and context. Consequently, we created two tools that play flexible, mutually supportive roles to enable design. SageBrush provides users with an interface for constructing graphic designs and customizing graphics found with SageBook. Brush also enables users to compose graphical queries to be searched using Book.

Another central theme of our approach is the use of automated design knowledge in SAGE to provide new display capabilities, to enhance the usability of graphic design interfaces, and to provide design expertise when needed by users. These are realized in several ways.

First, SAGE enables users to create a wide variety of *integrative* displays, which coordinate multiple spaces, graphemes, and visual properties to show the relationships among several data attributes or data sets. This is possible because SAGE recognizes and parses the structure and semantics of sketches that users construct.

Second, knowledge enables a system to automatically design a graphic when requested by users. This can occur when users do not know how to represent data (i.e. they lack expertise in general or for a specific problem) or when they want to compare alternative designs with the ones they have created.

Third, SAGE reduces the work of designing a graphic by completing it automatically when partially specified. This often eliminates the need for users to assign data to elements of the graphic, select graphical properties once objects are specified, or perform other repetitive selections.

Fourth, SAGE makes it possible to search displays created previously based on meaningful criteria: the data and graphic elements they contain. Without this knowledge, Book would be limited to browsing graphics based on file attributes.

There are many research problems remaining, especially for supporting users with limited graphics expertise. First, the operation of any automatic presentation system depends on the existence of data characterizations [8]. In this research, data characterizations were already present in the database or spreadsheet. We will be exploring ways to infer them or obtain them interactively.

Second, although SAGE considers user information-seeking goals or tasks [1,8,9], no attempt was made to provide users with the ability to specify these. We are considering creating a goal-selection interface so users can convey their intentions as design directives.

Finally, there are numerous new graphic design problems to address, including the design of interactive mechanisms for manipulating data displays, displays of large data sets, and graphical techniques such as animation and 3D. See [7] for a more complete discussion of research problems in this area.

REFERENCES

1. Casner, S. M. A Task-Analytic Approach to the Automated Design of Information Graphic Presentations. *ACM Transactions on Graphics*, 10, 2 (Apr. 1991), 111-151.
2. Fischer, G. Cognitive View of Reuse and Redesign. *IEEE Software*, (July, 1987), 60-72.
3. Mackinlay, J. D. Automating the Design of Graphical Presentations of Relational Information. *ACM Transactions on Graphics*, 5, 2 (Apr. 1986), 110-141.
4. Marks, J. W. Automating the Design of Network Diagrams. Ph.D. thesis, Harvard University, 1991.
5. Myers, B. A., Goldstein, J., and Goldberg, M. A. Creating Charts by Demonstration. *Proceedings SIGCHI'94 Human Factors in Computing Systems,* Boston, MA, ACM, April, 1994.
6. Navin-Chandra, D. *Exploration and Innovation in Design: Towards a Computational Model.* Springer-Verlag, 1991.
7. Roth, S. F. and Hefley, W.E. Intelligent Multimedia Presentation Systems: Research and Principles. In Mark Maybury (Ed.) *Intelligent Multimedia Interfaces,* AAAI Press, 1993, pp. 13-53.
8. Roth, S. F. and Mattis J. Data Characterization for Intelligent Graphics Presentation. *Proceedings SIGCHI'90 Human Factors in Computing Systems*, Seattle, WA, ACM, April, 1990, pp. 193-200.
9. Roth, S. F. and Mattis, J. Automating the Presentation of Information. *Proceedings IEEE Conference on AI Applications*, Miami Beach, FL, Feb. 1991, pp. 90-97.
10. Roth, S. F., Mattis, J., and Mesnard, X. Graphics and Natural Language Generation as Components of Automatic Explanation. In Sullivan and Tyler (Ed.), *Intelligent User Interfaces*, Addison-Wesley, Reading, MA, 1991, 207-239.
11. Tufte, E. R. *The Visual Display of Quantitative Information.* Graphic Press, Cheshire, CT, 1983.

Reflections on. . .

Interactive Graphic Design Using Automatic Presentation Knowledge

Stephen Roth

The first few papers in this section show that the early work in this area was concerned with the problem of representing knowledge computationally and developing mechanisms to use this knowledge to automate presentation design. In contrast, the goal of the work reported in this paper was to take a first step in exploring how people might actually use this technology. We were concerned with developing a useful product concept and identifying research problems needed to produce it. Our initial goal was to explore user interface approaches to enable people to both obtain help from intelligent presentation design systems and convey their visualization requests as they worked on their information-seeking tasks.

We have continued to focus on the theme of developing a complete product concept for automatic presentation technology in our recent work on general data exploration environments. Our goal has been to apply automated visualization techniques to support the ongoing process of analysis for people working in information-intensive domains. This requires being able to use SAGE to generate visualizations as needed without disrupting their analysis work. Although it is still important that SAGE-generated visualizations help users view relationships in data, they must also enable users to

- manipulate data visually to acquire new information by filtering, reorganizing, aggregating, transforming, controlling the level of detail, and navigating through information.
- use visualizations to communicate and collaborate both synchronously and asynchronously.
- use visualizations as interfaces for controlling or interacting with the objects they represent, typically as interfaces to applications.

Our recent work has focused on embedding the process of creating visualizations in a comprehensive user interface environment, called Visage, for working in information-intensive domains. Visage provides an "information-centric" approach to UI design, in which every graphical object representing data is fully interactive. Therefore, it can be manipulated to perform a set of operations common to the entire environment (e.g., drag and drop, drill down, aggregation, selection, painting). The environment enables SAGE-generated visualizations to be copied and dragged into briefing slides, where they maintain their interactive behavior even as part of presentations. Furthermore, we are developing visual query interfaces that enable users to navigate through data using a combination of direct manipulation operations and query construction, both coordinated with SAGE-generated visualizations.

A second major application of the SAGE technology is as the graphics component of a multimedia presentation planning system called AutoBrief, which summarizes important patterns and changes in data sets using coordinated text and graphics. There are two needs for interactivity in this context. First, as with the generation of visualizations in Visage, Autobrief's generated text and graphic summaries must themselves be vehicles by which people further manipulate and explore the data. Second, they must serve as interfaces for follow-up questions. Our recent multimedia work continues this theme of empowering automatically generated presentations with interactive capabilities to support data exploration.

REFERENCES

Derthick, M.; Kolojejchick, J. A.; and Roth, S. F. 1997. An Interactive Visual Query Environment for Exploring Data. In *Proceedings of the Symposium on User Interface Software and Technology—UIST '97*, Vancouver, November, 1997. 189–198.

Kerpedjiev, S.; Carenini, G.; Roth, S. F.; and Moore, J. D. 1997. Integrating Planning and Task-Based Design for Multimedia Presentation. In *Proceedings of the International Conference on Intelligent User Interfaces (IUI'97)*, Orlando, FL, January, 145–152.

Kolojejchick, J. A.; Roth, S. F.; and Lucas, P. 1997. Information Appliances and Tools in Visage. *IEEE Computer Graphics and Applications* 17(4) July/August: 32–41.

Roth, S. F.; Chuah, M. C.; Kerpedjiev, S.; Kolojejchick, J. A.; and Lucas, P. (in press). Towards an Information Visualization Workspace: Combining Multiple Means of Expression. *Human-Computer Interaction Journal*, 12(1,2): 131–185.

SECTION IV

Automated Layout

The physical format and layout of a presentation often conveys the structure, intention, and significance of the underlying information and therefore plays an important role in presentation consistency, coherency, and effectiveness. The layout of media objects has a strong influence on the attentional structure of multimodal discourse. The user's focus of attention can be guided by using a functional layout that reflects intended communicative effects.

In the age of intelligent multimedia interfaces, it is unreasonable to expect that a human layout specialist's participation would be required for each and every screen that the user sees. Multimedia objects are too dynamic and come too fast to have the layout of every visual presentation designed manually.

As the complexity of multimedia presentation systems and interfaces increases, the role of automatic layout has become more important. Many multimedia content providers are not necessarily expert graphic artists, so the capture and deployment of good layout principles can provide for presentations what spell and grammar checkers do for text.

In most industrial applications, such as multimedia presentation generation, flowchart design, electronic publishing, and Internet access, the inherent layout design and realization tasks crucially rely on efficient, effective, flexible, and adaptive user interfaces. This has created an urgent need to build advanced tools for passive and active viewing, based on powerful features like customized/customizable display layouts at appropriate and convenient levels of abstraction.

Significant work has been done on automated graphical and multimedia layout with the realization that the task is difficult. In practice, the design of an efficient layout strategy for multimedia presentations—treated as a search and optimization problem—has proved to be a complicated computational process. In addition to the complexity of any single layout, multimedia layout also makes strong demands for flexibility, including the demands for multiple pagination strategies, varying and prioritized optimization criteria, and heterogeneous user-specific and application-specific, geometric-topologic, and semantic-pragmatic layout constraints.

The research underlying layout systems covers a broad spectrum of heterogeneous layout mechanisms, ranging from traditionally specified specialized algorithms to general AI-based tools. Procedural pagination and layout techniques comprise the large set of graph-drawing algorithms and dynamic programming-based methods. Search and optimization mechanisms include numerical optimization (e.g., linear and integer programming), heuristic and stochastic search, constraint satisfaction, physical simulations (e.g., simulated annealing), and genetic algorithms.

Grammar-driven approaches formulate layout requirements and styles as rules of a multidimensional (relational or graph layout) grammar. Knowledge-based layout systems encode general layout expertise by means of a declarative knowledge representation using rule-based, constraint-based, and case-based formalisms, coupled with efficient problem-solving mechanisms for the computation of the layout.

The following five papers each focus on three different aspects of layout: text layout (Hovy and Arens), informational graphics (Christensen, Marks, and Shieber), and graphics-text combinations (Feiner; Graf; Weitzman and Wittenburg); each employs a different mechanism to achieve a layout within their domain. Together, they provide a representative overview of automated layout during the last decade.

One of the first attempts to create an automated system for the layout of combinations of multiple media is presented by Feiner's graphical interface design system, GRIDS, which was developed in the context of the COMET project at Columbia University. GRIDS is constructed as an experimental rule-based system to investigate approaches to the automatic display layout of text and illustrations. Here the layout process is guided by the concept of graphical design grids, which are generated automatically with respect to information about the input material (e.g., scaling and cropping factors), the user profile, display restrictions, and legibility rules. After creating a prototype layout based on these rules, an actual instance of a layout is produced by scaling and placing display objects. A first prototype version of the testbed system was implemented using OPS5 augmented with LISP.

The second paper addresses the problem of automatically generating formatted text. Text is not the key idea but only a medium of sufficient structural richness (e.g., so-called text devices like display, footnotes, indentation, enumeration, etc.) to provide a framework for demonstrating how you can match the intended semantics of these text devices with the text content to be formatted. Hovy and Arens use Rhetorical Structure Theory (RST) to represent the structure underlying the text design process and then show how that representation can be exploited to derive an effective layout of text items. To achieve this, each text device is identified with a specific communicative function, then used as the basis for creating a layout pattern realized concretely using LaTeX.

In the third paper, Graf describes the constraint-based layout manager, LayLab, developed as an integral component of the multimedia presentation system WIP. The design of a compact and aesthetically pleasing layout is treated as a multidimensional satisfaction problem, articulated as a general finite discrete search problem and an optimization problem. LayLab's kernel consists of two dedicated constraint solvers: a finite domain constraint solver and an incremental hierarchical solver, integrated as a multilayered layout constraint engine. The constraint engine is triggered from a common metalevel consisting of layout rules and defaults. Individual display fragments are placed on an automatically generated grid. The underlying constraint language is able to encode graphical design knowledge expressed by semantic/pragmatic, geometrical/topological, and temporal relations; it also supports the use of prioritized constraints. In addition to constraint-based positioning, LayLab includes an automatic grid generator, a semantic-based typographer, and an interaction handler. Overall, LayLab demonstrates how rhetorical structure can be automatically deployed via constraint processing to influence the intentional and attentional state of the user.

Many types of informational graphics use text labels adjacent to visual features for annotation. If the text for explaining graphical elements is generated dynamically in an adaptive interface, a layout component must ensure the clarity of graphical displays by positioning the text labels in such a way that they do not obscure important display features.

Using an empirical approach, Christensen, Marks, and Shieber address the problem of placing text labels on diagrams as a combinatorial optimization problem known as the *point-feature label placement* (PFLP) problem. Within a classical framework defined by a search space and objective function, the authors consider label placement on geographic maps and diagrams, where the major difficulty is simultaneously placing labels in the correct position while maintaining legibility. The objective function assigns to each potential labeling as an element of the search space a value that corresponds to the relative quality of that labeling. Finding an optimal solution for such a layout problem by exhaustive search is known to be intractable. The empirical study uses a greedy algorithm to quickly generate an initial solution and then provides two heuristic improvement algorithms (one based on a variant of gradient descent and the other on simulated annealing), which are compared to provide insight into the time-versus-quality trade-off in solving PFLP problems. The experiments argue for the use of simulated annealing over the other alternatives, even for time-critical applications that require on-line layout.

In the final paper of this section, Weitzman and Wittenburg describe a grammar-based approach to automatic multimedia layout. In particular, Relational Grammars with semantic attributes are used to encode layout knowledge. Relational Grammars are higher-dimensional extensions to string-based grammars that can deal with arbitrary semantic relations among information objects. The context-free rewrite rules are annotated by semantic attributes that are used to generate code for creating media objects. The layout process based on Relational Grammars consists of three steps: parsing, syntax-directed translation, and constraint resolution. A bottom-up, nondeterministic parser is used to analyze the input set of content objects as well as the domain-dependent relations that hold between them. Ambiguity in derivations may lead to alternative layout solutions. Given a derivation tree, the translation phase determines a set of media objects to be created and a set of spatial and temporal constraints to be installed. Each terminal rule of the grammar installs local constraints between the media elements of the rule body. Rules for creating composite layout structures then link these smaller constraint networks together. As in Graf's LayLab system, the DeltaBlue constraint propagation algorithm is used as a basis for the final constraint satisfaction phase, which determines the actual numerical values for spatial positioning. Weitzman and Wittenburg show that it is possible to use the same input, but different layout grammars, to achieve unique styles of presentation. They consider the characteristics of the output medium as part of the input to the parser and thus make the layout sensitive to the output requirements (e.g., a large high-resolution display versus a small hand-held digital assistant).

Despite the significant work on automated layout over the past several years and the commercial proliferation of a variety of multimedia content and authoring tools, very little of this research has been exploited. The layout of typical presentation tools is usually determined statically in rigid patterns that are incapable of any adaptation to content or coordination of media. Also missing are any coherent integration of high-level authoring tools that provide support for intent-based layout facilities and any content-based reuse strategies that exploit the semantics and pragmatics of the presentation.

Most of the relevant work on automated layout concentrates on single media types—for example, in the context of graphics generation—and has not supported the interaction between layout design and content planning. Furthermore, investigations have mainly been concerned with syntactic aspects of layout, whereas the communicative function has only been treated in a rudimentary way.

Unsurprisingly, at least in retrospect, a certain pattern of underlying software architecture is developing, typified by the comparison of the treatment of automated layout as either a classical search and optimization problem or a constraint satisfaction problem. In both cases, a clear separation exists between knowledge about valid layouts and knowledge about improvements to a layout. This separation provides a framework both for structuring the articulation of layout semantics (layout intent, semantics, and pragmatics of interacting objects) and for structuring the problem-solving process to exploit those semantics. The development of sophisticated layout modules will be expedited by further exploitation of this evolving software architecture. As it matures, it is likely to provide stability and robustness for the development of commercial multimedia authoring tools.

A GRID-BASED APPROACH TO AUTOMATING DISPLAY LAYOUT

Steven Feiner

Department of Computer Science
Columbia University
New York, NY 10027

Abstract

A research testbed is described for exploring the automated layout of graphical displays. We address the problem of determining the size and position of the objects displayed to a user. Our approach is based on the graphic design concept of a design grid. A design grid is a set of proportionally-spaced vertical and horizontal lines that control the position and size of the objects being laid out. The system first generates a grid intended for a set of possible displays, based on information about the kind of material to be displayed, the user, and the display hardware. The grid is next used, in conjunction with further information about the kinds of objects to be presented, to create a prototype display layout. This prototype display layout determines how each actual set of objects will be sized and positioned in the displays presented to the user.

Keywords: user interface design, graphical layout, design grids

1. Introduction

Recent experiments in interface design have explored the use of direct manipulation graphical editors to lay out an application's displays [HANA80; FEIN82; WONG82; BUXT83; GREE85; OLSE85; HOLL86; MYER86]. Ideally, these systems allow a user to design an interface that has exactly the visual appearance that he or she desires. They have shown some dramatic results in allowing users, both programmers and nonprogrammers, to design certain kinds of interfaces in less time than it would take using conventional methods.

There are several problems, however, with the editor-based approach to interface design. First, most users are unfortunately not experienced graphic designers, let alone interface designers. That the system does exactly what its designer wants is therefore not enough: the designer has to want the right interface to begin with. It is true, however, that by making it easier to create and modify an interface, successive refinement is encouraged. Therefore, the designer may be more willing to change the interface in response to user pressure (or their own attempts to use it). Early editor-based systems provided only the simplest of layout assistance, such as the user-specified layout grids of IGD [FEIN82]. In contrast, more recent projects, such as Peridot [MYER86] and Designer [HOLL86], have begun to address this problem by monitoring the designer's actions and offering rule-based suggestions to help the user craft a better display.

Second, although the information to be presented and its general format may be known in advance, there may be a large, heterogeneous user community and a diversity of situations under which the material is to be viewed. One common approach attempts to take this into account in the initial design phase by providing a fixed set of different display types. Unfortunately, this may still result in grouping users and situations in overly large equivalence classes. Users and situations differ in seemingly small, but important, ways and our systems should be able to adapt to these.

Finally, there are many situations, such as command and control, and maintenance and repair, in which diverse, and sometimes unexpected, information must be presented on the fly. Here, timely presentation of information is essential, yet there may be no time for the presentation to be developed in advance.

In recognition of these problems, a number of researchers have investigated automated generation of both the form and content of graphical presentations, representative of which are [FRIE84; FEIN85a; MACK86]. There is a host of difficult problems associated with tasks such as determining what information is to be presented, when it is to be presented, what format it will be presented in, and what kind of user input will be accepted. In contrast, the system described here concentrates only on the layout of separately generated information. Thus, we assume that the specific material to be laid out will be provided as input.

2. Automating layout

At the core of the graphics layout problem that we are investigating is the task of determining the positions and sizes of a set of graphical objects. In the work described here, we use information about the objects to be displayed, the user, and the display. We intentionally ignore the possibility of interactions between layout generation and content generation.

This work is supported in part by the Defense Advanced Research Projects Agency under Contract N00039-84-C-0165 and the New York State Center for Advanced Technology under Contract NYSSTF-CAT(87)-5.

Our implementation requires that objects to be laid out are nonoverlapping upright rectangles. Even with these restrictions a layout problem may be quite costly to solve. Beach [BEAC85] has pointed out that determining whether an arbitrary set of nonoverlapping rectangular objects can fit on a display is *NP*-complete, as is finding the minimum size rectangle in which the objects can be packed. Although the layout resulting from a space minimization strategy alone may be quite space-efficient, it may also be difficult to use and understand. The challenge is to develop a set of constraints and evaluation criteria that will result in the generation of effective layouts, while simultaneously restricting the possibilities that must be considered. Happily, there are proven approaches to display layout in which arbitrary sizing and placement of objects are expressly prohibited.

3. Grid-based layout

Grid-based layout has provided a particularly influential and effective framework for graphic design [HURL78; MULL81]. In this design technique, the designer divides the design space with a rectangular *design grid*, whose lines are positioned in proportions based on the size of the space, the material being laid out, and the purpose for which the layout is designed. When layout is performed using the grid, objects are typically sized and positioned so that they are aligned with the grid lines and occupy an integral number of grid fields both horizontally and vertically.

Design grids often consist of a set of regularly spaced vertical and horizontal lines that describe a set of equal-sized rectangular grid *fields*. The fields are separated vertically and horizontally by equal-sized spaces and the entire array of fields is surrounded on the display by top, bottom, and side margins. In general, fields need not be of equal size, but there are many designers who follow these restrictions, in some cases further constraining the fields to be square.

Grid-based layout has been used extensively for magazine and newspaper design. In these applications, a single grid is developed for the generic material to be laid out and then is used for each page. The concept of the design grid has been adapted by Friedell [FRIE84] for positioning groups of icons and by Beach [BEAC85] for table layout. In Beach's system, a table is laid out from a user-provided specification of its contents, which includes the column and row position of each item in the table. Given these relative item positions, a constraint-based system determines the position and size of the columns and rows, guided by a style sheet specified for the layout.

Our system generates the original grid itself and completely determines the mapping of objects to positions in the grid. First a grid is created, based on information about the material to be laid out, the display, and the user. In part the information consists of a grammar, discussed later, describing the kind of material to be presented in actual displays. The actual objects that will be encountered in a particular display may be thought of as instances of these general classes of objects whose properties and relationships are input during the grid design phase. The system currently supports pictures, text blocks, and headings, which the user must further specialize by designating limits on their expected size and contents.

Next, the grid that the system produces is used in conjunction with information about the material to generate a *prototype display layout*. This prototype is then used to determine how to lay out input instances of the objects described by the display grammar to form actual displays.

By generating a grid first and using it to produce multiple layouts, we gain one of the important advantages of grid-based design: consistency. Each layout of a set is not optimized as an individual design problem, but bears a visual relationship to the others. Not only do we gain efficiency in not having to redesign each display afresh, but the use of a common layout format visually enforces the relationship between the displays. Furthermore, the regular spacing of the grid, and hence the regular sizes and positions of the objects embedded in it, also helps achieve a coherent, consistent look for an individual display [MULL81].

4. Designing the grid

Our system is a rule-based testbed that embodies a vastly simplified version of one of many possible approaches to display layout. It begins by determining the size of the individual grid field that will serve as the building block from which a grid of uniform-sized fields will be constructed. The field's size is derived from information about the pictures and text to be laid out and the user's position.

The distance at which the display will be viewed is used, in conjunction with legibility rules, to determine the point size to be used to set body text. This in turn determines the leading or vertical space between successive lines of type. The point size and leading for headings is determined similarly. Rules for legibility further determine an appropriate line length and hence the width of a text block. Information about the expected character count of textual material that will be included in the displays allows the system to determine an approximate number of lines, and hence an expected height for the text block.

The input includes a normalized size for the pictures. This normalized size specifies the minimum width and height that the picture must have in order to be understandable when viewed at a set distance. In conjunction with the viewer's distance it determines the actual minimum size at which the picture must be reproduced.

In the uniform-size grid field design scheme adopted, the field size is determined by the size of the smallest picture or text block to be laid out, further constrained so that the field is tall enough to hold an integral number of lines of text. In the layout style espoused by [MULL81], and currently enforced by our system, the ascender of the topmost line of type in a field is set flush with the top of the field, while the descender of the bottommost line of type in the field is set flush with bottom of the field. All lines of type are separated vertically by the previously determined leading. The vertical space between the grid fields must also hold an integral number of lines of text, although it includes leading above and below the first and last text lines respectively. This approach allows a passage of text to span multiple vertical grid fields, while still maintaining the same relationship to the top and bottom lines in each full grid field. The result of these constraints can be seen in the figures presented below.

If a picture does not exactly span an integral number of grid fields, it must be further scaled and/or cropped. In previous work, we explored the automated design of sequences of pictures that explain how to perform actions in a 3D world [FEIN85b]. Each of these pictures included information about the extent that bounds the essential material in the picture that must be displayed. The pictures discussed here are assumed to have this information. Cropping thus involves uniform scaling of the material in the extent if the aspect ratio will correctly span full grid fields or actual expansion of the extent vertically or horizontally. An interesting issue not addressed here is whether additional information or background should be shown by expanding the extent or whether the picture can be generated with an aspect ratio that takes into account knowledge of the grid design.

The horizontal space between horizontally adjacent grid fields must be wide enough to separate objects, such as columns of text, from each other. Furthermore, the array of grid fields containing the text and pictures is offset from the top, bottom, and sides of the display by margins. The display size is given as part of the input to the system. The size of the margins are currently set according to a standard ratio. Since proportionally-spaced fonts are used and the exact text being set is not yet known when the grid is being defined, there is some leeway in adjusting the width of the grid fields in conjunction with the margins and grid field horizontal spacing. Thus, extra slack can be distributed among the horizontal space between fields, the margins, and the width of the grid fields. Figure 1 shows the grid designed for a display whose size is indicated by the outermost rectangle. This is a scaled-down version of a grid designed for an 8½" by 11" display to be viewed at a distance of 20". Note that the lines of the grid are not actually drawn in the finished display.

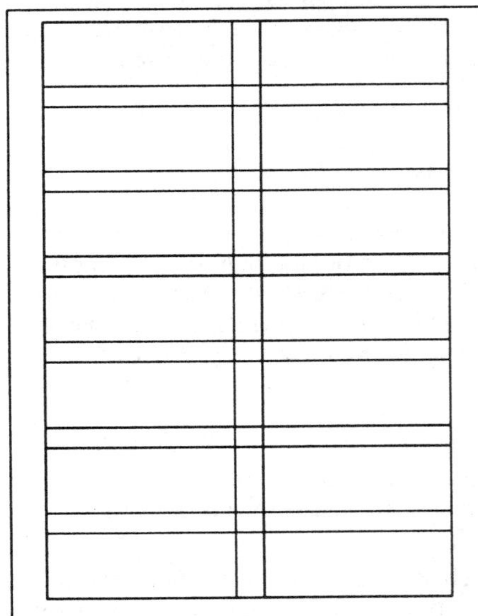

Figure 1: A scaled-down version of a grid designed for an 8½" by 11" display to be viewed at 20". The outermost rectangle defines the display's boundaries.

5. Prototype display grammar

The input used in designing the grid describes subclasses of pictures, text blocks, and headings by specifying bounds on their expected size (number of characters for text blocks and heads and normalized size for pictures). These are prototypes of the objects that will actually be laid out. In addition, these prototypes may be grouped together to define aggregates. Different kinds of groups may be specified, indicating the relationships that hold between their members. Groups are currently constrained to form a single hierarchy with arbitrarily deep nesting. In practice, however, display layouts (as opposed to the complex diagrams that they may contain) do not seem to evidence very deep nesting.

Our current system allows distinguishing whether a group's objects form an ordered or unordered set. For example, a collection of pictures may be an unordered set, while a set of pairs of pictures and text illustrating the steps of a maintenance and repair task may form a sequence. Groups are also used to perform alternation and repetition. Groups thus function as the operators at the internal nodes of a syntax tree whose leaves are the various kinds of pictures, text blocks, and headings from which a display may be constructed.

At the highest level, the entirety of the material to be displayed is organized as a single group. This may be thought of as a *prototype display grammar*, an example of which is shown pictorially in Figure 2. The prototype display grammar defines the underlying logical structure of a class of actual displays whose contents will be input later. The next step is to develop a prototype display layout.

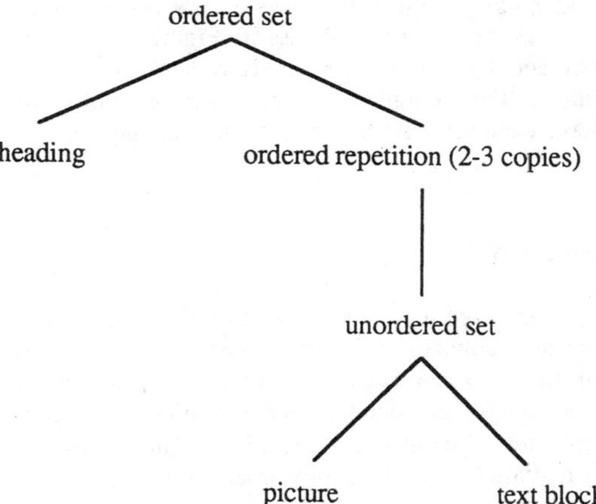

Figure 2: A pictorial representation of a prototype display grammar.

6. Designing a prototype display layout

We have designed a set of rules for each of the different kinds of grouping strategies that determine how their components should be laid out. For example, all of the elements in a sequence will be laid ordered either vertically or horizontally across the page.

The layout algorithm employs a generate and test strategy, traversing the prototype tree bottom-up from the leaves. At each node a set of layout alternatives is generated, based on the layout of its children. The first (and current) algorithm employed initially excludes from generation only alternatives that exceed the bounds of the grid. It generates the entire space of design alternatives before selecting an alternative for each node. The evaluation criteria with which we are experimenting favor designs in which identical elements in a sequence are laid out similarly, and in which horizontal and vertical layout approaches alternate down a branch.

7. Laying out an actual display

Creating a prototype display layout does not produce any graphical output. After the prototype display layout has been created, it can be used to determine the layout of one or more actual displays, based on a description of the input objects of which they are composed. This input consists of a list of object instances, the prototype class with which each is associated, and the actual contents of each instance (which must be consistent with the originally provided descriptions of their prototypes). Each object is then sized and positioned using information generated for its class during the creation of the prototype display layout. Members of sequential groups are processed in sequence to allow the layout of later objects to depend on the positions and sizes of earlier ones.

Figure 3a shows the grid of Figure 1 populated with a set of objects that are accepted by the prototype display grammar of Figure 2. In the current implementation the pictures are grey tone rectangles whose size and placement are determined by the system, while text is represented by hardwired sentences that the system positions and generates in the appropriate font, point size, and leading. Figure 3b shows the display without the grid visible, as the viewer would see it. Figure 4 shows the same set of objects laid out in different sized displays with different grids. All of the figures are generated for an observer at 20" and have been scaled down to ¼ of their actual size.

8. Implementation

The majority of the layout system is implemented in OPS5, a production system language [FORG81]. The drawing routines are written in Lisp and generate a human-readable intermediate file that forms a device-independent representation of the grid and the specific sets of picture and text that are laid out using it. The intermediate file is further processed for interactive display on a bitmapped workstation. It can also be automatically converted to PostScript [ADOB85], which was done to produce the figures included in this paper.

Eventually, we intend to lay out actual pictures and text generated by a companion project [FEIN88]. Therefore, there has been no emphasis on providing other than a program interface for specifying the information needed to build the grid or to describe the contents of a display.

9. Conclusions

We have described the beginnings of a testbed system for investigating the automated layout of graphical displays. The work described here is a preliminary implementation of one part of an architecture for generating both layout and information content automatically [FEIN88]. It has been used to explore the rule-based generation and use of a graphic design grid that governs the display layout process. Because the system is intended to be provided with the actual items to be laid out, it is not responsible for choosing the high-level display design style that determines the identities of these objects.

The current implementation has a number of serious limitations which we intend to address. Many of these are caused by the graphic design rules that the system uses, which are extremely rudimentary and often vastly oversimplified. For example, a number of decisions, such as font choice, are stated a priori. As well, the system has no concept of design basics such as visual balance or rhythm. One area of particular interest is that of design compromises. For example, if the minimum legible point size for a given viewer distance and font causes a block of text to be set so large that it won't fit on a small display, the system currently fails to develop a design, instead of producing an inferior one.

Nonhierarchical layout constraints are not currently provided, so there is no way to indicate that the same layout decisions should be used in disjoint parts of a display. Thus, two groups whose components have identical descriptions may be laid out in totally different ways. As well, the primitives implemented so far must be augmented to include input as well as output primitives.

We are also trying to develop strategies for prototype layout design that involve more careful pruning of the layout alternatives generated, backtracking to avoid the exponential growth of the design search space, and improved criteria for evaluating design alternatives. Although the current system can handle only an extremely small subset of designs, it was intended to provide a framework in which to develop ideas that could help point the way toward future, more powerful systems.

10. Acknowledgements

Mary Jones helped critique some of the system's first layouts and provided valuable suggestions for improvements, most of which still remain to be made. The Hewlett-Packard Company, through its AI University Grants Program, generously donated the equipment on which the testbed is being developed.

References

[ADOB85] Adobe Systems Inc. *PostScript Language Reference Manual.* MA: Addison-Wesley, 1985.

[BEAC85] Beach, R. *Setting Tables and Illustrations with Style.* Ph.D. Thesis, Dept. of Computer Science, University of Waterloo, Ontario, 1985. (Xerox PARC Report CSL-85-3, May 1985).

[BUXT83] Buxton, B. "Toward a Comprehensive User Interface Management System." *Computer Graphics*, 17:3, July 1983, 35-42.

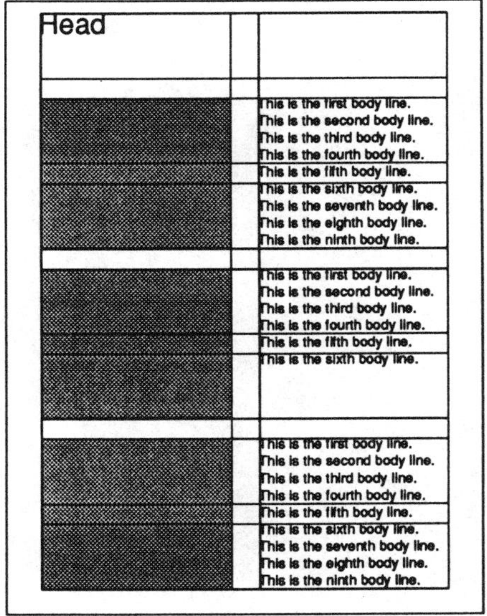

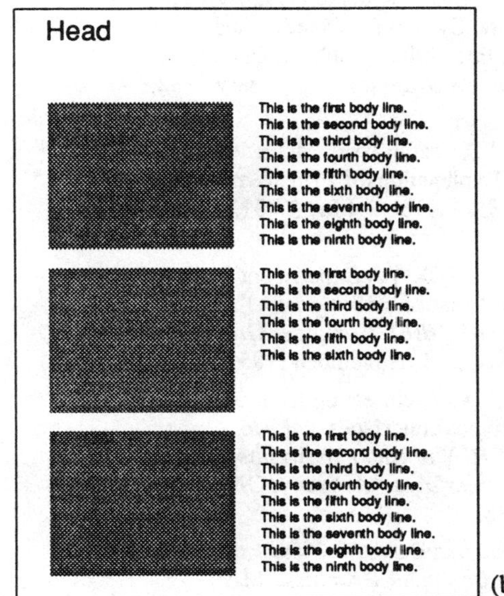

Figure 3: (a) The grid of Figure 1, populated with a set of objects accepted by the prototype display grammar of Figure 2. (b) The display as presented to the user.

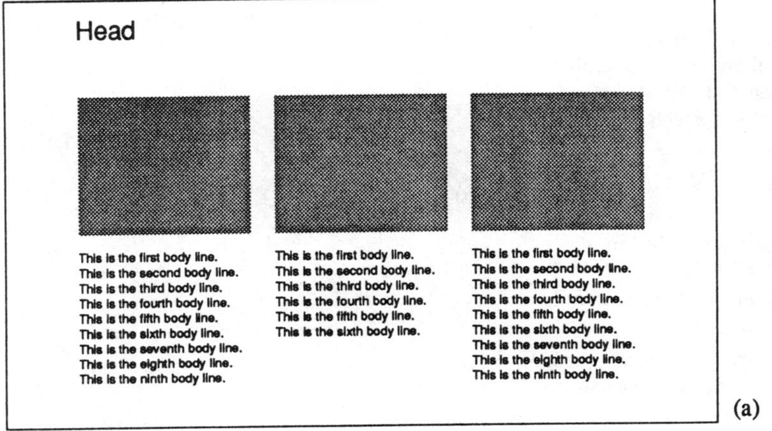

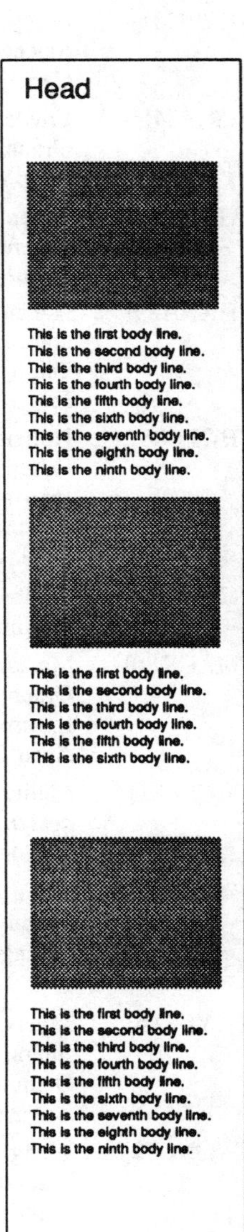

Figure 4: (a) The layout designed for a 14" by 8½" display. (b) The layout designed for a 4¼" by 22" display.

[FEIN82] Feiner, S., Nagy, S., and van Dam, A. "An Experimental System for Creating and Presenting Interactive Graphical Documents." *ACM Trans. on Graphics*, 1:1 January 1982, 59-77.

[FEIN85a] Feiner, S. "Research Issues in Generating Graphical Explanations." *Proc. Graphics Interface '85*, Montreal, May 27-31, 1985, 117-123.

[FEIN85b] Feiner, S. "APEX: An Experiment in the Automated Creation of Pictorial Explanations." *IEEE Computer Graphics and Applications*, 5:11, November 1985, 29-38.

[FEIN88] Feiner, S. "An Architecture for Knowledge-Based Graphical Interfaces." *Proc. ACM/SIGCHI Workshop on Architectures for Intelligent Interfaces*, Monterey, CA, Mar 29 - Apr 1, 1988.

[FOLE82] Foley, J. and van Dam, A. *Fundamentals of Interactive Computer Graphics*. MA: Addison-Wesley, 1982.

[FORG81] Forgy, C. *OPS5 User's Manual*. Computer Science Technical Report CMU-CS-81-135, Carnegie-Mellon University, July 1981.

[FRIE84] Friedell, M. "Automatic Synthesis of Graphical Object Descriptions." *Computer Graphics*, 18:3, July 1984, 53-62.

[GREE85] Green, M. "The University of Alberta Use Interface Management System." *Computer Graphics*, 19:3, July 1985, 205-213.

[HANA80] Hanau, P. and Lenorovitz, D. "Prototyping and Simulation Tools for User/Computer Dialogue Design." *Computer Graphics*, 14:3, July 1980, 271-278.

[HOLL86] Hollan, J., Hutchins, E., McCandless, T., Rosenstein, M., and Weitzman, L. "Graphical Interfaces for Simulation." In W. Rouse, ed., *Advances in Man-Machine Systems*, vol. 3, Greenwich, CT: Jai Press, 1986.

[HURL78] Hurlburt, A. *The Grid*. NY: Van Nostrand Reinhold Co., 1978.

[MACK86] Mackinlay, J. "Automating the Design of Graphical Presentations of Relational Information." *ACM Trans. on Graphics*, 5:2, April 1986, 110-141.

[MULL81] Müller-Brockmann, J. *Grid systems in graphic design*. Niederteufen, Switzerland: Verlag Arthur Niggli, 1981.

[OLSE85] Olsen Jr., D., Dempsey, E., and Rogge, R. "Input/Output Linkage in a User Interface Management System." *Computer Graphics*, 19:3, July 1983, 191-197.

[MYER86] Myers, B. and Buxton, B. "Creating Highly-Interactive and Graphical User Interfaces by Demonstration." *Computer Graphics*, 20:4, August 1986, 249-258.

[WONG82] Wong, P., and Reid, E. "FLAIR – User Interface Dialog Design Tool." *Computer Graphics*, 16:3, July 1982, 87-98.

Reflections on. . .

A Grid-Based Approach to Automating Display Layout

Steven K. Feiner

The system described in this paper was intended to be the first version of a spatial layout component for multimedia presentations, which would ultimately determine the size and position of text, graphics, and virtual interaction devices. Over the year following the paper's publication, I rewrote the system's original OPS5 and Lisp code in CLIPS and C to gain efficiency and clarity, and christened it GRIDS (Graphical Interface Design System) (Feiner 1991). When my group and Kathy McKeown's group began our collaboration on what was to become the COMET multimedia generation system (see Feiner and McKeown (1991) Section II in this collection), I reserved work on GRIDS for myself. As things turned out, however, I never found the time to extend GRIDS to support the layout needs of COMET's media generators or to build the application program interfaces to incorporate it into COMET. Instead, we developed a simple layout component for COMET that positioned monolithic text and illustration areas and left COMET's IBIS graphics generation system (see Seligmann and Feiner (1991), Section III in this collection) with the task of laying out the subparts of a hierarchical illustration.

At the heart of what GRIDS borrows from the grid-based graphic design process that inspired it is the notion of *two-phase* design. Although this was a fundamental theme of the conceptual architecture for knowledge-based multimedia generation systems proposed in (Feiner 1991), it was never incorporated in COMET. The key idea here is that a flexible prototype design for a general class of presentations is created in the first design phase and is then applied to any number of actual presentations in the second phase. This avoids the need to plan similar presentations from scratch and at the same time preserves a consistent look among presentations. To accomplish this, GRIDS is initially presented with the logical structure of a class of presentations, expressed as a simple grammar that encodes the range of possible presentations, such as the relationships among elements, the maximum number of characters in a text block, or the minimum size required for a particular kind of picture to be legible at a normalized distance. GRIDS then creates a design grid and method for using it that can lay out any presentation that obeys the grammar, much as a graphic designer may create a single design grid to lay out all issues of a magazine.

GRIDS was limited in the kinds of designs that it could synthesize because it did not have a general-purpose, numeric-constraint-satisfaction system. The simplistic generate-and-test approach that it used also made it time consuming to generate layouts for more than a relatively small number of objects (although many real-world design examples fall well within this range). Both of these general issues have been addressed in more recent systems, such as IMPROVISE (Zhou and Feiner 1997), which uses a hierarchical decomposition partial-order planner and a numeric constraint solver to perform a variety of graphics generation and layout tasks.

REFERENCES

Feiner, S. 1991. An Architecture for Knowledge-Based Graphical Interfaces. In Sullivan, J., and Tyler, S. (eds.), *Intelligent User Interfaces*, 259–279. Reading, MA: Addison-Wesley.

Zhou, M., and Feiner, S. 1997. Top-Down Hierarchical Planning of Coherent Visual Discourse. In *Proceedings of the 1997 International Conference on Intelligent User Interfaces*, 129–136. New York: Association for Computing Machinery.

Automatic Generation of Formatted Text

Eduard H. Hovy* and Yigal Arens†

Information Sciences Institute of USC
4676 Admiralty Way
Marina del Rey, CA 90292-6695
hovy@isi.edu, arens@isi.edu

Abstract

Few texts longer than a paragraph are written without appropriate formatting. To ensure readability, automated text generation programs must not only plan and generate their texts but be able to format them as well. We describe how work on the automated planning of multisentence text and on the display of information in a multimedia system led to the insight that text formatting devices such as footnotes, italicized regions, enumerations, etc., can be planned automatically by a text structure planning process. This is achieved by recognizing that each formatting device fulfills a specific communicative function in a text, and that such functions can be defined in terms of the text structure relations used as plans in a text planning system. An example is presented in which a text is planned from a semantic representation to a final form that includes English sentences and LaTeX formatting commands, intermingled as appropriate.

The Problem: Text Layout

No paper is submitted to this conference without a heading, section titles, and occasional italicized text; and most of them contain itemized lists, footnotes, indented quotations, boldfaced terms, and other formatting devices.

Why? The reason is clear: each such formatting device carries its own idiosyncratic meaning, and writers select the device that best serves their communicative intent at each point in the text.

A more interesting question is: How? That is, how do writers know what device to use at each point? How is device selection integrated with the text production process in general? Can the two processes be automated — can a text production system be made to plan not only the content and structure of the text but also the appropriate textual formatting for it?

The answer is yes, and this paper describes an experiment that demonstrates this ability.

Though manuals of style (such as [CMS 82, APA 83, Van Leunen 79]) may seem relevant, they contain little more than precise descriptions of the preferred forms of textual devices in fact. Their recommendations of use, when provided, are not detailed enough to help in the selection process itself. Instead, our approach to this problem builds upon ideas and techniques proven useful for multisentence text generation (specifically, text planning) and multimedia communication planning (specifically, the problem of best integrating different media, such as language, diagrams, tables, maps, etc., into a single coherent display. In research on these two questions, we came to realize that the problem of text formatting forms a natural point midway between pure text planning on the one hand and pure multimedia display planning on the other: though text formatting devices have features that make them resemble different media (two-dimensional offset in some cases, highlighting in others, etc.), they remain essentially textual. This similarity enabled us to extend some of the previous work on text planning done at USC/ISI (see [Hovy 88, Moore & Paris 89]) over the past several years to perform not only standard text structure planning but also text formatting.

The next section describes our characterization of text formatting devices. The section that follows it describes how we extended our text planner to handle the requirements of text layout, including an example of the generation, from a semantic representation, of a formatted segment of an Air Traffic Control manual — the type of document which would be difficult to comprehend without appropriate textual devices. The final section provides a description of the definition of additional text formatting devices and discusses shortcomings in the relevant theories.

*This author was supported in part by the Rome Air Development Center under RADC contract FQ7619-89-03326-0001.

†This author was supported by the Defense Advanced Research Projects Agency under Strategic Computing program contract no. MDA-903-87-C-0641.

Textual Devices

In the course of our work on automated modality selection (described in some detail in [Arens & Hovy 90]), we noticed an interesting fact: not only are the different text layouts and styles (plain text, itemized lists, enumerations, italicized text, inserts, etc., which we here call **Textual Devices**) used systematically in order to convey information, but *it is possible to define their communicative semantics precisely enough for them to be used in a text planner*. What's more, the systematicity holds across various types of texts, genres, and registers of formality. It is found in books, articles, advertisements, papers, letters, and even memos. The information these devices convey supplements the primary content of the text.

As a result, we believe that one can treat the different textual devices as different communication modalities. That is to say, the same type of reasoning that goes into the central data-to-modality allocation problem (the problem of deciding when and how to choose between using a picture, a table, or a sentence, etc.), goes into deciding whether to generate a straight paragraph or to use an enumerated list or a table or an insert. The reasoning is based, in large measure, on the contents to be conveyed to the reader. The process of device selection, like that of modality selection in general, consists of choosing one or more devices whose characteristics are suited for conveniently expressing essential portions of the contents.

As is the case with modalities in general, we find that textual devices are distinguished along several independent dimensions; we identify three broad classes: *Depiction*, *Position*, and *Composition*. In all three cases, the communicative function of text devices is to delimit a portion of text for which certain exceptional conditions of interpretation hold.

1. Depiction:

Depiction involves selecting an appropriate letter string to express the text. Examples of different depictions are:

Parentheses: Usually indicates that the parenthesized text is tangential to the main text. Used mainly for clause-sized text bodies.

Font switching: Indicates special importance of the delimited text, either that it is a new term being introduced, that it is of central importance, or that it is a foreign expression. This includes the use of boldface, underlining, and doubled emphasis (italicization *when the surrounding text is* not *italicized*).

Capitalization: Indicates that the text string names (identifies) a particular entity. Used mainly for single-word text bodies.

Quotation marks: Usually used to signal that the text body was written by another author, and occasionally used to indicate that the meaning of the text body is different than a standard interpretation would yield.

2. Position:

Repositioning involves moving the text block relative to the surrounding text on the page. Examples:

Inline: The non-distinguished normal case.

Offset (horizontal repositioning): Indicates either that the text block is authored by someone else (e.g., a long quoted paragraph, indented) or that it summarizes material that is especially relevant, as with an indented paragraph.

Separation (vertical repositioning): Indicates that the text block addresses a single point (as with paragraphs) or that it identifies or summarizes the subsequent text (as with or headings or titles).

Offpage: Offpage text provides material (usually of explanatory import) that is tangential to the main text, as with an appendix, footnote, or sidebar.

3. Composition:

Compositional devices impose an internal structure on the affected text body. Examples are:

Itemized list: A set of entities/discourse objects on the same level of specificity with respect to the subject domain, but that (in general) contain too much material to be expressed as a simple list within a single sentence. (This list is an example.)

Enumerated list: A set of entities/discourse objects on the same level of specificity with respect to the domain, which are, furthermore, ordered along some underlying dimension, such as time, distance, importance.

Term definition: A pair of texts separated by a colon or similar delimiter, in which the first text is the name of a discourse object and the second defines it or expresses some other fact related to it. (The typical form is "Term: Text string"; each entry in this itemization of Composition types is an example of Term Definition.)

From these definitions, it is clear that selecting an appropriate textual device (or combination of such) relies in large measure on the author's ability to accurately characterize the meaning expressed by the specific portion of text as well as its relationship to the surrounding text. That is, in order to know when to use a footnote, an itemized list, or an enumeration, for example, the author must be able to match the communicative function of the block of text *in its current context* against the communicative semantics of the textual devices so as to select the appropriate one. After all, the same sentence can properly be a footnote in one text and a parenthesized part of the text proper in another: the difference depends on how the text as a whole is organized to achieve its communicative purpose.

Thus (ignoring until Section such issues as textual prominence and style), there are three parts to the problem: the underlying semantic content to be communicated, the textual structure in which this meaning is couched, and the textual devices available for expression. With respect to semantics, we take a standard approach (namely, using frame-like representation structures that contain terms from a well-specified ontology). In order to define the communicative semantics of textual devices, we employ a theory of text structure that describes how coherent texts achieve their communicative purposes. We turn next to recent work on text structure planning.

Background: Text Planning

There is more to building coherent text than the mere generation of single sentences. At the very least, one has to delimit the content of each sentence and specify their order of appearance. Texts only achieve their communicative functions when they are coherent — when the reader is able to build up an understanding not only of each individual sentence but also of how each sentence relates to the whole. In order to produce coherent paragraphs, one requires an understanding of the interrelationships between the parts of a paragraph. For example, the following paragraph is simply not coherent, because the logical interrelationships between the sentences are not respected rhetorically:

> At the very least, one has to delimit the content of each sentence. Texts only achieve their communicative functions when they are coherent. One has to specify the order of appearance of each sentence. There is more to building coherent text than the mere generation of single sentences.

The question "What makes text coherent?" has a long history, going back at least to [Aristotle 54]. A number of researchers have recognized that in coherent text successive pieces of text are related in particular ways, and have provided different sets of interclause relations (see, for example, [Hobbs 79, Grimes 75, Shepherd 26, Reichman 78]). After an extensive study of several hundred texts of different types and genres,[Mann & Thompson 88] identified 25 basic rhetorical relations, which they claimed suffice to represent all intersentential relations that hold within normal English texts. Some relations are PURPOSE, ELABORATE, SEQUENCE, and SOLUTIONHOOD, the first three of which are typically signaled by "in order to", "for example", and "then" respectively (the last has no cue phrase). Their theory, called Rhetorical Structure Theory (RST), holds that the relations are used recursively, relating ever smaller blocks of adjacent text, down to the single clause level; it holds that a paragraph is only coherent if all its parts can eventually be made to fit under one overarching relation. Thus each coherent paragraph can be described by a tree structure that captures the rhetorical dependencies between adjacent clauses and blocks of clauses. The RST relations subsume most of the rhetorical relations proposed by previous researchers; recent attempts at more encompassing taxonomies that synthesize several hundred relations from linguists, computational linguists, philosophers, and other interested parties appear in [Hovy 90].

Within the past few years, a number of computational research projects have addressed problems that involve automatically generating coherent multisentence paragraphs that achieve a given communicative goal. Almost all of these use a tree of some kind to represent the structure of the paragraph. An ongoing effort at ISI, involving one of the authors, uses RST relations (and extensions of them) which are represented and formalized as plans in a top-down hierarchical planning system reminiscent of the Artificial Intelligence planning system NOAH [Sacerdoti 77]. The structure planner functions between some application program (such as an expert system) and the sentence generator Penman [Penman 89, Mann & Matthiessen 83]. From the application program, the planner accepts one or more communicative goals along with a set of semantic representations of relevant material which can be used to form the text. During the planning process, the structurer assembles the input entities into a tree that embodies the paragraph structure, in which nonterminals are RST relations and terminal nodes contain the input material. It then traverses the tree, noting the linking phrases at tree branches and submitting the leaves to Penman to be generated in English. The planning process is described in much more detail in [Hovy 88].

Extending the Planner: An Example of Layout Planning

The RST text structure planner (linked to Penman) has been used in several domains, most recently to plan and generate paragraphs of text about the procedures to be followed by air traffic controllers. The host system, ARIES [Johnson & Harris 90], is being developed in the context of an automatic programming project, and is intended to perform many air traffic control operations automatically.

In our example, the structurer is activated with the goal to describe the procedure to be followed by an air traffic controller when an aircraft is "handed over" from one region to the next. The underlying representation for this example consists of a semantic network of 18 instances, defined in terms of 27 air traffic do-

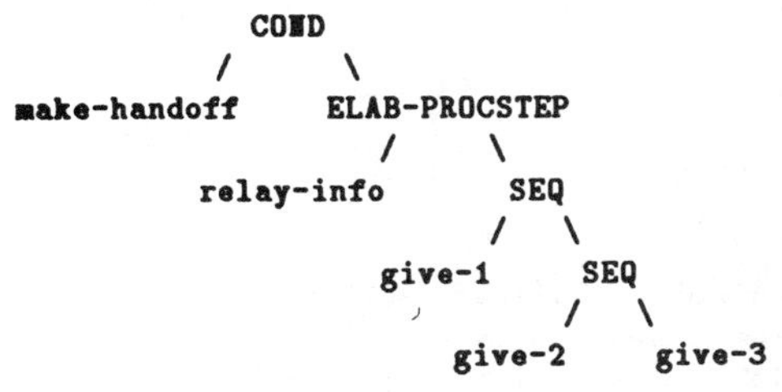

Figure 1: RST tree for ATC domain.

main concepts and 8 domain relations, implemented as frames in the Loom knowledge representation system [MacGregor 88].

The planner finds the RST-based plans CONDITION, ELABORATE-PROCESSSTEP, and SEQUENCE, and builds the paragraph tree shown in Figure 1. The leaves of this tree are reformulated in Penman's input language and the text generated is:

```
When making a handoff, the transferring
controller relays information to the
receiving controller in the following
order.  He gives the target's position.
He gives the aircraft's identification.
He gives the assigned altitude and
appropriate restrictions.
```

Though the text closely mirrors that of the actual Air Traffic Control Manual [ASA 89], the differences in formatting are significant; and these differences make the manual much more readable. The manual contains headings, term definitions signaled by italicized terms, enumerated lists, etc.

We have recently embarked on a study of several instructional texts, including recipes, school textbooks, and manuals for cars, sewing machines, and video players. An early conclusion is that certain textual formatting devices are highly correlated with specific configurations of the underlying text structure tree. For example, a series of nested SEQUENCEs, such as appears in Figure 1, is usually realized in the text as an enumerated list. Exceptions occur (in general) only when the individual items enumerated are single words (in which case the whole list is realized in a single sentence) or when there are few enough of them to place in a paragraph in-line (though usually in this case the keywords *first*, *second*, etc., are added).

On the assumption that we can capture most of the reasons for using such formatting devices as enumerations on the basis of RST alone, we augmented the text plan SEQUENCE in order to include explicit formatting commands and adapted the structure planner accordingly (namely, to ignore formatting commands when building the sentence generator inputs and finally to append the formatting commands and the sentence generator's output in the order mandated by the tree). For the formatting command we used LaTeX forms [Lamport 86] such as `\begin{enumerate} \item \end{enumerate}`. Although our implementation was done within the framework of our specific generation technology, we believe a similar augmentation could be performed with most if not all the text planners being developed at this time. The resulting tree (with formatting commands indicated) is shown in Figure 2. The text generated is:

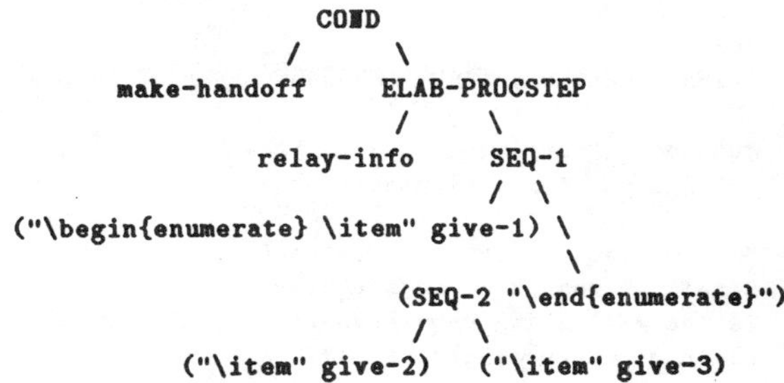

Figure 2: Augmented RST tree for ATC domain.

```
When making a handoff, the transferring
controller relays information to the
receiving controller in the following
order.  \begin{enumerate} \item He gives
the target's position.  \item He gives
the aircraft's identification.  \item He
gives the assigned altitude and appro-
priate restrictions.  \end{enumerate}
```

Note that due to the asymmetry of the LaTeX formatting command (i.e., the `\begin` and `\end` statements at either end), we had to create two SEQUENCE text plans, one for the top of a sequence and one for its recursive continuation. The relevant parts of the two SEQUENCEs are shown in Figure 3. The asterisk in the Nucleus and Satellite fields indicates to the planner the position in which to include the semantic content which eventually becomes the text.

The final text, as planned from the semantic representation, is produced and formatted directly by the system as follows:

> When making a handoff, the transferring controller relays information to the receiving controller in the following order.
> 1. He gives the target's position.
> 2. He gives the aircraft's identification.
> 3. He gives the assigned altitude and appropriate restrictions.

This example illustrates the planning of only a single formatting command. Despite its rather extreme

```
Name: SEQUENCE-1
Results:
 ((BMB SPEAKER HEARER (SEQUENCE-OF ?PART ?NEXT)))

Nucleus: ("\begin{enumerate} \item" *)     <-----
Satellite: (* "\end{enumerate}")           <-----

Nucleus requirements/subgoals: (...)
Satellite requirements/subgoals: (...)
Nucleus+Satellite requirements/subgoals: (...)
Nucleus growth points: (...)
Satellite growth points:
 (...
  (BMB SPEAKER HEARER (SEQUENCE-OF-2 ?NEXT ?FOLL)))

Order: (NUCLEUS SATELLITE)
Relation-phrases: ("" "then" "next")
Activation-question: "..."
```

```
Name: SEQUENCE-2
Results:
 ((BMB SPEAKER HEARER (SEQUENCE-OF-2 ?PART ?NEXT)))

Nucleus: ("\item" *)                       <-----
Satellite: ("\item" *)                     <-----

Nucleus requirements/subgoals: (...)
Satellite requirements/subgoals: (...)
Nucleus+Satellite requirements/subgoals: (...)
Nucleus growth points: (...)
Satellite growth points: (...)

Order: (NUCLEUS SATELLITE)
Relation-phrases: ("" "then" "next")
Activation-question: "..."
```

Figure 3: Top and recursive SEQUENCE text plans. (Details elided due to space limitations.)

simplicity, however, the example is sufficient to demonstrate that as long as one can characterize textual formatting devices in terms of particular structural configurations of the text tree, one can include appropriate formatting commands of several types into the generated output.

We next outline the definition of other textual devices in terms of text structure theories such as RST and point out some limitations of this idea.

Semantics of Textual Devices

The insight that the communicative semantics of text formatting devices can to a significant extent be stated in terms of text structure is a powerful one. Two major limitations should however be borne in mind: first, that there are additional factors that determine the use of most formatting devices, and second, that the representational power of current theories of text structure is still very limited.

Various types of additional factors affect the use of formatting devices. These range from the style of the author and the amount of visual prominence the author wishes to accord a text block, all the way to limitations on the text length. In current work at USC/ISI and the University of Nijmegen, we are attempting to systematize the various factors that play a role and to represent them in a single formalism that makes clear their nature and interrelationships [Vossers, Arens, & Hovy 91]. This work studies four major groups of factors — the nature of the communication, the goals of the author, the essential features of the information to be conveyed, and the capabilities of the reader — which together control the actual types of expressive media used (including normal text, formatting devices, and line diagrams).

With respect to defining how footnotes, sidebars, italicized regions, etc., really function in a text, we are well aware that precise definitions of the various devices are limited by the descriptive power of the particular theory of text structure employed. Such theories as RST, among the best available at the present time, still do not provide a great deal of detail and descriptive adequacy. But they do at least enable one to capture the essential functionality of the following textual devices:

- **Enumeration:** As described in the example above, the text structure relation SEQUENCE can generally be formatted as an enumerated list. The enumeration follows the sequence of the relation, which is planned in expression of some underlying semantic ordering of the items involved, for example time, location, etc.
- **Itemization:** The textual structure that relates a number of items without any underlying order is the RST relation JOINT, which can be realized by an itemized list (unless the items are small enough to be placed into a single sentence).
- **Appendix, footnote, and parentheses:** These are three devices that realize the same textual relation, namely BACKGROUND. They differ in the amount of material included in the relation's Satellite.
- **Section title or heading:** This device realizes the textual relation IDENTIFICATION, which links an identifier with the body of material it heads. A section or subsection is appropriate when the IDENTIFICATION is combined with a SEQUENCE chain that governs the overall presentation of the text.

For some textual devices, no text structure relation

has been identified by discourse linguists. For example, the Quotation device realizes the linguistic relation Projection (that which links a sayer to what is said; see [Halliday 85]), which is not included in RST, Conjunctive Relations, or Hobbs's or Dahlgren's theories. Other textual devices work on a level too detailed for text coherence theories, since they operate on individual words within a clause; text structure theories typically relate independent clauses only and provide no intraclausal links. And unlike the case for Projection, no purely linguistic constructs exist to handle them either. Thus text formatting devices such as italicization and capitalization for word definition or emphasis cannot at this time be represented. (Members of the Penman and EES projects at USC/ISI are currently building a new text planner with a network of considerably more detailed plans, in order to help address this problem of lack of expressive delicacy, a problem that also impinges on the syntactic realization of text.)

An additional shortcoming with our approach is the fact that we embed LaTeX commands literally into the RST plans. The text structure planner thus has no ability to reason about the implications of its formatting. Better would be to develop an abstract representation of textual devices which, when included in the text plans, would be realized into LaTeX (or Scribe, or any other formatting language) commands at the time the content is realized into English.

However, despite the problems with definitional delicacy, we are able to represent many of the textual devices listed above within the existing text structuring relations, which are all related to more or less well-understood text plans and communicative goals. To this extent, then, the insight that text formatting devices can be defined in terms of text structure relations (as described here) enables the automatic planning of appropriately formatted multisentence texts, a new and very useful capability.

Acknowledgments

Thanks to Bill Swartout for the idea of using LaTeX to illustrate the point, to Richard Whitney for implementation help, and to Lewis Johnson for ARIES.

References

[APA 83] *Publication Manual of the American Psychological Association* (third edition). 1983. Washington: American Psychological Association.

[Arens & Hovy 90] Arens Y., and Hovy, E.H. 1990. How to Describe What? Towards a Theory of Modality Utilization. In Proceedings of the 12th Annual Conference of the Cognitive Science Society, 487-494.

[Aristotle 54] Aristotle. The Rhetoric. In *The Rhetoric and the Poetics of Aristotle*, W. Rhys Roberts (trans). New York: Random House.

[ASA 89] ASA, Inc. 1989. *Airman's Information Manual.* Aviation Supplies and Academics.

[CMS 82] *The Chicago Manual of Style* (thirteenth edition). 1982. Chicago: University of Chicago Press.

[Grimes 75] Grimes, J.E. 1975. *The Thread of Discourse.* The Hague: Mouton.

[Halliday 85] Halliday, M.A.K. 1985. *An Introduction to Functional Grammar.* Baltimore: Edward Arnold Press.

[Hobbs 79] Hobbs, J.R. 1979. Coherence and Coreference. *Cognitive Science* 3(1):67-90.

[Hovy 88] Hovy, E.H. 1988. Planning Coherent Multisentential Text. In Proceedings of the 26th ACL Conference, 163-169.

[Hovy 90] Hovy, E.H. 1990. Parsimonious and Profligate Approaches to the Question of Discourse Structure Relations. Presented at the 5th International Workshop on Text Generation, Pittsburgh.

[Johnson & Harris 90] Johnson, W.L. and Harris, D. 1990. Requirements Analysis Using ARIES: Themes and Examples. In Proceedings of the 5th Knowledge Based Software Engineering Conference, 79-84. Tech Report no. RL-TR-91-11, Rome Laboratory.

[Lamport 86] Lamport, L. 1986. *LaTeX User's Guide and Reference Manual.* Reading: Addison-Wesley.

[MacGregor 88] MacGregor, R. 1988. A Deductive Pattern Matcher. In Proceedings of the 6th National Conference on Artificial Intelligence (AAAI-88), 696-701.

[Mann & Matthiessen 83] Mann, W.C. and Matthiessen, C.M.I.M. 1983. Nigel: A Systemic Grammar for Text Generation. Research Report RR-83-105, USC/ISI.

[Mann & Thompson 88] Mann, W.C. and Thompson, S.A. 1988. Rhetorical Structure Theory: Toward a Functional Theory of Text Organization. *Text* 8(3):243-281.

[Moore & Paris 89] Moore, J.D. and Paris, C.L. 1989. Planning Text for Advisory Dialogues. In Proceedings of the 27th ACL Conference, 67-75.

[Penman 89] *The Penman Documentation.* 5 unpublished volumes, USC/ISI.

[Reichman 78] Reichman, R. 1978. Conversational Coherency. *Cognitive Science* 2(1):283-327.

[Sacerdoti 77] Sacerdoti, E. 1977. *A Structure for Plans and Behavior.* Amsterdam: North-Holland.

[Shepherd 26] Shepherd, H.R. 1928. *The Fine Art of Writing.* New York: The Macmillan Co.

[Van Leunen 79] Van Leunen, M.-C. 1979. *A Handbook for Scholars.* New York: Alfred A. Knopf.

[Vossers, Arens, & Hovy 91] Vossers, M., Arens, Y., and Hovy, E.H. 1991. On the Automated Control of Communications Involving Text, Formatting, and Line Diagrams. Master's thesis, University of Nijmegen. Forthcoming.

Reflections on. . .

Automatic Generation of Formatted Text

Eduard Hovy and Yigal Arens

Although the nature of text formatting places it somewhere between text generation and multimedia proper, the text devices outlined in this paper (such as itemize and enumerate environments, italicized and boldfaced text segments, and headings, quotations, footnotes, and other text block offsets) do not appear to be manageable simply by adopting techniques from text planning and multimedia presentation planning independently. What is required is both the development of the foundational theories upon which text and multimedia presentation structures depend, and a greater understanding of how these theories interrelate to determine the use of textual devices with appropriate communicative semantics.

In contrast to the other papers in this section and to the other work by the authors, this aspect of information presentation has enjoyed very little attention. This is rather surprising since you might expect that the automated specification of suitable formatting for text would be given a high priority in today's world of increasingly sophisticated natural language text planners and generators and ubiquitous desktop publishing software. To our knowledge, the only similar work has been performed by the company Cognitive Systems, Inc., in their report generation software. It must therefore be that all other (semi-) automated text production facilities either have assembled a set of ad hoc routines for structuring text or do not care to publish their theories and methods.

It is, however, inconceivable that text generators of the future will not be called upon to determine where and how to employ the textual devices. When they need to signal text structure (for example, itemizations and enumerations), theories such as Rhetorical Structure Theory (RST) will provide some theoretical motivation; when they need to signal theme and focus (for example, italics and underlining), the work of text linguists on the information structure of text will be relevant; to place and interrelate text blocks and non-text material, they require methods of the kind outlined in the papers by Feiner and Weitzman and Wittenburg (this section). The fact that theories of discourse structure, information structure, and information placement are still in their infancy does not mean that they do not already provide insights that can profitably be exploited to guide good text formatting. We look forward to the time when the potential and interestingness of this corner of multimedia generation is recognized and text formatting theories and planners are developed.

Constraint-Based Graphical Layout of Multimodal Presentations

Winfried H. Graf

German Research Center for Artificial Intelligence (DFKI) GmbH
Stuhlsatzenhausweg 3, 66123 Saarbrücken, Germany
graf@dfki.uni-sb.de

Abstract

When developing advanced multimodal interfaces, combining the characteristics of different modalities such as natural language, graphics, animation, virtual realities, etc., the question of automatically designing the graphical layout of such presentations in an appropriate format becomes increasingly important. So, to communicate information to the user in an expressive and effective way, a knowledge-based layout component has to be integrated into the architecture of an intelligent presentation system. In order to achieve a coherent output, it must be able to reflect certain semantic and pragmatic relations specified by a presentation planner to arrange the visual appearance of a mixture of textual and graphic fragments delivered by mode-specific generators. In this paper we will illustrate by the example of *LayLab*, the layout manager of the multimodal presentation system *WIP*, how the complex positioning problem for multimodal information can be treated as a constraint satisfaction problem. The design of an aesthetically pleasing layout is characterized as a combination of a general search problem in a finite discrete search space and an optimization problem. Therefore, we have integrated two dedicated constraint solvers, an incremental hierarchy solver and a finite domain solver, in a layered constraint solver model, which is triggered from a common metalevel by rules and defaults. The underlying constraint language is able to encode graphical design knowledge expressed by semantic/pragmatic, geometrical/topological, and temporal relations. As graphical constraints frequently have only local effects, they are incrementally generated by the system on the fly.

1 Introduction

Due to the growing complexity of information that has to be communicated by current AI systems, there comes an increasing need for building sophisticated intelligent user interfaces that take advantage of a coordinated combination of different modalities, e.g., natural language, graphics, animation, and virtual realities to produce a flexible and efficient information presentation (cf. also [41, 1, 30]).

When developing advanced visual user interfaces composing coordinated text and graphics as in the system *WIP* (Knowledge-based Presentation of Information), the question of laying out such multimodal presentations in an appropriate format becomes increasingly important. Here, the graphical communication of multimodal information plays a crucial role.

As with many other interesting AI design problems, the determination of a complex layout can be viewed as a discrete combinatorial problem, i.e., finding in a finite discrete search space a point satisfying set of constraints. In contrast to other configuration tasks, e.g., hardware design, an optimal layout of a multimodal presentation has to satisfy certain additional aesthetic criteria. We treat layout as a *constraint satisfaction problem* (CSP) that can be solved efficiently by consistency techniques to prune the search space a priori.

Therefore, this paper details a constraint-based approach for processing design-relevant graphical knowledge for automatic layout, either as a formalism for specifying basic design principles such as gridding, alignment, symmetry, etc., or as a mechanism for propagating obligatory, optional, and default constraints to position individual layout fragments on a graphic design grid (cf. [15, 16]).

So, the arrangement of an aesthetically pleasing layout is characterized as a combination of a general search problem in a finite discrete search space and an optimization problem. Both problems are addressed by an advanced constraint solver model comprising two dedicated solvers for handling different kinds of graphical constraints defined on constraint hierarchies and finite domains.

We will illustrate the use of these constraint techniques by the example of *LayLab*, *WIP*'s experimental layout manager. The task of the knowledge-based presentation system *WIP* is the generation of a variety of multimodal documents from an input consisting of a formal description of the communicative intent of a planned presentation. *WIP* generates illustrated texts that are customized for the intended audience and situation (see also [47, 1, 46]).

A fundamental goal of our work is to construct a universal framework for automatic layout management, as an integrated component of a multimodal presentation system, that makes intelligent use of human visual abilities and generation parameters, such as user stereotypes, output devices, etc., whenever arranging multimodal objects in any kind of presentation. Thus, from the functional viewpoint the main task of a knowledge-based layout manager is to convey certain semantic and pragmatic relations specified by a presentation planner by the arrangement of graphics and text fragments delivered by mode-specific generators, i.e., to determine the size of the layout elements and the exact coordinates for positioning them on the document page.

2 Related Research

As graphics hardware becomes more and more sophisticated, computer-based graphical communication achieves a crucial role in intelligent user interfaces. While much research in this area has focused on the automatic synthesis of graphics for either presenting relational information (cf. [26]) and realistic depictions of 3D objects as in [39, 37], the automatic layout design of graphical presentations is relatively unexplored.

Some interesting early efforts in automating layout include Eastman's work on a *General Space Planner* that addressed the task of arranging objects (e.g., furniture) in a space subject to given constraints (cf. [4], chap. III). Feiner's *GRIDS* (GRaphical Interface Design System) was constructed as an experimental system to investigate approaches in the automatic display layout of text, illustrations, and later virtual input devices (cf. [11]). In contrast to, e.g., *WIP*, the generation of the contents is separated from that of the style of a presentation. The current version of the testbed system has been implemented using an OPS5-like production language. The layout process is guided by the concept of a graphical design grid. Other approaches using computer-based grids, modeled by a human designer, can be found in the system *VIEW* (cf. [13]) for synthesizing graphical object depictions from high-level specifications and by [5] for low-level table layout, whose high-level topology was specified by the user as a matrix.

Since constraint satisfaction techniques have become more sophisticated during the last decade, and with the growing availability of advanced graphics hardware, there has been an upward trend in applying constraint techniques to user interface design. Thus, most of the related work on applications of constraint languages and systems has been done in the area of computer graphics and graphical interfaces, especially geometric layout (e.g., [7, 21]).

A pioneering system in both constraint satisfaction and interactive graphics was *Sketchpad* (cf. [43]) written by Sutherland at MIT in 1963. Using the Sketchpad system allowed a user to create complex objects by sketching primitive graphical entities and specifying constraints on them. Many of these ideas have been explored by Borning in the *ThingLab* system at Xerox PARC [6], a graphical constraint-oriented simulation laboratory implemented in Smalltalk-80. Later versions of ThingLab were concerned with extensions supporting constraint hierarchies, incremental compilation, and graphical facilities for defining new kinds of constraints (e.g., [8, 12]). Both systems exploit numeric techniques such as relaxation for solving constraint networks containing cycles, in contrast to symbolic techniques, e.g., used in Steele's constraint language (cf. [42]). Other research activities in constraint-based graphics include the systems *Juno* [34], *IDEAL* [45], *Magritte* [14], *Bertrand* (cf. [23]), and the work of Cohen et al. on constraint-based tiled windows (cf. [9]).

An increasing number of interface-design systems mostly based on a graphical editor have been developed during the last years to make the interface design process more efficient and comfortable than with conventional techniques. Here, constraints provide a means of stating layout requirements, e.g., the *Peridot* system deduces constraints automatically as the user demonstrates the desired behaviour (cf. [33]).

Other representative research related to in this paper has concentrated more on the theoretical background of constraint languages (see also [23]) including *constraint logic programming* (cf. [19]). One example is *CHIP* (cf. [10, 44]), a new logic language developed at the ECRC in Munich, combining the declarative aspects of logic programming with the efficiency of consistency techniques. A special feature is its facility of solving constraints defined over finite domains that enables CHIP to solve a variety of discrete combinatorial search problems.

3 Multimodal Layout

Design is a central skill in many human tasks such as layout of multimodal presentations. In general, we have to distinguish functional versus art design. In our context, design means the arrangement of an efficient and expressive presentation subject to given restrictions, e.g., regarding filled versus empty space and non-overlapping, that further satisfies some aesthetic and functional criteria, such as transparency, legibility, objectivity, or credibility.

Layout design is essentially influenced by ideas and approaches known from general graphics design (e.g., [3, 20]). So, we will transfer the graphical presentation problem as it is defined in [26] to *multimodal objects* (i.e., textual, graphic, or virtual objects) and tackle it with graphical techniques. Thus, the *multimodal presentation problem* is to synthesize a multimodal design that effectively expresses a set of semantic and pragmatic relations and their structural properties. As we will not treat content issues of automatic presentations here, presentation design means the arrangement of the outer form of a document. According to (cf. [26]), a design can be judged to be effective when it can be interpreted accurately or quickly, when it has visual impact, or when it can be realized in a cost-effective manner.

Beach (cf. [5]) has shown that the general layout problem formalized as a random packing problem, i.e., determining whether an unordered set of non-overlapping rectangular table entries can be arranged into a minimum space, is strongly *NP-complete* and thus, there is no general and efficient algorithm for solving it. So even the question of finding an aesthetically pleasing layout for multimodal documents under certain outward restrictions seems to be intractable. The problem becomes linear in time only if we use additonal constraints to reduce the design space for arrangement, e.g., sufficient grid structures.

3.1 The Grid-based Approach

Basic formal design aspects have been addressed by several graphical techniques such as typographic grids (see [32, 38]). The grid partitions a 2D plane into smaller rectangular units of mostly equal size, so-called 'universal' grid fields, using horizontal and vertical lines. The fields are separated by an intermediate space depending on the size of the type characters and the illustrations. A grid-based approach builds a logical and constant basis for the designer, but does not limit his creativity. So, a grid can be treated as an ordering system for efficiently designing functional (i.e., uniform, coherent, and consistent) layouts. This method is also used in Feiner's expert system for automatically laying out displays containing text and pictures.

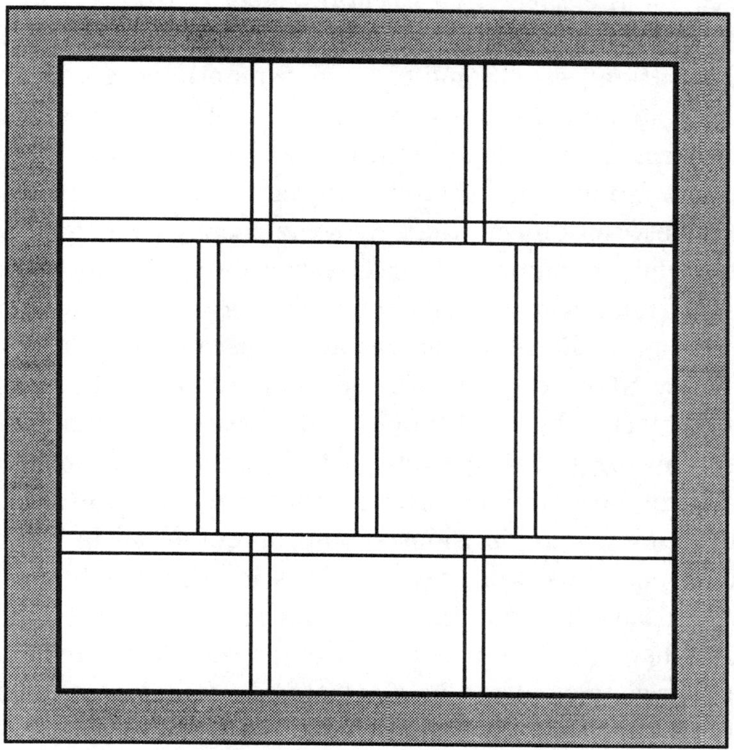

Figure 1: Structure of a Superimposed Design Grid

The granularity of the grid can be determined by the number of grid fields. To gain more flexibility the concept of *superimposed grids*, i.e., a multiple set of grids comprising different type areas (e.g., combining an odd and even number of columns) for one document page based on the information to be presented, has become useful for major newspapers (cf. Fig. 1). The design of an optimal grid for a specific presentation is a difficult task, including decisions about the dimensions of the type area, its divisions, and its margins. For a variation of the selected grid, a priori knowledge about the typographic elements is a necessary prerequiste.

3.2 Classifying Multimodal Relationships

The logical structure of a multimodal document is essentially characterized by functional dependencies between the different document parts, e.g., a mixture of text and graphics, which may describe actions themselves. In empiric psychological studies [48] have observed that there is large variability of layout patterns, such as pictures sandwiched within text, surrounding the text, superimposed over the text, and interspersed throughout the text, when placing illustrations with respect to corresponding text.

Semantic and pragmatic relationships between graphic and textual fragments are represented by *WIP*'s presentation planner (cf. [2]) by means of so-called *rhetorical relations* based on the *rhetorical structure theory (RST)* proposed in [29] for text planning. Examples of RST relations are 'sequence', 'contrast', 'elaboration', 'organization', 'motivation', etc. Some of these semantic-pragmatic coherence relations between major document parts can be easily reflected by graphic constraints representing topological arrangement facilities for visualization.

Relationships among multimodal layout objects on a document can be classified into, *local* relations between objects that are semantically connected and *global* relations regarding the whole document. Local relationships correspond to the topology while global ones are related to the geometric process. These relationships have to be considered in order to achieve a coherent and consistent presentation.

So, the general layout process follows the strategy of building larger units from groups of objects connected by local topological relations first and to ultimately arrange these units following global relations. This approach favors the idea of arranging identical structures in a similar way. By that, we can express the basic design principle, that the same layout decisions should be employed in different parts of a presentation. This concept also addresses the question of rhythm and visual balance.

As a well-designed layout is determined by its visual clarity, semantic dependencies and contradictions in the information to be presented are reflected by building larger units of locally connected layout elements. In contrast to local relationships, global relationships handle larger units of topological arranged objects by basic design strategies.

Graphical layout of multimodal presentations comprises most features of visual interface design, including the overall display layout, use of color and grey levels, as well as the placement of the individual layout elements with respect to their internal semantic relations. A well-designed expressive and effective layout is determined essentially by its clarity, consistency, and attractive aesthetic appearence. Visual clarity of a presentation can be achieved by using a visual organization of information that emphasizes the underlying logical structure. Therefore, a few global design rules regarding similarity, proximity, closure, and good continuation have been stated by different Gestalt psychologists (e.g., [3]). For placing the designed presentation elements in the overall context, basic layout principles that concern gridding, proportion, and balance have been established.

4 Encoding Graphical Knowledge via Constraints

A central idea underlying automatic layout is the incorporation of causal geometric knowledge into the layout design process in order to achieve a deep encoding of perceptual criteria, i.e., design strategies can be used for generating the layout of every kind of multimodal presentation independent of the current domain.

We will address the problem of encoding this very heterogeneous types of design relevant knowledge, e.g., graphical and psychological information about perceptual criteria expressing horizontal versus vertical alignment, grouping, symmetry, similarity, and ordering by using constraint formalisms.

To influence the interface design and to determine the graphical style of the multimodal presentation, application domain-specific knowledge as well as common-sense knowledge about basic design heuristics have to be encoded. But some of the layout issues can only be settled by basic design heuristics or individual preferences.

4.1 Constraint Representation

Layout as a configuration task can be viewed as a combinatorial problem, in a finite discrete search space. The main problem consists of finding any solution that satisfies all topological and geometrical restrictions with regard to certain aesthetic criteria. So, the design of an optimal layout can be treated as a combination of a general search problem with an optimization problem.

In the following, we will view layout as a Boolean CSP. That is, one has a set V of variables $v_1, \ldots, v_n$ each to be instantiated in an associated domain D_i and a set of Boolean constraints limiting the set of allowed values for specified subsets of the variables. There are various forms of definitions for the terminus 'constraint'. Informally, a constraint expresses desired relations among one or more objects. In this paper, we will stay to a general definition for CSP given by [27, 28] as a formula in first-order predicate logic restricted to unary and binary predicates:

$$\begin{aligned}(\exists x_1)(\exists x_2)\ldots(\exists x_n) \quad & (x_1 \in D_1)(x_2 \in D_2)\ldots(x_n \in D_n) \\ & P_1(x_1) \wedge P_2(x_2) \wedge \ldots \wedge P_n(x_n) \wedge \\ & P_{12}(x_1, x_2) \wedge P_{13}(x_1, x_3) \wedge \ldots \wedge P_{n-1,n}(x_{n-1}, x_n).\end{aligned}$$

Here P_{ij} is only included in the wff if $i < j$ since it is assumed that $P_{ji}(v_j, v_i) = P_{ij}(v_i, v_j)$. Intuitively, a constraint definition comprises a declarative representation of the relation and a set of procedures that can be invoked by the underlying constraint solver to fufill it. We will treat these procedures as methods in an object-oriented sense that can alternately try to satisfy the constraint.

The declarative semantics of constraint languages allow one to specify graphical objects while avoiding extraneous concerns about the realization of the drawing algorithms. Another major advantage is their ability to describe complex objects simply and naturally. So, constraint networks provide an elegant mechanism to declaratively state design-relevant knowledge about heterogenious geometrical and topological relationships, characterizing properties between different kinds of multimodal objects that can be maintained by the underlying system. They can be easily used to specify layout requirements in graphical environments in order to guarantee local circumscriptions of the presentation like format restrictions, margins, distances, and non-overlapping, or to maintain consistency among objects on the whole document. Furthermore, our approach uses constraint programming techniques to declaratively represent aesthetic knowledge, e.g., basic design principles expressing perceptual criteria, as well as to compute the precise position and size of a set of multimodal elements.

With regard to the definition above, layout planning as a CSP can be formalized in the following manner: the position of each layout item is a variable, with an associated domain that contains an infinite number of n-tuples of real values. Those domains can be described intensionally by constraints, e.g., specifying the boundaries of the connected subspaces permitted for that item. Constraints, e.g. ",The header has to be placed in the upper left corner," must also be expressed intensionally by algebraic equations and inequalities on the values of the constraint variables. Moreover, one might have p-ary relations such as "Text-1 must be between Graphics-2 and Graphics-3".

Layout constraints can be classified as *semantic/pragmatic*, *geometrical/topological*, and *temporal*. Semantic and pragmatic constraints essentially correspond to coherence relations like the RST relations described above. They can be compiled into graphic constraints that specify perceptual criteria concerning the organization of the visual elements, such as the sequential ordering (horizontal versus vertical layout), alignment, grouping, symmetry, or similarity. Geometrical and topological constraints refer to absolute and relative constraints. Furthermore, we can classify constraints in absolute ones that fix geometric parameters to constant values (e.g., absolute coordinates) and in those that relate a geometric parameter of one object to another (e.g., relative distance). Temporal relations are used in the case of animated presentations to represent temporal, spatial information.

Elementary constraints of the constraint language are defined by the arithmetic functions of the underlying Symbolics Lisp system. *Primitive constraints* represent elementary local relations, e.g., 'beside', 'connect', or 'under', expressing basic geometric relations. These constraints are specified by sets of mathematical equations (e.g., two objects that are constrained to touch at specific points) or by sets of inequalities (e.g., one object is constrained to lie inside another). The primitive constraints can be aggregated to more complex *compound constraints* , specifying the visualization of semantic-pragmatic relations such as 'contrast' or 'sequence'.

To give an example of a typical compound constraint in a predicate logic-like notation, let's have a look at a section of the representation of the 'contrast' constraint, i.e., to contrast two different objects. This definition specifies how the particular stylistic feature, to place contrasting things adjacent to each other in a row or column, is built into the constraint representation. The corresponding constraint network is illustrated in Fig. 2.

$$
\begin{aligned}
\textbf{CONTRAST}\ & (\mathrm{G}_1, \mathrm{G}_2) \leftrightarrow \\
& \mathrm{G}_1 \equiv \mathrm{pkt}(\mathrm{x}_{\mathrm{G}_1}, \mathrm{y}_{\mathrm{G}_1}, \mathrm{wi}_{\mathrm{G}_1}, \mathrm{he}_{\mathrm{G}_1}) \wedge \\
& \mathrm{G}_2 \equiv \mathrm{pkt}(\mathrm{x}_{\mathrm{G}_2}, \mathrm{y}_{\mathrm{G}_2}, \mathrm{wi}_{\mathrm{G}_2}, \mathrm{he}_{\mathrm{G}_2}) \wedge \\
& [\mathtt{EQUAL}(y_{G_1}, y_{G_2}) \wedge \mathtt{BESIDE}(x_{G_1}, \mathtt{wi}_{G_1}, x_{G_2}) \\
& \vee \\
& \mathtt{EQUAL}(x_{G_1}, x_{G_2}) \wedge \mathtt{UNDER}(y_{G_1}, \mathtt{he}_{G_1}, y_{G_2})]
\end{aligned}
$$

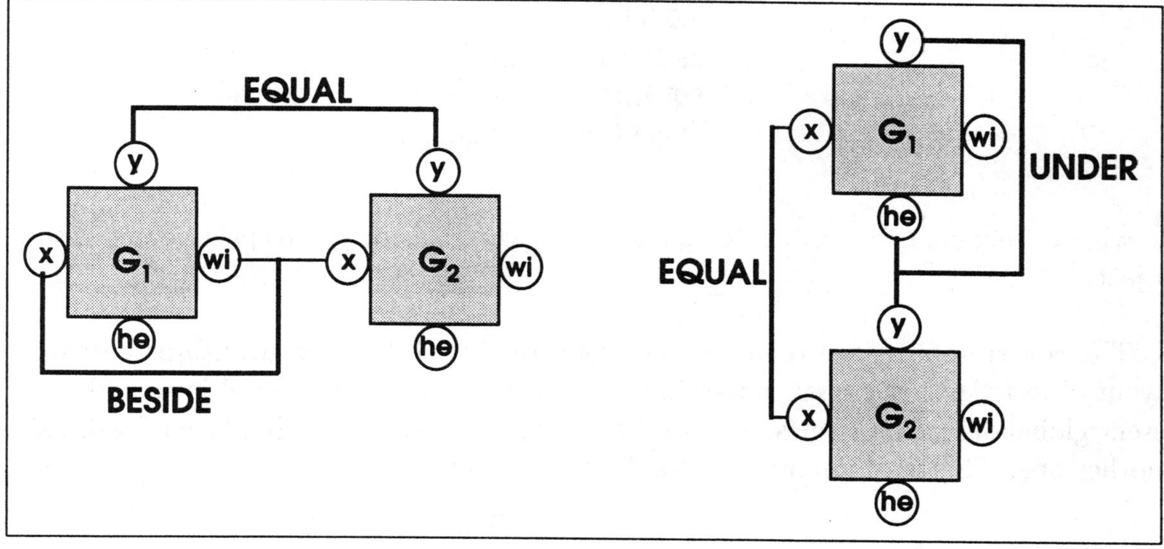

Figure 2: Constraint Network of the Definition Above

Since the ordering of the constraints in the definition is significant for their ranking, the stronger constraints have to preceed the weaker ones. E.g., according to the definition above, the layout manager will use a horizontal alignment in preference to a vertical one if a contrast-constraint has to be satisfied.

In graphical synthesis tasks like layout, constraints frequently have only local effects, i.e., the set of variables that are relevant to a solution and must be assigned values, changes dynamically as layout fragments are incrementally generated by a presentation system during problem solving. So, we have to distinguish *static constraints* that are related to a fixed set of variables and *dynamic constraints* that are generated on the fly (cf. [31]).

Another form of dynamic constraints concerns those in which the number of layout elements belonging to one relation is not known a priori (e.g., 'sequence'). The definition of a dynamic constraint for two sequentially related graphics-text blocks B_1 and B_2 is given by the following logical formula:

$$
\begin{aligned}
\textbf{SEQUENCE}\ (\mathrm{B}_1,\mathrm{B}_2) \leftrightarrow\ & \\
& \mathrm{B}_1 \equiv \mathrm{pkt}(\mathrm{x}_{\mathrm{B}_1},\mathrm{y}_{\mathrm{B}_1},\mathrm{wi}_{\mathrm{B}_1},\mathrm{he}_{\mathrm{B}_1})\wedge \\
& \mathrm{B}_2 \equiv \mathrm{pkt}(\mathrm{x}_{\mathrm{B}_2},\mathrm{y}_{\mathrm{B}_2},\mathrm{wi}_{\mathrm{B}_2},\mathrm{he}_{\mathrm{B}_2})\wedge \\
& [\mathtt{EQUAL}(x_{B_1},x_{B_2})\wedge \\
& \mathtt{UNDER}(y_{B_1},\mathtt{he}_{B_1},y_{B_2})\wedge \\
& \mathtt{EQUAL}(y_{B_1},\mathtt{?succ\text{-}y})\wedge \\
& \mathtt{BESIDE}(\mathtt{?succ\text{-}x},\mathtt{wi}_{B_1})] \\
& \vee \\
& [\mathtt{EQUAL}(y_{B_1},y_{B_2})\wedge \\
& \mathtt{BESIDE}(x_{B_1},\mathtt{wi}_{B_1},x_{B_2})\wedge \\
& \mathtt{EQUAL}(x_{B_1},\mathtt{?succ\text{-}x})\wedge \\
& \mathtt{UNDER}(\mathtt{?succ\text{-}y},\mathtt{he}_{B_1})],
\end{aligned}
$$

where ?succ-x, ?succ-y denote the x- and y-variables of the respective successor object.

The constraints regarded so far were concerned with local relationships between layout objects. Other global constraints refer to aggregated units of objects and represent global design strategies, e.g., that a unit should be preferably placed 'RightOf' another one. This is represented in the following way:

$$
\begin{aligned}
\textbf{RIGHT-OF}(X_1,X_2,X_3,X_4,X_5,X_6,X_7,X_8)\ \leftrightarrow\ & \\
& [(\mathtt{FDADD\ (FDMIN}\ X_1)\ X_4)\ \wedge\ \mathtt{;;;\ x2\text{-}min} \\
& (\mathtt{FDMAXRIGHT\ MIN}\ X_8\ X_2))\wedge\ \mathtt{;;;\ x2\text{-}max} \\
& (\mathtt{FDMIN}\ X_2)\wedge\ \mathtt{;;;\ y2\text{-}min} \\
& (\mathtt{FDDIFF\ (FDMAX}\ X_2)(\mathtt{FDDIFF}\ X_7\ X_3))]\ \mathtt{;;;\ y2\text{-}max} \\
& \wedge \\
& [(\mathtt{FDMIN}\ X_1)\wedge\ \mathtt{;;;\ x1\text{-}min} \\
& (\mathtt{FDDIFF\ (FDMAX}\ X_5)\ X_4)\wedge\ \mathtt{;;;\ x1\text{-}max} \\
& (\mathtt{FDMIN}\ X_2)\wedge\ \mathtt{;;;\ y1\text{-}min} \\
& (\mathtt{FDDIFF\ (FDMAX}\ X_6)(\mathtt{FDDIFF}\ X_3\ X_7))]\ \mathtt{;;;\ y1\text{-}max}
\end{aligned}
$$

Another problem addresses the handling of default constraints representing default assumptions, i.e., assigning a default value to a variable unless another value is known. To avoid trivial solutions to a constraint problem one has to express negative defaults explicitly.

4.2 Constraint Satisfaction

The constraint solving process ensures that all constraints will be satisfied when the individual layout elements are assembled into a complete layout. In problem solving, one has to decide generality versus efficiency. Since efficient constraint satisfaction is crucial when using constraints for graphical tasks, currently available universal constraint systems seem to be incovenient because of their increasing run time. Therefore, we have focused on tailoring specific solving algorithms for handling the large variety of design constraints to our needs, especially by extending or modifying approaches from recent work on constraint logic programming cf. [19]).

4.2.1 Handling of Constraint Hierarchies

Besides the semantic classification of local constraints outlined above, one often wants to prioritize the constraints in those which must be required and others which are preferably held and could be relaxed in the worst case. If the various constraints are given a priority, the most important and restrictive constraints can be satisfied first. A powerful way of expressing this layout feature is to organize the constraints in a hierarchy by assigning a preference scale to the constraint network. A set of constraints each labelled with a certain strength is called a *constraint hierarchy* (cf. [8]). We distinguish between *obligatory*, *optional* and *default constraints.* The latter state default values, which remain fixed unless the corresponding constraint is removed by a stronger one.

A typical example of using a constraint hierarchy in geometric layout is the problem of specifying the relative distance between two graphic elements, e.g., communicating a contrast relation. The adequate aesthetic criteria can be represented by the following constraints of different strength:

- An obligatory constraint that specifies that the distance between two graphics G_1 and G_2 has to be greater than zero.
- A disjunction of two optional constraints states that the graphics G_1 and G_2 are preferably to be aligned side by side or else one below the other.

For solving local constraints that are compiled from semantic/pragmatic RST relations between a set of layout objects, *SIVAS* (**S**ingle **VA**lue **S**olver), an incremental constraint solver that can handle constraint hierarchies, has been constructed.

The processing of constraint hierarchies is based on the *DeltaBlue algorithm* by Freeman-Benson (cf. [12]), an incremental algorithm that maintains an evolving solution to the constraint hierarchy as constraints are added and removed dynamically. DeltaBlue, as one instance of a spectrum of incremental hierarchical algorithms, has been constructed as an extension for *flat* constraint solvers that satisfy required constraints only. It is restricted to solving hierarchies of unique, non-cyclic constraints using a so-called *locally-predicate-better comparator* for finding an optimal solution.

The flat solver underlying *SIVAS* employs a *value inference* technique for constraint propagation of numeric constraints similar to Sketchpad and ThingLab. Using this technique, variables are labeled with constant values, and values of uninstantiated variables are determined from instantiated ones using constraints.

In contrast to hypermedia-based approaches to adaptive information presentation, in *WIP* the information to be presented is partially generated on the fly. Therefore, incrementality is also required in the automatic layout design. Therefore, *SIVAS* is able to dynamically generate layout constraints, i.e., to add constraints to and remove constraints from the network during runtime. That way, it achieves a high performance of the presentation design process by minimizing the cost of finding a new solution. It does this by exploiting knowledge of the previous solution.

4.2.2 Handling of Finite Domains

The high-level arrangement of larger units of layout elements on the design grid is accomplished by satisfying the global constraints that represent general geometric design strategies.

When processing global relations, we can impose the further restriction that the variable domains each consist of a finite number of discrete values, as we can treat the grid coordinates in the design space as finite domains. In this case, the constraining relations can be specified extensionally as the set of all p-tuples that fulfill the constraint.

FIDOS (**FI**nite **Do**main **S**olver) is an incremental solver for handling global graphical constraints that is based on a so-called *label inference* technique. Here, variables range over a set of values, and constraints are used to restrict these sets.

The complex space optimization problem can be efficiently solved by using consistency techniques based on the idea of a priori pruning. As the efficiency of standard backtracking algorithms suffers from its so-called thrashing behaviour, various intelligent inference techniques based on tree search procedures such as *delay* mechanisms (cf. [19, 10]), *check rules* and *looking ahead* (cf. [44]), *guarded rules* and *residuation* (cf. [40]) are surveyed to reduce or eliminate thrashing.

We have employed the *forward checking* technique known from the CHIP system (cf. [44]) based on the idea of a priori pruning, that is using constraints to reduce the search space before the discovery of a failure in contrast to conventional search techniques. Forward checking makes sure that each not-yet-assigned variable has at least one consistent value with the already assigned variables. This technique is well suited for early pruning of layout alternatives in order to efficiently satisfy global geometric constraints.

4.3 A Layered Constraint Solver Model

We have integrated these two special-purpose constraint solvers, *SIVAS* and *FIDOS*, for satisfying local topological and global geometrical relationships in a new architecture model that is organized hierarchically. Because it is very difficult and inefficient to represent design heuristics via constraints, we use rules and defaults on a metalevel to trigger the inference process. This model is proposed as a general framework for processing most of the layout-relevant graphical knowledge that can be encoded by means of constraints. Fig. 3 sketches the architecture of the layered constraint solver model. For a more detailed description refer to [24].

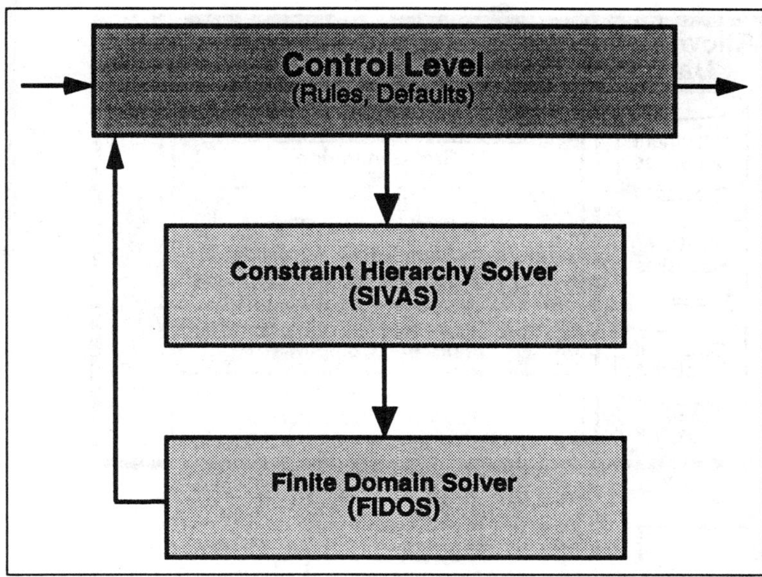

Figure 3: Model of a Layered Constraint Solver

5 The Architecture of the LayLab System

In the following, by the example of *LayLab WIP*'s layout manager, we propose a conceptual architecture for a knowledge-based layout component that automatically designs the graphical layout of multimodal presentations. Various modules are embedded in this archicture (see Fig. 4): a positioning component, an intelligent typographer, a document beautifier, an interaction handler, and a knowledge-base. Let's have a closer look at its major components.

To communicate information to the user in an effective way, a knowledge-based presentation system must be able to reflect certain semantic and pragmatic relations specified by a presentation planner to automatically determine the outward appearance of the visualization and verbalization results delivered by the graphics and text generator. That is the main task of the constraint-based *positioning component CLAY*. It exploits the two constraint solvers *SIVAS* and *FIDOS* outlined in section 4.2 to arrange the multimodal layout elements in the design space (see also [15, 16, 24]).

Since the placement process is essentially based on a graphic design grid as a framework for effective layout, we have constructed a rule-based *grid generation component* that automatically generates a set of superimposed grids, depending on different generation parameters such as output medium and user. Type area and text width are determined by legibility rules using default values for point size, font, distance, etc. Then, a uniform grid field is computed regarding the smallest picture or text block

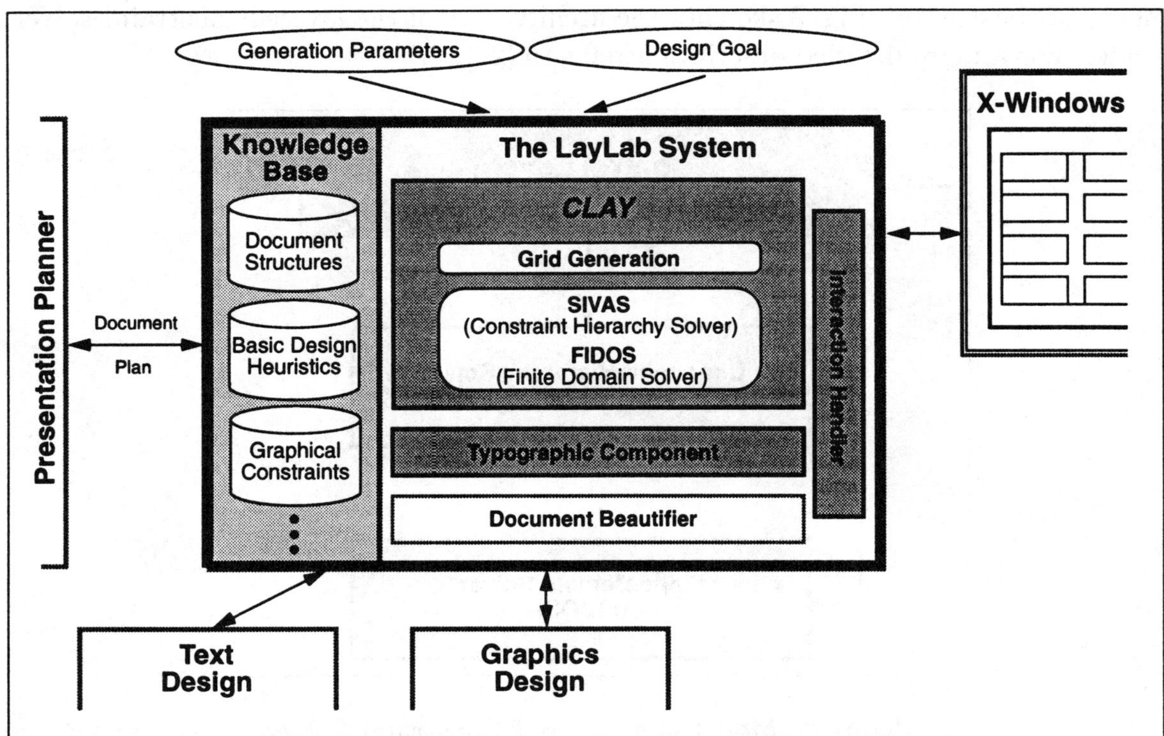

Figure 4: A Zoom into the Architecture of *WIP*'s Layout Manager Showing the Various Submodules

that holds an integral number of lines and scaling/cropping factors. If the grid is constructed, the individual design elements are adjusted to the size of the universal grid fields and fitted precisely into an integer number of fields, considering that the smallest grid field corresponds to the smallest text or graphic element to be presented (cf. also [25]).

The *typographic component* addresses the problem of laying out text. It must decide not only how to organize the text, but also how to shape it. With [18] who treat text layout as a planning task, we distinguish different textual devices such as plain text, itemized lists, indented paragraphs, enumerations, sidebars, footnotes, italicizations, quotation, inserts, etc. Relations between these textual devices are treated analogously to text-picture combinations via constraints.

The determination of the graphical style of the individual layout objects, including the choice of colors or grey levels, and the rendering of the entire document (e.g., design of the background) is performed by a *document beautification component* (cf. [36, 5]).

An *interaction handler* builds the interface to the hardware output medium (e.g., display) and presents the visualization and verbalization results of the mode-specific generators using special communication software (e.g., X-Windows).

LayLab's *knowledge base* contains information about document structures, rule-based representations of basic design heuristics as well as the graphical design constraints extensively illustrated before.

6 The Overall Layout Process

Considering this architecture, a complete layout design is achieved stepwise via a refinement process. Therefore, the design process is carried out in three phases with different levels of detail. We use the concept of a superimposed grid to simplify the initial construction phase by reducing the layout space (cf. section 3). In the first phase, a draft version of a skeletal page layout for uninstantiated text and graphics boxes is determined. Since at that stage of the process neither the text generator nor the graphics generator has produced any output, the layout manager only has information about the contents, the act structure and the selected mode combination which is available via a design record (cf. [46]). Therefore, the layout manager has at its disposal default assumptions to determine a skeletal version of an initial page layout based on uninstantiated text and graphics boxes. As soon as a generator has supplied any output, the corresponding box is instantiated and the incremental process of layout planning can start.

In that design phase we distinguish between local and global relationships. A low-level layout is determined based on local topological constraints that are compiled from semantic/pragmatic RST relations specified between layout fragments and describe their relative topology. Finally, the high-level layout is computed as a global geometrical arrangement. In this step, aggregated units of locally connected objects are placed on the grid using global relations to determine the explicit coordinates.

Frequently, a draft layout has to be revised because of design constraints or visual imbalances in the output presentation. When a partially instantiated layout entered in the design record is evaluated by the layout manager with a negative result, a dependency-based layout revision process is initiated, i.e., revising the skeletal layout after contents planning, or in the worst case, revising the planned contents due to graphical constraints. A larger example showing the temporal coordination of contents planning and layout design is reported in [1]. Fig. 5 shows a typical layout pattern generated by the system for a set of graphic objects with corresponding text blocks.

7 Integration and Implementation Aspects

The layout manager outlined above is integrated in the hierarchically organized architecture of the overall *WIP* system. This includes two parallel processing cascades for the incremental generation of text (cf. [17]) and pictures including depictions of 3D objects (cf. [37]) and is moderated by a presentation planner (cf. [2]) and the layout manager. So, there is a coordination of the contents generation and the for-

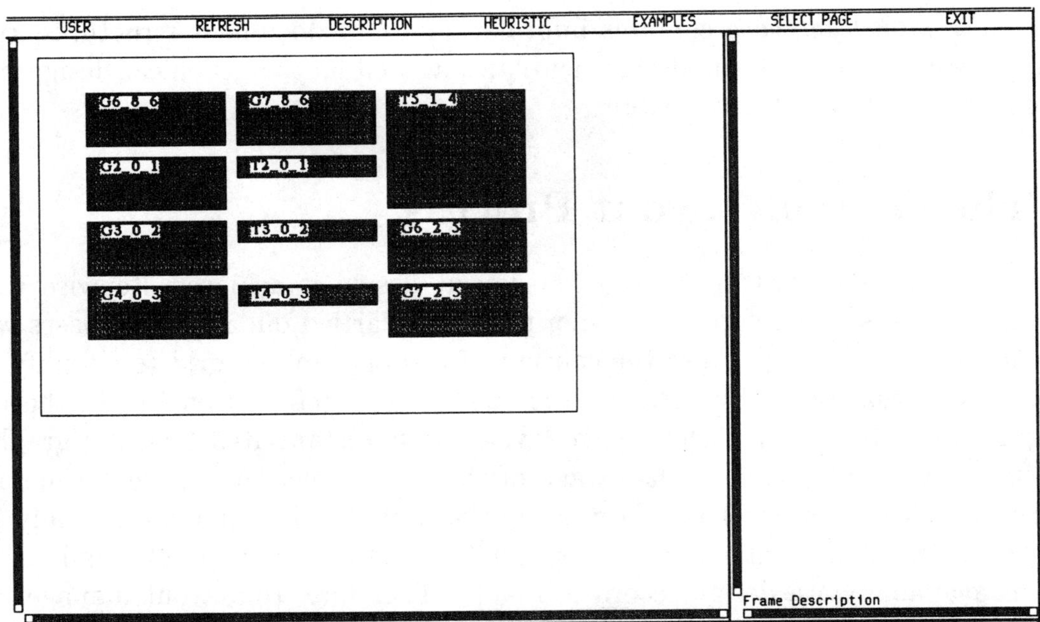

Figure 5: A Snapshot of a System Run

mat design process. A so-called *design record* is employed to exchange information about intermediate results of the current presentation generation between the various components. To achieve a coherent output with an optimal media mix, the single components of an intelligent user interface have to be interleaved. Therefore, the layout manager has to be integrated into the presentation planning process at an early stage to allow for an incremental refinement of the initial layout. The interplay of the various components is illustrated in a companion paper (see [1]).

The layout design process is influenced by most of *WIP*'s generation parameters as design objectives, resource limitations, output modes (incremental vs. complete only), and layout formats (e.g., hardcopy, screen display, slides), the costs of different modalities' activations, the user's individual preferences, and more.

LayLab, a stand-alone prototype version of *WIP*'s integrated layout manager, including *CLAY*, its constraint-based positioning component (see also [24]), has been implemented on a Symbolics XL 1200 Lisp machine and several MacIvory workstations under Genera 8.0 using Symbolics Common Lisp/CLOS and Flavors for object-oriented interface programming. The interaction handler and the typographer exploit features of the interface programming tools included in the Symbolics Lisp environment. These comprise window management utilities, which are compatible to the X-Windows system, and low-level text formatting routines. The constraint solvers *SIVAS* and *FIDOS* integrated in *CLAY* have been implemented by Wolfgang Maaß (for further information see [24]).

First evaluations of the constraint solving process achieved a high runtime efficiency. Currently, *CLAY* is transported to UNIX workstations and is going to be tested in other domains and environments (e.g., configuration of technical devices). The work on the intelligent typographic and document rendering component is still in progress. Preliminary demonstrators have already been implemented.

8 Conclusions and Future Work

The work presented in this paper reflects the problems surrounding intelligent layout design of multimodal presentations as well as the current interdisciplinary investigations in the area of graphics design and psychology. *LayLab*, a testbed system for laying out multimodal documents containing text and graphics elements with which it is provided by mode-specific generators has been discussed in terms of the *WIP* architecture. We hypothesized that increased flexibility of constraints, the semantic expressiveness of constraint hierarchies, and the efficiency gained from using the domain concept in combination with forward checking aim at a powerful problem solver for synthesis tasks like automatic layout.

Most of our current research is concerned with knowledge representation. We have to maintain the graphical constraints knowledge base in order to augment the primitive and non-primitive design constraints. Furthermore, we focus on a universal constraint-based representation of document structures and a declarative representation of design basics.

As our approach only allows a rudimentary treatment of design compromises and alternatives, we have to regard this feature by extending the underlying constraint language to complexer structures.

Since *WIP* will be enriched by further dynamic modalities such as animation in the future, the layout manager has to cope with that problem too.

Frequently, it is easier for experts in a specific domain (e.g., graphics designers) to express their expertises such as positive or negative constraints by graphical examples. Therefore, the construction of an automatic acquisition component that infers design constraints from graphical sketches will be required in order to allow a maintenance of the knowledge-base by the experts themselves (see also [22]). In that case, the system could learn new layout patterns by interactively criticizing old ones through the user.

Acknowledgements

The research reported in this paper has been carried out in the *WIP* project which is supported by the German Ministry for Research and Technology under contract ITW 8901 8. I would like to thank Wolfgang Wahlster, Steve Feiner, Elisabeth André and Thomas Rist for stimulating discussions about automating layout as well as Wolfgang Maaß and Dudung Soetopo who implemented a first prototype.

References

[1] E. André, W. Finkler, W. Graf, T. Rist, A. Schauder, and W. Wahlster. WIP: The automatic synthesis of multimodal presentations. In Maybury [30], pages 75–93. Forthcoming, also DFKI Research Report RR-92-46.

[2] E. André and T. Rist. The design of illustrated documents as a planning task. In Maybury [30], pages 94–116. Forthcoming, also DFKI Research Report RR-92-45.

[3] R. Arnheim, editor. *Towards a Psychology of Art.* University of California Press, Berkeley, 1966.

[4] A. Barr and E. Feigenbaum. *The Handbook of Artificial Intelligence*, volume 1. Pitman, London, England, 1981.

[5] R. Beach. *Setting Tables and Illustrations with Style.* PhD thesis, Dept. of Computer Science, University of Waterloo, Ontario, Canada, 1985.

[6] A. Borning. The programming language aspects of ThingLab, a constraint-oriented simulation laboratory. *ACM Transactions on Programming Languages and Systems*, 3(4):353–387, Oct. 1981.

[7] A. Borning and R. Duisberg. Constraint-based tools for building user interfaces. *ACM Transactions on Graphics*, 5(4):345–374, Oct. 1986.

[8] A. Borning, R. Duisberg, B. Freeman-Benson, A. Kramer, and M. Woolf. Constraint hierarchies. In *Proceedings of OOPSLA '87 (ACM Conference on Object-Oriented Programming Systems, Languages, and Applications)*, pages 48–60, Orlando, FL, Oct. 1987.

[9] E. Cohen, E. Smith, and L. Iverson. Constraint-based tiled windows. *IEEE Computer Graphics and Applications*, 6(5):35–45, 1986.

[10] M. Dincbas, P. Van Hentenryck, H. Simonis, A. Aggoun, T. Graf, and F. Berthier. The constraint logic programming language CHIP. In *Proceedings of the International Conference on Fifth Generation Computer Systems FGCS-88*, pages 693–702, Tokyo, Japan, Dec. 1988.

[11] S. Feiner. A grid-based approach to automating display layout. In *Proceedings of the Graphics Interface '88, Edmonton, Canada*, pages 192–197. Morgan Kaufmann, Los Altos, CA, June 1988.

[12] B. Freeman-Benson, J. Maloney, and A. Borning. An incremental constraint solver. *Communications of the ACM*, 33(1):54–63, 1990.

[13] M. Friedell. Automatic synthesis of graphical object descriptions. *Computer Graphics*, 18(3):53–62, 1984.

[14] J. Gosling. *Algebraic Constraints.* PhD thesis, Dept. of Computer Science, Carnegie Mellon University, 1983.

[15] W. H. Graf. Constraint-based processing of design knowledge. In *Working Notes of the AAAI-91 Workshop on Intelligent Multimedia Interfaces*, Anaheim, CA, U.S.A., July 1991.

[16] W. H. Graf and W. Maaß. Constraint-basierte Verarbeitung graphischen Wissens. In W. Brauer and D. Hernández, editors, *Proceedings of 4. Internationaler GI-Kongreß Wissensbasierte Systeme - Verteilte KI und kooperatives Arbeiten*, pages 243–253. Springer-Verlag, Berlin, Oct. 1991.

[17] K. Harbusch, W. Finkler, and A. Schauder. Incremental syntax generation with tree adjoining grammars. In W. Brauer and D. Hernández, editors, *Proceedings of 4. Internationaler GI-Kongreß Wissensbasierte Systeme - Verteilte KI und kooperatives Arbeiten*, pages 363–374. Springer-Verlag, Berlin, Oct. 1991.

[18] E. Hovy and Y. Arens. Automatic generation of formatted text. In *Proceedings of the 9th National Conference of the American Association for Artificial Intelligence*, pages 92–97, Anaheim, CA, U.S.A., July 1991.

[19] J. Jaffar and J.-L. Lassez. Constraint logic programming. In *Proceedings of the 14th ACM Symposium on Principles of Programming Languages*, pages 111–119, Munich, Germany, Jan. 1987.

[20] L. Koren and W. Meckler. *Graphics Design Cookbook: Mix and Match Recipes for Faster, Better Layouts.* Chronicle Books, San Francisco, CA, 1989.

[21] G. Kramer, J. Pabon, W. Keirouz, and R. Young. Geometric constraint satisfaction problems. In *Working Notes AAAI Spring Symposium 'Constraint-Based Reasoning'*, pages 242–251, Stanford University, CA, Mar. 1991.

[22] D. Kurlander and S. Feiner. Inferring constraints from multiple snapshots. Technical Report, Dept. of Computer Science, Columbia University, New York, NY, 1991.

[23] W. Leler. *Constraint Programming Languages: Their Specification and Generation.* Addison-Wesley, Reading, MA, 1988.

[24] W. Maaß. Constraint-basierte Plazierung in multimodalen Dokumenten am Beispiel des Layout-Managers in WIP. Master's thesis, Dept. of Computer Science, University of the Saarland, Saarbrücken, Germany, 1992.

[25] W. Maaß, T. Schiffmann, D. Soetopo, and W. Graf. LAYLAB: Ein System zur automatischen Plazierung von Text-Bild-Kombinationen in multimodalen Dokumenten. DFKI Document D-92-02, German Research Center for Artificial Intelligence (DFKI), Saarbrücken, Germany, 1991.

[26] J. Mackinlay. *Automatic Design of Graphical Presentations.* PhD thesis, Dept. of Computer Science, Stanford University, Stanford, CA, 1986.

[27] A. Mackworth. Consistency in networks of relations. *Artificial Intelligence*, 8(1):99–118, 1977.

[28] A. Mackworth. Constraint satisfaction. In S. Shapiro, editor, *Encyclopedia of Artificial Intelligence*, volume 1, pages 205–211. John Wiley & Sons, Chichester, England, 1988.

[29] W. Mann and S. Thompson. Rhetorical structure theory: Towards a functional theory of text organization. *Discourse Processes*, 9:57–90, 1986.

[30] M. T. Maybury, editor. *Intelligent Multimedia Interfaces.* AAAI Press, Menlo Park, CA, 1993. Forthcoming.

[31] S. Mittal and B. Falkenhainer. Dynamic constraint satisfaction problems. In *Proceedings of the 8th National Conference of the American Association for Artificial Intelligence*, pages 25–32, Boston, MA, U.S.A., July 1990.

[32] J. Müller-Brockmann. *Grid Systems in Graphic Design.* Verlag Arthur Niggli, Niederteufen, Switzerland, 1981.

[33] B. Myers. Using AI techniques to create user interfaces by example. In Sullivan and Tyler [41], pages 385–402.

[34] G. Nelson. Juno, a constraint-based graphics system. *Proceedings of the ACM SIGGRAPH '85*, 19(3):235–243, 1985.

[35] A. Ortony, J. Slack, and O. Stock, editors. *Communication from an Artificial Intelligence Perspective: Theoretical and Applied Issues.* Springer-Verlag, Berlin, 1992.

[36] T. Pavlidis and C. V. Wyk. An automatic beautifier for drawings and illustrations. *Computer Graphics*, 19(3):225–234, 1985.

[37] T. Rist and E. André. Incorporating graphics design and realization into the multimodal presentation system WIP. In T. Catarci, M. F. Costabile, and S. Levialdi, editors, *Advanced Visual Interfaces (Proceedings of the International Workshop AVI '92)*, World Scientific Series in Computer Science - Vol. 36, pages 193–207. World Scientific Press, Singapore, 1992. Also DFKI Research Report RR-92-44.

[38] R. Rüegg. *Basic Typography: Design with Letters.* ABC-Verlag, Zürich, Switzerland, 1989.

[39] D. Seligmann and S. Feiner. Automated generation of intent-based 3D illustrations. *Computer Graphics*, 25(3), July 1991.

[40] G. Smolka. Residuation and guarded rules for constraint logic programming. Research Report RR-92-13, German Research Center for Artificial Intelligence (DFKI), Saarbrücken, Germany, Mar. 1991.

[41] J. Sullivan and S. Tyler, editors. *Intelligent User Interfaces.* Frontier Series. ACM Press, New York, NY, 1991.

[42] G. J. Sussman and G. L. Steele. Constraints – a language for expressing almost-hierachical descriptions. *Artificial Intelligence*, 14(1):1–39, 1980.

[43] I. Sutherland. Sketchpad: A man-machine graphical communication system. In *IFIPS Proceedings of the Spring Joint Computer Conference*, pages 329–345, 1963.

[44] P. Van Hentenryck. *Constraint Satisfaction in Logic Programming.* MIT Press, Cambridge, MA, 1989. Revision of Ph.D. thesis, University of Namur, 1987.

[45] C. van Wyk. A high-level language for specifying pictures. *ACM Transactions on Graphics*, 1(2):163–182, 1982.

[46] W. Wahlster, E. André, S. Bandyopadhyay, W. Graf, and T. Rist. WIP: The coordinated generation of multimodal presentations from a common representation. In Ortony et al. [35], pages 121–144. Also DFKI Research Report RR-91-08.

[47] W. Wahlster, E. André, W. Graf, and T. Rist. Designing illustrated texts: How language production is influenced by graphics generation. In *Proceedings of the 5th Conference of the European Chapter of the Association for Computational Linguistics (EACL)*, pages 8–14. Berlin, 1991. Also DFKI Research Report RR-91-05.

[48] D. Willows and H. Houghton, editors. *The Psychology of Illustration, Vol. 1, 2.* Springer-Verlag, Berlin, 1987.

Reflections on. . .

Constraint-Based Graphical Layout of Multimodal Presentations

Winfried H. Graf

In the initial AVI '92 paper, we proposed a dedicated constraint approach toward graphical layout of multimodal presentations for the first time. Meanwhile, constraint processing has evolved into state-of-the-art technology in the area of graphical layout (cf. Hower and Graf 1996). Whereas our original paper was concerned with the layout of fully generated text/graphics documents, in our follow-up work, we have concentrated on a generalization of LayLab's hybrid constraint solver model with regard to dynamic multimedia presentations, including, for example, hyperstyle-like presentation parts and animated characters. Therefore, we have extended LayLab's previous architecture toward a full-fledged multimedia layout framework. Based on its central layout constraint engine, LayLab embeds major task-specific components to support on-line display layout, semantics-based typography, editing, interaction, and beautification by the help of constraints (Graf 1995).

We have extended the incremental constraint hierarchy solver SIVAS by indirect reference constraints to allow for dynamic input and user interaction (Graf & Neurohr 1995). Furthermore, the efficiency and expressiveness of the finite domain solver FIDOS has been enhanced by propagator constraints, typed constraints, and single/multiple-check constraints, as well as universal and existential quantification of constraints. In addition, we have introduced a new constraint primitive for the class of multimedia layout problems as well as dedicated heuristic search and optimization techniques. As the physical manifestation of multimedia presentations frequently conveys the communicative intention, rhetorical structure, and meaning of the underlying information, we have also addressed page layout itself as an important carrier of meaning, influencing the intentional and attentional state of the user (Graf 1996a, 1996b).

Besides the deployment of constraint-based layout technology, we have also focused on the gap between academic research prototypes and innovative products by applying the LayLab system to a diverse set of real-world application domains. For example, we have exploited FIDOS in an adaptive pagination tool for commercial yellow pages, called YPPS (Graf et al. 1996), that is already incorporated in the publishing process at two international telecommunication companies. Today YPPS is one of the first industrial graphics applications of constraint technology. Although multimedia technology is so popular that virtually everybody is using it, there seems to be no principled multimedia layout manager. In order to overcome this lack, we have recently proposed a standard reference model for an intelligent multimedia layout manager (Graf 1998). Our current work is concerned with empirical evaluations of layout techniques, layout of charts and tables, and the exploitation of constraint processing for intelligent net assistants.

REFERENCES

Graf, W. H. 1995. The Constraint-Based Layout Framework LayLab and Its Applications. In Cruz, I. F., Marks, J., and Wittenburg, K. (eds.), *Proceedings of the ACM Multimedia '95 Workshop on Effective Abstractions in Multimedia Layout, Presentations, and Interaction*, November 4, San Francisco. (*http://www.cs.tufts.edu/~isabel/mmwsproc.html*)

Graf, W. H. 1996a. Intent-Based Layout Design of Multimedia Presentations Using Constraints. Ph.D. dissertation, Dept. of Computer Science, University of the Saarland, Saarbrücken, Germany. (in German).

Graf, W. H. 1996b. Intent-Based Layout in Interactive Multimedia Communication. In Lee, J. (ed.), *Proceedings of the First International Workshop on Intelligence and Multimodality in Multimedia Interfaces*. Menlo Park, CA: AAAI Press.

Graf, W. H. 1997. Intelligent Multimedia Layout: A Reference Architecture for the Constraint-Based Spatial Layout of Multimedia Presentations. In Rist, T., Faconti, G., and Wilson, M. (guest eds.), *Computer Standards and Interfaces* (Special Issue on Intelligent Multimedia Presentation Systems), Vol. 18, Nos. 6 and 7, 515–524. Amsterdam: Elsevier Science.

Graf, W. H., and Neurohr, S. 1995. Constraint-Based Layout in Visual Program Design. In Haarslev, V. (ed.), *Proceedings of the 11th IEEE Symposium on Visual Languages*, 116–117. Los Alamitos, CA: IEEE Computer Society Press.

Graf, W. H.; Neurohr, S.; and Goebel, R. 1996. YPPS: A Constraint-Based Tool for the Pagination of Yellow-Page Directories. In Geske, U., and Simonis, H. (eds.), *Proceedings of the KI-96 Workshop on Declarative Constraint Programming*, 87–97. GMD-Studien 297, St. Augustin, Germany: GMD.

Hower, W., and Graf, W. H. 1996. A Bibliographical Survey of Constraint-Based Approaches to CAD, Graphics Layout, Visualization, and Related Topics. *Knowledge-Based Systems* 9(7): 449–469. Oxford, UK: Elsevier.

An Empirical Study of Algorithms for Point-Feature Label Placement

Jon Christensen
Harvard University
Cambridge, Massachusetts

Joe Marks
Mitsubishi Electric Research Laboratories
Cambridge, Massachusetts

Stuart Shieber
Harvard University
Cambridge, Massachusetts

Abstract

A major factor affecting the clarity of graphical displays that include text labels is the degree to which labels obscure display features (including other labels) as a result of spatial overlap. Point-feature label placement (PFLP) is the problem of placing text labels adjacent to point features on a map or diagram so as to maximize legibility. This problem occurs frequently in the production of many types of informational graphics, though it arises most often in automated cartography. In this paper we present a comprehensive treatment of the PFLP problem, viewed as a type of combinatorial optimization problem. Complexity analysis reveals that the basic PFLP problem and most interesting variants of it are NP-hard. These negative results help inform a survey of previously reported algorithms for PFLP; not surprisingly, all such algorithms either have exponential time complexity or are incomplete. To solve the PFLP problem in practice, then, we must rely on good heuristic methods. We propose two new methods, one based on a discrete form of gradient descent, the other on simulated annealing, and report on a series of empirical tests comparing these and the other known algorithms for the problem. Based on this study, the first to be conducted, we identify the best approaches as a function of available computation time.

CR Categories: H.5.2 [**Information Interfaces and Presentation**]: User Interfaces—*screen design.* 2.1 [**Artificial Intelligence**]: Applications and Expert Systems—*cartography.* I.3.5 [**Computer Graphics**]: Computational Geometry and Object Modeling—*geometric algorithms, languages, and systems.*

General Terms: algorithms, experimentation.

Additional Key Words and Phrases: label placement, automated cartography, stochastic methods, simulated annealing, heuristic search.

1 Introduction

Tagging graphical objects with text labels is a fundamental task in the design of many types of informational graphics. This problem is seen in its most essential form in the field of cartography, where text labels must be placed on maps while avoiding overlaps with cartographic symbols and other labels, though it also arises frequently in the production of other graphics (e.g., scatterplots). Although several techniques have been reported for automating various label-placement tasks, the positioning of labels is still performed manually in many applications, even though it can be very tedious.[1] Determining an optimal positioning of the labels is, consequently, an important problem.

In cartography, three different label-placement tasks are usually identified: labeling of area features (such as oceans or countries), line features (such as rivers or roads), and point features (such as cities or mountain peaks) (Imhof, 1962; 1975). While it is true that determining the optimal placement of a label for an isolated point feature is a very different task from determining the optimal placement of a label for an isolated line or area feature, the three placement tasks share a common

[1]Cook and Jones (1990) report that cartographers typically place labels at the rate of only 20 to 30 labels per hour, with map lettering contributing up to half of the time required for producing high-quality maps.

combinatorial aspect when multiple features are present. The complexity arises because the placement of a label can have global consequences due to label-label overlaps. This combinatorial aspect of the label-placement task is independent of the nature of the features being labeled, and is the fundamental source of difficulty in automating label placement. We therefore concentrate on point-feature label placement (PFLP) without loss of generality; in Section 5 of the paper we describe how our results generalize to labeling tasks involving line and area features.

The PFLP problem can be thought of as a combinatorial optimization problem. Like all such problems, two aspects must be defined: a *search space* and an *objective function.*

Search space. An element of the search space can be thought of as a function from point features to label positions, which we will call a *labeling*. The set of potential label positions for each point feature therefore characterizes the PFLP search space. For most of the published algorithms, the potential label positions are taken, following cartographic standards, from an explicitly enumerated set. Figure 1 shows a typical set of eight possible label positions for a point feature. Each box corresponds to a region in which the label may be placed. Alternatively, a continuous placement model may be used, for example by specifying a circle around the point feature that the label must touch without intersecting.

In certain variants of the PFLP problem, we allow a labeling to omit certain points and their labels (presumably those that are most problematic to label, or least significant to the labeling application). When this option is included, the PFLP problem is said to include *point selection.*[2]

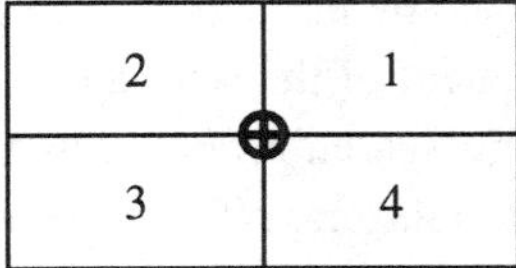

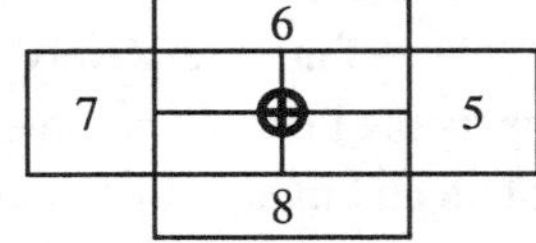

Figure 1: A set of potential label positions and their relative desirability. Lower values indicate more desirable positions.

Objective function. The function to be optimized, the objective function, should assign to each element of the search space (a potential labeling of the points) a value that corresponds to the relative quality of that labeling. The notion of labeling quality has been studied by cartographers, most notably by Imhof (1962; 1975). However, Imhof's analysis is descriptive, not prescriptive; coming up with an appropriate definition of the objective function for a general label-placement problem (that is, one that includes point, line, and area features) is a difficult task. Labeling quality can depend on many factors, including detailed "world knowledge" and characteristics of human visual perception. Many of the label-placement algorithms reported in the literature therefore incorporate sophisticated objective functions. A popular approach has been to use a rule-based paradigm to encode the knowledge needed for the objective function (Ahn and Freeman, 1984; Freeman and Ahn, 1987; Jones, 1989; Cook and Jones, 1990; Doerschler and Freeman, 1992). For the PFLP problem, however, a relatively simple objective function suffices. Our formulation of the objective function is due to Yoeli (1972).[3] In Yoeli's scheme, the quality of a labeling depends on the following factors:

- The amount of overlap between text labels and graphical features (including other text labels);
- A priori preferences among a canonical set of potential label positions (a standard ranking is shown in Figure 1); and
- The number of point features left unlabeled. (This criterion is pertinent only when point selection is incorporated into the PFLP problem.)

[2]In many types of production-quality maps, overplots are preferred to exercising point selection (Ebinger and Goulette, 1990).

[3]A recent study conducted by Wu and Buttenfield (1991) addresses the issue of placement preference for point-feature labels in more detail.

Figure 2 illustrates these factors. By specifying how to compute a numerical score for each of the criteria above, an objective function can be defined. Such a function assigns to each labeling a number that indicates its relative quality. We will assume that low scores correspond to better labelings, so that the goal of the search is to minimize the objective function.

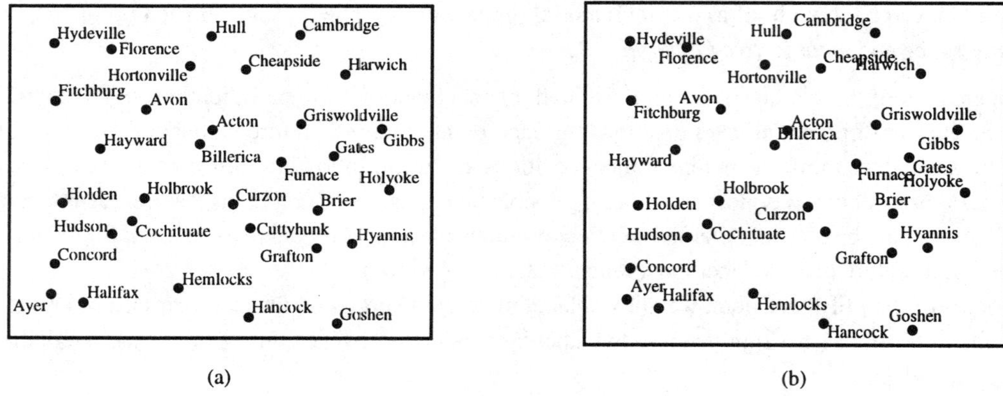

Figure 2: Good (a) and bad (b) labelings of the same map.

The PFLP problem is a combinatorial optimization problem defined by its search space and objective function; we wish to identify a general algorithm that is able to find a relatively good element of the search space. A natural issue to raise, before exploring possible search algorithms, is the intrinsic complexity of this search problem. In Section 2 we summarize some previous results that show that the problem and many of its interesting variants are NP-hard. Thus, any complete search algorithm will be impractical, any practical algorithm incomplete.[4] This characterization is borne out by previously published algorithms, which fall into two classes: exhaustive search algorithms and local search algorithms. We review these algorithms in Section 3. As expected, the exhaustive algorithms are computationally profligate, and therefore impractical for realistically sized labeling instances.

We also present two new algorithms for the PFLP problem in Section 3. The first is a local search technique based on a discrete form of gradient descent. Although it is also incomplete, its performance on problems with high label density and its efficiency make it attractive under certain circumstances. The second technique is a stochastic algorithm based on simulated annealing. An extensive empirical comparison of all the algorithms, the first comparative study of label-placement heuristics, is presented in Section 4;[5] it illustrates the advantages of the new methods and provides recommendations for selecting a labeling algorithm.

2 The Computational Complexity of PFLP

In this section, we review some recent results on the inherent complexity of PFLP that have implications for algorithm design. To demonstrate the inherent complexity of the problem (and, subsequently, to compare various algorithms for the task), we must decide upon a particular instance of search space and objective function. We begin with a relatively simple version of the problem. Once this simplified problem is shown to be NP-hard, it is straightforward to demonstrate that more complicated variants of the problem are also NP-hard.

Our initial statement of the PFLP problem assumes a discrete placement model comprising four equally favored candidate positions, those numbered 1 through 4 in Figure 1. Point selection is not allowed and the objective function to be minimized is the number of point features labeled with one or more overplots. This simplified PFLP problem statement is an optimization problem. In order to apply the theory of NP-completeness to PFLP, we formulate a corresponding decision problem. For any given PFLP problem instance, we can ask the question: Is there an admissible labeling, a labeling with a score of zero, in

[4]This holds, of course, only if $P \neq NP$, as is commonly believed.

[5]Brief summaries of this work have appeared elsewhere (Christensen et al. 1993; 1994).

which no labels overlap and no point features are obscured? The NP-completeness of this admissible-labeling problem has been established independently by at least three different teams of researchers (Kato and Imai, 1988; Marks and Shieber, 1991; Formann and Wagner, 1991). An algorithm for the PFLP optimization problem could always be used to solve the admissible-labeling problem: find an optimal labeling and check to see whether the cost is 0. Thus the PFLP optimization problem is at least as difficult as the admissible-labeling problem; in other words, the admissible-labeling result implies that optimal PFLP is NP-hard.

In spite of the apparent intractability of the basic problem, some simple restrictions can reduce the complexity dramatically. For example, a placement model that allows only two potential positions for each label results in a problem that is solved easily in polynomial time (Formann and Wagner, 1991). Similarly, the restricted set of problem instances in which no potential label position overlaps more than one other potential label position can also be solved efficiently.[6] However, these polynomially solvable subcases notwithstanding, the previous complexity results imply that PFLP problems likely to be of practical interest are NP-hard.

If label sizes are held steady, increasing the scale of a map makes more room for labels. This observation leads to the following question: how much must the scale be increased to permit an admissible labeling for a given PFLP problem instance? Formann and Wagner have developed an efficient algorithm for this problem that is guaranteed to find an admissible labeling with a map scale no more than twice optimal (Formann and Wagner, 1991).

The recent complexity results make it clear that practical variants of PFLP, including all those discussed in this paper, are almost certainly intractable. Thus the failure of previous researchers to find an exact, polynomial-time algorithm for PFLP is not surprising—it is extremely unlikely that anyone will ever discover such an algorithm. Instead, research efforts should be directed towards powerful heuristic methods that may not exhibit guaranteed performance bounds, but that may work acceptably in practice. Several such algorithms are described and compared in the next section.

3 Algorithms for PFLP

Previously proposed PFLP algorithms fall into two main classes: those that perform a potentially exhaustive global search for an acceptable or optimal labeling, and those that perform search on a local basis only.

3.1 Exhaustive search: naive or clever

Exhaustive search algorithms for constraint satisfaction are often categorized based on the manner in which backtracking is performed. As an example, consider an algorithm that enumerates points in a prescribed order and places each label in a position that is currently unobstructed. If, as the algorithm proceeds, a point cannot be labeled (either because there are no positions without conflict, or because all available positions have been tried), the algorithm returns to the most recently labeled point and considers the next available position. The algorithm continues in this way until an acceptable labeling is identified or until the entire search space has been exhausted. A variety of modifications can be made to this algorithm in the hope of improving its performance. Heuristics include variable ordering, value ordering, returning to the source of failure, and various pruning techniques (Korf, 1988).

Exhaustive search algorithms like these have formed the basis for numerous reported algorithms for label placement (Ahn and Freeman, 1984; Freeman and Ahn, 1987; Noma, 1987; Freeman, 1988; Jones, 1989; Cook and Jones, 1990; Ebinger and Goulette, 1990; Doerschler and Freeman, 1992; Consorti et. al, 1993). While these algorithms perform acceptably for relatively small problems, in practice the exponential nature of the search space quickly overcomes the heuristics for even moderately sized problems, making the approach of exhaustive search impractical as a general solution to the PFLP problem, regardless of the sophistication of the particular heuristic. Indeed, the widespread use of exhaustive search techniques for the combinatorial aspects of the label-placement problem is something of a mystery. Zoraster (1991) notes that part of the problem might be the inappropriate use of expert-system technology: whereas a rule-based approach is useful in general label placement for determining potential label positions and for evaluating candidate labelings, it suggests, misleadingly, that rule-based techniques—exhaustive search is easy to implement in a rule-based system—are useful for all aspects of label placement.

---

[6]Developing an efficient algorithm for this artificial problem is left as an exercise for the interested reader.

3.2 Greedy algorithms

A more practical approach to search results from avoiding the unbounded backtracking strategy of the exhaustive methods altogether. By limiting the scope of the search, more efficient algorithms can be devised. Of course, these algorithms may not find optimal solutions, but the hope is that a suitable trade-off between labeling quality and computational cost can be found.

Instead of undoing previously computed label placements, as with exhaustive search and its variants, any point whose label cannot be placed can be treated summarily: the point can be left out if point selection is allowed (Langran and Poiker, 1986), or it can be labeled even though a label overlap or feature obscuration results. (A third option, that of appealing to a human oracle for assistance, is noted by Yoeli (1972) as a practical alternative.) Such a "greedy algorithm" for PFLP yields behavior that is effective for a much more realistic space of problems, although the lack of backtracking certainly impairs the quality of the solutions that are found. For a greedy algorithm to be at all successful in identifying reasonable labelings, it is essential that heuristics for guiding the search, such as those mentioned in Section 3.1, be used. Even then, there is typically much improvement that can be made to the resulting labelings, as will be shown subsequently.

3.3 Discrete gradient descent

The quality of labelings produced by a greedy algorithm can be improved dramatically if the labelings are repaired subsequently by local alteration. This is the motivation for the gradient-descent algorithms presented below. A gradient-descent method is defined relative to a set of operations that specify ways in which one or more labels can be repositioned simultaneously. The basic idea of gradient descent is to choose from among the set of available operations the one that yields the most immediate improvement. By repeatedly applying the operation that most improves the labeling (or, equivalently, the operation that causes the most movement in the direction of the objective-function gradient), a new labeling can be computed that is significantly superior to the original. Again we present a straw man to exemplify the idea. Let the set of operations comprise those that move a single label arbitrarily from one potential position to another. An outline of the resulting algorithm, which we call *discrete gradient descent* is given below:

1. For each feature, place its label randomly in any of the available candidate positions.
2. Repeat until no further improvement is possible:
   (a) For each feature, consider moving the label to each of the alternative positions.
   (b) For each such repositioning, calculate the change in the objective function that would result if the label were moved.
   (c) Implement the single label repositioning that results in the most improvement. (Ties are resolved randomly.)

In practice the algorithm precomputes a table of costs associated with each possible repositioning. After each label positioning, only elements of the table that touch the old or new label positions are recomputed.

Local minima

The major weakness of the discrete gradient-descent algorithm is its inability to escape from local minima of the objective function. Figure 3 shows a typical example of a local minimum. (The examples of local minima in this section, and those discussed for the Hirsch and Zoraster algorithms, though artificially constructed, are idealized versions of local minima that arose during experimentation with actual maps.) In this case, the conflict can be resolved by moving the lower feature's label to its bottom-left position and the upper feature's label to its upper-right position. Unfortunately, making any single move has no effect on the value of the objective function, and, because the algorithm only accepts changes that show an immediate improvement, the algorithm is unaware of the possibility of accepting a neutral move in order to make an improvement. Adjusting the algorithm to allow it to make moves that do not affect the objective function might remedy this particular example, but is not sufficient in general. In the example of Figure 4, the current value of the objective function could be improved from four obstructed labels (Figure 4a) to three (Figure 4b) by moving the four middle labels to their left-most positions. However any one of these moves will initially result in an uphill step and an intermediate score of 5. To limit the incidence of such local minima, more sophisticated gradient-descent heuristics have been devised. Nevertheless, as we will see, even the simplest discrete gradient-descent method performs surprisingly well.

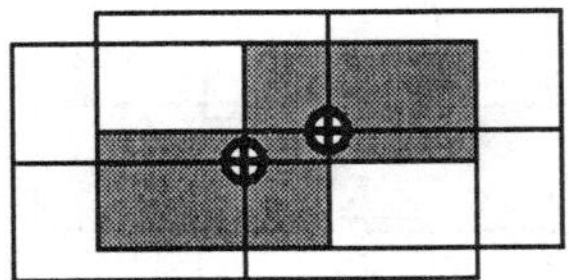

Figure 3: A local minimum of the discrete gradient-descent algorithm. The candidate label positions are marked with boxes, and the selected label positions are shaded.

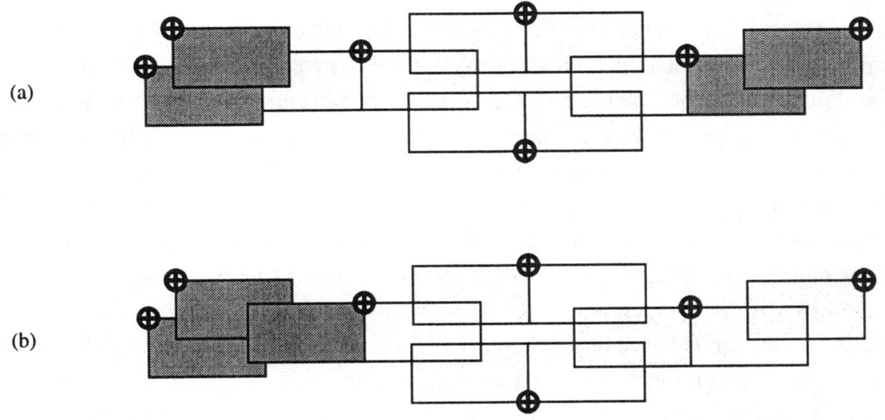

Figure 4: Another local minimum of the discrete gradient-descent algorithm (a) and an optimal configuration (b). The candidate label positions are marked with boxes, and selected label positions are shaded. Obstructed label positions are shaded dark.

3.4 Approximating the gradient with overlap vectors

Hirsch (1982) presents a more sophisticated gradient-descent method for PFLP.[7,8] Hirsch's algorithm uses a continuous placement model in which each point feature has an infinite set of potential label positions. The potential positions for a point touch, but do not intersect, a circle centered about the point; labels are allowed to slide continuously around a circle (see Figure 5a). When the label touches at the highest, lowest, left-most, or right-most points of the circle, it is considered to be in a special zone and is allowed to slide back and forth along the point of tangency (see Figure 5b).

Initially each label is placed in the special zone to the right of its point. Each label is then tested for overlaps with other labels and intersections with the circular boundaries of other points. For each conflict an overlap vector is computed based on the x and y extents of the overlap or intersected area. Each overlap vector is split between the two conflicting features and represents the movement required to eliminate a particular conflict. The sum of overlap vectors associated with each label is then calculated to give an aggregate vector that represents (in an intuitive sense) a good direction in which to move the label so as to eliminate the overlaps and intersections. In Figure 5c the overlap vectors are drawn in light gray, and the aggregate vectors in black. (For labels involved in only one conflict the single overlap vector and the aggregate vector are the same.)

---

[7]A more elaborate version of this approach is described in U.S. Patent #5,355,314 (Feigenbaum, 1994). The algorithm described therein differs from Hirsch's method in the following ways: in addition to repulsive forces from other labels and features, labels experience attractive forces from the cartographic features that they tag; labels initially start out very small and are grown to their full size over the course of the physical simulation; the coefficients in the various force formulae are set so that conflicts lead to a "marginally stable" system in which conflicted labels can be subjected to strong forces sufficient to escape some local minima; moving labels encounter frictional forces that help to dampen oscillations; and the Imhof standards for point-feature label preferences are incorporated through various algorithm-specific heuristics. This algorithm is currently in commercial use. Due to its recent publication, we were unable to include the algorithm in our comparative study.

[8]Mower (1986; 1993) describes an approach that shares characteristics of both Hirsch's algorithm (relaxation and constraint-propagation) and depth-first search (features are treated serially instead of in parallel as Hirsch does).

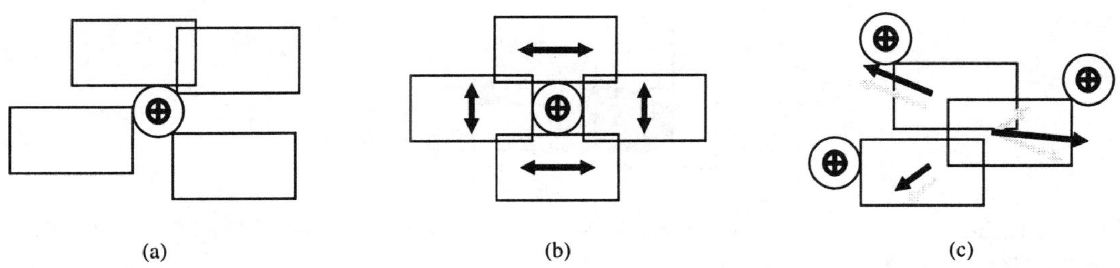

Figure 5: Some example potential label positions for Hirsch's algorithm (a), along with the special zones (b), and an example of overlap vectors (c).

Once an aggregate overlap vector has been calculated for each label, the algorithm seeks to move each label in the general direction of this vector in an effort to reduce the number of overlaps. The heuristic technique employed involves two styles of movement, an *incremental movement* around the circle and an *absolute movement*, which shifts the label directly to the point on the circle indicated by the overlap vector. Thus there are only two basic operations available for altering a labeling, but each operation is applied to all point features on a given round of application so that many labels may change positions simultaneously. The absolute movement repositions the label directly to the position indicated by the aggregate vector, regardless of the label's current position. The incremental movement, on the other hand, involves a series of heuristic rules that move the label in the direction of the aggregate overlap vector. Hirsch suggests alternating between the two movement styles, with more frequent application of the incremental movement.

The intuition behind the algorithm is best explained by an analogy with a physical system. The individual overlap vectors represent a "force" of repulsion between overlapping objects, the sum an aggregate force. Thus, through gradual movements, the system settles into a local minimum of the "energy" of the system. The overlap vectors approximate the gradient in the energy space. To allow some ability to exit from local minima, the absolute movements are designed to allow a jump from one energy state to another, hopefully lower one.

There are two sources of problems for Hirsch's algorithm. First, since the overlap vectors provide only an approximation of the gradient, they are subject to error. Second, like the discrete gradient-descent algorithm, Hirsch's algorithm is susceptible to getting stuck in local minima.

Gradient approximation errors

A typical dilemma is due to the summation of overlap vectors. When multiple labels overplot a single label, the magnitude of the calculated aggregate vector will often be unnecessarily large, leading to problems of overshooting during incremental movements.

Note also that Hirsch's overlap vectors each exhibit two degrees of freedom, whereas the labels are constrained to lie tangent to their associated circles. The result is that even in those cases where the accumulated overlap vector represents a favorable direction of movement, the particular manner in which a label is repositioned is often quite fragile. If a large component of the overlap vector points radially outward, for example, the location of the repositioned label is somewhat arbitrary.

Local minima

Hirsch's algorithm, like the discrete gradient-descent algorithm, can also get stuck in local minima. The nature of these minima is closely related to the specific heuristics the algorithm employs in response to various overlap situations. Figure 6 shows a problematic configuration. During applications of the incremental movement, the label is adjusted slightly up and down until it is centered between, but still conflicting with, the two labels above and below. During applications of the absolute-style movement, the horizontal component of the overlap vector dominates, and the label cycles between the left and right placements, missing the acceptable positions above and below the feature.

Compensating for the placement model

In order to compare the performance of Hirsch's algorithm against other PFLP algorithms, several issues relating to the placement model need to be addressed. The presence of a circular buffer surrounding each point feature handicaps the algorithm, disallowing free space that other algorithms are able to exploit, and forcing labels outward, thus increasing their effec-

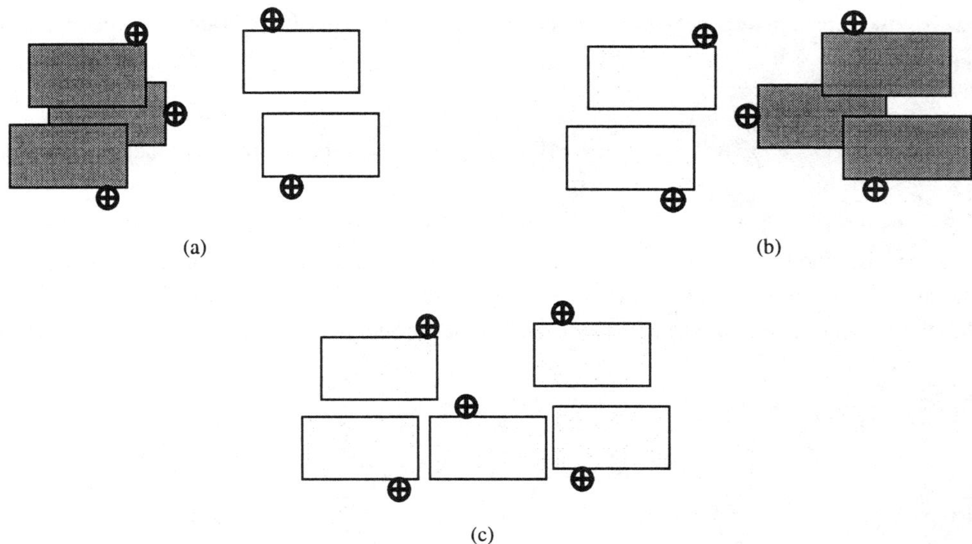

Figure 6: A local minimum of Hirsch's algorithm. The algorithm oscillates between configurations (a) and (b), unable to discover the preferred configuration (c).

tive dimensions. We considered two methods to compensate for this. First, we experimented with adjusting the label sizes for Hirsch's algorithm. We decreased the dimensions of each label such that the combined area of the placement circle and reduced label was equivalent to the area of the unmodified label. Second, we simply set the radius of the placement circle to zero. We found the latter method to perform slightly better on average, and included this variant of the algorithm in our comparisons.[9] A related issue involves the continuous nature of the placement model. Since this allows a larger and therefore less-constrained search space, this probably gives Hirsch's algorithm an advantage. Although this discrepancy is harder to resolve, a fairer comparison could be obtained by running the discrete algorithms with a 16- or 20-position placement model, as opposed to the four-position model used in the experiments. However, the results described in Section 4 render this point irrelevant.

3.5 Mathematical programming for PFLP

Next, we turn to an algorithm introduced by Zoraster (1986; 1990) that addresses the optimization nature of PFLP directly by applying mathematical programming techniques to its solution.[10] Zoraster begins by formulating PFLP as a 0-1 integer programming (ZOLP) problem:[11]

- Given K labels and N_k possible positions for each label, each potential label position is represented by a variable $X_{i,k}$, $1 \le i \le N_k$, and $1 \le k \le K$. (Point selection is achieved by specifying a special label "position" that indicates a deselected point.)
- Each $X_{i,k}$ has value 0 or 1, indicating the absence or presence, respectively, of a label in that position.
- One set of constraints expresses the requirement that each point be labeled exactly once: $\sum_{i=1}^{N_k} X_{i,k} = 1$ for $1 \le k \le K$.

[9]This is perhaps not surprising given the algorithm's predilection for label placements within special zones. Incremental movements tend to relocate labels into special zones, whereas only the absolute-style movements are able to move a label out of a special zone. Since the algorithm finishes with a series of 15 incremental movements, in practice nearly all labels finish in special zones.

[10]This algorithm is in commercial use in the oil industry to label drilling maps (Zoraster, 1990).

[11]Cromley (1986) has experimented independently with a slightly different ZOLP formulation of the label-placement problem.

- Given Q pairwise overlaps between possible label positions, a second set of constraints expresses the requirement that no two labels overlap: $X_{r_q, s_q} + X_{r'_q, s'_q} \leq 1$ for each potential overlap, $1 \leq q \leq Q$.

- The objective function is $\sum_{k=1}^{K} \sum_{i=1}^{N_k} W_{i,k} X_{i,k}$, where $W_{i,k}$ is a weighting that represents placement preferences.

Because ZOLP is itself NP-hard (Sahni, 1974), a complete, efficient algorithm for the PFLP problem recast in this way is still not possible, but heuristic techniques for ZOLP can now be applied to the PFLP problem. Zoraster combines Lagrangian relaxation, subgradient optimization, and several problem-specific heuristics in his solution. The primary insight of Zoraster's algorithm is to relax the overplot constraints and include them as additional penalty terms in the objective function. This gives:

- Minimize $\sum_{k=1}^{K} \sum_{i=1}^{N_k} W_{i,k} X_{i,k} + \sum_{q=1}^{Q} (X_{r_q, s_q} + X_{r'_q, s'_q} - 1) d_q$

- Still subject to $\sum_{i=1}^{N_k} X_{i,k} = 1$ for $1 \leq k \leq K$

In this modified objective function, the $d_q \geq 0$ are Lagrangian multipliers, one for each pairwise overplot constraint. Note that for a given set of Lagrangian multipliers, the minimum value of the objective function is easily identified by choosing the label-position variable with the smallest objective-function coefficient for each point feature. Although Lagrangian methods for ZOLP can be arbitrarily sophisticated, Zoraster's basic algorithm is a straightforward implementation of standard techniques (Fisher, 1981):

1. Compute and store the objective-function coefficient for each potential label position.
2. Generate a current labeling (CL) by picking the label position with the lowest objective-function coefficient for each point feature.
3. Initialize the active constraint set (ACS) to the empty set.
4. Repeat for 40 iterations or until a solution with no label conflicts is found:
   (a) Identify all pairwise constraints that CL violates and add any new ones to ACS. (The Lagrangian multiplier of each newly introduced constraint is zero initially, so adding a new constraint to ACS does not affect the objective-function coefficients.)
   (b) Make a local copy, CL', of CL.
   (c) Repeat for x iterations, where x is the lower of 400 or the number of iterations required to find a feasible solution with respect to the current ACS, plus an additional 100 iterations if a feasible solution is found in the first 400 iterations:[12]
      i. Update CL' by picking the label position with the lowest objective-function coefficient for each point feature.
      ii. Copy CL' to CL if it is better.
      iii. If a constraint in ACS is overconstrained (i.e., both conflicting label positions are occupied), the corresponding Lagrangian multiplier is increased, thus increasing the objective-function coefficients for the two label positions involved.
      iv. If a constraint in ACS is underconstrained (i.e., both conflicting label positions are not occupied), the corresponding Lagrangian multiplier is decreased, thus decreasing the objective-function coefficients for the two label positions involved.
5. Return CL.

[12]This inner loop constitutes the Lagrangian heuristic, with steps (iii) and (iv) constituting the subgradient optimization. Note that the Lagrangian heuristic will be solving relatively simplified versions of the full problem initially, because very few constraints will be included in ACS at first.

Local minima

If the algorithm were implemented exactly as described above, it would perform quite poorly. The algorithm exhibits two weaknesses: a pronounced sensitivity to local minima, and a tendency to fall into useless cyclic behavior.

To address the worst of these deficiencies, Zoraster recommends a series of modifications to the basic algorithm. The first modification he suggests is rescaling the size of the multiplier increments used in 4(c)iii and 4(c)iv. If a specified number of iterations have passed without improving the best solution seen, the algorithm is assumed to be in a region surrounding a local minimum of the objective function. By reducing the multiplier increments periodically, the algorithm is often able to identify improved minima.

Even with this modification, the algorithm tends to cycle about local minima, continuously re-evaluating a particular sequence of labelings. If two features have overlapping label positions, for example, and both are currently occupied, then the associated objective-function coefficients of both positions will be increased. This will make them less attractive over time and it is likely that both labels will be simultaneously moved to alternate positions. On subsequent iterations, both positions will still overlap but are now unoccupied so their associated coefficients will decrease. This will make both positions relatively more attractive to their respective features and it often occurs that they will be simultaneously reoccupied. This situation is illustrated in Figure 7. In order to avoid this particular type of cyclic behavior, Zoraster discriminates in the overconstrained case, applying the multiplier to only one of the objective-function coefficients; the choice between coefficients is made by examining whether the algorithm is currently in an odd- or even-numbered iteration. This second modification proves to be crucial to the success of the algorithm though it has no motivation or analogue in the mathematical formulation.

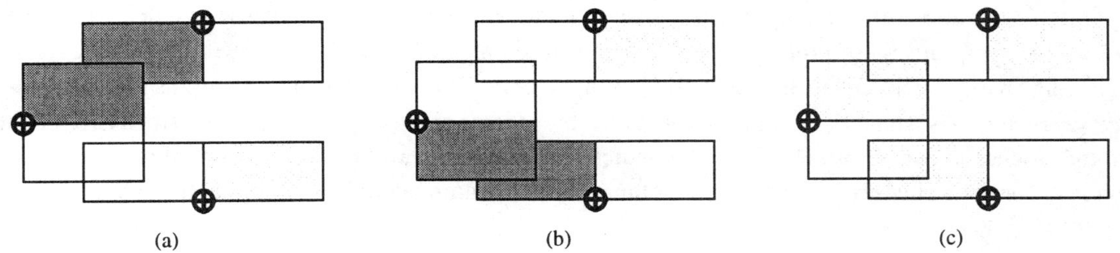

Figure 7: Stable and unstable configurations for Zoraster's approach. The conflict in configuration (a) causes the filled regions of the upper and left points to be disfavored, and the slack in the potential conflict between the lower and left points causes the unfilled regions for those two points to be favored. This leads eventually to modifying the configuration as in (b). This configuration, similarly, eventually leads back to the configuration in (a). The stable configuration (c) is never found.

A more insidious form of cycling can be caused by the intersection of more than two potential label positions. Overplots will gradually be discouraged, yet resolved overplots will result in underconstrained pairwise constraints, which in turn encourage surrounding labels to repopulate the contentious region. This situation is illustrated in Figure 8. Since the center candidate position overplot represents an underconstrained constraint, the left and right labels will be encouraged to move into the conflicted area, despite the fact that this will always introduce a conflict with the top label. As the number of label positions that overlap increases beyond three, the problem is exacerbated since label positionings are encouraged in regions that are often already dense with overplots. Zoraster attempts to address this deficiency by a third modification: arbitrarily pinning variables (i.e., fixing their values permanently) that are subject to four or more pairwise overplot constraints. If no feasible solution has been identified after 400 iterations of the Lagrangian heuristic, variables that are subject to more than three overplot constraints are pinned to zero. If after 600 iterations a feasible solution has still not been identified, the current (infeasible) solution is returned to the top level of the algorithm. This is equivalent to arbitrarily eliminating label positions in crowded areas of the map.

A fourth modification that attempts to control the algorithm's susceptibility to this weakness is the choice of multiplier increments. Zoraster recommends an initial overconstrained stepsize of $+\frac{1}{8}$ and an underconstrained stepsize of $-\frac{1}{16}$. The relative magnitudes of the stepsizes loosely represent the ability of a violated constraint to discourage subsequent reoccupation of a conflicted label position. Although Zoraster offers these values as empirical constants based on his experiments with a vari-

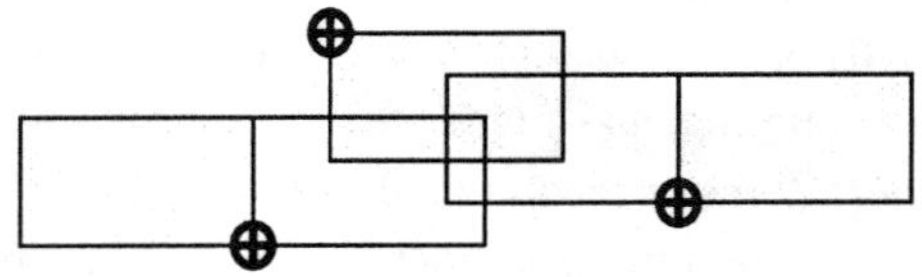

Figure 8: An unstable configuration for Zoraster's algorithm.

ety of different maps, optimal values are probably dependent on the density of the particular labeling problem. Indeed, we obtained better performance by using slightly modified parameter values and by making other subtle changes to the algorithm, as discussed elsewhere (Christensen et al., 1992).

3.6 Stochastic search

As we have seen, each of the local search methods can be trapped in local minima of the search space; the inherent intractability of the problem makes this inevitable for any practical algorithm. Nonetheless, we may still hope to improve upon the level of performance exhibited by these algorithms by examining more carefully the frailties that they exhibit.

The problems with the local search methods fall into two classes. First, there are systematic patterns on which the various algorithms get into trouble by getting trapped in local minima. As the number and density of points increases, the odds of seeing these patterns increase correspondingly, and performance may degrade. Second, the particular operations that the algorithms incorporate do not allow for jumping out of a local minimum once one is found. These two behaviors of *systematicity* and *monotonicity* are symptomatic of problems for which stochastic methods tend to work well. Stochastic methods, such as simulated annealing (Kirkpatrick, Gelatt Jr., and Vecchi, 1983; Černy, 1985) and genetic algorithms (Holland, 1975), attempt to resolve the problems of systematicity and monotonicity by incorporating a probabilistic or stochastic element into the search. Since the stochastic course of behavior is unpredictable, systematic artifacts of the algorithm can be eliminated, and allowance can be made for a suitably limited, nonmonotonic ability to jump out of local minima. It seems natural then to apply a stochastic method to the PFLP problem.

Simulated annealing for PFLP

Simulated annealing (Kirkpatrick, Gelatt Jr., and Vecchi, 1983; Černy, 1985) is essentially a stochastic gradient-descent method that allows movement in directions other than that of the gradient. In fact, the solution is sometimes allowed to get worse rather than better. Of course, such anarchic behavior is not tolerated uniformly. Rather, the ability of the algorithm to degrade the solution is controlled by a parameter T, called the temperature, that decreases over time according to an annealing schedule. At zero temperature, such negative steps are disallowed completely, so that the algorithm reduces to a descent method (though not necessarily along the gradient). At higher temperatures, however, a wider range of the space can be explored, so that regions surrounding better local minima (and perhaps even the global minimum) may be visited. The following outline describes the essential characteristics of a simulated-annealing algorithm for PFLP:

1. For each point feature, place its label randomly in any of the available potential positions.
2. Repeat until the rate of improvement falls below a given threshold:
   (a) Decrease the temperature, T, according to the annealing schedule.
   (b) Pick a label and move it to a new position.
   (c) Compute ΔE, the change in the objective function caused by repositioning the label.
   (d) If the new labeling is worse, undo the label repositioning with probability $P = 1.0 - e^{-\Delta E/T}$.

The implementation of a standard simulated-annealing algorithm involves four components: choice of an initial configuration, an appropriate objective function, a method for generating configuration changes, and an annealing schedule.

Initial configuration. As an alternative to starting with randomly placed labels, one could consider a "piggyback" method where simulated annealing is applied as a post-process to the results of another algorithm. In our experiments, however, this did not lead to either a significantly better solution or faster convergence.

Objective function. The choice of objective function affects the aesthetics of the layout, the quality of the solution, and efficiency of the search. Because simulated annealing is a statistical method that relies on a large number of evaluations for its success, the best objective functions are those for which ΔE can be computed quickly. The objective functions we chose counted the number of obstructed labels (if point selection was disallowed) or the number of deleted labels plus the number of obstructed labels. If point selection is allowed, we also considered an objective function that counts the number of pairwise overplots plus the number of deleted labels. This change in objective function does not noticeably change the performance of the annealing algorithm, but has the advantage of being significantly faster to compute.

Configuration changes. We have experimented with two strategies for choosing which label to reposition: the label can be chosen randomly from the set of all labels, or it can be chosen randomly from the set of labels that are currently experiencing a conflict. The second method isolates changes to those parts of the map that have conflicts, causing the algorithm to converge faster. When cartographic preferences that distinguish label positions are included in the problem, this simplification is no longer acceptable because the movement of unconflicted labels may affect the current value of the objective function. In the experiments reported here, the more time-consuming method of choosing from all available features was used.

Annealing schedule. The initial value of T was selected so that $P = \frac{2}{3}$ when $\Delta E = 1$. At each temperature a maximum of $20n$ labels are repositioned, where n is the number of point features. The temperature is then decreased by 10 percent. We employ a Metropolis-style algorithm, always accepting a suggested configuration change if it leads to a lower cost. If more than $5n$ successful configuration changes are made at any temperature, the temperature is immediately decreased. This process is repeated for at most 50 temperature stages. However, if the algorithm stays at a particular temperature for the full $20n$ steps without accepting a single label repositioning, then it stops with the current labeling as the final solution. We found the particular choice of annealing schedule to have a relatively minor affect on the performance of the algorithm as discussed in Section 4. This particular schedule was chosen to provide a reasonable trade-off between efficiency and solution quality; longer annealing schedules result in slightly improved solutions.

4 Comparison Experiments

In order to compare the effectiveness of this wide variety of algorithms for PFLP, we implemented six algorithms chosen from the set of non-exhaustive methods for PFLP. (Our experiments have shown that exhaustive methods are impractical for maps with as few as 50 point features.) The algorithms evaluated included a straw-man random-placement algorithm, in which label positions are assigned in a completely random fashion. This algorithm serves as an effective lower bound on algorithm performance. A greedy algorithm that serves as an efficient variant of the exhaustive methods described in Section 3.1 was also tested. The discrete gradient-descent algorithm was implemented, in addition to the algorithms of Hirsch and Zoraster. Finally, a stochastic algorithm utilizing simulated annealing was implemented. Each of the algorithms (except for Hirsch's) was allowed four candidate placement positions for labels. All candidate positions were taken to be equally desirable, i.e., preferences among different potential label positions were not considered (except where otherwise noted). A complete discussion of the implementation details for all of the algorithms is provided elsewhere (Christensen et al., 1992).

We began our comparison by testing the performance of each of the algorithms on randomly generated data, with and without point selection, to establish an overall ranking. To determine whether the relative performance of the algorithms was affected by the particular distribution, we then conducted similar tests on naturally occurring point-feature data. Next we ran a series of experiments on two gradient-descent variants in an attempt to improve on the best-seen solutions. Finally we investigated the effects of varying the annealing schedule of the simulated-annealing algorithm, and noted that the presence of cartographic preferences for candidate positions plays an important role in the usefulness of varying the annealing schedule. For this we conducted four additional trials, comparing the performance of three different annealing schedules while varying the use of point selection as well as the inclusion of cartographic preferences.

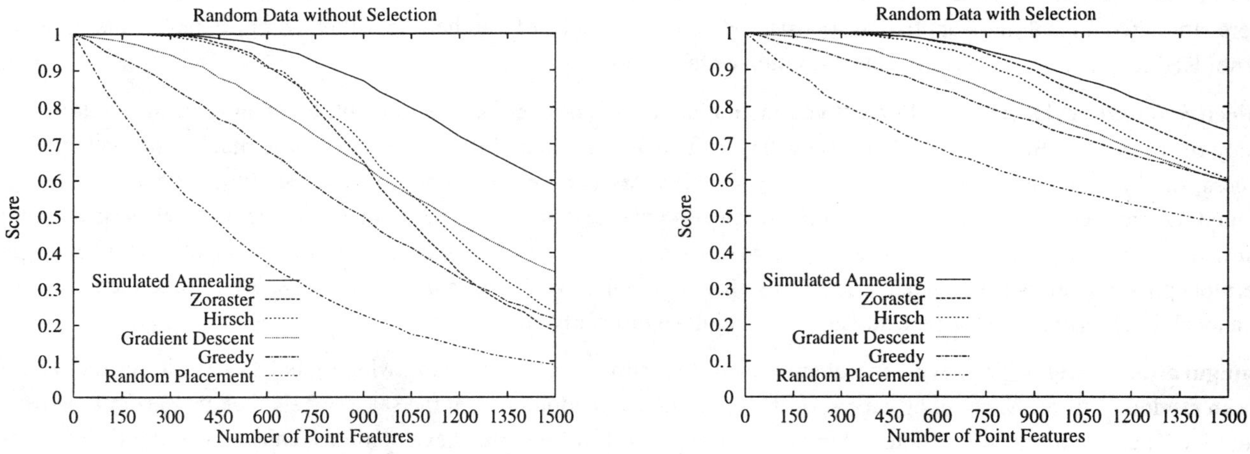

Figure 9: Results of empirical testing of six PFLP algorithms on randomly generated map data with point selection prohibited and allowed. The vertical axis shows the fraction of labels plotted without obstruction.

In the first group of tests, n point features with fixed-size labels (30 x 7 units) were randomly placed on a region of size 792 by 612. (These dimensions were selected subjectively in an effort to identify a typical map scale for an 11 by 8.5 inch page size.) Tests were run for n = 50, 100, 150, ..., 1500. For each problem size tested, 25 layouts were generated, a score was calculated equal to the fraction of labels placed without overplots, and the results were averaged to give a composite result for the algorithm at that problem size. No penalty was assessed for label positions that extended beyond the boundary of the region. These tests were then repeated with point selection allowed. For most of the algorithms (greedy, gradient descent, Zoraster, and simulated annealing) this was a natural extension. For the Hirsch algorithm, however, there was no straightforward method of allowing points to be deleted. In order to include Hirsch's algorithm in the point-selection comparisons, we developed a post-pass deletion heuristic, which seeks to clear the map of overplots with the fewest number of label deletions possible. This heuristic deletes the feature whose label has the greatest number of conflicts with other (non-deleted) labels. This process is repeated until the map is free from overplots. Although this algorithm is clearly non-optimal (it is straightforward to show that optimal PFLP is reducible to the problem of optimal label deletion, which is therefore NP-hard), we found it to be an acceptable heuristic in practice. The score was again the fraction of labels placed without conflict. Figure 9 shows the results of these experiments. As these graphs show, simulated annealing performs significantly better across the full range of problems considered. Other perspectives on these results are shown in Figures 10 and 11. Figure 10 shows a particular random map of 750 point features labeled by the six basic algorithms. Figure 11 illustrates the variance across 25 different problem instances, for maps involving 750 and 1500 point features.

Next, cartographic data for Massachusetts were used to test the algorithms on naturally occurring point-feature distributions obtained from the GNIS state file for Massachusetts (United States Geological Survey 1990). The algorithms were again scored based on the number of unconflicted labels, both with and without point selection. At each problem size, 25 layouts were generated by choosing randomly from the data file. For example at n = 350, each problem instance was generated by choosing 350 point features randomly from the GNIS data. Tests were run for n = 50, 100, 150, ..., 500. Figure 12 shows the results of these tests. Because the ratio of average label size to available map area is significantly larger for the Massachusetts examples, and also due to clustering of the point features, the performance of the algorithms deteriorates faster in the experiments involving Massachusetts data (Figure 12) as compared with the randomly generated data (Figure 9). Nonetheless, the overall rankings are preserved.

Though the simulated-annealing algorithm easily dominated the competing algorithms, we noted that the discrete gradient-descent algorithm performed surprisingly well given its simplicity, especially at high densities, where it outperforms all methods but simulated annealing. To investigate this approach in more detail, we implemented two related algorithms, "2-opt" and "3-opt" discrete gradient-descent algorithms, which consider the best sequence of two and three repositionings at each iteration.[13] A practical implementation of these algorithms is moderately complicated and requires a careful strategy for selective rescoring of repositionings at each iteration, supporting data structures for efficient search of a table of repositionings, and some clever record-keeping measures. Figure 13 shows the results of these new variants compared with the original discrete gradient-descent algorithm, the simulated-annealing algorithm and the random-placement algorithm. Although the "2-opt" and "3-opt" algorithms each improve on the performance of their predecessor, the degree of improvement grows less in each case, hinting towards an asymptote around the performance of the simulated-annealing algorithm. Further, even with a very careful implementation, the computational requirements of the 2-opt and 3-opt algorithms quickly become unreasonable as the number of candidate positions increases.

The next set of experiments investigated the effect of the annealing schedule on the performance of the simulated-annealing algorithm. We found that for very simple objective functions, e.g., the original four-position model without placement preferences, most potential label repositionings have no effect on the value of the objective function. For such spaces, a simple random descent (the equivalent of zero-temperature simulated annealing) performs nearly as well as simulated annealing at medium and even long schedules. This is seen in Figure 14. As the terrain of the search space becomes rougher, and involves a greater number of local minima, the utility of the annealing schedule is increased. Figure 15 shows that in experiments involving a four-position model with placement preferences, the performance of zero-temperature annealing drops roughly to that of the discrete gradient-descent algorithm.[14]

Computational resources required for the various algorithms vary dramatically, but not unexpectedly. As a rough indication of algorithm performance, Figure 16 depicts a scatterplot of running times for each of the algorithms running on a DEC 3000/400 AXP workstation. To the extent that these running times are representative of the intrinsic computational requirements of each algorithm, certain subsumption relationships can be derived. For example, Zoraster's algorithm lies to the lower right of the 3-opt discrete gradient-descent algorithm, indicating that it is both slower and exhibits inferior solutions. The 3-opt algorithm, in turn, is dominated by the simulated-annealing algorithm. Eliminating algorithms that are subsumed by other algorithms leaves a "staircase" of algorithms that, depending on requirements of time versus solution quality, would be preferred for a given task. At both densities shown, this staircase includes, in order of increased computation time and solution quality: random placement, the greedy algorithm, the original gradient-descent algorithm, Hirsch's algorithm at low densities, the 2-opt gradient-descent algorithm, and the simulated-annealing algorithm.

5 Conclusions

The point-feature label-placement problem is a graphics-design problem of practical importance and noted difficulty. Analysis of the computational complexity of the problem bears out its inherent difficulty; the search for good heuristic solutions thus becomes important. In this paper, we have proposed two new algorithms for PFLP—variants of discrete gradient descent and simulated annealing—and compared them with previously proposed algorithms. This empirical testing, which constitutes the first such comparative study, provides the basis for a graphic comparison of the time-quality tradeoff in label-placement algorithms, demonstrating that certain algorithms—3-opt gradient descent, Zoraster's, and Hirsch's algorithm, for instance—are subsumed by others in both speed and quality. The experiments also argue for the use of simulated annealing over the alternatives when solution quality is critical. For time-critical applications, the annealing schedule can often be shortened or eliminated altogether while still providing reasonable solutions. This result stands in contrast to previous empirical investigations of simulated annealing, which have shown that for a few NP-hard problems simulated annealing is competitive with customized heuristic techniques, but typically only when allowed to run for very long periods of time (Johnson et al., 1989; 1991). Simulated annealing has the additional advantage of being one of the easiest algorithms to implement. Table 1 gives the number of lines of code for each of the algorithms under our implementation, as an admittedly rough indication of implementation complexity.[15]

---

[13]We use these terms because of the similarity of these methods to the *k*-opt methods proposed for the NP-complete Traveling Salesman Problem (TSP). Variants of this method comprise the current best algorithms for the TSP (Johnson, 1990).

[14]Note that the performance of the gradient-descent algorithm appears to have increased relative to the original experiments. Because the original objective function yields a search space with many flat plateaus, the algorithm is often unable to find the edge of a plateau and terminates; the modified objective function yields virtually no plateaus and the algorithm is able to continue further before reaching a local minimum. A second reason for the improvement is the inclusion of preferences in the score metric. Since the score considers a larger dynamic range, the scale of the graph along the vertical axis is more compressed, resulting in a closer grouping of the algorithms. (Notice the relatively higher performance of random placement as compared with the previous trials.)

[15]Our implementation makes extensive use of function pointers to provide dynamic reconfiguration of the basic aspects of each algorithm. As a result, however, these numbers are undoubtedly higher than those that would occur in more straightforward implementations.

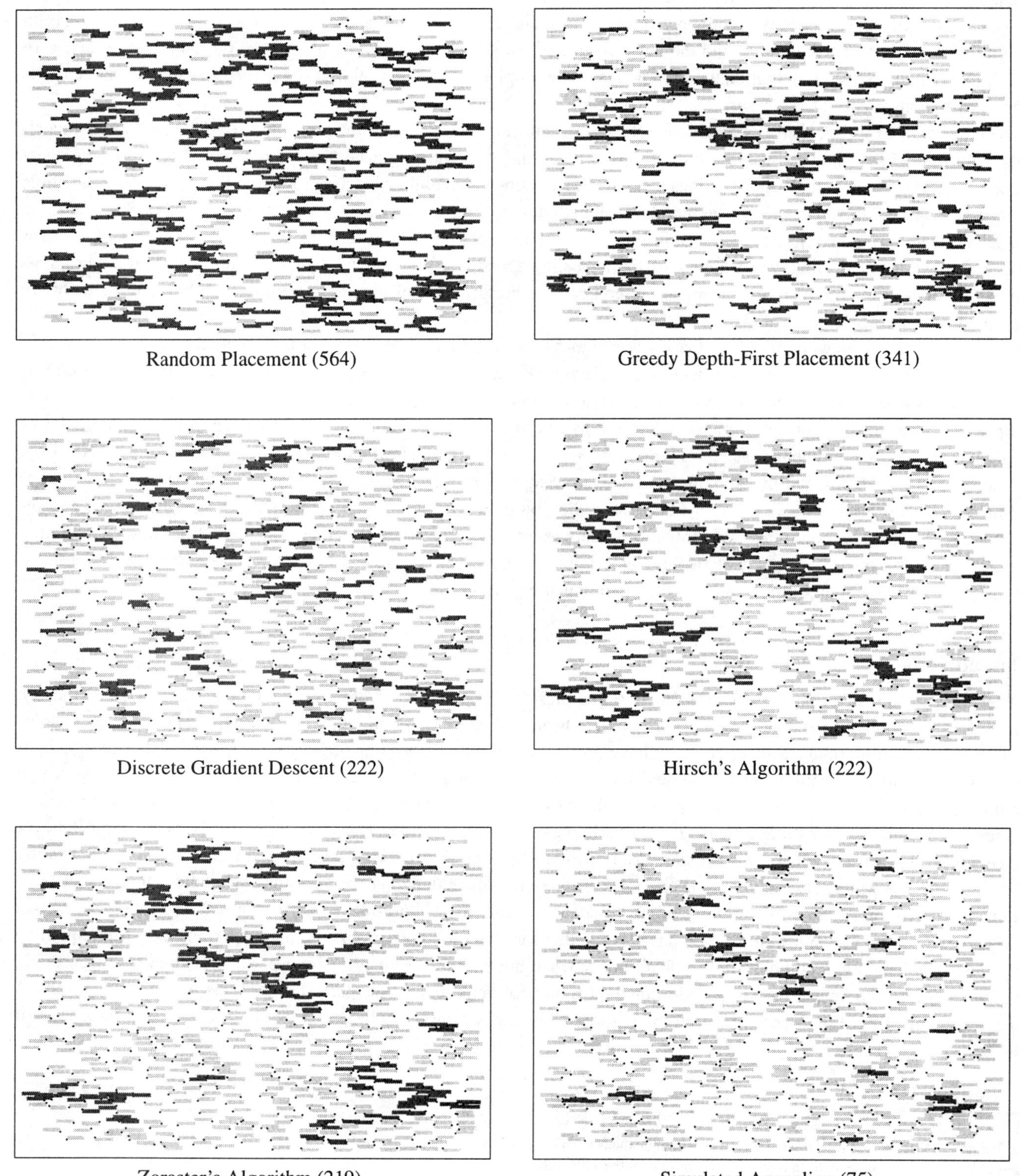

Figure 10: A sample map of 750 point features with labels placed by the six different algorithms. Labels printed in dark grey overplot other labels or points. Labels printed in light gray are free of overplots. Numbers in parenthesis indicate the final value of the objective function computed as the number of labels with overplots.

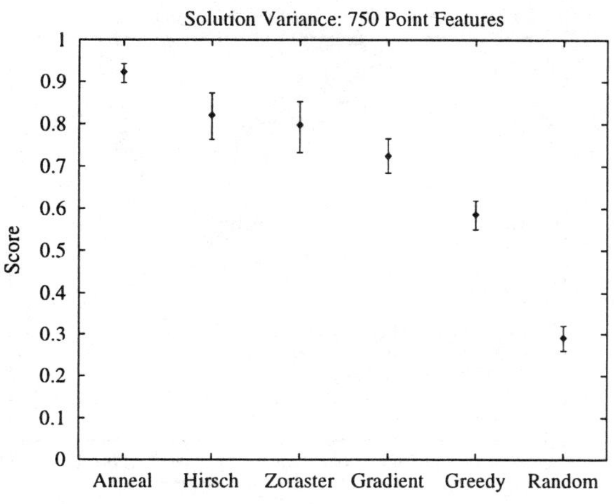

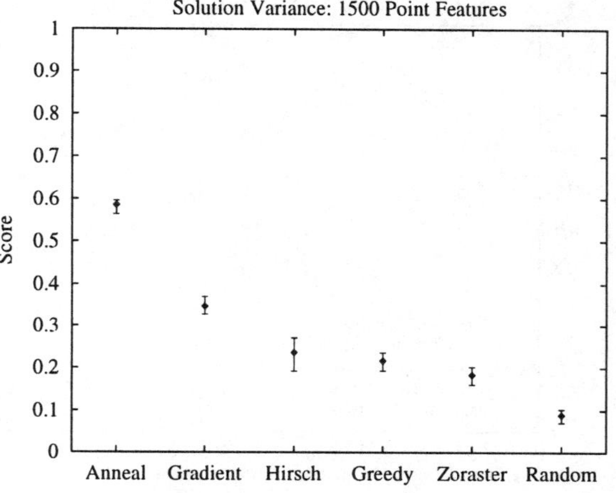

Figure 11: Range of results generated for 25 different labeling problems involving 750 and 1500 point features.

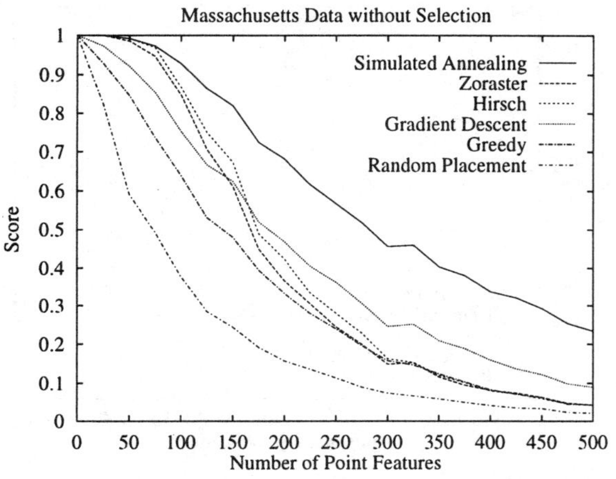

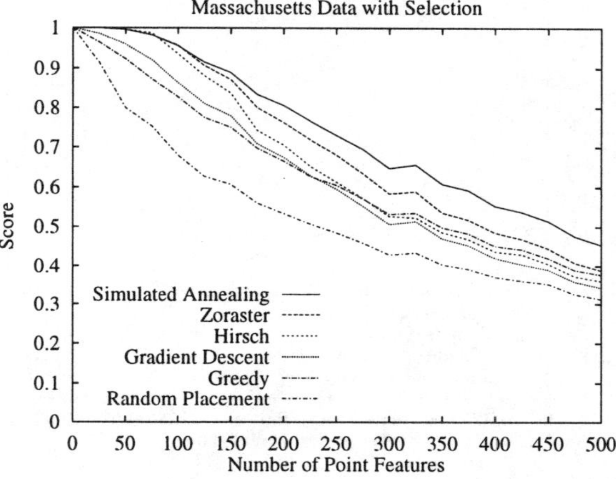

Figure 12: Results of empirical testing of six PFLP algorithms on GNIS data for Massachusetts with point selection prohibited and allowed.

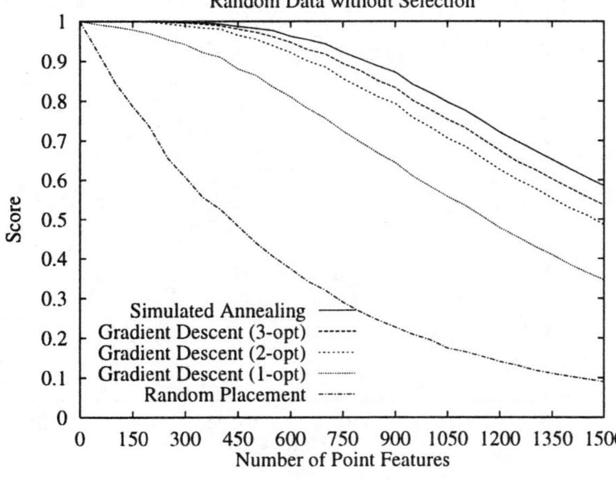

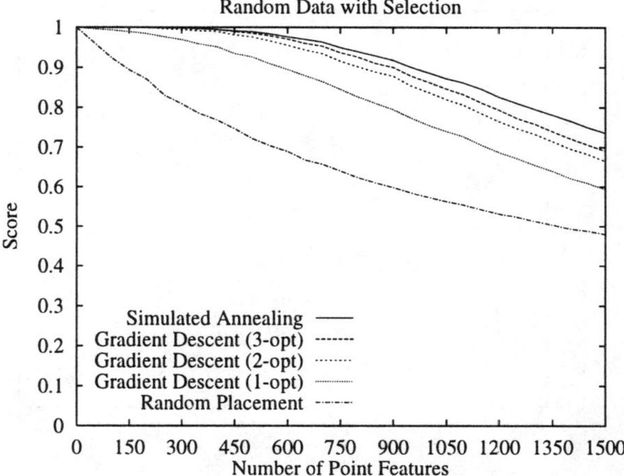

Figure 13: Results of empirical testing of discrete gradient-descent algorithms on randomly generated map data.

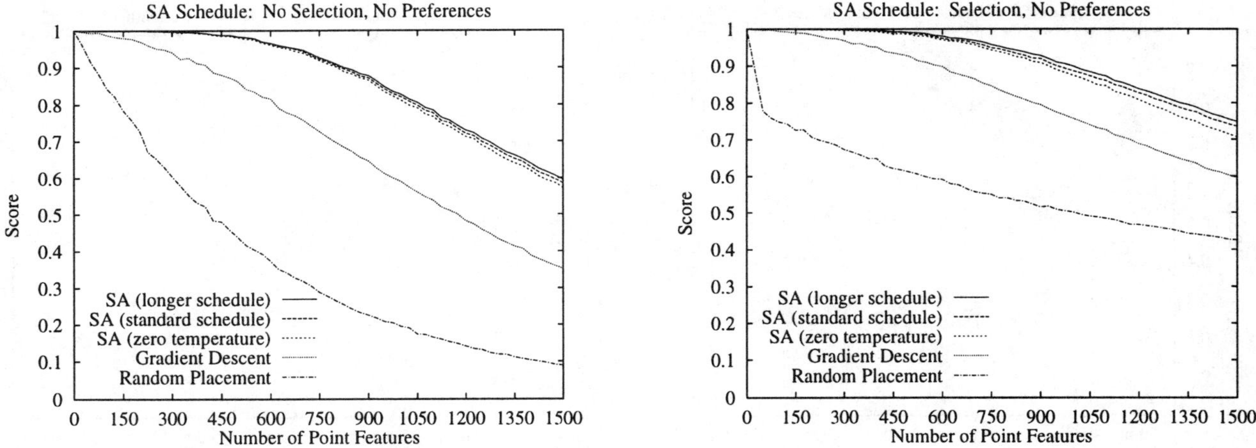

Figure 14: Comparison of annealing schedules against a gradient-descent algorithm without cartographic preferences.

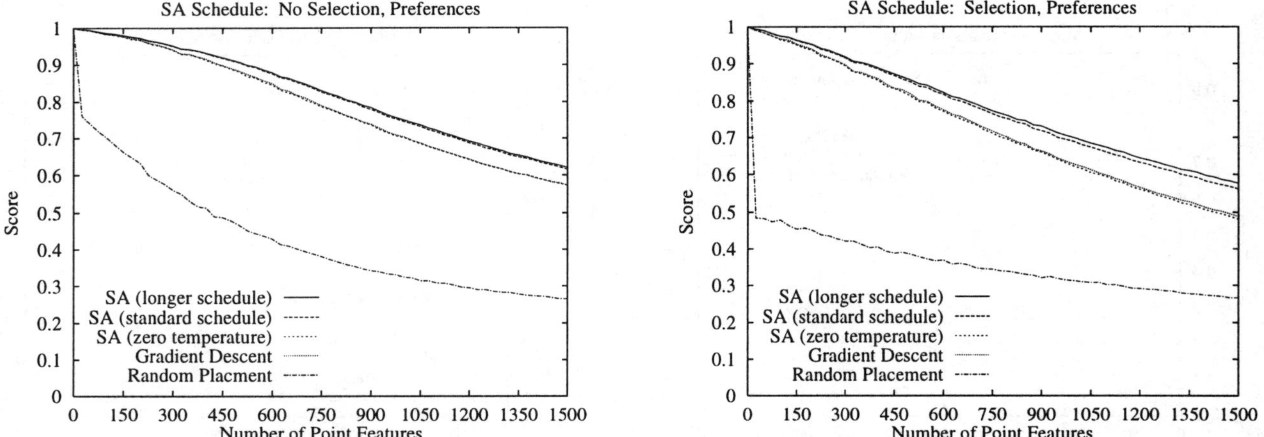

Figure 15: Comparison of annealing schedules against a gradient-descent algorithm with cartographic preferences. (Note that the lines corresponding to zero-temperature annealing and gradient descent lie very close together).

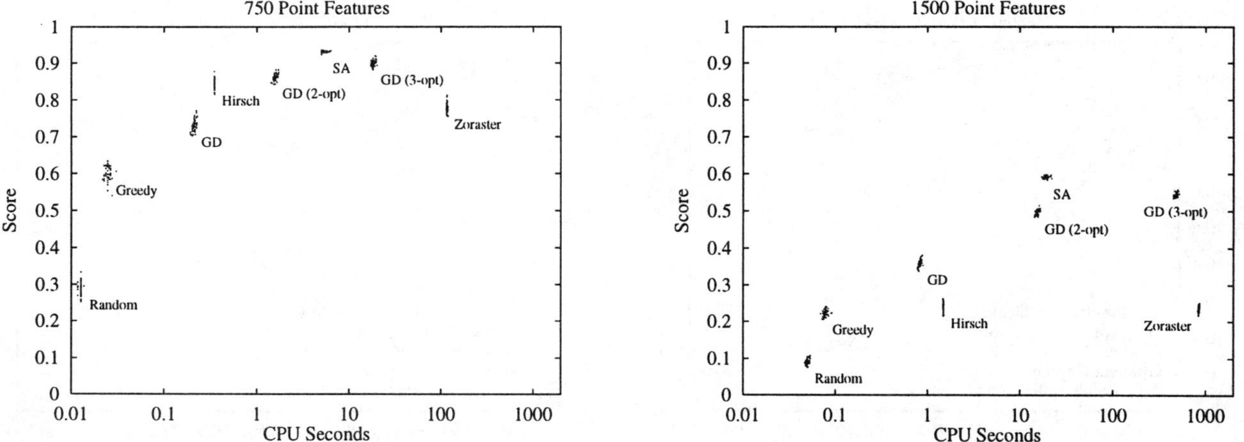

Figure 16: Running times for 50 different trials of 750 point features and 1500 point features. Note the logarithmic scale of the horizontal axis.

Algorithm	Lines of C code
Random Placement	20
Greedy	79
Gradient Descent (1-opt)	210
Simulated Annealing	239
Zoraster	346
Hirsch	381
Gradient Descent (2-opt)	1807
Gradient Descent (3-opt)	2284

Table 1: Lines of source code for label-placement algorithms

Unlike much of the previous work on label placement, the approach we have suggested cleanly separates the combinatorial-optimization aspect of the problem from the candidate-position modeling aspect. This way of stating the problem allows for the search algorithms discussed here to be used with more advanced cartographic positioning models. Modifying the algorithm to generate new sets of potential label positions, which is necessary to permit the labeling of line and area features, is accomplished easily, provided adequate models of line-feature (Ebinger and Goulette, 1990) and area-feature labeling (Carstensen, 1987; van Roessel, 1989) are available. Figure 17 shows a sample map involving all three feature types, as labeled by the simulated-annealing algorithm (Edmondson et al., 1995). Changing the objective function to allow for a priori placement preferences, sophisticated point selection, and complex interactions between labels and map symbology is also possible.

6 Acknowledgments

Much of this work was done while the second author was at Digital Equipment Corporation, Cambridge Research Laboratory. The research reported in this paper was funded in part by a contract with U S WEST Advanced Technologies, by Grants IRI-9157996 and 9350192 from the National Science Foundation, and by a grant from Digital Equipment Corporation. Andy Breeding, an information analyst at Digital Equipment Corporation, assisted us in the compilation of the bibliography. The authors wish to express their particular appreciation to the fourth anonymous reviewer for a very careful reading and many helpful suggestions, to Shawn Edmondson for his work on candidate-position algorithms for linear and area features, and to Tom Ngo for additional support.

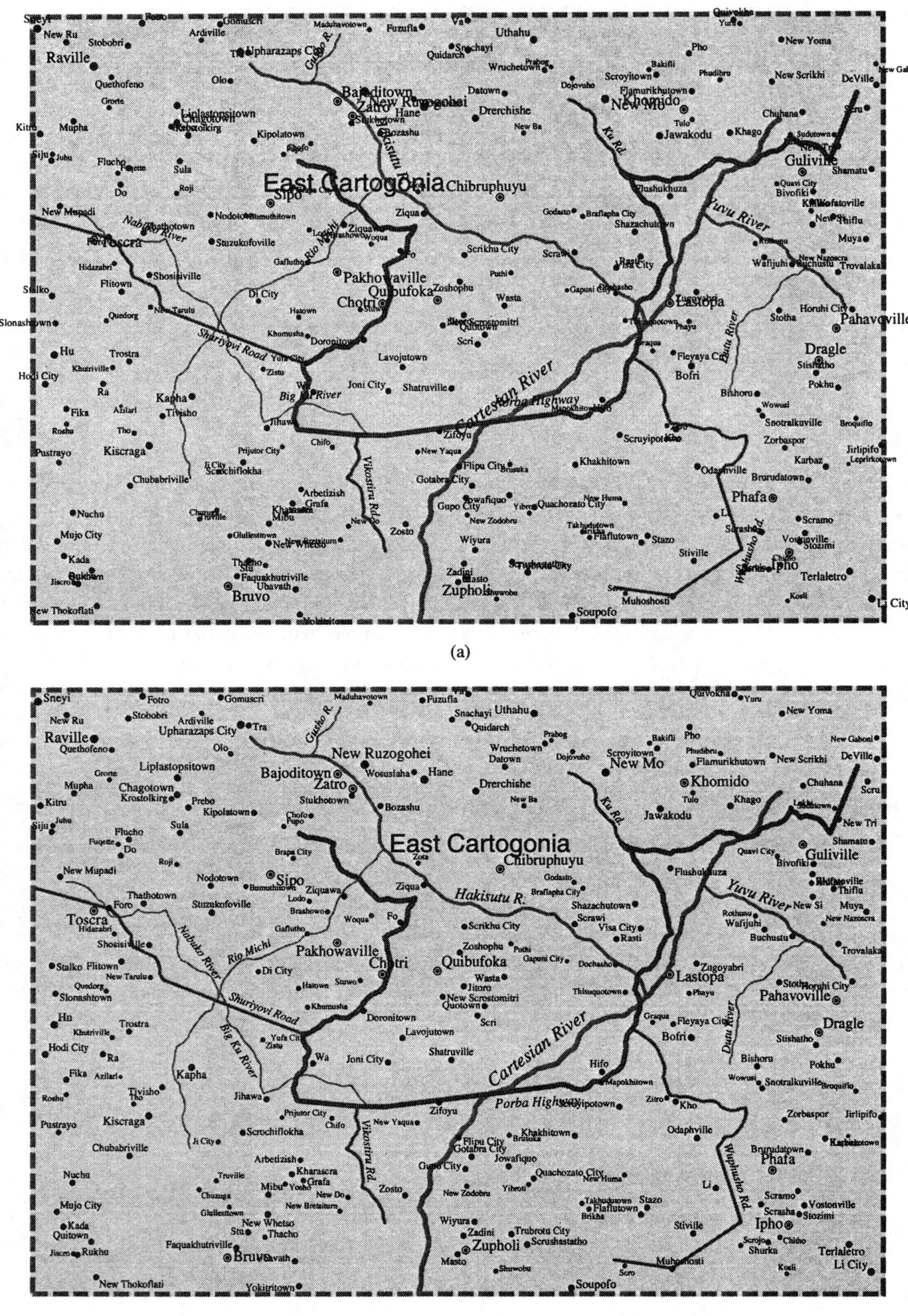

Figure 17: A map involving line, area, and point features labeled by the simulated-annealing algorithm. A random labeling is shown in (a). An intermediate configuration of the algorithm is shown in (b). The final labeling is shown in (c). The simulated-annealing algorithm converges from a random labeling to a final labeling in less than a second on a DEC 3000/400 AXP workstation.

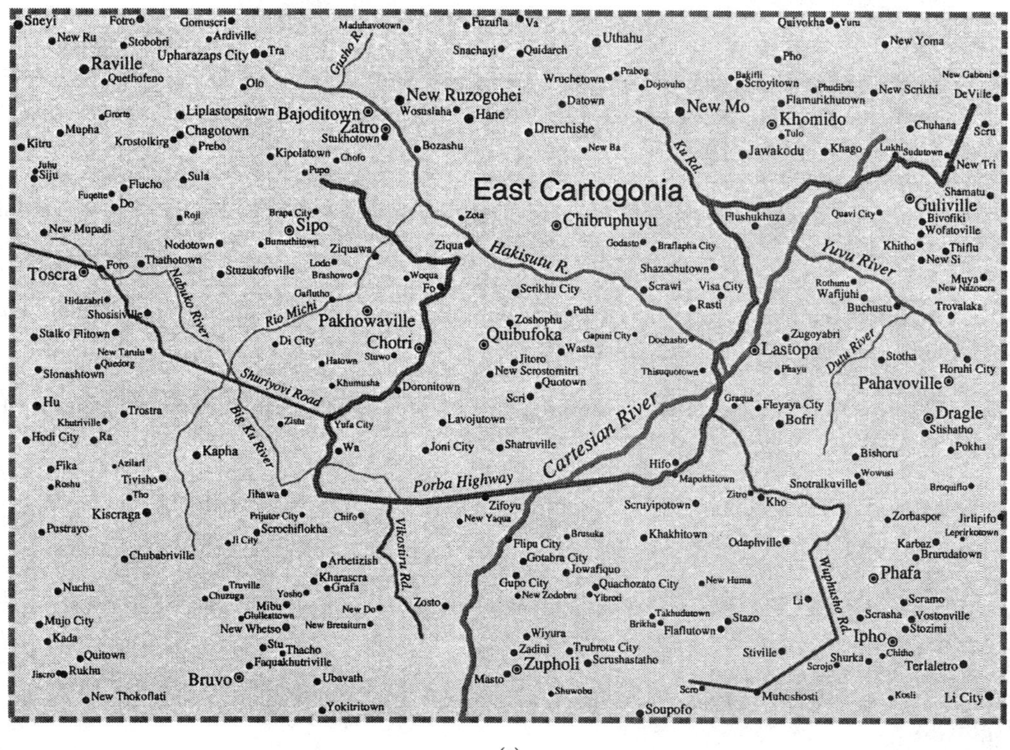

(c)

Figure 17: A map involving line, area, and point features labeled by the simulated-annealing algorithm. A random labeling is shown in (a). An intermediate configuration of the algorithm is shown in (b). The final labeling is shown in (c). The simulated-annealing algorithm converges from a random labeling to a final labeling in less than a second on a DEC 3000/400 AXP workstation.

References

Ahn, J. and H. Freeman. 1984. A program for automatic name placement. *Cartographica*, 21(2&3):101-109, Summer & Autumn. Originally published in *Proceedings of the Sixth International Symposium on Automated Cartography (Auto-Carto Six)*, Ottawa/Hull, October 1983.

Carstensen, L. W. 1987. A comparison of simple mathematical approaches to the placement of spot symbols. *Cartographica*,24(3):46-63.

Černy, V. 1985. A thermodynamical approach to the travelling salesman problem: An efficient simulation algorithm. *Journal of Optimization Theory and Applications*, 45:41-51.

Christensen, J., J. Marks, and S. Shieber. 1992. Labeling point features on maps and diagrams. Center for Research in Computing Technology, Harvard University, TR-25-92, December.

Christensen, J., J. Marks, and S. Shieber. 1993. Algorithms for cartographic label placement. *Proceedings of the American Congress on Surveying and Mapping '93*, February.

Christensen, J., J. Marks, and S. Shieber. 1994. Placing text labels on maps and diagrams. *Graphics Gems IV.* Academic Press, pages 497-504.

Cook, A. C. and C. B. Jones. 1990. A Prolog rule-based system for cartographic name placement. *Computer Graphics Forum*, 9:109-126.

Consorti, V., L.P. Cordella, and M. Iaccarino. 1993. Automatic lettering of cadastral maps. *Proceedings of the International Conference on Document Analysis and Recognition*, page 129-132, Tsukuba Science City, Japan, October.

Cromley, R. G. 1986. A spatial allocation analysis of the point annotation problem. In *Proceedings of the Second International Symposium on Spatial Data Handling*, pages 38-49, Seattle, Washington, July. International Geographical Union and International Cartographic Association.

Doerschler, J. S. and H. Freeman. 1992. A rule-based system for dense-map name placement. *Communications of the Association of Computing Machinery*, 35(1):68-79, January.

Ebinger, L. R. and A. M. Goulette. 1990. Noninteractive automated names placement for the 1990 decennial census. *Cartography and Geographic Information Systems*, 17(1):69-78, January.

Edmondson, S., J. Christensen, J. Marks, and S. Shieber. 1995. A general cartographic labeling algorithm. In preparation.

Feigenbaum, M. 1994. Method and apparatus for automatically generating symbol images against a background image without collision utilizing distance-dependent attractive and repulsive forces in a computer simulation. Assigned to Hammond Inc., Maplewood, New Jersey. U.S. Patent #5,355,314. Patent filed 11/5/93, received 10/11/94.

Fisher, M. L. 1981. The Lagrangian relaxation method for solving integer programming problems. *Management Science*, 27:1-18.

Formann, M. and F. Wagner. 1991. A packing problem with applications to lettering of maps. In *Proceedings of the Seventh Annual Symposium on Computational Geometry*, pages 281-288, North Conway, New Hampshire, July. ACM.

Freeman, H. and J. Ahn. 1987. On the problem of placing names in a geographic map. *International Journal of Pattern Recognition and Artificial Intelligence*, 1(1):121-140.

Freeman, H. 1988. An Expert System for the automatic placement of names on a geographical map. *Information Sciences*, 45:367-378.

Hirsch, S. A. 1982. An algorithm for automatic name placement around point data. *The American Cartographer*, 9(1):5-17.

Holland, J. H. 1975. *Adaptation in Natural and Artificial Systems*. University of Michigan Press, Ann Arbor.

Imhof, E. 1962. Die Anordnung der Namen in der Karte. *International Yearbook of Cartography*, 2:93-129.

Imhof, E. 1975. Positioning names on maps. *The American Cartographer*, 2(2):128-144.

Johnson, D. S. 1990. Local optimization and the traveling salesman problem. In *Proceedings of the 17th Colloqium on Automata, Languages, and Programming*, pages 446-461. Springer-Verlag.

Johnson, D. S., C. R. Aragon, L. A. McGeoch, and C. Schevon. 1989. Optimization by simulated annealing: An experimental evaluation; part I, graph partitioning. *Operations Research*, 37(6):865-892.

Johnson, D. S., C. R. Aragon, L. A. McGeoch, and C. Schevon. 1991. Optimization by simulated annealing: An experimental evaluation; part II, graph coloring and number partitioning. *Operations Research*, 39(3):378-406.

Jones, C. 1989. Cartographic name placement with Prolog. *IEEE Computer Graphics and Applications*, 9(5):36-47, September.

Kato, T. and H. Imai. 1988. The NP-completeness of the character placement problem of 2 or 3 degrees of freedom. *Record of Joint Conference of Electrical and Electronic Engineers in Kyushu*, 1138. In Japanese.

Kirkpatrick, S., C. D. Gelatt Jr., and M. P. Vecchi. 1983. Optimization by simulated annealing. *Science*, 220:671-680.

Korf, R. E. 1988. Search: A survey of recent results. In H. E. Shrobe, editor, *Exploring Artificial Intelligence: Survey Talks from the National Conferences on Artificial Intelligence*. Morgan Kaufmann, San Mateo, California, pages 197-237.

Langran, G. E. and T. K. Poiker. 1986. Integration of name selection and name placement. In *Proceedings of the Second International Symposium on Spatial Data Handling*, pages 50-64, Seattle, Washington, July. International Geographical Union and International Cartographic Association.

Marks, J. and S. Shieber. 1991. The computational complexity of cartographic label placement. Technical Report TR-05-91, Harvard University, March.

Mower, J. E. 1986. Name placement of point features through constraint propagation. In *Proceedings of the Second International Symposium on Spatial Data Handling*, pages 65-73, Seattle, Washington, July. International Geographical Union and International Cartographic Association.

Mower, J. E. 1993. Automated feature and name placement on parallell computers. In *Cartography and Geographic Information Systems,* 20(2):69-82.

Noma, E. 1987. Heuristic method for label placement in scatterplots. *Psychometrika*, 52(3):463-468.

Sahni, S. 1974. Computationally related problems. *SIAM Journal on Computing*, 3:262-279.

United States Geological Survey, National Mapping Division. 1990. Geographic Names Information System, November.

van Roessel, J. W. 1989. An algorithm for locating candidate labeling boxes within a polygon. *The American Cartographer*, 16(3):201-209.

Wu, C. V. and B. P. Buttenfield. 1991. Reconsidering rules for point-feature name placement. *Cartographica*, 28(1):10-27, Spring.

Yoeli, P. 1972. The logic of automated map lettering. *The Cartographic Journal*, 9(2):99-108, December.

Zoraster, S. 1986. Integer programming applied to the map label placement problem. *Cartographica*, 23(3):16-27.

Zoraster, S. 1990. The solution of large 0-1 integer programming problems encountered in automated cartography. *Operations Research*, 38(5):752-759, September-October.

Zoraster, S. 1991. Expert systems and the map label placement problem. *Cartographica*, 28(1):1-9, Spring.

An Empirical Study of Algorithms for Point-Feature Label Placement

Jon Christensen, Joe Marks, and Stuart M. Shieber

The placement of text labels on maps is a surprisingly difficult (NP-hard) layout task. It requires placing labels so that the visual association between labels and their respective features is unambiguous while simultaneously avoiding label-label and label-symbol overlaps that hinder legibility.

The text placement task is significant and interesting for two principal reasons. First, it is an important element of many graphical layout problems, albeit an oft ignored one. Naturally, it is a primary concern in automated cartography, but textual annotations are also important in a wide variety of other informational graphics, so the problem is pervasive. Second, the set of text placement methods that have been studied so far illustrates well the range and diversity of automatic approaches, artificially intelligent and otherwise, that can be brought to bear on graphical layout. Notably, traditional AI methods such as expert systems have not been particularly successful when applied to this problem (Zoraster 1991).

Search and knowledge representation are two important AI themes, and both are pertinent to research on layout in general and text placement in particular. Our paper was the first comprehensive and comparative survey of solutions to the search or optimization problem inherent in text placement. AI-flavored methods in our survey included variants of depth-first search, hill climbing, and simulated annealing (the latter two being applied for the first time to text placement); non-AI-flavored methods included physical relaxation and zero-one integer programming. However, before any search or optimization method can be applied in practice, you must also solve the knowledge representation problem of encoding good labeling practice in an objective function or procedure. This representation issue is considered at length in a companion paper (Edmondson et al. 1996) as well as in several of our references.

REFERENCES

Edmondson, S.; Christensen, J.; Marks, J.; and Shieber, S. 1996. A General Cartographic Labeling Algorithm. *Cartographica*, Vol. 33, No. 4, Winter 1996, 13–23.

Zoraster, S. 1991. Expert Systems and the Map Label Placement Problem. *Cartographica* 28(1) Spring: 1–9.

Grammar-based articulation for multimedia document design

Louis Weitzman[1,*], **Kent Wittenburg**[2,**]

[1] Meta Media Design, 49 Melcher Street, 4th Floor, Boston, MA 02210-1511, USA
[2] Computer Graphics & Interactive Media Research, Bellcore, 445 South Street, MCC 1A-332R, Morristown, NJ 07960–6438, USA

Abstract. This paper describes an approach to the problem of articulating multimedia information based on parsing and syntax-directed translation that uses Relational Grammars. This translation is followed by a constraint-solving mechanism to create the final layout. Grammatical rules provide the mechanism for mapping from a representation of the content and context of a presentation to forms that specify the media objects to be realized. These realization forms include sets of spatial and temporal constraints between elements of the presentation. Individual grammars encapsulate the "look and feel" of a presentation and can be used as generators of such a style. By making the grammars sensitive to the requirements of the output medium, parsing can introduce flexibility into the information realization process.

Key words: Automatic design – Grammar-directed design – Visual languages – Relational grammars – Parsing – Constraints

1 Introduction

A fully functioning multimedia system requires a wide range of stages to achieve effective automatic presentations. These include the processes of content selection, which identifies what to say; media allocation, which identifies in what media to say it; and media realization, which identifies how to say it in these media (Maybury 1993). However, to communicate effectively, adaptive multimedia systems must not merely present information, but must also present information that has been specifically designed for a given context and task. The dynamics of information in the future will require a more careful crafting of the documents we author. Information will constantly be changing, users will have different requirements, and display devices on which they view the information will require vastly different design solutions. At the same time, documents will be including more structured knowledge of their content. To support the dynamics of this information-rich environment and exploit the nature of these structured documents, we will need new techniques and paradigms for the automatic design and presentation of this information.

The research described here focuses on the media realization phase and describes a formalism, Relational Grammars, for encoding design knowledge along with a methodology – parsing, syntax-directed translation, and constraint resolution – as a realization procedure that may encode the same content differently under differing circumstances.

Kochhar et al. (1991) characterize the articulation of a designed artifact along the axis of automaticity, from completely manual to completely automatic. Relational Grammars (Wittenburg 1992, 1993; Wittenburg et al. 1991) provide a number of affordances along this axis, some of which have been explored in working prototypes. These paradigms include:

- Incremental improvement
- Graphic design completion
- Design verification and error checking
- Syntax-directed editing
- Structural zooming
- Automatic presentation

In a previous paper (Weitzman and Wittenburg 1993), we described an interactive improver-based paradigm that uses Relational Grammars to support the authoring phase of a design process. In this article, we apply this same formalism in the generation phase to support an automatic articulation of a multimedia document. This articulation includes graphic constraints (e.g., font specification), spatial constraints (e.g., relative positioning), and temporal constraints (e.g., sequence of presentation).

Our larger vision includes an authoring component that produces a grammar, rather than a finished, static document. The grammar can then be used dynamically, as described here, to present content selected through a variety of mechanisms.

As can be seen from Fig. 1, Relational Grammars play a central role in this vision. In the interactive paradigm, the improver-based grammar watches the user's authoring actions and suggests improvements, creates composite objects, and so on. In the automatic paradigm, the realization grammar, a product of the authoring process, maps from sets of content objects to multimedia documents.

* e-mail: weitzman@media.mit.edu
** e-mail: kentw@belcore.com
Correspondence to: L. Weitzman

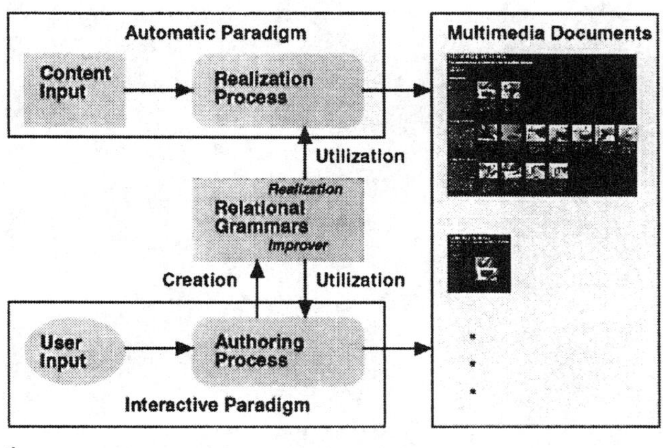

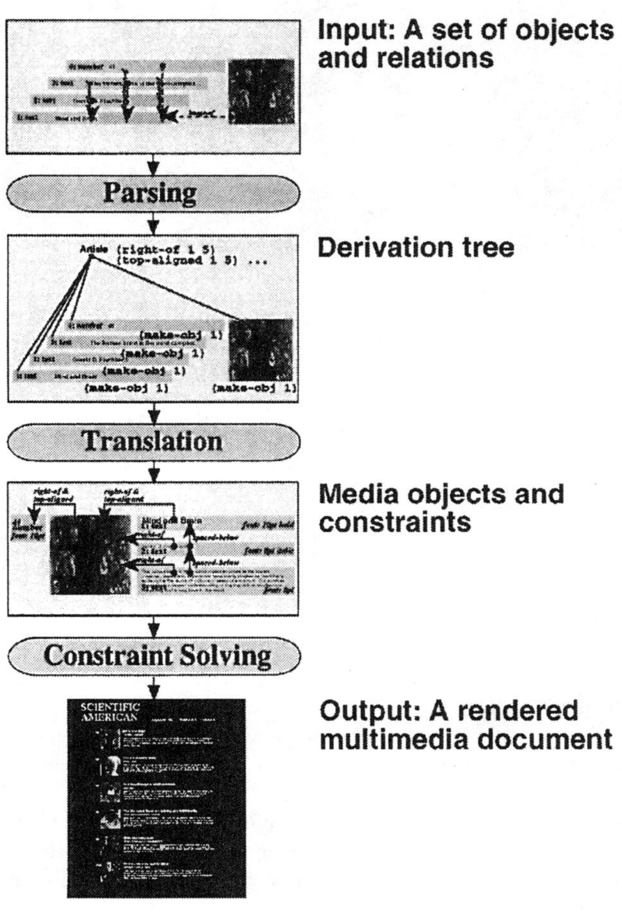

Fig. 1. Vision of an integrated environment for the interactive authoring and automatic articulation of multimedia documents
Fig. 2. Overview of the process of articulating the presentation of a multimedia document

This mapping can be sensitive to differing properties of the content or the context resulting in different realization options. In this article, we focus on only the realization grammar and the role of parsing in the realization process. Authoring of grammars and the relationship between the improver grammar and the realization grammar are issues we will address in future work.

Our language of design follows in the tradition of rule-based paradigms. One assumption this approach makes is that the domain knowledge can be encoded in the form of rules. In the domain of graphic design, layout designs are typically described in this manner. Existing publications can be analyzed, and the rules of their construction can be inferred and generalized by a designer to new domains such as multimedia documents. Some rules are generic and transcend single design layouts (e.g., equal sizing and alignment of similar elements), while other rules are specific to a particular design (e.g., vertical indentation for a particular layout).

After an overview of the architecture of our presentation system, we turn to a working example, a "home screen" of a multimedia on-line document. It takes its "look and feel" from the table of contents of a popular magazine. This first example, which describes the parameters of spatial and temporal layout, allows us to focus on the architecture of our realization system. We discuss the form of the input and the output of the realization process. Next, we provide examples of rules that articulate these particular design styles. We then move on to the realization of a dynamic presentation in which the grammar constrains the elements of the presentation both spatially and temporally. This exercise also serves as an example of how syntax-directed translation can achieve differing results depending on characteristics of the output display. Related work in automated layout and multimedia presentation is compared. Finally, we conclude with future directions of this research.

2 Architectural overview

Relational Grammars with semantic attributes provide a mechanism for the articulation phase of the larger multimedia presentation problem. An overview of the system architecture is presented in Fig. 2. Given a representation of the content to be communicated by some design, we create one or more instances of a fully articulated design. Here we are not concerned with the important problem of accessing and filtering information. The assumption is that the information to be presented has already been chosen, and that the relationships between the elements are known. Another process, or the user, first selects the information to be presented. The system parses content elements and relations to build a derivation tree. In the first example, this corresponds to the hierarchical composition of the set of articles and headers to be included in the home screen.

Depending on the needs and purpose of the application, the hierarchical structure represented by the parse tree may not have to be constructed dynamically by a parser. The alternative is to assume that an authoring phase produces the hierarchical structures manually. The advantage of using parsing is that more primitive elements can serve as the starting point, allowing the parser to do a certain amount of selection and/or error correction in assembling pre-existing pieces. Various designs can be articulated, which might require different hierarchical structures. If, however, parsing is not required, and a content authoring phase can supply the hierarchical structure in the form of an abstract syntax tree, the remaining pieces of our proposed architecture still remain applicable.

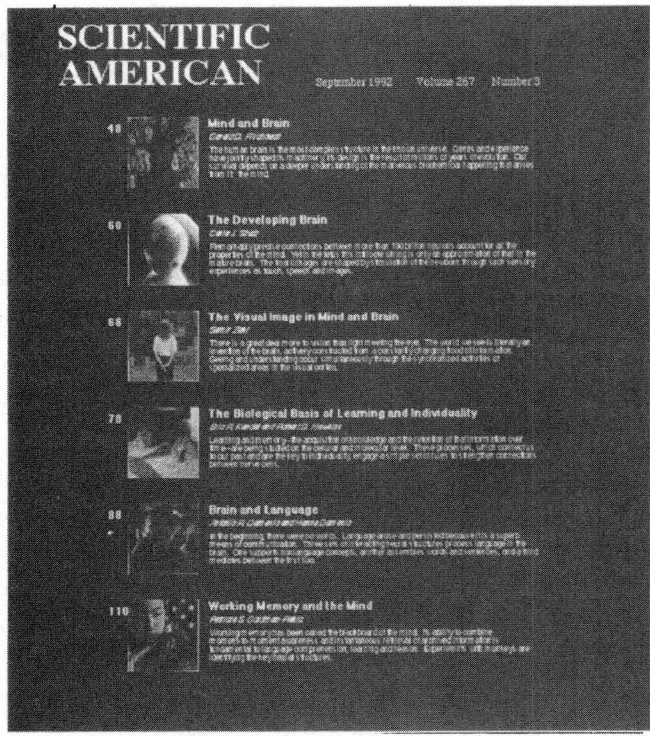

3

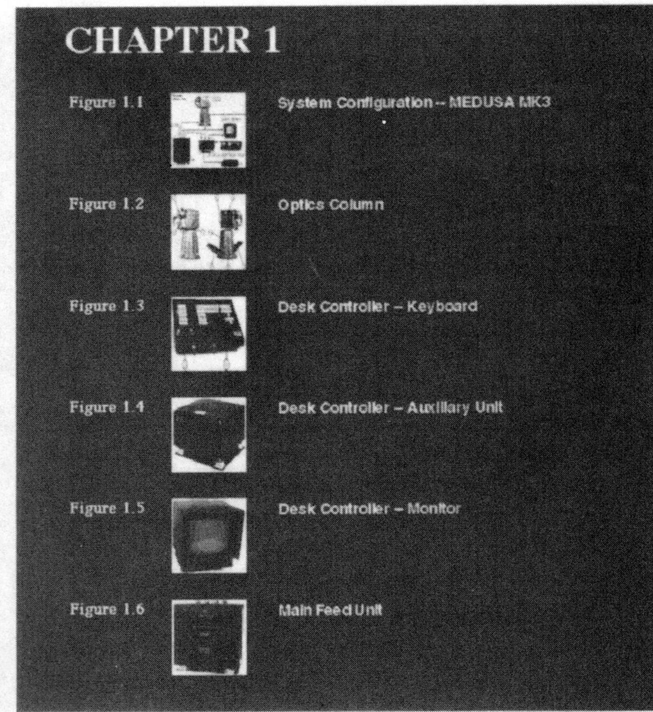

5

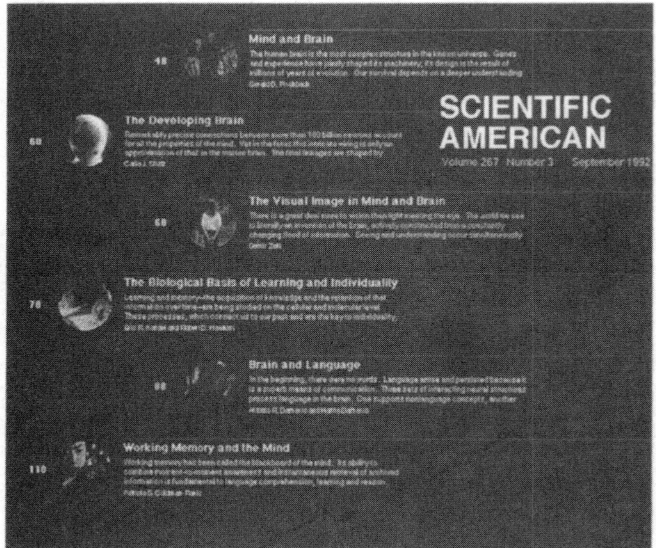

4

Fig. 3. Automatic layout of a Scientific American table of contents in the traditional style

Fig. 4. Automatic layout of a Scientific American table of contents (the same input as in Fig. 3) in the style of Wired magazine's table of contents

Fig. 5. Automatic layout of an on-line training manual in the traditional style of Scientific American. Variations of the basic rules parse the articles even though information (such as authors and descriptions) is missing

Given a derivation tree, a translation phase is invoked. Following in the tradition of syntax-directed translation (Aho et al. 1986), each grammar rule has an associated set of attributes that are used to compute the output forms from a syntactic derivation tree. Here the output determines a set of media objects to be created and a set of spatial and temporal constraints to be installed. Through familiar methods of computing inherited and synthesized attributes, the semantic output of the parse tree is produced. A constraint resolution procedure is then invoked to solve the constraints among media objects that, in this case, determine the actual numerical values for spatial positioning. Finally, the media objects are rendered on the display.

3 Examples of spatial layout

Figures 3–5 illustrate the results of our system in the realm of spatial layout and graphical style. Figures 3 and 4 use the same content, but different grammars, to achieve unique styles of presentation. Figure 3 is an automatically generated on-line version of the table of contents modeled directly from an issue of Scientific American (1992). Figure 4 uses the grammar based on another publication's style to present the same information. [This layout is based on a grammar derived from Wired (1994).] Figure 5 illustrates different contents that use the same grammar as in Fig. 3. However, note that Fig. 5 has less information (i.e., no authors or descriptions). The grammar in question contains rule variants that permit successful parses even though such content differences exist.

4 The articulation components

We use Fig. 3 as our running example in the following discussion of the sequence of processing steps in our articulation process.

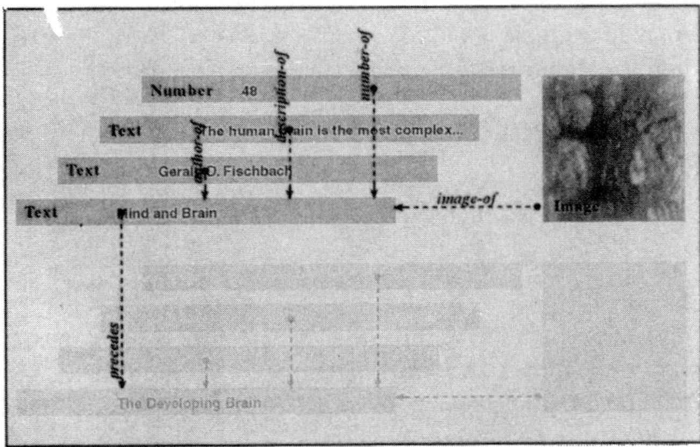

Fig. 6. An example of partial input to the parser for the on-line magazine example. The input is a set of primitive objects (text, numbers, images) and the relations between the objects (*author-of, description-of, page-of, image-of, precedes*)

4.1 Input to the parser

The input to the parser is a set of content objects, as well as the domain-dependent relations that hold between them. Conceptually, the input is a database, which can be thought of abstractly as a graph with primitive objects as nodes and relations as (hyper)arcs. In the on-line magazine example, we read in a file describing the content information and construct our own internal database. Figure 6 illustrates the form of the input data for the parser. For example, the figure indicates that "Gerald D. Fischbach" is in the *author-of* relation to "Mind and Brain." The basic types of objects that comprise the input to the parsing process include text, numbers, and images. In this example we order the articles as they are in the original publication (i.e., the *precedes* relation), but we could have used other relations to determine the presentation sequence, such as importance, type of article (e.g., lead with a general science article), highest priority based on user profile, etc.

4.2 Grammar

The input can be relatively unstructured and multidimensional, which means that it requires the use of grammar and parsing technologies that go beyond conventional 1D strings. Relational Grammars are extensions to string-based grammars in which composition relations other than just string concatenation are allowed. They belong to a wide-ranging family of higher-dimensional grammar frameworks, e.g., array, tree, or graph grammars (Rosenfeld 1990) or unification-based constraint grammars (Helm and Marriott 1991). While string grammars generate or compose expressions consisting of 1D arrays of symbols, these higher-dimensional grammars deal in structures characterized by, for example, geometric positions in 2D or 3D space, topological connectivity, or, as in the case at hand, arbitrary semantic relations holding among information objects.

The basic idea at the core of context-free higher-dimensional approaches is to enhance the classical definition of context-free string grammars by substituting other mathematical constructs for the expression class that comprises the input and output of each replacement step in a derivation. The general idea is summarized as follows:

Context-free higher-dimensional grammars:

$G = (N, T, S, P)$
N is a set of nonterminal labels
T is a set of terminal labels disjoint from N
S, a member of N, is the start label
P is a set of productions of the form
$A \rightarrow a$, where a, a replacement for a nonterminal A, is a composite mathematical construct such as an n-dimensional array, a tree, a graph, a set of relations over a multiset, and so on.

The expression class for Relational Grammars is a construct called an indexed multidimensional multiset (md-set). It is formally defined as an n-tuple (I, $R1 \ldots Rn$) such that $R1 \ldots Rn$ are relations, i.e., ordered tuples, on the indexed multiset of symbols I. In this application domain, the symbols are in fact a vocabulary of types of the content objects such as text, image, number, and so on. Examples of relations $R1 \ldots Rn$ are, in our running example, *author-of, description-of, page-of,* and *image-of.*

Productions for Relational Grammars must serve to determine replacement operations in a derivation over md-sets. Figure 7 shows a rule that is used repeatedly in the derivation behind Fig. 3. The context-free backbone corresponds to the rewrite rule:

Article $\rightarrow$ Text Text Text Number Image.

In the rule language, integers are simply an indexing method over the objects whose types are mentioned in the

```
(Defrule (Make-Article The-Grammar)
Article → Text Text Text Number Image
   0        1    2    3     4      5
(Author-Of 2 1)
(Description-Of 3 1)
(Page-Of 4 1)
(Image-Of 5 1)
(article-name 0) = 1
(article-image 0) = 5
:OUT
(right-of 1 5)
(right-of 2 5)
(right-of 3 5)
(right-of 5 4)
(top-aligned 1 5)
(top-aligned 5 4)
(spaced-below 2 1)
(spaced-below 3 2)
(set-font 1 10pt :bold)
(set-font 2 8pt :italic)
(set-font 3 8pt :plain)
(set-font 4 10pt :plain))
```

Fig. 7. The definition of the Make-Article rule. The conditions for rule matching include relations between the elements (e.g., author-of). Article is the resulting composite category that is created when the five basic categories (numbered 1 through 5) are matched and the indicated relations satisfied

context-free backbone: 0 indicates the left-hand-side rule element and $1 \ldots n$ represent the right-hand-side rule elements. These elements are technically unordered.

Besides forms for specifying the primary elements of a rule and their types, the rule language has three other kinds of forms as evidenced in Fig. 7: relational constraints, attribute assignments, and :OUT forms.

A relational constraint such as (*author-of* 2 1) is a requirement that the object matching rule element 2 (of type Text in this case) must stand in the *author-of* relation to the object matching rule element 1 (also of type Text). During parsing, relational constraints either have the effect of generating possible candidates for rule element matches or filtering candidate matches that have been proposed. We call the generating relations "expander relations." They must be binary, and the parser executes a query based on these relational expressions as it explores candidates to match rule elements. For example, the query (*author-of* :? i) might be executed when matching the rule in Fig. 7 to expand the match to the second right-hand-side element, assuming that i is an index to the input matching the first right-hand-side element. However, one might want to include further relational constraints (of any arity). A parser would execute such constraints as predicates. We use predicates in this application of Relational Grammars to check for global attributes of the presentation environment such as screen size.

Attribute assignments associate attributes of the left-hand-side of the rule with those on the right-hand-side. The form (article-name 0) = 1 indicates that the left-hand-side composite object referenced as 0 has an attribute article-name that is equated with the text-element 1. A distinguished class of attributes that we call "expander attributes" play a particular technical role in the parsing process and also in defining classes of Relational Languages. In brief, the issue has to do with whether to allow nonterminals to appear as direct arguments to expander relations. A "yes" answer requires dynamic updating of the input database, since composites built through parsing are not included in the input initially. Including relational constraints directly on composites is reasonable when using bottom-up parsing, but it complicates the definition of Relational Grammars as generative systems, since the *composition-of* relation must in principle be reversible. Further, significant problems are introduced for all forms of predictive parsing, as discussed in Wittenburg (1992). The alternative is to write grammars that state relational constraints only on individuals in the input set and use feature percolation to pass up bindings of these individuals as attribute values in derivations.

The idea, then, is to state expander relational constraints over attribute values rather than over the nonterminal composite objects themselves. For example, another rule used in our running example combines Article objects built with the rule in Fig. 7. It has relational constraint forms such as:

```
Article-group → Article Article
     0             1       2
...
(precedes (article-name 1)(article-name 2)

...
```

This rule states that the values of attributes article-name of two composite objects of type Article must stand in the *precedes* relation. Any such relations will be present in the original input.

The forms following :OUT in the rule definition represent an extension of Relational Grammars as previously conceived to include "semantic" attributes. Consistent with standard practice in compiler design, in which attributes are used to generate compiler code, here we use attributes to generate code for creating media objects. The numbers in these forms may be thought of as variables that by convention, are dereferenced to the media objects (rather than the input objects) associated with these rule elements. These :OUT forms serve the role of style specifications in the articulation process. Other more abstract specifications than, say, specific font sizes, could be used here.

See (Wittenburg 1992, 1993, 1996) for more details concerning Relational Grammars. Weitzman's thesis (Weitzman 1995) has the full set of rules used in this example.

4.3 Parsing

The parser's goal is to build one or more derivation trees that cover the input. In our current implementation, we use the bottom-up, nondeterministic algorithm presented in (Witten-

```
(Defrule (Make-Simple-Article The-Grammar)
Simple-Article → Text Text Image
     0              1    2    3
(Page-Of 2 1)
(Image-Of 3 1)
(article-name 0) = 1
(article-image 0) = 3
:OUT
(right-of 1 3)
(top-aligned 3 1)
(right-of 3 2)
(top-aligned 3 2)
(set-font 1 14pt :bold)
(set-font 2 10pt :bold))
```

Fig. 8. A variation of the Make-Article rule. This version needs only three input elements to produce the results shown in Fig. 5

burg et al. 1991) with an additional control feature that allows for termination as in a depth-first search, i.e., the parser returns as soon as a new derivation is found. Subsequently, parses may be sought until the search space is exhausted. The output of parsing is then one or more derivation trees, each of which yields an independent presentation.

Efficiency of parsing can be an issue with these grammars. The "connectivity" of the expander relation space affects how much work the parser must do before it exhaustively searches the entire space. The base case is one in which the expander relations simply replicate the linear structure of a string. In fact, our use of the *precedes* relation (we really mean *immediately-precedes*) in our running example is of this ilk. If a preprocessor can determine the linear sequence of content objects and index them with an expander relation such as *precedes*, then the parsing problem diminishes to parsing a string, which is known to have a low polynomial bound on complexity. Research continues in high-dimensional parsing to define other classes that are somewhere in between this base case and the most general case, for which we cannot guarantee a polynomial bound in our parsing algorithms. Of note are the results from the literature on graph grammars (Brandenburg 1989), which have shown a polynomial bound for a class of "context-free" graph grammars. Future work is called for in characterizing the nature of relation spaces that are useful in applying parsing technologies to multimedia generation.

As with other parsing domains, input that is not strictly covered by the grammar is another issue. One can take advantage of various methods for error correction that have been proposed in the parsing literature. So far, we have explored only the technique of adding rule variants to handle some of the underspecified cases. Figure 8 illustrates a variation of the rule shown in Fig. 7. Here, the rule matches with only three input elements and produces a Simple-Article that combines with other Simple-Articles and produces the output in Fig. 5.

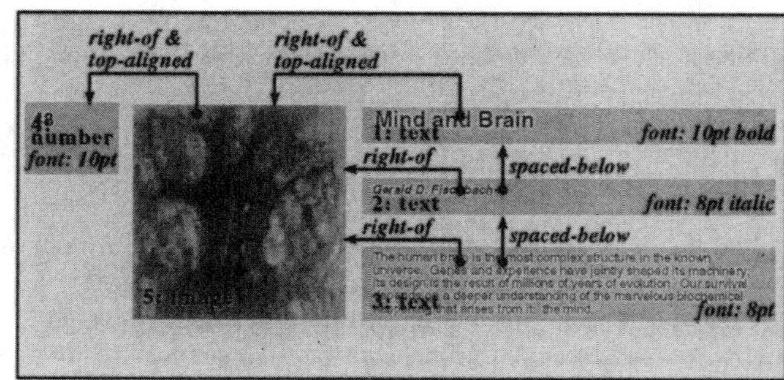

Fig. 9. A part of the translation for the presentation in Fig. 3 generated with the rule in Fig. 7. The translation has created media objects and installed spatial constraints that must subsequently be solved

4.4 Translation

When a derivation is found that covers all of the input, the set of :OUT forms is collected in a depth-first, left-to-right walk through the derivation tree. The Make-Article rule, in Fig. 7, includes a number of forms constraining spatial attributes (*right-of, top-aligned*, and *spaced-below*), as well as graphic (*set-font*) attributes. In this example, basic lexical items include an output form that creates the realized element in the presentation. Figure 9 illustrates these output constraints graphically.

In the current implementation, we use only synthesized attributes, i.e., the output attribute of each node of the derivation tree depends only on the values of attributes of nodes below (Knuth 1968), but we are extending the framework to incorporate inherited attributes as well. Another extension we have added in a preliminary form is to allow alternative :OUT forms for rules. That is, an *Article* object formed with one rule might be realized in more than one possible way. The generalization of this paradigm implies a search during the translation process itself, since more than one alternative realization might be tried and evaluated. See Brandenburg (1994) for a proposal of such an architecture in the context of graph layout.

4.5 Constraint solving

The use of a constraint-solving algorithm is a natural match with the rule formalism. Each rule installs only local constraints between the elements of the rule body. Rules for creating composite structures then create the constraints that link these smaller constraint networks together. The output forms of the final rule in the derivation then seeds this network with actual x and y values that are propagated during the constraint-satisfaction phase of the realization. In the final presentation, we allow the user to interact with the elements. In our on-line table-of-contents example, the user can move and resize individual elements, and the constraint system interactively maintains the proper relationships installed by the grammar.

The constraint-propagation system used is DeltaBlue developed at the University of Washington (Freeman-Benson et al. 1990; Maloney 1991). DeltaBlue is designed for non-cyclic constraint networks to be used in interactive applications with up to ~20 000 constraints.

In our experience, we generate considerably fewer constraints (i.e., in the neighborhood of 100 constraints). When specifying spatial positions, we construct constraints for every element's x and y positions, as well as their width and height. If temporal constraints are used to modify an element's visibility, we also produce constraints for an element's start time, duration, and end time. The default is that an element is always visible.

We assume that rule authors specify proper constraint networks. In this context, "proper" means networks that avoid cycles as well as over-constrained or under-constrained networks. Any tool that automatically generates the grammar's output constraints must ensure that these criteria are met when constructing constraint networks.

5 Examples of dynamic documents

In the previous examples, all output was constrained spatially. The following examples illustrate various ways in which grammars can produce dynamic presentations that go beyond the traditional static presentation of information. Dynamics are incorporated into the presentations by the grammars in the following ways:

1. Dynamic data types (e.g., quicktime movies, audio icons) are included in the lexicon of the presentations.
2. Temporal constraints are used between output elements to create an automatic sequence of pages presented to the viewer.
3. Hyperlinks are installed by the grammar to produce an interactive sequence of pages through which the viewer can navigate. One way to create hyperlinked documents is through the use of HyperText Mark-up Language (HTML) in conjunction with viewers such as National Center for Supercomputing Applications (NCSA) Mosaic (NCSA 1993).
4. Presentation elements are tapped into underlying simulations and reflect the state of that simulation by modifying their graphic attributes, such as visibility, color, size, and position.

Temporal constraints in this implementation are currently represented by intervals and their relationships to each other. These are based on the classic 13 relationships proposed by Allen (1983). This interval-based temporal logic includes the six relations of *before*, *meets*, *overlaps*, *during*, *starts*, and *finishes*, as well as their inverses and the relationship of *equality*. Our system constructs a constraint network based on the relative time of an element's presentation suggested by the grammar. Some examples of temporal constraints that can be used as rule output forms are listed here.

1. Two objects that share the same start time: (start-time= object1 object2)
2. Two objects that share the same end time: (end-time= object1 object2)
3. Two objects that share the same duration: (duration= object1 object2)
4. An object's end time equals another object's start time: (meets-in-time object1 object2)
5. The start time of an object is seeded with a value: (start-time object value)

The output forms "align" elements temporally, according to their start and end times. Using the same constraint satisfaction approach for spatial layout, the system identifies the relative time slots for realization. Then one presentation element is seeded with a specific presentation time, and the constraint system solves for the presentation times of the other elements. Given these temporal constraints, the system could automatically present the information over time.

The ability to modify the graphic attributes of presentation elements dynamically is based on the tapping mechanism developed in the Steamer project (Hollan et al. 1984) and generalized in the Icon Editor (Rosenstein and Weitzman 1990). Steamer visualized the complex process of steam propulsion. Elements in the interface were connected, or tapped, into a mathematical simulation of the process. This tapping mechanism included a mapping of values in the simulation to attributes that could be displayed in the interface and back again. By separating the interface from the simulation or process being visualized, elements could maintain a visual presentation of the component in the model, achieving a more general approach to interface construction.

For example, a pump might be connected to a simulation variable that would indicate the state of that pump. That state might be represented by a discrete value of *off*, *on* or *standby*. In Steamer, these states were mapped to graphic values that would modify the color of the pump from red to green to yellow, respectively. In addition, this tapping mechanism was bidirectional, mapping user input (e.g., mouse clicks) back into the simulation.

Here the simulation is simply the underlying presentation's abstract time value, an integer starting from 0. Typically, the user modifies this value by interacting with a horizontal slider. This action updates the presentation's time, which propagates to the other elements in the presentation, changing their visibility, position, color, etc. More complicated simulations could be generated by this approach. All that is necessary is that the grammar's output forms install the proper taps into the media objects created.

With the additional data types, constraints, links, and taps, the grammar can specify dynamic relationships between the elements of an automatic or user-controlled presentation. Here are a few examples of these presentations.

The first is based on a repair procedure (Henkenius 1993). This repair procedure is composed of three major steps, each containing a number of minor steps. Figure 10 shows the layout of the complete procedure on a large, high-resolution display. However, if we consider the characteristics of the output medium as part of the input to the parser, we can make the presentation sensitive to the output requirements. We make this property of the output display part of the parse input with the aid of the predicate mechanism of Relational Grammars.

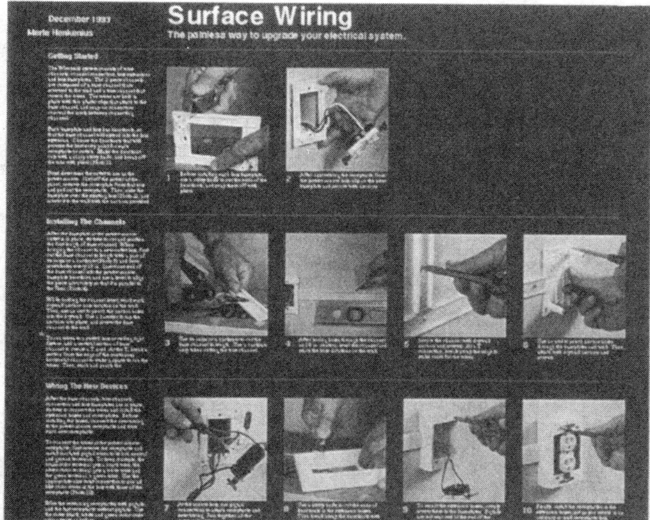

10

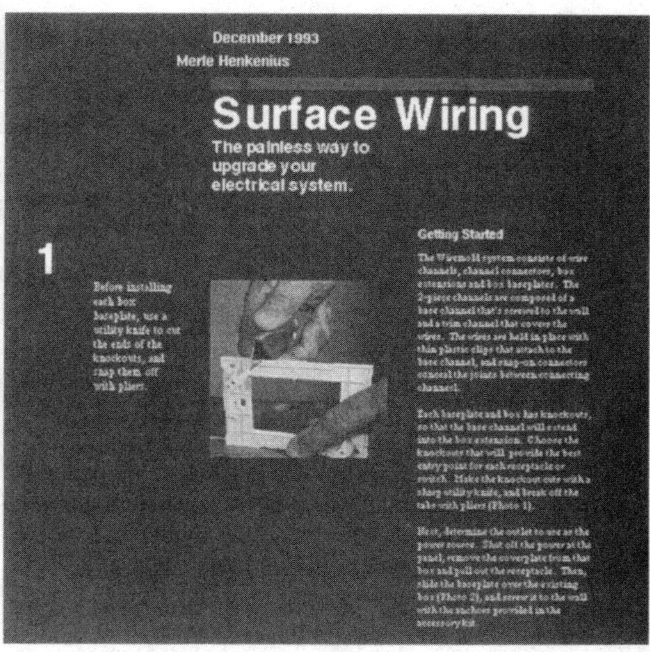

11

```
(Defrule (Make-Step Repair-Procedure-Grammar)
  Step → Image Text Number
   0       1    2     3
  (Description-Of 2 1)
  (Number-Of      3 1)
       ...
  :OUT
  ;;; geometric constraints

       ...

  ;;; tapping information
  (setf (visibility-tap 1) '*time*)
  (setf (visibility-tap 2) '*time*)
  (setf (visibility-tap 3) '*time*)
  (set-visible-range 1 (value 3) (value 3))
  (set-visible-range 2 (value 3) (value 3))
  (set-visible-range 3 (value 3) (value 3)))
```

12

Fig. 10. Presentation of a home repair procedure from Popular Mechanics magazine on a high-resolution display
Fig. 11. Presentation of the same home-repair procedure as in Fig. 10, but constrained temporally as well as spatially. The user can manually step through the procedure by interacting with the horizontal bar at the top of the page
Fig. 12. The definition of a rule that uses tapping to produce dynamic behavior. Here, tapping information is added to presentation elements that are subsequently controlled by the interactive slider in the presentation

That is, certain rules are fired only if a global predicate such as *large-display-p* is true; others are fired if it is not true.

For instance, if this repair procedure is being carried out by a person in the field with a hand-held digital assistant, the grammar can generate quite a different presentation. Figure 11 shows this alternative interpretation displaying the first step of the complete procedure. As part of the presentation, the horizontal bar at the top of the page becomes an active object that uses the tapping mechanism to control the presentation of elements. As the user interacts with the bar, the presentation's current time is modified. This in turn modifies the visibility of the individual elements. The display area of the device used to articulate the second presentation is much smaller than that of the first presentation. The grammar trades off the spatial resolution of the high-quality display with temporal resolution on the much smaller screen.

Figure 12 illustrates a grammar rule, Make-Step, that contributes output forms supporting the tapping mechanism for the presentation shown in Fig. 11. The composite formed in this rule is a simple Step composed of an image, its description and its number. The text on the right of the image in Fig. 11 is not part of this composite, but is part of a higher-level composite representing a sequence of steps for a subtask. In this rule, the three elements are tapped into the **time** variable, and the range of their visibility is based on an attribute of the Number element. This visibility range shows when an element should be presented on the screen.

The forms work as follows. The first three :OUT forms set the tap of three objects to the integer-valued **time** variable. The next three forms tie the range of visibility to exactly the number of the step in the procedure. This has the effect of making these objects visible only when their step values matches the current time.

A use of tapping to control graphic attributes, rather than a simple sequence, is illustrated in Fig. 13. This presentation illustrates the layered input of a personal pager that uses the

13

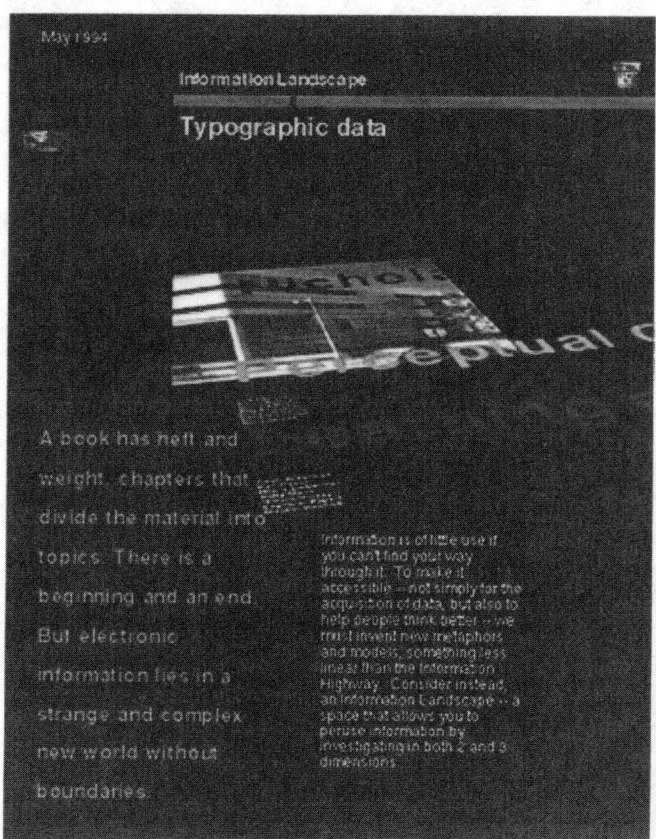

14

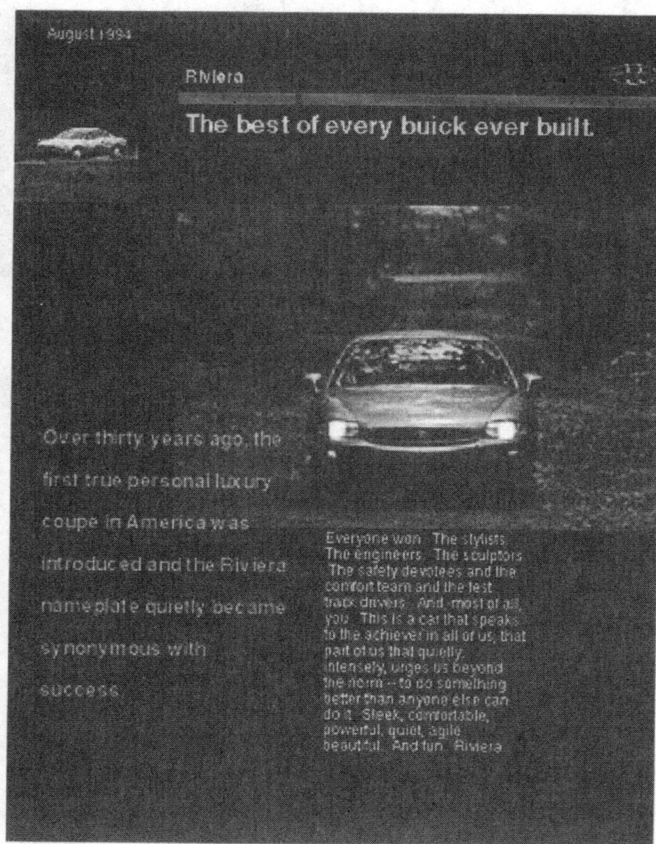

15

Fig. 13. Presentation of an exploding diagram of a personal pager. Individual pieces of information change their visibility, color, and position, depending on the current presentation focus set by the user with the interactive slider. (Images of SkyTel © All rights reserved)

Fig. 14. A high-resolution color presentation of research at the Visible Language Workshop. This spans three pages and includes QuickTime movies

Fig. 15. Advertising data using the same grammar as used in Fig. 14

dynamics of an exploding diagram. The interaction is again controlled through the use of the horizontal slider that progressively enables the visibility of the information, expands the position of the elements of the pager, and highlights relevant pieces of text. With different grammar rules, we could display this presentation with transparency to reveal the separate layers dynamically or we could display it with multiple small images to present the information in a storyboard (similar to the static presentation of this information in Fig. 13).

Other examples of design sensitivity to the delivery environment are shown in Figs. 14–16. Figures 14 and 15 exhibit the high-end articulation of a multimedia presentation. Figure 16 is the low-end. All use the very same grammar parameterized for three different end-delivery environments. Figures 14 and 15 incorporate different content, but reuse the same design suited for high-end multimedia workstations. The design consists of a few pages of information that incorporate Quicktime movies and audio icons. Figure 14 presents Information Landscape, a demonstration of work from the Visible Language Workshop shown at Technology, Entertainment and Design Conference (TED5) in Monterey, 1994. Figure 15 is a multimedia automobile advertisement. The nondeterministic grammar, however, offers other design results depending on the size of the display. There are three choices: a large vertical display as shown in Figs. 14 and 15, a National Television Standard Committee (NTSC) resolution display with horizontal aspect ratio, or a very small black-and-white display simulating a personal digital assistant (PDA). Figure 16 is an illustration of a PDA display with the same content as Fig. 14. Single pages on the large display occupy multiple pages on the small PDA display. In addition, input control on the large display is through the mouse interacting with the horizontal slider while pen-based input is used to navigate through the pages on the PDA.

Another way to support interaction dynamics is through the use of hypermedia links. This class of documents provides easy access to related information by simply clicking on links presented to the user. A popular way to generate these documents is by creating HTML files and viewing them within a browser such as NCSA Mosaic (NCSA 1993). Figure 17 illustrates an on-line table-of-contents "home page" presented in this way. The titles of articles in this example are linked to the actual on-line article (Wired WWW Server).

Input to this presentation is similar to the original table-of-contents examples in Figs. 3–5. In this example, however, the grammars support the generation of an HTML file. The hierarchy of the information is supported in the dynamics of the hyperlinked article. In addition, the grammar accommodates variation in the delivery environment based on its software capabilities. The graphically more limited delivery environment of an HTML viewer is taken into account.

6 Related work

It is important to note that the approach described in this paper addresses only a very specific part of the more general multimedia presentation problem: the problem of articulation. Our main concern is with the representation and articulation of multimedia design knowledge, not with the automatic inferencing of designs from first principles. Along the spectrum of artificial intelligence (AI) approaches vs. intelligent assistant (IA) approaches, this work falls more towards the IA side, particularly when it is combined with a tool for rule authoring that incorporates design assistance as discussed in Weitzman and Wittenburg (1993) and Weitzman (1995). While our approach may be less ambitious than the AI approaches, it has the distinct advantage of requiring less labor-intensive knowledge engineering and may be more likely to succeed in the short term.

As far as the mechanics of the generation system go, the main difference between comparable parts of other automatic generation systems and the work described here has to do with the nature of the rules and the approach to control. All the other rule-based systems of which we are aware use general forward- or backward-chaining inference rules. Metarules are typically used to constrain the search of the design space and a form of generate-and-test determines the appropriateness of a solution. More often than not, this aspect of these systems receives little attention in the literature, perhaps because adequate control mechanisms can be difficult to specify. We, however, use an independently motivated parsing algorithm that is enabled by our choice of Relational Grammars. The issue of control is thus folded into the more general problem of finding efficient parsing algorithms for higher-dimensional grammars, a continuing research topic. As progress is made on this front, the results can be incorporated into future versions of our system. In the meantime, authors of the rules used in our approach need not concern themselves with issues of control.

Work most closely related to our own includes "intelligent" multimedia presentation systems and user interface management systems.

6.1 Multimedia presentation systems

Today, many systems address the larger problem of multimedia presentation and include articulation as just one component of a larger system. COMET (Feiner and McKeown 1993) is a knowledge-based system that produces interactive and coordinated explanations that combine text with 3D graphics. It uses "media generators" that can communicate with each other to produce a presentation. The underlying generator within COMET, called IBIS (Seligmann and Feiner 1991), uses a rule-based approach that generates and tests its presentation alternatives. Each rule invokes a set of stylistic strategies that specify high-level visual effects (e.g., highlighting an object). These strategies are in turn realized by other, lower-level rules. Another general multimedia platform for generation is WIP (Andre et al. 1993). WIP approaches the problem of multimedia design as a planning problem to achieve coherent multimodal presentations of text and graphics. The articulation of the layout is the same constraint-satisfaction algorithm used in our research. They encode the graphical design knowledge through constraints that express semantic/pragmatic relations (alignment, grouping, symmetry or similarity) and geometrical/topological relations (absolute and relative position).

Coordination of complex temporal relationships has been attempted in some of the larger multimedia systems. Karp and Feiner (1990) examine these complex relationships in the context of building animations between elements of the presentation. This includes the temporal synchronization of special editing effects (e.g., cuts, wipes, fades, dissolves), camera control movements, and multiple views of the same information. As part of this more complete model, user interactions are also modeled. The use of temporal constraints in our system is a simple extension of the spatial constriants and is based upon Allen's categories of temporal logic (Allen 1983). We construct a constraint network based on the relative time of an element's presentation suggested by the grammar. Then, using the same constraint satisfaction approach for spatial layout, we identify the relative time slots for realization.

Other systems that automatically design artifacts are characterized by the fact that the domain can be expressed as a set of discrete rules that easily encode design knowledge. In architecture, this has been limited to applications in highly constrained specialties such as kitchen design (Oxman and Gero 1987) or simple floor plan layout (Mitchell et al. 1976). Other domains, like information graphics (Mackinlay 1986), also lend themselves to this approach. One example, ANDD (Marks 1990), is a system that automatically designs network diagrams. It is an effective rule-based system that designs and articulates network diagrams to communicate information represented in

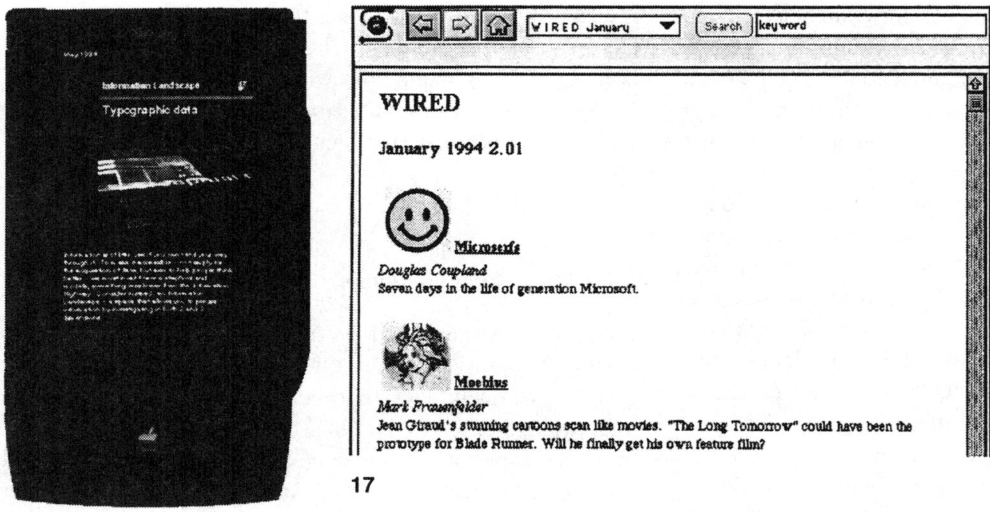

Fig. 16. A low-resolution presentation of the same information shown in Fig. 14. This presentation spans six pages and is designed to be viewed on a personal digital assistant (PDA)

Fig. 17. Presentation of a table of contents from Wired magazine with links in the Mosaic environment

arbitrary attributed graphs and is part of a multimedia explanation facility.

A specific technique for controlling design articulation is the use of the grid (Hurlburt 1978). Early research that focuses on articulation using the grid for the layout of information was done by Feiner (1988). This system uses information about the kind of material to be displayed, the user, and display hardware. The system then creates displays using more information about the kinds of objects to be presented. This system first generates a grid and then uses it in the presentation of information. In our work, we characterize the same categories of information, but the notion of a grid is implicitly represented in the output constraints of the grammar.

6.2 User interface management systems

To support the view that the end result of multimedia generation is a dynamic interface rather than a static page (or a static sequence of frames), we allow each presentation element to be connected to a value within an application or simulation. Then, each element in the interface has the potential to become dynamic by visualizing values within the application or simulation and/or modifying those values through user interaction. For example, in a multimedia training document, the simulation of a device to be repaired could control how the element is presented and how it behaves when the student interacts with the document. This behavior can be encoded in the output of the grammar constraints as illustrated in the example shown in Fig. 13.

The separation of interface from application is commonly taken by developers of user interface management systems (UIMS). It enhances modular development and supports automatic construction and reuse of interface elements. Early work in the visualization of simulations can be found in Steamer (Hollan et al. 1984) and the Process Visualization System (Foley and McMath 1986). This approach separates the dynamics of the application from the specific presentation to the user. Typical UIMS, in fact, support this same separation (Arens et al. 1988; Kim and Foley 1993; Wiecha et al. 1990). DON (Kim and Foley 1993) consists of an application model (containing both data and control models), a design process model supporting top-down iterative design and graphic design knowledge to support the layout process. An expert system, rule-based approach is used. ITS (Wiecha et al. 1990) is similar but emphasizes the usability of the style language by the interface designer. By making the underlying rule base more accessible, the designer has the ability to modify the rule base itself.

7 Future directions

In support of the design process, Relational Grammars have proven useful as the basis for a number of interaction paradigms. An open question is how much further they can be pushed to support the creative activity of design. This larger vision suggests a number of future research directions.

7.1 Parsing algorithms

We believe that further research on parsing algorithms in the service of multimedia articulation is called for. For example, depending on properties of the content database, deterministic (LR) algorithms for Relational Grammars may be possible, which of course would be more efficient than the one we are currently using. Research on such algorithms for multidimensional grammars continues. However, nondeterminism in parsing, along with the possibility of ambiguity in derivations, may play the role of generating more than one possible presentation, which could in turn be reviewed by a higher-level control structure in more "intelligent" applications. Still another idea is to use predictive parsers to help do some of the content selection (Wittenburg 1993, 1996).

7.2 Ambiguity in design

Traditionally, ambiguity in parsing is something to be avoided. However, in supporting a creative process, this may not be the case. Ambiguity should be viewed as beneficial and something that needs to be maintained until later design decisions have been able to disambiguate the designer's intention. These ambiguous interpretations can be viewed as alternative solutions in the larger design space. Building an environment to explore this space enabling better solutions is one of our goals.

7.3 Cooperative design

We have shown two distinct paradigms that use Relational Grammars for design support: completely automatic and improver-based. A different approach embraces both methods within a single paradigm. Cooperative CAD (Kochhar and Friedell 1990) is a technique that mixes automatic articulation with manual control. This cooperative paradigm puts the user in control to articulate design decisions manually, and also supports automatic design exploration by the system. Relational Grammars can provide a formalism for this approach.

7.4 Design by demonstration

The very nature of design suggests that the solution to the problem is not known a priori. In fact, as the design progresses, initial assumptions and decisions may be redefined or dropped altogether. This suggests that the language of a design, the basic vocabulary and the rules for combination, evolves as the solution is explored. What is important is having an environment that responds to these needs. A designer should be able to redefine rules and add new ones to support their design process. An area of research that can provide some insight is in programming-by-demonstration (Cypher 1993). With this approach, designers could modify an existing grammar or create new grammars without coding. This would help create a design environment in which nonprogrammers can modify the existing rule sets. A prototype of such a tool is discussed in Weitzman (1995).

7.5 New applications

Exploration of the use of Relational Grammars to support online training manuals and the design of dynamic presentations is a continuing research focus. In addition, as interest in the Internet continues to grow, it is becoming more apparent that we will need automated techniques to support the design and presentation of information. One interesting application for Relational Grammars is in the production of timely, personalized newspapers. Intelligent agents would retrieve information over the net and submit it to the grammar for automatic presentation.

Acknowledgements. We thank R. MacNeil, the late Professor M. Cooper, of the Visible Language Workshop, J. Hollan, and G. Furnas, formerly of Bellcore's Computer Graphics & Interactive Media Research Group, for their support of this research. The first author's was carried out at MIT's Media Lab sponsored in part by the News in the Future project, the Joint National Intelligence Development Staff (JNIDS), and the Alenia Corporation.

References

Aho AV, Sethi R, Ullman JD (1986) Compilers: principles, techniques, and tools. Addison-Wesley, Reading

Allen J (1983) Maintaining knowledge about temporal intervals. Commun ACM 26:832–843

Andre E, Finkler W, Graf W, Rist T, Schauder A, Wahlster W (1993) WIP: the automatic synthesis of multimodal presentations. In: Maybury M (ed) Intelligent multimedia interfaces. AAAI Press/MIT Press, Cambridge, pp 75–93

Arens Y, Miller L, Shapiro S, Sondheimer N (1988) Automatic construction of user-interface displays. Proceedings of the American Association of Artificial Intelligence, St. Paul, Minn., pp 808–813

Brandenburg F (1989) On polynomial time graph grammars. In: Goos G, Hartmanis J (eds) STACS 88: 5th Annual Symposium on Theoretical Aspects of Computer Science, Lecture notes on computer science 294, Springer, Berlin Heidelberg New York, pp 227–236

Brandenburg F (1994) Designing graph drawings by layout graph grammars. In: Tamassia R, Tollis IG (eds) Graph drawing: DIMACS International Workshop, Lecture notes in computer science 894, Springer, Berlin Heidelberg New York, pp 416–427

Cypher A, (1993) Watch what I do: programming by demonstration. MIT Press, Cambridge, Mass

Feiner S (1988) A grid-based approach to automating display layout. Proceedings of Graphics Interface '88, Edmonton, Canada pp 192–197

Feiner S, McKeown K (1993) Automating the generation of coordinated multimedia explanations. In: Maybury M (ed) Intelligent multimedia interfaces, AAAI Press/MIT Press, Cambridge, Mass., pp 117–138

Foley J, McMath C (1986) Dynamic process visualization, IEEE Comput Graph Appl 6:16–25

Foley J, Kim W, Kovacevic S, Murray K (1991) UIDE – an intelligent user interface design environment. In: Sullivan J, Tyler S (eds) Architectures for intelligent interfaces: elements and prototypes, Addison-Wesley, Reading pp 339–384

Freeman-Benson B, Maloney J, Borning A (1990) An incremental constraint solver. Commun ACM 33:54–63

Helm R, Marriott K (1991) A declarative specification and semantics for visual languages. J Vis Lang Comput 2:311–331

Henkenius M (1993) Surface wiring. Popular mechanics 170:63–66

Hollan J, Hutchins E, Weitzman L (1984) Steamer: an interactive inspectable simulation-based training system. AI Magazine 5:15–28

Hurlburt A (1978) The grid. Van Nostrand Reinhold, New York

Karp P, Feiner S (1990) Issues in the automated generation of animated presentations. Proceedings of Graphics Interface, Halifax, Canada, Canadian Information Processing Society, Toronto, pp 39–48

Kim W, Foley J (1993) Providing high-level control and expert assistance in the user interface presentation design. Proceedings of

INTERCHI'93, Amsterdam, The Netherlands, Association for Computing Machinery Press, New York, pp 430–437

Knuth DE (1968) Semantics of context-free languages. Math Syst Theor 2:127–146

Kochhar S, Friedell M (1990) User control in cooperative computer-aided design. Symposium on User Interface Software and Technology, Snowbird, Utah, Association for Computing Machinery Press, New York, pp 143–151

Kochhar S, Marks J, Friedell M (1991) Interaction paradigms for human-computer cooperation in graphical-object modeling, Proceedings of Graphics Interface '91, Calgary, Canada, Canadian Information Processing Society, Toronto, pp 180–191

Mackinlay J (1986) Automating the design of graphical presentations of relational information. ACM Trans on Graph 5:110–141

Maloney J (1991) Using constraints for user interface construction. PhD Dissertation, University of Washington, Technical Report 91–08–12, Seattle, Wash

Marks J (1990) A syntax and semantics for network diagrams. Proceedings of the IEEE Workshop on Visual Languages, Skokie, Ill., IEEE Computer Society Press, Los Alamitos, CA, pp 104–110

Maybury M (1993) Intelligent multimedia interfaces, AAAI Press/MIT Press, Cambridge, Mass

Mitchell W, Steadman J, Liggett R (1976) Synthesis and optimization of small rectangular floor plans. Environment and Planning B: Planning and Design 3:37–70

National Center for Supercomputing Applications (NCSA) (1993) Internet manuscript, mosaic@ncsa.uiuc.edu

Oxman R, Gero J (1987) Using an expert system for design diagnosis and design synthesis. Expert Systems 4:4–15

Rosenfeld A (1990) Array, tree, and graph grammars. In: Bunke H, Sanfeliu A (eds) Syntactic and structural pattern recognition: theory and applications, World Scientific, Singapore

Rosenstein M, Weitzman L (1990) Icon Editor: the specification of graphic behavior without coding. Proceedings of the 23rd Annual Hawaii International Conference on Systems Sciences, Kailua-Kona, Hawaii, IEEE Computer Society Press, Los Alamitos, CA, pp 523–530

Seligmann D, Feiner S (1991) Automated generation of intent-based 3D illustrations. Proceedings of ACM Siggraph Las Vegas, Association for Computing Machinery Press, New York, pp 123–132

Scientific American (1992) Special issue on Mind and brain 267:4

Weitzman L (1995) Architecture of information: interpretation and presentation of information in dynamic environments. PhD dissertation, MIT Media Laboratory, Cambridge, Mass

Weitzman L, Wittenburg K (1993) Relational grammars for interactive design. IEEE Symposium on Visual Languages, Bergen, Norway, IEEE Computer Society Press, Los Alamitos, CA, pp 4–11

Weitzman L, Wittenburg K (1994) Automatic presentation of multimedia documents using relational grammars. ACM Multimedia'94, San Francisco, Calif., Association for Computing Machinery Press, New York, pp 443–451

Wiecha C, Bennett W, Boies S, Gould J, Greene S (1990) ITS: a tool for rapidly developing interactive applications. ACM Trans Inform Syst 8:204–236

Wired (1994) 2.01:13

Wired WWW Server. http://www.wired.com

Wittenburg K (1992) Earley-style parsing for relational grammars. Proceedings of IEEE Workshop on Visual Languages, Seattle, Wash., IEEE Computer Society Press, Los Alamitos, CA, pp 192–199

Wittenburg K (1993) Adventures in multidimensional parsing: cycles and disorders. Proceedings of the 3rd International Workshop on Parsing Technology, Tilburg, The Netherlands, and Durbuy, Belgium, Tilburg University, Tilburg, The Netherlands, pp 333–348

Wittenburg K (1996) Predictive parsing for unordered relational languages. In: Bunt H, Tomita M (eds) Recent advances in parsing technologies. Kluwer Academic, Boston Dordrecht London

Wittenburg K, Weitzman L, Talley J (1991) Unification-based grammars and tabular parsing for graphical languages. J Vis Lang Comput 2:347–370

Grammar-Based Articulation for Multimedia Document Design

Louis Weitzman and Kent Wittenburg

Adaptive design is still an unsolved problem and is becoming more critical with the evolution of the World Wide Web and the added effort needed to support it. The web is fueling much of today's tool construction, and yet there is a long way to go, given the increasing complexity of the design process. Some of the tools and techniques that are moving in the direction of adaptive design include cascading style sheets, template-based design, and data-driven publishing. The "write once, publish anywhere" battle cry may be an unrealistic goal, but surely we can do better than starting from scratch each time.

So the need is greater than ever for tools to support adaptive design. Despite this need, we have seen little work emerging from the research community to support the one-to-many design goal. For more focused tasks, however, some progress has been made. Ryall et al. (1997) provides a nice example of the IA (intelligent assistant) approach in the context of graph layout design.

Since the publication of this work, there has been progress in consolidating higher-dimensional grammar formalisms. The forthcoming book *Theory of Visual Languages* collects papers from a 1996 Workshop on Theory of Visual Languages and includes formal work on a unifying theory of visual language formalisms (Marriott and Meyer 1998). It also includes a comprehensive survey of visual language specification, recognition, and applications (Marriott, Meyer, and Wittenburg 1998).

Unfortunately, neither of us have found ourselves in a position to build directly on the work presented in the paper here. Therefore, open questions still remain as to whether the particulars of our parsing/generation methods will scale up to realistically sized systems. One of the main stumbling blocks has to do with how content is represented. Our higher-order parsing operations are required if the content must be restructured with each design generated. If not, it may still be the case that the techniques for mapping of structures to constraint statements will prove useful. In addition, our vision of combining our design support tools (Weitzman and Wittenburg 1993) with the generation tools discussed in this paper has not been pursued, given the scale of the required effort and its prerequisite that the rule/template system already be in place.

REFERENCES

Marriott, K., and Meyer, B. 1998. The CCMG Visual Language Hierarchy. In Marriott, K., and Meyer, B. (eds.), *Theory of Visual Languages*. New York: Springer-Verlag, (in press).

Marriott, K.; Meyer, B.; and Wittenburg, K. 1998. A Survey of Visual Language Specification and Recognition. In Marriott, K., and Meyer, B. (eds.), *Theory of Visual Languages*. New York: Springer-Verlag, (in press).

Ryall, K.; Marks, J.; and Shieber, S. 1997. An Interactive System for Drawing Graphs. In North, S. (ed.), *Graph Drawing: GD '96, Lecture Notes on Computer Science 1190*, 387–394. Berlin/Heidelberg: Springer-Verlag.

SECTION V

User and Discourse Modeling

User modeling research looks for ways of enabling interfaces to adapt to their users—by constructing, maintaining, and exploiting user models, which are explicit representations of the properties of individual users. User modeling has been found to enhance the effectiveness and usability of interfaces in a wide variety of situations: it can be used to tailor information presentation to the user, to predict the user's future behavior, to help the user find relevant information, and to adapt interface features to the user. User models are complemented by discourse models, which contain the system's description of the syntax, semantics, and pragmatics of the interactive (possibly even multimodal) session as it proceeds. It seems commonly agreed that a discourse model should contain a syntactic and semantic description of the discourse segments; a record of the discourse referents; and the intentional, attentional, and rhetorical structure of the dialog, including a focus space stack, reference links (anaphoric, cataphoric, exophoric), and a description of the individual dialog contributions on the abstract level of dialog acts.

The first article by Elaine Rich is widely viewed as marking the beginning of user modeling as a field of research. Using the example of a book recommendation system, Grundy, this article introduces many issues and ideas that still deserve attention nearly two decades later. First, it introduces the notion of user stereotypes, which has been adopted by many subsequent researchers (e.g., Kobsa, Müller, and Nill, this section). A *stereotype* is a cluster of properties that often occur together (e.g., those associated with a scientist). Rich's representation of stereotypes is more differentiated than many later representations. For example, a user is assumed to possess a given property to a particular degree, and the system has a particular degree of confidence in such an ascription; each user is typically viewed as belonging to several distinct stereotypes; and the system is capable of long-term learning, adapting its stereotypes on the basis of experience with users.

Grundy performs most of the functions that are typical of the class of user modeling systems that recommend objects to users; for example, eliciting and interpreting evidence relevant to the user's evaluation standards and predicting the user's evaluations. More recent systems of this sort have tended to use more general decision-theoretic concepts for representing the user's evaluation standards and managing the uncertainty inherent in these tasks (see Jameson et al. (1995) for an overview and Linden et al. (1997) for a recent example).

The second paper by David Chin describes UCEgo, the intelligent agent component of the Unix Consultant (UC) natural language advisory system that helps users of varying expertise utilize Unix. By explicitly modeling user goals and plans, UCEgo enables UC to take the initiative: volunteering information, correcting user misconceptions, or rejecting unethical user requests. In the latter case, for example, if a user asks UC to delete another user's files, the system must reason between competing goals of wanting to help the user and wanting to preserve another's files. UCEgo uses goal hierarchies and goal precedence relations (implemented as daemons) to make these judgments. UCEgo takes as input user goals and plans from a goal analyzer (PAGAN) and user model (KNOME) as well as UC's own themes (internal agent motivations such as helping the user, self-preservation, and acting ethically), which give rise to specific goals (e.g., to preserve the UC program and Unix system) and, ultimately, to speech acts that are realized and communicated to the user. UC is able to detect and correct user misconceptions (e.g., if a user asks what a command option does when there is no such option, UC will tell the user it doesn't exist). UC also volunteers various kinds of information such as warnings, suggestions, and elaborations on yes/no questions (e.g., if a user asks if "rn" is used to rename files, UC will respond "No, rn is used to read news. To rename a file, use mv."). In conclusion, Chin demonstrates convincingly that an interface that knows more than its user can effectively reason about goals and plans (including detecting positive and negative goal interactions) to determine appropriate system actions. Accordingly, Chin's work, and user modeling in general, has strong ties to Section VII of this collection, "Agent Interfaces."

The next paper by Wolfgang Wahlster explores the role of user and discourse models for the disambiguation of natural pointing gestures in the intelligent multimedia interface XTRA. The XTRA system provides natural language access to an expert system, which assists the user in filling out a tax form. During the dialog, the relevant page of the tax form is displayed on one window of the screen so that the user can refer to regions and elements of the form by tactile gestures. XTRA was the first system that could analyze pars-pro-toto gestures, focusing gestures, and vague pointing gestures. It uses a unification-based approach to integrate the natural language and pointing input. The paper focuses on the disambiguation of a variety of deictic gestures exploiting user and discourse knowledge together with linguistic and domain constraints. It shows how XTRA exploits a user model during output generation to decide whether pointing is adequate for referring to an object. In addition, the model explicitly reasons about the appropriate type and granularity of a planned pointing gesture. The paper discusses how the user and discourse model influence the comprehension and production of multimodal dialog contributions and, conversely, how multimodal communication influences user and discourse modeling.

The subsequent paper by Alfred Kobsa, Dietmar Müller, and Andreas Nill represents two lines of research in user modeling. First, it gives an example of the use of a general user modeling shell, BGP-MS. User modeling shells have been developed to handle the common tasks of a user modeling component to support software reuse. BGP-MS is the most widely used shell (see Kobsa and Pohl (1995) for a more detailed description and the issue in which it appears for more information on user modeling shells). Two characteristic features are its logic-based representation formalism and its use of stereotype hierarchies. The latter builds upon the ideas in Rich's article (this section), but BGP-MS does without the quantitative gradations that are associated with Rich's stereotypes. This paper also gives a straightforward example of an adaptive hypertext system. Hypertext and hypermedia have proven to be a fruitful context for the application of user modeling techniques. The system KN-AHS illustrates some ways in which a hypertext system can construct a user model on the basis of a user's behavior and can adapt the form and content of its presentations on the basis of that model. An overview of adaptive hypertext systems has been provided more recently by Brusilovsky (1996).

In addition to inferring a model of the user by observing and reasoning about their actions, it is equally important to design output by taking into account the expected effects on the user's state. The paper by Johanna Moore and Cécile Paris argues convincingly that a natural language generation system must be able to reason about the intended effects of individual parts of the text on the hearer and about its own previous utterances. In addition, their discourse model includes an explicit representation of how the components of a generated text relate to one another rhetorically. In particular, they present an advanced text planner for explanation dialogs that interprets follow-up questions in the context of the ongoing advisory dialog.

The key feature of their approach is the explicit representation of the intentional and rhetorical structure of the dialog stored in a dialog history. By recording the planning process behind the generated text, the system can interpret and answer the user's follow-up questions in a context-sensitive way. The authors designed over 150 plan operators that encode knowledge about how intentions may be achieved via a set of rhetorical means, and their text planner can generate answers to a large variety of "why" and "how" questions using Penman as a realization component. The text planner described by Moore and Paris was generalized to a multimedia presentation planner in the WIP project described in the paper by Wahlster et al. included in Section II of this collection.

When a long and complex explanation is being given, users should have the opportunity to ask for clarification as soon as they lose track. In such a situation, it is not adequate to wait until the explanation is complete and then ask follow-up clarification questions, as described in the preceding paper by Moore and Paris. Rather, user interaction must be allowed as the explanation proceeds. In the next paper, Alison Cawsey describes her EDGE system that is concerned with tutorial explanatory dialogs combining text, graphics, and pointing actions.

The distinguishing feature of Cawsey's approach is that the explanations are planned incrementally, interleaving planning and execution. The EDGE system focuses on interactions that may take place in the middle of a long explanation and how they influence the way such an explanation develops. The system integrates content planning, discourse planning, and user modeling in a computational model of explanatory discourse. Cawsey's intelligent interface allows users to indicate that they are confused about the system's presentation at any point of an explanatory multimodal presentation, and the system attempts to repair that confusion before continuing. Assumptions about the user's knowledge are updated as the dialog progresses so that the detailed planning of an explanation can be tailored to the user. The incremental planning approach suggested by Cawsey implies that all remaining planning decisions will take into account the revised context after a clarification dialog.

The final two papers in this section exploit user and discourse models in the context of intelligent multimedia interfaces to complex applications. The distinguishing feature of the ALFresco interface described in the paper by Oliviero Stock is its combination of hypermedia capabilities with natural language and gestural input. ALFresco is an intelligent interface to an information system about Italian frescoes of the fourteenth century. Hypertext and video sequences can be retrieved by typed natural language queries coordinated with pointing gestures to images displayed on a touch screen. ALFresco combines generated and canned text when answering queries of the user. The generated text includes buttons that are linked to canned hypermedia presentations. The innovative idea is to represent as much knowledge about the frescoes as possible in a knowledge representation language in order to generate tailored explanations of the masterpieces but to use canned text for complex topics that cannot be represented in a declarative way given the limited expressive power of currently available formalisms. ALFresco combines these advanced input and output techniques with explicit user and discourse modeling, leading to a highly adaptive and flexible interface for multimedia information exploration.

The next article similarly explores multimedia interfaces but, in this case, to expert systems. John Burger and Ralph Marshall describe investigations into providing multimedia dialog driven in part by their experience with typed natural language interfaces that failed to take into consideration all interactions between systems and users (e.g., deictic references to windows or items on the screen). The authors found that different users prefer different types of input mechanisms (e.g., menus versus typed natural language), validating a requirement for generation of displays to facilitate alternative forms of input. The paper describes AIMI (An Intelligent Multimedia Interface), a generalization of the King Kong portable natural language interface, and exemplifies AIMI in action, interpreting multimedia input and automatically tailoring multimedia output. The paper describes influences on presentation design (e.g., content and size of the message, its purpose, available means of communication). An interesting aspect of AIMI is that, unlike previous systems in which deictic references were built into the grammar (see, e.g., Neal et al. from Section I of this volume), one canonical form is used to represent both multimedia input and output. For example, typed input, menu selection, and mouse clicks are translated into a common KL-ONE representation. Further, an explicit model of user attention and intention is acquired, represented, and exploited as the interaction proceeds.

Collectively, these papers advance important ideas and techniques for building, maintaining, and using models of user and discourse context. Issues explored include stereotypical and individual user models, detection and correction of user misconceptions, plan-based interfaces that enable incremental and mixed initiative interaction, and the extension of user and discourse models for multimodal dialog. The area remains rich with unexplored research issues such as the appropriate degree of explicit versus implicit model acquisition, the role of user and discourse shells, the degree and control of interface adaptivity, and the ethics associated with individual model construction and management.

Scientific advances and innovative applications of user and discourse models have the potential for profound impact on the way users learn, decide, act, and play in the future.

REFERENCES

Brusilovsky, P. 1996. Methods and Techniques of Adaptive Hypermedia. *User Modeling and User-Adapted Interaction* 6(2–3): 87–129.

Jameson, A.; Schäfer, R.; Simons, J.; and Weis, T. 1995. Adaptive Provision of Evaluation-Oriented Information: Tasks and Techniques. In Mellish, C. S. (ed.), *Proceedings of the Fourteenth International Joint Conference on Artificial Intelligence*, 1886–1893. San Francisco: Morgan Kaufmann.

Kobsa, A., and Pohl, W. 1995. The BGP-MS User Modeling System. *User Modeling and User-Adapted Interaction* 4(2): 59–106.

Linden, G.; Hanks, S.; and Lesh, N. 1997. Interactive Assessment of User Preference Models: The Automated Travel Assistant. In Jameson, A., Paris, C., and Tasso, C. (eds.), *User Modeling: Proceedings of the Sixth International Conference*, UM97, 67–78. Vienna: Springer.

User Modeling via Stereotypes*

ELAINE RICH

The University of Texas at Austin

This paper addresses the problems that must be considered if computers are going to treat their users as individuals with distinct personalities, goals, and so forth. It first outlines the issues, and then proposes stereotypes as a useful mechanism for building models of individual users on the basis of a small amount of information about them. In order to build user models quickly, a large amount of uncertain knowledge must be incorporated into the models. The issue of how to resolve the conflicts that will arise among such inferences is discussed. A system, Grundy, is described that builds models of its users, with the aid of stereotypes, and then exploits those models to guide it in its task, suggesting novels that people may find interesting. If stereotypes are to be useful to Grundy, they must accurately characterize the users of the system. Some techniques to modify stereotypes on the basis of experience are discussed. An analysis of Grundy's performance shows that its user models are effective in guiding its performance.

1. INTRODUCTION

Scene I

Someone walks into a large library, tells the librarian that he is interested in China, and asks for some books. What sort of books does the librarian recommend? That depends. Is the person a small child who just saw a TV show about China and wants to see more pictures of such an exotic place? Is the person a high school student doing a term paper? Or maybe a prospective tourist? Or a scholar interested in Eastern thought? Can the person read Chinese? The librarian needs to know these things before he can point the reader to the right books. Some of what he needs to know he'll know before he even thinks about it, such as the approximate age of the person. Some things he'll assume until he has evidence to the contrary, such as that the person does not read Chinese. To find out other things, he'll ask a few specific questions. Only after he has a rough model of the person he's talking to can he answer the question.

Scene II

The phone rings in the information division of a large pharmaceutical firm. The caller wants information about a drug the company makes. What sort of information should be provided? That depends. Is the caller a doctor, a patient, or an FDA representative? To provide the right information, the person answering the phone needs to know some facts about the caller.

The scenes above illustrate some kinds of situations in which people need to form a *model* of the person with whom they are dealing before they can behave appropriately. They form their model by collecting a few specific pieces of information and then invoking the knowledge they have about the groups to which the current person belongs, such as scholar or medical patient.

As computers come to be used by a larger number of people to help perform a great variety of tasks, it is becomming more and more important for them to be easy for people to use. There are many factors than can contribute to the ease of use of a computer system, ranging from the good design of input devices such as terminals to the speed of the system's response, the appropriateness of its response, and the naturalness of its input and output languages. Appropriate models of the users of a system can be an important contribution because they can simultaneously affect several of those factors, such as speed and quality of response and habitability of the language interface.

Most systems that interact with human users contain, even if only implicitly, some sort of model of the creatures they will be dealing with. For example, the central assumption behind the mini-max strategy used by game playing programs is that the opponent is trying to win and will therefore make his best possible move. Although it is almost always valid to assume that the opponent wants to win, it is much less often true that he will therefore make the best move. He may, and probably does, have idiosyncracies of style or strategy that preclude that. Of course, human players know that and watch for evidence of such quirks in their opponents.

The term "user model" can be used to mean several different things. The three major dimensions along which user models can be classified are:

—Are they models of a canonical user or are they models of individual users?
—Are they constructed explicitly by the user himself or are they abstracted by the system on the basis of the user's behavior?
—Do they contain short-term, highly specific information or longer-term, more general information?

There are other significant differences between the systems using these various types of user models, but they follow from these major differences. Systems with a single model of a canonical user can have that model permanently embedded within themselves, whereas systems with models of individual users must build the model on the fly, and so must make explicit the ways in which the

*This research was sponsored in part by the Defense Advanced Research Projects Agency (DOD), ARPA Order No. 3597, monitored by the Air Force Avionics Laboratory Under Contract F33615-78-C-1551, while the author was at Carnegie-Mellon University. The author was supported by a grant from the Xerox Corporation.

The views and conclusions contained in this document are those of the author and should not be interpreted as representing the official policies, either expressed or implied, of the Defense Advanced Research Projects Agency or the US Government.

model influences the performance of the overall system. Systems that extract the user model from the user's behavior must grapple seriously with the issues of incorrect or conflicting information arising from the inferences that led to the model. Systems with explicitly stated user information can, on the other hand, avoid many of those issues. Systems that deal with short-term knowledge must deal successfully with the problem of detecting when things change, while longer-term systems may be able to finesse that issue. But as these differences reduce to the three outlined above, they do not need to be focused on explicitly.

The work described here has concentrated on user models in one corner of this space. Models of individual users were built because of the facility for personalization that they provide that is lacking in a canonical user model. Implicitly constructed models were used because of the inherent inaccuracy and the annoyance of requiring users to construct their own models of themselves. The choice of position along the third dimension was much less clear cut. Both short-term knowledge (such as the topic currently being discussed or the goal now being pursued) and long-term knowledge (such as the level of the user's knowledge about the problem domain or goals that are likely to be pursued) can be important to the performance of an interactive system. But it appeared likely that different techniques would be appropriate for dealing with the two types of knowledge. Models of long-term user characteristics were chosen because very little work has been done with them, while short-term user models were already being explored, particularly in the context of natural language understanding. So the rest of this work will deal explicitly with the issues involved in individual user, implicit, long-term user modeling.

2. A BRIEF DISCUSSION OF IMPLICIT, INDIVIDUAL USER, LONG-TERM USER MODELING

A user modeler is significant only insofar as it communicates with a larger performance system in which it is embedded. This suggests that the issues that must be tackled in order to implement a user model and to integrate it usefully into a system are the structure of the user modeler itself and the links between the user modeler and the rest of the system.

2.1. The User Modeler and the Links into It

The first major issue that a user modeler must confront is how to build models of users. In building a model of a person, the obvious first step is to collect some facts about the person, as, for example, his age or his experience with computers. However useful this approach is, through, it is severely limited in its effectiveness for two reasons. One is that it might take a lot of questions to accumulate all the knowledge the system needs. The other reason is that the person may not always be able to provide accurate answers, either because he doesn't know, as for example, a student talking about his incorrect knowledge, or because he doesn't want to talk about it, as for example whether someone's grandmother is interested in reading books about homosexuality. To deal with situations such as these, systems must be able to infer information about their users based on a small number of explicitly stated facts.

There is a lot of evidence in the psychological literature to support the assertion that people are not reliable sources of information about themselves. Nisbett and Wilson (1979) describe a number of experiments that suggest that people are very bad at introspecting and then reporting on their cognitive processes. A different source of unreliability in self-description is suggested by the work of McGuire and Padawer-Singer (1976). They present evidence in support of the assertion that, when asked to describe themselves, people are heavily influenced by the social groups in which they find themselves. People seem to mention those characteristics that distinguish them from the other people in the group. This clearly introduces an element of unreliability into such descriptions since it is difficult to control or measure which groups a person is identifying with at a particular instant.

All of these experiments suggest that it is important that a user modeler not rely too heavily on answers to specific questions in building models of individuals. The most obvious way to build a user model without asking many questions is to make direct inferences from a user's behavior to a model of him. For example, if the base system performs some action which the user said was not what he wanted, the system should look at the reasons that it performed that action and conclude that it is likely that at least one of these reasons is wrong, at least for this user. But even this mechanism of drawing explicit inferences from the user's behavior is not always sufficient, since it may require many interactions between the system and the user to build a user model with enough information in it to be of significant use.

2.1.1. Stereotypes. A major technique people use to build models of other people very quickly is the evocation of *stereotypes*, or clusters of characteristics. So, for example, one might know that if someone is a judge, he or she is probably over forty, well-educated, reasonably pro-establishment, fairly affluent, honest, and well-respected in the community. Although not all of these attributes are necessarily true of any particular judge, a person would tend to assume them until shown otherwise. Besides our everyday belief that we possess such stereotypes, there is also lore, in such areas as education, that something like stereotypes is necessary. (Highet, 1950).

In addition, there has been a lot of discussion in the psychology literature about the nature of sterotypes. For a review of much of this work, see Hamilton (1979). There are many theories about why people use stereotypes, but one of the most certain explanations is that people use stereotypes as a means for dealing with the fact that the world is far more complex than they can deal with without some form of simplification and categorization. One of the ways in which stereotypes help to simplify the world is that they have a strong effect on what characteristics of a person are attended to and remembered. As a result, they will tend to be confirmed by experience since potentially disconfirmatory evidence will be ignored. (See, for example, Cantor & Mischel, 1979, and Snyder & Uranowitz, 1978.)

When computer systems use stereotypes, they may be able to avoid some of the pitfalls that plague the human use of stereotypes. Computers will not develop any emotional attachment to their steotypes and so, to whatever extent that contributes to the inadequacies of stereotypes, computers will be immune. There are, however, very direct limitations on the cognitive ability of any individual computer system, although these limitations are not identical to those of people. So we shall have to discover to what extent a computer system's stereotypes can be altered on the basis of experience and to what extent perception is sufficiently biased that such learning is not possible. On the other hand, computer systems are definitely superior to people in that they can explicitly use stereotypes in certain situations and not in others.

Of course, a computer cannot help but be at a loss compared to a human in quickly sizing up a person on the basis of superficial characteristics, if for no other reason than that it can neither see him (to determine his age, type of clothing, or sex) nor hear him (to determine where he comes from or his self-assurance). But it does have available, because of the way communication between man and machine takes place, some information that a person would not have. For example, if a user types quickly, he is probably either a secretary, a computer scientist, a newspaper reporter, an author, etc.

In order for a system to be able to use stereotypes effectively, it must have two kinds of information. It must know the stereotypes themselves—the collections of characteristics or *facets*. A user can be characterized by a set of facets, each of which contains a value (or values). The particular set of facets used will, of course, be determined by the domain and purpose of the system as a whole, but could include such things as level of expertise with the system, specific concepts dealt with by the system that are of particular interest, or specific system tasks that are of particular concern. Stereotypes are simply collections of facet-value combinations that describe groups of system users.

A system that is going to use stereotypes must also know about a set of *triggers*—those events whose occurrence signals the appropriateness of particular stereotypes. So, for example, if a user immediately uses an advanced construct in a system, that should serve as a trigger for the "expert-user" stereotype, which should then be *activated*. When a stereotype is activated, the predictions it makes about various characteristics should be incorporated into the model of the user.

Stereotypes, as used in this context, are also very similar to scripts (Schank, 1977), frames (Minsky, 1975), and schemas (Bobrow & Norman, 1975). All these mechanisms provide a means of representing partial descriptions of frequently occurring situations. This is done by specifying a collection of the significant aspects of a situation while omitting mention of the nonsignificant ones. In the case of scripts, the aspects mentioned are events. In the case of stereotypes, the aspects are personality characteristics. Looked at in this light, stereotypes are just another instance of the increasingly well-understood phenomenon that people interpret many of their experiences in terms of stored expectations for those experiences. Another way of looking at the wide applicability of this sort of structure is that although all situations are not identical, neither are they all completely dissimilar.

As suggested by the need for the generalization relationship between stereotypes, the stereotypes in use by a given system may range from very general ones, such as man or woman, which might be appropriate in a wide variety of domains, to very specific ones, such as reader of good mysteries, which are appropriate only for specific systems and domains. All of these can contribute to the system's model of an individual user.

The use of stereotypes, then, when combined with the ability to record explicit statements by the user about himself and to make direct inferences about a user from his behavior, may provide a powerful mechanism for creating computer systems that can react differently to different users.

2.1.2. The USS. The core of the user modeler is its model of an individual user. This model, called the *User Synopsis* or USS, is built by combining the direct information provided by the user, direct inferences from the user's actions, and predictions made by stereotypes that are deemed appropriate for this user. The information in the USS can then be used to guide the rest of the system.

2.1.3. Probabilistic Inference. Very little of the information in the USS is known for sure to be true, since it arises almost entirely from probabilistic rather than certain inferences. Some behaviors suggest specific characteristics, while others suggest the appropriateness of a particular stereotype, which then suggests particular characteristics. This is very similar to the situation that arises in medical diagnosis, as described in Shortliffe, (1976), and the way these inferences should be handled by a user modeler is very similar to the way they are handled in MYCIN.

Because of the uncertain nature of behaviorally inferred knowledge, a user modeling system must associate with each piece of information that it possesses a rating representing how confident it is that that information is correct. So stereotypes actually consist of a set of (attribute, value, rating) triples. The situation in the User Synopsis is even more complicated. In order to be able to resolve the conflicts that will inevitably arise, the system should remember why it believes the things it believes. So the USS consists of a set of (attribute, value, rating, justifications) quadruples.

Notice that both stereotypes and the USS contain ratings. In both cases, the ratings indicate confidence in the associated fact. In the case of stereotypes, the ratings represent confidence that any person who fits the stereotype will exhibit a particular characteristic. In the case of the USS, the ratings indicate the confidence the system has in its belief that a particular fact is true of a particular user.

2.2. Links Out of the User Modeler

The other major aspect of user modeling is how the user models, once they are built, are used to guide the performance of the rest of the system. In other words, how are the links out of the user modeler to the base system, the language understander, and the language generator used? The solution to this problem depends heavily on the structure of the particular system in question. Some general guidelines are discussed in Rich (1979).

If both of these issues, compiling a user model and using that model effectively, can be dealt with successfully, performance systems should be able to significantly improve the level of service they provide to their users.

2.3. Choice of Task Domain

In order to have a forum in which to explore these issues and to be able to make a convincing case that some solutions have been found, it was deemed necessary to tackle the issues in the context of a specific task domain and actually to build a system into which the solutions to the issues could be incorporated. Although the actual task chosen is not important, it is important that it satisfy the two principle criteria that determine appropriateness of this sort of user model. These criteria are:

—The system should be one that will be used by a heterogenous group of users. If the set of possible users is highly homogeneous, then it is much more efficient to simply build in a model of a canonical user.

—The system should be one that has a nontrivial amount of flexibility in its operation. If it does not, then it does not need the additional information of a user model to tell it what to do.

The task that was chosen for this experiment is to suggest to users novels that they might like to read. In other words, to play librarian. This task meets both of the above criteria. Almost everyone reads novels at least occasionally. And the task is highly flexible; any one of a large number of books could be selected. So this looked like a good forum for the exploration of the issues raised by individual user modeling.

3. AN OVERVIEW OF GRUNDY

The main purpose of this section is to provide an overview of Grundy, a system that plays librarian. The best way to view the task of the system is that is should come as close as possible to simulating the performance of a good librarian at a public library when a patron walks in the door looking for something to read over the weekend. If the librarian already knows him, she[1] will be able to provide some suggestions right away. This will happen almost all the time, for example, in a small town library where the librarian knows everyone. If, on the other hand, the librarian doesn't know him, she will first size him up quickly. How old is he? How well educated does he appear to be? Is he a man or a woman? Even those clues will probably not be enough, though, so she will have to ask a few questions. Maybe she'll ask him what the last book that he read and liked was. Or maybe who his favorite author is. Then she'll start recommending books. Based on his reaction to the first few suggestions, she'll modify her view of him if necessary and continue making suggestions until he is satisfied. Grundy will try to do as well as it can it performing this task. Clearly, it has several limitations. It cannot see the user. That eliminates many of the librarian's initial clues. And many questions that the librarian might ask would be very difficult for the system to use effectively. In order to get any information out of the user's response to the question about the last book he read, the system would have to know a much larger number of books than it is ever likely to know. So, although the system will try to perform the same task as the librarian, it will not try to copy exactly her performance. Rather it will try to perform the task using the techniques best suited to the system's strengths and weaknesses.

The rest of this section attempts to provide an overview of Grundy, and simultaneously an exposition of some of the issues involved in user modeling. It presents a dialogue between a user and the system, annotated to explain what the system knows and what it is trying to do at each stage. The lines printed in upper case were typed by the system; those in lower case were typed by the user.

PLEASE TYPE IN YOUR NAME

John Greene

YOU HAVEN'T USED THIS SYSTEM BEFORE, HAVE YOU?

no

> The system can now activate two stereotypes. The first, ANY-PERSON, will be activated for any new user. It predicts middle of the road values along almost all dimensions. Of course, it predicts them with very low ratings so that they can immediately be superseded by specific information. It can also activate the

[1]This is not to suggest that readers are necessarily male and that librarians are female. But in order to make this description readable, it is necessary to use different pronouns for the two people. No political statement is intended.

MAN stereotype on the basis of the name "John." It will activate both of these stereotypes and construct an image of its total current knowledge of the user before it tries to do anything else.

Then it will try its first task designed to tell it as much as possible about the user.

OK

I'D LIKE TO KNOW WHAT SORT OF PERSON YOU THINK YOU ARE. PLEASE TYPE IN A FEW SINGLE WORDS THAT YOU THINK CHARACTERIZE THE MOST IMPORTANT ASPECTS OF YOURSELF

unconventional open direct honest humorous persistent adventurous

I DON'T KNOW THE WORD UNCONVENTIONAL

I DON'T KNOW THE WORD OPEN

I DON'T KNOW THE WORD DIRECT

WOULD YOU LIKE TO TRY SOME MORE WORDS?

Since it didn't get the complete picture the user was trying to convey, it gives him another chance.

yes

OK GO AHEAD

relaxed jewish friendly playful thoughtful eccentric

At this point, Grundy believes it knows quite a lot about John. Because he is male, it believes he has a fairly high tolerance for violence and suffering, as well as a preference for thrill, suspense, fast plots, and a negative interest in romance. Because of stereotypes evoked by "humorous," "friendly," and "playful" it thinks he's quite optimistic. It thinks he's interested in conflicts such as art-vs-science, exploration, God, and what it means to be human. It thinks he has particular sympathy for such strengths as kindness, courage, honesty, and perceptiveness.

HAVE YOU EVER READ EARTH ANGELS BY SUSAN CAHILL?

To select a book to recommend, it picks one of the facets of John which has both a non-middle-of-the-road value and a fairly high rating. Then it rates all the books suggested by that facet by comparing them to John along all dimensions. It got this suggestion from the belief that he is politically liberal (which it believes from "Jewish").

no

Grundy selects, from the things it knows about the book, those things that it thinks will make John like it.

YOU MIGHT LIKE IT.
IT IS ABOUT A GIRL WHO GOES TO CATHOLIC ELEMENTARY SCHOOL, HIGH SCHOOL, AND COLLEGE, THEN GOES ON TO BECOME A NUN, BUT FINALLY BACKS OUT A FEW DAYS BEFORE FINAL VOWS.
A MAJOR CONFLICT IN IT IS THE RELATIONSHIP OF MAN TO GOD.
ONE OF THE MAJOR STRENGTHS OF ONE OF THE MAIN CHARACTERS IS INTELLIGENCE.
ONE OF THE MAJOR STRENGTHS OF ONE OF THE MAIN CHARACTERS IS INDEPENDENCE.
IT IS POLITICALLY LIBERAL.
IT HAS A BIT OF ROMANCE.
IT HAS A MEDIUM-FAST MOVING PLOT.
DOES THAT SOUND GOOD?

no

Grundy needs to find out where it went wrong. It knows the reasons it thought John would like the book. It asks about them to see which if any of them is incorrect. The order in which it asks about them is determined by an *a priori* rating of how likely that reason is to be the problem and the current rating of the related characteristics of John. It asks about things it is least sure of first.

WAS IT BECAUSE OF THE DEPTH OF THE CHARACTER DEVELOPMENT? (EITHER TOO MUCH OR NOT ENOUGH)

no

WAS IT BECAUSE OF THE AMOUNT OF ROMANCE? (EITHER TOO MUCH OR NOT ENOUGH)

no

WHERE YOU BOTHERED BY THE POLITICAL POSITION ESPOUSED BY THE BOOK?

no

AREN'T YOU INTERESTED IN THE RELATIONSHIP OF MAN TO GOD?

no

It has found the problem. There may, of course, be other problems, but since a primary goal of a system like this is to ask as few questions as possible, it stops asking now. If there are other problems, it will discover them later.

Although John is not interested in the relationship of man to God, it was not unreasonable for Grundy to have throught he was, since he said he was Jewish, and the mention of a religious group frequently (though not always—it may refer to an ethnic group) indicates an interest in religious ideas. But now Grundy changes its belief to reflect this more specific information.

DO YOU WANT SOME MORE SUGGESTIONS?

yes

HAVE YOU EVER READ ZEN AND THE ART OF MOTORCYCLE MAINTENANCE BY ROBERT PIRSIG?

It selected this based on the personality characteristic "living in a separate world," which it got from "eccentic." It also matched on several other dimensions, such as an interest in the conflict of art-vs-science.

yes

DID YOU LIKE IT?

yes

Grundy now has some additional information about John. It goes through all the characteristics of this book and makes direct inferences about John based on them.

HAVE YOU EVER READ THE CRYING OF LOT 49 BY THOMAS PYNCHON?

It also generated this one based on "separate world."

no

YOU MIGHT LIKE IT.
IT IS A HUMOROUS WELL-WRITTEN NOVEL OF SOUTHERN CALIFORNIAN INSANITY.
ONE OF THE MAJOR WEAKNESSES OF ONE OF THE MAIN CHARACTERS IS LIVING IN A DIFFERENT WORLD FROM THE REST OF MANKIND.
ONE OF THE MAJOR STRENGTHS OF ONE OF THE MAIN CHARACTERS IS INTELLIGENCE.
ONE OF THE MAJOR STRENGTHS OF ONE OF THE MAIN CHARACTERS IS ABILITY TO COPE WITH WHATEVER HAPPENS.
IT HAS ALMOST NO ROMANCE.
IT IS MILDLY PHILOSOPHICAL.
DOES THAT SOUND GOOD?

yes

GOOD

DO YOU WANT SOME MORE SUGGESTIONS?

no

OK THEN. BYE.

4. STEREOTYPES IN GRUNDY

4.1. Stereotypes and Stereotype Structures

A *stereotype*, as mentioned above, is a collection of frequently occuring characteristics of users. Figure 1 contains some sample stereotypes used by Grundy. A bit of explanation of the values contained in those stereotypes is in order. The simple linear scales (Thrill, Tolerate–sex, Tolerate–violence, Tolerate–suffering, Romance, Education, Sex--open, and Piety) have values ranging from −5 to +5. The numbers associated with each value of the list-valued facets (e.g.

FACET	VALUE	RATING
Activated-by	*Athletic-w-trig*	
Genl	*ANY-PERSON*	
Motivations		
Excite	3	600
Interests		
Sports	4	800
Thrill	5	700
Tolerate-violence	4	600
Romance	−5	500
Education	−2	500
Tolerate-suffering	4	600
Strengths		
Physical-strength	4	900
Perseverance	3	600
	SPORTS-PERSON	

FACET	VALUE	RATING
Activated-by	*Feminist-w-trig*	
Genl	*ANY-PERSON*	
Genres		
Woman	3	700
Politics	Liberal	700
Sex-open	5	900
Piety	−5	800
Political-causes		
Women	5	1000
Conflicts		
Sex-roles	4	900
Upbringing	3	800
Tolerate-sex	5	700
Strengths		
Perseverance	3	600
Independence	3	600
Triggers	Fem-woman-trig	
	FEMINIST	

Figure 1. Some Sample Stereotypes.

Strengths, Genres) also range from −5 to 5. Ratings range from 0 to 1000, with higher numbers indicating greater degrees of certainty.

Stereotypes can contain any number of characteristics; they will almost never contain values for all the characteristics that the system understands. For example, the FEMINIST stereotype contains values for the facets PIETY and

TOLERATE-SEX, which the SPORTS-PERSON stereotype does not. But SPORTS-PERSON contains values for the facets THRILL and TOLERATE-SUFFERING, which FEMINIST does not. But since usually more than one stereotype will be active for a particular user, it will be possible to build up a fairly complete picture of a user even though the individual stereotypes contain only partial information.

The stereotypes about which the system knows are arranged in a directed acyclic graph (DAG) formed by the partial ordering relation "generalization of." This is important because it allows information not to have to be represented identically in many different stereotypes. For example, Figure 2 shows a piece of the stereotype DAG containing the stereotypes for religious people. It represents the fact that there are many characteristics shared by Christians, regardless of denomination, and others shared by all religious people regardless of religion. This generality DAG can be used to focus the attention of the system on the events that are the most likely to be of significance.

The most general node of any stereotype structure is the stereotype ANY-PERSON. It provides default values for all facets, but provides them with very low ratings. These values can be used to prevent the system from doing anything that might be offensive until it learns enough about the individual user to know his particular inclinations. It is a cross between a model of a canonical user and a lower bound on the user's tolerance for things.

This notion of a canonical or representative person with respect to whom individual characteristics can be compared has been useful in at least one other system. Carbonell (1979) describes a system for describing personality traits as goal structures and then using the personality traits to understand stories. He describes personality traits as changes to the goal structure one would attribute to an average person. Thus a miserly person would rate the "preserve money" goal higher than another person would. This mechanism of representing individuals as departures from a norm has two significant advantages. It provides a frame of reference and it corresponds well to the conversational notion of default. If someone's "preserve money" goal is exactly what one would normally expect, a storyteller (or a system user or a conversationalist) will not usually mention it. If it is mentioned, it will be because the value is different from what one would otherwise expect. In either case, the system's model is likely to be correct.

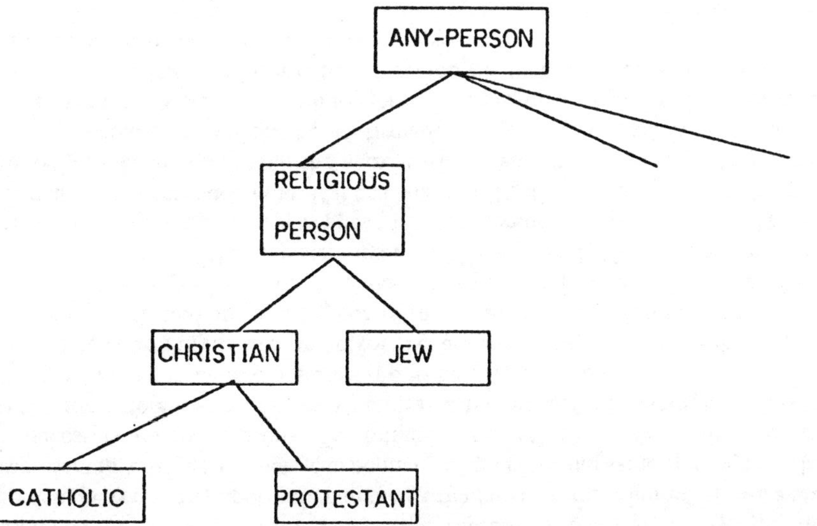

Figure 2. A Piece of the Stereotype DAG.

Although it is usually true that stereotypes will share the values of their generalizations, it is not always so. For example, although religious people can reasonably be expected to be quite pious, Jewish people are much less likely to be so than other religious groups. So the information in the JEWISH stereotype overrides some of the information in the RELIGIOUS stereotype. The algorithm for incorporating stereotype information into the USS must then handle this override. The most extreme case of overriding of general information by specific occurs with respect to the ANY-PERSON stereotype, most of whose information will eventually be overridden by other stereotypes once the system gets to know the user. This use of general information accompanied by specific overrides when necessary has also been useful in other systems (see Carbonell, 1979 or Charniak, 1977).

It is important that the structure used to represent the generality relationships among stereotypes be a DAG rather than a tree to make it possible to represent the fact that some stereotypes may have more than one immediate generalization. For example, Grundy has a stereotype of a MARXIST. That stereotype has two generalizations, each representing different aspects of a Marxist's position: LEFT-WING-PERSON and RADICAL. It is unfortunate that this structure is necessary since it complicates many of the algorithms that the user modeler uses to maintain the user synopsis.

The generality structure of stereotypes in the user modeler's data base is merely a DAG and not a lattice because, although there is a least upper bound (ANY-PERSON), there is no greatest lower bound. The stereotypes that are active at any particular time do, however, form a lattice with the user synopsis representing a single user, as the greatest lower bound. This has no effect on the algorithms used to move around in the structure, however.

4.2. Activating Stereotypes

Stereotypes can be activated as a result of almost any kind of action. A stereotype is activated by instantiating one of its triggers. A trigger is an object associated with a particular situation. In addition to its name, it contains the name of the stereotype to be activated and the rating (a number between 0 and 1000) to be assigned to the stereotype. The rating represents the probability that the stereotype is actually appropriate in the particular situation. Figure 3 shows a few representative triggers. There can be many triggers for the same stereotype. This is necessary for two reasons. The ratings to be assigned to the stereotype may differ for different situations in which it is activated and it is useful to be able to tell what situation caused a stereotype to be activated.

Each currently active stereotype has associated with it a list of the triggers that have activated it. If a trigger is instantiated, the action will depend on whether that trigger has been instantiated before. If it has, no further action will result. If it has not, then the stereotype will be activated. Here again, the action depends on what has already happened. If the stereotype has not previously been activated, it is activated now. If it has and is still active, then two things happen: its rating increases and both the current trigger and the earlier triggers get their ratings increased to reflect the confirmation they have just received. If, on the other hand, the stereotype is no longer active, the situation must be re-examined on the basis of the new information to decide whether the balance of the evidence is in favor of or opposed to the stereotype.

	NO-TV-TRIG	(Besides asking for characteristic words, the other thing Grundy can do to find out about users is to ask them about TV. This trigger is activated if the user says he does not watch TV.)
FACET	*VALUE*	
Stereotype	NON-TV-PERSON	(this stereotype suggests that a person is likely to be educated and serious)
Rating	800	(maybe this person is not really a non-TV person. Maybe he just can't afford to buy one.)

	SCI-ED-TRIG	(This trigger is associated with the SCIENTIST stereotype and will be activated whenever the SCIENTIST stereotype is activated.)
FACET	*VALUE*	
Stereotype	EDUCATED-PERSON	
Rating	900	
Reasons	SCIENTIST	

Figure 3. Some Sample Triggers.

The major action involved in the activation of a stereotype is updating the user synopsis to reflect the new information. This involves going through each of the facets for which information is predicted by the stereotype, seeing what information is already there and why, and deciding what the value should be, based on both the new and the old information. If the stereotype was not already active, this will always be done. If it was, then it may be necessary to propagate its change in rating to all the predictions it makes. But it is only necessary to do that if the rating change is significant. So its new rating will be compared to its rating the last time changes were propagated. If the difference is greater than an appropriate threshold the changes will be propagated.

The amount a stereotype influences the value of a facet is a function of both the rating of the stereotype and the strength with which the stereotype predicts the value of the facet, as well as the other evidence already present about the facet. There is no explicit priority given to earlier inferences over later ones, but because the earlier ones will tend to determine the course of later interactions, questions, and observations, they will end up having a more pronounced effect than will later inferences.

Stereotypes can be activated whenever their triggers are instantiated. Triggers can be instantiated almost any time. The three major types of situations in which they are instantiated in Grundy are:

—As part of a specific task designed to solicit information about the user, such as the tasks that ask about descriptive words or TV watching. For example, associated with each word that the system understands to characterize users is a list of triggers to be instantiated if that word is used.

—As a result of a facet in the USS being given a particular value. For example, if the gender facet is assigned the value male, then the MAN stereotype will be activated as a result of a trigger associated with the facet.

—As a result of another stereotype being activated. When a stereotype is activated all of its generalizations are also activated. This means that information that is common to all the specializations of a given stereotype can be represented just once in the most general stereotype to which it applies. In addition, stereotypes may contain triggers that will be instantiated whenever the stereotype is. The stereotypes indicated by the triggers will then be activated too. This is useful if the fact that someone is a member of one class suggests that he is also a member of another. For example, the scientist stereotype suggests the atheist stereotype. The ratings of the additional stereotypes will be a function of the rating of the stereotype that caused them to be invoked and the rating of the trigger that activated them. In other words, it represents the probability that the first stereotype is appropriate and, given that it is, that the other stereotype is too.

There are other situations that could arise in other contexts, for example:

—In a system with a natural language front end, stereotypes could be triggered by the use of arbitrary words, phrases, or grammatical constructions.
—In a system with a specific set of commands that the user can issue, stereotypes can be triggered by the use of particular commands.
—Stereotypes could be triggered by any other information that the system has about the user. For example, his account number might indicate his status in some way.

The thing that all of these situations have in common is that they are specific situations that the system must recognize individually and handle. So to associate stereotypes with the situations, all that is necessary is to build some structure in which the appropriate triggers are linked to the relevant situation (another piece of information for each entry in the lexicon, or command table, or user account list, or facet description, for example). Then whenever the system processes a situation, it also checks for associated triggers.

4.3. Combining Stereotypes to Form the USS

As mentioned earlier, the central structure in a user modeling system is the USS, the model of an individual user. The USS is built by combining all of the knowledge the system has or can infer about the user. Figure 4 shows an example of a USS built by Grundy. It was constructed on the basis of the user having told Grundy that she is a feminist and an intellectual. Notice that some facets contain values predicted by a single stereotype, while others have been affected by more than one. Sometimes (as in the case of SEX-OPEN) the stereotypes reinforced each other's predictions. Other times (as in the case of PIETY) the values predicted by the various stereotypes conflicted. When such conflicts occur, an appropriate value must be computed for the USS, and its associated rating must be computed to indicate the lack of confidence that the conflict suggests. In the case of linear facets such as PIETY, the value stored in the USS will be a weighted average (weighted by rating) of the values predicted by all the relevant stereotypes. For other types of facets, other conflict resolution mechanisms are appropriate. For some symbolic facets, the value selected will be the most specific object that is a generalization of all the suggested values. As the complexity of the values which facets are allowed to assume grows, the sophistication of the conflict-resolution rules will also have to grow. It is significant that even such simple rules as these enabled Grundy to perform quite well (see Section 7.1).

FACET	*VALUE*	*RATING*	*JUSTIFICATIONS*
Gender	female	1000	Inference-female name
			WOMAN
Nationality	USA	100	ANY-PERSON
Education	5	900	INTELLECTUAL
Seriousness	5	800	INTELLECTUAL
Piety	−3	423	WOMAN
			FEMINIST
			INTELLECTUAL
Politics	Liberal	910	FEMINIST
			INTELLECTUAL
Tolerate-sex	5	700	FEMINIST
Tolerate-violence	−5	597	WOMAN
Tolerate-suffering	−5	597	WOMAN
Sex-open	5	960	FEMINIST
			INTELLECTUAL
Personalities	4	646	WOMAN
Opt-pes	0	100	ANY-PERSON
Plot-intr	0	100	ANY-PERSON
Plot-speed	−2	475	EDUCATED-PERSON
Suspense	0	100	ANY-PERSON
Thrill	−4	839	WOMAN
			INTELLECTUAL
Romance	3	696	WOMAN
Confusion	3	570	EDUCATED-PERSON
Real-fant	0	100	ANY-PERSON
Comedy	0	100	ANY-PERSON
Genres			
Literature	4	700	INTELLECTUAL
Women	3	700	FEMINIST
Political-causes			
Women	5	1000	FEMINIST
Strengths			
Perceptiveness	2	570	EDUCATED-PERSON
Intelligence	4	800	INTELLECTUAL
Independence	3	600	FEMINIST
Perseverance	3	600	FEMINIST
Sympathy	2	497	WOMAN
Kindness	2	497	WOMAN
Weaknesses			
Reason	3	600	INTELLECTUAL
Conflicts			
Difference	3	600	INTELLECTUAL
Upbringing	3	800	FEMINIST
Sex-roles	4	900	FEMINIST
Propriety	2	497	WOMAN
Love	2	497	WOMAN
Motivations			
Learn	4	700	INTELLECTUAL
Interests			
Ideas	4	900	INTELLECTUAL

Figure 4. A Sample User Synopsis.

5. EXPLOITING THE USER MODEL

5.1. How Grundy Exploits the USS

The raison d'etre of a user model is to provide guidance to an underlying system in the performance of its task. Grundy's task is to suggest appropriate novels and the USS guides the execution of that task in three ways. It enables the system to focus on a fairly small set of potentially appropriate books; it provides a way of evaluating each of those books in detail in order to select the best one to recommend; and it provides a way of selecting which of the selected book's many attributes would be of interest to a particular user.

For each recommendation it makes, Grundy performs the following set of actions:

1. It builds a set of all of the facets of the USS which have a fairly high rating and a non-middle-of-the-road value. This is the set of salient characteristics of the user.
2. It randomly selects one facet from the set. It then builds a set of books to consider by selecting those books with specific attributes suggested by the chosen user characteristic. For example, if the EDUCATION facet were being used and it contained a high value, then books with high PHILOSOPHY and LITERARY-MERIT values would be included in the initial set. This step constitutes the attention-focusing function of the USS.
3. Once the set of possible books is assembled, each of them is compared facet by facet to the USS in order to decide which book is the best match. This step exploits the evaluation capability of the USS.
4. Having selected a book to recommend, Grundy must decide what to say to the user about the book, since it knows much more than most people would want to hear. The USS is used again, this time to filter the most interesting of the book's features so that they can be presented

From this discussion it should be clear that a user model can serve a variety of functions even to an underlying system as simple as Grundy.

5.2. How Grundy Does Not Exploit the USS

Because of the simplicity of the overall Grundy system, there are several areas in which it does not exploit the USS. These include:

—Deciding how to phrase things (for example, as a function of the user's educational level). Grundy's sentence generation mechanisms are so simple that they have no use for any outside information.

—Deciding what questions to ask the user about himself. This is a problem because most of the time Grundy gets enough information from its first question ("Tell me some words that describe yourself."). In a few limited situations, additional information will be sought specifically to correct what Grundy perceives to be a misconception on its part about the user. If, for example, a book is rejected by the user because of its political position and Grundy believed that the user would like the book because of its politics, it will ask the user a direct question in order to ascertain for sure his political position.

—Interpreting things the user says to the system. Because of the limited natural language facility possessed by Grundy, statements by the user are restricted to single words. There is little room for exploitation of additional knowledge of any sort in interpreting such simple statements.

These limitations in the ways Grundy exploits the user model arise from limitations within the Grundy system itself rather than from inherent limitations in the applicability of user models. See Rich (1979), for a fuller discussion of these issues, particularly the potential for the use of user models in conjuntion with a natural language understander.

6. LEARNING

6.1. Hierarchical Memory

The knowledge in a system like Grundy is divided into three sections, as a function of its scope of relevance. First there is the knowledge about the domain in which the system operates. That information is true and relevant to all users and all dialogues (although of course not all of it will be relevant to any one dialogue, it could be). At the next level is the knowledge about an individual user. That knowledge is relevant each time that user interacts with the system. At the narrowest level is the information that is relevant to this dialogue only.

In order to provide access to the appropriate parts of the system's knowledge at the appropriate times, it is necessary to arrange the system's knowledge hierarchically. Whenever the system wants to access some information, it looks first to see if that information exists in the dialogue-specific memory. If it is not there, it looks in the user-specific memory. And if it is not there, it looks in the universal memory. This hierarchical search is embedded in the data-base access routines, so it is transparent to the rest of the system. To record information, it is necessary to specify which memory the information should be stored in. This mechanism has the advantage that it is possible to override universal knowledge with more specific knowledge without permanently erasing the global knowledge.

At the end of the session, all the information in the user memory is written into a file corresponding to the user. That file will be retrieved whenever that user returns to the system. The universal memory can be written out to form a new universal file. And the dialogue memory can be forgotten.

6.2. Adapting Stereotypes

In addition to learning models of individual users, it is important for a user modeling system to be able to modify its data base of stereotypes. This importance arises from the almost total lack of real data on which to base the initial construction of the stereotypes. To bias a system forever with the prejudices of its designer would place an undue burden on it (although even those pure prejudices would probably be significantly better than nothing). In addition, computers have a significant advantage over people with respect to the user of stereotypes—they are not emotionally committed to them and thus are able to change them as warranted by experience. This advantage certainly ought to be exploited.

Almost all events that occur when a stereotype is active can shed some light on the correctness of the stereotype and its triggers. If the user behaves in a way predicted by the stereotype, it lends confirmation both to the appropriateness of that prediction and to the appropriateness of the triggers that caused the stereotype to be activated. If, on the other hand, the user exhibits a behavior that conflicts with a prediction of an active stereotype, then either the prediction is inappropriate or the triggers that caused the stereotype to be activated are inappropriate (or possibly both). It should be noted that this does not necessarily mean that the stereotype or the triggers are wrong. They may correctly predict a strong likelihood to which the current user is merely one of the exceptions. When a conflict does occur, however, the system cannot tell exactly why it arose. It can merely conclude that there is less evidence for the predictions than there was before the conflict. Because it also cannot know which of its inferences is the source of the problem (either the triggers or the stereotype itself or both), it must unreinforce all of them by lowering their ratings. If some of the inferences are in fact correct, they will be reinforced in other situations and so will be retained by the system. The inferences that are not correct will eventually be eliminated.[2] It is because of this spurious unreinforcement that may occur that it is particularly necessary that reinforcement occur whenever a prediction is borne out by experience. Otherwise it might be reasonable to simply do nothing when the system is already on the right track and to modify the data base only when it is suggesting erroneous conclusions.

A major issue that arises in adapting the stereotypes and triggers on the basis of experience is how much to change them each time a significant event occurs. If they are changed too much then it is too easy for a few atypical users to excessively contort the system. If, however, change is too slow, then it will require a great many users for whom the data base is inaccurate before significant change can occur. Ideally, the weight to be given to a new piece of information would be a function of how much information has already been accumulated. At the outset, a new piece of information would be weighted heavily compared to the old value. As more and more information accumulates to support the old value, a new piece of information would be given less and less weight. Unfortunately, to implement this approach accurately requires storing, along with each prediction in the system, a measure of that amount of data that has accumulated in support of it. That is a heavy overhead. One possible compromise is to use the rating as an estimate of the amount of supporting data. It is not always a very good estimate, though. For example, there might be a lot of evidence supporting the assertion that half the members of a particular class possess a given characteristic. And there might be much less evidence evidence in support of another prediction that eighty percent of the members of that class possess a second characteristic. But the rating of the former will be lower than the rating of the latter. Fortunately, the very nature of the adaptation process is flexibility. And in addition, all the quantities being manipulated are approximations at best. So using the rating of a prediction to serve a dual purpose as a measure of confidence of a prediction as well as an estimate of the amount of information behind the prediction is not an unreasonable compromise.

An even simpler compromise, and the one actually used in Grundy, is to weight the old value by a constant factor. This avoids the problem of having the weight depend on the rating (which may, as was just noted, be unrelated to the amount of evidence that has accumulated). It does, of course, fail to weight according to the evidence at all. If the initial values were unrelated to the appropriate values, this would not be a reasonable approach, since in order to avoid wild fluctuations, the weight assigned to the old value must be large, and so it takes a long time, even at the beginning, for change to occur. But if the initial values are reasonable, this method does provide the slow change that is appropriate.

The actual mechanisms used by Grundy to modify its stereotypes and triggers can then be described as follows. Whenever an inference or a fact is recorded in the USS, stereotypes and triggers can be modified. At present, only numerical values are altered. This includes both the values for the linear numerical scales as well as the values associated with the symbolic attributes of the list facets (such as GENRES and INTERESTS).

Each fact or inference suggests a value for a particular facet in the USS. Every stereotype that has contributed to the value already contained in the USS for that facet may be modified, as well as all triggers that have activated those stereotypes. For each of these stereotypes one of three cases arises. In the first, the stereotype and the newly acquired information neither confirm nor conflict, so nothing is done. In the second, the stereotype predicts a value that confirms the newly acquired information. If that happens, the value contained in the stereotype will be modified by the value suggested by the new knowledge according to the following formula:

$$\text{New-Stereotype-Value} = \frac{\text{Old-Stereotype-Value} * \text{Constant} + \text{New-Info-Value}}{\text{Constant} + 1}$$

The rating to be assigned to this prediction is recomputed as follows:

$$\text{New-Stereotype-Rating} = \text{Old-Stereotype-Rating} + \frac{\text{New-Info-Rating}}{\text{Old-Stereotype-Rating}}$$

[2]In order to eliminate inferences from the system, it is necessary to have a threshold below which inferences are too trivial to bother with and then to compare ratings to this threshold whenever they are changed. Although this is straightforward, it has not been implemented in Grundy.

Note that the rating modification formula makes it easy to increase low ratings, but more difficult to increase already high ones. Then the rating of each of the triggers that activated the stereotype is modified according to the formula:

$$\text{New-Trigger-Rating} = \text{Old-Trigger-Rating} + \frac{\text{New-Info-Rating}}{\text{Old-Trigger-Rating}}$$

The other situation that may arise is that a stereotype's prediction may conflict with the new information. In that case, the new value will be computed using the same formula given above. But the ratings will be decreased by the modification value, rather than increased as in the case of a confirming piece of new knowledge.

Thus values will tend to move in the direction suggested by the bulk of the other evidence available, and ratings will increase with confirming evidence and decrease with conflicting indications.

6.3. Creating New Stereotypes

The next step in the learning process after the modification of existing stereotypes is the creating of new ones. This could be done after a system had enough models of individual users to be able to abstract patterns from them. The construction of new stereotypes can be done using straightforward pattern classification techniques in very much the same way that TIERESIAS (Davis, 1977) builds models that describe classes of rules it has learned. Such stereotypes would have the same advantages that such automatically constructed models provide to TIERESIAS, principally lack of vulnerability to the prejudices of the system designer. This step has not actually been taken in Grundy, since it has not yet had enough experience on which to draw.

7. THE PERFORMANCE OF GRUNDY

In order to collect evidence that Grundy is successfully exploiting user models, twenty-three people were observed using the system. By the end of this experiment, Grundy knew about 153 words, 90 stereotypes, and 115 triggers. Some of these were added during the course of the experiment as they were suggested by some of the dialogues. The use Grundy made of this information was by no means uniform. Some things were very heavily used (the MAN stereotype, for example), while others were rarely if ever used.

7.1. Grundy's Success at Recommending Novels

Although building the ideal novel recommending program was not the primary goal of this research, it is important to establish that Grundy exhibits some form of intelligent action in order to show that the user modeling techniques are effective. In order to measure the system's success, a small experiment was conducted at the end of each conversation Grundy had with a user. Some books were selected randomly from the data base, and several characteristics of those books were also chosen randomly. The books were then suggested to the user. It was then possible to compare Grundy's rate of success at recommending books that looked good to the users both when it was exploiting the user model and when it was not. Table 1 shows the results of the comparison. It shows the number of good suggestions (i.e. the user said he might like) and the number of bad ones (i.e. the user said he would not like) in both the controlled and random modes. The data clearly demonstrate that the user models do contribute significantly to Grundy's performance as a novel recommender.

TABLE 1
Grundy's Success Rate

	CONTROLLED	RANDOM
GOOD	102	54
BAD	39	60

7.2. Learning in Grundy

As has already been discussed, it is important that the stereotypes and triggers that form the bulk of the data base of a user modeling system be able to change to reflect the actual body of users of the overall system. On the other hand, it is important that no single user be allowed to have a momentous effect on a system's global view of the class of all users. So in running Grundy with about twenty users, only the most commonly invoked stereotypes could be expected to change significantly. The most frequently activated stereotype was the MAN stereotype, and it did show interesting and significant change over the period Grundy was run. For example, the stereotype initially predicted that men would like books that are very fast-moving and full of suspense. The values of both of these characteristics decreased considerably on the basis of Grundy's experience with its users. Both of these changes can easily be explained by the difference between the group the stereotype was originally intended to characterize (all adult male Americans) and the group it was actually applied to in practice (some adult male intellectuals). The people who used the system, although they were men and did seem to like fast-moving, exciting books, also tended to like philosophical novels and literary classics, which tend to be much calmer. Thus by the end of the experiment, Grundy had a more accurate picture of the men it was encountering than it had had at the outset. This suggests that the learning mechanisms are capable of causing at least some sorts of improvement in the stereotype data base of a user modeling system.

7.3. The Effectiveness of Stereotypes

In looking at the results of Grundy's attempts to use stereotypes to build useful models of people, one is reminded of one important characteristic of stereotypes and thus of systems that use them. Although a stereotype may often provide highly appropriate and useful information about a person, it is, at best, an expression of a tendency and not an absolute truth. One example will serve to illustrate this point clearly.

Several stereotypes in Grundy predict that people who fit them will be interested in the conflict "art-vs-science." Those predictions caused Grundy to believe, correctly, that several users were interested in that conflict and thus to recommend books involving it. But one person, who fit three stereotypes that predict an interest in that conflict said, on the second questionnaire, that he was definitely not interested in it. Figure 5 shows all the situations in which Grundy believed the user was interested in art-vs-science.

This example just serves as a reminder of the great usefulness of stereotypes, but, at the same time, their fallibility.

User	Stereotypes that Predicted An Interest	Is the User Interested?
4	Intellectual, Contemplative, Scientist	yes
6	Intellectual	yes
7	Intellectual, Contemplative	yes
8	Intellectual	yes
9	Contemplative	yes
10	Intellectual, Artist	yes
11	Intellectual	yes
13	Intellectual	yes
20	Intellectual	yes
22	Scientist, Artist, Contemplative	NO

Figure 5. An Illustration of the Fallibility of Stereotypes.

7.4. Conclusion

Grundy is not a perfect novel recommender nor is it a perfect user model builder. But it does a respectable job at both tasks. Thus the techniques it demonstrates can be seen to be useful and to provide at least a start along the path of discovering the right way to build and exploit user models.

8. CONCLUSION

The goals of this research were to discover the usefulness of individual user models to performance systems and to explore the appropriateness of some specific techniques (principally the use of stereotypes) to the task of building such models. Although it is always difficult to generalize from a single system to the class of all systems, the experience with Grundy suggests both that user models can be of significant benefit and that the use of stereotypes to build those models can be highly productive. A more detailed study of all of these issues can be found in Rich (1979).

REFERENCES

Bobrow, D. G. & Norman, D. A. Some principles of memory schemata. In D. G. Bobrow & A. Collins (eds.), *Representation and Understanding*. New York: Academic Press, 1975.

Cantor, N. & Mischel, W. Traits as prototypes: Effects on recognition memory. *Journal of Personality and Social Psychology*, 1977, 35, 38–48.

Carbonell, J. Jr. *Subjective understanding: Computer models of belief systems*. PhD Thesis, Yale Univ. Computer Science Dept., 1979.

Charniak, E. A framed painting: The representation of a common sense knowledge fragment. *Cognitive Science*, 1977, 1, 355–394.

Davis, R. Interactive transfer of expertise: Acquisition of new inference rules. Proceedings of the 5th International Joint Conference on Artifical Intelligence, 1977, 321–328.

Hamilton, D. L. A cognitive-attributional analysis of stereotyping. In L. Berkowitz (ed.), *Advances in Experimental Psychology*, 1979.

Highet, G. *The Art of Teaching*. Vintage, 1950.

McGuire, W. J. & Padawer-Singer, A. Trait salience in the spontaneous self-concept. *Journal of Personality and Social Psychology*, 1976, 33, 743–754.

Minsky, M. A framework for representing knowledge. In P. H. Winston (ed.), *Psychology of Computer Vision*. New York: McGraw-Hill, 1975.

Nisbett, R. E. & Wilson, T. D. Telling more than we know: Verbal reports on mental processes. *Psychological Review*, 1977, 84, 231–259.

Rich, E. A. *Building and exploiting user models*. PhD Thesis, Carnegie-Mellon Univ. Computer Science Dept., 1979.

Schank, R. C. & Abelson, R. P. *Goals, Plans, Scripts and Understanding: An Enquiry into Human Knowledge Structures*. Lawrence Erlbaum Associates, 1977.

Shortliffe, E. H. MYCIN: *Computer-Based Consultations in Medical Consultations*. American Elsevier, 1976.

Snyder, M. & Uranowitz, S. W. Reconstructing the past: Some cognitive consequences of person perception. *Journal of Personality and Social Psychology*, 1978, 36.

Reflections on. . .

User Modeling via Stereotypes

Elaine Rich

Twenty years ago, I wanted to combine the storage capabilities of computers with the data-filtering ability of people. Even back then, a couple of decades before the World Wide Web, it was clear that computers would come to know (or more accurately, store) more and more information. But who cares, unless we can figure out a way to extract just what we want from the mass of material that's there?

To try to solve that problem, I did some very informal studies of question-answering strategies in several very different domains. One simple idea jumped out. People use stereotypes of other people and, by and large, those stereotypes work fairly well in helping them formulate appropriate responses to questions. For example, there were movies I would recommend to my roommate but not my grandmother (although that particular distinction is less clear cut in the 90s than it was in the 70s).

To test the idea of stereotypes as a way to filter information, I built Grundy, a system that recommended novels to people. Grundy ran on a DEC PDP10 computer. Before I could let someone sit down for a session with Grundy, I had to arrange to get my job priority bumped up so that Grundy got a lot more than its fair share of the cycles. I couldn't think of any other way to produce reasonable response time since experimental subjects don't generally want to work in the middle of the night. But when it was time for Grundy to review its experiences and update its stereotypes, I waited until 3 A.M. and let Grundy take over the whole machine. To review experiences with fewer than 100 subjects and fewer than 50 stereotypes, Grundy had to consume half the total computing resources of a leading computer science department. I guess I wasn't real surprised when people weren't rushing to copy the idea, despite the fact that the stereotypes in Grundy worked.

Now, 20 years later, the machine on my desk can do that kind of processing in a flash. With that problem solved and with the need for some kind of effective filtering mechanism far greater than it was in Grundy (which, after all, only had less than a couple hundred books to choose from), why aren't stereotypes in widespread use outside the research lab? I'm not sure, but I can think of one good reason and one bad reason. The bad reason is that the word *stereotype* still connotes prejudice, not accumulated experience. But that's not the real problem. The real problem is that stereotypes work by matching characteristics of users against descriptions of items in a database. Learning a few key characteristics of each user isn't hard. But the descriptions of the items in the database have to come from someplace. In Grundy, I read the books and built the descriptions by hand. That took a lot of time (but reading novels was a good way to escape real dissertation work, so I didn't mind).

However, if stereotypes are going to be practical in real systems, the descriptions will have to be constructed automatically. For some properties, such as the level of reading difficulty, this is easy. For others, such as Grundy's attribute, plot-speed, this is a lot more difficult. But it's not impossible. For example, recent work on empirical properties of texts has shown that you can learn a lot from word frequencies. My hope is that, over the next several years, techniques for automatically extracting descriptions for everything from individual texts and images to entire web sites will develop to the point that it will become practical to exploit the idea of stereotypes to help users find what they really want in the sea of on-line materials we all swim in every day.

CHAPTER 9

INTELLIGENT INTERFACES AS AGENTS

DAVID N. CHIN
Department of Information and Computer Sciences
University of Hawaii at Manoa

ABSTRACT

An intelligent interface cannot just respond passively to its user's commands and queries. It must be able to take the initiative in order to volunteer information, correct user misconceptions, or reject unethical user requests. To do these things, a system must be an intelligent agent. UCEgo is the intelligent agent component of UC (UNIX Consultant), a natural-language system that helps the user solve problems in using the UNIX operating system. UCEgo provides UC with its own goals and plans. By adopting different goals in different situations, UCEgo creates and executes different plans, enabling it to interact intelligently with the user. UCEgo adopts goals from its *themes*, adopts subgoals during planning, and adopts *metagoals* for dealing with goal interactions. It also adopts goals when it notices that the user either lacks necessary knowledge or has incorrect beliefs. In these cases, UCEgo plans to volunteer information or correct the user's misconception, as appropriate.

This research was supported in part by the Office of Naval Research, under grant N0014-48-C-0732; the Defense Advanced Research Projects Agency (DoD), under DARPA Order No. 4871, monitored by Space and Naval Warfare Systems Command under contract N00039-84-C-0089; the National Science Foundation under grant #85-14890; and Hughes Aircraft grant #442427-59868.

9.1 INTRODUCTION

There has been some debate concerning whether intelligent interfaces should be structured as agents or whether it is better to think of them as tools with intelligently organized direct-manipulation options available for the user. In the interface-as-agent view, the interface is seen as a separate entity that mediates between the user and the machine. The user tells the interface what to do, and then the interface acts on these instructions. In the competing interface-as-tool view, the interface is seen as directly representing the machine. The interface merely facilitates the user's direct manipulation of the machine. In this view, all user actions should have immediate, directly perceptible results.

Proponents of the interface-as-tool view point out that the agent view requires that the interface have a well-defined model of the dialogue between the user and the interface. This is difficult because dialogue models are poorly understood and users tend to have difficulty trying to learn the nature of the dialogue. Misunderstandings by users concerning the nature of the dialogue can lead to problems. For example, users may expect one of their entries to constitute an order to the interface, whereas the interface models the entry as a mere statement of fact (or vice-versa). Such misunderstandings are less likely in the direct-manipulation model because users usually see the effects of their actions immediately. Also, the similarity between user-interface dialogues and human-human dialogues tends to set up faulty expectations concerning the capabilities of the interface in the user's mind. Finally, the interface-as-agent view is too unconstrained since it allows the interface to perform unexpected actions as an agent.

On the other hand, the interface-as-agent proponents argue that dialogue is a natural interaction mode, and they point out that most computer operating systems have been successfully based on implicit dialogue models. However the strongest argument for viewing the interface as an agent relates to the added flexibility needed by intelligent interfaces. This paper will show that intelligent interfaces often need to behave as agents at least part of the time. In particular, whenever the interface has greater knowledge than the user, the interface may need to take the initiative (i.e., perform unexpected actions) in order to correct the user, volunteer information, or suggest alternative courses of action. This paper will expand on the argument that intelligent interfaces need to be agents and will describe a natural-language interface that implements some of these ideas.

9.2 CONSULTATION PROGRAMS

An intelligent interface cannot just respond passively to its user's instructions and queries. Rather, it must be able to take the initiative in its dialogue with the user. For example, consider a hypothetical intelligent interface that provides help in using the UNIX[1] operating system. A user would be able to ask such a system in English (or some other natural language) for advice about how to do things, for definitions of terminology, or for advice in solving problems. The consultant program would then provide solutions in English like a real human consultant would. Also like a human consultant, such a program may need to take the initiative during the consultation. For instance, consider the following user interaction with the hypothetical consultation program:

User: What is chin's phone number?

Program: I'm sorry, I do not know that. To find out, type 'finger chin'.

In the above interaction, the program does not know the answer to the user's query. A system that was not capable of taking the initiative in the consultation dialogue would simply inform the user that it failed to find an answer and then await further instructions from the user. However a more intelligent interface might make the additional suggestion shown above. Here, the program has *volunteered* additional information to the user about how to find out chin's phone number using the UNIX **finger** command. The ability to take the initiative in order to volunteer information is especially critical for consultation systems, because, by definition, such systems know more about their domains of expertise than their users, who may not even know enough to ask the right questions. So, an intelligent consultation system needs to be able to take the initiative in order to volunteer critical information that its user may not even know was pertinent.

Another example showing why an intelligent system needs to take the initiative in the dialogue with the user is shown below:

User: What does ls −v do?

Program: It lists the contents of your current directory.

The hypothetical program gives an answer that is literally correct, since the **ls** command actually ignores inappropriate flags such as $-v$. However, a consultant that provides only the above answer has failed to correct the user's incorrect preconception that the **ls** command has a $-v$ flag. So, although the user did not specifically ask whether **ls** has a $-v$ flag, a good consultant would not fail to provide the information that in fact **ls** does not have such a flag. Such a response is shown in the next dialogue:

User: What does ls −v do?

Program: There is no −v option for ls.

This is a better answer even though it does not literally answer the user's question. In deciding to ignore the user's direct question and shift its attention to the user's misconception, the program has taken the initiative in the dialogue. This shows that a good consultant cannot just passively respond to the user; rather, it must have its own agenda.

In the previous dialogue, the better answer requires that the program realize that the user has a misconception. To do this, the system must first infer that the user believes that **ls** has a $-v$ option and then realize that the user's belief conflicts with the program's knowledge. So, in general, a good consultant system must also model the user's knowledge and beliefs.

Even after a consultant system realizes that the user has a misconception, it must decide how to deal with the misconception. In the example of the $-v$ flag, the system decides that it should inform the user of the facts in order to correct the user's misconception. In other cases, the system may choose to ignore the misconception, as in the following scenario:

User: How can I delete someone else's file when I don't have write permission on the file?

Program: I will not help you delete someone else's file, because that is unethical.

In the user's statement above, the user has assumed that one needs write permission on the file to delete it. This is not true. Rather, one needs write permission on the parent directory to delete the file. Regardless of what is the correct precondition, the program decides not to help the user because of ethical considerations. This also means that the program decides not to correct the user's misconception, so as to avoid helping the user delete someone else's file. This is an example of a decision by a consultant program to be uncooperative.

Of course a good consultant program cannot arbitrarily decide to be uncooperative. In the previous case, the decision to be uncooperative should be based on the fact that the user's goal of deleting someone else's file conflicts with the program's goal of preserving all users' files. In such cases, the program's goal of preserving files should win out over the program's desire to help the user who asked the question. These sorts of goals and goal interactions are needed to guide a consultant system properly.

9.3 INTELLIGENT AGENTS

The examples in the previous section have shown that a good computer consultation system cannot be a passive system that just answers the user's

[1] UNIX is a trademark of Bell Laboratories.

queries and follows the user's instructions literally. Rather, the consultant system must often take the initiative. This is because consultant systems should have greater knowledge in their field of expertise than users. As in the example in the previous section, the consultant may sometimes need to take the initiative to correct a user's misconceptions. Also, the consultant may need to take the initiative to provide needed information that the user did not explicitly ask for. Often the user does not even realize that such information is pertinent and so would never ask for it. A computer consultant system needs to have the human-like capability of taking the initiative in a dialogue rather than always responding to the user passively.

Previous efforts in natural-language systems that take the initiative have resulted in programs capable of *mixed-initiative* dialogues. Among the first of these, the SCHOLAR system [Carbonell70b; Carbonell70a] for CAI (Computer-Aided Instruction), could take the initiative to test the user on facts in its knowledge base. It also allowed the user to query the system about facts in its knowledge base. This type of mixed-initiative works only for limited situations, such as mutual quizzing. A system based on answering or generating quiz questions cannot be adapted to help the user solve problems, volunteer information pertinent to the user's problems, or detect misconceptions evident from the user's questions (as opposed to wrong answers from the user).

Each of the above approaches works to provide programs the capability to take the initiative in limited situations. However, neither approach is general enough to cover other types of situations where a program should take the initiative. For example, neither approach would allow a program to take the initiative to correct a user misconception.

The approach that I take is to view the program as an *agent*. That is, a consultation system should be viewed as a system that can perform actions. For a natural-language consultation system, acting consists of mostly *speech acts* [Austin62;Searle69], that is, acting by communicating with the user. Within this paradigm, taking the initiative in a dialogue translates into acting without the guidance of the user. An agent that has this capability of taking the initiative is called an *autonomous agent*.

A *rational agent* is an agent that behaves rationally. In AI programs, much as in popular psychology, this usually means that a program's behavior is determined by reasonable plans and goals and that the program attributes reasonable plans and goals to other rational agents. For example, PAM [Wilensky78] understood stories involving rational agents by analyzing the goals and plans of the characters. Also, TALE-SPIN [Meehan76] used plans and goals to create simple stories with rational agents as characters. In the problem-solving domain, robot planning programs (e.g., [Fikes71; Sacerdoti74]) have shown that planning is a good paradigm for programming robots as rational agents. In the realm of conversation, [Hobbs80] has argued that human conversation fits such a paradigm. So, a program that contains reasonable plans and goals and whose behavior is determined by those plans and goals can be considered a rational agent.

Within the planning paradigm, a *rational autonomous agent* is one that contains plans and goals that allow the agent to take the initiative in appropriate situations. The central problem in building autonomous agents is determining which situations require the agent to take the initiative. For a rational autonomous agent that is based on the planning paradigm, this problem translates to the problem of determining appropriate goals for the planner. Such a process is called *goal detection* [Wilensky83].

After a rational autonomous agent, henceforth called an *intelligent agent*, has detected appropriate goals, it is up to the planner of the intelligent agent to formulate a plan to satisfy these goals and then carry out the plan. Much work has been done in AI in the area of planning where the goals of the planner are provided by the operator. For example, [Newell72] formulated means-ends analysis as a general strategy for achieving given ends or goals. However, the all robot-planning programs assumed that the goals are given by the users. Likewise, in TALE-SPIN the programmer provided the initial goals of the characters. For story understanding, PAM was able to recognize a character's goals when directly stated in the narrative, or when the goal could be inferred from the characters' stated actions based on the assumption that the actions were part of the character's plan. As [Carbonell82] points out, none of these systems have systematically addressed the problem of goal detection, which is essential for building intelligent agents.

This paper will address the problem of building a natural-language computer consultation system that behaves as an intelligent agent. The UC (UNIX Consultant) system embodies such an intelligent agent.

9.4 UC, THE UNIX CONSULTANT

UC (UNIX Consultant) is an interactive natural-language consultant system for the UNIX operating system. UC is able to provide information about how to do things in UNIX, definitions about UNIX or general operating system terminology, and help in debugging problems with using UNIX. A short overview of UC follows. For more details on UC, the reader is referred to [Chin87], [Wilensky86], and [Wilensky84].

In a typical UC session, the user types questions in English to UC, and UC responds to the user in English. A schematic diagram of the flow of information among UC's various components is shown in Figure 9.1.

The input to UC is analyzed by the ALANA language analysis component of UC, which produces a semantic representation of the input. This representation is in the form of a KODIAK network (a semantic network representation language developed at Berkeley [Wilensky87]). Next, UC's concretion mechanism performs concretion inferences [Wilensky83; Norvig83] based on the semantic network. Concretion is the process of inferring more specific interpretations of the user's input than might strictly be correct on a logical basis. Such inferences might be motivated by the context of the utterance or

FIGURE 9.1
FLOW OF INFORMATION AMONG UC COMPONENTS

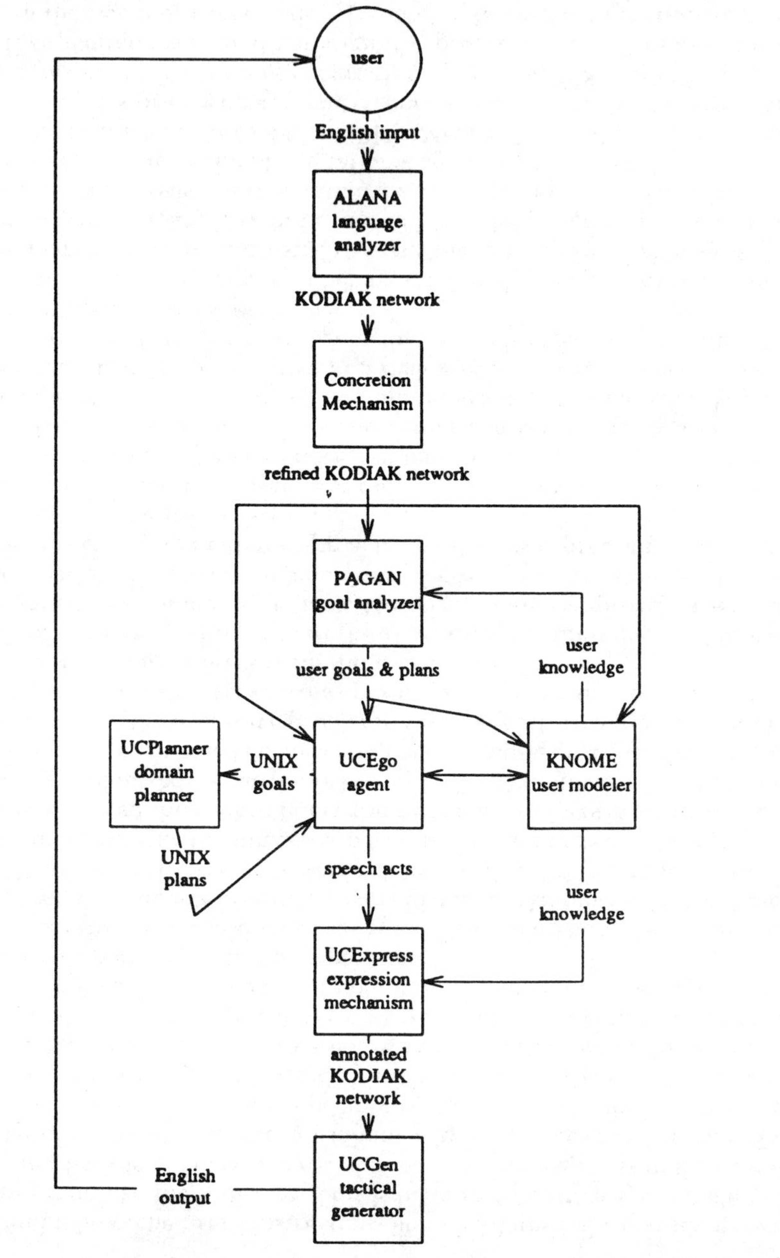

by culturally accepted usage biases. After concretion, the modified KODIAK network is passed to PAGAN, UC's goal analysis component. PAGAN deduces the user's actual goals. This includes inferring the user's high-level goals as well as the user's immediate goals. PAGAN also handles phenomena such as indirect speech acts.

After the initial analysis of the user's input, the UCEgo component of UC decides how UC should respond. UCEgo is the component of UC that implements an intelligent agent. It first determines what UC's own goals should be, then formulates a plan to achieve these goals, and finally carries out this plan. UCEgo detects its own goals based on the present situation, which may include varied factors such as the user's goals and the user's utterances, as well as UC's own goals, knowledge, and internal state.

Part of UCEgo's response may involve calling on the services of the UCPlanner component of UC. UCPlanner is a UNIX domain planner that creates plans for doing things in UNIX. Another component of UC that may be called by UCEgo is UCExpress. UCExpress uses the process of answer expression to refine the communicative plans produced by UCEgo. First, UCExpress prunes extraneous concepts from the answer, either when the user already knows the concepts or when the concepts are already part of the conversational context. Next UCExpress uses specialized formats such as similes and examples to express information to the user in a clear and concise manner. The result of UCExpress's processing is an annotated KODIAK network that is ready for generation into English by the UCGen tactical-level generator.

Another important part of UC is KNOME, the user-modeling component. KNOME encodes the knowledge and beliefs of the user. It also deduces what the user knows and believes, based on UC's conversation with the user. KNOME also models the extent of UC's own knowledge of UNIX. This is useful in differentiating between actual user misconceptions and cases in which UC's knowledge base is incomplete.

This paper will concentrate on the UCEgo component of UC and how it detects the right goals for UC in appropriate situations. By detecting the right goals, UC can respond intelligently to the user.

9.5 GOAL DETECTION

The central problem in building an intelligent agent is how to detect appropriate goals for the agent, goals that can then be used to guide the agent's actions. This process is called *goal detection* [Wilensky83].

Although considerable work has been done in the area of planning, very few planning systems have addressed the problem of how to detect appropriate goals for planning. In almost all planning systems, the high-level goals are provided by the human operators of the planners. An exception is described by [Allen79], whose system simulated a train station ticket agent. It detected goals based on an analysis of obstacles to a user's plans. By addressing these obstacles, the system could volunteer information that the user would need to achieve the user's plan. This approach addresses only a fraction of the general problem of goal detection. An analysis of obstacles to the user's plan does not address how these obstacle-related goals might interact with the system's other goals. Also, analyzing obstacles would not lead a system to detect user misconceptions and detect the goal of correcting the misconceptions. Even in terms of volunteering useful information to the user, an analysis of obstacles to a user's plans does not address the problem of when the system should volunteer an alternative plan.

The PANDORA planner [Faletti82] detected its own goals. It detected goals when actual or projected states conflicted with goals or plans and when certain frames describing situations were activated. For example, the goal of "find out about the world" was attached to the morning frame, which meant that PANDORA would try to read a newspaper in the morning. However, except for very simple frames, PANDORA did not address the problem of when is it proper to invoke frames and their associated goals. Also, because PANDORA existed in a self-contained simulated world, it did not address the problem of detecting goals when the system must interact with real users.

Schank and Abelson advocate *themes* as the origin of goals [Schank77]. However, themes give rise to only very high-level goals, such as being rich. Their theory does not explain how a program might proceed from these very high-level goals to lower-level goals, such as the goal of possessing a quarter that one sees on the sidewalk as opposed to a quarter that one sees in someone else's hand.

Once an agent has determined its goals, the relatively better-understood process of planning can be applied to satisfy them. The following sections describe how goals are detected by UCEgo.

9.6 TYPES OF SITUATIONS

In general, an agent may detect new goals whenever there is a change in an agent's environment or internal state. Any combination of factors in the agent's environment or internal state that leads to a new goal for the agent is called a *situation* after the terminology of [Wilensky83]. This section will classify the kinds of situations that lead UCEgo to detect new goals.

Since UC is a computer consultation system, UCEgo's environment is limited to a dialogue with the user on the subject of the UNIX operating system. So for UCEgo, situations are composed of combinations of UC's internal state, the user's statements, and information that might be derived from the user's statements, such as the user's plans and goals and the user's knowledge and beliefs. UC's internal state includes UC's domain knowledge, UC's own goals, and UC's *themes* [Schank77].

The situations that give rise to goals in the UC domain can be divided into five main classes:

1. themes → goals,
2. plans → subgoals,
3. goal interactions → metagoals,
4. gaps in the user's knowledge → goals,
5. user misconceptions → goals.

Themes can be considered as the internal motivations of an agent, so they are a prime source of new goals. Another source of goals is the planning process. As an agent plans for goals, the resulting plans may produce subgoals that the agent will need to adopt and plan to satisfy. When an agent has several goals, these goals may interact, giving rise to a *metagoal* [Wilensky83] which is a goal for dealing with the interaction among other goals.

Themes, plans, and goal interactions are universal sources of goals in that they are common to all intelligent agents. The other two sources of goals are somewhat more particular to a consulting environment. In a consulting environment, situations commonly arise wherein the state of the user's knowledge base (as deduced from conversing with the user) is not consistent with the consultant's knowledge base. One kind of inconsistency is detected when the consultant determines that the user lacks some necessary knowledge. Another kind of inconsistency is found when the consultant determines that the user's knowledge base conflicts with its own knowledge base, that is, that the user has a misconception. Both of these classes of situations are concerned with the user's knowledge, since the main task of a consultant is to impart information to the user. In other types of programs, a different focus may lead to other situation classes.

In UCEgo, each situation class is represented by a single KODIAK network pattern, which is used as the left-hand side of an *if-detected demon* [Chin87]. When a piece of KODIAK network matches such a pattern, the network is considered to represent a situation of the class, and the demon adds a new goal (also represented as a piece of KODIAK network) to UC's memory.

Unlike situation classes, goals in UC are explicitly represented in KODIAK using the has-goal relation, which has two aspectuals: *goal* and *planner*. A goal is modeled as a relation between an individual (planner) and some state (**goal**) that that individual wishes to achieve. There is no absolute category of goals, since a state cannot be said to be a goal unless some individual can be said to have that goal. This is not to say that there are not some states (e.g., having lots of money) that are habitually thought of as being goals. However, habitual goals encompass only a fraction of what is meant by the term *goal*. Almost any state can be a goal, provided only that some individual wishes to achieve that state. Thus treating goals as aspectuals of HAS-GOAL relations does capture the meaning of the term *goal*.

9.7 GOALS FROM THEMES AND PLANS

UCEgo has a number of themes that give rise to goals. These include life themes as well as role themes. An example of a life theme is UCEgo's stay-alive theme. This theme gives rise to the recurrent background goals of preserving the UC program and preserving the UNIX system. The stay-alive theme is also an instance of the *preservation theme* [Wilensky83], since it gives rise to preservation goals. An example of a role theme is UCEgo's consultant role theme. This gives rise to the recurrent goals of helping the user and being polite to the user. The goal of being polite is a background goal, since UCEgo does not attempt to plan for it immediately. On the other hand, the goal of helping the user is a foreground goal, because UC immediately tries to find ways to help the user.

Since all goals that arise from themes are detected when UC first starts up, it might seem that attributing these goals to themes is extraneous. However, themes are really quite useful. First of all, themes provide a relative-importance ordering for goals, which is useful in case of goal conflicts (see Section 9.8). This relative importance metric for goals can be used as the basis for a more complete theory that provides a calculus of goal values for an agent. Second, themes provide a means of organizing goals into related groups. For example, if UC were to provide other functions besides a UNIX Consultant, then the goals that arise from its consultant role theme could be added when UC starts working as a consultant and removed when UC stops working as a consultant.

The goals that arise from themes usually give rise to yet more goals, called subgoals, during the planning phase of UCEgo. In fact, all of UC's goals can ultimately be traced back to UC's themes, either directly or as subgoals of other goals that can be traced back to UC's themes.

9.7.1. Goals from Themes

When UC first starts up, it has a number of themes. These immediately give rise to goals for UC. The themes that have been found to be important for UC include the stay-alive and ethics life themes, and the consultant role theme. Other systems may find that different themes will be useful. Certainly, systems that are not consultation systems will have a different role theme than UC's consultant role theme.

The consultant role theme represents UC's job of being a UNIX consultant. It motivates UC to behave as a consultant to help the user. Therefore, the consultant role theme leads UCEgo to adopt the recurrent goal of helping the user. This goal is a recurrent goal, since once UC has helped the user, UC continues to have the goal of helping the user. Unlike other goals that arise from themes, the goal of helping the user is not a background goal. This means that UCEgo is constantly planning how to satisfy this goal.

Another aspect of being a consultant involves being polite to the client. So the consultant role theme leads UCEgo to adopt the recurrent background goal of being polite to the user. This goal is a recurrent goal, since UC never stops being polite to the user. It is also a background goal, since UCEgo does not try to plan how to be polite to the user. Instead, when a situation arises in which UC should be polite, this goal will become activated. Such social situations include greetings, farewells, and apologies.

TABLE 9.1
THEMES THAT GIVE RISE TO GOALS IN UC

Theme	goal
UC-consultant role theme	UC help user
	UC be polite to user
UC-stay-alive life-theme	preserve UC program
	preserve Unix system
UC-ethics life-theme	UC act-ethically

The ethics life theme represents UC's desire to act ethically. It gives rise to UC's goal of ACT-ETHICALLY. Since UC cannot perform actions except for communicative acts, UC only has to worry about performing unethical communicative actions. For example UC worries about providing information to the user that will help the user perform an unethical act. In such situations, UCEgo detects a conflict between UC's goal of helping the user (from the consultant role theme) and UC's goal of ACT-ETHICALLY. Such goal interactions are described further in Section 9.8.

The stay-alive life theme is an instance of the preservation theme [Wilensky83], from whence arise preservation goals. This particular preservation theme represents UC's desire to preserve itself. As a result, it leads UC to adopt the goals of preserving the UC program and preserving the UNIX system on which UC runs. Other preservation goals that need to be taken into account in planning how the user should do things in UNIX (e.g., preserving the user's files and preserving the privacy of the user's files) are handled by UC's UNIX domain planner ([Luria85, Luria88]).

Themes in UC and the goals that they give rise to are summarized in Table 9.1.

9.7.2. Situations Leading to Subgoals

Except for goals that UC adopts from its themes, all of UC's other goals are subgoals or, less frequently, metagoals. This section will show how UCEgo adopts subgoals and will describe some of the subgoals found in UC. Other subgoals are introduced when appropriate in later sections.

Subgoals are created as part of the planning process. Many of UCEgo's plans contain steps that call for the achievement of a state. When UCEgo adopts such a plan, it adopts the subgoal of achieving that state.

An example of a particular subgoal is shown in Figure 9.2. The double circle represents an if-detected demon, and the arrows radiating inward toward the double circle represent the left-hand-side of the daemon, whereas the arrows radiating outward represent the right-hand-side of the daemon. This daemon allows UCEgo to adopt the user's goal of knowing something. It is triggered by a class of situations that consists of two parts:

1. UC has the goal of helping someone (UC-HAS-GOAL3).
2. That person wants (HAS-GOAL0) to know (KNOW2) something.

When UCEgo encounters a matching situation, it asserts that a plan for (PLANFOR3) helping (HELP1) the user (PERSON4) is to satisfy (SATISFY1) the subgoal of having the user know (KNOW2) what the user wants to know. This situation is a very common one for UC, because UC's users usually want to know something about UNIX.

UC's goal of acting ethically motivates another class of situations in which UCEgo detects a subgoal. When someone wants to know how to alter someone else's file, an if-detected demon detects the subgoal of preventing that person from knowing how to alter someone else's file. More formally, the situation consists of five relations:

1. UC has the goal of acting ethically.
2. Someone (*?p1*) wants to know:
3. A plan for altering a file (altering includes the subclass of deleting).
4. The owner of the file is someone, *?p2*.
5. The owner (*?p2*) differs from the alterer (*?p1*).

FIGURE 9.2
IF-DETECTED DEMON FOR DETECTING THE SUBGOAL OF HAVING THE USER KNOW

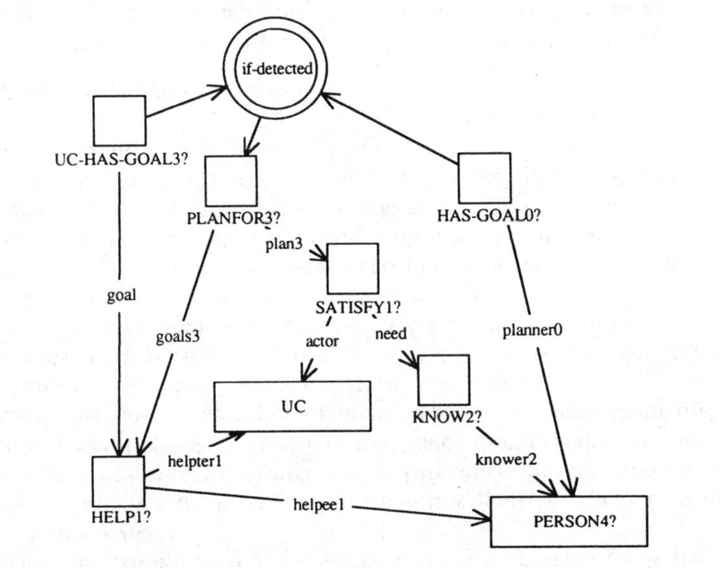

When UCEgo detects such a situation, it asserts that a plan for acting ethically is to adopt the subgoal of preventing the first person from knowing how to alter the second person's file. Normally this type of situation occurs when the user asks UC how to alter someone else's file. UC should not help the user perform unethical actions, so in such cases, UC should not provide the user with such information. However this conflicts with UC's normal mode of operation in which UC adopts the user's goal of knowing in order to help the user. This results in an internal goal conflict for UC. Section 9.8 describes such goal interactions and how they are resolved.

In a sense, the meaning of high-level goals such as help-the-user, or act-ethically is defined by the set of situation classes in which UC adopts subgoals of these high-level goals. UC can only act to satisfy high-level goals when particular situations lead UC to adopt specific subgoals. It might seem that such high-level goals are superfluous, since one can always leave the high-level goals out of the situation and UC would continue to adopt the subgoals when appropriate. However, high-level goals serve several important functions. First, high-level goals help to organize related situations and subgoals. By removing a particular high-level goal from the system, one can disable an entire class of related situations or subgoals. Second, high-level goals allow the system to provide explanations about why it performed certain actions. When UC refuses to help the user delete someone else's file, it explains that it will not help because it is unethical. Finally, high-level goals help the system resolve conflicts between subgoals (see Section 9.8.2).

9.8 METAGOALS

Correcting user misconceptions or providing suggestions to the user do not necessarily require that the system have explicit goals of its own. Those types of responses can be provided by simpler systems that do not have goals and plans. However, a system based on planning for goals is more flexible, because it can much more easily handle interactions among goals. Goals can interact either negatively by conflicting or positively by overlapping. When UCEgo detects a situation where goals conflict or overlap, it creates a new goal for dealing with the goal interaction. Goals for dealing with other goals are called *metagoals* [Wilensky83].

Metagoals are not distinguished from other goals in the UC program either by representational differences or by differences in their processing. Of course, in discussing goals it is useful to make a distinction between metagoals and subgoals because these types of goals tend to originate from different kinds of situations and tend to have different subject areas.

Metagoals are also useful for controlling the planning and plan execution process. In UC, metagoals control when UCEgo tries to find out information for the user in situations in which UC does not know the information. Also, when UCEgo cannot find a prestored plan to satisfy one of UC's goals, UCEgo adopts the metagoal of knowing a plan for finding out a plan to satisfy this goal. This is an example of *metaplanning* [Wilensky83], since UC is planning to create a plan that is used to find another plan. For more details on metaplanning in UCEgo, see [Chin87].

9.8.1. Mutual Inclusion

Metagoals are used to deal with both positive and negative interactions between goals. One way in which goals can interact positively is through *mutual inclusion* [Wilensky83]. This describes situations in which a planner has the same or similar goals for different reasons. In such situations, the planner can merge the goals into a single goal. This saves resources, because the planner no longer has to plan several times nor execute many similar plans.

When UCEgo finds that it has two goals that are similar, it adopts the metagoal of merging the redundant goals. The redundant goals may actually be identical, or they may be just similar enough to be merged successfully into a single goal. For example, consider what happens when the user asks UC, "Is **cp** used to copy files?" and UC answers, "Yes."

In processing this query, UC's goal analysis component, PAGAN, deduces that the user's goal is to know whether **cp** is a plan for copying files. PAGAN also deduces that this goal has two possible parent goals (one or both of which might hold):

1. The user wants to know the effects of the **cp** command.
2. The user wants to know how to copy files.

To see why this added level of goal analysis is necessary, consider the slightly different query, "Is **cp** used to create files?" The answer to this query is *no*. However this is not a very good answer. In fact, any human consultant who only replied *no* in this case would be labeled uncooperative. The reason *no* is not a good answer for this query, whereas *yes* is a reasonable answer for the first query is because the *no* answer only superficially addresses the user's goals. It only addresses the user's immediate goal, to know whether or not **cp** is used to create files; it does not address either of the two possible goals that motivate that goal: The user wants to know the effects of the **cp** command, or the user wants to know how to create files, or both. To provide a more cooperative answer in such situations, UCEgo volunteers additional information by addressing the user's higher-level goals as well as the user's immediate goal. Volunteering information in such cases is described in Section 9.10.4.

The second query shows that UCEgo sometimes needs to address all of the user's goals rather than just the user's immediate goal. However, if UCEgo were to address all of the user's goals in the first query, it would end up providing three very similar, indeed redundant, answers to the user. UCEgo might approach this problem of redundant answers in one of two ways. It could always handle only the user's immediate goal and then volunteer more information only if it discovers that satisfying the user's immediate goal does not contribute to satisfying the higher-level goals that motivate the immediate goal. The problem with this approach is that it is fairly difficult to tell whether satisfying the immediate goal helps to satisfy the underlying goals. In fact, a planner will usually have to plan to satisfy the underlying goals before it can make such a judgment.

Since a planner must often plan for the underlying goals anyway, UCEgo uses the strategy of always planning to satisfy all of the user's goals and then noticing when these goals overlap to prevent redundant answers. Figure 9.3 shows the if-detected daemon that notices situations with potential goal overlap. Whenever UC has two different goals (UC-HAS-GOAL1 and UC-HAS-GOAL2) of wanting the user (PERSON1) to know something, and the answer (ANSWER-FOR1 and ANSWER-FOR2) for those queries are similar (implemented by the procedural test, UC-test-similar), then UCEgo adopts the metagoal (UC-HAS-GOAL3) of merging the redundant goals (MERGE-REDUNDANT-GOALS).

The procedural test, UC-test-similar, checks to see if the two goals are similar enough to be merged. It first matches the two answers to see if they are the same. If so, then the two goals can be merged. It also has knowledge that certain types of relations are similar enough that they convey essentially the same information. For example, HAS-EFFECT and PLANFOR are similar enough to be merged, provided of course that they relate similar concepts.

An example of merging goals occurs during the processing of the user query, "Is cp used to copy files?" By adopting all three potential user goals, UCEgo detects the three goals:

1. UC wants the user to know whether **cp** is used to copy files.
2. UC wants the user to know the effects of the **cp** command.
3. UC wants the user to know a plan for copying files.

UCEgo cannot tell that these goals are similar until after it has deduced the referent of the descriptions in UC's goals. For instance, the referent for the goal of knowing the effects of the **cp** command is an HAS-EFFECT rela-

FIGURE 9.3
IF-DETECTED DEMON FOR DETECTING OVERLAPPING GOALS

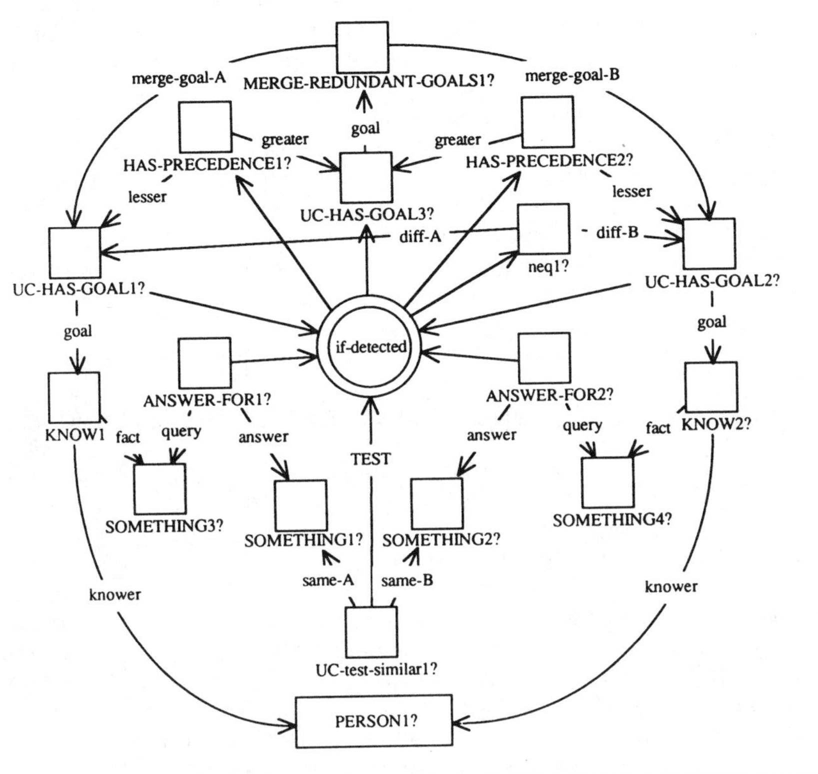

tion, whereas the referent of the goal of knowing a plan for copying files is a PLANFOR relation. These are similar albeit different relations, so they are candidates for merging. Since they both relate a UNIX-CP-COMMAND to a COPY-FILE-EFFECT, UC-test-similar decides that they can indeed be merged. Another type of similarity is found when one answer is contained in the other. In this example, the answer for the goal of knowing whether **cp** is a plan for copying files is the HAS-TRUTH-VALUE relation relating the truth value, *true,* and the proposition that the **cp** command is a plan for copying files. When comparing this answer, only the propositional content is compared. Eventually, all three goals are merged by discarding all but the immediate goal.

The final answer is shortened to just *yes,* rather than "Yes, **cp** is used to copy files." This is done since the proposition, "**cp** is a plan for copying files," is already part of the context (it is part of the user's query). Such processing is done by the UCExpress component [Chin87].

9.8.2. Goal Conflict

Goals can interact negatively by conflicting. When UCEgo detects a situation in which UC has two goals that conflict with one another, UCEgo adopts the metagoal of resolving the goal conflict. A frequent type of goal conflict situation is found when a planner wants both to achieve some state and to prevent that state from occurring. UCEgo detects such situations with the if-detected demon shown in Figure 9.4.

An example of a goal conflict situation is when the user asks UC, "How can I delete UC?" In this case, the usual flow of processing leads UCEgo to adopt the user's goal of having the user know a plan for deleting the UC program. This subgoal can be traced back to UC's goal of helping the user, which in turn arose from UC's consultant role theme (see Section 9.7.1).

In parallel to this, UCEgo also has a stay-alive life theme, which gives rise to UC's goal of preserving the UC program, that is, the UC executable file rather than the UC process—if UC wanted to preserve its process, it might refuse to tell the user how to exit UC. This goal is a *background goal* [Chin87], which means that UCEgo does not actively attempt to plan for the goal. Rather, the goal is considered only when UCEgo detects a relevant situation, such as in the present example. Whenever someone wants to know

FIGURE 9.4
IF-DETECTED DEMON FOR DETECTING GOAL CONFLICT

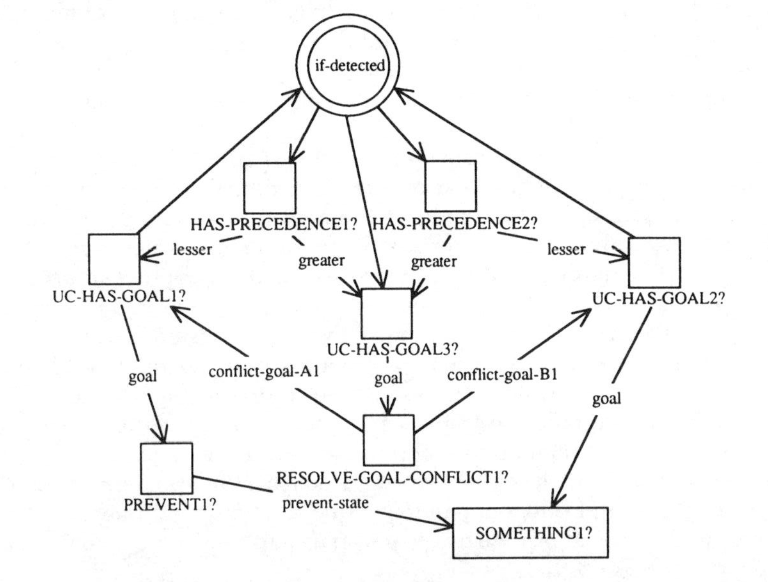

how to alter something that UC wishes to preserve, UCEgo adopts the subgoal of preventing the user from knowing how to do that. In this example, the user wants to delete (a specific kind of altering) the UC program, which UC wants to preserve. So, UCEgo adopts the subgoal of preventing the user from knowing how to delete the UC program.

At this point, these two lines of processing interact with a goal conflict. On the one hand, UC wants to help the user and hence wants the user to know how to delete it. On the other hand, UC wants to preserve the UC program and hence wants to prevent the user from knowing how to delete it. The goals of wanting the user to know and wanting to prevent the user from knowing serve to activate the conflict-detection demon shown in Figure 9.4. Activating the demon gives UC the goal of resolving the conflict. In this case, the metaplan of abandoning the lower-priority goal (helping the user) is used to resolve the conflict. To determine which goal is less important, UCEgo first searches for a direct precedence relationship (represented by a HAS-PRECEDENCE relation) between the two goals. If such a relation does not exist, then the search is expanded to include the causal parents of the goals. The search continues until the ultimate sources of the goals, which are usually UC themes, are included in the check for relative precedence relations. Since goal conflicts usually involve goals that originate from different UC themes and because all of UC's themes have an a priori relative precedence, UC-resolve-conflict is almost always able to decide which goal to abandon in order to resolve the conflict. In this case, UC's stay-alive life theme has greater apriori precedence than UC's consultant role theme, so UC abandons the lower-priority goal of helping the user by telling the user how to delete UC.

9.9 HANDLING USER MISCONCEPTIONS

User misconceptions are commonly encountered in systems like consultant programs where the system knows more than the user. A user is said to have a misconception when the user's beliefs conflict with what the consultation system knows. In order to respond properly in such cases, the consultant system must first determine that the user's beliefs conflict with what the system believes and then correct the user's misconception.

There has been considerable research on user misconceptions, both theoretical work on the types of misconceptions and concrete implementations of systems that can detect and correct some kinds of user misconceptions [Mays80, Webber83, Kaplan83, McCoy85, McCoy89, Marburger86, Quilici89]). However, none of these treat the interface as an intelligent agent. UC's agent approach allows greater flexibility in making principled decisions about when UC might wish to correct a user's misconception. For example, UC will decide that it should not correct a user's misconception when it would help the user do something that UC opposes.

9.9.1. Detecting Misconceptions in UC

User misconceptions are detected by UC during the processing of the user's query. Currently, UC handles only relational misconceptions, that is, misconceptions in which the user believes a relation holds between two objects when, in fact, such a relation cannot hold or does not happen to hold between those particular objects. UC does not handle object-oriented misconceptions, such as those for which [McCoy85] discusses correction strategies.

In processing the user's query, UC checks to see whether all relations mentioned by the user in the user's query have a counterpart in UC's knowledge base. For example, if the user asks, "What does ls −e do?" then UC's parser/understander understands part of this as a HAS-OPTION relation relating an instance of the **ls** command and an instance of the *−e* option. While looking for the effects of the command, UC finds that there is no corresponding HAS-OPTION relation between the **ls** command and the *−e* option in UC's knowledge base. At this point, UC suspects that the user may have a misconception.

In order to see whether the user actually has a misconception or whether UC just lacks information about this particular option of this command, UC checks with the KNOME subcomponent [Chin87, Chin89], which models the limitations of UC's knowledge base using *metaknowledge*. If KNOME has metaknowledge that UC knows all the options of this command, then UC knows that the user has a misconception. On the other hand, if the options of this command are not covered by KNOME's metaknowledge, then UC cannot assume that the user has a misconception. Instead, UC must assume that it lacks information about this command/option combination.

9.9.2. Correcting Misconceptions

After UC has determined either that the user has a misconception or that UC lacks knowledge, UCEgo decides how UC should reply to the user. When the user has a misconception, UCEgo tries to correct this misconception by denying that what the user mistakenly believes is the case. On the other hand, if UC determines that it lacks information, then UCEgo apologizes to the user for not knowing the answer to the user's query. These two types of responses are shown in the UC session of Figure 9.5.

In the first query, UC corrects the user's misconception that **who** has a *−b* option. It does this by first noticing that the user's usage of "who −b" translates into a *has-option* relation between a *UNIX-who-command* and a *-b option*. There is no equivalent *has-option* relation in UC's knowledge base, so UC suspects a possible user misconception. To see if this is the case or if UC just lacks knowledge about this particular option, UC consults the metaknowledge stored in KNOME. The appropriate metaknowledge in this case is the fact that UC knows all the options of all simple commands. Since **who** is a simple command, and since the *-b option* is not listed among the options

FIGURE 9.5
UC SESSION SHOWING DIFFERENT UC RESPONSES TO POSSIBLE MISCONCEPTIONS

 # What does who -b do?

who does not have a -b option.

 # What does ruptime -t do?

I'm sorry, I do not know that.

---

of UNIX-*who-command* in UC's knowledge base, KNOME can infer that there is no such option for **who**. Next, UCEgo decides that UC should correct the user's misconception by denying the existence of a $-b$ option for **who**.

On the other hand, in the second query, UC professes ignorance about the $-t$ option of the **ruptime** command. As in the previous query about **who**, UC detects a possible misconception when it does not find a $-t$ option listed for **ruptime** in its knowledge base. However, in this case, **ruptime** is a complex command, so the previous metaknowledge does not apply. There is no metaknowledge about the options of complex commands (due to not enough programming by UC's implementors rather than any inherent limitation of UC), so UC cannot tell if **ruptime** has a $-t$ option. In order to be polite, UCEgo apologizes to the user for not knowing.

9.10 FILLING GAPS IN USER KNOWLEDGE

A major difference between programs that purport to be consultants or tutors and typical application programs is the fact that consultant/tutor programs typically know more about their domain than their users. This leads to problems when users of a consultant system do not know enough to ask the right questions. A tutoring system can usually avoid this problem by properly structuring tutoring sessions or by not providing the user with opportunities for unconstrained inquiry. A consultant system, however, cannot utilize either of these methods. It must be able to handle unconstrained inquiries from the user in its domain and be prepared to deal with users that do not know enough to ask the right questions.

One type of difficulty encountered by consultant systems in dealing with users occurs when the user lacks some information that is useful for the user's task. In such cases, the consultant should volunteer the information rather than waiting for the user to ask for it. Volunteering the information solves the bottleneck problem that occurs when the user never asks for needed information because the user does not realize than the information is necessary.

9.10.1. Different kinds of Volunteered Information

In order to be able to volunteer information, a consultant system must do three things:

1. Determine that it would be helpful for the user to know some information.
2. Deduce whether the user already knows the information.
3. Inform the user when the system believes that the user does not know the information or when the system wants to remind the user of the information.

The kinds of information that might be volunteered by a consultant can be divided into three types: *warnings*, *suggestions*, and *elaborations*. Warnings are provided when the consultant believes there is a potential problem for the user. Suggestions are given to present alternatives and methodological hints to the user. Elaborations involve providing additional information that is relevant to the user's query. Each type of volunteered information is described in greater detail below.

9.10.2. Warnings

A consultant system should consider providing a warning to the user when the consultant believes that there may be a problem with the user's plans. Two factors come into play when deciding whether to give a warning. The first factor is the likelihood that the problem will actually occur. For example, if the user wants to print a file, the user's plan may fail if there is a power blackout or if the printer is out of ink. The chances of a problem caused by a power blackout are so unlikely that giving such a warning would be unreasonable. On the other hand, it may be reasonable to warn the user about the printer being out of ink if the consultant knows that the printer is currently low or out of ink or if this particular printer is so heavily used that it frequently runs out of ink.

Another factor in deciding whether to give a warning to the user is the consultant's belief about whether the user is already aware of the potential problem. Being aware of the problem implies that the user knows both that there is a potential problem with this type of plan and that this problem may arise in this case. If the consultant believes that the user is already aware of the potential problem, then the consultant does not need to warn the user. If the consultant believes that the user knows about this class of problem but might not apply this knowledge in this particular case, then the consultant should remind the user with a warning. In some cases, the potential problem may be important enough that the consultant may wish to remind the user even though the user is already aware of the problem.

Common warnings include telling the user about a plan's preconditions that are commonly violated and telling the user about a plan's deleterious sideeffects. An example of warning the user about a commonly violated precondition is:

User: How can I delete the directory named misc?

UC: Type 'rmdir misc.' However, rmdir works only if the directory is empty.

In the example, UC warns the user about a precondition of the **rmdir** plan, namely that the directory must be empty. This precondition is commonly violated, hence it is something that should be mentioned to the user. This can be contrasted to other preconditions of **rmdir,** such as the need for write permission on the directory containing the directory to be deleted. This precondition is much less frequently violated, so it need not be mentioned to the user. Such frequency information is stored as *concerns* [Luria87] by the UNIX domain planning component of UC. When the UNIX domain planner creates a plan, it passes along to UCEgo those preconditions that have a high degree of concern. UCEgo then decides whether to warn the user about the precondition, depending on whether or not KNOME believes that the user already knows that this type of problem may arise in this such plans. Since KNOME does not model the user's ability to apply general knowledge to individual cases, UCEgo can only assume that, if the user knows about this problem in general, then the user will know that it applies in this specific case. So UCEgo provides a warning only when KNOME believes that the user does not know about the precondition to the plan.

Warnings about a plan's deleterious side effects are handled in a similar fashion. The UNIX domain planner stores concerns about the side effects of plans and returns them along with the plan that it produced. In the following example, UC warns the user about one of **mv**'s deleterious side effects, namely that **mv** will overwrite files:

User: How can I move the file named new to the file named old?

UC: Type 'mv new old'. However, be careful, since if the file named old exists, it will be deleted.

9.10.3. Suggestions

Suggestions are provided by a system to present alternative plans to the user and to present methodological hints to the user. A trace of a UC dialogue in which UC volunteers a suggestion to the user is shown in Figure 9.6.

Since UC was not programmed with direct access to UNIX, UC does not know who is on the system. Hence UC apologizes to the user in order to be polite. However, UC does know how the user can find out who is on the system, namely by using the **who** command. So, if UC believes that the user does not already know about the **who** command, UC will suggest this plan to the user. If UC were expanded to allow direct access to UNIX, then UC would not only tell the user who is on the system, but it would also volunteer information about the **who** command if UC did not believe that the user already knows about **who**.

Figure 9.7 shows the demon that detects the subgoal of having the user know how to find out something that the user wishes to know when the user

FIGURE 9.6
UC SESSION SHOWING UC VOLUNTEERING A SUGGESTION TO THE USER

 # Who is on the system?

I'm sorry, I do not know that.
To find out, type 'who'.

FIGURE 9.7
IF-DETECTED DEMON THAT SUGGESTS HOW TO FIND OUT INFORMATION

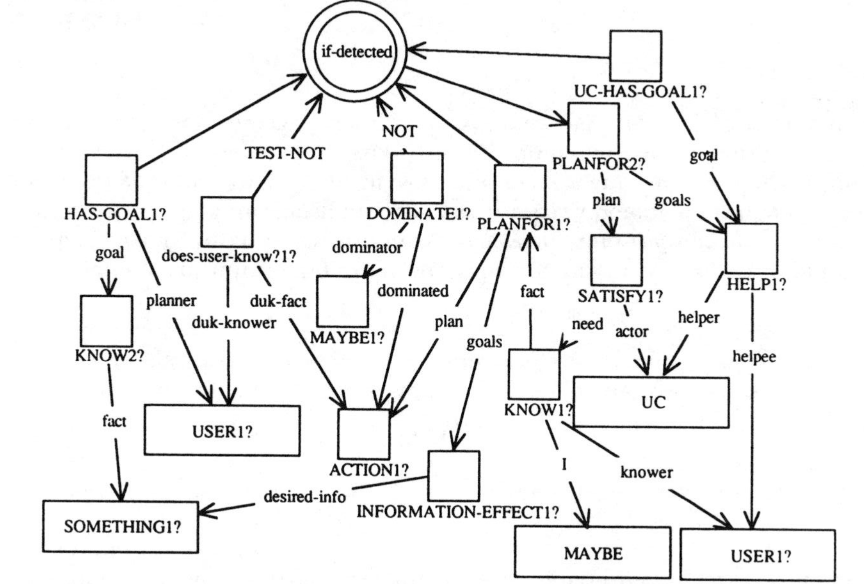

does not know this particular plan for finding out the required information (obviously, the user does know one plan for finding out, namely, ask UC).

This demon is activated in the following situations:

1. UC wants to help the user (UC-HAS-GOAL1).
2. The user wants to know something (HAS-GOAL1).
3. There is a specific (tested by the NOT DOMINATE1 test)[2] plan for finding out (INFORMATION-EFFECT1) the information.
4. The user does not know the plan (tested by the TEST-NOT, does-user-know?1, which represents a call to KNOME).

In such situations, the daemon asserts that a plan for helping the user is to adopt the subgoal of having the user know the plan for finding out the information.

The previous example shows how UCEgo proceeds when it fails to find a plan for a goal. It adopts the metagoal of finding a plan for that goal. In this case, UC does not know who is on the system, so it adopts the metagoal of knowing a plan for finding out who is on the system. UC's UNIX domain planner returns the plan of using the **who** command, which UC cannot use because it does not have direct access to UNIX. However, UC can suggest this plan to the user who does have access to UNIX and so can use the plan. The if-detected demon shown in Figure 9.7 suggests the plan (for helping the user) of adopting the subgoal of having the user know the **who** plan. Note that the daemon only suggests this plan if KNOME believes that the user does not already know about **who**. After all, it is possible that the user does know **who**, but instead decided to ask UC in order to find out the information (a plan that fails in this case). Some other examples of the same type are shown in Figure 9.8.

The last example shows a *reminder*-type suggestion. Reminders are given when the system believes that the user already knows some information but also that the user is likely to forget or ignore the information. In such cases, the system issues a reminder. In this example, KNOME believes that the user already knows about filing printer output in the boxes, so normally UCEgo would abandon the goal of suggesting that to the user. However, in this case it is likely that the user will shirk this duty, so UCEgo decides to provide the suggestion as a reminder.

In general, to issue a reminder-type suggestion requires that a system perform the following:

FIGURE 9.8
UC SESSION SHOWING SUGGESTIONS BY UC

\# *What is Chin's office?*

I'm sorry, I do not know that.
To find out, type 'finger chin'.

\# *What is the inode of the file named junk?*

I'm sorry, I do not know that.
To find, type 'ls -i'.

\# *How can I print a file on the laser printer?*

Use lpr -Plz.
Don't forget to file the printer output in the boxes.

1. Detect some useful information for suggestion to the user.
2. Determine that the user is likely to forget or ignore the information.
3. Inform the user if the system believes that the user needs to be reminded of the information.

Whether a user is likely to forget or ignore information is represented in UC in a fashion similar to concerns [Luria87]. Facts that users are likely to forget or ignore are marked as needing reminders. Since UC will provide a reminder-type suggestion regardless of whether the user already knows the information, there is not the need to check for this as there is in other types of suggestions. On the other hand, UC does need to check whether it has direct evidence during the current session that the user is cognizant of the information. So, if the user has mentioned the information previously or if UC has previously reminded the user of the information, then UC does not provide a reminder-type suggestion to the user.

9.10.4. Elaborations

Elaborations are given when the user asks a simple yes/no question and the system volunteers more information than a simple yes/no answer. This type of volunteered information has been termed *overanswering* by [Wahlster83], who implemented overanswering in the HAM-ANS natural- language system. An example of elaboration produced by UC is shown in Figure 9.9.

Elaborations such as this require the system to recognize that the user not only has the goal of knowing whether **rn** is used to rename files but also that this goal is a subgoal of two possible parent goals, namely knowing the effects of the **rn** command and knowing how to rename files. In UC,

[2] The NOT designation allows encoding situations involving the absence of certain relations. The DOMINATE relation is a trick to allow the specification of additional category memberships for any node, or in this case, node ACTION1's lack of membership in the MAYBE category (which indicates that a concept is hypothetical).

FIGURE 9.9
UC SESSION SHOWING AN ELABORATION IN UC'S RESPONSE TO THE USER

 # Is rn used to rename files?

No, rn is used to read news.
To rename a file, use mv.

these deductions are made by UC's goal analysis component, PAGAN. After PAGAN has deduced the user's goals, UCEgo proceeds by adopting all of the user's possible goals. In cases where the answer is *yes*, both potential parent goals are satisfied by the simple answer of *yes*, so all three goals can be merged into a single goal (see Section 9.8.1), and no elaboration is needed. However, in Figure 9.9, a *no* answer satisfies only the user's immediate goal of knowing whether **rn** is used to rename files, and it does not satisfy either possible parent goal. In such cases, UCEgo proceeds to process both parent goals and produces answers to satisfy both. The parent goal of knowing the effects of the **rn** command is addressed by, "rn is used to read news." The other parent goal of knowing how to rename files is answered with, "To rename a file, use mv." When KNOME believes that the user already knows one of these elaborations, only the other elaboration is given to the user.

This goal-based approach to elaboration can be compared to the overanswering methodology of HAM-ANS. HAM-ANS used specific strategies such as filling optional deep case slots in the case frame associated with a verb used in the user's request. The problem with such non–goal-based approaches is that they are prone to volunteering information that the user may not actually be interested in. For example, when the user asks HAM-ANS, "Has a yellow car gone by?" HAM-ANS elaborates upon the *where* case-slot to produce the answer, "Yes, one yellow one on Hartungstreet." This is a good answer if the user were actually interested in where the yellow car passed by. However, if the user were interested in how long ago the car passed by, then an elaborative answer like, "Yes, fifteen minutes ago," would be much better. Likewise, if the user were interested in following the yellow car, then a better answer would be, "Yes, north on Hartungstreet."

In order to choose between such different elaborations, an analysis of the user's goals is needed. For example, if the user had prefaced the question by the statement, "My friend is supposed to pick me up here," then an analysis of the user's goals would show that the user is probably more interested in how long ago the yellow car passed by. On the other hand, if the user is a police officer chasing a vehicle, then the user is probably interested in following the yellow car. So, deciding how to elaborate a yes/no answer requires a goal-based elaboration strategy such as the one used in UC.

Besides being useful for deciding exactly how to elaborate a *yes/no* answer, a goal-based strategy also tells the system whether it is useful to elaborate at all. For example, when the user asks UC, "Is compact used to compact files?" then a simple answer of *yes* is quite sufficient. There is no need for UC to elaborate on this answer because it addresses all of the user's possible parent goals.

9.11 CONCLUSIONS

This paper demonstrates that an intelligent interface that knows more than its user needs to be an intelligent agent in order to respond properly to its user. An intelligent agent based on goals and plans is the most flexible, because such a system can more easily detect positive and negative goal interactions. Within this planning paradigm, the key problem for building an intelligent agent is how to *detect* the right goals for the agent in appropriate *situations*. Once an agent has adopted appropriate goals, planning to satisfy those goals is a better-understood problem.

ACKNOWLEDGMENTS

The work described in this paper was done at the University of California, Berkeley, as part of my Ph.D. thesis. I wish to thank Robert Wilensky, who supervised this work. I also wish to thank the past and present members of BAIR (Berkeley Artificial Intelligence Research) who have contributed in various ways to the UC project.

REFERENCES

[Allen79] Allen, J. F. 1979. *A Plan-Based Approach to Speech Act Recognition.* Ph.D. thesis, Department of Computer Science, University of Toronto. Also available as Technical Report 131, University of Toronto.

[Austin62] Austin, J. L. 1962. *How to Do Things with Words.* London: Oxford University Press.

[Carbonell70a] Carbonell, J. R. 1970. An Artificial-Intelligence Approach to Computer Assisted Instruction. *IEEE Transactions on Man-Machine-Systems,* MMS-11 (4), 190–202.

[Carbonell70b] Carbonell, J. R. 1970. *Mixed-Initiative Man-Computer Instructional Dialogues.* Ph.D. thesis, Massachusetts Institute of Technology. Also available as *Technical Report 1971,* Bolt Beranek and Newman.

[Carbonell82] Carbonell, J. G. 1982. Where Do Goals Come From? In *Proceedings of the Fourth Annual Conference of the Cognitive Science Society,* Ann Arbor, August, pp. 191–194.

[Chin87] Chin, D. N. 1987. *Intelligent Agents as a Basis for Natural Language Interfaces.* Ph.D. thesis, University of California, Berkeley. Also available as *Technical Report UCB/CSD 88/396,* Computer Science Division, University of California, Berkeley.

[Chin89] Chin, D. N. 1989. Knome: Modeling What the User Knows in UC. In Kobsa, A., and Wahlster, W. eds. *User Models in Dialog Systems.* Berlin: Springer-Verlag, pp. 74–107.

[Faletti82] Faletti, J. 1982. PANDORA-A Program for Doing Commonsense Planning in Complex Situations. In *Proceedings of the Second Annual National Conference on Artificial Intelligence,* Pittsburgh, August, pp. 185–188.

[Fikes71] Fikes, R. E., and Nilsson, N. J. 1971. STRIPS: A New Approach to the Application of Theorem Proving to Problem Solving. *Artificial Intelligence,* 2 (3–4), 189–208.

[Hobbs80] Hobbs, J. R., and Evans, D. A. 1980. Conversation as Planned Behavior. *Cognitive Science,* 4 (4), 349–377.

[Kaplan83] Kaplan, S. J. 1983. Cooperative responses from a Portable Natural Language Database Query System. In Brady, M., and Berwick, R. C. eds. *Computational Models of Discourse.* Cambridge, MA: MIT Press.

[Luria85] Luria, M. 1985. Commonsense Planning in a Consultant System. In *Proceedings, 1985 IEEE International Conference on Systems, Man, and Cybernetics,* Tucson, pp.602–606.

[Luria87] Luria, M. 1987. Expressing Concern. In *Proceedings of the 25th Annual Meeting of the Association for Computational Linguistics,* Stanford, CA, July, pp. 221–227.

[Luria88] Luria, M. 1988. *Knowledge Intensive Planning.* Ph.D. thesis, University of California, Berkeley.

[Marburger86] Marburger, H. 1986. A Strategy for Producing Cooperative Nl Reactions in a Database Interface. In *Proceedings of AIMSA-86,* Wana, Bulgaria.

[Mays80] Mays, E. 1980. Failures in Natural Language Systems: Applications to Data Base Query Systems. In *Proceedings of the National Conference on Artificial Intelligence,* Stanford, CA, August, pp. 327–330.

[McCoy85] McCoy, K. F. 1985. *Correcting Object-Related Misconceptions.* Ph.D. thesis, University of Pennsylvania, Department of Computer and Information Science, Moore School. Also available at *Technical Report MS-CIS-85-57.*

[McCoy89] McCoy, K. F. 1989. Highlighting a User Model to Respond to Misconceptions. In Kobsa, A., and Wahlster, W. eds. *User Model in Dialog Sytems.* Berlin: Springer-Verlag, pp. 233–254.

[Meehan76] Meehan, J. R. 1976. *The Metanovel: Writing Stories by Computer.* Ph.D. thesis, Yale University. Also available as *Yale University Computer Science Research Report #74* and through New York: Garland Publishing, 1980.

[Norvig83] Norvig, P. 1983. Frame Activated Inferences in a Story Understanding Program. In *Proceedings of the Eighth International Joint Conference on Artificial Intelligence,* Karlsruhe, West Germany, August, pp. 624–626.

[Newell72] Newell, A., and Simon, H. A. 1972. *Human Problem Solving.* Englewood Clifts, NJ, Prentice-Hall.

[Quilici89] Quilici, A. 1989. Recognizing and Responding to Plan-Oriented Misconceptions. In Kobsa, A., and Wahlster, W. eds. *User Models in Dialog Systems,* Berlin: Springer-Verlag, pp. 108–132.

[Schank77] Schank, R. C., and Abelson, R. P. 1977. *Scripts, Goals, and Understanding.* Hillsdale, NJ: Lawrence Erlbaum.

[Sacerdoti74] Sacerdoti, E. D. 1974. Planning in a Hierarchy of Abstraction Spaces. *Artificial Intelligence,* 5 (2), 115–135.

[Searle69] Searle, J. R. 1969. *Speech Acts; An Essay in the Philosophy of Language.* Cambridge, England: Cambridge University Press.

[Wahlster83] Wahlster, W., Marburger, H., Jameson, A., and Busemann, S. 1983. Over-answering Yes-No-Questions: Extended Responses in a Nl Interface to a Vision System. In *Proceedings of the Eighth International Joint conference on Artificial Intelligence,* Karlsruhe, West Germany, August, pp. 643–646.

[Webber83] Webber, B. L., and Mays, E. 1983. Varieties of User Misconceptions: Detection and Correction. In *Proceedings of the Eighth International Joint Conference of Artificial Intelligence,* vol. 2, pp. 650–652, Karlsruhe, West Germany, August.

[Wilensky84] Wilensky R., Arens, Y., and Chin, D. N. 1984. Talking to Unix in English: An Overview of UC. *Communications of the ACM,* 27 (6), 574–593.

[Wilensky78] Wilensky, R. 1978. *Understanding Goal-Based Stories.* Ph.D. thesis, Yale University. Also Available as *Yale University Computer Science Research Report #140,* New Haven.

[Wilensky83] Wilensky, R. 1983. *Planning and Understanding: A Computational Approach to Human Reasoning.* Reading, MA: Addison-Wesley.

[Wilensky86] Wilensky, R., Mayfield, J., Albert, A., Chin, D. N., Cox, C., Luria, M., Martin, J., and Wu, D. 1986. UC—A Progress Report. *Technical Report UCB/CSD 87/303.* Computer Science Division, University of California, Berkeley.

[Wilensky87] Wilensky, R. 1987. Some Problems and Proposals for Knowledge Representation. *Technical Report UCB/CSD 87/351.* Computer Science Division, University of California, Berkeley.

Reflections on. . .

Intelligent Interfaces as Agents

David N. Chin

This paper was first presented at the 1988 Workshop on Architectures for Intelligent Interfaces. At that time, there was a strenuous, ongoing debate regarding whether a "direct-manipulation" model or an "intermediary" model (termed the "interface-as-agent view" in the paper) was more appropriate as the basis for human-computer interaction. The direct-manipulation model provides interfaces (typically graphical) that the user can "manipulate," that is, actions by the user on the interface are translated by the interface into changes in the underlying system. For example, dragging a file icon onto a trash can icon is translated into removal of the file. An ideal direct-manipulation interface is "natural" in that actions on the "model world" of the interface parallel real-world actions, and "invisible" in the sense that the user does not realize that the interface is translating the user's actions into system actions. On the other hand, a user must *tell* an intermediary-style interface what to do (using a command language that might be a natural language), thus forcing the user to acknowledge the existence of the interface as an intermediary between the user and the system. At the time, many human-computer interface designers felt that graphical, direct-manipulation interfaces represented a major advancement over command language interpreters and their intermediary-style interaction. They advocated a pure, invisible, model-world interface with no intermediary-style interaction.

This paper argued that an *intelligent* interface must be able to take the initiative in order to volunteer information, correct user misconceptions, or reject unethical requests. Most users do not expect a model world to volunteer suggestions—only agents do that, and the only agents familiar to people are intermediaries. For instance, users would be quite surprised if a program that they have been directly manipulating for a long time suddenly tells them, "You are using me incorrectly." Users can much more easily accept suggestions when volunteered by intermediary agents. At the time, these arguments sparked many lively discussions because they provided a cogent advocacy for a new kind of intelligent intermediary interaction based on interfaces as agents.

Since then, proponents on both sides have tempered their views. Interfaces can and do provide a mixture of direct-manipulation and intermediary styles of interaction. In addition, the interface-as-agent view has evolved into today's software agents (also called softbots). There are differences between the UC agent system described in this paper and more recent software agents. Whereas UC acted as an intermediary between the user and a knowledge base about the Unix operating system, most other software agents are intermediaries to the much more complex and variable world of the Internet. Furthermore, not all software agents use UC's goal/planning approach to agent architecture, and many provide direct-manipulation interfaces in place of or in addition to UC's intermediary-style, natural language interface. However, this paper, with its strong advocacy of intelligent agent interfaces and its architectural description of one of the very first fully implemented software agents, was certainly influential in the development and popularization of modern software agents.

CHAPTER 3

USER AND DISCOURSE MODELS FOR MULTIMODAL COMMUNICATION

WOLFGANG WAHLSTER
Computer Science Department,
German Research Center for Artificial Intelligence,
University des Saarlandes

ABSTRACT

In face-to-face conversation humans frequently use deictic gestures parallel to verbal descriptions for referent identification. Such a multimodal form of communication is of great importance for intelligent interfaces, because it simplifies and speeds up reference to objects in a visual context. Natural pointing behavior is very flexible, but possibly ambiguous or vague, so that without a careful analysis of the discourse context of a gesture there would be a high risk of reference failure. The subject of this paper is how the user and discourse models of an intelligent interface influence the comprehension and production of natural language with coordinated pointing, and conversely how multimodal communication influences the user model and the discourse model.

This research was partially supported by the German Science Foundation (DFG) in its Special Collaborative Programme on AI and Knowledge-Based Systems (SFB 314).

After a brief description the deixis analyzer of our XTRA system, which handles a variety of tactile gestures, including different granularities, inexact pointing gestures, and pars-pro-toto deixis, we present some empirical results of an experiment that investigates the similarities and differences between natural pointing in face-to-face communication and simulated pointing using our system. This paper focuses on consequences of this investigation for our present work on an extended version of the deixis analyzer and a gesture generator currently under development. We show how gestures can be used to shift focus and how focus can be used to disambiguate gestures. Finally, we discuss how the user model affects the decision of the presentation planning component to use a pointing gesture, a verbal description, or both, for referent identification.

3.1 INTRODUCTION

In face-to-face conversation humans frequently use *deictic gestures* (e.g., the index finger points at something) parallel to verbal descriptions for referent identification. Such a *multimodal* form of communication can improve human interaction with machines, because it simplifies and speeds up reference to objects in a visual world.

The basic technical prerequisites for the integration of pointing and natural language are fulfilled by high-resolution bit-mapped displays and window systems for the presentation of visual information; various pointing devices such as mouse, light-pen, joystick, and touch-sensitive screens for deictic input; and the DataGlove™[Zimmerman87] or even image sequence analysis systems for gesture recognition. But the remaining problem for artificial intelligence is that explicit meanings must be given to natural pointing behavior in terms of a formal semantics of the visual world.

Unlike the usual semantics of mouse clicks in direct manipulation environments, in human conversation the region at which the user points is not necessarily identical with the region to which he or she intends to refer. Following the terminology of Clark, we call the region at which the user points, the *demonstratum*; the descriptive part of the accompanying noun phrase, the *descriptor* (which is optional); and the region to which he or she intends to refer, the *referent* [Clark83]. In conventional systems there exists a simple one-to-one mapping of a demonstratum onto a referent, and the reference resolution process does not depend on the situational context. Moreover, the user is not able to control the granularity of a pointing gesture, since the size of the predefined mouse-sensitive region specifies the granularity.

Compared to that, natural pointing behavior is much more flexible, but also possibly ambiguous or vague. Without a careful analysis of the *discourse context* of a gesture there would be a high risk of reference failure, as a deictic operation does not cause visual feedback from the referent (e.g., inverse video or blinking as in direct manipulation systems).

The subject of this paper is how the user and discourse models of an intelligent interface influence the comprehension and production of natural language with coordinated pointing to objects on a graphics display and conversely how multimodal communication influences the user and discourse models.

Figure 3.1 outlines the basic architecture of an intelligent interface with multimodal input and output. For the sake of clarity, we have omitted all aspects of processing components and knowledge base that are not relevant to the topic of this paper.

Before we review previous research on the combination of natural language and pointing and describe some current approaches related to our work, let us briefly introduce the basic concepts of user and discourse models.

FIGURE 3.1
THE BASIC ARCHITECTURE OF AN INTELLIGENT MULTIMODAL INTERFACE

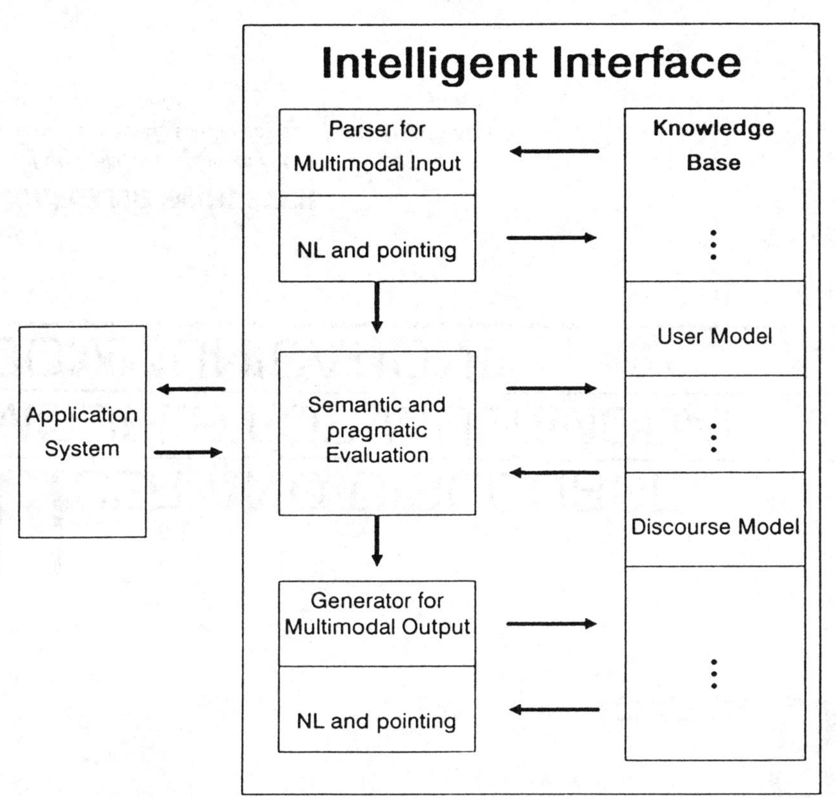

3.2 USER MODELS AND DISCOURSE MODELS

A reason for the current emphasis on user and discourse models [Wahlster86, Kobsa89] is the fact that such models are necessary prerequisites in order for a system to be capable of exhibiting a wide range of intelligent and cooperative dialogue behavior. Such models are required for identifying the objects to which the dialogue partner is referring, for analyzing a nonliteral meaning and/or indirect speech acts, and for determining what effects a planned utterance will have on the dialogue partner. A cooperative system [Wahlster84] must certainly take into account the user's goals, plans, and prior knowledge about the domain of discourse, as well as misconceptions the user may possibly have concerning the domain.

We use the following definitions [Wahlster88]:

- A *user model* is a knowledge source containing explicit assumptions about all aspects of the user that may be relevant to the dialogue behavior of the system.
- A *user modeling component* is that part of a dialogue system that performs the following functions:

1. To incrementally build up a user model
2. To store, update, and delete entries in it
3. To maintain the consistency of the model
4. To supply other components of the system with assumptions about the user

- A *discourse model* is a knowledge source that contains the system's description of the syntax, semantics, and pragmatics of a dialogue as it proceeds.
- A *discourse modeling component* is that part of a dialogue system that performs the following functions:

1. To incrementally build up a discourse model
2. To store and update entries in it
3. To supply other components of the system with information about the structure and content of previous segments of the dialogue

It seems commonly agreed upon that a discourse model should contain a syntactic and semantic description of discourse segments, a record of the discourse entities mentioned, the attentional structure of the dialogue including a focus space stack, anaphoric links, and descriptions of individual utterances on the speech act level. However, there seem to be many other ingredients needed for a good discourse representation that have not yet been determined in current discourse theory.

An important difference between a discourse model and a user model is that entries in the user model must often be explicitly deleted or updated, whereas in the discourse model entries are never deleted (except for phenomena related to forgetting). Thus according to our definition above, a belief revision component is an important part of a user modeling component.

This does not imply that the discourse model is static and only the user model is dynamic. The discourse model is also highly dynamic (consider, e.g., focus shifting), but it lacks the notion of logical consistency that is important for belief revision and default reasoning in a user modeling component. The discourse model is like an annotated trace of the various levels of the system's processing involved in understanding the user's utterances and generating its own dialogue contributions.

3.3 RELATED WORK ON DEICTIC INPUT

Although in an intelligent multimodal interface the "common visual world" of the user and the system could be any graphics or image, most of the projects that combine pointing and natural language focus on business forms or geographic maps.

To the best of our knowledge, Carbonell's work on SCHOLAR represents the first attempt to combine natural language and pointing in an intelligent interface [Carbonell70]. SCHOLAR, a tutoring system for geography, allowed simple pointing gestures on maps displayed on the terminal screen. NLG [Brown79] also combined natural language and pointing using a touch screen to specify graphics with inputs like (1).

(1) Put a point called A1 here <touch>.

Woods and his co-workers developed an ATN editor and browser that can be controlled by natural-language commands and accompanying pointing gestures at the networks displayed on the screen [Woods79].

In SDMS [Bolt80] the user can create and manipulate geometric objects by natural language and coordinated pointing gestures. The first commercially available multimodal interface combining verbal and nonverbal input was NLMenu [Thompson86], where the mouse could be used to rubber band an area on a map in sentences like (2).

(2) Find restaurants, which are located here <pointing> and serve Mexican food.

All approaches to gestural input mentioned so far in our brief review were based on a simple one-to-one mapping of the demonstratum onto a referent and thus have not attacked the central problems of analyzing pointing gestures.

Recently, several research groups have more thoroughly addressed the problems of combining nonverbal and verbal behavior. Several theoretical studies and empirical investigations about the combination of natural language and pointing have been published [Hayes86, Hinrichs87, Reilly85]. Working prototype systems have been described, which explore the use of complex pointing behavior in intelligent interfaces.

For example, the TACTILUS subcomponent[1] of our XTRA system [Kobsa86], which we will describe below in more detail, handles a variety of *tactile gestures*, including different granularities, inexact pointing gestures, and *pars-pro-toto deixis*. In the final case, the user points at an embedded region when actually intending to refer to a superordinated region.

In the DIS-QUE system [Wetzel87] the user can mix pointing and natural language to refer to student enrollment forms or maps. The deictic interpreter of the T^3 system [Scragg87] interacts with a natural language interpreter for the analysis of pointing gestures indicating ship positions on maps. In addition it can utilize continuing or repeated deictic input. CUBRICON [Neal91] is yet another system that simultaneously handles input in natural language and pointing to icons on maps, using language to disambiguate pointing and using pointing to disambiguate language.

While the simultaneous utilization of both verbal and nonverbal channels provides maximum efficiency, most of the current prototypes do not use truly parallel input techniques, since they combine *typed* natural language and pointing. In these systems the user's hands move frequently back and forth from the keyboard to the pointing device. Note, however, that multimodal input makes even natural-language interfaces without speech input more acceptable (fewer keystrokes) and that the research on typed language forms the basis for the ultimate speech-understanding system.

3.4 A CLASSIFICATION OF TACTILE POINTING GESTURES

For a study of the semantics and pragmatics of pointing, it is important to distinguish between two types of gestures:

- Pointing at *graphic models of objects* in the domain of discourse (e.g., geographic maps, icons for an office environment). In this case, the *detailed structure* of an icon is not relevant for the interpretation of a pointing gesture. For example, pointing at the lid of the trash icon causes the same effect as pointing at the can.
- Pointing at *objects* of a visual domain (e.g., forms, texts, graphics, formulas, images). In principle, *every pixel* on the screen can be a *separate reference object* in this case. For example, in our XTRA system (see Section 3.5 following) gestures can refer to all parts of the tax forms.

[1] In 1984 in the proposal for the XTRA project, I described the basic architecture of a flexible multimodal interface with a gesture analysis component. Since 1985, we have been working on the integration of pointing and natural language. The current version of TACTILUS was designed and implemented by J. Allgayer.

Today, most multimodal interfaces combining natural language and pointing belong to the first category (see Section 3.3 preceding). In this case, the interpretation and generation of pointing gestures are much easier than in the second category.

On the other hand, many of the subtleties of natural pointing come into their own only in the second case (see also [Schmauks87]). Moreover, that category covers a much wider range of possible applications.

Another fundamental distinction, which is independent from the classification introduced above, is whether the system deals with a static or a dynamic visual domain:

- Pointing at *fixed* and *static* visual objects on the screen (e.g., an icon for an airport on a map, a region of a tax form). In this case pointing gestures refer to *directions*, *locations*, or *objects*.
- Pointing at *dynamic* and *animated* visual objects on the screen (e.g., an animated ship icon on a map, a moving car in an image sequence). The pointing gestures can refer to *events* (e.g., "This U-turn was not allowed").

One limitation of the current prototypes is that the presented visual material is fixed and finite, so that the system builder can encode its semantics into the knowledge base. While some of the recent NL interfaces respond to queries by generating graphics, they are not able to analyze and answer follow-up questions about the form and content of these graphics, since they do not have an appropriate representation of its syntax and semantics. Here one of the challenging problems is the *automatic formalization of synthetic visual information* as a basis for the interpretation of gestural input.

3.5 XTRA: AN INTELLIGENT MULTIMODAL INTERFACE TO EXPERT SYSTEMS

XTRA (eXpert TRAnslator) is an intelligent multimodal interface to expert systems that combines natural language, graphics, and pointing for input and output. As its name suggests, XTRA is viewed as an intelligent agent, namely a translator that acts as an intermediary between the user and the expert system. XTRA's task is to translate from the high-bandwidth communication with the user into the narrow input/output channel of the interfaces provided by most of the current expert systems.

The present implementation of XTRA provides natural language access to an expert system, which assists the user in filling out a tax form. During the dialog, the relevant page of the tax form is displayed on one window of the screen, so that the user can refer to regions of the form by tactile gestures. As shown in Figure 3.2, there are two other windows on the right part of the display, which contain the natural language input of the user (upper part) and the system's response (lower part). An important aspect of

FIGURE 3.2
THE COMBINATION OF NATURAL LANGUAGE, GRAPHICS, AND POINTING IN XTRA

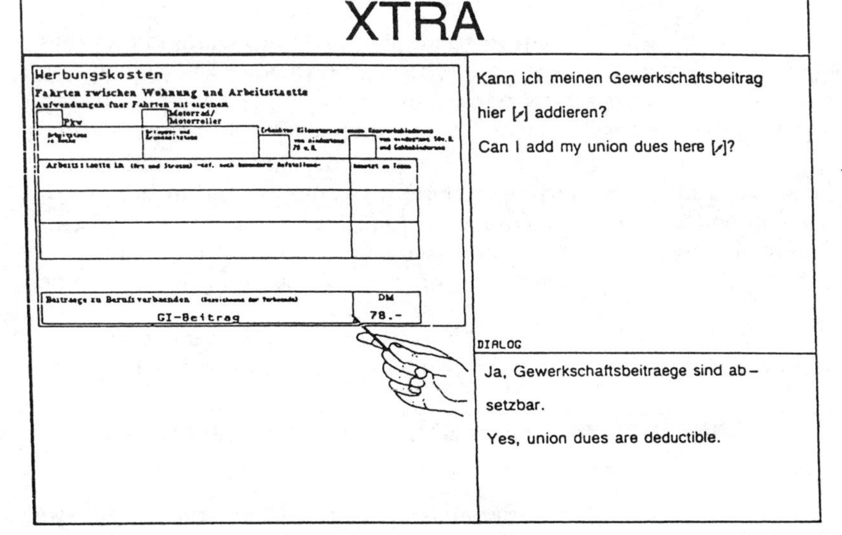

the communicative situation realized in XTRA is that the user and the system share a common visual field—the tax form. As in face-to-face communication, there is no visual feedback after a successful referent identification process. Moreover, there are no predefined 'mouse-sensitive' areas, and the forms are not specially designed to simplify gesture analysis. For example, the regions on the form may overlap, and there may be several subregions embedded in a region of the form.

XTRA uses a unification-based parser for German, which is distinguished from similar parsers in that it is able to parse multimodal input. As Figure 3.3 shows, XTRA's parser treats pointing gestures as terminal symbols in the input stream. These symbols are then mapped onto the preterminal category "deictic."

In its full generality, the parsing of multimodal input is a complicated subject in its own right, and even a modest exposition of this topic would be beyond the scope of the present paper.

The syntax and semantics of the tax form are represented as a directed acyclic graph, called *organization graph*. It contains links to concepts in a terminological knowledge base encoded in SB-ONE, a representation language in the KL-ONE paradigm. The nodes of the organization graph represent various types of regions of the form, and the edges describe relations such as "geometrically embedded" or "conceptual part of." Four types of nodes are used in this graph:

- *Value regions*, where data can be entered by the user (e.g., the region where the number 78 has been typed in; see Figure 3.2)
- *Label regions*, which provide captions for value regions and framed regions (e.g., the string DM above the number 78 in Figure 3.2)
- *Framed regions*, which highlight rectangular parts of the form (e.g., the box containing the string DM in Figure 3.2)
- *Abstract regions* as aggregations of conceptually related, but not necessarily adjacent parts of the form (e.g., the column of three boxes above the DM box in Figure 3.2)

In addition to the direct interpretation of a gesture, where the demonstratum is simply identical to the referent, TACTILUS provides two other types of interpretation. In a pars-pro-toto interpretation of a gesture the demonstratum is geometrically embedded within the referent. In this case, the referent is either a framed region that contains smaller regions, or an abstract region. An extreme case of a pars-pro-toto interpretation in the current domain of XTRA is a situation where the user points at an arbitrary part (pars in Latin) of the tax form intending to refer to the form as a whole (pro toto in Latin). Another frequent interpretation of gestures is that the demonstratum is geometrically adjacent to the referent: the user points, for instance, below or to the right of the referent. Reasons for this may be inattentiveness or the attempt to gesture without covering up the data in a field.

The user first chooses the granularity of the intended gesture by selecting the appropriate icon from the pointing mode menu or by pressing a combination of mouse buttons and then performs a tactile gesture with the pointing device symbolized by the selected mouse cursor. The current implementation supports four pointing modes (see Figure 3.4):

- Exact pointing with a pencil
- Standard pointing with the index finger
- Vague pointing with the entire hand
- Encircling regions with the '@'-sign

The deixis analyzer of XTRA is realized as a *constraint propagation* process on the organization graph described above. A pointing area of a size corresponding to the intended granularity of the gesture is associated with each available pointing mode. A plausibility value is computed for each referential candidate of a particular pointing gesture according to the ratio of the size of the part covered by the pointing area to the size of the entire region. The

FIGURE 3.3
A CHART PRODUCED BY XTRA'S PARSER FOR MULTIMODAL INPUT

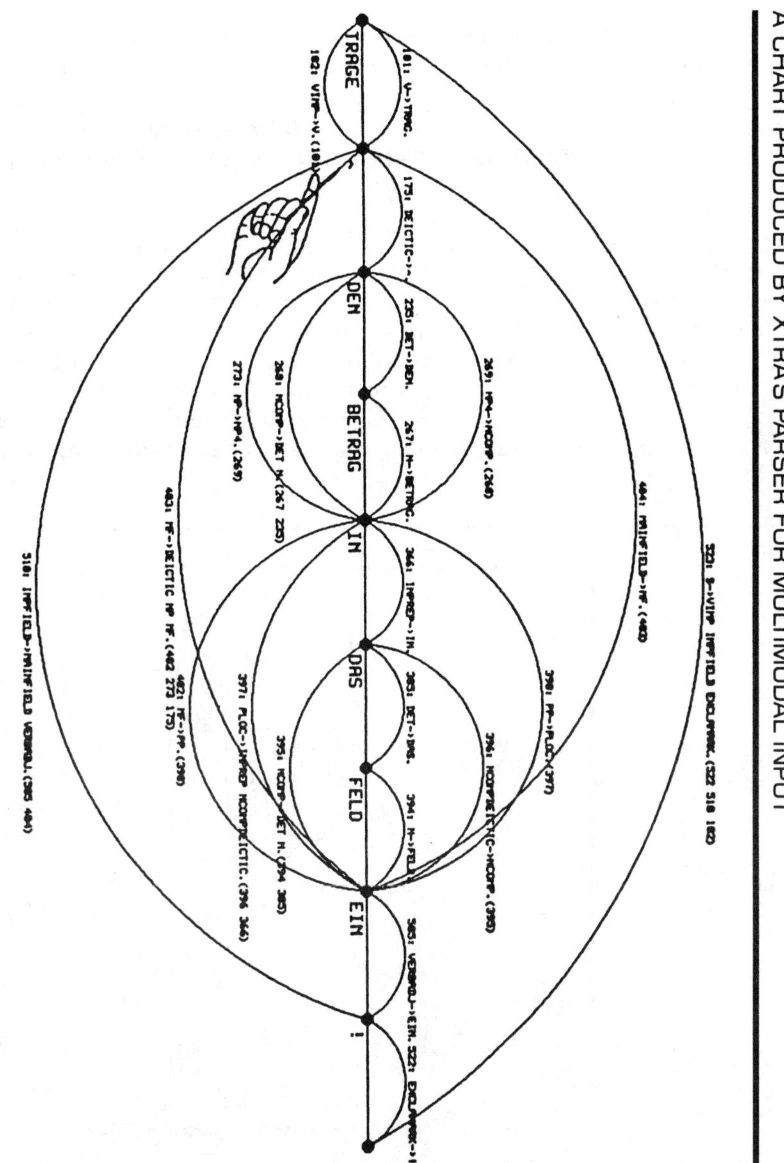

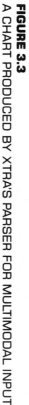

FIGURE 3.4
THE POINTING MODE MENU

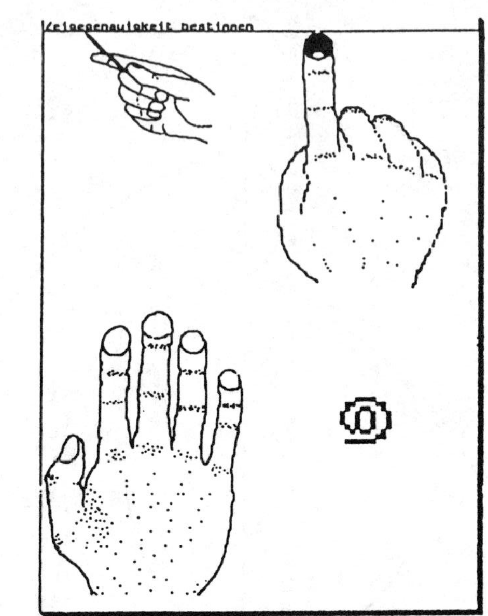

result of the propagation process is a list of referential candidates consisting of pairs of region names and plausibility values.

Since pointing is fundamentally ambiguous without the benefit of contextual information, this list often contains many elements. Therefore, TACTILUS uses various other knowledge sources of XTRA (e.g., the semantics of the accompanying verbal description, case frame information, the dialog memory) for the disambiguation of the pointing gesture (see [Allgayer86] and [Kobsa86] for further details).

3.6 NATURAL VERSUS SIMULATED POINTING: SOME EMPIRICAL RESULTS

In order to evaluate the strengths and limitations of the deixis analyzer described above, an experiment[2] was carried out. The main objective of the experiment was to investigate the *similarities* and *differences* between the following:

- *Natural pointing* in face-to-face communication with an advisor
- *Simulated pointing* using the TACTILUS component of the XTRA interface

In this experiment, 32 subjects were asked to fill in two pages of the German income tax forms using data about a fictitious person. The information about this person was provided by the experimenter in textual form.

While the first page of the tax form was presented as a hard copy and was filled out using a pencil, the second page was displayed on the screen of a Lisp machine and was filled out using TACTILUS. The complete experiment consisting of 16 hours of dialog sessions was video- and audiotaped.

The tape transcriptions consist of an analysis of both the spoken and typed or written expressions and the accompanying gestures along with their temporal interdependency.

1200 gestures were identified and classified along the following dimensions (selection only):

device ::= pencil | finger | hand | mouse arrow (screen only)
movement ::= point | underline | encircle
exactness ::= precise | borderline | vague
directness ::= tactile | visual (hardcopy only)
location ::= exact | above | below | left | right

Considering first the data for which there was no marked difference between natural and simulated pointing, two main results of the experiment should be noted:

- The low frequency (< 1%) of the following types of pointing gestures:
  using the hand/hand icon as a pointing device
  encircling
- The high frequency of pointing *below* the demonstratum.

Let us now turn to the results of the first part of the experiment, where the subjects used a pencil to fill in a hard copy of the tax form. The most important findings for natural pointing were the following:

- The high frequency of underlining (about 30%). The data showed the following order of frequency for the dimension "type of movement": point > underline > encircle.
- The preference of the subjects for using the pencil as a pointing device.

[2] It should be noted that in what follows we present only some preliminary results and that the final evaluation of all the data obtained from the experiment is not yet available. The experiment was designed by M. Wille with the help of D. Schmauks and Th. Pechmann.

- The high frequency of pointing at the borderline of the demonstratum (about 36%).
- The frequency of using pointing device for focusing (see Section 3.7).
- The large percentage of visual pointing gestures (about 60%) as compared to tactile pointing gestures.

An encouraging result of the experiments with TACTILUS was that after a short training period (1–2 mins) even subjects without any computer experience were able to use the system to perform the specified task. There were two important observations in this part of the experiment:

- The low frequency of underlining (1.6%)
- A greater number of gestures (830) than in the natural setting (370)

It is quite clear that the higher frequency of pointing in the dialog sessions with TACTILUS can be explained by the fact that in this setting the subjects had the additional task of positioning the input cursor, which required extra pointing.

Most of the design decisions for TACTILUS were supported by the findings from the experiment. It became evident that the important prerequisites for truly natural interaction in a multimodel mode are the following:

- *Context-sensitive interpretation* of pointing gestures (i.e., no one-to-one mapping of the demonstratum onto the referent)
- A *user model* and *discourse model* together with *assertional* and *terminological knowledge* for the interpretation of *ambiguous* pointing gestures

In addition, it was concluded that the ability to deal with a variety of tactile gestures, including different granularities and inexact pointing, to evaluate pointing gestures *below* the demonstratum and to cope with pars-pro-toto deixis is a positive feature of the current implementation that should be extended in future versions of the system.

On the other hand, the data suggest that in our current work on an improved version of TACTILUS the hand icon should be removed and that we need not make an effort to extend the mechanisms for the interpretation of encircling gestures (e.g., by allowing circles around arbitrary polygons), since these options were used extremely seldom. It also became clear that the interpretation of focusing gestures must be included in an improved version of the system, since this use of pointing was often observed in the natural setting but could not be handled by TACTILUS.

The high frequency of visual pointing gestures on the 2D tax forms showed that the 3D analysis of the position and orientation of the pointing device (e.g., by using a DataGlove™) is a promising direction for further improvements of the current system. With two DataGloves and the option to type with the gloves or to use speech input, truly parallel input becomes possible.

Finally, some comments are in order concerning the extent to which these findings may be generalized. The situation investigated in this study was highly restricted. The study was limited to 2D demonstrata with a permanent location. 3D and moving objects were excluded as targets for pointing actions. Another limitation of the present study concerned the nature of the experimental task, which was basically data entry. There is a large variety of situations in which people use deictic gestures that could not be studied in the present experiment.

3.7 THE INFLUENCE OF POINTING GESTURES ON THE DISCOURSE MODEL

In the experiment reported above, pointing was used not only for referent identification but also to mark or change the *dialogue focus*, for example, to control or shift *attention* during comprehension. As we noted in section 3.2, focus is an important notion in a discourse model, since it influences many aspects of language analysis and production. For example, focus can be used to disambiguate definite descriptions and anaphora [Grosz81].

Figure 3.5 gives an example of the disambiguation of a definite description using a focusing gesture. Without focus the definite description 'the A' is ambiguous in the given visual context, since three objects are visible which could be referred to as 'A' (one in each row of the table displayed in Figure 3.5). Together with the gesture of pointing at row Y, which marks this row as a part of the immediate focus, the definite description can be disambiguated, since there is only one 'A' in the focused row.

As in the case of gestures for referent identification, the effect of a focusing gesture can also be produced by a *verbal paraphrase*. For the example presented in Figure 3.5, a meta-utterance like 'Now let's discuss the entries in row Y' would have the same effect on the discourse model and help to disambiguate the subsequent definite description.

As we noted earlier, without a discourse context most pointing gestures are ambiguous. In the example above, we have seen that a discourse context can be established not only by verbal information but also by gestures. Thus there is a twofold relation between gestures and focus. Gestures can be used to shift focus, and focus can be used to disambiguate gestures.

From this it follows that in *simultaneous pointing actions* two communicative functions of pointing can be combined: focus shifting and reference. The following two types of simultaneous pointing can be identified:

- One-handed input:

  Focusing act: For example, the pencil is put down on the form, so that it points to a particular region on the form.

FIGURE 3.5
FOCUSING GESTURE DISAMBIGUATING THE QUESTION "WHY SHOULD I DELETE THE 'A'"

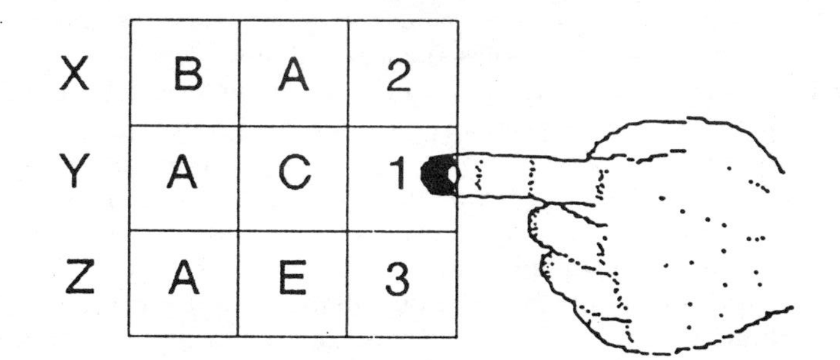

Referential act: A subsequent pointing gesture refers to an object in the marked region.

- Two-handed input (see also [Buxton86]):

  Focusing act: For example, the index finger of one hand points to a region of the form.

  Referential act: The index finger of the other hand points to an object in the marked region.

Figures 3.6 and 3.7 illustrate the use of focusing gestures for the disambiguation of referential gestures. Note that in both situations displayed in Figures 3.6 and 3.7 the index finger points at the same location on the form and that the utterances combined with these referential gestures are identical. The cases shown in both figures differ only in the location of the pencil used for focusing.

Let us explore the processing of these examples in detail. Since the referential gesture with the index finger is relatively inexact, TACTILUS computes a large set of possible referents. The head noun, "numbers," of the verbal description that accompanies the pointing gesture imposes two restrictions on this set of possible referents. Since there are only four numbers displayed on the part of the form shown in Figures 3.6 and 3.7, the semantics of the noun restricts the solution space to the power set of {3, 4, 7, 5}, and the plural implies that only sets with at least two elements are considered in this power set. Finally, the position of the index finger on the form makes the interpretations {3, 7, 5}, {3, 4, 5}, {3, 4, 7} and {4, 5, 7} implausible, so that the resulting set of plausible referential readings becomes {{3, 4}, {4, 5}, {3, 4, 7, 5}}, where {3, 4, 7, 5} is a typical example of a pars-pro-toto reading.

FIGURE 3.6
SIMULTANEOUS POINTING GESTURES

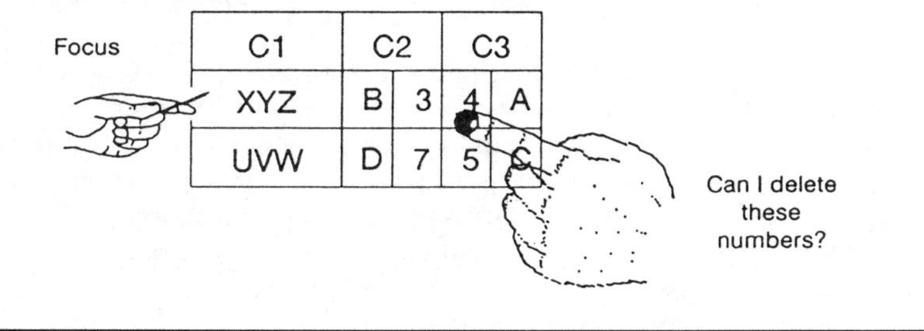

This means that there remain three possible interpretations before we consider the focusing gesture. It is worth noting that this is one of the cases where the combination of verbal and nonverbal information in one reference act does not lead to an unambiguous reading. Here information from the discourse model helps to clarify what is meant. In Figure 3.6 the pencil points at the row beginning with XYZ, so that this row and all its parts become focused. Now the intersection of the set of plausible referents and the currently focused objects results in the unique interpretation {3, 4}. Similarly, in Figure 3.7 the pencil is pointing at the block of columns called 'C3', so that the intersection of the focused elements with the results of the referential analysis is again a unique interpretation, namely {4, 5}, but it differs from the set of referents found for the gestural input shown in Figure 3.5. These examples once again emphasize the basic premise of our work, that pointing gestures must be interpreted in a highly context-sensitive way and that all approaches supposing a one-to-one mapping of the demonstratum onto the referent will fail in complex multimodal interactions.

FIGURE 3.7
SIMULTANEOUS POINTING GESTURES WITH DIFFERENT FOCUS

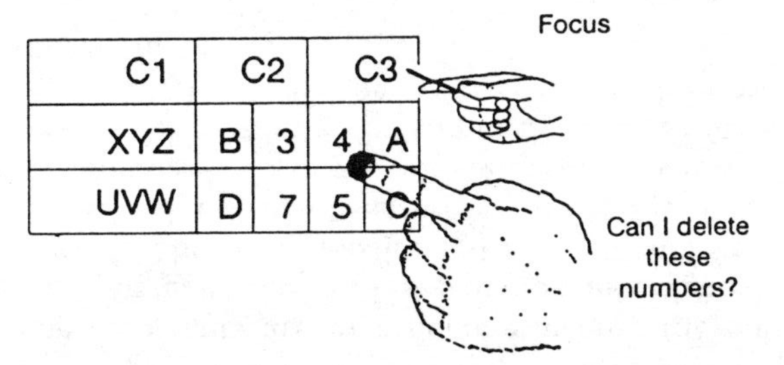

FIGURE 3.8
INTRINSIC INTERPRETATION OF 'REPLACE THE BOX BY THE RIGHT CIRCLE'

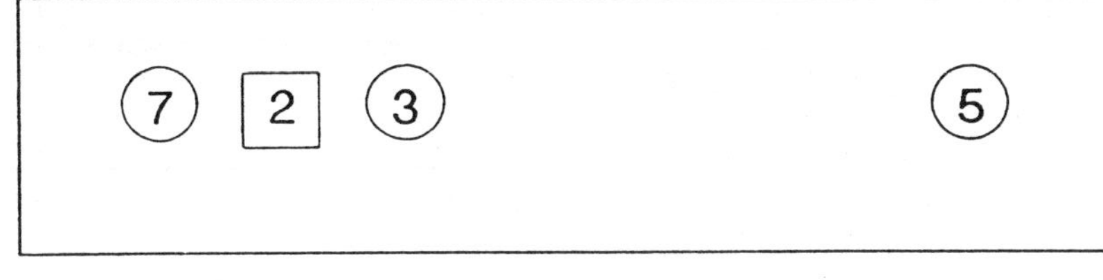

As we have seen, each focusing gesture modifies the discourse model. Another example of the impact of such focus information on the comprehension process is the effect of gestures on the selection of the *intrinsic* or *extrinsic use of spatial relations*. It is well known that the interpretation of spatial expressions depends on the selected frame of reference (for a more complete discussion of the intrinsic versus extrinsic use of spatial prepositions see [Retz-Schmidt88]).

One way to establish a reference frame is to use an intrinsic orientation. For example, consider the interpretation of the definite description 'the right circle' in Figure 3.8. Since there are three circles in the shared visual world of the user and the system, the interpretation of 'right' is crucial for finding the correct referent. In this case, the normal reading direction selecting from left to right forms the basis for an intrinsic interpretation as a default, selecting Circle 5 as the referent of the noun phrase.

Another way to establish a frame of reference is the use of a certain point of view for the extrinsic interpretation of spatial relations. The pointing gesture at Box 2 shown in Figure 3.9 overrides the default interpretation used for Figure 3.8. The focus information in the discourse model resulting from the gesture should cause the system to favor an interpretation

FIGURE 3.9
EXTRINSIC INTERPRETATION OF 'REPLACE THE BOX BY THE RIGHT CIRCLE'

where 'the right circle' refers to Circle 3. In this example, the position of the pointer induces a reference frame for the interpretation of the spatial description.

Note that in this situation the pointing gesture at Box 2 is redundant with respect to the referent identification process for the noun phrase 'the box'. Because only one box is visible, a unique referent can be determined without considering discourse information.

3.8 USER MODELING FOR PRESENTATION PLANNING

As we noted at the outset, an intelligent interface should be able not only to analyze multimodal input, but also to generate multimodal output. The design of XTRA's generator allows the simultaneous production of deictic descriptions and pointing actions [Reithinger87]. Because an intelligent interface should try to generate cooperative responses, it has to exploit its user model to generate descriptions tailored to users with various levels of expertise.

One important decision that a multimodal presentation planner has to make is whether to use a pointing gesture or a verbal description for referent identification. Let us use an example from our tax domain to explore the impact of the user model on this decision.

Suppose the system knows the concept 'Employee Savings Benefit' and an entry in the user model says that the current dialog partner seems to be unfamiliar with this concept. When the system plans to refer to a field in the tax form, which could be referred to using 'Employee Savings Benefit' as a descriptor, it should not use this technical term but a pointing gesture to the corresponding field. This means that in the conversational context described (3) would be a cooperative response, whereas (4) would be uncooperative.

(3) You can enter that amount here [↗] | in this [↗] field.

(4) You can enter that amount as employee savings benefit.

To summarize that point, if the system knows that a technical term which could be used to refer to a particular part of the tax form visible on the screen is not understandable to the user, it can generate a pointing gesture, possibly accompanied by a mutually known descriptor.

In the following, we discuss a particular method of user modeling, called *anticipation feedback*, that can help the system to select the right granularity of pointing when generating multimodal output. Anticipation feedback loops involve the use of the system's comprehension capability to simulate the user's interpretation of a communicative act that the system plans to realize [Wahlster86]. The application of anticipation feedback loops is based on the implicit assumption that the system's comprehension procedures are similar to those of the user. In essence, anticipation on the part of the system means answering a question like (5).

(5) If I had to analyze this communicative act relative to the assumed knowledge of the user, then what would be the effect on me?

If the answer to this question does not match the system's intention in planning the tested utterance, it has to replan its utterance, as in a generate-and-test loop. Figure 3.10 shows an extremely simplified version of a multimodal description planning process with an anticipation feedback loop for user modeling. Let us assume that the generator decided to plan a deictic description of an object X, to which the systems intends to refer. The result of the description planning process is a an expression Y of the functional-semantic structure (FSS) together with planned gesture. The FSS is a surface-oriented semantic representation language used on one of the processing levels of the how-to-say component of XTRA's generator.

This preliminary deictic description is fed back into the system's analysis component, where the referent identification component together with the gesture analyzer TACTILUS try to find the intended discourse object. If the system finds that the planned deictic description refers unambiguously to X, the description is fed into the final transformation process before it is outputted. Otherwise, an alternative FSS and/or pointing gesture has to be found in the next iteration of the feedback process (Figure 3.10).

Now let us use a concrete example to follow the feedback method as it goes through the loop. Suppose that the system plans to refer to the string 'Membership Fees' in the box shown in Figure 3.11. Also assume that the presentation planner has already decided to generate an utterance like 'Delete this [↗]' together with the pointing gesture shown in Figure 3.12.

For a punctual pointing gesture the system chooses the pencil as a pointing device. In this case, the exact position of the pencil was selected according to XTRA's default strategy described in [Schmaucks88]: the pencil is below the entry, so that the symbol does not cover it.

When this pointing gesture is fed back into the gesture analyzer of the referent identification component, the set of anticipated reference candidates might be {'Fees', 'e', 'Membership Fees'} containing only elements that can be 'deleted' (the current version of TACTILUS does not deal with characters or substrings of a string). Since the system has detected that the planned gesture is ambiguous, it starts replanning and then selects the index finger icon as a pointing gesture with less granularity (Figure 3.12). This time, the result of the feedback process is unambiguous, so that the system can finally perform the pointing action.

FIGURE 3.10
AN ANTICIPATION FEEDBACK LOOP FOR PRESENTATION PLANNING

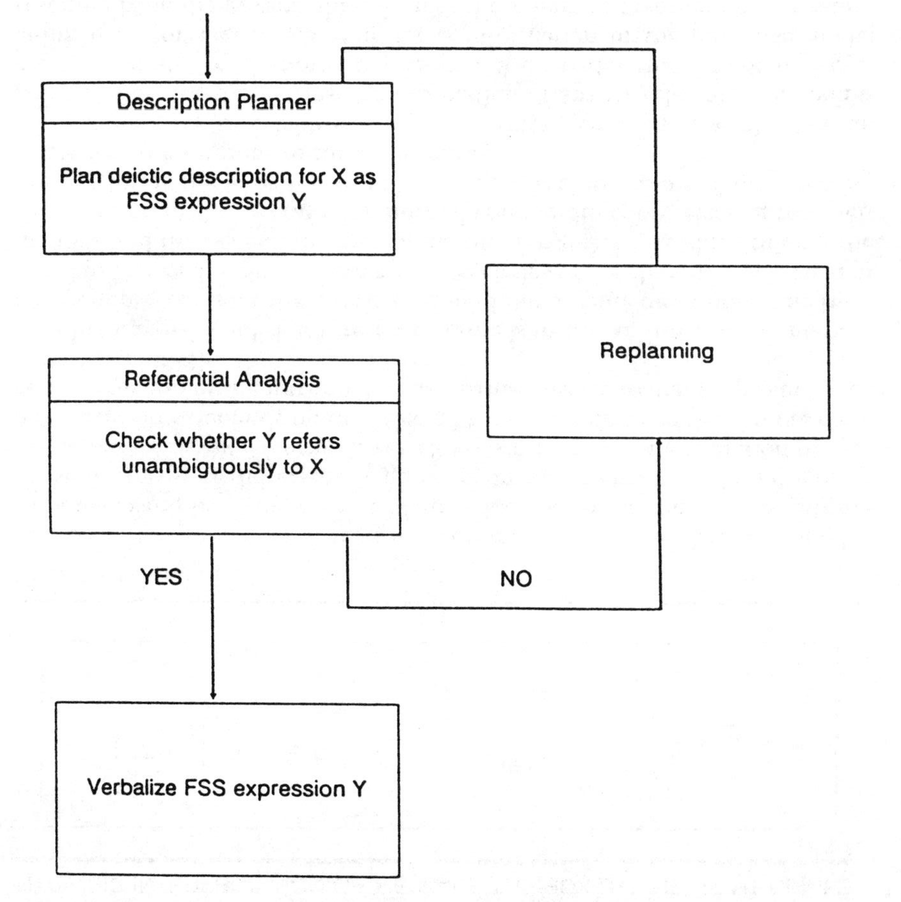

FIGURE 3.11
PLANNED POINTING GESTURE

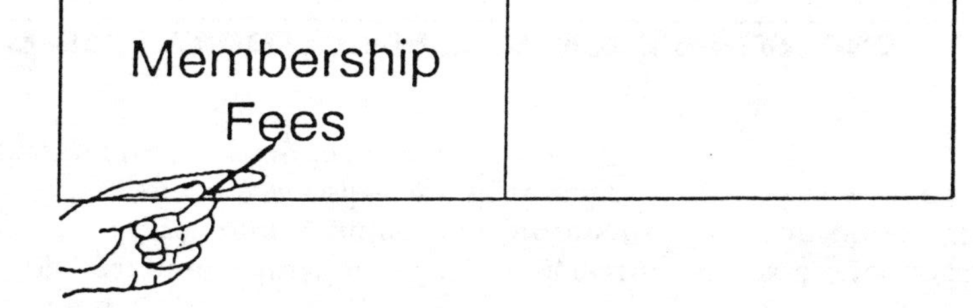

FIGURE 3.12
POINTING GESTURE AFTER REPLANNING

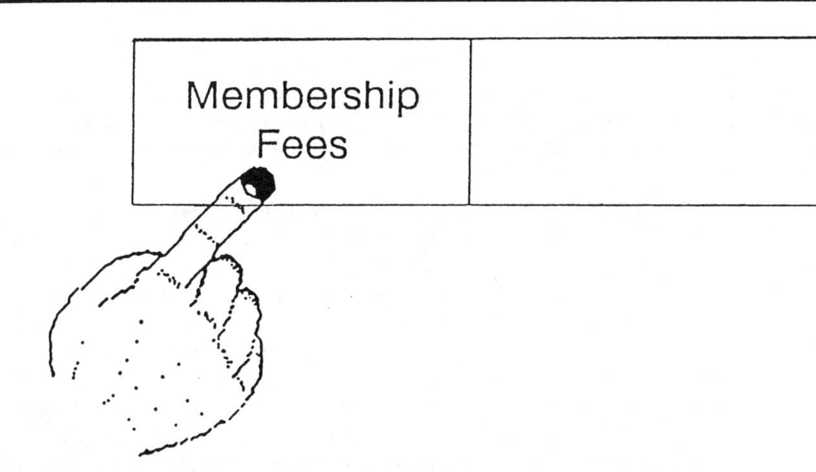

3.9 CONCLUSIONS

We have shown how the user and discourse models of an intelligent interface influence the comprehension and production of natural language with coordinated pointing to objects on a graphics display, and conversely how multimodal communication influences the user model and the discourse model.

First, we described XTRA as an intelligent interface to expert systems that handles a variety of tactile gestures, including different granularities, inexact pointing, and pars-pro-toto deixis, in a domain- and language-independent way. Then we discussed several extensions to the XTRA's deixis analyzer and presented our approach to generating multimodal output.

We showed how gestures can be used to shift focus and focus can be used to disambiguate gestures, so that simultaneous pointing actions combine two communicative functions: focus shifting and reference. We explored the role of user modeling for presentation planning and described how the user model can be exploited to generate multimodal descriptions tailored to the user's level of expertise.

Finally, we discussed anticipation feedback as a particular method of user modeling that can help the system to select the right granularity of pointing when generating multimodal output.

Some of the questions that have to be answered through future research on intelligent multimodal interfaces are the following:

- How can we deal with pointing gestures which refer to events? When there are dynamic and animated objects on the screen, the restriction of current prototypes, that is, that the presented visual material is fixed and static, is no longer viable.
- How can we handle pointing in 3D space? In the current systems the deictic space is two-dimensional and all objects are completely visible, so that tactile pointing is always possible.
- How can we cope with complex pointing actions, for example, a continuous movement of the index finger (underlining something, specifying a direction or a path) or a quick repetition of discrete pointing acts (emphatic pointing, multiple reference)?

REFERENCES

[Allgayer86] Allgayer, J., and Reddig, C. 1986. Processing Descriptions Containing Words and Gestures—A System Architecture. In Rollinger, C.-R. (ed.), *Proceedings GWAI/ÖGAI 1986*. Berlin: Springer, pp. 119–130.

[Bolt80] Bolt, R. A. 1980. Put-That-There: Voice and Gesture at the Graphics Interface. *Computer Graphics*, 14, 262–270.

[Brown79] Brown, D. C., Kwasny, S. C., Chandrasekaran, B., and Sondheimer, N. K. 1979. An Experimental Graphics System with Natural-Language Input. *Computer and Graphics*, 4, 13–22.

[Buxton86] Buxton, W., and Myers, B. A. 1986. A Study in Two-Handed Input. In *Proc. CHI'86 Human Factors in Computing Systems*, New York: ACM, pp. 321–326.

[Carbonell70] Carbonell, J. R. 1970. *Mixed-Initiative Man-Computer Dialogues*. BBN Report No. 1971. Cambridge, MA: Bolt, Beranek and Newman.

[Clark83] Clark, H. H., Schreuder, R., and Buttrick, S. 1983. Common Ground and the Understanding of Demonstrative Reference. *Journal of Verbal Learning and Verbal Behavior*, 22, 245–258.

[Grosz81] Grosz, B. 1981. Focusing and Description in Natural Language Dialogues. In Joshi, A., Webber, B., and Sag, I. (eds.) *Elements of Discourse Understanding*. New York: Cambridge Univ. Press, pp. 84–105.

[Hayes86] Hayes, P. J. 1986. Steps towards Integrating Natural Language and Graphical Interaction for Knowledge-based Systems. *Proceedings 7th European Conference on Artificial Intelligence*, Brighton, Great Britain, pp. 436–465.

[Hinrichs87] Hinrichs, E., and Polanyi, L. 1987. Pointing The Way: A Unified Treatment of Referential Gesture in Interactive Discourse. *Papers from the Parasession on Pragmatics and Grammatical Theory at the 22nd Regional Meeting*, Chicago Linguistic Society, Chicago, pp. 298–314.

[Kobsa86] Kobsa, A., Allgayer, J., Reddig, C., Reithinger, N., Schmauks, D., Harbusch, K., and Wahlster, W. 1986. Combining Deictic Gestures and Natural Language for Referent Identification. In *Proceedings 11th International Conf. on Computational Linguistics*, Bonn, Germany, pp. 356–361.

[Kobsa89] Kobsa, A., and Wahlster, W. (eds.), 1989. *User Models in Dialog Systems*. New York: Springer.

[Neal91] Neal, J. G., and Shapiro, S. C. 1991. Intelligent Multi-Media Interface Technology. In present volume.

[Reilly85] Reilly, R., (ed.) 1985. *Communication Failure in Dialogue: Techniques for Detection and Repair.* Dublin, Ireland: Deliverable 2, Esprit Project 527, Educational Research Center, St. Patrick's College.

[Reithinger87] Reithinger, N. 1987. Generating Referring Expressions and Pointing Gestures. In Kempen, G. (ed.) *Natural-Language Generation*, Dordrecht: Kluwer, pp. 71–81.

[Retz-Schmidt88] Retz-Schmidt, G. 1988. Various Views on Spatial Prepositions. In *AI Magazine*, 9 (2) 95–105. Also appeared as: Report No. 33, SFB 314, University of Saarbrücken, Computer Science Department.

[Schmauks87] Schmauks, D. 1987. Natural and Simulated Pointing. In *Proceedings 3rd European ACL Conference*, Copenhagen, Denmark, pp. 179–185.

[Schmauks88] Schmauks, D., and Reithinger, N. 1988. Generating Multimodal Output—Conditions, Advantages, and Problems. In *Proceedings 12th International Conference on Computational Linguistics*, Budapest, Hungary, pp. 584–588.

[Scragg87] Scragg, G. W. 1987. *Deictic Resolution of Anaphora*. Unpublished paper, Franklin and Marshall College, P.O. Box 3003, Lancaster, PA 17604.

[Thompson86] Thompson, C. 1986. Building Menu-Based Natural Language Interfaces. *Texas Engineering Journal*, 3, 140–150.

[Wahlster84] Wahlster, W. 1984. Cooperative Access Systems. *Future Generation Computer Systems*, 1, 103–111.

[Wahlster86] Wahlster, W., and Kobsa, A. 1986. Dialog-Based User Models. In Ferrari, G. (ed.), *Proceedings of the IEEE*, 74 (7), 948–960.

[Wahlster88] Wahlster, W. 1988. Distinguishing User Models from Discourse Models. In Kobsa, A., and Wahlster, W. (eds.) *Computational Linguistics*. Special Issue on User Modeling, 14 (3), 101–103.

[Wetzel87] Wetzel, R. P., Hanne, K. H., and Hoepelmann, J. P. 1987. *DIS-QUE: Deictic Interaction System-Query Environment.* LOKI Report KR-GR 5.3/KR-NL 5, Stuttgart, Germany: Fraunhofer Gesellschaft, IAO.

[Woods79] Woods, W. A., et al. 1979. *Research in Natural Language Understanding*. Cambridge, MA: Annual Report, TR 4274, Bolt, Cambridge, MA: Beranek and Newman.

[Zimmermann87] Zimmermann, T. G., Lanier, J., Blouchard, C., Bryson, S., and Harvill, Y. 1987. A Hand Gesture Interface Device. *Proceedings CHI'87 Human Factors in Computing Systems*, New York: ACM, pp. 189–192.

Reflections on. . .

User and Discourse Models for Multimodal Communication

Wolfgang Wahlster

XTRA was the first multimodal interface that could analyze and generate a large variety of continuous deictic gestures combined with natural language text. XTRA's gesture generator, ZORA, exploited the bidirectional nature of the knowledge about the semantics of gestures for checking whether a planned gesture will establish an unambiguous reference to the intended domain object. Thus, XTRA's gesture generator, ZORA, used our gesture analyzer, TACTILUS, for the anticipation of the user's gesture interpretation process. In the parallel VITRA project that dealt with the incremental natural language description of image sequences, we generalized this approach of an anticipation feedback loop for procedural user modeling to mental images. The system tried to predict changes in the listener's mental image and compared these with the intended effects of a planned output, possibly leading to a revision in VITRA's verbalization process (Schirra and Stopp 1993).

XTRA's approach of using the unification of typed feature structures in order to integrate the semantics of typed NL input and deictic gestures has been generalized recently in the QuickSet system (Johnston et al. 1997) to the full spectrum of gestural input.

After an empirical validation (Schmauks and Wille 1991), we have further generalized the results of XTRA in a number of follow-up projects that integrate speech input or output with complex gestures. FLUIDS provides a Java-based multimodal interface to a real-time traffic control system that accepts coordinated gestures and commands of an operator over a World Wide Web presentation visualizing the traffic flow on digital maps.

In our PPP project, the lifelike character PPP Persona uses two-handed gestures to control the attentional structure of a multimodal presentation. Particular relations between the objects focused by pointing gestures are introduced by coordinated speech output (e.g., "this button controls this LED"). The presentation planner of PPP decides when and how to point and automatically synchronizes the generated pointing behavior with the speech output by processing the qualitative and metric temporal constraints specified in the presentation strategies. An interesting feature of the pointing behavior of the Persona agent is that it can use a magnifying glass as a pointer, in addition to the conventional pointing stick, to shift the level of detail of the demonstratum.

MOFA is a multimodal route advisor system for car drivers that accepts continuous speech input coordinated with deictic gestures on digital maps. Like XTRA, the MOFA system developed at DFKI (Deutsches Forschungszentrum für Künstliche Intelligenz) for Siemens can disambiguate natural pointing gestures by exploiting semantic and contextual information extracted from the spoken input. An interesting feature of MOFA is that the system can not only analyze natural gestures in localization tasks but can also use pointing for the direct manipulation of graphical objects triggering actions in the application domain. When MOFA uses the mouse as an input device, the analysis of referential gestures can rely just on the mouse trajectories, whereas for triggering gestures additional clicking events must be evaluated. However, when MOFA's touch screen is used for gestural input, complex contextual constraints have to be processed to distinguish between these completely different kinds of gestures.

REFERENCES

Johnston, M.; Cohen, P. R.; McGee, D.; Oviatt, S.; Pittman, J. A.; Smith, I. 1997. Unification-Based Multimodal Integration. In Cohen, P, and. Wahlster, W. (eds.), *Proceedings of the ACL-EACL'97 Joint Conference*, Madrid, 281–288.

Schirra, J., and Stopp, E. 1993. ANTLIMA—A Listener Model with Mental Images. In *Proceedings of IJCAI-93,* Chambery, France, 175–180.

Schmauks, D., and Wille, M. 1991. Integration of Communicative Hand Movements into Human-Computer Interaction. *Computers and the Humanities* 25: 129–140.

KN-AHS: An Adaptive Hypertext Client of the User Modeling System BGP-MS

Alfred Kobsa, Dietmar Müller, Andreas Nill

Dept. of Information Science, Univ. of Konstanz
P.O. Box 5560-D73, 78434 Konstanz, Germany
{kobsa,mueller,nill}@inf-wiss.uni-konstanz.de

Abstract[1]

This paper describes the automatic adaptation of hypertext to the user's presumed domain knowledge in the KN-AHS system, and the support that the user modeling shell system BGP-MS can provide for this adaptation. First, basic hypertext concepts will be introduced and reasons given for why hypertext should adapt to the current user (especially to his/her state of knowledge). A brief overview of those representation and inference components of BGP-MS that are used by KN-AHS will then be provided, followed by a description of its adaptive user interface. The interaction between the adaptive hypertext system and the user modeling system will be investigated in detail based on a possible dialog with a user. Finally, the inter-process communication between KN-AHS and BGP-MS will be described and related work discussed. The aim of this work was to demonstrate the feasibility of user modeling with BGP-MS in a "normal" hardware and software environment that is frequently found in the workplace.

1. Hypertext and adaptive hypertext

1.1 Hypertext

Hypertext consists of any number of objects[2] that can be linked with one another in a network structure. Therefore, hypertext is not necessarily read in linear (i.e., sequential) order like conventional text, but can be read in a non-linear order by navigating within the hypertext node network. This non-linear linkage of objects represents the basic characteristic of hypertext [cf. Seyer 1991, Kuhlen 1991].

Gaining information in a non-linear form is not new (see e.g. information search in encyclopedias). As opposed to printed media, however, the representation of information in electronic form allows the user to directly and comfortably traverse contextual connections. Hypertext has therefore been able to enjoy an increased importance in the last few years, especially as a basis for on-line help systems and electronic encyclopedias.

The user-friendliness of many hypertext systems is rooted in their usage of intuitively understandable direct-manipulative interfaces [cf. Kuhlen 1991, Shneiderman & Kearsly 1989]. The user has the possibility of directly manipulating graphical objects with a pointer (e.g. a mouse) without having to use complicated commands. The effect of these actions can be seen immediately on the screen. Direct manipulation can be used, for example, to reach a different node from the node currently shown on the screen. The usual graphical objects used in such navigating operations include mouse-sensitive text passages (hotwords) or buttons (more on this in Section 3). Other important hypertext components are glossaries, indices, and graphical representations of the hypertext structure, which all offer important meta-information about the basic text objects. Recent research supplements associative navigation by controlled navigation and by search techniques from the field of Information Retrieval, in order to increase the search efficiency [cf. Kuhlen 1991].

1.2 Adaptive Hypertext

Two major problems arise when working with hypertext systems:

• *Orientation and navigation problems*: When navigating in hypertext, users are frequently uncertain as to how to reach their goals. Since users can choose any course within hypertext, they run the risk of losing their orientation. Navigation aids that take users' goals into account may be helpful. Kaplan et al. [1993] showed empirically that navigation suggestions based on knowledge about the objectives and the navigation behavior of previous users as well as the goals of the current user can significantly accelerate the current user's search for information.

• *Comprehension problems*: Since hypertext is frequently read by users with differing knowledge and experience levels, it may at the same time be too difficult and too detailed for laypersons, and too redundant for experts. Boyle & Encarnacion [1993] showed empirically that an automatic adaptation of hypertext to the user's state of knowledge significantly improves text understanding as well as partially improving search speed.

The system KN-AHS[3] deals with the second problem and adapts hypertext objects to the current user's state of knowledge. In contrast to other adaptive hypertext systems, the realization of KN-AHS took advantage of existing software products. TOOLBOOK [Asymetrix 1989], a widely available hypertext shell system, offered us a powerful tool for the implementation of the hypertext and its user interface. The user modeling shell system BGP-MS offered a wide variety of representation and inference possibilities that ensure flexible adaptation. Both tools run as independent software systems on a PC platform and interact via inter-process communication.

---

[1] This work was supported by the German Science Foundation (Grant Ko-1044) and the Univ. of Konstanz (Grant AFF 17/92).

[2] The objects in a hypertext base are not only text documents but can also include non-textual data (tables, graphs, animation, etc.). If an audiovisual component is involved, then the term 'hypermedia' is used.

[3] KN-AHS stands for KoNstanz Adaptive Hypertext System.

2. User modeling using BGP-MS

Over the last few years, researchers have tried to develop so-called 'user modeling shell systems', since programming user modeling components in application systems is very time-consuming. By using these shell systems, integrated mechanisms and methods are made available which are often needed in user modeling components.

One of these shells is BGP-MS[4], which is currently under development. From the perspective of the application system, BGP-MS can be regarded as a "black box" that receives information about the user and answers questions posed by the application system concerning current assumptions about the user. In order to realize its adaptive dialog behavior that is oriented on the user's state of knowledge, KN-AHS utilizes certain services of BGP-MS. The following sections will gradually present the BGP-MS components that are used, and explain their functionality with regard to the adaptation of hypertext by means of examples[5].

2.1 Communication between the application and BGP-MS

The user modeling component of KN-AHS is not integrated into the application (as is the case for user modeling components in virtually all other user-adaptive systems), but is rather an independent process that communicates with the application. Observations based on user actions will be reported to BGP-MS by the hypertext system (cf. Fig. 1, part a). The application can ask BGP-MS questions about the user (b) and BGP-MS can in return report its current assumptions concerning the user (c).

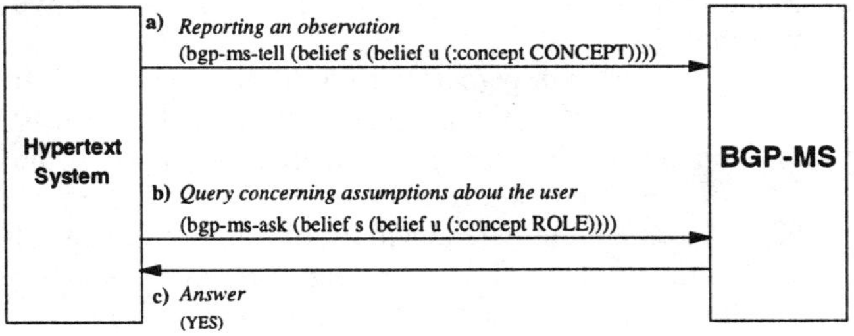

Fig. 1: Communication between the application and BGP-MS

2.2 Partitions for collecting different types of assumptions

BGP-MS utilizes the partition mechanism SB-PART [Scherer 1990], which allows different types of assumptions about the user to be represented simultaneously, but still separately. These assumptions include, for example, assumptions concerning the user's knowledge or goals, assumptions concerning application-relevant characteristics of user subgroups (so-called 'stereotypes'), or the domain knowledge of the user modeling component.

Partitions can be ordered in an inheritance hierarchy, where subordinate partitions inherit the contents of superordinate ones. Fig. 2 shows a simple partition hierarchy, as is currently used in our adaptive hypertext. The depicted partitions can be divided into three groups:

- The *individual user model* consists of the partitions SBUB (System Believes User Believes), which contains BGP-MS's assumptions about the user's knowledge, and

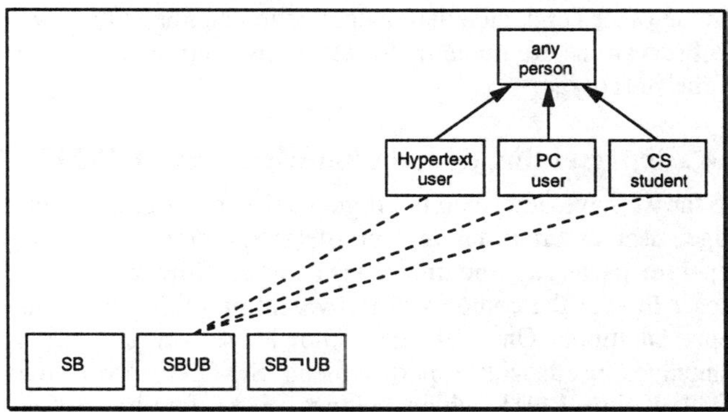

Fig. 2: Partition hierarchy in SB-PART

SB¬UB, which contains BGP-MS's assumptions about what the user does not know.
- The *stereotypes* for user subgroups are ordered hierarchically. We assume for our application that the stereotype "any person" is available, which includes only general information, i.e. knowledge available to any user. All other stereotypes include typical characteristics of users with various fields of specialization, namely hypertext users, PC users, and computer science students[6]. They inherit the contents from the general stereotype.
- The *domain knowledge* in BGP-MS, which is included in the partition SB (= System Believes).

2.3 Stereotype mechanisms

BGP-MS allows the user model developer to define so-called 'stereotypes' that contain application-relevant characteristics of user subgroups. The programmer can also define the conditions under which a user will be assigned to these subgroups, and those under which an existing assignment should be withdrawn. BGP-MS contains a stereotype managing mechanism that analyzes observations received from the application and checks the activation and retraction conditions of all stereotypes. It will then enter

[4] BGP-MS stands for Belief, Goal and Plan Maintenance System [Kobsa 1990].

[5] A more comprehensive description of BGP-MS can be found in [Kobsa & Pohl, 1994].

[6] This type of stereotype hierarchy -- a kernel with several specializations -- has been investigated several times in connection with the use of UNIX commands [Hanson et al. 1984, Sutcliffe & Old 1987]. The model is also referred to as 'lettuce model' because of its graphical form in Venn diagrams [Kobsa 1990].

inheritance links between the individual user model and those stereotypes that become active, and delete links to stereotypes that become deactivated. More than one stereotype can be active at the same time, if allowed by the user model programmer. He/she can also define the frequency of stereotype revision.

The broken lines in Fig. 2 represent the possible inheritance relationships with the stereotypes hypertext user, PC user and CS student. Since only "positive knowledge" is contained in the stereotypes of KN-AHS at the time being, a connection to SB¬UB is not possible. Several stereotypes can be active simultaneously, since the readers (such as all authors of this paper) can be both hypertext and PC users. On the other hand, an existing connection can be withdrawn if observations are made that meet the retraction conditions of the stereotype.

2.4 Representing domain knowledge in BGP-MS

So far we have described the organization of system knowledge, user assumptions and pre-defined stereotypes using separate partitions and inheritance links. Now we take a closer look at the contents of individual partitions and their representation. One of the knowledge representation languages used within partitions is SB-ONE [Profitlich 1989, Kobsa 1991], which belongs to the family of KL-ONE type languages. The following simplified description of the language elements is sufficient for the purposes of this paper.

The two most important representational elements in KL-ONE type languages are concepts (depicted as ovals in Fig. 3) and role relationships between concepts (depicted as small circles). For the purposes of KN-AHS, two types of concepts are distinguished: field concepts, which represent small fields of knowledge, and terminological concepts, which represent technical terms. In Fig. 3, 'UM-Shell', 'GUMS', 'BGP-MS', 'KL-ONE', 'SB-ONE', 'CLASSIC' and 'BACK' are field concepts. 'ROLE' and 'CONCEPT' are terminological concepts. The role 'associated-concept' (the only role used in KN-AHS) defines the relationship between fields and their associated terminology.

Super- and subordinations are also found for concepts, where the subordinated concept inherits all role relationships of the superordinated concept. The field concepts 'SB-ONE' and 'BGP-MS' in Fig. 3 inherit all roles of the field concept 'KL-ONE', and thereby all associated terminological concepts.

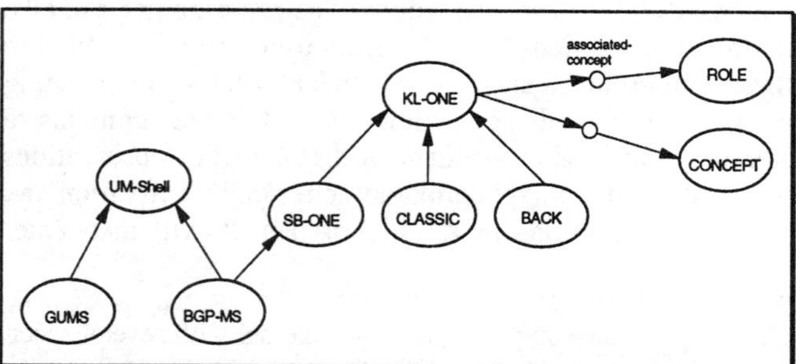

Fig. 3: Detail of the concept hierarchy in the partition 'System Believes' (SB)

2.5 User model acquisition and inferences

Messages that an application communicates to BGP-MS may express various types of information about the user's knowledge. KN-AHS only takes assumptions about the user's conceptual knowledge into account when adapting hypertext documents. Its messages to BGP-MS are therefore restricted to information on whether the user is familiar or unfamiliar with certain concepts. These "primary assumptions" about the user become entered into the partitions SBUB and SB¬UB, respectively. Primary assumptions will be compared with all stereotype activation and deactivation conditions in regular pre-set intervals. As an effect, inheritance links between stereotype partitions and the partition SBUB may be entered or erased.

The user model developer may also define inference rules that become executed after each new entry into the individual user model. The inferences used in KN-AHS are based on domain knowledge that is represented in SB. They take sub- and superfield relationships and the "associated-concept" relationship between fields and their respective terminology into account, and comprise the following rules:

a) Sub- and superfield relationships
   - a1) If a minimum percentage P1 of direct subfields of a field were reported to be known/unknown, then all its subfields are known/unknown.
   - a2) If a minimum percentage P2 of direct subfields of a field were reported to be known/unknown (where P1 can be different from P2), then the superfield is also known/unknown.

b) Relationships between fields and their respective terminology
   - b1) If a minimum percentage P3 of the terminological concepts of a field were reported to be known/unknown, then all terminological concepts of the field are known/unknown.
   - b2) If a minimum percentage P4 of the terminological concepts of a field were reported to be known/unknown (where P3 can be different from P4), then the field is also known/unknown.

Conflicts can arise between the observations made by the application and assumptions inferred in BGP-MS. If this is the case, then the inferred assumptions will have a lower priority and will be discarded from the partition. Dependency management between premises and consequences will not be able to be considered until sometime in the future.

3. The adaptive hypertext system KN-AHS

In this section, we will first describe the functionality of the user interface of KN-AHS. We will focus especially on reviewing the direct-manipulative actions that are available to the user. Then the assumptions will be described that KN-AHS draws about the user and reports to BGP-MS, as well as the kind of hypertext adaptation that it performs

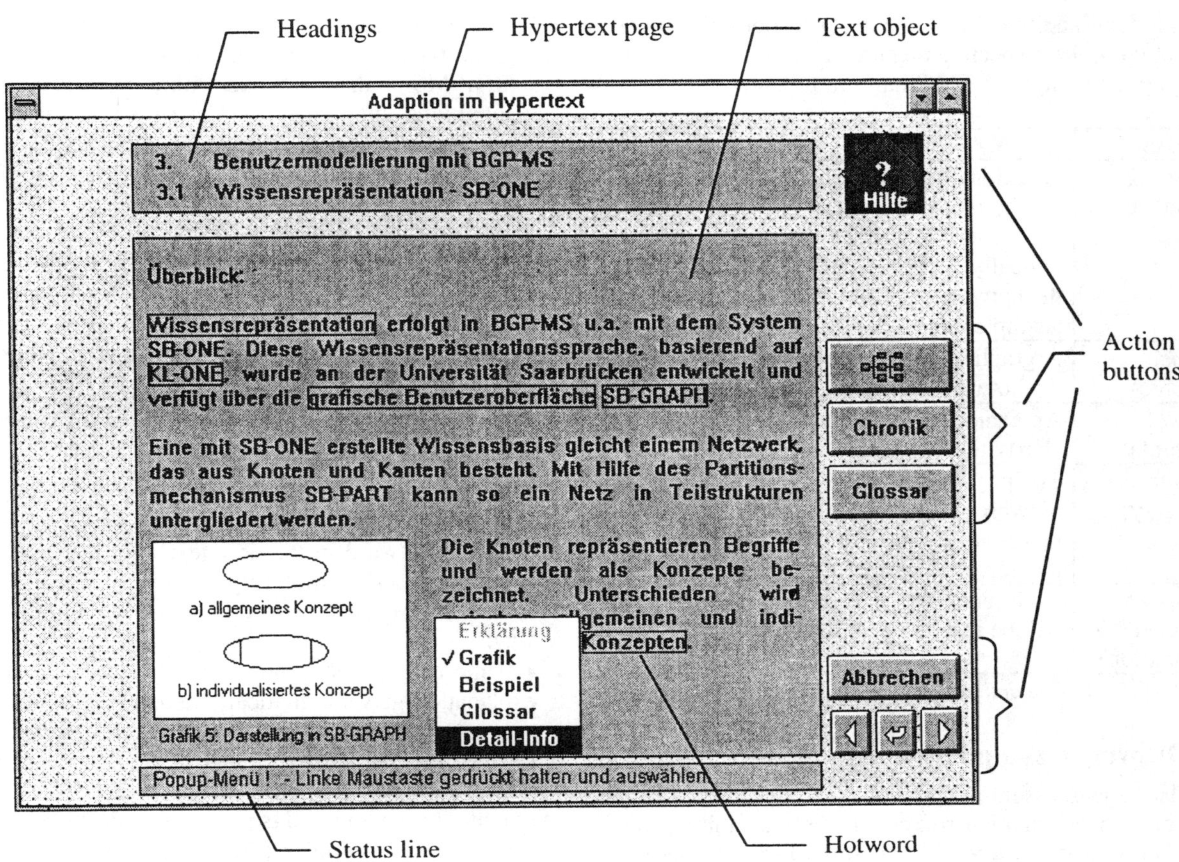

Fig. 4: Selecting additional information on a hotword

after consulting BGP-MS on the presumable conceptual knowledge of the user. Finally, the adaptive behavior of KN-AHS as well as its interaction with BGP-MS will be illustrated by an example of a possible user dialog.

3.1 The user interface

Fig. 4 shows an example of the user interface of KN-AHS. Special attention was paid to awakening interest and curiosity, and to stimulate users to navigate through the hypertext. It was also important that the interface should be largely self-explanatory. Users should be able to correctly predict the outcome of each possible action. This is especially important if assumptions about their knowledge are formed on the basis of their actions.

In a simplified form, the hyperdocument can be divided into four areas:

- *Headings*: This box informs the users of their whereabouts (i.e., the current chapter).
- *Text object*: This area is the core of the hypertext page. The reader can receive information in the form of text and graphics (if the text object is longer than a screen page, then a vertical scroll bar will be automatically inserted). So-called 'hotwords' can be found within this area, i.e. mouse-sensitive text passages such as the boxed text elements 'Wissensrepräsentation' (knowledge representation), 'KL-ONE', 'Konzepten' (concepts) etc. in Fig. 4. The actions that the user can perform on these hotwords will be described further below.
- *Status line*: The status line is found on the lower screen edge below the text object. It offers the user additional information about possible actions for each hotword.
- *Action buttons*: These are found on the right side of the screen. Starting here, the user can "jump" to other areas within the hypertext, for example (from top to bottom)
  - to a context-sensitive help text,
  - to a graphically represented table of contents,
  - to the dialog history, which includes a list of the already-viewed text objects to which the user can return on demand,
  - to the glossary, which is context-independent.

Other buttons are also available that enable the reader to jump to a previous or following page, as well as to the front-runner page of the one depicted on the screen.

When the user moves the mouse cursor across a hotword, the form of the mouse cursor indicates the available actions for the hotword. The user may (a) jump to another text object that provides detailed information on the hotword; or (b) request additional information with a pop-up menu, namely an explanation, a graphic, an example, a glossary definition, or additional details. Table 1 lists in greater detail the additional information that is available in KN-AHS via this pop-up menu. An example can be found in Fig. 4, where the user clicked on the hotword 'Konzepten'.

Some kinds of additional information may not be available for a hotword; the respective menu entries then turn to grey in the pop-up menu (like 'Erklärung' in Fig. 4).

Menu entry	Effect
Erklärung (Explanation)	Additional information which explains the hotword *in context* will be inserted near the hotword to ensure a terminologically supportive effect. In some cases the hotword may also become replaced by a simpler term or expression.
Grafik (Graphic)	A graphic appears which should illustrate the hotword.
Beispiel (Example)	An example will be displayed that should clarify the hotword.
Glossar (Glossary)	The page of the glossary that contains the hotword will be displayed. A context-independent definition or description of the hotword can be found there.
Detail-Info (Detailed information)	Additional details related to the hotword will be inserted near the hotword.

Table 1: Effects of the options in the hotword pop-up menu.

3.2 Drawing assumptions about the user

KN-AHS draws assumptions about the user's knowledge based on two information sources: namely an initial interview, and some of the hypertext actions which the user may perform.

In the initial interview, questions are posed to the user that refer to his membership in clearly separable user subgroups (like 'computer science student'), and his exposure to PCs, hypertexts, etc. The user's replies become communicated to BGP-MS, which can activate initial stereotypes for the user (see Section 2.3). If the user decides to skip this interview, BGP-MS will only activate the 'any person' stereotype.

Certain actions that the user may perform afterwards in the hypertext give rise to assumptions about his familiarity with individual concepts:

- If the user requests an explanation, a graphic, an example or a glossary definition for a hotword, then he is assumed to be unfamiliar with this hotword.
- If the user unselects an explanation, a graphic, an example or a glossary definition for a hotword, then he is assumed to be familiar with this hotword.
- If the user requests additional details for a hotword, then he is assumed to be familiar with this hotword.

With each hotword for which more information can be requested, the corresponding SB-ONE concept that represents this technical term in BGP-MS is associated. When KN-AHS draws an assumption about the user's familiarity with a hotword, KN-AHS notifies BGP-MS that the corresponding concept is known or unknown to the user. An example can be found in Fig. 1, in which KN-AHS informs BGP-MS that the user is familiar with the concept 'CONCEPT' after it made the assumption that the user is familiar with the hotword 'Konzepten'.

BGP-MS is also equipped with a component that draws assumptions about the user based on the user's actions [Pohl et al. 1994]. Instead of drawing assumptions itself and communicating them to BGP-MS, KN-AHS could therefore also inform BGP-MS about the actions that the user performed, and let BGP-MS draw the assumptions. However, since the concept names in BGP-MS must be anyway known to KN-AHS in order that it can ask BGP-MS about the user's familiarity with them (see Section 3.3), this option was not chosen in order to avoid redundancy.

3.3 Adapting the document based on the user's conceptual knowledge

When the user switches to a new text object, KN-AHS aims at adapting it to the user's presumed conceptual knowledge. For each hotword in the new text object, it asks BGP-MS about the user's familiarity with the corresponding SB-ONE concept. The hotword is then treated in the following way:

- If the user is unfamiliar with the associated concept, an explanation gets automatically added to the hotword. (The very same adaptation would take place if the user had selected the 'explanation' entry in the pop-up menu for this hotword). Also, an icon that symbolizes an available graphic for the hotword is placed near the hotword.
- If the user is familiar with the hotword, more details are automatically added after the hotword.
- If no information is available from BGP-MS concerning the user's familiarity with the hotword, then the hotword is not changed.

Possibly icons that signal the availability of examples and glossary information may be added in the future for hotwords that are unknown to the user. However, this may raise the danger of the hypertext becoming visually overloaded on the terminal screen.

3.4 An example of an adaptation step

In this section we present an example that shows how adaptation in hypertext can be performed based on reader actions. We will specifically concentrate on the interplay between hypertext components and the user modeling system.

The user in Fig. 4 would like to learn more about the hotword 'Konzept' and asks for 'Detail-Info' (detailed information). The displayed screen page will be expanded and the desired information will be shown. Because of this user action, the hypertext application reports to BGP-MS that the user is familiar with the associated concept 'CONCEPT' (see Section 2.4). BGP-MS enters the term in the partition SBUB, carries out inferences in the knowledge base and starts the stereotype mechanism in pre-set intervals (see section 2.3).

Fig. 5 shows another text object that the reader could possibly encounter later in the hypertext session. It is interesting to note that detailed information for the hotword

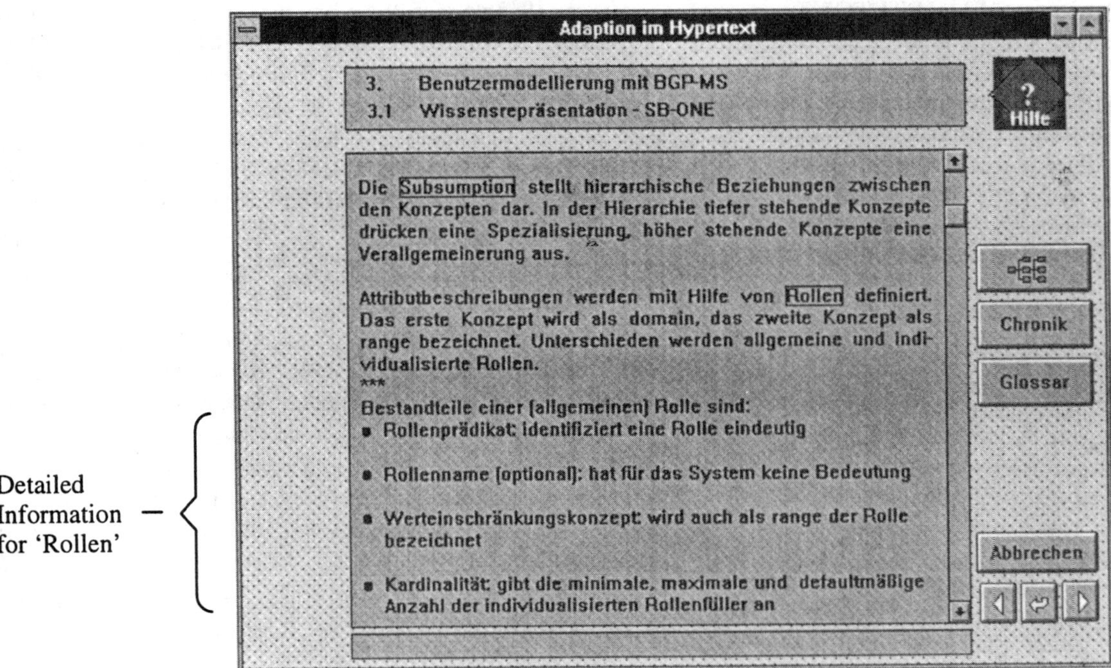

Fig. 5: Automatic addition of detailed information for the hotword 'Rolle'

'Rollen' is already provided, even though the user did not explicitly request more information.

How did that happen? Before switching pages the hypertext system asked BGP-MS whether or not the user was familiar with the expandable hotwords shown on the newly requested page. BGP-MS checked the individual user model and informed the hypertext application[7]. The concept 'ROLE' was reported as known (i.e., included in SBUB), and the hotword 'Rollen' was therefore automatically supplemented by detailed information. One reason why the concept 'ROLE' is contained in SBUB could be that rule b1 in section 2.5 fired after the concept 'CONCEPT' was entered in this partition.

4. Discussion and related work

The aim of this work was to demonstrate the feasibility of user modeling with BGP-MS in a "normal" hardware and software environment that is frequently used in the workplace. The basic architecture that we described -- application and user modeling system are independent processes that communicate via inter-process communication -- is quite unique. Only Orwant [1994] proposes a related framework (which is located on the level of a computer network however).

Some work already exists in the area of adaptive hypertext documents. The system that seems most closely related to KN-AHS is MetaDoc [Boyle & Encarnacion 1993]. It is also PC based and uses adaptation techniques that are similar to those in KN-AHS. Both its hypertext and its user-modeling component are "self-made". In comparison to MetaDoc, KN-AHS clearly profits from the greater expressiveness of the BGP-MS user modeling shell, which allows for the representation of hierarchically structured knowledge domains (instead of MetaDoc's flat "concept islands"), for inferences based on this hierarchy of knowledge domains, for more complex stereotype hierarchies than those of MetaDoc, and for more flexible stereotype activation rules. The adaptive range of KN-AHS goes somewhat beyond MetaDoc in that also graphics (and in the future possibly examples) become automatically included in the hypertext. A minor but noteworthy difference is that KN-AHS will only adapt the hypertext when the user switches to a *new* text object; it will never change a hotword in the current text as a result of an action that the user performed on a different hotword in the current text object since this seems to violate the constancy principle of software ergonomics.

Other related systems are ANATOM-TUTOR [Beaumont 1994] and ΥπADAPTερ [Böcker et al. 1990], which present hypertext-based tutorials on anatomy and Common Lisp, respectively. Both systems use self-made hypertext components. ANATOM-TUTOR contains a self-made user modeling component, while ΥπADAPTερ employs the MODUS user modeling shell [Schwab 1989], which is functionally included. Both systems are active tutorial systems and not only hypertext browsers like KN-AHS. They therefore have additional adaptive characteristics (e.g., ΥπADAPTερ exploits the user model for topic selection and presentation) and additional sources of information

---

[7] Possible answers are 'known' or 'unknown' (if the corresponding concept is included in SBUB or SB¬UB) as well as 'no statement possible' (if neither is the case).

about the user (e.g., ANATOM-TUTOR receives information about the user through a quiz). The adaptation of hypertext contents consists in adding or omitting information based on the assumptions about the user's knowledge (and also the user's preferences and learner type in the case of ϒπADAPTερ).

5. Hardware and Software Environment

KN-AHS has been implemented under MS-DOS 6.2 and MS WINDOWS 3.1 on a PC platform. TOOLBOOK 1.5, a popular hypertext shell system from Asymetrix Corporation has been used to construct the hypertext. The BGP-MS user modeling shell was developed (and will be further enhanced) in Common Lisp on SUN workstations. The relevant parts were ported to Golden Common Lisp 4.3, which also runs under MS WINDOWS.

The communication between the hypertext system and BGP-MS was realized using the inter-process communication system KN-IPCMS[8]. The current PC version exploits the DDE functionality[9] that is also supported by TOOLBOOK and Golden Common Lisp. KN-IPCMS is a platform-independent message-oriented communication protocol that allows both for synchronous and for asynchronous communication. In the interaction between KN-AHS and BGP-MS, observations made by KN-AHS will be transferred asynchronously. This means that KN-AHS and BGP-MS run concurrently, i.e. the user model management will largely be performed while the user is reading the current text object. Questions posed to BGP-MS will however be handled synchronously and will have priority over incoming observations.

References

Asymetrix Corporation 1989. *Using TOOLBOOK®: A Guide to Building and Working with Books (Version 1.5).* Washington.

Beaumont, I. 1994. User Modelling in the Interactive Anatomy Tutoring System ANATOM-TUTOR. *User Modeling and User-Adapted Interaction.* In press.

Boyle, C., and Encarnacion, A. O. 1993. An Adaptive Hypertext Reading System. *User Modeling and User-Adapted Interaction.* In press.

Böcker, H.-D.; Hohl, H. and Schwab, Th. 1990. *ϒπADAPTερ: Individualizing Hypertext.* In: D. Diaper et al., eds.: Human-Computer Interaction - INTERACT '90. North-Holland, Amsterdam, The Netherlands.

[8] KN-IPCMS stands for KoNstanz InterProcess Communication Management System.

[9] DDE (Dynamic Data Exchange) is a communication protocol under MS WINDOWS that defines how WINDOWS applications can exchange messages and data, and helps application programs communicate with one another, as long as they can support DDE as well.

Hanson, S. J.; Kraut, R.E.; and Farber, J.M. 1984. Interface Design and Multivariate Analysis of UNIX command use. *ACM Transactions on Office Information Systems* 2(1):42-57.

Kaplan, C.; Fenwick, J.; Chen, J. 1993. Adaptive Hypertext Navigation Based on User Goals and Context. *User Modeling and User-Adapted Interaction* 3(3):193-220.

Kobsa, A. 1990. Modeling the User's Conceptual Knowledge in BGP-MS, a User Modeling Shell System. *Computational Intelligence* 6:193-208.

Kobsa, A. 1991. *Utilizing Knowledge: The Components of the SB-ONE Knowledge Representation Workbench.* In: J. Sowa, ed.: Principles of Semantic Networks: Exploration in the Representation of Knowledge. San Mateo, CA: Morgan Kaufmann.

Kobsa, A., and Pohl, W. 1994: The User Modeling Shell BGP-MS. *User Modeling and User-Adapted Interaction.* Submitted.

Kuhlen, R. 1991. *Hypertext. Ein nicht-lineares Medium zwischen Buch und Wissensbank.* Berlin: Springer.

Orwant, J. 1994. Heterogenous Learning in the Doppelgänger User Modeling System. *User Modeling and User-Adapted Interaction.* Submitted.

Pohl, W.; Kobsa, A.; and Kutter, O. 1994. User Model Acquisition Heuristics Based on Dialog Acts. WIS Report 6, Dept. of Information Sc., Univ. of Konstanz, Germany.

Profitlich, H. J. 1989. SB-ONE: Ein Wissensrepräsentationssystem basierend auf KL-ONE. Master Thesis, Dept. of Computer Science, Univ. of Saarbrücken, Germany.

Scherer, J. 1990. SB-PART: Ein Partitionsmechanismus für die Wissensrepräsentationssprache SB-ONE. Master Th., Dept. of Comp. Sc., Univ. of Saarbrücken, Germany.

Schwab, T. (1989): Methoden zur Dialog- und Benutzermodellierung in Adaptiven Computersystemen. Ph.D. Thesis, Dept. of Comp. Sc., Univ. of Stuttgart, Germany.

Seyer, P.C. 1991. *Understanding Hypertext: Concepts and Applications.* Blue Ridge Summit, PA: Windcrest Books.

Shneiderman, B.; Kearsley, G. 1989. *Hypertext hands-on! An Introduction to a New Way of Organizing and Accessing Information.* Reading, MA: Addison-Wesley.

Sutcliffe, A. G., and Old, A. C. 1987. Do Users Know They Have User Models? Some Experiences in the Practise of User Modeling. In: H.-J. Bullinger and B. Shackel, ed.: Human-Computer Interaction: INTERACT'87. North-Holland, Amsterdam, The Netherlands.

KN-AHS: An Adaptive Hypertext Client of the User Modeling System BGP-MS

Alfred Kobsa, Dietmar Müller and Andreas Nill

At the time of its publication in 1994, this paper was original for two reasons:

1. It advocated the separation of user modeling systems and application systems and presented BGP-MS, a concrete implementation of a dedicated user modeling process on a widely used hardware platform that operates concurrently with application systems.
2. It demonstrated the usefulness of BGP-MS in a then fairly novel type of user-adaptive application, namely, a hypertext system with dynamic content adaptation, KN-AHS.

Independent user modeling systems and user-adaptive hypertext systems have both progressed considerably since this time. BGP-MS (BGP) has meanwhile become a networkwide user modeling server that is accessible via TCP/IP (Fink et al. 1997; Pohl and Höhle 1997). The proprietary interprocess communication described in our paper has been replaced by KQML (Finin et al. 1994). Security and privacy mechanisms are currently being added. Another user modeling server that has meanwhile been developed for the Internet is described in (Orwant 1995). First standardization efforts have recently been started (Kobsa).

Adaptive hypertext and hypermedia has meanwhile become a full-fledged research area (Brusilovsky 1996; Brusilovsky et al. 1998). More than 20 systems have been developed, and two adaptive WWW courses are already used in academic syllabi. Some empirical evidence already shows that adaptive navigation support in hypermedia systems is indeed useful, particularly in educational contexts (Brusilovsky and Pesin 1995; Specht 1997; Weber and Specht 1997). For *content* adaptation as performed in KN-AHS, this still remains to be shown. Our own attempts to replicate the positive experimental results in (Boyle and Encarnacion 1994) using a derivative of KN-AHS in the area of gymnastics exercises for the spine have remained largely unsuccessful (Höferlin 1995; Mast 1995).

REFERENCES

BGP-MS home page. (includes software). (*http://zeus.gmd.de/hci/projects/bgp-ms/*)

Boyle, C., and Encarnacion, A. O. 1994. Meta Doc: An Adaptive Hypertext Reading System. *User Modeling and User-Adapted Interaction* 4(1): 1–19.

Brusilovsky, P. 1996. Methods and Techniques of Adaptive Hypermedia. *User Modeling and User-Adapted Interaction* 6(2–3): 87–129.

Brusilovsky, P.; Kobsa, A.; and Vassileva, J. (1998). *Adaptive Hypertext and Hypermedia Systems*. Dordrecht, Netherlands: Wolters Kluwer.

Brusilovsky, P., and Pesin, L. 1995. Visual Annotation of Links in Adaptive Hypermedia. In *CHI'95 Conference Companion*, Denver, CO, 222–223.

Finin, T.; Fritzson, R.; McKay, D.; and McEntire, R. 1994. KQML as an Agent Communication Language. In *Third International Conference on Knowledge and Information Management*, 456–463. New York: ACM Press.

Fink, J.; Kobsa, A.; and Schreck, J. 1997. Personalized Hypermedia Information through Adaptive and Adaptable System Features: User Modeling, Privacy, and Security Issues. In Mullery, A., Besson, M., Campolargo, M., Gobbi, R., and Reed, R. (eds.), *Intelligence in Services and Networks: Technology for Cooperative Competition*, 459–467. Berlin-Heidelberg: Springer-Verlag. (*http://zeus.gmd.de/~kobsa/papers/1997-IS&N'97-kobsa.ps*)

Höferlin, G. 1995. KN-AHS: Empirische Untersuchung des Adaptiven Hypertextsystems. Master's thesis, Dept. of Information Science, University of Konstanz, Germany.

Kaplan, C.; Fenwick, J.; Chen, J. 1993. Adaptive Hypertext Navigation on User Goals and Context. *User Modeling and User-Adapted Interaction* 3: 193–220.

Kobsa, A. A Standard for the Performatives in the Communication between Applications and User Modeling Systems. (*http://zeus.gmd.de/~kobsa/rfc.ps*)

Mast, R. 1995. KN-AHS: Konzeption und Realisierung eines Adaptiven Hypertextsystems. Master's thesis, Dept. of Information Science, University of Konstanz, Germany.

Orwant, J. 1995. Heterogeneous Learning in the Doppelgänger User Modeling System. *User Modeling and User-Adapted Interaction* 4(2): 107–130.

Pohl, W., and Höhle, J. 1997. Mechanisms for Flexible Representation and Use of Knowledge in User Modeling Shell Systems. In Jameson, A., Paris, C., and Tasso, C. (eds.), *User Modeling: Proceedings of the Sixth International Conference 1997*, 403–414. Vienna: Springer.

Specht, M. 1997. Adaptive Methoden in Computerbasierten Lehr/Lernsystemen. Ph.D. thesis, Dept. of Psychology, University of Trier, Germany.

Weber, G., and Specht, M. 1997. User Modeling and Adaptive Navigation Support in WWW-Based Tutoring Systems. In Jameson, A., Paris, C., and Tasso, C. (eds.), *User Modeling: Proceedings of the Sixth International Conference,* 289–300. Vienna: Springer.

Planning Text for Advisory Dialogues: Capturing Intentional and Rhetorical Information

Johanna D. Moore*
University of Pittsburgh

Cécile L. Paris†
USC/Information Sciences Institute

To participate in a dialogue a system must be capable of reasoning about its own previous utterances. Follow-up questions must be interpreted in the context of the ongoing conversation, and the system's previous contributions form part of this context. Furthermore, if a system is to be able to clarify misunderstood explanations or to elaborate on prior explanations, it must understand what it has conveyed in prior explanations. Previous approaches to generating multisentential texts have relied solely on rhetorical structuring techniques. In this paper, we argue that, to handle explanation dialogues successfully, a discourse model must include information about the intended effect of individual parts of the text on the hearer, as well as how the parts relate to one another rhetorically. We present a text planner that records this information and show how the resulting structure is used to respond appropriately to a follow-up question.

1. Introduction

Explanation systems must produce multisentential texts, including justifications of their actions, descriptions of their problem-solving strategies, and definitions of the terms they use. Previous research in natural language generation has shown that schemata of rhetorical predicates (McKeown 1985; McCoy 1989; Paris 1988) or rhetorical relations (Hovy 1991) can be used to capture the structure of coherent multisentential texts. Schemata are scriptlike entities that encode standard patterns of discourse structure. Associating a schema with a communicative goal allows a system to generate a text that achieves the goal. However, we have found that schemata are insufficient as a discourse model for advisory dialogues. Although they encode standard patterns of discourse structure, schemata do not include a representation of the intended effects of the components of a schema, nor how these intentions are related to one another or to the rhetorical structure of the text. While this may not present a problem for systems that generate one-shot explanations, it is a serious limitation in a system intended to participate in a dialogue where users can, and frequently do, ask follow-up questions.

In this paper, we argue that to participate in explanation dialogues successfully, a generation system must represent and reason about the intended effect of individual parts of the text on the hearer, as well as how the parts relate to one another rhetorically. We present a text planner that constructs explanations based on the intentions of the speaker at each step and that notes the rhetorical relation that holds between each pair of text spans. By recording the planning process behind the system's utterances as well as the user's utterances in a dialogue history, our system is able to reason about its previous utterances both to interpret and to answer users' follow-up questions. We describe the plan language employed and the plan structure built by our system and provide an example of how this structure is used in responding appropriately to a follow-up question. Additional examples appear in Moore and Swartout (1989) and Moore (in press).

2. Motivation: A Naturally Occurring Advisory Dialogue

When we began our work on interactive explanations, we gathered samples of naturally occurring dialogues from several sources: transcripts of electronic dialogues between system users and operators collected by Robinson (1984), protocols of programmers interacting with a mock program enhancement advisor, and tape recordings of office-hour interactions between first-year computer science students and teaching assistants. A portion of a dialogue extracted from the office-hour interactions appears in Figure 1.

In this dialogue, a student and a teaching assistant are discussing a programming assignment that involves writing a procedure to swap the values stored at two locations in the C programming language. The student is confused about how to write the procedure because he does not understand that C is a call-by-value language, and so he must pass the addresses of the two variables to be swapped. In the teacher's response in turn 8, she explains that in C one cannot change the value of a variable defined outside of a procedure. She justifies this by saying that C is call-by-value and then goes on to define this term. The student then asks "What's call-by-value?" (turn 9). To respond appropriately to this question, the teacher must realize that she has defined call-by-value in abstract terms as part of her previous explanation and that her first attempt was not fully understood. In this dialogue, the instructor recovers from this failure by giving a very specific example of how call-by-value works (turn 10). The teacher explains call-by-value differently the second time because she realizes that she has tried to explain this once before, and that the strategy she used the first time was not sufficient.

Note that giving a very general description of a concept is a good first strategy. General definitions are an efficient way to convey knowledge because if the hearer understands a general definition, it covers a wide range of cases. Giving example(s) first would be a bad approach because this strategy requires the hearer to form the correct generalization from the example(s). Unless the examples are numerous enough and well chosen, this may be difficult to achieve (Klausmeier 1976). However, when a general description is not understood by itself, examples provide effective elaboration and may help the hearer assimilate the general description (Charney, Reder, and Wells 1988). In the sample dialogue, because the teacher knows that she has already given a general description in turn 8, she can give a very specific example in turn 10.

Another characteristic of advisory dialogues is exemplified in this sample. Advice-seekers often ask questions such as "Why?" and "How come?". To interpret such questions, the system must have a representation of what it has said just prior to the query, so that it can determine what the user could be asking about.

3. Limitations of Previous Approaches

There are two main approaches to text generation. In attempting to construct a system capable of participating in dialogues like the one above, we found that neither approach could be directly applied to this task. Here we describe the limitations of these approaches for our purposes.

* Department of Computer Science and Learning Research and Development Center, University of Pittsburgh, Pittsburgh, PA 15260. E-mail: jmoore@cs.pitt.edu
† USC/Information Sciences Institute, 4676 Admiralty Way, Marina del Rey, CA 90292-6695. E-mail: paris@isi.edu

STUDENT I can't figure out how to write the SWAP procedure in C. [1]

TEACHER You write a procedure called SWAP that takes the addresses of the two variables to be swapped as its arguments. [2]

STUDENT I did that. [3]

⋮

[Student shows teacher his program code.]

⋮

TEACHER Here [points to call to SWAP in the main program], when you call SWAP, you have to pass the *addresses* of the variables you want swapped. [4]

STUDENT Why? [5]

TEACHER Because otherwise the procedure just swaps its local copies of the arguments. [6]

STUDENT How come? [7]

TEACHER You cannot change the value of a variable defined outside a procedure unless you pass its address. This is because C is call-by-value. That means that when you pass an argument to a procedure in C, the procedure makes a copy of the argument, and does its work on that copy. The value of the variable passed in as an argument remains unchanged. [8]

STUDENT What's call-by-value? [9]

TEACHER OK, suppose in our main program we have a variable V with value 3, and a procedure called PLUS-ONE that takes one argument, call it A. Now when we call PLUS-ONE(V) what actually happens is that the value of V, which is 3, is copied to A. So A equals 3 and our procedure adds 1 to A, so A now equals 4. The original variable V that appeared in the call to PLUS-ONE does not change. V still equals 3. [10]

STUDENT So, how can I ever write a procedure that swaps two values? [11]

TEACHER You write a procedure that takes addresses of variables as its arguments. When you call it, you pass the pointers to the variables to be swapped. So you write SWAP(&X,&Y). The & sign means take the address of the variable. When you say &X, the address of X is copied to a temporary variable, and SWAP uses the temporary copy of the address. But the address always points to the same place, namely the location where X is held. So SWAP will operate on X, using a copy of X's address, rather than operating on a copy of X. [12]

STUDENT Oh, okay. [13]

Figure 1
Portion of a naturally occurring advisory dialogue.

3.1 Planning with Speech Acts

Work by Cohen and Perrault (1979), Appelt (1985), and Cohen and Levesque (1990) demonstrated that planning techniques could be useful in text generation. These researchers provide a formal axiomatization of illocutionary actions that may be used to reason about the beliefs of the hearer and speaker and the effects of surface speech acts on these beliefs. To use this approach in a generation process, the system first generates hypotheses about what combinations of actions to perform. For efficiency, Appelt (1985) uses simplified versions of the axioms (called **action summaries**) encoded in NOAH-style plan operators (Sacerdoti 1977) to generate these hypotheses. Theorem-proving is then used to determine if a series of proposed actions will have the desired effect on the hearer's mental state. The systems that have been built within this framework to date (Cohen 1978; Appelt 1985) plan short (one- or two-sentence) texts to achieve the speakers' goal(s).

In this approach, the **intentional structure** describing the speaker's purposes and the relationships between them (Grosz and Sidner 1986) is explicitly represented. However, this approach does not represent or use rhetorical knowledge about how speech acts may be combined into larger bodies of coherent text to achieve a speaker's goals. It assumes that appropriate axioms could be added to generate longer texts, and that the text produced will be coherent as a byproduct of the planning process. However, this has not been demonstrated.

Moreover, we believe that building a system to produce multisentential texts directly from the logics proposed by proponents of this approach would prove to be computationally infeasible. We see two problems. First, this approach requires the system to acquire and maintain a correct, detailed model of the hearer's beliefs. Sparck Jones (1989) has questioned not only the feasibility of acquiring such a model, but also of verifying its correctness, and the tractability of utilizing such a model to affect a system's reasoning and the generation of responses. Second, all of the formal axiomatizations espoused by proponents of this approach are based on extensions to first-order logic. In the general case, theorem-proving in first-order logic is undecidable. To be fair, some proponents of this approach, e.g. Cohen and Levesque (1990), claim to provide a specification *of* an agent, and do not claim that the axiomatization should be used directly as a specification *for* the implementation of an agent. Heuristics are clearly needed in order to make an implementation based on such a formalism tractable. Our approach employs rhetorical strategies as compiled knowledge about what actions may be used to satisfy certain intentions. In fact, our operators have much in common with Appelt's action summaries.

3.2 The Schema-Based Approach

To produce the longer bodies of text required for advisory dialogues in an efficient manner, other researchers turned to an approach that makes use of script-like structures, **schemata**, to generate coherent multisentential texts achieving a given communicative goal. Schemata, originally proposed by McKeown (1985), represent standard patterns of discourse structure by encoding the set of communicative techniques that a speaker can use for a particular discourse purpose. Schemata are made up of **rhetorical predicates** that characterize the means that speakers use to achieve their goals and delineate the structural relations between propositions in a text. Linguists, e.g., (Shepherd 1926; Grimes 1975), found that rhetorical predicates tend to occur in certain combinations, and McKeown further observed that certain combinations are more appropriate than others depending on the discourse purpose. For example, she found that speakers frequently describe objects by:

1. Identifying the object as a member of some generic class and giving attributive or functional information about the object.
2. Providing analogical, constituent, or additional attributive information about the object.
3. Providing examples of the object.

To encode these standard patterns of discourse structure, McKeown devised several schemata that represent combinations of rhetorical predicates. For example, the above pattern is embodied in the IDENTIFICATION **schema**, shown in Figure 2. By associating each rhetorical predicate with an access function for an underlying knowledge base,

Identification Schema[1]

Identification (class & attributive/function)
{Analogy/Constituency/Attributive/Renaming/Amplification}*
Particular-illustration/Evidence+
{Amplification/Analogy/Attributive}
{Particular-illustration/Evidence}

Sample Definition Generated using Identification Schema:

(1) A ship is a water-going vehicle that travels on the surface. (2) Its surface-going capabilities are provided by the DB attributes DISPLACEMENT and DRAFT. (3) Other DB attributes of the ship include MAXIMUM_SPEED, PROPULSION, FUEL (FUEL_CAPACITY and FUEL_TYPE), DIMENSIONS, SPEED_DEPENDENT_RANGE and OFFICIAL_NAME. (4) The DOWNES, for example, has MAXIMUM_SPEED of 29, PROPULSION of STMTURGRD, FUEL of 810 (FUEL_CAPACITY) and BNKR (FUEL_TYPE), DIMENSIONS of 25 (DRAFT), 46 (BEAM), and 438 (LENGTH) and SPEED_DEPENDENT_RANGE of 4200 (ECONOMIC_RANGE) and 2200 (ENDURANCE_RANGE).

Figure 2
TEXT identification schema and sample generated text (from McKeown [1985], pp. 210–212).

these schemata can be used to guide both the selection of content and its organization into a coherent text. Figure 2 also shows a sample text generated from a knowledge base of naval concepts using the IDENTIFICATION schema. McKeown identified four schemata, each of which could be used to achieve one or more discourse purposes.

As shown in Figure 2, schemata contain many options and alternatives. To instantiate a schema, its components are filled in sequentially by using the access functions to search the underlying knowledge base for information that satisfies the rhetorical predicates. In McKeown's theory, each entry in the schema can be filled by an instantiated predicate or a full schema of the same name. So, for example, in the IDENTIFICATION schema, the first entry can either be satisfied by an instance of the IDENTIFICATION predicate, or a recursive instantiation of the IDENTIFICATION schema itself.

McKeown found that schemata alone were not sufficient to constrain the generation process. To overcome this, when a schema indicates that more than one choice is possible, McKeown's system appeals to constraints on the shift of focus of attention (Sidner 1979). These constraints guide the selection of the information that fits in best with the previous discourse. Since McKeown's seminal work, many other researchers have used schemata as the basis for producing multisentential texts. In many cases, these researchers found that schemata provided only a partial solution, and they have identified additional factors that control the generation process: Paris (1988) uses information about the user's knowledge of domain concepts to tailor descriptions of complex physical objects to a particular user; McCoy (1989) uses object perspectives and a user model to provide corrective responses to users' misconceptions about objects; and Hovy (1988) uses pragmatic and stylistic information to produce different accounts of the same incident.

1 The "{}" indicate optionality, "/" indicates alternative, "+" indicates that the item may appear one or more times, and "*" indicates that the item may appear zero or more times.

SYSTEM	What characteristics of the program would you like to enhance?	[1]
USER	Readability and maintainability.	[2]
SYSTEM	You should replace (SETQ X 1) with (SETF X 1). SETQ can only be used to assign a value to a simple-variable. In contrast, SETF can be used to assign a value to any generalized-variable. A generalized-variable is a storage location that can be named by any access function.	[3]

Figure 3
Partial dialogue.

3.2.1 Inadequacies of Schemata for Advisory Dialogue. Like others, we found that schemata were not sufficient to handle the issues we wished to investigate. When we attempted to use schemata for our purposes, two main problems arose. First, schemata lack an explicit representation of the intentional structure of the text being produced, and therefore are missing the information needed to recover from explanatory failures. Second, we found that schemata are too rigid to handle certain of the opportunistic phenomena we observed in naturally occurring dialogues. We discuss these two problems in more detail.

Lack of Intentional Structure. As we have seen, schemata encode standard patterns of discourse structure. However, they do not include an explicit representation of the effects that individual components of a schema are intended to have on the hearer, or of how these intentions relate to one another or to the rhetorical structure of the text. This presents a serious problem for a system that must participate in a dialogue where users can ask follow-up questions like the ones we saw in the sample dialogue of Figure 1. If a system does not keep a record of the intentions behind its utterances, it cannot determine what went wrong when the user indicates that an explanation was not completely understood, nor provide an alternative explanation to correct the problem.

To allow a system to handle follow-up questions that may arise if the user does not fully understand an explanation, a generation facility must be able to determine what portion of the text failed to achieve its intended purpose. If the generation system only knows the *top-level* communicative goal that was being achieved by the text (e.g., to make the hearer know a concept, or to make the hearer want to perform an action), and not what effect the individual parts of the text were intended to have on the hearer or how they fit together to achieve this top-level goal, its only recourse is to use a different strategy to achieve the top-level goal. It is not able to re-explain or clarify any *part* of the explanation.

We illustrate this important point by working through an example taken from an actual dialogue with a system called the Program Enhancement Advisor (PEA) (Neches, Swartout, and Moore 1985). (Note that, for precisely the reasons we describe in this paper, PEA does *not* employ schemata to generate its utterances. We describe PEA's text planner in Section 5.) As shown in Figure 3, PEA begins its interaction with the user by asking what characteristics of the user's program are to be enhanced and then suggests changes that will improve these aspects of the program. Now consider what a schema that could produce the system's utterance in turn 3 of the sample dialogue in Figure 3 would look like. One schema that would suffice, which we have called the *Recommend-Replacement Schema*, is shown instantiated in Figure 4.

System's Utterance

(1) You should replace (SETQ X 1) with (SETF X 1). (2) SETQ can only be used to assign a value to a simple-variable. (3) SETF can be used to assign a value to any generalized-variable. (4) A generalized-variable is a storage location that can be named by any access function.

Recommend-Replacement Schema (Instantiated)

(Recommendation (replace-setq-with-setf)) (1)
(Compare&Contrast-Attributive)
(Attributive SETQ use assign-value-to-simple-variable) (2)
(Attributive SETF use assign-value-to-generalized-variable) (3)
(Identification generalized-variable storage-location (4)
(restrictive named-by access-function))

Figure 4
Hypothetical schema representation of system's utterance.

This schema begins with a RECOMMENDATION of a replacement act, followed by a COMPARE & CONTRAST predicate that highlights the important difference(s) between the replacee and the replacer.[2] Instead of using a simple predicate, we instantiate the COMPARE & CONTRAST predicate using a schema that expands into two ATTRIBUTIVE predicates and an IDENTIFICATION predicate that defines a term introduced in the second ATTRIBUTIVE.

Note that this schema indicates *what* to do *when*, i.e., recommend the action and contrast the replacee with replacer, but it does not say *why* this information is being presented. For example, the schema does not indicate that, by contrasting SETQ with SETF, the speaker is trying to persuade the hearer to do the replace act. Nor does it indicate that the text produced by the IDENTIFICATION predicate appears because the speaker is trying to make the hearer know about the concept `generalized-variable`. In addition, the relationships between these intentions are not represented. To make clear what is missing, we have represented in Figure 5 the intentional structure of this text using Grosz and Sidner's (1986) notions of dominance and satisfaction-precedence. In Grosz and Sidner's theory (1986, p. 179), if an action that satisfies one intention, I_1, is intended to provide part of the satisfaction of another intention, I_2, then I_2 *dominates* I_1. I_1 *satisfaction-precedes* I_2 whenever I_1 must be satisfied before I_2. The representation shown in Figure 5 makes it clear that the expert system's (E) top-level intention (I_0) is to get the user (U) to intend to replace (SETQ X 1) with (SETF X 1), and this intention dominates E's intentions to recommend this act (I_1) and to persuade U to perform it (I_2). In addition, for this schema, the recommendation (I_1) must be satisfied before the persuade (I_2) is attempted.

A schema can be viewed as the result of a "compilation" process where the *rationale* for all of the steps in the process has been compiled out. What remains is the top-level communicative goal that invoked the schema (in this case something like *Get the user to adopt the goal of replacing* SETQ *with* SETF), and the sequence of actions (i.e. instantiated

2 The first step of the schema is to identify commonalities of the two entities being contrasted. In McKeown (1985), this step is optional if no commonalities exist. We have changed this definition slightly to render this step optional if the speaker believes these commonalities are known to the hearer. This is the case here, so the instantiated schema does not contain this step.

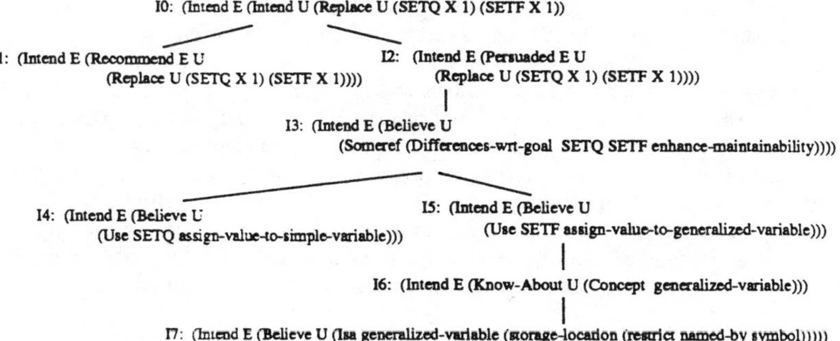

Figure 5
Intentional structure of system's utterance.

rhetorical predicates that cause sentences to be generated) that are used to achieve that goal. All of the intermediate structure shown in Figure 5 has been lost.[3]

Because of this compilation, schemata provide a computationally efficient way to produce multisentential texts for achieving discourse purposes. They are "recipes" of rhetorical actions that encode frequently occurring patterns of discourse structure. Using schemata, the system need not reason directly about how speech acts affect the beliefs of the hearer and speaker, nor about the effects of juxtaposing speech acts. The system is guaranteed that each schema will lead to a coherent text that achieves the specified discourse purpose.

However, this compilation is also a disadvantage. If the hearer does not understand the utterance produced by a schema, it is very difficult for the system to recover. In the example above, without understanding why the COMPARE & CONTRAST schema and IDENTIFICATION predicate are present in the instantiated structure, the system cannot determine how to proceed if the user does not immediately understand and accept the system's utterance. In the sample text under consideration, the COMPARE & CONTRAST occurs as part of the top-level schema in order to persuade the hearer to perform the recommended replacement action. This is represented in the intentional representation of Figure 5 by intentions I_2 and I_3 and the dominance relationship $dominates(I_2, I_3)$.

3 Note that the schema shown in Figure 4 would not be compiled directly from the structure shown in Figure 5. The schema would be compiled from an hierarchical text plan that included the intentions as well as the rhetorical methods and speech acts that are used to achieve the intentions. Figure 5 shows *only* the intentional structure.

If the text produced by the COMPARE & CONTRAST portion of the schema fails to persuade the hearer, the speaker should try other strategies for achieving this intention. For example, the speaker may paraphrase the reasoning that led to recommending this act, cite the advice of experts, or invoke authority. However, because information about intentions has been "compiled out" of the schema representation, the system cannot recover because it cannot determine which goal failed or what other linguistic strategies can be used to achieve the goal.

Note that the problem stems from the fact that, in general, there is not a one-to-one mapping from intentions to schemata or rhetorical predicates. For example, the COMPARE & CONTRAST schema can be used to persuade the hearer to perform a replacement action as in the example above, but it could also be used for several other purposes. This schema could be used to identify the differences between two objects so that the hearer can discriminate one from the other. It could also be used in a strategy where a new concept is defined by comparing it to a known concept. Thus, simply knowing that a COMPARE & CONTRAST schema (or predicate) appears in a text does not tell the system why that COMPARE & CONTRAST appears. As a result, if it fails to achieve its intended effect, the system cannot determine how to recover. To find alternative strategies, the system must know what goal it was trying to achieve!

Rigidity of Schemata. A second problem with schemata is that they are too rigid. In the naturally occurring dialogues we analyzed, we have often observed what appear to be opportunistic effects. One such effect we identified is the tendency of the explainer to define a concept immediately after mentioning that concept in the explanation. One possible reason for this is that the explainer only realizes that the hearer may not know that concept after a sentence including it has been planned or uttered. Recall that this occurred in the teacher–student dialogue in Figure 1 (turn 8). As another example, consider the following explanation given by a doctor when asked about the possible ways to treat migraine (italics indicate our present concern, not spoken emphasis).[4]

> Some of the possible ways that I approach migraine would be, depending on the frequency of your headaches, we would determine which approach I would recommend. [...] So, for example, say that you told me that you had three to four headaches [...] in the month, what I would recommend with that frequency is that you should be on something prophylactically. *Prophylactically basically means preventing the headache from occurring before it actually starts.* If you had infrequent headaches, maybe several times a year, [...] then I would recommend more something abortive. *That means that when the headache came on, I would treat you at that point.* I would rather, to help prevent side effects from you having to take a medicine on a daily basis, just try to abort them, if they were infrequent.

Because a new term can be introduced in virtually any statement, one could only handle this phenomenon in the schema-based approach by incorporating an optional IDENTIFICATION predicate for every term mentioned in the previous predicate after *every* entry in *every* schema. Note that this would be inefficient because if these predicates appear in the schema, the system must consider them (i.e., search for instantiations in the knowledge base and invoke the focusing mechanism) for *every* additional predicate added to the schema.[5] We believe that a more elegant and efficient approach is to use planning techniques that permit new goals to be posted as they arise and to be worked into an evolving text plan according to rules of discourse as represented in plan operators. The framework that we propose in this paper handles this type of opportunistic planning in a limited way. Suthers (1991) handles a wider array of opportunistic effects using data-driven plan critics to decide when additional information should be included.

3.3 Requirements for a Text Planner

Like others, e.g., Levy (1979) and Appelt (1985), we take the view that speakers have goals to affect the mental states of their hearers and must choose from among the linguistic resources available to them the ones that will satisfy these goal(s). We argued that an approach to text planning that attempts to reason directly about how speech acts can be combined into coherent multisentential texts to achieve a speaker's intentions is likely to be computationally infeasible. However, our discussion of schemata pointed out that we must be careful about what and how much is compiled out of our representations for the sake of efficiency. While we believe the schema-based approach to be correct in spirit, we think that too much information has been lost in schemata composed simply of rhetorical predicates.

Ideally, what we desire is an approach that:

- records enough information about the system's intentions and how those intentions were achieved, so that the system can reason about its own previous utterances to determine how to recover when its explanations are not understood, and
- is capable of producing texts in a computationally efficient manner.

To achieve these goals, we propose an approach to text planning in which plan operators encode knowledge about how intentions may be achieved via a set of techniques commonly found in natural discourse. Thus we require a plan language that links intentions to the rhetorical means for achieving them.

4. Linking Intentions and Rhetorical Structure

Two theories of discourse structure that make the connection between rhetorical relations and speaker intentions have been proposed: Hobbs' (1979, 1983, 1985) theory of coherence relations, and Mann and Thompson's (1988) Rhetorical Structure Theory. As we will see, Rhetorical Structure Theory can be adapted to a computational model in a fairly natural way, and in fact there is an implemented prototype of the theory (Hovy 1991). However, the straightforward operationalization that is used in this prototype suffers from a fundamental problem for our purposes. After discussing the two theories that link intention to rhetorical structure, we discuss this problem in detail. In Section 5, we describe how this problem may be solved and present a text planner that implements this solution.

4 This example is taken from transcripts gathered by Claudia Tapia and Johanna Moore at the University of Pittsburgh.

5 It is also unclear how we could represent this opportunistic strategy in the schema-based approach, since it is only when "unpacking" complex concepts such as `assign-value-to-generalized-variable` that the system recognizes that it will introduce the terms `assign`, `value` and `generalized-variable`. See Moore and Paris (1992) for more discussion about this topic.

4.1 Theoretical Background

Hobbs characterizes coherence in terms of a set of binary **coherence relations** between a current utterance and the preceding discourse. He identified four reasons why a speaker breaks a discourse into more than one clause and classified the relations accordingly. For example, if a speaker needs to connect new information with what is already known by the hearer, the speaker chooses one of the **linkage relations**, such as BACKGROUND or EXPLANATION. As another example, when a speaker wishes to move between specific and general statements, he or she must employ one of the **expansion relations**, such as ELABORATION or GENERALIZATION. According to Hobbs, how the speaker chooses to continue a discourse is equivalent to deciding which relation to employ. From the hearer's perspective, understanding why the speaker continued as he or she did is equivalent to determining what relation was used.

Hobbs originally proposed coherence relations as a way of solving some of the problems in interpreting discourse, e.g., anaphora resolution (Hobbs 1979). He defines coherence relations in terms of inferences that can be drawn from the propositions asserted in the items being related. For example, Hobbs (1985, p. 25) defines ELABORATION as follows:

> ELABORATION: S_1 is an ELABORATION of S_0 if the hearer can infer the same proposition P from the assertions of S_0 and S_1.

Here S_1 represents the current clause or larger segment of discourse, and S_0 an immediately preceding segment. S_1 usually adds crucial information, but this is not part of the definition, since Hobbs wishes to include pure repetitions under ELABORATION.

Hobbs' theory of coherence is attractive because it relates rhetorical relations to the functions that speakers wish to accomplish in a discourse. Thus, Hobbs' theory could potentially tell a text planner what kind of rhetorical relation should be used to achieve a particular goal of the speaker. For example, Hobbs (1979) notes two functions of ELABORATION. One is to overcome misunderstanding or lack of understanding, and another is to "enrich the understanding of the listener by expressing the same thought from a different perspective." However, note that such specifications of the speaker's intentions are not an explicit part of the formal definition of the relation. For this reason we have chosen an alternative theory of text structure, Rhetorical Structure Theory (RST) (Mann and Thompson 1988), as a basis for our text planning system.

In contrast to Hobbs' coherence relations, the definition of each **rhetorical relation** in RST indicates constraints on the two entities being related as well as constraints on their combination, *and a specification of the effect that the speaker is attempting to achieve on the hearer's beliefs or inclinations.* Thus RST provides an explicit connection between the speaker's intention and the rhetorical means used to achieve those intentions. As an example, consider the RST definition of the MOTIVATION relation shown in Figure 6. As shown, an RST relation has two parts: a **nucleus (N)** and a **satellite (S)**.[6] The MOTIVATION relation associates text expressing the speaker's desire that the hearer perform an action (the nucleus) with material intended to increase the hearer's desire to perform the action (the satellite). For example, in the text below, (1) and (2) are related by MOTIVATION:

> (1) Come to the party for the new President. (2) There will be lots of good food.

6 This is an oversimplification. In fact, there are a small number of RST relations, e.g., SEQUENCE and JOINT, that are **multinuclear** and can relate more than two pieces of text.

relation name: MOTIVATION
constraints on N: Presents an action (unrealized with respect to *N*) in which the Hearer is the actor.
constraints on S: none
constraints on N + S combination: Comprehending S increases the Hearer's desire to perform the action presented in N.
effect: The Hearer's desire to perform the action presented in N is increased.

Figure 6
RST relation—MOTIVATION.

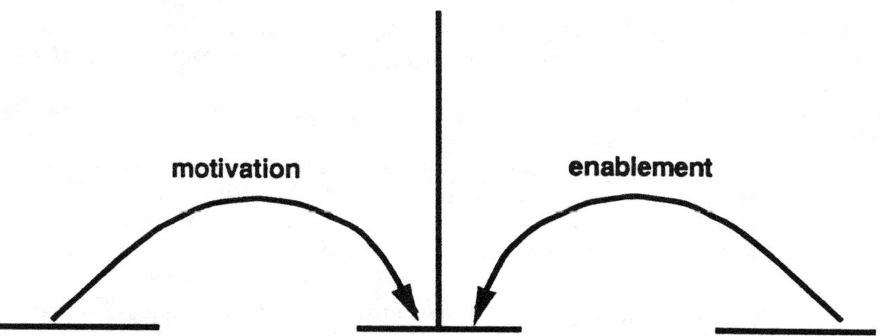

Figure 7
Graphical representation of an RST schema.

The nucleus of the relation is that item in the pair that is most essential to the writer's purpose. In the example above, assuming that the writer's intent is to make the hearer go to the party, clause (1) is nuclear. In general, the nucleus could stand on its own, but the satellite would be considered a non sequitur without its corresponding nucleus. In our example, without the recommendation to *come to the party* the satellite in (2) is out of place. Moreover, RST states that the satellite portion of a text may be replaced without significantly altering the intended function of the text. The same is not true for the nucleus. For example, replacing (2) above with:

> (2′) All the important people will be there.

does not greatly change the function of the text as a whole. However, replacing the recommendation in the nucleus, e.g.,

> (1′) Don't go to the party.

significantly alters the purpose of the text.

RST relations may be combined into **schemata** that define how a text can be broken down into smaller units. Each schema contains a nucleus and zero or more satellites related to the nucleus by one of the RST relations. RST schemata do not constrain the ordering of the nucleus and satellites, and relations may occur any number of times within a schema. Furthermore, the schemata are recursive; text serving as a satellite in one schema may itself consist of a nucleus and any number of satellites. A graphical depiction of one schema defined by Mann and Thompson (1988) appears in Figure 7. This schema consists of a nucleus and two satellites: one providing `MOTIVATION` for the material in the nucleus, and the other providing `ENABLEMENT` for the material in the nucleus.

4.2 Using RST in Text Generation

Although originally intended for generation, until recently RST was used primarily as a tool for analyzing texts in order to investigate various linguistic issues. The analyst breaks the text down into parts called **text spans** and then tries to find an RST relation that connects each pair of spans until all pairs are accounted for. To determine whether or not a relation holds between two spans of text, the analyst checks to see whether the constraints on the nucleus and satellite hold and whether it is plausible that the writer desires the condition specified in the Effect field. All of the text is given. One need only determine whether or not the constraints are satisfied.

Using RST in a constructive process, such as generating a response to a question, is a very different task. For example, in order to produce text that will succeed in getting the hearer to perform an action, a system must determine what (if any) information in its knowledge base could be used to increase the hearer's desire to perform the action (`MOTIVATION`), what information could be used to increase the hearer's ability to perform the action (`ENABLEMENT`), how much of this information to present, in what order, at what level of detail, etc. Moreover, the theory states that the nucleus and satellite portions of a text may occur in any order, relations may occur any number of times, and a nucleus or satellite may be expanded into a text employing any other relation at any point. In order to use RST, a text generation system must have control strategies that dictate how to find such knowledge in the knowledge base, when and what relations should occur, how many times, and in what order.

Mann (1984) suggested that goal pursuit methods used in artificial intelligence could be applied to RST for text generation. Schemata can be viewed as means for achieving the goals stated as their effects, and the constraints on relations as a kind of precondition to using a particular schema. However, much work must be done to formalize the constraints and effects of the RST relations and schemata in order to use RST in a text generation system.

One attempt at formalization was made by Hovy (1991), who operationalized a subset of the RST relation definitions for use as plan operators in a text structuring process. Hovy's structurer employs a top-down planning mechanism to order a given set of input elements into a coherent text. To form plan operators from RST relation definitions, Hovy maps the intended effect of the relation to the `Results` field of the corresponding operator. In Hovy's system, the contents of the `Results` field are viewed as the communicative goal(s) that may be achieved by using the associated relation, and the relation name as the rhetorical strategy that achieves the goal(s). The constraints on the nucleus, satellite, and their combination that are specified in the relation definition become subgoals in Hovy's operators. The relation name is also included in the plan operator (and in the evolving plan) so that appropriate connectives can be inserted in the final text.

Figure 8 shows the RST relation definition for the `CIRCUMSTANCE` relation, and Figure 9 shows Hovy's characterization of this relation as a plan operator. Note from this figure that Hovy's operator includes fields called **growth points**. These post optional subgoals, which will be expanded if information satisfying these goals appears in the

relation name: `CIRCUMSTANCE`
constraints on N: none
constraints on S: presents a situation (not unrealized)
constraints on N + S combination:
S sets a framework in the subject matter within which Hearer is intended to interpret the situation presented in N.
effect: The Hearer recognizes that the situation presented in S provides the framework for interpreting N.

Figure 8
RST relation—`CIRCUMSTANCE`.

Name: CIRCUMSTANCE
Results:
((BMB SPEAKER HEARER (CIRCUMSTANCE-OF ?X ?CIRC)))
Nucleus + Satellite requirements/subgoals:
((OR (BMB SPEAKER HEARER (HEADING.R ?X ?CIRC))
(BMB SPEAKER HEARER (TIME.R ?X ?CIRC))))
Nucleus requirements/subgoals:
((BMB SPEAKER HEARER (TOPIC ?X)))
Nucleus growth points:
(BMB SPEAKER HEARER (ATTRIBUTE-OF ?X ?ATT))
Satellite requirements:
((BMB SPEAKER HEARER (TOPIC ?CIRC)))
Satellite growth points:
((BMB SPEAKER HEARER (ATTRIBUTE-OF ?CIRC ?VAL)))
Order: (NUCLEUS SATELLITE)
Relation phrases: (" ")

Figure 9
Hovy's RST plan for `CIRCUMSTANCE` (from Hovy [1991] p. 90).

set of input items to be expressed. As Hovy (1991, p. 94) points out, RST operators with growth points can be viewed as schemata, and this is how they are used in his implementation. He also argues that by viewing growth points as "suggestions" rather than "injunctions," the RST operators can be used in a more "open-ended" approach to planning. Hovy (1991, p. 98) goes on to suggest a range of criteria that a planner might use to determine when additional material should be included/excluded, but these have not been implemented.

The operator in Figure 9 says that in order to achieve the state where the speaker believes that the hearer and speaker mutually believe that `?CIRC` is a circumstance of some event `?X`, the speaker can state `?X` (this will be the result of posting the nucleus subgoal `(BMB SPEAKER HEARER (TOPIC ?X)))`, and then state the circumstantial information (this will be the result of posting the satellite subgoal `(BMB SPEAKER HEARER (TOPIC ?CIRC)))`. The constraints on the Nucleus + Satellite check that whatever is bound to the variable `?CIRC` either stands in a `HEADING.R` or `TIME.R` relation to the event bound to `?X`.[7] Using this operator, Hovy's structurer can generate portions of

7 This particular operator was used in a naval application where the main events were ship movements

text such as:

Knox is en route to Sasebo. Knox is heading SSW.

The second sentence (the satellite) stands in a CIRCUMSTANCE relation to the first sentence (the nucleus). Typically, this text would be only a portion of a larger paragraph.

4.3 A Problem with the Straightforward Operationalization of RST

Above we have argued that, in order for a system to be able to participate in dialogues, it must have an explicit representation of the intentional structure of its own utterances. Further, we have seen that RST provides a link between intentions and rhetorical relations, and that RST can be adapted in a straightforward manner for use in a text-structuring task by encoding the specification of the intended effect of an RST relation as the goal that the plan operator can be used to achieve, and the constraints on relations as the subgoals that must be satisfied.

However, in our efforts to use RST to construct a text plan that includes both the intentions of individual segments of the text and an indication of the rhetorical relations between segments, we found such an operationalization to be inadequate in the general case. More specifically, we found that there is an important distinction between two previously identified classes of RST relations that must be taken into account when attempting to use RST for text planning. Mann and Thompson (1988, pp. 256–257) break the RST relations into two classes: **presentational** and **subject matter**. Presentational relations are those whose intended effect is to increase some inclination in the hearer, such as the desire to act (MOTIVATION), or the degree of positive regard for (ANTITHESIS), the degree of belief in (EVIDENCE), or the degree of acceptance of (JUSTIFY) the information presented in the nucleus. In contrast, the intended effect of a subject matter relation is that the hearer recognize that the relation in question holds "in the subject matter." For example, VOLITIONAL-CAUSE relates two text spans if the speaker intends the hearer to recognize that the situation presented in the satellite is a cause for the volitional action presented in the nucleus.

The Effects of the presentational relations can be adopted in a straightforward manner as intentions for plan operators. However, the Effects of the subject matter relations are not sufficient for representing speakers' intentions. The Effects of subject matter relations capture the speaker's intention to make the hearer understand a piece of subject matter, but do not indicate *why* the speaker is presenting this information. Consider again the CIRCUMSTANCE relation in Figure 8. The specified effect of this relation is that the hearer knows some circumstance of the situation presented in the nucleus. As we have seen from Hovy's work, this relation is typically used to provide information about the time of an event, the location of an object, etc. But in order to participate in a dialogue, the system must know more than the fact that it intended to convey the time of an event or location of an object: it must know *why* it intended to convey that. We illustrate the problem with an example.

Consider the hypothetical fragment of task-oriented dialogue shown in Figure 10, in which a system is instructing a user in how to take apart a physical device. The system tells the user to remove the cover. In order to increase the user's ability to perform the act, the system employs an ENABLEMENT relation that tells the user what tool to use. Then, *in order to help the user find the appropriate tool*, the system tells the user where the tool is located, a CIRCUMSTANCE. Now, suppose that we have a text planner

---

and the circumstances that were important to report were heading and time. The operator could be generalized to a wider range of circumstances.

SYSTEM Remove the cover. You'll need the Phillips screwdriver. It's in the top drawer of the toolbox. Do you have it? [1]

USER No. [2]

Figure 10
Fragment of hypothetical task-oriented dialogue.

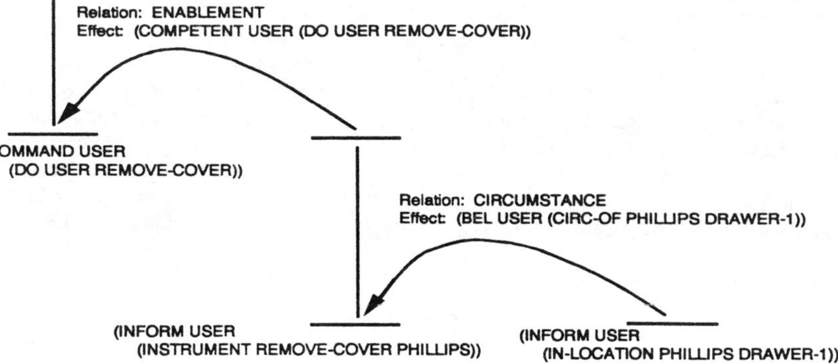

Figure 11
RST tree for system's utterance.

that only records the RST relations used and the speech acts they relate, as shown in Figure 11. Since each RST relation has a relation name as well as an Effect, these have both been recorded on the arcs representing the relations.

Now, let us consider how to respond to the user's "No" in the sample dialogue. Clearly the user is indicating an inability to locate the Phillips screwdriver, i.e., either she or he is unable to identify the referent of the term "Phillips screwdriver," or there is no Phillips screwdriver in the toolbox. For the sake of this example, let us assume that the hearer is unable to identify the referent. In terms of building a system that can participate in such dialogues, there are two problems with the representation shown in Figure 11. First, as the user indicates that he or she cannot identify the Phillips screwdriver, it is clear that the portion of the text that failed is the part that attempts to uniquely identify the Phillips screwdriver, namely the text generated in the CIRCUMSTANCE satellite: *It's in the top drawer of the toolbox.* However, it is difficult for a system to determine that this is the portion of text that failed, since the only intention represented is that the system wants the hearer to know that the screwdriver being in the toolbox is a circumstance of the Phillips screwdriver. The system has no representation of *why* this bit of circumstantial information is being conveyed.

Second, even if the system could identify this as the offending portion of the plan tree, it is very limited in terms of recovery strategies. In this case, the system's only recourse is to try to find different ways of achieving the subgoal (BEL USER (CIRCUMSTANCE-OF PHILLIPS ?CIRC)), i.e., other operators that have this effect but post different subgoals, or by finding different pieces of information that satisfy the constraints on the operator of Figure 9, i.e., alternative bindings for the variable ?CIRC, which is currently bound to (IN-LOCATION PHILLIPS DRAWER-1). But it is likely that the location of the Phillips screwdriver is the only piece of circumstantial information relevant to identifying the screwdriver.[8] So presenting other circumstantial information that may be stored in the knowledge base (e.g., when it was purchased, or how long it has been in the toolbox) is almost certainly not relevant and should not be mentioned here. But how can the system tell what is relevant without knowing *why* circumstantial information is being presented? What is missing from the representation in Figure 11 is a critical piece of information indicating that the speaker is presenting the circumstantial information because she or he intends this information to allow the hearer to identify the tool. (We could denote this intention as (KNOW USER (REF PHILLIPS))).

One may argue that the system could recover by trying other operators that implement the ENABLEMENT relation. But again, there are two problems. First, there may not be any other such operators whose constraints are satisfied in this situation. That is, perhaps the only way to remove the cover without damaging it is to use a Phillips screwdriver. Second, even if there were other operators for implementing the ENABLEMENT relation, the system is not behaving intelligently. It will never be able to figure out that it can recover by telling the user some attributive information about the object it is trying to identify, e.g., *The Phillips screwdriver has a yellow handle and a cone-shaped head.* This is because such a text would be produced by an ELABORATION-OBJECT-ATTRIBUTE relation, not a CIRCUMSTANCE relation. Again, this problem arises because the representation lacks the crucial piece of intentional information: (KNOW USER (REF PHILLIPS)), as well as the information that once the Phillips screwdriver has been mentioned, the rhetorical continuations that can be used to help achieve the intention (KNOW USER (REF PHILLIPS)) are CIRCUMSTANCE, ELABORATION-OBJECT-ATTRIBUTE, CONTRAST (one could identify an object by contrasting it with an object known to the user), etc.

The argument ultimately hinges on the observation that, in the case of the subject matter RST relations, the mapping between intentions and rhetorical relations is *not* a one-to-one mapping. In fact, the mapping is many-to-many. This is similar to the argument we made earlier with respect to schemata of rhetorical predicates. Because the mapping of intentions to rhetorical predicates is not one-to-one, intentions cannot be recovered from a record of the rhetorical predicates used to produce a text.

With respect to subject matter relations, we have just shown that an intention such as (KNOW USER (REF PHILLIPS)) may be achieved by a variety of different rhetorical relations. Similarly, a given subject matter relation may be used in service of several different intentions. For example, the CIRCUMSTANCE relation can be used when the speaker wants the hearer to identify the referent of a description (*"It's in the toolbox."*) or know a precondition for an action ("You want flight 101. *It leaves at 8:00 pm.*") In addition, the CIRCUMSTANCE relation is used when the speaker wants the hearer to know how entities are temporally or spatially related. ("He volunteered as a classical music announcer. *That was in 1970.* He left to go to graduate school. *That would've been 1973.*")

Contrast this with the presentational RST relations where the mapping between intention and rhetorical relation *is* a one-to-one mapping. For example, if the speaker's goal is to "increase the hearer's desire to perform the action presented in the nucleus," then whatever text is used to achieve this goal, it stands in a MOTIVATION relation to the nucleus.

8 This is because the knowledge base search originally retrieved this as the information that is most relevant to helping this hearer identify the Phillips screwdriver.

Because of this dichotomy between the two classes of RST relations, we conclude that any approach to discourse structure that relies solely on rhetorical relations or predicates and does not explicitly encode information about intentions is inadequate for handling dialogues. Hovy's (1991) approach suffers from this problem.[9] Moreover, as Moore and Pollack (1992) argue, a straightforward approach to revising such an operationalization of RST by modifying subject matter operators to indicate associated intentions cannot succeed. Such an approach "presumes a one-to-one mapping between the ways in which information can be related and the ways in which intentions combine into a coherent plan to affect a hearer's mental state." We have just shown examples indicating that no such mapping exists.

5. A Text Planner for Advisory Dialogues

In this section we present a text planner that constructs explanations based on the intentions of the speaker at each step and the linguistic means available for realizing these intentions. Given a goal representing the speaker's intention, our planner finds the linguistic resources available for achieving that goal. These linguistic resources can be either speech acts, which are directly satisfiable, or rhetorical strategies indicating how what can be said next relates to what has already been said. While planning, our system records both the intentions behind text spans and the rhetorical relation that holds between each two text spans.

This approach improves upon Hovy's work in two ways. First, as we have seen, Hovy's operationalization of RST relations into plan operators conflates intentional and rhetorical structure. In contrast, our plan language preserves an explicit representation of both intentional and rhetorical knowledge, and thus is more suitable for participating in dialogues. Second, our text planning system is able to select the content to include in its explanations in addition to structuring that content. Recall that Hovy's system is given a set of input elements to express. Like Appelt (1985, pp. 6–10), we believe that the tasks of choosing what to say and choosing a strategy for saying it cannot be divided. They are intertwined and influence one another in many ways. What knowledge is included in a response greatly depends on the speaker's intention and the linguistic strategy chosen to achieve it. For example, the information to be included when describing an object by drawing an analogy with a similar object will be quite different from the information to be included in describing the object by discussing its components. At the same time, which strategy is chosen to satisfy an intention must depend on what knowledge is available. For example, whether the system chooses to draw an analogy will depend on whether an analogous concept familiar to the hearer is available in the system's knowledge sources. In our text planner, decisions are made locally each time alternative strategies for achieving a (sub)goal are considered. The content of the text is not selected a priori.

5.1 The Plan Language

To enable our planner to construct text plans that explicitly capture the intentional and rhetorical structures of the text it produces, we distinguish two types of goals:

- **Communicative goals**. These represent the speaker's intentions to affect the beliefs or goals of the hearer. They are denoted as states, such as the

9 To be fair, the goal of Hovy's work was to show that RST could be used to order a set of input propositions into a coherent text. He did not set out to provide a system that could participate in a dialogue.

state in which the hearer believes a certain proposition, has a goal to perform an action, or has the knowledge necessary to perform an action. The presence of a communicative goal in a text plan does not cause any text to be generated directly. Achieving goals of this type leads to the posting of linguistic goals.

- **Linguistic goals**. These correspond to the linguistic means available to speakers for achieving their communicative goals. They lead to the generation of text and are of two types: **speech acts** and **rhetorical goals**. In our system, we assume that speech acts, such as `INFORM` or `RECOMMEND`, can be straightforwardly mapped into utterances that form part of the final text.[10] They are considered primitives by the text planner. Rhetorical goals, such as `MOTIVATION` and `CIRCUMSTANCE`, cannot be achieved directly and must be refined into one or more subgoals. The strategies for achieving them may post further communicative goals or speech act goals in order to express satellite information in a text. They are intended to establish rhetorical links between text spans, and often cause connective markers to be generated in the final text.

We distinguish these two types of goals for two reasons. First, the distinction is necessary to handle the many-to-many mapping between intentions and rhetorical strategies for achieving them. Table 1 summarizes the mapping between intentions and rhetorical relations we have identified in generating the texts necessary for our application. These mappings have been encoded in our library of plan operators. In this table, the presentational RST relations appear above the double line. As shown, there *is* a one-to-one mapping between these relations and speaker intentions. However, note that for the subject-matter relations that appear below the double line, there is *not* a one-to-one mapping between rhetorical relations and speaker's intentions. In general, there may be many different rhetorical strategies for achieving any given intention. For example, as discussed above and indicated in Table 1, the intention `(KNOW ?h (REF ?object-descriptor))` can be achieved by telling the hearer circumstantial information about the object (`CIRCUMSTANCE`), by contrasting the object with an object known to the user (`CONTRAST`), or by telling the hearer some of the attributes or parts of the object (`ELABORATION-OBJECT-ATTRIBUTE` or `ELABORATION-WHOLE-PART` respectively). Moreover, the mapping in Table 1 makes it clear that a particular rhetorical strategy may serve many intentions. For example, `CONTRAST` may be used to identify the referent of a description, to define a new term, to identify the differences between entities, to make the hearer believe that a method is the best one for achieving a domain goal, etc. As we will see, operators in our plan language achieve intentions by posting rhetorical subgoals and/or speech acts.

The second reason for separately and explicitly representing the two types of goals is so that the completed plan structure will contain an explicit representation of the speaker's intentions as well as a record of the speech acts and rhetorical strategies used to achieve them. As we have argued above, it is essential that the intentional structure of a text be recorded so that the system may respond to the user's follow-up questions. In addition, having the rhetorical structure explicitly noted in the text plan allows the text generator to include discourse markers in the final text in a straightforward manner. Such markers enhance the coherence of the text and aid the reader in understanding the text as a whole, by helping him or her understand how

10 Here we are using the term "speech act" where Appelt (1985) would use "surface speech act."

Table 1
Intention to rhetorical relation mapping.

Intention	Rhetorical Relation	
(PERSUADED ?h ?proposition) (PERSUADED ?h (DO ?h ?act)) (COMPETENT ?h (COMPREHEND ?h ?x)) (COMPETENT ?h (DO ?h ?act))	EVIDENCE MOTIVATION BACKGROUND ENABLEMENT	**Presentational Relations**
(KNOW ?h (REF ?desc))	CIRCUMSTANCE CONTRAST ELABORATION-OBJECT-ATTRIBUTE ELABORATION-WHOLE-PART	**Subject Matter Relations**
(KNOW-ABOUT ?h ?concept)	CIRCUMSTANCE CONDITION CONTRAST ELABORATION-GENERAL-SPECIFIC ELABORATION-OBJECT-ATTRIBUTE ELABORATION-SET-MEMBER ELABORATION-SPECIFIC-GENERAL ELABORATION-WHOLE-PART PURPOSE SEQUENCE	
(BEL ?h (REF (DIFFS ?x ?y) ?d))	CONTRAST	
(BEL ?h (STEP ?act ?goal))	ELABORATION-GENERAL-SPECIFIC ELABORATION-PROCESS-STEP SEQUENCE	
(BEL ?h ?proposition)	CONTRAST ELABORATION (all types)	
(BEL ?h (METHOD-FOR ?goal ?method))	CONDITION CONTRAST MEANS SEQUENCE	
(BEL ?h (BEST-METHOD-FOR ?goal ?method))	CONCESSION CONDITION CONTRAST OTHERWISE	

the parts of the text relate to one another (Brewer 1980; Cahour, Falzon, and Robert 1990; Ehrlich and Cahour 1991; Goldman and Durán 1988; Levy 1979; Meyer, Brandt, and Bluth 1980).[11] In a system such as ours, sets of connectives are associated with each rhetorical relation, and one can be chosen based on features of the final text being produced (e.g., whether or not a sentence boundary occurs between nucleus and satellite, etc.). The system need not reason directly about the relationships between the effects of speech acts to determine a suitable connective—a process we believe to be much more computationally intensive.

5.2 Representing Plan Operators

Our plan language provides operators for achieving the two types of goals presented in the previous section. Each operator consists of:

- **an effect:** a characterization of the goal that this operator can be used to achieve. This may be a communicative goal, such as *The speaker intends to*

11 Note that rhetorical structure is not the only source of discourse markers. They may be used to mark shifts in attentional structure, discourse segment boundaries, or aspects of the exchange structure in interactive discourse (Grosz and Sidner 1986; Redeker 1990; Schiffrin 1987).

achieve the state in which the hearer believes a proposition or a linguistic goal, such as *Establish motivation between an act and a goal* or *Inform the user of a proposition*.

- **a constraint list:** a list of conditions that should be true in order for the operator to have the intended effect. Constraints may refer to facts in the system's domain knowledge base, information in the user model, information in the dialogue history, or information about the evolving text plan.
- **a nucleus:** a subgoal that is most essential to achievement of the operator's effect. Every operator must contain a nucleus.
- **satellites:** additional subgoal(s) that may contribute to achieving the effect of the operator. An operator can have zero or more satellites. When present, satellites may be required or optional. Unless otherwise indicated, a satellite is assumed to be required.

5.2.1 Representing Mental States. Before providing examples of operators encoded in the plan language, we introduce the representational primitives used to express the knowledge contained in plan operators. The 12 predicates listed here were sufficient to represent the communicative goals that were needed to produce responses to the range of questions handled by the PEA system. Development of other application systems in a range of domains using the text planner described here is underway, and experience with these systems will help us determine whether this set of mental states is sufficient or must be extended (Carenini and Moore 1993; Rosenblum and Moore 1993).

We express information about agents' mental states in the following terms. In the notation below, constants are denoted by symbols written in all uppercase letters, e.g., `DO`, and typed variables are denoted by lowercase symbols beginning with a "?", e.g., `?agent`.

1. `(KNOW-ABOUT ?agent (CONCEPT ?c))`: The agent knows of the existence of the concept `?c`. This does not imply that the agent knows any particular properties of the concept, its subconcepts, the instances of this concept, or how this concept is used in problem solving.
2. `(KNOW ?agent (REF ?description))`: The agent can identify the real world entity described by `?description`.
3. `(BEL ?agent (?predicate ?e1 ?e2))`: The agent believes that the two-place predicate holds between entities `?e1` and `?e2`.
4. `(BEL ?agent (SOMEREF (?predicate ?arg1 ?arg2 ...?argN-1)))`: The agent believes that there exists some entity(ies) satisfying the N-ary predicate, i.e., there is some referent of this N-ary predicate.
5. `(BEL ?agent (REF (?predicate ?arg1 ?arg2 ...?argN-1) ?referent))`: The agent believes that the referent satisfies the N-ary predicate. This notation is used when $N > 2$. When $N = 2$, we use the notation shown in 3 above.
6. `(GOAL ?agent ?goal)`: The agent has adopted the specified domain goal. In this expression, `?goal` must be a nonprimitive domain action, i.e., a goal that requires further refinement before it can be achieved.
7. `(GOAL ?agent (DO ?agent ?action))`: `?agent` has adopted a goal to perform the specified action. The action must be a primitive in the domain.
8. `(PERSUADED ?agent (DO ?agent ?act))`: The agent is persuaded to perform the action at some unspecified time in the future. This is how we have chosen to represent the RST effect *Increase the hearer's desire* to perform an action.
9. `(PERSUADED ?agent (ACHIEVE ?agent ?goal))`: The agent is persuaded to adopt the goal.
10. `(PERSUADED ?agent ?proposition)`: The agent is persuaded that `proposition` is true. This is how we have chosen to represent the RST effect *Increase the hearer's belief* in a proposition.
11. `(COMPETENT ?agent (DO ?agent ?act))`: The agent knows the information necessary to perform the primitive domain action.
12. `(COMPETENT ?agent (ACHIEVE ?agent ?goal))`: The agent knows a method for achieving the nonprimitive domain action ?goal.

Representing Communicative and Linguistic Goals. Communicative goals represent the speaker's intention to produce a certain effect on the hearer's mental state, e.g., to make the hearer believe some proposition or adopt a goal to perform a certain action. In the plan language, communicative goals are written simply in terms of mental states of the hearer. When a goal of the form `(BEL ?hearer ?proposition)` appears in a text plan, it should be read as *The speaker intends to achieve the state where ?hearer believes ?proposition*. When `(BEL ?hearer ?proposition)` appears in the effect field of an operator, it indicates that the operator is capable of having this effect on the hearer's mental state.

To achieve a communicative goal, operators post linguistic (rhetorical and speech act) subgoals. Rhetorical goals are of the form `(relation-name arg1 ...argN)`, where `relation-name` is one of the relations defined in RST. An expression of this form represents a goal to establish the rhetorical relation between the entities listed as arguments. For example, `(MOTIVATION REPLACE-SETQ-WITH-SETF ENHANCE-READABILITY)` indicates the speaker's rhetorical goal to establish that the domain goal `ENHANCE-READABILITY` is motivation for the act `REPLACE-SETQ-WITH-SETF`.

Communicative and rhetorical goals are eventually refined into primitive actions that can be executed to cause changes in the hearer's mental state. In our planning formalism, we treat speech acts as primitive. Speech act goals thus appear at the leaf nodes of text plans. There are currently four speech acts in our system: `INFORM`, `ASK`, `RECOMMEND`, and `COMMAND`.

Finally, there are two special forms in the plan language: `FORALL` and `SETQ`. These may appear in the nucleus or satellite fields of plan operators. `FORALL` has the form

```
(FORALL ?variable-name ?goal).
```

A `FORALL` clause in a nucleus or satellite field causes an instance of the goal, `?goal`, to be posted for each possible binding of the variable named by `?variable-name`. `?goal` may be a communicative goal, a rhetorical goal, or a speech act. Its specification must contain an occurrence of the variable named by `?variable-name`. An example of this special form appears in the nucleus of the plan operator in Figure 14.

The `SETQ` special form is expressed as:

```
(SETQ ?variable-name ?expression).
```

`SETQ` causes the variable named `?variable-name` to be bound to the result of evaluating the expression `?expression`. This special form is useful for assigning values to variables that will be used in later steps of the nucleus or satellites. An example appears in the operator in Figure 16.

Representing Operator Constraints. Constraints on the user's knowledge and goals are expressed using the notation given above for representing the hearer's mental states. Any of the expressions described above can appear in the constraint list of an operator. For example, if the expression

```
(KNOW-ABOUT USER (CONCEPT STORAGE-LOCATION))
```

appears in the constraint field of an operator, it indicates that in order to use the operator (without making assumptions), the hearer should be familiar with the concept `STORAGE-LOCATION`.

Constraints on the expert system's knowledge are of the form `(?predicate ?arg1 ...?arg-N)`, where `?predicate` is an N-ary predicate referring to the expert system's domain knowledge. Since the expert system's knowledge base is made up of several complex data structures, predicates are not tested by a simple unification process. Instead an access function must be written for each predicate in order to test if an instantiated predicate is true, or to find acceptable bindings when a predicate contains variables in some argument positions. The range of predicates over the domain knowledge is quite large, and therefore we will not enumerate them here. We provide English paraphrases of knowledge base constraint predicates wherever they appear in examples.

Finally, constraints may refer to the dialogue history or the status of the current text plan under construction. There are currently two types of constraints in this category. First, there are constraints that indicate whether the operator can be used in nucleus or satellite position in a text plan. The clause `(NUCLEUS)` in the constraint field of an operator, indicates that this operator can be used to expand the nucleus branch of a text plan. Likewise, the clause `(SATELLITE)` indicates that the operator can be used to expand a satellite branch.

Second, there are constraints on the focus of attention. We are currently using a simple implementation of local focus rules based on the work of Sidner (1979) and McKeown (1985). We have found the need for two such constraints in the operators we have encoded thus far:

- `(CURRENT-FOCUS ?entity)`: indicates that the operator can be used if `?entity` is currently in focus.
- `(IN-POTENTIAL-FOCUS-LIST ?entity)`: indicates that the operator can be used if `?entity` is on the list of items that have just been mentioned, and therefore could become the next focus.

5.2.2 Operationalizing RST Schemata. Given these notational conventions, let us consider how we operationalize an RST schema in our plan language. In general, several operators are required to represent the knowledge in an RST schema. For example, Figures 12, 14, and one of Figures 15 or 16 operationalize a portion of the RST schema

In Plan Language Notation:

```
EFFECT: (GOAL ?hearer (DO ?hearer ?act))
CONSTRAINTS: (NUCLEUS)
NUCLEUS:
    (RECOMMEND ?speaker ?hearer (DO ?hearer ?act))
SATELLITES:
    (((PERSUADED ?hearer (DO ?hearer ?act)) *optional*)
     ((COMPETENT ?hearer (DO ?hearer ?act)) *optional*))
```

English Paraphrase:

To make the hearer want to do an *act*,
IF this text span is to appear in nucleus position, THEN
  1. Recommend the *act*
AND optionally,
  2. Achieve state where the hearer is persuaded to do the *act*
  3. Achieve state where the hearer is competent to do the *act*

Figure 12
Plan operator for recommending an act.

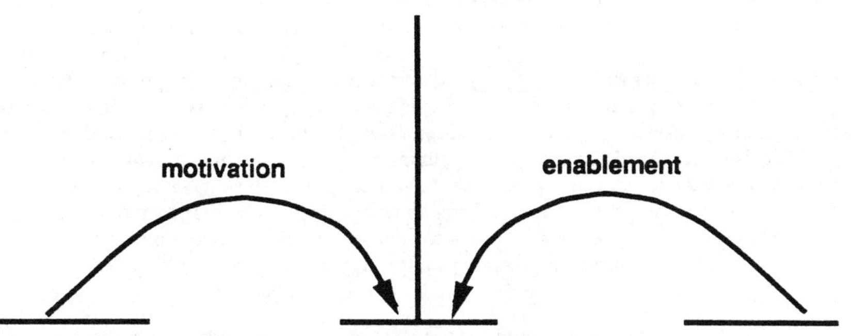

Figure 13
Graphical representation of an RST schema.

depicted in Figure 7, repeated in Figure 13 for the reader's convenience. The operator shown in Figure 12 says that one way of achieving the state where the hearer has the goal of performing an action is to recommend the act (the nucleus), and, optionally, to post a subgoal to achieve the state where the hearer is persuaded to perform the recommended act (the first satellite), and, optionally, to post a subgoal to achieve the state where the hearer has the knowledge necessary to perform the act (the second satellite). `RECOMMEND` is considered a primitive in our system, and can be mapped directly into a specification for the sentence generator. Therefore no operators are needed to achieve it.

However, the system does require operators for achieving the two satellite subgoals. Figure 14 shows an operator that can be used to achieve the first satellite. Informally, this plan operator states that if an act is a step in achieving some goal(s) of

In Plan Language Notation:

```
EFFECT: (PERSUADED ?hearer (DO ?hearer ?act))
CONSTRAINTS: (AND (STEP ?act ?goal)
                  (GOAL ?hearer ?goal)
                  (MOST-SPECIFIC ?goal)
                  (CURRENT-FOCUS ?act)
                  (SATELLITE))
NUCLEUS: (FORALL ?goal
                  (MOTIVATION ?act ?goal))
SATELLITES: nil
```

English Paraphrase:

To achieve the state in which the hearer is persuaded to do an *act*,
IF the *act* is a step in achieving some *goal(s)* of the hearer,
AND the *goal(s)* are the most specific along any refinement path
AND *act* is the current focus of attention
AND the planner is expanding a satellite branch of the text plan
THEN motivate the *act* in terms of those *goal(s)*.

Figure 14
Plan operator for persuading user to do an act.

the hearer, the speaker can persuade the hearer to perform the action by motivating the action in terms of those goals. This plan operator thus indicates that the communicative goal of persuading the hearer to do an act can be achieved by using the rhetorical strategy MOTIVATION. This operator thus links the intention with the rhetorical means used to achieve it.

Finally, the system needs an operator that can achieve a MOTIVATION subgoal. In our current operator library, there are several such operators. Two of these are shown in Figures 15 and 16. The operator in Figure 15 is very general and can be used to motivate any action in terms of a hearer goal that the act may help to achieve. It posts a subgoal to make the hearer believe that the act is a step in achieving the goal. In the simplest case, this subgoal will be refined directly into a surface speech act that informs the hearer of this fact. The operator in Figure 16 is a more specific operator and can be used only when the act to be motivated is a replacement (e.g., replace SETQ with SETF). In this case, one strategy for motivating the act is to compare the object being replaced and the object that replaces it with respect to a goal of the hearer.

The three operators shown in Figures 12, 14, and 15 together form one operationalization of a portion of the RST schema shown in Figure 13. Referring back to this schema and the definition of the RST relation MOTIVATION shown in Figure 6, the reader will note that these three operators can be used to produce the nucleus and the MOTIVATION satellite portion of the schema. To complete the operationalization of the full schema shown in Figure 13, we must also provide operators to refine the second optional satellite, (COMPETENT ?hearer (DO ?hearer ?act)). For the sake of brevity, we have omitted these operators here.

There are three important points to note about our operationalization. First, operators like the one shown in Figure 14 provide an explicit link between speaker intentions and the rhetorical means that achieve them. In the case of this particular operator, there is actually a one-to-one mapping between the intention (*Achieve state where*

```
EFFECT: (MOTIVATION ?act ?goal)
CONSTRAINTS: (AND (STEP ?act ?goal)
                  (GOAL ?hearer ?goal))
NUCLEUS: (BEL ?hearer (STEP ?act ?goal))
SATELLITES: nil
```

Figure 15
Plan operator for motivating any action by stating the shared goals that act is a step in achieving.

```
EFFECT: (MOTIVATION ?act ?goal)
CONSTRAINTS: (AND (STEP ?act ?goal)
                  (GOAL ?hearer ?goal)
                  (ISA ?act REPLACE))
NUCLEUS: ((SETQ ?replacee (FILLER-OF OBJECT ?act))
          (SETQ ?replacer (FILLER-OF GENERALIZED-MEANS ?act))
          (BEL ?hearer
               (SOMEREF (DIFFERENCES-WRT ?replacee ?replacer ?goal))))
SATELLITES: nil
```

Figure 16
Plan operator for motivating a replace act by describing differences between replacer and replacee.

hearer is persuaded to do an act) and the rhetorical strategy for achieving it (MOTIVATION). However, as Table 1 shows, this is not the case for subject matter relations. By providing operators that explicitly link intentions with rhetorical strategies, our system can handle the many-to-many mapping between intentions and the communicative strategies that achieve them. So, to return to the Phillips screwdriver example, our system would have several plan operators for achieving the intention: (KNOW ?hearer (REF ?description)). One plan operator would indicate that a rhetorical strategy for achieving this goal is to tell the hearer the location of the object (CIRCUMSTANCE), another would indicate that another way to achieve the goal is to tell the hearer the identifying attributes of the object (ELABORATION-OBJECT-ATTRIBUTE), etc.

Second, operators like the one shown in Figure 14 contribute to the computational efficiency of the system. These operators encode knowledge about the rhetorical strategies that may be used to satisfy particular intentions. Other operators, e.g., the MOTIVATION operators shown in Figures 15 and 16, encode different methods for realizing these rhetorical strategies in different situations. Thus we have provided a plan language that preserves an explicit representation of the intention behind each portion of the text, while maintaining the efficiency advantages that originally motivated the use of schemata of rhetorical predicates or relations for natural language generation.

Third, as illustrated by the two alternative operators for achieving a MOTIVATION subgoal shown in Figures 15 or 16, in our plan language we can represent very general strategies that are applicable across domains, as well as very specific strategies that may be necessary to handle the idiosyncratic language used in a particular domain. While one may argue that the operator in Figure 16 could be replaced by a more general, domain-independent operator, this does not obviate the need for domain-specific communication strategies. Rambow (1990) argues that domain-specific communication knowledge must be used (whether implicitly or explicitly) in all planned communication, and advocates that **domain communication knowledge** be represented explicitly. In our plan language, some types of domain-specific communication strategies can be represented in plan operators. When there are multiple operators capable of achieving a given effect, the constraint mechanism controls which operators are deemed appropriate in a given context. Note, however, that we do not wish to claim that a top-down planning formalism that maps speakers' intentions to rhetorical and speech acts can or should be used to generate all text types. In particular, Kittredge, Korelsky, and Rambow (1991) have shown that RST cannot account for the structure of report texts. Moreover, they argue that report generation does not require reasoning about the speaker's intentions to affect the mental attitudes of the hearer. For report generation, they advocate a data-driven approach in which domain communication knowledge plays a central role.

5.3 Constraints Integrate Multiple Sources of Knowledge

Operators contain applicability constraints that specify the knowledge that must be available and the state of the text-planning process that must exist if the operator is to be used. These constraints integrate multiple sources of knowledge; they may refer to the expert system's knowledge bases, the user model, the dialogue history, or the evolving text plan. To our knowledge, our text planner is unique in its explicit representation of constraints from all of these knowledge sources.

It is important to recognize that in our formalism, constraints do more than just limit the applicability of an operator. They also specify the type of knowledge to be included in an explanation, so that the process of satisfying constraints causes the planner to *find* information that will be included in the text. Thus, the selection of information to be presented and the determination of how to present that information are truly integrated in our planning model.

For example, when attempting to apply the operator shown in Figure 14, the variables `?act` and `?hearer` will be bound. What is not yet determined is which domain goals should be used to motivate the act. Checking to see if the first three constraints on this operator are satisfied causes the planner to search its knowledge sources to find acceptable bindings for the variable `?goal`. The first constraint, `(STEP ?act ?goal)`, says that there must be some domain goal(s) that the act is a step in achieving. Satisfying this constraint requires the planner to search the expert system's domain planning knowledge for such goals. The second constraint, `(GOAL ?hearer ?goal)`, further specifies that any such domain goals must be goals of the hearer (user). To check this constraint, the system must inspect the user model. The third constraint requires that `?goal` be the most specific goal along any refinement path satisfying the first two constraints.

The last two constraints of the operator in Figure 14 refer to the evolving text plan. The fourth constraint, `(CURRENT-FOCUS ?act)`, says that this operator can be used when the act is the current focus of attention. The fifth and final constraint, `(SATELLITE)`, says that this operator can only be used when the planner is working on a satellite branch of the current text plan.

In our system, constraints are treated differently depending on the knowledge source to which they refer. We consider the expert system's domain knowledge to be complete and correct. Therefore, constraints referring to the expert system's knowledge bases are considered "rigid." If any one of these constraints fails to be satisfied, the operator is rejected from consideration immediately. In contrast, we do not assume that the system's model of the user is either complete or correct. Thus, constraints referring to the user's knowledge state are treated more loosely. They specify what the user should know in order to understand the text that will be produced by the operator. However, when selecting an operator, if the user model contains no information relevant to a particular constraint, the planner may simply assume that the constraint is satisfied. When it does so, the assumption is recorded in the plan structure so that this assumption can be questioned if the explanation is not understood.

In the current implementation, constraints on the dialogue history and evolving text plan are rigid. However, we are exploring the idea of treating these as preconditions, since, if they are not true in a given situation, they could be made true by generating some additional text. For example, if a constraint such as `(IN-POTENTIAL-FOCUS-LIST ?act)` is not true, it can be made true by using rhetorical techniques to introduce `?act`, if it is a new topic, or to return to `?act`, if it has been mentioned before. User model constraints can also be treated as preconditions in cases where the system has the underlying knowledge to support explanations that could make them true. We would like to provide our text planner with the ability to choose between making an assumption or planning text to satisfy a user model constraint. Modifying the architecture to support this type of reasoning is relatively straightforward. The more difficult problem is to identify heuristics that guide the text planner in making the most effective choices. When we incorporate the notion of preconditions into our plan operators, we will make a distinction between constraints that the system can try to satisfy and those that must already be satisfied before the operator can be applied. This distinction was first made by Litman and Allen (1987) and later by Maybury (1992).

5.4 The Planning Mechanism

An overview of the explanation generation facility and its relation to other components in the system is shown in Figure 17. The text planner produces a plan for an explanation using the operators in its plan library. The planning process begins when a communicative goal is posted. This may come about in one of two ways. First, in the process of performing a domain task, the expert system may need to communicate with the user, e.g., to ask a question or to recommend that the user perform an action. To do so, it posts a communicative goal to the text planner. Alternatively, the user may request information from the system. In this case, the **query analyzer** interprets the user's question and formulates a communicative goal. Note that a communicative goal such as *Achieve the state where hearer knows about concept c* is really an abstract specification of the response to be produced.

When a goal is posted, the planner identifies all of the potentially applicable operators by searching its library for all operators whose effect field matches the goal. To make this search more efficient, plan operators are stored in a discrimination network based on their effect field. For each operator found, the planner then checks to see if all of its constraints are satisfied. Those operators whose constraints are satisfied (or, in the case of user model constraints, can be assumed to be satisfied) become candidates for achieving the goal.

From the candidates, the planner selects an operator based on several factors, including what the user knows (as indicated in the user model), the conversation that has occurred so far (as indicated in the dialogue history), the relative specificity of the candidate operators, and whether or not each operator requires assumptions to be made. The knowledge of preferences is encoded into a set of selection heuristics. A discussion of the selection process is beyond the scope of this paper; see Moore (in press) for details. Once a plan operator has been selected, it is recorded in the current plan node as the selected operator, and all other candidate plan operators are recorded in the plan node as untried alternatives. If the operator chosen requires any assumptions to be made, they are also recorded in the plan node. The planner then

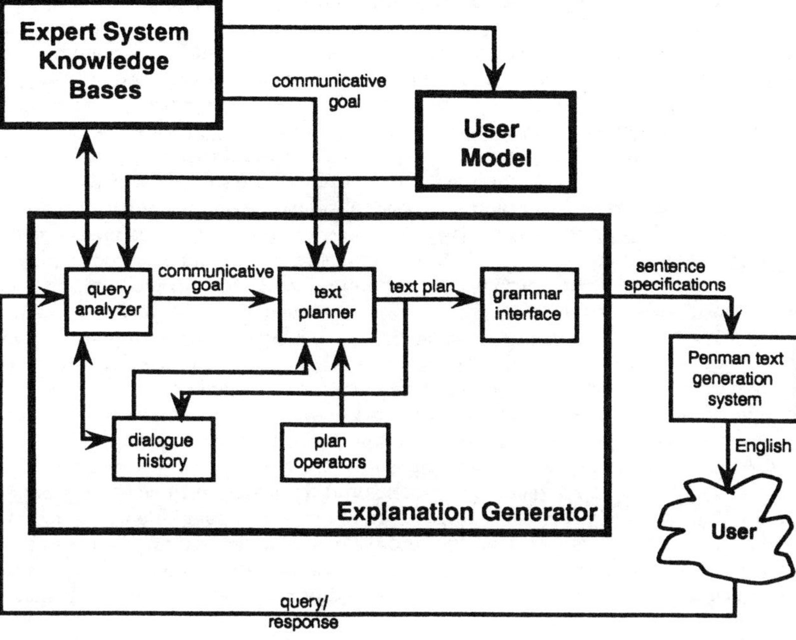

Figure 17
Architecture of explanation system.

expands the selected plan operator by posting its nucleus and required satellites as subgoals to be refined.

Recall that in Section 4.2 we noted that a text generator must decide on the ordering of the text spans it produces. When instantiating an operator, the planner must decide on the ordering of the subgoals in the nucleus and satellite. There are really two ordering issues: (1) for each satellite, the planner must determine whether that satellite should appear before or after the nucleus, and (2) whenever there are multiple subgoals in a set of satellites, the planner must determine the order of these subgoals.

In our current framework, the second type of ordering knowledge is compiled into our text-planning strategies. That is, subgoals should be expanded in the order in which they appear in the plan operator. This is the approach taken by most systems employing schemata, e.g., McKeown (1985); Paris (1991b), and is also common in systems that make use of linear planners, e.g., Cawsey (1993); Hovy (1991); Maybury (1992). Again, this leads to computational efficiency, since the planner does not have to reason about ordering among sibling subgoals. However, some flexibility is lost. We plan to investigate this tradeoff in our future work.

To solve the first ordering problem, we appeal to ordering information provided by RST. Although RST does not strictly constrain ordering, Mann and Thompson (1988) have observed that, for some relations, one ordering is significantly more frequent than the other. In RST, these ordering observations are treated as "strong tendencies" rather than constraints. For example, in an EVIDENCE relation, the nuclear claim usually precedes the satellite that provides the evidence for the claim; in contrast, in a BACKGROUND relation, the satellite providing the background information necessary to understand the nuclear proposition usually precedes the nucleus. Our planner expands the nucleus before the satellite except for those relations that have been identified as having a typical order of satellite before nucleus.

Finally, the planner must decide when to expand optional satellites. In the current implementation, the planner has two modes, terse and verbose. In terse mode, no optional satellites are expanded. In verbose mode, each satellite is checked against the user model, and those that do not duplicate the user's existing knowledge are expanded. For example, the plan operator in Figure 12 has two satellites. The first satellite calls for persuading the hearer to perform the act. The second satellite calls for making the hearer competent to perform the act and would, if expanded, provide any information the hearer needs to know in order to be capable of performing the act. These satellites are both marked "optional," indicating that it would be sufficient to simply state the recommendation. In verbose mode, the planner will check each of these satellites against the user model. To avoid expanding the first satellite, the user model would have to contain information indicating that the user already has the goal of performing the recommended act. However, note that this would never be the case, since if it were, the system would not be planning text to make the hearer adopt the goal of doing the act. That is, it would not be expanding this operator in the first place. The second satellite provides a more interesting example. In verbose mode, if the user model indicates that the user knows how to perform replacement actions, the second satellite will not be expanded, since the system believes that the user has the knowledge necessary to perform the recommended act.

The planner maintains an agenda of pending goals to be satisfied. When instantiating a plan operator, it creates a new node for the nucleus subgoal and puts it into a list. The planner then expands each of the required satellites and adds them to this list. If the satellite is one that should precede the nucleus, the new satellite node is appended to the front of the list. Otherwise, it is appended to the back of this list. The planner then considers each of the optional satellites. For each of the ones it decides to expand, the planner creates a new node and adds it to the appropriate end of the list. The list is then appended to the *front* of the agenda of goals to be expanded. In this way a text plan is built in depth-first order.

When a speech act is reached, the system constructs a specification that directs the realization component, Penman (Mann and Matthiessen 1985; Penman Natural Language Generation Group 1989), to produce the corresponding English utterance. The system builds these specifications based on the type of speech act, its arguments, and the context in which it occurs.[12] As the planner examines each of the arguments of the speech act, new goals may be posted as a side effect. If one of the arguments is a concept that the user does not know (as indicated in the user model), a satellite subgoal to define this new concept is posted. In addition, if the argument is a complex data structure that cannot be realized directly by English lexical items, the planner will have to "unpack" this complex structure, and, in so doing, will discover additional concepts that must be mentioned. Again, if any of these concepts is not known to the user, subgoals to explain them are posted. An example of this phenomenon is given

12 Bateman and Paris (1989, 1991) are investigating the problem of phrasing utterances for different types of users and situations.

SYSTEM	What characteristics of the program would you like to enhance?	[1]
USER	Readability and maintainability.	[2]
SYSTEM	You should replace (SETQ X 1) with (SETF X 1). SETQ can only be used to assign a value to a simple-variable. In contrast, SETF can be used to assign a value to any generalized-variable. A generalized-variable is a storage location that can be named by any accessor function.	[3]

Figure 18
Sample dialogue.

in the next section. In this way, our system can *opportunistically* define a new term when the need arises. Contrast this approach to the schema-based approach described earlier. Recall that handling this type of phenomenon with schemata would require that the definition of each schema explicitly include an optional Identification predicate after *every* entry in *every* schema.

Planning is complete when all subgoals in the text plan have been refined to speech acts. It is important to note that text planning proceeds in such a way that speech acts are planned *in the order in which they will appear in the final text*. This provides two advantages. First, the text plan is a record of the system's utterances in the order in which they are generated. Because our text plans also include the intentional structure of the final text, focus information can be derived from a completed text plan, and there is no need to maintain a separate data structure for managing focus information. Second, by doing the planning in this manner, the planner can easily be extended for incremental generation in which planning and realization are interleaved.

6. Participating in Explanatory Dialogues: An Example

In this section, we provide an example illustrating how our system constructs a text plan for recommending an action. We contrast the text plan produced by our system with the schema representation we showed in Figure 4, and show how the text plan may then be used to handle two follow-up questions. See Moore (in press) for a more detailed discussion of the planning process and additional examples.

Let us return to the sample dialogue with the PEA system that was shown in Figure 3 and that we include again in Figure 18 for the reader's convenience. In this dialogue the user indicates a desire to enhance the readability and maintainability of his or her program. To enhance maintainability, the expert system determines that the user should replace SETQ with SETF. To recommend this transformation, the expert system posts the communicative goal (GOAL USER (DO USER REPLACE-1)) to the text planner. This goal says that the speaker would like to achieve the state where the hearer has adopted the goal of performing the act REPLACE-1.

A plan operator capable of satisfying this goal was shown in Figure 12. The nucleus is expanded first, causing (RECOMMEND SYSTEM USER (DO USER REPLACE-1)) to be posted as a subgoal. RECOMMEND is a speech act goal that can be achieved directly, and thus expansion of this branch of the plan is complete. Focus information—the current focus and the potential focus list—is also updated at this point. In this case, the current focus is the act REPLACE-1 and the potential focus list includes the participants in this act, i.e., USER, SETQ, and SETF.

Next, the planner must expand the satellites. Since both satellites are optional in this case, the planner must decide which, if any, are to be posted as subgoals. For the purposes of this example, assume that the planner is in verbose mode and that the user model indicates that the user has the knowledge necessary to perform replacement acts (i.e., he or she knows how to use the text editor). Thus, only the first satellite will be expanded, posting the communicative subgoal to achieve the state where the user is persuaded to perform the replacement, i.e., (PERSUADED USER (DO USER REPLACE-1)). A plan operator for achieving this goal using the rhetorical relation MOTIVATION was shown in Figure 14.

When attempting to satisfy the constraints of the operator in Figure 14, the system first checks the constraint (STEP REPLACE-1 ?goal). This constraint states that, in order to use this operator, the system must find a domain goal, ?goal, which REPLACE-1 is a step in achieving. To find such goals, the planner searches the expert system's problem-solving knowledge. A detailed discussion of the expert system framework we use is beyond the scope of this paper. However, it is important to note that the type of explanation capability we are describing in this paper places stringent requirements on the way domain knowledge is represented and used in reasoning. Interested readers may find a thorough treatment of this topic in Swartout (1983), Clancey (1983), Neches, Swartout, and Moore (1985), Swartout, Paris, and Moore (1991), and Moore and Paris (1991).

In this example, the applicable expert system goals, listed in order from most to least specific, are:

```
apply-SETQ-to-SETF-transformation
apply-local-transformations-whose-rhs-use-is-more-general-than-lhs-use
apply-local-transformations-that-enhance-maintainability
apply-transformations-that-enhance-maintainability
enhance-maintainability
enhance-program
```

Thus, six possible bindings for the variable ?goal result from the search for domain goals that REPLACE-1 is a step in achieving.

The second constraint of the current plan operator, (GOAL ?hearer ?goal), is a constraint on the user model stating that ?goal must be a goal of the hearer. Not all of the bindings found so far will satisfy this constraint. Those that do not will not be rejected immediately, however, as we do not assume that the user model is complete. Instead, they will be noted as possible bindings, and each will be marked to indicate that, if this binding is used, an assumption is being made, namely that the binding of ?goal is assumed to be a goal of the user. The selection heuristics can be set to tell the planner to prefer choosing bindings that require no assumptions to be made.

In this example, since the user is employing the system to enhance a program and has indicated a desire to enhance the readability and maintainability of the program, the system infers the user shares the top-level goal of the system (ENHANCE-PROGRAM), as well as the two more specific goals ENHANCE-READABILITY and ENHANCE-MAINTAINABILITY. Of these two more specific goals, only ENHANCE-MAINTAINABILITY is on the refinement path leading to the act REPLACE-1. Therefore, the two goals that completely satisfy the first two constraints of the operator shown in Figure 14 are ENHANCE-PROGRAM and ENHANCE-MAINTAINABILITY. Finally, the third constraint indicates that only the most specific goal along any refinement path to the act should be chosen. This constraint encodes the explanation principle that, in order to avoid explaining parts of the reasoning chain that the user is familiar with, when one goal is a subgoal of another, the goal that is lowest in the expert system's refinement structure, i.e., most specific, should be chosen. Note that ENHANCE-MAINTAINABILITY is a refinement of ENHANCE-PROGRAM. Therefore, ENHANCE-MAINTAINABILITY is now the preferred candidate binding for the variable ?goal.

The last two constraints of the operator are also satisfied: REPLACE-1 is the current focus, and the operator is being used to expand a satellite branch of the text plan.

The plan operator is thus instantiated with ENHANCE-MAINTAINABILITY as the binding for the variable ?goal. The selected plan operator is recorded as such, and all other candidate operators are recorded as untried alternatives.

The nucleus of the chosen plan operator is now posted, resulting in the subgoal (MOTIVATION REPLACE-1 ENHANCE-MAINTAINABILITY). The plan operator chosen for achieving this goal is the one shown in Figure 16. This operator motivates the replacement by describing differences between the object being replaced and the object replacing it with respect to the user's goal, i.e., by posting the subgoal (BEL USER (SOMEREF (DIFFERENCES-WRT-GOAL SETF-FUNCTION SETQ-FUNCTION ENHANCE-MAINTAINABILITY))). Although there are many differences between SETQ and SETF, only the differences relevant to the domain goal at hand (ENHANCE-MAINTAINABILITY) should be expressed.

The relevant differences are determined in the following way. From the expert system's problem-solving knowledge, the planner determines what roles SETQ and SETF play in achieving the goal ENHANCE-MAINTAINABILITY. In this case, the system is enhancing maintainability by applying transformations that replace a specific construct with one that has a more general usage. SETQ has a more specific usage than SETF, and therefore the comparison between SETQ and SETF should be based on the generality of their usage. Thus, the goal:

```
(BEL USER (SOMEREF (DIFFERENCES-WRT-GOAL SETQ-FUNCTION
                                         SETF-FUNCTION
                                         ENHANCE-MAINTAINABILITY)))
```

posts the single subgoal

```
(BEL USER (REF (DIFFERENCE SETF-FUNCTION SETQ-FUNCTION) USE)).
```

To satisfy this goal, the system uses an operator that informs the user that SETQ can be used to assign a value to a simple variable, and contrasts this with the use of SETF. Focus information is again updated at this point. SETF becomes the current focus, and USE, ASSIGN-TO-GV and its arguments, VALUE and GENERALIZED-VARIABLE, become potential foci.

Finally, the text planner expands the speech act

```
(INFORM SYSTEM USER (USE SETF-FUNCTION ASSIGN-TO-GV))
```

in order to form a specification for the surface generator. In doing so, the system must express the complex concept ASSIGN-TO-GV where

```
ASSIGN-TO-GV = (ASSIGN (OBJECT VALUE)
                       (DESTINATION GENERALIZED-VARIABLE)).
```

When expressing processes such as ASSIGN, the system expresses the process itself, as well as the participants (e.g., OBJECT) involved in and circumstances (e.g., DESTINATION) surrounding the process. In this case, to express the concept ASSIGN-TO-GV, the system will express the assignment action, the object being assigned (i.e., VALUE), and the destination of the assignment (i.e., GENERALIZED-VARIABLE). To understand the final utterance that will be generated, the listener must know the concepts ASSIGN, VALUE, and GENERALIZED-VARIABLE.

When building specifications for complex processes such as ASSIGN-TO-GV, the planner checks each of the fillers (e.g., VALUE, GENERALIZED-VARIABLE) of the roles (e.g., OBJECT, DESTINATION) of the concept (e.g., ASSIGN) to determine if the user knows that filler. If so, the planner can simply mention that filler concept by name in the generated text. If, on the other hand, the user model does not indicate that the user is familiar with the concept to be mentioned, the planner must either make an assumption that the user knows the concept (if the planner is in terse mode) or post a subgoal to make the hearer know this concept to the front of its current agenda (if the planner is in verbose mode).

In the current example, recall that the planner is in verbose mode and further suppose that the user model indicates that the user knows the following concepts:

```
CAR-FUNCTION
CDR-FUNCTION
SETQ-FUNCTION
CAR-OF-CONS
CDR-OF-CONS
SIMPLE-VARIABLE
ASSIGN
VALUE
```

Thus, the user model indicates that the user knows the concepts ASSIGN and VALUE but has no indication that the user knows the concept GENERALIZED-VARIABLE. As a result, the system posts a subgoal to make the user know this concept, i.e., (KNOW-ABOUT USER (CONCEPT GENERALIZED-VARIABLE)). Since GENERALIZED-VARIABLE is a member of the potential focus list, no special care need be taken to introduce it. This goal can thus be achieved by elaborating on the previous text to define this new term. This is done with a plan operator that describes concepts by stating their class membership and describing their attributes.

The text plan for response 3 of the sample dialogue is now completed, and it is shown in its entirety in Figure 19. Contrast this text plan with the instantiated schema representation for the same utterance shown in Figure 4. Note that in addition to representing rhetorical relations between portions of the text (e.g., MOTIVATION, CONTRAST, and ELABORATION) that are analogous to the rhetorical predicates contained in the schema, the text plan includes the intentional structure of the text (as shown in Figure 5). Although in this case the text span boundaries coincide with the text segment (as defined by Grosz and Sidner) boundaries, this need not always be the case. In RST, a text span is either a minimal unit or a schema application made up of one or more relations between minimal units. The minimal unit is "essentially a clause, except that clausal subjects and complements and restrictive relative clauses are considered parts of their host clause rather than as separate units" (Mann and Thompson 1988, p. 248). Thus, at least at the lowest level of analysis, text spans can be determined on the basis of syntactic structure alone. For Grosz and Sidner, intentions are the basic determiner of discourse segmentation. A segment must have an identifiable **discourse segment purpose (DSP)**, and embedding relationships between segments are a surface reflection of relationships among their associated DSPs (Grosz and Sidner 1986, pp. 177–178). Therefore, text spans and text segments are based on quite different criteria.

In a text plan produced by our system, any subtree headed by a communicative goal (i.e., an intention) corresponds to a discourse segment in Grosz and Sidner's theory. A segment may consist of more than one span. In such cases, the spans will be connected by subject matter RST relations. Such a case would arise, for example, if the system needed to inform the hearer of a procedure involving several steps. The subtree for the entire procedure would be associated with an intention, and the spans stating the steps would be related to one another by SEQUENCE relations. To construct

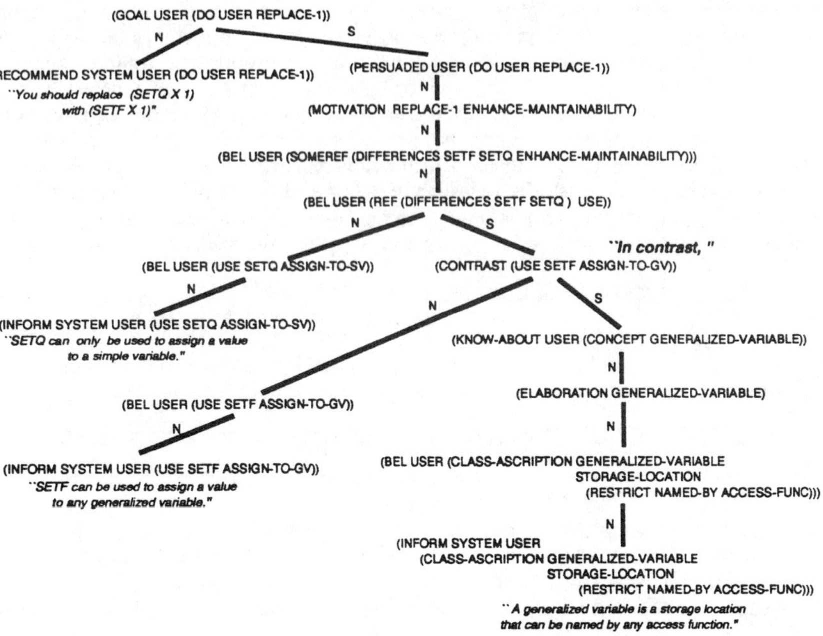

Figure 19
Completed text plan for recommending replace SETQ with SETF.

plan operators for our system based on sample texts, we first segment the texts based on intentional structure. We then identify the rhetorical structure and relate it to the intentional structure. In our formalism, rhetorical techniques are viewed as linguistic strategies for achieving communicative intentions.

In our system, after a text plan like the one shown in Figure 19 is constructed, it is recorded in the system's dialogue history and passed to the grammar interface, which translates the hierarchical text plan into a sequence of sentence specifications suitable for the sentence generator. In the process of this translation, the system decides where to place sentence boundaries and which, if any, connective markers to include. We currently use a simple set of heuristics that make these decisions based on the rhetorical relation between two text spans. To determine sentence boundaries, we have divided the space of RST relations into those that may appear within a clause complex and those that must start a new sentence. To choose connectives, we have associated a small set of possible connectives with each rhetorical relation. Some connectives are suitable for starting new sentences, while others are suitable for constructing complex sentences. If the system finds more than one suitable connective for expressing an RST relation, the first one is chosen.

Thus, in translating the text plan shown in Figure 19 into response 3, we see that `MOTIVATION`, `CONTRAST`, and `ELABORATION` cause a sentence break. Although not shown in this example, other relations, e.g., `MEANS`, cause a complex sentence to be formed. In addition, the `CONTRAST` relation is expressed explicitly via the connective "In contrast," whereas the `MOTIVATION` and `ELABORATION` relations do not cause any connectives to be added. The heuristics we have described here are clearly too simplistic, and we are currently working on more sophisticated techniques for linearizing our text plans. However, note that the information recorded in our text plan is already useful in making these decisions, and we believe this information will also facilitate more complex strategies.

6.1 Recovering From Failure: Avoiding Repetition

After the system has produced its recommendation, suppose that the user asks

[USER] What is a generalized variable? [4]

Recall that, from our analysis of naturally occurring dialogues such as the one shown in Figure 1, we observed that advice-seekers frequently ask such questions.

The query analyzer interprets this question and formulates the communicative goal: `(KNOW-ABOUT USER (CONCEPT GENERALIZED-VARIABLE))`. At this point, the explainer must recognize that this goal was attempted by the last sentence of the previous explanation and was not fully achieved. Failure to do so might lead to simply repeating the description of a generalized variable that the user did not understand. Note that this is precisely what would occur if we had generated the previous explanation using the schema shown in Figure 4. From the schema, the system would not be able to recognize that part of the text previously generated was intended to make the user know about generalized variables. A schema to define a term would thus be triggered and it would give the same answer as was previously generated. Even if a schema-based system were to keep track of the information it already mentioned so that it could avoid literally repeating the same content, it would still not be capable of generating a new text, *taking into consideration the fact that a goal was previously attempted but failed*. The same argument can be made about a system that generates explanations based solely on "RST plans" of the type used in Hovy's (1991) structurer.

By examining the text plan of the previous explanation recorded in the dialogue history, our system is able to determine whether the current goal (resulting from the follow-up question) is a goal that was previously attempted, as it is in this case. This time, when attempting to achieve the goal, the planner must select an alternative strategy. **Recovery heuristics** are responsible for selecting an alternative strategy when responding to such follow-up questions (Moore and Swartout 1989; Moore in press). One of these indicates that when the goal is to make the user know a concept, a good recovery strategy is to give examples.

In the current case, the user model indicates that there are examples of the concept `GENERALIZED-VARIABLE` that the user is familiar with, namely `CAR-OF-CONS` and `CDR-OF-CONS`. Thus, the strategy of giving examples can be applied to yield the following system response:

[SYSTEM] For example, the car of a cons is a generalized variable named by the access function `CAR`, and the cdr of a cons is a generalized variable named by the access function `CDR`. [5]

Providing an alternative explanation would not be possible without the explicit representation of the intentional structure that underlies the generated text recorded in our text plans. To avoid repetitions, the system must realize what goals it has tried to achieve in the previous discourse and what strategies it used to achieve them. Then, if the same goal is posted later in the discourse, the system can realize that its previous strategy was not successful and can employ an alternative strategy.

A similar situation would arise if the user were to indicate that he or she has not been persuaded to replace SETQ with SETF, e.g., with an utterance such as:[13]

[USER] I don't see why I should replace SETQ with SETF. [4′]

This would cause the query analyzer to post a goal to persuade the user to perform this act. Once again, the system must recognize that it has already attempted to persuade the user to perform the act by contrasting the usage of SETQ with the usage of SETF. Since this strategy did not succeed, it must be able to persuade the user in a different way. From the information recorded in the text plan in Figure 19, our system can determine that it has already tried to persuade the user to do the replacement. Since MOTIVATION is a presentational RST relation, the system has no other strategies for achieving the persuade goal. However, it does have several other rhetorical strategies for MOTIVATION. One of these is to provide a trace of the expert system's reasoning and could be used to generate the following explanation:

[SYSTEM] I'm trying to enhance the maintainability of the program [5′]
by applying transformations that enhance maintainability.
A transformation enhances maintainability if the usage of
the construct on its right hand side is more general than
usage of the construct on its left hand side. The usage of
SETF is more general than the usage of SETQ.

Again, a schema-based system would not be able to recover correctly from this failure. As we argued earlier, because the schemata do not record the intentions of the schema components, the system cannot determine that it contrasted SETQ with SETF in order to persuade the user to perform the replacement, and thus would not know what part of the schema to replan nor what other strategies to try.

7. Comparison to Related Work

Building on our work, Maybury (1992) devised a system to plan "communicative acts." Like Appelt (1985, p. 9), Maybury's system makes use of a hierarchy of linguistic actions. At the highest level, Maybury has added rhetorical acts (e.g., describe, explain, convince). The next two levels correspond to the top two levels of Appelt's hierarchy: illocutionary acts (e.g., inform, request), and locutionary acts (assert, ask, command).[14] The actions at each level in the hierarchy have been encoded into plan operators that are used in a process of hierarchical decomposition (Sacerdoti 1977) to refine rhetorical acts through illocutionary acts into locutionary acts.

An example operator from Maybury's system is shown in Figure 20. This is a rhetorical operator that can be used to define an entity by giving its "logical definition" (the entity's genus and differentia.) Note that operators in Maybury's language contain both a "header" and an "effects" field. The header field designates the type of act (e.g., define, inform) associated with the operator, whereas the effects field specifies the effect(s) that this act is expected to have on the hearer's mental state. To cause the planner to generate a text, a "discourse controller" posts a goal to cause an effect in the hearer's mental state, such as KNOW-ABOUT(USER, KC-135). This goal is matched against the effects field of operators in the plan library, and one is chosen. Therefore, at the top level, Maybury's system has a record of the intention causing the text to be produced. But now consider what happens during goal refinement. When an operator is instantiated, the clauses in its decomposition field are posted as subgoals. Note from Figure 20 that in Maybury's operator language expressions in the decomposition field are not subgoals to affect the hearer's mental state. Rather, they are linguistic actions such as define, inform, and assert. Unless these actions are locutionary, they become subgoals. To achieve an action subgoal, the planner matches the subgoal against the *header* field of operators in the plan library. When an operator is chosen, the propositions in the effects field are recorded, and the actions in the decomposition become further subgoals.

So, in fact Maybury's system does *not* have a record of the intentional structure behind the text it is producing. There are two problems. First, except at the top level, planning is done by matching against the header field of operators, *not against the effects field*. Because there are multiple effects listed for most of the operators, the system cannot know which one is the *intended* effect! Maybury's system thus cannot distinguish between intended effects and side effects. It is crucial that agents be able to distinguish their intentions from the side effects of their actions in order to recover from plan failures (Davis 1979; Bratman 1987). Therefore, Maybury's system does not have the knowledge necessary for recovering from failures, as our system does.

A second problem with Maybury's text plans is that they do not capture the relationship between intentions, i.e., that some intentions are in the plan because they in turn serve other intentions that appear higher in the plan tree. Once again, this is because Maybury's system simply records all the effects of each action. It is impossible to tell from the sets of effects at each level of the decomposition how effects are related to one another. Grosz and Sidner (1986) argue that such relations between intentions are a crucial part of intentional structure. Contrast Maybury's plans with those produced by our system. Our text plans explicitly represent the intended effects of actions and the relationships between these intentions. While we believe that it is useful to represent additional effects of operators, it is crucial to distinguish intended effects from side effects. Therefore, we argue that while Maybury's approach does indeed represent the effects of all of the "communicative acts" in his plans, it does *not* capture intentional structure and therefore cannot be used to recover from communication failures.

In related work, Cawsey (1993) built a system called EDGE that allows the user to interrupt with clarification questions while a text is being generated. EDGE plans extended tutorial explanations about the structure and input/output behavior of simple electrical circuits. This system is novel because it addresses issues of conversation management, such as turn-taking and topic control. The system separates discourse planning rules from content planning rules for this purpose. EDGE plans an explanation at a high level, following a specified curriculum. This plan is fleshed out as the dialogue progresses, causing sentences to be generated. After each sentence is generated, the system pauses to allow the user to supply feedback by choosing an item from a menu.

The EDGE discourse planner maintains an agenda indicating the topics that will be covered later in the explanation. Based on this agenda, the system can recognize when the user is asking about a topic that will be covered eventually, and can make

13 We do not currently allow users to ask questions phrased in such a manner because we do not have a sophisticated natural language understanding component. Instead, we have implemented a direct manipulation interface that allows users to use the mouse to point at the noun phrases or clauses in the text that were not understood or accepted. To approximate the query above, the user could highlight the system's original recommendation to replace SETQ with SETF, and select "Why?" from the menu that appears. As a result of interpreting this "Why?", the system posts the communicative goal (PERSUADED USER (DO USER REPLACE-1)); see Moore and Swartout (1990) for more details.

14 Appelt has two layers below locutionary acts that are not included in Maybury's system: concept activation and utterance acts.

NAME	define-by-logical-definition
HEADER	Define(*speaker*, *hearer*, *entity*)
CONSTRAINTS	$\exists c$ Superclass(*entity*, *c*)
PRECONDITIONS	
ESSENTIAL	$\exists c$ Superclass(*entity*, *c*)$\wedge$ KNOW-ABOUT(*speaker*, *c*)
DESIRABLE	$\neg$ KNOW-ABOUT(*hearer*, *entity*)
EFFECTS	$\forall x \in$ superclasses(*entity*)
	KNOW(*hearer*, Superclass(*entity*, *x*))$\wedge$
	$\forall y \in$ differentia(*entity*)
	KNOW(*hearer*, Differentia(*entity*, *y*))
DECOMPOSITION	Inform(*speaker*, *hearer*, Logical-Definition(*entity*))

Figure 20
A plan operator for defining (from Maybury [1992]).

comments such as *We'll be getting to that in a moment*. If this is not the case, or if the user insists, EDGE answers the user's question immediately. Once the interruption has been addressed, EDGE alters its subsequent explanation plan based on what took place during the interruption, and proceeds with its explanation as specified in the overall explanation plan. To resume from interruptions coherently, the discourse planning rules that manage the conversation include markers and meta-comments (e.g., *Anyway, I was talking about...*).

Because of its extended explanation plan and its discourse management rules, EDGE can handle interruptions in ways that are beyond the current capability of our system. However, as Cawsey points out, EDGE is based on a largely syntactic model of dialogue structure, and the system does not explicitly represent *why* different dialogue actions are selected. The effects that dialogue operators are intended to have on the user's knowledge and goals are not represented. EDGE content plans are much like schemas and therefore suffer from the limitations we discussed in Section 3.2.1. If a user fails to understand a text produced by a content plan, the system's only recourse is to try another strategy to achieve the top-level content goal, e.g., "describe how an entity works." Moreover, the content plans of EDGE are domain-specific, and are not based on general rhetorical techniques. Because rhetorical structure is not represented, the system cannot choose connective markers or use other rhetorical devices that make text easier to comprehend. For these reasons, EDGE cannot handle the types of phenomenon our system handles.

It is also important to note that, because we are dealing with expert and advisory applications, our system must be able to manage a dialogue whose structure emerges dynamically as the user asks questions. In advisory interactions, the system presents the user with a recommendation or result and only provides explanations when the user requests them. It is not appropriate for the system to plan extended explanations, testing the user's understanding and elaborating without provocation. Therefore, Cawsey's approach, which relies on the fact that the system has an extended explanation plan to follow, cannot be used directly.

It is clear, however, that our approach and Cawsey's are complementary, and that a complete system would need to incorporate aspects of both. In particular, our system should be augmented to include conversation management operators in order to manage topic shifts, to handle interruptions, and to generate meta-comments about the discourse itself.

8. Status and Future Directions

The text planner presented in this paper is implemented in Common Lisp and can produce the text plans necessary to participate in the sample dialogue described in this paper and several others; see Moore (in press) and Paris (1991a). We currently have over 150 plan operators that can answer the following types of questions:

- Why?
- Why *conclusion*?
- Why are you trying to achieve *goal*?
- Why are you using *method* to achieve *goal*?
- Why are you doing *act*?
- How do you achieve *goal* (in the general case)?
- How did you achieve *goal* (in this case)?
- What is a *concept*?
- What is the difference between *concept1* and *concept2*?
- Huh?

The text planner is being incorporated into several knowledge-based systems and two intelligent tutoring systems currently under development. Two of these systems are intended to be installed and used in the field. This will give us an opportunity to evaluate the techniques proposed here and extend the system as appropriate. It has also been employed in Reithinger's (1991) system for incremental language generation, and serves as the basis of the presentational planner for WIP, a multimedia system that plans text and graphics to achieve communicative goals (Wahlster et al. 1991). Finally, it is the basis for a text planner capable of generating explanatory texts that integrate examples with their surrounding context (Mittal and Paris 1993). This integration would not be possible without our system's explicit representation of the intentions for generating portions of the text and the rhetorical strategies used to achieve them.

We have begun to investigate how the discourse history should be indexed and exploited to control the dialogue and affect subsequent responses in more general ways. As reported here, the dialogue history is used primarily to determine how to interpret and answer follow-up questions (e.g., *Why?*, *How come?*), and to determine how to respond when the user asks a question that has already been answered or indicates that an explanation was not understood (*Huh?*). In Carenini and Moore (1993) and Rosenblum and Moore (1993) we discuss additional ways in which prior explanations can affect the generation of the current utterance.

We currently do not allow the user to return to a previous topic (e.g., once the system has moved on to a new topic, *Let's go back to replacing SETQ with SETF ...*), or to introduce new goals into the dialogue (e.g., *Well, now suppose I wanted to enhance efficiency ...*). In order to allow the user to change topics and introduce new goals at will, the system will need to be able to track the user's shifting goals and attention. Sidner (1985) and Carberry (1987) have proposed approaches for tracking the topic of conversation in task-oriented dialogues. However, their approaches rely on the assumption that the topic of conversation closely follows the structure of the domain task. Litman and

Allen (1987) identified types of subdialogues in task-oriented interactions, including clarifications and corrections, in which topic shift deviates from task structure, and they devised a plan recognition model for handling such subdialogues. Our system currently handles what Litman and Allen call **clarification subdialogues**. We believe that our model could be extended to handle other types of subdialogues, and that the text plans recorded in our dialogue history will aid in more general discourse management tasks than the ones we currently address. To perform these tasks, our system must understand how the previous responses stored in its discourse history relate to one another. That is, we must address issues of how to build a representation of the intentional structure of the dialogue that is emerging across conversational turns (Grosz and Sidner 1986) and to track global focus (Grosz 1977). In addition, we will need communicative strategies for managing the dialogue, e.g., strategies for introducing a topic, strategies for returning to a topic, etc.

9. Conclusions

We have presented an approach to natural language generation that extends previous theories and implementations in order to enable a computational system to play the role of a dialogue participant in an advisory setting. We began by illustrating the types of phenomena that are prevalent in advisory dialogues. We argued that, in order to participate in such dialogues, a system must be capable of reasoning about its own previous utterances. Follow-up questions must be interpreted in the context of the ongoing conversation, and the system's previous contributions form part of this context.

We claimed that to handle explanation dialogues successfully, a discourse model must include the intended effect of individual parts of the text on the hearer, as well as a representation of how the parts relate to one another rhetorically. Through principled arguments and detailed examples, we showed that previous approaches to multisentential text generation, which do not explicitly represent the intentional structure of their utterances, cannot be used for advisory dialogues. We presented our approach to text generation in which the system reasons about and records the intentions behind each text span as well as the rhetorical means used to achieve them. Finally, we demonstrated how this record can be used to overcome some of the limitations of earlier approaches.

Acknowledgments

The research described in this paper was supported in part by the Advanced Research Projects Agency under a NASA Ames cooperative agreement Number NCC 2-520. Johanna Moore is currently supported by grants from the Office of Naval Research Cognitive and Neural Sciences Division (Grant Number N00014-91-J-1694), the National Science Foundation Research Initiation Award (Grant Number IRI-9113041), and the National Library of Medicine. Cécile Paris gratefully acknowledges the support of the Advanced Research Projects Agency under the contract DABT63-91-C-0025 and the National Science Foundation (Grant Number IRI-9003078) while writing this paper.

The authors would like to thank William Swartout, who has advised us on this work since its inception and has also given us useful comments on this paper. We would also like to thank Martha Pollack for her help in clarifying some of the ideas presented in this paper, and Giuseppe Carenini, Violetta Cavalli-Sforza, Vibhu Mittal, Richmond Thomason, and Arlene Weiner, who provided useful comments on earlier drafts of this paper. Finally, we are indebted to the anonymous reviewers whose detailed and insightful comments greatly improved the final version of this paper.

References

Appelt, Douglas E. (1985). *Planning English Sentences*. Cambridge University Press.

Bateman, John A., and Paris, Cécile L. (1989). "Phrasing a text in terms the user can understand." In *Proceedings, Eleventh International Joint Conference on Artificial Intelligence*, 1511–1517. Detroit, MI.

Bateman, John A., and Paris, Cécile L. (1991). "Constraining the deployment of lexicogrammatical resources during text generation: Towards a computational instantiation of register theory." In *Functional and Systemic Linguistics: Approaches and Uses*, edited by Eija Ventola, 81–106. Mouton de Gruyter.

Bratman, Michael (1987). *Intentions, Plans, and Practical Reason*. Harvard University Press.

Brewer, W. F. (1980). "Literacy theory, rhetoric, and stylistics: Implications for psychology." In *Theoretical Issues in Reading Comprehension*, edited by R. J. Shapiro, B. C. Bruce, and W. F. Brewer, 221–239. Lawrence Erlbaum.

Cahour, Béatrice; Falzon, Pierre; and Robert, Jean Marc (1990). "From text coherence to interface consistency: A psycholinguistic approach." In *Work with Display Units 89*, edited by L. Berlinguet and D. Berthelette. Elsevier Science Publishers B.V.

Carberry, Sandra M. (1987). "Pragmatic modeling: Toward a robust natural language interface." *Computational Intelligence*, 3(3), 117–136.

Carenini, Giuseppe, and Moore, Johanna D. (1993). "Generating explanations in context." In *Proceedings, International Workshop on Intelligent User Interfaces*, edited by Wayne D. Gray, William E. Hefley, and Dianne Murray, 175–182. ACM Press.

Cawsey, Alison (1993). *Explanation and Interaction: The Computer Generation of Explanatory Dialogues*. MIT Press.

Charney, Davida H.; Reder, Lynne M.; and Wells, Gail W. (1988). "Studies of elaboration in instructional texts." In *Effective Documentation: What We Have Learned from Research*, edited by Stephen Doheny-Farina, 48–72. MIT Press.

Clancey, William J. (1983). "The epistemology of a rule-based expert system: A framework for explanation." *Artificial Intelligence*, 20(3), 215–251.

Cohen, Philip R. (1978). *On knowing what to say: Planning speech acts*. Doctoral dissertation, Department of Computer Science, University of Toronto.

Cohen, Philip R., and Levesque, Hector (1990). "Rational interaction as the basis for communication." In *Intentions in Communication*, edited by Philip R. Cohen, Jerry Morgan, and Martha E. Pollack, 221–255. MIT Press

Cohen, Philip R., and Perrault, C. Raymond (1979). "Elements of a plan-based theory of speech acts." *Cognitive Science*, 3, 177–212.

Davis, Lawrence H. (1979). *Theory of Action*. Prentice Hall.

Ehrlich, Marie-France, and Cahour, Béatrice (1991). "Contrôle métacognitif de la compréhension: cohésion d'un texte expositif et auto-évaluation de la compréhension." *Bulletin de Psychologie*, XLIV(399), 147–155. Special edition edited by E. Cauzinille and J. Beaudichon.

Goldman, Susan, and Durán, Richard P. (1988). "Answering questions from oceanography texts: Learner, task, and text characteristics." *Discourse Processes*, 1, 373–412.

Grimes, Joseph E. (1975). *The Thread of Discourse*. Mouton.

Grosz, Barbara J. (1977). "The representation and use of focus in dialogue understanding." Technical Report 151, SRI International, Menlo Park, CA.

Grosz, Barbara J., and Sidner, Candace L. (1986). "Attention, intention, and the structure of discourse." *Computational Linguistics*, 12(3), 175–204.

Hobbs, Jerry R. (1979). "Coherence and coreference." *Cognitive Science*, 3(1), 67–90.

Hobbs, Jerry R. (1983). "Why is discourse coherent?" In *Coherence in Natural Language Texts*, edited by F. Neubauer, 29–69. H. Buske.

Hobbs, Jerry R. (1985). "On the coherence and structure of discourse." Technical Report CSLI-85-37, Center for the Study of Language and Information, Leland Stanford Junior University, Stanford, California.

Hovy, Eduard H. (1988). *Generating Natural Language Under Pragmatic Constraints*. Lawrence Erlbaum.

Hovy, Eduard H. (1991). "Approaches to the planning of coherent text." In *Natural Language Generation in Artificial Intelligence and Computational Linguistics*, edited by Cécile L. Paris, William R. Swartout, and William C. Mann, 83–102. Kluwer Academic Publishers.

Kittredge, R.; Korelsky, T.; and Rambow, O. (1991). "On the need for domain communication knowledge." *Computational Intelligence*, 7(4), 305–314.

Klausmeier, Herbert J. (1976). "Instructional design and the teaching of concepts." In *Cognitive Learning in Children*, edited by J. R. Levin and V. L. Allen. Academic Press.

Levy, David M. (1979). "Communicative

goals and strategies: Between discourse and syntax." In *Syntax and Semantics. Volume 12: Discourse and Syntax*, edited by P. Cole and J. L. Morgan, 183–210. Academic Press.

Litman, Diane J., and Allen, James F. (1987). "A plan recognition model for subdialogues in conversations." *Cognitive Science*, 11, 163–200.

Mann, William C. (1984). "Discourse structures for text generation." In *Proceedings, Tenth International Conference on Computational Linguistics*, 367–375. Stanford, CA.

Mann, William C., and Matthiessen, Christian M. I. M. (1985). "A demonstration of the Nigel text generation computer program." In *Systemic Perspectives on Discourse: Selected Papers from the Ninth International Systemics Workshop*, edited by R. Benson and J. Greaves, 50–83. Ablex.

Mann, William C., and Thompson, Sandra A. (1988). "Rhetorical structure theory: Towards a functional theory of text organization." *TEXT*, 8(3), 243–281.

Maybury, Mark T. (1992). "Communicative acts for explanation generation." *International Journal of Man-Machine Studies*, 37(2), 135–172.

McCoy, Kathleen F. (1989). "Generating context sensitive responses to object-related misconceptions." *Artificial Intelligence*, 41(2), 157–195.

McKeown, Kathleen R. (1985). *Text Generation: Using Discourse Strategies and Focus Constraints to Generate Natural Language Text.* Cambridge University Press.

Meyer, B. J. F.; Brandt, D. M.; and Bluth, G. J. (1980). "Use of top-level structure in texts: Key for reading comprehension in ninth-grade students." *Reading Research Quarterly*, 16, 72–102.

Mittal, Vibhu O., and Paris, Cécile L. (1993). "Automatic documentation generation: The interaction between text and examples." In *Proceedings, Thirteenth International Joint Conference on Artificial Intelligence (IJCAI)*, Chambery, France.

Moore, Johanna D. (In press.) *Participating in Explanatory Dialogues: Interpreting and Responding to Questions in Context.* MIT Press.

Moore, Johanna D., and Paris, Cécile L. (1991). "Requirements for an expert system explanation facility." *Computational Intelligence*, 7(4), 367–370.

Moore, Johanna D., and Paris, Cécile L. (1992). "Exploiting user feedback to compensate for the unreliability of user models." *User Modeling and User-Adapted Interaction*, 2(4), 331–365.

Moore, Johanna D., and Pollack, Martha E. (1992). "A problem for RST: The need for multi-level discourse analysis." *Computational Linguistics*, 18(4), 537–544.

Moore, Johanna D., and Swartout, William R. (1989). "A reactive approach to explanation." In *Proceedings, Eleventh International Joint Conference on Artificial Intelligence*, 1504–1510. Detroit, MI.

Moore, Johanna D., and Swartout, William R. (1990). "Pointing: A way toward explanation dialogue." In *Proceedings, National Conference on Artificial Intelligence*, 457–464. Boston, MA.

Neches, Robert; Swartout, William R.; and Moore, Johanna D. (1985). "Enhanced maintenance and explanation of expert systems through explicit models of their development." *IEEE Transactions on Software Engineering*, SE-11(11), 1337–1351.

Paris, Cécile L. (1988). "Tailoring object descriptions to the user's level of expertise." *Computational Linguistics*, 14(3), 64–78.

Paris, Cécile L. (1991a). "Generation and explanation: Building an explanation facility for the explainable expert systems framework." In *Natural Language Generation in Artificial Intelligence and Computational Linguistics*, edited by Cécile L. Paris, William R. Swartout, and William C. Mann, 49–81. Kluwer Academic Publishers.

Paris, Cécile L. (1991b). *The Use of Explicit User Models in Text Generation: Tailoring to a User's Level of Expertise.* Frances Pinter.

Penman Natural Language Generation Group (1989). The Penman User Guide. Available from USC/Information Sciences Institute, 4676 Admiralty Way, Marina del Rey, CA.

Rambow, Owen (1990). "Domain communication knowledge." In *Proceedings, Fifth International Workshop on Natural Language Generation*, 87–94. Pittsburgh, PA

Redeker, Gisela (1990). "Ideational and pragmatic markers of discourse structure." *Journal of Pragmatics*, 14, 367–381.

Reithinger, Norbert (1991). *Eine parallele Architektur zur inkrementellen Generierung multimodaler Dialogbeiträge.* Doctoral dissertation, Technischen Fakultät der Universität des Saarlandes, Saarbrücken, Germany.

Robinson, Jane J. (1984). "Extending grammars to new domains." Technical Report ISI/RR-83-123, USC/Information Sciences Institute.

Rosenblum, James A., and Moore, Johanna D. (1993). "Participating in instructional dialogues: Finding and exploiting relevant prior explanations." In *Proceedings, World Conference on Artificial Intelligence in Education.*

Sacerdoti, Earl D. (1977). *A Structure for Plans and Behavior.* Elsevier.

Schiffrin, Deborah (1987). *Discourse Markers.* Cambridge University Press.

Shepherd, H. R. (1926). *The Fine Art of Writing.* Macmillan.

Sidner, Candace L. (1979). *Toward a computational theory of definite anaphora comprehension in English discourse.* Doctoral dissertation, Massachusetts Institute of Technology, Cambridge, MA.

Sidner, Candace L. (1985). "Plan parsing for intended response recognition in discourse." *Computational Intelligence*, 1(1), 1–10.

Sparck Jones, Karen (1989). "Realism about user modelling." In *User Models in Dialog Systems*, edited by Alfred Kobsa and Wolfgang Wahlster, 341–363. Symbolic Computation Series, Springer-Verlag.

Suthers, Daniel D. (1991). "Task-appropriate hybrid architectures for explanation." *Computational Intelligence*, 7(4), 315–333.

Swartout, William R. (1983). "XPLAIN: A system for creating and explaining expert consulting systems." *Artificial Intelligence*, 21(3), 285–325.

Swartout, William R.; Paris, Cécile L.; and Moore, Johanna D. (1991). "Design for explainable expert systems." *IEEE Expert*, 6(3), 58–64.

Wahlster, Wolfgang; André, Elisabeth; Graf, Winfried; and Rist, Thomas (1991). "Designing illustrated texts: How language production is influenced by graphics generation." In *Proceedings, European Chapter of the Association for Computational Linguistics*, 8–14. Berlin.

Planning Text for Advisory Dialogues: Capturing Intentional and Rhetorical Information

Johanna D. Moore and Cécile L. Paris

The main contribution of our research was to show that schemata of rhetorical relations or predicates cannot be used as the sole means of controlling discourse structure in an interactive dialog system. The basic problem is that such representations of a discourse do not fully specify the intentional structure of that discourse. Intentional structure is crucial for responding effectively to questions that address a previous utterance: without a record of what an utterance was intended to achieve, it is impossible to handle feedback indicating that the hearer does not fully understand or accept that utterance. The planner described here overcomes this limitation by representing information about the intended effect of individual parts of the text on the hearer as well as how the parts relate to one another rhetorically. This planner was originally developed as the basis for an interactive expert system explanation component (Moore 1995). However, because of the decoupling of intentional and rhetorical structures and the explicit reasoning about intention, it has been used and extended to address a wide range of issues in intelligent information presentation, including the generation of coordinated multimedia instructions (Wahlster et al. 1993), the production of descriptions that incorporate appropriate examples (Mittal and Paris 1993), and the generation of multilingual instructions from an underlying task model (Paris and Vander Linden 1996). In addition, others have developed a system based on the same principles to generate instructional hypermedia (De Carolis and Pizzutilo 1997).

Despite its usefulness, the discourse planning model we developed had several limitations: (1) it relied on a customized planning algorithm with procedural semantics for the purpose of solving specific text planning problems (e.g., guaranteeing a legal RST structure), (2) the action description language blurred the distinction between action and effect, and (3) the expressive power of action descriptions was limited (e.g., actions could have only one effect). To overcome these limitations, Young, Moore, and Pollack (1994) built on research coming from the AI planning community to develop a new algorithm that introduces action decomposition into a partial-order causal link planner. The algorithm is implemented in a discourse planner called Longbow, which is currently being used to generate tutorial dialogs, for example, (Freedman and Evens 1996), and to provide textual guidance to support understanding of novel visualizations (Mittal et al. 1995).

REFERENCES

De Carolis, B., and Pizzutilo, S. 1997. From Discourse Plans to User Adapted Hypermedia. In *Proceedings of the Sixth International Conference on User Modeling*, 37–40.

Freedman, R., and Evens, M. 1996. Generating and Revising Hierarchical Multi-Turn Text Plans in an ITS. In *Proceedings of the 3rd International Conference on Intelligent Tutoring Systems*, 632–640.

Mittal, V., and Paris, C. 1993. Automatic Documentation Generation: The Interaction between Text and Examples. In *Proceedings of IJCAI'93*, Chambery, France, 1158–1163.

Mittal, V.; Roth, S.; Moore, J. D.; Mattis, J.; and Carenini, G. 1995. Generating Explanatory Captions for Information Graphics. In *Proceedings of IJCAI'95*, Montreal, Canada, 1276–1283.

Moore, J. D. 1995. *Participating in Explanatory Dialogues: Interpreting and Responding to Questions in Context*. Cambridge, MA: MIT Press.

Paris, C., and Vander Linden, K. 1996. An Interactive Support Tool for Writing Multilingual Manuals. *IEEE Computer* 29(7): 49–56.

Wahlster, W.; André, E.; Finkler, W.; Profitlich, J.; and Rist, T. 1993. Plan-Based Integration of Natural Language and Graphics Generation. *Artificial Intelligence* 63(1–2): 387–428.

Young, R. M.; Moore, J. D.; and Pollack, M. E. 1994. Towards a Principled Representation of Discourse Plans. In *Proceedings of the 16th Annual Conference of the Cognitive Science Society*, 946–951. Hillsdale, NJ: Lawrence Erlbaum.

Planning interactive explanations

ALISON CAWSEY

Computing Science Department, University of Glasgow, 17 Lilybank Gardens, Glasgow, UK

Human verbal explanations are essentially interactive. If someone is giving a complex explanation, the hearer will be given the opportunity to indicate whether they are following as the explanation proceeds, and if necessary interrupt with clarification questions. These interactions allow the speaker to both clear up the hearer's immediate difficulties as they arise, and to update assumptions about their level of understanding. Better models of the hearer's level of understanding in turn allow the speaker to continue the explanation in a more appropriate manner, lessening the risk of continuing confusion.

Despite its apparent importance, existing explanation and text generation systems fail to allow for this sort of interaction. Although some systems allow follow-up questions at the end of an explanation, they assume that a complete explanation has been planned and generated before such interactions are allowed. However, for complex explanations interactions with the user should take place as the explanation progresses, and should influence how that explanation continues.

This paper describes the EDGE system, which is able to plan complex, extended explanations which allow such interactions with the user. The system can update assumptions about the user's knowledge on the basis of these interactions, and uses this information to influence the detailed further planning of the explanation. When the user appears confused, the system can attempt to fill in missing knowledge or to explain things another way.

1. Introduction

There are many computer applications which have to give explanations to the user. These include help systems, which may explain how to use some complex command; expert systems, which may explain their recommendations or diagnoses; and tutorial systems, which may explain some complex concept to the user.† In many cases the information required may be extensive and involve many potentially unknown concepts, so there is a strong possibility that the user may not understand a particular presentation. In order to improve such explanations it is therefore necessary both to try and prevent such misunderstandings happening in the first place (by choosing an appropriate presentation for the particular user), and to provide a framework where misunderstandings can be dealt with when they occur.

Until recently most of the work on improving the acceptability and understandability of explanations has concentrated on the first of these—tailoring an explanation (or description) to a particular user based on assumptions about what the user knows (e.g. Weiner, 1980; Paris, 1987; Wallis & Shortliffe, 1985). However, there is no guarantee that this approach will result in a satisfactory explanation, as the assumptions made about the user's knowledge are unlikely to be accurate. It is therefore important that we are able to deal with the user's misunderstandings when they occur, and also to update any assumptions about the user's knowledge as an explanation progresses. The user should be involved in a dialogue and be able to indicate what they have understood (or not) and ask clarification questions when confusions arise.

Although several authors have noted the importance of dialogue in human explanation and advice giving, and proposed that computational advice and explanation systems should be similarly interactive (e.g. Pollack *et al.*, 1982; Gilbert, 1987), most existing systems, as Moore (1990) observes, still treat explanation and advice giving as a "one-shot" process. Moore's own work is a notable exception, placing importance on allowing clarification questions to be asked at the end of an explanation, and answered in the context of this preceding explanation. The "explanatory dialogue" then consists of an initial explanation, and a sequence of follow-up clarifications. However, although this approach is appropriate for short, fairly simple explanations, it is not sufficient for long and complex explanations. When a complex explanation is being given the user (or explainee) must have the opportunity to ask for clarification as soon as they "lose track" of the explanation, and not wait until the explanation is complete. This allows the system (or explainer) both to clear up the immediate confusion, and to adjust any assumptions about their level of understanding. This in turn enables the system to continue the explanation in a more appropriate manner.

The system described in this paper (referred to as the EDGE system, or Explanatory Discourse GEnerator) aims, therefore, to show how an extended explanation may be generated which allows interactions with the user as the explanation proceeds. The particular type of explanations considered in order to explore these issues are *tutorial* explanations of *how something works*. Such explanations are normally quite complex, and involve numerous interactions between explainer and explainee. A fragment of an explanation generated by the system (during an evaluation session with a user) is given in Figure 1.

In common with Moore (1990), the approach taken in this work is to view the generation of an explanation as a simple planning problem—a sequence of linguistic

---

S: OK, we're going to be explaining how the heat detector works.
   Do you know what the heat detector circuit is like?
U: **No**
S: A heat detector circuit is a sort of potential divider circuit.
U: **What does a heat detector circuit do?**
S: I'll be getting on to that in a minute.
   Do you know what the potential divider circuit does for different inputs?
U: **No**
S: Oh well, let's go through what the potential divider circuit does.
   When it has one low (fully conducting) input resistance (near 9V rail) and one high (not conducting) input resistance (near 0V rail) then the output voltage is high (9V)...

FIGURE 1. Fragment of interactive explanation generated by EDGE system.

† Note that we are using the term "explain" in a fairly general sense, meaning "to make clear or intelligible", and not limited to giving justifications.

(or graphical†) actions must be found to achieve some communicative goal.‡ However, unlike Moore we use two levels of planning. One level is concerned with planning the content of the explanation, while the other level is concerned with organizing the dialogue with the user. Both these aspects of discourse planning depend on the system's assessment of the discourse situation. For example, choices in content planning depend on the system's assumptions about the user's knowledge, while choices in dialogue planning depend on the rôles of the system and user. As the explanation depends on possibly changing aspects of the discourse situation, the explanation is planned incrementally, interleaving planning and execution. The system does not decide either on the details of what to say or the order in which it is said until it has to, and when confusions occur it can attempt either to fill in missing knowledge or to re-explain concepts that were misunderstood.

The rest of this paper will describe the system in more detail. However, first the background to the system will be given. This consists of a discussion of related work in several fields, and a description of the initial empirical analyses of human explanatory dialogues.

2. Related work

As far as we know there have been no previously published attempts to generate interactive tailored explanations of the sort that we are concerned with here. However, there is a huge amount of research relevant to explanation and dialogue in general. The EDGE system therefore takes ideas from many different research areas. This section briefly reviews some of the more important areas, indicating how each contributes to EDGE.

The section is organized in three main parts. In the first, work relevant to organizing and selecting the content of an explanation is discussed; in the second, different approaches to dialogue structure are introduced; and in the third, ways of updating assumptions about the user's knowledge.

2.1. SELECTING AND ORGANIZING THE INFORMATION

Within artificial intelligence there are two main areas concerned with selecting and ordering information to be conveyed. The first, concerned primarily with the *coherence* of the presentation, is the fast-growing area of text planning. The second relevant area is in the very different field of intelligent tutoring systems, where there has been recent interest in how to plan an individual curriculum (or sequence of lessons), given assumptions about the user's (student's) knowledge.

2.1.1. Text planning

Within computational linguistics there has been interest recently in how coherent multi-sentence descriptions may be generated. Two main approaches have dominated, the first using *schemàta* to constrain the overall organization of the text, and the second using *planning operators* to generate a sequence of utterances given particular communicative goals.

In a *schema*-based approach (McKeown, 1985) standard patterns of discourse structure are encoded which capture the organization of a wide range of texts (such as definitions and descriptions), and these patterns are used to constrain the organization of a generated text given some information to convey. These patterns are based on sequences of general purpose *rhetorical predicates,* (such as *identification, attribute, comparison* and *evidence*), and are obtained by detailed analysis of many texts. For example, one of the patterns which McKeown (1985) identified as being commonly used in giving definitions was the *constituency* schema. Roughly speaking, this involved first *identifying* the object, then presenting the *constituents* of the object, giving characteristic information about each in turn, and finally presenting additional *attributive* information about the object being defined.

Paris (1987) extended McKeown's work by considering how these common patterns of text structure depend on the expertise level of the intended reader. From an analysis of adult and children's encyclopaedias she showed that device descriptions aimed at a relative expert followed the *constituency schema* mentioned above, while those aimed at those with less expertise are given largely in terms of a *process* description based on causal links explaining the behaviour of the device. By combining process and constituency schemata depending on assumptions about the user's knowledge her system could generate descriptions tailored to the user.

Schema-based approaches have the problem that they fail to provide an explanatory account of *why* a particular text type is structured in a particular way, and as a result are not easy to adapt to particular situations. In order to generate texts applicable to a new situation, new texts must first be analysed in detail to determine the appropriate schema. Plan-based accounts aim to overcome this problem partially by associating particular general text structures with the communicative goals that they are used to achieve (Moore, 1990; Moore & Paris, 1990; Maybury, 1990). Moore, for example, attempts to base her text planner on a theory of *rhetorical relations* which links the relations between sections of a text to the communicative goal that the text is intended to achieve (Mann & Thompson, 1987). For example, a *motivation* relation may exist between sections of a text where the goal is to convince the hearer to carry out some action. These relations are encoded as planning operators (with the *effect* of the operator corresponding to the communicative goal the associated relation is used to achieve) and used in a simple hierarchical planning system which both determines what to say (given the communicative goal) and how it should be structured. Moore makes the point that this representation (unlike schemata) enables the system to reason about its own explanation, as the goals of the different parts of the explanation are all explicit. This enables follow-up questions to be dealt with intelligently, including *repairing* a misunderstood explanation by re-explaining things another way.

Moore's system is important in emphasizing the importance of dialogue and replanning in explanation generation. However, as her system was designed to generate short explanations in the context of an interaction with an expert system she focuses on the dialogue which results from the follow-up questions asked by the user after a planned explanation is complete. She does not consider the interactions

† In the domain chosen (explaining how things work) graphical actions, such as pointing at a diagram, are vital to an explanation. Although this research does not focus on how these may best be generated, the system does allow a limited range of such actions.

‡ In the EDGE system the overall communicative goal is always to get the user to understand some complex concept, such as how a device works. Moore (1990) considers a wider range of communicative goals, such as persuading the user to take some action, but the basic approach remains the same.

which may take place in the middle of a long explanation, or how they influence the way such an explanation develops. Also, while her system is able to choose between alternative explanation strategies depending on the knowledge of the user, she does not consider how the understandability of an explanation may depend on *prerequisite* relations between the concepts being explained.

The next section will introduce a research area which has paid more attention to planning a presentation based on relationships between concepts in the domain, and which has had to consider interactions with the user in the middle of a planned sequence of teaching actions.

2.1.2. *Curriculum planning*

In the last few years there have been several attempts to produce systems that will plan an individualized curriculum, or sequence of lessons, given knowledge of a particular student's understanding in some domain. Although these are concerned with the organization of information at a much higher level than text generation systems (with terminal actions corresponding to entire lessons rather than single utterances), many of the ideas apply to the generation of interactive explanations. In particular, this work has considered how the presentation of information should depend on prerequisite relations between concepts, and what to do when a step in a partially completed lesson plan fails.

One of the first attempts was the planner developed by Peachey and McCalla (1986). Planning operators could be defined for teaching different concepts or skills in a particular domain. An operator described the prerequisite concepts which should be known in order for the concept to be effectively learned, the effect of the operator on the user's knowledge and an action that could be invoked in order to teach that skill. Possible teaching actions proposed included giving a lecture, playing a game or presenting a simulation.

Given a skill to be made known and assumptions about the user's prior knowledge a simple STRIPS-like planner (Fikes *et al.*, 1972) could be invoked to plan a curriculum for that user. The result of this planning process would be a representation of alternative partially ordered sequences of teaching actions. Of course, the effects of any teaching action cannot be guaranteed, so an important feature of the system was the ability to re-invoke the planner to repair the curriculum plan if checks on the user's understanding indicated that the desired concepts had not been learned.

Other recent curriculum planning systems include those by MacMillan *et al.* (1988), Lesgold (1988) and Murray (1989). Murray's system is perhaps the most interesting. He uses four levels of planning: planning lesson objectives using domain-dependent knowledge; planning the presentation; planning to deal with interruptions; and meta-planning based on preferences in the planning process. Murray therefore provides a more explicit model of how to deal with student initiative within a planning framework.

These systems illustrate the use of prerequisite relations between concepts to plan some complex presentation; the importance of checking understanding and replanning; and the use of several levels of planning dealing with different aspects of the problem. Each of these features of curriculum planning is equally applicable to the planning of an extended explanation, and the EDGE model shares many features with these systems. However, planning an extended interactive explanation involves new problems, such as how to organize the dialogue with the user and how to use the dialogue in order to update and check assumptions about the user's knowledge. The next two sections will therefore discuss these issues.

2.2. CHOOSING DIALOGUE ACTIONS

For an explanatory dialogue system it is important to consider how to select and organize interactions with the user, and how to respond to user initiative within a system-driven explanation. There are several relevant areas of research. Within the field of intelligent tutoring systems there has been some work carried out on tutorial dialogues, where the system is controlling some question–answer session in order to instruct the student. Within linguistics and sociolingusitics there has been much research on the organization of human discourse, while within computational linguistics discourse models have been developed based on the goals and plans of the participants. Each of these areas is relevant to the design of an explanatory dialogue system, and each has influenced the EDGE model.

2.2.1. *Tutorial dialogues*

The EDGE system is particularly concerned with *tutorial* explanatory dialogues, so previous work on tutorial dialogues is very relevant. Work in this area has been mainly concerned with emulating the cababilities of human tutors in testing and instructing a student through a question–answer dialogue. A tutorial dialogue system must consider both how to select appropriate topics to question the user about, and how to respond to the user's perceived errors and misconceptions. The WHY system, for example (Stevens & Collins, 1977), based topic selection on traversing a *script* representing a physical process being taught, questioning the user on each stage in the process. The system could respond to the user's errors by invoking dialogue rules which aimed to get the user to realize the consequences of their misconceptions, emulating a *Socratic* dialogue style. The system therefore tried to get users to thank about their errors, rather than just correcting them.

Other notable systems include the GUIDON system (Clancey, 1983) and MENO tutor (Woolf & McDonald, 1984) and its later developments (e.g. Woolf & Murray 1987). Woolf and Murray, for example present general discourse schemata for controlling a tutorial dialogue, including a remediation schema which describes what actions to take when the user makes an error. This schema involves first acknowledging any ***grain of truth*** in the answer, then giving information which aimed to make the user realize why the answer was wrong. This might include giving an example, an analogy or showing the consequence of the error.

These early systems all assume that the system dominates and controls the dialogue (as is the case in the EDGE system). More recent work (e.g. Baker, 1989) has aimed to provide a framework for more complex types of tutorial dialogue where teacher and student have more equal roles. However, practical systems have not yet been developed based on this, and the EDGE system is closer in some respects to the earlier work where the system was dominant. The system borrows ideas from this work (such as having remediation strategies for responding to user/student errors) but extends it in various ways. In particular, the system shows how the content of the dialogue may be planned, how user initiative can be dealt with in the context of such a planned dialogue and how assumptions about the user may be updated. The EDGE system can also be used to generate interactive explanations of other types (than tutorial) where testing the user's understanding, for example, may be inappropriate.

2.2.2. *Discourse analysis*

Another area of research which provides insights into how dialogues should be organized comes from work on discourse analysis—and in particular the tradition started by Sinclair and Coulthard (1975), which considers the characteristic high-level organization of particular types of discourse. Sinclair and Coulthard show how the normal structure of classroom discourse may be described using rules similar to rules of syntax. They use five categories of discourse unit in their description, with rules relating the type of discourse items in one category to possible combinations of types of items in the category below. The five categories proposed are the following: the *lesson* (or in other discourse types the *interaction*), the *transaction* (on some topic), the *exchange*, the *move* and the *linguistic act*.

The EDGE dialogue planner uses the last four of these categories, focusing on the organization of the transaction (and in particular the *informing* transaction) and of different types of exchanges. Sinclair and Coulthard, for example, show that an informing transaction consists of an opening boundary exchange, an informing exchange and a closing boundary exchange. The informing exchange (as defined by them) may in turn involve what they term *pupil-elicit* exchanges (where the student asks a question) and *teacher-elicit* exchanges (where the teacher asks a question), as well as informing statements and feedback from the student. The organization of the different types of exchanges is in turn described in terms of types of move, such as *initiating* and *response* moves.

A variant of this basic framework has been previously applied in work on natural language dialogue systems (Wachtel, 1986; Ferrari & Reilly, 1986), where the discourse structure is used to provide expectations concerning the user's input. However, it has not previously been used for the *control* of a dialogue. Many of the details of the framework have had to be adapted, but the basic categories and hierarchical structuring have proved useful for defining the structure of (and therefore controlling) explanatory dialogues. Explicitly defining dialogue structures in this way allows for a range of different dialogue types (e.g. tutorial *vs* advisory) to be defined independent of other aspects of the system.

2.2.3. *Plan-based models of discourse*

The "syntactic" models of discourse described above can be compared with McKeown's schemata describing text structure. Although they do capture the organization of particular types of discourse they do little to explain *why* the discourse has that structure or to relate it to the communicative goals of the speaker.

Within computational linguistics there have been a number of research projects that aimed to show how actions in a dialogue relate to the goals and intentions of the participants. For example, Allen & Perrault (1980) showed how the intentions behind utterances could be analysed by representing knowledge about both dialogue actions (such as speech acts) and domain actions (such as the action of boarding a train) as planning operators. The *request* speech act was represented as a planning operator with the *effect* that the hearer wants to carry out the requested action, while the *board train* action was represented as an operator with the precondition that the agent was at the right location, and the effect that the agent was on the train. Their system could reason about utterances like "What platform does the train to Edinburgh leave from?" and infer that the speaker probably wants to board the train to Edinburgh.

More recent work in this area has considered in more detail how speech acts should be represented, how plans may be best inferred from sequences of utterances, and how joint plans should be represented. Much of this work is described in (Cohen *et al.*, 1990).

Unlike the work above, the EDGE dialogue planning rules do not make explicit the effect of different speech acts on the mental state of the hearer, but rather define when different higher-level dialogue actions (such as types of exchanges) should be used. The rules are based on normal discourse conventions adapted from the more syntactic models of discourse discussed in the last section, and provide an efficient and practical approach to the flexible generation of fairly complex dialogues. However, the EDGE system's distinction between content and dialogue planning rules is similar to the distinctions between domain and discourse planning operators referred to above.†

2.3. UPDATING A USER MODEL

In an explanatory dialogue it should be possible to guess what the user knows, and update these guesses or assumptions based on the interactions with the user. We will therefore briefly review work on user modelling. As the EDGE system is only concerned with using the user's *knowledge* (and not his goals or preferences), and as we do not explicitly address the problem of inferring student misconceptions we will only be concerned with *overlay* modelling where the user's knowledge is represented as a subset of the expert's.

One important technique for guessing what the user may know (or other aspects of a user model) is through the use of stereotypes (Rich, 1979). Here a user is assigned to some class (e.g. technican) and assumed to have the typical attributes of that class. A simple version of the approach is to assign the user to a class representing their level of expertise, and label concepts in the domain according to their difficulty (or strictly speaking, the level of expertise at which they are normally learned). Then users in classes more expert than the concept's difficulty level may be assumed to know the concept, and users below that level may be assumed not to (given no evidence to the contrary). This provides a very simple, but reasonably effective way of guessing the user's knowledge and has been used in a number of recent systems (Chin, 1988; Sleeman 1985).

However, where there are interactions with the user the more important issue is perhaps how to update and revise this model as the dialogue progresses. This should be based on several sorts of interactions: from the user's utterances (e.g. Kass & Finin, 1987); from the system's utterances and the user's response (or lack of

† The main difference is that the EDGE system's content goals refer to concepts that the system wants the user to understand, while domain goals usually refer to a physical state of affairs which some agent wants.

response); from questions asked by the user; and from questions answered by the user. It should also be possible to make implicit inferences based on the relationships between concepts in the knowledge base. These different sources of information are discussed by Wahlster and Kobsa (1989), for example.

The EDGE user modelling component uses both stereotype information and interactions with the user. Initial "guesses" about the user's knowledge based on his stated level of expertise are revised based on interactions as the explanatory dialogue progresses.

3. Human explanatory dialogues

The details of the EDGE model are based on a simple prior analysis of human explanatory dialogues. Eleven different experts were each asked to explain how a set of eight simple electronic circuits worked. The resulting (verbal) explanations were recorded and later transcribed and analysed. Seven of the experts explained to a "real" novice, who might interrupt, and who could be questioned about their understanding. Each expert explained to a different novice. The remaining four experts explained to a passive observer, with no interaction between the two. (This enabled the analysis of explanation content separate from the dialogue). Altogether, 52 interactive explanations (involving a novice) and 32 non-interactive explanations were obtained.

From these analysed explanations it was possible to derive a schema or grammar representing the typical organization of the explanation content in this particular domain, and to make a number of observations about the dialogue. The following sections will first discuss the organization of the content of the explanations, and then go on to discuss features of the dialogue.

3.1. THE STRUCTURE OF THE CONTENT OF THE EXPLANATIONS

Texts may be classified in many ways. For example, sections of the text may be classified according to the type of information being conveyed. This is essentially the approach of "story grammar" analyses (Rumelhart, 1975) where terms like *setting* and *event* are used. Another approach is to classify the rhetorical relations that exist between text sections (Mann & Thompson, 1987), such as *evidence, summary* and *background.* Yet another type of analysis relevant to the analysis of explanations considers what different explanation strategies are being used to convey information. For example, a concept may be explained through *examples,* by giving an *analogy,* by referring to a more general concept (*classification*) or simply by conceptual *decomposition.*†

In order to understand the organization of an explanation it is useful to consider all these types of analysis/categorization, as each relates to a different aspect of explanation structure. Attempting to describe texts using a single level of description leads to the mixing of different types of category, such as schemata involving both explanation strategies (e.g. analogy), content (e.g. causal-event) and rhetorical predicates (e.g. illustration) (McKeown, 1985; Paris, 1987). Yet a causal event may be described using an analogy and serve as an illustration of some other concept.

The explanations in the corpus were analysed primarily in terms of the organization of the *content* of the explanation, using terms like *causal-event, process* and *behaviour* to classify items in the texts. However, the analysis also considered what rhetorical relations and explanation strategies appeared to be being used. Figure 2 gives an example uninterrupted explanation from the corpus which illustrates the typical structure of the explanations. In terms of content the first line *identifies* the circuit as a kind of potential divider circuit. Lines 2–4 give a description of the *components* of the circuit, while line 5 describes its *function.* Lines 6–11 describe the *processes* that occur when light falls on the circuit in terms of *causal-events* (such as light falling causing resistance to change). Finally line 12 summarizes the overall *behaviour* of the device. In terms of rhetorical relations we can hypothesize that lines 1–5 provide *background* information to the explanation of how the circuit works (lines 6–11) while there appears to be a *summary* relation between lines 6–11 and line 12. Explanation strategies used include *classifying* the circuit as an instance of a known class (in line 1) and giving *example* process descriptions in lines 8–9 and 10–11 to illustrate how the circuit works.

Figure 3 shows a simplified grammar representing the different possible sequences of types of information in the analysed explanations,† along with the rhetorical relations and explanation strategies which seemed to be being used. All except two of the uninterrupted explanations followed the basic pattern indicated by the rules, and though the dialogues were harder to analyse (given extensive user interruptions) the majority had the same basic form. As far as possible the terms used in the content grammar rules reflect what sort of information is being conveyed. However, the term *structure* is used rather loosely to include background descriptive information about the device, including details of its components.

As well as the content structuring rules the figure shows what rhetorical relations and explanation strategies seem to be being used. For example, there is a

1. Well, this here looks to be a potential divider circuit
2. and it contains two components
3. one of which is a light-dependent resistor
4. and the other is a variable resistor.
5. The purpose of this circuit is to provide a varying output voltage on this line here.
6. The idea is that when light falls on this light-dependent resistor its resistance changes,
7. so therefore because the resistance of this series circuit has changed the voltage at this point here can change.
8. So, when light falls on the LDR the resistance of this part of the circuit is very low
9. and so this voltage here is a high voltage.
10. In darkness the resistance of the LDR is large
11. and so the voltage at this point drops to a low value.
12. So, we can get a high or low output depending on how much light is falling on the light-dependent resistor.

FIGURE 2. Example uninterrupted human explanation.

† These explanation strategies have often been associated with rhetorical relations. For example, the purpose of one section of text may be to provide an *example* illustrating another. However, in analysing explanations it appears more useful to look at these separately as strategies for getting concepts across, rather than as functional relations between text sections.

† Note that any item in the rules should be considered optional, the rules just constraining the order of information presentation—some "explanations" included simply a process or behaviour description. "+" indicates items that may be repeated, such as describing each component in a system.

Content structuring rules	Rhetorical relations	Explanation strategies
How-it-works→ Description, Process$^+$, Behaviour	Background Summary	Examples
Structure→ Identification, Components, Functions.	Elaboration?	Classificiation
Structure→ Similarity, Component$^+$, (differences)	Compare–Contrast	Analogy
Components→ Constituency Component$^+$	Background?	Decomposition
Component→ Identification Behaviour	Background	Decomposition
Process→ Causal-event$^+$	Sequence	Decomposition
Behaviour→ Causal-event$^+$	Joint?	Examples

FIGURE 3. Describing text structure.

relationship of *background* between the *process* description and the *structure* of the device, while the second *structure* rule is using an *analogy* with a related device. These relations and explanation strategies show how different types of content function in relation to one another. For example, the *causal-event* type may serve in different roles, such as an *example* in illustrating the behaviour of a device or as part of a *sequence* of events demonstrating an overall process.

It is worth briefly contrasting the results of this analysis with the more wide ranging analyses of Paris and McKeown (McKeown, 1985; Paris, 1987). Although they have much in common, with the initial device description (captured in the *structure* rule) largely consistent with, say, McKeown's *constituency* and proposed *analogy* schemata, we differ from Paris who observed constituency and process descriptions to be alternatives depending on the knowledge of the hearer. In our corpus, where the speaker was given the specific goal of explaining how something worked, the constituency/analogy description appeared as background information necessary in order to make sense of the process description, occurring before it, with its inclusion dependent on the user's knowledge.

A comprehensive account of text structure should represent the constraints on each level of description (content *vs* relations *vs* explanation strategy), how each interacts with the others and thus constrains the organization of the whole text. However, such a full account will be left to further work. The most important level of description for our purposes is captured in the content structuring rules, and it is these that we focus on in the initial system. Only one type of rhetorical relation is explicitly considered, and that is the *background* relation. This is related to *prerequisite* relations which exist between concepts being explained, and so is vital if explanations are to be generated which depend on the user's knowledge. In particular, the analysis suggests that a prerequisite to understanding a causal explanation of a device's behaviour includes a knowledge of the component behaviours, as well as general knowledge of the class and function of the device. The EDGE system represents these prerequisite topics as preconditions in content planning rules, and therefore can generate explanations where this background information is only included if not already believed to be understood.

3.2. THE STRUCTURE OF THE DIALOGUE

The seven sets of interactive explanations analysed varied widely in the dialogue style adopted by the participants. Some experts adopted a tutorial rôle, taking the students step by step through some reasoning. Others adopted a simple informative rôle, giving an explanation and dealing with any clarification questions. Still others adopted a co-operative rôle, allowing the novice to contribute steps of the explanation on an equal basis to the expert.

Depending on the different rôles adopted by the participants different dialogue features occurred (some being illustrated in Figure 4). Common to all the dialogues were the presence of:

Opening and closing exchanges or statements, whereby the beginnings and ends of topics and conversations were negotiated or marked. These are present in some form in all types of dialogue, but the form depends heavily on the participants rôles. For example, in a formal tutorial rôle the expert may indicate explicitly what he is about to say (as illustrated in Figure 4) without giving the novice any opportunity to change the topic.

Checking moves and acknowledgements, where the expert paused, and gave the user the opportunity to indicate whether they were following. Again, all dialogues provide some opportunities for the hearer to indicate if they are following, though in a tutorial context this may be more obvious, as indicated in the figure.

Clarification questions. These occurred both in the middle of an explanation, interrupting its flow, and at the end of an explanation. We therefore distinguish in Figure 4 between interrupting clarifications and follow-up clarifications. Clarification questions of some kind were present in almost all the dialogues, the exceptions being dialogues where a simple circuit was being explained to a relatively knowledgeable novice.

Where the expert adopted an explicit tutorial rôle there were also:

Tutorial questions and responses, where the expert explicitly tested the novice's understanding and responded to any perceived errors in the novice's reply.

The EDGE dialogue model attempts to incorporate these different features within a common discourse planning framework, allowing variation depending on the participants rôles. The overall structure of the dialogue can be described using a modified version of the hierarchical model of discourse structure suggested by Sinclair and Coulthard (1975), mentioned in Section 2.2.2. *Transactions* on some

Opening exchange:
E: What I'm goint to do is to get you to explain this last circuit to me. Before I do that I better say briefly what a comparator is.

Closing exchange:
N: OK
E: Is that sufficient?
N: I think I know what's going on with it.

Checking moves and acknowledgements:
E: . . . as variable depending on the value of the resistance.
N: OK
E: I can just write a relationship, this is I1, the output voltage is I1 times R.
N: Right.

Follow-up clarifications:
E: In this circuit we have an output whose voltage depends on the amount of light falling on the LDR. And the more light falls on here, the more it will conduct so the higher the voltage will be here.
N: What does LDR stand for?
E: Light-dependent resistor.
N: What's this bit?
E: That's a variable resistor, . .

Interrupting clarifications:
E: These components here, you might consider them as being both resistors. Two variable resistors. I can write down a relation for resistance. .
N: You'll have to tell me what a resistance is.
E: A resistor is just . . . (clarification sub-dialogue describing resistance)
N: I see, or at least, I think I see.
E: Well, in this circuit here there are just two resistors, . . .

Tutorial exchanges:
E: Yeah, what's going to happen to the resistance between here and here?
N: It's going to be low.
E: So what's going to happen to the voltage here, if you have a very low resistance?
N: It's going to tend to a high limit.

FIGURE 4. Types of exchange in explanatory dialogues.

topic generally begin with some opening exchange, then involve a number of tutorial and informing exchanges and interrupting clarification sequences, and finally end with a closing exchange. The structure of the different types of exchanges can be described in terms of types of moves, which in some cases consisted of several distinct linguistic acts. The definitions of these different types of exchanges allows each of the above dialogue features to be incorporated in the model. For example, closing exchanges are defined to allow for the possibility of follow-up questions, while informing exchanges involve pausing for acknowledgements for the user which provides a form of checking move and allows the user to interrupt with some clarification question.

Within this basic framework different dialogue styles may be defined depending on the rôle of the system. For example, given a formal tutorial rôle the system will structure topic-opening exchanges so that the user is told what will follow, but not be given the opportunity to change the topic. Given a non-tutorial (e.g., advisory) rôle the system will not select tutorial exchanges, and will structure opening and closing exchanges differently. The system does not currently allow dialogue styles where the participants rôles are equal, or the user is dominant. Allowing this type of dialogue would require both a more complex dialogue model and more flexible input mechanism for the user, who can currently only input questions, replies and acknowledgements through menus provided by the system. The practical development of an interactive explanation system which does not assume that the system is dominant will be left for further work.

4. Planning understandable explanation content

Having examined the organization of human explanatory dialogues, and reviewed some relevant research areas, the remaining sections will present the EDGE computational model of explanatory discourse. This first section will be concerned with planning the overall content of the explanation. This will be followed by a section describing the planning of the dialogue with the user (and how this interacts with the content planning), a section describing how misunderstandings are dealt with in the explanatory dialogue, and a section on how the discourse context (e.g. assumptions about user's knowledge) is updated through the interactions and influences the development of the explanation.

The EDGE content planner is concerned with generating *understandable* explanations by both capturing *prerequisite relations* between concepts being explained, and alternative strategies for explaining those concepts. General rhetorical relations are not treated explicitly as appear of more marginal importance for the type of tutorial explanations considered. The content structuring rules given in Figure 1 were reformulated in terms of planning rules. Given a particular concept such as *how-it-works* or *behaviour*, one or more planning rules were defined which represented both the prerequisite knowledge required (as *preconditions* of the rule) and the sub-steps involved in conveying the concept (as *subgoals* of the rule). *Constraints* on planning rules represent the situations in which the particular rule may be successfully applied, such as only using an analogy-based planning rule if the analogous concept is known. The *effect* of a content planning rule is not represented explicitly as it is highly uncertain—a content planning operator which has the goal (`how-it-works (device)`) has the effect that system assumes the user knows how the device works IF the interaction with the user during the explanation do not suggest otherwise. The user modelling component will determine whether this is the case.

Figure 5 illustrates six of these content planning rules (denoted c-plans).† The first is a top-level strategy for explaining how a device works. Prerequisite knowledge involves knowing the *structure* of the device, which includes (in our definition of the term) knowledge of the device type and components. This information may either be conveyed directly, using the third rule, or can be conveyed by a comparison with a similar device, using the second rule. The fourth rule describes how the

† Note that in the representation used the first bracketed expression represents arguments to the planning rule which will be instantiated to particular values. Items in other bracketed expressions will normally be each evaluated in this context using normal LISP evaluation. Some of the details of the presentation and content of the planning rules have changed since earlier papers.

```
c-plan how-it-works (device)
  preconditions: structure (device)
  subgoals: c-goal process (device)
            c-goal behaviour (device)

c-plan structure (device)
  constraints: device-analogy (device)
               know-user
                   ((list 'structure (device-analog device)))
  subgoals: c-goal compare-structure (device (device-analog device))

c-plan structure (device)
  subgoals: c-goal identify (device)
            c-goal components (device)
            c-goal function (device)

c-plan components (device)
  subgoals: c-goal constituency (device)
            forall component in (components device)
                   (c-goal behaviour (component))

c-plan component (device)
  preconditions: know-user identify-diagram (device)
  subgoals: c-goal behaviour (device)

c-plan identify-diagram (device)
  subgoals: call point-at ((device-position device)))
            d-goal teaching . exchange ((list 'identify-diagram device))
```

FIGURE 5. Example content planning rules.

components of a device are explained by first giving the *constituency* (i.e. mentioning what components the circuit is made up of) then describing each component in turn. Describing a component (fifth rule) involves identifying it on the diagram (if not already recognized) and then giving its behaviour. The last rule in the figure illustrates a mixture of discourse and graphical actions in the rule to *identify* a component on a diagram.

In general explanation planning involves using content planning rules (c-plans) to try and satisfy content goals (or c-goals) and dialogue planning rules (d-plans) to satisfy dialogue goals (d-goals). Content goals will be concepts to be made known, while dialogue goals will be things like types of exchages which are to be used. Initially one or more goals will be placed on an agenda. Goals on this agenda will be partially ordered, and planning will proceed by repeating the following basic planning step:

1. A goal is selected from the agenda. The selection depends on the partial ordering of the agenda, and *focus* constraints (c.f. McKeown, 1985, Grosz & Sidner, 1986) which attempt to link domain objects referred to in the new goal to domain objects referred to in the goals which resulted in the preceding text.
2. If the goal is immediately executable (i.e., a graphical or linguistic action) it is executed.
3. If the goal is an iterative goal (forall..) new goals are put on the agenda in the obvious manner.

Otherwise:

(a) A planning rule is selected to try and satisfy that goal. The selection of the planning rule (from available alternatives) depends on the constraints on the rules and a default ordering reflecting the specificity of the rule.
(b) New goals are put on the agenda based on the preconditions and subgoals of this planning rule. Ordering constraints are imposed so that preconditions will be executed before subgoals.

Preconditions in content planning rules (such as `know-user behaviour (ldr)`) are treated as follows. Initially they are placed on the agenda along with subgoals, even if the system believes that they are already satisfied. This is because the system can "change its mind" about the user's knowledge. However, when they are taken off the agenda, then if they are already satisfied then they are thrown out. If they are not already satisfied then the subgoals of the goal are obtained and placed on the agenda with *c-goal* type goals replaced with *know-user* goals to mark them as prerequisites, to be explained only if now already known.

Suppose the system is planning how to explain how a "light unit" works, and the only goal on the agenda is the content goal:

```
(1) c-goal how-it-works (light-unit)
```

In the current system there is only one planning rule which can be used to try and satisfy this goal—the first rule in Figure 5. Prerequisite and subgoals would therefore be put on the agenda, as follows, with ordering constraints that the first (prerequisite) goal be executed before the others:

```
(2) know-user structure (light-unit)
    c-goal process (light-unit)
    c-goal behaviour (light-unit)
```

The system next selects which rule to use to explain the background *structure* of the device. If no analogous device is known then the third rule in Figure 5 is selected, resulting in a new agenda:

```
(3) know-user identify (light-unit)
    know-user components (light-unit)
    know-user function (light-unit)
    c-goal process (light-unit)
    c-goal behaviour (light-unit)
```

Assuming that the system believes that the user already knows the *identification* (or circuit type) of the light unit, the *constituency* of the light-unit and the *behaviour* of the resistor, then after several more planning steps (using the next three rules in Figure 5) the agenda will become:

```
(4) know-user identify-diagram (ldr)
    know-user behaviour (ldr)
    know-user function (light-unit)
    c-goal process (light-unit)
    c-goal behaviour (light-unit)
```

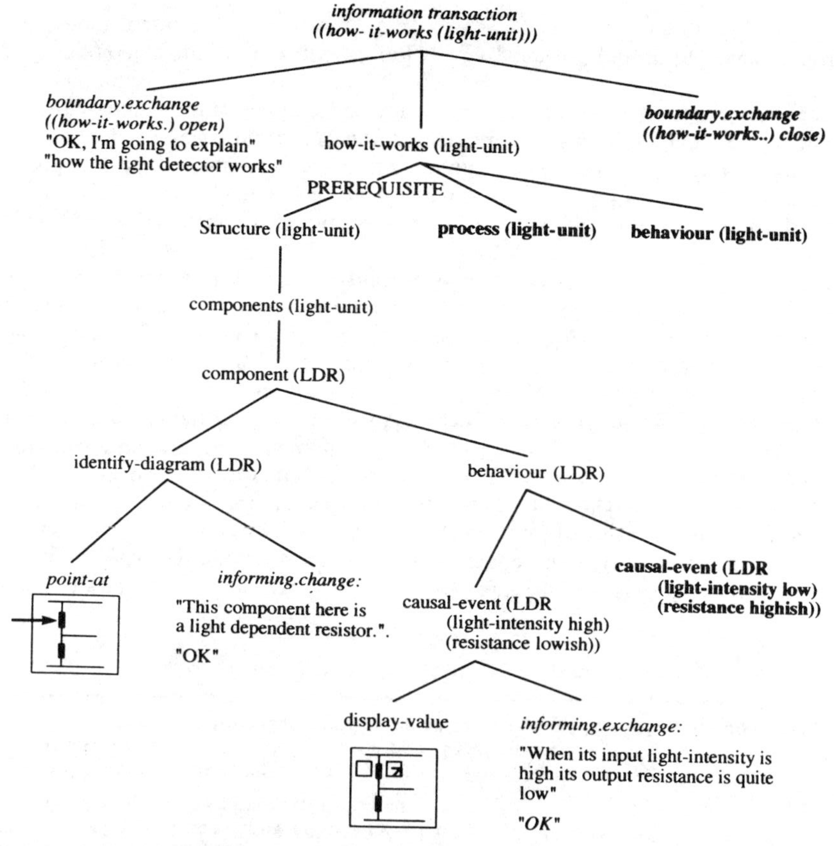

FIGURE 6. Partial interactive explanation plan.

Next, the identify-diagram rule will be selected, and the system will execute the actions of pointing at the diagram and have an exchange with the user about the diagram. This will often involve simply informing them that the indicated component is a light dependent resistor and waiting for them to indicate that they understand this.† (The selection of exchanges is explained further in the next section.) Content planning continues in this manner until the agenda is empty and therefore the full explanation generated.

An example section of the discourse plan (or discourse model) is given in Figure 6. This plan includes dialogue goals (such as a transaction and a number of exchanges) in *italic* font. These will be discussed further in the next section. Goals in bold font are not fully expanded, and will still be on the agenda. The plan illustrates both lingustic and graphical actions at the beginnings of an explanatory dialogue.

The approach to text planning described above enables background information to be missed out if assumed already known by the user, and different explanation strategies to be used depending on the knowledge of the user. However, as it stands it fails to make explicit the different general purpose explanation strategies which are used, or the rhetorical relations implicit in the text. This will be an important area for further work.

5. Structuring the dialogue

So far the system described can be used to plan what to say depending on the user's knowledge. The plan is developed incrementally, not committing to goal orderings or detailed expansions until necessary. The rest of the system is concerned with the interactions with the user—how to organize the overall dialogue, how to clear up misunderstandings that occur and how to monitor aspects of the changing situation (such as assumptions about the user's knowledge) and to use this in developing the plan of what to say.

First, the basic dialogue planning mechanism will be described. As mentioned earlier, as well as the content planning rules, there is a set of dialogue planning rules (denoted d-plans) which are used to structure *transactions* on the topic, *exchanges* with the user and *moves* within that exchange. These are loosely based on Sinclair and Coulthard's (1975) model of classroom discourse mentioned in Sections 2 and 3, but adapted to deal with a range of more informal tutorial and advisory styles. Normally a transaction will consist of a number of exchanges, which will consist of a number of moves.

Figure 7 illustrates some of the rules used. The first rule is used to organize opening and closing exchanges around topic discussions, while the second and third are used to structure particular types of exchanges depending on the system's rôle and the user's assumed knowledge. To illustrate the use of these rules (and the interaction with content planning), we will assume that the initial rôle assigned to

```
d-plan informing.transaction (topic)
  subgaols: d-goal boundary.exchange (topic 'open)
            d-goal teaching.exchanges (topic)
            d-goal boundary.exchange (topic 'close))

d-plan boundary.exchange (topic type)
  constraints: equal (type 'open)
               system-role ('formal-tutorial)
  subgoals: d-goal frame.move (type)
            d-goal focussing.move (topic type)

d-plan teaching.exchange (prop)
  constraints: maybe-knows-user (prop)
               system-role ('tutorial)
  subgoals: d-goal teacher-elicit.exchange (prop)
```

FIGURE 7. Example dialogue planning rules.

† Note that sentence level generation is managed simply by selecting from a set of templates and filling in object names or pronouns (depending on focus). User input in the system comes from menus, but is given in **bold** font in the examples.

the system is *formal-tutorial* which is a sub-type of *tutorial*, and that the following goal has been placed on the agenda:

```
(5) d-goal informing.transaction (how-it-works (light-unit))
```

The system uses the first rule in Figure 7 and puts the following goals on the agenda (in a fixed order):

```
(6) d-goal boundary.exchanges ((how-it-works (light-unit)) open)
    d-goal teaching.exchange ((how-it-works (light-unit)))
    d-goal boundary.exchange ((how-it-works (light-unit)) close)
```

Next the system will try and plan the opening boundary exchange. As its rôle is *formal-tutorial* the second planning rule in Figure 7 will be used, and a *frame* move (Sinclair and Coulthard's term for a topic opening discourse marker,)† and a *focusing* move (a meta-comment on the following discourse) selected, which after further planning will result in the following utterance:

(7) "OK, I'm going to explain how the light detector works."

Once the opening boundary exchange has been generated the *teaching exchanges* goal is taken off the agenda. This teaching.exchanges rule (not illustrated) causes content planning to be initiated. In this example this is done by putting the following goal onto the system's agenda:

```
(8) c-goal how-it-works (light-unit)
```

Content planning then continues as described in the previous section until a dialogue goal is encountered. This may be a *teaching* exchange, or an *UM-elicit* exchange. The latter is used when the system needs to know whether or not the user knows some concept in order to make a planning decision, and so plans an exchange to find this out.

Suppose the following goal is taken off the agenda:

```
(9) d-goal teaching.exchange ((identify-diagram (ldr)))
```

Teaching exchanges may be either *informing* exchanges where the system gives some information and waits for an acknowledgement, or *teacher-elicit* exchanges, where the system asks the user a question to test their knowledge. The latter are selected when the system thinks the user "maybe" knows the relevant concept, and its rôle is tutorial. However, if a simple informing exchange is selected then after further planning the following utterance is generated:

(10) "This component here is a light dependent resistor."

This utterance will immediately follow a pointing action, resulting from the other subgoal of the *identify-diagram* planning rule in Figure 5, and will be followed by a pause, allowing the user to indicate if they are following. Figure 6 illustrates a

† Discourse markers (or clue words) are words like "Now", "OK", "Well" and "Anyway" which carry no propositional content but tell the hearer something about what is to follow and its relation to the preceding discourse.

S: OK, I'm going to go through how a light detector unit works.	*Opening exchange* **How-it-works (light-unit)**
A light detector unit is a sort of potential divider circuit. U: **OK.**	*Informing exchange* **Device-type (light-unit)**
S: This component here is a light dependent resistor. U: **OK.**	*Informing exchange* **Identify-diagram (LDR)**
S: Do you know what it does? U: **No**	*UM-elicit exchange* **Behaviour (LDR)**
S: OK, what do you think its output resistance is when it has a high input light intensity? U: **Low-fully conductive**	*Elicit exchange* **Causal-event (LDR (light-intensity high) (resistance lowish))**
S: No, not quite, it's actually quite low.	
......	
OK, Is that enough about how the light detector works? U: **Yes**	*Closing Exchange* **How-it-works (light-unit)**
S: OK	

FIGURE 8. Different exchanges in a simple explanation.

(slightly simplified) discourse plan which includes the utterances given above in (7) and (10), as well as the point action.

In order to generate dialogues which depend on the system's rôle a simple hierarchy of rôle types are defined. The most general rôle type is the *information giving* rôle which has sub-types *advisory* and *tutorial.* In turn the tutorial rôle type has sub-types for informal and formal styles of tuition, which influence the degree of initiative allowed the user. Constraints on dialogue planning rules refer to these rôles as we saw in the example, and influence both the realization and the selection of different types of exchanges. For example, *teacher-elicit* exchanges are not allowed in the advisory rôle, while if the rôle is not *formal-tutorial* then topic opening boundary exchanges will include (at least) a checking move to see if the user is happy with the proposed topic.

Figure 8 illustrates a sample dialogue with a variety of types of exchange within it, given the formal tutorial style. These do not include clarification sequences which will be the subject of the next section.

6. Dealing with misunderstandings

So far we have seen how the content of an explanation can be planned, and how a simple dialogue may be organized around that planned content. This allows the system to introduce and close topics by planning opening and closing exchanges, to check on the user's understanding (through teaching and *UM-elicit* exchanges) and to give the user the opportunity to interrupt to ask clarifications or to indicate they are not following (whenever the system is pausing in an exchange with the user).

But what happens when the user indicates that they do not understand, or when the system determines this by questioning the user? The system must then work out how to fix that misunderstanding and how to continue the rest of the explanation (if this is not complete).

This section will consider three cases. In the first, the user asks a clarification question in the middle of the explanation. The issue we will consider here is how the remaining discourse is resumed following the interrupting clarification sequence. In the second, the user just signals that they do not understand, but does not identify the area of difficulty (or only does in general terms). The main problem here is how to guess at the likely problem and then either re-explain things another way or fill in missing information. In the third, the system detects some misunderstanding based on the user's reply to questions, and has to plan some appropriate remedial response.

6.1. CLARIFICATION QUESTIONS

At various points in the explanation the system will pause waiting for user input. For example, in an *informing* exchange the system may pause to give the user the opportunity to indicate whether they understand, while in a *teacher-elicit* exchange the system will pause expecting a reply to a question. At any such points the user may "interrupt" with a clarification question. These clarification questions are not freely composed by the user, but must be selected from a menu.† The questions are mapped directly to goals in the content planning system, so, for example, a "*what does an LDR do*?" question would be mapped to a `(c-goal behaviour (LDR))` goal.‡

Given a clarification goal, the system will check the agenda of explanation goals to see if the question is about to be answered anyway, and if so whether there is prerequisite information which should be discussed first. If this is the case then the user is told that the question will be answered later, and given the opportunity of abandoning the question.

However, assuming the clarification goes ahead, the system must deal with the question and then resume any planned explanation in a coherent manner. In order to make clear the scope of the interruption (so that the user knows what is happening in the dialogue), discourse markers are added around the clarification sequence—in particular the end of the interrupting sequence is marked with "Anyway" and possibly a meta-comment describing what the system was in the middle of explaining. A special "interruption" discourse planning rule is used in order to add such markers and meta-comments. This is given in Figure 9, along with a short example clarification generated by the system.§

Of course, in human dialogues the continuing explanation following an interruption will normally follow on quite naturally from the "interrupting" sequence. It is not always apparent where the interrupting clarification ends and the "main" explanation resumes. In order to make the interrupting sub-dialogue cohere better

† As well as asking questions from a fixed menu of questions relevant to the text, the user could click on items in the diagram and obtain a menu of relevant questions. This latter facility was given because in human dialogues the context of the questions was frequently the diagram rather than the past explanation—hearer's would be working out the behaviour of the circuit for themselves, using the diagram as context, so questions might be unrelated to the immediately preceding text.

‡ This is obviously an oversimplification, as in general the interpretation of a question should depend on its context (Moore, 1990).

§ Note that in this and later examples the user's *acknowledgements* (i.e. "OK" responses following *inform* actions from the system) are not displayed. These were illustrated in Figure 8.

```
(d-plan interrupting.transaction (topic old-topic)
  subgoals: boundary.exchange (topic 'open-sub-topic)
            teaching.exchanges (topic)
            boundary.exchange (topic old-topic 'resuming)
```

S: . . . so the output voltage is high.
U: **What does an LDR do?**
S: Well, when its input light intensity is high then its output resistance is quite low. When its input resistance is low then its output resistance is quite high. Anyway, I was in the middle of going through how the light detector circuit works. When the . . .

FIGURE 9. Interruption discourse rule and example discourse fragment.

with the following discourse the EDGE system uses the following two strategies. The first is to use the partial order of goals on the agenda, and attempt to make the sub-topic chosen next follow on from the user's clarification topic. This is done by attempting to select a goal from the agenda where the items in focus in that goal overlap with the item(s) in the user's clarification question. If this is possible then the system does not explicitly mark the topic resumption with a meta-comment, as there is no longer a sharp shift between the interrupted and continuing discourse. The second strategy is simply to repeat part of the interrupted discourse. This was frequently observed in the human dialogues analysed, and is currently used when the system had just asked a question when the user interrupted, so that the user is reminded of the system's question and that a reply to it is still expected!

As well as influencing the immediately following discourse, the clarification sequence will influence the detailed planning of the remaining explanation, since the user model will have been updated during the clarification sequence. This is discussed further in Section 7.

6.2. GUESSING THE PROBLEM

Sometimes people are not able to say exactly why they do not understand an explanation. They may signal that they are not following by saying, "I don't understand", "What?" or, in face-to face interaction, by just looking puzzled. In all these cases it is up to the explainer to guess at the problem and attempt to either re-explain things another way or to patch the explanation by filling in more background knowledge. This type of explanation repair has been discussed by Moore (1990). However, Moore only allows the repair at the end of a complete explanation. In general people may signal that they do not understand at any point in an exlanation, as illustrated in Figure 10, taken from the corpus of human dialogues. The EDGE system allows the user to indicate that they are confused at any point (when the system is pausing), and attempts to repair this confusion before continuing.

So that the system can guess at potential problems and explain things in other ways, the explanation plan includes (as in Moore's system):

- The set of assumptions made when expanding a goal in the plan.
- Any alternative plan operators which could have been used at that point in the planning process.

E: This is an OPAMP, a feature of which is, well there's two significant features. One is that its inputs make very little difference to the circuit they are attached to, they take a small current, so they do not actually effect this. So the potential divider here always moves, with only this attached to it this will always give you a voltage between here and here and it won't disturb anything.
N: I don't understand.
E: This circuit, this wire here, does not disturb the circuit. It takes a very small current, so therefore—remember, we were talking about the earlier circuits with two resistors—if there was a lot of current going down here. . .
. . . The other thing that it does is amplifies the difference between its inputs.

FIGURE 10. Human clarification and resumption of explanation.

By looking at assumptions which were made (e.g. assuming that the user knew some particular background knowledge), and alternative strategies which could be used, the system can do two things. It can guess at missing background knowledge which should have been included in the explanation, and patch the explanation by offering to explain that to the user, or it can replan an explanation using alternative strategies, and present the modified explanation to the user. Unlike Moore's system, the system checks with the user that a possible repair is appropriate before attempting it. Figure 11 illustrates a simple example repair where the system guesses that the user does not have the necessary background knowledge about a potential divider circuit, so after checking with the user that this is in fact the case, attempts to fill in this missing knowledge.

S: . . then its output voltage is high.
U: **What?**
S: Don't you know what a potential divider circuit does?
U: **No.**
S: OK, when the potential divider circuit has a high resistance (R1) and a low resistance (R2) then its output voltage is low. When it has a low resistance (R1) and a high resistance (R2) then its output voltage is high. Anyway, suppose the light detector has a low input. .

FIGURE 11. Example, explanation, repair.

6.3. ATTEMPTING REMEDIATION

The final example of explanation repair considered is where the system itself deduces that the user has a problem and gives a remedial response. This is particularly important when the system is adopting a *tutorial* rôle. In the EDGE system, problems are identified in a relatively simple way by explicitly asking the user questions to check their understanding. Sets of remediation strategies are defined for dealing with particular types of errors in replies.

This type of response in dialogue has been extensively discussed in work on tutorial dialogues (Section 2.2.1), and the EDGE system attempts to incorporate some of the strategies presented in this work. The general strategy is to provide extra information by which the user might be able to understand their mistake, and then ask the question again. The extra information may be a simple analogy, or some reasoning steps which show how the correct answer could be reached. Giving indirect remedial responses such as these (rather than simply presenting the user with the correct answer) encourages the user to think more about the question and to understand their error.

The system defines remediation planning rules in a similar manner to normal content planning rules. For example, two rules are defined for dealing with incorrect responses to questions about device behaviour. In the first (applicable when the behaviour of a similar device is known to the user) an analogy (or rather comparison) is given and the question asked again. In the second the behaviour of the device is explained in terms of its component behaviours, and the question asked again. This strategy is applicable when the behaviour of the device can be "decomposed" into simpler steps known to the user. Figure 12 illustrates an example dialogue taken from scripts of users using the system which includes each of these types of remediation sequences.

The remediation strategies currently used are chosen so that a user should be able to indirectly *infer* the correct answer to a question given the remedial information. However, the system does not currently attempt to guess at the particular misunderstandings or gaps in knowledge leading to incorrect responses (as discussed in the last section). Further developments should therefore attempt to extend the

S: What's the output voltage (V2) of the heat detector circuit going to be when the input heat intensity is high (hot)?
U: **Low (0V).**
S: Wrong, not quite,
A heat detector circuit is much like a light detector circuit only:
—Its output voltage depends on the input light intensity.
—It has a thermistor instead of a light-dependent resistor.
The component here is a thermistor.
Let's go through what a thermistor does.
When the input heat intensity (H1) of the thermistor is high (hot) the output resistance (R1) will be quite low.
When it is low (cold) the output resistance (R1) will be quite high.
So, what's the output voltage (V2) of the heat detector circuit going to be when the input heat intensity is high (hot)?
U: **Quite high (towards 9V).**
S: Precisely, very good, it's quite high (towards 9V).
Anyway, we were in the middle of explaining how the low heat warning device works if it has the following inputs: heat intensity high.
What's the output voltage (V5) of the comparator going to be when the input voltage (V2) is quite high (towards 9V).
U: **Quite high.**
S: Wrong, not quite,
OK, maybe we better go through what a comparator does when it has a highish input voltage.
Suppose the input voltage is quite high.
When the operational amplifier has one medium (about 4.5V) input voltage (V3) and one quite high input voltage (V2) then the output voltage (V5) is low (0V).
Anyway, we were in the middle of explaining how the low heat warning device works if it has the following inputs: heat-intensity high.
U: **What's a comparator.**
S: OK, this circuit section here is a comparator.

FIGURE 12. Example dialogue fragment involving remediation sequences.

model of remediation to use such specific hypotheses about the user's missing or erroneous knowledge.

6.4. CONCLUSION

This section has illustrated some of the problems involved in dealing with user misunderstandings in the context of a complex explanation. This involves being able to guess at possible problems, to select appropriate "remedial" information, and to resume an interrupted explanation in a coherent manner. The EDGE system begins to show how this is possible within an interactive explanation system, and evaluation of the system (Section 8) indicates that the strategies are helpful. However, further work on integrating and extending the ideas is required before we can claim to have a full account of explanation repair.

7. Monitoring and responding to the changing situation

In any dialogue the discourse situation will be continually changing in largely unpredictable ways. It is clear that that changing situation should influence the way the dialogue proceeds. However, in an extended interactive explanation there may also be an overall unchanging explanatory goal. There is therefore a tradeoff between planning out in detail how to satisfy that goal, and reacting locally to changes in the current situation.

In the EDGE system the explanation is only partially planned in advance. At any point in the explanation the future plan will consist of a few high level sub-goals, but no details on how they are to be realized. Changes in the context part way through an explanation will therefore influence how the remaining explanation develops, as remaining planning decisions will take into account that revised context. This approach does have disadvantages—it is impossible to guarantee an "optimal" plan or to anticipate interactions between subgoals of the plan. However, for the type of explanations considered here these problems appear not to be that important. There are few interactions between subgoals, and, given the fact that the information about the user's knowledge is unreliable and changing, it is much more important to deal with explanation repair than to attempt to try to produce an "ideal" explanation in the first place. That "ideal" explanation would only work reliably if our assumptions about the user happen to be correct, and if we had a perfect model of how they learned.

In explanation generation there are numerous aspects of the discourse situation which could be considered, such as the participants' goals, social rôles and knowledge, and the current discourse focus. The EDGE system attempts to consider:

The current focus. The system records the objects currently in focus and uses this to influence the order material is presented (c.f. McKeown, 1985). The representation of focus is based simply on the arguments to planning rules, and may include domain objects, discourse goals and propositions. The current focus is represented by the stack of focus "spaces" based on the goal structure of the discourse (Grosz & Sidner, 1986).

The system's rôle. The dialogue will depend on the roles of the participants (e.g. tutorial or advisory), as mentioned in Section 3 and 5. This rôle may shift in an extended explanation. In the EDGE system an initial attempt has been made to model these rôle shifts based on the degree to which the user initiates dialogue sequences rather just than passively answers questions.

The user's knowledge. Assumptions about the user's knowledge are updated as the dialogue progresses (discussed further below) and influence choices in both the content of the discourse and the dialogue moves chosen.

Dialogue exchange	Inference
System tells user X, user acknowledges	User maybe knows X
System asks user X, user replies correctly	User knows X
System asks user X, user replies incorrectly	User doesn't know X
System asks user if she knows X	User's reply
User asks X	User doesn't know X

FIGURE 13. Direct rules for inferring what the user knows.

The most important aspect of the discourse situation considered in the current system is the set of assumptions about the user's knowledge. These are updated on the basis of direct inferences from the interactions with the user and indirect inferences based on relations between concepts in the domain and on stereotype information. These two types of inference rules are illustrated in Figures 13 and 14. Initially, assumptions about the user's knowledge come from the stereotype (or class) assigned to the user, which indicates the level they have reached in learning about electronics. Each concept in the domain is labelled with its level of difficulty, giving the stage at which it is normally learned. So given the user's level and the concept difficulty, it is possible to guess whether a concept is known (c.f. Chin, 1988). Given an interaction with the user more direct (and certain) inferences can be drawn which in turn allow further indirect inferences. The direct inferences may cause the initial stereotype to be changed, such as from intermediate to novice if the user asks a number of "simple" questions. This is done by maintaining a simple

Condition	Inference
All sub-concepts known/unknown	Parent concept known/unknown
All sub-concepts known or maybe known	Parent concept maybe known
Concept difficulty greater than level of expertise of user	Concept probably unknown
Concept difficulty less than level of expertise of user	Concept maybe known
Parent concept known/maybe known	Sub-concepts maybe known

FIGURE 14. Indirect rules for inferring what the user knows.

score related to the average difficulty of the questions asked and answered by the user.

Suppose, for example, the system was about to describe the components of the light detector circuit. The current estimate of the user's general expertise is "intermediate" so the system assumes the user already knows about fixed resistors. However there is some evidence that the stereotype intermediate is too high. If the user now asks the system to identify the fixed resistor on the diagram the system concludes that they do not know this fairly simple concept, and as a result of this changes the user's assumed expertise level to novice. The question is answered, but the system no longer assumes that the user knows all about resistors. In continuing the dialogue the system will go on to describe the "behaviour" of the fixed resistor (i.e. it has fixed output resistance) which it would not otherwise have mentioned.

In the example above the system would also use the changed focus resulting from the user's question to influence the order of the continuing explanation. So, the fact that the user asked about the fixed resistor means that the system attempts to continue talking about the fixed resistor, rather than (say) talking about the light-dependent resistor before returning again to mention further facts about the fixed resistor.

8. Evaluating the approach

In order to begin to assess the EDGE system as a practical approach to explanation generation the system was evaluated with a small number of users taken from the author's department. These users found the interactive explanations instructive and largely coherent. However, as no comparative evaluation was carried out, with alternative architectures, it is unclear which features of the system contributed most to this conclusion. The main value of the evaluation was therefore in revealing some possible problems with the approach.

The first problem concerned the user modelling rules, which did not appear to act very well. User's frequently guessed answers to questions based on little real understanding, or asked questions purely out of curiosity as to how the system would reply, rather than actual lack of understanding. The latter at least might be partly an artefact of the somewhat unrealistic experimental situation, but it remains unclear as to whether the simple user modelling rules used in the system can be effective. This emphasises again the need for explanation repair, in the absence of a reliable user model.

A second problem became apparent when a user who had virtually no knowledge of the basic concepts of electricity used the system. The system was not able to explain these concepts or to recover from basic misunderstandings. Dealing with this problem requires more than simply adding in more concepts to the knowledge base. Circuit models appropriate to students at different stages of learning may need to be qualitatively different, as White and Frederiksen (1986) have suggested.

Finally, although the meta-comments on the discourse were generally helpful, the users sometimes got "lost" and could not see why the system was saying something or asking a question. In human discourse, pauses and intonation are widely used to prevent this, as well a more subtle topic shifting. Restricted channel (and in

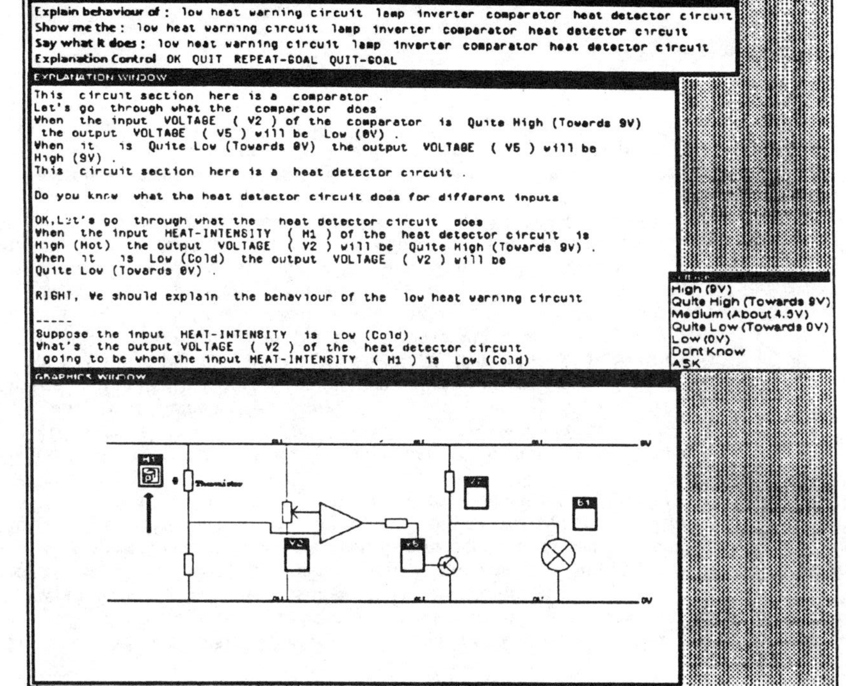

FIGURE 15. Example display.

particular, text-based) interactive communication is still a little understood area, so it is difficult to know how discourse signals are best adapted to the new medium.

Figure 12 gave a section of an explanatory dialogue from one of the evaluation sessions, while Figure 15 gives an example screen showing the interface in the evaluated version of the system. The circuit displayed in this figure is the same as that explained in Figure 12. The display shows clearly some of the graphical actions and menus associated with system.

9. Conclusion and further work

This paper has presented an approach to generating interactive extended explanations. The basic approach is based on two levels of planning: content planning and dialogue planning. Content planning is concerned with deciding what to say depending on assumptions about the user's knowledge, while dialogue planning is concerned with managing any interactions with the user. The explanation is planned incrementally, so changing assumptions about the user (or other aspects of context) influence the detailed planning of the explanation. More detail on the approach is available in (Cawsey, in press).

The EDGE system is very much an experimental system, working in a restricted domain. Although preliminary results suggest that the basic approach is both computationally feasible and helpful to users, there is much further work to be done on the details of the approach.

The EDGE content planner is fairly limited, being based on domain specific rules rather than on general rhetorical or explanation strategies. Further work should therefore focus on developing a clean, domain-independent approach to content planning which makes explicit the different types of constraint on the organization and selection of content. This might take as starting point the work by Moore (1990) and by Maybury (1990). Initial explorations suggest that it will not be sufficient simply to use a domain knowledge base and fully domain-independent text planning rules. We also need some general knowledge of how particular *types* of knowledge (such as processes and events) are related.

Although the EDGE dialogue planner is effective in generating coherent and appropriate dialogue actions, it fails to make fully explicit *why* different dialogue actions are selected, being based on a largely syntactic model of dialogue structure. Effects of particular dialogue actions on the user's knowledge are not explicitly defined, but built into the functions that execute particular speech acts. Further work should therefore consider whether more explictly plan-based models of dialogue (as discussed in Section 2.2.3) may be used effectively for the generation of flexible extended dialogues of this type.

A variety of repair strategies are available in the EDGE system for dealing with user misunderstandings. However, no comprehensive computational account of these kinds of repair has been developed. This should take into account the different kinds of problem and misunderstanding that occur, how they are recognized, and what techniques are available to clear up the misunderstanding.

Finally, there are many open questions concerning the user model. As we have already noted, the rules for updating the user model need further testing and development. However, further work is also required on how the explanation should be best tailored to the user's knowledge. Although the use of prerequisite relations between topics is undoubtedly important, it remains difficult to determine exactly what the important background material for a particular topic is.

In conclusion then, we believe that the approach presented here provides a useful framework for the generation of interactive explanations for a variety of computer applications. However, the system described is only an experimental system which illustrates the basic ideas, and work is needed to both develop the approach and to test it in new domains and in more realistic applications.

This research was carried out while the author was at the Department of Artificial Intelligence, University of Edinburgh, funded by a studentship and fellowship from the Science and Engineering Research Council. I would like to thank all my colleagues at Edinburgh for their input to this work (including those who spent time explaining circuits or testing my system). I would also like to thank Karen Sparck Jones and my anonymous reviewers for their helpful comments on this paper.

References

Allen, J. F. & Perrault, C. F. (1980). Analysing intention in utterances. *Artificial Intelligence*, **15**, 143–178.

Baker, M. (1989). A model for tutorial dialogues based on critical argument. In D. Bierman, J. Breuker, & J. Sandberg. *Artificial Intelligence and Education*. pp. 2–8, Amsterdam: IOS.

Cawsey, A. (in press). *Explanation and Interaction: The Computer Generation of Explanatory Dialogues*. Cambridge, MA: The MIT Press.

Chin, D. (1988). KNOME: Modelling what the user knows in UC. In A. Kobsa, & W. Wahlster, *User Models in Dialogue Systems*. pp. 74–107, Berlin: Springer-Verlag.

Clancey, W. (1983). *Knowledge-based tutoring: The GUIDON system*. Cambridge, MA: Press.

Cohen, P. R., Morgan, J. L. & Pollack, M. E. (1990). *Intentions and Communication*. Cambridge MA: MIT Press.

Ferrari, G. & Reilly, R. (1986). A two level dialogue representation. *Proceedings of COLING '86*, pp. 42–45, Bonn, 25–29 August.

Fikes, R. E., Hart, P. E. & Nilsson, N. J. (1972). Learning and executing generalised robot plans. *Artificial Intelligence*, **3**, 251–288.

Gilbert, N. G. (1987). Advice, discourse and explanations. *Proceedings of the third Alvey Explanation Workshop*, University of Manchester. (Available from the Department of Trade and Industry, London, UK).

Grosz, B. J. & Sidner, C. (1986). Attention, intentions, and the structure of discourse. *Computational Linguistics*, **12**, 175–204.

Kass, R. & Finin, T. (1987). Rules for the implicit acquisition of knowledge about the user. *Proceedings of the Sixth National Conference on Artificial Intelligence*, pp. 295–300, Seattle, WA, 13–17 July.

Lesgold, A. (1988). Towards a theory of curriculum design for use in intelligent instructional systems. In H. Mandl & A. Lesgold, Eds. *Learning Issues for Intelligent Tutoring Systems*. pp. 114–137, New York: Springer Verlag.

MacMillan, S. A., Emme, D. & Berkowitz, M. (1988). Instructional planners: lessons learned. In J. Psotka, L. D. Murray & S. A. Mutter, Eds. *Intelligent Tutoring Systems: Lessons Learned*. pp. 17–27, Hillsdale, NJ: Lawrence Erlbaum.

Mann, W. C. & Thompson, S. A. (1987). Rhetorical structure theory: description and construction of text structures. In G. Kempen, Ed. *Natural Language Generation: New Results in Artificial Intelligence, Psychology and Linguistics*. pp. 85–95, Dortrecht: Nijhoff.

Maybury, M. T. (1990). *Planning multi-sentential English text using communicative acts*. Ph.D. thesis, Computer Laboratory, University of Cambridge. (published as technical report RADC-TR-90-411, Rome Air Development Center).

McKeown, K. R. (1985). *Test Generation: Using discourse Strategies and Focus Constraints to Generate Natural Language Text*. Cambridge: Cambridge University Press.

Moore, J. D. (1990). *A reactive approach to explanation in expert and advice-giving systems*. Ph.D. thesis (published as Technical Report ISI-SR-90-251, USC/Information Sciences Institute).

Moore, J. D. & Paris, C. L. (1990). Planning text for advisory dialogues. *Proceedings of the 27th Annual Meeting of the Association for Computational Linguistics*, pp. 203–211, Vancouver, Canada, 26–29 July.

Murray, B. (1989). Control for intelligent tutoring systems: a blackboard-based dynamic instructional planner. In D. Bierman, J. Breuker & J. Sandberg, Eds, *Artificial Intelligence and Education*. pp. 150–168, Amsterdam: IOS.

Paris, C. L. (1987). Combining discourse strategies to generate descriptions to users along a naive/expert spectrum. *Proceedings of the Tenth International Joint Conference on Artificial Intelligence*, pp. 626–632, Milan, Italy, 23–28 August.

Peachey, D. R. & McCalla, G. I. (1986). Using planning techniques in intelligent tutoring systems. *International Journal of Man–Machine Studies*, **24**, 77–98.

Pollack, M. E., Hirschberg, J. & Webber, B. L. (1982). User participation in the reasoning processes of expert systems. *Proceedings of the Second National Conference on Artificial Intelligence*, pp. 358–361, Pittsburgh, PA, 18–20 August.

Rich, E. (1979). User modelling via stereotypes, *Cognitive Science*, **3**, 329–345.

Rumelhart, D. E. (1975). Notes on a schema for stories. In D. G. Bobrow, & A. Collins, Eds. *Representation and Understanding*. pp. 211–238, New York: Academic Press.

Sinclair, J. McH. & Coulthard, R. M. (1975). *Towards an analysis of discourse: The English Used by Teachers and Pupils.* Oxford: Oxford University Press.

Sleeman, D. (1985). UMFE: A user modelling front end subsystem. *International Journal of Man-Machine Studies,* **23,** 71–88.

Stevens, A. L. & Collins, A. (1977). *The goal structure of a socratic tutor.* Technical report no. 3518, Bolt, Beranek and Newman Inc.

Wachtel, T. (1986). Pragmatic sensitivity in natural language interfaces and the structure of conversation. *Proceedings of COLING* '86, pp. 35–41, Bonn, Germany, 25–29 August.

Wallis, J. W. & Shortliffe, E. H. (1985). Customized explanations using causal knowledge. In B. G. Buchanan & E. H. Shortliffe, Eds. *Rule Based Expert Systems: The MYCIN Experiments of the Stanford Heuristic Programming Project.* pp. 371–390, Reading, MA, London: Addison Wesley.

Wahlster, W. & Kobsa, A. (1989). User models in dialog systems. In A. Kobsa, & W. Wahlster, Eds. *User Models in Dialog Systems.* pp. 5–34, Berlin: Springer Verlag.

Weiner, J. L. (1980). BLAH, a system which explains its reasoning. *Artificial Intelligence,* **15,** 19–48.

White, B. Y. & Frederiksen, J. R. (1986). Intelligent tutoring systems based on qualitative model evolutions. *Proceedings of the Fifth National Conference on Artificial Intelligence,* pp. 313–319, Philadelphia, PA, 11–15 August.

Woolf, B. & McDonald, D. D. (1984). Context-dependent transitions in discourse. *Proceedings of the Third National Conference on Artificial Intelligence,* pp. 355–361.

Woolf, B. & Murray, T. (1987). A framework for representing tutorial discourse. *Proceedings of the Tenth International Conference on Artificial Intelligence,* pp. 189–192, Milan, Italy, 23–28 August.

Planning Interactive Explanations

Alison Cawsey

In this paper, I presented a system (and general framework) for generating extended explanations. The system was based on an analysis of human verbal explanations, and thus the explanations were designed to be interactive and adaptive: a dialog with the user was allowed as an explanation progressed, and the detailed content of the explanation was adapted given an updated model of what the user knew. Further, explanations involved a mixture of graphical and text-based actions planned in a uniform manner, starting from a single communicative goal. I'll reflect briefly on a number of key assumptions in the approach:

1. *The design of an explanation system should be based on an analysis of human explanations.* Although I still believe that an analysis of human explanations provides important insights, I feel that it is not a good idea to apply a model based on human texts or dialogs too literally. For example, hypertext now provides a well-understood mechanism for enabling a reader to interact with a text and ask for clarificatory or follow-up information. More recent work (Reiter, Mellish, and Levine, Section II of this volume) has looked at how hypertext may be dynamically generated, and that seems the best way forward for many practical systems, especially given the recent dominance of the WWW in providing access to information.
2. *Explanations should be interactive.* Although it is clear that a user should be able to interact with explanatory material in some way, we have to consider further the nature of this interaction. It is easy to provide hypertext links—but will the user get lost? It is easy to intersperse material with questions that check the user's understanding—but should we force the user to answer these questions? These questions apply not just to "intelligent" systems but to dumb help systems and computer-aided learning material as well.
3. *Explanations should be adaptive.* In principle, an explanation that is tailored to the user, and adapts to changing assumptions about their needs and prior knowledge, must surely be a good thing. Yet adaptivity is something where a little is a dangerous thing. If we can get it right, then great. If we don't quite make it, then we may lose consistency and options and end up with something worse than the equivalent nonadaptive system. We need more empirical work to determine which user characteristics are important in tailoring material and which are irrelevant.
4. *Explanations can be planned using hierarchical expansion planning, starting from a single communicative goal.* Although this has proved a successful approach, used in many more recent systems, it has fundamental limitations. Real applications involve many interacting communicative goals, and the communication processes are not well enough understood to formulate these in a precise planning framework. We need to explore alternative problem-solving methods for planning explanatory material, perhaps adapting the varied problem-solving and knowledge acquisition methods used by the expert systems community.

Overall, I believe we need to look at alternative architectures for planning such explanations and to focus more on real usability issues rather than assuming that adaptive, interactive systems based on human dialogs are necessarily the most appropriate. More practical systems must be developed and evaluated for further progress.

Natural Language and Exploration of an Information Space: the ALFresco Interactive System

Oliviero Stock*
IRST - Istituto per la Ricerca Scientifica e Tecnologica
38050 Povo, Trento, Italy
e-mail: stock@irst.it

Abstract

In traditional natural language systems, the channel of communication between the user and the system was a narrow and constraining device. In many areas natural language-based information access requires the possibility for the user of exploring the domain and a system's comfortable habitability. The present work presents a rationale for building intelligent interfaces that combine natural language and hypermedia as new means for human-computer interaction and in particular gives an outline of a prototype of this kind, built for the exploration of Italian frescoes: the ALFresco interactive system.

1 Introduction

Natural language interface design has for a long while been based on the teletype approach. The channel of communication between the user and the system was a narrow and constraining device. On the other hand, certainly not all the necessary techniques for understanding "pure" natural language, especially in the pragmatics field, seem to be advanced enough to reproduce this traditional way of communicating.

In recent times an innovative approach has emerged [Arens *et al.*, 1989], that acknowledges that a larger bandwidth communication between user and computer can be established, in particular by exploiting graphics. Intelligent multimodal systems have been developed for interfacing a user with a dynamic process such as the simulation of the operations inside a factory [Cohen *et al.*, 1989], a simulated battlefield [MacLaughlin and Shaked, 1989] or the activities of U.S. Navy ships [Arens *et al.*, 1988]. In such applications, the advantage of integrating multiple media in output is obvious, for example, to explain sequences of operations or to display the status of a complex process. Similarly for input, pointing to images on a screen may individuate the objects involved in some desired action [Wahlster, 1988; Hollan *et al.*, 1988]. Very recently some projects of multimodal information presentation have combined graphics and language in output in a new creative way [Feiner and McKeown, 1990; Wahlster *et al.*, 1991].

A different and nowadays quite popular technology is hypertext. The generalization of the idea of hypertext to multimediality gives rise to the concept of hypermedia:, "a style of building systems for information representation and management around a network of multimedia nodes connected together by typed links" [Halasz, 1988]. Hypermedial systems promote a navigational, explorative access to multimodal information: the user, browsing around the network, is at the same time both exploring the network and searching for useful information.

Multimodality and hypermediality provide the possibility of realizing intelligent interfaces that amplify capabilities we have in nature. The present work presents a rationale for building intelligent interfaces that combine natural language and hypermedia as a new means for human-computer interaction and gives an outline of a prototype of this kind, built for the exploration of Italian frescoes: the ALFresco interactive system.

2 Combining hypermedia and NLP

The main reason for trying to integrate two approaches that have up to now represented independent lines of research is that there are a number of advantages that accrue in both directions. Integrating NL with hypermedia facilities provides the following advantages: from the NL perspective: a means for organizing heterogeneous and unstructured information, for favouring the direct manipulation of all objects integrated with language, and for facilitating explorative behaviour; from the hypermedia perspective: a solution to the problem of disorientation and of the cognitive overhead of having too many links; from an unbiased point of view that looks at all this as an independent new approach: the offer of a high level of interactivity and system habitability in which each modality overcomes the constraints of the other, resulting in the whole being more than the sum of the parts.

We shall briefly discuss these points.

Many of the problems that prevent NL systems from providing useful interfaces stem from the current inability to handle the difficulties, lack of knowledge and mis-

*The various modules of ALFresco were realized by the NLP interface group at IRST. The group currently includes G. Carenini, E. Franconi, A. Lavelli, B. Magnini, F. Pianesi, M. Ponzi, C. Strapparava, and previously also F. Cecconi and V. Samek-Lodovici. Many of the ideas reported here have emerged working with them. G. Carenini, M. Ponzi and C. Strapparava have given a particular contribution to the present work.

understandings that arise during dialogs. Hypermediality has the virtue of offering a powerful means for organizing highly heterogeneous and unstructured information, a kind of knowledge not easily handled by natural language systems (and AI systems in general). For example, in situations in which an AI application has a formal representation of only a subpart of the relevant domain knowledge, it is not possible to generate natural language text about information not explicitly represented in the system. A possible solution is the dynamic generation of hypertextual (possibly hypermedial) nodes pointing to a canned hypermedia network about those areas of the domain that have not been formally represented. Direct manipulation of images, buttoned text etc., integrated with the natural language channel is a powerful concept. On the interaction strategy side the crucial point is to integrate an exploration modality in the environment. With this a user finds it easy to move around, see what is available here and there, possibly follow some exploration path, without being necessarily constrained by any definite goal.

Looking at interaction from the hypermediality point of view, one of the major problems is *disorientation*, as pointed in [Conklin, 1987]. Hypermedia offer more degrees of freedom, more dimensions in which one can move, and hence a greater potential for the user to become lost or disoriented; the user has the problem of having to know where she is and how to get to some other place that she knows (or thinks) exists in the network.

A solution is the integration of a query facility within the system, providing a way of jumping inside the network without having to follow the predefined paths through it. [Halasz, 1988] identifies two kinds of queries:

1. *content queries* allow retrieval of all objects (nodes or links) that satisfy some requirements;
2. *structure queries* allow retrieval of a subnetwork matching a given pattern.

NL can be the best way for handling such queries, if we assume that the system has some information about the knowledge presented by the different nodes and about the semantics of the structure of the network. But there is more to it than just adding queries to a hypertext system.

The hypertext research community has begun to acknowledge the importance of user modeling. [Conklin, 1987] points out that a common difficulty arising in interacting with a hypermedia system is the *cognitive overhead* caused by the number of links that may be followed from each node. It would be very useful to be able to tell which links the specific user is less likely to follow, in order not to display them all (or to display them with a lower degree of relevance). User modelling has a long history and great power in NLP, basically to represent the communicative context in which a sentence is uttered [Kass and Finin, 1988; Kobsa *et al.*, 1986]. So, for instance in generation, a text can be naturally tailored (at all levels, from the rhetorical to the lexical choices) for the intended reader, yielding an effective communicative act [Hovy, 1988; Paris, 1987].

The handling of initiative shifts and of different attitudes on the side of the user is of basic importance for the improvement of human-computer interaction. When a user encounters a system that she has never used before she is very unlikely to have a clear idea of how to formulate a problem so that the system understands it. It is also possible that the user does not have enough information about the domain to be able to produce *any* clear problem formulation. We believe that at least in typically "explorative" and "individually creative" domains, a substantial environment habitability is of the utmost importance, and does greatly benefit from a global, even if approximates user model rising through dialog. The combination of the relative freedom provided by a natural language interface (with the power of making complex and precise requests and answers) and a visual presentation (with direct manipulation possibility) of some organized subdomains has immense potential impact. And of course the user can interleave precise requests with concrete exploration of "the surroundings". This last aspect needs original studies on the Cognitive Science side. One step in this direction is [Slack and Conati, 1991].

3 A note on discovering art

Hypertextual systems for museums are presently quite common, but they provide limited possibilities. The main weakness lies in what we have emphasized before: the difficulty of expressing a precise complex request, the lack of possibility of pursuing a particular goal through conversation, etc. It is well known that even without entering in the complex and subtle world of art *understanding*, art curiosity develops as a function of two factors: a) the cumulative effect of information (especially information answering free requests by the person or giving some limited further hints, relevant to her inclination); b) fruition of an art work when the person experiencing it is prepared and anticipates it. Art curiosity grows slowly and autonomously and imposing more data or experiences than the person is prepared to cope with has no positive effect at all. Only by combining information and perception with a sensation of driving the game and enjoying circumscribed moments of mere exploration, can a user experience the possible development of an interest in art. A typical consequence might be that you take a trip just to go and see one painting that you saw before among others and did not even notice.

Now, in the design of an artificial system that provides an environment for a user interested in art, the same concepts must be exploited. Also to be noted, as far as the modality of language communication is concerned, is the fact that *written* language is acceptable even if not the most desirable solution: a user interested in this domain (as opposed to a generic user of an automatic counter at a train station) is likely to know how to use a keyboard.

4 ALFresco

ALFresco is an interactive system for a user interested in frescoes. It runs on a SUN 4 connected to a videodisc unit and a touchscreen. The particular videodisc in use includes images about Fourteenth Century Italian frescoes and relevant monuments[1]. The system, besides un-

[1]The videodisc "Italian Art History" was provided by Rizzoli SpA; we take this occasion to thank them.

derstanding and using language, shows images and combines film sequences. Images are active in that the user may refer to items by combining pointing with the use of linguistic demonstratives. The system's linguistic output includes buttons that allow the user to enter in an hypertextual modality. The dialog may cause zooming into details or changing the focus of attention onto other frescoes.

The overall aim is not only to provide information, but also to promote other masterpieces that may attract the user. ALFresco will eventually provide a proposal for a cultural tour appropriate for the particular user, through further negotiation with her.

The system is based upon domain knowledge represented in different ways:

- a KB expressed in a KLOne-like language called YAK (a.k.a. KRAPFEN) [Franconi, 1990]. YAK is a hybrid system, whose terminological component consists of a tangled hierarchy in which generic concepts and roles are defined. The assertional box consists of instances that are represented as frames (in the spirit of LOOM, [MacGregor and Bates, 1987]) connected to the terminological box by a realizer that builds in the terminological hierarchy the most specific generic concept to which the particular instance belongs. The KB is used for defining everything the system can reason about: frescoes, monuments, painters, contents of frescoes, towns etc. and provides the base for ALFresco's deductive inference capabilities;
- a NoteCards hypermedia network (see below) containing unformalized knowledge such as art critics' opinions on the paintings and their authors.

Monodirectional pointers link instances or features in the knowledge base to images and film fragments stored in the videodisc. Bidirectional pointers connect knowledge base entities to regions of images.

At this point an explanation is due. Fourteenth Century frescoes have a content that almost always is centered on a sacred scene. The scene includes an event that can be reasonably well described (for instance the event "annunciation" performed by the angel Gabriel to Mary, in which the contents of the message is another event, namely the forthcoming birth of Jesus) and includes a number of well identified recurring characters: humans, animals, saints, angels etc.

The contents that we represent are the contents of the foreground of the paintings, while nothing is said about the background where the artist could have expressed any real world scene. In this particular context the indexabilty of the objects and the related concept of the granularity of internal representation are quite easily made clear to the user at the beginning of the interaction.

NL and hypermedia are integrated both in input and output. In input, our efforts have been focussed on combining the interpretation of NL deictic references with pointing to images displayed on a touch screen. For instance, the user can ask a question such as: *"Who is this person?"* while touching the image of a persòn appearing in the currently displayed fresco. Both the linguistic and the graphical deixes may be ambiguous, but usually the correct integration of the information provided by the two channels allows the identification of the intended reference. In output, images and generated text with buttons are yielded that offer entry points for further hypertextual exploration. A sketch of the ALFresco system architecture is shown in Figure 1 and in the following subsections we shall give an outline of the main components of the system.

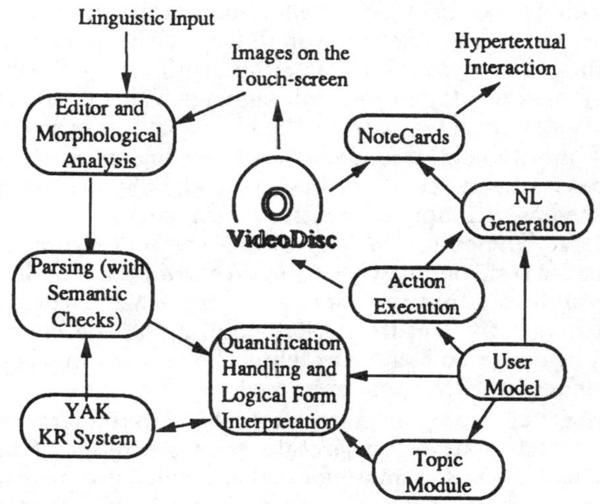

Figure 1: ALFresco architecture

An English version of a dialog fragment (taken from a real session with ALFresco) oriented to requests of information follows:

U: *I would like to know if A.L. ever painted a work that represents a sacred scene with an angel.*

S: *Yes, by example, A Lorenzetti, the Annunciation. The angel is the Arcangel Gabriel.*

U: *Who is this person?* [pointing at Mary on the touch screen]

S: *Mary.*

U: *Can you show me an enlargement containing it?*

S: [The system shows an enlargement]

U: *Was the author influenced by someone?*

S: *For example by Giotto*

U: *Where did this master see the light?* [meaning "where was he born"]

S: *Colle di Vespignano*

U: *Show me a detail with this scene.* [pointing to some place about the centre of the scene]

S: [The system shows the detail]

U: *In what town was A.L. born?*

S: *Siena*

U: *Show it to me.*

S: [the system shows a small film segment about Siena]

U: *I would like to see a fresco of the master in a monument of the town.*

S: [the system shows a film segment about a large fresco, "the Effects of Good Government", and outputs the name with a "description" button.]

At this point the user presses that button and a generated text is issued. Clicking on buttons the user can move inside an hypertext with comments written by art critics, or see related images, or explore the network. At any point it is possible to resume the dialog.

4.1 Parser

As far as sentence analysis is concerned, ALFresco is based on the WEDNESDAY 2 parser, (described in [Stock, 1989]). It is a chart-based parser able to cope with a large number of linguistic phenomena, including declarative, imperative and interrogative sentences, complex relative clauses (and other phenomena connected with so-called long distance dependencies), idiomatic expressions, various kinds of ellipses, constituent coordination, etc. One relevant capability of the parser is its ability to analyze idiomatic forms, with all the flexibility they may display in natural language. This characteristic is strictly integrated in the chart-based approach.

A morphological analyzer works on-line while the user types the sentence on the keyboard, thereby providing an immediate building of inactive lexical edges for the chart parser. The editor through which the sentence is input behaves transparently: for instance words can be deleted guaranteeing that the edges are reorganized accordingly. An important feature is that pointing to the currently displayed fresco can occur while the user is entering the sentence, in correspondence to demonstratives.

In general, the parser *per se* would output a large number of alternative interpretations of a sentence (this is particularly unfortunate for Italian, which is a freer word order language than English and in which even simple sentences can be ambiguous from a syntactic point of view). Through continuous interactions with the conceptual knowledge co mponent via a lexical semantic analysis component the possible functional relations are filtered; this permits greatly reducing the number of alternative representations of the sentence.

Another vital aspect for an interactive system that must allow good habitability and integration of modalities is the capability of treating elliptical forms. Also the solution to this problem is built into the chart approach (see [Lavelli and Stock, 1990]). The following dialogue fragment:

U: *Did Giotto portray St.Francis in a work located in Assisi?*
S: *Yes, for example in the Sermon to the birds.*
U: *Gioacchino in a fresco located in Padova?*

results in the last sentence being interpreted as *Did Giotto portray Gioacchino in a fresco in Padova?*.

4.2 Semantic interpretation

As far as semantic interpretation is concerned, multimediality made it necessary to have a layered and modular approach. In some recently developed systems a multilevel semantics approach has been proposed, in which various levels of formalization, each with its own particular functionality, correspond to successive levels of abstraction of logical-linguistic phenomena [Scha, 1983; Stallard, 1986]. A level bound to lexical semantics can be individuated (usually denoted as EFL, English-oriented formal language) and a level of meaning representation (usually denoted as WML, world model language; see Figure 2). Meaning representation is therefore as much as possible independent from the application domain. In ALFresco the interpretation modules' task is to present a meaning representation of the sentence that can be used by the various modules of the system.

The interpretative phase has several functions: in the first place it computes quantifiers' scopings. The algorithm is based on the concept of Cooper storage as in [Hobbs and Shieber, 1987] and on a) lexical classification of quantifiers; b) syntactic and surface order characteristics; c) presence of disambiguating expressions. It solves definite expressions such as determinative NP's, demonstratives (for example deriving from pointing actions), pronouns, by interacting with the topic module. It interprets the sentence dynamically, exploiting the semantics of operators, quantifiers, verbal modifiers, various levels of coordination and so on. The resulting representation is intensional, i.e. it is possible to abstract it in relation to time and context. The integration with temporal and contextual interpretation modules is currently under investigation.

```
(indef x (indef y
        (and (monument y)
         (has-place nil y (definite (town z))))
        (and (fresco x)
         (has-place nil x y)
         (made-by nil x (definite (painter w)))))
      (want nil speaker (see nil nil x)))
```

Figure 2: A WML form for *"I would like to see a fresco of the master in a monument of the town."*

In our case, without passing to a DBL form (Data Base Language in [Scha, 1983]) WML expressions are selectively and dynamically mapped into YAK's assertional language. In the process the topic module (see below) is called in.

4.3 The Topic Module and pointing

In a multimedial dialog system, the topic module must integrate global focus strategies, local focus approaches and deictic reference techniques. The main points of ALFresco's topic module [see [Samek-Lodovici and Strapparava, 1990] are the following.

ALFresco basically structures discourse in turns, with confirmations of referents from previous turns into the current one. The user normally refers to entities bound to particular frescoes. So the basic idea is to combine a) Grosz's idea of factoring the search for referents into topic-spaces [Grosz, 1977]: our topic-spaces are typically built around frescoes; and b) Hajicova's approach consisting in letting the entities that have been mentioned slowly fade away unless they are mentioned again with a certain functional role [Hajicova, 1987].

The system relies on two stacks: 1) a stack of turns, where each turn contains the referents inserted or confirmed by the user or by ALFresco , and 20 a stack of Topic Units, in which each Topic Unit contains all the referents inserted by the user or by the system while discussing a particular fresco.

As far as the deictic context is concerned, in our case it changes whenever a new fresco is displayed on the screen. Similarly to XTRA [Wahlster, 1988], [Kobsa *et al.*, 1986] we associate the accessible entities with the regions they occupy on the screen. Regions overlap significantly (e.g. the region of the "annunciation" and the region of the angel Gabriel in Giotto's Annunciation). As in CUBRICON [Neal and Shapiro, 1988], the ALFresco topic module permits both the use of linguistic input to solve ambiguous touches and the use of touches to solve ambiguous linguistic input. More generally, both a touch and a linguistic expression may be ambiguous and yet yield a unique referent through mutual constraint.

4.4 The user's interest model

The user's interest model consists of an activation network, the nodes of which are associated with ordered sets of individual concepts. The grouping of the individuals is performed according to a measure of domain-dependent pragmatic closeness; whenever a set is activated, all the entities composing it are considered somehow relevant. Each set represents an *interest area* and is identified by particular concepts or individuals represented in YAK. The individuals that belong to an area and their relative relevance (represented by the ordering) are computed on the basis of their proximity to the identifier of the area (if it is an individual) or to its instances (if it is a terminological concept). The process that builds the interest areas interprets the A-box as a graph in which the nodes are the individual concepts and the edges connect an individual to those individuals filling one of its roles or having a role filled by it.

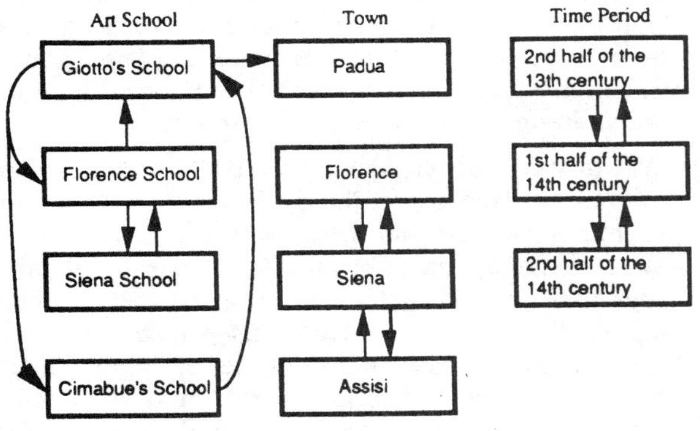

Figure 3: Some interest areas

The dynamic information represented by the model consists in the activation level associated with the interest areas. A node receives a certain amount of activation whenever one of the individuals it contains is referred to by the user or the system. The intensity of these activation impulses depends on how explicitly the individual is mentioned. After each user query, activation impulses are propagated through the network.

Figure 3 shows a simplified activation network relative to the domain of ALFresco. The areas are grouped in structures that represent interest dimensions, i.e. classes of entities that are likely to be at the centre of the user's interest. The dimensions currently used in the user model correspond to the T-box concepts defining *art schools, towns* and *time periods*. The weighted links connecting different areas can represent different kinds of pragmatic closeness: for instance, a link between two areas of the Towns dimension represents geographic closeness. "Geographic closeness" is intended as a pragmatic relation, with consequences relative for instance to the possibility that the user considers a trip from one town to another.

The generator makes use of the user's interest model. For instance, it asks the latter which is the most relevant area of a certain dimension of interest, and the model returns the main element associated with the most active area of that dimension.

4.5 Actions performed by the system

The actions performed by ALFresco are realized exploiting the media the system is based upon: a) the system can show one or more images or pieces of film, b) give some punctual answer to a question by replying with instances such as the title and location of a painting, or dates etc., or, finally, c) give a more complex description of a fresco or some other entities, through natural language. All three different media allow the user to interact with them by direct manipulation. A higher level, *ad hoc*, pragmatic component decides how to react in the given dialogic situation, considering the type of request, the context, the model of the interest of the user, the things already shown or said to the user and so on. We shall focus our attention on the language generator. There are three main aspects:
1) the semantic/pragmatic component and its interactions with the other modules of the dialog system (user model in particular); 2) the syntactic realization component; 3) the integration of NLG and hypertext techniques.

The communicative goal of the generation component, providing information about instances of the domain (i.e. frescoes), is achieved by execution of rhetorical schemata [McKeown, 1985].

The schemata's task is to select and order appropriate attributes, generic-classes, values, instances (Figure 4) from a set of possible alternatives; the process of selection is driven by both an *a priori*, strongly domain-dependent ordering between the KB items and a sequence of queries to the KB. For instance, the selection of the comparative-attribute for a fresco starts by asking the KB for other instances with a *similar* value for the *content* attribute (the first in an *a priori* ordering) and values for the other attributes subsumed by concepts stemming from the user modeling module; if the KB returns one instance, this is used as a comparative-instance and the selection process ends, if it returns more than one instance another *a priori* ordering (this time between the instances) is exploited; in both cases the content would be the comparative-attribute. When no instance is returned, the selection process iterates on other attributes.

The user modeling component provides a relevance criterion for operating selections between the individual concepts described in the assertional box of the knowledge representation system. After this phase of determination of the rethorical schemata and of the particular contents, the syntactic realization component is called in.The algorithm works on a unification based formalism in a bottom-up, head driven fashion [Pianesi, 1991] and yields complex natural language sentences.

4.6 Integrating NL Generation and hypertextual techniques

The system's answer is a hypermedia node containing a (possibly generated) text with links to both the hypermedia network and images from the videodisc. In particular, the output of the NL generation component is passed to the hypermedia module which transforms the plain text into a hypertextual entry point to the underlying hypermedia network. Buttons pointing to hypermedial information are associated to individual contents selected by rethorical schemata.

The hypermedia module is based on the NoteCards system, a general hypermedia environment developed at Xerox PARC. We chose Notecards for its powerful programmer's interface to a Lisp environment and general tailorability. The system provides an extremely flexible environment in which it is possible to integrate many of the different kinds of interaction that can take place in the exploration of a complex set of knowledge.The primitive constructs of the system are ***cards*** and ***links***:

- Cards are usually displayed on the screen as standard Xerox Lisp windows containing a piece of text. NoteCards allows for the creation of new card types.
- Links are used to interconnect individual cards into networks; they are displayed as icons inside the substance of a card. Clicking the mouse in such an icon retrieves the destination card and executes the associated actions (usually the card is displayed on the screen).

The tailorability of NoteCards has been exploited in ALFresco in the implementation of virtual (dynamically constructed) links that connect text cards to images and fragments of films stored in the videodisc.

ALFresco's generated text appears as a card providing the user with a dynamic entry-point both to images from the videodisc and to a static base of hypertextual information. Figure 4 shows the card produced in relation to the last point in the dialog of section 4. The canned texts accessible through buttons deal with particularly complex topics (such as comparisons between styles as they are elaborated by art critics) definitely outside the expressive scope of current KR systems.

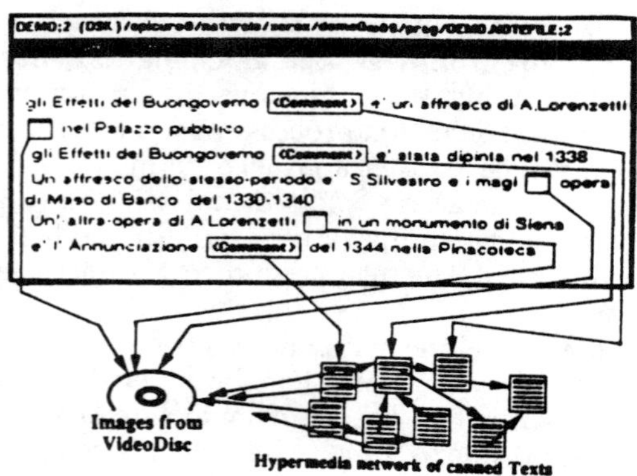

Figure 4: *"The Effects of Good Government is a fresco by A.L. in the Public Palace. The Effects of Good Government was painted in 1338. A fresco from the same period is S. Silvestro and the Holy Kings by Maso di Banco, painted in 1330-1340. Another work by A.L. in a monument of Siena is the Annunciation, of 1344 in the Pinacoteca".*

Presenting the user with a mix of generated and canned text in general can be misleading; in fact the unaware user might: a) make references to canned text (the system is unable to understand) and b) overestimate the system's capabilities. The use of graphic containers overcomes this problem making clear the difference between the two kinds of text: canned text has to be presented in an evocative graphical format, such as a simulated open book.

Another important aspect is the *Browser construct*. Browsers are constructs containing a structural diagram of a network of cards with different types of links visualized in different dashing styles. Browser cards can be automatically computed by the system and, when generated, have an active behaviour: i.e. it is possible to click on a node of the displayed network in order to access the corresponding card. The user can refer to this overall structure in her exploration.

Two general problems, connected with the rationale of section 2 are worth discussing:

1. User modeling connected to linguistic communication may suggest the possibility of applying the same model to the control of hypertextual communication. Anyway, it is not clear whether a simple user model (such as that of ALFresco) could really improve the efficiency of hypertextual interaction: it might be the case that only very sophisticated (and yet not understood) modeling techniques can help hypertext exploration when another powerful means for focusing a request (i.e. natural language) is available in the same environment.
2. Would it be advantageous that the model of interest (to be used in the language-centered modality) is changed as the user browses through the network? We feel that given a) the limited accuracy of current user models and b) the fact that hypertext modality on its own would only be used in a very limited way to explore the surroundings or have a general bird eye's view of the domain, it may be wrong to constrain the behaviour of the whole system in that way. It seems to us better not to modify the user model through the hypertext modality thereby minimizing any consequences for the natural language-centered interaction.

5 Conclusions

We have discussed the combination of natural language dialog and hypermediality within an artificial intelligence view of information exploration. The habitability of a system that provides an active integration of the two paradigms is greatly enhanced and a number of interesting issues that amplify more traditional possibilities arise. The exploratory dialog system ALFresco has been presented: an NL and hypermedial system connected to a videodisc that gives information about Italian frescoes of the Fourteenth Century. The system as described here is implemented in Xerox Common Lisp and runs on a Sun 4 connected to a videodisc unit.

Many points are to be explored: among the extensions we intend to pursue the idea that the system can in the end provide through further negotiation a suggestion for a personal cultural-touristic itinerary. We believe that this area is of great potential because cultural tourism is increasing material relevance, especially in Italy, but also because it is an area that requires a shift from a mass-oriented, impersonal perspective toward an individual-oriented, creative opportunity for all. In general, we think that the integration of hypermediality with AI and NLP technology opens a wide range of new perspectives for the development of intelligent interfaces and that it will ultimately lead to an innovative paradigm for man-machine interaction.

Acknowledgements

We would like to thank Jon Slack for many helpful discussions and Luigi Stringa for encouraging an integrated view of AI at IRST.

References

[Arens *et al.*, 1988] Y. Arens, L. Miller, S.C. Shapiro, and N.K. Sondheimer. Automatic construction of user interface displays. In *Proc. AAAI-88 Conference*, St. Paul, Minnesota, 1988.

[Arens *et al.*, 1989] Y. Arens, S. Feiner, J. Hollan, and R. Neches. *Proc. of the IJCAI Workshop on a New Generation of Intelligent Interfaces.* Detroit, 1989.

[Cohen *et al.*, 1989] P.R. Cohen, M. Dalrymple, D.B. Moran, F.C.N. Pereira, , J.W. Sullivan, R.A. Gargan Jr, J.L. Schlossberg, and S.W. Tyler. Synergetic use of direct manipulation and natural language. In *Proc. of CHI'89 Conference*, Austin, Texas, 1989.

[Conklin, 1987] J. Conklin. Hypertext: An introduction and survey. *IEEE Computer*, 20(9), 1987.

[Feiner and McKeown, 1990] S. Feiner and K. McKeown. Coordinating text and graphics in explanation generation. In *Proc. AAAI-90 Conference*, Boston, Mass., 1990.

[Franconi, 1990] E. Franconi. The YAK manual: Yet Another KRAPFEN. Technical Report 9003-01, IRST, Trento, Italy, 1990.

[Grosz, 1977] B. Grosz. The representation and use of focus in dialogue understanding. Technical Report 151, SRI Project 5844, SRI, Menlo Park, CA, 1977.

[Hajicova, 1987] E. Hajicova. Focusing: a meeting point of linguistics and artificial intelligence. In P. Jorrand and V. Sgurev, editors, *Artificial Intelligence II: Methodology, Systems, Applications.* Elsevier Science Publishers, 1987.

[Halasz, 1988] F.G. Halasz. Reflections on NoteCards, seven issues for the next generation of hypermedia systems. *Communications of the ACM*, 13(7), 1988.

[Hobbs and Shieber, 1987] J.R. Hobbs and S.M. Shieber. An algorithm for generating quantifier scopings. *Computational Linguistics*, 13(1-2), 1987.

[Hollan *et al.*, 1988] J. Hollan, E. Rich, W. Hill, D. Wroblenski, W. Wilker, K. Wittenburg, and J. Grudin. An introduction to HITS: Human Interface Tool Suite. Technical Report ACA-HI-406-88, MCC, Austin, Texas, 1988.

[Hovy, 1988] E. Hovy. *Generating Natural Language under Pragmatic Constraints.* Erlbaum Lawrence Associates, 1988.

[Kass and Finin, 1988] R. Kass and T. Finin. Modeling the user in natural language systems. *Computational Linguistics*, 14(13), 1988.

[Kobsa *et al.*, 1986] A. Kobsa, J. Allagyer, C. Reddig, N. Reithinger, D. Schmauks, K. Harbusch, and W. Wahlster. Combining deictic gestures and natural language for referent identification. In *Proc. COLING 86*, Bonn, Germany, 1986.

[Lavelli and Stock, 1990] A. Lavelli and O. Stock. When something is missing: Ellipsis, coordination and the chart. In *Proc. COLING 90*, Helsinki, Finland, 1990.

[MacGregor and Bates, 1987] R.M. MacGregor and L. Bates. The LOOM Knowledge Representation Language. Technical Report ISI/RS-87-188, USC/Information Sciences Institute, Marina del Rey, CA, 1987.

[MacLaughlin and Shaked, 1989] D.M. MacLaughlin and V. Shaked. Natural language text generation in semi-automated forces. Technical Report 7092, BBN, Cambridge, Mass., 1989.

[McKeown, 1985] K.R. McKeown. *Text Generation.* Cambridge University Press, 1985.

[Neal and Shapiro, 1988] J.G. Neal and S.C. Shapiro. Intelligent multimedia interface technology. In *Proc. of the Workshop on Architectures for Intelligent Interface Technology*, Monterey, CA, 1988.

[Paris, 1987] C.L. Paris. Combining discourse strategies to generate descriptions to users along a naive/expert spectrum. In *Proc. of IJCAI 87*, Milano, Italy, 1987.

[Pianesi, 1991] F. Pianesi. X-bar theory and deep structure: a tabular bottom-up generator. Technical Report 9104-11, IRST, Trento, Italy, 1991.

[Samek-Lodovici and Strapparava, 1990] V. Samek-Lodovici and C. Strapparava. Identifying noun phrase references, the topic module of the ALFRESCO system. In *Proc. ECAI 90*, Stockholm, Sweden, 1990.

[Scha, 1983] R. Scha. Logic foundation for question answering. Technical Report MS 12.331, Philips Research Labs, Einhoven, The Netherlands, 1983.

[Slack and Conati, 1991] J.M. Slack and C. Conati. Modeling interest: exploration of an information space. Technical Report 9101-03, IRST, Trento, Italy, 1991.

[Stallard, 1986] D. Stallard. A terminological simplification transformation for nl question answering system. In *Proc. of the 24th Meeting of the ACL*, New York, 1986.

[Stock, 1989] O. Stock. Parsing with flexibility, dynamic strategies and idioms in mind. *Computational Linguistics*, 15(1), 1989.

[Wahlster *et al.*, 1991] W. Wahlster, E. Andre', W. Graf, and T. Rist. Designing illustrated texts: How language production is influenced by graphics generation. In *Proc. 5th Conf. of the European Chapter of ACL*, Berlin, 1991.

[Wahlster, 1988] W. Wahlster. User and discourse models for multimodal communication. In J.W. Sullivan and S.W. Tyler, editors, *Architectures for Intelligent Interfaces: Elements and Prototypes.* Addison-Wesley, 1988.

Natural Language and Exploration of an Information Space: The ALFresco Interactive System

Oliviero Stock

The work on ALFresco has developed in several ways since the time of the initial article's publication (see also (Stock and the NLP Group 1993)). Some of the main points follow. Multimodal dialog management has been at the center of our interest (the architecture is sketched in Figure 1), with a strong emphasis on cohesion.

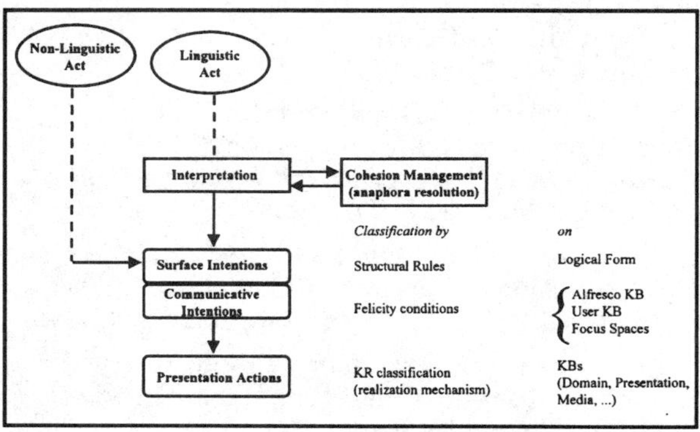

FIGURE 1. ALFresco Architecture

The key for multimodal interaction is provided by the uniform use of felicity conditions (Stock et al. 1997), the rules that govern the relations between the interactional exchanges and communicative intentions. In substance, we have proposed a level of multimodal acts representation roughly corresponding to what, for strictly linguistic dialogs, is the illocutionary act.

Dialog cohesion management is described in (Zancanaro et al. 1997) and is based on an adaptation of the centering model, here developed for dialogs in a multimodal environment. Its tasks are (1) to resolve anaphoras, (2) to build a dialog structure based on cohesion, and (3) to manage focus spaces.

The use of a graphical feedback of the dialog cohesion status to the user was presented in (Zancanaro et al. 1993). This visual representation reassures the user at a glance on the system's interpretation (as such, it takes the place of a paraphraser) and allows cooperative recovery from discourse misconceptions by means of a series of "intuitive actions" when this interpretation is not the one the user meant.

In general, a tighter integration of different modes of exploration—language oriented and navigational—has been accomplished. I think this is a very fruitful concept that can lead to various applications. The study of the involved cognitive aspects is of great importance here. Lab experiments with implemented prototypes and simulated systems will make all of us understand better this kind of amplification of human communicative capabilities.

REFERENCES

Stock and the NLP Group. 1993. AlFresco: Enjoying the Combination of NLP and Hypermedia for Information Exploration. In Maybury, M. (ed.), *Intelligent Multimedia Interfaces*, 197–224. Cambridge, MA: AAAI/MIT Press.

Stock, O.; Strapparava, C.; and Zancanaro, M. 1997. Explorations in an Environment for Natural Language Multimodal Information Access. In Maybury, M. (ed.), *Intelligent Multimedia Information Retrieval*, 381–398. Cambridge, MA: AAAI/MIT Press.

Zancanaro, M.; Stock, O.; and Strapparava, C. 1993. Dialog Cohesion Sharing and Adjusting in a Multimodal Interactive Environment. In *Proceedings of IJCAI 93, Thirteenth International Joint Conference on Artificial Intelligence*, Chambery, France, 1230–1236.

Zancanaro, M.; Stock, O.; and Strapparava, C. 1997. Multimodal Interaction for Information Access: Exploiting Cohesion. *Computational Intelligence* 13(4): 439–464.

Chapter 8

The Application of Natural Language Models to Intelligent Multimedia

John D. Burger and Ralph J. Marshall

Abstract

One of the features that distinguishes intelligent multimedia interfaces from more static approaches such as preconfigured hypertext, is the ability to reason about how to present information to the user and how to interpret user input in the context of the ongoing dialog between human and computer. In this chapter, we describe an intelligent multimedia interface tool, and the internal mechanisms used to support this intelligent behavior. The central idea behind this work is the extension of existing work in natural language understanding to handle multimedia conversations. By incorporating context tracking and a knowledge representation, we are able to automate many of the interface decisions without seriously limiting the scope of the interactions.

1. Why Develop an Integrated Multimedia Interface?

An earlier project at The MITRE Corporation involved augmenting the MACPLAN[1] mission planning expert system with the KING KONG[2] natural language shell. It was during that work we reached the conclusion that it was not practical to have an intelligent interface that only accounted for part of the users' interaction with the underlying system. Since KING KONG was intended solely as a natural language interface tool, we decided to adapt and extend its communication models to attack the more encompassing problem of a complete interface. This project was known as AIMI,[3] and forms the basis of the ideas we present in this chapter.

1.1. A Brief Description of MACPLAN

MACPLAN was an expert system designed to assist human planners in the task of devising cargo transportation schedules and routes (see [Kissmeyer and Tallant 1989] for details). It included a series of graphic displays that showed the selected routes and resource flows in the current plan, and both menus and a simple ATN-based natural language interface for issuing commands. The system focused around a small set of graphic displays that supported most of the planning and data entry work.

The goal of the KING KONG integration effort, was to replace the ATN-based parser with a full-fledged dialog system which would provide a much wider range of features to the users. The most important of the capabilities provided by KING KONG were the ability to issue commands and ask questions not anticipated by the menu designers, perform anaphoric reference resolution, and handle deictic introduction of items for later reference. However, we deliberately intended the port of KING KONG to be an extension to the existing MACPLAN interface rather than a complete replacement, since many of the graphic displays were popular with the users.

Users were initially disappointed by the rather low success rate of the natural language interface, but once they understood its limitations they found the ability to use anaphoric reference and deictic reference to be a decided improvement over the previous parser. However, when the users learned to take advantage of the context mechanism, they ran into the problem that it was only tracking user actions involving the language interface. Since the graphic interface was more natural for many types of interactions, users continued to rely on it to a large extent. They were confused by the fact that selecting an item on the screen only introduced it into the dialog context in certain circumstances, and we were never able to satisfactorily explain the distinction to them.

---

[1] MACPLAN is an acronym for "Military Airlift Command Planner".

[2] KING KONG is not an acronym.

[3] AIMI is an acronym for "An Intelligent Multimedia Interface". Part of this work was funded through Rome Laboratories under Air Force Contract number F19628-89-C-0001.

1.2. Lessons Learned

The MACPLAN experience convinced us that many of the advanced context-tracking mechanisms in KING KONG are of limited practical advantage if the system does not track the entire set of interactions between the system and users. Since there didn't appear to be a good way (short of extensive modification to the existing MACPLAN interface code) to improve the communication between the two systems, we concluded that the proper solution was to build an interface tool that could accommodate *all* of the necessary communication channels. By extending the internal dialog support tools of KING KONG to a complete multimedia interface system we were able to develop a seamless interface that was cognizant of all the activities performed by the user and could respond appropriately in a much wider range of situations.

Another important conclusion we reached during the MACPLAN work is that most casual computer users (especially those who do not touch-type) would much rather select from a limited set of menu options than have to enter a long command in text, even if the natural language system does an excellent job of interpreting their sentences. This reinforced the need for an interface tool that is not restricted to producing static displays, but rather one that is able to generate responses that can form the basis for follow-up queries or commands.

1.3. A Brief Description of AIMI

Rooted in the work discussed above, AIMI'S project goals were to develop a portable intelligent multimedia/multimodal interface. By *portable*, we mean that much of the processing done by the system is independent of any particular back end system. The intent was to be able to connect AIMI to a new back end with minimum effort. (We use the phrases *front end* and *back end* to distinguish the interface from the underlying system with which the user wishes to interact.) AIMI reasons in detail about the meaning of user input, using a number of AI approaches discussed below. Similarly, when presenting information to the user, the system is able to intelligently choose among the presentation alternatives available to it and then design the most appropriate presentation. Currently, AIMI'S repertoire of modalities includes natural language, maps, mouse gestures, business charts, specialized interactive inspectors, still images, and non-speech audio.

Despite the existence of multiple communication modalities, AIMI deals with the meaning of input and output without respect to any particular modality. This is because many of the mechanisms developed for the KING KONG system have been generalized to allow for the intelligent processing of communication in general, regardless of the medium of the communication. Some of these mechanisms include a meaning representation component, an intentional context model that tracks the user's goals, and an attentional context model that tracks the entities introduced into the mutual focus of attention of the user and the interface. As we shall see, these mechanisms, as well as the presentation planning components of the system, do most of their reasoning at a level that is removed from the domain of the back end and the mode of input or output. This allows new input and output capabilities to be more easily added to the system. In addition, the interface front end can be more easily ported among different back end systems.

2. What We Mean by Knowledge Representation

As discussed above, many of the mechanisms of an intelligent interface can benefit from a rich and explicit representation of knowledge, including a system's representation of input and output. For example, in AIMI, at the heart of the representation machinery, there is a terminological reasoner that stores predicate subsumption hierarchies, as in KL-ONE (see Brachman and Schmolze [1985]). The information in these hierarchies can be used in virtually every processing step that is performed on input and output, from understanding the input, to discourse processing, evaluation and the selection of how to present the response.

The meanings of input and output events can be encoded as expressions in a sorted first-order language (with generalized quantifiers) whose predicates are drawn from the terms in the subsumption hierarchy. For example, the English sentence "London is reachable with what all-weather aircraft from airports in Scotland?" is represented in AIMI by the following expression:

```
(WH x (LAMBDA y
          (AND  (AIRCRAFT y)
                (AC-TYPE y All-Weather)))
      (EXISTS z (LAMBDA w
                  (AND  (AIRPORT w)
                        (AIRPORT-IN-COUNTRY w Scotland)))
        (REACHABLE London x z)))
```

In this example, the LAMBDA-terms are sorts, *à la* λ-abstraction, and WH is a generalized quantifier that is used to encode the meanings of Wh-terms such as "what" and "where" (see Bayer and Vilain [1991]). Again, the predicates in this expression, for instance AIRCRAFT and REACHABLE, correspond to terms in the knowledge representation's subsumption hierarchies. Examples of related approaches include such systems as KRYPTON, BACK, and KL-TWO [Brachman et al. 1985; van Luck et al. 1987; Vilain 1985]. Many kinds of knowledge are represented in AIMI using this logical language, including the system's model of the user's goals. Most of the system's reasoning is done at the level of expressions in this language, and is thus independent of the medium of the original input.

Given a meaning language such as that just described, a system can make use of a planner to determine how to accomplish goals expressed in the meaning language. This combination allows for a strong distinction between what to do and how to accomplish it. This enables a system to be more sensitive to factors external to a user's actual commands, and accomplish a given command in different ways, depending on such things as the user's implicit goals, the status of the display, the system's display capabilities, and other external information. Similarly, a system may satisfy its own goals in different ways. For example, when an anomalous situation occurs, a system may choose between a warning dialog box and an audio indication such as a siren.

Another useful feature of an explicit knowledge representation and a meaning language, is that it allows for an appropriate level of communication between sub-modules in an interface. This is especially useful when incorporating an existing interface component into a larger interface, for example, a self-contained map display system. The connection between the existing component and the rest of the interface can be in the high-level terms of the knowledge representation.

Finally, a rich and explicit meaning representation language allows more easily for "self referentiality", that is, for the user and the interface itself to refer to the artifacts of their interactions, such as graphical presentations. Such a capability is described in more detail in section 6.

3. Knowledge Representation and Intelligent Interfaces

In order to effectively separate the user interface from the application, there must be methods for interpreting input and generating output that are not specific to the domain of the application. One convenient way to achieve this separation is to develop general purpose reasoning mechanisms for communication that extract the necessary domain-specific information from an instantiated knowledge representation. We feel that the style of knowledge representation outlined in Section 2 is suitable for organizing the information needed to generate both text and graphics. Using a single data source in this fashion helps to ensure that communication is consistent across modes and also enables the interface to select the most appropriate mode with fewer constraints on what can be said or understood.

3.1. Knowledge-Based Presentation Planning

A reasonable amount of research has been done on the problem of automating the design of information graphics, which is one requirement of a system like AIMI. Most of these approaches (see [Roth and Mattis 1990a] for one example) require a taxonomy of data types used by the system so that the design module can make decisions about appropriate ways to display a given set of data. While one can always build such a taxonomy into the system, using an existing knowledge representation that supports inheritance computations and automatic classification of data points eliminates the need for a separate component.

While a complete description of the methods for generating automatic displays is beyond the scope of this chapter, a brief description of one popular approach will serve to demonstrate the benefit of having a knowledge representation (and optionally an associated natural language component).

The basic notion behind automatic design of charts is that there is a generally accepted syntax and semantics of graphical displays that people rely on in order to decode a given presentation. For example, the syntactic restrictions on bar charts require that all of the bars have the same scale and baseline, and that the height (or length) of the bar is used to represent differing values for corresponding items. Finding a valid interpretation of these charts requires that we agree on the semantics of the bars as well. The height should correspond in a direct fashion to the value represented, and the value should be some measurement of amount. For example, a bar chart that attempts to represent the starting dates of events is semantically invalid because dates are points in time, not amounts. On the other hand, lengths of events are amounts and thus can be represented with bars. See Roth and Hefley [this volume] for a more comprehensive introduction to the issues of automatic graphic design.

While the specific requirements of a given automated designer will vary, most will need to ask questions about the data such as:

- Is this field quantitative or qualitative?
- Is there any natural ordering among the data points?
- Are any data points missing or unknown?
- How are data points from this set to be labeled?

Questions like these can be supported by the knowledge representation mechanisms used by AIMI, making it easy to include such a design component in the system without extensive modifications.

Another important use of a type taxonomy is the ability to store domain-specific information about preferred display methods. For example, if a system processes information about various countries, it may be desirable to attach an icon representing the flag of a given nation to the corresponding node in the taxonomy. When a presentation that includes a list of countries is being planned, the design can make use of the icons as appropriate. While the specific icon, color, or pattern to be associated with a data type is not something the presentation module should have built into it, the general knowledge that some data sets will be able to provide such information can be used to generate more effective graphics.

It should be noted that the requirements of presentation design at this level do not require the services of a full-blown knowledge representation. A more restricted taxonomy that simply classifies the data sets and provides a place to attach additional type-specific information is sufficient. Thus, the advantages of automatic presentation design can still be had even if the system has no other need for the sort of knowledge representation advocated here.

3.2. The Added Value of a Natural Language Generator

While we have just seen that an integrated knowledge representation can be used to support the generation of multimedia displays at run time, the quality of those displays can be further enhanced by the presence of an associated natural language generation facility. Labels need to be generated for the data points, chart axes, legends, and so on, and the resulting displays will be vastly improved by the use of natural language rather than computer-generated code words.

There are two broad types of text generation that will benefit the user: simple label generation, and full-text description. Generating reasonable names and labels for various chart elements can be done by associating a name generator with various concepts in the knowledge representation hierarchy. This will allow the chart to contain labels such as **Imogen Cunningham** rather than **Person-32**—an obvious improvement that does not require a large investment in additional code.

A more complete natural language generator can provide several additional levels of functionality. Presenting answers in text is often the most appropriate mode of communication. Such answers can also be communicated in speech if the system decides that it is the best channel under the circumstances. If the text generation is supported by the core system (rather than produced by a black-box approach) the interface can perform appropriate reasoning and control over the output as required for a system that is a well-meshed set of communication channels and not just a collection of display modules. For a more comprehensive exposition of the use of natural language generation in multimedia interfaces, see Maybury [this volume].

4. Context Models

Many natural language systems utilize various *context models* while processing. Although such models were initially formulated for linguistic interactions, they often prove to be of sufficient generality to accommodate non-linguistic interactions as well [Neal and Shapiro 1991; Wahlster 1991; Burger and Marshall 1991]. The notion of a *discourse* is central to such systems, and underlies much of the intelligent assistance that they are able to provide to their users. Discourse is broadly construed as the sequence of interactions, be they linguistic, graphic, or gestural, between a system and its user. By contextualizing the user's input and the system's output in the light of earlier interactions, a wide range of cooperative behavior can be provided that is focused on the task the user is trying to accomplish.

Many approaches to modeling this sort of discourse are based on the work of Grosz and Sidner [1986]. For purposes of this discussion, their model attempts to capture the interrelations between the discourse's *intention* structure, which models the respective goals of the discourse participants, and the *attentional* structure, which reflects the foci of the participants' attention.

Each of the interactions between the user and the back end system is associated with an intention (roughly, a goal) that the user and the back end system share. Each intention is represented as a logical expression in the sort of meaning representation language described in section 2. The relationships among intentions are also represented, for example, subgoal/supergoal. In addition, a context model must represent the attentional state of a discourse. Such a representation can be composed of a number of focus spaces (as described in Grosz and Sidner [1986]), each containing representations of the entities introduced explicitly during a particular segment of a discourse, or that become salient while interactions in that segment are produced or interpreted. Each focus space is associated with a particular intention; since it consists of the entities introduced by the utterances associated with that intention, a focus space contains only entities that are salient in the context of a particular goal.

An interface's intentional model can be used to disambiguate user input, and to understand *why* a user is doing something. An intention model as described here relies on the assumption that each interaction in a discourse is to be understood as contributing, directly or indirectly, to the satisfaction of a particular intention. Thus, an important part of discourse processing is the *recognition* of the intention motivating a particular utterance. We will not describe methods for accomplishing such recognition, but a number of algorithms exist.[4] Using this recognition of the goals underlying a user's input, an interface can engage in a number of cooperative behaviors, including disambiguating the input, providing information other than that directly requested (see [Schaffer Sider and Burger 1992]), and warning the user if her underlying assumptions are incorrect (see Schaffer Sider [1990]).

Maintaining the interface's attentional model involves identifying those entities that have been introduced into the discourse by each interaction, and adding them to the internal focus spaces appropriately. Simple models may merely keep a global focus space ordered by recency [Neal and Shapiro 1991], while others may segment the focus space, often in terms of the intentional state of the discourse (for example, [Schaffer Sider and Burger 1992]). Information from the attentional model is often used in natural language systems to resolve referring expressions, and this translates quite straightforwardly to the incorporation of deictic gestures. For example, in a mixed modality interface, a user may point to items with a mouse, such as a city on a map, and then refer to them with natural language: "Send the plane there." This is a more general approach than those that incorporate the pointing gesture into the natural language grammar [Neal and Shapiro 1991], as it allows pointing gestures to be used in conjunction with other modalities, such as menu selections. Thus the user could point to the city, and then select the **Destination** command from a menu.[5]

Natural language systems often also use the attentional model when generating output to decide when to use referring expressions. Again, this notion translates to multimodal output quite straightforwardly. If an interface knows that a particular city has previously been displayed on a map, and later output refers to that city again, the system may merely be able to highlight the city, rather than generate new output. This often leads to smoother and less disjointed interactions between the user and the system.

Later, we shall describe other instances of the usefulness of context models such as these in interfaces without natural language.

5. Reasoning About the Dialog

One of the things necessary for an *intelligent* multimedia interface is the ability to determine how to communicate with the user at any given point in time. A number of factors should influence that decision:

- What is to be communicated?
- How much is to be said?
- Is this a question or a response, and should it be available for follow-up?
- What do we expect the user to do as a result of receiving this message?
- What communications channels are available?
- Which channels does the user prefer?

[4] See, for example, Carberry [1988], Kautz [1987], or Schaffer Sider and Burger [1992].

[5] For greater detail on the use of deictic gestures in both input and output, see Wahlster [1991].

- What modes of communication have we been using so far?

While taking full account of each of the above points is well beyond the scope of existing artificial intelligence technology, there are limited ways for the answers to each of the above questions to influence the choice we make. We will expand on the reasoning applied to each of these questions in the following sections.

5.1. Content of the Message

The range of interesting communication that can occur between the user and a system is primarily determined by the area of expertise of the underlying application. We make the strong assumption that computing the answer, including any attendant data reduction or amplification, is the responsibility of the back end system. While the interface should provide facilities that make it easy for the user to ask follow-up questions or to request a modified version of the answer, we have made no attempt to do any such data analysis in the front end. This philosophy can be contrasted with the tighter integration between presentation and domain knowledge found in systems such as TEXPLAN (see Maybury [this volume]).

In many systems, the format of the response that is generated is either completely determined by the question or the user is required to specify it as part of the initial query. Since one main purpose of an intelligent interface is to support relatively unstructured dialog while assuming much of the burden of selecting appropriate methods of presentation, having the ability to generate responses based on the *answer* as well as the *question* is essential.

5.2. Purpose of the Message

While the general guidelines for determining how the purpose should influence the form are easy to derive, applying them appropriately in different conversational contexts is important. Consider the following cases:

Yes/no response: This answer is probably going to be transitory, and most communication channels will be able to convey it effectively. Thus, printing "Yes" in response to a typed question or having the system generate a euphonious sound in response to mouse input are typically the best choices. Note that even here the input mode is important for determining how to respond.

Detailed listing of facts: As the size and level of complexity of the message increase, certain communications channels will be more or less able to convey a response effectively. Selecting the appropriate channel (audio for rapidly changing non-quantitative information, graphics for more static information) can best be done by weighing what the user is currently doing against the absolute best mode of conveying this particular answer.

Request for data entry: This may range from asking the user to select a file name to filling in a large set of values in a form. Here the method of eliciting the answer may consist of presenting a list of possible choices (if only a few responses are valid), providing a graphical presentation that allows the user to browse a directory structure, or presenting a blank input window for typing in a name. However, since the user must eventually provide a response, the format of the question should assist the user in specifying the answer. This means that linear, computer-driven methods (such as telephone menus) should be avoided if possible.

Alarm: Here the system needs to weigh the importance of the alarm, any other alarms that may also be active at the moment, and the probable focus of attention of the user. A well-known example concerns the problem of alerting airplane pilots to dangerous situations—if too many alarms are sounding simultaneously no real communication is possible. Also, if the user of a multi-screen display has been recently providing input to a particular screen the visual alarms should obviously appear on that device, and possibly move when the system detects that the user is focusing on another display. This ability can be greatly aided by the attentional context tracking mechanisms described in section 4.

5.3. Available Means of Communication

Clearly, the way a given message will be conveyed to the user depends heavily on the physical means at the system's disposal. While this is an obvious point, it means that the system must make its decisions in a manner that does not rely on knowing the choices in advance. The available hardware may change from user to user, session to session, or even within a session if equipment is subject to faults and subsequent repairs. Also, the system should make an effort to check the suitability of each available channel for the current audience. By marking some channels as inappropriate or less effective the system can accommodate handicapped users to a limited extent without a radical modification.

5.4. Tailoring the Message to the Intended Recipient

While accommodating physical limitations of a particular user is important, in general, we want to try to adapt to the preferences of the user in more subtle ways as well. For example, if a given user is a slow typist, we would want to downgrade input choices that require extensive typing and thus tend to prefer more mouse- or voice-based methods. However, since these are merely preferences and not simple on/off switches, the system will still decide to prompt the user for typed input if the amount of information expected is large or if it is otherwise impractical to elicit it through other means. While it is possible to consider deriving these preference settings automatically by monitoring the user, there is no need for a complicated user preference learning subsystem in order to offer this level of customization.

5.5. Maintaining the Flow of the Conversation

One of the problems with using the preceding criteria as the sole means of choosing how to express each new utterance is that a conversation composed of apparently randomly selected types of communication is quite disorienting. If the user is currently selecting items from a menu, any response or request for further input should weigh the fact that the user is currently looking at a given screen and holding the mouse, thus hopefully avoiding generating text on a distant window. Also, since the user is not simply engaging in isolated acts of communication, we want each response to contain as many possible ways for the user to select part of it for further detail, amplification, or otherwise use it to continue the discourse. Having a discourse model that tells us what goals the user is currently pursuing allows us to compare the advantage of these sorts of active responses with the potential benefits of more passive but also more appropriate methods of response.

6. The Interface as a Domain

An important goal of intelligent interface design ought to be to create a unified presentation to the user of the information known to the system. This includes the information relevant to the interface itself, as well as the domain of the underlying system. When using an interface, users should usually not see two entities, the interface and the back end. They should see one unified entity. Accordingly, it should be as easy for the user to ask Which graphs display aircraft speeds?" as it is to ask "What is the speed of each aircraft?" A properly designed user interface should be well-integrated with the underlying domain, and thus can be the target of questions and operations in much the same way as the back end system. This follows from the philosophy that user interfaces are not ends in themselves; rather they exist to facilitate the work of the user on the tasks that he *really* needs to accomplish. Since that work usually involves significant operations on the interface objects, those manipulations should benefit from the strengths of the interface.

Accordingly, interface objects should be first-class citizens in the knowledge representation described in section 2. Windows, graphs, images; all of these should be available for discussion by the user. In particular, when information is presented to the user, the means of presentation can be introduced into the discourse model. Thus, if the user asks "How much does each employee earn?" and the answer is presented in a bar chart, the user can then say "Print that chart".

A recent trend in interface design is to decouple the interface from the back end system (for example, Foley et al. [1988] and Weicha and Boies [1990]). This is done for purposes of modularity, so that large changes in the back end do not necessitate large changes to the interface. This is quite appropriate, but, unfortunately, often results in the artificial distinction between the front and back end discussed above. We feel that the use of a declarative knowledge representation to model the back end *and* the interface gives the system the necessary modularity and also results in a more integrated product.

7. Examples

7.1. A Multimedia Dialog

The following example dialog is taken from a user's interaction with a back end mission planning system via the AIMI interface. It is a real example of AIMI's capabilities, and illustrates many of the issues of interface design we have discussed above..

At this point in the dialog, the user has already indicated that she wants to plan a mission from Alconbury to Oceana. AIMI has responded by presenting two views of the mission. One is a detailed, form-based "inspector" that we will not deal with here. The other representation of the unfolding mission is displayed on a simple cartographic system, as shown in Figure 1, and comprises the two endpoints of the mission, labeled, with an arrow drawn between them. In this example, bracketed text describes an action by the user or system, while unbracketed text is natural language input and output.

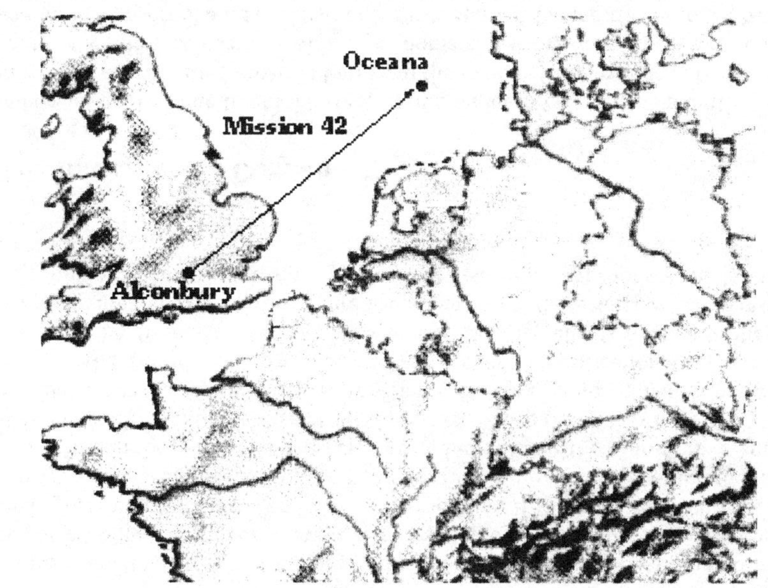

Figure 1. AIMI's Cartographic Representation of the Mission

What AC Are Appro... Text Print Kill		
F4C	F4D	F4E
F4G	F111E	F111F
F-15	F-15E	F-16

Figure 2. A "Flat List"

User: What AC are appropriate for the mission?

System: [A "flat list", or menu-like window, appears, displaying the names of several aircraft—see Figure 2]

User: [Clicks on F-4C in the flat list] What is its speed?

System: An F-4C has a speed of 260 meters-per-second
No F-4Cs are stationed at Alconbury

User: What are the speeds of the planes?

System: [Displays a bar chart—See Figure 3]

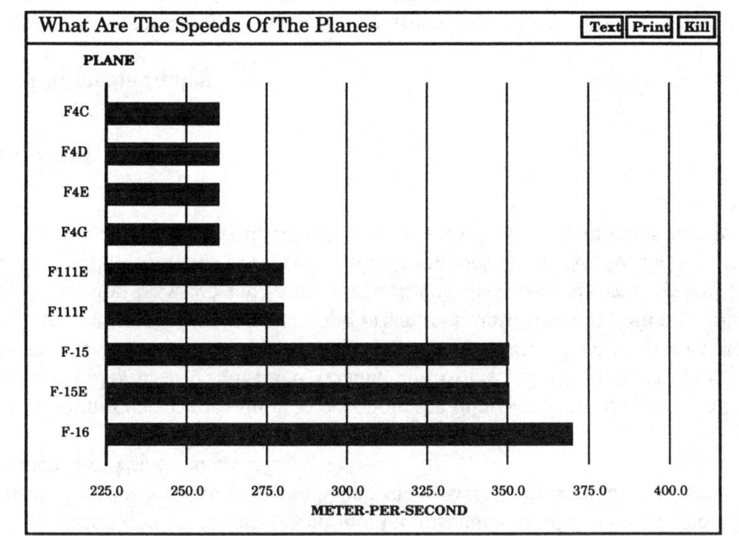

Figure 3. A Bar Chart

User: [Clicks on **Text** button of bar chart]

System: An F-4C has a speed of 260 meters-per-second, an F-4D has a speed of 260 meters-per-second, an F-4G has a speed of 260 meters-per-second, an F-4E has a speed of 260 meters-per-second, an F-111E has a speed of 280 meters-per-second, an F-111F has a speed of 280 meters-per-second, an F-15 has a speed of 350 meters-per-second, an F-15E has a speed of 350 meters-per-second and an F-16 has a speed of 370 meters-per-second

User: Print the chart

System: [Prints a hardcopy of the bar chart]
User: What bases have F-16s?
System: [Adds and highlights three bases on the map—See Figure 4][6]
User: [Drags the mission endpoint to one of the three highlighted airbases]
System: Düsseldorf is the source of Mission 42

7.2. Commentary

A number of features are demonstrated by the previous example. One thing that should be made clear is that, although the "flat list" of Figure 2 appears to be a menu, clicking on one of the items does not do anything but introduce the corresponding entity into the discourse. All of the textual items in the charts generated by AIMI are similarly mouseable, including the labels on the bar chart (Figure 3). After the user introduces an entity into context, the system resolves later references to it using the attentional context mechanisms described in section 4. This ability allows the user to more naturally integrate gestural and textual input, as in the question "What is its speed?" The system resolves references such as "the mission" and "the planes" in the same way.
After the system answers that question, it gives the user some additional information: "No F-4Cs are stationed at Alconbury". This unsolicited output is called a *cooperative response.* The system uses the intentional context mechanisms described in section 4 (and in further detail by Schaffer Sider [1990]) to reason about the user's goals in asking the question. This allows the system to infer that the user is considering using F-4Cs in the mission being planned. However, a necessary condition of this goal is violated, namely that the chosen airbase has the aircraft available. The system decides to inform the user of this problem using a natural language utterance.[7]

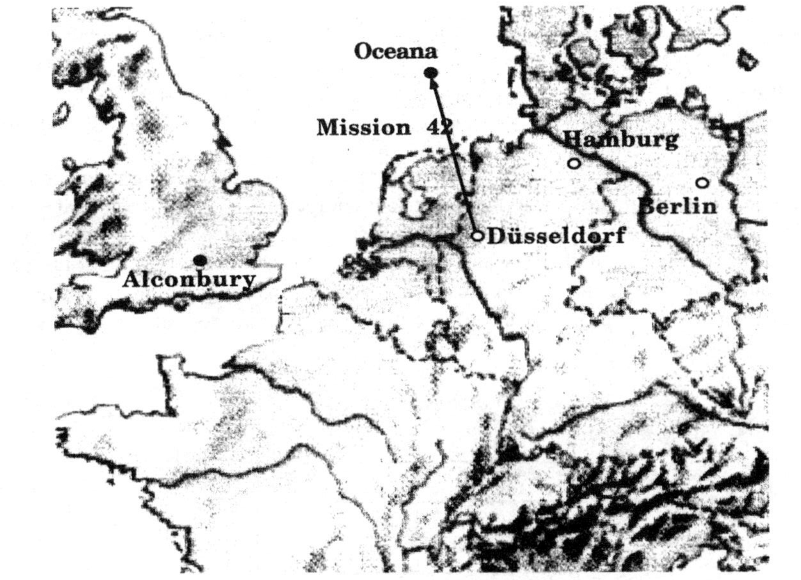

Figure 4. Highlighting Airbases, and Changing the Source of the Mission

Note that the direct answer to the question "What is its speed?" could have been presented as a bar chart, just as were the nine aircraft speeds in the following exchange. Of course, AIMI's knowledge about graphical design tells it that a bar chart with only one bar is a very poor chart indeed. However, without the ability to generate natural language output, the system would have been forced to generate just such a chart.

Correspondingly, the set of nine aircraft speeds could have been realized as natural language. AIMI examined this presentation alternative when answering the original question, and determined that the bar chart was a more perspicuous realization than text (the reader will presumably agree). However, when the user clicks on the **Text** button of the bar chart, the system is forced to re-realize the underlying information as text. As well as being able to force the system to generate text output, the user ought to be able to choose various other graphic alternatives as well (a table, for example).

6When AIMI highlights graphic objects such as the three airbases, the system blinks them briefly.

7In point of fact, AIMI always uses natural language when giving the user unsolicited information (except for alarms). Presenting a graphical representation of such information was deemed to be too likely to be disorienting.

Just as the **Text** button forces the system to re-realize the information as text, rather than a bar chart, so the command to "Print that chart" causes the system to re-realize the information on a printer.[8] In this case, the type of graphic remains the same, a bar chart, but the device changes, from a color monitor to a black-and-white printer. The system actually re-designs the bar chart in this case, as the display capabilities of these two devices may be different, and re-renders it as POSTSCRIPT code. Also note that the user is able to refer to artifacts of the discourse with natural language, in this case "that chart". As discussed in Section 6, graphic presentations are introduced into the discourse just as are domain entities such as "the planes".

The system's use of the map to answer the question about airbases (Figure 4) is a good example of how a knowledge representation can aid response generation. Here, the system had at least three alternatives to choose from: text, a flat list, as in Figure 2, and the map. The latter was not an alternative for the information in Figure 2, because AIMI's knowledge representation informed it that the aircraft were not cartographic entities. The airbases are, of course, and the system's design knowledge was used to determine that a cartographic representation was to be preferred to a flat list, while text is usually used only as a last resort.

When the user drags the mission endpoint in Figure 4, she is able to take advantage of the fact that most of AIMI's presentations are designed to be interactive. When possible, changes in the graphical realization of information made by the user are translated into changes to the underlying information. Of course, when taken to its extreme, this would allow the user to stretch the bars in Figure 3, thus altering the speeds of the aircraft stored in the underlying database. Currently, such interactions are not allowed.

7.3. Tailoring the Response to the Situation

As noted above, there are a number of factors that must be considered by the system when deciding how to convey a given piece of information. This section shows two examples of how the format of the response can differ depending on the anticipated use.

[8]Clicking on the **Print** button has exactly the same meaning.

These examples are taken from a travel reservation information system. While this domain has not actually been modeled by AIMI, the decisions and resulting graphs are representative of the processing actually performed by the system. We assume that the intentional model for this domain includes (at least) two distinct high-level goals: selecting a particular train for travel between New York and Washington, D.C., and maintaining the database of travel schedules.

When Do Trains ... Text Print Kill

New York	Washington
8:00 am	**10:59 am**
8:20 am	11:41 am
9:00 am	**11:59 am**
9:40 am	12:35 pm
10:00 am	**12:55 pm**
11:00 am	**1:55 pm**
11:20 am	2:49 pm
Noon	**2:55 pm**

Bold MetroLiner Service
Roman Normal Service

Figure 5. The Answer as a Table

Figure 5 shows one possible response to the question "When do trains leave from New York for Washington?" Since the node corresponding to "database maintenance" in the intention model has been marked as favoring exact information over the ability to perceive trends or make comparisons, the system has decided to present the response in a table. This makes it easy to check the times for correctness, something that would be difficult or impossible with a more graphical response.

Note that if this response were being generated on a screen, most of the items in the table could be mouse-sensitive, allowing the user to continue the dialog from this point. For example, since the user is understood to be maintaining the database rather than using it to make a reservation, mousing on one of the times would most likely indicate that it should be changed. Thus, in this context the system's response to the mouse click would be to post the goal of allowing the user to modify the value. Similarly, clicking on one of the city names could allow the user to enter a new city, effectively asking the same question about a different pair of cities. It is because the system knows what it is presenting, and what question it is answering, that it can support follow-up interactions of this sort.

However, the system is also capable of generating a noticeably different type of response to the same question asked in a different context. If the intentional mechanism has concluded that the user is trying to select a particular train for making reservations, AIMI could present an interval bar chart (Figure 6) indicating when each train leaves and arrives. This would allow the user to base the selection on preferred time of travel, length of trip, or price (since MetroLiner service is more expensive than standard coach seating).

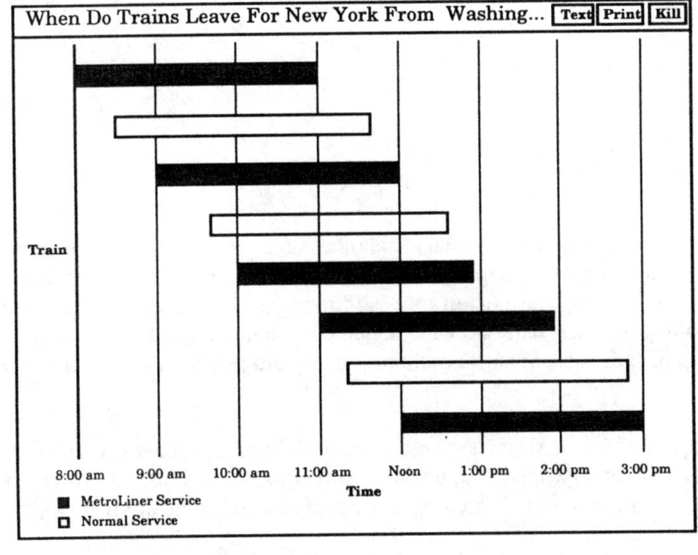

Figure 6. The Answer as a Bar Chart

The important point here is that the system does not have a single response that it generates for a given type of question, and it does not necessarily use the same format even if the same question is asked in two different settings. The extra levels of reasoning that are performed by the system independent of the particular domain allow us to provide this flexibility without having to tailor the machinery to each new domain. We believe that this capability is a strong indication of the need for knowledge-based infrastructure in multimedia interfaces.

8. Conclusion

In this chapter we have presented our vision of a system that can support an integrated multimedia dialog between computer and human. We feel that these interactions are similar in many respects to the text dialogs that have been the focus of linguistic study over a long period of time, and that we should thus adapt results from that field to this more general problem.

Building the reasoning machinery of the interface around a knowledge representation and the associated planning and context tracking mechanisms allows us to achieve many of the same results in multimedia that are already common in natural language systems. We are able to convert input in various surface forms (typed text, menu selections, and mouse clicks) into a canonical form that can be processed without becoming bogged down in the specifics of the original communication. This facility also allows us to generate responses and goals in the same abstract form, and then present them via any of the available and appropriate output methods.

Not only does this distinction between surface form and internal semantics allow us to multiplex the various communications channels, but it provides a modular system that can incorporate new methods of interaction simply by adding the appropriate tools to transform between their raw, mode-specific data and the actual information content. Since each such module is responsible for this transformation, there is no need to devise a monolithic interpretation and response planning scheme; each module is free to use whatever approaches are best suited.

Tracking the complete conversation is important, not only to provide a more consistent view to the user, but also because it allows us to use intentional context models to derive some insight into what the user appears to be doing at a given moment. This information, even at a coarse level of refinement, can be used to help select appropriate means of response without requiring that the user explicitly indicate what "mode" they are in.

Finally, we feel that the ability to model the interface itself is an important contribution of our method. By removing the distinction between the underlying application and the interface at this level we can greatly improve the user's ability to accomplish the job at hand.

While we would like to have had more opportunity to refine the specifics of this system, we were able to accomplish enough to convince ourselves that this is a viable approach to managing the complexity of an intelligent multimedia interface. It is clear that it would be unwise to ignore the long history of investigation into what constitutes effective communication merely because color graphics have been added to an interface.

Reflections on. . .

The Application of Natural Language Models to Intelligent Multimedia

John Burger

Work on AIMI grew out of research at MITRE into intelligent natural language interfaces. King Kong was a symbolically intensive NL interface, with explicit algorithmic phases for syntactic parsing, semantic interpretation, response generation, and discourse processing, among others. It was necessary to extend the purely NL system to other sorts of output (initially) and eventually to different input modes as well.

The research goals included a desire (perhaps naive, in retrospect) to push an explicit, first-order predicate calculus semantic representation as far as possible, to include graphs and other kinds of output, and mouse gestures and such for input. We were also very interested in using an explicit discourse representation to mediate between different modalities for both input (e.g., mouse gestures and pronouns) and output (highlighted graphic elements and generated deictic references).

In particular, we felt it was very important to handle anaphoric reference in a natural and flexible fashion. Other approaches had included, for example, adding explicit, optional mouse gestures to a syntactic grammar. We decided instead to generalize the system's existing discourse representation to handle this sort of phenomenon. The discourse model tracked both intentional and attentional foci, and the result was indeed quite flexible—it was simple, for example, to add the interface artifacts generated by the system, such as graphs and sounds, to the attentional model, allowing further NL inputs to refer to these artifacts with pronouns and deictic gestures.

I feel that AIMI represented a very interesting approach to intelligent multimedia, coming as it did from a natural language interface background. However, like many such hand-tooled systems, past and present, the system suffered from an inherent brittleness, with many hard-coded behaviors. Adding novel kinds of modalities required some investment of time and expertise, and many other extensions, such as the addition of languages other than English, would have required substantial effort. Dissatisfaction with the lack of generality of purely algorithmic approaches led the MITRE natural language group (*http://www.mitre.org/resources/centers/advanced_info/g04h/nl-index.html*) to explore nonsymbolic approaches to language processing. This has taken us into corpus-based information extraction and similar ventures, finding substantial success using machine learning approaches to syntax, semantics, and discourse (Aberdeen et al. 1995). This has enabled us to rapidly build information extraction systems for such tasks as broadcast news analysis (Maybury et al. 1997) and foreign language information extraction.

In general, these approaches allow fairly general system architectures to automatically acquire language processing knowledge with a modicum of human intervention or hard-coded expertise. In many cases, the systems can be extended and adapted by users, with example-driven approaches rather than by system developers. These non- and partially symbolic approaches are extremely flexible and robust, for a variety of shallow language processing tasks. It remains to be seen, however, whether such approaches can also be applied to deeper, interpretation-intensive tasks, such as are typically required for intelligent interfaces.

REFERENCES

Aberdeen, J.; Burger, J.; Day, D.; Hirschman, L.; Robinson, P.; and Vilain, M. 1995. Description of the Alembic System Used for MUC-6. In *Proceedings of the Sixth Message Understanding Conference*, Columbia, MD, November 6–8. Advanced Research Projects Agency Information Technology Office. San Francisco: Morgan Kaufmann.

Maybury, M.; Merlino, A.; and Morey, D. 1997. Broadcast News Navigation Using Story Segments. In *ACM International Multimedia Conference*, Seattle, WA, November 8–14. New York: ACM Press. 381–391.

SECTION VI

Model-Based Interfaces

Designing interfaces is recognized as both a complex and resource-consuming task, and yet it can make or break applications. The complexity of interface design is a consequence of the nature of human-computer interaction; it is only partially understood and requires the multidisciplinary design talents of experts in human factors, computer science, device technology, and media design. Interfaces are typically deployed in diverse environments: input and output devices of varying capabilities (e.g., displays with ranging size, resolution, and color depth); wide ranges of the nature of frequency of use; and users of varying perceptual and cognitive abilities.

Originally, toolkits and User Interface Management Systems (UIMSs) were developed to address these challenges. Graphical user interface toolkits are software libraries of interface components such as windows, menus, and dialog boxes. Toolkits can enhance interface builder productivity through the reuse of existing designs and by facilitating design consistency among toolkit components. One disadvantage, however, is that they mix interface code with application code. In contrast, UIMSs aim to separate application from interface functionality (e.g., dialog control, presentation, and behavior), providing interface consistency and cost savings through (interface and application) code reuse and developer tools.

The papers in this section describe tools and techniques that assist the designer, decreasing the time and the expertise required to create interfaces. In contrast to current user interface toolkits, these papers separate dialog control from application code and presentation and style decisions from the toolkit code libraries. And in contrast to user interface management systems, they provide interface developers with finer-grained distinctions and more powerful design tools. Research has emphasized more precise definitions of interface functions in order to support declarative expression and modularization.

As many of the ideas in intelligent user interfaces find roots in the development of intelligent tutoring systems, it is fitting that the first article in this section begins with a description of the Steamer system by James Hollan, Edwin Hutchins, and Louis Weitzman. One key aim of Steamer was to enable the understanding of complex dynamic systems through the use of graphical interfaces that "approximate the models experts seem to use in reasoning about the system and which have the potential of supporting the development of useful reasoning models." The authors describe how "dynamic graphical explanations" could be designed to closely resemble an expert's qualitative explanation of steam plant behavior. The authors, however, also point out how different graphical depictions are appropriate for individuals with differing levels of expertise. The user can browse through a hierarchy of 100 complex diagrams depicting the propulsion system and its components at multiple levels of detail. The authors' design is supported by one of the first object-oriented *graphics editors*, which enables the incremental design and refinement of complex graphical displays even by non-programmers by using a graphical interface design tool.

(Most of the Steamer diagrams were created by a retired boiler technician with no prior computer science experience. Training at navy schools confirmed this result for instructors.) The graphics editor enables the composition of complex flow diagrams from selected diagrams depicting "observing gauges" or domain objects like pumps or valves and the interfacing of them to the underlying mathematics simulation models. For representing knowledge about the domain, the authors utilize a *procedures editor*, which provides the user with graphical access to generic components, procedures, and engineering principles for knowledge capture. This "smart" editor detects collisions in step sequences and includes "presenters," which can, for example, discuss an object's physical connections, energy connections, or information connections. These tools both make the propulsion domain more inspectable and promise to decrease the entry level and cost for development of complex interfaces.

The second paper by James Foley, Christina Gibbs, Won Chul Kim, and Srdjan Kovacevic describes the User Interface Design Environment (UIDE), a knowledge-based system to assist in user interface design and implementation. By representing user interface design knowledge as objects, their attributes, and the actions and associated pre- and postconditions of those actions, the authors demonstrate how functionally equivalent interfaces can be generated (transformed) from common specifications. This transformation enables a designer to quickly implement and test families or "equivalence classes" of interface designs. The authors detail an Interface Definition Language (IDL) for interface specification (not to be confused with the IDL associated with Common Object Request Broker Architecture or COBRA), which enables the formal specification of concepts such as the currently selected object, the currently selected command, and so on. Such formal representations are readily extensible to automated consistency and performance testing and runtime help.

Just as UIDE enables application developers to improve the design process beyond user interface management systems, the third paper by Charles Wiecha, William Bennett, Stephen Boies, John Gould, and Sharon Greene describes the ITS architecture, which separates applications into four layers: application actions, dialog control, style rules (specifications of presentation and behavior), and style program (primitive toolkit objects composed by style rules). These layers correspond to differing roles in application development, namely, application programmer, application expert, style expert, and style programmer. The authors illustrate how an interface of a prototypical airline reservation system can be generated using their approach. For example, the dialog layer is used to encode dialog actions such as choices among several items and associated application actions (e.g., view flights, make a reservation), lists, or forms. Style rules then convert these dialog actions into a tree structure, capturing layout structure (e.g., horizontal, vertical display) as well as other presentational attributes (e.g., fonts, color, size). Style rules can also modify ordering, for example, to group like choices. They illustrate the use of their tool to automatically generate interfaces for a kiosk application.

Whereas the primary focus of the preceding two papers was on automatically generating application menu and dialog boxes, the next paper by Pedro Szekely, Ping Luo, and Robert Neches reports on the HUMANOID system, which provides a more expressive model that enables interface designers to construct a broader range of application interfaces (e.g., to complex, real-time, heterogeneous data). HUMANOID supports the representation of abstraction, iteration, and conditional constructs and provides the designer with the ability to declaratively model how an interface should look (presentation) and behave (dialog). After defining the application model, HUMANOID selects among presentation and dialog behavior templates, which are then further refined by the developer. A designer's interface enhances ease of use by ensuring that all aspects of models are visible and changeable and that model and example views are coordinated; it also supports a spreadsheet paradigm for specifying formulas that define the values of input data. The design process is further advanced by allowing designers to delay design commitments and to work on separate elements of the interface semi-independently. The resulting declarative models can be used by automated design critics and automated help generation tools.

In contrast to HUMANOID, the paper by Angel Puerta, Henrik Eriksson, John Gennari, and Mark Musen reports on the Mecano model-based interface generator that uses domain models instead of data models to generate interfaces. By substituting a domain model for a data model, the interface designer is not required to perform any dialog specification, and Mecano can generate complete dynamic behavior specifications even for interfaces with hundreds of components. Mecano is illustrated in a medical domain; users can participate in design layout decisions and design revisions.

A final short paper by Jean Vanderdonckt describes the automatic generation of user interfaces in the specific area of interactive business applications. Vanderdonckt first describes an object-oriented, semantically linked (e.g., specializes, is-similar-to, contradicts), multipurpose, high-level style guide (the *corpus ergonomicus*), consisting of 3,700 guidelines and principles mined from style guides, recommendation reports, articles, human factors books, and standards. Pertinent guidelines are then extracted from this corpus and represented in the SEGUIA tool as strategies in a first-order predicate logic expert system for semi- or fully automated generation of the presentation of the interface. SEGUIA thus assists the designer in interface widget selection and layout tasks. Finally, an on-line hypermedia ergonomics guide, SIERRA, enables the designer/programmer to consult, select, apply, and check application usability during the application development life cycle.

Taken together, these papers make several key contributions. First, they move toward declarative specifications of interfaces, refining the distinctions among models and processes associated with the domain, the application, the user-machine dialog control, and the presentation. Second, they promise increased portability and ease of evolution as maintenance and extension is done within a more formal framework. Finally, they enable new forms of designer support, such as automated design critique, refinement, and implementation.

A number of open research issues remain. Foremost among these is that interface builders will only be as good as the expressiveness of the underlying representation. What representations can balance expressiveness with simplicity, efficiency, and ease of use? What and when is the appropriate role of the user in the design process and, related, the appropriate mix of automated versus mixed initiative design? What are the actual benefits of applying such an approach in terms of timeliness and quality of interface designs? Compelling answers to these questions are necessary if we are to realize the fundamental advances promised by model-based interfaces.

STEAMER:

An Interactive Inspectable Simulation-Based Training System

James D. Hollan

Edwin L. Hutchins

Louis M. Weitzman

Navy Personnel Research and Development Center
San Diego, California 92152

Abstract

The Steamer project is a research effort concerned with exploring the use of AI software and hardware technologies in the implementation of intelligent computer-based training systems. While the project addresses a host of research issues ranging from how people understand complex dynamic systems to the use of intelligent graphical interfaces, it is focused around the construction of a system to assist in propulsion engineering instruction. The purpose of this paper is to discuss the underlying ideas which motivated us to initiate the Steamer effort, describe the current status of the project, provide a glimpse of the directions we plan to pursue in the future, and discuss the implications of Steamer for AI applications in other instructional domains.

Introduction

Since we are firmly convinced that ideas like people have histories and can only be fully understood in the context of those histories, we will begin by discussing the underlying ideas that motivated us to initiate the Steamer effort. They include the following:

- **Mental Models**

  We were and still are caught up in the notion of mental models and of how important it is to better understand the models people use to think and reason about complex dynamic physical systems and devices. Without richer and more detailed understandings of the nature of these models instructional applications are going to be severely limited.

- **Graphical Interfaces for Interactive Inspectable Simulations**

  We believe that graphical interfaces to simulations of physical systems deserve extensive exploration. They make possible new types of instructional interactions by allowing one to control, manipulate, and monitor simulations of dynamic systems at many different hierarchical levels. The key idea in Steamer is the conception of *an interactive inspectable simulation.* We have consistently sought to make the system inspectable. This includes not only providing graphical views of the system but also allowing one to inspect various aspects of the procedures for operating the system. Interactive inspectable simulations have the potential of being major mechanisms for supporting the development of understandings of *process.*

- **Conceptual Fidelity**

  We are very much concerned with graphically depicting models that attempt in a fundamental sense to approximate those that experts employ to reason about a physical system. We want to focus on the conceptual rather than physical fidelity of the system to gain a deeper appreciation for how one might support and encourage the development of the mental models people need to understand and reason about dynamic physical systems.

- **Implementation Philosophy**

  From the first we wanted to build a non-toy system and to keep the tools we constructed as generic as possible. We felt very strongly that in order to establish the credibility of these ideas in the training community, we needed a usable system which addressed a real training problem in a complex training domain. It had to be more than a demonstration of the technology's potential and it had to cover that domain. Also, we have tried to keep the focus beyond just implementing Steamer but on the more general questions associated with teaching people to understand complex dynamic systems.

We hope these underlying ideas are still evident after the many design, pragmatic, and political decisions that comprise the making of a system like Steamer.

An Overview of Steamer

The Choice of Domain

The fundamental research goal of the Steamer project is to evaluate the potential of new AI hardware and software technology for supporting the construction of computer-based training systems. Just as Papert (1980) holds that one cannot think about thinking without thinking about thinking about something, one cannot evaluate technology in the abstract. We choose to work in the area of propulsion engineering for a number of pragmatic and scientific reasons.

1. There is a critical need for improvement in training in this area in the Navy. Thus, it has wide visibility, and we saw the potential for adequate research funding.

2. Alternative forms of training are quite expensive. A high-fidelity simulator costs about 7 million dollars. This has allowed us to explore hardware alternatives that currently are expensive, but which we anticipate will be much less expensive in the near future.

3. We had access to a detailed mathematical simulation model of a common (1200 psi) steam propulsion system. This permitted us to focus on the interface, tutorial, and explanation issues which are our major interest.

4. We wanted to work in a nontactical area for both personal and pragmatic reasons.

5. We wanted to focus on the use of graphical interfaces to support the development of useful mental models.

6. It seemed engineering domains provided the most instructional leverage from the use of these techniques. Since engineering is an area concerned with designed systems and physical mechanisms, it appeared to be promising for exploring the nature of mental models.

A steam propulsion system is an exceedingly complex physical system. The propulsion spaces account for about one third of the space in most Navy ships. There are thousands of components interconnected by miles of pipes. The operation of the plant is supervised by an engineering officer of the watch and controlled by a team of 16 to 25 individuals who operate in the most trying of circumstances. They often work long hours in a hot, dirty, and quite dangerous environment. Frequently, an individual must cover more than one watch station in a seemingly unending sequence of watches (6 hours on / 6 hours off). The status of the plant is primarily revealed by observing gauges depicting important operational parameters, although operators also make use of other forms of evidence as indicators of plant status, particularly how the plant *sounds* and *feels*. It takes years of instruction and experience to be able to understand and competently operate a propulsion plant. In addition, rich robust mental models of the plant are needed to be able to respond to the myriad casualty conditions that can and do arise.

The Steamer Graphical Interface

A principal intuition behind Steamer is that it could be quite valuable to be able to provide a color graphics interface to a simulation of a propulsion plant so one could view and manipulate the plant at a number of different hierarchical levels. Overall control of the system is accomplished by means of the multi-paned window interface depicted, in Figure 1. This interface provides a view of the overall status of the plant, the ability to make major transitions of plant state, controls for running the

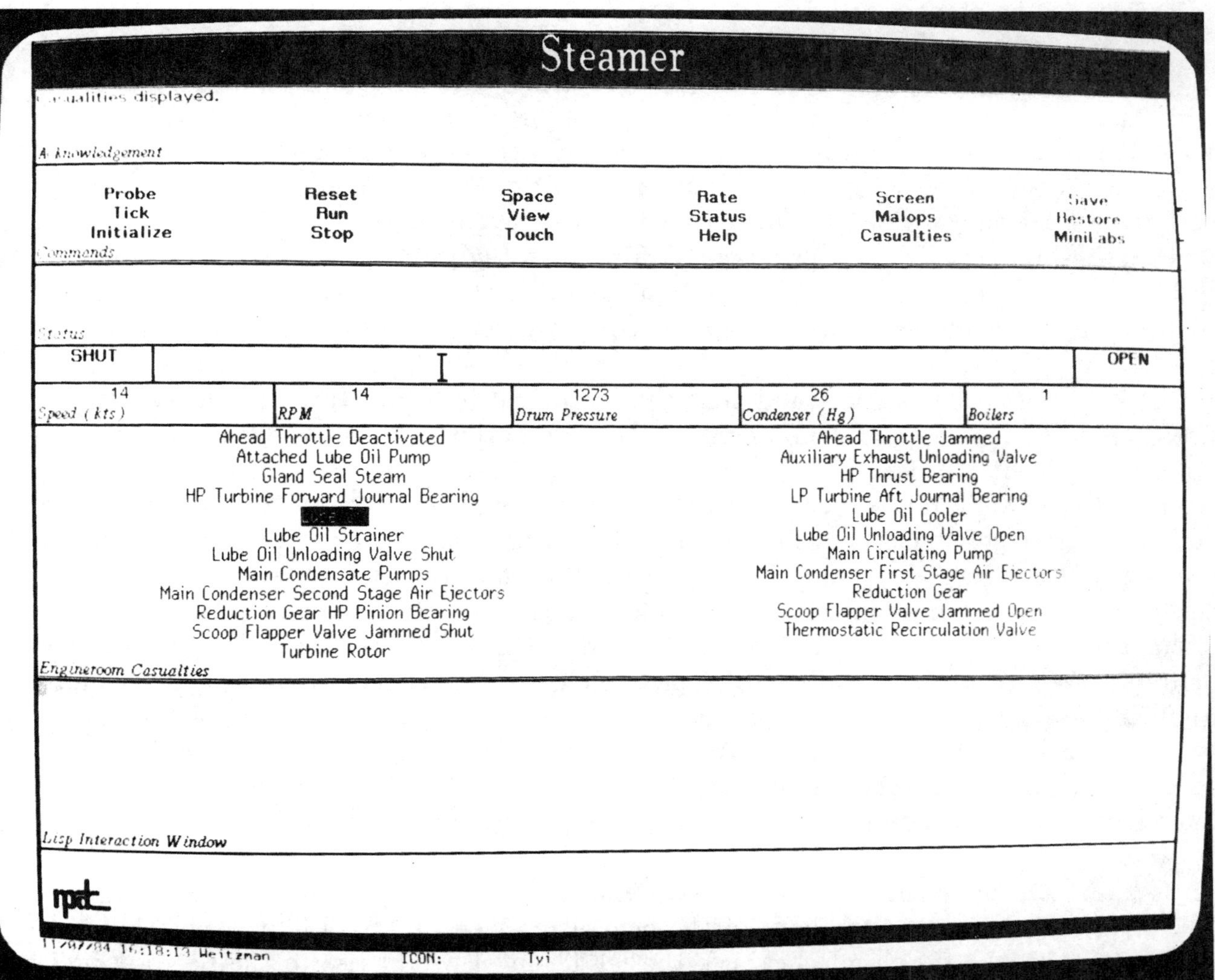

Figure 1. Steamer Interface. This interface is used to select views of the plant to be displayed on the color screen, to control the mathematical model, and to impose casualties. It also provides basic plan status information and the ability to control the throttle. Most control of the plant is accomplished by "touching" icons of the color screen with the mouse.

mathematical simulation, the ability to impose casualties, and access to a large number of diagrams of the plant.

In the current system we have one hundred color views available and have devised a quite powerful object-based graphics editor for modifying and expanding this set of views. The views range from high-level fairly abstract representations of the plant like the *Basic Steam Cycle* depicted in Figure 2, to views of subsystems such as *Make-Up and Excess Feed* shown in Figure 3. Other views show gauge panels which depict sets of gauges quite like actual gauge panels in a ship, as in Figure 4, and diagrams specifically constructed to reveal aspects of the system not normally available in a real plant but which might be beneficial for understanding some particular aspect of plant operation.

It is important to understand that this graphical interface functions in two ways. First, it reflects the state of components in the simulation. Thus, it reveals that a particular component is operating or not by means of changes in color or other graphical features of the iconic representation on the color screen. For example, a pump's state is depicted as green if it is operating and red if it is off. The interface also allows one to view many aspects of the plant that one cannot normally witness in a real plant. One can, for example, see flow rates in pipes. This information provides more than just state information. It can make much of the causal topology of the system more directly apparent. We think the ability to depict such characteristics of the plant is quite important for assisting an individual attempting to build a mental model of the operation of the plant. The second function of the graphical interface is to permit control of the components within the simulation. This control is provided by pointing to components with a mouse pointing device and clicking on them.

As an example, consider the Make-Up and Excess Feed Diagram depicted in Figure 3. If one were to increase the level of the deaerating feed tank (DFT)[1] (by pointing to a high position in the tank and clicking), the DFT's level would rise to the position indicated. As a result of this change in tank level, the Excess-feed Valve would go fully open and flows would increase through that portion of the system. Thus, the graphical interface allows both the monitoring of the state of the plant and also its manipulation. It is important to note the potential instructional significance of allowing students not only to interact with things that exist in the real plant (e.g., valves), but also of allowing students to manipulate things which one could not directly manipulate, e.g., DFT levels, which potentially can be of import to supporting the development of an understanding of the operation of a system.

1. The deareating feed tank is a storage tank intended to accomodate fluctuations in demand for water above.

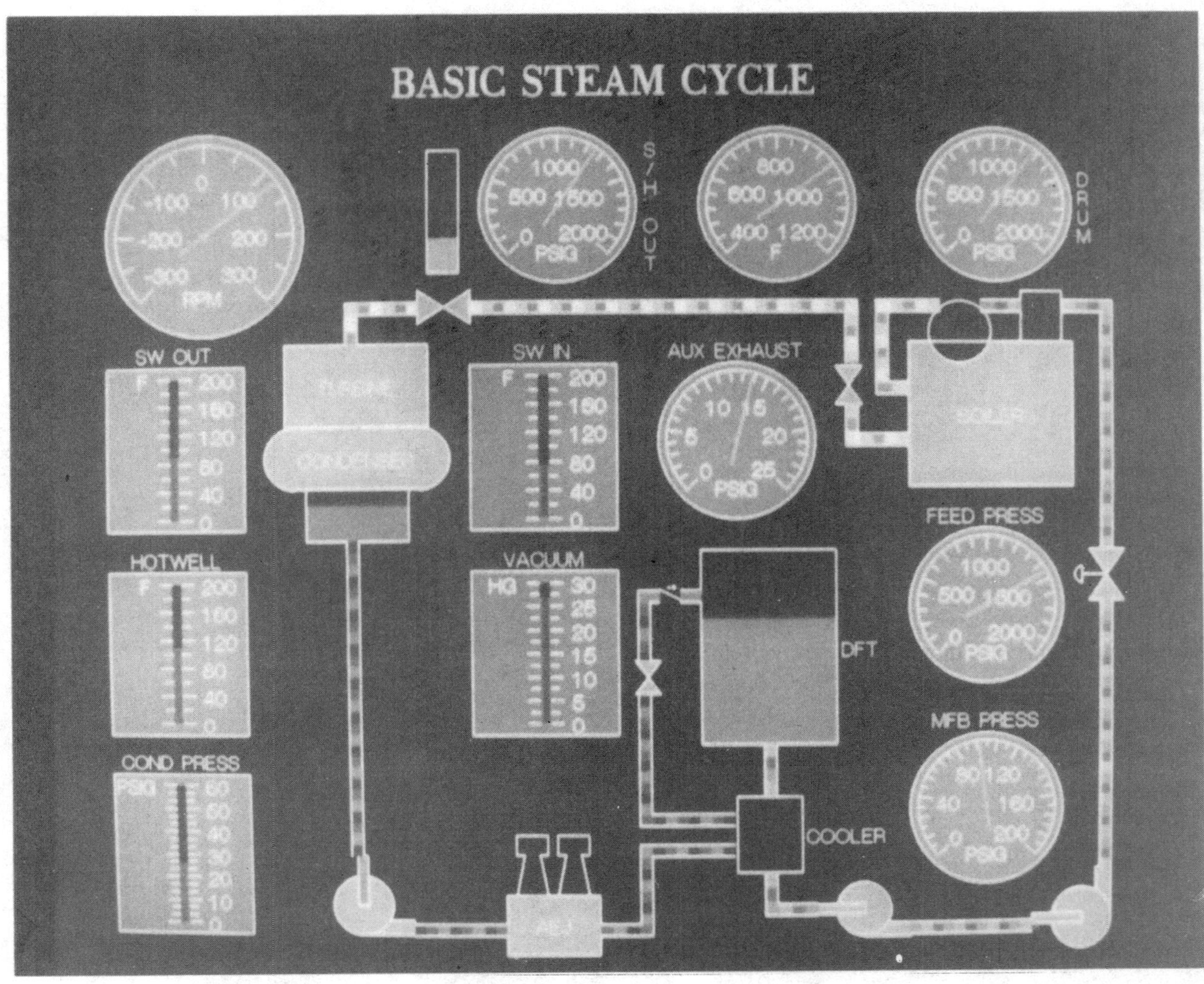

Figure 2. Basic Steam Cycle. This is a high level view of the whole steam plant. One of the important aspects of Steamer is the ability to depict the propulsion system at many different levels.

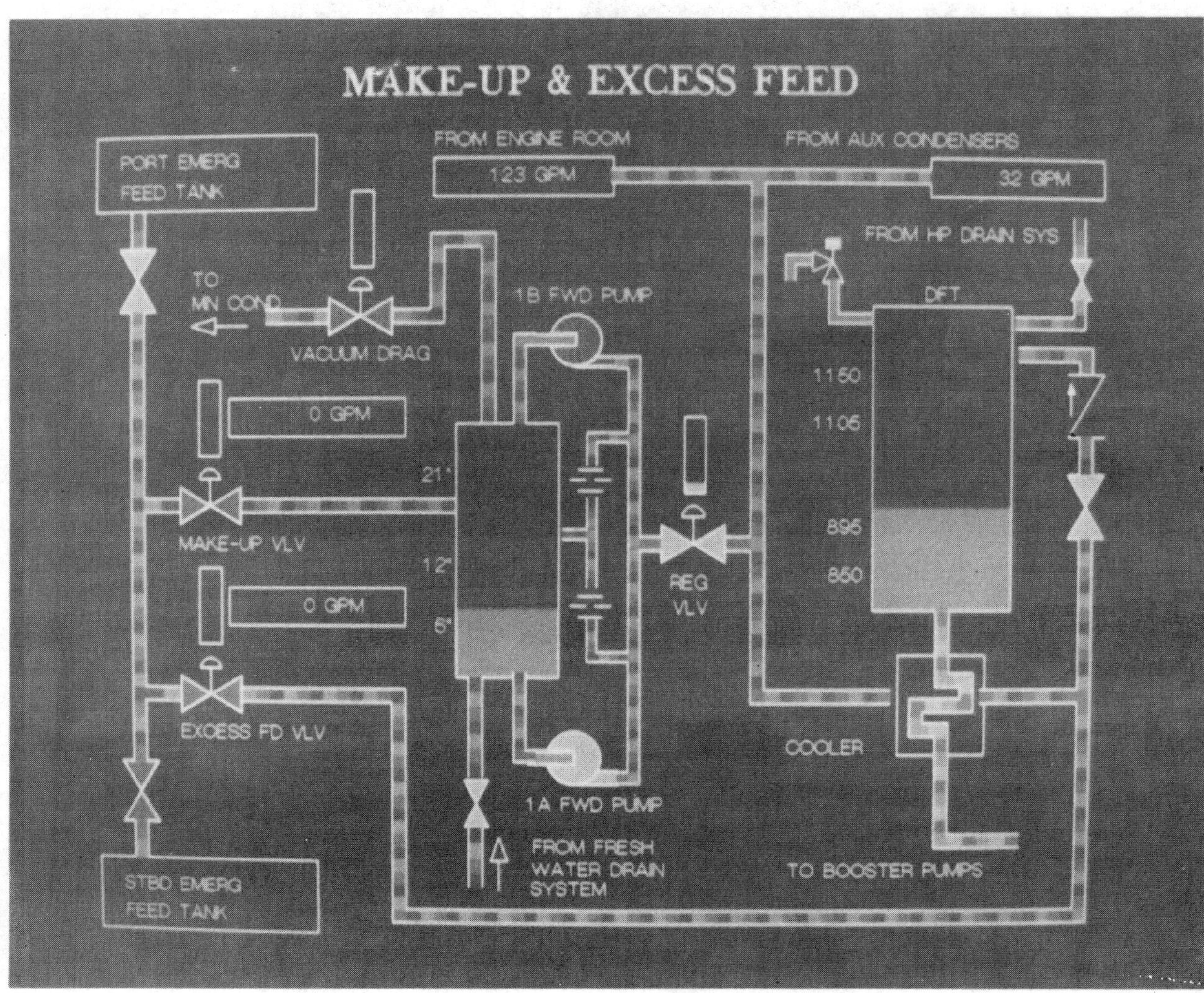

Figure 3. Make-Up and Excess Feed. This diagram provides a more detailed view of a subsystem. Adequate coverage of the plant has required approximately 100 diagrams.

One aspect of the graphical interface arising from our concern with mental models and conceptual fidelity is the ability to provide the user with depictions which approximate the models experts seem to use in reasoning about the system and which have the potential of supporting the development of useful reasoning models. The ability to provide dynamic interactive graphical interfaces is one of the real virtues and powers of the new *display engines*. Their high-resolution bit-mapped displays make possible a very different form of explanation which one might term *dynamic graphical explanations*.

These forms of graphical explanation can be of considerable benefit in revealing important aspect of normally opaque systems. For example, one portion of a steam propulsion system that is quite difficult to understand is the automatic boiler control system. This part of a propulsion plant is a complex system of negative feedback circuits that senses variables such as steam pressure, steam flow, and supply of combustion air and fuel in order to control the rate of firing of a boiler. The internal behavior of the system is characterized by the propagation of pneumatic signals in a world of multiple dynamic equilibria. Normally in a propulsion plant, this system would be viewed by means of a set of gauges like those depicted in Figure 4. The flow of casuality and the nature of the response of the system to various perturbations is very difficult to see in the readings of the gauges. Furthermore, in this system the first derivative of the signal is more important than the absolute value of the signal. Thus, what matters is not the actual level of the signal but whether the signal is, in any particular instant, rising, falling or steady. We created a *signal* or *derivative icon* to depict this information explicitly.

Figure 5 shows how this icon would appear at various points in time if it were reflecting the variable whose values are shown on the associated graph. This icon can be used to depict graphically the rate of change of a variable.

We have used the signal icon to create a series of diagrams to assist in explaining the behavior of an automatic boiler control system. Dynamic systems are particularly difficult to explain in language, in part, because of the serial nature of language. However, relationships that are difficult to describe unambiguously in words are often easily depicted graphically. Putting a layer of interface computation between a user and a quantitative model provides a graphical qualitative view of the underlying model. Such a qualitative graphical interface can operate as a *continuous explanation* of the behavior of the system being modeled by allowing a user to more directly apprehend the relationships that are typically described by experts. In a number of views we have instrumented the control air lines with signal icons to reveal the pneumatic signals that are being transmitted. A typical use of these views is to make some throttle change and then single-step the model and watch the transmission of signals. What evolves

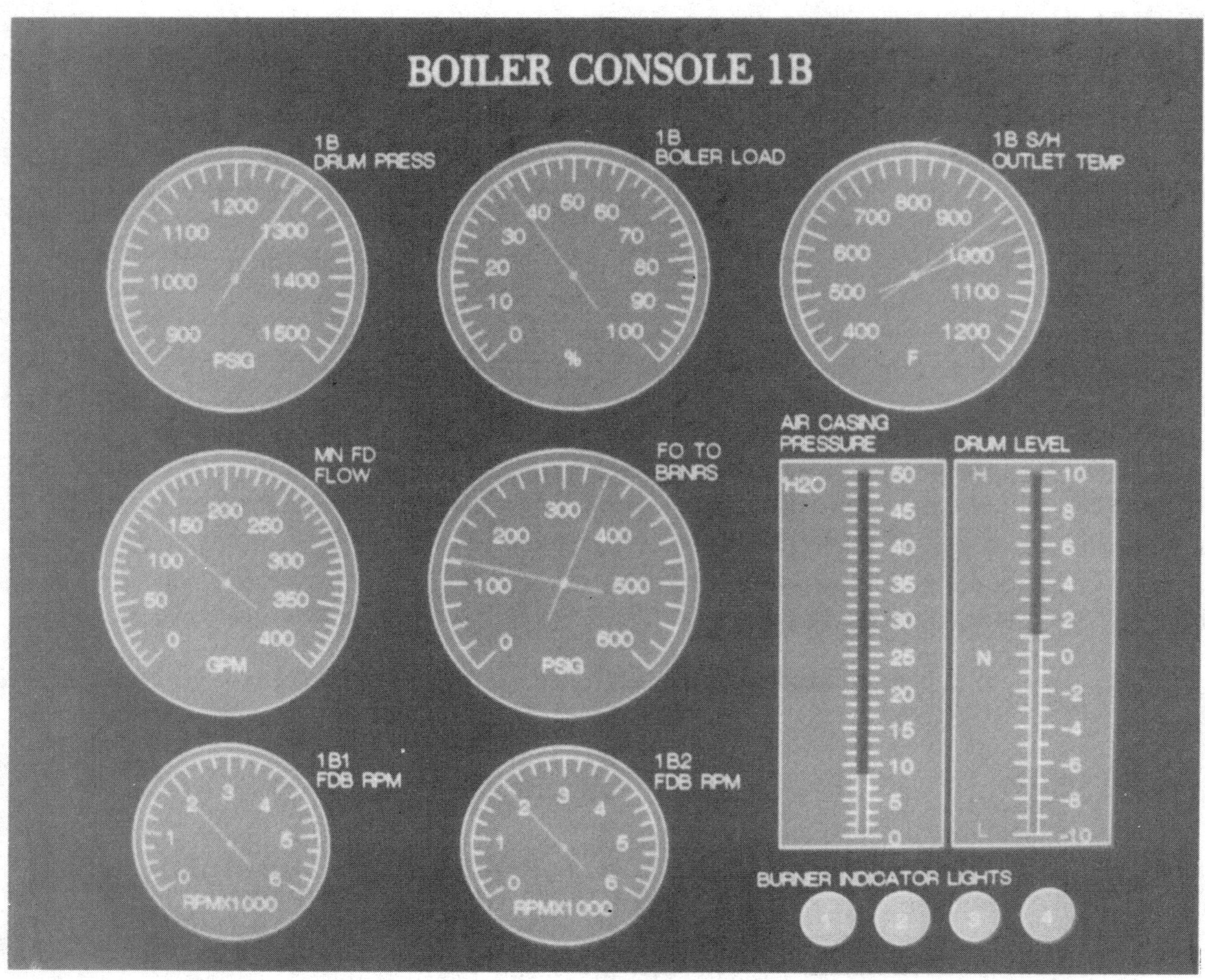

Figure 4. Boiler Console 1B. Traditional gauge panels like this boiler console panel can also be depicted.

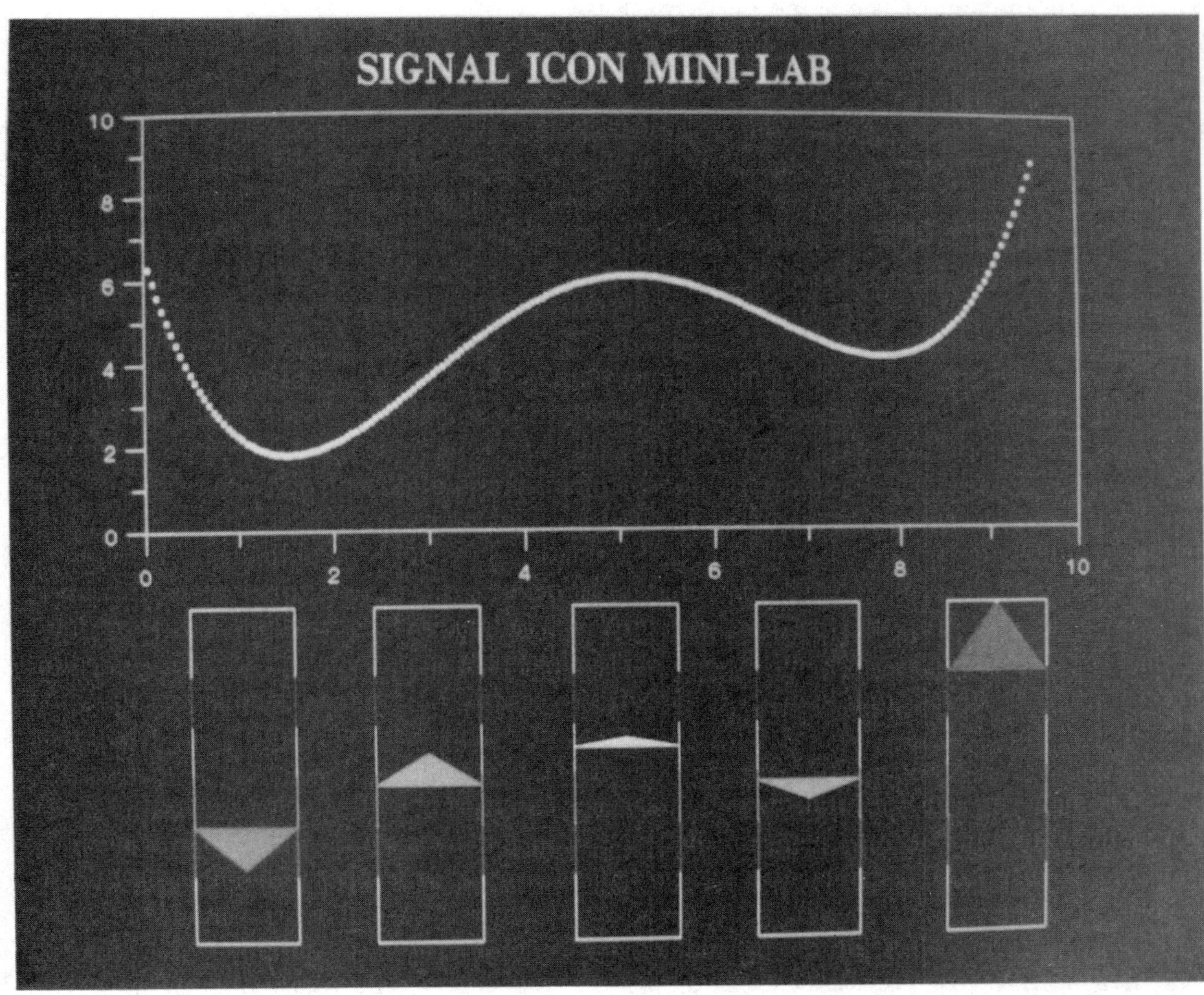

Figure 5. Signal Icon. These signal icons depict rate of change of the variable shown in the graph. We have used them to make visible aspects of automatic control systems which are difficult to see with traditional gauges.

is a graphical description of the plant's behavior which closely resembles an expert's qualitative explanation of the same perturbation.

It should be clear that these various graphical depictions are appropriate for use by people with very different levels of knowledge about the automatic combustion control system.

The gauge panel is appropriate for an expert who has a rich understanding of the system and needs very little support for his model. A series of signal icons arrayed in an order to fit a causal explanation is more appropriate for someone just developing an understanding of the system. An integrated view with both signal icons and normal gauges provides information to support a bridging from the causal depiction to operational gauge panel displays.

The Steamer Graphics Editor: A flavor is worth a thousand pictures

In order to build and modify the large number of views required to adequately cover the complex propulsion domain, we have implemented an object-based graphics editor.

Figure 6 depicts the user interface to the editor. A user interacts primarily by choosing options from this display and positioning and critiquing graphical icons on the color display.

In order to give you a bit of feel for the graphics editor, we will go through some events in a scenario of constructing a diagram. We choose the icons from a menu of available icons (See Figure 6). The available icons consist of basic graphical primitives (lines, circles, etc.), various indicators (dials, columns, graphs, etc.), and a large set of icons specifically designed to depict objects in the propulsion domain (a variety of pumps, valves, pipes, and electrical components).

A sampler of icons is provided in Figure 7. The user interacts by choosing items from menus and positioning the icons on the color screen. His major actions are *pointing* and *selecting*. When he selects an object and points to a position for it, he immediately gets a specific instantiation of the object with many characteristics defaulted (e.g. the color of a dial, its minimum and maximum values, the number of divisions on its scale, etc.). Then through a process of incremental refinement, he critiques the

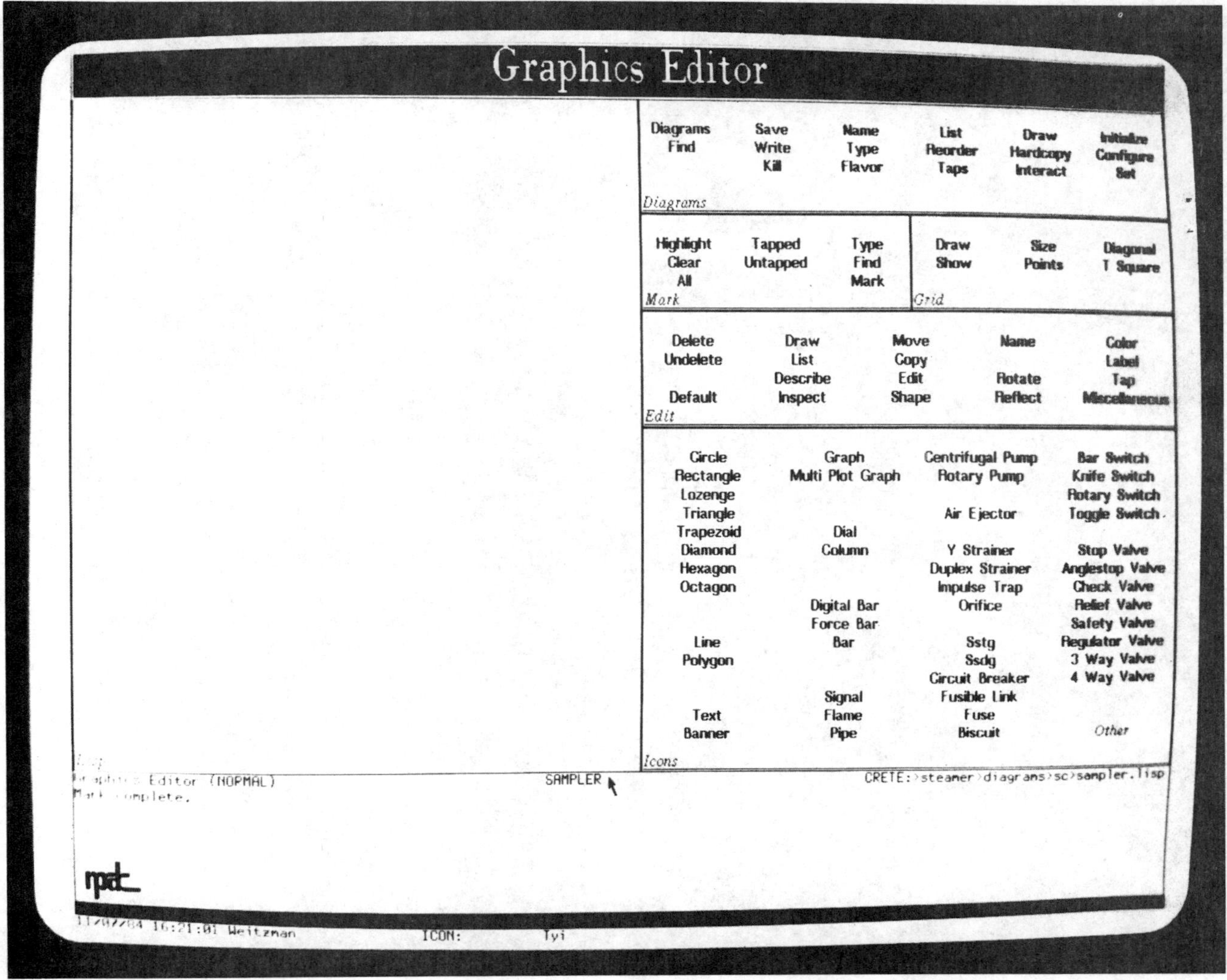

Figure 6. Graphics Editor Interface. The editor is a powerful facility for creating graphical interfaces to control the underlying simulation and to reflect the state of its components.

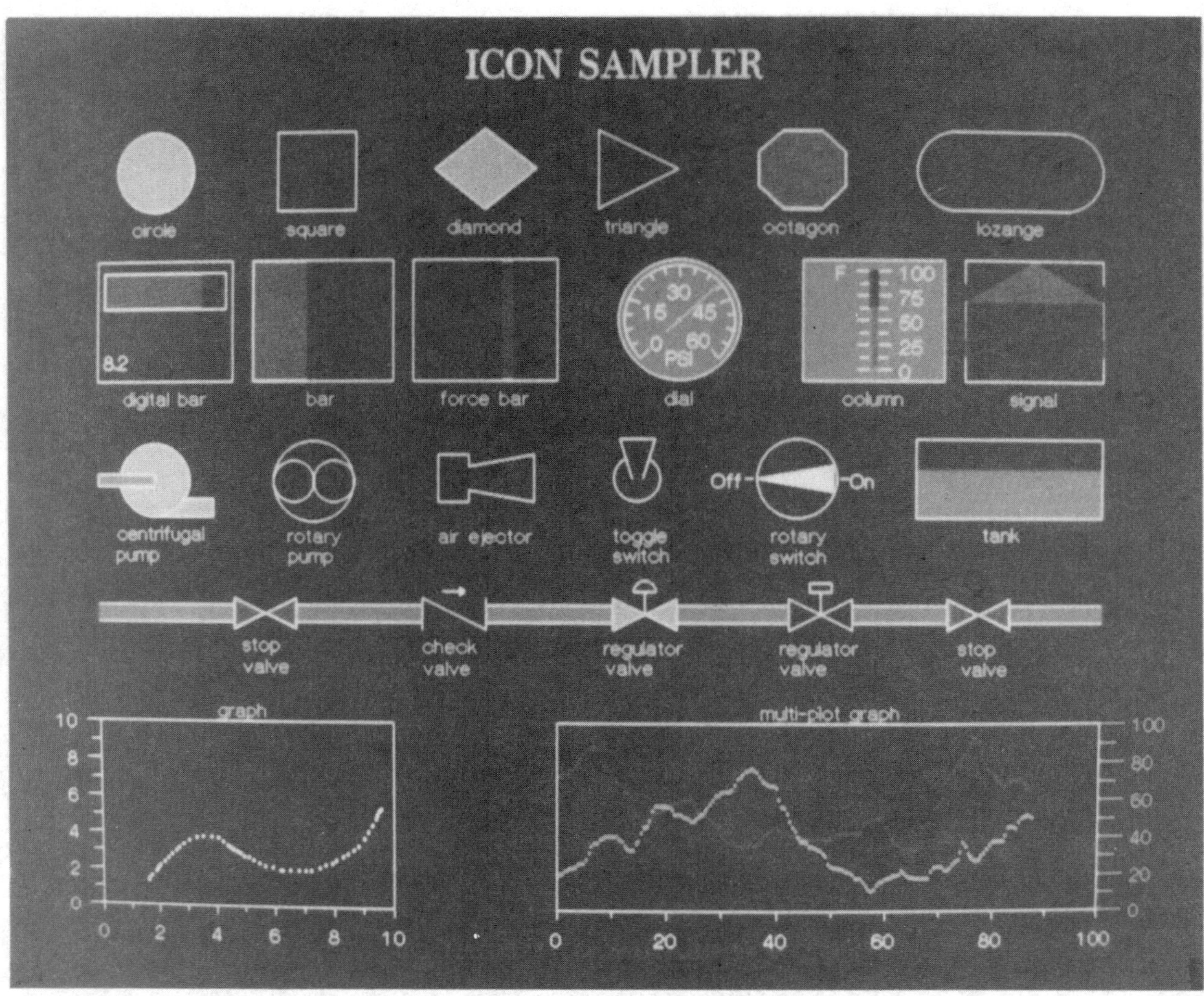

Figure 7. Sample Icons. Icons are implemented using the object oriented flavors system of ZetaLISP.

display, reformulates it and eventually makes it into what he wants. We think this form of interchange is very important. It seems quite natural and allows both the machine and the person to do what each does best. The critique is facilitated by requiring only the choice of different values for parameters which have not defaulted to the required values. What is created as a result of this interaction is not just the color graphic depiction of a diagram, but a program which contains a number of dynamic entities capable of responding to messages and of providing graphical support to an interactive instructional system. The editor then is a facility which makes it possible for a nonprogrammer to create some fairly complex pieces of LISP code.

For purposes of demonstration, consider creating a "dial" for use in a Steamer diagram. You would click on dial on the black and white screen. The cursor would then be taken to the color screen where you would position and size the dial. You immediately would get a default dial on the screen. Then, one would critique that dial by changing its parameters (position, size, scale, font, color, label, etc.) to match those required.

Figure 8 shows some characteristics of a dial that would get created by this simple interaction. Not only are all of the specific details of the dial created, but also, as a particular type of object, it inherits a large collection of messages from the objects out of which it is composed.

A dial, like the other graphical icons, is thus a dynamic object created out of a mixture of more basic elements which can be instantiated to meet the needs of particular applications. It is capable of responding to a variety of commands (messages) to perform specific actions. These messages make possible a very powerful generic interface ability which has been exceedingly useful in building Steamer.

Once satisfied with the visual characteristics of a diagram, the user then must tie the components to an underlying simulation or real-time interface. We refer to this process as *tapping.* By selecting an object and clicking on the "tap" in the graphics editor display, you would be provided with a pop-up menu to facilitate the association of the icon to variables in the mathematical simulation. Here you can specify not only the variable(s) whose value(s) will be reflected by the icon, but also the variable(s) in the math model which can be changed as a result of clicking on the icon. The editor provides a variety of mapping options to simplify translation from an underlying variable type (say logical) to appropriate messages to the object (say "ON" or "OFF"). In addition to associating icons with the mathematical simulation, one can also associate diagrams and the icons which compose them with what we term *model augments.* An augment allows additions to correct inadequacies of the simulation model, it supports

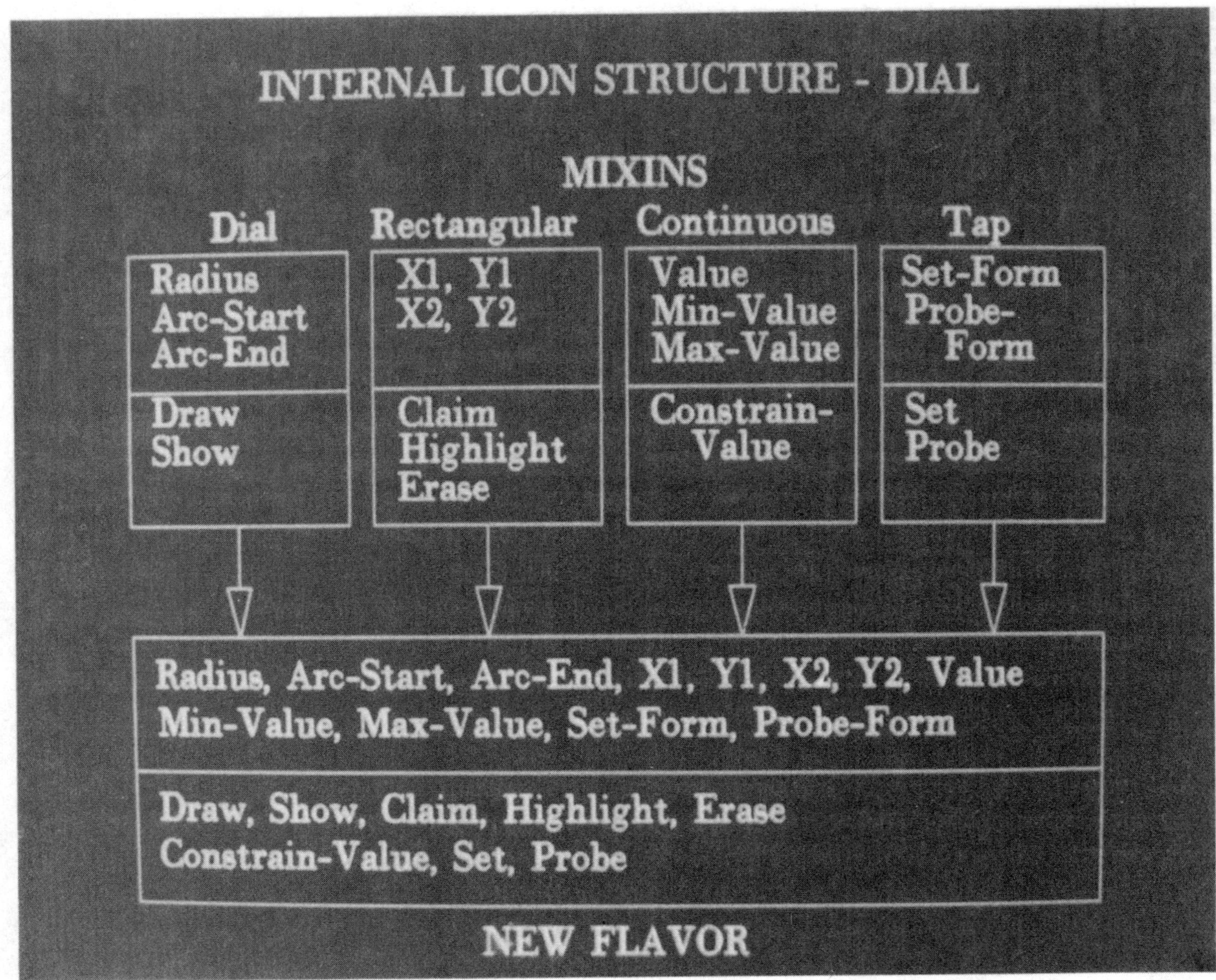

Figure 8. Internal Structure of the Dial Icon. Each icon is a message-receiving object composed by mixing together flavors. A subset of the 8 flavors used in a dial icon and the 40 instance variables and 122 messages that the flavors contribute is represented in this figure.

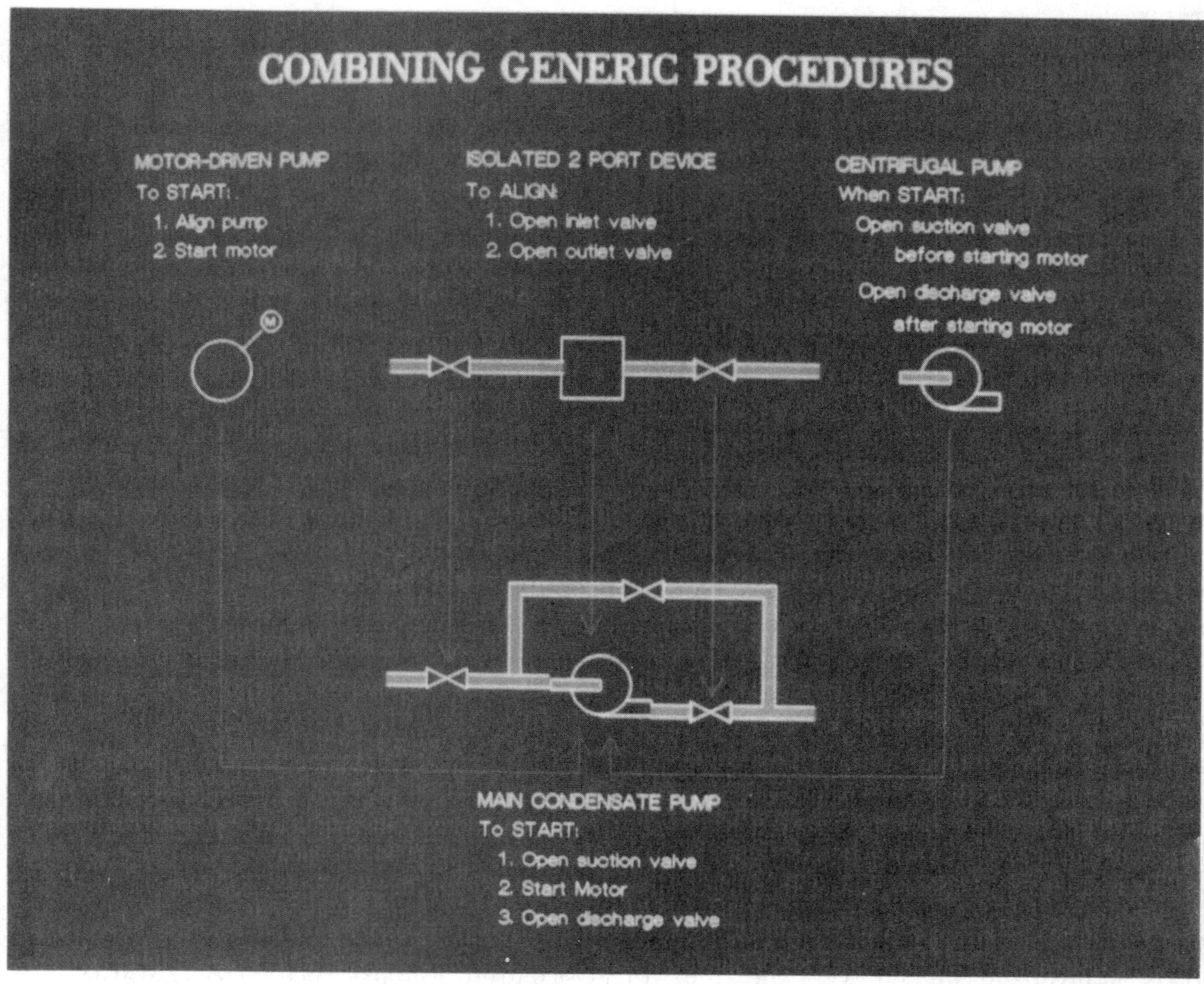

Figure 9. Composition of a Procedure from Generic Components. We are exploring techniques for composing procedures from generic components and for providing principled explanations.

the writing of more complex tapping code, and it provides stand-alone simulations for diagrams.

An example of the first augment is depicting flows. Flows are not represented in the Steamer math model. It is quite easy though to tie a section of pipe to a function in the augment which computes flow rate based on things which are represented. Typically one would check to see if there is a flow path through the section of pipe and then flow the pipe in proportion to the speed of the appropriate pump. We have also found augments valuable as a mechanism for implementing various mini-labs within Steamer to demonstrate important physical principles involved in the propulsion domain. In many cases the model augment provides the total mathematical model for a mini-lab and runs independent of the large simulation model.

The editor then is a complete system for constructing diagrams and interfacing them to an underlying mathematical model. It has gone through a long period of evolution and refinement. In its present state, it is very usable by computer-naive individuals. In fact, most of the diagrams in Steamer have been originated or refined by a retired boiler technician with more than 20 years of propulsion plant experience, but with no previous computer experience. In a number of tryouts of Steamer in Navy schools, we have found that a short period of training is all that is required for instructors to begin to be able to use the editor productively. The only problematic thing is tapping diagrams into the math model. Our subject matter expert now has no problem if an appropriate variable representing a component is available. However, for more complicated tappings like those involved in pipes, where one must write a bit of LISP code or where a stand-alone model is required, we must provide programming support.

The graphics editor is an extremely general and powerful tool with potential applications ranging far beyond Steamer. In designing and implementing the graphics editor we have capitalized on the very flexible object-oriented *Flavors System* of ZetaLISP. This editor has been used to create all of the Steamer diagrams. We have also used it in some quite different domains to explore its generality. For example, in collaboration with one of our colleagues at UCSD, Dave Rumelhart, the editor has been used to build a graphical interface to a number of parallel distributed models of cognition. In many ways the problems facing a researcher when implementing such models are much the same that we face in Steamer. When there is a complex dynamic system which needs to be understood, researchers can benefit from graphical views of that system at various hierarchical levels. Having a powerful tool like the editor available when actively developing a simulation model can be incredibly valuable. In addition, there are a wide variety of other potential applications of the graphics editor. For example, it would be very valuable for process control applications where one might tie icons to a real-time interface rather than an underlying simulation.

Where is the AI in Steamer?

One might view Steamer as being fundamentally a Cognitive Science rather than an AI research enterprise since we are primarily concerned with how people understand and reason about complex dynamic systems and how interactive graphical interfaces might support the development of useful mental models. On the other hand, we think Steamer is a most important AI application because it called for a very careful look at what aspects of AI technology are ready for application to the design and implementation of computer-based instructional systems. One of the most important AI technologies is the programming environment within which we work. The support provided by this *exploratory programming environment* has made it possible to successfully pursue the construction of a system like Steamer. The system could not have been constructed without the powerful programming tools which AI programming environments make available. Our work has been accomplished within the ZetaLISP environment (Weinreb & Moon, 1981). For an excellent description of a similar exploratory programming environment see Sheil's (1983) recent article.

Of course, using AI tools, either those associated with programming environments or even our use of a truth-maintenance system (McAllester, 1982) for maintaining the consistency of a database of assertions about plant state and student knowledge, doesn't make a project into an AI venture. Most of the genuine AI aspects of Steamer derive from our interest in knowledge representation. We have been very concerned with how one might represent the knowledge involved in the propulsion domain. Much of this has involved efforts to elicit and represent the types of models that human experts use in reasoning about propulsion plant components and procedures (Williams, Hollan, & Stevens, 1982). Considerable effort, thought, and code have gone into issues of representation. We have been concerned with representing the information required to adopt various perspectives on the plant and to maintain a flexible model of the state of the plant and of the student. This is very much the current focus of our efforts. What might be perceived as slowness in getting to this portion of the development is a necessary result of not building a toy system. It would have been easy not to fully complete the earlier graphical phases of the project or to settle for something less than good coverage of the complete propulsion plant or a less general graphics editor.

We would like to give you some examples of the knowledge representation aspects of the project that involve nongraphical aspects of our domain. When you spend from 50 million to a few billion dollars for a Navy ship, you also get an extensive users manual. One form of this manual contains a list of procedures, called the Engineering Operational Sequencing System (EOSS), for operating the plant. This set of manuals, which would fill a good sized book case, contains all of the procedures needed to run the ship's propulsion system. We have been attempting to represent these procedures in a form such that they can be executed and explained at different hierarchical levels. In some sense we face similar problems when creating the views needed to adequately cover the graphical representation of the propulsion domain. We have come to a similar solution: the creation of an editor. This editor, a *Procedures Editor,* makes available sets of generic components, generic procedures, and engineering principles. It allows for the composition of procedures not by writing down their steps, but by performing mappings from abstract generic components and procedures to particular instances.

Figure 9 depicts an example of the types of information that might be involved in the composition of a procedure. The identification of abstract devices and generic components is very much a research activity. That activity requires a deep knowledge of the domain, an appreciation for the generic models that experts use, and the ability to iteratively refine, extend, and reformulate those models which sufficiently cover the EOSS procedures. This is complicated because no such principled process was followed in constructing the existing EOSS procedures. They are a mixture of engineering constraints, rules of thumb, and historical accidents. We are attempting to identify the types of generic components which range from very abstract and general objects (e.g., two-port devices) to less general components (e.g., positive displacement pumps). The editor permits the user to instantiate particular instances of generic procedures and associate the steps that are derived with various underlying engineering principles. The editor provides considerable support for this process. For example, it detects collisions in orderings of steps and allows their resolution. Currently we are discussing what would be the most convenient form of interface to provide for the editor. In some ways a graphical interface seems appealing. In fact, some of the information could be gathered with and support the process of using the graphics editor. For example, knowledge about abstract pumps with suction and discharge valves could be represented. When the user places a pump into a diagram with the graphics editor, the system could assist in making an identification of the associated suction and discharge valves.

An initial version of the procedures editor has recently come to life and is starting to meet our needs for putting procedures into the system. It will make it possible to represent procedures in such a way that intelligent use can be made of them by providing the necessary representations to permit the system to adopt different viewpoints on portions of the propulsion system. One might, for example, view a particular pump as an instance of a *positive displacement pump* or as a component of a *pumping station*. We are developing a frame-based representation system that supports multiple perspectives and permits integration of the vast amount of structural, functional, topological, and graphical information contained within Steamer.

We have also been experimenting with a growing number of interpreters, which we call *presenters,* for allowing Steamer to talk about the propulsion system. Thus, a presenter might take an object and discuss how it is connected to other objects in the system in terms of its physical connections, energy connections, or information connections. Procedures also are objects in the representational system and can be talked about from a variety of perspectives. For example, the system can discuss the components of a procedure, salient procedural fragments which occur in many other procedures (e.g., the securing of an isolation valve or the establishment of a flow path), or the engineering principles which jointly conspire to constrain the ordering of the steps within a given procedure. Considerable work remains to be accomplished in this area, but currently, we think the procedures editor may turn out to be as valuable and powerful as our graphics editor.

In summary, we think there are a number of factors which distinguish Steamer from traditional AI efforts. Most derive from our fundamental cognitive science perspective on creating a training system that will help students come to understand and reason about a complex dynamic system. The effort, at this point, has been dominated not by attempting to build an expert system to replace a person, but rather by a deep commitment to graphics, to interactive graphical forms of support for understanding, to a concern with how to make more and more of the propulsion domain inspectable, and with the creation of generic tools (like the graphics editor) that allow nonprogrammers to create a significant portion of interactive inspectable training systems. These efforts have forced us to be very concerned with explanation as a primary goal rather than something that might be tacked onto the end of an expert system to help it recruit faith in its inferences. The types of principled explanations that we need can only derive from a rich and powerful representation of the generic components and procedures that seem to allow a human expert to parse and understand the tremendous complexity of the propulsion domain.

Directions for the Future

We are moving in essentially five directions in the future:

- We plan to continue the development of an integrated representation system to tie together the many different types of knowledge currently represented.

- We will work on providing Steamer with a consistent interface to create a central point of view and a consistent means of controlling the growing variety of things the system can do and that can be done to it. In short, we want to provide Steamer with a *style* and *consistent personality.*

- We will pursue the extension of generative and reactive aspects of Steamer. In particular, we will be providing the diagrams with a form of instructional augmentation containing the information needed to support mixed-initiative interactions with the diagrams. We need to be able to represent consistently the important things that a diagram might reveal to a student, to provide a mechanism for posing questions to the student which might be answered not by typing but by doing things to the diagram, and to provide mechanisms for monitoring a student's behavior while attempting to answer questions. For example, in the *Make-Up and Excess Feed diagram* (Figure 3) there are important control relationships between when and how far valves open, based on the levels of the tanks in the system. The system might, for example, ask the student to manipulate the diagram to get the Excess-Feed Valve fully open. In our initial evaluation of the system, we have found that having a student put forth hypotheses in this way results in the crossing of an important instructional and motivational threshold.

- We plan to pursue the implementation of an expanded student model. Presently we have only explored a very limited differential model which notates a student's knowledge of engineering principles. There is much that remains to be done here.

- Finally, in a related project, NPRDC's group plans to pursue a generalization of the graphics editor to include the ability to construct a simulation model interactively. The general notion here is to provide default behaviors for objects analogous to the current provision of default visual characteristics. This *Behavior Editor* will allow the user to critique the behavior associated with an object in much the same way he or she can currently critique graphical characteristics. We would like to see the extent to which a nonprogrammer can construct a simulation program by means of the same sorts of interactions that currently allow a user of our graphics editor to construct a graphical interface.

Conclusions, Concerns, and Counsel

We have tried to provide a brief overview of our current and projected efforts with Steamer. More importantly, we have attempted to point out what we see as the underlying ideas in the project:

- **Mental Models;**
- **Graphical Interfaces to Interactive Inspectable Simulations;**
- **Conceptual Fidelity; and**
- **Implementation Philosophy.**

We think we are just now seeing the introduction of the requisite hardware, software, and cognitive theory to permit principled instructional applications. We are quite convinced that the major constraints on progress currently are our knowledge of cognition and the methods with which to represent the vast amount and myriad types of domain knowledge needed to support instruction. We are also convinced that we will see more and more Steamer-like systems in the future. They provide the opportunity for a qualitatively different and superior form of training which focuses on providing the interactions needed to build up useful mental models and understandings of complex dynamic physical systems. Such systems can also increase the amount of supervised practice available to students by orders of magnitude.

The great promise of the application of artificial intelligence software and hardware technologies to the solution of problems in a variety of domains is a refrain heard often these days. We are both encouraged and fearful of the attention AI is currently receiving. We are encouraged because we too see tremendous promise in the technology and in the types of explicit computational accounts of cognition emerging from AI and the other cognitive sciences. There is a danger that real developments, substantive though they may be, will fall far short of inflated expectations. Such a turn of events could result in a backlash against AI similar to that suffered by computer-based instruction in the past decade.

It does not require an intellectual historian to see the parallels between the current interest in AI and early interest in computer-based instruction. It was some two decades ago that people first began to advocate the potential of computer technology to provide and improve instruction. Unfortunately, most actual instructional applications of the technology have fallen far short of its promise. We have argued elsewhere that one primary reason is that it is perhaps too easy to see the potential of the technology for instructional applications. It seems to require very little exposure to computation before most people are aware of its instructional potential. Without an appreciation for how much tacit knowledge underlies good instruction performed by human instructors, how difficult it is to make that tacit knowledge explicit, and what kinds of software and hardware are required to support its delivery, it is easy to visualize the potential without really knowing what might be required to make it a reality. As we mentioned earlier, within computer-based instruction we think we are just now beginning to see the kinds of hardware, software, and most importantly, the explicit computational formulations of cognitive theory essential to principled instructional applications. Without these requisite tools and theories, the types of instructional applications have and will continue to fall far short of the technology's potential. We also are particularly fearful that important research breakthroughs will be used inappropriately to sell aspects of the technology which, while still ripe for further research progress, are not yet ready for application. This could result in a slowing down of important research and development at a time when it should be accelerated.

We also would like to give some counsel on the application of AI to other instructional domains based on our experience with Steamer. In addition to warning about overzealous and uninformed advocates, we would like to put forth the following observations and recommendations:

1. We think it is tremendously important not to rush into applications. Premature application of a fragile technology will instill the same kinds of negative attitudes that premature applications of computer-based instruction did.

2. It is exceedingly important to provide sufficient basic research funding to make possible the development of a strong technological base to support future applications. Here we commend a recent letter to the editor in Science to your attention. Lindamood (1983), puts forth the novel thesis that the primary impact of the Japanese Fifth Generation Project may be *managerial* rather than *technological.* In particular he focuses on the nature of funding of that research endeavor and points out what may be the primary fault of US research funding: *over specifying and overmanaging the research endeavor*. This is typically done in the hopes of obtaining early application results but seems more likely to result not in early application but only poor science.

3. There is a real need for additional centers of excellence for providing a strong scientific and technological base. It is vital that mechanisms for transitioning the more promising results also be established as part of these centers. Interdisciplinary centers with ties to academia, industry, and the military are particularly important.

4. Very careful consideration should be given to the choice of a few well-funded initial demonstration systems. Such systems are very important for establishing the credibility of the best research ideas and can serve as important guide posts for subsequent efforts. Given the shortage of experienced people in AI and cognitive science, this seems a particularly wise approach.

5. Finally, much thought and research needs to be addressed to methods for evaluating these new AI-based instructional systems. There are some tremendously hard problems involved. Here we want to include not only the traditional view of evaluation but also evaluations of how these systems effect the communities within which they are placed. Powerful technologies sometimes have unanticipated beneficial or detrimental consequences. An evaluation of an application of this technology that considers only effects on the problem the technology is intended to solve may miss important consequences of the use of the technology.

Acknowledgements

The senior author of this paper, James Hollan, initiated the the Steamer effort five years ago in collaboration with Mike Williams (then at NPRDC and now at IntelliGenetics). Al Stevens of Bolt Beranek and Newman (BBN) joined the collaboration shortly thereafter. Since that time, a significant amount of the effort has been conducted under contract to BBN and a number of people have been involved in the project. At NPRDC, the Steamer Project currently involves the efforts of James Hollan, Edwin Hutchins, and Louis Weitzman. The BBN side of the effort presently includes Bruce Roberts, who in many ways is the principal software architect of Steamer, Terry Roe (a retired boiler technician chief with 22 years of propulsion operational experience who serves as our subject matter expert and although employed by BBN works with us in San Diego) and the part-time efforts of Albert Boulanger, and Glenn Abrett. Also over the years, we have been most fortunate to have received the capable assistance of Larry Stead (the original implementor of the Steamer Graphics editor; now with Symbolics), Ken Forbus (MIT) and Brian Smith (then at MIT and now at Xerox Parc).

References

Lindamood, G. E. (1983) Japanese Computer Project. *Science,* 221:1008.

McAllester, D. A. (1982) Reasoning utility package user's manual. AI Memo 667, Massachusetts Institute of Technology.

Papert, S. (1980) *Mindstorms: Children, computers, and powerful ideas.* New York: Basic Books.

Sheil, B. (1983) Power tools for programmers. *Datamation,* 29:131-144.

Weinreb D. & Moon D. (1981) *LISP Machine Manual.* Cambridge, MA: MIT Artificial Intelligence Laboratory.

Williams, M., Hollan, J., & Stevens A. (1983) Human reasoning about a simple physical system, In Gentner, D., & Stevens, A. (Eds.) *Mental Models.* Hillsdale, New Jersey: Erlbaum.

Steamer: An Interactive Inspectable Simulation-Based Training System

Jim Hollan

The Steamer project evolved out of discussions with Mike Williams and Al Stevens in the late 1970s. I had just arrived at UCSD (University of California at San Diego) and Mike and Al were recent UCSD graduates. We were all very interested in how interactive graphical representations could help people understand complex dynamic systems. It was Mike's training as a naval officer and the potential of research funding from the Navy that directed us to focus on steam propulsion as a domain.

Steamer developed from a zeitgeist of exciting ideas that surrounded us throughout the project. The "Naive Physics Manifesto" of Pat Hayes in 1978 and qualitative reasoning notions arising in the early work of Johan deKleer and Ken Forbus were central. Our perspective on this developing zeitgeist was later shared at an Office of Naval Research-funded workshop on mental models at UCSD, led by Dedre Gentner and Al Stevens. Mike, Al, and I presented a paper, "Human Reasoning about a Simple Physical System." Many others presenting at that workshop (John Seely Brown, Andy diSessa, Johan deKleer, Ken Forbus, and Don Norman) influenced the development of Steamer. Also of considerable import to the project was the commercial availability of Lisp machines. These wonderful machines provided both the development and delivery environments for Steamer. It is with both nostalgia and loss that I look back on that powerful integrated development environment.

In reflecting about Steamer, my main reaction is how very fortunate we were to attract so many great people. Ed Hutchins worked with us from the early days and supported the project with his absolutely unique abilities as a cognitive anthropologist with considerable computational expertise. Larry Stead was involved from the beginning and was the author of the Steamer graphics editor, the centerpiece of the effort. Bruce Roberts joined us early on and provided his knowledge representation experience and consummate Lisp programming style. Ken Forbus was a graduate student at MIT and worked with us during those early days. His feedback minilab greatly influenced our thinking about the importance of qualitative simulation. We were also quite fortunate to be able to find boiler technician chief Terry Rowe. He was unique in being a navy chief who could work with a bunch of Ph.D. researchers. His more than twenty years of experience in propulsion was vital to the effort. He is likely the only person whose first exposure to computation was on a Lisp machine.

There were many other people involved in the project at NPRDC, UCSD, BBN (Bolt, Beranek and Newman), and Xerox Parc. In many cases, their subsequent work followed from work on Steamer. Louie Weitzman's Ph.D. work at MIT evolved from his early designer system that was derivative from the Steamer graphics editor and a central part of a suite of tools (HITS) we were putting together while I directed the Microelectronics and Computer Technology Corporation's Human Interface Lab. Even my present work on Pad++, a multiscale interface environment, owes much to Steamer. In addition to the exciting people, my other major reflections are just how naive we were to take on the scale of project we did and how proud I am of what we accomplished. I thank all those involved.

A KNOWLEDGE-BASED USER INTERFACE MANAGEMENT SYSTEM

James Foley, Christina Gibbs, Won Chul Kim, Srdjan Kovacevic

Department of Electrical Engineering and Computer Science
George Washington University
Washington, DC 20052

ABSTRACT
A knowledge base which defines a user-computer interface is described. The knowledge base serves as input to a user interface management system, which implements the user interface. However, the knowledge base represents user interface design knowledge at a level of abstraction higher than is typical of user interface management systems. In particular, it represents objects, actions, attributes of objects, an object class hierarchy, and pre- and post-conditions on the actions. The knowledge base can be algorithmically transformed into a number of functionally equivalent interfaces, each of which is slightly different from the original interface. The transformed interface definition can be input to the UIMS, providing a way to quickly experiment with a family of related interfaces.

KEYWORDS: User Interface Design Tool, User Interface Management System, Expert System, Knowledge Base.

INTRODUCTION

We are developing the User Interface Design Environment (UIDE), a system to assist in user interface design and implementation. Figure 1 shows the overall organization of UIDE, the heart of which is a knowledge base representation of the conceptual design of a user interface, consisting of:

- the class hierarchy of objects which exist in the system (only single inheritance is currently supported)
- properties of the objects
- actions which can be performed on the objects
- units of information required by the actions
- pre- and post-conditions for the actions.

The knowledge base can be used for at least six different purposes:

- To represent the conceptual design of a user interface.
- To transform the knowledge base, and hence the user interface it represents, into a different but functionally-equivalent interface.
- To implement the user interface via a User Interface Management System (UIMS).
- To check the interface design for consistency and completeness.
- To evaluate the interface design with respect to speed of use (using a Key-stroke Model type of analysis [CARD80, CARD83]) and ease of learning (using a GOMS style analysis [KIER85]).
- To provide run-time help to the user.

UIDE currently achieves the first three purposes. Accordingly, this paper focuses on the structure of the knowledge base and how it supports these three purposes, and also describes the concept of user interface transformations.

UIDE goes beyond the capabilities of the typical User Interface Management System (UIMS) [OLSE84], which requires the designer to work at the syntactic and lexical levels of design and hence to focus on command names, screen and icon design, menu organization, sequencing rules, and interaction techniques. UIDE provides a higher-level conceptual design tool. This has many benefits. The designer is allowed to work at a higher level of abstraction. The user interface designer can request the UIMS to implement a syntax such as prefix, postfix, or "nofix" (free-form syntax with automatic prompting for missing information). This eliminates concerns about inconsistent syntax specified using tools such as BNF or ATNs, because the designer is working at a higher level of specification. The UIMS can effect changes from one syntactic structure to another, relieving the designer of the tedium of syntactic-level specifications. Or, the UIMS can be allowed to choose appropriate syntactic and lexical constructs, both for input and for output. For example, the automatic design concepts of MacKinlay [MACK86] can in the future be applied to screen and dialogue box design.

We have developed a Simple User Interface Management System (SUIMS), which accepts as input the knowledge

Algorithms to Evaluate User Interface Design
Library of User Interface Designs
Semantic (Action) Routines for the Application
Interactive Interface to UIDE
Current User Interface Design
User Interface Management System
Transformation Algorithms
User Interface Designer
End User

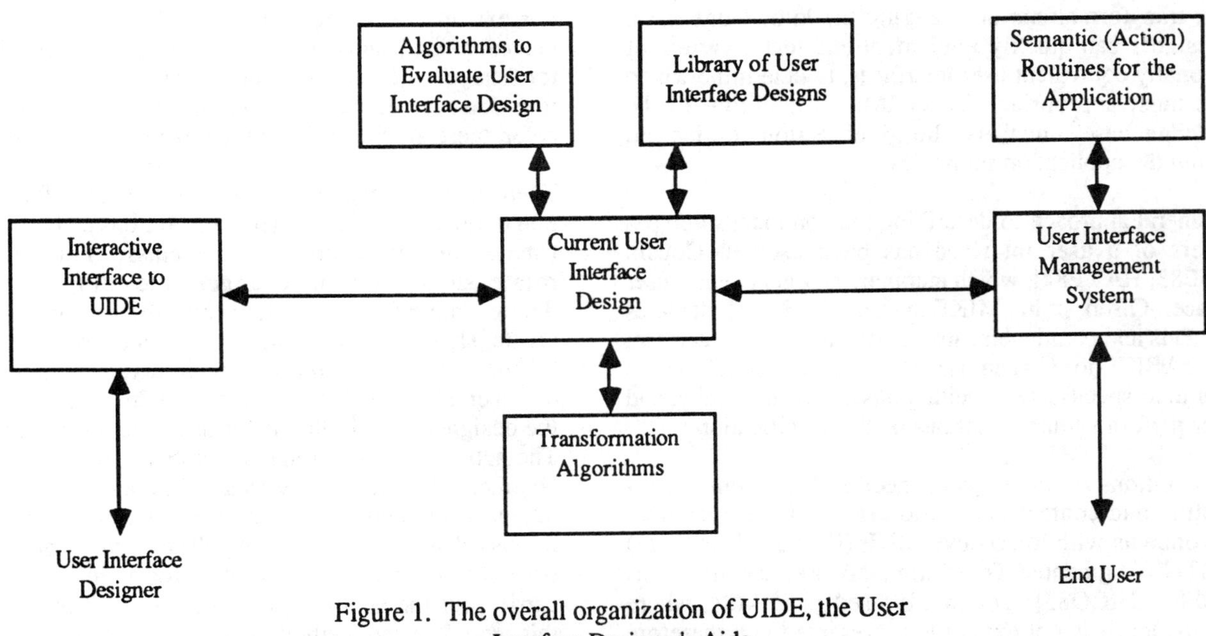

Figure 1. The overall organization of UIDE, the User Interface Designer's Aide

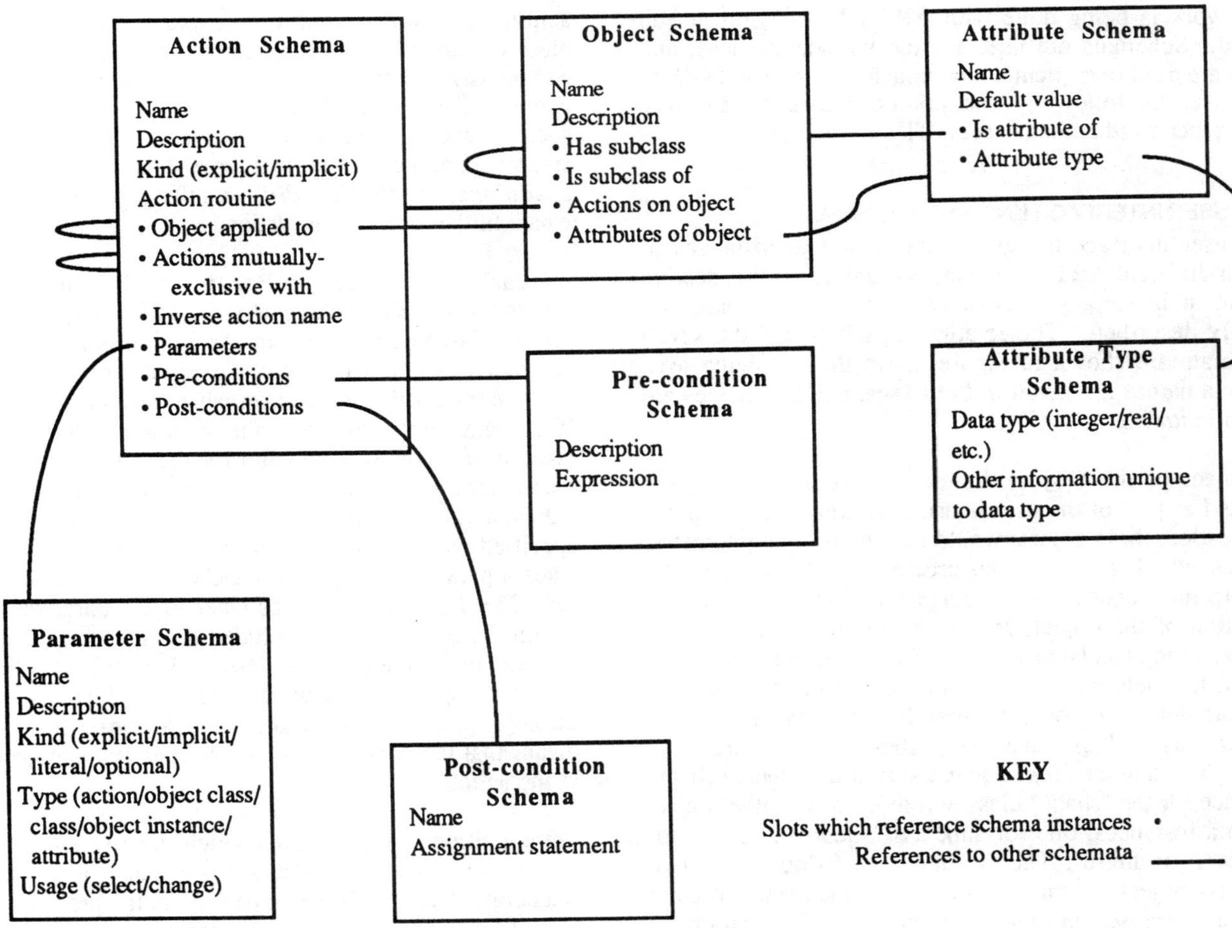

Action Schema
Name
Description
Kind (explicit/implicit)
Action routine
• Object applied to
• Actions mutually-exclusive with
• Inverse action name
• Parameters
• Pre-conditions
• Post-conditions
Object Schema
Name
Description
• Has subclass
• Is subclass of
• Actions on object
• Attributes of object
Attribute Schema
Name
Default value
• Is attribute of
• Attribute type
Pre-condition Schema
Description
Expression
Attribute Type Schema
Data type (integer/real/ etc.)
Other information unique to data type
Parameter Schema
Name
Description
Kind (explicit/implicit/ literal/optional)
Type (action/object class/ class/object instance/ attribute)
Usage (select/change)
Post-condition Schema
Name
Assignment statement
KEY
Slots which reference schema instances •
References to other schemata

Figure 2. Schemata and their relations.

base and implements the user interface it describes. By applying transformations or changing the knowledge base, the designer can quickly implement and test a variety of functionally equivalent user interfaces, to determine which one is most appropriate. The UIMS, in addition to the knowledge base, must also be given action routines to carry out the application semantics.

Our general approach to describing the commands and parameters of a user interface has been used in Cousin [HAYE83, HAYE84], which automatically generates a user interface. Olsen, in his MIKE system [OLSE86], declares commands and parameters, also generating a user interface. Neither MIKE nor Cousin uses pre- and post-conditions as part of their specification, neither has a class hierarchy, and neither performs transformations on the specification.

The operations on the objects specify all the units of information and context needed to carry out the operation. This contrasts with lower-level BNF (Backus-Naur Form) and ATN (Augmented Transition Network) specifications [GREE86, JACO83] commonly-used in UIMSs, where this knowledge is not explicitly represented and therefore cannot be used to assist in designing or implementing the interface.

The work is being done with ART [INFE87], on a Sun 3/160. Schemata are used for the knowledge base, and rules are used to implement the transformations and UIMS. However, the following description of the knowledge base uses generic rather than exact ART terminology.

THE USER INTERFACE KNOWLEDGE BASE

The user interface design is represented as instances of seven different ART schemata, or frames. In this section the most important slots of each of the schemata are briefly described. The relationships between the seven schemata are shown in Figure 2. In the following text, schema names are given in **bold face**, and slot names are given in *italics*.

Instances of the **Object Schema** represent the objects defined as part of the user interface design. In a graphics application, these objects would be the different geometric shapes which the user can create, modify, delete, etc. Within this schema, the *Description* slot is a textual description of the object, created by the user interface designer, which can be provided to the user at run time in response to a help request. The *Has subclass* and *Is subclass of* slots define the object hierarchy. For example, if an object class "shape" has two subclasses, "square" and "triangle", then the *Has subclass* slot of the object schema instance for the "shape" class will refer to two other object schema instances, one for subclass "square" and one for subclass "triangle". The *Is subclass of* slots in the two subclass object schema instances will each refer to class "shape". *Actions on object* is a relation linking an object schema instance to the action schema instances for those actions which can be applied to that object class. *Attributes of object* is a relation linking the object schema instance to the attribute schema instances for the object. For example, if objects of class "shape" can be created, moved, rotated, and deleted, then the object schema instance for "shape" will refer to action schema instances for these four actions. If shapes have an angle of rotation and a color, these are the attribute schema instances linked to.

There is an instance of the **Action Schema** for each action defined in the user interface. Actions can affect an attribute, an object, or an object class. For instance, a rotate_shape action changes the angle attribute, delete_shape would delete an object instance, and create_shape would create an instance of object class "shape." The *Description* is again textual, created by the designer and available for run-time help (and for review by the designer, should the intent of the action be forgotten). The action *Kind* is normally "explicit", but is changed to "implicit" if a Currently-selected Command transformation has been applied to the action. (This transformation is discussed in the next section.) The *Action routine name* provides the link to the run-time procedure which actually carries out the action. (In object-oriented programming, this would be the method name.) *Object applied to* is the inverse of *Actions on object* in the **Object Schema**. The *Actions mutually-exclusive with* slot refers to all actions which cannot be available at the same time as this action. This slot is used to organize menus: mutually exclusive commands, such as "turn x on" and "turn x off", can be assigned the same menu slot. *Inverse action* is the name of the action which is the inverse of this action, if such an action exists. This slot assists in implementing an undo command. The final three slots, *Parameters, Pre-conditions*, and *Post-conditions*, refer to schema instances which further describe the action.

For each action there is a **Parameter Schema** instance for each parameter, or unit of information, required by the action. The text slot*Description Kind* describes how the parameter is given its value: "explicit" means the value must be obtained from the user when the action is invoked. If the parameter is given a value with a separate command (such as a set_color command for the color attribute), the parameter kind is "implicit", while a parameter which has a default value is "optional". Such a parameter need not be specified when the user invokes an action. "Literal" indicates a parameter with a specific value, such as the color red. The *Type* slot indicates whether the parameter is an action, an object class, an object instance, or an attribute. A value of "change" in the *Usage* slot indicates that the parameter specifies a new value (as would be the case for the angle parameter of a rotate_shape action), while "select" means that the parameter is used to specify the object used in the action.

Pre-conditions are predicates which must be true in order for an action to be enabled and thus available to the user for selection. Any variables can be used in the pre-conditions. In addition, some specific variables having to do with the number of instances of different types of objects are also provided. Post-conditions are asserted following the execution of the action with which they are associated. A post-condition is one or more statements which assign values to the variables used in the pre-conditions. Pre- and post-conditions specify just enough of the application's semantics to allow context-sensitivity in presenting menus, giving context-sensitive help, and for the very limited understanding of the semantics which is necessary for the transformations.

A **Pre-condition Schema** is instantiated for each term in an action's pre-condition: for the pre-condition A and B, there will be one instance for A and another for B. The *Description* explains what the pre-condition means, and is used to generate the following types of explanations to the user at run-time:

- If the user is working with a command-line interface and has entered the name of a command which is not available because one or more of its pre-conditions are not satisfied, then the explanation to the user of why the command has been rejected includes the description of each false conjunctive term in the pre-condition.
- If the user asks for detailed help about a command, the description is given as part of the explanation of the command (along with the general description of the command and its parameters).

The actual *Expression* of the pre-condition is represented in a form which can be conveniently evaluated at run-time, to determine whether the pre-condition is true or false.

A **Post-condition Schema** instance exists for each variable which is changed when an action is performed. The *Assignment statement* is represented in a form which can be conveniently performed at run-time.

The types of information encoded and used in the pre- and post-conditions include:

- The number of objects of a particular object class which are in existence. A creation command increments this number as a post-condition; a deletion command decrements the number.
- The number of objects of different object classes which have been selected as belonging to the Currently selected Set.
- The existence of a currently selected command.
- The existence of a value for a parameter.
- Any variables established by the interface designer.

Examples of these are given in the next section.

Each attribute of an object, such as color, angle of rotation, etc. is described by an instance of the **Attribute Schema**, which includes an optional *Default value* for the attribute. This default is used when an instance of the object is created and the attribute is an "optional" parameter of the creation action. The *Attribute type* is a link to what is essentially a data type descriptor, analogous to the data typing of Pascal or C. The **Attribute Type Schema** records the attribute *Data type* as being integer, real, enumerated, etc., and gives other information which is specific to the data type. For example, the possible values of an enumerated data type are given.

USER INTERFACE TRANSFORMATIONS

A user interface designer typically develops and evaluates a number of alternative conceptual designs. Some of the alternatives will be slight variations on one another, while other designs will be quite different. We can automatically generate a set of alternative conceptual designs which are slight variations on one another. This is done via transformations which are applied to the user interface knowledge base, and are in the spirit of program transformations. Each transformation automatically creates a new user interface design with the same functionality as the original, but with a slightly different user view of the functionality. This automatic generation of alternatives saves designer effort. The transformations include factoring (sometimes called orthogonalization), special cases of which are the creation of a currently-selected object (CSO), a currently-selected command, and a currently-selected attribute value; establishing a currently-selected set (CSS) as a generalization of the CSO concept; establishing initial default values; specializing and generalizing commands based on object and command hierarchies; modifying the scope of certain types of commands; and consolidating commands based on pre-condition and post-condition equivalence.

A user interface transformation maps one user interface into another, by operating on the knowledge base representation of the interface. Interface transformations allow the designer to create a family of functionally-equivalent user interface designs for one application program and to test the effects of different design strategies. First the basic interface specifications are entered into the knowledge base - the objects, their attributes, and the actions acting on them. Once this base design is established, our system helps the designer explore alternative ways to structure the semantics of the application. Several generic design strategies have been implemented [FOLE87a] as transformation algorithms. For instance, to change the squares and triangles example mentioned above to use the CSO paradigm, the Factor Object Transformation would be applied. To obtain separate creation actions, one for triangle and one for square, the Specialize Transformation would be applied to the create_shape action.

In this section, the Currently-selected Set transformation is discussed. See [FOLE87b, FOLE87c] for details of other transformations. The transformations are implemented with ART rules which modify, delete, or instantiate the seven types of schema. The following set of actions, expressed here in the Interface Definition Language (IDL) [GIBB87] which we developed for specifying interfaces, will be used to illustrate the effect of the CSS transformation on the knowledge base.

initial: number(shape) = 0

pre-condition: true

create_shape(p: position, c: color, a: angle, object_type: shape_class)
post-condition: number(shape)=number(shape) + 1

pre-condition: number (shape) ≠ 0
rotate_shape(obj: shape, a: angle)
post-condition: none

pre-condition: number(shape) ≠ 0
delete_shape(obj: shape)
post-condition: number(shape) = number(shape) - 1

In this example, pre- and post-conditions based on the number of instances of shape objects are used to specify when the rotate_shape and delete_shape actions are available.

The currently selected set transformation factors a particular class of object out of the actions which operate on that object class. When the object to operate on is factored from an action, a currently selected object (CSO) or currently selected set (CSS) is established. An action for selecting a CSO is added, with a post-condition asserting that a CSO exists. A pre-condition, requiring that a CSO must exist before the action can be invoked, is added to actions which operate on instances of the object class which has been factored. A post-condition is added to actions which create a new instance of the class, asserting that a CSO exists. Actions which delete an object of the class being factored have a post-condition added asserting that a CSO no longer exists.

A currently selected set (CSS) can be created by the CSS transformation. A CSS is a set of selected objects which can be operated on by a succession of actions. The user selects the set of objects, and each action requested by the user is applied to each member of the CSS. The CSS transformation adds commands to add an object to the CSS, remove an object from the CSS, and clear the CSS. The command to add an object to the CSS has a post-condition which increases the size of the CSS by one, and decreases by one the size of the remaining, non selected set of objects (called the NSS in the following). A pre-condition, requiring that the CSS be non-empty, is added to actions which operate on instances of the object class which has been factored. A post-condition is added to actions which create a new instance of the class, asserting that the CSS has size one. Actions which delete an object of the class being factored have a post-condition added asserting that the CSS is empty.

The following set of actions results when the previous example is transformed to have a CSS:

initial: number(shape) = 0
initial: number(CSS_shape) = 0 {CSS (Currently Selected Set) initially empty}
initial: number(NSS_shape) = 0
{NSS (Non-Selected Set) initially empty}

{to add to CSS, must be some non selected shapes}
pre-condition: number(NSS_shape) ≠ 0
add_to_CSS_shape(obj: shape)
post-condition: number(CSS_shape) = number(CSS_shape) + 1
post-condition: number(NSS_shape) = number(NSS_shape) - 1

pre-condition: number(CSS_shape) ≠ 0
remove_from_CSS_shape(obj: shape)
post-condition: number(CSS_shape) = number(CSS_shape) - 1
post-condition: number(NSS_shape) = number(NSS_shape) + 1

pre-condition: number(CSS_shape) ≠ 0
clear_CSS_shape()
{all currently selected shapes become non selected shapes}
post-condition: number(NSS_shape) = number(NSS_shape) + number(CSS_shape)
post-condition: number(CSS_shape) = 0

pre-condition: true
create_shape(object_type: shape, p: position, c: color, a:angle)
{creation increases the number of shapes}
post-condition: number(shape) = number(shape)+1
{when a shape is created, the existing CSS, if any, is deselected, thus adding to the NSS}
post-condition: number(NSS_shape) = number(NSS_shape) + number(CSS_shape)
{size of the CSS after creation action is 1: the newly-created shape}
post-condition: number(CSS_shape) = 1

{in order to rotate a shape, it must first be selected}
pre-condition: number(CSS_shape) ≠ 0
rotate_shape(obj: shape **implicit**, a: angle)
{shape to rotate is implicit in the CSS}
post-condition: none

pre-condition: number(CSS_shape) ≠ 0
delete_shape(obj:shape **implicit**)
{shape to delete is implicit in the CSS}
{deletion decreases the total number of shapes}
post-condition: number(shape) = number(shape) - number(CSS_shape)
post-condition: number(CSS_shape) = 0
{deleting CSS empties it}

Other transformations work in similar ways, and are not described here in as much detail. In each case, schemata for actions, parameters, pre-conditions, and post-conditions are added, removed, or modified. The class hierarchy specialization transformation adds specialized actions in place of a general action. For instance, create_triangle and create_square actions replace the create_shape action seen in the previous examples. Class hierarchy generalization does the opposite. Attribute value specialization adds specialized actions for each value of an enumerated attribute. If color in the above example can be red, green, or blue, then create_shape could be replaced with create_shape_red, create_shape_green, and create_shape_blue. Attribute value generalization does the opposite.

The currently selected command transformation adds a set_command action with a post-condition asserting that the command has been selected. The actual action has a pre-condition added requiring that the command be selected. The object naming transformation adds a name parameter to the parameter list of every action which refers to an object, and adds an action to change an object's name.

The transformations are useful to generate design alternatives, as described here. They are also useful to formally specify exactly what is meant by currently-selected object, currently-selected command, etc. In addition, all interfaces which can be created by applying successive transformations form an equivalence class of interfaces. We have developed a canonical form representation to characterize each equivalence class in a standard way.

CONCLUSIONS

A knowledge base description of a user interface has been implemented and used as the basis for transforming the knowledge base and for implementing a user interface via a User Interface Management System. As we extend the knowledge base with additional schemata and slots, we will add to UIDE consistency and performance checking and run-time help capabilities.

REFERENCES

CARD80 Card, S., T. Moran, and A. Newell, The Keystroke-Level Model for User Performance Time with Interactive Systems, *Communications of the ACM* 23(7), July 1980, pp. 398-410.

CARD83 Card, S., T. Moran, and A. Newell, *The Psychology of Human-Computer Interaction*, L. Erlbaum Associates, Hillsdale, NJ, 1983.

FOLE82 Foley, J., and A. van Dam, *Fundamentals of Interactive Computer Graphics*, Addison-Wesley, Reading, Mass., 1982.

FOLE87a Foley, J., Transformations on a Formal Specification of User-Computer Interfaces, *Computer Graphics* 21(2), April 1987, pp. 109-113.

FOLE87b Algorithms to Transform the Formal Specification of a User-Computer Interface, Proceedings INTERACT '87, 2nd IFIP Conference on Human-Computer Interaction, Elsiver Science Publishers, Amsterdam, 1987, pp.1001-1006.

FOLE87c Foley, J., C. Gibbs, W. Kim, and S. Kovacevic, *Formal Specification and Transformation of User-Computer Interfaces*, Report GWU-IIST-87-10, Department of EE&CS, George Washington University, Washington DC 20052, 1987.

GIBB86 Gibbs, C., W. C. Kim, and J. Foley, *Case Studies in the Use of IDL: Interface Definition Language*, Report GWU-IIST-86-30, Dept. of EE&CS, George Washington University, Washington, DC 20052, 1986.

GREE86 Green, Mark, A Survey of Three Dialogue Models, *Transactions on Graphics* 5(3), July 1986, pp. 244-275.

HAYE83 Hayes, P and Szekely, P., Graceful Interaction Through the COUSIN Command Interface, *International Journal of Man-Machine Studies* 19(3), September 1983, pp. 285-305.

HAYE84 Hayes, P., Executable Interface Definitions Using Form-Based Interface Abstractions, In *Advances in Computer-Human Interaction*, H.R.Hartson, Ed., Ablex, NJ, 1984.

INFE87 Inference Corporation, *ART Reference Manual*, Inference Corporation, Los Angeles, CA, 1987.

JACO83 Jacob, R.J.K., Using Formal Specifications in the Design of a Human-Computer Interface, *Communications of the ACM* 26(4), April 1983, pp. 259-264.

KIER85 Kieras, D. and P. Polson, An Approach to the Formal Analysis of User Complexity, *International Journal of Man-Machine Studies*, 22(4), April 1985, pp. 365-394.

MACK86 MacKinlay, J., Automating the Design of Graphical Presentations of Relational Information, *ACM Transactions on Graphics*, 5(2), April 1986, pp. 110-141.

OLSE84 Olsen, D., W. Buxton, R. Ehrich, D. Kasik, J. Rhyne, and J. Sibert, A Context for User Interface Management, *IEEE Computer Graphics and Applications* 4(12), December 1984, pp. 33-42.

OLSE86 Olsen, D. MIKE: The Menu Interaction Kontrol Environment,*Transactions on Graphics* 5(4), October 1986, pp. 318-344.

ACKNOWLEDGEMENTS

The intellectual environment for this work was provided by the Graphics and User Interface Research Group at GWU, while financial support was provided by the National Science Foundation (Grant DMC-8420529), and the Department of EE&CS Industrial Liaison Program.

Reflections on. . .

A Knowledge-Based User Interface Management System

James Foley

Models—that is, abstract representations—of user interfaces have much potential. With this paper, we endeavored to describe one such model. Subsequent papers (referenced in the following) further refine the model, develop interactive tools for acquiring the model, support runtime graphical and textual help, provide GOMS analysis of an interface based on the model, and provide automated design and automatic runtime execution. Just as we were influenced by prior research work in this area, subsequent work has sometimes been influenced by these papers. At least one popular runtime help system shares many features with Sukaviriya's work.

The successes seen in data-oriented systems—database management systems, web publication systems—suggest that the basic directions are reasonable. The metadescriptions of CORBA provide a partial model and considerable infrastructure that could serve to support UIDE-style services. More progress is likely, with further successes probably to come in restricted application domains before we see more general solutions. Overall, I conclude that good progress was made but that we need more work to define a sufficiently robust user interface model and to create widely useful and usable design-time and runtime software environments for creating general-purpose user interfaces from abstract models.

REFERENCES

Byrne, M.; Wood, S.; Sukaviriya, P.; Foley, J.; and Kieras, D. 1994. Automating Interface Evaluation. In *Proceedings CHI'94—SIGCHI 1994 Computer Human Interaction Conference*, 232–237.

deBaar, D.; Foley, J.; and Mullet, K. 1992. Coupling Application Design and User Interface Design. In *Proceedings CHI'92 Computer Human Interaction Conference*, 259–266.

Foley, J.; Kim, W.; Kovacevic, S.; and Murray, K. 1989. The User Interface Design Environment—A Computer Aided Software Engineering Tool for the User-Computer Interface. *IEEE Software, Special Issue on User Interface Software* 6(1): 25–32.

Foley, J., and Sukaviriya, P. 1995. History, Results, and Bibliography of the User Interface Design Environment (UIDE), an Early Model-Based System for User Interface Design and Implementation. In Paterno, F. (ed.), *Interactive Systems: Design, Specification, and Verification*, Chapter 1, 3–10. Berlin: Springer.

Frank, M., and Foley, J. 1994. A Pure Reasoning Engine for Programming by Demonstration. In *Proceedings of UIST'94, ACM Symposium on User Interface Software and Technology*, 95–101.

Gieskens, D., and Foley, J. 1992. Controlling User Interface Objects through Pre- and Postconditions. In *Proceedings ACM CHI'92 Computer Human Interaction Conference*, 189–194.

Kim, W., and Foley, J. 1993. Providing High-Level Control and Expert Assistance in User Interface Presentation Design. In *Proceedings ACM INTERCHI 1993*, 430–437.

Sukaviriya, P., 1988. Dynamic Construction of Animated Help from Application Context. In *Proceedings ACM UIST '88 Conference*, 190–203.

Sukaviriya, P., and Foley, J. 1990. Coupling a UI Framework with Automatic Generation of Context-Sensitive Animated Help. In *Proceedings SIGGRAPH 1990 Symposium on User Interface Software and Technology (UIST '90)*, 152–166.

Sukaviriya, P.; Foley, J.; and Griffith, T. 1993. A Second Generation User Interface Design Environment: The Model and the Runtime Architecture. In *Proceedings ACM INTERCHI 1993*, 375–382.

ITS: A Tool for Rapidly Developing Interactive Applications

CHARLES WIECHA, WILLIAM BENNETT, STEPHEN BOIES, JOHN GOULD, and SHARON GREENE
IBM T.J. Watson Research Center

The ITS architecture separates applications into four layers. The action layer implements back-end application functions. The dialog layer defines the content of the user interface, independent of its style. Content specifies the objects included in each frame of the interface, the flow of control among frames, and what actions are associated with each object. The style rule layer defines the presentation and behavior of a family of interaction techniques. Finally, the style program layer implements primitive toolkit objects that are composed by the rule layer into complete interaction techniques. This paper describes the architecture in detail, compares it with previous User Interface Management Systems and toolkits, and describes how ITS is being used to implement the visitor information system for EXPO '92.

Categories and Subject Descriptors. D.2.2 [**Software Engineering**]: Tools and Techniques—*software libraries, user interfaces*; H.1.2 [**Models and Principles**]: User/Machine Systems—*human factors*; H.4 [**Information Systems Applications**]: General; I.3.6 [**Computer Graphics**]: Methodology and Techniques—*device independence, ergonomics, interaction techniques, languages*; K.6.1 [**Management of Computing and Information Systems**]: Project and People Management—*systems analysis and design, systems development*; K.6.3 [**Management of Computing and Information Systems**]: Software Management—*software development, software maintenance.*

General Terms: Design, Human Factors, Languages, Management, Standardization

Additional Key Words and Phrases: Management systems, user interface

1. INTRODUCTION

Application developers today face a problem of great complexity. Because of the diversity of users and of their equipment, applications must run in many different configurations. They must support displays of varying size, resolution, and color depth. Different types of input devices are required, from keyboards to touch screens. Applications must run in different countries and be able to reformat messages in varying lengths in each language. Messages should be available in large font sizes for vision-impaired users. Interface style should be consistent with other applications running on similar hardware. Style should at the same time conform to guidelines being developed by many organizations for presentation and interaction behaviors.

Historically, two types of layered architectures have been developed in attempts to provide the required flexibility in applications: User Interface Management Systems (UIMS) and toolkits. UIMS separate the application from its interface. Back-end computations are separated from dialog control and style. Style, however, is often treated in a single interface layer. Toolkits separate style from the application. Dialog control remains in the back end while the implementation of interaction techniques is hidden in a code library.

ITS is a four-layer architecture with separate tools for back-end computation, dialog control, definition of interface style, and implementation of graphic primitives used in the style. We begin by reviewing previous work done in UIMS and toolkits. Then we show how the layers of the ITS architecture combine the benefits of both UIMS and toolkits. After describing each layer of the architecture we show how ITS is being used to implement the visitor information system for EXPO '92 in Seville.

2. RELATED WORK

2.1 User Interface Management Systems

User Interface Management Systems, by analogy to Data Base Management Systems, divide applications into two layers. An application layer implements the underlying computations, while an interface layer implements the details of interface presentation and interaction. According to the traditional Seeheim [18] architecture, the interface layer defines the connection to the application, dialog flow of control, and presentation style. The application layer is structured as a set of callback routines executed in response to user actions or external interrupts.

The goals of separating the application from its interface are well documented [9, 10], and include reusing a given application in multiple interfaces, consistency among a family of applications that run using a common interface, and independent tools for application and interface developers. We believe previous UIMS have had limited success in meeting these goals because of two problems: They have not sufficiently decomposed the interface layer, and they have provided inadequate tools for interface designers.

The Seeheim model calls for separate dialog control and presentation components in the interface layer. Much of the previous work on UIMS has focused on the dialog component. Less attention has been paid to presentation. Previous systems sometimes represented presentation and dialog in a single layer. Serpent [20], for example, allows for control over style by composing primitive graphic objects into compound interaction techniques. However, this composition is specified together with dialog control flow.

In other systems, work has only recently begun to refine the presentation layer. One example is UIDE [6]. UIDE refines dialog into several layers for application data objects, commands, and control. Recent work focuses on new layers for intelligent control over presentation style [7]. The UofA* UIMS [22] separates dialog control from interface style. Interface style is generated automatically.

Portions of this paper have previously appeared in the proceedings of the 1989 and 1990 ACM Symposia on User Interface Software and Technology.
Authors' address: IBM T.J. Watson Research Center, P.O. Box 704, Yorktown Heights, NY 10598. email: wiecha@ibm.com

The rules that control style, however, are not exposed in a layer of their own. Rather, the interface designer tunes the interface once it has been automatically generated.

For those systems that do allow designer control over style, two approaches have been taken: manual editing with WYSIWYG or constraint-based editors, and automatic generation using executable style rules. An early example of the editing approach is the WYSIWYG form editor in Cousin [10]. Using such a tool, a designer may position command buttons or menu items and link them to application actions by direct manipulation.

Early editors supported only static screen designs. They specified *what* objects should appear and unconditionally *where* they should be located. These editors are inadequate for developing applications that must meet criteria of portability across hardware, end-user language, and type of user. An application that runs even in just two languages such as English and Spanish has different layouts driven by the translation of its messages. If it must run on displays of different resolutions or under a window system with resizable windows, its layout must change even more dramatically.

Work on interface workbenches has begun to respond to these challenges. More recent systems [3, 11] are based on layout constraints. Constraints describe *how* to reflow objects when window size or other variables change. However, constraints still do not capture *when* and *why* objects should appear, that is, the specifications in a style guide or the designer's knowledge that led to the given layout. Such knowledge is required if each screen is not to be designed individually or if the design is to be altered automatically under changing conditions.

Examples of systems that automatically generate interfaces include APEX [5], APT [15], Jade [25], and ITS [2, 26]. These systems all have the goal of encoding interface style in a set of executable rules. One dimension that helps distinguish among them is the intended role of their rules relative to an interface designer using the system. We can distinguish between design formulation and execution. Formulation involves making decisions such as what gridding to use in screen layout or what color values are appropriate for representing concepts such as errors, values, or prompts. Execution involves being able to apply these decisions automatically by executing style rules. APEX, for example, stresses the formulations of style. It consists of metarules for constructing style. In contrast, a graphic artist or human factors engineer formulates the design in ITS. Style rules are the language for representing and executing that design. The usability of the style language for designers is therefore of much greater concern in ITS than in previous work.

2.2 Toolkits

Toolkits differ from UIMS in the architectural separation that they make between application and interface. Toolkits are code libraries of common interface components such as standard windows, dialog boxes, menus, and dials. Applications developed using toolkits do not separate code for user interaction from the rest of the application. As in conventional applications, toolkit applications control internally the selection of interaction techniques and the sequencing of the user's dialog with them. To use a menu rather than a text entry field, for example, the programmer must change application code. To allow the user to interact nonmodally with a set of menus rather than step sequentially through them also requires changes to application code. In most UIMS both the selection and control of interaction techniques are external to the application.

Tookits do remove the composition and implementation of interaction techniques from applications. Thus a window may be composed of a hierarchy of objects including title bar, resize icon, and scrollbar. To the application programmer the window is created and manipulated as a single object. The implementation of each of these objects is also hidden in code reused from the toolkit. Thus the useful abstraction that toolkits offer application programmers is in the implementation of interaction techniques, not in their selection or design.

Historically, toolkits evolved out of the window system community in a variety of environments. The best known examples are MacApp [19] and the several X toolkits, Xtk [27], Atk [17], and Interviews [14]. Some of these toolkits gained quick commercial success because of their reduction of the complexity of programming interfaces.

The second factor driving their success is the growing interest in interface consistency and standards. By hiding the composition of interaction techniques from application programmers, toolkits control the implementation of interface style. An application that requests a window will by default get the toolkit standard definition of that window automatically.

Toolkits have two major problems in supporting the growing interest in consistency and standards. First, new interaction techniques can usually be composed only by programming. To create an analog clock object, for example, one must write a new toolkit object that instantiates, sizes, and positions a set of more primitive objects for clock hands and numbers. Nonprogramming graphic artists and human factors engineers therefore still lack appropriate tools to create styles themselves.

Toolkits are also poor tools for supporting consistency since they do not capture the rules governing when to use each interaction technique. These rules, an essential part of style, are contained only in hardcopy style guides. Such guides have now been published for a variety of styles, including the MacIntosh [1], Open Look [23], OSF/Motif [16], and Common User Access [12].

Hardcopy style guidelines are specifications for the presentation and interaction behavior of user interfaces. They may include general design philosophy, such as "adopt an object-action style" or "keep the user in control of the application at all times." Guidelines may also include more specific rules for implementing the interface, such as "the first item in a pull-down bar must appear below and one character to the right of the action bar item that leads to it." Based on informal observations of experience at IBM and elsewhere, guidelines are difficult to interpret by programmers and omit important details necessary for the complete definition of a style.

3. THE ITS ARCHITECTURE

3.1 Overview

The ITS architecture has four layers as shown in Figure 1. Actions read and write data values without concern for dialog control (when or in what sequence they will be called). They do not change depending on whether, or how many,

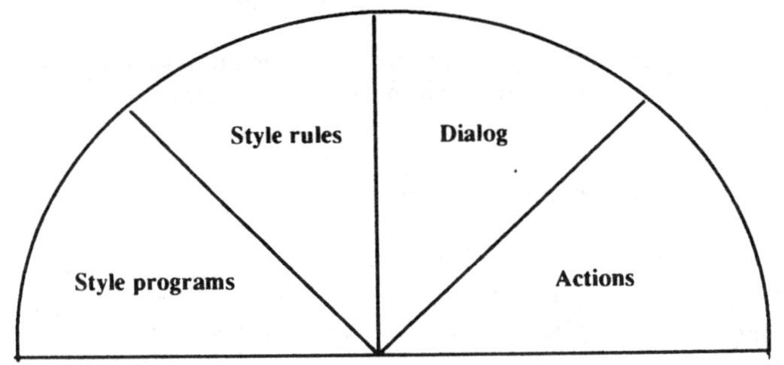

Fig. 1. Architecture of ITS applications.

views are attached to the data values they compute. The style of those views may change independently as well, for example, from tables to graphs. Actions are written in C.

Dialog is specified in the next layer of the system. Dialog includes the content of logical *frames* and the control flow among them. Separating dialog from actions allows actions to be reused in different applications. An airline reservation system intended for public access, for example, might not include some functions that are available to reservations agents. The dialog written for the reservations agent would have *frames* for those additional functions and the control flow necessary to access them. Two versions of the application can be created by writing different dialogs without having to change the actions themselves.

So far the application is not committed to a style, screen layout, language, or window system. The rule layer composes style programs into interaction techniques for each object in the dialog. An example of one type of style decision is whether to represent a *choice* the user must make as a radio button menu or action bar. These decisions are made automatically by a set of executable style rules. Style rules are written, and are open to modification, by interface designers. Style can be changed at any time by the appropriate selection of the rule base to be used in a given application.

Style rules are executed at compile time. Run-time changes in the dialog are managed by the style program layer. Example style programs include routines for text formatting, tree layout, row and column table layout, circular menus, raster images, scalable border decorations, and selectable hot spots on maps or images. Style programs can be added to the toolkit as required.

Style programs commit the application to screen layout, including the size and line wrapping of individual items. Layout is initially decided as each frame is drawn at run-time. Layout can later change when, for example, the user resizes a window.

3.2 Combining UIMS and Toolkit Layering

The split between actions and dialog in Figure 1 corresponds to the familiar separation between the application and its interface in previous UIMS. The remaining three layers further divide the interface into style-independent dialog

```
:frame id=main
  :choice purpose=overview, message="Select an item to"
    :ci message="View flights for today", activate=check_today
    :ci message="View future flights", activate=check_by_date
    :ci message="Make a reservation", activate=reserve
  :echoice
:eframe
```

Fig. 2. Dialog for opening frame of example airline reservations kiosk.

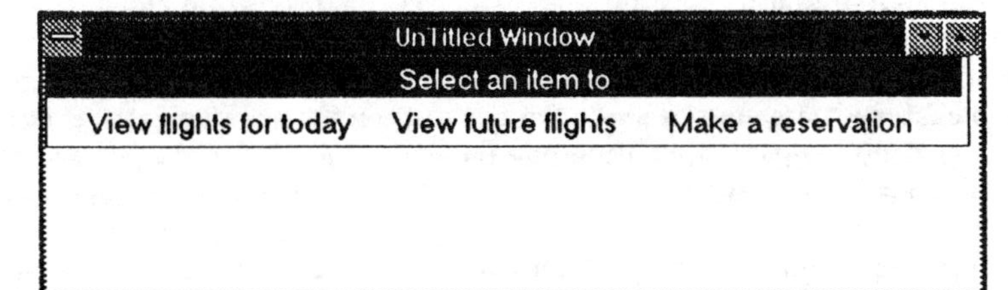

Fig. 3. Opening frame of the airlines reservation example shown in one possible style.

control, definition of style, and implementation of the toolkit objects used in creating styles. To understand the benefits of this layering consider a simple example, which might appear in an airlines reservation kiosk. Figure 2 shows the opening *frame* of dialog for the kiosk. The *frame* appears in one style as shown in Figure 3. *Choice* and *choice item* (*ci*) statements are keywords in the dialog language. *Messages* provide descriptive text that can be used variously as titles, prompts, or defaults under control of style rules. The dialog branches to the *frame* named by the *activate* attribute when the user *executes* an item.

To appear as shown in Figure 3, one or more style rules must fire and transform the *choice* into the tree shown in Figure 4. The rules introduce additional nodes for components of the menu not coded in the dialog. The style rules add a *title* and an object that arranges children horizontally (in this case the choice items). Style rules also decorate each node with attributes controlling presentation (such as color, font, margins, horizontal and vertical layout) and interaction behavior.

Splitting the interface into separate layers for style-independent dialog, rule base, and toolkit has three benefits. First, the dialog remains independent of style. Dialog can be mapped into any style simply by firing the appropriate rule. Second, interface designers now control style rather than application programmers. Application designers build dialogs only from style-independent objects such as *choice*. The rule layer represents the selection criteria for all interaction techniques. As we have seen, this knowledge is not captured in executable form in toolkit applications, only in hardcopy style guides.

The third consequence of the ITS architecture is that new interaction techniques can be composed by style rules from existing toolkit objects. In conventional toolkits, new interaction techniques are also composed from existing objects, but usually by programming. The example menu here was constructed

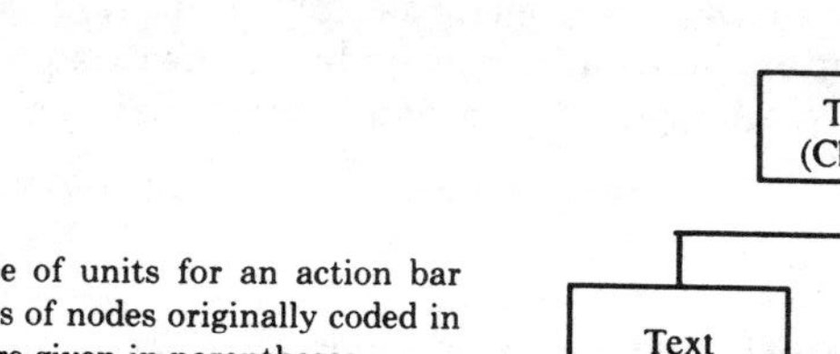
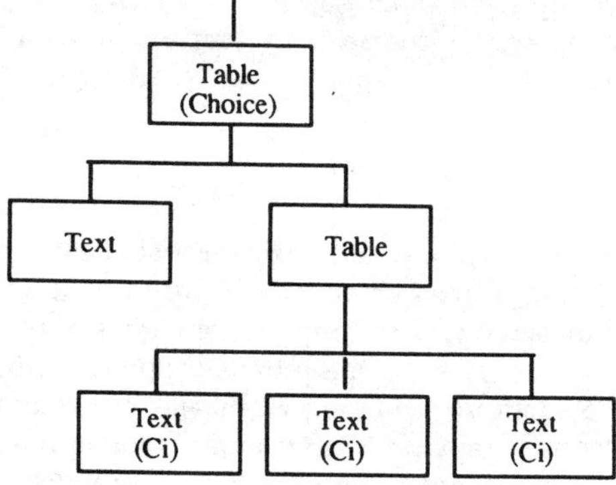

Fig. 4. Tree of units for an action bar menu. Types of nodes originally coded in the dialog are given in parentheses.

from only three toolkit objects: text, raster icons, and tabular layout. The style decisions on how to compose them into the final menu are made entirely by rules.

Since the menu is created by rules, a "menu" object is never added to the toolkit. The menu exists only as the coordinated behavior of the primitive objects. Since the toolkit need contain only primitive objects, programmers themselves have less need to implement new objects as style changes. As a result, interface designers enjoy control over style independent both of application and of toolkit programmers.

New objects are added to the toolkit whenever an interaction technique cannot be built simply by composing existing objects. Of course, these new objects are then available for reuse in composing other interaction techniques that may wish to build upon them.

3.3 Usability of Design Tools by Nonprogrammers

If application and style designers are to be truely independent from programmers, their dialog and rule languages must be highly usable. A financial analyst should be able to create a tax application, or an airline route planner a crew-scheduling application, with minimal application or style programming support. We want to give application and style experts executable tools to engage them as first class participants in application design. Currently their role is often restricted to providing input to systems analysts or programmers implementing widgets in a toolkit. Without appropriate software tools, admonitions toward user-driven design will remain only that.

Each layer in the ITS architecture corresponds to one of four roles in application development: application programmer, application expert, style expert, and style programmer. Of course, these roles may be played by one or several people as appropriate to the particular application.

An application expert is familiar with some problem domain, such as the airline industry, and wants to implement an application in that domain. The application expert typically is neither trained in programming, nor part of an information systems department. Traditionally the application expert interacts with a systems analyst to produce a design specification. Later, the specification is implemented by application programmers. Application designs produced by the analyst are not executable, but usually are represented as natural language or pseudocode algorithms. These incomplete specifications create opportunities for costly design errors. In ITS the application expert is the dialog author.

The style expert has had perhaps the poorest tool support in traditional application development. A style expert may be a graphic artist or human factors engineer. Style experts in the past have worked by drafting design guidelines or evaluating prototypes. They have had no separable work product, such as an executable style definition. Since they have had to influence designs indirectly through software developers, they have had difficulty having significant impacts. Rules give them direct control over style in ITS.

4. THE ACTION LAYER

A dialog depends on actions to implement the semantics of application functions. Actions are separated from dialog to create a library of reusable functions, to reduce the complexity of the dialog itself, and to allow changes in back-end computations independent of the interface. To communicate, the dialog and actions must share both data and control.

4.1 Data Sharing between Actions and Interface

Actions read values from data tables and return results to the same or other fields in tables. All communication between the application and interface occurs by passing values stored in data tables (see Figure 5). The collection of all data tables active in an application is called the data pool.

A particular instance of a data table is stored only once in the data pool. As in the Andrew Toolkit or Smalltalk Model-View-Controllers [13], any number of dialog objects may refer to a data table. Thus the same data may be shown in both tabular and graphical form if it is viewed simultaneously by two dialog objects. Whenever a value is changed by an action or by the user, all dialog objects representing it will be notified automatically. Each object then updates the display in whatever way is appropriate. The actions themselves have no knowledge of the number or type of dialog objects viewing the tables they manipulate in the data pool.

The update mechanism that sends style program messages about changed values is a hybrid of program-initiated and automatic notification [24]. Actions take the initiative in setting a bit in the data pool to indicate they have changed a field. This change flag is then propagated to style programs automatically by the dialog manager. Further, only those views of the changed field that are currently visible on the screen receive update notices. Others redraw only when they become visible.

4.2 Calling Actions

Control lies with the dialog manager until a user event triggers a call to an action. These events include *frame initialization* and *termination, selection, keyboard entry,* and *execution.* When called, the action is passed the event type and current dialog object. The events and parameters define the ITS architecture for actions. An action must be able to respond to one or more events. Otherwise actions are

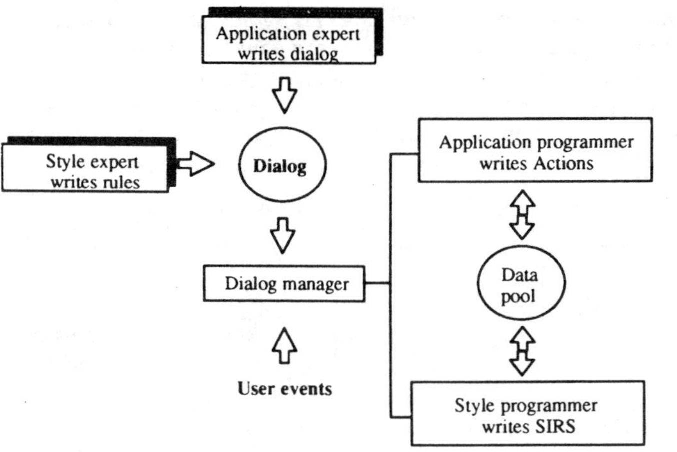

Fig. 5. The dialog manager calls actions in response to user events. Actions read and write values in the data pool. Change flags in the data pool trigger update notices to all style programs currently displaying the changed values.

conventional C library functions. In the OS/2 version of ITS they are typically stored in dynamically linked libraries and demand loaded.

This "external" model of control [10] can be interrupted asynchronously by an action that independently notices an error or other condition requiring user action. The action causes an interrupt by marking an arbitrary field in the data pool as changed. The resulting update notices may cause the dialog manager to branch to an error frame or to call other actions to correct the error.

5. THE DIALOG LAYER

The application expert in ITS is responsible for defining the *content* of the interface in the dialog layer. *Content* consists of two parts: tables that describe the data to be stored in the data pool and frames that define the application dialog itself.

5.1 Data Tables

Application actions receive input from the data pool and write output back to the data pool. ITS organizes these values using two data structures: *forms* and *lists*. A single set of *fields* is called a *form*; a set of *forms* is called a *list*. Both structures can be drawn, of course, in any number of styles not necessarily similar to physical forms and lists.

The application expert defines the structure of the data pool by writing table definitions. Tables are templates for the *fields* in each *list* and *form*. One or more instances of a table can be created in the pool under dialog control. Each instance is called a *generation* of the data object. Multiple *generations* are particularly useful when *frames* are called recursively and need private data spaces.

```
:form table=flight_info
  :fi field=destination, rangename=cities, size=20
  :fi field=departure_time, size=10
  :fi field=departure_date, size=20
  :fi field=airline, rangename=airlines, size=20
  :fi field=number_stops, size=5
:eform

:list listname=flights, numrecords=10
  :li field=destination, rangename=cities, size=20
  :li field=departure_time, size=10
  :li field=departure_date, size=20
  :li field=airline, rangename=airlines, size=20
  :li field=number_stops, size=5
:elist
```

Fig. 6. Data definition file. A form is a named collection of fields. A list is an array of forms with "numrecords" elements.

Tables for the airlines reservation example are shown in Figure 6. Each *field* has a name and an optional set of descriptive attributes. The *datatype* may be used by style rules in selecting appropriate interaction techniques for the *field*. The *size* attribute can be used in estimating the screen space required for the *field*. A *message* can be used as a title or prompt if no *message* is given in the dialog file.

Tables describe the data in a family of applications. Attributes given in the tables are inherited by a dialog when it refers to each *field*. Thus a family of dialogs may be built using the same table definitions and reuse attributes coded only once in the table.

5.2 Dialog

The dialog layer defines the content of a set of *frames* and the flow of control among them. Traditionally, application programs have fully controlled the sequencing of user dialog. Input and output statements were intermixed with those performing application computations. The application decided when and in what order interaction would take place. Nearly all UIMS remove control of dialog sequencing from the application and place it instead either in a central dialog manager [10] or in a distributed set of interaction objects that jointly regulate user interactions [21].

As we saw in Figure 2, control branches to the frame named by the *activate* attribute when the user executes a dialog statement. *Activated* frames are put on a run-time stack and popped from the stack as the user returns from them. Since the user can follow multiple dialog paths simultaneously, perhaps by interacting in different windows in parallel, the stack is really a tree of *frame* activations.

The *attachto* attribute controls where a *frame* is added to the execution stack. According to its intended lifetime in the dialog a *frame* may be attached near the root or near the leaves of the tree. For example, *frames* that are attached at the root of the stack exist until the user explicitly terminates them or leaves the application. *Frames* that are attached to lower branches of the stack terminate when any *frame* above them terminates. Since generations of *forms* and *lists* in the data pool are also linked to nodes in the stack, a *frame* may be bound to different data depending on where it appears in the stack.

Name	Description
Session	Indicates the start of a tag file or complete tag set.
Frame	Indicates the start of a group of conceptually related dialog blocks.
List	Indicates the start of a set of related items, e.g., a set of employees in an organization.
Li	List item. Specifies a field that should be included in a list built by an enclosing list tag.
Form	The start of a form, e.g., a related collection of fields.
Fi	Form item. Names a field to be included in a form built by an enclosing form tag.
Choice	Indicates the start of a set of alternatives to be chosen by the user.
Ci	Choice item. Specifies one of the choice items in the list enclosed by a Choice tag.
Info	Information block. A static panel of help information.
Ii	Information item. An item in a help panel.

Fig. 7. Objects used to specify dialog content.

Name	Values	Definition
Action	⟨action name⟩	Name of the action to call on frame entry, item selection, or execution.
Activate	⟨frame id⟩	Transfers control to frame "id" when an item is selected.
Purpose	Elaboration Example Feedback Group Help Instructional Overview Useraction Warning	Specifies the intention of the application expert in creating the frame. Can be used by style to set colors, titles, or controls appropriately.
Structure	Continuum Scale Order Set Points Label Disjoint	Description of the underlying nature of the data contained in the field. Used to choose appropriate interaction techniques.
UserCan	Delete Filter Hide Modify Search Select Show Sort	Specifies the actions the user can perform on the specified field.

Fig. 8. Selected dialog attributes.

Next, the application expert defines the content of each *frame* in the dialog. To simplify the application expert's job, we chose a small fixed set of dialog objects. These objects are listed in Figure 7. Each statement may include a number of attributes, some of which are listed in Figure 8. Attributes are used to specify the *actions* executed, *values* set, and *messages* displayed by each dialog object.

```
:frame id=check_today, action=getlist,
        listname=flights, value=flights.dta
  :list listname=flights, number=5
    :li field=destination, message="To"
    :li field=departure_time, message="Departure"
    :li field=airline, message="Carrier"
    :li field=number_stops, message="Stops"
  :elist
  :frame message="To search for selected flights"
    form table=flight_info
      :fi field=destination, message="Enter destination city"
    :eform
    :choice purpose=useraction
      :ci message="Ok", action=select_flights,
          table=flight_info, listname=flights
    :echoice
  :eframe
:eframe
```

Fig. 9. Frame for viewing and selecting flights in example airline reservation kiosk.

UnTitled Window
Select an item to
View flights for today View future flights Make a reservation

To	Departure	Carrier	Stops
New York	10:00	USAir	2
Atlanta	12:25	Delta	0
Chicago	09:15	American	1
Portland	10:20	Continental	0
Boston	18:30	TWA	1

To search for selected flights
Enter destination city
Ok

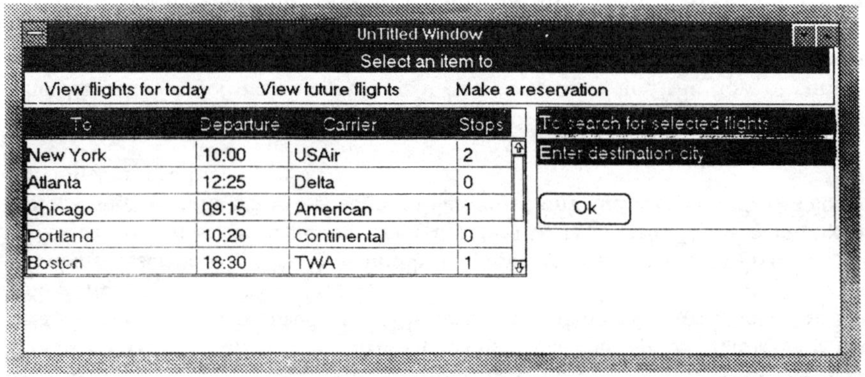

Fig. 10. Flight list and controls for selecting particular flights in the example airline reservation kiosk.

Figure 9 shows how these objects have been used to display a list of flights in the airline reservation example. The *frame* is shown in one possible style in Figure 10.

The *frame* contains a *list* showing four of the five *fields* defined for "flights" in the data definition file. Each *field* is coded on a list item (*li*) statement. The list items define the *fields* displayed in each *record* of the list. Five *records* will be presented to the user at a time. *Lists* and *forms* defined in the dialog file are views onto data values themselves, which are stored in the data pool. All views of "flights" will be synchronized by update messages from the dialog manager whenever any of them modify the data pool.

The *subframe* in Figure 9 groups a *form* and *choice* into a control for selecting particular flights. "Select_flights" will be called when the user *executes* "Ok." The action uses all nonnull fields of the table "flight_info" as search keys into the "flights" list. It replaces "flights" with the set of *records* satisfying the search. Dialog manager update messages then cause all views of the list to be redrawn.

6. THE RULE LAYER

What is style? One definition of style is a coordinated set of decisions on the appearance and behavior of the interaction techniques used in a family of applications. Three dimensions of this definition are important: (1) it refers to both the output and the input characteristics of interaction techniques, (2) it considers both style in the small (individual techniques) and in the large (a coordinated set of decisions), and (3) it applies to more than one application.

For a family of applications, both consistency and identity of style are important. Consistency means that similar functions in an interface, such as choosing a single item from a list of mutually exclusive options, are represented and interact with the user similarly wherever found in an interface. Consistency does not mean that such a function is identical throughout the interface, just that where appropriate the technique is similar and where differences exist, those differences have meaning.

Consider Grudin's example of a potentially destructive menu operation [8]. In his example, when a menu appears it defaults to the last item executed by the user. This helps the user repeat nondestructive operations such as copy or select. If, however, the last item executed was delete, then the menu defaults to another item. Grudin argues that this is an example of desirable, though inconsistent, behavior. We believe, rather, that this is consistent behavior. Consistency can mean a hierarchy of default rules and subrules for special cases. In our view, users will in fact perceive the consistency in behavior of dangerous operations even if that behavior differs from the default rule.

ITS represents the range of general to special cases as such a hierarchy of rules. In ITS, the different types of *choices* are represented with one or more rules that describe how they are similar, together with subrules that give the particular characteristics of each one of them.

What we call identity is perhaps as important as consistency. Identity is the customer's requirement of being able to create styles that users associate with their applications. Interface style is now an area of competitive advantage in itself. The identity of excellent styles is becoming strategically important to the success of our customers.

ITS style rules support each of these requirements. They control both presentation and interaction in style. They support style in the large by representing not just individual interaction techniques but the *conditions* under which each of them should be used. And they are an open architecture that allows customers to modify standard styles and create entirely new styles of their own.

6.1 The Rule Mechanism

Each rule has a *conditions* part and a *results* part. The *conditions* determine when a rule will be executed. *Conditions* may test the type of dialog statement (e.g., *choice, list, form*). Any dialog attribute can also be tested so that, for example, a rule will fire only for those *choices* that have *kind* = *1_and_only_1*. Other *conditions* may test for particular numbers or kinds of children. Thus a rule for

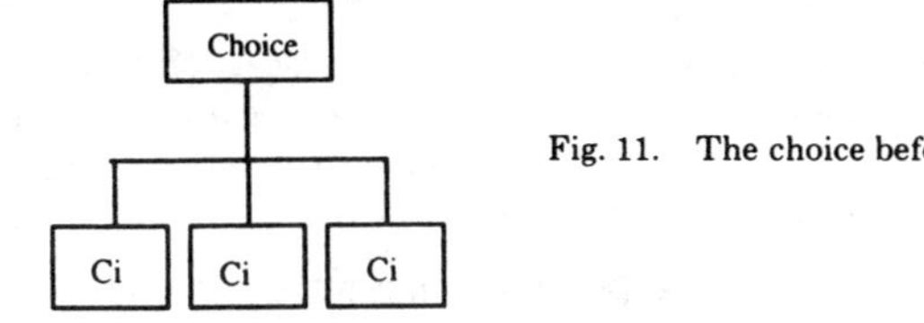

Fig. 11. The choice before style matching.

forms may fire only when a *form* has fewer than ten *fields*. Another rule that uses less screen space might fire when there are more than ten *fields*.

All of these *conditions* can be applied to a dialog object's children. A rule for *frames* that contain images can test for the presence of an image and can refer to the child that matches that test in the *results* part of the rule. That child might be positioned specially, or it might be assigned attributes to draw or interact with it differently than the other children.

All of a rule's tests must succeed for the rule to be considered for execution. Thus the current rule language supports only conjunctive *conditions*. Our experience to date does not suggest the need for more sophisticated conditionality including both conjunctive and disjunctive *conditions* within a single rule. Cases where the same *results* should occur for two different *conditions* can be handled by two rules with similar *results*. The language does support a null *condition* to catch all cases not otherwise coded. Thus if the rule base handles only the *1_and_only_1 kind* of *choice*, all others can be matched by a single rule with null *conditions*.

Five types of *result* statements can be nested with a rule:

—*Units*: to create and modify the dialog structure,
—*Set or Conditions*: to control the execution of nested rules,
—*Kids*: to collect or match on characteristics of the children of the dialog block being matched,
—*Attributes*: to set default values for style attributes, and
—*Content*: to generate dialog under style control.

6.2 Creating and Modifying Dialog Structure

Let us begin with structure. We have seen that the application expert codes a *choice* as shown in Figure 2. The set of allowed *choice items* are coded on separate *ci* statements. Before it has been matched by a rule, only the abstract *choice* exists as shown in Figure 11. The job of the style rule is now to refine this structure into one such as shown in Figure 12 by giving a template to control how each dialog node will be represented.

As style experts, assume we want all *choices* to be menus (rather than, say, entry fields). Structurally, a menu is simply a set of *choice items* arranged vertically or horizontally, perhaps under a *title*. Additional nodes are required beyond those shown in Figure 11 for the *title* and to group the *choice items* together.

Figure 13 shows a rule for creating simple menus. The *conditions* statement matches only on the type of dialog object, in this case all *choices*. The nested set

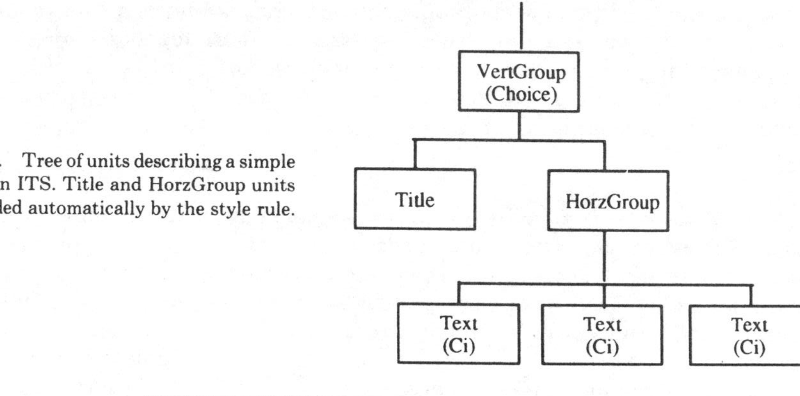

Fig. 12. Tree of units describing a simple menu in ITS. Title and HorzGroup units are added automatically by the style rule.

```
:conditions source=choice
    fire for all choices
  :unit type=VertGroup
    the block arranges the title vertically
    above the set of items
    :unit type=Title
    :eunit
    :unit type=HorzGroup
    the item is replicated for all children of
    the choice, i.e. all ci statements
      :unit type=Message, replicate=all
      :eunit
    :eunit
  :eunit

:econditions
```

Fig. 13. Style rule creating a simple menu with title.

of *units* describes the structure of the *choice* for this style. Thus the menu has a parent node that controls the layout of the *title* relative to the *choice items.* The child *unit* is *replicated* for all of the *ci* statements in Figure 11.

Unit structure is created by taking the rule as a template. Several *units* in the rule may derive from a given dialog object. For example, the single *choice* node in Figure 2 is redefined into a *vertgroup, title,* and *horzgroup unit* in Figure 13. Dialog attributes from the *choice* are assigned to all three *units* that derive from it. In this way style programs have ready access to all dialog attributes.

This is very helpful when the dialog node is bound to an object in the data pool. Then all *units* derived from it are bound to the same object. They are simply multiple views of the same data. Each *unit* will get update messages about changes to the data, but can decide to respond to them in very different ways.

Each parent *unit* handles the layout of its immediate children. Thus the *vertgroup unit* aligns the *title* above the set of *choice items,* and the nested *horzgroup* aligns the individual *items* horizontally. Vertical and horizontal directions themselves are defined by the *fillorder* attribute. *Fillorder* equals *colsfirst* in a *vertgroup* type and *rowsfirst* in a *horzgroup* type.

```
:conditions source=choice
    still match on all choices
  :unit type=VertGroup
    :unit type=Title
    :eunit
    pick the best one of the following subrules
    :set apply=best
    when only one choice item can be selected at a time
    (1_and_only_1), refine each item into separate dingbat
    icon and text for the radio buttons
    :conditions kind=1_and_only_1
      :unit type=VertGroup
        :unit type=HorzGroup, replicate=all
          :unit type=Dingbat
          :eunit
          :unit type=Message
          :eunit
        :eunit
      :eunit
    :econditions
    in the default case, each choice item is simply a text label
    as before
    :conditions
      :unit type=HorzGroup
        :unit type=Message, replicate=all
        :eunit
      :eunit
    :econditions
    :eset
  :eunit

:econditions
```

Fig. 14. Style rule creating a radio button menu or a simple menu, according to the kind attribute.

Now override this default rule to draw single-option choices as radio buttons. These *choices* should still have *titles,* but we now want the *items* to be stacked vertically. Each *choice item* should now include an *icon* for the button (called a *dingbat* by typesetters) and a *message.* Figure 14 shows the revised rule. The outer *conditions* statement still matches on all *choices.* The top *vertgroup* and *title units* are the same for both types of menu. *Choices* coded with *kind* equal to *1_and_only_1* are refined with separate *units* for the *icon* and *message.* Separate *units* are required since they will be decorated with different attributes. The *message* string, unlike the *icon,* redraws itself in reverse video when the user tracks into an *item.*

6.3 Matching on Characteristics of Children

In mapping from dialog to style, rules can change the order of children. The style expert may want to group all *items* together that *activate* other *frames.* Say, for instance, all *items* that transfer control to another *frame* should come first and have an urgent *background* color. The revised rule to do this is shown in Figure 15.

```
:conditions source=choice

    Name the set of kids that transfer control "go_kids".
    These are just the ci statements that have activate attrib-
    utes

  :kids name=go_kids, present=activate
  :unit type=VertGroup
    :unit type=Title
    :eunit
    :unit type=VertGroup

    each ci with an activate attribute is drawn as a text label
    with arrow icon to its right

      :unit type=HorzGroup, replicate=go_kids
        :unit type=Message
        :eunit
        :unit type=icon, shape=down_arrow
        :eunit
      :eunit

    other ci's are simply drawn as text items

      :unit type=Message, replicate=rest
      :eunit
    :eunit
  :eunit

:econditions
```

Fig. 15. Style rule reordering kids so that choice items that transfer control (i.e., have activate attributes) appear before others. In addition, they are drawn with an icon emphasizing that they are branches.

The *kids* statement collects groups of children that meet its *conditions*. In Figure 15 the rule again matches all *choices*. Any *choice items* that have *activate* attributes (*present=activate*) are included in the "go_kids" group. The name is simply an internal label used to refer to the set later in the rule.

Replicate names a set of children that should be refined using a given subtree of *units*. So, in Figure 15, the rule first *replicates* over the members of the "go_kids" group and then over the remaining children. *Rest* is a keyword that means all children not named in any group of *kids*. The *items* that transfer control are refined into three *units*: a *message*, an *icon* reminding the user that the *item* transfers control, and a parent horizontal group. Other *items* are drawn simply as *messages*.

6.4 Setting Default Values for Style Attributes

Style attributes control the appearance and behavior of *units*. Some of the attributes supported in the current system are listed in Table I. They control space and layout negotiations between parent and child *units*, presentation including font and colors, and interaction including the mapping between *physical* and *logical* events. Attributes are parameters to the style programs that render *units* on the screen. The style programs themselves are named on each *unit* by its *techid* attribute.

Table I. Selected Style Attributes Currently Supported in ITS

Name	Values	Definition
AnswerWidth	Children SelfCalc SelfFixed PopAdjust	Compute the width (depth) of this unit by summing the requests of the child units, by a nonstandard method, by using fixed estimates, or by combining the child requests and then adjusting them.
Layout	Count Space	How units should be fit into available space. By Count fits a given number of units, e.g., 3×4, into the space. By Space flows as many units as will fit into the available space, then wraps to the next vertical or horizontal free space.
TopMargin	⟨integer⟩	Number of screen units in top (bottom, left, or right) margin.
TechId	⟨program⟩	Name of the Style Program (P) that will draw this unit.
NomWidth	⟨integer⟩	Estimate of the Width (Depth) of this unit in screen units.

Attributes are assigned to *units* by labeling the *unit* with a *type*. Some of the style *types* we have used so far include *title*, *dingbat*, *message*, *horzgroup*, and *vertgroup*. Each *type* defines a set of attribute *values*. The set of attributes is the same for all *types*; only their *values* change among the *types*. Thus *prompt* and *title* may have a different font, horizontal justification, and color values. The *icon type* may be drawn with a raster style program, rather than the text formatter used by *prompt* and *title*. Justification and color attributes, however, can still be coded.

Style experts can create default attribute *values* and then override them later in subrules. The parent/child hierarchy of *units* defines the scope over which a *type's values* are defined. Most *types* are defined at the root of the dialog and are global. Those that are overridden at lower levels are changed only within the subtree where they are overridden.

Assume that several rules have refined the flight reservation frame in Figure 9 into the *unit* tree shown in Figure 16. Figure 17 shows how the *session* rule assigns defaults at the root node. Another rule has overridden the *font* for *title* below the *choice*. Note that the override occurs just for that individual *choice*. Other *choices* that may not have triggered the rule making this override will draw their *titles* as given in the root definition.

Two features of this design are significant. First, attributes inherit within each *type* independently of whether any *units* are actually assigned the *type*. Thus a style expert can write rules that define and override *title* attributes without concern for which interaction techniques may or may not actually use *title*. Attributes and *units* are defined separately.

Second, the *unit* hierarchy allows each parent to control *types* for its subtree. This can be done no matter how many levels exist between the *unit* that defines the *type* and the *unit* that uses it. For example, we may want the color of *titles* in a dialog box to be different from other *titles* on the screen. Pop-up dialog boxes, new windows, or areas of an existing window are all ways of representing *frames*. One of a set of alternative *frame* rules will be selected as the best match

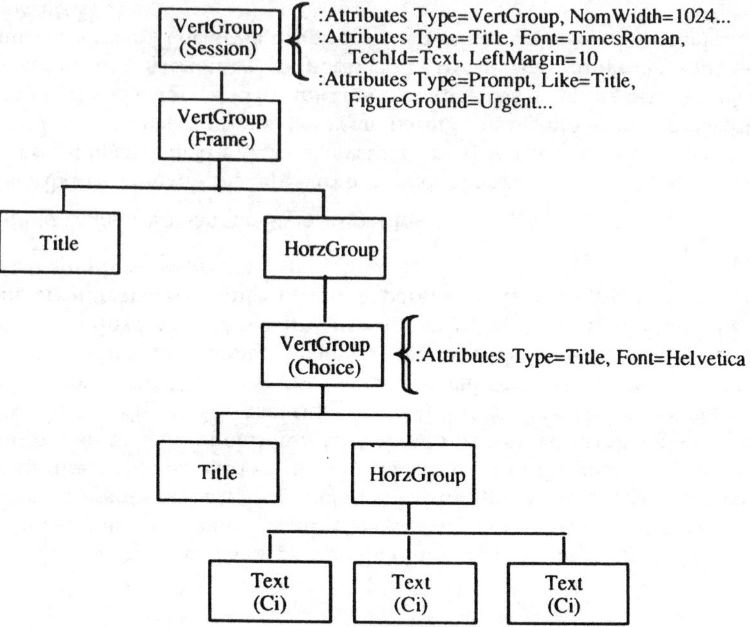

Fig. 16. The dialog tree after frame, nested subframe, and choice rules have fired. The font of titles has been overridden in this subframe.

```
:conditions source=session
    Start by defining default attributes for types used in this style. These
    defaults will be attached to the unit at the session, i.e. root, level.
    They will then inherit to lower units according to the type of each
    unit.
  :Attributes type=VertGroup, NomWidth=1024...
  :Attributes type=Title, Font=TimesRoman, TechId=text, LeftMargin=10, ...
  :Attributes type=Prompt, Like=Title, FigureGround=Urgent, ...
    Then define the unit structure for the session. We don't want titles
    here, so just create a single unit.
  :unit type=VertGroup
  :eunit
:econditions
```

Fig. 17. Any rule may assign default attributes. Those defaults are saved at the node that matches the rule: Defaults at the session level, as here, are global to the style.

for each *frame* statement in the dialog. This winning rule can override *title* colors set at higher levels of the dialog tree. The new color then is inherited by *titles* within the *frame*. Therefore, *titles* created by the same *choice* rule within different *frames* can take on different colors.

```
:conditions source=frame
  :unit type=VertGroup
      frames have titles above the set of frame contents
    :unit type=Title
    :eunit
    :unit type=HorzGroup
      Frame contents are arranged horizontally. The type isn't
      assigned here, but in other rules that match later on the spe-
      cific frame contents.
      :unit replicate=all
      :eunit
    :eunit
      each frame has Help and Quit buttons added automatically
      by the rule. The choice will be matched itself later as any
      other block.
    :content
      :choice purpose=useraction
        :ci message=Help, activate=AppHelp
        :ci message=Quit, action=shutdown
      :echoice
    :econtent
  :eunit
:econditions
```

Fig. 18. This rule creates Help and Quit buttons automatically in each frame.

6.5 Generating Dialog within Style

Finally, style rules can themselves generate dialog and delay committment to its style. A rule, for example, can add standard command buttons to each *frame* automatically. The rule in Figure 18 codes the same *choice* statements that could be used by an application expert to create Help and Quit buttons. Thus the *frame* rule does not have to say how they should appear, just that they should appear in each *frame*. The appropriate *choice* rule will fire later to create the button style. This technique has been used to generate "Yes" and "No" *choice items* for fields with Boolean data types. Rules have also automatically generated pull down menus for text entry *fields* where a fixed set of values is allowed for the *field*.

7. THE STYLE PROGRAM LAYER

7.1 Space Negotiations

Style programs, like actions, must respond to a standard set of messages from the dialog manager. The most important messages are sent to request screen space estimates, to paint to the screen, and to inform the style program when the user indicates *activation, selection,* or *execution*. The style expert can set attributes that control whether style programs receive each message or take the default response.

The problem in space negotiation is to request and then allocate screen space for each *unit* based on its requirements and the requirements of its children.

Space negotiation is a three-step process that balances performance with the need for high-quality layout. The first step is to determine the space requirements of each *unit*. The second, and optional, step is for the parent to adjust the space required for children. The third step assigns a specific location to each object that will be displayed.

Space requirements are determined by a depth first, left-to-right traversal of a *frame*. The first step occurs when moving downward. During this phase each *unit* is asked to respond with its own space requirements. Many *units* defer this question until their children have responded to it first. The second step of space allocation occurs during the upward search (looking for the next right-hand sibling) of each subtree. During this step each *unit* is asked to integrate and possibly adjust the space requirements of its children. An example would be a *unit* asking for enough space to give each of its children the same depth as that of the deepest child.

Space assignment is done by a second tree traversal. During this phase each *unit* receives its screen assignment, both location and size. This process is top down. From its allocation, each *unit* reserves what it requires and allocates the remaining space to its children. Each *unit* can, of course, have a different policy for allocating space.

7.2 Other Operations

Each of the above processes place their results only in documented attributes on the *unit* tree. This means that these results are publicly visible and hence are easily available for reuse. One such use is to be queried by children needing to make their own space or drawing decisions. For example, a text object that wants to set its font size relative to a parent can respond to a repaint message by setting its size as some increment on the size attributes in the parent block.

Mouse tracking or touch-paint location also benefits from standardized attribute definitions. The run-time manager can provide a default tree traversal for correlating mouse position with a displayed object. In ITS this default mapping is determined by the smallest display rectangle surrounding the mouse position. As such, mouse event mapping is similar to that in the X toolkit. However, alternative mappings are often required, as when a parent wants to redirect a mouse event to a child different than the one directly under the mouse (as in the Andrew toolkit). An attribute on each *unit* determines whether the *unit* wants to assume responsibility for pointer correlation within its borders. ITS thus combines a strong default method and the flexibility to override this method with alternative ones.

8. THE EXPO 92 VISITOR INFORMATION SYSTEM

To test the ITS application development tools, we are using them to build a visitor information system for the 1992 EXPO in Seville, Spain. ITS allows us to build this system iteratively as a series of progressively more complete prototypes. These prototypes are functioning applications and test each layer of ITS: actions, dialog, style rules, and style programs.

8.1 What Is the EXPO Visitor Information System?

The EXPO visitor information system will offer information and services to an estimated 20 million visitors from April through October, 1992. Information to be provided includes maps and directions for navigating around the two square kilometer site, up-to-the-minute schedules of events, and background information on countries and organizations participating in EXPO. In addition, the system will provide visitors with services beyond those traditionally found in information kiosks. These include person-to-person and group electronic messaging, automated restaurant reservations, public opinion polling, and locators for lost family members. Since we also believe the kiosk should be fun to use, it will provide a variety of standalone and networked games for use during offpeak hours.

8.2 What Are the Requirements for the EXPO Visitor Information System?

Developing a style for EXPO is a good test for ITS since both the application and the developers pose difficult challenges. The application must support several languages, including several dialects of Spanish, as well as English, French, and German. Most visitors will be extremely inexperienced computer users. Since we expect them to spend only a very few minutes at the information system, it must be operable with little or no training. To be visually attractive it must be of world-class graphic design quality and operate with multiple types of media: high-quality text, graphics, and images.

The developers, too, pose challenges the ITS tools must help meet. Our development team is distributed between two locations in Seville and New York. ITS must help integrate application functions developed in both locations. In addition, we maintain working prototypes in other locations for demonstration, including Madrid and visitor centers on the EXPO construction site. These prototypes must be attractive enough even in early versions to promote the desired image of a quality product in the works.

8.3 Dialog and Actions

The starting *frame* of the application is shown in Figure 19. Its appearance in the EXPO style is shown in Figure 20. The user can take an electronic walk through EXPO by selecting hotspots in maps and images at the left of the screen, take an opinion poll, draw a picture using a finger-painting program (Figure 21), send or receive electronic mail (Figure 22), or make a restaurant reservation.

In Figure 19, the "startexpo" and "stuff_caption" actions are called when the *frame* initially appears on the screen. "Startexpo" reads several data files to initialize the image network and opinion poll. "Stuff_caption," when called with the *frame initialize* message, sets up the caption of the current image in the image title area. Later, when "stuff_caption" is called with *select* messages, it replaces the caption with short titles describing each hotspot as they are selected on the image. Since no actions are coded on the messaging or opinion poll choice items, when *executed* they simply transfer control to the *frames* given by their *activate* attributes.

The image network panel is built from a *form* and two *lists* grouped together as a *subframe*. *Version = fit* is recognized by style rules to fit the *subframe* into

```
:frame id=basic_frame, level=a, action=startexpo, listname=nav_list,
      table=eachframe
  :choice message="Explore picture or", purpose=navigation, version=icon
    :ci message=Poll, value="opinion.bmp", activate=opinion_poll
    :ci message=Paint, value="paint.bmp", activate=finger_painting
    :ci message=Meals, value="meals.bmp", activate=reservations
    :ci message=Read,  value="read.bmp", activate=read_message
    :ci message=Send, value="send.bmp", activate=send_message
    :ci message=Vote, value="vote.bmp", activate=voting
  :echoice

  :frame version=fit, purpose=group
    :form version=almost
      :fi table=eachframe, field=ndx_title, purpose=overview
      :fi table=imagetext, field=label, purpose=feedback
    :eform

    :list listname=hotlist, datatype=image, number=11, table=eachframe,
      field=pic_file, message=the picture, action=stuff_caption
      :li field=index, action=newimage
    :elist

    :list listname=piclist,number=5, datatype=set_of_image
      :li field=small_pic_file,action=poptoimage
    :elist
  :eframe

  :frame purpose=navigation
    :choice structure=disjoint, purpose=useraction
      :ci message='Empezar en espanol', action=lang_and_size,value=spn
      :ci message="Let's Start in English", action=lang_and_size,value=eng
    :echoice
  :eframe
:eframe
```

Fig. 19. Dialog statements of the beginning EXPO frame as coded by the application expert. A choice block allows the user to select an EXPO service. Value attributes on choice items name the icon to be displayed with each choice. A form gives title and caption information for the image and its list of hotspots. A second list displays the route the user has traversed through the tree of images about EXPO.

the left-hand two-thirds of the screen and to be sure it appears there regardless of the order in which it is coded in the dialog statements. *Purpose = group* indicates to this style that all contents of the *subframe* are related, and hence they are drawn together on a gray background with no separating gaps or lines. *Structure = disjoint* is coded, in contrast, on the *choice* between Spanish and English. The EXPO style therefore separates these *choice items* visually on the screen.

Within the image *subframe*, the *form* contains two *form items* for the image title and caption. *Version* and *purpose* attributes are used here to guide style in choosing appropriate fonts, margins, and separating lines between the title and caption. The *list* with *datatype* = image contains the image and its set of hotspots. The image file name is found in the *field* "pic_file" in the *table* "eachframe." An image's hotspots are stored as *records* of the *list*. Each *record* contains *fields* for

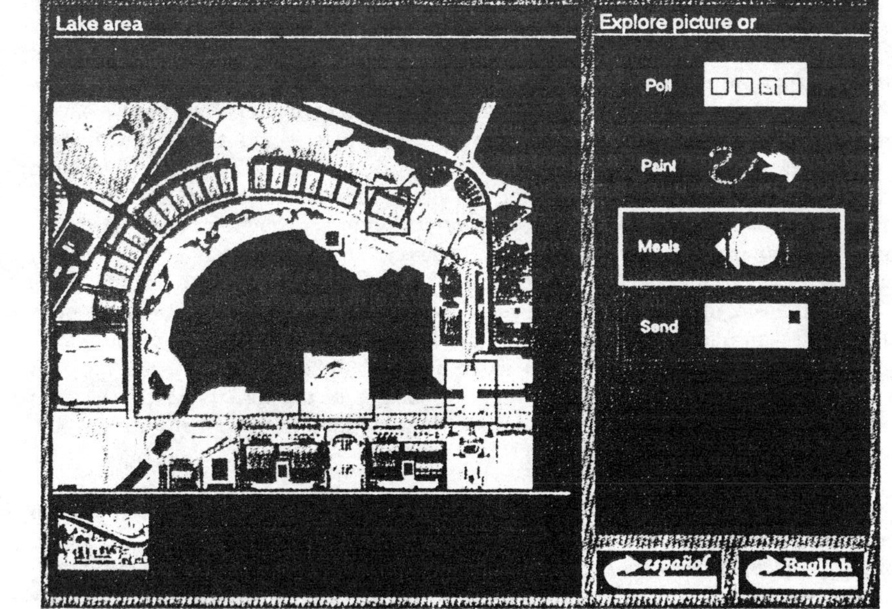

Fig. 20. Maps and images with selectable hotspots provide an electronic walk through EXPO.

the position and size of the hotspot. These *fields* are used by a style program to size and position the hotspot on the image.

To help users navigate, miniature pictures show the path of images taken from the root of the network. In Figure 19, the *list* with *datatype* = set_of_image stores this breadcrumb trail. This *list* is simply a view of the internal picture stack maintained by the "newimage" action. Each time "newimage" is called by *executing* a hotspot, it pushes a small picture file name onto the stack. "PopToImage," the action coded on *items* in the breadcrumb *list*, pops the stack to return directly to any image on the path to the root.

Note that all navigation through the image network is coded within a single *frame* in the dialog. No *activate* attributes transfer control outside that *frame* when users pick hotspots or pop the image stack. Rather, actions simply modify the contents of the data pool to point to new images and hotspots. Update messages propagated by the dialog manager to style programs cause repaints of only those parts of the screen that need to change to show the new image. All of the borders, title bars, and menu controls remain unchanged by these repaints. The effect minimizes disruption for the user.

8.4 Style Programs Needed to Implement EXPO

Eight different style programs are needed to control the screen in Figure 20. A text formatter draws titles, menus, command buttons, and explanatory text.

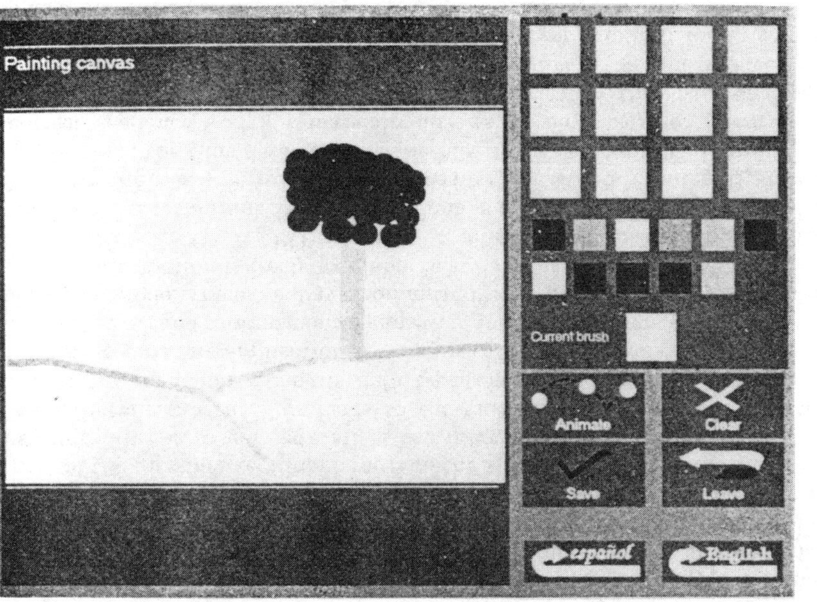

Fig. 21. Finger painting using a touch screen.

Pictures are displayed from true color images mapped offline to a 256-entry color table. Drop shadows and other decorative borders are computed from scalable bitmap definitions so they can wrap around units of any size. Selectable hotspots are computed from position data and superimposed over images. The same style program that highlights each hotspot is wrapped around the small images below the picture and around each selectable menu item. To cause all items to highlight when the user touches anywhere on the screen, a style program at the root of the screen's *unit* tree propagates finger down and up events to all interested *units* below it. Finally, rectangular layout is controlled by a style program using a gridded design [4]. In gridding, style experts specify the number of columns in a *frame*. *Units* within that *frame* are sized as multiples of the column width. A gridded *frame*, by having only a small number of *unit* sizes, typically looks more balanced than one with arbitrary sizes.

The text, gridded frame layout, picture, and drop shadow programs were reused from the toolkit. The programs for positioning hotspots, drawing their borders, and propagating touch events were added during the implementation of EXPO.

8.5 EXPO 92 Rules

The structure of the map *frame* is shown schematically in Figure 23. *Units* shown in bold correspond to the original content coded by the application expert in Figure 19. Other *units* are added automatically by style to control layout, to

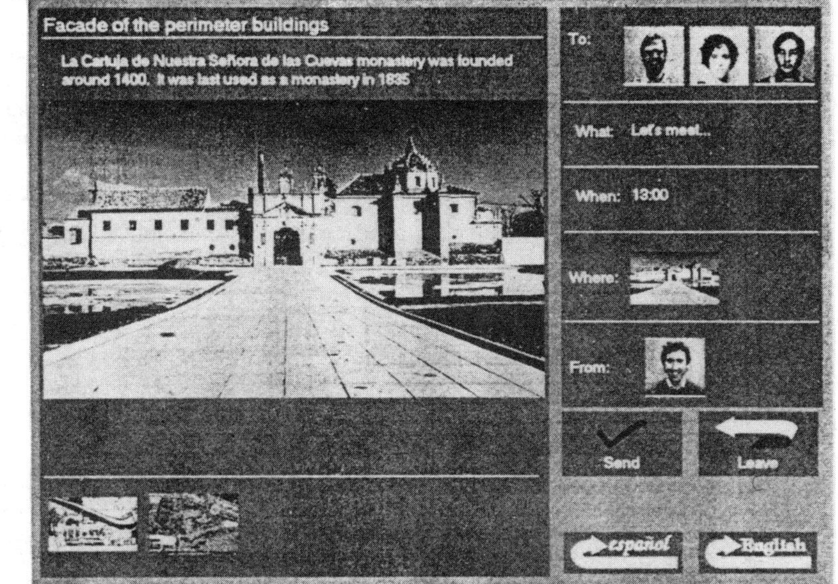

Fig. 22. Sending a message to family members. The "where" field of the message at right tracks the currently displayed image. "When" and "what" fields are set by graphical dialogs appearing in the image area.

refine original content nodes into more elaborate structure, and to create content not originally coded by the application expert.

Unit 1 in Figure 24 is the *frame* coded by the application expert. This root *unit* controls the entire group of hotspots contained within the *frame*. Hotspots are controlled from the root of the *frame* so they are all drawn and erased together wherever the touch occurs.

Units 2, 3, and 4 are created automatically by the rule in Figure 24 to control the placement of the image and language buttons within the *frame*. *Unit* 2 creates a horizontal group across the entire screen. *Unit* 3 at the left contains the image *subframe* (*unit* 5) and its three children, *units* 6 through 8. *Unit* 4 is a vertical group of the remaining *frame* contents. The buttons for changing languages are forced to the bottom of this right-hand column. Each of these objects are further refined by the firing of appropriate rules elsewhere in the style.

9. DISCUSSION

9.1 Layering not Separation

User Interface Management Systems traditionally have been used to build generic interface controls such as menus, buttons, and scroll bars. Large "client areas" have been left as terra incognita, into which the application has been allowed to

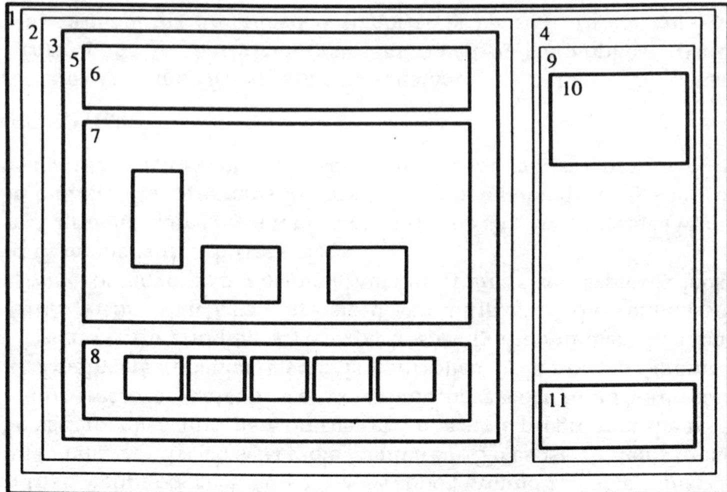

Fig. 23. Structure of map frame. The rule moves the image to the left of the screen as unit 7. Selectable hotspots are positioned by unit 7 according to locations provided by the application. Other frame contents are arranged vertically as children of unit 9. Only units in bold are coded by the application expert; others are added automatically by style rules to control layout and behavior.

write at will to handle more application-specific interaction techniques. Thus, the modularity gained by defining an interface externally from the application is lost for large segments of the interface. This is true because the application defines the style of interaction within the client area. Changes to the style of that part of the interface require changes to the application.

The alternative is to generate all of the interface within the UIMS and to eliminate the client area. This leads to the view that information about the application, in particular about its data types, is not hidden from style rules. Rather than separating application from style, ITS applications delay commitment to style. Delayed commitment means that application layers are not allowed to talk about style. Once we have committed to a particular style, however, application information is freely available to style rules and programs.

As an example, in the EXPO visitor information system users can select the time of day for a restaurant reservation. Time is a data type defined within the EXPO application as a pair of integer ranges for hours and minutes. By recognizing the use of the time data type, a style rule draws the hours and minutes in the correct sequence and automatically inserts a colon between them as is common in digital clocks. If the dialog further indicates that a given usage of time is for display only (by coding *usercan* = *show*), the rule reduces the separation between the *fields*, since space is no longer required for selectable hotspots around them.

:conditions source=frame

Start by naming the contents of the frame that we want to handle specially, these include the buttons to change languages (purpose=navigation)...

:kids name=bottom, source=frame, purpose=navigation

...and the image panel that should fit into the left side of the screen.

:kids name=fits, version=fit

Then define the unit tree for the frame.

:unit type=Group

Type=Group creates a unit to control the group of all hotspots on the screen. Draw messages are sent to each one from here, at the root of the frame, so they all appear and disappear together.

:unit type=HorzGroup

The horizontal group arranges an image panel at the left of the screen...

```
:unit type=VertGroup
  :unit replicate=fits
  :eunit
:eunit
:unit type=VertGroup
```

...then rest of the frame contents are stacked vertically at the right side of the screen.

:unit type=vertgroup, extradepth=accept

This extra vertical group accepts extra depth, while the language buttons below reject it. That forces them to the bottom of the screen.

```
      :unit replicate=rest
      :eunit
    :eunit
```

Buttons for changing languages come at the bottom of the right hand column.

```
    :unit replicate=bottom, extradepth=reject
    :eunit
  :eunit
:eunit
:econditions
```

Fig. 24. Style rule for location finder frame in EXPO. Other rules will fire for the individual contents of the frame, including the list for hotspots and the choices for personal services and languages.

9.2 Comparison with General-Purpose Production Systems

Style rules are not simple to write and understand in ITS. They are, however, much simpler to write and understand than general-purpose expert system languages such as OPS-5. ITS rules are specialized for generating interfaces in their syntax for the structure of interaction techniques, in the simple depth-first traversal used to match blocks in an application, and in the strategies supported for resolving conflicts among multiple rules that may match a given block.

The nonprocedural syntax is the most notable feature of how rules specify *units* in an interaction technique. Rules do not say how to transform dialog into specific styles. Instead, rules require the style expert to say only what the final structure should look like. The job of the ITS system is to transform the application expert's abstract tree into that style.

To be usable, the process of executing rules must also be simple. General-purpose expert systems execute rules until no new elements are added to working memory and all rules that match working memory elements have been fired. To simplify the process ITS considers each *unit* only once during a depth-first traversal of the dialog. The rule cycle consists of three steps: (1) select the next *unit* in the depth-first traversal, (2) fire one or more rules that match the selected *unit* according to a conflict resolution strategy described below, and (3) replace the *unit* with the refined subtree created by the rules just fired. Since each *unit* is replaced in the tree with a subtree refined according to the current style, rules often add new *units* that are visited for matching themselves later on. In this way rules control children but not siblings or parents of a selected node.

A typical style file contains different rules for each type of dialog statement. In addition, each statement (such as a *choice*) typically has several variant styles depending on the attributes coded on it by the application expert. *Choices*, for example, may appear differently depending on their *kind*, *purpose*, or *emphasis* attributes. How are conflicts resolved and the appropriate rule selected?

Two kinds of conflict resolution have been implemented in ITS: Execute the best rule that matches the *unit* under consideration, and execute all rules that match it in the order from most general to most specific. These two possibilities allow both for selection among competing alternatives (execute the best rule) and execution of a series of rules that progressively override defaults or make independent decisions (execute all matching rules in sequence).

The scope over which conflict resolution takes place is also more constrained in ITS than in general expert systems. ITS rules are organized into a hierarchy of sets. A set of alternative rules for *choices* might be nested inside a single set. This set itself would be contained in a set of sets for other attributes that rules might match on such as the *emphasis* or *state* of a data value. The organization of the two sets is shown graphically in Figure 25. Consider how a dialog *choice* will be processed by these rules. *Apply = each* tells the top-level set to fire each the two sets nested beneath it. As many rules in the left-hand set as match should be executed, since they make decisions on orthogonal attributes. Only one of the rules in the right-hand set should fire, since each applies to a different type of object.

9.3 Other Application Experience

In addition to EXPO '92 we have focused our application work on workbenches for the application expert. Two dialog workbenches are currently being built. One presents the dialog as a spreadsheet whose rows are dialog statements and columns contain attributes. The dialog is edited by typing into cells of the matrix or by selecting from ranges of values automatically maintained about the dialog being built.

The second workbench is based on two abstractions of the dialog: the control graph of *activations* among *frames* and the dialog tree within each *frame*. A *frame* can be selected from the control graph and its tree drawn in another window.

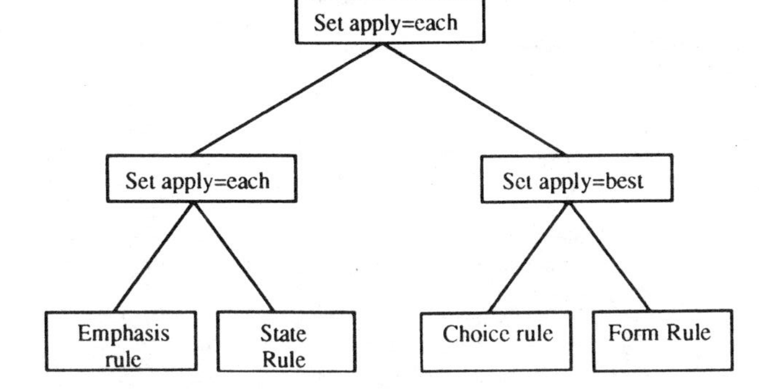

Fig. 25. Tree of sets of style rules.

Details of each object in the *frame* are shown in attached panels as the mouse tracks into nodes in the tree.

The two workbenches are complementary in that the first is a good tool for editing "in-the-small;" the second helps to view the overall structure of the dialog "in-the-large." We hope to combine them soon into an integrated tool.

9.4 Feedback into Improved Rules

We have described the benefits of generating interfaces automatically. Executable style rules greatly reduce the time required to build an interface. Given an excellent style, they also can improve the quality of an interface over that produced by untrained designers. But it is often argued that automatic style will not beat the quality of interfaces individually handcrafted by excellent designers. Is it not a good idea to allow designers to hand-tune automatically generated designs to bring them up to snuff?

While it is tempting to do so, it is a bad idea for two reasons. First, styles need to be tuned when they are missing knowledge that could have caused them to generate a better design in the first place. By manually tuning the output of the rule-base we would miss an opportunity to add the missing knowledge. No one else would benefit from our work.

Second, we ourselves would benefit from our hand-tuning only temporarily. The next time we modified the application, and regenerated its interface, we would have the opportunity to hand-tune the style again. Since maintenance is a fact of life, we need instead to write the new rules that let us use the improved style as often as needed.

Nonetheless, style workbenches do have a role in aiding interface design. Understanding and modifying the behavior of styles can be complex problems. A workbench could help by searching for rules whose behavior might be altered by style changes. The workbench could also provide visual examples of the results produced by firing rules. Direct manipulation changes to these displays, for example, to change the font of a title could be used together with prompts for entering the appropriate conditions of the changed rule.

9.5 Using Applications in Different Styles

We used to talk about writing styles that were truly separate from applications. These generic styles would work with all applications. We now believe that, while possible, this is not always desirable. This shift of view is captured by the shift from speaking about a separation between application and style in favor of a delayed commitment to style.

Styles with rules that match only on the fixed set of dialog statements and attributes (Figure 7 and Figure 8) work equally well when used with any application. These statements and attributes are standard components of all applications and so styles can be secure in matching on them.

Styles with rules that match also on application data types will not work equally well when used with any application. They have specialized knowledge about how to interact with particular types of data. On the other hand, they need not work any less well with other applications than do the generic styles. For an application with data types not matched by the style with application-specific rules, the generic rules will still fire. Rules that select for particular types of application data only improve a style.

9.6 Behavioral Experience

To understand the usability of our tools outside of our immediate group we have concentrated on two activities: teaching classes on interface design using ITS and transferring ITS to external customers. This experience has focused so far on the action and dialog layers, rather than the rule and style program layers. To date, we have taught ITS to roughly 25 people from within and outside IBM and from widely varying backgrounds. These classes are week-long, hands-on working sessions where students arrive with their own design problems and leave with working interfaces.

ITS has also been transferred to one customer external to IBM. A major insurance company has sent several of its programmers and style experts to our course. Subsequently, these programmers, working independently, successfully coded all of the actions and dialog for several prototype applications at their home locations.

CONCLUSIONS

We have described the four layers of the ITS architecture. The action layer implements back-end application functions. The dialog layer defines the content of the user interface, independent of its style. Content specifies the objects included in each frame of the interface, the flow of control among frames, and what actions are associated with each object. The style rule layer defines the presentation and behavior of a family of interaction techniques. Finally, the style program layer implements an extensible toolkit of objects that are composed by the rule layer into complete interaction techniques. Example style programs include routines to format text, render raster images, and arrange units in gridded rectangular layouts.

Our experience has shown that ITS is capable of implementing highly interactive applications. Highly interactive applications respond intimately to user actions based on the current application state. They require a tighter coupling between the application and interface than was provided by early UIMS. ITS provides this coupling by allowing actions to update the data pool on any user event and by reflecting these updates to all views of the changed data automatically.

Our experience has also suggested a number of extensions to both the dialog and rule layers. Many of the rules in the EXPO style, for example, match on the type of *list* or *form* being rendered. Examples include the time data type discussed above, as well as "labeled images" (an image together with descriptive text), "messages" (fields in an email message), and restaurant reservations.

The dialog layer will be extended with a more powerful type language. A type hierarchy will allow new types to be created as extensions of existing ones. The message type, for example, might be defined as a specialization of a flat collection of fields. Structured types will also be supported to help group fields in complex data such as messages and reservations.

The style rule layer will be extended at the same time to support the new type mechanism. The matching algorithm currently recognizes a type only by exact match. To avoid a proliferation of rules specific to single data types, the algorithm will be extended to recognize generalizations of a type if no rules are otherwise found. An instance of the message type, for example, might be matched by a more general rule for a flat collection of fields if no rule is given specifically for messages.

ACKNOWLEDGMENTS

The ITS System has been developed by the combined efforts of our entire group, including Chris Cesar, Tom Cofino, Lauretta Jones, Joe Kesselman, Rich Mushlin, Susan Spraragen, and Jacob Ukelson.

The EXPO '92 visitor information system is being developed jointly with Paco Curbera, Angel Llopis, Javier Martinez, Juan Rojas, and Luis Sopena of IBM's Madrid Scientific Center.

REFERENCES

1. Apple Computer, Inc. *Human Interface Guidelines: The Apple Desktop Interface.* Apple Programmers and Developer's Association. Renton, Wash, 1986.
2. Bennett, W., Boies, S., Gould, J., Greene, S., and Wiecha, C. Transformations on a dialog tree: Rule-based mapping of content to style. In *Proceedings of the ACM SIGGRAPH Symposium on User Interface Software and Technology* (Williamsburg, Va., Nov. 13–15). ACM, New York, 1989, pp. 67–75.
3. Cardelli, L. Building user interfaces by direct manipulation. In *Proceedings of the ACM SIGGRAPH Symposium on User Interface Software* (Banff, Alberta, Canada, Oct. 17–19). ACM, New York, 1988, pp. 152–166.
4. Feiner, S. A grid-based approach to automating display layout. In *Proceedings of Graphics Interface '88* (Edmonton, Canada, June). Morgan Kaufmann, Palo Alto, Calif., 1988, pp. 192–197.
5. Feiner, S. An experiment in the automated creation of pictorial explanations. *IEEE Comput. Graph. Appl. 5*, 11 (1985). 29–37.
6. Foley, J., Gibbs, C., Kim, W., Kovacevic, S. A knowledge-based user interface management system. In *Proceedings of CHI 1988* (Washington, D.C., May 15–19). ACM, New York, 1988, pp. 67–72.
7. Foley, J. Personal communication, 1989.

8. GRUDIN, J. The case against user interface consistency. *Commun. ACM 32,* 10 (Oct. 1989), 1164–1173.
9. HARTSON, H. R., AND HIX, D. Human-computer interface development: Concepts and systems for its management. *ACM Comput. Surv. 21,* 1 (1989), 5–92.
10. HAYES, P., SZEKELY, P., AND LERNER, R. Design alternatives for user interface management systems based on experience with COUSIN. In *Proceedings of CHI '85* (San Francisco, April 14–18). ACM, New York, 1985, pp. 169–175.
11. HUDSON, S. Graphical specification of flexible user interface displays. In *Proceedings of the ACM SIGGRAPH Symposium on User Interface Software and Technology* (Williamsburg, Va., Nov. 13–15). ACM, New York, 1989, pp. 105–114.
12. IBM CORP. *Systems Application Architecture, Common User Access Panel Design and User Interaction.* SC26-4351-0. Dec. 1987.
13. KRASNER, G., AND POPE. S. A cookbook for using the model-view-controller user interface paradigm in Smalltalk-80. *J. Object Oriented Program.* (Aug./Sept. 1988).
14. LINTON, M., VLISSIDES, J., AND CALDER, P. Composing user interfaces with interviews. *IEEE Comput. 22,* 2 (1989), 8–22.
15. MACKINLAY, J. Applying a theory of graphical presentation to the graphic design of user interfaces. In *Proceedings of the ACM SIGGRAPH Symposium on User Interface Software* (Banff, Alberta, Canada. Oct. 17–19). ACM, New York, 1988, pp. 179–189.
16. OPEN SOFTWARE FOUNDATION. *OSF/Motif Style Guide, Revision 1.0.* Open Software Foundation, Cambridge, Mass.
17. PALAY, A., HANSEN, W., KAZAR, M., SHERMAN, M., WADLOW, M., NEUENDORFFER, T., STERN, Z., BADER, M., AND PETERS. T. The Andrew toolkit: An overview. Tech. Rep. Carnegie Mellon Univ. Information Technology Center.
18. PFAFF, G., ED. *User Interface Management Systems.* Springer-Verlag, Berlin, 1985.
19. SCHUMUCKER, K. *Object-Oriented Programming for the Macintosh.* Hayden Books, Hasbrouck Heights, N.J., 1986.
20. SEI. Serpent, a user interface management system overview, version 1. Tech. Rep. 89-UG-2. Carnegie Mellon Univ./Software Engineering Institute, Feb. 1989.
21. SIBERT, J., HURLEY, W., AND BLESER, T. An object-oriented user interface management system. In *Proceedings of SIGGRAPH '86* (Dallas, Tex., Aug. 19–22). ACM, New York, 1986, pp. 259–268.
22. SINGH, G., AND GREEN, M. Chisel: A system for creating highly interactive screen layouts. In *Proceedings of the ACM SIGGRAPH Symposium on User Interface Software and Technology* (Williamsburg, Va., Nov. 13–15). ACM, New York, 1989, pp. 86–94.
23. SUN MICROSYSTEMS AND ATT. *Open Look, Graphical User Interface Application Style Guidelines.* Addison-Wesley, Reading, Mass.,
24. SZEKELY, P. Separating the user interface from the functionality of application programs. Ph.D. thesis, Dept. of Computer Science, Carnegie-Mellon Univ., 1988.
25. VANDER ZANDEN, B., AND MYERS, B. Automatic, look-and-feel independent dialog creation for graphical user interfaces. In *Proceedings of CHI '90* (Seattle, Wash., April 1–5). ACM, New York, 1990, pp. 27–34.
26. WIECHA, C., AND BOIES, S. Generating user interfaces: Principles and use of ITS style rules. In *Proceedings of the ACM SIGGRAPH Symposium on User Interface Software and Technology* (Snowbird, Utah, October 3–5). ACM, New York, 1990, pp. 21–30.
27. *X Toolkit Intrinsics Programming Manual, The X Window System Series,* vol. 4. O'Reilly and Associates, Sebastobol, Calif., 1989.

ITS: A Tool for Rapidly Developing Interactive Applications

Charles Wiecha

The EXPO '92 Guest Services System, an extremely early prototype of which is described in this paper, went on to be what is still today perhaps the largest example of a public information and services kiosk network. Used by an estimated 10 million people during the six-month duration of EXPO '92 in Spain, it consisted of a network of 231 stations linked by Europe's largest fiber-optic local area network on a site containing over 100 pavilions. Visitors to the EXPO could navigate a pictorial tour of the EXPO and pavilion contents, make reservations at over 25 restaurants, send and receive voice-based e-mail to friends and family using addressing written just-in-time on their magnetic entry tickets, read a daily news service, and take opinion polls. ITS allowed us to continue the iterative refinement of the application throughout EXPO, distributing a new version of the application on average every week. Significant changes were made to navigation in reservations, for example, as a direct result of field observations noting where users encountered trouble. Without an automated approach to maintaining style separate from content, these changes would have been much more difficult during live operations. ITS also allowed the coordinated development of the application between two separate groups in New York and Seville, Spain.

Following EXPO, ITS was used in a series of commercial applications, including a kiosk network for unemployment claims submission and job search in Illinois and Colorado, a desktop application for electronic commerce in the corporate market, and an application currently being rolled out in automobile dealerships that allows for real-time and competitive bidding for car loan transactions. All of these applications have shared the goal of "direct customer access," that is, allowing access to successively more sophisticated transactions by end users without customer service intermediaries. Direct customer access depends on a new level of usability due to the complexity of the services being accessed and the lack of any opportunity to provide advance training to the end user.

Our success in transferring the ITS technology to mainline software development groups in IBM has been more limited. We believe there are two reasons for this. The first reason is related to the decomposition of interface design into multiple layers. With a rule-based approach to generating a user interface, there is naturally an "explanation" problem of tracing how particular style decisions were made by the rule base and understanding how they resulted in the final interface. Further, at runtime, there are a number of data models, each potentially with several attached viewers. The distributed nature of this implementation creates another explanation problem of tracking which events are leading to which updates. To build and maintain such a complex system is challenging and may place demands on developers that are hard to meet in practice.

The second reason for limited transfer is that the architecture of a UIMS such as ITS that separates interface development into multiple roles conflicts with the expectations and structure of conventional development groups. Our roles are in support of an iterative style of development that negates the separation of architecture and testing from implementation. The jump to iterative development is perhaps more difficult than adopting new tools for content and style. With the advent and more widespread adoption of Internet-time iterative development, there will perhaps be more demand and opportunity for ITS-like tools.

BEYOND INTERFACE BUILDERS: MODEL-BASED INTERFACE TOOLS

Pedro Szekely, Ping Luo and Robert Neches

USC/Information Sciences Institute
4676 Admiralty Way
Marina del Rey, CA 90292
(310) 822-1511
E-mail: szekely@isi.edu, ping@isi.edu, neches@isi.edu

ABSTRACT

Interface builders only support the construction of the menus and dialogue boxes of an application. They do not support the construction of interfaces of many application classes (visualization, simulation, command and control, domain-specific editors) because of the dynamic and complex information that these applications process. HUMANOID is a model-based interface design and construction tool where interfaces are specified by building a declarative description (model) of their presentation and behavior. HUMANOID's modeling language provides simple abstraction, iteration and conditional constructs to model the interface features of these application classes. HUMANOID provides an easy-to-use designer's interface that lets designers build complex interfaces without programming.

KEYWORDS: UIMS, Design Process, Interface Builders, Model-Based Interface Tools.

INTRODUCTION

Most tools for interface construction support the construction of the menus and dialogue boxes of an application, but provide little or no support for constructing the main application displays that show application-specific objects and let end-users manipulate those objects. Most applications have interface requirements that go far beyond the menus and dialogue boxes that can be constructed using interface builders:

1. *Data with complex structure.* Most visualization applications (e.g., TreeViz [3]) visualize complex data structures with arbitrary levels of nesting.
2. *Heterogeneous data.* Applications typically process several kinds of data (different types of notes in a music editor, different kinds of shapes in a drawing editor), which require different presentations, and which require different input behaviors for convenient manipulation.
3. *Variable amounts of data.* Applications typically process variable amounts of data that could come from data bases or other programs (visualization, command and control, simulation) or data constructed interactively by the user (specialized editors).
4. *Time varying data.* Applications often process data that changes at run-time (command and control, simulation), or allow users to change the data (specialized editors). These applications typically show several views of the data, which must be kept coordinated and up-to-date.

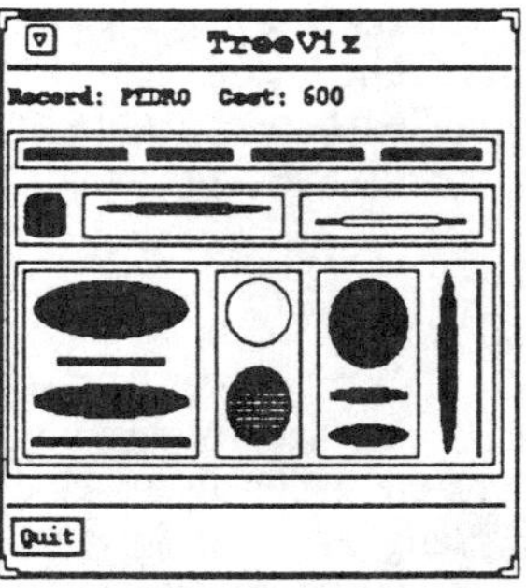

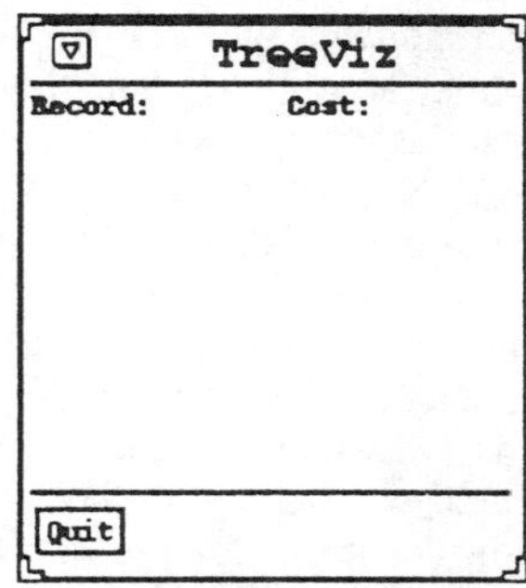

Figure 1. TreeViz, a visualization tool for hierarchical information (left), and the portions of that interface that can be constructed using interface builders (right).

Figure 1. illustrates the main shortcoming of most interface building tools. The left hand side of the figure shows the display of TreeViz [3], a simple visualization application for visualizing hierarchical data. In this example, TreeViz is visualizing the cost to maintain the computers in an organization. The shapes represent different classes of members of the organization, the shading represents different kinds of computer, and the size of the areas represents the cost to maintain the computer. The right hand side of the figure shows the portions of this interface that can be specified using an interface builder. If interface builders do not support the construction of the interface for even a simple application such as TreeViz, much less do they support the interface for the application classes mentioned above. The TreeViz display cannot be specified with an interface builder because the number of objects shown varies at run-time, the shape and shading of the objects depend on attributes of the data, and the layout is recursively defined.

The challenge for interface construction tools is to embody them with a richer and more expressive model of interfaces, while making them intuitive and easy to use for designers. Interface builders do not meet this challenge. They are intuitive and easy to use, but are not expressive enough.

This paper describes a tool called HUMANOID that meets

this challenge. The HUMANOID modeling language supports the specification of most aspects of an interface (presentation, behavior and dialogue). The main contribution of HUMANOID lies in the nature of the modeling language and the way in which it is delivered to designers in an intuitive and easy-to-use interface.

HUMANOID's modeling language has abstraction, composition, iteration and conditional constructs designed to support the modeling of interfaces with the characteristics mentioned above (numbered 1-4). The abstraction mechanism allows the specification of *presentation templates* to present all the instances of a class of objects, and *behavior templates* to specify how the presented objects can be manipulated. The composition construct allows presentation templates to be composed in order to define the presentation of data with complex structure (1). The conditional constructs support the presentation of heterogeneous data (2). Coupled with the iteration construct, the abstraction and composition constructs allow the specification of presentations of variable amounts of heterogeneous data (3). Finally, the modeling language uses a data-dependency mechanism similar to spreadsheet formulas to specify the dependencies between data and presentations in order to support automatic presentation update of time varying data (4).

This paper is organized as follows. The next section presents an overview of HUMANOID's modeling language and the desiderata for the designer's interface, followed by a related work section. The body of the paper discusses the main constructs of the modeling language, the designer's interface facilities for using the modeling constructs, and shows how to construct the TreeViz interface from scratch. The paper closes with current status and conclusions.

HUMANOID OVERVIEW

HUMANOID is a model-based system. Interfaces are specified by constructing a declarative model of how the interface should look and behave. A standard run-time support module is included in every application to execute the model, that is, to construct the application displays and interpret input according to the information in the model.

The Humanoid Modeling Language

HUMANOID provides a declarative modeling language that factors the design of interfaces into five semi-independent dimensions [12]: *1. Application semantics:* represents the objects and operations of an application. The application semantics defines the domain of discourse of the interface, and is referenced by the dimensions of the model that define the presentation, behavior and dialogue sequencing of the interface. *2. Presentation:* defines the visual appearance of the interface. *3. Behavior:* defines the input gestures (e.g. mouse clicks) that can be applied to presented objects, and their effects on the state of the application and the interface. *4. Dialogue sequencing:* defines the ordering constraints for executing commands and supplying inputs to commands. *5. Action side-effects*: defines actions executed automatically when commands or command inputs change state (e.g., making a newly created object the current selection).

Only the first three dimensions will be discussed in detail in this paper. Details on the last two appear elsewhere [12].

The Designer's Interface to Humanoid

The designer's interface to HUMANOID supports a very tight design/evaluate/redesign cycle. The typical screen of a designer's workstation (Figure 2.) contains windows showing different views of the design model (windows labeled `Part Editor`, `Presentation Template`

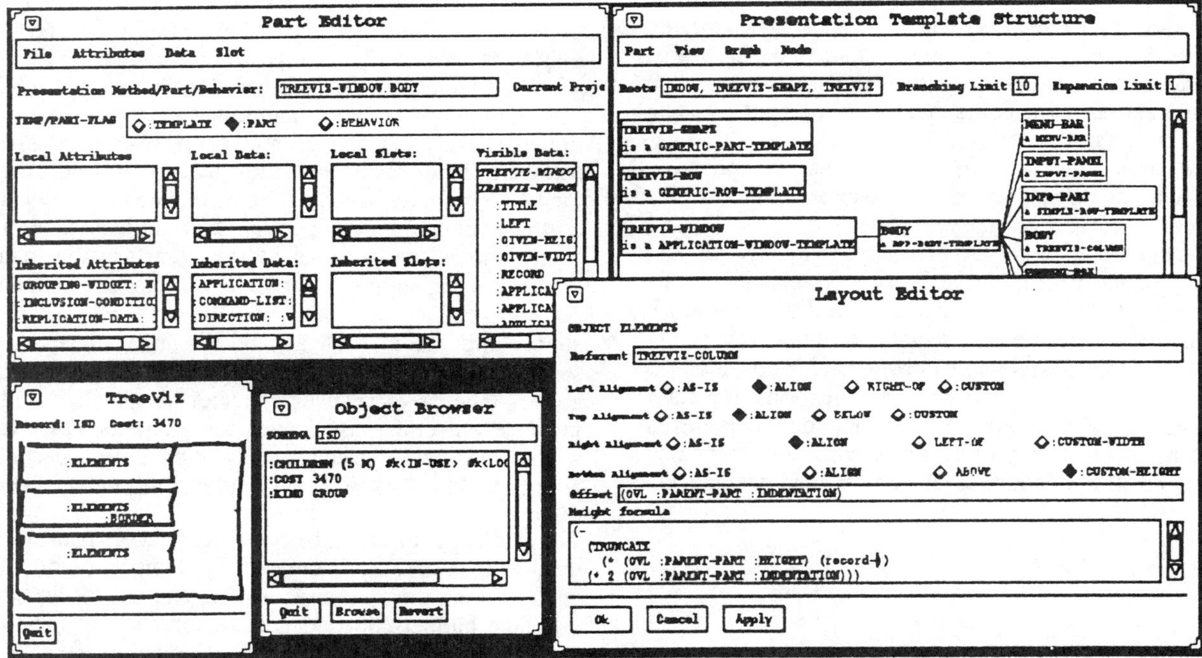

Figure 2. Snapshot of a screen showing a typical configuration of windows during a design session with Humanoid.

`Structure` and `Layout Editor`), windows showing the application data structures (`Object Browser`), and windows showing the interfaces that HUMANOID generates from the model (`TreeViz`). These windows are explained in more detail later in the paper.

The designer's interface was designed according to the following desiderata:

All features of the design should be visible and changeable by designers so that designers can control all aspects of an interface design.

Example interfaces are editable views of the model. HUMANOID capitalizes on the idea that people understand problems better when they can interact both with a symbolic representation and with illustrative examples of it [15]. So, HUMANOID shows designers views of the model (symbolic representation) and interfaces generated from the model (examples). Designers can refine the model by editing the example interfaces produced from the model.

All views of the design are linked together to help designers understand and edit the model. This requirement manifests itself in several features of HUMANOID.

- HUMANOID provides facilities to map from example features to model elements and vice-versa. Designers can point to an element of the design, and ask HUMANOID to highlight the portions of the example displays that it controls. Conversely, designers can point to a feature of an example display and ask to see the portions of the model that generated it.
- All example interfaces are kept up-to-date after every modification to the design model (even if the design is not fully specified), helping designers to immediately see the consequences of their modeling decisions. Conversely, when designers perform a refinement by demonstration they can immediately see HUMANOID's interpretation of the example in one of the design views.

RELATED WORK

Interface design and construction tools can be compared along expressivity and usability dimensions. The expressivity dimension defines the class of interfaces that can be specified, where as the usability dimension captures the level of expertise that designers need to use the tool.

At the low end of the expressivity spectrum are interface builders [9], with essentially a single modeling construct: instantiation. Designers can create instances of a predefined set of classes of interface building blocks, and set the values of their parameters. Interface builders can only be used to specify the menus and dialogue boxes of an application, but not the main application displays.

At the high end of the expressivity spectrum are programming languages, which allow programmers to create arbitrarily sophisticated interfaces by writing programs (procedural models of interfaces). Close to the programming end of the spectrum are object-oriented systems like Unidraw [13] which provide classes for building specific kinds interfaces. Even though Unidraw greatly facilitates the programming of graphical editors, the task still requires extensive programming skills.

The usability dimension generally goes in the opposite direction. Low expressivity tools like interface builders are easy to use, and high expressivity tools like programming languages or object-oriented frameworks are hard to use.

Demonstrational Tools

Demonstrational tools such as Lapidary [5] and Druid [10] are an attempt to move up the expressivity spectrum while remaining in the high end of the usability spectrum. Lapidary, for instance, lets designers demonstrate examples of a boxes and arrows application where the arrows should remain attached to the boxes, and constructs "box" and "arrow" classes with the appropriate constraints so that instances remain connected. The generalizations that demonstrational tools make are typically not shown to designers. In the cases where designers can view the generalizations (e.g. Lapidary), there are no tools to help designers understand the relationship between features of the examples and features of the generalizations. Hence, designers find it hard to understand the generalizations.

HUMANOID differs from these tools in that the model (generalizations) plays a primary role. The demonstrational capabilities of HUMANOID are weak compared to Lapidary and Druid, but HUMANOID derives its strength from its modeling power, and the combination of explicit model and example views to construct the models.

Other Model-Based Approaches

Most model-based systems score high in expressivity, but low in usability.

UIDE [2] is a model-based interface tool whose application and dialogue sequencing models are similar to HUMANOID's, but whose presentation model is relatively impoverished compared to HUMANOID's. UIDE does not have a sophisticated designer's interface so its usability is low. UIDE's approach to usability is automation. The richness of UIDE's model enables the construction of tools like Cartoonist [11] that generates animated help, and DON that generates dialogue boxes [4]. UIDE emphasizes model analysis tools such as consistency checkers [1] and keystroke analysis [2]. Since HUMANOID's and UIDE's models are similar, the complementary advantages of both systems could be integrated in a single tool.

ITS [14] can also be characterized as a model-based system. ITS has a presentation model similar to HUMANOID's, but its dialogue and application models are less expressive. ITS does not score high in usability due to its textual specification language, but it is a production quality system.

Having reviewed related work, we now focus on how HUMANOID's modeling language and designer's interface are used to build interfaces.

APPLICATION MODEL

The first step in designing an interface is to model the application functionality, i.e., the objects and the commands that the application provides. In HUMANOID, these are formally modeled in an object-oriented way, by specifying the types and slots of each object. Commands are modeled by specifying their inputs, preconditions, and a call-back procedure. Other more advanced features of the application model are discussed elsewhere [12].

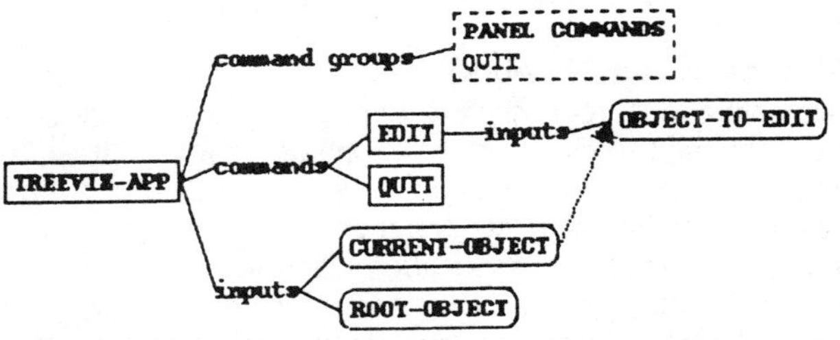

Figure 3. The application model of TreeViz.

Figure 3. shows the TreeViz application model. To start off the design we decided that there should be a `QUIT` command, and an `EDIT` command to edit the information contained in any record in the hierarchy. There is an input `ROOT-OBJECT` to store the root record of the hierarchy to be shown. We made the dialogue sequencing decision that there should be a notion of current selection, and that the `EDIT` command edits the current selection. Accordingly, we defined another global input called `CURRENT-OBJECT`, and tied the `OBJECT-TO-EDIT` input of the `EDIT` command to `CURRENT-OBJECT`. We also made a presentation decision by stating that `QUIT` belongs to the `PANEL COMMANDS` group, which tells HUMANOID which commands to present as a panel of command buttons.

If we were using an interface builder we would have started the design of the interface differently. We would have drawn a QUIT button at the bottom of the screen, and tied it to a callback procedure. We would have drawn the RECORD and COST labels at the top of the screen, but would not have been able to tie them to anything (Figure 1, right).

This is all that we could have done using an interface builder. As mentioned above, the main display of TreeViz cannot be specified using interface builders. We would not have been able to specify the `EDIT` command because we want a "double click" over the display area showing a record, rather than a screen button to invoke it. Interface builders have no provisions for such invisible behaviors.

The application model has several advantages over the interface builder approach:

- *HUMANOID generates a default interface for an application from the application model.* This default interface is very similar to the one constructed with an interface builder. It contains a menu-bar, an input panel, a blank area for the main application area, and a command panel at the bottom. In addition, HUMANOID provides facilities to customize the layout and other aspects of the interface to make it look as desired.
- *The application model makes all aspects of the design visible,* where as interface builders only allow designers to talk about elements that have an explicit representation on the end-user's interface. The application model allows designers to express "hidden" notions, such as the `EDIT` command and the dialogue sequencing constraints.
- *The application model can also be used by automated design critics and automatic help generation tools* as illustrated by the UIDE system [1,2,4,11].

After having defined an initial version of the application model, the designer can proceed to refine the default interface to specify the presentation and behavior of the main application area or to fine-tune the default interface.

The next sections describe the refinement process that HUMANOID supports. If we were using an interface builder, we would proceed to drop into a programming language, because the interface builder support ends when the construction of the main application areas starts.

PRESENTATION TEMPLATES

In HUMANOID, designers model the presentation of an application incrementally. They first identify the major elements of the display and define presentation templates for them, which initially are just names for the display elements. Designers then proceed to define the characteristics of each display element, such as the data it presents, its parts, and its layout. For example, in TreeViz we see that the display is composed of three major elements: shapes (rectangles, ovals, etc.), columns and rows (Figure 1), so we proceed to define presentation templates for them called `TreeViz-Shape`, `TreeViz-Column` and `TreeViz-Row` (Figure 4).

A *presentation template* is an abstraction to model the characteristics of display elements. At run-time presentation templates are used as rubber-stamps to create as many instances of a display element as needed. Presentation templates represent the following information:

- *Is-A*: a presentation template can be defined as a refinement of an existing template, by modifying any of the attributes listed below.
- *Input data*: the type of information that can be displayed using a presentation template.
- *Widget*: the graphical object produced by a presentation template. It can be a primitive graphical object (line, icon, text, etc.) a toolkit primitive (menu, button, etc.), or a layout management widget (column, row, table, graph, etc.)
- *Applicability conditions*: predicates identifying the contexts where the template is appropriate.
- *Parts*: the decomposition of a complex display into simpler displays. Each part is modeled in terms of the input data it ought to present, and a default template for presenting the data. HUMANOID uses that default template as a starting point for a search for the most appropriate template to display the part, based on the applicability conditions of other templates in the model.
- *Behaviors*: the input behaviors that can be invoked from the display elements specified by the presentation template.

HUMANOID provides specialized editors to construct presentation templates and to specify all their attributes. The window in Figure 2. labeled `Presentation`

Template Structure shows the part decomposition of templates. The boxes represent templates and the links represent parts. The window labeled Part Editor shows all the attributes of a selected part in the Presentation Template Structure window.

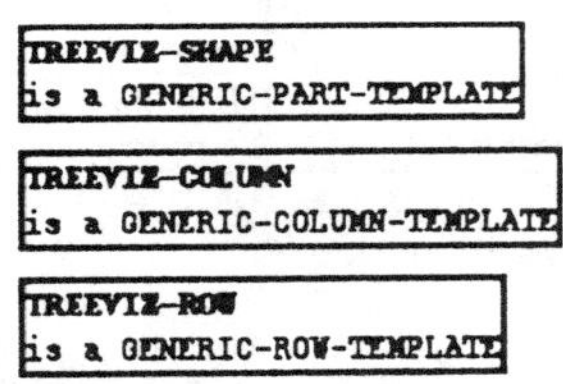

Figure 4. Initial definitions of the templates to construct the main application area of the TreeViz interface.

Figure 4. shows the initial template definitions to construct the main application area of TreeViz. We defined these templates as specializations of library templates that best approximate their desired effect (e.g. TreeViz-Column specializes Generic-Column-Template). We did not specify a particular shape for the TreeViz-Shape because we do not know yet what shape to use, and we want the shape to depend on the attributes of the record displayed in it. We will later need to use the conditional construct to specify this aspect of the interface. The ability to defer commitments on this issue is an example of the flexibility afforded by HUMANOID's model-based approach.

Adding Parts To Templates

In the case of TreeViz our next concern is to define the hierarchical decomposition of the display. In HUMANOID, we do this by adding parts to templates.

HUMANOID provides two ways to add parts to a template, by editing the model, or by editing an example generated from the model. To add a part by editing the model, the designer selects a template in the Presentation Template Structure window, and obtains a dialogue box to specify the name and the default presentation template for the part. To add a part by editing an example, the designer first specifies the template either by selecting it in the presentation model view, or by selecting a portion of the display in the example. Then, the designer selects the default presentation template for the part from a palette of library templates (like in an interface builder), and draws the part in the example window. When a part is specified by example, information about its size and location is incorporated into the model.

The facilities for adding parts illustrate the power of the coordinated model and example view approach. It is more convenient to select the part's parent in the model view because it shows all features of the model. The examples typically do not show the internal geometry management nodes of the display hierarchy. Also, small elements of the display which overlap each other are difficult to select. On the other hand, specifying the size and location of a new part is more conveniently done in the example window.

Our design of TreeViz proceeds by adding parts to the TreeViz-Column template. We need to add a BORDER part to show some kind of border around the column, and an ELEMENTS part to specify the contents of the column.

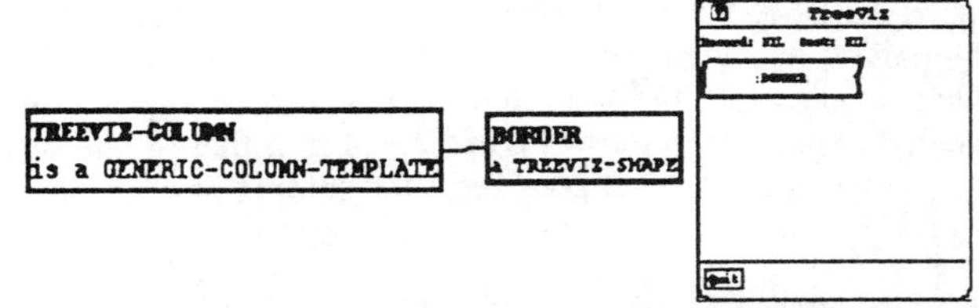

Figure 5. Once the BORDER part is added to TreeViz-Column, the generated example shows it.

Figure 5. shows the effects of adding the BORDER. We chose TreeViz-Shape as the default presentation template for the BORDER part so that the border shows the record associated with TreeViz-Column. HUMANOID shows the BORDER part as a sketch because the TreeViz-Shape template is not fully defined (it does not define a widget). The border's size is incorrect because we have not specified it yet (it should be the same size as the column).

The example illustrates how HUMANOID lets designers work in small incremental steps, without requiring them to fully define an aspect of the interface in order to get something on the screen. After adding the border we can work on any of the missing aspects of the interface. We can fix the border layout, define the conditions for choosing the appropriate shape, add the ELEMENTS part, or define the input behavior.

Suppose we add the ELEMENTS part. To fully specify it we need to specify what data it presents, what presentation template it uses for presenting its data, and how to get the part replicated as required by the data to be presented.

Specifying Part Input Data

Once a part is added to a template, it is necessary to specify the data that it should present. In general, the data presented in a part is a function of the data presented in its parent or ancestors further up the display hierarchy. These functions are typically defined by snippets of code that perform simple computations (e.g., accessing a slot value of an object, applying application-specific functions, concatenating strings, performing arithmetic). For example, in TreeViz, the ELEMENTS part presents the children of the record presented in its parent.

HUMANOID's interface for defining the values of input data of parts resembles the interface for entering formulas in a spreadsheet [7]. HUMANOID gives the designer a menu of commonly used functions and a type-in area for entering a *formula*, as these snippets of code are called in HUMANOID. Designers construct the formulas via a combination of type-in, menu-selection and pointing to enter references to other model elements (such as the input data of a template or an input of a command).

In the TreeViz example we use the spreadsheet interface to specify the value of the RECORD input data of the ELEMENTS part. We first choose the "get slot value" function from the menu, and then we point to relevant model elements to specify the object and the slot: we point to the RECORD input data of TreeViz-Column to specify that we want to access a slot of the record stored in the parent, and then we point to the CHILDREN slot in a window showing and example of a record (e.g. window labeled Object Browser in Figure 2.). From these pointing operations, HUMANOID constructs the snippet of code (g-value* (w+ :record) :children).

The spreadsheet paradigm for constructing the formulas that define the values of input data has two important benefits:

- Many computer users without programming expertise are familiar with spreadsheets, and can use them effectively.
- The recording of dependencies via references enables HUMANOID's automatic redisplay facility. When data referenced in a formula changes, HUMANOID can identify and update the affected portions of the display.

If we were using a conventional toolkit to build TreeViz, we would need to program both the propagation of data down the display hierarchy, and worry about bookkeeping for display update, say, in case a child of a record is deleted. Using HUMANOID we specified data propagation in a simple way, and we did not worry about display update at all.

Specifying Layout

Interface builders provide easy to use facilities to specify the layout of dialogue boxes. Designers simply drag and stretch the objects in the work area as needed, aided by alignment features (grids, gravity, dialogue-boxes) to neatly align the objects. Interface builders cannot be used to specify the layout of most application main displays because the objects to be laid out are computed by the application at run-time. It is necessary to specify *methods* for laying out objects rather than specifying the coordinates of concrete objects, as interface builders let designers do.

HUMANOID has a library of templates of commonly used layout methods such as rows, columns, tables and graphs. Designers use these templates by defining their templates as specializations of them (e.g., TreeViz-Column as a specialization of Generic-Column-Template). However, in many graphical interfaces, layouts different from the default ones are needed. In that case, the designer can use the layout specification facilities of HUMANOID.

Figure 2. showed a HUMANOID dialogue box for defining custom layouts. It is similar to the dialogue boxes provided in drawing editors and interface builders to define the alignment of parts, except that it is used to define the layout between two parts of a template (part and parent, or siblings), rather than two concrete objects. The dialogue box provides options for common cases (e.g., making the left side of object A be the left side of object B), and provides a custom option to allow designers to enter arbitrary formulas, should they need to. When entering arbitrary formulas, the spreadsheet paradigm is available to make it easy to enter references to other model elements.

In our TreeViz application we need to define the layout of the BORDER and ELEMENTS parts of TreeViz-Column. The BORDER part should be the same size as its parent, and we specify this by choosing the four "align" options in the

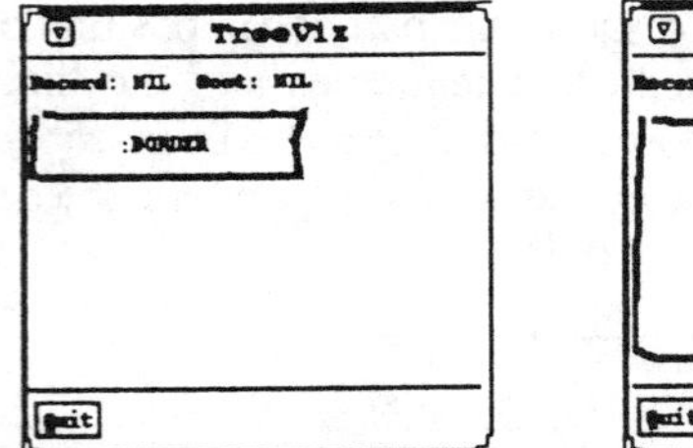

Figure 6. TreeViz examples before and after the layout of BORDER is defined.

Layout Editor dialogue box. Figure 6. shows the TreeViz example after the layout of the border is defined. We will postpone defining the layout of the ELEMENTS until we specify how to get the ELEMENTS part replicated.

The main benefits of HUMANOID's layout mechanism are:

- HUMANOID's library contains commonly used layout managers (row, column, table and graph).
- Custom layouts can be defined using dialogue boxes similar to the alignment facilities of interface builders.

If we were writing the TreeViz interface with a conventional toolkit, we would need to write some kind of recursive function to compute the layout. In HUMANOID, because it uses a constraint system [8], we specified the layout using simple formulas, entered with the spreadsheet interface. The constraint system solves the formulas to produce the correct layout, even when the window is resized.

BEHAVIOR TEMPLATES

TreeViz provides a good example of the kinds of input behavior required for manipulating the presentations of the main displays of an application. When the user moves the mouse over the visualization area, TreeViz shows, at the top of the window, a summary of the record that the mouse is pointing at. As the mouse moves, crossing the boundaries between regions, the information at the top of the window changes. When an interface is constructed using conventional toolkits, such input behaviors need to be programmed. Using HUMANOID, such behaviors can be specified by merely filling in options in a dialogue box.

HUMANOID's behavior model is based on Myers' Interactor model [6]. Myers identified seven classes of parameterized interactors that can be used to model the input behavior of a very large class of mouse and keyboard-based direct manipulation interfaces: *menu-interactor, move-grow-interactor, new-point-interactor, angle-interactor, text-interactor, trace-interactor* and *gesture-interactor*. Each interactor has between 10 and 20 parameters to specify the operation of the interactor.

We model the TreeViz behavior using a *menu-interactor*, whose menu elements are the leafs of the display tree (Myers' notion of an menu interaction is very general). Each time the mouse moves to a new leaf element, the menu interactor calls a standard action. Using the spreadsheet interface, we specify this action to set the application global input called CURRENT-OBJECT (Figure 3.) to the value of the RECORD input data of the leaf element pointed at with the mouse. The automatic update mechanism ensures that the screen is updated appropriately.

HUMANOID's behavior model has several benefits:

- Designers without programming experience can model application-specific behaviors of the kind that would require extensive programming if implemented in a traditional interface toolkit.
- The behavior model is separate from presentation, allowing designers to explore presentation and behavior features semi-independently. For example, in TreeViz the behavior works correctly even though the presentation model is not fully defined (neither the layout or the graphics of the visualization are defined). Once the presentation model is refined the behavior will still work, without modification.

ITERATION

A common concern in the design of many interfaces is to specify the presentation of variable amounts of data. HUMANOID provides an iteration construct, called *part replication*, to support this. It works by designating one of the input data of a part to be the index of the iteration construct. The run-time value of the index input data is expected to be a list. HUMANOID will instantiate (replicate) the part once for each element of the index input data. Each replication will be displayed using the default presentation template of the part. However, the conditional constructs (see next section) allow the specification of conditions to choose a different template for each replication depending on the attributes of the value of its index input data.

HUMANOID's iteration construct is very easy to use. The designer just needs to select one of the input data of a part, and designate it as the replication index.

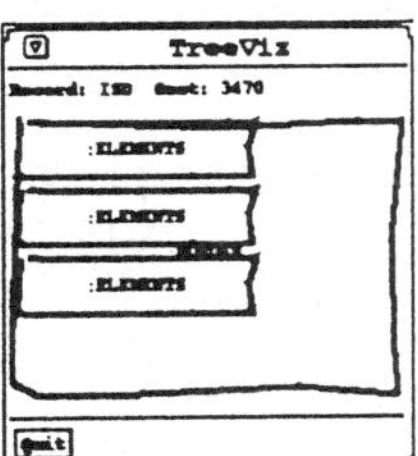

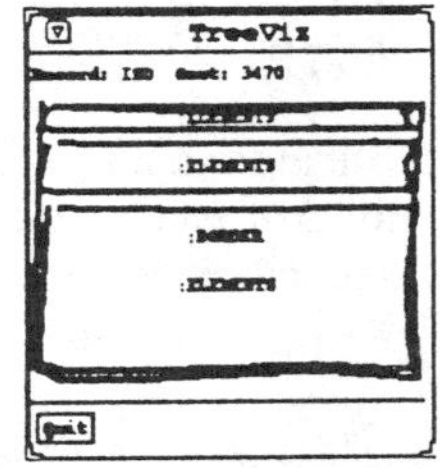

Figure 7. Left: TreeViz example showing the effects of replication (before the size of the ELEMENTS is specified). Right: TreeViz after the sizes are specified.

In TreeViz we use the iteration construct to specify that the ELEMENTS part of TreeViz-Column should be replicated for each of the children of the record stored in the parent. In section "Specifying Part Input Data" we specified that the record input data of ELEMENTS gets all the children of the parent's record. The only thing we need to do now is to designate RECORD as the replication index. Figure 7. shows the effect of specifying the replication. The ELEMENTS part got replicated 3 times because the parent's record has 3 children. Since TreeViz-Column is a kind of column template, the elements appear in a column.

We now need to fix the size of the ELEMENTS part. The width of each element is equal to the width of its parent, and we specify this by selecting the "align" options for "Left Alignment" and "Right Alignment" in the Layout Editor dialogue box (Figure 2). The height of each element is the height of its parent multiplied by the ratio of the COST slot of the element's record and the COST slot of the parent's record. We specify this formula using the "custom height" option for "Bottom Alignment" and use the spreadsheet facilities to enter references to the COST slot of the objects involved.

The notable aspect of HUMANOID's iteration construct is that it is simple, yet powerful. In addition, should the input data used as replication index change value a run-time, HUMANOID will automatically reconstruct the display.

Our TreeViz interface is almost finished. We now need to specify the actual shapes to be used to display each record. We do that using the conditional constructs.

CONDITIONALITY

One problem designers often face is to make presentations sensitive to the attributes of the data to be displayed. HUMANOID provides two conditional constructs to support this. The conditional constructs are designed to make it convenient to specify two common cases: hiding and showing display elements, and choosing different presentations based on the attributes of an object.

The *inclusion condition* of a part is a formula to determine whether the part appears in the display. The part is instantiated and included in the display if and only if the formula's value is true.

The *substitutions* of a template are a list of condition and template pairs that specify alternative templates to display the template's data. Substitutions can themselves have substitutions, so they form a hierarchy. When asked to display a part, HUMANOID searches the substitution hierarchy of the default template of the part to find the deepest substitution whose condition is true.

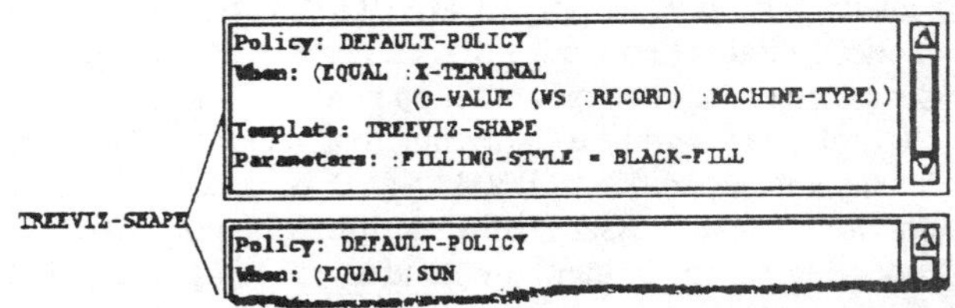

Figure 8. Substitution hierarchy used in TreeViz to specify different presentations based on the attributes of a record.

Figure 8. shows a portion of the substitution hierarchy we used in TreeViz to specify different presentations for records depending on the MACHINE-TYPE slot of the record. If the MACHINE-TYPE of a record is X-TERMINAL, then the shape should be black. Similar substitutions for other machine types and substitutions for person classes yields the finished TreeViz display shown in Figure 1.

HUMANOID provides an interactive interface to visualize and edit substitution hierarchies such as the one shown in Figure 8. Designers can add and delete nodes from the graph, and obtain dialogue boxes to edit all the attributes.

The conditional constructs of HUMANOID have several benefits. Conditionals can be added in a modular and incremental way (by adding part inclusion conditions, or adding nodes to the substitution hierarchy). Also, the use of spreadsheet paradigm to specify the conditions makes it easy for designers to define the conditions, and allows HUMANOID to automatically update displays, even if the update involves searching a substitution hierarchy again because the values of conditions changed. Once again, interface builders do not support conditional presentations, and achieving the same results through programming is much more work.

CURRENT STATUS

HUMANOID is implemented using CommonLisp, X windows and Garnet[8]. It has been used to implement the interfaces for three large applications: a logistics analysis system, a knowledge base development environment, and the HUMANOID designer's interface, which continues to be under active development.

CONCLUSIONS

HUMANOID integrates the traditional model-based approach of systems like UIDE, with the easy to use approach of interface builders and demonstrational tools. This yields a tool with the following benefits:

- *Expressivity.* Designers can specify the main windows of applications, not just menus and dialogue- boxes.
- *Ease of use.* Many aspects of HUMANOID increase ease of use: simple abstractions, all aspects of models are visible and changeable, model and example views are coordinated, spreadsheet paradigm for specifying snippets of code.
- *Support for the design process.* HUMANOID supports the design process by allowing designers to work top-down, to delay design commitments and to work on separate aspects of the interface semi-independently
- *Framework for the incorporation of more design-time and run-time support tools.* HUMANOID's explicit design model contains knowledge that can be used by automated design critics and automated help generation system. For example, a system like Cartoonist that generates animated help could be added to HUMANOID because the model contains the necessary information. In addition, the modeling language can be extended to incorporate other support tools (e.g. tools for task analysis).

ACKNOWLEDGMENTS

The research reported in this paper was supported by DARPA through Contract Numbers NCC 2-719 and N00174-91-0014. We wish to thank David Benjamin and Brian Harp for useful comments on drafts of this paper.

REFERENCES

[1] R. Braudes, A Framework for Conceptual Consistency Verification, D.Sc. Dissertation, Dept. of EE&CS, The George Washington University, Washington, DC 20052, 1990.

[2] J. Foley, W. Kim, S. Kovacevic and K. Murray, UIDE - An Intelligent User Interface Design Environment, in J. Sullivan and S. Tyler (eds.) Architectures for Intelligent User Interfaces: Elements and Prototypes, Addison-Wesley, Reading MA, 1991, pp. 339-384.

[3] B. Johnson, TreeViz: Treemap Visualization of Hierarchically Structured Information. In Proceedings CHI'92. May, 1992, pp. 369-370.

[4] W. Kim and J. Foley, DON: User Interface Presentation Design Assistant, In Proceedings UIST'90. October, 1990, pp. 10-20.

[5] B. A. Myers, B. Vander Zanden and R. B. Dannenberg. Creating Graphical Interactive Application Objects by Demonstration. In Proceedings UIST'89. November 1989, pp.95-104.

[6] B. A. Myers. A New Model for Handling Input. ACM Transactions on Informations Systems, 8(2). July 1990, pp. 289-320.

[7] B. A. Myers. Graphical Techniques In A Spreadsheet For Specifying User Interfaces. In Proceedings CHI'91. April, 1991, pp. 243-256.

[8] B. A. Myers, et. al. The Garnet Reference Manuals. Technical Report CMU-CS-90-117-R2, School of Computer Science, Carnegie Mellon University, Pittsburgh, PA 14212. May 1992.

[9] Neuron Data, Inc. 1991. Open Interface Toolkit. 146 University Ave. Palo Alto, CA 94301.

[10] G. Singh, C. H. Kok and T. Y. Ngan. Druid: A System for Demonstrational Rapid User Interface Development. In Proceedings UIST'90. October 1990, pp. 157-177.

[11] P. Sukaviriya and J. Foley, Coupling a UI Framework with Automatic Generation of Context-Sensitive Animated Help. In Proceedings of UIST '90. October 1990, pp. 142-146.

[12] P. Szekely, P. Luo, and R. Neches. Facilitating the Exploration of Interface Design Alternatives: The HUMANOID Model of Interface Design. In Proceedings CHI'92. May, 1992, pp. 507-514.

[13] M. Vlissides and M. A. Linton. Unidraw: A Framework For Building Domain-Specific Graphical Editors. ACM Transactions on Information Systems 8(3), July 1990. pp. 237-268.

[14] C. Wiecha, W. Bennett, S. Boies, J. Gould and S. Greene. ITS: A Tool For Rapidly Developing Interactive Applications. ACM Transactions on Information Systems 8(3), July 1990. pp. 204-236.

[15] M. D. Williams. What Makes RABBIT Run? Int. J. Man-Machine Studies, 21, 1984, pp. 333-352.

Beyond Interface Builders: Model-Based Interface Tools

Pedro Szekely, Ping Luo, and Robert Neches

The main contribution of the HUMANOID system was to show the benefits of using models to facilitate the construction of sophisticated user interfaces. In the early nineties, when the HUMANOID system was developed, interface builders were the most widely used tools for constructing interfaces. Ease of use notwithstanding, interface builders operate at the lowest level of the interface design process (the widget level), providing very little assistance for the high levels of interface design dealing with task decomposition and dialogue design. The interface builders of the late nineties, such as the Java Beans development tools, are similar in spirit. The universe of building blocks is now open-ended, including any component that adheres to the Java Beans specification. These tools also provide assistance in tieing together the components of a window and in defining their behavior. The greater power of the Java Beans tools depends on simple models of the properties, behavior of components, and the facilities of the Java language to query and manipulate these models at runtime.

Our HUMANOID was an early exploration of the capabilities that can be derived from sophisticated models of application data, presentation, and dialogue components. As described in this paper, our results were very encouraging. These results led to a collaboration with UIDE to work on a new system called Mastermind (Szekely et al. 1996) that combined the best features of HUMANOID and UIDE. Our goal was to build an interface design and construction environment using more comprehensive models, representing a wide variety of interface design concerns ranging from tasks to presentations and interaction techniques. This goal was too ambitious. The problems of modeling tasks in detail, representing the relationship between presentations (displays) and tasks, were harder then expected, and it was hard to use these models to drive the behavior of an interface.

After disappointing early results in building comprehensive models that cover a wide range of interface design aspects and a wide range of applications, we shifted our attention to building narrow-focus models and tools. The recent work of Frank and Szekely (1998) focuses on interfaces for constructing small, yet richly structured objects (e.g., rules for automatically handling email, database queries, air campaign objectives, tax forms). The modeling language is an extended BNF grammar that defines the structure of the objects. This modeling language is simple, yet covers an interesting range of applications. The level of support of our tools is very deep. The system can construct different styles of interfaces automatically, tailored to different platform capabilities and user and application contexts.

Based on almost 10 years of experience with model-based user interface construction tools, we argue that it is more profitable to work on focused models. We are no longer building model-based systems to construct interfaces similar to those that can be constructed using interface builders and arguing about the relative benefits of the approaches. The capabilities and quality of the interfaces generated from the focused models is unquestionable. The effort required to build similar interfaces using traditional means would be prohibitive.

REFERENCES

Szekely, P.; Sukaviriya, P.; Castells, P.; Muthukumarasamy, J.; and Salcher, E. 1996. Declarative Interface Models for User Interface Construction Tools: The Mastermind Approach. In Bass, L., and Unger, C. (eds.), *Engineering for Human-Computer Interaction*, 120–150. New York: Chapman & Hall.

Frank, M., and Szekely, P. 1998. Adaptive Forms: An Interactive Paradigm for Entering Structured Data. In *Proceedings of the 1998 International Conference on Intelligent User Interfaces*, San Francisco, January 6–9, 153–160.

Model-Based Automated Generation of User Interfaces

Angel R. Puerta, Henrik Eriksson, John H. Gennari, and Mark A. Musen

Medical Computer Science Group
Knowledge Systems Laboratory
Departments of Medicine and Computer Science
Stanford University
Stanford, CA, 94305-5479
{puerta,eriksson,gennari,musen}@camis.stanford.edu

ABSTRACT[1]

User interface design and development for knowledge-based systems and most other types of applications is a resource-consuming activity. Thus, many attempts have been made to automate, to certain degrees, the construction of user interfaces. Current tools for automated design of user interfaces are able to generate the static layout of an interface from the application's data model using an intelligent program that applies design rules. These tools, however, are not capable of generating the dynamic behavior of the interface, which must be specified programmatically, and which constitutes most of the effort of interface construction. Mecano is a model-based user-interface development environment that uses a domain model to generate both the static layout and the dynamic behavior of an interface. A knowledge-based system applies sets of dialog design and layout rules to produce interfaces from the domain model. Mecano has been used successfully to completely generate the layout and the dynamic behavior of relatively large and complex, domain-specific, form- and graph-based interfaces for applications in medicine and several other domains.

INTRODUCTION

In recent years there has been significant progress in providing automated assistance to user-interface developers. Commercially available interface builders, user-interface management systems, and interface toolkits provide considerable savings to developers in time and in effort needed to produce a new interface (deBaar, Foley, & Mullet 1992).

Even with these commercial tools present, the amount of effort and low-level detail involved in constructing interfaces is substantial. Therefore, researchers are investigating techniques to automate more portions of the interface design process. One promising area is that of model-based user-interface development (Puerta 1993; Szekely, Luo, & Neches 1993). In this approach, developers work with high-level specifications (models) of the interface to define dialog and layout characteristics. Model-based systems facilitate the automation of interface design tasks. A successful approach has been to use the application's data model to generate the static layout of an interface (deBaar, Foley, & Mullet 1992; Janssen, Weisbecker, & Ziegler 1993).

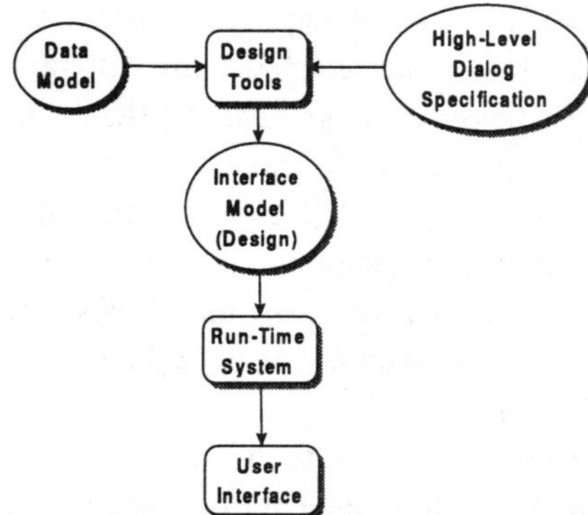

Figure 1. Generic framework for automated interface-generation environments that employ data models. The interface design is produced by tools that examine a data model and a dialog specification. The design may be represented implicitly or explicitly (as an interface model). The run-time system implements the design.

Figure 1 shows a generic framework for automated interface generation environments that employ data models. An intelligent design tool examines the data model and applies a set of design rules to produce a static design of an interface. Because the data model is shared between the interface design and the target application design, both designs can be coupled, and changes to the application design can be propagated easily to the interface design. The dynamic behavior of the interface, however, must be specified separately. This process can take many forms such as using a graphical editor to construct dialog Petri nets (Janssen, Weisbecker, & Ziegler 1993), to assigning sets of pre- and postconditions to each interface object (Gieskens & Foley 1992). Although working with

1. This work has been supported in part by grants LM05157 and LM05305 from the National Library of Medicine, and by gifts from Digital Equipment Corporation. Dr. Musen is recipient of NSF Young Investigator Award IRI-9257578.

high-level dialog specifications is helpful to interface developers, it does not automate the design of dynamic behavior. For large interfaces, editing the dialog specifications is still a time-consuming task involving the definition of hundreds of actions and conditions, some of which may conflict with each other.

The Mecano Approach

Current data-model approaches do not exploit the relationships among objects in the model to generate the dynamic behavior of an interface. In addition, a data model is application-specific. In the Mecano approach, we aim to use domain models from which dynamic interface behavior can be generated, and that are also sharable across a range of applications.

In this paper, we present Mecano, a model-based interface development environment that uses domain models instead of data models to generate interfaces. A domain model is a high-level knowledge representation that captures all the definitions and relationships of a given application domain. A domain model extends the data model for the application. By substituting the data model in Figure 1 for a domain model, Mecano does not require any dialog specification editing and can generate complete dynamic behavior specifications even for large interfaces with hundreds of components.

The rest of this paper is organized as follows. We first review related work and present an overview of Mecano, including a definition and illustration of domain models. Then, we show how various cases of dynamic behavior can be generated from domain models by using an example from the medical domain. Next, we explain how end users are able to participate in the layout design of interfaces generated in Mecano and how design revisions can be conducted. We conclude by analyzing this approach and summarizing the results.

RELATED WORK

There are three types of systems documented in literature that relate closely to the Mecano approach: (1) systems that use textual specifications to generate dialogs, (2) systems that combine the use of data models and high-level dialog specifications, and (3) systems that directly manipulate an interface model to produce an interface.

One of the earliest efforts to generate dialogs via textual descriptions is COUSIN (Hayes and Szekely 1992). It generates menus and fill-in forms from a specification of commands and their parameters. Mickey (Olsen 1989) uses an extended version of Pascal to describe contents, parameters, and behavior of direct-manipulation of interfaces. ITS (Wiecha et al. 1989) separates dialog and style into two different layers and allows the specification of the dialog layer through a command language and the definition of styles through a rule set. Given the textual description for a dialog, ITS reasons about the style rule set to generate the interface. The UofA* (Singh and Green 1991) system generates the presentation and dialog through a command language. These systems, in general, help the developer by providing tools to design dialogs at a high-level of abstraction, but they do not automate the design process beyond that point.

Among the first examples of the use of data models to derive static layouts for interfaces is HIGGENS (Hudson and King 1986). It allows a developer to view abstractly the interface by examining the data models, but it lacks an automatic generator for the actual interface.

The UIDE environment includes a tool for static layout generation from an extended data model (deBaar, Foley, & Mullet 1992). The specification of dynamic behavior, however, must be achieved by defining sets of pre- and postconditions (Gieskens and Foley 1992) for each one of the interface objects. The GENIUS environment (Janssen, Weisbecker, & Ziegler 1993) uses an entity–relationship data model along with a graphical editor for dialog specifications to generate interfaces. The data model, which can be edited graphically, provides the basis for the definition of the interface components and their layout. The graphical editor allows the review of *dialog nets,* a variation of Petri nets, that define the actions of the interface objects and the conditions that preclude or follow those actions.

Systems that employ data models have the advantage of sharing the data model with the target application, thus coupling the design of both. They cannot automate dynamic dialog design from the data model and have problems scaling up because of their approach to specifying dialogs. For example, the use of pre- and postconditions in large interfaces can cause conflicts among the conditions and may necessitate the development of conflict-resolution strategies.

Systems that generate interfaces by manipulating interface models include HUMANOID (Szekely, Luo, & Neches 1993) and DON (Kim and Foley 1993). HUMANOID defines an elaborate interface model that includes components for the application, the presentation, and the dialog. Developers construct application models and HUMANOID picks among a number of *templates* of interfaces to display the interface. The developer can then refine the behavior of the interface by editing the dialog model. HUMANOID assists, but does not automate, the generation of dynamic behavior specifications, and requires considerable additional developer effort to generate interfaces that do not conform to its templates, as is the case with most complex interfaces. DON uses a presentation model that allows developers to explore designs and that provides expert assistance in the generation of designs. DON does not have a dynamic behavior component for automatic generation of dialogs.

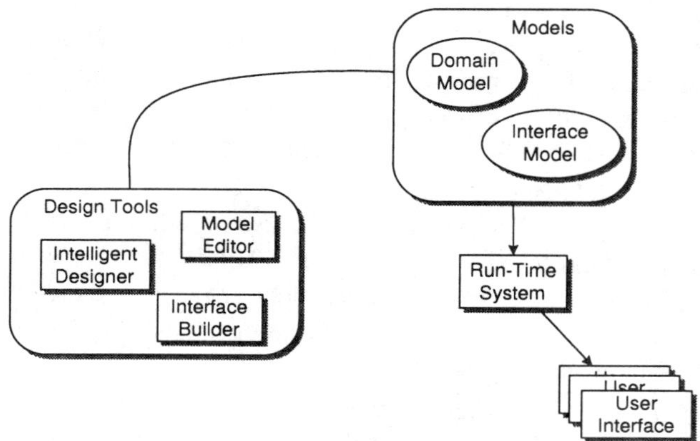

Figure 2. The main components of Mecano. The intelligent designer operates on a domain model, as opposed to a data model, to produce interface designs.

OVERVIEW OF MECANO

The main components of the Mecano environment are shown in Figure 2. Mecano follows the general architecture of Figure 1, replacing the data model with a domain model. The design tools include a model-editing tool, an intelligent designer tool, and an interface builder, which in our case is provided by the supporting platform, the NeXT environment.

The framework for user-interface development with Mecano calls for a developer to start by employing the model editor (Gennari 1993) to visualize and review a domain model (described later in this paper). The domain model is shared with the target application. Therefore, an interface developer need not build one for a given domain from scratch. Instead, the normal process is to revise an existing one. Once a domain model is deemed satisfactory, it is input to the intelligent designer (Eriksson, Puerta, & Musen 1994), a tool that produces a dynamic dialog specification and a preliminary layout for the interface. The layout can then be refined using NeXT's Interface Builder. Both the dialog and layout output by the intelligent designer are stored declaratively in an interface model. This model contains all facets of an interface design including interface objects, presentation, dialog, and behavior.

The design defined in the interface model is implemented by a run-time system. Mecano's run-time tools have the capability of implementing form- and graph-based interfaces with many types of objects, from simple ones, such as menus and push-buttons, to complex ones, such as list browsers and domain-specific graphical editors. The run-time tools implement the dynamic behavior of the interface according to the specifications in the interface model.

The overall design process in Mecano is iterative. The resulting interfaces may have deficiencies that require editing the domain model and regenerating the interface. In such cases, the intelligent designer keeps track of layout customizations that may have been made in the previous generation and reapplies these customizations as appropriate.

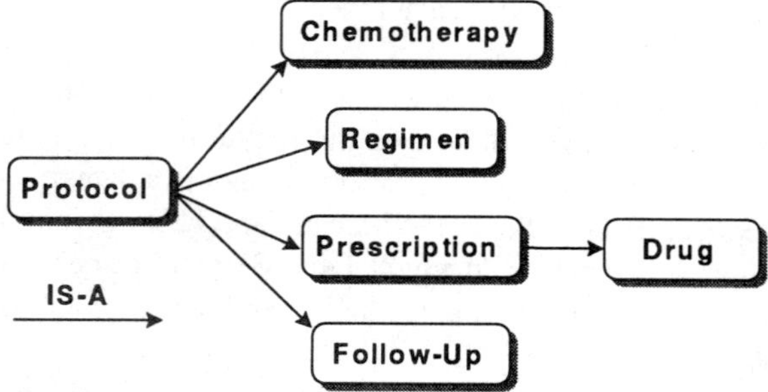

Figure 3. Partial view of a medical domain model for therapy (protocol) administration (IS-A view). The hierarchy of classes is used to generate the interface-navigation schema for windows and other objects.

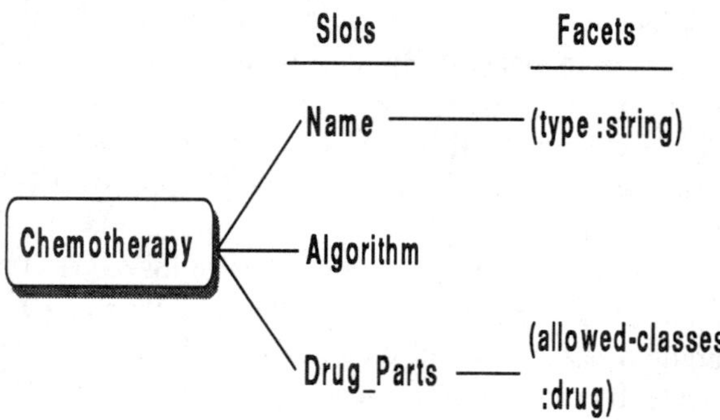

Figure 4. Partial view of the slots and facets (properties) for the *chemotherapy* class. Facets can define *allowed-classes* relationships among classes. These relationships are used to generate specifications for interface-object groupings in windows. Other facets like *type* are important to determine static layout (e.g., appropriate widget for a type *string* object)

Domain Models

A domain model is a representation of the objects in a domain and their interrelationships. Domain models in Mecano are constructed using a frame-based representation language that defines class hierarchies (Gennari 1993). Each *class* in the hierarchy can have a number of *slots* and each slot defines a number of properties (called *facets*) Figures 3 and 4 show partial views of a model for the medical domain of therapy administration (called protocol administration).

There are two important relationships in domain models. The *is-a* relationship (see Figure 3) determines the class hierarchy and is used by the intelligent designer in Mecano to specify the interface-navigation schema among windows and other objects. The *part-of* relationship (see Figure 4) is

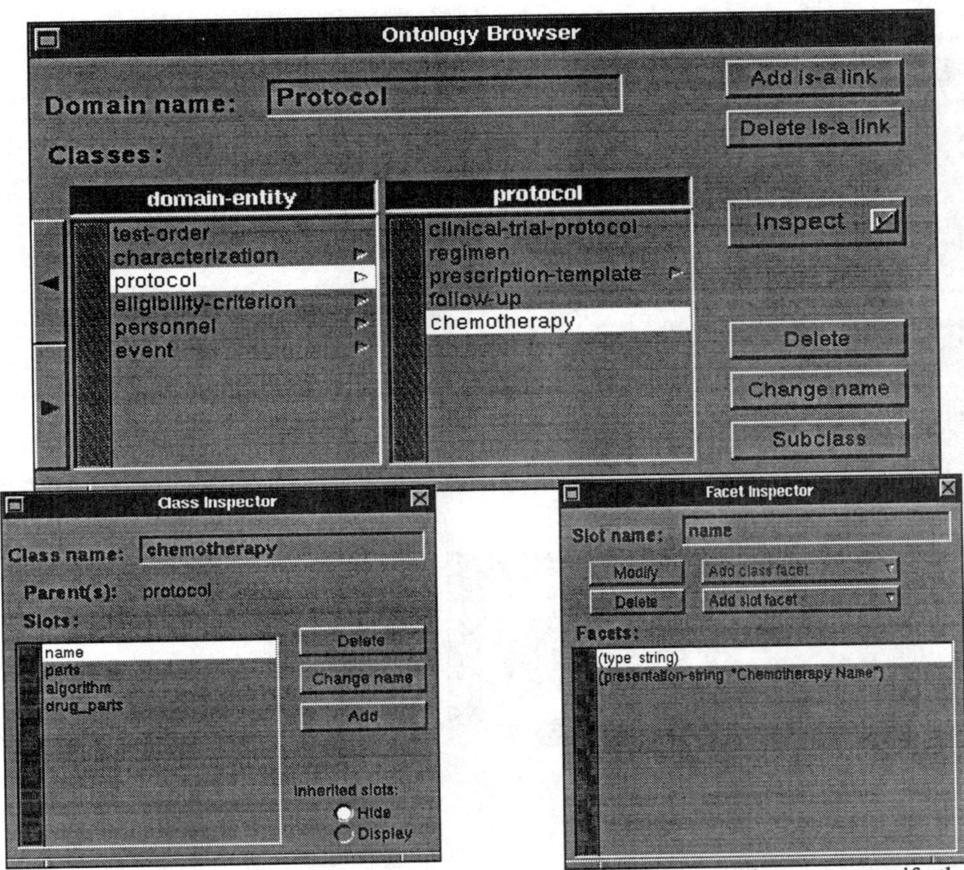

Figure 5. Editing the domain model. Using browsers and inspectors, the developer can specify the *class hierarchy* (top window) and the *slots* and *facets* (properties) of each class.

used to determine object groupings by windows. Other important facets include, for example, *type*, *cardinality*, *min* and *max* of a slot, which are used in the specification of the static layout (e.g., what widget should be used for the slot; size of a numeric input field). In fact, the application's data model is completely included in the domain model. Therefore, all the design rules of an intelligent design tool that may be applied to a data model can be applied to a domain model. In the next section, we illustrate the use of domain models to generate a therapy administration application.

GENERATION OF DIALOG SPECIFICATIONS FROM DOMAIN MODELS

Before dialogs can be generated, a domain model must be prepared with the model editor shown in Figure 5. The domain model is shared with the target application. Thus, a coupling of application design and interface design is established. Developers can build domain models incrementally, and can prototype interfaces early in the development process because Mecano supports iterative design. More importantly, it is not necessary to build domain models from scratch for every application. A domain model for medical therapy planning can be reused, with minor variations, in other applications. This is a significant advantage of Mecano over systems that design from data models because data models are difficult to reuse across applications.

Once edited, the domain model is used to generate dialog specifications. These specifications have two levels in Mecano:.

- High-level dialog defines all interface windows, assigns interface objects to windows, and specifies the navigation schema among windows in the interface.

- Low-level dialog defines specific dialog elements (widgets) to each interface object created at the high level and specifies how the standard behavior of the dialog element is modified for the given domain.

High-Level Dialog Generation

The elements of the high-level dialog specification are generated by examining the class hierarchy of the domain

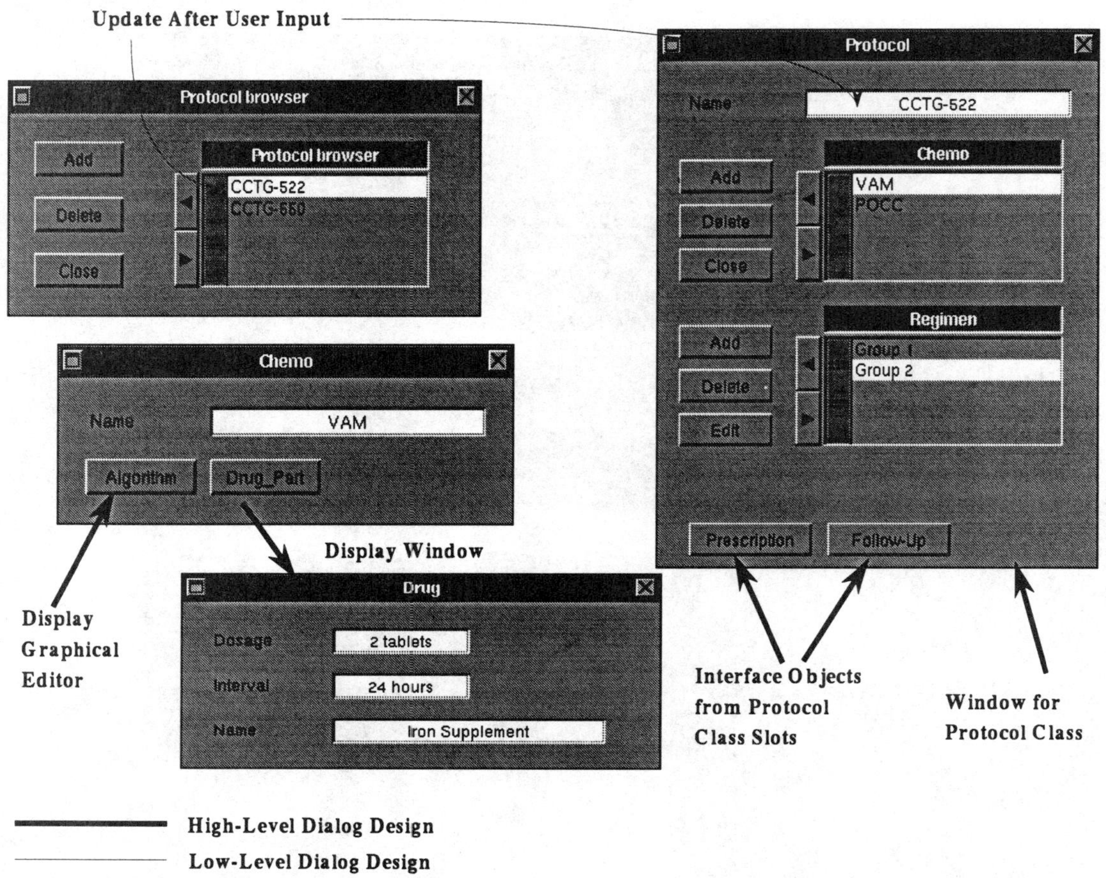

Figure 6. Interface generated from the partial domain model in Figures 3 and 4. Legends indicate generated dialog at high- and low-level design times. An interface generated from the full domain model for medical therapy contains over 60 windows and hundreds of dialog elements (widgets). The dynamic behavior of such interface can be generated automatically from a domain model.

model (see Figure 3) and the slots of each class (see Figure 4). Figure 6 shows an interface generated from the partial domain model shown in Figures 3, and 4. The complete medical domain model for therapy administration generates an interface with over 60 windows and hundreds of widgets. Note that the dialog for window navigation is established during high-level dialog design but that it can be refined, or augmented, at low-level dialog design time. The procedure to generate a high-level dialog design is as follows:

- Each class in the hierarchy is assigned a window.

- Window navigation is established by searching the class hierarchy for links indicated by the *allowed-classes* facet in the domain model. For example, the *Drug* window shown in Figure 6 is accessed from the *Chemo* window because the Drug class is an allowed class for the slot *Drug_Part*.

- Each window is assigned one *interface object* per slot in the class. After generation, the developer has the option of customizing the interface by splitting windows multiple objects into two or more windows. Interface objects are assigned actual widgets during low-level dialog design.

Low-Level Dialog Generation

Elements of the low-level dialog specification are generated by examining the facets (properties) defined for each slot in the domain model (see Figure 4). The process has these steps:

- Each interface object defined at high-level design time is assigned a dialog element (widget) by examining the facets of the corresponding slot in the domain model. For example an object of *type string* is assigned a text field, an object of *type Boolean* is assigned a check-box widget, and an object of *type string* and *cardinality multiple* (i.e., the object can be multiple-valued) is assigned a list browser.

- Each dialog element may be assigned *actions* beyond the standard behavior of the dialog element by examining the facets of the corresponding slot in the domain model. Examples of dialog-element actions include disabling editing in other dialog elements, and updating values in other dialog elements after a user input action (see Figure 6).

Note that the specification of dialog-element actions is one of the important operations that cannot be automated in systems that rely on data models for interface generation.

GENERATION OF DOMAIN-SPECIFIC GRAPHICAL EDITORS

One of the important capabilities in Mecano is the generation from domain models of domain-specific, nodes-and-links graphical editors useful to describe procedures such as flowcharts. Consider the following slot information for the class *Protocol*:

```
(slot algorithm
    (type :procedure)
    (allowed-classes :xrt :chemotherapy :drug))
```

When the intelligent dialog designer examines this slot during low-level dialog design, it assigns a graphical editor as the dialog element for that slot due to the type *procedure* defined for that slot. It also defines three graphical objects to be used during editing, one for *x-ray therapies* (xrt), one for *chemotherapies (chemo),* and one for *drugs*. Figure 7 shows a graphical editor generated from the above slot definition.

PARTICIPATORY LAYOUT DESIGN AND DESIGN REVISION

A crucial concern with any system that automatically generates interfaces is how it allows the developer to review and change the generated design. In Mecano, there are two types of revisions: layout and dialog.

The intelligent designer tool uses a layout algorithm to produce a *preliminary* layout of the interface objects. The philosophy in Mecano is to be able to involve the end user in the process of custom-tailoring a layout. For example, for the medical treatment application shown in this paper, the interface developer works together with a physician to review and custom tailor the preliminary layout with an interface builder (see Figure 2). Our experience is that this revision—in the case of the interface derived from the full model—may take between two and a half to four hours for the 65 windows included in that application (including layout and dialog revisions, and needed interface regenerations). Custom-tailoring information is kept on a database so that if the interface needs to be regenerated because of incremental changes to the domain model (as it is often the case), the customizations can be reapplied to the newly generated interface. Substantial revisions of the domain model, however, invalidate the information on the customization database.

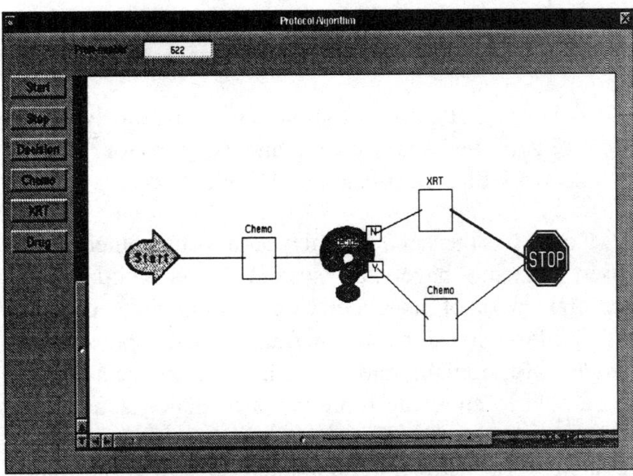

Figure 7. A graphical editor to draw medical treatments generated from a domain model. Both the drawing objects and their connectivity behavior are determined by the intelligent designer tool in Mecano.

The working sessions with the end user—in this paper's example, a physician—are also used to discover difficulties with the dialog design and incompleteness in the information displayed in the interface. Dialog design customizations can be made by editing directly the interface model (see Figure 2) and do not require a regeneration of the interface. On the other hand, for the interface to be able to display additional dialog elements, changes must be made to the domain model to define needed slots or classes. Such changes do require the interface be regenerated. Overall, the Mecano policy is to understand the interface design process as iterative and to support the introduction of custom changes without creating duplicate work.

ANALYSIS AND CONCLUSIONS

We have described a user-interface development environment that generates automatically presentation and dialog specifications for domain-specific, form- and graph-based interfaces. The strong points of this system are:

- Generation of both the static layout and the dynamic behavior of domain-specific, form- and graph-based interfaces, including relatively large and complex ones, for multiple domains (e.g., medical treatment, elevator configuration).

- Use of the application's domain models, which includes the application's data model, for interface generation considerably augments automation capabilities over systems utilizing only a data model.

• Support of participatory layout design involving end users of the applications, and support for iterative design without duplication of work.

Mecano has the same central weakness that other model-based systems have: the system is as good as the expressiveness of its underlying models. We continue researching extensions to our frame-based representation language for domain models and interface models in order to be able to automate more types of dialog actions. In particular, we are concerned with how to generate complex sequences of actions (commands) at low-level dialog design time. We are also working on the run-time system of Mecano to implement new types of widgets. Furthermore, the interface generation approach from domain models is most useful for domain-specific interfaces with a relatively fixed user dialogue (such as the medical forms shown in the figures in this paper). For other types of interfaces, it will be necessary to examine other types of models (such as a model of the user's task) to be able to generate automatically interface specifications. We are currently working on developing such task models as components of our generic interface model.

Overall, Mecano provides a framework for assisting the development of interfaces and for the study of interface models and the relationships between domain characteristics and user interface presentation and dialog.

ACKNOWLEDGMENTS

We wish to thank Tom Gruber for his helpful comments.

REFERENCES

de Baar, D.J.M.J., Foley, J.D. and Mullet, K.E. 1992. Coupling Application Design and User Interface Design. In *Proceedings of Human Factors in Computing Systems, CHI'92*. Monterey, California, May 1992, pp. 259–266.

Eriksson, H., Puerta, A.R. and Musen, M.A. 1994. Generation of Knowledge-Acquisition Tools from Domain Ontologies. In *Proceedings of the Eighth Banff Knowledge Acquisition for Knowledge-Based Systems Workshop.* Banff, Alberta, Canada. pp. 7.1–7.20.

Gennari, J.H. 1993. *A Brief Guide to Maître and MODEL: An Ontology Editor and a Frame-Based Knowledge Representation Language.* Stanford University, Knowledge Systems Laboratory, Report KSL-93-46, Stanford, California. June 1993.

Gieskens, D.F. and Foley, J.D. 1992. Controlling User Interface Objects through Pre- and Postconditions. In *Proceedings of Human Factors in Computing Systems, CHI'92*. Monterey, California, May 1992, pp. 189–194.

Hayes, P. and Szekely, P. 1992. Graceful Interaction through the {COUSIN} Command Interface. *International Journal of Man-Machine Studies*, **19**(3), pp. 285–305.

Hudson, S.E. and King, R. 1986 A Generator of Direct Manipulation Office Systems. *ACM Transactions on Information Systems*, **4**(2), pp. 132–163.

Janssen, C., Weisbecker A. and Ziegler J. 1993. Generating User Interfaces from Data Models and dialog Net Specifications. In *Proceedings of Human Factors in Computing Systems, INTERCHI'93*. Amsterdam, The Netherlands, April 1993, pp. 418–423.

Kim, W.C. and Foley, J.D. 1993. Providing High-Level Control and Expert Assistance in the User Interface Presentation Design. In *Proceedings of Human Factors in Computing Systems, INTERCHI'93*. Amsterdam, The Netherlands, April 1993, pp. 430–437.

Olsen, D.R. 1989. A Programming Language Basis for User Interface Management. In *Proceedings of Human Factors in Computing Systems, CHI'89*. Austin, Texas, May 1989, pp. 171–176.

Puerta A.R. 1993. The Study of Models of Intelligent Interfaces. In Proceedings of the 1993 International Workshop on Intelligent User Interfaces. Orlando, Florida, January 1993, pp. 71–80.

Singh, G. and Green, M. 1991. Automating the Lexical and Syntactic Design of Graphical User Interfaces: The UofA* UIMS. *ACM Transactions on Graphics*, **10**(3), pp. 213–254.

Szekely, P., Luo, P. and Neches, R. 1993. Beyond Interface Builders: Model-Based Interface Tools. In *Proceedings of Human Factors in Computing Systems, INTERCHI'93*. Amsterdam, The Netherlands, April 1993, pp. 383–390.

Wiecha, C., Bennett, W., Boies, S., Gould, J. and Greene, S. 1989. ITS: A Tool for Rapidly Developing Interactive Applications. *ACM Transactions on Information Systems*, **8**(3), pp. 204–236.

Model-Based Automated Generation of User Interfaces

Angel R. Puerta

The main contribution of Mecano was to incorporate the use of domain models, or ontologies, into the model-based interface development framework. Paradoxically, it was this same feature that unveiled the limitations of the Mecano approach. Domain models allowed us to generate not only the static layout but also significant portions of the dialog of an interface. This was possible, thanks to the much greater expressiveness of a domain ontology over a traditional data model. Many groups had employed data models before to support automated generation of interfaces, and that limited them to producing static layouts only. Mecano was used to build a number of form- and graph-based medical and military interfaces.

However, soon after we embarked on the ambitious project of generalizing the Mecano approach beyond forms, we found ourselves hitting the proverbial wall. We reasoned that our interface models must be comprehensive—go beyond domain representations and incorporate all relevant aspects of an interface design, including user tasks, presentations, dialogs, and users. In this we succeeded by creating a new modeling language for interfaces. We supported that language with an open client/server architecture that would allow multiple tools and environments to communicate with, operate on, and edit the interface model.

But the design space for interfaces exploded under this framework. The computational force and knowledge bases required to automate the design of interfaces, in the ample sense of the word, was unattainable. We questioned then the whole purpose of an environment like Mecano with its drive toward automating significant portions of the design process for an interface. The result was a new, redirected effort to build a model-based development environment with the same aim of Mecano, developing interfaces from a declarative model but with a significantly different philosophy. Instead of automation, we looked for ways to support interface designers. Instead of large knowledge bases and complex inferencing strategies to make design decisions, we built interactive tools for developers to do what they do best: design interfaces. Instead of using interface models as a driving mechanism for an expert system, we used them to organize and visualize interface design knowledge.

Our successor to Mecano, called MOBI-D (model-based interface designer) (Puerta and Maulsby 1997; Puerta 1997), is now a much different product. MOBI-D supports a user-centered design methodology that involves end users in the design process. It is task oriented (as opposed to domain oriented) and is an interactive environment, not an automatic one. Of course, we support the automation of menial or tedious tasks, but we do not try to take control away from designers. This is certainly a marked departure from previous efforts in model-based development—a new philosophy that other groups around the world are now starting to adopt. Thus, Mecano showed us the power of added expressiveness in an interface model. It also showed us the limits of automation and pointed us to a new path and a new paradigm.

REFERENCES

Puerta, A. 1997. Model-Based Development Tools. *IEEE Software*, 14(4): 40–47.

Puerta, A., and Maulsby, D. 1997. MOBI-D: A Model-Based Development Environment for User-Centered Design. In *Proceedings of CHI-97 (Extended Abstracts)*, Atlanta, GA, March, 4–5.

AUTOMATIC GENERATION OF A USER INTERFACE FOR HIGHLY INTERACTIVE BUSINESS-ORIENTED APPLICATIONS

Jean Vanderdonckt

Facultés Universitaires Notre-Dame de la Paix, Institut d'Informatique
Rue Grandgagnage, 21, B-5000 NAMUR (Belgium)
Tel. : +32 (0)81-72.49.75 - Fax. : +32 (0)81-72.49.67 - Telex : 59.222 FacNamB
Email : jvanderdonckt@info.fundp.ac.be

ABSTRACT

The goal of this work is to prove that a designer can be able to generate as systematically as possible a first sketch of the presentation for an ergonomical user interface in the specific area of highly-interactive business-oriented applications. It basically consists of three foundations : (i) the *corpus ergonomicus*, a multi-purpose high-level styleguide; (ii) the SEGUIA tool which is able to assist the designer in the selection and layout tasks ; (iii) the SIERRA tool which an on-line hypermedia documenting linguistic ergonomic criteria and guidelines defined in the corpus ergonomicus. This work is integrated in the TRIDENT project which is a methodology and a supporting environment for developing highly-interactive business-oriented applications.

KEYWORDS

Business-oriented applications, Computer-aided generation, Criteria, Guidelines, Layout, Selection, Styleguide.

INTRODUCTION

"Business-oriented applications" mainly deal with database applications found in office automation, data management, financial accounting, and administrative works. The adjective "highly-interactive" means that the user interface provides enhanced mechanisms for data manipulation, navigation, visualisation, and input/output. The user interface can become "ergonomic" if relevant guidelines, ergonomic recommendations and visual design principles are explictly included in a design methodology. The "automatic generation" attempts to provide a computer-aided design methodology supported with tools which automatically generate a workable and visible user interface from both the functional and operational requirements.

DESCRIPTION

The work basically consists of three parts : the *corpus ergonomicus*, the SEGUIA tool, and the SIERRA tool. These parts show the feasability of user interface generation by computer-aiding the designer's activities.

THE *CORPUS ERGONOMICUS*

The *corpus ergonomicus* is a high-level multi-purpose styleguide of about 3,700 guidelines and principles collected from styleguides, recommendations reports, articles, human factors books and standards [4]. These guidelines are uniformly organized according to a consistent object-oriented model. This model is composed of a numerical reference, a synthetic title, a complete natural language statement, a list of 900 bibliographical references, a design criteria, positive and negative examples with screen captures, exceptions, an evaluation criteria. All guidelines are connected together with typed links such as : is similar to, is dissimilar to, is conflicting with, inherits from, is inherited by, generalizes, specializes, preceeds, follows,...

Guidelines are sorted by importance according to eight design criteria : compatibility, consistency, user workload, adaptability, dialogue control, significance, user guidance, and error management [1]. These linguistic ergonomic criteria are defined along six levels of Nielsen's linguistic model of interaction : goal, pragmatic, semantic, syntactic, lexical, alphabetic, and physical [5]. Five Shneiderman's evaluation criteria are used : time to learn specific functions, speed of task performance, rate of errors, subjective user satisfaction, and human retention of commands over time [6]. Each guideline is related to interaction styles combined from: natural language, query language, command language, questions/answers, menu selection, form filling, function keys, direct manipulation, multi-windowing, graphic interaction, and multimedia interaction.

Each guideline is also expressed in terms of abstract interaction objects. These objects are hierarchically divided into six classes: action objects (e.g. menu bar, items), static objects (e.g. label, separator), scroll objects (e.g. scroll arrow, bar), control objects (e.g. radio box, button, list box), dialogue objects (e.g. window, dialogue box, panel) and feedback objects (e.g. messages, progress indicators). This taxonomy results from a cross-platform analysis of interaction objects and allow easy transportation and reusability.

THE *SEGUIA* TOOL

SEGUIA is an expert system for automatically generating user interfaces. Useful and relevant guidelines are extracted from the corpus and embedded as strategies in a first-order predicate logic expert system for deriving the presentation of the interface. This tool is implemented with Aion for Windows 3.1. This includes :

- an intelligent automatic selection of elementary and composite abstract interaction objects from a data model, a user model and a dialogue model. This selection requires selection rules which can be graphically depicted with a decision-tree technique for clearly visualizing and understanding why a particular interaction object has been chosen. SIERRA can be used as : an advice-giving system or a generation system with two modes :
  1. *full automatic generation* : all data instances of the concerned application are mapped into interaction objects instances without the designer's mediation;
  2. *computer-aided generation* : the designer follows step by step the selection process, can stop it and modify it. This mode basically provides forward chaining, backward chaining, and bidirectional chaining;
- an automatic composite objects (windows, dialog boxes, panels...) creation by selecting usable presentation units and types (minimal, maximal, input/output, functional, grouped and free) from an activity chaining graph and others cited models;
- an automatic interaction objects placer (layout) trying to optimize three dimensions in visual design: localization (where a particular object is placed), sizing (how objects are sized, justified, aligned) and arrangement of interaction objects (which logical sequence or predefined format is to be followed). Two strategies (i.e. two-column based and right/bottom) are introduced, defined according to fifteen mathematical geographic relations (e.g. alignment, centration, uniformization, balance). Comparing the strategies show that dynamic strategies are more successfull than static ones for complex cases;
- semi-automatic menu bar, pull-down menus generation with balanced hierarchy and user-adapted depth and breadth tree;
- semi-automatic message builder with appropriate and consistent wording.

Generating the elements of the presentation component is compatible with the definition of TRIDENT's architecture in terms of thre different objects : application objects, control objects, and presentation objects [2].

THE *SIERRA* TOOL

SIERRA is an interactive hypermedia guide providing facilities to the designer/programmer for guidelines consulting, selecting, applying, checking, application usability controlling during the application development life-cycle. Implemented with Multimedia Viewer V2.0 for Windows, SIERRA is context-sensitive with SEGUIA. The implementation of the whole corpus ergonomicus is currently studied with references to design criteria and abstract interaction objects mentioned above. This tool supports a multi-document environment where each document consists of a particular existing styleguide or standard (e.g. Apple Human Interface Guidelines, Smith & Mosier report, MIL-STD-1472D, IBM CUA). This leads to the study of reusable templates for documenting on-line styleguides and standards. Guidelines are connected with hypermedia links with different attributes :

- a relation type establishing the link range : intra-level, intra-section, intra-division,... ;
- a reference type : from one guideline to another, from one guideline to a section, a level or a division;
- a nature : simple (if one-to-one relation) or multiple (if one-to-many relation);
- a direction stating the orientation validity of the link : unidirectional or bidirectional;
- a link type compatible with the corpus : is similar to, is dissimilar to, is conflicting with, inherits from, is inherited by, generalizes, specializes, preceeds, follows,...

Future works and investigations include the comparison of automatic placement strategies, the implementation of SIERRA as a general-purpose usability guidance and help tool, the extension of interaction objects typology to multimedia objects, and the reduction of the corpus to a day-to-day minimal corpus for teaching and understanding ergonomical aspects.

REFERENCES

1. Bastien, Ch. and Scapin, D.L., A Validation of Ergonomic Criteria for the Evaluation of the Human-Computer Interfaces, in *International Journal of Man-Machines Studies*, Vol. 4, No. 2, 1992, pp. 183-196.
2. Bodart, F., Hennebert, A.-M., Leheureux, J.-M. , Sacre, I., and Vanderdonckt, J., Architecture Elements for Highly-Interactive Business-Oriented Applications, in Lecture Notes in Computer Science, Vol. 753, L. Bass, J. Gornostaev and C. Unger (eds.), Springer-Verlag, Berlin, 1993, pp. 83-104.
3. Bodart, F., Lesuisse, R., and Vanderdonckt, J., A Proposition for Layered Ergonomic Criteria in Design/-Evaluation, In *Proc. HCI International '93* (Orlando, August 8-13, 1993), p. 19.
4. Bodart, F. and Vanderdonckt, J. Expressing Guidelines into an Ergonomical StyleGuide for Highly Interactive Applications, in *Adjunct Proc. of INTERCHI'93* (Amsterdam, April 24-29, 1993), ACM Press, pp. 35-36.

5. Nielsen, J., A Virtual Protocol Model for Computer-Human Interaction, in *International Journal of Man-Machine Studies*, vol. 24, no. 3, 1986, pp. 301-312.
6. Shneiderman, B., Designing the User Interface, Strategies for Effective Human-Computer Interaction, Addison-Wesley, Reading, 1987.
7. Vanderdonckt, J. and Bodart, F., Encapsulating Knowledge for Intelligent Automatic Interaction Objects Selection. In *Proc. of INTERCHI'93* (Amsterdam, April 24-29, 1993), pp. 424-429.

Automatic Generation of a User Interface for Highly Interactive Business-Oriented Applications

Jean Vanderdonckt

During the last decade, we investigated the area of automated generation of user interfaces (UI) in the Trident project (Bodart et al. 1995). Several shifts of focus were observed:

1. *A shift from a model-based approach to task-based approach.* Model-based approaches for automatically generating a UI from information contained in one or several models have been largely investigated and proved feasible. Among these models, the task model rapidly appeared as a fundamental starting point, as it describes how a user could or should carry out an interactive task with the application. In a task-based approach, this task model is exploited to derive as automatically as possible a UI model, which is in turn used for generating the final UI code.
2. *Generation of an abstract UI rather than a concrete one.* In a task-based approach, the derived UI model consists in depicting the UI widgets hierarchy in terms of abstract interaction objects (AIOs) rather than in terms of concrete interaction objects (CIOs) (Vanderdonckt and Bodart 1993). This abstraction allows some autonomy of the UI with respect to a target computing platform and multiple cross-platform generations.
3. *Computer-aided design of UIs (CADUI) progressively replaces automated generation of UIs.* In the last method, a UI is (blindly) generated from various sources (e.g., models in a model-based approach, parameters, user profile) without any designer intervention during the generation process. Conversely, in the first method, a UI is incrementally built by letting a designer choose among propositions made by the system. For example, the SEGUIA system (Vanderdonckt 1997) suggests to designers which AIO to select for which type of information to input/display, and how widgets can be laid out in a usable fashion. SEGUIA is able to generate the complete presentation (e.g., windows, dialog boxes, buttons, icons, combination boxes) for a UI related to a business-oriented domain.
4. *The shift from a belief that automated generation would be usable enough for all kind of circumstances to a proof that it is worthwhile only under precise conditions.* In the past, automated generation was hoped as a good way to obtain a usable final UI instantly. It has been shown that the usability of a generated UI highly depends on the quality of information (e.g., in specifications, models). Even after refining it, there is still an obvious difference between a system-generated UI and a UI produced by a human factors expert. Nevertheless, automated generation of a user interface and, today, CADUI are viewed to be efficient in circumstances where a UI should be available very rapidly and when the resources (e.g., time, money, availability) required by a human factors expert clearly outweighs the cost of producing it with a system.

REFERENCES

Bodart, F.; Hennebert, A.-M.; Leheureux, J.-M.; Provot, I.; Vanderdonckt, J.; and Zucchinetti, G. 1995. Key Activities for a Development Methodology of Interactive Applications. In Benyon, D. and Palanque, P. (eds.), *Critical Issues in User Interface Systems Engineering*, Chapter 7, 109–134. Berlin: Springer-Verlag. (*http://www.info.fundp.ac.be/cgi-bin/pub-spec-paper?RP-96-025*)

Bodart, F., and Vanderdonckt, J. (eds.). 1996. Design, Specification and Verification of Interactive Systems '96. In *Proceedings of 3rd Eurographics Workshop on Design, Specification, Verification of Interactive Systems DSV-IS'96*, June 5–7, Namur, Belgium. Eurographics Series. Vienna: Springer-Verlag. (*http://www.info.fundp.ac.be/~jvd/dsvis/order96.html*)

Vanderdonckt, J. 1995. Accessing Guidelines Information with SIERRA. In Nordbyn, K., Helmersen, P. H., Gilmore, D. J., and Arnesen, S. A. (eds.), *Proceedings of Fifth IFIP TC 13*

International Conference on Human-Computer Interaction INTERACT'95, June 27–29, Lillehammer, 311–316. London: Chapman & Hall. (*http://www.info.fundp.ac.be/cgi-bin /pub-spec-paper?RP-95-020*)

Vanderdonckt, J. (ed.). 1996. Computer-Aided Design of User Interfaces. In *Proceedings of 2nd International Workshop on Computer-Aided Design of User Interfaces CADUI'96* June 5-7, Namur, Belgium: Presses Universitaires de Namur. (*http://www.info.fundp.ac.be /~jvd/dsvis/cadui96.html*)

Vanderdonckt, J. 1997. Conception Assistée de la Présentation d'une Interface Homme-Machine Ergonomique pour une Application de Gestion Hautement Interactive [Computer-Aided Presentation Design of an Ergonomic User Interface for a Highly Interactive Business-Oriented Application]. Ph.D. thesis, Facultes Universitaires Notre-Dame de la Paix Namur (FUNDP) Namur, Belgium.

Vanderdonckt, J., and Bodart, F. 1993. Encapsulating Knowledge for Intelligent Automatic Interaction Objects Selection. In Ashlund, S., Mullet, K., Henderson, A., Hollnagel, E., and White, T. (eds.), *Proceedings of ACM Conference on Human Aspects in Computing Systems InterCHI'93*, April 24–29, Amsterdam, 424–429. Reading, MA: Addison-Wesley. (*http://www.info.fundp.ac.be/cgi-bin/pub-spec-paper?RP-93-005*)

SECTION VII

Agent Interfaces

The dream of a volitional entity performing delegated tasks was envisioned in early writings about robots and precedes even the modern computer. A recent resurgence in the use of agents to enhance interaction has driven and been driven by technical advances as well as by a need to address growing system complexity and an increasingly varied user population. Technical advances have included the development of knowledge interchange and agent communication languages (e.g., KQML (Finin et al. 1994)), which enable human-agent and agent-agent communication and coordination (e.g., requests, tasking, negotiation). Advances in agent competencies coupled with advanced interface components (e.g., speech, facial animation) makes anthropomorphic agent emulation feasible. The papers in this section therefore represent agents that perform tasks on behalf of users as well as those that create interfaces possessing anthropomorphic communicative abilities (e.g., integrated speech, gesture, and facial displays).

The first contribution by Patti Maes investigates the use of computers as personal assistants who reduce work and information overload. Maes's paper explores such tasks as managing mail, scheduling meetings, filtering electronic news groups, and recommending entertainment (e.g., books, music). Interface agents supporting these tasks learn (1) from observing and imitating user behavior, (2) from user feedback, (3) directly from user-supplied examples, and (4) from other agents. In one example, the Maxims mail agent uses simple caricatures (e.g., working, pleased, confused) to convey the agent's state to the user. These agents not only recommend actions but indicate a level of confidence in the recommendation based on memory-based learning and use this and user-defined thresholds to determine when to recommend actions versus doing them. In the NewT news filtering application, a user gives positive or negative feedback on selected articles by indicating the author, source, or highlighted word or paragraph. In the Ringo system, agents use "social filtering" to detect correlations among users. After discovering which other users have values most similar to the current user (e.g., positive ratings of albums of a particular artist or books of a particular genre), the agent uses these to make recommendations of items not rated by the user. For example, if a user rates Luther Vandross albums highly, they will be matched with users that have similar evaluations, and the agent will recommend albums that the user has not rated but that other users with similar tastes have rated highly. (In fact, recommender systems have diversified and proliferated (Resnick and Varian 1997).) Maes argues that the resulting agents are both more *competent*, as they incrementally accumulate knowledge about the user, and more *trusted*, as they build up a model of the agent's competencies and limitations while interacting with the user.

The second article by Gerard Fischer, Kumiyo Nakakoji, Jonathan Ostwald, Gerry Stahl, and Tamara Sumner indicates how expert critics embedded in domain-oriented design environments can facilitate a design process by fostering reflection or change in the designed artifact. Using examples from their HYDRA-KITCHEN design environment, the authors present the complementary roles of generic, specific, and interpretive critics. Within the system, the user has access to a construction and specification component as well as a case-based catalog of previous designs. The evolving kitchen design is presented graphically together with an argumentation illustrator, which hierarchically presents issues, answers, and arguments supporting or refuting answers (e.g., doors should not be adjacent to stoves to avoid fire hazards). Critiquing, or evaluating, is a rule-based process motivated by the fact that design knowledge is typically incomplete and evolving, the problem is only partially specified and dynamic, and the knowledge required to complete the task is distributed among experts. When concluding, the authors point to the application of their critiquing environment to other domains. As is evident in this kitchen design critic, users will expect expert agents to assist in the formulation or execution of increasingly complex tasks.

Agents and agent communication languages might be used not only to support task performance but also to enable integration of complex software systems. The article by Phil Cohen, Michael Johnston, David McGee, Sharon Oviatt, Jay Pittman, Ira Smith, Liang Chen, and Josh Clow describes QuickSet, a handheld pen/voice interface to facilitate the setup of distributed interactive simulations. Using the Open Agent Architecture (OAA), the authors integrate a broad range of interface components or agents (e.g., speech, gesture, natural language, multimodal integration) via a facilitator that performs tasks such as routing, triggering, and dispatching via the Interagent Communication Language. An important design consideration motivating their approach is the desire to have communicative modalities compensate for each other's weaknesses. To enable multimodal integration, the authors present a unification operation over typed feature structures that combines consistent but partial information (e.g., using a gesture and spoken command to move an object). The authors emphasize the importance of their OAA approach (based on a distributed, Prolog-based blackboard architecture) in terms of system modularity, scalability, distribution, and integration with legacy systems. The authors describe valuable lessons learned from transitioning QuickSet—for example, the need to have full functionality overlap among speech, gesture, and direct manipulation input in noisy environments as well as weaknesses with current agent architecture (e.g., the need to separate data and control from the facilitator to avoid a bottleneck).

The article by Nagao and Takeuchi similarly integrates several interface components (speech, dialog processing, facial animation) to enable an anthropomorphic interface. Their aim is to reduce the stress of interaction and lower the complexity of understanding system results. The authors point to facial expressions as a rich communication channel for conveying emotional and conversational signals. They map several classes of system state (e.g., "thinking," "listening," "incredulity") onto 26 facial displays (e.g., "closing eyes," "eyebrow raising," "eyebrow lowering"). They further present a speech dialog system integrated with a facial animation system including a plan recognition component. States of the recognition system (e.g., understanding, syntactic error, ambiguity) result in utterances generated with consistent facial displays. For example, if the speaker's request exceeds the system's knowledge, it displays a facial shrug and replies, "I cannot answer such a question." A complex facial model of visemes is finely coordinated with synthesized phonemes. A controlled ablation experiment with 32 subjects investigated conversations held with facial displays versus those with short phrases substituted (e.g., "I am not confident") while inquiring about Sony computer product information. The authors found the conversations with facial displays to be smoother. They also found that early interaction with facial displays improves subsequent interaction even if subsequent conversation uses no facial displays.

The final article by Justine Cassell and colleagues reports on a system that generates coordinated facial expression, hand gesture, speech, and intonation for automatically animating conversations between multiple humanlike agents. A dialog planner generates both text and intonation patterns that mark theme (or topic) and rheme (or focus). The text, intonation, and turn-taking dynamics then drive generators of facial expressions, lip motion, eye gaze, head motion, and hand gestures. Arm, wrist, and hand motions are coordinated to ensure semantically meaningful communication. The authors detail and illustrate these mechanisms using a synthesized, fully animated conversation between a bank teller and a client. These models can be used as is or further refined by a human animator, thus saving significant time and effort and ensuring humanlike relationships between verbal and nonverbal behavior in creating animated agents.

As is evident across these papers, agents provide benefits such as simplifying, speeding up, and improving the quality of task performance. Interface agents enable more natural, multimodal interaction and draw directly on human perceptual and conversational abilities. Making machines more user centered—learning from, adapting to, and more effectively supporting the user—affords the possibility of increasing the acceptance, decreasing the stress, and enhancing the performance of the user.

Agent interfaces remain in their infancy. Many unexplored or underexplored topics include dealing with the psychology of human-agent interaction, supporting mixed initiative, designing architectures (components, connectors, constraints, representations) that enable more integrable and evolvable interfaces, and addressing social issues such as privacy and trust that stand in the way of adoption of these devices by mainstream users.

REFERENCES

Finin, T.; Fritzson, R.; McKay, D.; and McEntire, R. 1994. KQML as an Agent Communication Language. In *Proceedings of the Third International Conference on Information and Knowledge Management (CIKM'94)*, November. New York: ACM Press.

Resnick, P., and Varian, H. R. (guest eds.). 1997. Recommender Systems. *Communications of the ACM*, 40(3): 56–89. (*http://www.acm.org/cacm/MAR97/marchtoc.html*)

Agents that **Reduce Work and Information Overload**

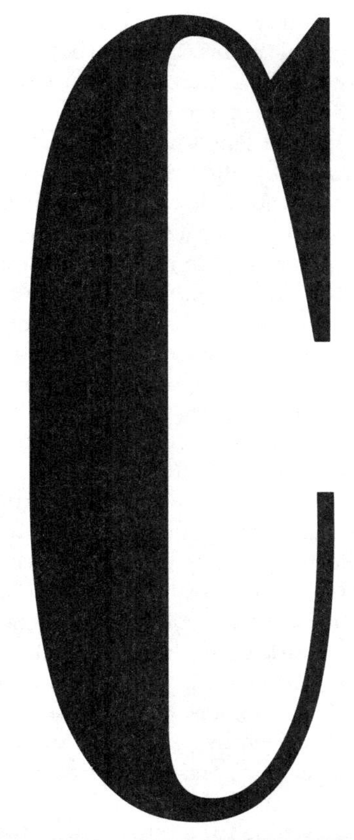

Pattie Maes

Computers are becoming the vehicle for an increasing range of everyday activities. Acquisition of news and information, mail and even social interactions and entertainment have become more and more computer based. At the same time, an increasing number of untrained users are interacting with computers, and this number will continue to rise as technologies such as hand-held computers and interactive television become popular.

Unfortunately, these technological developments are not in line with a change in the way people interact with computers. The currently dominant interaction metaphor of *direct manipulation* [21] requires the user to initiate all tasks explicitly and to monitor all events. This metaphor will have to change if untrained users are to make effective use of the computer and networks of tomorrow.

Techniques from the field of AI, in particular so-called "autonomous agents," can be used to implement a complementary style of interaction, which has been referred to as *indirect management* [9]. Instead of user-initiated interaction via commands and/or direct manipulation, the user is engaged in a cooperative process in which human and computer agents both initiate communication, monitor events and perform tasks. The metaphor used is that of a *personal assistant* who is *collaborating with the user* in the same work environment. The assistant becomes gradually more effective as it learns the user's interests, habits and preferences (as well as those of his or her community). Notice that the agent is not necessarily an interface between the computer and the user. In fact, the most successful interface agents are those that do not prohibit the user from taking actions and fulfilling tasks personally (see Figure 1).

Agents assist users in a range of different ways: they hide the complexity of difficult tasks, they perform tasks on the user's behalf, they can train or teach the user, they help different users collaborate, and they monitor events and procedures.

The set of tasks or applications an agent can assist in is virtually unlimited: information filtering, information retrieval, mail management, meeting scheduling, selection of books, movies, music, and so forth.

This article focuses on a novel approach to building interface agents. It presents results from several prototype agents that have been built using this approach, including agents that provide personalized assistance with meeting scheduling, email handling, electronic news filtering and selection of entertainment.

Approaches to Building Agents

The idea of employing agents in the interface to delegate certain computer-based tasks was introduced by visionaries such as Nicholas Negroponte [19] and Alan Kay [8]. More recently, several computer manufacturers have adopted this idea to illustrate their vision of the interface of the future (cf., videos produced in 1990-1991 by Apple, Hewlett Packard, Digital and the Japanese FRIEND21 project). Even though a great amount of work has gone into the modeling and construction of agents, currently available techniques are still far from being able to produce the high-level, humanlike interactions depicted in these videos. Two main problems have to be solved when building software agents. The first problem is that of *competence:* how does an agent acquire the knowledge it needs to decide when to help the user, what to help the user with and how to help the user? The second problem is that of *trust:* how can we guarantee the user feels comfortable delegating tasks to an agent? Two previous approaches for building interface agents can be distinguished. Neither one provides a satisfactory solution to these problems.

The first approach consists in making the end-user program the interface agent. Malone and Lai's Oval (formerly Object-Lens) system [12] has "semi-autonomous agents" which consist of a collection of user-programmed rules for processing information related to a particular task. For example, the Oval user can create an email sorting agent by creating a number of rules that process incoming mail messages and sort them into different folders. Once created, these rules perform tasks for the user without having to be explicitly invoked by the user. Similarly, one can buy "agents" that can be programmed by the user to provide information filtering services (e.g., selecting any new article that mentions MIT Media Lab).

The main problem of this approach is that it does not deal with the competence criterion in a satisfactory way. The approach requires too much insight, understanding and effort from the end-user, since the user has to recognize the opportunity for employing an agent, take the initiative to create an agent, endow the agent with explicit knowledge (specifying this knowledge in an abstract language), and maintain the agent's rules over time (as work habits or interests change).

Trusting the agent is less of a problem in this approach, provided that the user trusts his or her own programming skills. However, the programs we write typically behave differently than expected, even when we trust our programming skills.

The second approach, called the "knowledge-based approach," consists in endowing an interface agent with extensive domain-specific background knowledge about the application and the user (called a domain model and user model, respectively). This approach is adopted by the majority of people working in AI on intelligent user interfaces [25]. At runtime, the interface agent uses its knowledge to recognize the user's plans and to find opportunities for contributing to them. For example, UCEgo [1] is an interface agent designed to help a user solve problems in using the Unix operating system. The UCEgo agent has a large knowledge base about how to use Unix, incorporates goals and meta-goals, and does planning (e.g., UCEgo can volunteer information or correct the user's misconceptions).

Both competence and trust constitute problems in the knowledge-based approach. The first problem related to competence is that the approach requires a huge amount of work from the knowledge engineer. A large amount of application-specific and domain-specific knowledge has to be entered into the agent's knowledge base. Little of this knowledge or the agent's control architecture can be used when building agents for other applications. The second problem is that the knowledge of the agent is fixed once and for all. It cannot be customized to individual user habits and preferences. The possibility of providing an agent with all the knowledge it needs to always comprehend the user's sometimes unpredictable actions is questionable.

In addition to the competence problem, there is also a problem with trust. It is probably not a good idea to give a user an interface agent that is very sophisticated, qualified and autonomous from the start. Schneiderman has argued convincingly that such an agent would leave the user with a feeling of loss of control and understanding [18]. Since the agent has been programmed by someone else, the user may not have a good model of the agent's limitations, the way it works, and so forth.

Training a Personal Digital Assistant

In our work, we explore an alternative approach to building interface agents that relies on machine learning techniques. A similar approach has been reported upon by Dent *et al.* [4]. The hypothesis tested is that, under certain conditions, an interface agent can "program itself" (i.e., it can acquire the knowledge it needs to assist its user). The agent is given a minimum of background knowledge, and it learns appropriate "behavior" from the user and from other agents. The particular conditions that have to be fulfilled are: (1) the use of the application has to involve a substantial amount of repetitive behavior (within the actions of one user or among users), and (2) this repetitive behavior is potentially different for different users. If the latter condition is not met (i.e., the repetitive behavior demonstrated by different users is the same), a knowledge-based approach might prove to yield results faster than a learning approach. If the former condition is not met, a learning agent will not be able to learn anything (because there are no regularities to learn in the user's actions).

The machine learning approach is inspired by the metaphor of a personal assistant. Initially, a personal assistant is not very familiar with the habits and preferences of his or her employer and may not even be very helpful. The assistant needs some time to become familiar with the particular work methods of the employer and organization at hand. However, with every experience the assistant learns, either by watching how the employer performs tasks, by receiving instructions from the employer, or by learning from other more experienced assistants within the organization. Gradually, more tasks that were initially performed directly by the employer can be taken care of by the assistant.

The goal of our research is to demonstrate that a learning interface agent can, in a similar way, become gradually more helpful and competent. In addition, we attempt to demonstrate that the learning approach also presents a satisfactory solution to the trust problem. If the agent gradually develops its abilities—as is the case in our approach—the user is also given time to gradually build up a model of how the agent makes decisions, which is one of the prerequisites for a trust relationship. Furthermore, the particular learning approach adopted allows the agent to give "explanations" for its reasoning and behavior in a language the user is familiar with, namely in terms of past examples similar to the current situation. For example, "I thought you

Figure 1. The interface agent does not act as interface or layer between the user and the application. It behaves as a personal assistant that cooperates with the user on the task. The user is able to bypass the agent.

Figure 2. The interface agent learns in four different ways: (1) it observes and imitates the user's behavior, (2) it adapts based on user feedback, (3) it can be trained by the user on the basis of examples, and (4) it can ask for advice from other agents assisting other users.

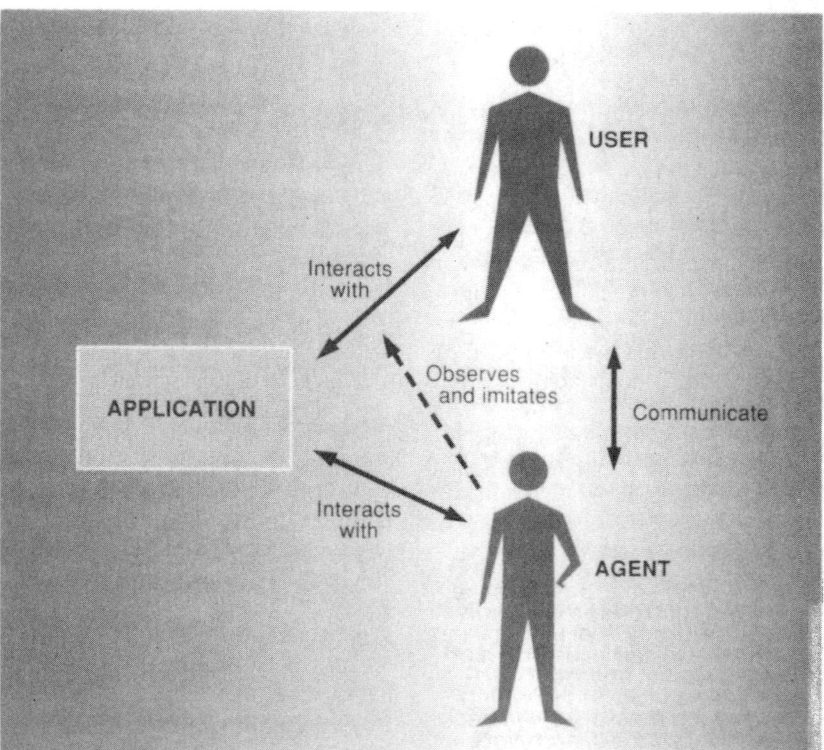

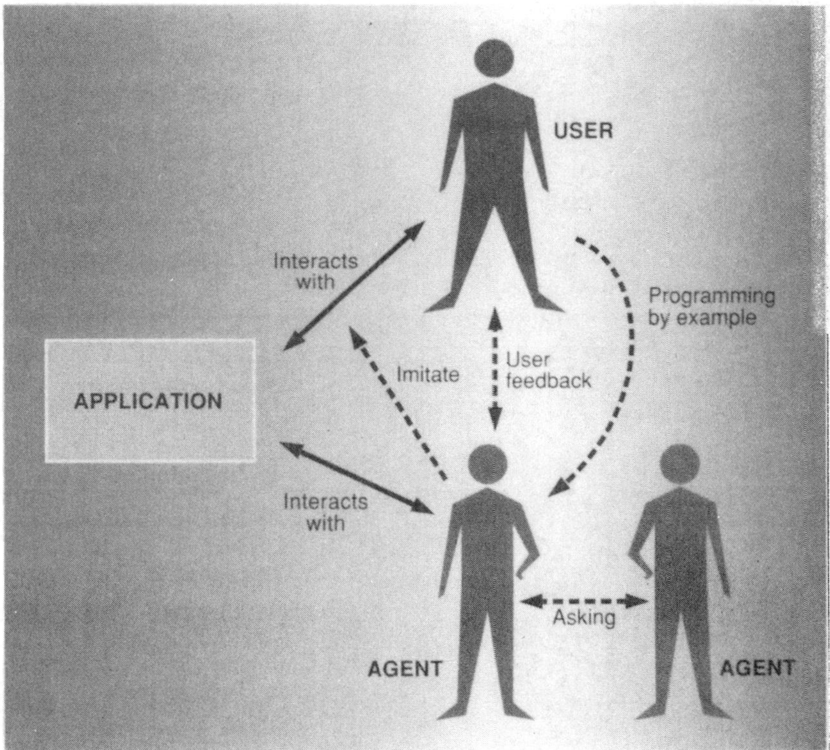

might want to take this action because this situation is similar to this other situation we have experienced before, in which you also took this action" or "because assistant Y to person Z also performs tasks that way, and you and Z seem to share work habits."

Finally, we believe the learning approach has several advantages over the previous two approaches. First, it requires less work from the end-user and application developer. Second, the agent can more easily adapt to the user over time and become customized to individual and organizational preferences and habits. Finally, the approach helps in transferring information, habits and know-how among the different users of a community. The results described in a later section support all of these hypotheses and predictions.

A learning agent acquires its competence from four different sources (see Figure 2). First, the interface agent learns by continuously "looking over the shoulder" of the user as the user is performing actions. The interface agent can monitor the activities of the user, keep track of all of his or her actions over long periods of time (weeks or months), find regularities and recurrent patterns and offer to automate these. For example, if an email agent notices that a user almost always stores messages sent to the mailing list "intelligent-interfaces" in the folder `pattie:email:int-int.txt`, then it can offer to automate this action the next time a message sent to that mailing list is read. Similarly, if a news filtering agent detects some patterns in the articles the user reads, then it can offer similar articles to the user when it discovers them.

A second source for learning is direct and indirect user feedback. Indirect feedback happens when the user neglects the suggestion of the agent and takes a different action instead. This can be as subtle as the user changing the order in which he or she reads incoming messages, not reading some articles suggested by the agent, or reading articles not suggested by the agent. The user can also give explicit negative feedback for actions automated by the agent ("don't do this again" or "I dislike this article").

Third, the agent can learn from examples given explicitly by the user. The user can train the agent by giving it hypothetical examples of events and situations and telling the agent what to do in those cases. The interface agent records the actions, tracks relationships among objects, and changes its example base to incorporate the example that it is shown. For instance, the user can teach a mail clerk agent to save all messages sent by a particular person in a particular folder by creating a hypothetical example of an email message (which has all aspects unspecified except for the sender field) and dragging this message to the chosen folder. Similarly, the user can instruct a news filtering agent by giving it examples of (partially specified) articles (e.g., "select any article in which the word MIT appears").

Finally, a fourth method used by the interface agent to acquire competence is to ask for advice from agents that assist other users with the same task (and that may have built up more experience). If an agent does not know itself what action is appropriate in a certain situation, it can present the situation to other agents and ask "what action they recommend for that situation." For example, if an email message arrives that has been sent by Nicholas Negroponte, then the email agent can ask other agents what to do with that message. If a majority of the other agents recommends that the message has high priority and should be presented to the user for reading right away, then the agent can offer this recommendation to its user, even though the agent never previously observed the user deal with messages from Nicholas Negroponte. Rather than averaging the recommendations of all other agents in the community, a user might also inform his or her agent to accept suggestions from one or more specific agents which assist specific users. For example, if one person in the lab is an expert in the use of a particular piece of software, then other users can instruct their agents to accept advice about that software from the agent of that expert user.

Additionally, the agent can learn from experience which agents are good sources for suggestions. It can learn to trust agents that in the past

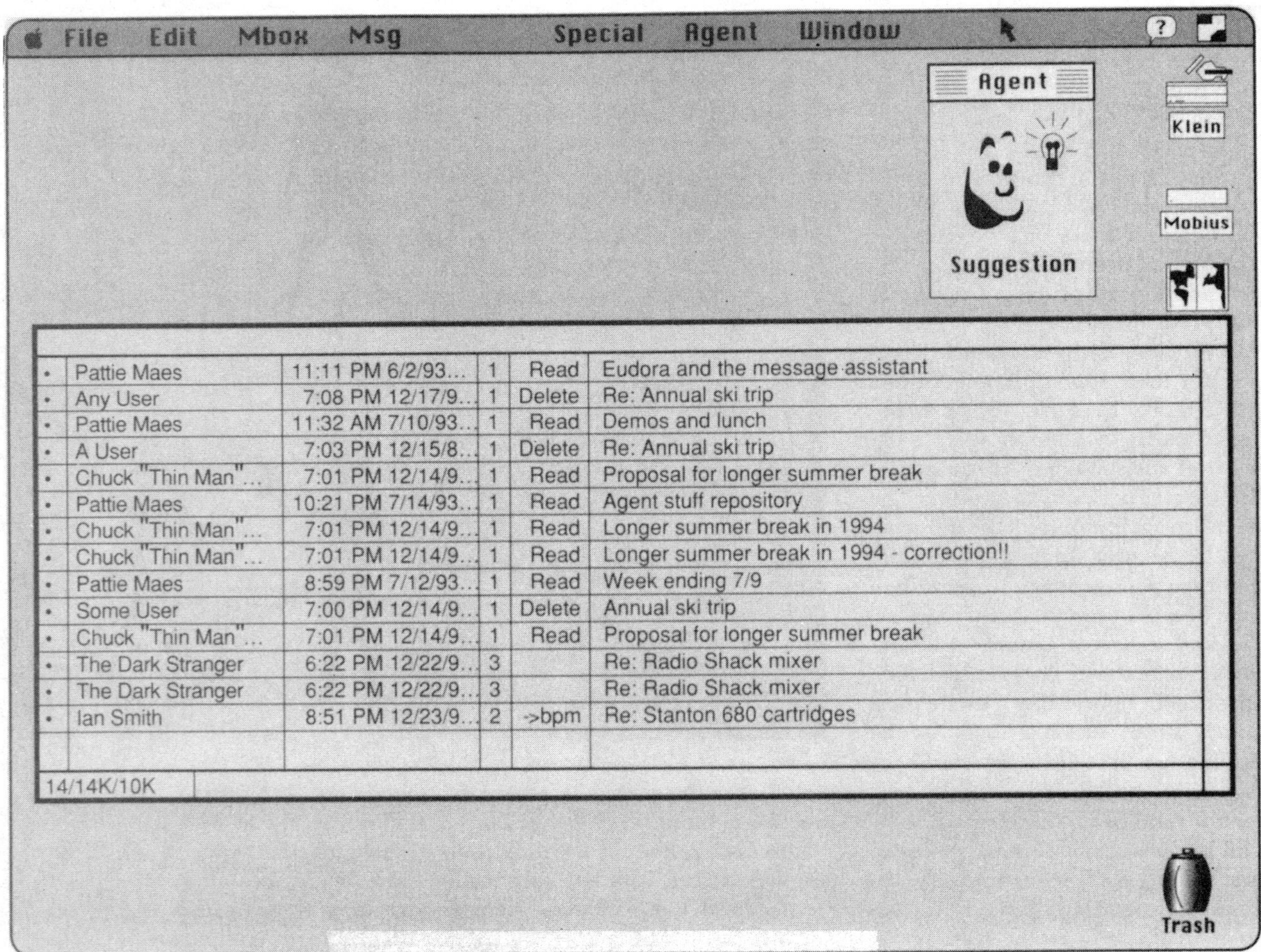

Figure 3. The email agent makes recommendations to the user (middle column). It predicts what actions the user will perform on messages, such as which messages will be read and in which order, which messages will be deleted, forwarded, archived, and so on.

have proven to recommend actions the user appreciated. The entertainment selection agent discussed next uses this technique to learn which other users have entertainment tastes similar to its user's tastes, and thus are good sources of suggestions.

Some Examples of Existing Agents

Four agents have been built using the learning approach previously discussed:

- An agent for electronic mail handling
- An agent for meeting scheduling
- An agent for electronic news filtering (Usenet Netnews).
- An agent that recommends books, music or other forms of entertainment

The choice of these domains was motivated by our dissatisfaction with the ways these tasks are currently handled. Many valuable hours are wasted dealing with junk mail, scheduling and rescheduling meetings, searching for relevant information among heaps of irrelevant information, and browsing through lists of books, music, and television programs in search of something interesting.

Electronic Mail Agent

Maxims [13] is an agent that assists the user with email. Maxims learns to prioritize, delete, forward, sort and archive mail messages on behalf of the user (Figures 3 and 4). Maxims is implemented in Macintosh Common Lisp. It communicates with the commercial email package Eudora [6] using Apple Events. The main learning technique used by Maxims is memory-based reasoning [24]. The agent continuously "looks over the shoulder" of the user as the user deals with email. As the user performs actions, the agent memorizes all of the situation-action pairs generated. For example, if the user saves a particular message after having read it, the mail agent adds a description of this situation and the action taken by the user to its memory of examples. Situations are described in terms of a set of features, which are currently handcoded. In this domain, the agent keeps track of the sender and receiver of a message, the Cc: list, the keywords in the Subject: line, whether the message has been read or not, whether it is a reply to a previous message, and so on.

When a new situation occurs that can be due to the user taking an action or due to some external event such as a message arriving, the agent will try to predict the action(s) of the user, based on the examples stored in its memory. The agent compares the

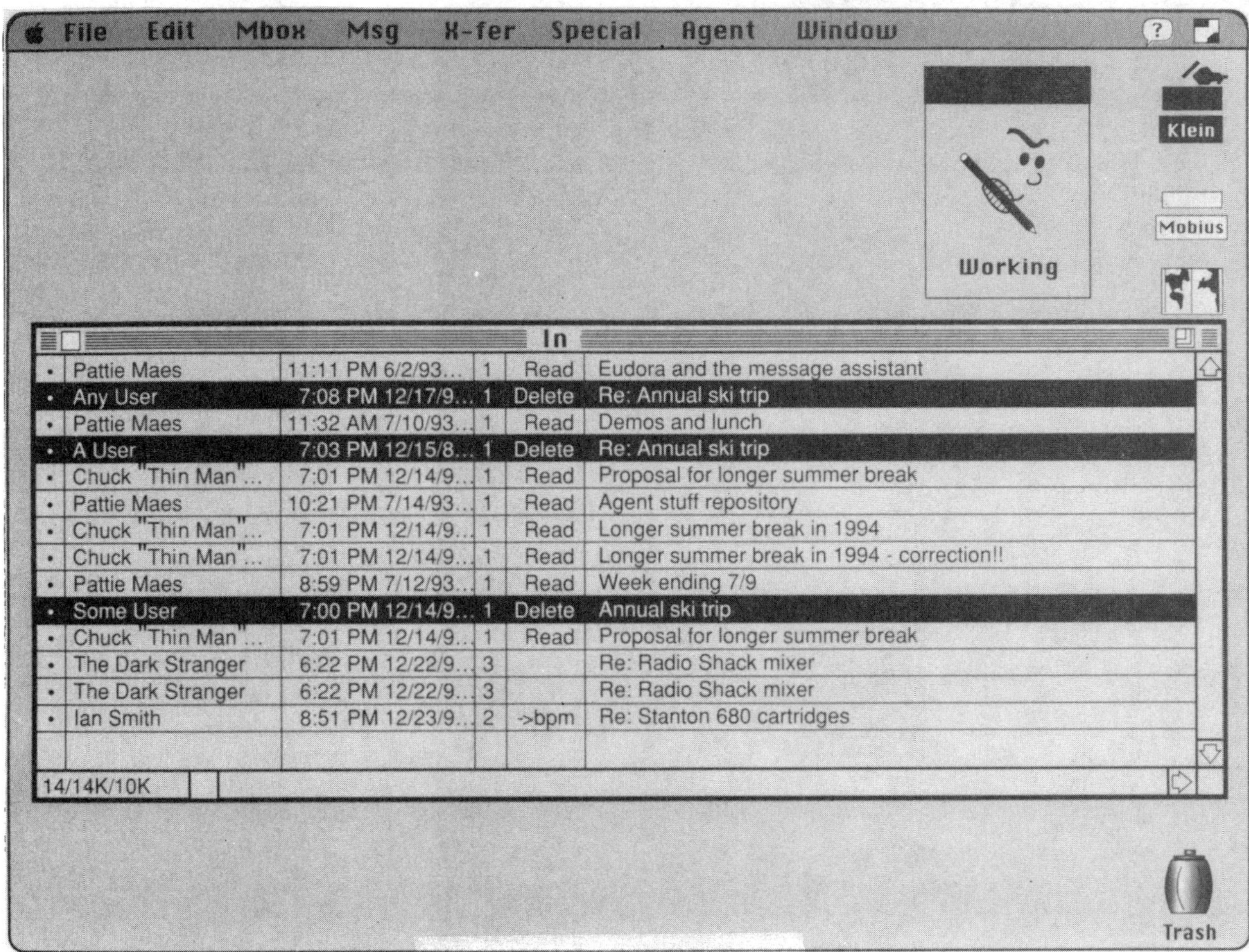

Figure 4. The user can select some of the suggestions made by the agent and ask the agent to execute them.

new situation with the memorized situations and tries to find a set of nearest neighbors (or close matches). The most similar of these memorized situations contribute to the decision of which action to take or suggest in the current situation. The distance metric used is a weighted sum of the differences for the features that make up a situation. Some features carry more weight than others. The weight of a feature is determined by the agent. Occasionally (e.g., at night), the agent analyzes its memory and determines the correlations between features and actions taken. For example, the agent may detect that the "from" field of an email message is highly correlated to whether its user reads the message, while the "date" field is not correlated. The detected correlations are employed as weights in the distance metric.

The agent does not only predict which action is appropriate for the current situation. It also measures its confidence in each prediction. The confidence level is determined by whether or not all the nearest neighbors recommended the same action, how close/distant the nearest neighbors are, and how many examples the agent has memorized (a measure of the accuracy of the correlation weights).

Two thresholds determine how the agent uses its prediction. When the confidence level is above the "do-it" threshold, then the agent autonomously takes the action on behalf of the user. In that case, it writes a report for the user about the action it automated. The user can ask the agent for its report of automated actions any time. If the confidence level is above the "tell-me" threshold, then the agent will offer its suggestion to the user, but will wait for the user's confirmation to automate the action. The user is responsible for setting the "tell-me" and "do-it" thresholds for actions at levels where the user feels comfortable. For example, if the user feels paranoid about the agent autonomously deleting messages, then the user can set the "do-it" threshold for that action at a maximum.

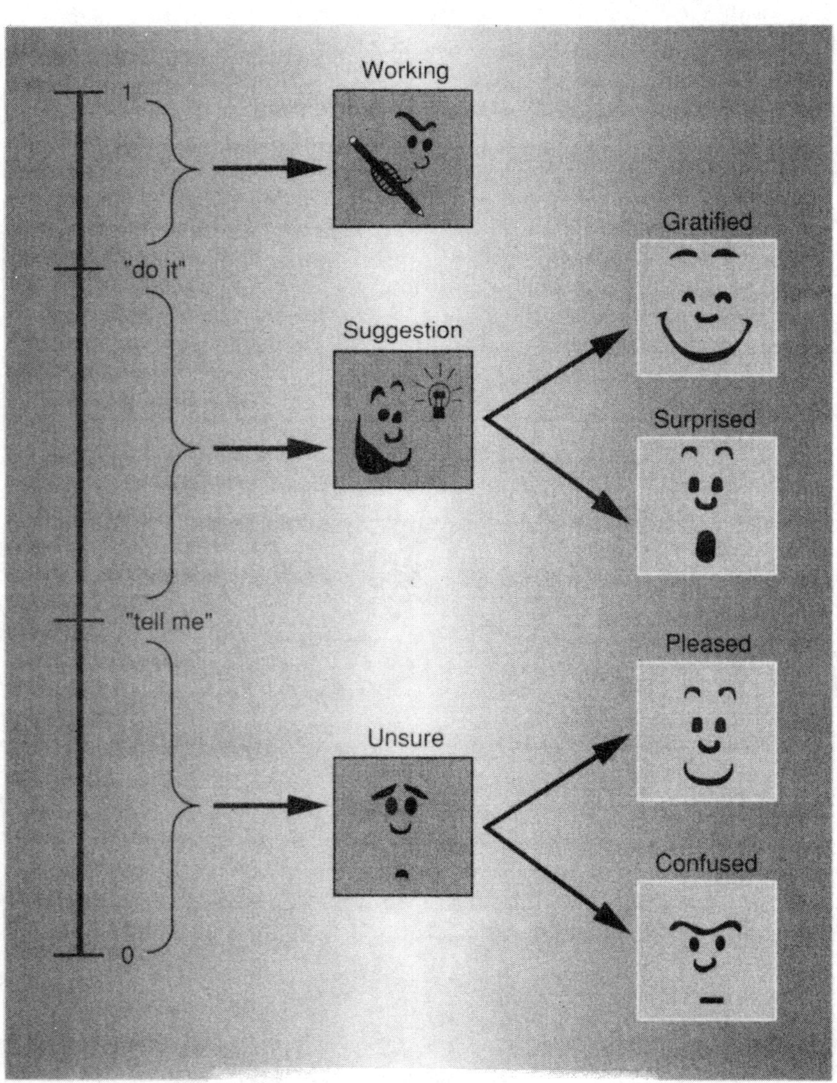

Figure 5. Simple caricatures convey the state of the agent to the user.

The agent communicates its internal state to the user via facial expressions (see Figure 5). These appear in a small window on the user's screen. The faces have a functional purpose: they make it possible for the user to get an update on what the agent is doing "in the blink of an eye." There are faces for "thinking" (the agent is comparing the current situation to memorized situations), "working" (the agent is automating an action), "suggestion" (the agent has a suggestion), "unsure" (the agent does not have enough confidence in its suggestion), and so forth. The "pleased" and "confused" face help the user gain information about the competence of the agent (if the agent never offers its suggestion, but it always shows a pleased face after the user takes an action, then clearly the "tell-me" threshold should be lowered. The agents have deliberately all been drawn as simple cartoon faces, in order not to encourage unwarranted attribution of human-level intelligence.

The Maxims agent gradually gains competence by observing the user and acquiring more examples. In order to deal with this slow start problem, two additional competence acquisition schemes exist. First of all, it is possible for the user to instruct the agent explicitly. If the user does not want to wait for the agent to pick up a certain pattern, then the user can create a hypothetical situation and show the agent what should be done. This functionality is imple-

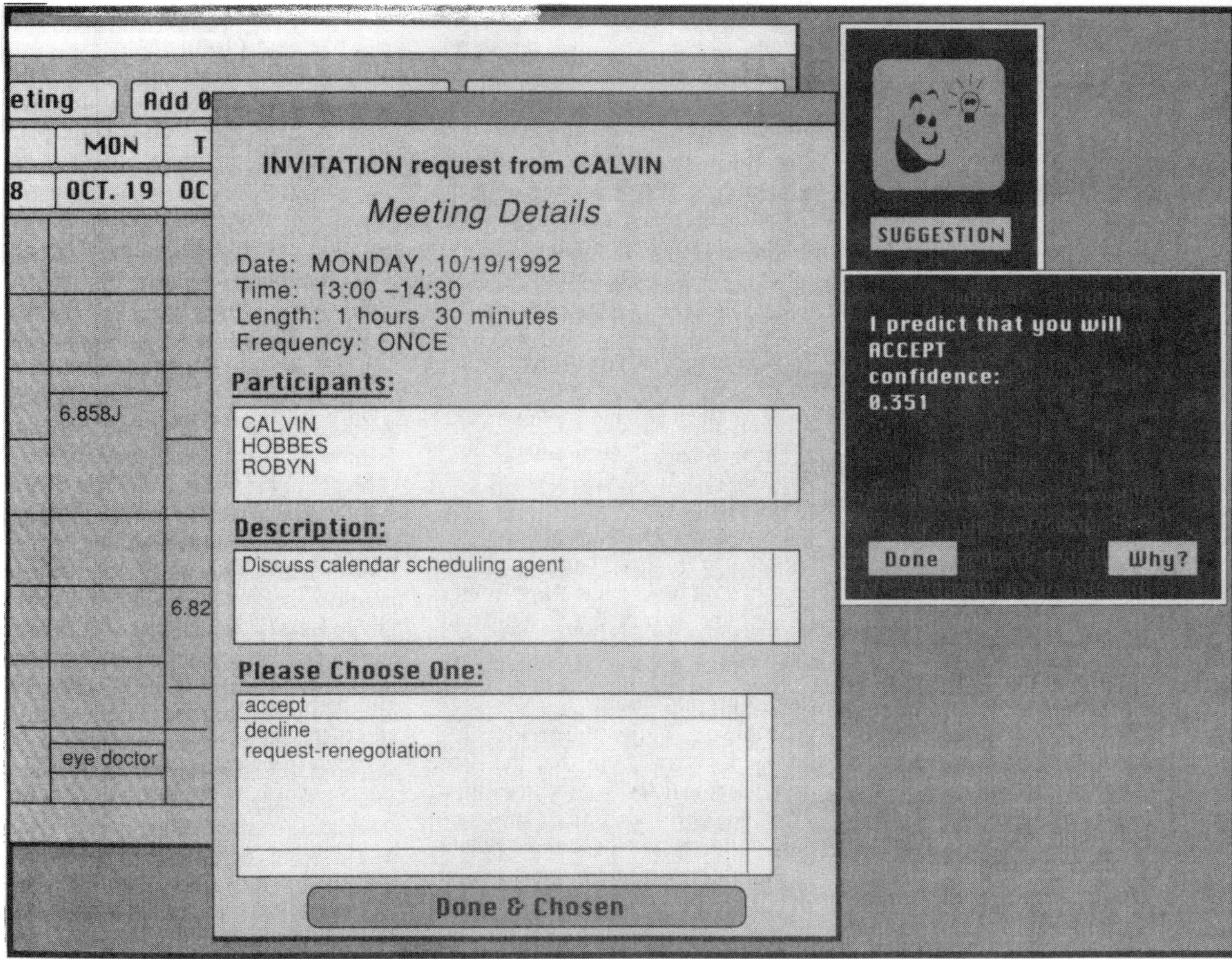

Figure 6. The calendar agent offers its suggestion to the user. The user can accept, take a different action or ask for an explanation.

mented by adding the example to the agent's memory, including "wildcards" for the features not specified in the hypothetical situation. For instance, the user can create a hypothetical message from Negroponte and show the agent that message has high priority. The new situation-action pair will match all situations in which an email message has been received from Negroponte. By varying the way in which such hypothetical examples are treated when selecting an action and when compiling statistics, both *default* and *hard-and-fast rules* can be implemented within the memory-based learning framework [11].

A second method that allows the agent to start from more than scratch is multiagent collaboration. When the agent does not have enough confidence in its prediction (confidence that is less than the "tell-me" threshold), it asks for help from other agents assisting other users with email. The agent sends part of the description of the situation to other agents via email and awaits their response. For example, if a new Media Lab user/agent pair receives a message from Negroponte, then that agent will ask other agents what it should do with that message. Some other agents will recommend that the message is important and should be immediately presented to the user for reading. The agent will make a prediction based on the different suggestions that are returned. The agent gradually learns which other agents are trustworthy sources of information for certain classes of problems. Every agent models how much it trusts other agents' advice. The trust level is increased or decreased when the action eventually taken by the user is compared with the recommendations (and confidence levels) of peer agents. The multiagent communication is an excellent method for transfer of information and competence among different users in a workgroup.

Meeting Scheduling Agent

The learning agent just described is generic. It can be attached to any application, provided the application is scriptable and recordable. The same agent was attached to a meeting scheduling software package [10, 11]. The resulting agent assists a user with the scheduling of meetings (accept/reject, schedule, reschedule, negotiate meeting times, etc.). The meetings scheduling agent is again implemented in MCL (see Figure 6). Meeting scheduling is another example of a task that fulfills the criteria for learning interface agents: the behavior of users is repetitive, but nevertheless very different for individual users. Some people prefer meetings in the morning, others in the afternoon. Some group meetings, others spread them out. Different people have different criteria for which meetings are important, which meeting initiators are important (and should be accommodated), and so on. The learning interface agent approach is ideally suited for assisting the user in a very personalized way by automating the scheduling task according to the unique habits of the user.

Both the Maxims agent and the meeting scheduling agent have been tested by real users. The results of these user tests are very encouraging. Users are eager to try out interface agents. They welcome whatever help they can get with their work overload. Users reported they felt comfortable delegating tasks to the agents. The tests revealed it is important to provide the agent with an extensive set of features to describe situations. The more features the agent has, the better the agent performs. The useless features eventually become disregarded by the agent (the weights become 0 because they do not correlate with certain actions). The tests also revealed that several areas need further improvement. First, the agents have to be made to run faster, and second, users requested they be able to instruct the agent to forget or disregard some of their behavior. Figure 7 shows some of the results obtained with the meeting scheduling agent. The agent's confidence in correct predictions increases with time, while its confidence in wrong predictions tends to decrease.

Figure 7. Typical results from a learning meeting scheduling agent. The confidence level in correct predictions increases with time, while the confidence level in wrong predictions tends to decrease.

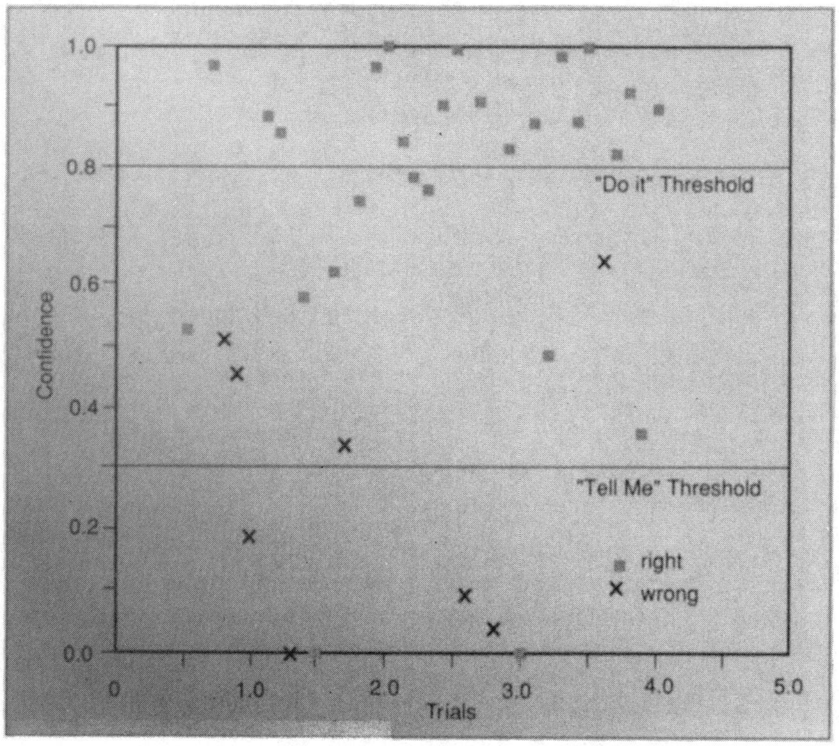

News Filtering Agent

Probably one of the more widely useful agents is an agent that helps the user select articles from a continuous stream of news [22, 23]. As more and more information becomes available on the network (see World Wide Web, on-line news feeds, etc.), users become more and more desperate for tools that will help them filter this stream of information and find articles of interest to them.

NewT is a system that helps the user filter Usenet Netnews. It is implemented in C++ on a Unix platform. A user can create one or many "news agents" and train them by means of examples of articles that should or should not be selected. For example, Figure 8 shows four agents (and icons) created by a user: one for business news, one for political news, one for computer news and one for sports news. An agent is initialized by giving it some positive and negative examples of articles to be retrieved. The agent performs a full text analysis (using the vector-space model [20] for documents) to retrieve the words in the text that may be relevant. It also remembers the structured information about the article, such as the author, source, assigned indices, and so forth. The user can also program the agent explicitly and fill out a set of templates of articles that should be selected (e.g., select all articles by Michael Schrage in the *Los Angeles Times*).

Once an agent has been bootstrapped, it will start recommending articles to the user. The user can give it positive or negative feedback for articles or portions of articles recommended. For example, the user can highlight a word or paragraph and give selective positive or negative feedback. The user can also select the author or source and give positive and negative feedback.

This will increase or decrease the probability that the agent will recommend similar articles in the future. The current implementation only performs content filtering, in the sense that the agent tries to correlate the positive and negative feedback with the contents of the article. It does not perform "social filtering," which would mean agents of different users would exchange recommendations with one another. However, a weaker form of social filtering is implemented in the NewT system: a user can train an agent for a while and then create a duplicate of that agent and give it to another user.

The NewT agents were tested by a group of 12 users. A larger group is using the system on a daily basis. As is the case with the other agent systems previously described, the NewT agents are not meant to automate all of the user's news interests. The agents are able to recommend articles to the user that concern topics (or authors or sources) in which the user has shown a continued interest. The user is still responsible for browsing the news sources to find less predictably interesting articles. Once such articles have been discovered, the user can train the agent to select those kinds of articles in the future. Again, the results obtained with the news agents were very promising. Users liked using the system and found it very useful. The main limitation of the system is its restriction to keywords only. However, if a method for deeper semantic analysis of texts becomes available (e.g., as a result of natural language understanding research), this deeper representation can be learned by using the same statistical learning techniques as are currently used for relevant keywords.

Entertainment Selection Agent

A fourth and final application area is entertainment selection. Of all four applications discussed, this one might have the best potential to become the next "killer application." Currently, critics publish reviews and recommendations which are meant for a large, general audience, but no individualized mechanisms exist to help people select movies, books, television and radio shows based on their personal tastes. However, as soon as

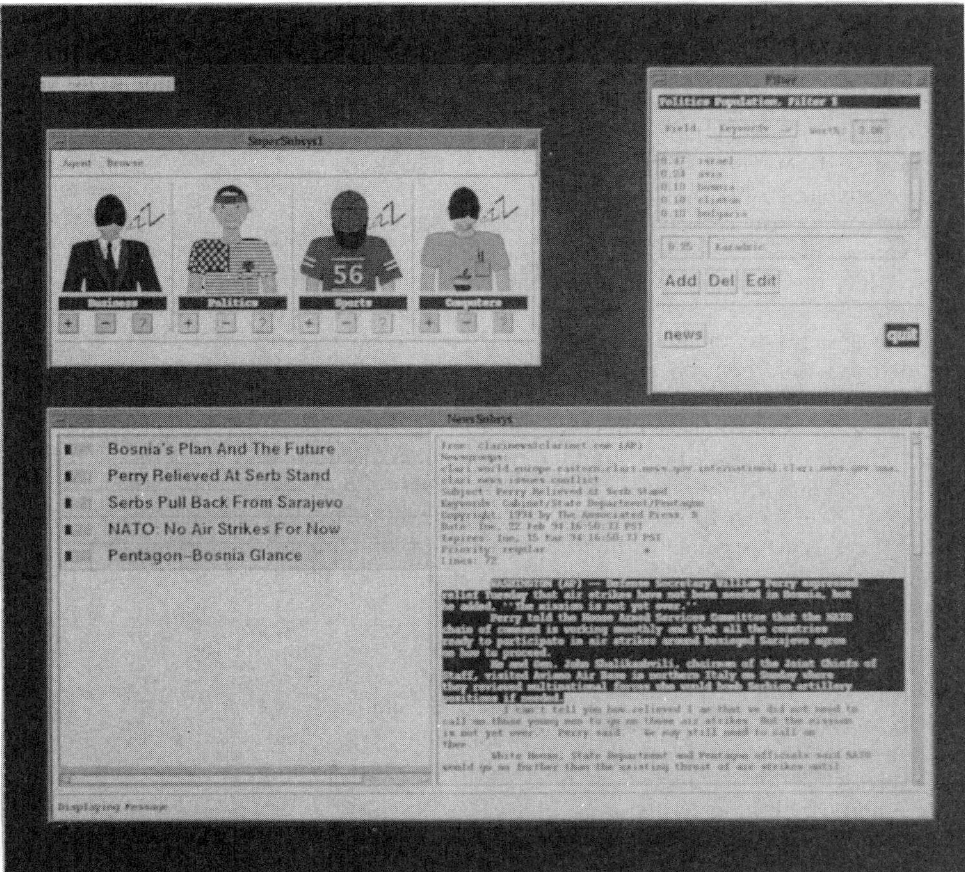

Figure 8. The NewT personalized news filtering system. A user can create a set of agents that assist the user with the filtering of an on-line news source. The agents are trained by means of positive and negative examples of articles to be selected or not selected, respectively.

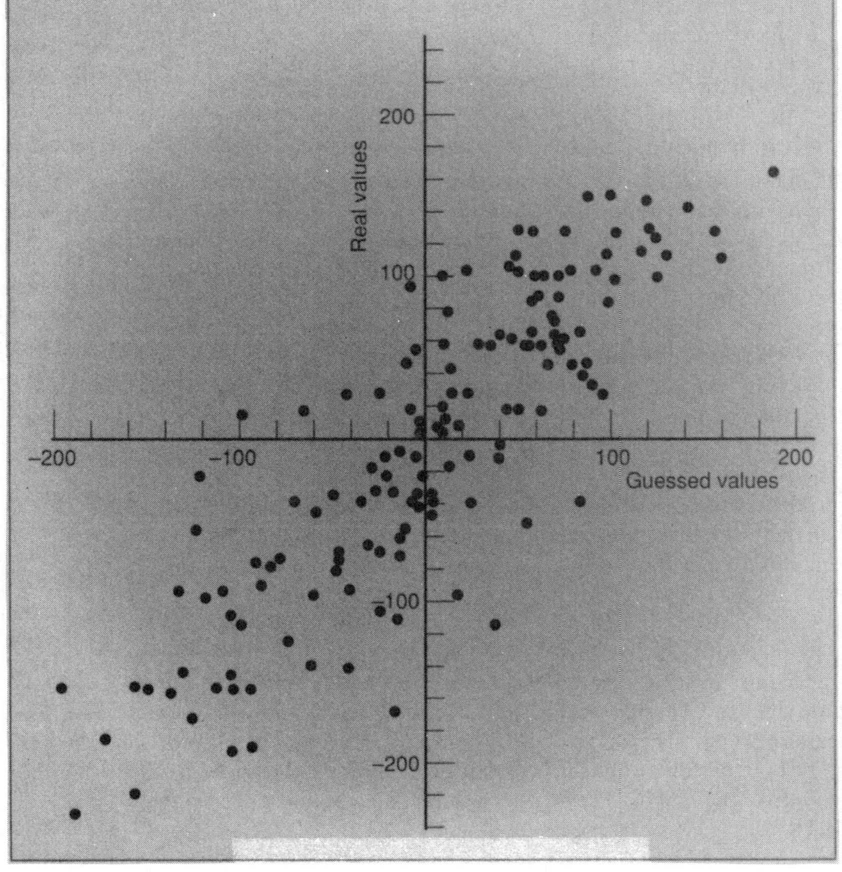

Figure 9. Results obtained with the entertainment selection agents. The Y-axis represents actual values assigned by users to items. The X-axis represents values guessed by the agents based on correlations among users.

entertainment becomes more interactive, agents can offer personalized, "readership of one" recommendations and critiques. Ringo is a personalized music recommendation system implemented on Unix platform in Perl. A similar system was built for recommending science fiction books [7]. The agents in these system use "social filtering." They do not attempt to correlate the user's interests with the contents of the items recommended. Instead, they rely solely on correlations between different users.

In these systems, every user has an agent that memorizes which books or music albums its user has evaluated, and how much the user liked them. Then, agents compare themselves with other agents. An agent finds other agents that are correlated, that is, agents that have values for similar items and whose values are positively correlated to the values of this agent. Agents accept recommendations from other correlated agents. Basically, what this means is that, if user A and user B have related musical tastes, and A has evaluated an album positively which B has not yet evaluated, then that album is recommended to user B. The actual algorithm is slightly more complex in the sense that agents combine the recommendations from a collection of related agents, rather than a single related agent. Figure 9 illustrates some of the results obtained.

One problem with this approach is how to bootstrap the whole system, so that enough data is available for the agents to start noticing correlations and make recommendations. A second problem is that users can end up relying too much on the recommendation system, and may not enter into the system any new items that they discovered themselves.

In order to deal with both of these problems, "virtual users" are created that represent a particular taste, (e.g., a virtual "Madonna fan" user, who has high ratings for all Madonna albums and no other ratings, or a virtual "cyberspace fan" user, who rates all books on cyberspace highly and has no other ratings). Similarly, a virtual user can be created for a publishing company, like the "MIT Press fan" who rates all MIT Press books highly. By entering such virtual user data into the system, the agent system can bootstrap itself, and agents for actual users can correlate themselves with virtual users.

Discussion

As computers are used for more tasks and become integrated with more services, users will need help dealing with the information and work overload. Interface agents radically change the style of human-computer interaction. The user delegates a range of tasks to personalized agents that can act on the user's behalf. We have modeled an interface agent after the metaphor of a personal assistant. The agent gradually learns how to better assist the user by:

- Observing and imitating the user
- Receiving positive and negative feedback from the user
- Receiving explicit instructions from the user
- Asking other agents for advice

These agents have been shown to tackle two of the hardest problems involved in building interface agents. The agents are *competent:* they become more helpful, as they accumulate knowledge about how the user handles certain situations. They can be *trusted:* the user is able to gradually and incrementally build up a model of the agent's competencies and limitations.

Even though the results obtained with this first generation of agents are encouraging, many open questions for future research remain. Some of these are user interface issues: Should there be one or many agents? Should agents use facial expressions and other means of personification? What is the best metaphor for interface agents? Other questions are more algorithmic and technical: How can we guarantee the user's privacy, especially if agents communicate with one another about their users? How can heterogeneous agents, built by different developers and using different techniques, collaborate? How can a system of incentives be devised, so that users are motivated to share the knowledge their experienced agents have learned? Most importantly, from a legal standpoint, should a user be held responsible for his or her agent's actions and transactions?

Acknowledgments
Beerud Sheth, Robyn Kozierok, Yezdi Lashkari, Max Metral, Carl Feynman, Upendra Shardanand, Cecile Pham and Henry Lieberman were responsible for many of the concepts and for the implementation of the four prototype agents discussed. Christie Davidson, Yezdi Lashkari and Henry Lieberman helped in the preparation of the article. ◼

About the Author:
PATTIE MAES is an assistant professor at the MIT Media Laboratory. Her research interests are in the areas of Artificial Intelligence, Artificial Life and Human-Computer Interaction. In particular, she is interested in modeling and building autonomous agents. **Author's Present Address:** The Media Laboratory, MIT Building E15-305B, 20 Ames St, Cambridge, MA 02139; email: pattie@media.mit.edu.

References

1. Chin, D. Intelligent interfaces as agents. In J. Sullivan and S. Tyler, eds., *Intelligent User Interfaces.* ACM Press, N.Y., 1991.
2. Crowston, K. and Malone, T. Intelligent software agents. *BYTE, 13,* 13 (Dec. 1988), 267–271.
3. Cypher, A. EAGER: Programming repetitive tasks by example. In *Proceedings of CHI'91.* ACM Press, N.Y., 1991, pp. 33–39.
4. Dent, L. Boticario, J. Mc Dermott, J. Mitchell, T. and Zabowski, D. A personal learning apprentice. In *Proceedings of the National Conference on Artificial Intelligence.* MIT Press, Cambridge, Mass., 1992.
5. Don, A. Anthropomorphism: From Eliza to Terminator 2, panel description. In *Proceedings of CHI'92.* ACM Press, N.Y., 1992, pp. 67–70.
6. Dorner, S. Eudora Reference Manual. Qualcomm Inc., 1992.
7. Feynman, C. Nearest neighbor and maximum likelihood methods for social information filtering. Internal report, MIT, Dec. 1993.
8. Kay, A. Computer software. In *Sci. Amer. 251,* 3 (Mar. 1984), 191–207.
9. Kay, A. User Interface: A personal

view. In B. Laurel, ed., *The Art of Human-Computer Interface Design.* Addison-Wesley, Reading, Mass., 1990.

10. Kozierok, R. and Maes, P. A learning interface agent for scheduling meetings. In *Proceedings of ACM SIGCHI International Workshop on Intelligent User Interfaces.* ACM Press, N.Y., 1993, pp. 81–88.

11. Kozierok, R. A learning approach to knowledge acquisition for intelligent interface agents. SM Thesis, Department of Electrical Eng. and Computer Science, MIT, May 1993.

12. Lai, K. Malone, T. and Yu, K. Object Lens: A "spreadsheet" for cooperative work. *ACM Trans. Office Inf. Syst. 6,* 4 (Apr. 1988), 332–353.

13. Lashkari, Y., Metral, M. and Maes, P. Collaborative interface agents. In *Proceedings of the National Conference on Artificial Intelligence.* MIT Press, Cambridge, Mass., 1994.

14. Laurel, B. Interface agents: Metaphors with character. In B. Laurel, ed., *The Art of Human-Computer Interface Design.* Addison-Wesley, Reading, Mass., 1990.

15. Lieberman, H. Mondrian: A teachable graphical editor. In A. Cypher, ed., *Watch what I do: Programming by Demonstration,* MIT Press, Cambridge, Mass., 1993.

16. Maes, P. and Kozierok, R. Learning interface agents. In *Proceedings of the AAAI'93 Conference.* MIT Press, Cambridge, Mass., pp. 459–465.

17. Myers, B. *Creating User Interfaces by Demonstration.* Academic Press, Boston, Mass., 1988.

18. Myers, B., ed. Demonstrational interfaces: Coming soon? In *Proceedings of CHI'91.* ACM Press, N.Y., 1991, pp. 393–396.

19. Negroponte, N. *The Architecture Machine; Towards a more Human Environment.* MIT Press, Cambridge, Mass., 1970.

20. Salton, G. and McGill, M. *Introduction to Modern Information Retrieval.* McGraw-Hill, N.Y., 1983.

21. Schneiderman, B. Direct manipulation: A step beyond programming languages. *IEEE Comput. 16,* 8 (Aug. 1988), 57–69.

22. Sheth, B. and Maes, P. Evolving agents for personalized information filtering. In *Proceedings of the Ninth Conference on Artificial Intelligence for Applications.* IEEE Computer Society Press, 1993.

23. Sheth, B. A learning approach to personalized information filtering. SM Thesis, Department of Electrical Eng. and Computer Science, MIT, Feb. 1994.

24. Stanfill, C. and Waltz, D. Toward memory-based reasoning. *Comm. ACM 29,* 12, (Dec. 1986), 1213–1228.

25. Sullivan, J.W. and Tyler, S.W., eds. *Intelligent User Interfaces.* ACM Press, N.Y., 1991.

This research is sponsored by Apple Computer, by the NSF under grant number IRI-92056688, and by the News in the Future Consortium of the MIT Media Laboratory.

Reflections on. . .

Agents That Reduce Work and Information Overload

Patti Maes

In 1991, I started the Software Agents research group at the MIT Media Laboratory. The mission of the group was to build software that a user can delegate tasks to. Our intuition was that as computers get used by more people for more daily activities, our relationship to software will have to change. The dominant metaphor for Human-Computer Interaction is that of a tool. Just like a hammer, most software just sits there and waits until a user picks it up to do something. Our vision was to create software that would have a sense of the user's goals and interests, that would be continually running, and that would actively assist the user whenever it could by either offering suggestions or even automating actions on behalf of the user. The goal of the group was to develop the techniques to build such software agents and to evaluate whether indeed they did work.

In the past six years, we have built such software for a range of applications. We have built "eager assistant" agents, which "look over the shoulder" of the user, find patterns in the user's behavior, and then offer to automate them. We have built information filtering agents, which learn a person's interests and suggest relevant new information. We have built "remembrance" agents, which log everything a user does and then later help the user remember past actions, people, and situations. We have built "matchmaking" agents, which take the initiative to introduce people to each other that have similar interests. Finally, and most recently, we have built agents that buy and sell on behalf of users, actively negotiating on the user's behalf.

We built working prototypes of all of these agents and tested these systems, sometimes with as few as six users, other times with as many as 20,000. Overall, we consider our new approach to be a success. Results from the prototypes were very positive, and several similar commercial software agents are now available. In the process, we learned some important lessons about what ultimately makes an agent successful, that is, accepted and used by people on a daily basis. Specifically, we learned that it is not so much the underlying algorithms that represent the hardest challenge but rather the design of the user interface between the agent and the user.

In order for an agent to be really useful, the user needs to be able to trust the agent. Some important lessons we learned are that, first, the user profile (the model of the user's goals and interests, which the agent maintains) should be easily accessible and editable by the user. Second, the agent's way of operating has to be understandable (at some level) by the user. As a consequence, using complex algorithms to drive the agent's behavior typically fails. For example, we had to simplify our initial designs for complex AI-based buying and selling agents because users did not trust the agents (because they could not sufficiently predict their behavior). Third, it is important to integrate the agent into existing interfaces that the user already uses rather than to build a separate agent-user interface. For example, when building a personal newspaper agent, it is better to have the agent highlight relevant articles in the existing newspaper interface rather than have it present its personalized news selection in a separate interface. By doing so, there is less risk of the user relying too much on an (imperfect) agent, which, for example, could result in "tunnel vision" in the case of a newspaper agent.

REFERENCES

See papers at *http://lcs.www.media.mit.edu/groups/agents /research.html.*

Embedding critics in design environments

GERHARD FISCHER, KUMIYO NAKAKOJI,[1] JONATHAN OSTWALD,[2] GERRY STAHL[3] and TAMARA SUMNER

University of Colorado, Boulder, Colorado 80309-0430, USA (email: gerhard@cs.colorado.edu)

Abstract

Human understanding in design evolves through a process of critiquing existing knowledge and consequently expanding the store of design knowledge. Critiquing is a dialogue in which the interjection of a reasoned opinion about a product or action triggers further reflection on or changes to the artifact being designed. Our work has focused on applying this successful human critiquing paradigm to human-computer interaction. We argue that computer-based critiquing systems are most effective when they are embedded in domain-oriented design environments, which are knowledge-based computer systems that support designers in specifying a problem and constructing a solution. Embedded critics play a number of important roles in such design environments: (1) they increase the designer's understanding of design situations by pointing out problematic situations early in the design process; (2) they support the integration of problem framing and problem solving by providing a linkage between the design specification and the design construction; and (3) they help designers access relevant information in the large information spaces provided by the design environment. Three embedded critiquing mechanisms—generic, specific, and interpretive critics—are presented, and their complementary roles within the design environment architecture are described.

1 Introduction

Human understanding in design evolves through a process of critiquing (Fischer et al., 1991) existing knowledge and consequently expanding and refining the state of knowledge. Our work has focused on applying this human critiquing paradigm to human-computer interaction. Our experience with this approach is based on several years of system prototyping, the integration of cognitive and design theories, and empirical evaluation of these systems. Based on these experiences, we conclude that computational critiquing systems are most effective at supporting human designers when embedded in domain-oriented design environments (Fischer, 1992).

In section 2, we explain why the critiquing paradigm is essential for supporting the complex activity of design. Using illustrations from critiquing systems we have built, we demonstrate in section 3 how embedding in design environments enhances the computational critiquing process. Examples of our embedded critiquing system are drawn from HYDRA-KITCHEN, a residential kitchen design environment we have built. Section 4 explains three embedded critiquing mechanisms we have designed, implemented, and studied, called generic, specific and interpretive critics. Finally, in section 5 we assess some of the benefits of these embedded critiquing mechanisms.

[1] Also at: Software Engineering Laboratory, Software Research Associates, Inc., 1-1-1 Hirakawa-cho, Chiyoda-ku, Tokyo 102, Japan.
[2] Also at: Nynex Science and Technology Center, White Plains, New York, USA.
[3] Also at: School of Environmental Design, University of Colorado, Boulder, Colorado 80309, USA.

2 The critiquing approach

Critiquing is a dialogue in which the interjection of a reasoned opinion about a product or action triggers further reflection on or changes to the artifact being designed. For example, a kitchen designer might critique a kitchen floor plan in terms of building code violations, efficiency, safety concerns, or eventual resale value. An agent—human or machine—capable of critiquing in this sense is a *critic*. Computer-based critics are made up of sets of rules or procedures for evaluating different aspects of a product; sometimes each individual rule or procedure is referred to as a critic (Fischer et al., 1991).

2.1 Importance of human critiquing

Human critiquing plays an important role in design both in the growth of human knowledge and in terms of error elimination. By "human critiquing" we mean subjecting our designs and products to the scrutiny of other people, be they peers, domain specialists, or society in general.

Complex design activities prohibit an individual from knowing everything that is relevant; in addition, expertise is frequently controversial. Complex design situations can therefore be characterized by a "symmetry of ignorance" (Rittel, 1984), and the knowledge needed to solve a design problem is distributed among designers and their clients (Rittel & Webber, 1984). Critiquing is an important method for working within such a framework of distributed knowledge because it fosters a maximum of participation to activate as much of the distributed design knowledge as possible. In kitchen design, the designer and the homeowner take turns proposing ideas and criticizing each other's sugges ions. In this way, the often tacit knowledge (Polanyi, 1966) that each party has can come into play and complement the other's partial grasp of the design problem.

Critiquing is ubiquitous. It is, for example, at the heart of the scientific method. Popper (1965) theorized that science advances through a cycle of conjectures and refutations. Scientists formulate hypotheses and put forth these conjectures for scrutiny and refutation by the scientific community. Besides contributing to the growth of knowledge, this critiquing cycle of conjectures and refutations is essential for creating a shared understanding within the scientific community and providing a stable base for future growth in scientific knowledge.

Critics play an important role in making designers aware of breakdown situations (Fischer, 1993). Petroski (1985) noted the importance of failure in the growth of engineering knowledge. For instance, when an airplane crashes, the Federal Aviation Adminstration sends a team of specialists to the site to determine the cause of the accident. In essence, these specialists are critiquing the plane's design and construction and current aviation practices. Over the years, this practice has contributed much to the growth of aviation knowledge in terms of both airplane design and improved safety regulations (Chambers & Nagel, 1985). In turn, this growth in knowledge contributes toward future error elimination; that is, planes with the same defect are repaired and aviation regulations are improved to prevent similar crashes.

The activity of critiquing plays an important role in engineering, science, and design in general. It produces many benefits, including the growth of knowledge, error elimination and the promotion of mutual understanding of all participants. Through the critiquing process, designers gain a better understanding of the design problem by hearing the different points of view of other design participants. In our work, we have taken this successful human critiquing paradigm and shown how it can be effectively applied to enhance human-computer interaction. In the remainder of this paper, the term "critiquing" will refer to computer-based critiquing systems.

2.2 Applying computer-based critiquing to design

Our design environments are *cooperative problem-solving systems* (Fischer, 1990) in which the computer system helps users design solutions themselves as opposed to having an expert system

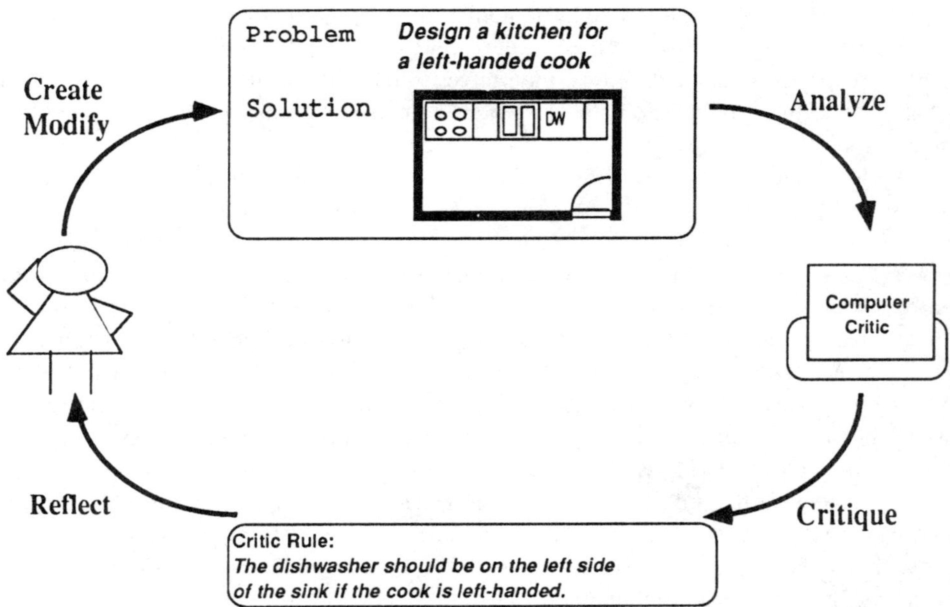

Figure 1 A cooperative problem-solving system has two agents—a human designer and a computer-based critic. Both agents contribute what they know about the domain to solving some problem. For the critiquing systems discussed in this paper, the human's primary role is to generate and modify solutions; the computer's role is to analyse these solutions and produce a critique for the human to consider in the next iteration of this process

design solutions for them. As illustrated in Figure 1, critiquing is integral to cooperative problem-solving systems. The core task of critics is to recognize and communicate debatable issues concerning a product. Critics point out problematic situations that might otherwise remain unnoticed. Many critics also advise users on how to improve the product and explain their reasoning. Critics thus help designers avoid problems and learn different views and opinions. Critiquing systems *augment* the ability of human designers to evaluate their solutions; decisions concerning whether or not to follow the critic suggestions are left up to the designers.

Critiquing systems are well suited for design tasks in complex problem domains in which the traditional expert systems or automated design approaches have proven inadequate. Such design tasks have the following characteristics: (a) knowledge about the design domain is *incomplete* and *evolving;* (b) the problem requirements can be specified only partially; and (c) necessary design knowledge is *distributed* among many design participants.

2.2.1 Knowledge about the design domain is incomplete and evolving

Some domains, such as user interface design (Lemke & Fischer, 1990) and lunar habitat design (Stahl, 1993), are not sufficiently understood; that is, creating a complete set of principles that exhaustively captures their domain knowledge is impossible. Complex problem domains are continually changing as new design knowledge is gained and old design knowledge becomes obsolete. For example, user interface design principles have certainly changed to accommodate the shift from primarily character-based user interfaces to sophisticated graphical user interfaces. Any system supporting design in complex domains must be able to evolve with the domain.

Expert systems and automated design approaches are infeasible in these complex situations in which all the potential relevant background knowledge cannot be articulated (Winograd & Flores, 1986). Because autonomous expert systems leave the human out of the decision process and all "intelligent" decisions are made by the computer, these systems require *a priori* a comprehensive knowledge base covering all aspects of the tasks being performed. Most expert systems also fail to adequately support the evolution of domain knowledge. First, expert systems typically do not support the addition of knowledge by domain experts, and instead rely on knowledge engineers to acquire this knowledge from domain experts and subsequently codify it for the specific system. Second, expert systems have shown themselves to be brittle (Rittel & Webber, 1984); that is, a small shift in the problem domain can render an expert system's knowledge base obsolete and inoperative (Buchanan & Shortliffe, 1984).

An important aspect of embedded critiquing systems is their incremental nature; they do not need a large or comprehensive rule-base to be effective. Because critics are structured to be independent entities, adding or modifying a critic does not affect the behavior of the remaining critics. Parts of the critiquing system can remain operational and continue to support the design process while other parts undergo evolutionary change. In the HYDRA-KITCHEN system we have prototyped a "generic" critiquing mechanism that is knowledgeable about commonly accepted design principles and standard design practices. These principles are found in textbooks and training programs and are recognized by professional kitchen designers as being important aspects of producing a "good" floor plan. Although this general knowledge base is insufficient for automating the design of kitchen floor plans or for making a detailed analysis of the appropriateness of the design for a particular client, the generic critiquing system provides designers with valuable feedback concerning their floor plan designs. One study involving both amateur and expert kitchen designers showed that HYDRA's generic critics helped both categories of designers, even though its rule-base contained only 24 critic rules (Fischer et al., 1989).

2.2.2 The problem requirements can be specified only partially

Design problems are ill-defined: they cannot be precisely specified before attempting a solution (Rittel & Webber, 1984). Problem specifications reflect the designer's understanding of the problem framing and the problem solution. Researchers in situated cognition (Lave, 1988) and design (Schoen, 1983) have shown that designers arrive at solutions by iteratively reframing the problem—adjusting and refining their understanding of the problem framing and problem solution to reflect decisions made, means that may be chosen, materials available, and other changes in the context. Thus, problem specifications are not only incomplete, they are also dynamic in nature.

The expert system approach is based on the assumption that the problem to be solved can be fully articulated to the system *a priori*. The system can return a solution only if given a complete and accurate problem specification. Furthermore, changes in the problem specification can completely invalidate the expert system's proposed solution. Thus, expert systems are inadequate in ill-defined domains with partial and evolving problem specifications.

We have constructed a critiquing mechanism that supports design as a process of problem reframing. This "specific" critiquing mechanism enables only those critics pertinent to the current partial specification, and as such embodies domain knowledge concerning situation-specific design characteristics that not every design will share. In kitchen design, professional designers elicit this situation-specific knowledge from their customers using predefined questionnaires; the answers to these questionnaires form part of the kitchen specification. In HYDRA-KITCHEN, as the designer changes the problem specification, the "specific" critiquing mechanism brings different sets of critics to bear upon the design. This mechanism supports the coevolution of problem framing and problem solving by making explicit the relationship between the partial problem specification and the current design solution.

2.2.3 Necessary design knowledge is distributed among many design participants

Design domains such as network design are so large and complicated and have so many subdomains that no single person can know all there is to know (Fischer, 1991). In such complex domains, the necessary design knowledge is distributed among many participants and most design work is done by teams whose members have different areas of expertise (Hackman & Kaplan, 1974; Johansen, 1988). When designing in ill-defined domains, there are no "optimal" solutions (Simon, 1981). Conflicts in opinion about how to proceed often arise due to differences in the designers' areas of expertise, their personal styles, and their particular problem framing. Often, such conflicts are resolved and design proceeds after designers present reasoned arguments supporting their opinions for discussion and negotiation.

Our critiquing systems support design as a deliberative and interpretative process. Critiquing systems contain a collection of critics that embody different areas of domain expertise, different design styles, and often diverging opinions. Our "interpretive" critiquing mechanism supports designers with varying interests and differing areas of expertise to work together by allowing design knowledge to be defined and bundled into personal or topical groupings. Using this mechanism, designers can examine their design from many different perspectives in which each perspective brings different design knowledge and critics to bear upon the current design.

All of our critiquing mechanisms—generic, specific and interpretive—support design as a deliberative process. Besides simply pointing out a potential flaw in the design, these critics offer a reasoned opinion as to why their suggestion should or should not be followed. This interaction style typifies cooperative problem-solving systems: it is the role of the critiquing system to bring relevant design knowledge to the designer's attention; it is the role of the designer to evaluate the trade-offs and make the final decisions.

3 Embedding critics in integrated design environments

Our early research focused on building and evaluating general purpose (i.e., not domain-oriented) critiquing mechanisms (Fischer et al., 1991). During later work, we became interested in building domain-oriented design environments (Fischer, 1992). In the last few years, we have merged these two research interests by embedding critiquing mechanisms into domain-oriented design environments. This embedding enhances both the richness of the critiquing process and the ability of our design environments to support the complex activity of design. This section discusses early critiquing systems we have built and how they contributed to the development of the multifaceted architecture, HYDRA, for design environments. A scenario using HYDRA-KITCHEN illustrates how the embedded critiquing mechanisms integrate the various components in the design environment.

3.1 Analyses of early critiquing systems

Critical analyses of our early stand-alone critiquing systems (Fischer et al., 1991) and systems built by others (Burton & Brown, 1982; Silverman, 1992), combined with empirical evaluations, led us to realize that the challenge in building critiquing systems is not simply to provide feedback: the challenge is to say *the right thing at the right time.* Our analyses identified several shortcomings in early critiquing systems that hindered their ability to say the "right" thing at the "right" time:

- lack of domain orientation;
- insufficient facilities for justifying critic suggestions;
- lack of an explicit representation of the user's goals;
- no support for different individual perspectives;
- timing problems with critic intervention strategies.

3.1.1 Lack of domain orientation

LISP-CRITIC (Fischer, 1987) allows programmers to request suggestions on how to improve their code. The system proposes transformations that make the code more cognitively efficient (i.e., easier to read and maintain) or more machine efficient (i.e., faster or smaller). However, the lack of domain orientation limits the depth of critical analysis the critiquing system can provide. Without domain knowledge, critic rules cannot be tied to higher level concepts; LISP-CRITIC can answer questions such as whether the Lisp code can be written more efficiently, but it cannot assist a user in deciding whether the code can solve a specific problem.

3.1.2 Insufficient facility for justifying critic suggestions

FRAMER (Lemke & Fischer 1990) enables designers to develop window-based user interfaces on Symbolics Lisp machines. FRAMER's knowledge base contains design rules for evaluating the completeness and syntactic correctness of the design as well as its consistency with interface style guidelines. Evaluations of FRAMER showed (1) that many users did not understand the consequences of following the critic's advice or why the advice was beneficial to solving their problem, and (2) that when users do not understand why a suggestion is made, they tend to blindly follow the critic's advice whether or not it is appropriate to their situation. FRAMER provided short explanations to address this problem. However, in design there are not always simple answers; access to argumentative discussions detailing the pros and cons of a particular suggestion are necessary (Rittel & Webber, 1984).

3.1.3 Lack of an explicit representation of the user's goals

JANUS (Fischer et al., 1989) is a step toward addressing the previous shortcomings. JANUS allows designers to construct kitchen architectural floor plans. It contains two integrated subsystems: a domain-oriented kitchen construction kit and an issue-based hypermedia system containing design rationale. Critics respond to problems in the construction situation by displaying a message and providing access to appropriate rationale in the hypermedia system. However, these critics often give spurious or irrelevant advice resulting from the lack of an explicit representation of the user's task. The only task goal built into JANUS is one of building a "good" kitchen; that is, a kitchen that conforms to commonly accepted standards and design practices. With an explicit model of the designer's intentions for a *particular* design, critics can be selectively enabled based on this model and provide less intrusive and more relevant advice.

3.1.4 No support for different individual perspectives

It is not possible to anticipate all the knowledge necessary for a critiquing system to say the "right" thing in every design situation. Design domains are continually evolving as new knowledge is gained. JANUS-MODIFIER (Fischer & Girgensohn, 1990) was developed to respond to this problem by making the domain knowledge (including critics) end-user modifiable. But being able to add new knowledge is not sufficient; different users must be able to organize and manage design knowledge and critics to reflect *their* perspectives on design. Design environments need to support interpretation of a problem from many perspectives (technical, structural, functional, aesthetic, personal), and critique accordingly.

3.1.5 Timing problems with critic intervention strategies

A number of systems (Fischer et al., 1985; Burton & Brown, 1982) investigated critic intervention strategies, which determine when and how a critic should signal a potential problem. This research focused on studying *active* versus *passive* intervention strategies. Active critics continually monitor user actions and make suggestions as soon as a problematic situation is detected. Passive critics are explicitly invoked by users to evaluate their partial design.

A protocol analysis study (Lemke & Fischer, 1990) showed that passive critics were often not activated early enough in the design process to prevent designers from pursuing solutions known to be suboptimal. Often, subjects invoked the passive critiquing system only after they thought they had completed the design. By this time, the effort of repairing the situation was expensive. In a subsequent study using the same design environment, an active critiquing strategy was shown to be more effective by detecting problematic situations early in the design process.

However, our interactions with professional designers showed that active critics are not a perfect solution either: they can disrupt the designer's concentration on the task at the wrong time and interfere with creative processes. Interruption becomes even more intrusive if the critics signal breakdowns at a different level of abstraction compared to the level of the task users are currently engaged. For example, if the designer is currently concerned about where the refrigerator should

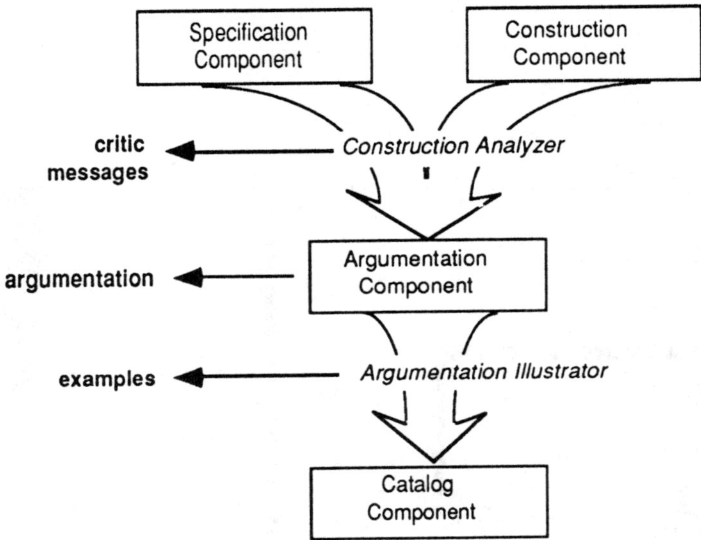

Figure 2 The critiquing process with HYDRA. The links between the components—the *Construction analyser* and the *Argumentation illustrator*—are crucial for exploiting the synergy of the integration.

be located in a kitchen floor plan, then a critic suggestion that a double-bowl sink is better than a single-bowl sink is probably inappropriate and distracting at this point in time.

What is needed is a critiquing system that: (1) alerts designers to problematic solutions; (2) avoids unnecessary disruptions; and (3) allows users to control the critic's intervention strategy. Embedding critics in design environments allows users to *control* critic intervention through interaction with the construction, specification, and perspective design components built into the design environment.

3.2 HYDRA: *A multifaceted architecture for design environments*

Design environments are computer programs that support designers in concurrently specifying a problem and constructing a solution. Design environments provide information repositories to store domain knowledge and allow designers to accumulate additional domain-knowledge through interaction with the environment.

HYDRA (Figure 2 represents its components schematically; Figure 3 provides a screen image) contains design creation tools in the form of a construction component and a specification component Design information repositories are provided in the form of argumentation and catalog knowledge bases. The architecture is *multifaceted* because these components provide multiple representations of both the current design and underlying domain knowledge. The critiquing mechanisms integrate these facets in the design environment architecture. The various representations are managed by the following four components:

- The *construction component* is the principal medium for modelling a design. It provides a palette of domain-oriented design units, which can be arranged in a work area using direct manipulation. Design units represent primitive elements in the construction of a design, such as sinks and stoves in the domain of kitchen design. Critics can be tied to these domain-oriented design units and to relationships between design units.
- The *specification component* allows designers to describe abstract characteristics of the design they have in mind. The specifications are expected to be modified and augmented during the design process, rather than to be fully articulated at the beginning. The specification provides the system with an explicit representation of the user's goals. This information can be used to

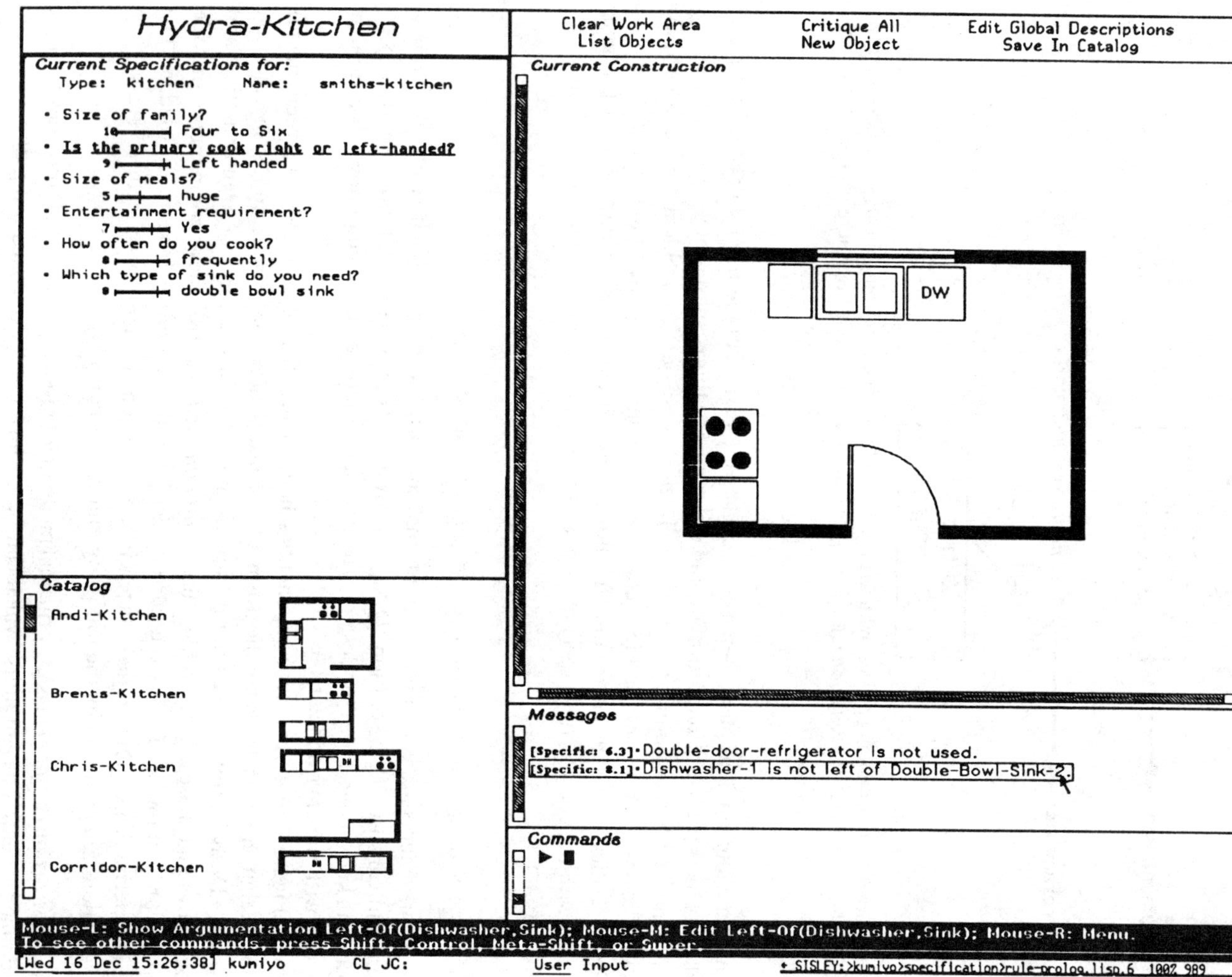

Figure 3 Screen image of HYDRA-KITCHEN. The "Current Specification" window shows a summary of currently selected answers using the specification component. An indicator attached to each of the selected answers allows users to assign weights of importance to the specified item in order to set priorities. The "Catalog" window shows previous kitchen designs that can be examined or reused. The "Current Construction" window shows a partial construction being built using components provided in a palette of kitchen design units (not shown). The "Messages" window is used to present critic notification messages. The number attached to the critic message is a weighted measure indicating the relevance of the fired critic.

tailor both the critic suggestions put forth and the accompanying explanations to the user's task at hand.

- The *argumentative hypermedia component* contains design rationale based on the procedural hierarchy of issues (PHI) structure (see Figure 5) (McCall, 1987; Conklin & Begeman, 1988). The PHI structure consists of issues, answers, and arguments about decisions made during the course of design. Users can annotate and add argumentation as it emerges during the design process. Argumentation is a valuable component in a critic's explanation; it identifies the pros and cons of following a critic suggestion and helps the user to understand the consequences of following a suggestion.
- The *catalog component* provides a collection of previously constructed designs. These illustrate examples within the space of possible designs in the domain and support reuse (Prieto-Diaz & Freeman, 1987) and case-based reasoning (Kolodner, 1991). Catalog entries are also important components in a critic's explanation. Often, a critic does not suggest a course of action but instead points out a deficiency in the current design; catalog entries can then be used as specific examples illustrating sample solutions that address a deficiency noted by a critic.

This architecture derives its power from the *integration* of its components. When used in combination, each component augments the value of the others in a synergistic manner. The components of the architecture are integrated by two linking mechanisms (see Figure 2). Together, these linking mechanisms support the critiquing process by providing critic messages, explanatory argumentation, and illustrative examples:

- The *construction analyser* is the core critiquing component in HYDRA. This mechanism analyses the design construction for compliance with the currently enabled set of critic rules. When a lack of compliance is detected, the critic signals a breakdown and provides entry into the exact place in the argumentative hypermedia component in which the appropriate explanation is located.
- The *argumentation illustrator* can retrieve both positive and negative catalog examples to illustrate the problematic situation detected by the *construction analyser*. Providing specific examples is essential, because the explanation given in the form of argumentation is often highly abstract and conceptual. Concrete design examples that match this explanation assist designers in understanding the potential problem, assessing the design situation, and devising a solution.

In addition to the construction and argumentation components of its predecessor JANUS, HYDRA supports a specification component (Fischer & Nakakoji, 1991) and a catalog of designs. The specification format is based on questionnaires used by professional kitchen designers to elicit their customers' requirements, such as the kitchen owner's cooking habits and family size. Each component in HYDRA contains design knowledge that can be used by an embedded critiquing mechanism to overcome the deficiencies of the stand-alone systems previously described.

As mentioned in section 2.2, we have studied three classes of embedded critiquing mechanisms: generic, specific and interpretive critics. These mechanisms embody different types of design knowledge, and correspond to three dimensions of embedding. *Generic critics* are embedded in the construction and use domain knowledge concerning desirable spatial relationships between design units to detect problematic situations in the partial design construction. *Specific critics* are embedded in the partial specification and take advantage of additional knowledge in the partial specification to detect inconsistencies between the design construction and the design specification. *Interpretive critics* are embedded in a perspective mechanism that enables designers to create topical groupings of critics and design knowledge; such groupings support designers in examining their artifacts from different viewpoints. The argumentation and catalog components provide rich sources of domain knowledge that all three mechanisms use in their explanation process when communicating with the designer.

The following section provides a scenario depicting how kitchen designers work within the HYDRA environment. The scenario describes the three critiquing mechanisms, and it illustrates the benefits derived from embedding these mechanisms in the multifaceted architecture.

3.3 Scenario illustrating generic, specific and interpretive critics

Imagine that Bob, a professional kitchen designer, has been asked to design a kitchen for the Smith family. The partial specification of the Smith's kitchen is articulated using HYDRA, as shown in Figure 3.

Bob begins working on a floor plan in the construction area. He moves the dishwasher next to the cabinet. Bob's action triggers a *generic critic*, and the message "The dishwasher is too far from the sink" is displayed. Generic critics reflect knowledge that applies to all designs, such as accepted standards, building codes, and domain knowledge based on physical principles. Often, this generic knowledge can be found in textbooks, training curricula, or by interviewing domain practitioners. Bob highlights the critic's message and elects to see its associated argumentation. The argumentation explains that plumbing guidelines require the dishwasher to be within one meter of the sink. Bob follows the critic's suggestion and moves the dishwasher next to the right side of the sink (for details, see Fischer et al., 1991).

This action triggers a *specific critic* with the rule "If you are left-handed, the dishwasher should be on the left side of the sink". Specific critics reflect design knowledge that is tied to situation-specific physical characteristics and domain-specific concepts that not every design will share. These critics are constructed dynamically from the partial specification to reflect current design goals. This particular critic rule was activated because Bob specified that the primary cook is left-handed (see Figure 3). Bob examines the supporting argumentation "Having the dishwasher to the left of the sink creates an efficient work flow for a left-handed person". Bob decides this is an important concern and puts the dishwasher on the left side of the sink.

Then Bob remembers that the Smiths are remodelling mainly to increase their property value in anticipation of selling in two years. So Bob decides to examine his design from a resale-value perspective. When Bob switches to the resale-value perspective, an *interpretive critic* is triggered with the ruie "The dishwasher should be on the right side of the sink". Interpretive critics support design as an interpretive process by allowing designers to interpret the design situation from different perspectives according to their interests. In this perspective, the critic about the dishwasher and sink has been redefined and its associated rationale has been modified. Now the argumentation says "Optimizing your kitchen for left-handed cooks can adversely affect the house's resale value since most kitchen users are right-handed". Bob decides that enhancing the Smiths' resale value is the more important consideration and moves the dishwasher. As long as he remains in the resale-value perspective, Bob will be informed by the critics whenever they detect a feature negatively affecting resale value. Additionally, the critics will provide Bob access to argumentation concerning designing for resale.

4 Three embedded critiquing mechanisms

This section describes in detail three embedded critiquing mechanisms—*generic, specific* and *interpretive.* Examples of how these three critic styles are deployed were illustrated in the previous scenario. In all three mechanisms, critic knowledge is captured by rules with condition and action parts. The *condition* clause checks whether a certain situation exists in the current design construction. The *action* clause notifies the designer that a particular situation has been detected. Figure 4 illustrates a condition-action critic rule in which the condition checks if the stove is away from the window; the action part notifies the designer that "the stove is not away from the window".

For all three mechanisms, the basic critiquing process consists of the following phases: (1) the set of appropriate critic rules to be enabled is identified; (2) the design construction is then analysed for compliance with the currently enabled set of critic rules; (3) when a lack of compliance is detected, the critic signals a possible problem and provides entry into the argumentative hypermedia component in which the appropriate explanation is located; and (4) concrete catalogue examples that illustrate the explanation given in the form of argumentation can

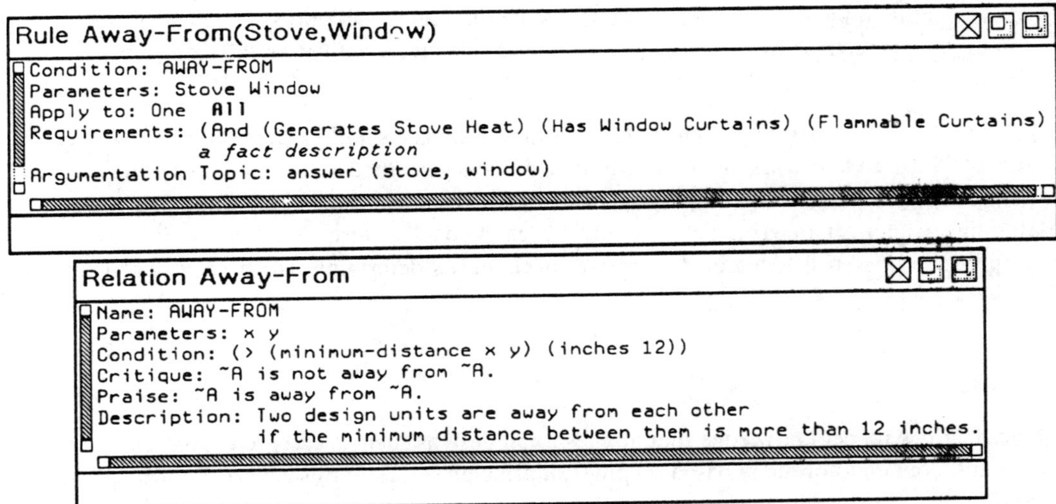

Figure 4 The "stove should be away from the window" critic rule and the definition of the "away-from" spatial relation

Table 1 The critic mechanisms—generic, specific and interpretive—differ in how they enable critic rules, the rules' scope of applicability, and the types of design knowledge each mechanism is best suited to represent

	How enabled	*Applicability*	*Design knowledge*	*Example*
Generic	Enabled by placing design units into the construction area	All designs	Standards	Cabinets should be 150 cm above floor
			Physical principles	Heat ignites flammable objects
Specific	Enabled by the partial specification	Specific design	Situation characteristics	Cook is left-handed and 150 cm in height
			Abstract domain concepts	Efficiency; safety
Interpretive	Enabled by the currently active design perspective	Specific perspective	Multiple interpretations of domain concepts	Cabinet height: convenient for cook
				Cabinet height: desirable for resale value

optionally be delivered (Fischer et al., 1991). As illustrated in Table 1, the three critic mechanisms differ mainly in terms of how they enable critic rules and in the types of design knowledge embodied in their rules.

- *Generic critics* (Fischer et al., 1991) are enabled by the placement of design units into the construction area. These critics apply to all designs containing the design unit to which the critics are attached. Generic critics reflect knowledge that is applicable to all designs, such as accepted standards or regulations or domain knowledge based on physical principles (see Table 1).
- *Specific critics* (Nakakoji, 1993) are constructed dynamically to reflect the designer's goals as they are stated explicitly in the specification component. These critics apply only to the design situation currently under construction. Specific critics reflect design knowledge that is tied to situation-specific physical characteristics and domain-specific concepts that not every design will share.
- *Interpretive critics* (Stahl, 1993) provide a mechanism for supporting design as an interpretive process; that is, they are a response to the recognition that domain concepts such as "cabinet height" and "efficiency" can have more than one definition or interpretation depending upon the

current situation and the designer. Interpretive critics allow designers to view their work from multiple perspectives by creating, managing and selectively activating different sets of design knowledge.

Specific examples illustrating each of these critic mechanisms will be discussed below. Generic critics will be used to discuss the basic critiquing process described at the beginning of this section. The three mechanisms for embedded critics differ from one another primarily in how they determine which set of critic rules should be enabled. The discussion of specific critics and interpretive critics will focus on how these mechanisms determine which critics are currently enabled.

4.1 Generic critics

Generic critics reflect knowledge that applies to all designs such as accepted standards, building codes and domain knowledge based on physical principles. Often, this generic knowledge can be found in textbooks, training curricula, or by interviewing domain practitioners. A generic critic representing an accepted kitchen design standard is the cabinet height critic. Kitchen designers agree that unless more specific information regarding the primary cook is known, the top cabinets should be placed 150 cm above the floor. A generic critic reflecting domain knowledge based on safety principles is the "stove should be away from the window" rule shown in Figure 4. This rule reflects the principle that objects that generate heat (e.g., the stove) should not be placed under flammable objects (e.g., the curtains on the window).

Generic critics in HYDRA are implemented as object-oriented methods of appliances and other design units in the design construction. When the design construction is altered, all design units implicated by the changes evaluate their critic methods. These methods are defined and parameterized by the information in property sheets such as those shown in Figure 4. For example, the rule box shown defines a generic critic for stoves. This method checks that the stove is "away from" all windows in the construction area.

The condition away-from is defined in the relation property sheet as taking two objects and evaluating whether or not the minimum distance between them is greater than 12 inches. The corresponding message for display if this condition is not met is the critique: the first object "is not away from" the second object.

The critic defined in the rule sheet applies this relation to the stove as the first parameter and sequentially to each window in the construction as the second parameter. The definition specifies that this rule shall be applied to windows (Apply to: All) because stoves should be away from all windows to prevent fires. Other critic rules specify only that there should exist at least one object in the construction (Apply to: One) that matches the condition relation with the first parameter—for example, the dishwasher should be near at least one sink.

Further requirements can be specified for the applicability of the critic rule. These applicability requirements make use of domain concepts like "generates heat", "has curtains" and "is flammable". In the example rule, a stove has to be away from a window only if the stove generates heat (e.g., it is not a microwave), if the window has curtains, and if the curtains are flammable. Finally, the definition of the critic lists a topic in the argumentation issue-based that will be displayed if this critic fires and the user selects the critic message.

All generic critics in HYDRA are defined through property sheets like these for rules and relations. Using these property sheets, designers are able to modify the definitions of existing critics and to create additional critics.

Critics inform designers of potentially problematic situations by using a three-tiered approach that involves simple notification, supporting argumentation and specific examples. First, the critic signals the designer of a potentially problematic situation with a simple initial notification message. The form of this initial notification message is defined by the critique phrase in the spatial relation definition. The critic shown in Figure 4 would display the message "Stove-1 is not away from

Window-1". Variables in the notification string are resolved into specific design units by the critic rule using the spatial relation. Associating notification messages with the spatial relations allows these messages to be shared by many critic rules. The downside of this approach is that the notification message signals only that a spatial relation was detected and does not report why this is significant.

As discussed in section 3.1, our work has shown that such "one-shot" notifications, which merely identify a situation, are inadequate. Critics that support design as an argumentative process (Rittel & Webber, 1984) should be capable of presenting different alternatives and opinions and each alternative's corresponding advantages and disadvantages. The critiquing systems use the argumentation component of HYDRA to provide the second tier of explanation, thereby "making argumentation serve design" (Fischer et al., 1991).

Each critic rule has an associated link into the argumentation component where issues pertaining to the situation identified by the critic are discussed. For the critic in Figure 4, the associated link is found in the slot "Argumentation Topic: answer (stove, window)". The designer can view the critic's associated design rationale by selecting the initial notification message displayed in the Message area (Figure 3). Because design rationale contains design issues accompanied by positive and negative argumentation, critic explanations in this form help the designer understand why the current design situation may be significant or problematic.

Sometimes designers may not understand the arguments made in the design rationale or they may understand the arguments but not know what action to take. In these situations, providing designers with specific examples can be helpful. The third tier of critic explanation delivers specific examples upon request that illustrate the issue being discussed. Designers can select an issue in the argumentation and request to see a positive example or a counter example. As illustrated in Figure 4, critic conditions are associated with argumentation issues. When the designer requests to see an example of a specific issue, the *argumentation illustrator* (see Figure 5) takes the critic condition associated with the selected argumentation issue and searches the catalog component for examples that fulfill the condition.

4.2 Specific critics

In HYDRA specification knowledge is related to: (1) situation-specific physical characteristics such as the size and shape of the kitchen or the owner's height; (2) specified requirements such as "a dishwasher should be included"; and (3) abstract domain concepts such as safety and efficiency. The specification issues were derived from questionnaires used by professional kitchen designers (Nakakoji, 1993).

Specific critics evaluate the construction situation for compliance with the partial specification. They reduce the intrusiveness of a critiquing system by narrowing the enabled critics to those that are relevant to the task at hand as determined from the partial specification. Specification-linking rules (Fischer & Nakakoji, 1991) are used to dynamically identify the set of specific critics to be enabled.

The specification consists of issue/answer pairs (see Figures 3 and 6). A specification linking rule represents a dependency between an issue/answer pair in the specification and associated pro and con arguments in the argumentation component. As shown in Figure 6, a specification linking rule connects the argumentation issue "Where should the stove be located?" with the specification item "Is safety important to you?" The shared domain distinction "safety" is used to establish a dependency between this particular specification item and the argumentation issue.

A critic condition is associated with each answer in the specification, and a domain distinction is associated with each argument. Domain distinctions are a vocabulary for expressing domain concepts such as safety or efficiency. Whenever the designer modifies the specification, the critiquing system recompiles the specification-linking rules to reflect the newly relevant domain distinctions. In this way, critiquing criteria are tied to a representation of the partially articulated goals of a specific design project.

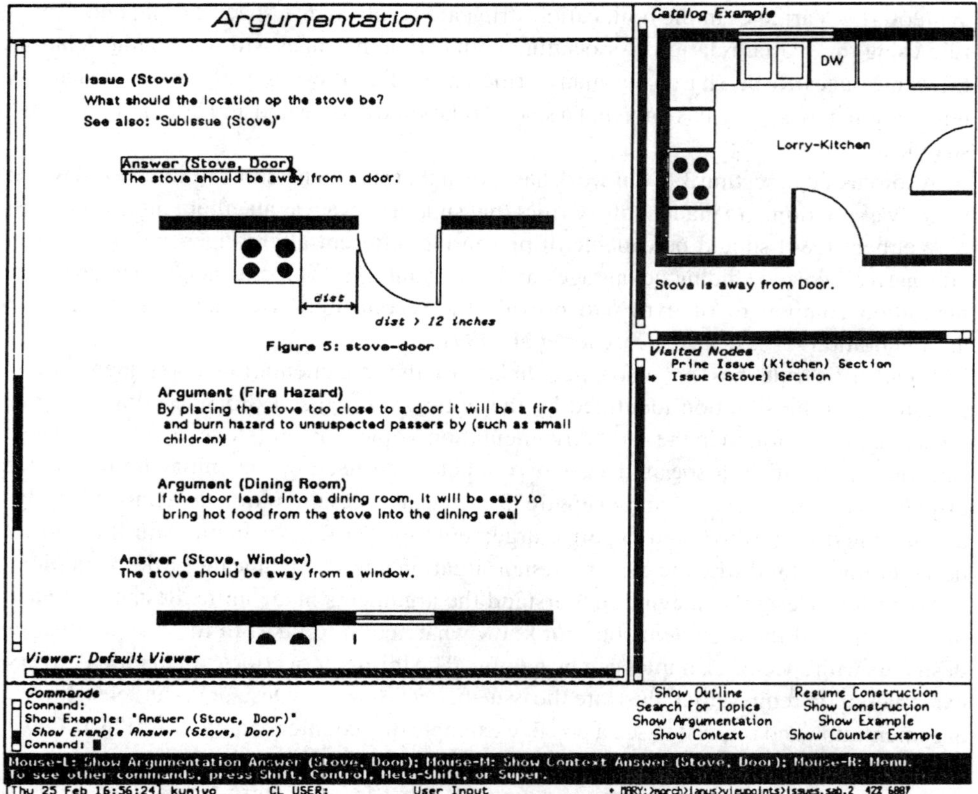

Figure 5 Argumentation consists of issues, answers and arguments supporting or refuting answers. The designer can view the stove-away-from-window critic's associated design rationale by selecting the initial notification message displayed in the Message area (e.g. "Stove-1 is not away from Window-1") of Figure 3. The arguments shown explain why many kitchen designers believe windows and stoves should not be adjacent. Choosing the menu item "Show Example" causes example designs that illustrate the answer advocated in the argumentation to be delivered to the designer.

The operation of the specification-linking rules can best be conveyed with an example. Assume the designer knows that the kitchen owners have young children and he specifies that having a safe (child-proof) kitchen is very important (Figure 6). The domain distinction associated with this specification item is "safety". In the argumentation, answers (e.g., "the stove should be away from all doors") are associated with critic conditions (e.g., "away-from stove door"). Pro and con arguments are associated with domain distinctions. In Figure 6, the domain distinction "safety" is associated with the pro argument and the domain distinction "efficiency" is associated with the con argument.

Specification-linking rules link the domain distinctions activated in the specification with the appropriate critic condition. First, the argumentation is analysed until the domain distinction activated in the specification (safety) is found. If the domain distinction is associated with a pro argument, then a specification-linking rule is created with the form: domain distinction implies critic condition. If the domain distinction is associated with a con argument, then a specification-linking rule is created with the form: domain distinction implies not critic condition. The specification-linking rules "safety implies stove away-from door" and "efficiency implies stove not away-from door" can be derived from the example in Figure 6. Whenever the designer modifies the specification, the critiquing system recomputes the specification-linking rules. For the partial specification shown in Figure 6, specification-linking rules supporting the notion of safety will be constructed. The right side of the specification rules are the enabled critic conditions used to evaluate the design construction for adherence to the current specification.

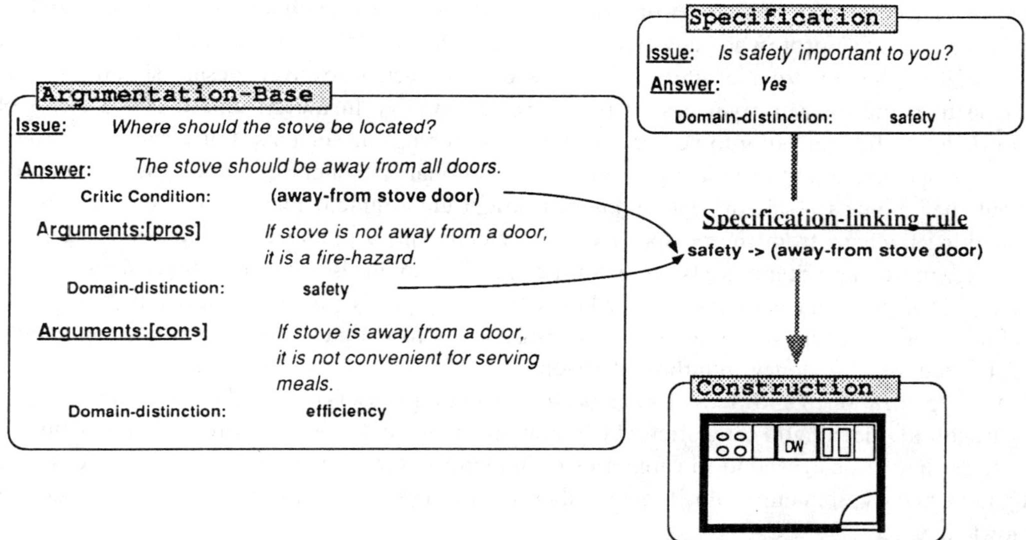

Figure 6 Derivation of the Specification-Linking rules. The domain distinction associated with a specification item is paired with a matching pro or con argument in the hypermedia issue base. The critic condition associated with an answer is linked with the domain distinction to form a specific critic rule.

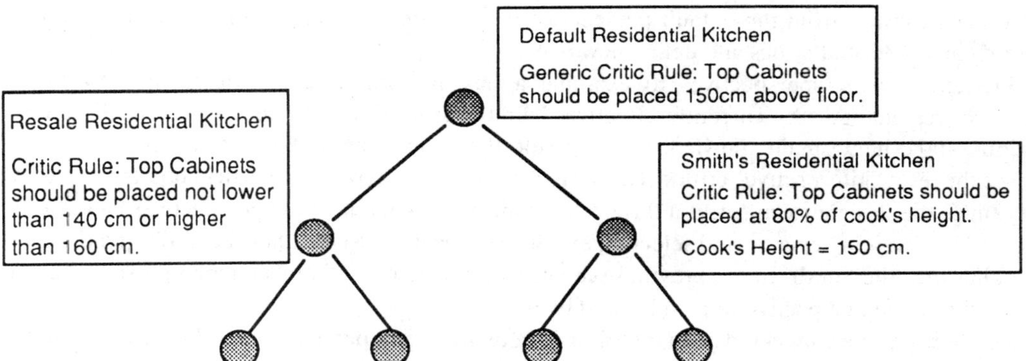

Figure 7 Perspectives are arranged in an inheritance network. Three perspectives—a "default kitchen", "Smith's kitchen" and a "resale kitchen"—are shown. The preferred placement of the top cabinets depends on the perspective selected. The critic rule analysing the placement of the top cabinets is redefined within each of the three perspectives.

Often, conflicts between specific critics arise. The designer could have specified that he was concerned with both safety and efficiency. For example, having the stove to the left of the refrigerator may be efficient, but it may also be less safe if this places the stove next to the door. Using the specification component, the designer cannot only state which concepts are of interest, he can also articulate his level of interest by weighting specification items. The critiquing system uses these weights to help prioritize critic activity. When a critic fires, it displays an importance weight next to the initial notification message that reflects the weights assigned to the specification items that enabled the particular critic rule (see Figure 3). The designer can then take these relative weights into account when deciding to respond to the critic messages.

4.3 Interpretive critics

Design can be viewed as an interpretive process (Stahl, 1993). Designers and their clients interpret the design situation according to personal backgrounds, experiences, and concerns. This means that there cannot be a unique set of domain knowledge that is adequate for all people and all interests. We have prototyped a design environment (Stahl, 1992) with *perspectives* (Bobrow & Goldstein, 1980) to provide alternative views or approaches to given design situations. The perspectives mechanism organizes all the design knowledge in the system. It allows items of knowledge to be bundled into personal or topical groupings or versions. For instance, a resale-value perspective might include critics and design rationale pertinent to homeowners concerned about their home's resale appeal. A kitchen design environment might have perspectives for evaluating kitchens from the perspective of an electrician, a plumber, an interior designer, a realtor, a mortgage writer or a city inspector. Perspectives could also be defined for individuals who have special preferences or for specific kitchens. A perspective for the Smith's kitchen would include design rationale for its unique set of design decisions so that any future modifications could be checked for consistency with those decisions.

The organization of knowledge by perspectives encourages users to view the knowledge in terms of structured, meaningful categories which they can create and modify. It provides a structure of contexts that can correspond to categories meaningful in the design domain. This can ease the cognitive burden of manipulating large numbers of alternative versions of critics and other design knowledge.

Interpretive critics are the result of interactions between the perspectives structure and the critic mechanisms (Figure 7). Critics are associated with design perspectives. The perspectives provide a mechanism for creating, managing and selectively activating different sets of critics along with their related design knowledge, such as spatial relations, domain distinctions, palette items and argumentation. A perspective can incorporate critics from other perspectives, including generic and specific critics from the default perspective (see Figure 7). Additionally, a perspective may modify any inherited critics and define new ones.

Designers switch perspectives to examine a design from different viewpoints. Switching perspectives changes the currently effective definitions of critics, the terms used in these definitions, and other domain knowledge. As a result, the critics adapt to the different perspectives—hence the term "interpretive" critics. The designer always works within a particular perspective. At any time, the designer can select a different perspective by name. New perspectives can also be created by assigning a name and selecting existing perspectives to be inherited. Bob, the designer working with the Smiths in the previous scenario, could create a Smith's kitchen perspective and select the resale perspective to be inherited by it.

Perspectives are connected in an inheritance network; a perspective can modify any knowledge inherited from its parents or it can add new knowledge. Consider the inheritance network shown in Figure 7. Suppose that in the default perspective there is a rule that checks "if the top cabinets are 150 cm above the floor". In the Smith's kitchen perspective the rule that determines cabinet height is based on the cook's height. This *same* critic rule will be evaluated differently in the three different perspectives because it is defined in terms of the spatial relationship whose definition varies. Similarly, either the rule or the spatial relationship in the rule could be defined indirectly in terms of something in the argumentation issue-base, such as the answer to an issue requesting the primary cook's height. Critics and the design knowledge on which they are based can be adapted to interpret designs differently in many ways: by inheritance, by modification of inherited objects, or by addition of new objects into a perspective.

Interpretive critics based on perspectives provide a mechanism for refining the critiquing process that is orthogonal to the specific critics. Specific critics fine-tune the generic critics that embody general domain knowledge, relating them to the design choices specified for a given project. Whereas the set of generic and specific critics may be extensible in the sense that new critics can be added from time to time, the perspectives mechanism provides for multiple definitions of these sets to exist simultaneously so that individual designers can fluidly adopt varying viewpoints on designs. This provides a means for structuring new critics and other knowledge representations as they emerge during use of the design environment and systematically retaining this knowledge for use in future projects.

5 Benefits of embedding: increasing the shared context

Computational media offer great capacity for storing large volumes of information and support for managing dynamic information spaces (Norman, 1993). Computational media can integrate diverse information sources such as reference materials, solutions tc previous design problems, and collections of design rationale. However, access to large information spaces creates a new problem for designers; information overload. In situations of information overload, the critical resource for designers is not information, but rather the attention with which to process information. Simon (1981) argued with convincing examples that a design representation suitable for a world in which the scarce factor is information may be exactly the wrong one for a world in which the scarce factor is attention. When presenting people with information, the primary concern is to present items that are relevant to the task at hand (Fischer & Nakakoji, 1991). Critics embedded in design environments exploit a rich notion of the designer's task at hand, or context, to provide relevant information to designers.

Design environments support a cooperative problem-solving process in which the designer determines the context of design by manipulating interface objects (such as graphical objects and form-based objects) in the construction, specification and perspective components. Objects in the construction component define a construction context that provides generic critics with a representation for the task at hand. Values and priorities for specification objects define a specific context that allows specific critics to compute relevant information for the particular task as specified by the designer. The perspective mechanism determines an interpretive context that enables collections of critics and their associated argumentation.

The context defined by the construction, specification and perspective situations allows the system to provide information relevant to a dynamic representation of the task at hand that is shared by the designer and the design environment. This shared context enables precise intervention by critics, reduces annoying interruptions, and increases the relevance of information delivered to designers. Critics embedded in design environments benefit the design process by increasing the designer's understanding of design situations, by pointing out significant design situations that might have been overlooked, and by locating relevant information in very large information spaces.

5.1 Increasing the designer's understanding of design situations

The solution of a design problem necessarily involves coming to a deeper understanding of the problem through attempts to solve it. Design problems cannot be clearly defined "up front", before any attempt at a solution is made. New requirements emerge during the design process (Schoen, 1983; Rittel, 1984; Fischer et al., 1992) that cannot be identified until portions of the artifact have been designed or implemented. These aspects of design create the following dilemma: (1) one cannot gather information meaningfully unless the problem is understood; (2) one cannot understand the problem without having a concept of the solution in mind; and (3) one cannot understand the problem without information about it.

Problem framing and problem solving are *mutually enabling* design processes because each informs the other. Design methodologists such as Schoen (1983) and Rittel (1984) stress the strong interrelationship between problem framing and problem solving. They characterize design problems by the need for designers to impose a discipline, or framing, on the problem to reduce the complexity of the situation to a manageable level. Problem framing is the process of determining the boundaries (or framework) of a problem, such as determining the "givens" of the problem, the assumptions under which the designer operates, and the criteria for evaluating a solution. Each move toward a design solution tests the problem framing, potentially exposing conflicting or unrealistic goals. Critics embedded in design environments support designers in creating and modifying the problem framing throughout the design process—not just in the beginning. Critics support a design process where "understanding the problem is the problem".

In this view of design, in which problem framings and problems solutions coevolve, each action by the designer has the potential to alter the understanding of the problem, which in turn can influence subsequent actions. Our goal is to support design as a cooperative problem-solving dialogue between the designer and the evolving design situation.

5.2 Pointing out significant design situations

By seeing design as a "reflective conversation with the situation" (Schoen, 1983), action is governed by nonreflective thought processes and proceeds until it breaks down. A *breakdown* (Fischer, 1993) occurs when the designer realizes that nonreflective action has resulted in unanticipated consequences—either good or bad. Schoen described this realization as "the situation talks back". Reflection is used to repair the breakdown, and then (nonreflective) situated action continues. The hallmark of reflection-in-action is that it takes place within the *action present*—within the time period during which the decision to act has been made but the final decision about how to act has not. This is the time period during which reflection can still make a difference in what action is taken.

Schoen's theory of design is based on designers interacting with traditional media, and the back-talk from the situation is determined solely by the designer's skill, experience and attention. Computational technology, such as critics embedded in design environments, afford a new type of back-talk from the design situation. Computational design situations can actively point out breakdowns to designers. This active design support enables designers to hear the situation talk back in situations that might have remained mute in passive media.

Reflection-in-action, as supported by embedded critics, is an ongoing cycle of action, break-down and reflection. Designers act when they shape the design situation. They establish a shared context with the design environment by manipulating interface objects in the construction, specification or perspective components. Breakdowns are triggered by critics embedded in the design environment that detect situations that indicate the designer might need to reflect. Based on the shared context, critics support reflection by delivering information relevant to the breakdown situation. Argumentative information helps designers understand the breakdown situation, and the catalog contains design solutions that provide examples of how other designers have resolved similar problems.

The scenario illustrates how embedded critics support design as a reflective conversation with the situation. In the scenario, critics triggered two consecutive breakdowns. In the first, the construction situation talked back to Bob when his actions violated a generic kitchen design principle that "the dishwasher should not be too far from the sink". After some reflection, he moved the dishwasher nearer to the sink to comply with the critic. However, this action created a new breakdown situation. A specific critic signalled a breakdown to remind Bob that his actions were inconsistent with his partial specification; that is, his placement of the sink might not be optimal for left-handed cooks. This breakdown led him to reflect on his goals; instead of altering the design construction, Bob reformulated his partial specification.

5.3 Locating relevant information in large information spaces

Making information relevant to the task at hand poses many challenges for the design of interactive computer systems, particularly for problems in which the need for information is critical and yet precise information needs cannot be known in advance of attempts to solve the problem. Our design environments that support design in complex domains are high-functionality computer systems; that is, they provide a large amount of functionality and are built on large information bases. Such systems provide more information and functionality than a single person can master (Draper, 1984). Two factors contribute to this behaviour: (1) the effort of finding information often outweighs the perceived benefits of doing so; and (2) users are not aware that the information even exists. Both factors can be related to the discrepancy between the designer's perception of an information space and the actual information contained in a high-functionality system (see Figure 8).

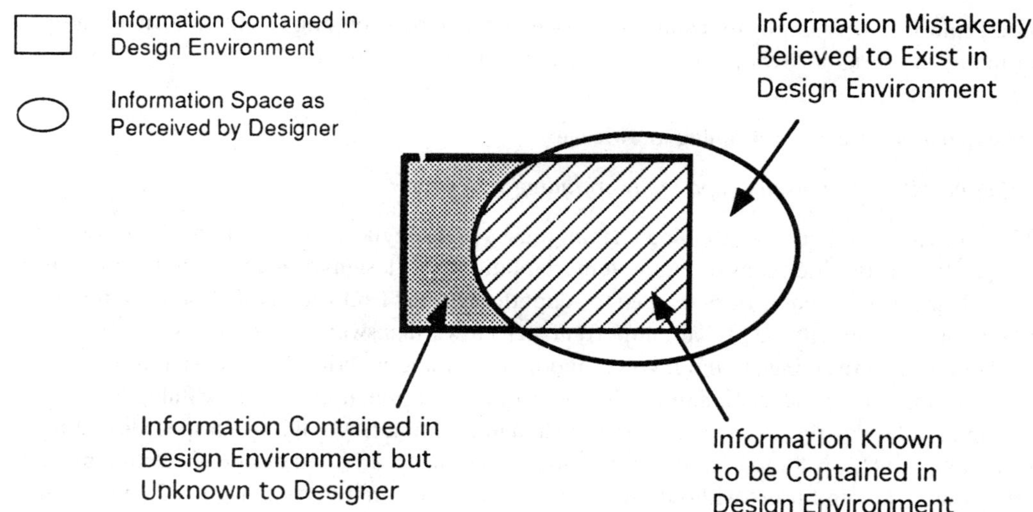

Figure 8 Large information spaces contain more information than a single person can know exists. The oval represents the information a designer perceives to be in the design environment. The square represents the information actually contained in the design environment. This figure illustrates that the designer's perception includes information that does not exist in the design environment, and does not include some information that actually exists in the design environment.

Designers are often unwilling to disrupt the design process to search for information in large information spaces, even if they know the information exists. In addition, designers may not know when they *need* information. Embedded critics save designers the trouble of explicitly querying the system for information. Critics notify designers of situations indicating the need to reflect (breakdowns) and provide access to information fueling reflection. The context of the breakdown situation serves as an implicit query that enables embedded critics to deliver relevant information. Designers benefit from needed information without having to explicitly ask for it.

Embedded critics can also deliver relevant information (Nakakoji, 1993) about which designers were unaware (see Figure 8). Critics provide the designer with a pointer into part of the system's information space with which the designer needs to become aware. The designer can further browse the unfamiliar portion of the information space starting from the entry point provided by the critic.

Critics afford *learning on demand* (Fischer, 1991) by letting designers access new knowledge in the context of actual problem situations; users are informed (1) when they are getting into trouble, (2) when they are missing important information, and (3) when they come up with problematic solutions. Learning on demand is a promising approach for the following reasons: (1) it contextualizes learning by integrating it into work rather than relegating it to a separate design phase; (2) it lets designers see for themselves the usefulness of new knowledge for actual problem situations, thereby increasing the designers' understanding of their situations; and (3) it makes new information relevant to the task at hand, thereby leading to better decision making, better products, and better performance.

Critics exploit the shared context of breakdown situations to compute what information is relevant to the task at hand. In the scenario, each critic's notification message was linked to information in the argumentation component. For the "dishwasher not too far from the sink" issue, the designer was reminded of plumbing requirements he might have known about but did not remember in the context of the design situation. The "left-handed" specific critic identified information the designer had previously been unaware of: that the recommended positions of the sink and dishwasher are dependent upon whether the cook is right- or left-handed. The interpretive critic (enabled by adapting a Resale Perspective) informed Bob of additional information about which he had previously been unaware. Now that he is aware of this "resale" value concern, Bob could explore further implications of a resale perspective by browsing related information or by continuing his design process, where he will be informed on demand.

6 The dynamic nature of critiquing knowledge

6.1 Supporting designers in adapting the critiquing system

To be successful, embedded critiquing systems must adapt to reflect changes in the design domain. Two questions arise when considering system adaptation: will designs be *able* to adapt the system as required, and will designers be *motivated* to adapt the system? End-user modifiability components and design environment "seeds" are important steps toward answering these questions.

Adapting the critiquing system involves modifying or adding critic rules, design units, design unit relations and critic explanations in the form of argumentation and catalog examples. Sometimes, adapting the system is as simple as changing parameters or filling out specialized forms. Girgensohn (1992) explored end-user modifiability in domain-oriented design environments. His work showed that end-users without any formal training in computer science need considerable environmental support in the form of explanatory help, critics that support modification processes, task decomposition agendas, and computer-supported object classification to effect significant system changes. Even with this extensive environmental support, none of the subjects in his user studies were able to complete the adaptations without intervention from the study supervisor. Girgensohn's research has demonstrated that enabling designers to adapt their systems is a very difficult problem which requires further research in the areas of demonstration components, domain-oriented knowledge representations, and adaptive user modelling components. The HERMES project is exploring a different approach toward achieving end-user modifiability by building into the design environment an English-like end-user programming language (Stahl et al., 1992).

6.2 "Seeding" the critiquing system with domain knowledge

Whereas ongoing adaptation of embedded critiquing systems is in the hands of designers solving design problems, system builders must create the original conditions that enable and motivate this evolution process to occur. Specifically, system builders must provide initial environments in the form of a seed.

We cannot offer an easy-to-follow prescription for successful seed building. Seed building requires a deep understanding not only of the application domain, but also of the *practice* (Ehn, 1989) of the people who will use the system. System builders cannot hope to attain such an understanding without, at least to some extent, becoming domain experts themselves. But this is generally infeasible. For useful seeds to be built, system-building must be based on a process of mutual education (Greenbaum & Kyng, 1991) between system builders, who know about building software design environments, and domain designers, who understand the practice of design in the target application domain. The goal of this mutual education process is to establish a shared understanding of what domain knowledge a seed should contain so that it will immediately support the practice of designers within that domain.

6.3 Accumulating design knowledge through critics

Embedded critics play the crucial role of "knowledge attractors" in domain-oriented design environments. Design knowledge surfaces during reflection-in-action, when designers reflect upon the source of breakdowns and devise courses of action for resolving the breakdowns. User observations in using specific critics revealed that when designers were fired a critic rule, they often argued for or against the associated argument and were motivated to describe the reason by articulating pro or counter arguments to the argumentation (Nakakoji, 1993). The incomplete nature of design knowledge guarantees the argumentation is never complete. Designers who arrive at an innovative resolution to a breakdown may add their arguments to the existing rationale, enriching the information space contained in the design environment.

7 Conclusions

Although this paper focuses primarily on a single design environment built for residential kitchen design, the HYDRA-KITCHEN system, other ongoing research in our group has demonstrated that embedded critiquing systems have broad applicability to a variety of domains and that embedded critiquing systems can be applied to complex, new domains with few accepted design rules and practices, and non-spatially-oriented domains.

The interpretive critiquing mechanism is being explored in the domain of lunar habitat design (Stahl, 1993). Unlike kitchen design, lunar habitat design is a completely new domain with few design rules and no standardized vocabulary. In domains with few standards, negotiation, argumentation and interpretation are increasingly important aspects of design. This aspect of the lunar habitat design domain led us to extend our critiquing systems to include interpretive mechanisms.

The Voice Dialog Design Environment tests the applicability of critiquing systems to non-spatial domains. The system supports the design and simulation of applications with phone-based interfaces (Repenning & Sumner, 1992). In this domain, design units include audio prompts, voice menus and telephone touch-tone input. Relations between design units are temporal in nature; that is, design units occur before or after certain events in the execution sequence. This design environment is part of a joint research project between the University of Colorado and voice dialogue application designers at US WEST Advanced Technologies (Sumner et al., 1991).

We have demonstrated how embedding critic mechanisms in design environments overcomes many deficiencies found in stand-alone critiquing systems. The generic, specific and interpretive critics we have explored correspond to three dimensions of embedding. Generic critics are embedded in the construction context because they are enabled by the placement of design units in the work area. Specific critics are embedded in the partial specification by being dynamically constructed from domain distinctions tied to specification items; they reduce the intrusiveness of generic critics by narrowing the enabled critics to those that are relevant to the partially specified task at hand. Interpretive critics are embedded in the network of perspectives that supports the evolution of alternative viewpoints on designs; using these critics, designers are able to consider their designs critically from multiple perspectives. The beneficial role of human critiquing in science, design and engineering had been socially recognized long before the advent of computational critiquing systems. Our approach of embedding critics into integrated design environments is an important step toward applying the critiquing paradigm to create more useful and usable knowledge-based computer systems.

Acknowledgements

The authors thank the members of the Human-Computer Communications group at the University of Colorado, who contributed to the conceptual framework and the system discussed in this paper. The research was supported by the National Science Foundation under grants No. IRI-8722792 and IRI-9015441, by the Colorado Advanced Software Institute, by US WEST Advanced Technologies, by the NYNEX Science and Technology Center, and by Software Research Associates, Inc. (Tokyo, Japan). We especially wish to thank Barbara Gibson at Kitchen Connection in Boulder, Colorado, for sharing her expertise in kitchen design.

References

Bobrow, DG and Goldstein, I, 1980. "Representing design alternatives" In: *Proceedings of AISB Conference*, AISB, Amsterdam.

Buchanan, B and Shortliffe, E, 1984. "Human engineering of medical expert systems" In: B Buchanan and E Shortliffe (Eds), *Rule-Based Expert Systems: The MYCIN Experiments of the Stanford Heuristic Programming Project*, Addison-Wesley, Reading, MA, pp 599–612.

Burton, R and Brown, JS, 1982. "An investigation of computer coaching for informal learning activities" In: D Sleeman and JS Brown (Eds), *Intelligent Tutoring Systems*, Academic Press, London, pp 79–98.

Chambers, AB and Nagel, DC, 1985. "Pilots of the future: Human or computer?" *Commun. ACM* **28** (11) 1187–1199.

Conklin, J and Begeman, M, 1988. "gIBIS: ` hypertext tool for exploratory policy discussion" *Trans. Office Infor. Syst.* **6** (4) 303–331.

Draper, SW, 1984. "The nature of expertise in UNIX" In: *Proceedings of INTERACT'84, IFIP Conference on Human-Computer Interaction*, pp 182–186, Elsevier, Amsterdam.

Ehn, P, 1989. *Work-Oriented Design of Computer Artifacts* (2nd ed.), Arbetslivscentru, Stockholm.

Fischer, G, 1987. "A critic for LISP" In: *Proceedings of the 10th International Joint Conference of Artificial Intelligence*, pp 177–184, Milan, Italy.

Fischer, G, 1990. "Communication requirements for cooperative problem solving systems" *Information Syst.* **15** (1) pp 21–36.

Fischer, G, 1991. "Supporting learning on demand with design environments" In: *Proceedings of the International Conference on the Learning Sciences*, pp 165–172, Evanston, IL.

Fischer, G, 1992. "Domain-oriented design environments" In: *Proceedings of 7th Annual Knowledge-Based Software Engineering (KBSE-92) Conference*, pp 204–213, McLean, VA.

Fischer, G, 1993. "Turning breakdowns into opportunities for creativity" In: E Edmonds (Eds), *Creativity in Cognition*, Penrose Press.

Fischer, G and Girgensohn, A, 1990. "End-user modifiability in design environments" In: *Proceedings of CHI'90*, pp 183–191, ACM Press.

Fischer, G, Grudin, J, Lemke, AC, McCall, R, Ostwald, J, Reeves, BN and Shipman, F, 1992. "Supporting indirect, collaborative design with integrated knowledge-based design environments" *Human Computer Interaction* (Special Issue on Computer Supported Cooperative Work) **7** (3).

Fischer, G, Lemke, AC, Mastaglio, T and Morch, A, 1991. "The role of critiquing in cooperative problem solving" *ACM Trans. Infor. Syst.* **9** (2) 123–151.

Fischer, G, Lemke, AC, McCall, R and Morch, A, 1991 "Making argumentation serve design" *Human Computer Interaction* **6** (3–4) 393–419.

Fischer, G, Lemke, AC and Schwab, T, 1985. "Knowledge-Based Help Systems" In: *Proceedings of Human Factors in Computing Systems, CHI'85 Conference Proceedings*, pp 161–167, San Francisco, CA.

Fischer, G, McCall, R and Morch, A, 1989. "Design environments for constructive and argumentative design" In: *Proceedings of CHI'89*, pp 269–275, ACM Press.

Fischer, G and Nakakoji, K, 1991. "Making design objects relevant to the task at hand" In: *Proceedings of AAAI-91, Ninth National Conference on Artificial Intelligence*, pp 67–73, AAAI Press/The MIT Press.

Girgensohn, A, 1992. *End-User Modifiability in Knowledge-Based Design Environments*, Unpublished Ph.D Dissertation, Department of Computer Science, University of Colorado at Boulder. (Also available as TechReport CU-CS-595-92.)

Greenbaum, J and Kyng, M, 1991. *Design at Work: Cooperative Design of Computer Systems*, Lawrence Erlbaum.

Hackman, JR and Kaplan, RE, 1974. "Interventions into group process: An approach to improving the effectiveness of groups" **5** 459–480.

Johansen, R, 1988. *Groupware: Computer Support for Business Teams*, Free Press.

Kolodner, J, 1991. "Improving human decision making through case-based decision aiding" **12** (2) 52–68.

Lave, J, 1988. *Cognition in Practice*, Cambridge University Press.

Lemke, AC and Fischer, G, 1990. "A cooperative problem solving system for user interface design" In: *Proceedings of AAAI-90, Eighth National Conference on Artificial Intelligence*, pp 479–484, AAAI Press/ The MIT Press.

McCall, R, 1987. "PHIBIS: Precedurally Hierarchical Issue-Based Information Systems" In: *Proceedings of the Conference on Architecture at the International Congress on Planning and Design Theory (New York)*, American Society of Mechanical Engineers.

Nakakoji, K, 1993. *Increasing shared knowledge of design tasks between humans and design environments: The role of a specification component*, PhD Dissertation Thesis, Department of Computer Science, University of Colorado at Boulder.

Norman, DA, 1993. *Things That Make Us Smart*, Addison-Wesley.

Petroski, H, 1985. *To Engineer is Human: The Role of Failure in Successful Design*, St. Martin's Press.

Polanyi, M, 1966. *The Tacit Dimension*, Doubleday.

Popper, KR, 1965. *Conjectures and Refutations*, Harper & Row.

Prieto-Diaz, R and Freeman, P, 1987. "Classifying software for reusability" **4** (1) 6–16.

Repenning, A and Sumner, T, 1992. "Using agentsheets to create a voice dialog design environment" In: *Proceedings of Symposium on Applied Computing (SAC'92)*, pp 1199–1207, ACM Press.

Rittel, H, 1984. "Second generation design methods" In: N Cross (Ed.) *Developments in Design Methodology*, pp 317–327, Wiley.

Rittel, H and Webber, MM, 1984. "Planning problems are wicked problems" In: N Cross (Ed.) *Developments in Design Methodology*, pp 134–144, Wiley.

Schoen, DA, 1983. *The Reflective Practitioner: How Professionals Think in Action*, Basic Books.

Silverman, B, 1992. "Survey of expert critiquing systems: Practical and theoretical frontiers" *Comm. ACM* **35** (4) 106–127.

Simon, HA, 1981. *The Sciences of the Artificial* (2nd ed.), The MIT Press.

Stahl, G, 1992. *Toward a Theory of Hermeneutic Software Design*, No. CU-CS-589-92, Computer Science Department, University of Colorado at Boulder.

Stahl, G, 1993. "Supporting interpretation in design" *J. Architecture and Planning Research* (Special Issue on Computational Representations of Knowledge) (Forthcoming).

Stahl, G, McCall, R and Peper, G, 1992. "A hypermedia inference language as an alternative to rule-based expert systems" (Submitted to Expert Systems ITL Conference).

Sumner, T, Davies, S, Lemke, AC and Polson, PG, 1991. *Iterative Design of a Voice Dialog Design Environment*, Technical Report No. CU-CS-546-91, Department of Computer Science, University of Colorado at Boulder.

Winograd, T and Flores, F, 1986. *Understanding Computers and Cognition: A New Foundation for Design*, Addison-Wesley.

Embedding Critics in Design Environments

Gerry Stahl, Jonathan Ostwald, Tamara Sumner, Kumiyo Nakakoji, and Gerhard Fischer

Although this paper was written in response to a specific request of *The Knowledge Engineering Review*, it stands as one of the best summary statements of our central line of research over several years in the Human-Computer Communications research group (together with its summary version, (Fischer et al. 1993)). It ties together the following claims:

- Software systems to support the work of professionals gain computational power by incorporating *domain-specific* knowledge and functionality.
- *Domain-oriented design environments* incorporate multiple interconnected components in order to integrate tools for doing design work with tools for maintaining design rationale and other information sources.
- *Computational critics* can perform useful functions to support design activities of professionals, such as deciding when specific rules of thumb apply, noting potential problems, and pointing to sources of useful information.
- For critics to be effective, they must be *embedded* in design environments where they can assess the state of work on a design artifact and initiate the delivery of information that is relevant to the task a designer is performing.

The ideas presented in the article were explored further by the authors and other members of our group. Nakakoji (1993; Nakakoji and Fischer 1995) provides a detailed discussion of the interaction between construction and specification in the KID system described in the article, as well as demonstrating an implementation of specific critics. Stahl (1993a, 1993b) explores the philosophic and design methodological motivation for mechanisms in design environments to support human interpretation, including an end-user scripting language to define interpretive critics. Sumner (1995; Sumner et al. 1997) weighs the pros and cons of a toolbelt (component-based) alternative to a domain-oriented design environment (an integrated software application). Her system for voice dialog designers experimented with flexible intervention strategies for critics, including a selection of sets of critics; this proved particularly useful for experienced domain designers, whereas the critics discussed in the article were more effective as learning-on-demand mechanisms for less experienced designers because they delivered highly contextualized information. Ostwald (1995, 1996) addressed the knowledge acquisition problem with an environment to support shared understanding between system designers and domain experts.

Our research group has since evolved into the Center for LifeLong Learning and Design (L^3D; see *http://www.cs.colorado.edu/~l3d*), an interdisciplinary effort to design software that supports the integration of working and learning (Fischer et al. 1996). Our idea of critiquing has been generalized into a three-layer model: the work process takes place within a software environment so that its state can be represented computationally; there are multiple rich information spaces that include domain knowledge and local community history; various mechanisms (including critics) actively map from the work state to timely and relevant information. This more general model is appropriate to web-based systems, where globally distributed information sources can be incorporated. This helps to address a serious issue we have encountered with design environments: the need to keep information up-to-date. Domain-specific systems are expensive to build, largely due to the effort to acquire, formalize, and maintain domain knowledge. Our current research investigates how to make the web more interactive so that user communities can build and evolve web knowledge bases with minimal support from system developers (Fischer et al. 1996). This raises important social as well as technical research issues about supporting communities of practice with intranet-based organizational memories.

REFERENCES

Fischer, G.; Lindstaedt, S.; Ostwald, J.; Schneider, K.; and Smith, J. 1996. Informing System Design through Organizational Learning. In *Proceedings of the International Conference on Learning Sciences (ICLS'96)*, 52–59.

Fischer, G.; McCall, R.; Ostwald, J.; Reeves, B.; and Shipman, F. 1994. Seeding, Evolutionary Growth and Reseeding: Supporting Incremental Development of Design Environments. In *Human Factors in Computing Systems, CHI'94 Conference Proceedings*, 292–298.

Fischer, G.; Nakakoji, K.; Ostwald, J.; Stahl, G.; and Sumner, T. 1993. Embedding Computer-Based Critics in the Contexts of Design. In *Human Factors in Computing Systems, InterCHI'93 Conference Proceedings*, 157–164.

Nakakoji, K. 1993. Increasing Shared Understanding of a Design Task between Designers and Design Environments: The Role of a Specification Component. Ph.D. dissertation, Dept. of Computer Science, University of Colorado.

Nakakoji, K., and Fischer, G. 1995. Intertwining Knowledge Delivery and Elicitation: A Process Model for Human-Computer Collaboration in Design. *Knowledge-Based Systems Journal, Special Issue on Human-Computer Collaboration in Design* 8(2–3): 94–104.

Ostwald, J. 1995. Supporting Collaborative Design with Representations for Mutual Understanding. In *Human Factors in Computing Systems, CHI'95 Conference Companion*, 69–70.

Ostwald, J. 1996. Knowledge Construction in Software Development: The Evolving Artifact Approach. Ph.D. dissertation, Dept. of Computer Science, University of Colorado.

Stahl, G. 1993a. Interpretation in Design: The Problem of Tacit and Explicit Understanding in Computer Support of Cooperative Design. Ph.D. dissertation, Dept. of Computer Science, University of Colorado.

Stahl, G. 1993b. Supporting Situated Interpretation. In *Proceedings of the Cognitive Science Society: A Multidisciplinary Conference on Cognition*, 965–970.

Sumner, T. 1995. Designers and Their Tools: Computer Support for Domain Construction. Ph.D. dissertation, Dept. of Computer Science, University of Colorado.

Sumner, T.; Bonnardel, N.; and Harstad, B. 1997. The Cognitive Ergonomics of Knowledge-Based Design Support Systems. In *Human Factors in Computing Systems, CHI '97 Conference Proceedings*, 83–90.

Multimodal Interaction for Distributed Interactive Simulation

Philip R. Cohen, Michael Johnston, David McGee, Sharon Oviatt, Jay Pittman, Ira Smith, Liang Chen and Josh Clow
Center for Human Computer Communication
Oregon Graduate Institute of Science and Technology
P.O.Box 91000
Portland, OR 97291-1000 USA
Tel: 1-503-690-1326
E-mail: pcohen@cse.ogi.edu
http://www.cse.ogi.edu/CHCC

ABSTRACT

This paper presents an emerging application of Artificial Intelligence research to distributed interactive simulations, with the goal of reducing exercise generation time and effort, yet maximizing training effectiveness. We have developed the QuickSet prototype, a pen/voice system running on a hand-held PC, communicating via wireless LAN through an agent architecture to NRaD's[1] LeatherNet system, a distributed interactive training simulator built for the US Marine Corps. The paper describes our novel multimodal integration strategy offering mutual compensation among modalities, as well as QuickSet's agent-based infrastructure, and provides an example of multimodal simulation setup. Finally, we discuss our applications experience and lessons learned.

KEYWORDS: multimodal interfaces, agent architecture, gesture recognition, speech recognition, natural language processing, distributed interactive simulation.

1. INTRODUCTION

In order to train personnel more effectively, the US Government is developing large-scale military simulation capabilities. Begun as SIMNET in the 1980's [Thorpe, 1987], these distributed, interactive environments attempt to provide a high degree of fidelity in simulating combat equipment, movement, atmospheric effects, etc. Numerous workstation-based simulators that share a replicated and distributed database are networked together worldwide to provide a computational substrate. A rather ambitious goal for 1997 is to be able to create and simulate a large scale exercise, in which there may be on the order of 50,000 entities (e.g., a vehicle or a person). A major goal of the Government, as well as of the present research, is to develop technologies that can aid in substantially reducing the time and effort needed to create scenarios.

The Simulation Process

There are four general phases of user interaction with these simulations: creating entities, supplying their initial behavior, interacting with the entities during a running simulation, and reviewing the results. In the first phase, a user "lays down" or places forces on the terrain that need to be positioned in realistic ways, given the terrain, mission, available equipment, etc. In addition to positioning these entities at the start of a simulation, the user needs to supply them with behavior, which may involve complex maneuvering, communication, etc. While the simulation is being run, human controllers may observe ongoing events, and change the behavior of those entities to react appropriately to those events. Finally, after a simulation is run, a user will often want to review and query the resulting simulation history. This paper discusses the first two of these phases, while our current and future research addresses the remaining two.

2. THE SIMULATION INTERFACE

Our contribution to the distributed interactive simulation (DIS) effort is to rethink the nature of the user interaction. As with most modern simulators, DISs are controlled via graphical user interfaces (GUIs). However, for a number of reasons, GUI-based interaction is rapidly losing its benefits, especially when large numbers of entities need to be created and controlled. At the same time, for reasons of mobility and affordability, there is a strong user desire to be able to create simulations on small devices (e.g., PDA's). This impending collision of trends for smaller screen size and for more entities requires a different paradigm for human-computer interaction with simulators.

[1] NRaD = US Navy Command and Control Ocean Systems Center Research Development Test and Evaluation (San Diego).

3. QUICKSET

To address these simulation interface problems, we have developed QuickSet (see Figure 2) a collaborative, handheld, multimodal system for configuring military simulations based on LeatherNet [Clarkson and Yi, 1996], a system used in training platoon leaders and company commanders at the USMC base at Twentynine Palms, California. LeatherNet simulations are created using the ModSAF simulator [Courtmanche and Ceranowicz, 1995] and can be visualized in a wall-sized virtual reality CAVE environment [Cruz-Neira et al., 1993; Zyda et al., 1992] called CommandVu. In addition to LeatherNet, QuickSet is being used in a second effort called ExInit (Exercise Initialization), that will enable users to create brigade-level exercises.

A major design goal for QuickSet was to provide the same user interface for handheld, desktop, and wall-sized terminal hardware. We believe that only gesture and speech-based interaction comfortably span this range. However, rather than provide just one of these modalities, QuickSet offers both because it has been demonstrated that there exist substantive language, task performance, and user preference advantages for multimodal interaction over speech-only and gesture-only interaction with map-based tasks [Oviatt, 1996; Oviatt, in press].

QuickSet offers speech and pen-based gesture input on multiple 3-lb hand-held PCs (Fujitsu Stylistic 1000), which communicate via wireless LAN through the Open Agent Architecture (OAA) [Cohen et al., 1994], to ModSAF, and to CommandVu. With this highly portable device, a user can create entities, establish "control measures" (e.g., objectives, checkpoints, etc.), draw and label various lines and areas, (e.g., landing zones) and give the entities behavior; see Figure 1, where the user has said "M1A1 platoon follow this route <draws curved line >."

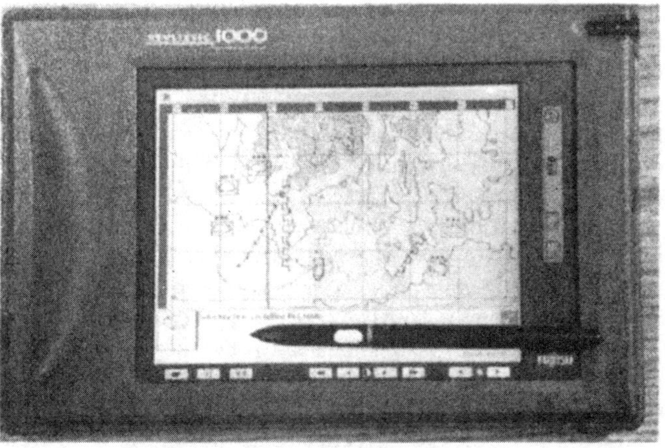

Figure 1: QuickSet running on a wireless handheld PC. The user has created numerous units, fortifications and objectives.

In the remainder of the paper, we describe the system components, the multimodal interface architecture, and the agent infrastructure that integrates both the components of QuickSet, as well as the military applications. We discuss its application, and finally lessons we have learned, particularly about the agent architecture.

4. SYSTEM ARCHITECTURE

Architecturally, QuickSet uses distributed agent technologies based on the Open Agent Architecture[2] for interoperation, information brokering and distribution. An agent-based architecture was chosen to support this application because it offers easy connection to legacy applications, and the ability to run the same set of software components in a variety of hardware configurations, ranging from standalone on the handheld PC to distributed operation across numerous workstations and PCs. Additionally, the architecture supports mobility in that lighter weight agents can run on the handheld, while more computationally-intensive processing can be migrated elsewhere on the network. The agents may be written in any programming language (here, Quintus Prolog, Visual C++, Visual Basic, and Java), as long as they communicate via the Interagent Communication Language (see below). The configuration of agents used in the Quickset system is illustrated in Figure 2. The architecture is described in detail in Section 6. A brief description of each agent, relevant to the user interface portions of the QuickSet system follows.

QuickSet interface: On the handheld PC is a geo-referenced map of the region such that entities displayed on the map are registered to their positions on the actual terrain, and thereby to their positions on each of the various user interfaces connected to the simulation. The map interface agent provides the usual pan and zoom capabilities, multiple overlays, icons, etc. The user can draw directly on the map, in order to create points, lines, and areas. The user can create entities, give them behavior, and watch the simulation unfold from the hand-held. When the pen is placed on the screen, the speech recognizer is activated, thereby allowing users to speak and gesture simultaneously.

Speech recognition agent: The speech recognition agent used in QuickSet is built on IBM's VoiceType Application Factory. The recognizer uses an HMM-based continuous speaker-independent speech recognition technology for PCs under Windows 95/NT and OS/2. Currently, it produces a single most likely interpretation of an utterance. One copy of this agent runs on every PC in the QuickSet system.

Gesture recognition agent: OGI's gesture recognition agent collects and processes all pen input from the PC screen or tablet. The recognizer sends an n-best list of possible interpretations to the facilitator, who forwards the recognition results to the multimodal integration agent. A gesture recognition agent runs on each PC in the Quickset architecture. A more detailed description of the gesture recognition agent is in Section 6.

[2] Open Agent Architecture is a trademark of SRI International

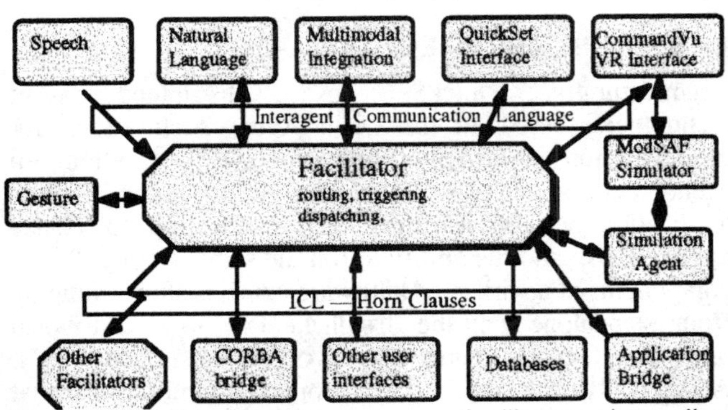

Figure 2: The blackboard serves as a facilitator, channeling queries to agents who claim they can solve them.

Natural language agent: The natural language agent currently employs a definite clause grammar and produces typed feature structures as a representation of the utterance meaning. Currently, for this task, the language consists of noun phrases that label entities, as well as a variety of imperative constructs for supplying behavior.

Multimodal integration agent: The multimodal interpretation agent accepts typed feature structure meaning representations from the language and gesture recognition agents. It unifies those feature structures together, producing a multimodal interpretation. A more detailed description of multimodal interpretation is in Section 5.

Simulation agent: The simulation agent, developed primarily by SRI International [Moore et al., 1997], but modified by us for multimodal interaction, serves as the communication channel between the OAA-brokered agents and the ModSAF simulation system. This agent offers an API for ModSAF that other agents can use.

Web display agent: The Web display agent can be used to create entities, points, lines, and areas, and posts queries for updates to the state of the simulation via Java code that interacts with the blackboard and facilitator. The queries are routed to the running ModSAF simulation, and the available entities can be viewed over a WWW connection using a suitable browser.

Other user interfaces: When another user interface connected to the facilitator, subcribes to and produces the same set of events as others, it immediately becomes part of a collaboration. One can view this as human-human collaboration mediated by the agent architecture, or as agent-agent collaboration.

CommandVu agent: Since the CommandVu virtual reality system is an agent, the same multimodal interface on the handheld PC can be used to create entities and to fly the user through the 3-D terrain. For example, the user can ask "CommandVu, fly me to this platoon <gesture on the map>."

Application bridge agent: The bridge agent generalizes the underlying applications' API to typed feature structures, thereby providing an interface to the various applications such as ModSAF, CommandVu, and Exinit. This allows for a domain-independent integration architecture in which constraints on multimodal interpretation are stated in terms of higher-level constructs such as typed feature structures, greatly facilitating reuse.

CORBA bridge agent: This agent converts OAA messages to CORBA IDL (Interface Definition Language) for the Exercise Initialization project.

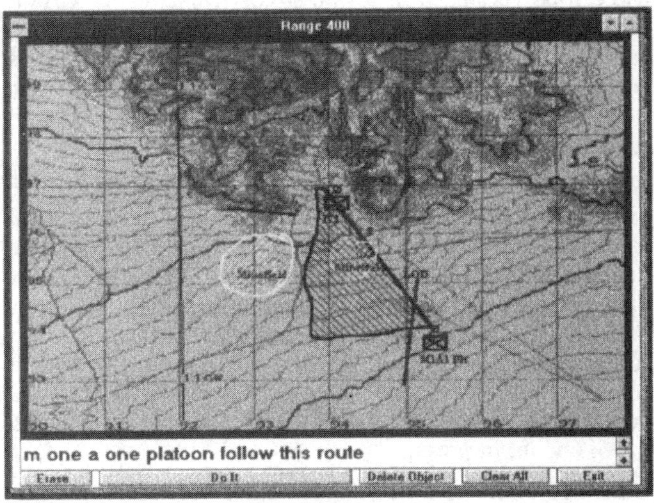

Figure 3: The QuickSet interface as the user establishes two platoons, a barbed-wire fence, a breached minefield, and issues a command to the platoon in the southeast to follow a specified route.

To see how QuickSet is used, we present the following example.

4. EXAMPLE

Holding QuickSet in hand, the user views a map from the ModSAF simulation, and with spoken language coupled with pen gestures, issues commands to ModSAF. For example, to create a unit in QuickSet, the user would hold the pen at the desired location and utter: "red T72 platoon" resulting in a new platoon of the specified type being created. The user then adds a barbed-wire fence to the simulation by drawing a line at the desired location while uttering "barbed wire." Similarly a fortified line is added. A minefield of an amorphous shape is drawn and is labeled verbally, and finally an M1A1 platoon is created as above. Then the user can assign a task to the new platoon by saying "M1A1 platoon follow this route" while drawing the route with the pen. The results of these commands are visible on the QuickSet screen, as seen in Figure 3, as well as on the ModSAF simulation, which has been executing the user's QuickSet commands (Figure 4). They are also visible in the CommandVu 3D rendering of the scene.

Since any recognizer will make mistakes, the output of the gesture recognizer is not accepted as a simple decision. Instead the recognizer produces a set of probabilities, one for each possible interpretation of the gesture. The identities and types of objects, units, points, lines, and areas that have been drawn, tapped on, or encircled by the pen, as well as their recognition probabilities, are sent to the blackboard. Through triggers, the multimodal interpretation agent is sent these candidate interpretations.

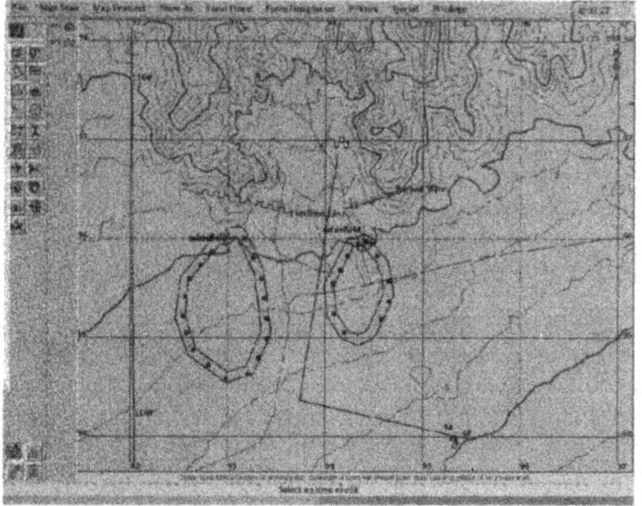

Figure 4: The ModSAF interface showing the forces and obstacles created from QuickSet.

In combining the meanings of the gestural and spoken interpretations, we attempt to satisfy an important design consideration, namely that the communicative modalities should compensate for each other's weaknesses [Cohen, 1992; Oviatt, 1992]. Here, we deliberately show an early version of QuickSet because it illustrates graphically that the unification-based multimodal integration process discussed in Section 7 has ruled out the higher-scoring area interpretation of the gesture (the shaded region in Figure 3) in favor of the unifying interpretation of the gesture as a linear route ("dog-legged" line in Figure 4), which was sent to ModSAF.[3] In response to this multimodal command, the automated platoon follows the route, sidesteps the minefields, breaches the fortifications, and engages in combat at the destination.

More detail on the gesture agent, multimodal integration, and agent architecture are provide below, since these artificial intelligence technologies are novel contributions of our effort.

6. GESTURE RECOGNITION

In order increase accuracy, QuickSet's pen-based gesture recognizer consists of both a neural network [Pittman, 1991] and a set of hidden Markov models. The digital ink is size-normalized, centered in a 2D image, and fed into the neural network as pixels. The ink is smoothed, resampled, converted to deltas, and given as input to the HMM recognizer. The system currently recognizes 68 pen-gestures (including units, lines of various types, objectives, etc.), and new ones are being added continually.

[3] In the present version of the system, the ultimate interpretation is reflected on the QuickSet screen

Both recognizers provide the same coverage (they recognize the same set of gestures). These gestures, some of which are illustrated in Figure 5, include various military map symbols (platoon, mortar, fortified line, etc.), editing gestures (deletion, grouping), route indications, area indications, taps, etc. The probability estimates from the two recognizers are combined to yield probabilities for each of the possible interpretations. The inclusion of route and area indications creates a special problem for the recognizers. Both recognizers recognize shape (although they see the shape in different data formats).

But as Figures 5 and 6 show, route and area indications may have a variety of shapes. This problem is further compounded by the fact that we want the recognizer to be robust in the face of sloppy writing. More typically, sloppy forms of various map symbols, such as those illustrated in Figure 6, will often take the same shape as some route and area indications. A solution for this problem can be found by combining the outputs from the gesture recognizer with the outputs from the speech recognizer, as is described in the following section.

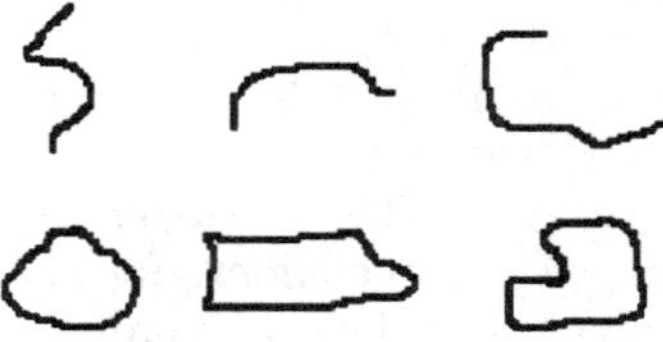

Figure 5: Pen drawings of routes and areas. Routes and areas do not have signature shapes that can be used to identify them.

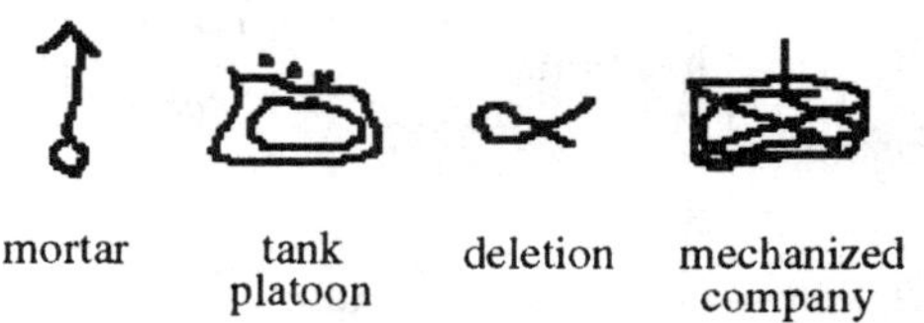

Figure 6: Typical pen input from real users. The recognizer must be robust in the face of sloppy input.

7. A UNIFICATION-BASED ARCHITECTURE FOR MULTIMODAL INTEGRATION

One the most significant challenges facing the development of effective multimodal interfaces concerns the integration of input from different modes. The major contribution of the present work is an architecture in which speech and gesture can compensate for errors in the other modality.

To model this integration, we utilize a unification operation over typed feature structures [Carpenter 1990, 1992; Calder 1987]. Unification is an operation that determines the consistency of two pieces of partial information, and if they are consistent combines them into a single result. As such, it is ideally suited to the task at hand, in which we want to determine whether a given piece of gestural input is compatible with a given piece of spoken input, and if they are compatible, to combine the two inputs into a single result that can be interpreted by the system.

The use of feature structures as a semantic representation framework facilitates the specification of partial meanings. Spoken or gestural input which partially specifies a command can be represented as an underspecified feature structure in which certain features are not instantiated. For example, if a given speech input can be integrated with a line gesture, it can be assigned a feature structure with an underspecified location feature whose value is required to be of type *line*.

The spoken phrase 'barbed wire' is assigned the feature structure in Figure 7.

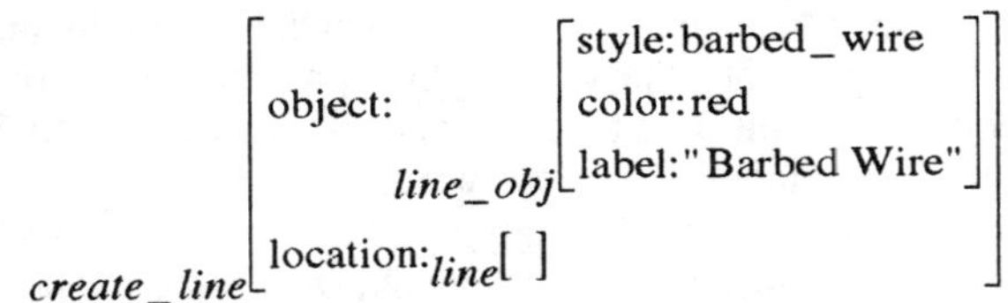

Figure 7: Feature Structure for 'barbed wire'

Since QuickSet is a task-based system directed toward setting up a scenario for simulation, this phrase is interpreted as a partially specified creation command. Before it can be executed, it needs a location feature indicating where to create the line, which is provided by the user's drawing on the screen. The user's ink is likely to be assigned a number of interpretations, for example, both a point interpretation and a line interpretation, which are represented as typed feature structures (see Figures 8 and 9). Interpretations of gestures as location features are assigned the more general *command* type which unifies with all of commands taken by the system.

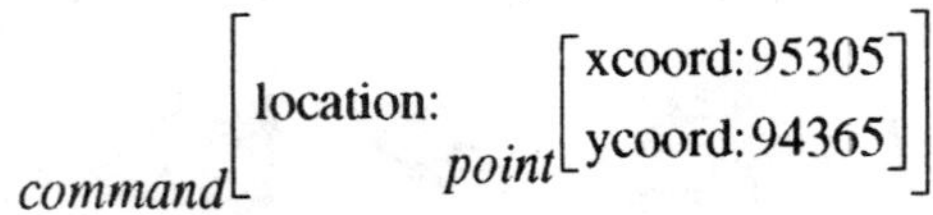

Figure 8: Point Interpretation of Gesture

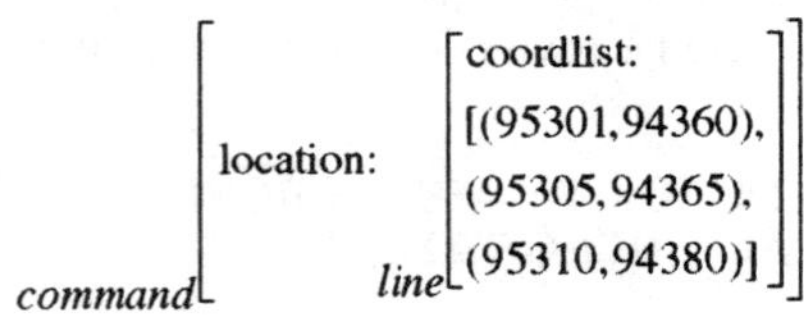

Figure 9: Line Interpretation of Gesture

The task of the integrator agent is to field incoming typed feature structures representing interpretations of speech and of gesture, identify the best potential interpretation, multimodal or unimodal, and issue a typed feature structure representing the preferred interpretation to the bridge agent, which will execute the command.

In the example case above, both speech and gesture have only partial interpretations, one for speech, and two for gesture. Since the speech interpretation (Figure 7) requires its location feature to be of type *line*, only unification with the line interpretation of the gesture will succeed and be passed on as a valid multimodal interpretation (Figure 10).

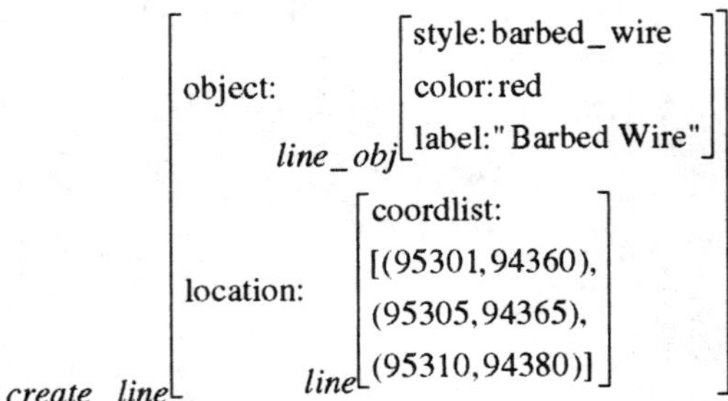

Figure 10: Feature Structure for Multimodal Line Creation

The ambiguity of interpretation of the gesture was resolved by integration with speech, which in this case required a location feature of type *line*. If the spoken command had instead been 'M1A1 Platoon', intending to create an entity at the indicated location, it would have selected the point interpretation of the gesture in Figure 8.

Similarly, if the spoken command described an area, for example an 'anti tank minefield', it would only unify with an interpretation of gesture as an area designation. In each case the unification-based integration strategy compensates for errors in gesture recognition through type constraints on the values of features.

Gesture also compensates for errors in speech recognition. In the open microphone mode, spurious speech recognition errors are more common than with click-to-speak, but are frequently rejected by the system because of the absence of a compatible gesture for integration. For example, if the system recognizes 'M1A1 platoon', but there is no overlapping or immediately preceding gesture to provide the location, the speech will be ignored. The architecture also supports selection among the n-best speech recognition results on the basis of the preferred gesture recognition. In the future, n-best recognition results will be available from the recognizer, and we will further examine the potential for gesture to help select among speech recognition alternatives.

COMPARISON WITH OTHER MULTIMODAL INTEGRATION EFFORTS

Systems capable of integration of speech and gesture have existed since the early 80's. One of the first such systems was the "Put-That-There" system [Bolt 1980]. However, in the sixteen years since then, research on multimodal integration has not yielded a reusable scalable architecture for the construction of multimodal systems that integrate gesture and voice. There are four major limiting factors in previous approaches to multimodal integration:

(i) The majority of approaches limit the bandwidth of the gestural mode to simple deictic pointing gestures made with a mouse [Brison and Vigouroux (ms.); Cohen 1992; Neal and Shapiro 1991; Wauchope 1994] or with the hand [Koons et al 1993].

(ii) Most previous approaches have been primarily language-driven, treating gesture as a secondary dependent mode [Neal and Shapiro 1991, Cohen 1992; Brison and Vigouroux (ms.), Koons et al 1993, Wauchope 1994]. In these systems, integration of gesture is triggered by the appearance of expressions in the speech stream whose reference needs to be resolved, such as definite and deictic noun phrases (e.g. 'this one', 'the red cube').

(iii) None of the existing approaches provide a well-understood generally applicable common meaning representation for the different modes.

(iv) None of the existing approaches provide a general and formally-well defined mechanism for multimodal integration.

Our approach to multimodal integration overcomes these limiting factors in that a wide range of continuous gestural input is supported, and integration may be driven by either mode. Typed feature structures are used to provide a clearly defined and well-understood common meaning representation for the modes, and multimodal integration is accomplished through unification. Vo and Wood [1996] present an approach to multimodal integration similar in spirit to that presented here in that it accepts a variety of gestures and is not solely speech-driven. However, we believe that unification of typed feature structures provides a more general, formally well-understood, and reusable mechanism for multimodal integration than the frame merging strategy that they describe. Cheyer and Julia [1995] sketch a system based on Oviatt's [1996] results and the Open Agent Architecture [Cohen et al., 1994], but describe neither the integration strategy nor multimodal compensation.

8. AGENT INFRASTRUCTURE

Major considerations in designing QuickSet have been: interoperation with legacy systems running in a heterogeneous computing environment, modularity, network transparency and distributed operation, scalability, and collaboration. A requirement of the infrastructure was that it be able to respond fast enough to provide near real-time performance from a multimodal user interface running on a small, handheld PC. The entire architecture had to run standalone on a 486/100Mhz PC, but be able to be reconfigured rapidly when more computing resources were available on a LAN.

The Open Agent Architecture satisfies most of these requirements. The architecture is based on FLiPSiDE [Schwartz, 1993], an enhanced distributed Prolog-based blackboard architecture. In the traditional blackboard model, individual knowledge sources (agents) communicate by posting and reading messages on a common blackboard. An agent will periodically poll the board to see if there are any posted goals (from other agents) it can solve; when an agent needs help, it can post a goal to be solved, then retrieve the answer when it appears on the board. The OAA model enhances this with a facilitator agent resident on the blackboard. This facilitator stores the blackboard data, identifies agents that can solve particular posted goals and routes requests to the appropriate agents.

All communication among the agents takes place through the facilitator agent. In addition to the standard blackboard operations of posting and reading, agents in an OAA can send queries to the facilitator agent and they can request the facilitator to set triggers on itself, or to route triggers to agents who can satisfy the trigger's conditions. These requests are expressions in an Interagent Communication Language (ICL) consisting of Horn clauses.

When an agent registers with the facilitator agent, it supplies a list of goals it can solve as an argument. The facilitator will add the agent to its list of available knowledge sources, recording the goals in the supplied parameter list. The current semantics of this registration are those of an assertion followed by a conditional offer. That is, not only is the registering agent asserting that it can solve the goals in the argument list, it is also offering to do so whenever requested by the facilitator.

Whenever a goal to be solved is posted to the blackboard, the facilitator routes the goal to those registered agents that have claimed to be able (and willing) to solve it. These solution-requests use synchronous communication — the agent posting the solve will block until a solution (or failure) is reported by the facilitator. The OAA also provides an asynchronous query facility —allowing the agent who posts the request to continue local computation while waiting for a response. Through the use of triggers, the agent can request that the facilitator notify it when an event has occurred, where an event can be any phenomenon in the distributed system describable in the ICL. In particular, the event in question could be the appearance of a solution to an asynchronous request posted earlier. Most of the QuickSet integration is based on asynchronous agent interaction, thereby allowing multiple agents to engage in interactions with centralized agents (e.g., the simulation agent) without blocking or waiting for others. This is particularly important for user interfaces, which must respond to speech and gesture input within a very short time window, even while the system's responses to prior inputs are being computed.

Although this architecture is derived from FliPSiDe, it omits Schwartz' considerable effort devoted to locking of the blackboard. (Similar considerations were vital in the early blackboard systems [Fennel and Lesser, 1977].) The architecture is similar to that of KQML/KIF [Finin et al., 1994; Genesereth and Ketchpel, 1994] in its use of a brokered architecture, an agent communications language and a logically-based propositional content language. We employ many fewer speech act types (and have argued that in fact, KQML should only have a small number of communication acts as well [Cohen and Levesque, 1995; Smith and Cohen, 1996]) and use a subset of first-order logic, where that effort uses KIF. The OAA has provided an effective framework for integrating legacy applications. By linking in an agent library written in the application's native language, the application can become a full-fledged agent, potentially capable of participating in multiagent systems. To date, the architecture has been sufficient for our initial experiments, but needs to be revised significantly for data and interaction intensive applications.

8. CONCLUDING REMARKS

Below we characterize how QuickSet has been applied and what we have learned from this research, development and technology transition experience.

Applications

QuickSet has been delivered to the US Navy and US Marine Corps. for use at Twentynine Palms, California, where it is primarily used to set up training scenarios and to control the virtual environment. The system was also used by the US Army's 82 Airborne Corps. at Ft. Bragg during the Royal Dragon Exercise. There, QuickSet was deployed in a tent, where it was subjected to noise from explosions, low-flying jet aircraft, generators, etc. Not surprisingly, it readily became apparent that spoken interaction with QuickSet would not be feasible. To support usage in such a harsh environment, a complete overlap in functionality between speech, gesture, and direct manipulation was desired. The system has been revised to accomodate these needs.

Finally, QuickSet is now being extended for use in the ExInit simulation initialization system for DARPA's STOW-97 (Synthetic Theater of War) Advanced Concept Demonstration. In this version, QuickSet runs either on a Pentium Pro or on the handheld unit, with the agent architecture interoperating with a collection of CORBA servers (written by MRJ Corp. and Ascent Technologies) that decompose high-level units into their constituents, and that perform terrain reasoning, and other "back-end" functions. The multimodal integration here is used to create and position the high level units, and to mark up boundaries, objectives, and obstacles on a map.

Lessons learned

Much was learned from the effort to date about the scalability of agent architectures and about multimodal user interfaces. Although a conceptually reasonable first step, the implementation of the OAA agent architecture lacked necessary features for supporting robust interaction and collaboration. First, it had no features for authentication, or for locking, as in FliPSiDe. Thus, one user's agents could interfere with another's. This was addressed through better identification of the user behind each agent. In an environment where there is one multimodal integration agent on the network, this approach prevents one user's speech from being combined with another user's gesture. Second, the implementations in Prolog and C were not multi-threaded. Thus, when multiple users were rapidly creating units, the simulator agent would lose data and only create the last of the units received. Finally both control and data were routed through the blackboard to the various agents. This works well when the amount of data is relatively small, but will not scale for multimedia applications. Rather, data and control paths should be separated. Research is ongoing at OGI to redesign an agent architecture that overcomes the above limitations.

Regarding the multimodal interface itself, QuickSet has undergone a "proactive" interface evaluation in that high-fidelity "wizard-of-Oz" studies were performed in advance of building the system that predicted the utility of multimodal over unimodal speech as an input to map-based systems [Oviatt, 1996; Oviatt et al., 1997]. For example, it was discovered there that multimodal interaction would lead to simpler language than unimodal speech. Such observations have been confirmed when examining how users would create linear features with CommandTalk [Moore, 1995], a unimodal spoken system that also controls LeatherNet. Whereas to create a "phase line" between two three-digit <x,y> grid coordinates, a user would have to say: "create a line from nine four three nine six one to nine five seven nine six eight and call it phase line green," a QuickSet user would say "phase line green" while drawing a line. Given that numerous difficult-to-process linguistic phenomena (such as utterance disfluencies) are known to be elevated in lengthy utterances and also to be elevated when people speak locative constituents [Oviatt, 1996; Oviatt in press], multimodal interaction that permits' pen input to specify locations offers the possibility of more robust recognition.

In summary, we have developed a handheld system that integrates numerous artificial intelligence technologies, including speech recognition, gesture recognition, natural language processing, multimodal integration, distributed agent technologies, and reasoning. The multimodal integration strategy allows speech and gesture to compensate for each other, yielding a more robust system. We are currently engaged in evaluation experiments to quantify the benefits of this approach. The system interoperates with existing military simulators and virtual reality environments through a distributed agent architecture. QuickSet has been deployed for the US Navy, US Marine Corps, and the US Army, and is being integrated into the DARPA STOW-97 ACTD. We are currently evaluating its performance, interacting with the end users of the system in the various services, and will begin to collect field usage data during future exercises.

ACKNOWLEDGMENTS

This work is supported in part by the Information Technology and Information Systems offices of DARPA under contract number DABT63-95-C-007, in part by ONR grant number N00014-95-1-1164, and has been done in collaboration with the US Navy's NCCOSC RDT&E Division (NRaD), Ascent Technologies, MRJ Corp. and SRI International.

REFERENCES

Bolt, R. A. 1980. "Put-That-There":Voice and gesture at the graphics interface. *Computer Graphics*. 14.3, pp. 262-270

Calder, J. 1987. Typed unification for natural language processing. In E. Klein and J. van Benthem (Eds.), Categories, Polymorphisms, and Unification. Centre for Cognitive Science, University of Edinburgh, Edinburgh, pp. 65-72.

Brison, E. and N. Vigouroux. (unpublished ms.). Multimodal references: A generic fusion process. URIT-URA CNRS. Universitб Paul Sabatier, Toulouse, France.

Cheyer, A., and L. Julia. 1995. Multimodal maps: An agent-based approach. *International Conference on Cooperative Multimodal Communication (CMC/95)*, May 1995. Eindhoven, The Netherlands. pp. 24-26.

Carpenter, R. 1990. Typed feature structures: Inheritance, (In)equality, and Extensionality. In W. Daelemans and G. Gazdar (Eds.), *Proceedings of the ITK Workshop: Inheritance in Natural Language Processing,* Tilburg University, pp. 9-18.

Carpenter, R. 1992. *The logic of typed feature structures.* Cambridge University Press, Cambridge.

Clarkson, J. D., and J. Yi. 1996. LeatherNet: A synthetic forces tactical training system for the USMC commander. *Proceedings of the Sixth Conference on Computer Generated Forces and Behavioral Representation.* Orlando, Florida, 275-281.

Cohen, P. R. The Role of Natural Language in a Multimodal Interface. *Proceedings of UIST'92,* ACM Press, NY, 1992, 143-149.

Cohen, P.R., Cheyer, A., Wang, M., and Baeg, S.C. An Open Agent Architecture. *Proceedings of the AAAI Spring Symposium Series on Software Agents* (March 21-22, Stanford), Stanford Univ., CA, 1994, 1-8.

Cohen, P. R. and Levesque, H. J. Communicative actions for artificial agents. In *Proceedings of the International Conference on Multiagent Systems,* AAAI Press, Menlo Park, California, 1995.

Courtt manche, A.J. and Ceranowicz, A. ModSAF Development Status. *Proceedings of the Fifth Conference on Computer Generated Forces and Behavioral Representation,* Univ. Central Florida, Orlando, 1995, 3-13.

Cruz-Neira, C. D.J. Sandin, T.A. DeFanti, "Surround-Screen Projection-Based Virtual Reality: The Design and Implementation of the CAVE," *Computer Graphics,* ACM SIGGRAPH, August 1993, pp. 135-142.

Fennell, R. D., and Lesser, V. R., Parallelism in artificial intelligence problem solving: A case study of HEARSAY-II, *IEEE Transactions on Computers C-26(2),* 1977, 98-111.

Finin, T. and Fritzson, R. and McKay, D. and McEntire, R. KQML as an agent communication language, *Proceedings of the Third International Conference on Information and Knowledge Management (CIKM'94),* ACM Press, New , November, 1994.

Genesereth, M. and Ketchpel, S., Software Agents, *Communications of the ACM, 37(7),* July, 1994, 100-105.

Koons, D.B., C.J. Sparrell and K.R. Thorisson. 1993. Integrating simultaneous input from speech, gaze, and hand gestures. In Mark T. Maybury (ed.) *Intelligent Multimedia Interfaces.* AAAI Press/ MIT Press, Cambridge, MA, pp. 257-276.

Moore, R. C., Dowding, J, Bratt, H., Gawron, M., and Cheyer, A. CommandTalk: A spoken-language interface for battlefield simulations, Proc. of the 3rd Applied Natural Language Conference, Wash. DC, 1997.

Neal, J.G. and Shapiro, S.C. Intelligent multi-media interface technology. In J.W. Sullivan and S.W. Tyler, editors, *Intelligent User Interfaces,* chapter 3, pages 45–68. ACM Press Frontier Series, Addison Wesley Publishing Co., New York, New York, 1991.

Oviatt, S. L., Pen/Voice: Complementary multimodal communication, Proceedings of SpeechTech'92, New York, February, 1992, 238-241.

Oviatt, S.L., Multimodal interfaces for dynamic interactive maps. *Proceedings of CHI'96 Human Factors in Computing Systems* ACM Press, NY, 1996, 95-102.

Oviatt, S.L. Multimodal interactive maps: Designing for human performance, *Human Computer Interaction,* in press.

Oviatt, S. L, A. DeAngeli, and K. Kuhn. Integration and synchronization of input modes during multimodal human-computer interaction. *Proceedings of the Conference on Human Factors in Computing Systems (CHI '97),* ACM Press, NY, 1997, 415-422.

Pittman, J. A. Recognizing handwritten text *Human Factors in Computing Systems (CHI'91),* 1991, 271-275.

Schwartz, D.G. Cooperating heterogeneous systems: A blackboard-based meta approach. Technical report 93-112, Center for Automation and Intelligent Systems Research, Case Western Reserve University, Cleveland, Ohio, April 1993. Ph.D. thesis.

Smith, I. A. and Cohen, P. R. Toward a Semantics for an Agent Communications Language Based on Speech-Acts *Proceedings of the Thirteenth National Conference in Artificial Intelligence* (AAAI 96), AAAI Press, 24-31.

Thorpe, J. A. The new technology of large scale simulator networking: Implications for mastering the art of warfighting 9th *Interservice Training Systems Conference,* 1987, 492-501.

Vo, M. T. and C. Wood. 1996. Building an application framework for speech and pen input integration in multimodal learning interfaces. *International Conference on Acoustics, Speech, and Signal Processing,* Atlanta, GA.

Wauchope, K. 1994. Eucalyptus: Integrating natural language input with a graphical user interface. Naval Research Laboratory, Report NRL/FR/5510--94-9711.

Zyda, M. J., Pratt, D. R., Monahan, J. G., and Wilson, K. P., NPSNET: Constructing a 3-D virtual world, Proceedings of the 1992 Symposium on Interactive 3-D Graphics, March, 1992.

Reflections on...

Multimodal Interaction for Distributed Interactive Simulation

Phil Cohen

The QuickSet system reported here represents the convergence of three strands of prior research—multimodal interaction with simulators, multimodal interaction via pen and voice, and multiagent architectures. Our research on multimodal interaction with simulators began with the Shoptalk system, developed between 1986 and 1989 (Cohen, Section I of this volume; Cohen 1992). That system demonstrated how natural language (via keyboard and speech) could be integrated with direct manipulation and graphical user interface technologies to produce an interface that allowed the strengths of each mode to compensate for the weaknesses of the other. With this system, users could state rules for operating manufacturing equipment, ask questions (including follow-ups), compare the results of multiple scenarios, and control the simulation time, using a combination of natural language and direct manipulation. One variant of Shoptalk that was developed was Miltalk, a multimodal map-based system for military simulation that allowed users to create and inquire about military simulations, using a combination of spoken language and pointing gestures.

The second strand of research woven into QuickSet is Oviatt's exploration of multimodal interfaces that incorporate both spoken language and pen-based gestures (Oviatt Section VIII of this volume; Oviatt 1997; Oviatt et al. 1997). Based on a high-fidelity interface simulation, it was shown that multimodal interaction with map-based systems results in simpler and easier-to-process language, faster and less error-prone task performance, and clear user preference over speech-only interaction. In addition, typical patterns of integration and synchronization of pen and speech were identified (Oviatt et al. 1997). As a result of these extensive user tests, the design of QuickSet was informed at the start about effective styles of multimodal interaction with maps.

The final strand is that of multiagent architectures. QuickSet is based on the Open Agent Architecture (OAA) (Cohen et al. 1994), a facilitated architecture that itself derives from prior work on distributed Prolog-based blackboard systems (Schwartz 1993) and is comparable to current facilitated architectures based on KQML (Finin et al. 1994). The design of QuickSet takes heavy advantage of the OAA's ability to interoperate different platforms (Unix and PC) such that various agents (such as a military simulator or 3-D virtual reality system) can be operating on a Unix platform, with the user interface agents operating primarily on PCs. As a result, QuickSet scales immediately from wearable to wall-sized PCs. Because of the OAA's use of a centralized facilitator, QuickSet immediately becomes a heterogeneous collaborative system with a replicated architecture. However, not being multithreaded, the OAA cannot properly handle concurrent access by multiple users. This and other problems with OAA are currently being addressed in our new prototype, the Adaptive Agent Architecture.

REFERENCES

Cohen, P. R. 1992. The Role of Natural Language in a Multimodal Interface. In *Proceedings of the 5th Annual ACM User Interface Software Technology (UIST'92) Conference*. Monterey, CA: Academic Press. 143–149.

Cohen, P. R.; Cheyer, A.; Wang, M. Q.; and Baeg, S. C. 1994. An Open Agent Architecture. In *Working Notes of the AAAI 1994 Spring Symposium on Software Agents*, March, Stanford University.

Finin, T.; Fritzson, R.; McKay, D.; and McEntire, R. 1994. KQML as an Agent Communication Language. In *Proceedings of the Third International Conference on Information and Knowledge Management (CIKM'94)*, November. New York: ACM Press.

Oviatt, S. L. 1997. Multimodal Interactive Maps: Designing for Human Performance. *Human-Computer Interaction, Special Issue on Multimodal Interfaces*. 12(1–2): 93–130.

Oviatt, S. L.; DeAngeli, A.; and Kuhn, K. 1997. Integration and Synchronization of Input Modes during Multimodal Human-Computer Interaction. In *Proceedings of Conference on Human Factors in Computing Systems: CHI '97*, 415–422. New York: ACM Press.

Schwartz, D. G. 1993. Cooperating Heterogeneous Systems: A Blackboard-Based Meta Approach. Ph.D. thesis, Center for Automation and Intelligent Systems Research, Case Western Reserve University, Cleveland, OH, Technical Report 93-112, April.

SPEECH DIALOGUE WITH FACIAL DISPLAYS: MULTIMODAL HUMAN-COMPUTER CONVERSATION

Katashi Nagao and **Akikazu Takeuchi**
Sony Computer Science Laboratory Inc.
3–14–13 Higashi-gotanda, Shinagawa-ku, Tokyo 141, Japan
E-mail: {nagao,takeuchi}@csl.sony.co.jp

Abstract

Human face-to-face conversation is an ideal model for human-computer dialogue. One of the major features of face-to-face communication is its multiplicity of communication channels that act on multiple modalities. To realize a natural multimodal dialogue, it is necessary to study how humans perceive information and determine the information to which humans are sensitive. A face is an independent communication channel that conveys emotional and conversational signals, encoded as facial expressions. We have developed an experimental system that integrates speech dialogue and facial animation, to investigate the effect of introducing communicative facial expressions as a new modality in human-computer conversation. Our experiments have showen that facial expressions are helpful, especially upon first contact with the system. We have also discovered that featuring facial expressions at an early stage improves subsequent interaction.

Introduction

Human face-to-face conversation is an ideal model for human-computer dialogue. One of the major features of face-to-face communication is its multiplicity of communication channels that act on multiple modalities. A channel is a communication medium associated with a particular encoding method. Examples are the auditory channel (carrying speech) and the visual channel (carrying facial expressions). A modality is the sense used to perceive signals from the outside world.

Many researchers have been developing multimodal dialogue systems. In some cases, researchers have shown that information in one channel complements or modifies information in another. As a simple example, the phrase "delete it" involves the coordination of voice with gesture. Neither makes sense without the other. Researchers have also noticed that nonverbal (gesture or gaze) information plays a role in setting the situational context which is useful in restricting the hypothesis space constructed during language processing. Anthropomorphic interfaces present another approach to multimodal dialogues. An anthropomorphic interface, such as Guides [Don *et al.*, 1991], provides a means to realize a new style of interaction. Such research attempts to computationally capture the communicative power of the human face and apply it to human-computer dialogue.

Our research is closely related to the last approach. The aim of this research is to improve human-computer dialogue by introducing human-like behavior into a speech dialogue system. Such behavior will include factors such as facial expressions and head and eye movement. It will help to reduce any stress experienced by users of computing systems, lowering the complexity associated with understanding system status.

Like most dialogue systems developed by natural language researchers, our current system can handle domain-dependent, information-seeking dialogues. Of course, the system encounters problems with ambiguity and missing information (i.e., anaphora and ellipsis). The system tries to resolve them using techniques from natural language understanding (e.g., constraint-based, case-based, and plan-based methods). We are also studying the use of synergic multimodality to resolve linguistic problems, as in conventional multimodal systems. This work will be reported in a separate publication.

In this paper, we concentrate on the role of nonverbal modality for increasing flexibility of human-computer dialogue and reducing the mental barriers that many users associate with computer systems.

Research Overview of Multimodal Dialogues

Multimodal dialogues that combine verbal and nonverbal communication have been pursued mainly from the following three viewpoints.

1. *Combining direct manipulation with natural language (deictic) expressions*

   "Direct manipulation (DM)" was suggested by Shneiderman [1983]. The user can interact directly with graphical objects displayed on the computer screen with rapid, incremental, reversible operations whose effects on the objects of interest are immediately visible.

   The semantics of natural language (NL) expressions is anchored to real-world objects and events by means of pointing and demonstrating actions and deictic expressions such as "this," "that," "here," "there," "then," and "now." Some research on dialogue systems has combined deictic gestures and natural language such as Put-That-There [Bolt, 1980], CUBRICON [Neal *et al.*, 1988], and ALFRESCO [Stock, 1991].

   One of the advantages of combined NL/DM interaction is that it can easily resolve the missing information in NL expressions. For example, when the system receives a user request in speech like "delete that object," it can fill in the missing information by looking for a pointing gesture from the user or objects on the screen at the time the request is made.

2. *Using nonverbal inputs to specify the context and filter out unrelated information*

   The focus of attention or the focal point plays a very important role in processing applications with a broad hypothesis space such as speech recognition. One example of focusing modality is following the user's looking behavior. Fixation or gaze is useful for the dialogue system to determine the context of the user's interest. For example, when a user is looking at a car, that the user says at that time may be related to the car. Prosodic information (e.g., voice tones) in the user's utterance also helps to determine focus. In this case, the system uses prosodic information to infer the user's beliefs or intentions. Combining gestural information with spoken language comprehension shows another example of how context may be determined by the user's nonverbal behavior [Oviatt *et al.*, 1993]. This research uses multimodal forms that prompt a user to speak or write into labeled fields. The forms are capable of guiding and segmenting inputs, of conveying the kind of information the system is expecting, and of reducing ambiguities in utterances by restricting syntactic and semantic complexities.

3. *Incorporating human-like behavior into dialogue systems to reduce operation complexity and stress often associated with computer systems*

   Designing human-computer dialogue requires that the computer makes appropriate backchannel feedbacks like nodding or expressions such as "aha" and "I see." One of the major advantages of using such nonverbal behavior in human-computer conversation is that reactions are quicker than those from voice-based responses. For example, the facial backchannel plays an important role in human face-to-face conversation. We consider such quick reactions as being situated actions [Suchman, 1987] which are necessary for resource-bounded dialogue participants. Timely responses are crucial to successful conversation, since some delay in reactions can imply specific meanings or make messages unnecessarily ambiguous.

   Generally, visual channels contribute to quick user recognition of system status. For example, the system's gaze behavior (head and eye movement) gives a strong impression of whether it is paying attention or not. If the system's eyes wander around aimlessly, the user easily recognizes the system's attention elsewhere, perhaps even unaware that he or she is speaking to it. Thus, gaze is an important indicator of system (in this case, speech recognition) status.

   By using human-like nonverbal behavior, the system can more flexibly respond to the user than is possible by using verbal modality alone.

We focused on the third viewpoint and developed a system that acts like a human. We employed communicative facial expressions as a new modality in human-computer conversation. We have already discussed this, however, in another paper [Takeuchi and Nagao, 1993]. Here, we consider our implemented system as a testbed for incorporating human-like (nonverbal) behavior into dialogue systems.

The following sections give a system overview, an example dialogue along with a brief explanation of the process, and our experimental results.

Incorporating Facial Displays into a Speech Dialogue System

Facial Displays as a New Modality

The study of facial expressions has attracted the interest of a number of different disciplines, including psychology, ethology, and interpersonal communications. Currently, there are two basic schools of thought. One regards facial expressions as being expressions of emotion [Ekman and Friesen, 1984]. The other views facial expressions in a social context, regarding them as being communicative signals [Chovil, 1991]. The term "facial displays" is essentially the same as "facial expressions," but is less reminiscent of emotion. In this paper, therefore, we use "facial displays."

A face is an independent communication channel that conveys emotional and conversational signals, encoded as facial displays. Facial displays can be also regarded as being a modality because the human brain has a special circuit dedicated to their processing.

Table 1 lists all the communicative facial displays used in the experiments described in a later section. The categorization framework, terminology, and individual displays are based on the work of Chovil [1991], with the exception of the emphasizer, underliner, and facial shrug. These were coined by Ekman [1969].

Table 1: Communicative Facial Displays Used in the Experiments. (Categorization based mostly on Chovil [1991])

Syntactic Display	
1. Exclamation mark	Eyebrow raising
2. Question mark	Eyebrow raising or lowering
3. Emphasizer	Eyebrow raising or lowering
4. Underliner	Longer eyebrow raising
5. Punctuation	Eyebrow movement
6. End of an utterance	Eyebrow raising
7. Beginning of a story	Eyebrow raising
8. Story continuation	Avoid eye contact
9. End of a story	Eye contact
Speaker Display	
10. Thinking/Remembering	Eyebrow raising or lowering, closing the eyes, pulling back one mouth side
11. Facial shrug: "I don't know"	Eyebrow flashes, mouth corners pulled down, mouth corners pulled back
12. Interactive: "You know?"	Eyebrow raising
13. Metacommunicative: Indication of sarcasm or joke	Eyebrow raising and looking up and off
14. "Yes"	Eyebrow actions
15. "No"	Eyebrow actions
15. "Not"	Eyebrow actions
17. "But"	Eyebrow actions
Listener Comment Display	
18. Backchannel: Indication of attendance	Eyebrow raising, mouth corners turned down
19. Indication of loudness	Eyebrows drawn to center
Understanding levels	
20. Confident	Eyebrow raising, head nod
21. Moderately confident	Eyebrow raising
22. Not confident	Eyebrow lowering
23. "Yes"	Eyebrow raising
Evaluation of utterances	
24. Agreement	Eyebrow raising
25. Request for more information	Eyebrow raising
26. Incredulity	Longer eyebrow raising

Three major categories are defined as follows.

Syntactic displays. These are facial displays that (1) place stress on particular words or clauses, (2) are connected with the syntactic aspects of an utterance, or (3) are connected with the organization of the talk.

Speaker displays. Speaker displays are facial displays that (1) illustrate the idea being verbally conveyed, or (2) add additional information to the ongoing verbal content.

Listener comment displays. These are facial displays made by the person who is not speaking, in response to the utterances of the speaker.

An Integrated System of Speech Dialogue and Facial Animation

We have developed an experimental system that integrates speech dialogue and facial animation to investigate the effects of human-like behavior in human-computer dialogue.

The system consists of two subsystems, a facial animation subsystem that generates a three-dimensional face capable of a range of facial displays, and a speech dialogue subsystem that recognizes and interprets speech, and generates voice outputs. Currently, the animation subsystem runs on an SGI 320VGX and the speech dialogue subsystem on a Sony NEWS workstation. These two subsystems communicate with each other via an Ethernet network.

Figure 1 shows the configuration of the integrated system. Figure 2 illustrates the interaction of a user with the system.

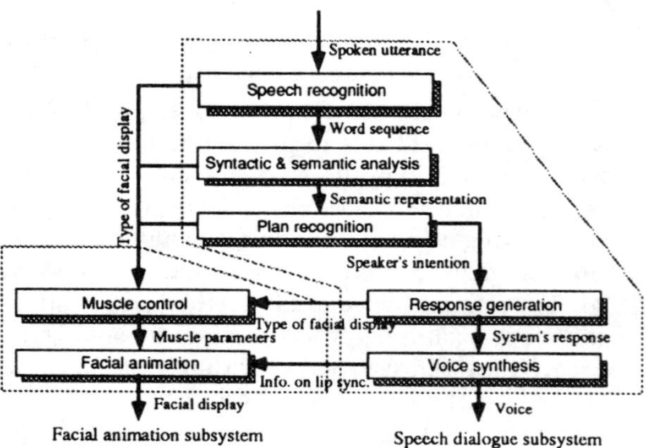

Figure 1: System Configuration

Facial Animation Subsystem

The face is modeled three-dimensionally. Our current version is composed of approximately 500 polygons. The face can be rendered with a skin-like surface material, by applying a texture map taken from a photograph or a video frame.

In 3D computer graphics, a facial display is realized by local deformation of the polygons representing the face. Waters showed that deformation that simulates the action of muscles underlying the face looks more natural [Waters, 1987]. We therefore use numerical equations to simulate muscle actions, as defined by Waters. Currently,

Figure 2: Dialogue Snapshot

the system incorporates 16 muscles and 10 parameters, controlling mouth opening, jaw rotation, eye movement, eyelid opening, and head orientation. These 16 muscles were determined by Waters, considering the correspondence with action units in the Facial Action Coding System (FACS) [Ekman and Friesen, 1978]. For details of the facial modeling and animation system, see [Takeuchi and Franks, 1992].

We use 26 synthesized facial displays, corresponding to those listed in Table 1, and two additional displays. All facial displays are generated by the above method, and rendered with a texture map of a young boy's face. The added displays are "Smile" and "Neutral." The "Neutral" display features no muscle contraction whatsoever, and is used when no conversational signal is needed.

At run-time, the animation subsystem awaits a request from the speech subsystem. When the animation subsystem receives a request that specifies values for the 26 parameters, it starts to deform the face, on the basis of the received values. The deformation process is controlled by the differential equation $f' = a - f$, where f is a parameter value at time t and f' is its time derivative at time t. a is the target value specified in the request. A feature of this equation is that deformation is fast in the early phase but soon slows, corresponding closely to the real dynamics of facial displays. Currently, the base performance of the animation subsystem is around 20–25 frames per second when running on an SGI Power Series. This is sufficient to enable real-time animation.

Speech Dialogue Subsystem

Our speech dialogue subsystem works as follows. First, a voice input is acoustically analyzed by a built-in sound processing board. Then, a speech recognition module is invoked to output word sequences that have been assigned higher scores by a probabilistic phoneme model. These word sequences are syntactically and semantically analyzed and disambiguated by applying a relatively loose grammar and a restricted domain knowledge. Using a semantic representation of the input utterance, a plan recognition module extracts the speaker's intention. For example, from the utterance "I am interested in Sony's workstation." the module interprets the speaker's intention as "he wants to get precise information about Sony's workstation." Once the system determines the speaker's intention, a response generation module is invoked. This generates a response to satisfy the speaker's request. Finally, the system's response is output as voice by a voice synthesis module. This module also sends the information about lip synchronization that describes phonemes (including silence) in the response and their time durations to the facial animation subsystem.

With the exception of the voice synthesis module, each module can send messages to the facial animation subsystem to request the generation of a facial display. The relation between the speech dialogues and facial displays is discussed later.

In this case, the specific task of the system is to provide information about Sony's computer-related products. For example, the system can answer questions about price, size, weight, and specifications of Sony's workstations and PCs.

Below, we describe the modules of the speech dialogue subsystem.

Speech recognition. This module was jointly developed with the Electrotechnical Laboratory and Tokyo Institute of Technology. Speaker-independent continuous speech inputs are accepted without special hardware. To obtain a high level of accuracy, context-dependent phonetic hidden Markov models are used to construct phoneme-level hypotheses [Itou *et al.*, 1992]. This module can generate N-best word-level hypotheses.

Syntactic and semantic analysis. This module consists of a parsing mechanism, a semantic analyzer, a relatively loose grammar consisting of 24 rules, a lexicon that includes 34 nouns, 8 verbs, 4 adjectives and 22 particles, and a frame-based knowledge base consisting of 61 conceptual frames. Our semantic analyzer can handle ambiguities in syntactic structures and generates a semantic representation of the speaker's utterance. We applied a preferential constraint satisfaction technique [Nagao, 1992] for performing disambiguation and semantic analysis. By allowing the preferences to control the application of the constraints, ambiguities can be efficiently resolved, thus avoiding combinatorial explosions.

Plan recognition. This module determines the speaker's intention by constructing a model of his/her beliefs, dynamically adjusting and expanding the model as the dialogue progresses [Nagao, 1993]. The model deals with the dynamic nature of dialogues by applying the following two mechanisms. First, preferences among the contexts are dynamically computed based on the facts and assumptions within each context. The preference provides a measure of the plausibility of a context. The currently most preferable context contains a currently recognized plan. Secondly, changing the most plausible context among mutually exclusive contexts within a dialogue is formally treated as belief revision of a plan-recognizing agent. However, in some dialogues, many alternatives may have very similar preference values. In this situation, one may wish to obtain additional information, allowing one to be more certain about committing to the preferable context. A criterion for detecting such a critical situation based on the preference measures for mutually exclusive contexts is being explored. The module also maintains the topic of the current dialogue and can handle anaphora (reference of pronouns) and ellipsis (omission of subjects).

Response generation. This module generates a response by using domain knowledge (database) and text templates (typical patterns of utterances). It selects appropriate templates and combines them to construct a response that satisfies the speaker's request.

In our prototype system, the method used to comprehend speech is a specific combination of specific types of knowledge sources with a rather fixed information flow, preventing flexible interaction between them. A new method that enables flexible control of omni-directional information flow in a very context-sensitive fashion has been announced [Nagao *et al.*, 1993]. Its architecture is based on *dynamical constraint* [Hasida *et al.*, 1993] which defines a fine classification based on the dimensions of satisfaction and the violation of constraints. A constraint is represented in terms of a clausal logic program. A fine-grained declarative semantics is defined for this constraint by measuring the degree of violation in terms of real-valued *potential energy.* A field of force arises along the gradient of this energy, inferences being controlled on the basis of the dynamics. This allows us to design combinatorial behaviors under declarative semantics within tractable computational complexity. Our forthcoming system can, therefore, concentrate on its computational resources according to a dynamic focal point that is important to speech processing with broad hypothesis space, and apply every kind of constraint, from phonetic to pragmatic, at the same time.

Correspondence between Conversational Situations and Facial Displays

The speech dialogue subsystem recognizes a number of typical conversational situations that are important to dialogues. We associate these situations with an appropriate facial display(s). For example, in situations where speech input is not recognized or where it is syntactically invalid, the listener comment display "Not confident" is displayed. If the speaker's request exceeds the range of the system's domain knowledge, then the system displays a facial shrug and replies "I cannot answer such a question." The relationships between conversational situations and facial displays are listed in Table 2.

Example Dialogue

Here is an example of a possible dialogue with the system[1]. **Un:** indicates user speech inputs, **Sn:** indicates voice responses delivered by the system to the user. Terms enclosed within square brackets illustrate the types of facial displays introduced in previous section. "Continuing" means that the system facial expression remains the same.

U1: Hello.

S1: [Attend and BOStory] Hi. This is Sony Computer Science Laboratory.

S2: [Continuing] I can answer any question about computer-related products.

U2: uh ...

S3: [NotConfident] I beg your pardon.

U3: I want to know about a personal computer.

S4: [Question] Do you want to know about a Sony personal computer?

U4: No, I don't.

S5: [Shrug] I cannot answer such a question.

U5: Please tell me about a Sony personal computer.

S6: [BOStory] Sony personal computer "QuarterL" is a standard IBM compatible notebook-style personal computer.

U6: What can I do with it?

S7: [BOStory] You can use all IBM PC software.

S8: [Continuing] For example, you can use a word processor, and a spreadsheet.

U7: Can I use UNIX with it?

S9: [BOStory] If you want to use UNIX,

---

[1] Actually, the system accepts and speaks only Japanese. The example is a translation.

Table 2: Relation between Conversational Situations and Facial Displays

CONVERSATIONAL SITUATION	FACIAL DISPLAY(S)
Recognition failure	NotConfident (Listener comment display "Not confident")
Syntactically invalid utterance	NotConfident
Many recognition candidates with close scores	ModConfident (Listener comment display "Moderately confident")
Beginning of a dialogue	Attend (Listener comment display "Indication of attendance")
Introduction to a topic	BOStory (Syntactic display "Beginning of a story")
Shift to another topic	EOStory (Syntactic display "End of a story") and BOStory
Clarification dialogue	Question (Syntactic display "Question mark")
Underline a remark	Underliner (Syntactic display "Underliner")
Answer "Yes"	SpeakerYes (Speaker display "Yes")
Answer "No"	SpeakerNo (Speaker display "No")
Out of the domain	Shrug (Speaker display "Facial shrug")
Answer "Yes" with emphasis	SpeakerYes and Emphasizer (Syntactic display "Emphasizer")
Violation of pragmatic constraints	Incredulity (Listener comment display "Incredulity")
Reply to "Thanks"	ListenerYes (Listener comment display "Yes") and Smile (Complementary display "Smile")
......	....

S10: [Underliner] I recommend you get a workstation.

U8: Tell me about a workstation.

S11: [EOStory and BOStory] Sony workstation "NEWS" is a high-performance laptop workstation.

S12: [Continuing] Its CPU is an R3081 RISC processor, and its processing speed of 37 MIPS is the fastest in this class.

U9: Is it large?

S10: [SpeakerNo and Emphasizer] No, it isn't.

S11: [BOStory] "NEWS" is 32.4 cm in width, 36.4 cm in depth, and 6.9 cm in height.

U10: Is it light?

S12: [SpeakerYes and Emphasizer] Yes, it is.

S13: [BOStory] The weight of "NEWS" is 4.5 kg.

U11: How much?

S14: [BOStory] "NEWS" costs 700,000 yen.

U12: What does the personal computer cost?

S15: [EOStory and BOStory] "QuarterL" costs 398,000 yen.

U13: Thank you.

S16: [ListenerYes and Smile] You are welcome.

S17: [Continuing] It's my pleasure.

U2 is an example of noisy inputs. The system could not recognize the expression and displayed the facial backchannel NotConfident and replied "I beg your pardon." In **U3**, there is missing information about personal computer maker. So, the system enters a clarification dialogue **S4**, showing the Question display. In this case, the system tried to drive the user into the domain with which the system is familiar. However, the user refused to agree with the system by utterance **U4**, then the system revealed its discouragement by showing a facial shrug. In **U8**, the user changes the topic, by asking for workstation information. The system recognizes this by comparison with the prior topic (i.e., personal computers). Therefore, in response to question **S11**, the system displays EOStory and subsequently BOStory to indicate the shift to a different topic. The system also manages the topic structure so that it can handle anaphora and ellipsis in utterances such as **U9**, **U10**, and **U11**.

Experimental Results

To examine the effect of facial displays on the interaction between humans and computers, experiments were performed using the prototype system. The system was tested on 32 volunteer subjects. Two experiments were prepared. In one experiment, called **F**, the subjects held a conversation with the system, which used facial displays to reinforce its response. In the other experiment, called **N**, the subjects held a conversation with the system, which answered using short phrases instead of facial displays. The short phrases were two- or three-word sentences that described the corresponding facial displays. For example, instead of the "Not confident" display, it simply displayed the words "I am not confident." The subjects were divided into two groups, **FN** and **NF**. As the names indicate, the subjects in the **FN** group were first subjected to experiment **F** and then **N**. The subjects in the **NF** group were first subjected to **N** and then **F**. In both experiments, the subjects were assigned the goal of enquiring about the functions and prices of Sony's computer products. In each experiment, the subjects were requested to complete the conversation within 10 minutes. During the experiments, the number of occurrences of each facial display was counted. The conversation content was also evaluated based on how many topics a subject covered intentionally. The degree of task achievement reflects how it is preferable to obtain a greater number of visit more topics, and take the least amount of time possible. According to the frequencies of appeared facial displays and the conversational scores, the conversations that occurred during the experiments can be classified into two types. The first is "smooth conversation" in which the score is relatively high and the displays "Moderately confident," "Beginning of a story," and "Indication of attendance" appear most often. The second is "dull conversation," characterized by a lower score and in which the displays "Neutral" and "Not confident" appear more frequently.

The results are summarized as follows. The details of the experiments were presented in another paper [Takeuchi and Nagao, 1993].

1. The first experiments of the two groups are compared. Conversation using facial displays is clearly more successful (classified as smooth conversation) than that using short phrases. We can therefore conclude that facial displays help conversation in the case of initial contact.

2. The overall results for both groups are compared. Considering that the only difference between the two groups is the order in which the experiments were conducted, we can conclude that early interaction with facial displays contributes to success in the later interaction.

3. The experiments using facial displays **F** and those using short phrases **N** are compared. Contrary to our expectations, the result indicates that facial displays have little influence on successful conversation. This means that the learning effect, occurring over the duration of the experiments, is equal in effect to the facial displays. However, we believe that the effect of the facial displays will overtake the learning effect once the qualities of speech recognition and facial animation have been improved.

The premature settings of the prototype system, and the strict restrictions imposed on the conversation inevitably detract from the potential advantages available from systems using communicative facial displays. We believe that further elaboration of the system will greatly improve the results. The subjects were relatively well-experienced in using computers. Experiments with computer novices should also be done.

Concluding Remarks and Further Work

Our experiments showed that facial displays are helpful, especially upon first contact with the system. It was also shown that early interaction with facial displays improves subsequent interaction, even though the subsequent interaction does not use facial displays. These results prove quantitatively that interfaces with facial displays help to break down the mental barrier that many users have toward computing systems.

As a future research direction, we plan to integrate more communication channels and modalities. Among these, the prosodic information processing in speech recognition and speech synthesis are of special interest, as well as the recognition of users' gestures and facial displays. Also, further work needs to be done on the design and implementation of the coordination of multiple communication modalities. We believe that such coordination is an emergent phenomenon from the tight interaction between the system and its ever-changing environments (including humans and other interactive systems) by means of situated actions and (more deliberate) cooperative actions. Precise control of multiple coordinated activities is not, therefore, directly implementable. Only constraints or relationships among perception, conversational situations, and action will be implementable.

To date, conversation with computing systems has been over-regulated conversation. This has been made necessary by communication being done through limited channels, making it necessary to avoid information collision in the narrow channels. Multiple channels reduce the necessity for conversational regulation, allowing new styles of conversation to appear. A new style of conversation has smaller granularity, is highly interruptible, and invokes more spontaneous utterances. Such conversation is closer to our daily conversation with families and friends, and this will further increase familiarity with computers.

Co-constructive conversation, that is less constrained by domains or tasks, is one of our future goals. We are extending our conversational model to deal with a new style of human-computer interaction called *social interaction* [Nagao and Takeuchi, 1994] which includes co-constructive conversation. This style of conversation features a group of individuals where, say, those individuals talk about the food they ate together in a restraurant a month ago. There are no special roles (like the chairperson) for the participants to play. They all have the same role. The conversation terminates only once all the participants are satisfied with the conclusion.

We are also interested in developing interactive characters and stories as an application for interactive entertainment. We are now building a conversational, anthropomorphic computer character that we hope will entertain us with some pleasant stories.

ACKNOWLEDGMENTS

The authors would like to thank Mario Tokoro and colleagues at Sony CSL for their encouragement and helpful advice. We also extend our thanks to Nicole Chovil for her useful comments on a draft of this paper, and Satoru Hayamizu, Katunobu Itou, and Steve Franks for their contributions to the implementation of the prototype system. Special thanks go to Keith Waters for granting permission to access his original animation system.

REFERENCES

[Bolt, 1980] Richard A. Bolt. 1980. Put-That-There: Voice and gesture at the graphics interface. *Computer Graphics*, 14(3):262–270.

[Chovil, 1991] Nicole Chovil. 1991. Discourse-oriented facial displays in conversation. *Research on Language and Social Interaction*, 25:163–194.

[Don *et al.*, 1991] Abbe Don, Tim Oren, and Brenda Laurel. 1991. Guides 3.0. In *Proceedings of ACM CHI'91: Conference on Human Factors in Computing Systems*, pages 447–448. ACM Press.

[Ekman and Friesen, 1969] Paul Ekman and Wallace V. Friesen. 1969. The repertoire of nonverbal behavior: Categories, origins, usages, and coding. *Semiotica*, 1:49–98.

[Ekman and Friesen, 1978] Paul Ekman and Wallace V. Friesen. 1978. *Facial Action Coding System*. Consulting Psychologists Press, Palo Alto, California.

[Ekman and Friesen, 1984] Paul Ekman and Wallace V. Friesen. 1984. *Unmasking the Face*. Consulting Psychologists Press, Palo Alto, California.

[Hasida *et al.*, 1993] Kôiti Hasida, Katashi Nagao, and Takashi Miyata. 1993. Joint utterance: Intrasentential speaker/hearer switch as an emergent phenomenon. In *Proceedings of the Thirteenth International Joint Conference on Artificial Intelligence (IJCAI-93)*, pages 1193–1199. Morgan Kaufmann Publishers, Inc.

[Itou *et al.*, 1992] Katunobu Itou, Satoru Hayamizu, and Hozumi Tanaka. 1992. Continuous speech recognition by context-dependent phonetic HMM and an efficient algorithm for finding N-best sentence hypotheses. In *Proceedings of the International Conference on Acoustics, Speech, and Signal Processing (ICASSP-92)*, pages I.21–I.24. IEEE.

[Nagao and Takeuchi, 1994] Katashi Nagao and Akikazu Takeuchi. 1994. Social interaction: Multimodal conversation with social agents. In *Proceedings of the Twelfth National Conference on Artificial Intelligence (AAAI-94)*. The MIT Press.

[Nagao *et al.*, 1993] Katashi Nagao, Kôiti Hasida, and Takashi Miyata. 1993. Understanding spoken natural language with omni-directional information flow. In *Proceedings of the Thirteenth International Joint Conference on Artificial Intelligence (IJCAI-93)*, pages 1268–1274. Morgan Kaufmann Publishers, Inc.

[Nagao, 1992] Katashi Nagao. 1992. A preferential constraint satisfaction technique for natural language analysis. In *Proceedings of the Tenth European Conference on Artificial Intelligence (ECAI-92)*, pages 523–527. John Wiley & Sons.

[Nagao, 1993] Katashi Nagao. 1993. Abduction and dynamic preference in plan-based dialogue understanding. In *Proceedings of the Thirteenth International Joint Conference on Artificial Intelligence (IJCAI-93)*, pages 1186–1192. Morgan Kaufmann Publishers, Inc.

[Neal *et al.*, 1988] Jeannette G. Neal, Zuzana Dobes, Keith E. Bettinger, and Jong S. Byoun. 1988. Multimodal references in human-computer dialogue. In *Proceedings of the Seventh National Conference on Artificial Intelligence (AAAI-88)*, pages 819–823. Morgan Kaufmann Publishers, Inc.

[Oviatt *et al.*, 1993] Sharon L. Oviatt, Philip R. Cohen, and Michelle Wang. 1993. Reducing linguistic variability in speech and handwriting through selection of presentation format. In *Proceedings of the International Symposium on Spoken Dialogue (ISSD-93)*, pages 227–230. Waseda University, Tokyo, Japan.

[Shneiderman, 1983] Ben Shneiderman. 1983. Direct manipulation: A step beyond programming languages. *IEEE Computer*, 16:57–69.

[Stock, 1991] Oliviero Stock. 1991. Natural language and exploration of an information space: the ALFRESCO interactive system. In *Proceedings of the Twelfth International Joint Conference on Artificial Intelligence (IJCAI-91)*, pages 972–978. Morgan Kaufmann Publishers, Inc.

[Suchman, 1987] Lucy Suchman. 1987. *Plans and Situated Actions*. Cambridge University Press.

[Takeuchi and Franks, 1992] Akikazu Takeuchi and Steve Franks. 1992. A rapid face construction lab. Technical Report SCSL-TR-92-010, Sony Computer Science Laboratory Inc., Tokyo, Japan.

[Takeuchi and Nagao, 1993] Akikazu Takeuchi and Katashi Nagao. 1993. Communicative facial displays as a new conversational modality. In *Proceedings of ACM/IFIP INTERCHI'93: Conference on Human Factors in Computing Systems*, pages 187–193. ACM Press.

[Waters, 1987] Keith Waters. 1987. A muscle model for animating three-dimensional facial expression. *Computer Graphics*, 21(4):17–24.

Speech Dialogue with Facial Displays: Multimodal Human-Computer Conversation

Katashi Nagao

In this short article, I present an overview of some work conducted since the paper. One item is called a social agent that has a face capable of various facial expressions and head gestures. This agent can participate in human-to-human conversations. Another is an evaluation of situated facial displays and eye contacts in game sessions in which two humans and a computer participate. Finally, I introduce an ongoing project related to the paper. The objectives of this project include the development of an interactive environment in which multiple social agents and humans are involved. An example application is the use of agents as corporate representatives. Each agent has its own expertise. Collaboration of multiple agents and multimodal interaction among agents and humans results in a flexible and natural conversational interface.

Extension: Social Agents

Many artificial intelligence and human-computer interaction researchers seek to create intelligent autonomous creatures that act like partners rather than tools. With such partners, we could depend on their assistance to achieve certain tasks, delegating to them the responsibility for working out the details, rather than invoking a series of commands that cause the system to carry out well-defined and predictable operations. Animated agents are one of the possible approaches to the creation of such computer systems. The agent has a face, body, mouth, eyes, and ears, perceives multimodal messages, and take actions based on them.

We presented an autonomous agent that participates in human conversation, called a *social agent* (Nagao and Takeuchi 1994). Its main characteristics are summarized by the following three points. First, a social agent has the important properties of socialness and autonomy. Autonomy allows agents to decide how to act in an ever-changing environment, whereas socialness allows them to behave both cooperatively and collaboratively. A social agent tries to contribute to human society by smoothing over communication obstacles. Second, human conversants often encounter miscommunication (misunderstanding others' intentions and beliefs) and fail to achieve their joint goals. Our social agent, therefore, is always concerned with detecting miscommunication. It is designed to overhear human-to-human conversations and explain the cause of misunderstandings. Third, a social agent interacts with humans through multimodal (verbal and nonverbal) communication channels, using speech, facial expressions, and head and eye movements. Using such humanlike behavior, a social agent can exist naturally in human social environments and participate in conversations.

Evaluation: Situated Facial Displays

Takeuchi and Naito (1995) reported another work related to the paper. They performed experiments using facial animation in a card game context and evaluated the role of facial characteristics and eye contact between two users and a computer. In the game sessions, a "computer with a face" works as an ally for one user and as an opponent against the other. The computer observes games between users and tries to offer advice to its partner using facial actions.

The effect of facial displays was evaluated through two types of experiments. One used facial animation whereas the other used an arrow marker to indicate card position. Users reacted differently according to the setting. The authors commented that facial displays have a specific role in conveying situation-dependent nuances.

Future Plan: A Multiparticipant Interactive Environment

Beyond traditional human-computer interaction, we are developing a multiuser/agent interactive environment. In this environment, the agents are a kind of social actor and take responsibility for certain social services through their interactions with humans. The new interactive environment involves more than two participants, either human or animated agent. Each agent must recognize every participant with his/her/its personality. There are no fixed roles. Turn taking is flexible and highly dependent on the conversational situation.

We are planning to develop an animated agent that is capable of multimodal interaction and a multiuser/agent interactive environment that includes multiple humans and agents as social service providers. Objectives of this project include:

- Development of a conversational interface based on agents that are provided with humanlike figures and behavior.
- Development of a multimodal integration method for auditory and visual interaction systems that handles low-level (signal-level) and high-level (symbol-level) information and their coordination.
- Exploration of a multiuser interaction environment that includes humans and agents.

REFERENCES

Nagao, K., and Takeuchi, A. 1994. Social Interaction: Multimodal Conversation with Social Agents. In *Proceedings of the Twelfth National Conference on Artificial Intelligence (AAAI-94)*, 22–28. Cambridge, MA: MIT Press.

Takeuchi, A., and Naito, T. 1995. Situated Facial Displays: Towards Social Interaction. In *Proceedings of the ACM Conference on Human Factors in Computing Systems (CHI'95)*, 450–455. New York: ACM Press.

ANIMATED CONVERSATION: Rule-based Generation of Facial Expression, Gesture & Spoken Intonation for Multiple Conversational Agents

Justine Cassell Catherine Pelachaud Norman Badler Mark Steedman
Brett Achorn Tripp Becket Brett Douville Scott Prevost Matthew Stone [1]
Department of Computer & Information Science, University of Pennsylvania

Abstract

We describe an implemented system which *automatically* generates and animates conversations between multiple human-like agents with appropriate and synchronized speech, intonation, facial expressions, and hand gestures. Conversations are created by a dialogue planner that produces the text as well as the intonation of the utterances. The speaker/listener relationship, the text, and the intonation in turn drive facial expressions, lip motions, eye gaze, head motion, and arm gesture generators. Coordinated arm, wrist, and hand motions are invoked to create semantically meaningful gestures. Throughout, we will use examples from an actual synthesized, fully animated conversation.

1 Introduction

When faced with the task of bringing to life a human-like character, few options are currently available. Either one can manually and laboriously manipulate the numerous degrees of freedom in a synthetic figure, one can write or acquire increasingly sophisticated motion generation software such as inverse kinematics and dynamics, or one can resort to "performance-based" motions obtained from a live actor or puppet. The emergence of low-cost, real-time motion sensing devices has led to renewed interest in active motion capture since 3D position and orientation trajectories may be acquired directly rather than from tedious image rotoscoping [34]. Both facial and gestural motions are efficiently tracked from a suitably harnessed actor. But this does not imply that the end of manual or synthesized animation is near. Instead it raises the challenge of providing a sophisticated toolkit for human character animation that does not require the presence nor skill of a live actor [2], thus freeing the skilled animator for more challenging tasks.

In this paper we present our system for *automatically animating conversations between multiple human-like agents with appropriate and synchronized speech, intonation, facial expressions, and hand gestures*. Especially noteworthy is the linkage between speech and gesture which has not been explored before in synthesizing realistic animation. In people, speech, facial expressions, and gestures are physiologically linked. While an expert animator may realize this unconsciously in the "look" of a properly animated character, a program to automatically generate motions must know the rules in advance. This paper presents a working system to realize interacting animated agents.

Conversation is an interactive dialogue between two agents. Conversation includes spoken language (words and contextually appropriate intonation marking topic and focus), facial movements (lip shapes, emotions, gaze direction, head motion), and hand gestures (handshapes, points, beats, and motions representing the topic of accompanying speech). Without all of these verbal and nonverbal behaviors, one cannot have realistic, or at least believable, autonomous agents. To limit the problems (such as voice and face recognition) that arise from the involvement of real human conversants, and to constrain the dialogue, we present the work in the form of a dialogue generation program in which two copies of an identical program having different knowledge of the world must cooperate to accomplish a goal. Both agents of the conversation collaborate via the dialogue to develop a simple plan of action. They interact with each other to exchange information and ask questions.

In this paper, we first present the background information necessary to establish the synchrony of speech, facial expression, and gesture. We then discuss the system architecture and its several subcomponents.

2 Background

Faces change expressions continuously, and many of these changes are synchronized to what is going on in concurrent conversation. Facial expressions are linked to the content of speech (scrunching one's nose when talking about something unpleasant), emotion (wrinkling one's eyebrows with worry), personality (frowning all the time), and other behavioral variables. Facial expressions can replace sequences of words ("she was dressed [wrinkle nose, stick out tongue]") as well as accompany them [16], and they can serve to help disambiguate what is being said when the acoustic signal is degraded. They do not occur randomly but rather are synchronized to one's own speech, or to the speech of others [13], [20].

Eye gaze is also an important feature of non-verbal communicative behaviors. Its main functions are to help regulate the flow of conversation, signal the search for feedback during an interaction (gazing at the other person to see how she follows), look for information, express emotion (looking downward in case of sadness), or influence another person's behavior (staring at a person to show power)[14].

People also produce hand gestures spontaneously while they speak, and such gestures support and expand on information con-

[1] The authors would like to thank Francisco Azuola, Chin Seah, John Granieri, Ioi Kim Lam, and Xinmin Zhao.

veyed by words. The fact that gestures occur at the same time as speech, and that they carry the same meaning as speech, suggests that the production of the two are intimately linked. In fact, not only are the meaning of words and of gestures intimately linked in a discourse, but so are their functions in accomplishing conversational work: it has been shown that certain kinds of gestures produced during conversation act to structure the contributions of the two participants (to signal when an utterance continues the same topic or strikes out in a new direction), and to signal the contribution of particular utterances to the current discourse. It is clear that, like facial expression, gesture is not a kinesic performance independent of speech, or simply a 'translation' of speech. Rather, gesture and speech are so intimately connected that one cannot say which one is dependent on the other. Both can be claimed to arise from a single internal encoding process ([8], [21], [27]).

2.1 Example

In this section of the paper we present a fragment of dialogue (the complete dialogue has been synthesized and animated), in which intonation, gesture, head and lip movements, and their inter-synchronization were automatically generated. This example will serve to demonstrate the phenomena described here, and in subsequent sections we will return to each phenomenon to explain how rule-generation and synchronization are carried out.

In the following dialogue, imagine that Gilbert is a bank teller, and George has asked Gilbert for help in obtaining $50. The dialogue is unnaturally repetitive and explicit in its goals because the dialogue generation program that produced it has none of the conversational inferences that allow humans to follow leaps of reasoning. Therefore, the two agents have to specify in advance each of the goals they are working towards and steps they are following (see section 4.1).

Gilbert: Do you have a blank check?
George: Yes, I have a blank check.
Gilbert: Do you have an account for the check?
George: Yes, I have an account for the check.
Gilbert: Does the account contain at least fifty dollars?
George: Yes, the account contains eighty dollars.
Gilbert: Get the check made out to you for fifty dollars and then I can withdraw fifty dollars for you.
George: All right, let's get the check made out to me for fifty dollars.

When Gilbert asks a question, his voice rises. When George replies to a question, his voice falls. When Gilbert asks George whether he has a blank check, he stresses the word "check". When he asks George whether he has an account for the check, he stresses the word "account".

Every time Gilbert replies affirmatively ("yes"), or turns the floor over to Gilbert ("all right"), he nods his head, and raises his eyebrows. George and Gilbert look at each other when Gilbert asks a question, but at the end of each question, Gilbert looks up slightly. During the brief pause at the end of affirmative statements the speaker (always George, in this fragment) blinks. To mark the end of the questions, Gilbert raises his eyebrows.

In saying the word "check", Gilbert sketches the outlines of a check in the air between him and his listener. In saying "account", Gilbert forms a kind of box in front of him with his hands: a metaphorical representation of a bank account in which one keeps money. When he says the phrase "withdraw fifty dollars," Gilbert withdraws his hand towards his chest.

2.2 Communicative Significance of the Face

Movements of the head and facial expressions can be characterized by their placement with respect to the linguistic utterance and their significance in transmitting information [35]. The set of facial movement clusters contains:

- *syntactic functions* accompany the flow of speech and are synchronized at the verbal level. Facial movements (such as raising the eyebrows, nodding the head or blinking while saying "do you have a blank CHECK") can appear on an accented syllable or a pause.
- *semantic functions* can emphasize what is being said, substitute for a word or refer to an emotion (like wrinkling the nose while talking about something disgusting or smiling while remembering a happy event: "it was such a NICE DAY.").
- *dialogic functions* regulate the flow of speech and depend on the relationship between two people (smooth turns[1] are often co-occurrent with mutual gaze; e.g at the end of "do you have a blank check?", both interactants look at each other).

These three functions are modulated by various parameters:

- *speaker and listener characteristic functions* convey information about the speaker's social identity, emotion, attitude, age (friends spend more time looking at each other while talking than a lying speaker who will avoid the other's gaze).
- *listener functions* correspond to the listener's reactions to the speaker's speech; they can be signals of agreement, of attention, of comprehension (like saying "I see", "mhmm").

2.3 Communicative Significance of Hand Gestures

Gesture too can be described in terms of its intrinsic relationship to speech. Three aspects of this relationship are described before we go on to speak about the synchronization of the two communicative channels.

First of all, four basic types of gestures occur only during speech ([27] estimates that 90% of all gestures occur when the speaker is actually uttering something).

- *Iconics* represent some feature of the accompanying speech, such as sketching a small rectangular space with one's two hands while saying "do you have a blank CHECK?"
- *Metaphorics* represent an abstract feature concurrently spoken about, such as forming a jaw-like shape with one hand, and pulling it towards one's body while saying "then I can WITHDRAW fifty dollars for you".
- *Deictics* indicate a point in space. They accompany reference to persons, places and other spatializeable discourse entities. An example might be pointing to the ground while saying "do you have an account at THIS bank?".
- *Beats* are small formless waves of the hand that occur with heavily emphasized words, occasions of turning over the floor to another speaker, and other kinds of special linguistic work. An example is waving one's left hand briefly up and down along with the phrase "all right".

In some discourse contexts about three-quarters of all clauses are accompanied by gestures of one kind or another; of these, about 40% are iconic, 40% are beats, and the remaining 20% are divided between deictic and metaphoric gestures [27]. And surprisingly, although the proportion of different gestures may change, all of these types of gestures, and spontaneous gesturing in general, are found in discourses by speakers of most languages.

There is also a semantic and pragmatic relationship between the two media. Gesture and speech do not always manifest the same information about an idea, but what they convey is always complementary. That is, gesture may depict the way in which an action was carried out when this aspect of meaning is not depicted in speech. For example, one speaker, describing how one deposits checks into a bank account, said "you list the checks" while she depicted with her hands that the deposit slip is to be turned over and turned vertically in order for the checks to be listed in the spaces provided on the back of the slip.

[1] Meaning that the listener does not interrupt or overlap the speaker.

Finally, the importance of the interdependence of speech and gesture is shown by the fact that speakers rely on information conveyed in gesture – sometimes even to the exclusion of information conveyed by accompanying speech – as they try to comprehend a story [9].

Nevertheless, hand gestures and gaze behavior have been virtually absent from attempts to animate semi-autonomous agents in communicative contexts.

2.4 Synchrony of Gesture, Facial Movements, and Speech

Facial expression, eye gaze and hand gestures do not do their communicative work only within single utterances, but also have interspeaker effects. The presence or absence of confirmatory feedback by one conversational participant, via gaze or head movement, for example, affects the behavior of the other. A conversation consists of the exchange of meaningful utterances and of behavior. One person punctuates and reinforces her speech by head nods, smiles, and hand gestures; the other person can smile back, vocalize, or shift gaze to show participation in the conversation.

Synchrony implies that changes occurring in speech and in body movements should appear at the same time. For example, when a word begins to be articulated, eye blinks, hand movement, head turning, and brow raising can occur and can finish at the end of the word.

Synchrony occurs at all levels of speech: the phonemic segment, word, phrase or long utterance. Different facial motions are characteristic of these different groups [13], [20]. Some of them are more adapted to the phoneme level, like an eye blink, while others act at the word level, like a frown. In the example "Do you have a blank check?", a raising eyebrow starts and ends on the accented syllables "check", while a blink starts and ends on the pause marking the end of the utterance. Facial expression of emphasis can match the emphasized segment, showing synchronization at this level (a sequence of head nods can punctuate the emphasis). Moreover, some movements reflect encoding-decoding difficulties and therefore coincide with hesitations and pauses inside clauses. Many hesitation pauses are produced at the beginning of speech and correlate with avoidance of gaze (the head of the speaker turns away from the listener) as if to help the speaker to concentrate on what she is going to say.

Gestures occur in synchrony with their semantically parallel linguistic units, although in cases of hesitations, pauses or syntactically complex speech, it is the gesture which appears first ([27]). At the most local level, individual gestures and words are synchronized in time so that the 'stroke' (most energetic part of the gesture) occurs either with or just before the phonologically most prominent syllable of the accompanying speech segment ([21], [27]). At the most global level, we find that the hands of the speaker come to rest at the end of a speaking turn, before the next speaker begins her turn. At the intermediate level, the phenomenon of co-articulation of gestural units is found, whereby gestures are performed rapidly, or their production is stretched out over time, so as to synchronize with preceding and following gestures, and the speech these gestures accompany. An example of gestural co-articulation is the relationship between the two gestures in the phrase "get the check MADE OUT TO YOU for fifty dollars and then I can WITHDRAW fifty dollars for you". During the phrase 'made out to you', the right hand sketches a writing gesture in front of the speaker. However, rather than carrying this gesture all the way to completion (either both hands coming to rest at the end of this gesture, or maintaining the location of the hands in space), the hand drops slightly and then pulls back towards the speaker to perform the 'withdraw' gesture. Thus, the occurrence of the phrase 'made out to you', with its accompanying gesture, affected the occurrence of the gesture that accompanied "withdraw".

3 Computer Animation of Conversation

3.1 Literature on Facial Control Systems

Various systems have been proposed to integrate the different facial expression functions. Most of the systems use **FACS** (Facial Action Coding System) as a notational system [17]. This system is based on anatomical studies, and describes any visible facial movements. An action unit **AU**, the basic element of this system, describes the action produced by one or a group of related muscles.

The multi-layer approach [19] allows independent control at each level of the system. At the lowest level (geometric level), geometry of the face can be modified using free form deformation techniques. At the highest level, facial animation can be computed from an input utterance.

In M. Patel's model [28] facial animation can also be done at different levels of representation. It can be done either at the muscle level, the **AU** level or the script level. For each **AU** the user can select starting and ending points of action, the intensity of action, the start and end tensions and the interpolation method to compute the in-between frames. An alternative approach is proposed by [11] with good results.

Building a user-interface, [37] propose a categorization of facial expressions depending on their communicative meaning. For each of the facial functions a list of facial displays is performed (for example, remembering corresponds to eyebrow action, eye closure and one side of mouth pull back). A user talks to the 3D synthetic actor. A speech system recognizes the words and generates an answer with the appropriate facial displays. Grammar rules, a small vocabulary set and a specific knowledge domain are part of the speech analysis system. The responses by the 3D actor are selected from a pre-established set of utterances. The appropriate facial displays accompanying the answer follow the analysis of the conventional situation (e.g. if the user's speech is not recognized the 3D actor will answer with a "not-confident" facial display).

3.2 Literature on Gesture Animation

The computer graphics literature is rather sparse on the topic of gesture animation. Animators frequently use key parameter techniques to create arm and hand motions. Rijpkema and Girard [33] created handshapes automatically based on the object being gripped. The Thalmanns [18, 26] improved on the hand model to include much better skin models and deformations of the finger tips and the gripped object. Lee and Kunii [22] built a system that includes handshapes and simple pre-stored facial expressions for American Sign Language (ASL) synthesis. Dynamics of arm gestures in ASL have been studied by Loomis et al [25]. Chen et al [10] constructed a virtual human that can shake hands with an interactive participant. Lee et al [23] automatically generate lifting gestures by considering strength and comfort measures. Moravec and Calvert [5] constructed a system that portrays the gestural interaction between two agents as they pass and greet one another. Behavioral parameters were set by personality attribute "sliders" though the interaction sequence was itself pre-determined and limited to just one type of non-verbal encounter.

4 Overview of System

In the current system, a model of face-to-face interaction is used to generate all of the behaviors implemented, from the informational status of intonation to the communicative function of head nods, gaze, and hand gestures. Additionally, however, this system implements two agents whose verbal and nonverbal behaviors are integrated not only within turns, but across speakers.

In the remaining parts of the paper we explain the different elements of Figure 1. We start from the top of the figure and work towards its bottom. Currently, gesture is generated by the dialogue

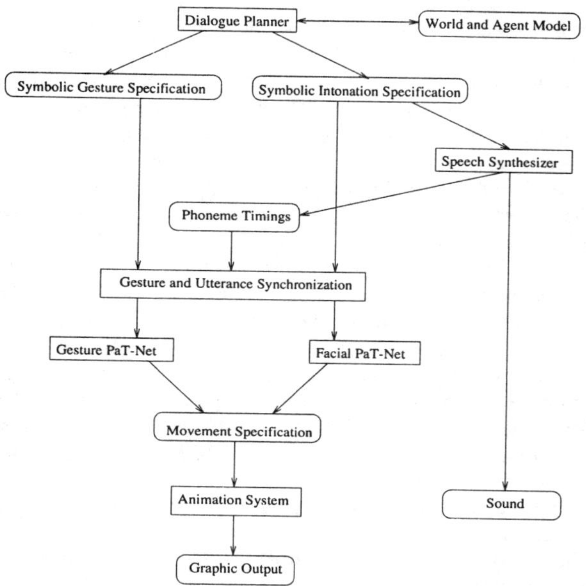

Figure 1: Interaction of components

planner, while facial expression and gaze are generated by the facial PaT-Net.

4.1 Dialogue Planner

The text of this dialogue is automatically generated on the basis of a database of facts describing the way the world works, a list of the goals of the two agents, and the set of beliefs of those two agents about the world, including the beliefs of the agents about one another [30], [7]. In this instance the two agents have goals that change over the course of the dialogue (Gilbert comes to have the goal of helping George get $50; George comes to have the goal of writing a check).

Text is generated and pitch accents and phrasal melodies are placed on generated text as outlined in [36] and [31]. This text is converted automatically to a form suitable for input to the AT&T Bell Laboratories TTS synthesizer ([24]). When the dialogue is generated, the following information is saved automatically: (1) the timing of the phonemes and pauses, (2) the type and place of the accents, (3) the type and place of the gestures.

This speech and timing information will be critical for synchronizing the facial and gestural animation.

4.2 Symbolic Gesture Specification

The dialogue generation program annotates utterances according to how their semantic content could relate to a spatial expression (literally, metaphorically, spatializeably, or not at all). Further, references to entities are classified according to discourse status as either new to discourse and hearer (indefinites), new to discourse but not to hearer (definites on first mention), or old (all others) [32]. According to the following rules, these annotations, together with the earlier ones, determine which concepts will have an associated gesture. Gestures that represent something (iconics and metaphorics) are generated for rhematic verbal elements (roughly, information not yet spoken about) and for hearer new references, provided that the semantic content is of an appropriate class to receive such a gesture: words with literally spatial (or concrete) content get iconics (e.g. "check"); those with metaphorically spatial (or abstract) content get metaphorics (e.g. "account"); words with physically spatializeable content get deictics (e.g. "this bank"). Meanwhile, beat gestures are generated for such items when the semantic content cannot be represented spatially, and are also produced accompanying discourse new definite references (e.g. "fifty dollars"). If a representational gesture is called for, the system accesses a dictionary of gestures (motion prototypes) that associates semantic representations with possible gestures that might represent them[2] (for further details, see [7]).

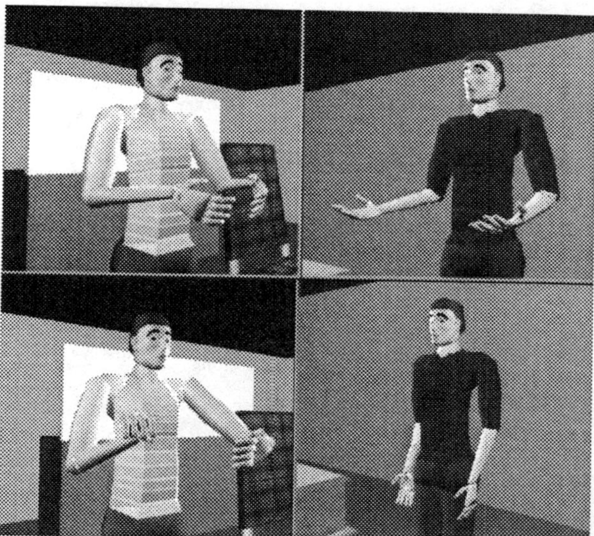

Figure 2: Examples of symbolic gesture specification

In Figure 2, we see examples of how symbolic gestures are generated from discourse content.

1. "Do you have a BLANK CHECK?"
    - In the first frame, an iconic gesture (representing a rectangular check) is generated from the first mention (new to hearer) of the entity 'blank check'.
2. "Will you HELP me get fifty dollars?"
    - In the second frame, a metaphoric gesture (the common *propose* gesture, representing the request for help as a proposal that can be offered to the listener) is generated because of the first mention (new to hearer) of the request for help.
3. "You can WRITE the check."
    - In the third frame, an iconic gesture (representing writing on a piece of paper) is generated from the first mention of the concrete action of 'writing a check'.
4. "I will WAIT for you to withdraw fifty dollars for me."
    - In the fourth frame, a beat gesture (a movement of the hand up and down) is generated from the first mention of the notion 'wait for', which cannot be represented spatially.

After this gestural annotation of all gesture types, and lexicon look-up of appropriate forms for representational gestures, information about the duration of intonational phrases (acquired in speech generation) is used to time gestures. First, all the gestures in each intonational phrase are collected. Because of the relationship between accenting and gesturing, in this dialogue at most one representational gesture occurs in each intonational phrase. If there is a representational gesture, its preparation is set to begin at or before the beginning of the intonational phrase, and to finish at or before the next gesture in the intonational phrase or the nuclear stress of the phrase, whichever comes first. The stroke phase is then set to coincide with the nuclear stress of the phrase. Finally, the relaxation is set to begin no sooner than the end of the stroke or the end of

[2] This solution is provisional: a richer semantics would include the features relevant for gesture generation, so that the form of the gestures could be generated algorithmically from the semantics. Note also, however, that following [21] we are led to believe that gestures may be more standardized in form than previously thought.

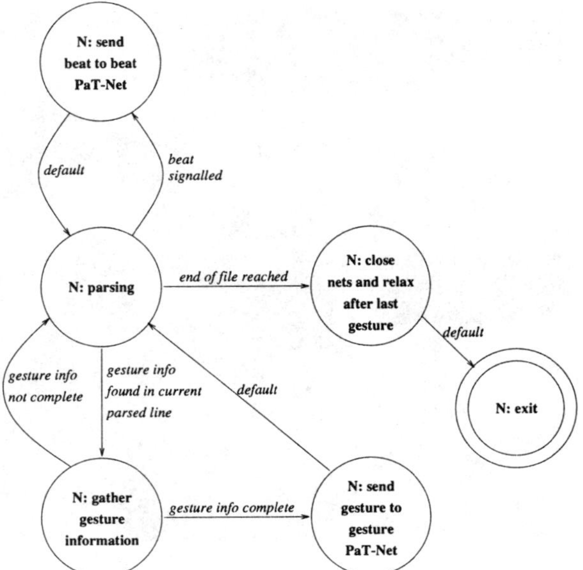

Figure 3: Pat-Net that synchronizes gestures with the dialogue at the phoneme level.

the last beat in the intonational phrase, with the end of relaxation to occur around the end of the intonational phrase. Beats, in contrast, are simply timed to coincide with the stressed syllable of the word that realizes the associated concept. When these timing rules have been applied to each of the intonational phrases in the utterance, the output is a series of symbolic gesture types and the times at which they should be performed. These instructions are used to generate motion files that run the animation system ([3]).

4.3 The Underlying Coordination Model

Interaction between agents and synchronization of gaze and hand movements to the dialogue for each agent are accomplished using Parallel Transition Networks (PaT-Nets), which allow coordination rules to be encoded as simultaneously executing finite state automata ([4]). PaT-Nets can call for action in the simulation and make state transitions either conditionally or probabilistically. Pat-Nets are scheduled into the simulation with an operating system that allows them to invoke or kill other PaT-Nets, sleep until a desired time or until a desired condition is met, and synchronize with other running nets by waiting for them to finish or by waiting on a shared semaphore.

In addition, the PaT-Net notation is object oriented with each net defined by a *class* with actions and transition conditions as *methods*. The running networks are instances of the PaT-Net class and can take parameters on instantiation. This notation allows Pat-Nets to be hierarchically organized and allows constructing new nets by combining existing nets or making simple modifications to existing nets.

Behaviors are implemented as specified in the following sections, with all head, eye and hand movement behavior for an individual encoded in PaT-Nets. A PaT-Net instance is created to control each agent with appropriate parameters. Then as agents' PaT-Nets synchronize the agents with the dialogue and interact with the unfolding simulation they schedule activity that achieves a complex observed interaction behavior.

4.4 Gesture Generator

The gesture PaT-Net sends information about the timing, shape, and position of the hands and arms to the animation system. The animation process produces a file of motions to be carried out by the two figures. Starting with a given gesture and its timing, speech rate and surrounding gestures constrain the motion sequence for a proper co-articulation effect. As depicted in Figure 3, upon the signalling of a particular gesture, parse-net will instantiate one of two additional PaT-Nets; if the gesture is a beat, the finite state machine representing beats ("beat-net") will be called, and if a deictic, iconic, or metaphoric, the network representing these types of gestures ("gest-net") will be called. This separation is motivated by the "rhythm hypothesis" ([38]) which posits that beats arise from the underlying rhythmical pulse of speaking, while other gestures arise from meaning representations. In addition, beats are often found superimposed over the other types of gestures, and such a separation facilitates implementation of superposition. Finally, since one of the goals of the model is to reflect differences in behavior among gesture types, this system provides for control of freedom versus boundedness in gestures (e.g. an iconic gesture or emblem is tightly constrained to a particular standard of well-formedness, while beats display free movement); free gestures may most easily be generated by a separate PaT-Net whose parameters include this feature.

Gesture and beat finite state machines are built as necessary by the parser, so that the gestures can be represented as they arise. The newly created instances of the gesture and beat PaT-Nets do not exit immediately upon creating their respective gestures; rather, they pause and await further commands from the calling network, in this case, parse-net. This is to allow for the phenomenon of gesture coarticulation, in which two gestures may occur in an utterance without intermediary relaxation, i.e. without dropping the hands or, in some cases, without relaxing handshape. Once the end of the current utterance is reached, the parser adds another level of control: it forces exit without relaxation of all gestures except the gesture at the top of the stack; this final gesture is followed by a relaxation of the arms, hands, and wrists.

Consider the following data from the intonation and gesture streams. Let us examine a gesture PaT-Net that acts on this input.

Intonation: Do you have a blank CHECK
Gesture: pr beat sk rx

In this example, the primary intonational stress of the phrase falls on 'check', but there is a secondary stress on 'blank'. The gesture line of the example shows that the preparation ('pr') of the gesture begins on 'have', that the stroke of the gesture ('st') falls on check, and that the gesturing relaxes ('rx') after 'check'. Because of the secondary stress on the new informational item 'blank', a beat gesture falls there, and it is found superimposed over the production of the iconic gesture.

Due to the structure of the conversation, where the speakers alternate turns, we assume similar alternation in gesturing. (Gesturing by listeners is almost non-existent [27].) For the purposes of gesture generation, phoneme information is ignored; however, utterance barriers must be interpreted both to provide an envelope for the timing of a particular gesture or sequence of gestures and to determine which speaker is gesturing. Timing information, given in the speech file, also allows the PaT-Net to determine whether there is enough time for a complete gesture to be produced. For example, the iconic gesture which accompanies the utterance *"Do you have a blank [check]?"* has sufficient time to execute: it is the only (non-beat) gesture occurring in the phrase, as shown above. However, if this timing is insufficient to allow for full gesture production, then the gesture must be foreshortened to allow for the reduced available timing (because beat gestures are produced by a separate PaT-Net system, they do not enter into questions of co-articulation).

The most common reason for foreshortening is anticipation of the next gesture to be produced in a discourse. In anticipatory co-articulation effects, most often the relaxation phase of the foreshortened iconic, metaphoric or deictic gesture and preparation phase of the next gesture become one. This process can be seen in the gestures accompanying the phrase *"Get the check [made out to you] for fifty dollars and then I can [withdraw] fifty dollars for you"*. "[Made out to you]" is produced .90 seconds into the phrase, and "[withdraw]" is generated at 1.9 seconds. This causes some foreshortening in the relaxation process during the first gesture, from which the second gesture is then produced.

Co-articulation constraints – synchronizing the gestures with intonational phrases and surrounding gestures – may actually cause the given gestures to be aborted if too little time is available for production given the physical constraints of the human model.

4.5 Gesture Motion Specification

The graphics-level gesture animation system accepts gesture instructions containing information about the location, type, timing, and handshape of individual gestures. Based on the current location of the hands and arms in space, the system will attempt to get as close as possible to the gesture goals in the time allowed, but may mute motions or positionings because it cannot achieve them in time (co-articulation effects). This animation system calls upon a library of predefined handshapes which form the primitives of hand gesture. These handshapes were chosen to reflect the shapes most often found in gesture during conversational interaction ([21]). The animation system also calls upon separate hand, arm and wrist control mechanisms.

The gesture system is divided into three parts: hand shape, wrist control, and arm positioning. The first, hand shape, relies on an extensible library of hand shape primitives for the basic joint positions, but allows varying degrees of relaxation towards a neutral hand position. The speed at which the hand may change shape is also limited to allow the modelling of hand shape co-articulation. Large changes in hand position are restricted as less time is allotted for the hand movement, forcing faster hand gestures to smooth together.

The wrist control system allows the wrist to maintain and change its position independently of what complex arm motions may be occurring. The wrist is limited within the model to a physically realistic range of motion. Wrist direction is specified in terms of simple directions relative to the gesturer, such as "point the fingers of the left hand forward and up, and the palm right".

The arm motion system accepts general specifications of spatial goals and drives the arms towards those goals within the limits imposed by the arm's range of motion. The arm may be positioned by using general directions like "chest-high, slightly forward, and to the far left".

The expressiveness of an individual's gesturing can be represented by adjusting the size of the gesture space of the graphical figure. In this way, parameters such as age (children's gestures are larger than adults') and culture (in some cultures gestures tend to be larger) can be implemented in the gesture animation.

4.6 Symbolic Facial Expression Specification

In the current system, facial expression (movement of the lips, eyebrows, etc.) is specified separately from movement of the head and eyes (gaze). In this section we discuss facial expression, and turn to gaze in the next section.

P. Ekman and his colleagues characterize the set of semantic and syntactic facial expressions depending on their meaning [15]. Many facial functions exist (such as manipulators that correspond to biological needs of the face (wetting the lips); emblems and emotional emblems that are facial expressions replacing a word, an emotion) but only some are directly linked to the intonation of the voice. In this system, facial expressions connected to intonation are automatically generated, while other kinds of expressions (emblems, for example) are specified by hand [29].

4.7 Symbolic Gaze Specification

Gaze can be classified into four primary categories depending on its role in the conversation [1], [12]. In the following, we give rules of action and the functions for each of these four categories (see Figure 4). The nodes of the Pat-Net they refer to is also indicated.

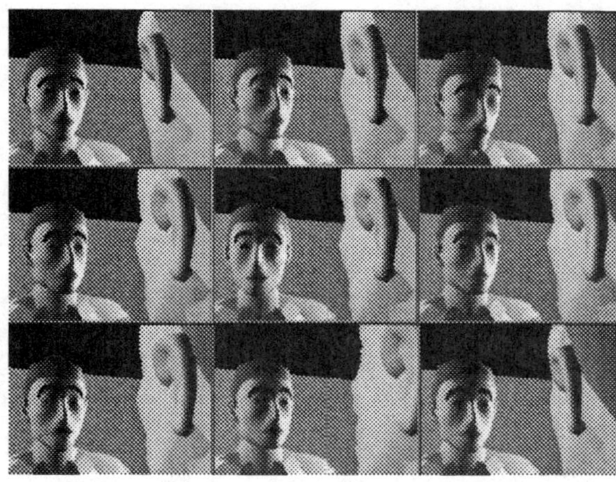

Figure 4: Facial expressions and gaze behavior corresponding to: "All right. <pause> You can write the check".

planning: corresponds to the first phase of a turn when the speaker organizes her thoughts. She has a tendency to look away in order to prevent an overload of information (`beginning of turn`). On the other hand, during the execution phase, the speaker knows what she is going to say and looks more at the listener. For a short turn (duration less than 1.5 sec.), the speaker and the listener establish eye contact (mutual gaze) [1] (`short-turn`).

comment: accompanies and comments speech, by occurring in parallel with accent and emphasis. Accented or emphasized items are punctuated by head nods; the speaker looks toward the listener (`accent`). The speaker also gazes at the listener more when she asks a question. She looks up at the end of the question (`utterance: question`). When answering, the speaker looks away (`utterance: answer`).

control: controls the communication channel and functions as a synchronization signal: responses may be demanded or suppressed by looking at the listener. When the speaker wants to give her turn of speaking to the listener, she gazes at the listener at the end of the utterance (`end of turn`). When the listener asks for the turn, she looks up at the speaker (`turn request`).

feedback: is used to collect and seek feedback. The listener can emit different reaction signals to the speaker's speech. Speaker looks toward the listener during grammatical pauses to obtain feedback on how utterances are being received (`within-turn`). This is frequently followed by the listener looking at the speaker and nodding (`back-channel`). In turn, if the speaker wants to keep her turn, she looks away from the listener (`continuation signal`). If the speaker doesn't emit a `within-turn` signal by gazing at the listener, the listener can still emit a `back-channel` which in turn may be followed by a `continuation signal` by the speaker. But the probability of action of the listener varies with the action of the speaker [14]; in particular, it decreases if no signal has occurred from the speaker. In this way the listener reacts to the behavior of the speaker.

4.8 Gaze Generator

Each of the dialogic functions appears as a sub-network in the PaT-Net. Figure 5 outlines the high-level PaT-Net for gaze control for a single agent. It contains the four dialogic functions, their nodes that define each function, and their associated actions. From the definitions given above, we extract the conditions and the actions characterizing the dialogic functions. For this current version of the program we do not differentiate head movement and eye movement.

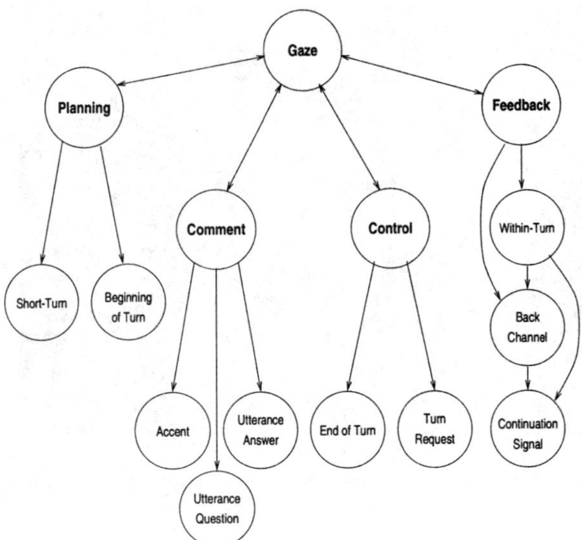

Figure 5: The gaze movement PaT-Net: actions are defined in the nodes; conditional and probabilistic transitions occur on arcs. All leaf nodes also branch back to the root node unconditionally.

That is the eyes follow the head. Moreover, in the literature this difference is rarely made. In what follows, we use "gaze" to refer to head and eye movement.

Each node is characterized by a probability. A person can have the floor talking or pausing, but loses it as soon as the other person starts talking. There are 3 possible states per person while having the floor. If Speaker has the floor: Speaker talks and Listener pauses, both of them are talking, or both of them are pausing. For each of these states, Speaker and Listener can gaze at each other or not. This gives us 12 possibilities, or 24 per dyad. We can then compute the probability of being in each of these states [6]. Most of the nodes of the Pat-Net can be characterized by a certain set of states. For example the occurrence of a "within-turn signal" as we defined it corresponds to the action: person1 looks at the person2 while having the floor and pausing. These state sets correspond to a sub-matrix. We compute the probability of each sub-matrix in relation to the particular state (having the floor and pausing) to arrive at a probability of occurrence. We do such a computation for all the other nodes of the Pat-Net. Probabilities appropriate for each agent given the current role as listener or speaker are set for the PaT-Net before it executes. At each turn change, the probabilities change values accordingly. This information is used to determine the rules and transitional probabilities for actions in Pat-Nets.

For each phoneme, the GAZE Pat-Net is entered. A transition is made on the node whose condition is true. If the probability of the nodes allows it, the action is performed. The action of the different nodes of the Pat-Net is illustrated in the following with the example:

`Gilbert: Get the chEck made OUt to you for fifty dollars` *<pause>* `And thEn` *<pause>* `I can withdrAw fifty dollars for you.`

planning: For the first few phonemes of the beginning of the example utterance [3](in our example it corresponds to "Get the ch"), the sub-network **planning** is applied. This utterance is not short so the node `short-turn` is not entered.

But the node `beginning-turn` is entered; the condition of being in a beginning of turn is true but its probability did not allow the action `speaker gazes away` to be applied. Therefore the speaker (Gilbert) keeps his current gaze direction (looking at George).

comment: In our example, on accented items ("chEck", "thEn" and "withdrAw"), the node `accent` of the sub-network **comment** is reached; the actions `speaker gazes at the listener` and `head nod` are performed by Gilbert. As before, the instantiation of an action depends on its probability. The system easily represents the parallel agent actions.

control: In our example at the end of the utterance[4] (corresponding to "fifty dollars for you" here) the sub-network **control** is entered. Two actions are considered. The node `end of turn` corresponds to action performed by the speaker: `speaker gazes at listener.` The other node `turn request` affects the listener; the action `listener gazes at the speaker and up` is performed.

feedback: The two intonational phrases of our example (*get the check made out to you for fifty dollars* and *and then*) are separated by a pause; this corresponds to a within-turn situation. The sub-network **feedback** is entered. If the probability allows it, the action `speaker gazes at the listener` is performed[5]. After a delay (0.2 sec., as specified by the program), the node `back-channel` is reached. Once more the program checks the probabilities associated with the actions. Two actions can happen: `listener gazes at the speaker` and/or `the listener nods.` In either case, the final step within the **feedback** sub-network is reached after some delay. The action `speaker gazes away from the listener` is then performed.

4.9 Facial Expression Generator

Facial expressions belonging to the set of semantic and syntactic functions (see section 4.6) are clustered into functional groups: lip shape, conversational signal, punctuator, manipulator and emblem. We use **FACS** to denote facial expressions. Each is represented by two parameters: *its time of occurrence* and *its type*. Our algorithm [29] embodies rules as described in Section 4.6 to automatically generate facial expressions, following the principle of synchrony.

The program scans the input utterance and computes the different facial expressions corresponding to these functional groups. The computation of the lip shape is made in three passes and incorporates coarticulation effects. Phonemes are associated to some characteristic shapes with different degree of deformability. For deformable elements, temporal and spatial constraints modify these shapes to consider their surrounding context. A conversational signal (movements occurring on accents, like the raising of an eyebrow) starts and ends with the accented word; while punctuator signal (movement occurring on pause, like frowning) happens on the pause. When a blink is one of these signals it is synchronized at the phoneme level. Other signals such as emblems and emotional emblems are performed consciously and must be specified by the user.

By varying the two parameters defining a facial expression, different speaker personalities can be obtained. For example a persuasive person can punctuate each accented word with raising eyebrows, while another person might not.

4.10 Gaze and Facial Motion Specification

The gaze directions generated in a previous stage can now be instantiated. As discussed earlier, the GAZE PaT-Net in Figure 5 is run for each agent at the beginning of every phoneme. Depending on the course taken through the GAZE network due to probabilistic branching and environmental state, the net may commit its agent to a variety of actions such as a head nod or a change in the gaze point. A change in the gaze is accomplished by supplying the human model with a 3D coordinate at which to look and a time in

[3]A beginning of a turn is defined as all the phonemes between the first one and the first accented segment.

[4]End of turn is defined as all the phonemes between the last accented segment and the last phonemes.

[5]In the case the action is not performed, the arc going to the node `back-channel` is immediately traversed without waiting for the next phonemic segment.

which to move – the scheduled motion then begins at the current point in the simulation and has the specified duration. A head nod is accomplished by scheduling a sequence of joint motions for the neck, supplying both the angle and the angular velocity for each nod cycle. Note that the gaze controller schedules motions as they are necessary by reacting to the unfolding simulation (in fact, it does this in semi-real time) and does not have to generate all motions in advance. This makes the gaze controller easy to extend and easy to integrate with the rest of the system.

Different functions may be served by the same action, which differ only in their timing and amplitude. For example, when punctuating an accent, the speaker's head nod will be of larger amplitude than the feedback head nods emitted by the listener. Different head nod functions may also be characterized by varying numbers of up/down cycles. The gaze direction is sustained by calling for the agent to look at a pre-defined point in the environment until a change is made by another action.

For facial expressions, the program outputs the list of **AUs** that characterize each phonemic element and pause [29].

After scanning all the input utterances, all the actions to be performed are specified. Animation files are output. The final animation is done by combining the different output files for the gesture, face and gaze in *Jack*.

5 Conclusions

Automatically generating information about intonation, facial expression, head movements and hand gestures allows an interactive dialogue animation to be created; for a non-real-time animation much guess-work in the construction of appropriate motions can be avoided. The resulting motions can be used as is – as demonstrated in the video – or the actions and timings can be used as a cognitively and physiologically justified guide to further refinement of the conversation and the participants' interactions by a human animator.

REFERENCES

[1] M. Argyle and M. Cook. *Gaze and Mutual gaze*. Cambridge University Press, 1976.

[2] N. I. Badler, B. A. Barsky, and D. Zeltzer, editors. *Making Them Move: Mechanics, Control, and Animation of Articulated Figures*. Morgan-Kaufmann, San Mateo, CA, 1991.

[3] N. I. Badler, C. Phillips and B. L. Webber. *Simulating Humans: Computer Graphics, Animation, and Control*. Oxford University Press, June 1993.

[4] Welton M. Becket. The *jack lisp api*. Technical Report MS-CIS-94-01/Graphics Lab 59, University of Pennsylvania, 1994.

[5] Tom Calvert. Composition of realistic animation sequences for multiple human figures. In Norman I. Badler, Brian A. Barsky, and David Zeltzer, editors, *Making Them Move: Mechanics, Control, and Animation of Articulated Figures*, pages 35–50. Morgan-Kaufmann, San Mateo, CA, 1991.

[6] J. Cappella. personal communication, 1993.

[7] Justine Cassell, Mark Steedman, Norm Badler, Catherine Pelachaud, Matthew Stone, Brett Douville, Scott Prevost and Brett Achorn. *Modeling the interaction between speech and gesture. Proceedings of the Cognitive Science Society Annual Conference*, 1994.

[8] Justine Cassell and David McNeill. Gesture and the poetics of prose. *Poetics Today*, 12:375–404, 1992.

[9] Justine Cassell, David McNeill, and Karl-Erik McCullough. Kids, don't try this at home: Experimental mismatches of speech and gesture. presented at the International Communication Association annual meeting, 1993.

[10] D. T. Chen, S. D. Pieper, S. K. Singh, J. M. Rosen, and D. Zeltzer. The virtual sailor: An implementation of interactive human body modeling. In *Proc. 1993 Virtual Reality Annual International Symposium*, Seattle, WA, September 1993. IEEE.

[11] M.M. Cohen and D.W. Massaro. Modeling coarticulation in synthetic visual speech. In N.M. Thalmann and D.Thalmann, editors, *Models and Techniques in Computer Animation*, pages 139-156. Springer-Verlag, 1993.

[12] G. Collier. *Emotional expression*. Lawrence Erlbaum Associates, 1985.

[13] W.S. Condon and W.D. Osgton. Speech and body motion synchrony of the speaker-hearer. In D.H. Horton and J.J. Jenkins, editors, *The perception of Language*, pages 150–184. Academic Press, 1971.

[14] S. Duncan. Some signals and rules for taking speaking turns in conversations. In Weitz, editor, *Nonverbal Communication*. Oxford University Press, 1974.

[15] P. Ekman. Movements with precise meanings. *The Journal of Communication*, 26, 1976.

[16] P. Ekman. About brows: emotional and conversational signals. In M. von Cranach, K. Foppa, W. Lepenies, and D. Ploog, editors, *Human ethology: claims and limits of a new disipline: contributions to the Colloquium*, pages 169–248. Cambridge University Press, Cambridge, England; New-York, 1979.

[17] P. Ekman and W. Friesen. *Facial Action Coding System*. Consulting Psychologists Press, Inc., 1978.

[18] Jean-Paul Gourret, Nadia Magnenat-Thalmann, and Daniel Thalmann. Simulation of object and human skin deformations in a grasping task. *Computer Graphics*, 23(3):21–30, 1989.

[19] P. Kalra, A. Mangili, N. Magnenat-Thalmann, and D. Thalmann. Smile: A multilayered facial animation system. In T.L. Kunii, editor, *Modeling in Computer Graphics*. Springer-Verlag, 1991.

[20] A. Kendon. Movement coordination in social interaction: some examples described. In Weitz, editor, *Nonverbal Communication*. Oxford University Press, 1974.

[21] Adam Kendon. Gesticulation and speech: Two aspects of the process of utterance. In M.R.Key, editor, *The Relation between Verbal and Nonverbal Communication*, pages 207–227. Mouton, 1980.

[22] Jintae Lee and Tosiyasu L. Kunii. Visual translation: From native language to sign language. In *Workshop on Visual Languages*, Seattle, WA, 1993. IEEE.

[23] Philip Lee, Susanna Wei, Jianmin Zhao, and Norman I. Badler. Strength guided motion. *Computer Graphics*, 24(4):253–262, 1990.

[24] Mark Liberman and A. L. Buchsbaum. Structure and usage of current Bell Labs text to speech programs. Technical Memorandum TM 11225-850731-11, AT&T Bell Laboratories, 1985.

[25] Jeffrey Loomis, Howard Poizner, Ursula Bellugi, Alynn Blakemore, and John Hollerbach. Computer graphic modeling of American Sign Language. *Computer Graphics*, 17(3):105–114, July 1983.

[26] Nadia Magnenat-Thalmann and Daniel Thalmann. Human body deformations using joint-dependent local operators and finite-element theory. In Norman I. Badler, Brian A. Barsky, and David Zeltzer, editors, *Making Them Move: Mechanics, Control, and Animation of Articulated Figures*, pages 243–262. Morgan-Kaufmann, San Mateo, CA, 1991.

[27] David McNeill. *Hand and Mind: What Gestures Reveal about Thought*. University of Chicago, 1992.

[28] M. Patel. *Making FACES*. PhD thesis, School of Mathematical Sciences, University of Bath, Bath, AVON, UK, 1991.

[29] C. Pelachaud, N.I. Badler, and M. Steedman. Linguistic issues in facial animation. In N. Magnenat-Thalmann and D. Thalmann, editors, *Computer Animation '91*, pages 15–30. Springer-Verlag, 1991.

[30] Richard Power. The organisation of purposeful dialogues. *Linguistics*, 1977.

[31] Scott Prevost and Mark Steedman. Generating contextually appropriate intonation. In *Proceedings of the 6th Conference of the European Chapter of the Association for Computational Linguistics*, pages 332–340, Utrecht, 1993.

[32] Ellen F. Prince. The ZPG letter: Subjects, definiteness and information status. In S. Thompson and W. Mann, editors, *Discourse description: diverse analyses of a fund raising text*, pages 295–325. John Benjamins B.V., 1992.

[33] Hans Rijpkema and Michael Girard. Computer animation of hands and grasping. *Computer Graphics*, 25(4):339–348, July 1991.

[34] Barbara Robertson. Easy motion. *Computer Graphics World*, 16(12):33–38, December 1993.

[35] Klaus R. Scherer. The functions of nonverbal signs in conversation. In H. Giles R. St. Clair, editor, *The Social and Physhological Contexts of Language*, pages 225–243. Lawrence Erlbaum Associates, 1980.

[36] Mark Steedman. Structure and intonation. *Language*, 67:260–296, 1991.

[37] Akikazu Takeuchi and Katashi Nagao. Communicative facial displays as a new conversational modality. In *ACM/IFIP INTERCHI'93*, Amsterdam, 1993.

[38] K. Tuite. The production of gesture. *Semiotica*, 93(1/2), 1993.

6 Research Acknowledgments

This research is partially supported by NSF Grants IRI90-18513, IRI91-17110, CISE Grant CDA88-22719, NSF graduate fellowships, NSF VPW GER-9350179; ARO Grant DAAL03-89-C-0031 including participation by the U.S. Army Research Laboratory (Aberdeen); U.S. Air Force DEPTH contract through Hughes Missile Systems F33615-91-C-000; DMSO through the University of Iowa; National Defense Science and Engineering Graduate Fellowship in Computer Science DAAL03-92-G-0342; and NSF Instrumentation and Laboratory Improvement Program Grant USE-9152503.

Animated Conversation: Rule-Based Generation of Facial Expression, Gesture and Spoken Intonation for Multiple Conversational Agents

Justine Cassell

This work was inspired by research in three previously distinct fields: psycholinguistics, dialog semantics, and computer graphics. In psycholinguistics, research by Cassell, Duncan, Kendon, McNeill, and others had shown that we structure our contributions to discourse not only by way of the speech we utter but also through the use of gesture and facial expression, and that these nonverbal modalities could be described through their relationship to intonation, discourse structure, and turn taking. In dialog planning, the pioneering work of Power (1979) had shown how conversational planning can be integrated with action planning, and work by Prevost and Steedman (1994) had defined a related discourse semantics and its grammatical relation to intonation contour. In computer graphics, research by Badler, Calvert, and the Thalmanns had resulted in animated models of the human body that could carry out realistic human movements and could be programmed using high-level input commands (such as "walk"). And research by Pelachaud had led to an animated face programmable at the level of facial action units and speech segments.

These three bodies of research led us to believe that it was time to connect an animated human figure with generators for hand gestures, facial expression, and speech with appropriate intonation. Our hope was that, ultimately, this figure could be used for human-computer interface, although the unreliability of the available speech recognition technology led us to first implement two humanoid figures that could converse with one another.

Not only was the research inspired by three fields but we hoped that it would in turn contribute to all of those fields. Indeed, once the implementation was complete, we realized that we had depended on an "additive" strategy for the interaction of verbal and nonverbal behaviors and that a "distributive" strategy would be preferable. That is, we initially believed that intonation might mark discourse structure, so might gesture, and so might gaze. In fact, when all three paraverbal channels are deployed to mark the same discourse function, the human figure looks like he is using his body too much. Similar issues arose in the subsequent inclusion of manual tasks during discourse; in this case, the hands were simultaneously required for both and conflicts inevitably arose. Subsequently, we have looked at how discourse structure might be marked by one of the verbal or nonverbal channels in a given context (Cassell and Prevost, in preparation). This insight led to a similar advance from the point of view of the computer graphics, namely, that commands sent to the eyes and hands should derive from the same control system, or Pat-Net (parallel transition network).

In subsequent research, we have turned to communicative gestures in other contexts (Noma and Badler 1997), to generalization of the conversational dialog planner, to a general-purpose modal theorem prover (Stone, to appear), and to using the multimodal humanlike agent for human-computer communication (Thorisson and Cassell 1996; Torres, Cassell, and Prevost 1997).

REFERENCES

Badler, N.; Phillips, C.; Webber, B. 1993. *Simulating Humans: Computer Graphics, Animation, and Control.* Oxford, England: Oxford University Press.

Calvert, T. 1991. Composition of Realistic Animation Sequences for Multiple Human Figures. In Badler, N., Barsky, B., and Zeltner, D. (eds.), *Making Them Move: Mechanics, Control and Animation of Articulated Figures*, 35–50. San Francisco: Morgan Kaufmann.

Cassell, J., and McNeill, D. 1991. Non-Verbal Imagery and the Poetics of Prose. *Poetics Today* 12(3): 375–404.

Cassell, J., and Prevost, S. (in preparation). Embodied Natural Language Generation: A Framework for Generating Speech and Gesture. *Computational Linguistics*.

Duncan, S. 1972. Some Signals and Rules for Taking Speaking Turns in Conversations. *Journal of Personality and Social Psychology* 23(2): 283–292.

Kendon, A. 1972. Some Relationships between Body Motion and Speech. In Siegman, A. W., and Pope, B. (eds.), *Studies in Dyadic Communication*. New York: Pergamon Press.

McNeill, D. 1992. *Hand and Mind: What Gestures Reveal about Thought*. Chicago: University of Chicago Press.

Noma, T., and Badler, N. 1997. A Virtual Human Presenter. In *Proceedings of IJCAI Workshop in Animated Interface Agents*, Nagoya, Japan, August.

Pelachaud, C.; Badler, N.; and Steedman, M. 1996. Generating Facial Expressions for Speech. *Cognitive Science* 20: 1–46.

Power, R. 1979. The Organisation of Purposeful Dialogues. *Linguistics* 17: 107–152.

Prevost, S., and Steedman, M. 1994. Specifying Intonation from Context for Speech Synthesis. *Speech Communication*. 15: 139–153.

Stone, M. (to appear). Representing Scope in Intuitionistic Deductions. *Theoretical Computer Science*.

Thorisson, K., and Cassell, J. 1996. Why Put an Agent in a Body: The Importance of Communicative Feedback in Human-Humanoid Dialogue. In *Proceedings of the Lifelike Computer Characters Workshop*, Snowbird, Utah, 44–45.

Torres, O.; Cassell, J.; and Prevost, S. 1997. Turn-Taking vs. Discourse Structure: How Best to Model Multimodal Conversation. In *Proceedings of the First International Conference on Human-Computer Conversation,* Bellagio, July.

SECTION VIII

Evaluation

This final section focuses on IUI evaluation. Community-wide evaluation using shared corpora and standardized tasks has been applied to several areas enabling intelligent interface technologies—most notably, community evaluations in speech and natural language processing (e.g., DARPA 1986, 1989, 1990, 1991, 1992; Hirschman and Thompson 1995), information extraction (e.g., MUC-3 1991, MUC-4 1992, MUC-5 1993, MUC-6 1995; Chinchor et al. 1993), and information retrieval (annual Text Retrieval and Evaluation Conferences (e.g., TREC-1)). Unfortunately, no community-wide evaluation measures, metrics, or methods have been developed or applied to IUIs. This section attempts to collect examples that might foster more rigorous development and widespread use of evaluation in the future. Ideally, evaluations should be user focused, feasible, and independent of specific task, as well as theory and technology neutral. Performed in a precise, comprehensive, and objective manner, evaluation can benchmark and chart progress, enable comparison of relative strengths and weaknesses of approaches, and thus serve as a guide for future investigations.

Evaluations can be either glass box (internal, component focused) or black box (comprehensive, end-to-end). Criteria for black-box evaluation include quantitative measures (e.g., time to perform tasks, accuracy of tasks, percent of interassessor agreement) as well as qualitative ones (e.g., user indication of utility, ease of use, naturalness). Glass-box evaluation can focus on specific knowledge sources or individual processing modules (e.g., multimedia input analysis, presentation layout) or higher-level tasks (e.g., including a user, data set, application, and task). It might focus on particular kinds of phenomena (e.g., ability to handle linguistic variability, graphical ambiguity). Another important aspect is whether the evaluation is measuring a metric or metrics against some benchmark or whether it is comparative (e.g., to human or other system performance). Ablation studies (e.g., removing or adding one interface module to measure effects) can prove valuable in gaining insight into the complex interrelationships of multifunctional interfaces. Important dimensions of the problem include considering human-human versus human-computer communication, spoken versus written communication, unimodal versus multimodal communication, and direct versus mediated communication. As the papers in this section illustrate, the evaluator and analyst have at their disposal a range of tools, such as Wizard-of-Oz experiments, simulations, and instrumentation of live environments to evaluate a variety of metrics using a range of evaluation methodologies (e.g., simulation based, corpus based, task based).

A variety of standard user interface evaluation approaches can serve as a starting point for IUI evaluation. Very low-cost approaches to evaluate interfaces include "heuristic evaluation," in which an expert physically or cognitively "walks through" the interface to perform a task (Nielsen and Molich 1990; Wharton et al. 1992). Although inexpensive, these techniques are ad hoc, providing neither a formal diagnostic nor a predictive model of usability. Subsequent work has looked at task-analytic, formal, or theoretical models, such as Goals, Operators, Methods, and Selectors (GOMS) (Gray et al. 1993), Cognitive Complexity Theory (CCT) (Kieras et al. 1995; Polson 1987), and Interacting Cognitive Subsystems (ICS) (Barnard 1987). For example, GOMS measures the amount of time an expert takes to execute a task without errors using an interface. CCT attempts to characterize the complexity of the interface for learning purposes by counting up production rules, and so on to attempt, for example, to measure acquiring interface mastery and transferability of skills from one interface to another. ICS attempts to model the mental resources the user employs in interacting with an interface. These efforts are the first steps toward methods that not only describe but prescribe interface functionality, enabling critique and/or synthesis of cognitively ergonomic interfaces with predictable user performance.

Unfortunately, these attempts currently focus on rather low-level events (e.g., keystrokes, mouse clicks) and don't address some of the more salient topics in IUIs, such as predicting the expected success of particular input devices, mixes of modality, distribution of initiative, or level of adaptivity in the interface. More recent efforts emphasize task-driven evaluation (Johnson et al. 1995). This is not to undervalue the potential benefits of such methods. An industrial application of GOMS by Bonnie John (1990) in a very time- and decision-constrained domain with no problem solving resulted in productivity gains saving millions of dollars. In fact, the first paper in this section attempts to provide a formal model for predicting the success of a broad range of pointing devices.

Evaluation has the potential not only to tell us where we are but to guide us where to go. In the first paper by Stuart Card, Jock Mackinlay, and George Robertson, the authors illustrate how human performance analysis and formal device modeling should play a direct role in the design of interfaces. Drawing on Mackinlay's earlier notions for display analysis (Section III of this volume), the authors formally model the semantics of input devices in an artificial language that includes primitives and composition operators (e.g., merge, connect). Using this language, represented (input) devices can be critiqued in terms of their expressiveness and effectiveness (e.g., footprint, pointing speed, precision, time to learn, error type, and frequency). As an illustration, the authors reason using their formalism to show when and why a mouse is a more effective input device than a head mouse in a text editing task, as well as how various muscle groups (e.g., neck, arm, and finger muscles) constrain the performance of input devices. Their approach enables designers to perform very low-cost design exploration (e.g., performance approximations) prior to expensive device prototyping.

Focusing specifically on natural language interfaces but with more general implications for intelligent interfaces, the second paper by Nils Dahlbäck, Arne Jönsson, and Lars Ahrenberg argues for the importance of Wizard-of-Oz studies to empirically discover the qualities of human-machine interaction as distinct from human-human communication. As in Oviatt's work described next, the authors utilize a simulation environment (ARNE-3), which includes a response editor with menu-accessible canned texts and templates, access to back-end systems, an editor for database query generation, and a time-stamped interaction log.

By collecting 150 dialogs using nine different real or simulated application domains with varying levels of "intelligence" and associated scenarios, the authors make several key observations. First, their human-machine dialogs have a simpler structure than human dialogs. Second, users and systems rely on "shared" conceptual models of the domain (in contrast to individualized user models). Third, users exhibit different behavior when dealing with computers versus humans (e.g., users are less likely to be polite in human-computer conversations, also implying increased use of indirect speech acts). On the other hand, some linguistic features—such as the type and frequency of anaphoric expressions used—change, and yet subjects do not appear to have these under conscious control. Some differences arise as a consequence of the channels available for communication (e.g., spoken versus written language).

In a calendar application, the authors were surprised to discover that, in spite of very slow response times, conversations remained coherent, including the use of anaphoric expressions. One speculation is that since both the dialog and calendar are displayed on the screen, this affects the dialog structure, indicating the need to perform evaluation that includes the entire multimedia interface context. The authors also observe that "speakers adapt to the perceived characteristics of [their] interlocutors."

The third paper by Sharon Oviatt describes an approach toward more robust interfaces by designing them to guide human input in a way that minimizes linguistic variability (e.g., disfluencies, prosody, and timing). Using high-fidelity simulations of applications, Oviatt describes a method to discover and quantify phenomena and to identify their causal basis through controlled experiments. Oviatt's experimental environment includes a programmer assistant who plays the role of the system and is enabled by automated simulation software that supports accurate and rapid responses by the assistant, including simulated errors to enhance realism. In this context, Oviatt investigates disfluent speech and hyperarticulation. Disfluencies include self-corrections, false starts, repetitions, and filled pauses (e.g., "uh," "um"). Oviatt notes that disfluencies occur at a higher rate in human-human than in human-computer speech. She further identifies that disfluencies increase with the length of utterances (possibly because of increased planning demands) but can be diminished by 30–40% by using structured interfaces that elicit shorter utterances. A sharp increase in disfluencies also occurs in spatial linguistic references, which can also be mitigated through the deployment of visual displays (e.g., maps) with a direct manipulation device (e.g., pen). Based on speech corpus analysis, Oviatt characterizes hyperarticulation by pause elongation (73% longer on average) and pause insertion (91% increase in frequency) as well as phonological alteration (e.g., first uttering "tweny" for 20 but subsequently clearly enunciating it as "twenty"). Oviatt outlines three methods to address hyperarticulate speech: (1) train recognizers on these phenomena, (2) design an error-handling recognizer to be invoked as part of a set of recognizers, and (3) avoid these altogether by effective design.

Using simulations, Oviatt identifies how users naturally switch input modalities to resolve failed recognition. She advocates using multimodal input to exploit this finding, enabling users to exploit their intuition for switching modalities but also taking advantage of the fact that the confusion matrices for alternate input modalities are complementary (e.g., spoken versus written). For example, in multimodal experiments, Oviatt found that users often select speech to describe sets of entities or to identify nonvisible entities, whereas simple graphic or gesture input is used to indicate locations, draw lines, and outline spatial areas (tasks difficult to perform with speech). In summary, Oviatt's methodology promises to facilitate the construction of spoken language systems through the use of simulation to identify the causal factors of speech variability, to model the drivers of their occurrence in the interface, and to exploit these factors to make interface design trade-offs that optimize system performance.

The final article by Marilyn Walker, Diane Litman, Candace Kamm, and Alicia Abella presents a general framework for evaluating spoken language systems that integrates many previous efforts in evaluation. Their framework, PARADISE (PARAdigm for Dialog System Evaluation), distinguishes evaluating what an agent and user accomplish from how they do it. PARADISE attempts to overcome limitations with current evaluation approaches, such as the inability to (1) generalize results to other tasks and environments, (2) calculate performance over subdialogs as well as dialogs, (3) correlate performance with external validation criteria and (4) normalize performance for task complexity. PARADISE uses a decision-theoretic approach that enables a weighted combination of performance measures, including task success as well as dialog efficiency (e.g., time, number of utterances) and dialog quality (e.g., response delay, inappropriate utterance ratio, repair ratio). A hierarchical task representation (using attribute value matrices) enables the calculation of performance of entire dialogs as well as subdialogs. Moreover, since the measures normalize for task complexity, agents performing different tasks can be compared. The paper illustrates the application of PARADISE in comparing the performance of two agents in a train timetable task.

For a variety of reasons, evaluation of IUIs is more complex than that of standard interfaces. Whereas intelligent interfaces are more active participants in an interaction (e.g., possibly critiquing, completing, or refining the actions performed by the human user), this increased participation adds new dimensions of evaluation issues, such as proper locus of control, task sharing, and the need for informative feedback to keep the user aware of what the machine is doing. All of this complexity needs to be balanced with the cost of performing evaluation, so a particular challenge is how we can develop and disseminate cost-effective evaluation methods and tools to support the designer and ultimately to enhance the experience for the user.

REFERENCES

Barnard, P. 1987. Cognitive Resources and Learning of Human-Computer Dialogues. In Carroll, J. M. (ed.), *Interfacing Thought: Cognitive Aspects of Human-Computer Interaction*. Cambridge, MA: MIT Press.

Chinchor, N.; Hirschman, L.; and Lewis, D. 1993. Evaluating Message Understanding Systems. *Computational Linguistics* 19(3) September: 409–450.

DARPA. 1986. *Proceedings of the DARPA Speech Recognition Workshop*. SAIC-86/1546.

DARPA. 1989. *Proceedings of the Second DARPA Speech and Natural Language Workshop*, Cape Cod, MA, October. San Francisco: Morgan Kaufmann.

DARPA. 1990. *Proceedings of the Third DARPA Speech and Natural Language Workshop*, Hidden Valley, PA, June. San Francisco: Morgan Kaufmann.

DARPA. 1991. *Proceedings of the Fourth DARPA Speech and Natural Language Workshop*, Pacific Grove, CA, February. San Francisco: Morgan Kaufmann.

DARPA. 1992. *Proceedings of the Fifth DARPA Speech and Natural Language Workshop*, Harriman, NY, February. San Francisco: Morgan Kaufmann.

Gray, W. D.; John, B. E.; and Atwood, M. E. 1993. Project Ernestine: A Validation of GOMS for Prediction and Explanation of Real-World Task Performance. *Human-Computer Interaction*, 8(3): 237–209.

Hirschman, L., and Thompson, H. 1995. Overview of Evaluation in Speech and Natural Language Processing; Introduction to Chapter 13. In Cole, R., Mariani, J., Liberman, M., Uszkoreit, H., Zaenen, A., and Zue, V. (eds.), *Evaluation in the Joint EC-US Survey of the State of the Art in Human Language Technology*. (*http://www.cse.ogi.edu /CSLU/HLTsurvey/HLTsurvey.html*)

John, B. 1990. Extensions of GOMS Analysis to Expert Performance Requiring Perception of Dynamic Visual and Auditory Information. In *Proceedings of ACM CHI '90 Conference on Human Factors in Computing Systems*, 107–115.

Johnson, P.; Johnson, H.; and Wilson, S. 1995. Rapid Prototyping of User Interfaces Driven by Task Models. In Carroll, J. (ed.), *Scenario-Based Design: Envisioning Work and Technology in System Development*, London: John Wiley & Sons. 209–246.

Kieras, D.; Wood, S.; and Meyer, D. 1995. Predictive Engineering Models Using the EPIC Architecture for a High-Performance Task. In *ACM CHI '95 Conference on Human Factors in Computing Systems*, 11–18.

MUC-3. 1991. *Proceedings of the Third Message Understanding Conference (MUC-3)*, San Diego, CA, May. San Francisco: Morgan Kaufmann.

MUC-4. 1992. *Proceedings of the Fourth Message Understanding Conference (MUC-4)*, McLean, VA, June. San Francisco: Morgan Kaufmann.

MUC-5. 1993. *Proceedings of the Fifth Message Understanding Conference (MUC-5)*, Baltimore, MD, August. San Francisco: Morgan Kaufmann.

MUC-6. 1995. *Proceedings of the Sixth Message Understanding Conference (MUC-6)*, Columbia, MD, November 6–8. Advanced Research Projects Agency Information Technology Office. San Francisco: Morgan Kaufmann.

Nielsen, J., and Molich, R. 1990. Heuristic Evaluation of User Interfaces. In *Proceedings of ACM CHI '90 Conference on Human Factors in Computing Systems*, 249–256.

Polson, P. 1987. A Quantitative Theory Of Human-Computer Interaction. In Carroll, J. M. (ed.), *Interfacing Thought: Cognitive Aspects Of Human-Computer Interaction*. Cambridge, MA: MIT Press.

TREC-1. 1993. First Text REtrieval Conference (TREC-1), NIST, Harmon, Donna K. (ed.). NIST Special Publication 500–207, March. (See also TREC-2 (500-215, March 1994), TREC-3 (500-525, April 1995), and TREC-4 (500-536, October 1996).)

Wharton, C.; Bradford, J.; Jeffries, R.; and Franzke, M. 1992. Applying Cognitive Walkthrough to More Complex User Interfaces: Experiences, Issues and Recommendations. In *Proceedings of CHI'92 Conference on Human Factors in Computing Systems*, Monterey, CA, 381–388. New York: ACM Press.

A Morphological Analysis of the Design Space of Input Devices

STUART K. CARD, JOCK D. MACKINLAY, and GEORGE G. ROBERTSON
Xerox Palo Alto Research Center

The market now contains a bewildering variety of input devices for communication from humans to computers. This paper discusses a means to systematize these devices through morphological design space analysis, in which different input device designs are taken as points in a parametrically described design space. The design space is characterized by finding methods to generate and test design points. In a previous paper, we discussed a method for generating the space of input device designs using primitive and compositional movement operators. This allowed us to propose a taxonomy of input devices. In this paper, we summarize the generation method and explore the use of device footprint and Fitts's law as a test. We then use calculations to reason about the design space. Calculations are used to show why the mouse is a more effective device than the headmouse and where in the design space there is likely to be a more effective device than the mouse.

Categories and Subject Descriptors: H.1.2 [**Models and Principles**]: User/Machine Systems—*human factors* J.6 [**Computer Applications**]: Computer-Aided Engineering—*computer-aided design*

General Terms: Design, Human Factors

Additional Key Words and Phrases: Design knowledge systematization, design rationale, design space, input devices, morphological analysis, semantics

1. INTRODUCTION

Human-machine interface technology has been developed to the point where it is appropriate to systematize existing research results and craft into a body of engineering and design knowledge. A case in point is the design of input devices. A bewildering variety of such devices now exists on the market, including typewriter keyboards, mice, headmice, pens and tablets, dialboxes, Polhemus sensors, gloves, and body suits. How can we make sense of this variety? How can we identify promising opportunities for new design? As part of their development, most engineering disciplines organize the designs that have emerged in terms of abstractions that give insight into the design space (e.g., [32]). This insight allows individual designs to be grouped into families, aids in the teaching of cumulated knowledge, suggests new designs, and may form the basis of toolkits for composing individual designs. In this paper we continue the development of a set of abstractions that provide one method for bringing order to knowledge about input devices.

Previous work on systematizing human-machine input devices has provided three lines of development: toolkits, taxonomies, and performance studies. We argue that a fourth line of development, a morphological design space analysis, can be used to integrate the results of this previous work.

Toolkits. User interface toolkits or user interface management systems help with a wide range of problems, including the construction, run-time execution, and post-run-time analysis of a user interface [33]. They may help systematize input device knowledge by providing a library of prebuilt input device modules [25, 27], architecture and specification techniques for combining these modules [2, 34], or postprocessing analysis tools [24]. Sometimes, as in [2], they even provide architectural models of input device interactions. But the device models implicit in user interface toolkits sketch only a limited picture of the design space of input devices and their properties. Even for the construction of interfaces, they present interface designers with many design alternatives but do little to help with the design decisions themselves. In order to achieve a systematic framework for input devices, toolkits need to be supported by technical abstractions about the user, the devices themselves, and the task they are used to perform.

Taxonomies. Two recent attempts have been made to provide taxonomies of the design space of input devices. Foley, Wallace, and Chan [15] focused on computer graphics subtasks. They classified input devices under the graphics subtasks they were capable of performing (e.g., the tablet and the light pen are capable of character recognition). They also reviewed experimental evaluations of input devices. Buxton and Baecker [4, 7] proposed a taxonomy of input devices classified according to the physical properties and the number of spatial dimensions they sense. The limitation of the Foley-Wallace-Chan scheme is that the categories, while reasonable, are somewhat ad hoc, and there is no attempt at defining a notion of completeness for the design space. The limitation of the Buxton and Baecker scheme is that it only includes continuous devices. In addition to the two taxonomies, Bleser and Sibert have designed a tool for selecting interaction techniques based on their characteristics [6]. Rather than abstracting the design space, the goal of their tool is to include most of the factors, including the physical packaging of an input device, in a design tool. The importance of attempts to make taxonomies of input devices is that they make progress in helping us to understand the design space—not only the devices that exist and their relationships, but also potential devices that might be invented.

Performance studies. Studies have been made of human performance with pointing devices. English and Engelbart [12] studied several devices and found the mouse the fastest device. Card, English, and Burr [9] confirmed these empirical results and discovered that pointing speed with the mouse is governed by Fitts's law [14] with a bandwidth similar to that of the hand. Subsequent studies have empirically compared speed and preference of various devices and confirmed and improved the use of Fitts's law [1, 13, 15, 17, 19, 20, 36]. Unfortunately, these studies have not always agreed, largely because some studies have not attempted to disentangle task, subject, and human performance variables. The performance studies have, however, established abstractions, including Fitts's relation [20], which, in turn, expresses the linkage between device performance and fundamental performance parameters of the human.

Morphological design space analysis. In this paper, we begin to relate this previous work by employing another technique, morphological design space analysis, in which we seek to comprehend different input device designs as points in a parametrically described design space. The goal is to find abstractions both for generating the design space and for testing the designs contained therein. In order to represent the designs as points in this design space, some parametric representation is determined that can represent the central idea of particular designs. The essence of this technique has previously been used by a small number of researchers/designers in the analytical study of other design spaces. Bertin [5] used a similar method in his study of the semiology of graphics and applied it to the graphical design of diagrams, networks, and maps. Zwicky [37] used a similar method to generate the design space of jet engines. In both cases, the result was insight into the properties of the design space as well as into the production of novel designs. Mackinlay [21, 22] applied the technique to human-computer interfaces. He formalized Bertin's analysis and used it to generate graphic designs automatically for the presentation of statistical data. Human psychophysical data were used to select from among those designs that accurately expressed the data, those that were the most effective in communicating it. Several researchers have since built on Mackinlay's analysis, either to extend it to new domains or to add more analysis of the user's tasks and goals (e.g., [11, 30]).

Mackinlay, Card, and Robertson [23] applied the morphological approach to the analysis of input devices. They built on results of the taxonomies to propose a parametric representation to be used in generating points in the input device design space. This paper continues that analysis, exploring how results from input device performance studies can be integrated on the test side of the generate-and-test paradigm to give additional insight into the design space. First, we summarize the representation of the design space, and then we discuss how figures of merit might be associated with it.

2. GENERATING THE DESIGN SPACE

Let us reflect, for a moment, on the role of input devices. An input device is part of the means used to engage in dialogue with a machine. Unlike human-human conversation, the dialogue is between fundamentally dissimilar agents, in terms of both perception and processing. Furthermore, it takes place under conditions (e.g., the persistence of displays) that are different from the evanescent, sequential, oral conversation that is often taken as the model for communication. Instead of words, the user may move the mouse and press buttons, and the machine may show highlighted animated diagrams.

The design of human-machine dialogues is, at least in part, the design of artificial languages for this communication. Mackinlay [21, 22], in work on the automatic generation of displays, suggested that each display could be thought of as a sentence in a formal language and that such sentences could be analyzed as to their ability to transmit an intended semantic meaning from the machine to the user. In the case of input devices, we can analyze the manipulations of an input device as sentences in a formal language of communication. In particular, we can try to analyze the sentences that are possible with an input device in terms of combinatoric operators. What are the primitive moves? What are the composition operators for combining primitive moves into complex sentences of moves? The combination of primitive moves and composition operators gives us a parametric abstract representation that represents the space of sentences it is possible to transmit. In a sense, this generates the design space of input devices. Input devices are those devices that allow some portion of these potential sentences actually to be realized and communicated from human to machine. Of course, the human has a communicative intention. This communicative intention must be encoded into the simple sentences of input device movements (the coding may be variable, depending on the situation of the moment) and then decoded by the application. In our analysis, we make the idealized assumption that functions of the application program express the semantics of the interaction. A radio, for example, may have a function *increment-volume-to* (*loudness*). A possible human intention may be expressible in terms of invoking this function. The job of an input device, such as a volume control knob, is to allow the user to make some combination of moves such that the moves can be interpreted as actually invoking the desired function with the desired parameters.

Conceptually, the most general case of human-machine interaction is the case of a human interacting with an embedded computer (e.g., the autopilot on an airplane). Such an interaction can be modeled as the interaction in an artificial language among at least three agents [8, 31]:

(1) a human,
(2) a user dialogue machine, and
(3) an application.

We can trace the semantics of an input device by tracing the mappings from human action through mappings inherent in the device and finally into changes in the parameters of the application.

There are two key ideas in modeling the language of input device interaction:

(1) a *primitive movement vocabulary*, and
(2) a set of *composition operators*.

The movement vocabulary gives the elementary sentences that can be expressed in the artificial language. The composition operators give methods of combining this vocabulary into a combinatorically richer set.

2.1 Primitive Movement Vocabulary

We begin with the observation inspired by Baecker and Buxton [4] that

> *basically, an input device is a transducer from the physical properties of the world into logical parameters of an application.*

Formally, we represent the input device as a six-tuple,

$$\langle \mathbf{M}, \mathbf{In}, \mathbf{S}, \mathbf{R}, \mathbf{Out}, \mathbf{W} \rangle,$$

where

- —**M** is a manipulation operator,
- —**In** is the input domain,
- —**S** is the current state of the device,
- —**R** is a resolution function mapping from the input domain set to the output domain set,
- —**Out** is the output domain set, and
- —**W** is a general-purpose set of device properties that describe additional aspects of how a device works (perhaps using production systems).

Generally, we assume somewhat idealized devices without stickiness, significant lags, noise, linearity problems, etc. But noise and linearity could be modeled through the **R** input-to-output mapping, and lag could be modeled through the **W** work properties mechanism.

Table I lists the various manipulation operators, **M**, possible for an input device. They are an extension of the physical properties suggested by Baecker and Buxton [4]. They represent all combinations of linear and rotary, absolute and relative, and position and force. Although other input devices are possible (based, say, on speech or heat), virtually all input devices use some combination of the properties listed in Table I.

Figure 1 illustrates the description of a simple set of radio controls, using our primitive movement vocabulary. The volume knob is rotated about the Z axis (conventionally assumed to be normal to the panel surface). It is a continuous device that maps using the identity operator from an input domain set of 0–270 degrees into the same set. The selector knob, on the other hand, maps from the set consisting of 0–90 degrees into the ordered sequence $\langle 0, 45, 90 \rangle$ degrees. Finally, the station knob is a dial that moves any number of turns to the right or to the left. It is presumed to connect to a slider that moves back and forth between 0 and 5 inches. The station knob is a relative device. It keeps turning after the slider is against one side and no longer moves. But, if the knob direction is reversed, then the slider reverses immediately. The volume knob, the selection switch, and the slider each go through another mapping into the parameters of an application.

Table I. Physical Properties Used by Input Devices

	Linear	Rotary
Position		
Absolute	Position **P**	Rotation **R**
Relative	Movement **dP**	Delta rotation **dR**
Force		
Absolute	Force **F**	Torque **T**
Relative	Delta force **dF**	Delta torque **dT**

2.2 Composition Operators

The example in Figure 1 also illustrates the notion of a composition operator. The output domain set of the station knob is mapped into the input domain set of the slider. This sort of composition operator is called a connection. There are three composition operators:

(1) merge composition,
(2) layout composition, and
(3) connect composition.

These operations are illustrated in Figure 2 for the mouse. *Merge composition* is the combination of two devices such that the resulting input domain set is the cross product of the input domains of the two devices. A mouse can be thought of as the merge composition of two orthogonal one-dimensional sliders. *Layout composition* is the collocation of two devices on different places of a common panel or space. The three buttons of a mouse and the XY sensors are all four layout-composed together to form the mouse. *Connect composition* occurs when the output domain of one device is mapped onto the input domain of another device. For the mouse, the output is connected to the input for the screen cursor. The screen cursor, of course, is not actually a physical device. This illustrates another point about the modeling scheme, namely, that devices do not have to be physical devices, but can also be virtual devices implemented in software, such as the cursor.

The modeling scheme uses a formalized notation, which we have not reproduced here, to keep track of mappings of movements of the input devices (signals, really) through various transformations into application-defined meanings. See [23] for more details.

2.3 The Design Space for Input Devices

The design space for input devices is basically the set of possible combinations of the composition operators with the primitive vocabulary. We graph a simplified partial visualization of this space in Figure 3. This is our equivalent to Foley, Wallace, and Chan's [15] and Buxton's [7] classifications. A

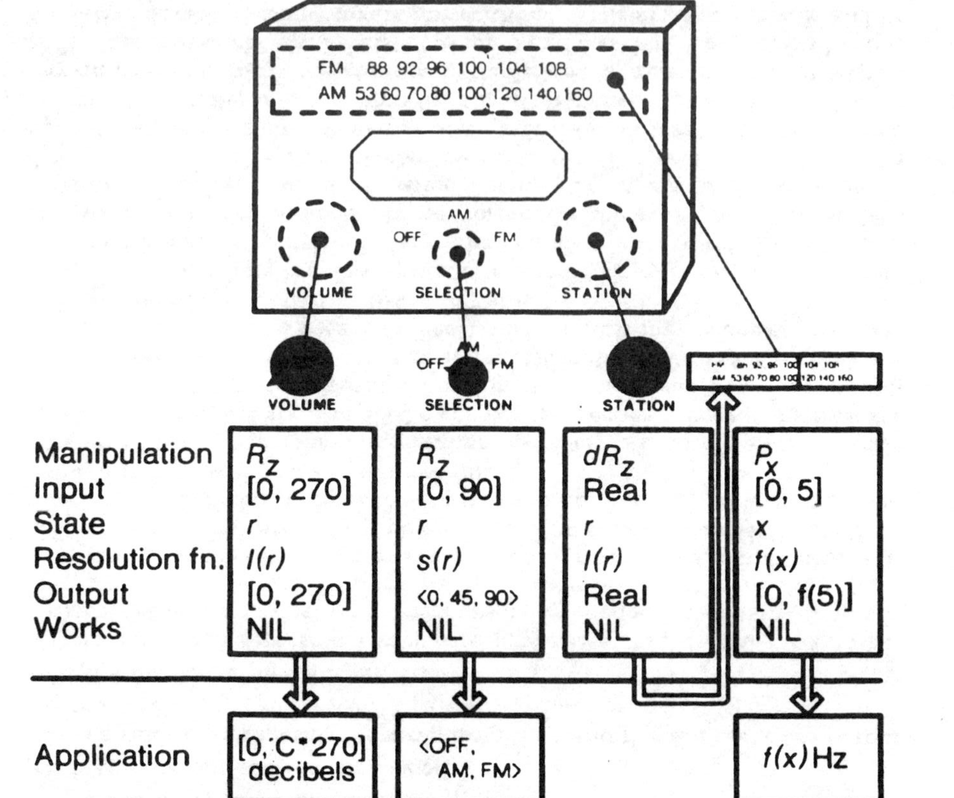

Fig. 1. Analysis of a simple radio. Two rotational devices are connected directly to the application. The third rotational device is connected to a positional device, which is then connected to the application.

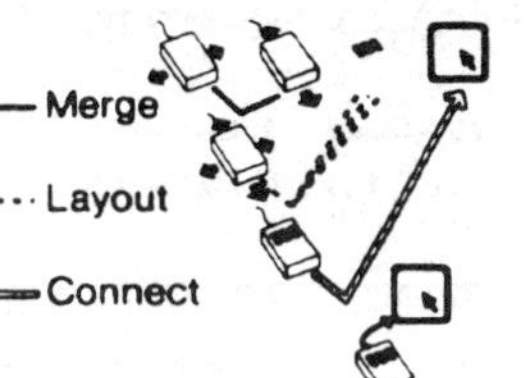

Fig. 2. Composition operators used in describing the mouse.

device is represented in the figure as a set of circles connected together. Each circle represents a transducer in the device, plotted according to the canonical physical property it transduces. Each line indicates a composition operator: connection composition (double-line arrow), layout composition (dotted

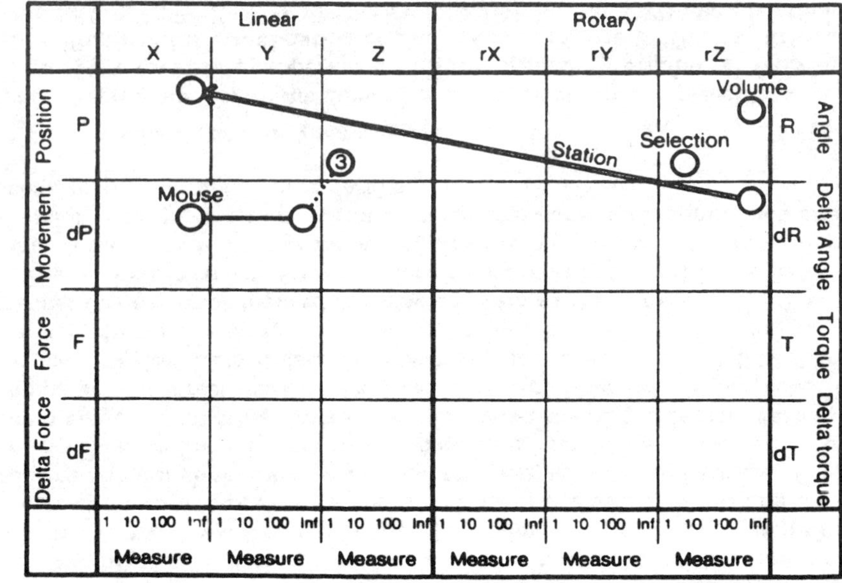

Fig. 3. Input device taxonomy. The diagram describes an input device taxonomy that is based on the analysis presented in this paper. Circles are used to indicate that a device senses one of the physical properties shown on the vertical axis along one of the linear or rotary dimensions shown on the horizontal axis. For example, the circle representing the radio volume control indicates a device that senses an angle around the Z axis. The position in a column indicates the number of values that are sensed (i.e., the measure of the domain set). For example, the circle representing the selection control represents a discrete device. Lines are used to connect the circles of composite devices. A black line represents a merge composition (such as the X and Y components of the mouse). The dashed line represents a layout composition (such as the three buttons on a mouse, represented by a circle with a 3 in it to indicate identical devices).

line), or merge composition (black line). It is important to note that each group of linked circles in Figure 3, which collectively represent a device, is only a single point in a very large design space and that variants in devices are possible (e.g., in the input or output domains or the mappings), which are below the level of detail visualized in the figure. These variants are, however, describable in the more formal notation of [23].

In Figure 3 we have plotted the devices of our radio example and the mouse to illustrate their use. The radio volume knob is in the cell for sensors of angles relative to the Z axis. It is located on the right side of the cell, showing that it is continuous. The selection knob is similar but is located nearer the left side, showing that it takes just a few values. The station knob is located in the cell for relative angle and is connected to a slider for the tuning mechanism. A mouse is depicted in the figure as a circle on X movement, a circle on Y movement, and a circle containing the number 3 on Z positioning. This indicates that the mouse is a layout composition of four diagram. Of course, many of these devices might be undesirable, but the point is that Figure 3 is a sufficiently rich depiction of the design space for input devices that it can be used both to classify nearly all existing devices and to generate ideas for new devices not yet invented. In particular, we have used our model of the input device design space to help design novel egocentric motion devices for virtual 3-D environments [23, 29].

3. TESTING POINTS IN THE DESIGN SPACE

Up to this point, we have described how to model the space of input device designs, including methods to help generate the space. We have shown that we can distinguish systematically among devices used in other taxonomies. But we also need to be able to test points in the design space in order to characterize regions of it. We need to be able to utilize results from performance studies of input devices. Following Mackinlay [21, 22], the mappings implied by specific input device designs can be evaluated according to two basic criteria: (1) *expressiveness* (the input conveys exactly and only the intended meaning) and (2) *effectiveness* (the input conveys the intended meaning with felicity).

In some design spaces, expressiveness is a major concern. For example, in the design of visual displays it may be relatively easy to generate a display that conveys an intended meaning, but difficult to prevent the display from conveying some unintended meaning as well (e.g., an arbitrarily ordered set of bars on the bar chart visually conveys an ordering relationship among the bars that is not intended). In the design of input devices, an expressiveness problem arises when the number of elements in the **Out** set does not match the number of elements in the **In** set to which it is connected. If the projection of the **Out** set includes elements that are not in the **In** set, the user can specify illegal values; and if the **In** set includes values that are not in the projection, the user cannot specify legal values. Perhaps the user wishes to convey the meaning of the system "Select pixel $x = 105$, $y = 32$" with a device that has a resolution of $\frac{1}{4}$ in (as for some touch panels). The user will not be able to express the request exactly, and there will be some loss of expressiveness, serious or not depending on the situation.

More interesting for input devices is effectiveness, and this is the aspect on which we will dwell. Assuming that it is possible to express the user's intention in a sentence in the repertoire of the input device, there is still the question of how well this can be done in terms of speed, errors, or other figures of merit for an input device (in a particular task for a particular user). Possible figures of merit include the following:

—*Desk footprint*. The amount of area consumed by the device on the desk.

—*Pointing speed* (really, *device bandwidth*). How quickly the device can be used to select a target. In addition to just the simple time difference, devices that are slower than the user's unaided hand put stress on the user, because the slower pointing time may reflect more difficult guidance by the user (e.g., error correction) and may make the user have to think about

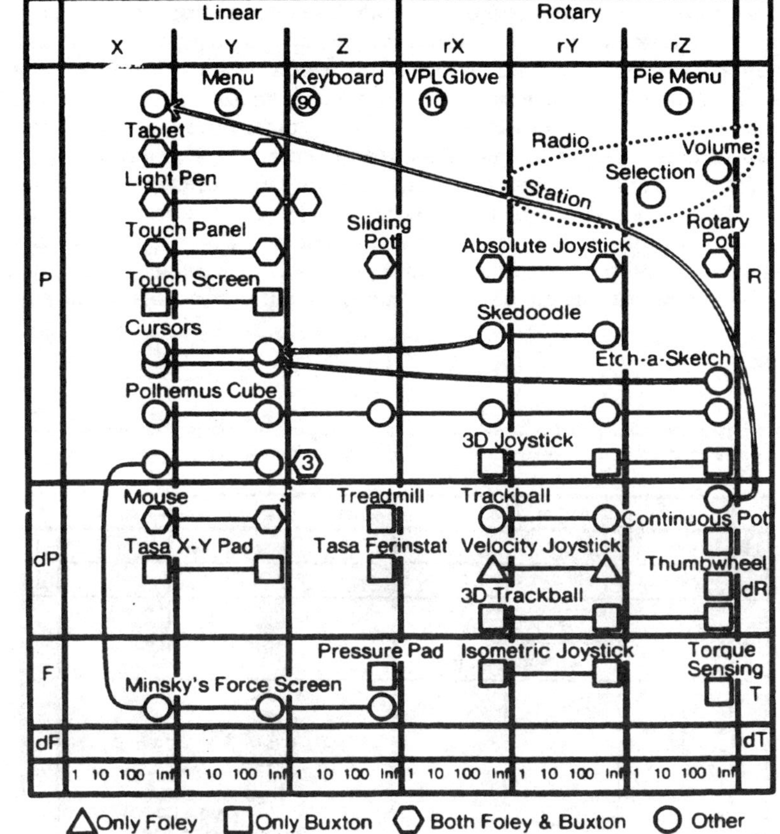

Fig. 4. A broad range of input devices plotted on the taxonomy. Devices previously classified by Foley, Wallace, and Chan [15] and by Baecker and Buxton [4, 7] are indicated by triangles, squares, and hexagons. Hexagons indicate devices included in both previous taxonomies. Other devices, indicated by circles, include the radio devices described previously and some unusual devices to demonstrate the generality of the taxonomy.

devices: one device that is itself the merge composition of two elementary devices sensing change in X and Y, and three other devices that are simple buttons. The placement of the X and Y circles to the right of the column indicates nearly continuous resolution. The location of the button circles to the left indicates controls with only two states.

To demonstrate the coverage of the taxonomy, we have reclassified the devices listed by Foley, Wallace, and Chan [15] and by Buxton and Baecker [4, 7] (see Figure 4). With the exception of voice, we have been able to position all of the devices considered so far. Furthermore, it is possible to generate potential new devices by placing circles in various cells of the operating the device consciously rather than unconsciously using the tool to manipulate the environment.

—*Pointing precision*. How small a target can conveniently be selected with the device.

—*Errors*. There are a number of interrelated metrics for errors: percentage of times a target is missed, the end-point distance from the target, and various statistical measures of distributions of these, such as the root mean squared error of a drawn line compared to a model line.

—*Time to learn*. The amount of practice required before a user is proficient with a device.

—*Time to grasp the device*. How long it takes to engage the device if the hands are doing something else.

—*User preference*. How well users like the device and whether they prefer it to other devices.

—*Cost*. The retail cost.

These figures of merit include human performance measures such as speed and errors, as well as pragmatic concerns such as desktop footprint, panel space, or cost. To illustrate how we can annotate the design space of input devices (and, in particular, the representation of it given in Figure 4), we discuss two of these figures of merit: footprint and bandwidth. It is footprint we choose because it is concrete and straightforward and, therefore, makes an easy example. It also illustrates how nonperformance pragmatic concerns are of importance.

3.1 Footprint

An input device requires a certain amount of space on a desk: its footprint. Desk space is a small, finite resource; hence, a small footprint is better than a large one. The actual footprint of some devices such as the mouse depends on the sequence of actions in an application. But, to estimate the space required, we can use an extreme task.

As an example, compare the relative desk footprint of different input devices for pull-down menus on the original Macintosh (12″ screen) and on the SuperMac (19″ screen). The mouse must be able to move from any place on the screen to the menu bar, which is at the extreme top of the screen. The footprint is, therefore, an image of virtually the entire screen in the movement of the device. Table II estimates the footprint for various devices. Three of the devices (light pen, on-screen touch pad, and rotary potentiometers) require no additional footprint (assuming that no footprint is needed to store the lightpen and that the potentiometers mount on the case). Two of the devices (trackball and joystick) have small footprints that are independent of screen size. Two of the devices (mouse and tablet) have footprints that vary dramatically as the screen size increases from 12″ to 19″. The *C:D* ratio for the mouse and tablet in Table II is the "control-display ratio." The traditional control-display ratio for a mouse is 1:2; that is, for each inch of control (mouse) movement, the display (cursor) moves two inches.

Table II. Footprint Estimates for Various Input Devices

Device	Footprint (in^2) 12″ screen	19″ screen
Light pen	0	0
On-screen touch pad	0	0
Rotary pots	0	0
Headmouse	0	0
Trackball (2″ × 2″)	4	4
Joystick (2″ × 2″)	4	4
Mouse (C : D = 1 : 2)	4	43
Tablet (C : D = 1 : 1)	69	173

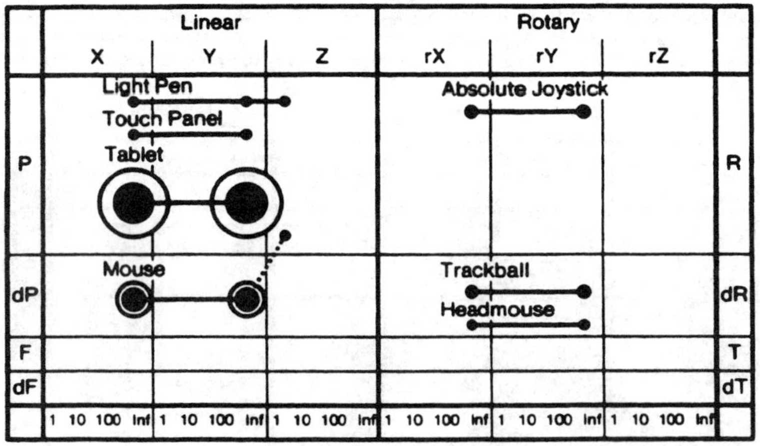

Fig. 5. Footprint of input devices for Macintosh pull-down menus. The filled circles describe the device footprint for the 12″ screen, and the open circles describe the device footprint for the 19″ screen.

In Figure 5 we have annotated our depiction of the input device design space, by using the area of the circle representing each sensor to indicate the footprint required. The filled circles are for a 12″ screen, and the open circles are for a 19″ screen. Black dots represent no additional footprint. Several facts about the design space of potential devices are evident from the diagram: (1) The tablet and the mouse are very expensive in footprint relative to other devices. (2) Going from 12″ to 19″ displays causes a major increase in footprint size for the mouse and tablet (unless the control-display ratio is changed). In fact, this dramatic increase in footprint for the mouse as a function of screen size is behind two innovations in mouse design: One of these, powermice (the control-display ratio changes as a function of velocity),

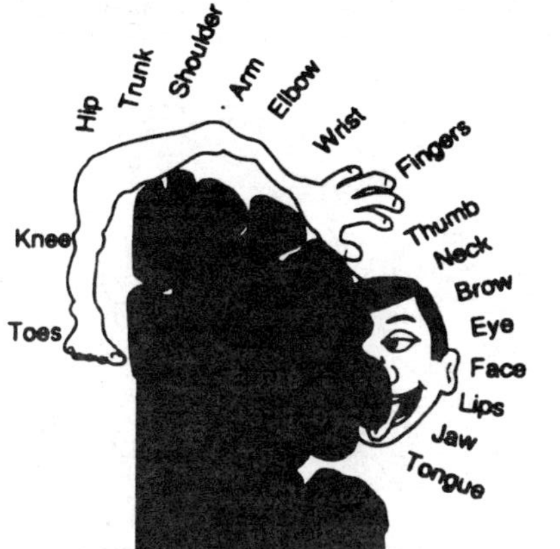

Fig. 6. Motor regions of the cerebral cortex, after [26].

sacrifices pointing speed to get a smaller footprint [16]. The other, higher-resolution mice, uses an improved sensor to get a smaller footprint without sacrificing speed.

3.2 Bandwidth

Now let us turn to another figure of merit, bandwidth. It is usually desirable for an input device to be as fast to use as possible, but speed of use is actually a joint product of all three elements in our model: (1) the human, (2) the application, and (3) the device. For the moment, we restrict ourselves to tasks that involve pointing at a target with a continuous device.

The speed and error performance of a particular device may depend on a number of subtleties such as the relationship between the geometry of the device and the geometry of the hand or coefficients of friction. But we can give a rough characterization of input device design effectiveness in terms of the following:

(1) human—the bandwidth of the human muscle group to which the input device transducer is attached;

(2) application—the precision requirements of the task to be done with the device; and

(3) device—the effective bandwidth of the input device.

Bandwidth of the human muscle group. Some groups of muscles can be controlled more finely than other groups of muscles. Figure 6 shows that more of the motor cortex is devoted to some groups of muscles (such as the fingers) than to others (such as the neck). Undoubtedly, the determinants of muscle performance are more complex than just simple cortical area; still, roughly speaking, those groups of muscles having a large area devoted to them are heuristically promising places to connect with input device transducers if we desire high performance. Of course, there are several factors to be taken into account (e.g., promising muscle groups may already be occupied with other tasks or be physically or socially inconvenient, or the task may only require crude control), but the point is that the muscle group that is connected to an input device may impose inherent bandwidth limitations on that device.

Figure 7 shows data from experiments by Langolf [18] and by Radwin, Vanderheiden, and Lin [28]. Subjects in Langolf's experiment performed a peg insertion task under the microscope for the curves marked finger and wrist, and the Fitts's dotting task [14] for the curve marked arm. Langolf observed the approximate muscle groups being used and made the observation that different muscle groups gave rise to different Fitts's law slopes. Subjects in Radwin, Vanderheiden, and Lin's experiment used a headmouse to select targets on a CRT. The figure plots the movement times observed in both experiments as a function of Fitts's Index of Difficulty,

$$MovementTime = K + (I_M \cdot I_D), \tag{1}$$

where K is a constant that depends on how the target is selected and how the trial is begun, I_M is the reciprocal of the bandwidth of the device, and I_D is the Fitts's Index of Difficulty,

$$I_D = \log_2 \frac{2D}{S}.$$

D is the distance to the target, and S is the width of the target. Bandwidth is measured in bits/s. The convenient units for I_M are ms/bit. Figure 7 gives a rough index for the bandwidth of different parts of the body.

Precision requirements of tasks. The user will deploy the input device in subtasks of the application. We can characterize an application by listing a selection of these tasks and by analyzing input device performance relative to this set of tasks. Table III gives some values from such an analysis for simple text editing. The target size (column (1) in the table) ranges from 5.5 cm for a typical paragraph to 0.069 cm for a period. Associated with each task, we have shown a calculation of Fitts's Index of Difficulty, I_D, in column (2). A technical difficulty is that eq. (1) has been shown to be inaccurate for pointing tasks with I_D below about 2 bits (very easy tasks) [35]. We can overcome this problem by using Welford's more accurate method for computing I_D:

$$I_D = \log_2 \left(\frac{D}{S} + .5 \right).$$

I_D ranges from 1.18 bits for pointing to a paragraph to 7.14 bits for pointing to a period. Since we do not have specific data on target distance, the calculation assumes a typical distance of half way from the center of a 19" screen to the side edge, that is, A = 9.7 cm. In a more refined analysis, actual empirical data could be used or different assumptions could be made.

Device bandwidth. Now consider the effectiveness of an input device for a given application. The input device is connected to a certain set of human

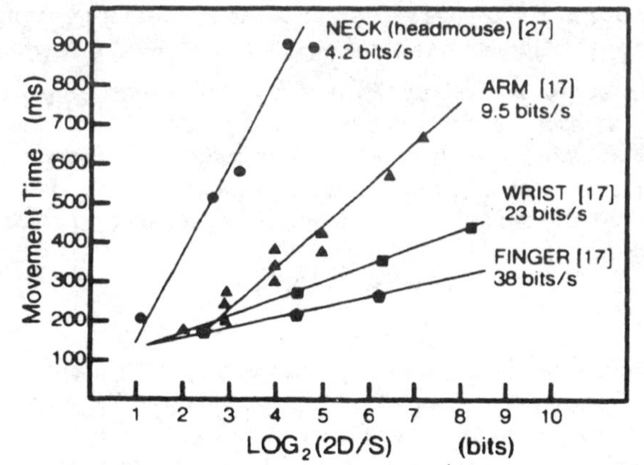

Fig. 7. Summary of Fitts's dotting experiments [18, 28].

Table III Fitts's Law Slopes for Various Devices

Target	(1) Size S^a (cm)	(2) I_D (bits)	Movement time (3) Mouse (ms)	(4) Headmouse (ms)	(5) Fingers (ms)
Paragraph[b]	5.5	1.18	113	280	30
Word[c]	2.3	2.24	220	540	56
Character[d]	0.41	4.59	440	1100	115
Period[e]	0.069	7.14	690	1710	179

[a] Based on 74 pixel/in. = 29.1 pixel/cm, as displayed on a Macintosh screen [3, p. 214].
[b] Estimated size based on 10 lines × 16 pixel/line = 160 pixels/29.1 pixel cm^{-1} = 5.5 cm.
[c] Based on 5.5 characters/word = 60 pixels.
[d] Based on character n = 12 pixels. Times Roman 12-point font on a Macintosh. (Examined and counted in MacDraw II.)
[e] Based on a 2-pixel-wide dot.

muscles. This determines an upper bound on the bandwidth of the device (as indexed by the Fitts's law slope). Of course, the device itself can degrade the achievable performance. Currently, empirical testing is required to check whether this is the case. But the performance of many devices is more or less set by the muscle groups with which the device is designed to connect. For the moment, we assume that this is so in order to compute the inherent limitations imposed on a device by the muscle group to which it is connected.

We would like to use Figure 7 to characterize a device according to what tasks are easy for it to perform. But, first, three technical details must be addressed. The lines in Figure 7 have intercepts near, but not exactly at, the origin. This reflects small details of the experimental conditions such as how the target is selected and how a trial is started. These vary slightly from line to line and make comparisons among the muscle groups more difficult. Therefore, for the purpose of our calculation, we set each of the intercepts exactly to zero. Second, since Langolf's measurements [18] were made using a serial task and since we are interested in discrete tasks, we have to adjust for the 2 ~ 3 bits/s higher value in continuous tasks [20]. We have, therefore, added 2 bits/s Langolf's measurements for the arm, wrist, and fingers. Third, we wish to adjust the slopes to use Welford's formulation of the Fitts's Index of Difficulty. Mackenzie's reanalysis of Fitts's data ([19, Table 2]) suggests that this would reduce the measured bandwidth by 0.3 ~ 0.4 bit/s. However, since this is relatively small in comparison to the adjustment already made for a discrete task, no additional adjustment seems warranted. The lines in Figure 8 now reflect our best estimate of bandwidth differences among the muscles. These normalizations are compatible with direct measurements on the mouse [9], which have been added to Figure 8.[1]

We now return to the question of which tasks are easy and which are hard to perform with a device. Of course, tasks with a high Fitts's Index of Difficulty are harder and those with a low Index of Difficulty are easier, but just as we can talk about days that are hot and days that are cold and reference these terms to approximate regions on the Fahrenheit temperature scale, we can find approximate regions on the Fitts's Index of Difficulty scale. We start by estimating the size thresholds where pointing tasks become easy and hard. The mouse is currently the dominant pointing device, so it makes a convenient comparative reference point. Subjectively, pointing to a word is a relatively easy target with a mouse. But pointing to targets smaller than an average word (of 5.5 characters = 2.3 cm) begins to be less than easy. So we take a word as the *hardest easy target*. This choice is supported by the fact that many mouse-based text editors have special features for selecting a word (e.g., double clicking anyplace within the word) partially so that the user can avoid the harder, more precise selections when possible. Pointing to a word at our assumed distance of $D = 9.7$ cm and $I_M = 96$ ms/bit for the mouse from Figure 8 takes[2]

$$
\begin{aligned}
MovementTime[\,hardest\ easy\ task\,] &= MovementTime[\,mouse,\ word\,]\\
&= I_M \cdot I_D\\
&= I_M \cdot \log_2 \frac{D}{S} + .5,\\
&= 96\ \text{ms/bit} \cdot \log_2\left(\frac{9.7}{2.3} + .5\right)\\
&= 96\ \text{ms/bit} \cdot 2.24\ \text{bit}\\
&= 220\ \text{ms}.
\end{aligned}
$$

[1] We have used data from our earlier experiments on the mouse, since these simulate a discrete text pointing situation. Recent experiments [19] get a lower bandwidth for the mouse, but use a continuous task and a mouse with variable gain.

[2] Most of the calculations in this paper are rounded to two significant digits (some tabulated intermediate values, such as I_D, are kept at three significant digits to lessen round-off errors).

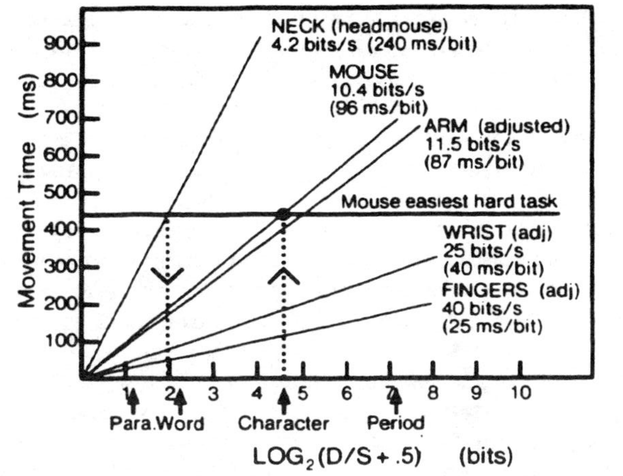

Fig. 8. Simplification of Figure 7 suitable for calculations.

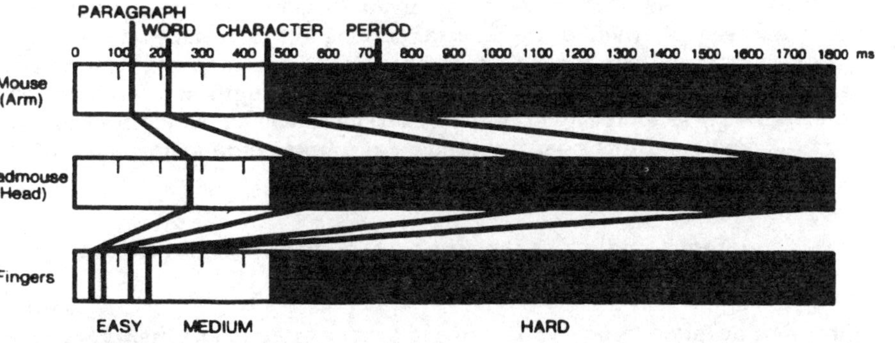

Fig. 9. Calculated effect of muscle group on task difficulty. The figure shows the time for the tasks in Table III for a perfect device connected to different muscle groups.

Therefore, we classify tasks that require less than 220 ms as *easy*. This relationship is shown in Figure 9.

Subjectively, pointing to a character is relatively hard with a mouse. But pointing to targets larger than a character (of typical width 12 pt = .41 cm on a Macintosh) begins to feel easy. So we take a character as the *easiest hard target*. Pointing to a character at our assumed distance takes 440 ms. We therefore classify tasks that require more than 440 ms as *hard*. The pointing tasks of Table III are classified in Figure 9a into easy, medium, or hard using this scheme.

We can use our classification to define the *precision* of a device. For the mouse, we define its precision to be the Fitts's Index of Difficulty I_D of the easiest hard task. For the mouse, this is the I_D of the character, or 4.59 bits. This line of reasoning can be extended to other devices, using the mouse as our standard.

> *We characterize the* precision *of a device as the I_D that requires the same amount of time as the* easiest hard task *of the mouse.*

On the basis of our assumption that the typical distance is $D = 9.7$ cm, we can reduce this computation to

$$\textit{Device precision} = \textit{Time}[\textit{hardest easy task for mouse}]/I_M = \frac{440 \text{ ms}}{I_M \text{ bits}}. \quad (2)$$

Of course, it is to be understood that differences in particular devices, systems, tasks, and users mean that these computations are approximate to a degree. Nonetheless, the comparisons we shall make are not very sensitive to the exact values selected for the parameters. Notice that, although we have used the mouse to set our definition of easy and hard tasks, the definition is not dependent on the mouse. The mouse is simply used as a convenient and familiar way to determine the approximate time boundaries of these categories.

The computation implied by this definition is depicted graphically by the dashed line in Figure 8. A line extending vertically from the I_D for the easiest hard task for the mouse intersects the mouse's Fitts's law slope. A line extending horizontally from this intersection point intersects the Fitts's law line from another muscle group or device. A line extending vertically down from this second intersection point determines the I_D for the target that could be pointed to in the same time as the easiest hard task for the mouse. This is taken as the precision of the device. A similar graphical computation can be used with this figure to determine comparisons between devices, such as: What sort of target could have been pointed to by a mouse in the time it takes a headmouse to point to a word?

3.3 Example 1: Effect of Muscle Groups on Input Devices

Now let us calculate the consequences of which muscle groups are used in building an input device. Compare the mouse (which uses a lot of arm and shoulder movement) to a headmouse, a plug-compatible replacement for the mouse based on neck movements. A headmouse has three ultrasonic sensors worn on the head like earphones, a transmitter mounted on the display, and plugs into the mouse port. Moving the head changes the XY coordinates of the mouse cursor in the appropriate manner.

We compute a comparison of the two devices based on the application tasks in Table III. Column (3) in Table III shows the time required to point to each task target with the mouse based on the approximation in Figure 8. For example, a word has an I_D of about 2.24 bits and requires about 220 ms to point to, as previously calculated.

Table IV. Characteristics of Input Devices

Property	Device (1) Mouse	(2) Headmouse	(3) Fingers
Bandwidth[a]	10.4 bits/s	4.2 bits/s	40.0 bits/s
I_M[b]	96 ms/bit	240 ms/bit	25 ms/bit
Device precision[c]	4.6 bits	1.8 bits	17.6 bits
Mouse-relative precision[d]	100%	39%	380%

[a] Data from Figure 8.
[b] $I_M = 1/\text{bandwidth}$.
[c] Device precision $= [I_{M(\text{mouse})}/I_{M(\text{device})}]\log_2(9.7\ \text{cm}/0.41\ \text{cm} + .5)$.
[d] Mouse-relative precision = device-precision/mouse-precision.

Column (4) shows the amount of time the headmouse requires to point to the same target, according to Figure 8. For a headmouse, pointing to a word requires

$$\begin{aligned} \mathit{MovementTime}[\mathit{headmouse}, \mathit{word}] &= 240\ \text{ms/bit} \cdot 2.24\ \text{bits} \\ &= 540\ \text{ms}. \end{aligned}$$

Figure 9b depicts graphically the amount of time required to point to each of the targets using the mouse as compared to the headmouse. The spectrum of pointing times is shifted to the right. Easy tasks become hard or moderate. The figure makes clear the penalty incurred by using the neck muscles with the headmouse instead of the arm muscles with the mouse: A user can point to a character with the mouse in about the same time it takes a user with the headmouse to point to a word.

Another effect of muscle group used can be seen by comparing the computed precision of the mouse and headmouse. Using eq. (2), the precision of the headmouse is 440 ms/(240 ms/bit) = 2.0 bits, as compared to the 4.6 bits we computed for the mouse earlier. This means that the mouse is more precise. To be concrete, it means that the headmouse could only point to a target with an $I_D = 1.8/4.6 = 39$ percent as great in the same amount of time.

It is interesting to calculate the performance that might be achievable if we were able to couple the high-performance fingers (whose bandwidth we have estimated at 40 bits/s in Figure 8) with the transducer of an appropriate input device. This computation is carried through in column (5) of Table III. Our characterization for the mouse, headmouse, and ultimate finger-operated devices is summarized in Table IV. The computed device precision for the fingers is 17.6 bits, almost four times as much as for the mouse. If such a device could be built, Figure 9c shows that all of the tasks, even the high-precision task of pointing to a single period, might be made into easy tasks. Whether this performance is practically achievable is unknown, but the calculation shows a region of promise in the design space. This is, of course, precisely the sort of speculation we wish to enable by systematizing the design space of input devices.

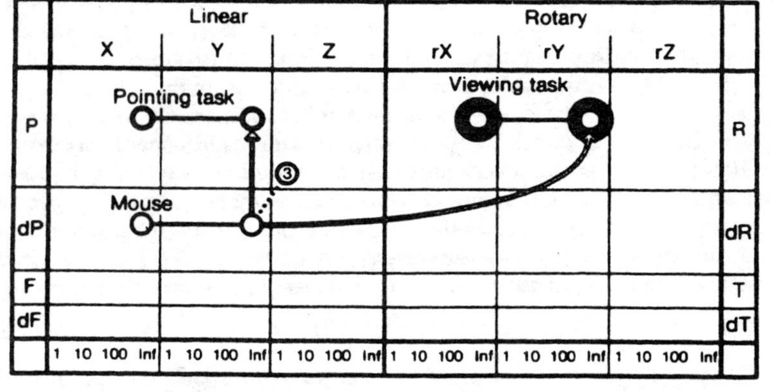

Fig. 10. Analysis of a virtual head movement device based on the mouse. White circles indicate device sensors, and gray circles indicate tasks. Size reflects the precision of the device, as defined in the text, or the precision required by the task. A smaller circle indicates higher precision, with the mouse and pointing corresponding to character precision and viewing to paragraph precision. When the white device circle is smaller than the gray task circle, the device is adequate for the task. According to the figure, the mouse can be used both for viewing and for pointing.

3.4 Example 2: Display Selection in a 3-D Information Environment using Mouse and Headmouse

We now apply the preceding analysis of device bandwidth to one of our designs for virtual input devices in a virtual workspace. In this design, the user is given a simulated head in a virtual 3-D environment. Moving the mouse forward and back rotates the virtual head up and down; moving the mouse left and right rotates the head to the left or to the right. The screen also contains a circle cursor fixed to its center that can be used to point into the virtual environment. The user points to an object by moving it to the cursor and pressing a mouse button. Thus, the user can accomplish two basic tasks with this arrangement: viewing the virtual world and pointing at objects.

Figure 10 shows the set of connected devices and tasks implied by this description. The mouse is connected to a 2-D rotational task for viewing the virtual world and a 2-D positional task for moving an object to the cursor. Devices and their projection onto tasks are shown with filled circles. The size of the circles approximate the precision of the devices and the difficulty of the

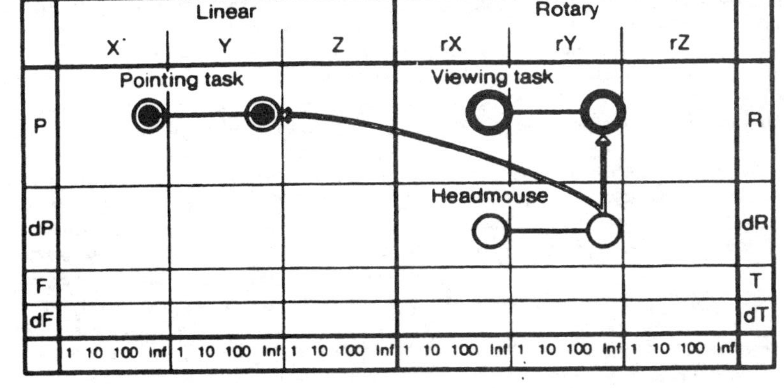

Fig. 11. **Analysis of a virtual head movement device based on the headmouse. According to the figure, the headmouse, with precision slightly larger than a word, is precise enough for viewing but not for pointing. Therefore, these two tasks need to be broken apart in the design if the headmouse is to be used.**

tasks. For purposes of the calculation, we have assumed that moving the virtual head to look around in the virtual 3-D world is roughly equivalent in difficulty to pointing to a paragraph, and that pointing to objects is roughly equivalent to pointing to a character, which is also the easiest hard task for the mouse. Since the task circles contain the filled circles projected from the mouse, it is clear that the mouse is precise enough for both tasks.

The headmouse seems like an obvious device for this application, but in fact, our analysis shows that it is appropriate for only half of the tasks. When we make the equivalent diagram for the headmouse in Figure 11, we see that the headmouse is matched to the viewing task, but it is not precise enough for the pointing task. If we want to use the headmouse, we should separate out the pointing task and put it on some other, more precise device. Incidentally, a similar analysis for editing would suggest that the headmouse is not very good for text editing because the transducer has been connected to a muscle with too little bandwidth for the precision of editing subtasks, such as pointing to a character.

4. CONCLUSION

In this paper we have illustrated a way of systematizing knowledge about input devices. We have provided a method for helping to generate points in the design space. We have shown how designs can be critiqued in terms of expressiveness and effectiveness, and have used two effectiveness metrics, footprint and bandwidth, to illustrate how regions of the space can be systematically analyzed.

The virtue of the present analysis is that it allows one to generate and calculate the consequences of interesting regions of the design space. This allows one to concentrate prototyping and engineering efforts in areas where analysis shows promising possibilities. For example, calculation shows that the headmouse is not likely to be successful for text editing for the fundamental reason that, despite the fact that the headmouse has an impressive transducer, this transducer is attached to a muscle group that does not have enough bandwidth to place the tasks of interest in the easy region. This analysis could be done in a short time on the back of an envelope and could make a strong prediction about whether an expensive research, development, and marketing effort is justified. One member of the lab refused to believe these calculations, claiming that the difference in pointing time between a headmouse and a mouse was purely a matter of users having had more practice with the mouse (this argument is obviously faulty because learning mainly affects the intercept of Fitts's law, not the slope). To prove his point, he was determined to spend eight hours the next day using the headmouse for text editing until he became as skilled with it as with a mouse. Not only did the differences continue to hold (as predicted), but he was also unable to move his neck for three days, much to the bemusement of his colleagues. We have purposely used a highly approximative style of calculation to illustrate the utility of rapid, simple analysis based on simple assumptions for gaining insight into the design space. More refined analyses could be pursued, perhaps in connection with an empirical study to test and advance these conclusions. But, even at the present level of approximation, the analyses have force, as our colleague discovered.

The present analysis also suggests a promising direction for developing a device to beat the mouse by using the bandwidth of the fingers. In fact, this analysis has been used by one of the authors to design novel input devices.

The design of human–machine interfaces, it has been argued, can be at least partially viewed as the design of artificial languages for communicating between human and machine. This paper has analyzed the basic semantics of one component of such artificial languages: input devices. Mackinlay [21, 22], as noted, has made a similar analysis of graphical presentations of data—communication in the other direction, from machine to human. Both studies have tried to work out a systematic description of the semantics of the messages to be communicated between human and machine. There are, of course, many additional complexities to human–machine communication that have not been dealt with (e.g., feedback, turn-taking, or animation), but the techniques used in these studies seem likely to be useful for future systematic treatments of other areas. In particular, it allows us to accumulate theory, empirical results, and design in a coherent framework.

Carroll [10] has called for a paradigm in human–computer interaction termed *usability-innervated invention* in which the analysis of human performance participates directly in the creation of computer-based artifacts, either through the explicit attempt to have new artifacts embody psychological claims ("psychology as the mother of invention") or through the analysis of the tasks the artifacts aid. We think morphological analyses of design spaces can play a role in such a paradigm and that the analyses can be used to integrate the results from several disciplines. For example, often we expect the operators for the generation of the design space to be computer-science oriented and the development and application of theories (or empirical analyses) for testing the space to be psychological. But Bertin's operators for generating the design space were largely semiotic and perceptual. In any case, the emphasis is on discovering the structure of the design space and its consequences.

REFERENCES

1. Albert, A. The effect of graphic input devices on performance in a cursor positioning task. In *Proceedings of the Human Factors Society-26th Annual Meeting* (Seattle, Wash., Oct. 25-28, 1982). Human Factors Society, Santa Monica, Calif., 1982, pp. 54-58.
2. Anson, E. The device model of interaction. *Comput. Graph. 16*, 3 (July 1982), 107-114. (Also, *SIGGRAPH '82 Proceedings.*)
3. Apple Computer. *Technical Introduction to the Macintosh Family.* Addison-Wesley, Reading, Mass., 1987.
4. Baecker, R. M., and Buxton, W., Eds. *Readings in Human-Computer Interaction: A Multidisciplinary Approach.* Kaufmann, Los Altos, Calif., 1987, pp. 357-365.
5. Bertin, J. *Semiology of Graphics.* University of Wisconsin Press, Madison, Wis., 1983. (Translation by W. J. Berg of 1973 edition of Semiologie graphique.)
6. Bleser, T. W., and Sibert, J. Toto: A tool for selecting interaction techniques. In *Proceedings of User Interface Software and Technology* (Snowbird, Utah, Oct. 3-5, 1990). ACM, New York, 1990, pp. 135-142.
7. Buxton, W. Lexical and pragmatic considerations of input structures. *Comput. Graph. 17*, 1 (Jan. 1983), 31-37.
8. Card, S. K. Human factors and artificial intelligence, In *Intelligent Interfaces: Theory, Research and Design*, P. A. Hancock and M. H. Chignell, Eds. Elsevier Science Publishers B.V., North-Holland, Amsterdam, 1989, pp. 270-284.
9. Card, S. K., English, W. K., and Burr, B. J. Evaluation of mouse, rate-controlled isometric joystick, step keys, and text keys for text selection on a CRT. *Ergonomics 21*, 8 (Aug. 1978), 601-613.
10. Carroll, J. M. Evaluation, description and invention: Paradigms for human-computer interaction. In *Advances in Computers*, vol. 29, M. C. Yovits, Ed. Academic Press, San Diego, Calif., 1989, 47-77.
11. Casner, S. M. A task-analytic approach to the automated design of graphic presentations. *ACM Trans. Graph. 10*, 2 (Apr. 1991), 111-151.
12. English, W. K., Engelbart, D. C., and Berman, M. L. Display-selection techniques for text manipulation. *IEEE Trans. Hum. Factors Electron. HFE-8*, 1 (March 1967), 5-15.
13. Epps, B., Snyder, H., and Mutol, W. Comparison of six cursor devices on a target acquisition task. In *Proceedings of the Society for Information Display* (San Diego, Calif., May 6-8, 1986). Society for Information Display, 1986, pp. 302-305.
14. Fitts, P. M. The information capacity of the human motor system in controlling amplitude of movement. *J. Exper. Psychol. 47*, 6 (June 1954), 381-391.
15. Foley, J. D., Wallace, V. L., and Chan, P. The human factors of computer graphics interaction techniques. *IEEE Comput. Graph. Appl. 4*, 11 (Nov. 1984), 13-48.
16. Jellinek, H., and Card, S. K. (1990). Powermice and user performance. In *CHI'90 Conference Proceedings* (Seattle, Wash., Apr. 1-5, 1990). ACM Press, New York, 1990, pp. 213-220.
17. Karat, J., McDonald, J., and Anderson, M. A comparison of selection techniques: Touch panel, mouse and keyboard. In *Human-Computer Interaction—INTERACT 84*, B. Shackel, Ed. Elsevier North-Holland, Amsterdam, 1985, pp. 189-193.
18. Langolf, G. D. Human motor performance in precise microscopic work. Ph.D. dissertation, Dept. of Indsutrial Engineering, Univ. of Michigan, Ann Arbor, Mich., 1973. (Also published by the MTM Association, Fairlawn, N.J., 1973.)
19. MacKenzie, I. S. Fitts' law as a performance model in human-computer interaction. Ph.D. thesis, Dept. of Education, Univ. of Toronto, Ontario, Canada, 1991.
20. MacKenzie, I. S. Fitts' law as a research and design tool in human-computer interaction. *Hum.-Comput. Interaction.* In press.
21. Mackinlay, J. Automatic design of graphical presentations. Ph.D. dissertation. Computer Science Dept., Stanford Univ., Calif., 1986. (Also Tech. Rep. Stan-CS-86-1038.)
22. Mackinlay, J. Automating the design of graphical presentations of relational information. *ACM Trans. Graph. 5*, 2 (Apr. 1986), 110-141.
23. Mackinlay, J. D., Card, S. K., and Robertson, G. G. A semantic analysis of the design space of input devices. *Hum.-Comput. Interaction 5*, 2-3 (1990), 145-190.
24. Olsen, D. R., and Halverson, B. W. Interface usage measurements in a user interface management system. In *Proceedings of the ACM SIGGRAPH Symposium on User Interface Software* (Banff, Alberta, Canada, Oct. 17-19, 1988). ACM, New York, 1988, pp. 102-108.
25. Olsen, D. R., et al. ACM SIGGRAPH workshop on software tools for user interface management. *Comput. Graph. 21*, 2 (April 1987), 71-147.
26. Penfield, W., and Rasmussen, T. *The Cerebral Cortex of Man: A Clinical Study of Localization of Function.* Macmillan, New York, 1990.
27. Pfaff, G. E.. *User Interface Management Systems.* Springer-Verlag, New York, 1985.
28. Radwin, R. G., Vanderheiden, G. C., and Lin, M. A method for evaluating head-controlled computer input devices using Fitts' law. *Hum. Factors 32*, 4 (Aug. 1990), 423-438.
29. Robertson, G. G. , Card, S. K., and Mackinlay, J. The cognitive coprocessor architecture for interactive user interfaces. In *Proceedings of the ACM-SIGGRAPH Symposium on User Interface Software and Technology* (Williamsburg, Va., Nov. 13-15, 1989). ACM, New York, 1989, pp. 10-18.
30. Roth, S. F., Mattis, J., and Mesnard, X. Graphics and natural language as components of automatic explanation. In *Intelligent User Interfaces*, J. Sullivan and S. Tyler, Eds. ACM Press, New York, pp. 207-239.
31. Sheridan, T. B. Supervisory control of remote manipulators, vehicles and dynamic processes: Experiments in command and display aiding. *Adv. Man-Machine Syst. Res. 1* (1984), 49-137.
32. Siewiorek, D., Bell, G., and Newell, A. *Computer Structures.* McGraw-Hill, New York, 1981.
33. Tanner, P. P., and Buxton, W. A. S. Some issues in future UIMS development. In *User Interface Management Systems*, G. E. Pfaff, Ed. Springer-Verlag, New York, 1985, pp. 67-79.
34. van den Bos, J. Abstract interaction tools: A language for user interface management systems. *ACM Trans. Program. Lang. Syst. 10*, 2 (July 1988), 215-247.
35. Welford, A. T. *Fundamentals of Skill.* Methuen, London, 1968.
36. Whitefield, D., Ball, R., and Bird, J. Some comparisons of on-display and off-display touch input devices for interaction with computer generated displays. *Ergonomics 26*, 11 (1983), 1033-1053.
37. Zwicky, F. The morphological approach to discovery, invention, research, and construction. In *New Methods of Thought and Procedure*, F. Zwicky and A. G. Wilson, Eds. Springer-Verlag, New York, 1967, 273-297.

Reflections on. . .

A Morphological Analysis of the Design Space of Input Devices

Jock D. Mackinlay and Stuart K. Card

Zwicky's morphological analysis breaks a subject matter such as input devices or jet engines into component parts (Zwicky 1967). The power of such an analysis comes from combining the components, either to describe existing items or to suggest new items. For design spaces, the approach tends to be inclusive, capturing poor designs along with good designs. It can become the generator in a "generate and test" search strategy. This is probably the reason this paper is part of this collection.

Although abstract and inclusive, a morphological analysis can have concrete, practical implications. For example, John Sibert read this paper and invented a new finger-mounted pointing device (Sibert and Cokturk 1997). An even more concrete impact has been to help the authors understand the repetitive stress impact of the current computer systems on their own bodies. In particular, the paper describes how to model the mappings from our bodies to user interface widgets such that you can quickly estimate the transfer function. Fitts' law tells us that rapid selection of small distant targets is difficult. Major damage can occur when this difficult task is repeatedly transferred through our input devices into our bodies. Unfortunately, our current user interfaces are full of small targets—window resize widgets, menus, toolbars, and so on. Furthermore, the distance to these targets has increased with the proliferation of larger screens. If you are a regular computer user, you must be ever vigilant to the signals of your body. A tingle in your fingers can lead to major arm or neck surgery if you do not change your behavior. Slow down your selection of targets. Take frequent breaks. Consider the placement and construction of your input devices. The morphology you protect may be your own.

REFERENCES

Sibert, J. L., and Cokturk, M. 1997. A Finger-Mounted, Direct Pointing Device for Mobile Computing. In *Proceedings of ACM UIST'97*, 41–42.

Zwicky, F. 1967. The Morphological Approach to Discovery, Invention, Research, and Construction. In Zwicky, F. and Wilson, A. G. (eds.), *New Methods of Thought and Procedure*, 273–297. New York: Springer-Verlag.

WIZARD OF OZ STUDIES — WHY AND HOW

Nils Dahlbäck, Arne Jönsson, Lars Ahrenberg

Natural Language Processing Laboratory
Department of Computer and Information Science
S-581 83 LINKÖPING, SWEDEN
Phone: +46 13 28 10 00
nda@ida.liu.se, arj@ida.liu.se, lah@ida.liu.se

ABSTRACT
We discuss current approaches to the development of natural-language dialogue systems, and claim that they do not sufficiently consider the unique qualities of man-machine interaction as distinct from general human discourse. We conclude that empirical studies of this unique communication situation is required for the development of user-friendly interactive systems. One way of achieving this is through the use of so-called Wizard of Oz studies. We describe our work in this area. The focus is on the practical execution of the studies and the methodological conclusions that we have drawn on the basis of our experience. While the focus is on natural language interfaces, the methods used and the conclusions drawn from the results obtained are of relevance also to other kinds of intelligent interfaces.

KEYWORDS: Design and evaluation, dialogue, natural language interfaces.

THE NEED FOR WIZARD OF OZ STUDIES

Dialogue has been an active research area for quite some time in natural language processing. It is fair to say that researchers studying dialogue and discourse have developed their theories through detailed analysis of empirical data from many diverse dialogue situations. In their recent review of the field, Grosz, Pollack and Sidner [12] mentions work on task-oriented dialogues, descriptions of complex objects, narratives, informal and formal arguments, negotiations and explanations. One thing which these studies have shown is that human dialogue is a very complex activity, leading to a corresponding complexity of the theories proposed. In particular it is evident that participants must rely on knowledge and reasoning capabilities of many different kinds to know what is going on in a dialogue.

When it comes to using data and theories to the design of natural language interfaces it has often been argued that human dialogues should be regarded as a norm and a starting-point, i.e. that a natural dialogue between a person and a computer should resemble a dialogue between humans as much as possible. But a computer is not a person, and some of the differences are such that they can be expected to have a major influence on the dialogue, thus making human-human data an unreliable source of information for some important aspects of design, in particular the style and complexity of interaction.

First let us look at some of the differences between the two dialogue situations that are likely to play a significant role. We know that language is influenced by interpersonal factors. To take one example, it has been suggested by R. Lakoff [18] and others that the use of so-called indirect speech acts is motivated by a need to follow "rules of politeness" (1. don't impose, 2. give options). But will a user feel a need to be polite to a computer? And if not, will users of NLIs use indirect requests in the search of information from a database? If not, do we need a component in our NLI for handling indirect requests? This is obviously an empirical question that can be answered only by studying the language used in such situations.

Indirect utterances are of course something more than just ways of being polite. There are other forms, such as omitting obvious steps in an argument - relying on the listener's background knowledge, and giving answers, not to the question, but by supplying information relevant to an inferred higher goal. But also the use of these will presumably vary with the assessed characteristics of one's dialogue partner.

In the case of keyboard input another important factor is that the communication channel is different form ordinary human dialogues. The fact that the dialogue will be written instead of spoken will obviously affect the language used. As pointed out by Cohen [3] "Keyboard interaction, with its emphasis on optimal packaging of information into the smallest linguistic "space", appears to be a mode that alters the normal organization of discourse."

Much of our language behaviour, on all levels, from pronunciation to choice of words and sentences, can be seen as a result of our attempts to find the optimal compromise between two needs, the need to make ourselves understood, and the need to reach this goal with as little effort as possible. It is a well established fact in linguistic research that we as speakers adapt to the perceived characteristics of our interlocutors. The ability to modify the language to the needs of the hearer seems to be present already at the age of four [21]. Language directed to children is different from language directed to adults, as is the case when talking to foreigners, brain-injured people etc. There are good reasons to believe that similar adjustments can and will be made when we are faced with the task of interacting with a computer in natural language. One important consequence of this is that goals in some dialogue research in computational linguistics such as 'Getting computers to talk like you and me' [20] or developing interfaces that will "allow the user to forget that he is questioning a machine"[10], are not only difficult to reach. They are misconceived.

Given these differences between the two types of dialogue and the well-founded assumption that they will affect the linguistic behaviour of the human interlocutors, it follows that the language samples used for providing the empirical ground should come from relevant settings and domains. In other words, the development of NLI-software should be based on an analysis of the language and interaction style used when communicating with NLIs. Since, as we just observed, users adapt to the language of their interlocutors, analysis of the language used when communicating with existing NLIs is of limited value in the development of the next generation systems. This is what motivates data collection by means of Wizard of Oz techniques, i.e. studies where subjects are told that they are interacting with a computer system through a natural-language interface, though in fact they are not. Instead the interaction is mediated by a human operator, the wizard, with the consequence that the subject can be given more freedom of expression, or be constrained in more systematic ways, than is the case for existing NLIs. (Some well-known studies based on a more or less 'pure' Wizard of Oz technique are those of Cohen [3], Grosz [11], Guindon [13], and Kennedy et al. [17]. For a review and discussion of these and other studies, see [5, 16]. [9] provides a review focused on speech systems)

Of course you cannot expect to gather all the data you need for the design of a given application system by means of Wizard of Oz studies, e.g. as regards vocabulary and syntactic constructions related to the domain. But for finding out what the application-specific linguistic characteristics are, or for gathering data as a basis for theories of the specific genre of human-computer interaction in natural language, the Wizard of Oz-technique seems to us to be the best available alternative.

The rest of this paper is concerned with a description of our work in the area of Wizard of Oz simulation studies. The focus is on the practical execution of the studies and the methodological conclusions that we have drawn on the basis of our experience. Some results on the characteristics of human-computer-interaction in natural language have been reported elsewhere [4, 5, 6, 7, 8, 16] and further work is currently in progress. Some of the major results obtained this far is that man-machine dialogues exhibit a simpler structure than human dialogues, making it possible to use simpler but computationally more tractable dialogue models; that the users and system rely on an conceptual model specific for the domain *but* common for all users, i.e. uses mutual knowledge based on community membership, to use the terminology of [2]. These results in turn suggest less need for dynamic user modelling but a larger need for dynamic focus management than has hitherto been assumed in the HCI/NLP communities.

SOME DESIGN ISSUES

To circumvent the risk of drawing general conclusions that in fact are only a reflection of the specific experimental setting used, we have striven to vary the type of background system, not only as regards the content or application domain, but also as regards the 'intelligence' of the system and the types of possible actions to perform by the person using it. This far we have collected approximately 150 dialogues, using nine different real or simulated background systems. Apart from the use of 'pure' natural language, in one case the dialogues also contain tables displaying the contents of the INGRES-database, and in two cases a limited use of graphics is possible.

Our aim is to simulate the interaction with a system in the case of an occasional or one-time user, i.e. a user who is unfamiliar with the system, but has some knowledge of the domain. We think that this is the most relevant user-category to study, as otherwise the user will be adapted to the system.

We have therefore tried to use background systems and tasks which follow these criteria. But it is not enough to have a reasonable background system and a good experimental environment to run a successful experiment. Great care should also be taken regarding the task given to the subjects. If we give them too simple a task to solve, we will not get much data to analyse, and if we give them too detailed instructions on which information they should seek from the system, there is a risk that what they will type is not their way of phrasing the questions but ours. Our approach has been to develop a so-called scenario, i.e. a task to solve whose solution requires the use of the system, but where there does not exist one single correct answer, and/or where there are more than one way to reach the goal. Fraser and Gilbert [9] in their simulations of speech-systems also propose the use of scenarios to achieve realistic interactions.

We have previously stressed some consequences of the fact that computers are different from people which has motivated the choice of Wizard of Oz simulations. But another consequence of this is that such simulations are very difficult to run. People are flexible, computers are rigid (or consistent); people are slow at typewriting, computer output is fast; computers never make small mistakes (e.g. occasional spelling errors), people make them all the time. The list could be made longer, but the conclusion is obvious. If we want our subjects to believe that they are communicating with a computer also after three exchanges, we cannot let the person

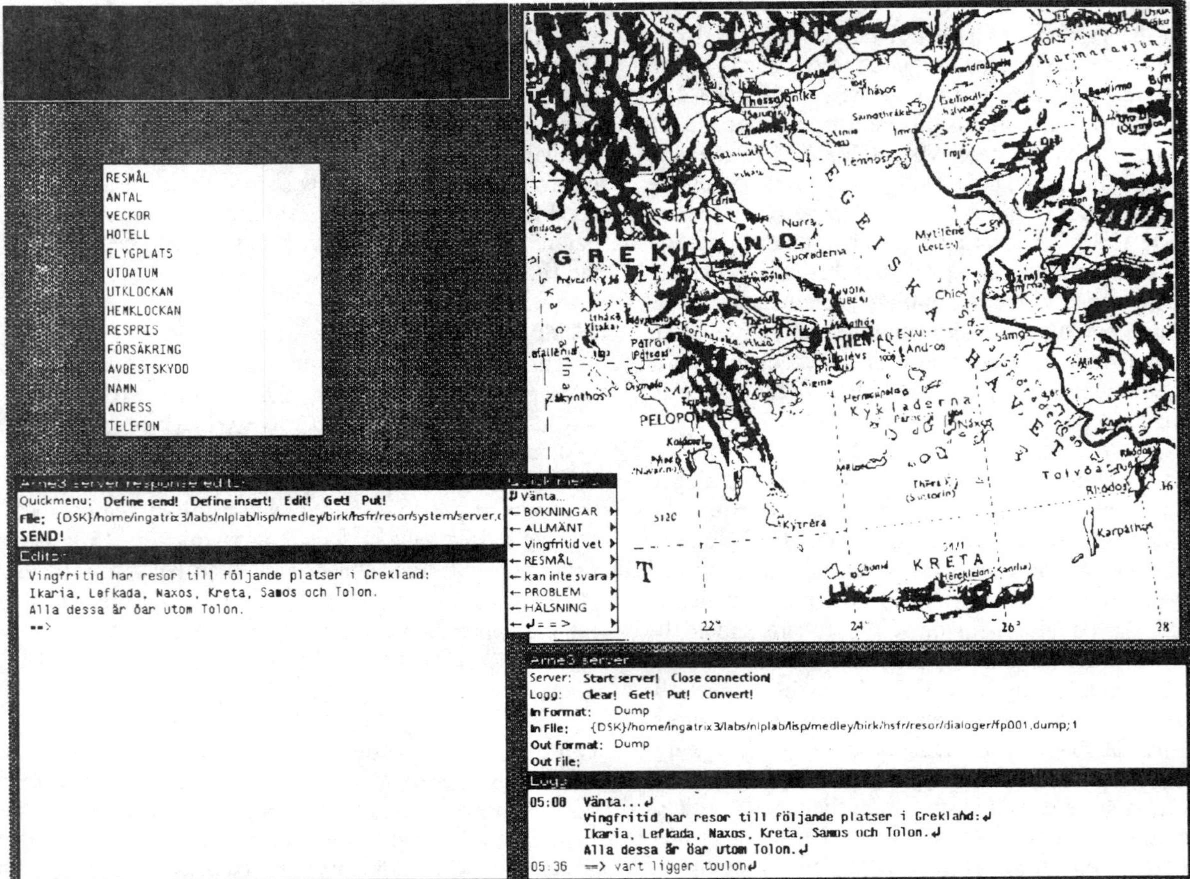

Figure 1: An overview of the simulation environment (The Wizards view.)

simulating the computer just sit and slowly write the answers on the screen. Therefore, to make the output from the wizard resemble that of a computer as far as possible as regards timing and consistency, we have developed an environment for conducting the experiments, currently running on SUN Sparc stations in the Medley Lisp environment. The background system can be a real system on the same or another computer, or it can be simulated too. The simulation environment will be the topic of the next section.

THE SIMULATION ENVIRONMENT *ARNE*

The simulation environment now exists in its third version, ARNE-3. Some of its main features are:

- response editor with canned texts and templates easily accessed through menus
- ability to access various background systems
- editor for creating queries to database systems
- interaction log with time stamps

The simulation environment is customized for each new application. An overview of the simulation environment is shown in figure 1, where the application is a Travel agency system holding information on holiday trips to the Greek archipelago. The environment in its base configuration consists of two parts, a log and a response editor, each accessed through its own window. The editor window can be seen in the lower left part of the screen, while the log window is found in the lower right part. Maps and other kinds of graphics can also be displayed.

In one scenario for the Travel system the subject can also order a holiday trip. The window in the upper left part of the screen is the template for the order. This is filled in by the wizard as the interaction proceeds. When the ordering window is completed, the subjects receives a confirmation in natural language of the ordered item. This is generated automatically by a Common Lisp function from the order template. This is in line with our general policy to automate as much as possible of the interaction.

The editor window is used to create responses to the subjects. When a response is ready it is sent to the subject and simultaneously logged in the log window. To speed up the response time the editor has a hierarchically organised set of canned texts which are easily reached through a set of menus, seen to the right in the editor window. Figure 2 shows the hierarchy of canned texts for the menu item Resmål (Eng: Resort). The wizard can stop at any point in the hierarchy and will thus provide more or less detailed information depending on how far the dialogue has developed. So, in the

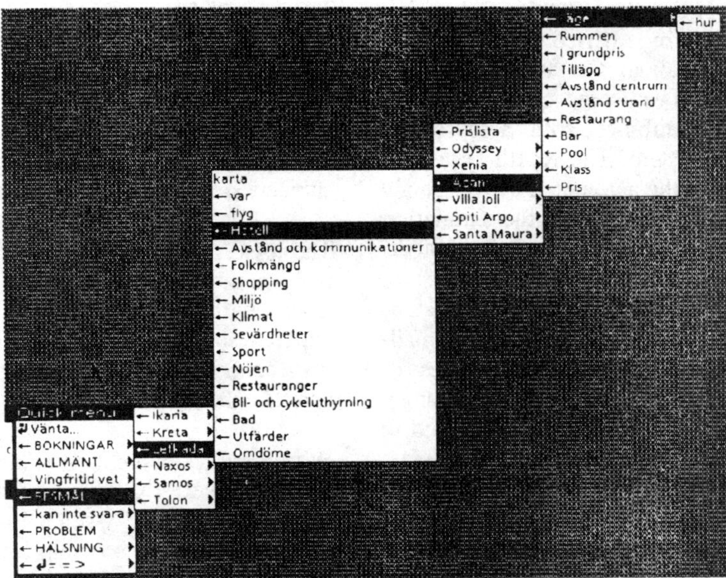

Figure 2: A menu hierarchy

example of figure 2, if the wizard stops at Lefkada, on the second level in the hierarchy, the subject will be provided with general information on Lefkada, while if the wizard stops at Adani, general information about hotel Adani on Lefkada is provided. The total amount of canned text available in this fashion is 2300 rows, where a row is everything between a full line of text to a single word. This corresponds to approximately 40 A4-pages. The text from the menus is entered into the editor window, to allow the wizard to edit the information, if necessary, before sending it to the subject.

Certain messages are so simple and also commonly used that they can be prompted directly to the subject without first passing the editor. These are also present in the quick menus. In the example there are two such quick responses, one is the prompt ==>, and the other is Vänta ... (Eng. "Wait ..."). The latter ensures that the subject receives an acknowledgement as soon as the input is acquired, meanwhile the wizard scans through the canned texts for an answer.

The simulation environment can also be connected to existing background systems. One example of this is the *Cars* simulations, where subjects could acquire information on properties of used cars from an Ingres database containing such information. The simulation environment in these simulations consisted of four different windows. Here there were two windows added for database access, one is the actual database interface and the other is a query command editor. As forming a SQL-query can take quite some time we needed to speed up that process. This is done in a similar way as the response generation namely by using hierarchically organised menus. The menus contain information that can be used to fill in a SQL-template.The editor used for this purpose is an instance of the same editor that was used for creating responses to the subject. Thus, the wizard need not learn a new system which again provides a more efficient interaction as the same commands and actions are used to carry out both tasks. The database access menus do not only contain SQL-query templates, but also entries for the objects and properties that are stored in the database. Thus the wizard can avoid misspelled words which would lead to a database access failure and a slow down of response time.

It is a time-consuming task to customize the simulation environment to a particular application. For some applications we have used some 20-40 pilot studies before being satisfied with the scenario and the performance of the simulation. But we believe that without such preparation, there is a large risk that the value of the results obtained is seriously diminished.

OUR EXPERIMENTAL DATA

We have conducted a number of Wizard of Oz-experiments using different background systems and scenarios.

Corpus 1

Corpus 1 was collected using the first versions of the simulation environment. This corpus contains dialogues with five real or simulated background systems.

The first system, PUB, was a library database then in use at our department, containing information on which books the department owned, and on which researchers room they were kept. Common bibliographic information was also obtainable. The C-line system was a simulated database containing information about the computer science curriculum at Linköping University. The scenario for the subjects was that they should imagine themselves working as study counsellors, their task being to answer a letter from a student with questions about the Master's program in computer science. Five dialogues were run in this condition.

In the third system, called HiFi, the user can order high quality HiFi equipment after having queried a simulated database containing information about the available equipment. The system can also answer some questions about which pieces can suitably be combined, so in a sense it is not a database but an expert system. The fourth system in this corpus is the first version of the automated travel agency encountered previously in the description of the simulation environment. In this version there were no graphics facilities.

The last system in corpus 1 is a simulated wine selection advisory system. It is capable of suggesting suitable wines for different dishes, if necessary within a specified price range. It could also tell whether two wines could be combined in the same meal.

The analysis of this corpus is presented in [5,7, 16] *general overview*, [4, 5, 8] *dialogue structure*, [5,6] *pronoun analysis*. [1] gives an overview of the NLI-project for which the analysis was used. [5] presents the most detailed analysis of both the dialogue structure and the pronoun patterns and also analyses the use of definite descriptions.

Corpus 2

The second corpus was collected using the refined Wizard of Oz-simulation environment presented here, and with a new set of scenarios.This corpus consists of totally 60 dialogues using two different background systems, the *Cars* database of used car models and a considerably revised and enlarged version of the travel system used in corpus 1. In this corpus half of the subjects could only obtain information from the system, whereas the other half of them also could order the trip as was the case in corpus 1. Dialogues where collected under two different conditions: one where the subjects knew that they were interacting with a person and one which was a real Wizard of Oz-simulation. We thus have 10 subjects in each cell. The analysis of this corpus is presently under way. Some results are used in [8].

SYSTEMS TRIED BUT NOT USED

We have found the simulation of database-dialogues fairly straightforward, as is the case with the simulation of systems where the user can perform more tasks, such as ordering equipment after having obtained information about the stock. But for some other kinds of systems we have encountered different kinds of problems, in some cases leading us to abandon the project of collecting the dialogues for a particular system.

One example of this was an EMYCIN based expert system, advising on tax issues in connection with the transfer of real estate. There were many reasons for our believing that this was a suitable system for our purposes. The domain is one with which we thought most people had some familiarity. Another reason was that rule-based expert systems such as this are a large and growing area and is considered one possible application domain for natural language interfaces.

The basic reason for not being able to use this promising application was that the system was only a prototype system that never was completed. Not only did it contain some bugs, but there were "holes" in its knowledge, i.e. some subareas for which no rules were implemented. It turned out to be impossible to create a scenario which guaranteed that the subjects kept themselves within the system's competence.

The lesson we learned from this was that if we shall use a real background system it must be well tested and functioning properly. Furthermore, the dialogue of EMYCIN-based expert systems is controlled by the system to an extent that it is difficult to simulate a more open dialogue where the user can take the initiative too.

With the development of bitmapped screens and mouses, it becomes interesting to study multi-modal interfaces where users can use both written input and direct manipulation. And if we make it possible for the user to use both modes, we can learn something about when the different interface methods are to be preferred. We therefore tried to use a computer-based calendar system developed at our department for this purpose. In the system you can book meetings with groups and individuals, deciding on the time and location. You can also ask the system about these meetings, and about the times when people or groups of people are not booked, for instance when planning a meeting with them. You can do this by writing in a calendar displayed in a window on the screen, but also using a limited natural language interface.

There were two major problems when designing this experiment. The first problem was to expand the ARNE environment so that it could handle graphics too. In the Calendar system we actually send the graphics on the net between the different work stations, which for obvious reasons gave long response times. This gave rise to some problems discussed below. In the later travel agency project we have therefore stored all the graphical information on the user's machine, and only send a signal from the wizard to this station tell which picture to display.

The second problem was deciding how to analyse the obtained data, and this we did not solve. If we lack well developed theories for dialogues in natural language, the case is even worse for this kind of multi-modal dialogues. The only thing we have been able to do thus far is to simply observe the users running the system. But even this simple data collection has given us one somewhat surprising observation concerning the effects of very slow response times on the dialogue structure. The interesting fact is that in spite of these long response times, the language used be the subjects still is coherent, with a number of anaphoric expressions, something which goes somewhat contrary to expectations, since one could assume that it is necessary for the user to have the dialogue 'on the top of his consciousness' to be able to use such linguistic devices. It is of course not possible here to give an explanation of this phenomenon, which in our opinion requires further investigation. But it is possible that the fact that both the dialogue and the calendar is displayed on the screen affects the dialogue structure.

Another system tried but not used was an advisory program for income tax return and tax planning that runs on IBM PCs. The reason for thinking that this was a suitable system for our experiments is of course the same as the one first one described above. One reason for not using it was that very little dialogue was necessary to use the program, apart from filling in the menus that correspond to various part of the tax forms. So it seems as if a natural language interface is not the preferred mode for such a system, but at most something which can supplement it. Another difficulty was with the scenario, as people are not willing to present their own income tax planning in an experiment and it is quite a complex task to learn a fictitious tax profile.

In one of our simulations we have tried to simulate also an advisory system. But there are some problems with this too, the most important being that it is difficult for the Wizard to maintain a consistent performance and give the same answers to similar questions from different users, and even from the same user. To some extent these problems can be overcome, but it seems to require longer development phases than for other kinds of systems.

Advisory system thus seem to give us two kinds of problems if we want to use them in Wizard of Oz studies. On the one hand, the simulation of the system is difficult to do, and if one wants to use a real system developed on existing shells, at least in some cases the dialogue is system driven to an extent that there seem to be little that can be gained from such a study.

To summarize, we can identify three parameters that must be given careful consideration: the background system, the task given to subjects, and the wizard's guide-lines and tools.

- If the background system is not simulated it should be fully implemented. A shaky prototype will only reveal that system's limitations and will not provide useful data. Furthermore, the system should allow for a minimum of mixed-initiative dialogue. A system-directed background system will give a dialogue which is not varied enough.
- The task given to subjects must be reasonably open, i.e. have the form of a scenario. Retrieving information from a database system and putting it together for a specific purpose can be fruitful. But, if the domain is so complex that it requires extensive domain knowledge, or the task is of a more private nature, then it is likely that the subjects try to finish their task as quickly as possible and again not provide enough dialogue variation. The specification of the task must allow for varied outcomes. Many different outcomes must be considered "correct" and there should be many ways to explore the background system to achieve a reasonable result.
- The simulation experiment must be studied in detail, from pilot experiments, before the real simulations are carried out. This information is used to provide knowledge to the wizard on how to act in various situations that he may encounter. Furthermore, the wizard needs a variety of pre-stored responses covering typical situations. Otherwise, besides slowing down the simulation, the ensuing variation will provide results that are less generalizable.

FOR AND AGAINST THE CHOSEN METHOD

We have conducted post-experimental interviews with all our subjects. The most important objective was of course to ascertain that they had not realized that the system had been simulated, and also to explain what we had done and why we had deceived them. (We also explained that the collected dialogue should be destroyed if they so wished.)

In the review of the Wizard of Oz method Fraser and Gilbert [9] argued, on ethical grounds, against deceiving subjects about the nature of their conversation partner. We do not want to deny that there are ethical problems here, but we think that they can be overcome, and that there are good reasons for trying to do so. As pointed out above it has been shown that there are differences in the language used when subjects think they communicate with a computer and when they think they communicate with a person. And, what is more important, the differences observed concern aspects of language over which subjects seem to have little conscious control, e.g. type and frequency of anaphoric expressions used. So at least if your interests concern syntax and discourse, we consider it important to make the subjects believe that they are communicating with a computer, simply because we do not think that subjects can role-play here and give you the data you need. And if, on the other hand, you find that subjects find it difficult to use the existing NLI, as for instance in [14], this amounts hardly to anything more than a demonstration of the limitations of existing technology.

So much for the need, but how about the ethics? We would claim that if one uses the practice developed within experimental social psychology of a debriefing session afterwards, explaining what you have done and why you found it necessary to do so, and furthermore that you tell the subjects that the data collected will be destroyed immediately if they so wish, you will encounter little problem. In our experiments we have done so, and we have so far only had a number of good laughs and interesting discussions with our subjects on their expectations of what a computer can and cannot do, but no one has criticized us for our 'lies'. Perhaps one reason for this is that none of the subjects felt that they had been put in an embarrassing situation. It is not exactly the same as Candid Camera.

Another possible critique is that one should study existing systems instead of simulated ones. But in this case we agree with Tennant's [22] conclusion that people can often adapt to the limitations of an existing system, and such an experiment does not therefore tell you what they ideally would need. It could also be argued that the human ability to adapt to the communicative capacity of the dialogue partner means that what we find is only the subjects adaptive responses to the wizard's conception of what an NLI should be able to do. But it is exactly for this reason that the wizards in our experiments have not been instructed to mimic any specific capacity limitations. At the present stage of development of NLI technology, we cannot say with any high degree of certainty what we will and will not be able to do in the future. Furthermore, it is extremely difficult to be consistent in role-playing an agent with limited linguistic or communicative ability, so, to make such an experiment you would need some way of making the restrictions automatically, for instance by filtering the input through a specific parser, and only understand those utterances that can be analysed by this parser. Furthermore, the fact that we have used different wizards for the different background systems guarantees at least that the language we find our subjects using is not the reflection of the idiosyncrasies of one single person's behaviour in such a situation.

The possible critique against the artificiality of the experimental setting can be levelled against another aspect of the method used, namely that the subjects are role-playing. They are not real users, and their motivation for searching information or ordering equipment is really not theirs. This is an argument that should be taken seriously. It is, however, our belief that the fact that the subjects are role-playing affects different aspects of their behaviour differently. If the focus of interest is for instance the goals and plans of the users, and the way that is manifested in the dialogue, the use of role-playing subjects should be made with caution. But if the focus is on aspects not under voluntary conscious control (cognitively impenetrable, to use Pylyshyn's, [19] term), the prospect is better for obtaining ecologically valid data. To take one specific example; if a user is just pretending to buy a holiday trip to Greece, she might not probe the alternatives to the extent that she would if she were in fact to buy it, simply because the goal of finishing the task within a limited time takes precedence. But it does not seem likely that the latter fact will affect the use of pronouns in a specific utterance, or the knowledge about charter holidays and Greek geography that is implicitly used in interpreting and formulating specific utterances.

CONCLUDING REMARKS

The present paper makes two points, one theoretical and one methodological. On the theoretical side we argue that it is natural for any human engaging in a dialogue to adapt to the perceived characteristics of the dialogue partner. Since computers are different from people, a necessary corollary from this is that the development of interfaces for *natural* dialogues with a computer cannot take human dialogues as its sole starting point, but must be based on a knowledge of the unique characteristics of these kinds of dialogues. Our own work has been concerned with natural-language interfaces, but the argument is of relevance for all kinds of intelligent dialogue systems.

The methodological point is simply that to acquire the relevant knowledge, we need high quality empirical data. But if the point is simple, gathering such data is not quite that simple. One way of doing so is by simulating intelligent interfaces (and sometimes also systems) using so-called Wizard of Oz-studies, i.e. having a person simulate the interface (and system). But even if the basic idea is simple, to acquire the required high-quality data a great deal of care and consideration need to be used in the design of such experiments. We have described our own simulation environment ARNE and some of our practical experiences, both positive and negative, form our research in this area, to illustrate some of the points that we consider important if such a research program is to contribute to the development of theoretically and empirically sound user friendly intelligent interfaces.

REFERENCES

1. Ahrenberg, Lars, Arne Jönsson & Nils Dahlbäck (1990) Discourse Representation and Discourse Management for Natural Language Interfaces, *Proceedings of the Second Nordic Conference on Text Comprehension in Man and Machine*, Täby, Stockholm.

2. Clark, Herbert H. & Catherine Marshall (1981) Definite Reference and Mutual Knowledge. In Joshi, Aravind, Webber, Bonnie, and Sag, Ivan (eds.) *Elements of Discourse Understanding*. Cambridge, Mass.: Cambridge University Press.

3. Cohen, Philip R. (1984) The pragmatics of referring and modality of communication, *Computational Linguistics*, **10**, pp 97-146

4. Dahlbäck, Nils (1991a) Empirical Analysis of a Discourse Model for Natural Language Interfaces, *Proceedings of the Thirteenth Annual Meeting of The Cognitive Science Society*, Chicago, Illinois.

5. Dahlbäck, Nils, (1991b) *Representations of Discourse, Cognitive and Computational Aspects*, PhD-thesis, Linköping University.

6. Dahlbäck, Nils (1992) Pronoun usage in NLI-dialogues: A Wizard of Oz study. To appear in Papers from the Third Nordic Conference on Text Comprehension in Man and Machine, Linköping April, 21-23, 1992.

7. Dahlbäck, Nils & Arne Jönsson (1989) Empirical Studies of Discourse Representations for Natural Language Interfaces, *Proceedings of the Fourth Conference of the European Chapter of the ACL*, Manchester.

8. Dahlbäck, Nils & Arne Jönsson (1992) An empirically based computationally tractable dialogue model, *Proceedings of the Fourteenth Annual Meeting of The Cognitive Science Society*, Bloomington, Indiana.

9. Fraser, Norman & Nigel S. Gilbert (1991) Simulating speech systems, *Computer Speech and Language*, **5**, pp 81-99.

10. Gal, Annie (1988) *Cooperative responses in Deductive Databases*. PhD Thesis, Department of Computer Science, University of Maryland, College Park.

11. Grosz, Barbara (1977) *The Representation and use of Focus in Dialogue Understanding*. Unpublished Ph.D. thesis. University of California, Berkely.

12. Grosz, Barbara J., Martha Pollack & Candace L. Sidner (1989) Discourse, In: Posner M. I. (Ed.) *Foundations of Cognitive Science*, Cambridge, MA: The MIT Press

13. Guindon, Raymonde (1988) A multidisciplinary perspective on dialogue structure in user-advisor dialogues. In Guindon, Raymoned (ed.) *Cognitive Science and its Applications for Human-Computer Interaction*. Hillsdale, N.J.: Erlbaum.

14. Jarke, M., Krause, J., Vassiliou, Y., Stohr, E., Turner, J. & White, N. (1985) Evaluation and assessment of domain-independent natural language query systems, *IEEE quarterly bulletin on Database Engineering*, Vol. 8, No. 3, Sept.

15. Jönsson, Arne (1991) A Dialogue Manager Using Initiative-Response Units and Distributed Control, P*roceedings of the Fifth Conference of the European Chapter of the Association for Computational Linguistics*, Berlin.

16. Jönsson, Arne & Nils Dahlbäck (1988) Talking to a Computer is not Like Talking to Your Best Friend. *Proceedings of The first Scandinivian Conference on Artificial Intelligence*, Tromsø, Norway.

17. Kennedy, A., Wilkes, A., Elder, L. & Murray, W. (1988) Dialogue with machines. *Cognition*, **30**, 73-105.

18. Lakoff, R.T. (1973) The Logic of Politeness; or minding your p's and q's. *Papers from the Ninth Regional Meeting, Chicago Linguistic Society*, pp 292-305.

19. Pylyshyn, Zenon (1984) *Computation and Cognition*, Cambridge MA: The MIT Press

20. Reichman, Rachel (1985) *Getting Computers to Talk Like You and Me*, MIT Press, Cambridge, MA.

21. Shatz, M. & Gelman, R. The development of communication skills: Modifications in the speech of young children as a function of listener. *Monographs of the Society for research in child development*.**38**, No 152.

22. Tennant, Harry (1981) *Evaluation of Natural Language Processors* Ph.D. Thesis. University of Illinois Urbana-Champaign.

Wizard of Oz Studies—Why and How

Nils Dahlbäck, Arne Jönsson, and Lars Ahrenberg

The paper was written at a time when empirical and situation-based approaches to developing NLIs (Natural Language Interfaces) and other kinds of IUIs were gaining increased attention. Our aim with the paper was to encourage that move, by providing some theoretical motivations for this approach and by sharing with other workers our practical experiences both of success and failure.

The shortest way of summarizing what has happened since the paper's publication is perhaps to say that the why is now unnecessary since the use of Wizard-of-Oz and other empirical methods is part and parcel of today's research agenda (though not necessarily for the reasons we give in the paper; the need became more or less obvious by the general progress in the field itself). The how of collecting and analyzing empirical data as a foundation for the development of intelligent interfaces is, however, still an important issue where there has been important progress in recent years, especially concerning the analysis of the collected data. The 1997 special issue of *Computational Linguistics* was devoted to empirical studies in discourse. The introduction by Walker and Moore provides an excellent overview of the current status of the field, also connecting it to similar work in other areas, e.g. (Cohen 1996). To be able to make full use of the empirical data available today, we believe that we need to know more about how to compare and contrast different dialog situations. We have tried to contribute to this by taking the first steps toward a multidimensional taxonomy for dialog situations (Dahlbäck 1997). But more work is clearly needed here.

One issue that has become more prominent in both IUI in general and NLP (Natural Language Processing) in particular is evaluation (Sparck Jones and Galliers 1996). Important here is, among other things, the development of a set of standard procedures and metrics (e.g., recall and precision and the Kappa statistic for measuring interater reliability). The Discourse Resource Initiative (Carletta et al. 1997), which aims at developing coding standards for dialog studies, and the sharing of tools and corpora, are other important steps toward placing the work on dialog systems on a firmer empirical ground.

The discussion here, as well as the original paper, has its focus on NLP and especially NLIs. But we believe that much of the work cited here can be adapted to other areas of IUI, for example, the work on different uses of empirical methods in different stages in the development of advanced user interfaces (Carletta et al. 1997; Walker and Moore 1997). In our own case, we have certainly been able to benefit from the experiences described in our paper, both in NLI design (Jönsson 1993), other areas of IUI (Höök et al. 1996), and other areas of NLP (Ahrenberg and Merkel 1996).

REFERENCES

Ahrenberg, L., and Merkel, M. 1996. Translation Corpora and Translation Support Tools—A Project Report. In Aijmer, K., Altenberg, B., and Johansson, M. (eds.), *Languages in Contrast*. Lund, Sweden: Lund University Press.

Carletta, J. 1996. Assessing Agreement on Classification Tasks: The Kappa Statistic. *Computational Linguistics*, 22(2): 249–254.

Carletta, J.; Dahlbäck, N.; Reithinger, N.; and Walker, M. (eds.). 1997. Standards for Dialogue Coding in Natural Language Processing. Dagstuhl Seminar Report, 167. (see also *http://www.georgetown.edu/luperfoy/Discourse-Treebank/dri-home.html*)

Cohen, P. R. 1996. *Empirical Methods for Artificial Intelligence*. Boston: MIT Press.

Dahlbäck, N. 1997. Towards a Dialogue Taxonomy. In Maier, E., Mast, M., and LuperFoy, S. (eds.), *Dialogue Processing in Spoken Language Systems*. Berlin: Springer-Verlag.

Höök, K.; Karlgren, J.; Wærn, A.; Dahlbäck, N.; Jansson, C.; Karlgren, K.; and Lemaire, B. 1996. A Glass-Box Approach to Adaptive Hypermedia. *Journal of User Modeling and User Adaptive Interaction* 6: 157–184.

Jönsson, A. 1993. A Method for Development of Dialogue Managers for Natural Language Interfaces. In *Proceedings AAAI'93*, Washington, DC, 190–195.

Sparck Jones, K., and Galliers, J. 1996. *Evaluating Natural Language Processing Systems*. Berlin: Springer-Verlag.

Walker, M., and Moore, J. 1997. Empirical Studies in Discourse. *Computational Linguistics*, 23(1): 1–12.

Multimodal Interaction

User-Centered Modeling for Spoken Language and Multimodal Interfaces

Sharon Oviatt
Oregon Graduate Institute of Science & Technology

By modeling difficult sources of linguistic variability in speech and language, we can design interfaces that transparently guide human input to match system processing capabilities. Such work will yield more user-centered and robust interfaces for next-generation spoken language and multimodal systems.

Historically, technology has driven the development of spoken language systems. However, successfully processing spontaneous speech and dialogue, especially in actual field settings, requires a considerably broader understanding of performance issues during human-computer spoken interactions. Inadequate research from this perspective has left a gap in our scientific knowledge, hindering our ability to support robust speech for real commercial applications. Here we look at recent research on user-centered modeling of human language and performance during spoken and multimodal interaction. We also will consider interface design aimed at next-generation systems.

Why can't speakers adapt?

Technologists developing speech and language-oriented systems tend to think that "users can adapt" to whatever they build. Typically, they rely on instruction, training, and practice with the system to encourage users to speak in a manner that matches system processing capabilities. However, human speech production involves a highly automatic set of skills organized in a modality-specific brain center. As a result, many of its features are not under full conscious control (for example, disfluencies, prosody, and timing). Moreover, even the most cooperative users face constraints on the extent to which they can adapt their speech to suit system limitations—such as the need to articulate with artificial pauses between words for an isolated word recognizer. Even when people concentrate on changing some aspect of their speech, such as deliberate pausing, as soon as they become absorbed with a real task, they quickly forget and slip back into their more natural and automatic style of delivery. My colleagues and I at the Center for Human-Computer Communication believe that a more promising and enduring approach to the design of spoken language systems would

- model the user- and modality-centered speech upon which the system must be built and
- design spoken interface capabilities that leverage from these existing, strongly engrained speech patterns.

This approach could substantially improve the commercial viability of next-generation systems for a wide range of real-world applications, especially communications devices and mobile technology.

User and modality-centered approach

Individual communication modalities, including spoken, written, keyboard, and others, shape the language transmitted within them. In a sense, communication channels physically constrain the flow and shape of human language just as a river bed directs the river's current. To be successful, technology based on human language input needs to be designed to accommodate the unique landmark features of the underlying input modality. In the case of speech—especially interactive speech, in which dialogue partners alternate turns—these landmark features include

- disfluencies,
- errors and repairs,
- confirmation requests and feedback,
- prosodic and nonverbal modulation of language,
- regulating turn-taking and dialogue control, and
- grammatically run-on constructions.

Unfortunately, current spoken language systems typically train on samples of read or noninteractive speech, which fail to represent these unique landmark features.

Variability in spoken language

Linguistic variability complicates the development of human language technology. Spoken language in particular is notoriously variable, verbose, and seemingly unruly. Since people focus on extracting meaning when they interact with others, they don't notice the fragmented and disfluent qualities of our utterances. Many people are quite surprised to see a literal transcription of what they just said. For example, consider this mailroom conversation:

Person A: "I thought you went, you were going to the Ashland Festival. . . the Ashland Shakespeare Festival."

Person B: "No, no, umm, that was the weekend, the weekend, remember?"

A: "Ohhh yes."

B: "We went to. . . it's uh, it's called Il Posto, Il Postino. Italian film with, uh, what's his name? The guy who played Mario?"

A: "Yeah, Massimo Troisi, uh, Troy-eee-zeee."

Like interactive conversations, spontaneous speech to computers is also fragmented, disfluent, and linguistically variable in ways that make it very different from formal textual language. During the exchange illustrated in Figure 1, the speaker first uses the map system's automatic locator to find Twin Lakes. As illustrated in the conversational exchange below, he then tries to add an open space to the map, but forgets to specify its intended location. After the system requests clarification, the user provides a lengthy and syntactically convoluted location description:

User: "Where is Twin Lakes?"

System: [map scrolls and highlights requested location]

User: "Add an open space."

System: "Please be more specific."

User: "Add an open space on the north lake to b. . . include the north lake part of the road and north."

Spoken input such as this—disfluent, repetitious, and syntactically ill-formed—would seriously challenge current speech technology.

Terminology

Disfluency: a spontaneous self-correction or repair that interrupts the smooth flow of an otherwise coherent sentence.

Prosody: fluctuations in stress and intonation across spoken words and sentences.

Syntactic ambiguity: the number of possible parse alternatives for assigning meaning to a grammatical sequence of words.

Word bigram perplexity: a measure of the average predictability of lexical items in a corpus, given information about word pair sequences within it.

Spiral error: a recognition system error that recurs on the same content item.

Hyperarticulation: a stylized and clarified form of pronunciation.

Hidden Markov Model: a probablistic transition state model used in the speech recognition process to produce phonemes as output.

For further discussion of Hidden Markov Models see

J. Makhoul and R. Schwartz, "State of the Art in Continuous Speech Recognition," *Voice Communication Between Humans and Machines*, D.B. Roe and J.G. Wilpon, eds., National Academy Press, Washington, D.C., 1994, pp. 165-198.

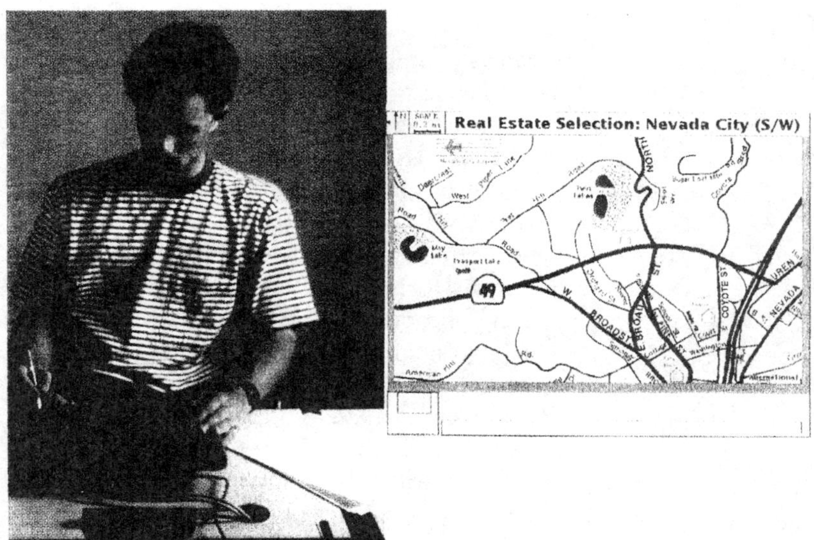

Figure 1. A user asks, "Where is Twin Lakes?" to invoke the map system's automatic locator.

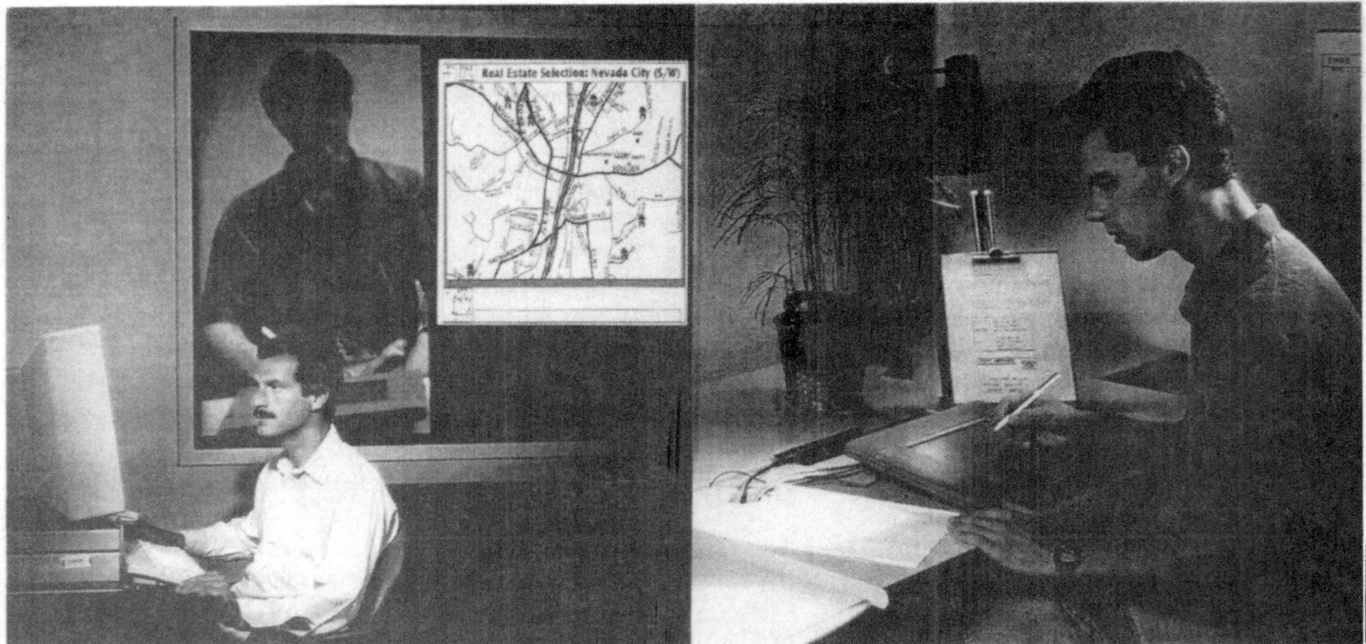

Figure 2. A test subject selects real estate during data collection (right panel), and a programmer assistant provides simulated system response (left panel).

Clearly, the demands on a user to plan the content and order of what to say while focused on a real interactive task plays a large role in generating these features of spontaneous speech. These same demands also trigger performance errors that must be repaired to prevent communication breakdown.

Managing linguistic variability

Interface techniques for successfully constraining spoken input have received the most scrutiny from the telecommunications industry in the course of automating telephone operator services.[1,2] This work emphasizes the need for realistic testing with simulated or fully functional systems. It also indicates that certain spoken language phenomena prove more amenable to channeling than others and that dramatic variations can occur in the successful elicitation of target language (city names, or digit strings, for example) depending on the type of system prompt.

Past research also shows that *linguistic convergence*—the tendency of people's speech patterns to gravitate toward those of their interactive partner—can serve to guide human spoken input during human-computer interaction. For example, a few studies have indicated that linguistic features like wordiness, lexical choice, and grammatical structure can be constrained through modeling and shaping techniques, with some system prompts more effective than others.[3] This approach has the advantage of not imposing any explicit constraints on users' behavior.

Our own research shows that many difficult sources of variability in human speech (wordiness, disfluencies, lexical composition, syntactic ambiguity, perplexity) can be reduced two to eight-fold by altering interface parameters such as presentation format, without necessarily sacrificing user acceptability.[4,5] Such work demonstrates the potential impact that basic interface design can have on managing spoken input and its processability.

We believe that modeling unique features of spontaneous interactive speech substantially assists in designing successful spoken interfaces. Our research has aimed to

- identify sources of variability in the speech stream at different linguistic levels,
- identify and model hard-to-process sources of variability with respect to current and near-term system processing capabilities, and
- discover interface techniques capable of effectively but transparently reducing these difficult sources of variability, thereby enabling more robust system processing.

With this approach, we wanted to support more robust spoken language systems by using models of users' preexisting language patterns rather than attempting to retrain strongly entrenched speech patterns. We also intended to design interfaces that effectively avoid difficult variability sources in speech, rather than having to excise or process them. We can build more robust spoken language systems as long as we can

- identify the underlying factors that cause hard-to-process sources of variability in speech;
- model the interface parameters that drive their observed frequency during human-computer interaction; and
- summarize the design trade-offs associated with different implementation decisions and use them to optimize system performance.

In this article, we concentrate on two hard-to-process spoken language phenomena—disfluent speech and hyperarticulation in response to system recognition failures.

Simulating planned systems

Our research primarily involves proactive and situated data collection for system design, which precedes building a fully functional system. To accomplish this, we used a semi-automatic simulation method in which a programmer assistant plays the role of the system. Figure 2 illustrates a test subject, using what he believes is a fully functional spoken language system, to select real estate (right panel); a remotely located programmer assistant who provides simulated system responses (left panel); and a view of videotaped data capture (left panel, large screen in background). As the subject works, the assistant tracks the subject's spoken input and simply clicks on predefined fields at a Sun Sparcstation to send system confirmations back to the subject.

We automated simulation software to support accurate and rapid responding by the assistant. For example, simulated recognition errors are delivered automatically by a random error generator, which can be preprogrammed to deliver different base-rates and types of recognition error distributed randomly across task content. Since we believe that users expect speedy interaction with a spoken language system, our simulation supports subject-paced interactions that average a 0.4 second delay between a subject's input and the system response. You can find technical details of the simulation method's capabilities and performance characteristics outlined elsewhere.[6]

High-fidelity simulations are the preferred method of designing and evaluating systems in the planning stages—they are relatively easy and inexpensive to adapt compared to building and iterating a complete system. They also let researchers and system designers alter a planned system's characteristics (multimedia input and output modes) in major ways and study the impact of important interface characteristics (the type and base-rate of system errors). In comparison, a particular system with fixed characteristics is less flexible and suitable as a research tool.

Simulation research can help designers evaluate critical performance trade-offs and make alternative system design decisions, which they must do to create more usable spoken language systems. Using simulation techniques lets researchers and designers quickly adapt and investigate system features, thus gaining a broader perspective on new classes of technology including human-language, multimodal, and multimedia systems.

With simulation research techniques, we can collect empirical data that

- reveals undiscovered phenomena of interest, such as landmark features of interactive speech, that spoken language systems will need to process;
- quantifies the prevalence of these spoken language phenomena;
- establishes their causal basis by isolating and manipulating factors that drive them; and
- interprets these phenomena in relation to performance and contextual factors that predict and help explain them, such as the interface characteristics influencing their rate of occurrence.

Disfluent talk to computers

Disfluencies in spontaneous speech arise from self-repairs that interrupt the smooth flow of an otherwise coherent linguistic construction. Examples of spoken disfluencies include

1. *Content self-corrections*—errors in task content that are spontaneously self-corrected, such as "west of, no, east of Seven Hills School."
2. *False starts*—a spontaneous rerouting of the grammatical structure of an utterance, such as "I want to. . . give me a hospital within 1.5 miles."

*Table 1. Spoken disfluency rates per 100 words.**

Type of Spoken Interaction	Disfluency Rate
Human-human speech	
Two-person telephone call	8:83
Three-person interpreted telephone call	6:25
Two-person face-to-face dialogue	5:50
One-person noninteractive monologue	3:60
Human-computer speech	
Unconstrained computer interaction	1:74/1:87/2:14
Structured computer interaction	0:78/0:87/1:70

* The human-computer disfluency rates represent verbal-temporal, computational-numeric, and visual-cartographic content, respectively (from left to right).

3. *Verbatim repetitions*—spontaneous repetition of a phoneme, syllable, word, or phrase while speaking, such as "Victor. . .Victorian museum."

4. *Filled pauses*—spontaneous nonlexical sounds that fill pauses in running speech, such as "uh" and "um."

Disfluencies are good examples of a spoken language feature that occurs frequently in task-oriented interactive speech, especially when planning demands are high.

Automatically correcting disfluencies

Because disfluent speech is widely recognized as a major challenge and source of failure for current spoken language systems, researchers address it in several ways. One computationally oriented approach searches for reliable methods to automatically detect and correct disfluent content during interactions with spoken language systems. This research focuses on identifying acoustic or prosodic cues for detecting self-repairs, either alone or in combination with syntactic, semantic, and pattern matching information.[7] This approach to automatically processing disfluencies seems a promising long-term effort. However, it also represents a difficult research problem that to date has not yielded a reliable and practical method for improving system recognition rates.

Interface design to avoid disfluencies

A second approach involves designing interfaces that substantially minimize disfluent speech. This approach assumes that if naturally occurring disfluency rates vary for different types of spoken interaction, then interface design might be an effective tool in successfully reducing disfluencies. This research focuses on

- empirically studying disfluencies and their properties during human-computer interaction, and modeling them quantitatively;
- identifying underlying cognitive factors that drive disfluencies; and
- designing techniques for structuring interfaces that can minimize disfluencies.

Table 1 summarizes the rate of disfluencies per 100 words in different kinds of spoken interaction. The data confirm that rates can vary by as much as 11-fold.[4,8] Table 1 also shows that disfluencies occur at higher rates in human-human than in human-computer speech and increase substantially during human-human telephone conversations.

Predicting disfluencies from utterance length

In human-computer interaction, several major disfluency findings stand out. First, spoken disfluencies respond strikingly to the increased planning demands of speaking progressively longer utterances. In fact, a large body of data based on several studies has shown that almost 80 percent of all the variance in spoken disfluencies during human-computer interaction is predictable simply by knowing an utterance's specific length.

The scatterplot in Figure 3 illustrates a linear model summarizing this relation, which broadly generalizes across tasks involving different content. In short sentences of one to six words, the disfluency rate averaged a minimal 0.66, whereas in moderate to lengthy sentences of seven to 18 words, this average increased to 2.81—a 326 percent increase. This relation probably results from the increasing cognitive load associated with planning the content and order of what to say, which rises progressively in longer utterances.

Designing a structured interface to minimize disfluencies

One effective interface technique to reduce spoken disfluencies involves designing a structured interface that successfully elicits brief utterances. An unconstrained format, which requires the speaker to self-structure and plan to a greater degree, will lead the same speaker in the same task to produce a substantially higher rate of disfluencies than a more structured format. Consider, for example, a structured form-based interaction that uses prompts like

Car pickup location:_______________

A highly structured format can reduce disfluencies to just 30 to 40 percent of those that would have occurred in an unconstrained interface.

As illustrated in Table 1, this structured format effect replicates across different communicative content and interfaces, including

1. verbal tasks, as illustrated in the car rental prompt;
2. numeric tasks, in which the user pays bills by speaking to a structured bank register; and
3. map-based real estate tasks, as illustrated previously in Figure 1.

In fact, using a structured presentation format can have a broad influence on simplifying natural language processing beyond reducing disfluent language. A structured format also can substantially reduce lexical variability, syntactic complexity and ambiguity, word bigram perplexity, and other problematic aspects of language. At the same time, users prefer this format by a factor of two to one.[5]

Predicting disfluencies from spatial content

Complex spatial tasks can precipitate higher disfluency rates than other domains, as shown in Table 1. For example, during map-based interactions, analysis of utterances matched on speaker and length revealed that disfluencies concentrate 50 percent more heavily on spatial location constituents than on baseline ones. Consider the following example of a self-corrected reversal of orientation:

User: "Place a boat dock on the east, no, west end of Reward Lake."

Even articulating relatively simple spatial location descriptions like this one elevates users' planning load and precipitates errors.

Designing a multimodal interface to minimize disfluencies

For complex spatial domains, such as map-based interactions, an effective interface technique for reducing spoken disfluencies would employ a multimodal interface with a direct, precise input mode such as a pen. Pen input generally indicates points, lines, and abstract areas more quickly and effectively than would a spoken spatial description. For example, in a multimodal interface, a user can point to the west end of Reward Lake and simply say "Boat dock."

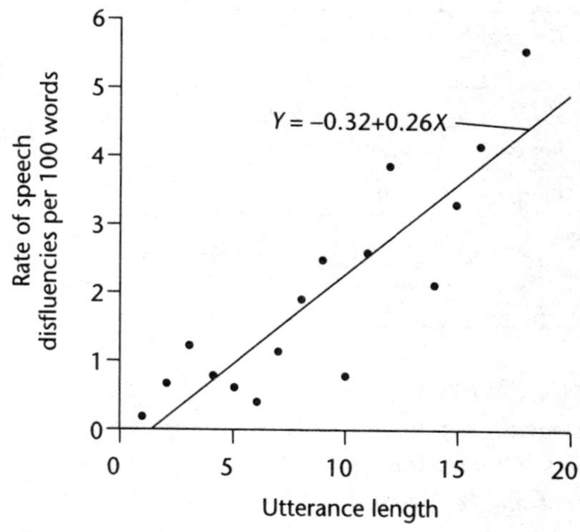

Figure 3. Linear regression model summarizing the increasing rate of spoken disfluencies per 100 words as a function of utterance length.

When interacting multimodally, users naturally tend to avoid articulating spatial information, instead conveying it with simple pen-based graphics, pointing, and gestures. When users are forced to speak spatial information, performance problems increase, including higher task-critical error rates, higher disfluency rates, longer and more complex syntactic constructions, and longer task completion time.[8] For map-based interactions, a multimodal interface reduces spoken disfluencies to just 50 percent of the rate that would have occurred for the same speaker completing the same task in a speech-only interface. Nearly all users (95 percent) prefer to interact with maps multimodally. The multimodal design of systems involving complex visual displays provides a good example of an interface strategy that effectively but transparently avoids difficult variability sources in human input, thereby enabling more robust system processing.

Hyperarticulation

Many researchers and corporate designers regard poor error handling to be a serious obstacle that prevents widespread commercialization of current recognition-based systems. This in part is because the widely advocated concept of designing for error has not been applied effectively to designing spoken language systems. Since speech technology is inherently error-prone, users can actually spend a substantial amount of time resolving errors, making graceful error handling essential.

Hyperarticulation provides a good example of a hard-to-process source of linguistic variability that occurs in task-oriented interactive speech when users try to resolve recognition errors with a system.[9] *Hyperarticulate* speech refers to a stylized

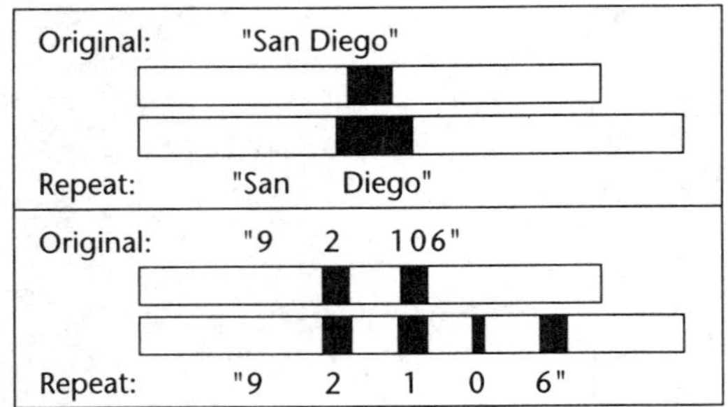

Figure 4. Pause elongation (top) and pause interjection (bottom) in matched original-repeat utterance pairs.

and clarified form of pronunciation and it has been associated with high rates of system recognition failure.

Current speech recognizers train on original error-free input, typically collected under unnatural and constrained task conditions—they omit training on hyperarticulated spoken repetitions elicited during real or simulated errors. As a result, hyperarticulate speech constitutes a difficult variability source that degrades speech recognizers' performance because it departs from the data they were trained on.

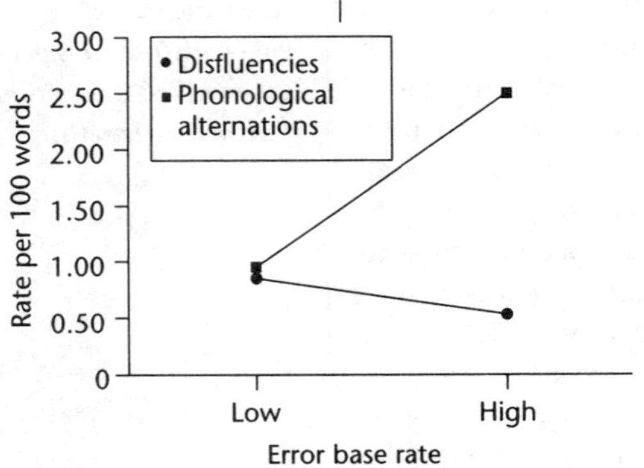

Figure 5. Rate of spoken disfluencies and phonological alternations per 100 words as a function of error base-rate.

In short, hyperarticulate speech is both users' natural reaction to system recognition failure, as well as a source of generating higher system error rates. That is, hyperarticulation has the potential to fuel a cycle of recognition failure. These factors may contribute to spiral errors in recognition-based systems—system errors that occur repeatedly on the same propositional content.[10] Spiral errors are a frustrating and consequential type of error. If the number of repetitions needed to resolve a spiral error becomes intolerable to the user, the user typically will quit the application.

Recognition technology design also contributes to the cycle of recognition failure. For example, one unfortunate property of Hidden Markov Models is the propagation of recognition errors—a misrecognized word can cause misrecognition of others in its vicinity.[11] Likewise, language models based on conditional probabilities can propagate recognition errors, because an error forces the language model into an incorrect state and increases the likelihood of an error on subsequent words.[12] Once an error occurs, the properties of spoken language technology and users' reactive hyperarticulations both play a role in perpetuating further errors, thereby hindering a graceful recovery.

Modeling hyperarticulate speech

In our research, we created a user-centered predictive model of how speakers systematically adapt their spoken language during human-computer error resolution. More specifically, we

- defined the type and magnitude of linguistic adaptations that occur when people try to resolve system recognition errors;
- modeled users' adapted language quantitatively, including phenomena at different linguistic levels (acoustic/prosodic, phonological, lexical, and input modality); and
- applied this information in designing better error avoidance and resolution techniques to support more robust processing in spoken language and multimodal systems.

We recently discovered that users' speech to computers becomes substantially lengthier and more clearly articulated during system error resolution. In comparing matched utterances involving the same speaker and same lexical content occurring immediately before and after a simulated recognition error, the total speech segment averaged 12 percent longer, total pause duration measured 73 percent longer, and 91 percent more pauses on average were interjected during repetitions following the error.[9]

Figure 4 illustrates two examples of these adaptations in repeat speech as a user repeats "San Diego" and the zip code "92106." In fact, the major difference between original and repeat speech is this relative increase in number and length of pauses.

Another major change is that speech during error resolution shifts from the relaxed and phonologically reduced style of conversational speech to a clear speech pattern. For example, in our study, speakers sometimes reduced *t* to the flap *d* sound during original input (saying "fordy" for 40), but repeated it as an unreduced *t* ("forty") during error correction. Speakers also don't reduce *nt* sequences when hyperarticulating, so during first input they omit the *t* sound in 20 ("tweny"), but clearly articulate it when repeating it during error resolution ("twenty"). In addition, they occasionally shift from a relaxed pronunciation with syllables omitted (saying "'leven" for 11) to articulating all segments when correcting it ("eleven").

Figure 5 illustrates that this shift toward clear-speech articulation also corresponds with a drop in spoken disfluencies during error resolution, an inverse relation accentuated during a high base-rate of errors.

Three solutions to hyperarticulate speech

Three methods can improve the performance of current spoken language systems on hyperarticulate speech. First, train recognizers on more natural samples of users' interactive speech to systems, including error resolution with the type and base-rate of errors expected in the target system. This approach entails collecting a more heterogeneous training corpus as a basis for recognition.

Second, design an error handling recognizer that could function as part of a coordinated suite of multiple recognizers and be swapped in and out at appropriate points during a system interaction. Building a successful recognizer of this kind depends on the availability of accurate data and quantitative models of hyperarticulation. Such a recognizer might work well in a form-based interface that has content-specific input slots, since reentry into the same slot would likely involve a correction.

Third, avoid hyperarticulate speech by designing a multimodal rather than a unimodal interface.

Designing a multimodal interface to avoid error

When users attempt to correct an error, sometimes a unidirectional shift occurs in their linguistic features toward hyperarticulate or clear speech. In other situations, they adapt their language in a linguistically contrastive manner to distinguish repeat speech from the original failed input. For example, during multimodal interaction users tend to shift input modes as they try to resolve system errors. In fact, compared with original error-free spoken input, this contrastive functional use of modes increases approximately three-fold during error resolution.[10] Figure 6 illustrates that the likelihood of shifting between input modes becomes more pronounced during repeated attempts to resolve spiral errors.

These data suggest that a multimodal rather than a speech-only interface design can avoid hyperarticulate speech and expedite error handling. First, multimodal system design can improve error avoidance, since users often act on good intuitions regarding a particular input mode's accuracy for conveying specific content. For example, they prefer to write, rather than speak, a foreign surname.[13] A flexible multimodal system can leverage people's natural ability to use input modes accurately and efficiently. Furthermore, the degree of error avoidance possible through multimodal interface design can be substantial. In one telecommunications application, for example, simply providing a second input mode could have prevented up to 86 percent of all task-critical errors.[10]

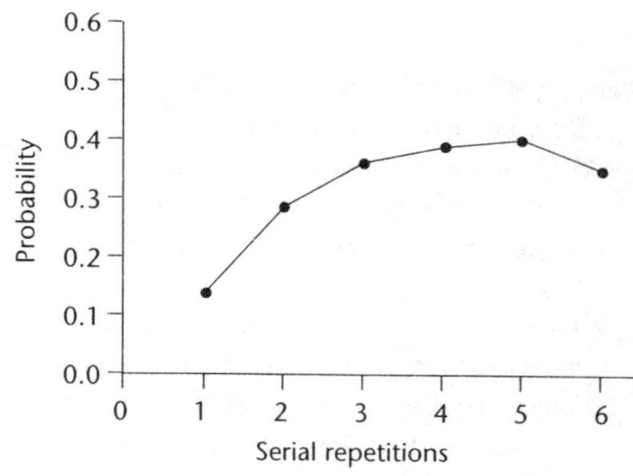

Figure 6. Probability of switching input modes at each serial repetition during a spiral error (1-6).

Second, a multimodal interface expedites recovery from recognition errors. Since the confusion matrices differ for the same content when spoken versus written, users' tendency to accelerate mode shifting during spiral errors could very effectively reduce a string of repeated failures.

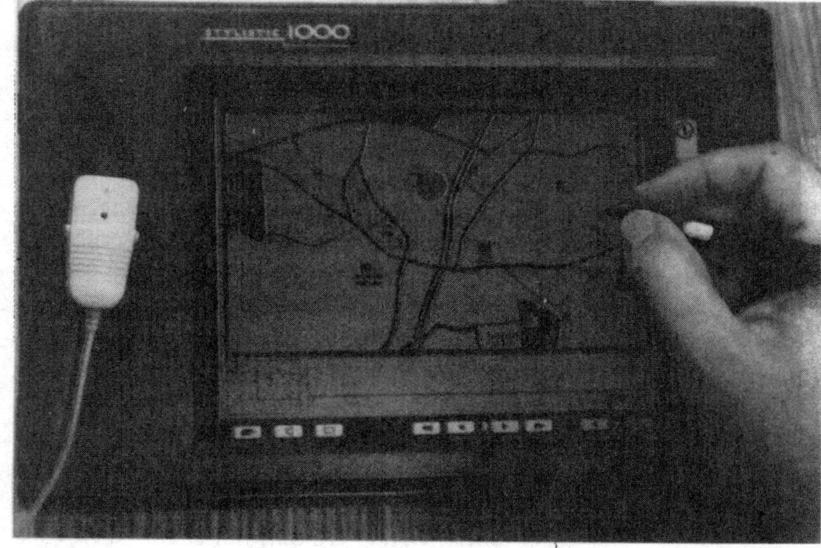

Figure 7. Multimodal pen and voice real-estate system on a hand-held PC.

Multimodal system development

The research reported here inspired the design and development of multimodal systems in our laboratory that support map-based applications ranging from real estate and healthcare selection to military simulation.[14] In these systems, the user communicates through the Fujitsu Stylistic 1000 shown in Figure 7, a wireless hand-held PC that provides both pen and speech recognition. The systems that we have developed integrate pen, voice, natural language, and multimodal interpretation subsystems via a distributed agent architecture.[15]

This agent architecture also allows the hand-held PC to control applications that reside else-

> **Recent Research on Spoken Language Systems**
>
> *Voice Communication Between Humans and Machines*, D.B. Roe and J.G. Wilpon, eds., National Academy Press, Washington, D.C., 1994.
>
> J.R. Rhyne and C.G. Wolf, "Recognition-Based User Interfaces," *Advances in Human-Computer Interaction*, H. R. Hartson and D. Hix, eds., Vol. 4, Ablex Publishing Corp., Norwood, N. J., 1993, pp. 191-250.
>
> R.L. Cole et. al, "The Challenge of Spoken Language Systems: Research Directions for the Nineties," *IEEE Trans. on Speech and Audio Processing*, Vol. 3, No. 1, pp. 1-21.
>
> *Survey on the State of the Art in Speech and Natural Language Processing*, R. Cole et al., eds., to be published by Cambridge University Press, Cambridge, Mass.

where on the Internet and that may operate in different software and hardware environments (for instance, virtual reality software running in Unix on Silicon Graphics hardware). The small size and wireless communication of the handheld PC, as well as its on-board multimodal interface involving spoken and pen-based input, effectively support mobile use in different environments.

Through a combination of spoken and gestural input, users of these multimodal systems can add entities to a map, edit or move entities currently displayed, ask questions about entities and related data, issue commands to control the map display, filter information in the database, or set up and activate scenarios. During multimodal interaction, users often select speech to describe sets of entities or to automatically locate entities not currently in view. In contrast, they typically use simple graphic or gestural input to indicate locations, draw lines (tracing irregular routes), and outline spatial areas—all ineffectively communicated when spoken. For instance, in a speech-only interface, military users typically speak location information using spatial coordinates with latitude and longitude designations. When they require a precise location, they typically must adjust these coordinates repeatedly until they achieve the correct location.

Spoken input: "Place a point at 1 5 2 0 3 4 and call it objective alpha. Cancel that. Put objective alpha at 1 5 1 0 3 6. Cancel that. Put objective alpha at 1 5 1 0 3 7."

In contrast, placing a dot on the required location and speaking the object's name is more precise and avoids repeated errors and self-correction:

Multimodal input: Objective alpha [•]

Our research team is currently developing a joint interpretation strategy based on parallel processing of spoken and pen-based signals to process multimodal input. In this approach, spoken language understanding compensates for ambiguity and potential errors in gestural interpretation and vice versa, through a statistically ranked unification of semantic interpretations.

Future directions

Many basic interface issues need to be resolved before technology can benefit fully from the natural advantages of speech—including the speed, ease, and interactive spontaneity that people experience when using it during human-human communication. Our work focuses on solving problems created by difficult spoken language phenomena, with the specific goal of using interface design to minimize their disruptive impact on system performance. One conclusion that emerges from this work is the potential performance and usability advantages of multimodal interface design—in terms of the expressive power, accuracy, efficiency, flexibility, ease of error handling, and resulting system robustness that multimodal interfaces can support. **MM**

Acknowledgments

This research has been supported in part by grants IRI-9213472 and IRI-9530666 from the National Science Foundation. We also would like to thank our corporate supporters: Apple Computer, AT&T/NCR, ATR Intl., CIC, ETRI, GTE Labs, Intel, Microsoft, NTT Data Communications, Scriptel, Southwestern Bell, Sun Microsystems, US West, and Wacom.

Special thanks to the many talented students and staff who have contributed to various aspects of this research, including Adam Cheyer, Antonella DeAngeli, John Dowding, David Fencsik, Martin Fong, Michael Frank, Jeremy Gaston, Martin Gottfried, Aaron Hallmark, Yi Han, Matt Heitz, Eric Iverson, Michael Johnston, Karen Kuhn, Gina Levow, Peggy Li, Jon Lindsay, Margaret MacEacheron, Elliott Moreton, Erik Olsen, James Pittman, Ira Smith, Robert vanGent, Michelle Wang, Lawrence Waugh, Dan Wilk, and Zak Zaidman. Thanks also to Phil Cohen and Etienne Barnard for helpful discussion and manuscript comments. Finally, sincere thanks to the generous people who volunteered to participate in this research as subjects.

References

1. D. Karis and K.M. Dobroth, "Automating Services with Speech Recognition over the Public Switched

Telephone Network: Human Factors Considerations," *IEEE J. of Selected Areas in Communications*, Vol. 9, No. 4, 1991, pp. 574-585.

2. J. Spitz, "Collection and Analysis of Data from Real Users: Implications for Speech Recognition/Understanding Systems," *Proc. 4th DARPA Workshop on Speech and Natural Language*, Morgan Kaufmann, San Mateo, Ca., 1991.
3. E. Zoltan-Ford, "How to Get People to Say and Type What Computers Can Understand," *Int'l. J. of Man-Machine Studies*, Vol. 34, 1991, pp. 527-547.
4. S.L. Oviatt, "Predicting Spoken Disfluencies During Human-Computer Interaction," *Computer Speech and Language*, Vol. 9, 1995, pp. 19-35.
5. S.L. Oviatt, P.R. Cohen, and M.Q. Wang, "Toward Interface Design for Human Language Technology: Modality and Structure as Determinants of Linguistic Complexity," *Speech Communication*, European Speech Communication Assoc., Vol. 15, 1994, pp. 283-300.
6. S.L. Oviatt, P.R. Cohen, M.W. Fong, and M.P. Frank, "A Rapid Semi-Automatic Simulation Technique for Investigating Interactive Speech and Handwriting," *Proc. Int'l Conf. on Spoken Language Processing*, J. Ohala et al., eds., University of Alberta Press, Edmonton, Canada, 1992, Vol. 2, pp. 1351-1354.
7. E. Shriberg, J. Bear, and J. Dowding, "Automatic Detection and Correction of Repairs in Human-Computer Dialog," *Proc. of the DARPA Speech and Natural Language Workshop*, Morgan Kaufmann, San Mateo, Ca., 1992, pp. 23-26.
8. S.L. Oviatt, "Multimodal Interactive Maps: Designing for Human Performance," to be published in *Human-Computer Interaction*, 1997.
9. S.L. Oviatt et al., "Modeling Hyperarticulate Speech During Human-Computer Error Resolution," *Proc. Int'l Conf. of Spoken Language Processing*, T. Bunnell and W. Idsardi, eds., Univ. of Delaware and A.I. duPont Inst., Vol. 2, 1996, pp. 801-804.
10. S.L. Oviatt and R. vanGent, "Error Resolution During Multimodal Human-Computer Interaction," *Proc. Int'l. Conf. on Spoken Language Processing*, T. Bunnell and W. Idsardi, eds., Univ. of Delaware and A.I. duPont Inst., Vol. 1, 1996, pp. 204-207.
11. J.R. Rhyne and C.G. Wolf, "Recognition-Based User Interfaces," *Advances in Human-Computer Interaction*, H. R. Hartson and D. Hix, eds., Vol. 4, Ablex Publishing Corp., Norwood, N. J., 1993, pp. 191-250.
12. F. Jelinek, "The Development of an Experimental Discrete Dictation Recognizer," *Proc. of the IEEE*, IEEE, New York, N.Y., 1985, 73, pp. 1616-1624.
13. S.L. Oviatt and E. Olsen, "Integration Themes in Multimodal Human-Computer Interaction," *Proc. Int'l Conf. on Spoken Language Processing*, K. Shirai et al., eds., Acoustical Society of Japan, Toyko, 1994, Vol. 2, pp. 551-554.
14. J.A. Pittman et al., "Quickset: A Multimodal Interface for Distributed Interactive Simulations," *Proc. of the 6th Conf. on Computer-Generated Forces*, Univ. of Central Florida, Orlando, Fla., 1996, pp. 217-224.
15. P.R. Cohen et al., "An Open Architecture," Working Notes of the AAAI Spring Symposium Series on Software Agents at Stanford, Ca., (Tech. Report SS-94-03, AAAI, Menlo Park, Ca.), 1994.

Reflections on...

User-Centered Modeling for Spoken Language and Multimodal Interfaces

Sharon L. Oviatt

During the late 1980s, I became interested in analyzing the linguistic and performance characteristics of different communication modalities. I was especially interested in how the structural properties of a communication mode influence the language transmitted within it, sometimes in quite profound ways. Having just abandoned academic psychology and gone to work in the natural language group of SRI's AI center, I also was interested in how technologically mediated communication differs from natural human communication patterns. I conducted a series of studies in which I collected and analyzed data on human-human versus human-computer communication, spoken versus written communication, direct versus mediated communication, unilingual versus interpreted communication, and unimodal versus multimodal communication. As a result, I became attuned to the unique landmark features of different communication modalities—especially those typical of spontaneous spoken language. I also developed a somewhat unique interdisciplinary perspective because of the cross-fertilization between my experiences with cognitive-empirical science and computational science.

During the early 1990s, I then had the opportunity to observe research progress in the DARPA-funded speech community, which stimulated my sense that work was needed on the *spontaneous* and *interactive* characteristics of spoken language with computers. I became interested in identifying *hard-to-process sources of variability* in spontaneous interactive speech, which led to my work on disfluent language (Oviatt 1995) and on interface design for managing linguistic variability during interaction with computers (Oviatt et al. 1994). While speech technology was developing rapidly, pen computing also began to emerge. I became intrigued with the potential complementarity of speech and pen input and began contemplating the advantages of building a *synergistic multimodal interface* capable of handling both spoken and pen-based input. At an NSF workshop on spoken language systems in 1992, I proposed that speech be viewed as just one input mode incorporated into more flexible and powerful multimodal interfaces—a view elaborated in my section on interactive multimodal systems in the subsequent workshop publication (Cole et al. 1995).

However, perhaps the most instrumental event in developing the research described in this paper was my collaboration with other colleagues in designing and building a semiautomatic simulation environment (Oviatt et al. 1992), which I have used extensively over the past five years as a tool for investigating interactive spoken, pen-based, and multimodal exchanges with computers. The resulting empirical foundation of data directly supported my ability to develop user-centered predictive models of spontaneous spoken and multimodal communication. In recent years, I have focused increasingly on multimodal communication, including the advantages of multimodal interface design for error handling (Oviatt et al. 1996; Oviatt and vanGent 1996) and for supporting interaction in visual-spatial domains (Oviatt, in press). Since writing this paper, I have continued to work on these aspects of multimodal interaction and on the integration and synchronization of input modes during multimodal interaction (Oviatt et al. 1997).

REFERENCES

Oviatt, S. L.; DeAngeli, A.; and Kuhn, K. 1997. Integration and Synchronization of Input Modes During Multimodal Human-Computer Interaction. In *Proceedings of ACM Conference on Human Factors in Computing Systems*, CHI'97. New York: ACM Press, 1997, 415–422.

PARADISE: A Framework for Evaluating Spoken Dialogue Agents

Marilyn A. Walker, Diane J. Litman, Candace A. Kamm and Alicia Abella
AT&T Labs—Research
180 Park Avenue
Florham Park, NJ 07932-0971 USA
walker,diane,cak,abella@research.att.com

Abstract

This paper presents PARADISE (PARAdigm for DIalogue System Evaluation), a general framework for evaluating spoken dialogue agents. The framework decouples task requirements from an agent's dialogue behaviors, supports comparisons among dialogue strategies, enables the calculation of performance over subdialogues and whole dialogues, specifies the relative contribution of various factors to performance, and makes it possible to compare agents performing different tasks by normalizing for task complexity.

1 Introduction

Recent advances in dialogue modeling, speech recognition, and natural language processing have made it possible to build spoken dialogue agents for a wide variety of applications.[1] Potential benefits of such agents include remote or hands-free access, ease of use, naturalness, and greater efficiency of interaction. However, a critical obstacle to progress in this area is the lack of a general framework for evaluating and comparing the performance of different dialogue agents.

One widely used approach to evaluation is based on the notion of a reference answer (Hirschman et al., 1990). An agent's responses to a query are compared with a predefined key of minimum and maximum reference answers; performance is the proportion of responses that match the key. This approach has many widely acknowledged limitations (Hirschman and Pao, 1993; Danieli et al., 1992; Bates and Ayuso, 1993), e.g., although there may be many potential dialogue strategies for carrying out a task, the key is tied to one particular dialogue strategy.

In contrast, agents using different dialogue strategies can be compared with measures such as inappropriate utterance ratio, turn correction ratio, concept accuracy, implicit recovery and transaction success (Danieli and Gerbino, 1995; Hirschman and Pao, 1993; Polifroni et al., 1992; Simpson and Fraser, 1993; Shriberg, Wade, and Price, 1992). Consider a comparison of two train timetable information agents (Danieli and Gerbino, 1995), where Agent A in Dialogue 1 uses an explicit confirmation strategy, while Agent B in Dialogue 2 uses an implicit confirmation strategy:

(1) User: I want to go from Torino to Milano.
Agent A: Do you want to go from Trento to Milano? Yes or No?
User: No.

(2) User: I want to travel from Torino to Milano.
Agent B: At which time do you want to leave from Merano to Milano?
User: No, I want to leave from Torino in the evening.

Danieli and Gerbino found that Agent A had a higher transaction success rate and produced less inappropriate and repair utterances than Agent B, and thus concluded that Agent A was more robust than Agent B.

However, one limitation of both this approach and the reference answer approach is the inability to generalize results to other tasks and environments (Fraser, 1995). Such generalization requires the identification of factors that affect performance (Cohen, 1995; Sparck-Jones and Galliers, 1996). For example, while Danieli and Gerbino found that Agent A's dialogue strategy produced dialogues that were approximately twice as long as Agent B's, they had no way of determining whether Agent A's higher transaction success or Agent B's efficiency was more critical to performance. In addition to agent factors such as dialogue strategy, task factors such as database size and environmental factors such as background noise may also be relevant predictors of performance.

These approaches are also limited in that they currently do not calculate performance over subdialogues as well as whole dialogues, correlate performance with an external validation criterion, or normalize performance for task complexity.

This paper describes PARADISE, a general framework for evaluating spoken dialogue agents that addresses these limitations. PARADISE supports comparisons among dialogue strategies by providing a task representation that decouples *what* an agent needs to achieve in terms of

[1]We use the term agent to emphasize the fact that we are evaluating a speaking entity that may have a personality. Readers who wish to may substitute the word "system" wherever "agent" is used.

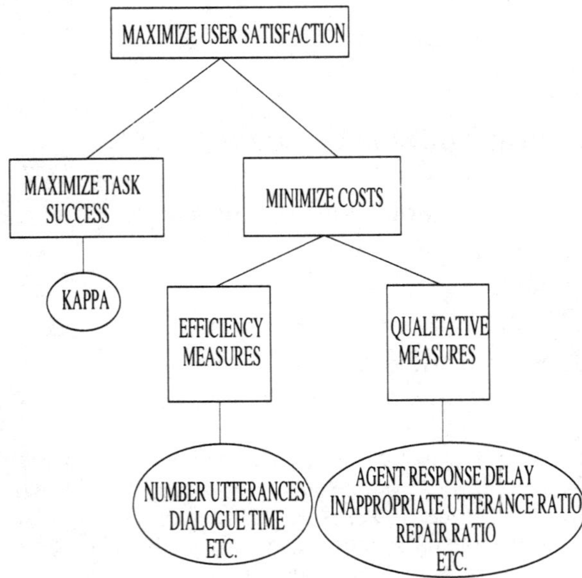

Figure 1: PARADISE's structure of objectives for spoken dialogue performance

the task requirements from *how* the agent carries out the task via dialogue. PARADISE uses a decision-theoretic framework to specify the relative contribution of various factors to an agent's overall *performance*. Performance is modeled as a weighted function of a task-based success measure and dialogue-based cost measures, where weights are computed by correlating user satisfaction with performance. Also, performance can be calculated for subdialogues as well as whole dialogues. Since the goal of this paper is to explain and illustrate the application of the PARADISE framework, for expository purposes, the paper uses simplified domains with hypothetical data throughout. Section 2 describes PARADISE's performance model, and Section 3 discusses its generality, before concluding in Section 4.

2 A Performance Model for Dialogue

PARADISE uses methods from decision theory (Keeney and Raiffa, 1976; Doyle, 1992) to combine a disparate set of performance measures (i.e., user satisfaction, task success, and dialogue cost, all of which have been previously noted in the literature) into a single performance evaluation function. The use of decision theory requires a specification of both the objectives of the decision problem and a set of measures (known as attributes in decision theory) for operationalizing the objectives. The PARADISE model is based on the structure of objectives (rectangles) shown in Figure 1. The PARADISE model posits that performance can be correlated with a meaningful external criterion such as usability, and thus that the overall goal of a spoken dialogue agent is to maximize an objective related to usability. User satisfaction ratings (Kamm, 1995; Shriberg, Wade, and Price, 1992; Polifroni et al., 1992) have been frequently used in the literature as an external indicator of the usability of a dialogue agent. The model further posits that two types of factors are potential relevant contributors to user satisfaction (namely task success and dialogue costs), and that two types of factors are potential relevant contributors to costs (Walker, 1996).

In addition to the use of decision theory to create this objective structure, other novel aspects of PARADISE include the use of the Kappa coefficient (Carletta, 1996; Siegel and Castellan, 1988) to operationalize task success, and the use of linear regression to quantify the relative contribution of the success and cost factors to user satisfaction.

The remainder of this section explains the measures (ovals in Figure 1) used to operationalize the set of objectives, and the methodology for estimating a quantitative performance function that reflects the objective structure. Section 2.1 describes PARADISE's task representation, which is needed to calculate the task-based success measure described in Section 2.2. Section 2.3 describes the cost measures considered in PARADISE, which reflect both the efficiency and the naturalness of an agent's dialogue behaviors. Section 2.4 describes the use of linear regression and user satisfaction to estimate the relative contribution of the success and cost measures in a single performance function. Finally, Section 2.5 explains how performance can be calculated for subdialogues as well as whole dialogues, while Section 2.6 summarizes the method.

2.1 Tasks as Attribute Value Matrices

A general evaluation framework requires a task representation that decouples *what* an agent and user accomplish from *how* the task is accomplished using dialogue strategies. We propose that an *attribute value matrix (AVM)* can represent many dialogue tasks. This consists of the information that must be exchanged between the agent and the user during the dialogue, represented as a set of ordered pairs of attributes and their possible values.[2]

As a first illustrative example, consider a simplification of the train timetable domain of Dialogues 1 and 2, where the timetable only contains information about rush-hour trains between four cities, as shown in Table 1. This AVM consists of four attributes (abbreviations for each attribute name are also shown).[3] In Table 1, these attribute-value pairs are annotated with the direction of information flow to represent who acquires the information, although this information is not used for evaluation. During the dialogue the agent must acquire from the user the values of DC, AC, and DR, while the user must acquire DT.

Performance evaluation for an agent requires a corpus of dialogues between users and the agent, in which users execute a set of scenarios. Each scenario execution has

[2] For infinite sets of values, actual values found in the experimental data constitute the required finite set.

[3] The AVM serves as an evaluation mechanism only. We are not claiming that AVMs determine an agent's behavior or serve as an utterance's semantic representation.

attribute	possible values	information flow
depart-city (DC)	Milano, Roma, Torino, Trento	to agent
arrival-city (AC)	Milano, Roma, Torino, Trento	to agent
depart-range (DR)	morning,evening	to agent
depart-time (DT)	6am,8am,6pm,8pm	to user

Table 1: Attribute value matrix, simplified train timetable domain

A1:	Hello, This is Train Enquiry Service.	DC,AC,DR,DT
	Please speak after the tone.	DC,AC,DR,DT
	Which information do you need?	DC,AC,DR,DT
U1:	I want to go from Torino to Milano.	DC,AC
A2:	Do you want to go from Trento to Milano?	DC,AC
	Yes or No?	DC,AC
U2:	No.	DC,AC
A3:	Do you want to leave from Trento?	DC
	Yes or No?	DC
U3:	No.	DC
A4:	Where do you want to leave from?	DC
U4:	I want to leave from Torino.	DC
A5:	Do you want to leave from Torino?	DC
	Yes or No?	DC
U5:	Yes.	DC
A6:	Do you want to go to Milano?	AC
U6:	Yes.	AC
A7:	At which time do you want to leave?	DR
U7:	I want to travel in the evening.	DR
A8:	Do you want to leave between 6 and 9 p.m.?	DR
	Yes or No?	DR
U8:	Yes.	DR
A9:	There is a train leaving at 8:00 p.m.	DT
	...	

Figure 2: Agent A dialogue interaction (Danieli and Gerbino, 1995)

a corresponding AVM instantiation indicating the task information requirements for the scenario, where each attribute is paired with the attribute value obtained via the dialogue.

For example, assume that a scenario requires the user to find a train from Torino to Milano that leaves in the evening, as in the longer versions of Dialogues 1 and 2 in Figures 2 and 3.[4] Table 2 contains an AVM corresponding to a "key" for this scenario. All dialogues resulting from execution of this scenario in which the agent and the user correctly convey all attribute values (as in Figures 2 and 3) would have the same AVM as the scenario key in Table 2. The AVMs of the remaining dialogues would differ from the key by at least one value. Thus, even though the dialogue strategies in Figures 2 and 3 are radically different, the AVM task representation for these dialogues is identical and the performance of the system for the same task can thus be assessed on the basis of the AVM representation.

2.2 Measuring Task Success

Success at the task for a whole dialogue (or subdialogue) is measured by how well the agent and user achieve the information requirements of the task by the end of the

[4]These dialogues have been slightly modified from (Danieli and Gerbino, 1995). The attribute names at the end of each utterance will be explained below.

B1:	Hello, This is Train Enquiry Service.	DC,AC,DR,DT
	Please speak after the tone.	DC,AC,DR,DT
	Which information do you need?	DC,AC,DR,DT
U1:	I want to travel from Torino to Milano.	DC,AC
B2:	At which time do you want to leave from Merano to Milano?	DC,AC,DR
U2:	No, I want to leave from Torino in the evening.	DC, DR
B3:	Do you want to leave from Torino between 6 and 11 p.m?	DC, DR
	Please answer Yes or No.	DC, DR
U3:	Yes.	DC, DR
B4:	A train leaves at 8 p.m.	DT
	...	

Figure 3: Agent B dialogue interaction (Danieli and Gerbino, 1995)

attribute	actual value
depart-city	Torino
arrival-city	Milano
depart-range	evening
depart-time	8pm

Table 2: Attribute value matrix instantiation, scenario key for Dialogues 1 and 2

dialogue (or subdialogue). This section explains how PARADISE uses the Kappa coefficient (Carletta, 1996; Siegel and Castellan, 1988) to operationalize the task-based success measure in Figure 1.

The Kappa coefficient, κ, is calculated from a confusion matrix that summarizes how well an agent achieves the information requirements of a particular task for a set of dialogues instantiating a set of scenarios.[5] For example, Tables 3 and 4 show two hypothetical confusion matrices that could have been generated in an evaluation of 100 complete dialogues with each of two train timetable agents A and B (perhaps using the confirmation strategies illustrated in Figures 2 and 3, respectively).[6] The values in the matrix cells are based on comparisons between the dialogue and scenario key AVMs. Whenever an attribute value in a dialogue (i.e., data) AVM *matches* the value in its scenario key, the number in the appropriate diagonal cell of the matrix (boldface for clarity) is incremented by 1. The off diagonal cells represent *misunderstandings* that are not corrected in the dialogue. Note that depending on the strategy that a spoken dialogue agent uses, confusions across attributes are possible, e.g., "Milano " could be confused with "morning." The effect of misunderstandings that *are* corrected during the course of the dialogue are reflected in the costs associated with the dialogue, as will be discussed below.

The first matrix summarizes how the 100 AVMs representing each dialogue with Agent A compare with the AVMs representing the relevant scenario keys, while the

[5]Confusion matrices can be constructed to summarize the result of dialogues for any subset of the scenarios, attributes, users or dialogues.

[6]The distributions in the tables were roughly based on performance results in (Danieli and Gerbino, 1995).

	KEY													
	DEPART-CITY				ARRIVAL-CITY				DEPART-RANGE		DEPART-TIME			
DATA	v1	v2	v3	v4	v5	v6	v7	v8	v9	v10	v11	v12	v13	v14
v1	**22**		1		3									
v2		**29**												
v3	4		**16**	4			1							
v4	1	1	5	**11**			1							
v5	3				**20**									
v6						**22**								
v7			2		1	1	**20**	5						
v8			1		1	2	8	**15**						
v9									**45**	10				
v10									5	**40**				
v11											**20**		2	
v12											1	**19**	2	4
v13											2		**18**	
v14											2	6	3	**21**
sum	30	30	25	15	25	25	30	20	50	50	25	25	25	25

Table 3: Confusion matrix, Agent A

	KEY													
	DEPART-CITY				ARRIVAL-CITY				DEPART-RANGE		DEPART-TIME			
DATA	v1	v2	v3	v4	v5	v6	v7	v8	v9	v10	v11	v12	v13	v14
v1	**16**		1		4				3	2				
v2	1	**20**	1			3								
v3	5	1	**9**	4	2		4	2						
v4	1	2	6	**6**			2	3						
v5	4				**15**				2	3				
v6	1	6				**19**								
v7			5	2	1	1	**15**	4						
v8		1	3	3	1	2	9	**11**						
v9	2				2				**39**	10				
v10									6	**35**				
v11											**20**	5	5	4
v12												**10**	5	5
v13											5	5	**10**	5
v14												5	5	**11**
sum	30	30	25	15	25	25	30	20	50	50	25	25	25	25

Table 4: Confusion matrix, Agent B

second matrix summarizes the information exchange with Agent B. Labels v1 to v4 in each matrix represent the possible values of depart-city shown in Table 1; v5 to v8 are for arrival-city, etc. Columns represent the key, specifying which information values the agent and user were supposed to communicate to one another given a particular scenario. (The equivalent column sums in both tables reflects that users of both agents were assumed to have performed the same scenarios). Rows represent the data collected from the dialogue corpus, reflecting what attribute values were actually communicated between the agent and the user.

Given a confusion matrix M, success at achieving the information requirements of the task is measured with the Kappa coefficient (Carletta, 1996; Siegel and Castellan, 1988):

$$\kappa = \frac{P(A) - P(E)}{1 - P(E)}$$

P(A) is the proportion of times that the AVMs for the actual set of dialogues agree with the AVMs for the scenario keys, and P(E) is the proportion of times that the AVMs for the dialogues and the keys are expected to agree by chance.[7] When there is no agreement other than that which would be expected by chance, $\kappa = 0$. When there is total agreement, $\kappa = 1$. κ is superior to other measures of success such as transaction success (Danieli and Gerbino, 1995), concept accuracy (Simpson and Fraser, 1993), and percent agreement (Gale, Church, and Yarowsky, 1992) because κ takes into account the inherent complexity of the task by correcting for chance expected agreement. Thus κ provides a basis for comparisons across agents that are performing *different* tasks.

When the prior distribution of the categories is unknown, P(E), the expected chance agreement between the data and the key, can be estimated from the distribution of the values in the keys. This can be calculated from confusion matrix M, since the columns represent the values in the keys. In particular:

$$P(E) = \sum_{i=1}^{n} \left(\frac{t_i}{T}\right)^2$$

[7] κ has been used to measure pairwise agreement among coders making category judgments (Carletta, 1996; Krippendorf, 1980; Siegel and Castellan, 1988). Thus, the observed user/agent interactions are modeled as a coder, and the ideal interactions as an expert coder.

where t_i is the sum of the frequencies in column i of M, and T is the sum of the frequencies in M ($t_1 + \ldots + t_n$).

P(A), the actual agreement between the data and the key, is always computed from the confusion matrix M:

$$P(A) = \frac{\sum_{i=1}^{n} M(i,i)}{T}$$

Given the confusion matrices in Tables 3 and 4, P(E) = 0.079 for both agents.[8] For Agent A, P(A) = 0.795 and κ = 0.777, while for Agent B, P(A) = 0.59 and κ = 0.555, suggesting that Agent A is more successful than B in achieving the task goals.

2.3 Measuring Dialogue Costs

As shown in Figure 1, performance is also a function of a combination of cost measures. Intuitively, cost measures should be calculated on the basis of any user or agent dialogue behaviors that should be minimized. A wide range of cost measures have been used in previous work; these include pure efficiency measures such as the number of turns or elapsed time to complete the task (Abella, Brown, and Buntschuh, 1996; Hirschman et al., 1990; Smith and Gordon, 1997; Walker, 1996), as well as measures of qualitative phenomena such as inappropriate or repair utterances (Danieli and Gerbino, 1995; Hirschman and Pao, 1993; Simpson and Fraser, 1993).

PARADISE represents each cost measure as a function c_i that can be applied to any (sub)dialogue. First, consider the simplest case of calculating efficiency measures over a whole dialogue. For example, let c_1 be the total number of utterances. For the whole dialogue D1 in Figure 2, c_1(D1) is 23 utterances. For the whole dialogue D2 in Figure 3, c_1(D2) is 10 utterances.

To calculate costs over subdialogues and for some of the qualitative measures, it is necessary to be able to specify which information goals each utterance contributes to. PARADISE uses its AVM representation to link the information goals of the task to any arbitrary dialogue behavior, by tagging the dialogue with the attributes for the task.[9] This makes it possible to evaluate any potential dialogue strategies for achieving the task, as well as to evaluate dialogue strategies that operate at the level of dialogue subtasks (subdialogues).

Consider the longer versions of Dialogues 1 and 2 in Figures 2 and 3. Each utterance in Figures 2 and 3 has been tagged using one or more of the attribute abbreviations in Table 1, according to the subtask(s) the utterance contributes to. As a convention of this type of tagging,

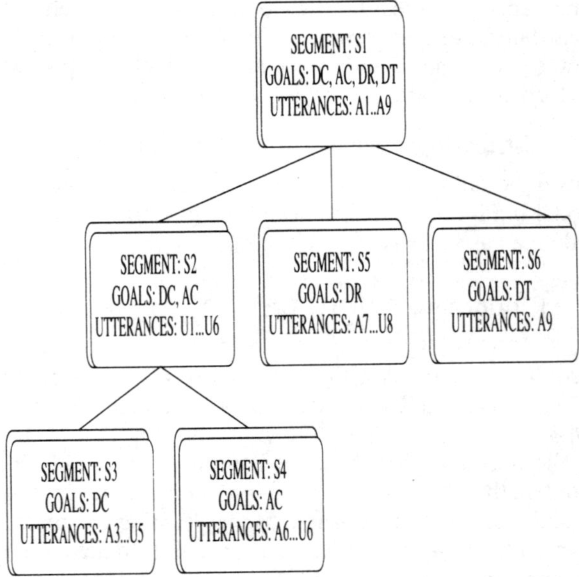

Figure 4: Task-defined discourse structure of Agent A dialogue interaction

utterances that contribute to the success of the whole dialogue, such as greetings, are tagged with all the attributes. Since the structure of a dialogue reflects the structure of the task (Carberry, 1989; Grosz and Sidner, 1986; Litman and Allen, 1990), the tagging of a dialogue by the AVM attributes can be used to generate a hierarchical discourse structure such as that shown in Figure 4 for Dialogue 1 (Figure 2). For example, segment (subdialogue) S2 in Figure 4 is about both depart-city (DC) and arrival-city (AC). It contains segments S3 and S4 within it, and consists of utterances U1 . . . U6.

Tagging by AVM attributes is required to calculate costs over subdialogues, since for any subdialogue, task attributes define the subdialogue. For subdialogue S4 in Figure 4, which is about the attribute arrival-city and consists of utterances A6 and U6, c_1(S4) is 2.

Tagging by AVM attributes is also required to calculate the cost of some of the qualitative measures, such as number of repair utterances. (Note that to calculate such costs, each utterance in the corpus of dialogues must also be tagged with respect to the qualitative phenomenon in question, e.g. whether the utterance is a repair.[10]) For example, let c_2 be the number of repair utterances. The repair utterances in Figure 2 are A3 through U6, thus c_2(D1) is 10 utterances and c_2(S4) is 2 utterances. The repair utterance in Figure 3 is U2, but note that according to the AVM task tagging, U2 simultaneously addresses the information goals for depart-range. In general, if an utterance U contributes to the information goals of N different attributes, each attribute accounts for 1/N of any costs derivable from U. Thus, c_2(D2) is .5.

Given a set of c_i, it is necessary to combine the dif-

[8] Using a single confusion matrix for all attributes as in Tables 3 and 4 inflates κ when there are few cross-attribute confusions by making P(E) smaller. In some cases it might be desirable to calculate κ first for identification of attributes and then for values within attributes, or to average κ for each attribute to produce an overall κ for the task.

[9] This tagging can be hand generated, or system generated and hand corrected. Preliminary studies indicate that reliability for human tagging is higher for AVM attribute tagging than for other types of discourse segment tagging (Passonneau and Litman, 1997; Hirschberg and Nakatani, 1996).

[10] Previous work has shown that this can be done with high reliability (Hirschman and Pao, 1993).

ferent cost measures in order to determine their relative contribution to performance. The next section explains how to combine κ with a set of c_i to yield an overall performance measure.

2.4 Estimating a Performance Function

Given the definition of success and costs above and the model in Figure 1, performance for any (sub)dialogue D is defined as follows:[11]

$$\text{Performance} = (\alpha * \mathcal{N}(\kappa)) - \sum_{i=1}^{n} w_i * \mathcal{N}(c_i)$$

Here α is a weight on κ, the cost functions c_i are weighted by w_i, and $\mathcal{N}$ is a Z score normalization function (Cohen, 1995).

The normalization function is used to overcome the problem that the values of c_i are not on the same scale as κ, and that the cost measures c_i may also be calculated over widely varying scales (e.g. response delay could be measured using seconds while, in the example, costs were calculated in terms of number of utterances). This problem is easily solved by normalizing each factor x to its Z score:

$$\mathcal{N}(x) = \frac{x - \overline{x}}{\sigma_x}$$

where σ_x is the standard deviation for x.

user	agent	US	κ	c_1 (#utt)	c_2 (#rep)
1	A	1	1	46	30
2	A	2	1	50	30
3	A	2	1	52	30
4	A	3	1	40	20
5	A	4	1	23	10
6	A	2	1	50	36
7	A	1	0.46	75	30
8	A	1	0.19	60	30
9	B	6	1	8	0
10	B	5	1	15	1
11	B	6	1	10	0.5
12	B	5	1	20	3
13	B	1	0.19	45	18
14	B	1	0.46	50	22
15	B	2	0.19	34	18
16	B	2	0.46	40	18
Mean(A)	A	2	0.83	49.5	27
Mean(B)	B	3.5	0.66	27.8	10.1
Mean	NA	2.75	0.75	38.6	18.5

Table 5: Hypothetical performance data from users of Agents A and B

To illustrate the method for estimating a performance function, we will use a subset of the data from Tables 3 and 4, shown in Table 5. Table 5 represents the results from a hypothetical experiment in which eight users were randomly assigned to communicate with Agent A and eight users were randomly assigned to communicate with Agent B. Table 5 shows user satisfaction (US) ratings (discussed below), κ, number of utterances (#utt) and number of repair utterances (#rep) for each of these users. Users 5 and 11 correspond to the dialogues in Figures 2 and 3 respectively. To normalize c_1 for user 5, we determine that $\overline{c_1}$ is 38.6 and σ_{c_1} is 18.9. Thus, $\mathcal{N}(c_1)$ is -0.83. Similarly $\mathcal{N}(c_1)$ for user 11 is -1.51.

To estimate the performance function, the weights α and w_i must be solved for. Recall that the claim implicit in Figure 1 was that the relative contribution of task success and dialogue costs to performance should be calculated by considering their contribution to user satisfaction. User satisfaction is typically calculated with surveys that ask users to specify the degree to which they agree with one or more statements about the behavior or the performance of the system. A single user satisfaction measure can be calculated from a single question, or as the mean of a set of ratings. The hypothetical user satisfaction ratings shown in Table 5 range from a high of 6 to a low of 1.

Given a set of dialogues for which user satisfaction (US), κ and the set of c_i have been collected experimentally, the weights α and w_i can be solved for using multiple linear regression. Multiple linear regression produces a set of coefficients (weights) describing the relative contribution of each predictor factor in accounting for the variance in a predicted factor. In this case, on the basis of the model in Figure 1, US is treated as the predicted factor. Normalization of the predictor factors (κ and c_i) to their Z scores guarantees that the relative magnitude of the coefficients directly indicates the relative contribution of each factor. Regression on the Table 5 data for both sets of users tests which factors κ, #utt, #rep most strongly predicts US.

In this illustrative example, the results of the regression with all factors included shows that only κ and #rep are significant ($p < .02$). In order to develop a performance function estimate that includes only significant factors and eliminates redundancies, a second regression including only significant factors must then be done. In this case, a second regression yields the predictive equation:

$$\text{Performance} = .40\mathcal{N}(\kappa) - .78\mathcal{N}(c_2)$$

i.e., α is .40 and w_2 is .78. The results also show κ is significant at $p < .0003$, #rep significant at $p < .0001$, and the combination of κ and #rep account for 92% of the variance in US, the external validation criterion. The factor #utt was not a significant predictor of performance, in part because #utt and #rep are highly redundant. (The correlation between #utt and #rep is 0.91).

Given these predictions about the relative contribution of different factors to performance, it is then possible to return to the problem first introduced in Section 1: given potentially conflicting performance criteria such as robustness and efficiency, how can the performance of Agent A and Agent B be compared? Given values for α and w_i, performance can be calculated for both agents

[11] We assume an additive performance (utility) function because it appears that κ and the various cost factors c_i are utility independent and additive independent (Keeney and Raiffa, 1976). It is possible however that user satisfaction data collected in future experiments (or other data such as willingness to pay or use) would indicate otherwise. If so, continuing use of an additive function might require a transformation of the data, a reworking of the model shown in Figure 1, or the inclusion of interaction terms in the model (Cohen, 1995).

using the equation above. The mean performance of A is -.44 and the mean performance of B is .44, suggesting that Agent B may perform better than Agent A overall.

The evaluator must then however test these performance differences for statistical significance. In this case, a *t* test shows that differences are only significant at the $p < .07$ level, indicating a trend only. In this case, an evaluation over a larger subset of the user population would probably show significant differences.

2.5 Application to Subdialogues

Since both κ and c_i can be calculated over subdialogues, performance can also be calculated at the subdialogue level by using the values for α and w_i as solved for above. This assumes that the factors that are predictive of global performance, based on US, generalize as predictors of local performance, i.e. within subdialogues defined by subtasks, as defined by the attribute tagging.[12]

Consider calculating the performance of the dialogue strategies used by train timetable Agents A and B, over the subdialogues that repair the value of depart-city. Segment S3 (Figure 4) is an example of such a subdialogue with Agent A. As in the initial estimation of a performance function, our analysis requires experimental data, namely a set of values for κ and c_i, and the application of the Z score normalization function to this data. However, the values for κ and c_i are now calculated at the subdialogue rather than the whole dialogue level. In addition, only data from comparable strategies can be used to calculate the mean and standard deviation for normalization. Informally, a comparable strategy is one which applies in the same state and has the same effects.

For example, to calculate κ for Agent A over the subdialogues that repair depart-city, P(A) and P(E) are computed using only the subpart of Table 3 concerned with depart-city. For Agent A, P(A) = .78, P(E) = .265, and κ = .70. Then, this value of κ is normalized using data from comparable subdialogues with both Agent A and Agent B. Based on the data in Tables 3 and 4, the mean κ is .515 and σ is .261, so that $\mathcal{N}(\kappa)$ for Agent A is .71.

To calculate c_2 for Agent A, assume that the average number of repair utterances for Agent A's subdialogues that repair depart-city is 6, that the mean over all comparable repair subdialogues is 4, and the standard deviation is 2.79. Then $\mathcal{N}(c_2)$ is .72.

Let Agent A's repair dialogue strategy for subdialogues repairing depart-city be R_A and Agent B's repair strategy for depart-city be R_B. Then using the performance equation above, predicted performance for R_A is:

$$\text{Performance}(R_A) = .40 * .71 - .78 * .72 = -0.28$$

For Agent B, using the appropriate subpart of Table 4 to calculate κ, assuming that the average number of depart-city repair utterances is 1.38, and using similar calculations, yields

$$\text{Performance}(R_B) = .40 * -.71 - .78 * -.94 = 0.45$$

Thus the results of these experiments predict that when an agent needs to choose between the repair strategy that Agent B uses and the repair strategy that Agent A uses for repairing depart-city, it should use Agent B's strategy R_B, since the performance(R_B) is predicted to be greater than the performance(R_A).

Note that the ability to calculate performance over subdialogues allows us to conduct experiments that simultaneously test multiple dialogue strategies. For example, suppose Agents A and B had different strategies for presenting the value of depart-time (in addition to different confirmation strategies). Without the ability to calculate performance over subdialogues, it would be impossible to test the effect of the different presentation strategies independently of the different confirmation strategies.

2.6 Summary

We have presented the PARADISE framework, and have used it to evaluate two hypothetical dialogue agents in a simplified train timetable task domain. We used PARADISE to derive a performance function for this task, by estimating the relative contribution of a set of potential predictors to user satisfaction. The PARADISE methodology consists of the following steps:

- definition of a task and a set of scenarios;
- specification of the AVM task representation;
- experiments with alternate dialogue agents for the task;
- calculation of user satisfaction using surveys;
- calculation of task success using κ;
- calculation of dialogue cost using efficiency and qualitative measures;
- estimation of a performance function using linear regression and values for user satisfaction, κ and dialogue costs;
- comparison with other agents/tasks to determine which factors generalize;
- refinement of the performance model.

Note that all of these steps are required to develop the performance function. However once the weights in the performance function have been solved for, user satisfaction ratings no longer need to be collected. Instead, predictions about user satisfaction can be made on the basis of the predictor variables, as illustrated in the application of PARADISE to subdialogues.

Given the current state of knowledge, it is important to emphasize that researchers should be cautious about generalizing a derived performance function to other agents or tasks. Performance function estimation should be done iteratively over many different tasks and dialogue strategies to see which factors generalize. In this way, the field can make progress on identifying the relationship between various factors and can move towards more predictive models of spoken dialogue agent performance.

[12] This assumption has a sound basis in theories of dialogue structure (Carberry, 1989; Grosz and Sidner, 1986; Litman and Allen, 1990), but should be tested empirically.

3 Generality

In the previous section we used PARADISE to evaluate two confirmation strategies, using as examples fairly simple information access dialogues in the train timetable domain. In this section we demonstrate that PARADISE is applicable to a range of tasks, domains, and dialogues, by presenting AVMs for two tasks involving more than information access, and showing how additional dialogue phenomena can be tagged using AVM attributes.

attribute	possible values	information flow
depart-city (DC)	Milano, Roma, Torino, Trento	to agent
arrival-city (AC)	Milano, Roma, Torino, Trento	to agent
depart-range (DR)	morning,evening	to agent
depart-time (DT)	6am,8am,6pm,8pm	to user
request-type (RT)	reserve, purchase	to agent

Table 6: Attribute value matrix, train timetable domain with requests

First, consider an extension of the train timetable task, where an agent can handle requests to reserve a seat or purchase a ticket. This task could be represented using the AVM in Table 6 (an extension of Table 1), where the agent must now acquire the value of the attribute request-type, in order to know what to do with the other information it has acquired.

U1:	I want to go from Torino to Roma	DC,AC
C1:	Approximately what time of day would you like to travel?	DR
U2:	What are the options?	DR
C2:	Morning or evening.	DR
U3:	Are those departure times?	DR
C3:	Yes.	DR
U4:	I'd like to leave in the morning.	DR
C4:	Train 702 leaves Torino Porto at 8 a.m.	DT
U5:	Please reserve me a seat on that train.	RT

Figure 5: Hypothetical Agent C dialogue interaction

Figure 5 presents a hypothetical dialogue in this extended task domain, and illustrates user utterance types and an agent dialogue strategy that are very different from those in Figures 2 and 3. First, Agent C in Figure 5 uses a "no confirmation" dialogue strategy, in contrast to the explicit and implicit confirmation strategies used in Figures 2 and 3. Second, Figure 5 illustrates new types of *user* utterances that do not directly further the informational goals of the task. In U2, the user asks the agent a wh-question about the DR attribute itself, rather than providing information about that attribute's value. Since U2 satisfies a knowledge precondition related to answering C1, U2 contributes to the DR goal and is tagged as such. In U3, the user similarly asks a yes-no question that addresses a subgoal related to answering C1. Finally, U5 illustrates a user request for an agent action, and is tagged with the RT attribute. The value of RT in the AVM instantiation for the dialogue would be "reserve."

Second, consider the very different domain and task of diagnosing a fault and repairing a circuit (Smith and Gordon, 1997). Figure 6 presents one dialogue from this domain.

1. C:	This is the circuit fix it shop.	ID,CB,RB,FT,FC,T
	How may I help you?	ID,CB,RB,FT,FC,T
2. U:	I want to fix a circuit.	ID,CB,RB,FT,FC,T
3. C:	What is the ID of the circuit?	ID
4. U:	Rs111.	ID
5. C:	I am familiar with that circuit.	CB
	The LED is supposed to be displaying alternately flashing one and seven.	CB
6. U:	The LED is off.	RB
7. C:	What is the switch at when the LED is off?	RB
8. U:	The switch is down.	RB
9. C:	Put the switch up.	RB
10. U:	Okay.	RB
11. C:	Put the knob to one zero.	RB
12. U:	Okay.	RB
13. C:	What is the LED displaying?	RB
14. U:	LED is displaying only a flashing seven.	RB
15. C:	Is there a wire between connector eight four and connector nine nine?	FT
16. U:	No.	FT
17. C:	Add a wire between connector eight four and connector nine nine.	FC
18. U:	Done.	FC
19. C:	What is the LED displaying?	T
20. U:	Alternately flashing one and seven.	T
21. C:	Is the one on the LED displaying for a longer period of time?	T
22. U:	No.	T
23. C:	Is the seven on the LED displaying for a longer period of time?	T
24. U:	No.	T
25. C:	Put the knob to zero.	T
26. U:	Okay.	T
27. C:	What is the LED displaying?	T
28. U:	Alternately displaying one and seven.	T
29. C:	Is the one on the LED displaying for a longer period of time?	T
30. U:	Yes.	T
31. C:	Put the switch down.	T
32. U:	The switch is down.	T
33. C:	What is the LED displaying?	T
34. U:	Nothing.	T
35. C:	The circuit is working correctly. Good-bye.	T

Figure 6: A circuit domain dialogue (Smith and Gordon, 1997), with AVM tagging

Smith and Gordon collected 144 dialogues for this task, in which agent initiative was varied by using different dialogue strategies, and tagged each dialogue according to the following subtask structure:[13]

- Introduction (I)—establish the purpose of the task
- Assessment (A)—establish the current behavior
- Diagnosis (D)—establish the cause for the errant behavior
- Repair (R)—establish that the correction for the errant behavior has been made
- Test (T)—establish that the behavior is now correct

Our informational analysis of this task results in the AVM shown in Table 7. Note that the attributes are almost identical to Smith and Gordon's list of subtasks. Circuit-ID corresponds to Introduction, Correct-Circuit-Behavior and Current-Circuit-Behavior correspond to Assessment,

[13]They report a κ of .82 for reliability of their tagging scheme.

Fault-Type corresponds to Diagnosis, Fault-Correction corresponds to Repair, and Test corresponds to Test. The attribute names emphasize information exchange, while the subtask names emphasize function.

attribute	possible values
Circuit-ID (ID)	RS111, RS112, ...
Correct-Circuit-Behavior (CB)	Flash-1-7, Flash-1, ...
Current-Circuit-Behavior (RB)	Flash-7
Fault-Type (FT)	MissingWire84-99, MissingWire88-99, ...
Fault-Correction (FC)	yes, no
Test (T)	yes, no

Table 7: Attribute value matrix, circuit domain

Figure 6 is tagged with the attributes from Table 7. Smith and Gordon's tagging of this dialogue according to their subtask representation was as follows: turns 1-4 were I, turns 5-14 were A, turns 15-16 were D, turns 17-18 were R, and turns 19-35 were T. Note that there are only two differences between the dialogue structures yielded by the two tagging schemes. First, in our scheme (Figure 6), the greetings (turns 1 and 2) are tagged with all the attributes. Second, Smith and Gordon's single tag A corresponds to two attribute tags in Table 7, which in our scheme defines an extra level of structure within assessment subdialogues.

4 Discussion

This paper presented the PARADISE framework for evaluating spoken dialogue agents. PARADISE is a general framework for evaluating spoken dialogue agents that integrates and enhances previous work. PARADISE supports comparisons among dialogue strategies with a task representation that decouples *what* an agent needs to achieve in terms of the task requirements from *how* the agent carries out the task via dialogue. Furthermore, this task representation supports the calculation of performance over subdialogues as well as whole dialogues. In addition, because PARADISE's success measure normalizes for task complexity, it provides a basis for comparing agents performing *different* tasks.

The PARADISE performance measure is a function of both task success (κ) and dialogue costs (c_i), and has a number of advantages. First, it allows us to evaluate performance at any level of a dialogue, since κ and c_i can be calculated for any dialogue subtask. Since performance can be measured over any subtask, and since dialogue strategies can range over subdialogues or the whole dialogue, we can associate performance with individual dialogue strategies. Second, because our success measure κ takes into account the complexity of the task, comparisons can be made across dialogue tasks. Third, κ allows us to measure partial success at achieving the task. Fourth, performance can combine both objective and subjective cost measures, and specifies how to evaluate the relative contributions of those costs factors to overall performance. Finally, to our knowledge, we are the first to propose using user satisfaction to determine weights on factors related to performance.

In addition, this approach is broadly integrative, incorporating aspects of transaction success, concept accuracy, multiple cost measures, and user satisfaction. In our framework, transaction success is reflected in κ, corresponding to dialogues with a P(A) of 1. Our performance measure also captures information similar to concept accuracy, where low concept accuracy scores translate into either higher costs for acquiring information from the user, or lower κ scores.

One limitation of the PARADISE approach is that the task-based success measure does not reflect that some solutions might be better than others. For example, in the train timetable domain, we might like our task-based success measure to give higher ratings to agents that suggest express over local trains, or that provide helpful information that was not explicitly requested, especially since the better solutions might occur in dialogues with higher costs. It might be possible to address this limitation by using the interval scaled data version of κ (Krippendorf, 1980). Another possibility is to simply substitute a domain-specific task-based success measure in the performance model for κ.

The evaluation model presented here has many applications in spoken dialogue processing. We believe that the framework is also applicable to other dialogue modalities, and to human-human task-oriented dialogues. In addition, while there are many proposals in the literature for algorithms for dialogue strategies that are cooperative, collaborative or helpful to the user (Webber and Joshi, 1982; Pollack, Hirschberg, and Webber, 1982; Joshi, Webber, and Weischedel, 1984; Chu-Carrol and Carberry, 1995), very few of these strategies have been evaluated as to whether they improve any measurable aspect of a dialogue interaction. As we have demonstrated here, any dialogue strategy can be evaluated, so it should be possible to show that a cooperative response, or other cooperative strategy, actually improves task performance by reducing costs or increasing task success. We hope that this framework will be broadly applied in future dialogue research.

5 Acknowledgments

We would like to thank James Allen, Jennifer Chu-Carroll, Morena Danieli, Wieland Eckert, Giuseppe Di Fabbrizio, Don Hindle, Julia Hirschberg, Shri Narayanan, Jay Wilpon, Steve Whittaker and three anonymous reviews for helpful discussion and comments on earlier versions of this paper.

References

Abella, Alicia, Michael K Brown, and Bruce Buntschuh. 1996. Development principles for dialog-based interfaces. In *ECAI-96 Spoken Dialog Processing Workshop*, Budapest, Hungary.

Bates, Madeleine and Damaris Ayuso. 1993. A proposal for incremental dialogue evaluation. In *Proceedings of the DARPA Speech and NL Workshop*, pages 319–322.

Carberry, S. 1989. Plan recognition and its use in understanding dialogue. In A. Kobsa and W. Wahlster, editors, *User Models in Dialogue Systems*. Springer Verlag, Berlin, pages 133–162.

Carletta, Jean C. 1996. Assessing the reliability of subjective codings. *Computational Linguistics*, 22(2):249–254.

Chu-Carrol, Jennifer and Sandra Carberry. 1995. Response generation in collaborative negotiation. In *Proceedings of the Conference of the 33rd Annual Meeting of the Association for Computational Linguistics*, pages 136–143.

Cohen, Paul. R. 1995. *Empirical Methods for Artificial Intelligence*. MIT Press, Boston.

Danieli, M., W. Eckert, N. Fraser, N. Gilbert, M. Guyomard, P. Heisterkamp, M. Kharoune, J. Magadur, S. McGlashan, D. Sadek, J. Siroux, and N. Youd. 1992. Dialogue manager design evaluation. Technical Report Project Esprit 2218 SUNDIAL, WP6000-D3.

Danieli, Morena and Elisabetta Gerbino. 1995. Metrics for evaluating dialogue strategies in a spoken language system. In *Proceedings of the 1995 AAAI Spring Symposium on Empirical Methods in Discourse Interpretation and Generation*, pages 34–39.

Doyle, Jon. 1992. Rationality and its roles in reasoning. *Computational Intelligence*, 8(2):376–409.

Fraser, Norman M. 1995. Quality standards for spoken dialogue systems: a report on progress in EAGLES. In *ESCA Workshop on Spoken Dialogue Systems Vigso, Denmark*, pages 157–160.

Gale, William, Ken W. Church, and David Yarowsky. 1992. Estimating upper and lower bounds on the performance of word-sense disambiguation programs. In *Proc. of 30th ACL*, pages 249–256, Newark, Delaware.

Grosz, Barbara J. and Candace L. Sidner. 1986. Attentions, intentions and the structure of discourse. *Computational Linguistics*, 12:175–204.

Hirschberg, Julia and Christine Nakatani. 1996. A prosodic analysis of discourse segments in direction-giving monologues. In *34th Annual Meeting of the Association for Computational Linguistics*, pages 286–293.

Hirschman, Lynette, Deborah A. Dahl, Donald P. McKay, Lewis M. Norton, and Marcia C. Linebarger. 1990. Beyond class A: A proposal for automatic evaluation of discourse. In *Proceedings of the Speech and Natural Language Workshop*, pages 109–113.

Hirschman, Lynette and Christine Pao. 1993. The cost of errors in a spoken language system. In *Proceedings of the Third European Conference on Speech Communication and Technology*, pages 1419–1422.

Joshi, Aravind K., Bonnie L. Webber, and Ralph M. Weischedel. 1984. Preventing false inferences. In *COLING84: Proc. 10th International Conference on Computational Linguistics.*, pages 134–138.

Kamm, Candace. 1995. User interfaces for voice applications. In David Roe and Jay Wilpon, editors, *Voice Communication between Humans and Machines*. National Academy Press, pages 422–442.

Keeney, Ralph and Howard Raiffa. 1976. *Decisions with Multiple Objectives: Preferences and Value Tradeoffs*. John Wiley and Sons.

Krippendorf, Klaus. 1980. *Content Analysis: An Introduction to its Methodology*. Sage Publications, Beverly Hills, Ca.

Litman, Diane and James Allen. 1990. Recognizing and relating discourse intentions and task-oriented plans. In Philip Cohen, Jerry Morgan, and Martha Pollack, editors, *Intentions in Communication*. MIT Press.

Passonneau, Rebecca J. and Diane Litman. 1997. Discourse segmentation by human and automated means. *Computational Linguistics*, 23(1).

Polifroni, Joseph, Lynette Hirschman, Stephanie Seneff, and Victor Zue. 1992. Experiments in evaluating interactive spoken language systems. In *Proceedings of the DARPA Speech and NL Workshop*, pages 28–33.

Pollack, Martha, Julia Hirschberg, and Bonnie Webber. 1982. User participation in the reasoning process of expert systems. In *Proceedings First National Conference on Artificial Intelligence*, pages pp. 358–361.

Shriberg, Elizabeth, Elizabeth Wade, and Patti Price. 1992. Human-machine problem solving using spoken language systems (SLS): Factors affecting performance and user satisfaction. In *Proceedings of the DARPA Speech and NL Workshop*, pages 49–54.

Siegel, Sidney and N. J. Castellan. 1988. *Nonparametric Statistics for the Behavioral Sciences*. McGraw Hill.

Simpson, A. and N. A. Fraser. 1993. Black box and glass box evaluation of the SUNDIAL system. In *Proceedings of the Third European Conference on Speech Communication and Technology*, pages 1423–1426.

Smith, Ronnie W. and Steven A. Gordon. 1997. Effects of variable initiative on linguistic behavior in human-computer spoken natural language dialog. *Computational Linguistics*, 23(1).

Sparck-Jones, Karen and Julia R. Galliers. 1996. *Evaluating Natural Language Processing Systems*. Springer.

Walker, Marilyn A. 1996. The Effect of Resource Limits and Task Complexity on Collaborative Planning in Dialogue. *Artificial Intelligence Journal*, 85(1–2):181–243.

Webber, Bonnie and Aravind Joshi. 1982. Taking the initiative in natural language database interaction: Justifying why. In *Coling 82*, pages 413–419.

PARADISE: A Framework for Evaluating Spoken Dialogue Agents

Marilyn A. Walker and Diane J. Litman

In the months since the paper's publication, we have applied PARADISE to two agents: ELVIS (Email Voice Interactive System) and TOOT, an agent for accessing Amtrak Train schedule information over the phone. In the following, we briefly describe experiments testing alternate dialog strategies and summarize our results using PARADISE. For more information about the measures used in these experiments and the results, see (Walker et al. 1997; Litman et al. 1997).

We tested two initiative strategies in ELVIS. The system initiative (SI) strategy controls the dialog by directing the user to select from a set of choices, whereas the mixed initiative (MI) strategy lets the user control the dialog. In (Walker et al. 1997), we report results from 12 users. Here we discuss results from 48 users. When we applied PARADISE to ELVIS experimental data to derive a performance equation, the significant factors were user perception of task completion (COMP, $p = .004$), elapsed time (ET, $p = .001$) and mean recognition score (MRS, $p < .0001$):

$$\text{Performance} = .20 * \text{COMP} + .45 * \text{MRS} - .23 * \text{ET}$$

COMP was significant (rather than Kappa) because users' perceptions sometimes differed from reality. The performance of the SI strategy was greater than that for MI, but performance for MI increased over successive tasks as users' expertise increased. We are continuing to explore how users' expertise affects performance.

Experiments with TOOT tested alternate dialog strategies for presenting information extracted from a web-based Amtrak schedule table. The strategies were linked to two conditions: (A) when there was no information that matched a user's query and (B) when there was too much matching information to present. For condition A, one strategy was to simply say there were no matching trains, whereas the alternate strategy involved automatically relaxing the time constraint. For condition B, alternate strategies were grouping and listing versus summarizing the range of trains. The performance equation derived from the application of PARADISE to experimental data for 12 TOOT users showed that COMP ($p < .05$), MRS ($p < .05$), and the number of user interruptions (barge-ins, $p < .05$) were significant factors:

$$\text{Performance} = .31 * \text{COMP} + .46 * \text{MRS} - .43 * \text{barge-ins}$$

A goal of PARADISE is to make generalizations about factors that contribute to performance in dialog agents by combining data across applications. Since we used the same set of measures in the two experiments, we can combine the data. We find that COMP ($p = .0001$), MRS ($p < .0001$), and ET ($p = .0004$) are significant for the combined set:

$$\text{Performance} = .23 * \text{COMP} + .43 * \text{MRS} - .21 * \text{ET}$$

Thus, the factors that are important over both applications are the same subset shown to be important in the ELVIS data. However, the relative magnitude of the COMP and ET factors increases, reflecting the stronger role that COMP plays in the performance model for TOOT. Interestingly, recognizer performance contributes more to user satisfaction than efficiency, even though it has often been assumed that users care more about efficiency. In addition, none of the efficiency measures were significant in TOOT. Our hypothesis is that users are more attuned to qualitative aspects of the dialog, particularly to the misunderstandings and requests for repetition that result from poor recognizer performance. Future work utilizing PARADISE should test this hypothesis as well as develop other generalizations about performance in spoken dialog agents.

REFERENCES

Litman, D. J.; Pan, S.; and Walker, M. A. (in submission). Evaluating Cooperative Response Strategies in a Web-Based Spoken Dialogue Agent.

Walker, M. A.; Hindle, D.; Fromer, J.; Di Fabbrizio, G.; and Mestel, C. 1997. Evaluating Competing Agent Strategies for a Voice Email Agent. In *Proceedings of EUROSPEECH 97, European Conference on Speech Communication*, Rhodes, Greece, 2219–2222.

Author Index

Keywords